# ADVERTISING AND
# PROMOTION

## AN INTEGRATED MARKETING COMMUNICATIONS PERSPECTIVE

**Belch & Belch: *Advertising & Promotion*** offers a seamless content and technology solution to improve student engagement and comprehension, automation of assignments and grading, and easy reporting to ensure that learning objectives are being met.

Connect® Marketing provides a wide array of tools and content to improve instructor productivity and student performance. In fact, the aggregated results of 34 Connect adoptions showed an 11% improvement in pass rates, a 16% improvement in retention, two times as many students receiving an A, and a 77% reduction in instructor grading time.

## Connect Performance Metrics

- Without Connect
- With Connect

*Data compiled from independent research studies at higher education institutions.*

Exam Scores: 74.7% / 80.4%
Pass Rates: 72.9% / 83.7%
Attendance Rates: 74.5% / 92.5%
Retention Rates: 71.1% / 87.5%

## Average Grade Distribution

With Connect: A B C D F
Without Connect: A B C D F

*Base: Seven control/test groups from six institutions.*
*Data compiled from independent research studies at higher education institutions.*

## Connect reduces time spent on administrative tasks...

Reviewing Homework: 60 minutes without Connect → 15 minutes with Connect

Giving Tests or Quizzes: 60 minutes without Connect → 0 minutes with Connect

Grading: 60 minutes without Connect → 12 minutes with Connect

## ...allowing for more time to focus on concept application and other learning.

**Without Connect**
- Time spent giving tests or quizzes: 20%
- Time spent on concept application and/or active learning: 40%
- Time spent reviewing homework: 40%

**With Connect**
- Time spent giving tests or quizzes: 0%
- Time spent reviewing homework: 10%
- Time spent on concept application and/or active learning: 90%

## Grade Distribution

Without LearnSmart:
- A 19.3%
- B 38.6%
- C 28.0%

With LearnSmart:
- A 30.5%
- B 33.5%
- C 22.6%

**58% more A's with LearnSmart**

## Student Retention Rate

Without LearnSmart: Dropout Rate 31%
With LearnSmart: Dropout Rate 20%

**35% fewer dropouts with LearnSmart**

## Student Pass Rate

Without LearnSmart: 57% / 43%
With LearnSmart: 30% / 70%

**25% more students passed with LearnSmart**

# CONNECT FEATURES

## Interactive Applications

Interactive Applications offer a variety of automatically graded exercises that require students to **apply** key concepts. Whether the assignment includes a *click and drag*, *video case*, or *decision generator*, these applications provide instant feedback and progress tracking for students and detailed results for the instructor.

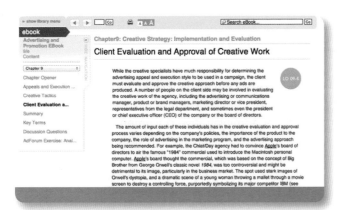

## eBook

Connect Plus includes a media-rich eBook that allows you to share your notes with your students. Your students can insert and review their own notes, highlight the text, search for specific information, and interact with media resources. Using an eBook with Connect Plus gives your students a complete digital solution that allows them to access their materials from any computer.

## Tegrity

Make your classes available anytime, anywhere. With simple, one-click recording, students can search for a word or phrase and be taken to the exact place in your lecture that they need to review.

## EASY TO USE

### Learning Management System Integration

McGraw-Hill Campus is a one-stop teaching and learning experience available to use with any learning management system. McGraw-Hill Campus provides single sign-on to faculty and students for all McGraw-Hill material and technology from within the school website. McGraw-Hill Campus also allows instructors instant access to all supplements and teaching materials for all McGraw-Hill products.

Blackboard users also benefit from McGraw-Hill's industry-leading integration, providing single sign-on to access all Connect assignments and automatic feeding of assignment results to the Blackboard grade book.

The **Best** of **Both Worlds**

## POWERFUL REPORTING

Connect generates comprehensive reports and graphs that provide instructors with an instant view of the performance of individual students, a specific section, or multiple sections. Since all content is mapped to learning objectives, Connect reporting is ideal for accreditation or other administrative documentation.

# ADVERTISING AND PROMOTION

## AN INTEGRATED MARKETING COMMUNICATIONS PERSPECTIVE

10e **George E. Belch & Michael A. Belch**

*Both of San Diego State University*

McGraw Hill Education

ADVERTISING AND PROMOTION: AN INTEGRATED MARKETING
COMMUNICATIONS PERSPECTIVE, 10E GLOBAL EDITION

10 9 8 7 6 5 4 3 2 1
CTP MPM
20  17  16  15  14

When ordering this title, use **ISBN 978-981-4575-11-9** or **MHID 981-4575-11-9**

Printed in Singapore

*To Our Families*
*and*
*Ramo (Coach) and Lorraine*
*and*
*Michael Andrew Anecharico*

# Dr. George E. Belch

George E. Belch is professor of marketing and chair of the marketing department at San Diego State University, where he teaches integrated marketing communications, strategic marketing planning, and consumer/customer behavior. Prior to joining San Diego State, he was a member of the faculty in the Graduate School of Management, University of California, Irvine. He received his PhD in marketing from the University of California, Los Angeles. Before entering academia, Dr. Belch was a marketing representative for the DuPont Company. He also worked as a research analyst for the DDB Worldwide advertising agency.

Dr. Belch's research interests are in the area of consumer processing of advertising information as well as managerial aspects of integrated marketing communications. He has authored or coauthored more than 30 articles in leading academic journals and proceedings, including *The Journal of Marketing Research, Journal of Consumer Research, International Journal of Advertising, Journal of Promotion Management, Journal of Advertising,* and *Journal of Business Research.* In 2000, he was selected as *Marketing Educator of the Year* by the Marketing Educators' Association for his career achievements in teaching and research. He also received the Distinguished Faculty Member Award for the College of Business Administration at San Diego State University in 1994 and 2003.

Dr. Belch has taught in executive education and development programs for various universities around the world. He has also conducted seminars on integrated marketing communications as well as marketing planning and strategy for a number of multinational companies, including Sprint, Microsoft, Qualcomm, MP3.com, Fluor Daniel, Square D Corporation, Armstrong World Industries, Sterling Software, and Texas Industries.

# Dr. Michael A. Belch

Michael (Mickey) A. Belch is a professor of marketing at San Diego State University and is also co-director of the Centre for Integrated Marketing Communications at San Diego State. He received his undergraduate degree from Penn State University, his MBA from Drexel University, and his PhD from the University of Pittsburgh.

Before entering academia he was employed by the General Foods Corporation as a marketing representative, and has served as a consultant to numerous companies, including McDonald's, Whirlpool Corporation, Senco Products, GTI Corporation, IVAC, May Companies, Phillips-Ramsey Advertising and Public Relations, and Daily & Associates Advertising. He has conducted seminars on integrated marketing and marketing management for a number of multinational companies and has also taught in executive education programs in France, Amsterdam, Spain, Chile, Peru, Argentina, Colombia, China, Slovenia, and Greece. He is the author or coauthor of more than 50 articles in academic journals and procedings in the areas of advertising, consumer behavior, and international marketing, including *The Journal of Advertising, Journal of Advertising Research, Journal of Business Research. Journal of Promotion Management,* and *International Journal of Advertising.* Dr. Belch is also a member of the editorial review board of the *Journal of Advertising* and the *International Journal of Advertising.* He received outstanding teaching awards from undergraduate and graduate students numerous times. He also received the Distinguished Faculty Member Award for the College of Business Administration at San Diego State University in 2007. He was recently awarded the Giep Franzen Fellowship from the University of Amsterdam.

# PREFACE

## THE CHANGING WORLD OF ADVERTISING AND PROMOTION

Nearly everyone in the modern world is influenced to some degree by advertising and other forms of promotion. Organizations in both the private and public sectors have learned that the ability to communicate effectively and efficiently with their target audiences is critical to their success. Advertising and other types of promotional messages are used to sell products and services as well as to promote causes, market political candidates, and deal with societal problems such as alcohol and drug abuse. Consumers are finding it increasingly difficult to avoid the efforts of marketers, who are constantly searching for new ways to communicate with them.

Most of the people involved in advertising and promotion will tell you that there is no more dynamic and fascinating field to either practice or study. However, they will also tell you that the field is undergoing dramatic transformations that are changing the ways marketers communicate with consumers forever. The changes are coming from all sides—clients demanding better results from their advertising and promotional dollars; lean but highly creative smaller ad agencies; sales promotion and direct-marketing firms, as well as interactive agencies, which want a larger share of the billions of dollars companies spend each year promoting their products and services; consumers who have changed the ways they respond to traditional forms of advertising; and new technologies that may reinvent the very process of advertising. We are experiencing perhaps the most dynamic and revolutionary changes of any era in the history of marketing, as well as advertising and promotion. These changes are being driven by advances in technology and developments that have led to the rapid growth of communications through interactive media, particularly the Internet, social media, and mobile devices.

Companies from outside the traditional advertising industry are rapidly changing the process of making and delivering advertising messages to consumers. Marketers are looking beyond traditional mass-media advertising to find new and more effective ways to communicate with their target audiences. They recognize there are numerous ways to reach their current and prospective customers and bring them into contact with their products and services. Many marketers view the Internet ads as a more cost-effective way to reach specific target markets and measure the results of their marketing efforts. Major changes are taking place in the way marketers are using the Internet for marketing communications, including new applications that facilitate interactive information sharing and collaboration and bilateral, as opposed to unilateral, communication. Web 2.0 developments mean that Internet users are no longer limited to the passive viewing of information and can interact with one another as well as companies and/or organizations. These applications have led to the development of social networking sites, video sharing sites, wikis, blogs, and online communities which have all experienced explosive growth. Just a few years ago Facebook, Twitter, YouTube, and LinkedIn did not even exist. Facebook now has more than 1 billion users, Twitter boasts over 500 million, and more than 4 billion videos are viewed each day on YouTube, including many of the TV commercials and other promotional videos created by marketers. Nearly every company or organization has a Facebook and Twitter page that they use to keep in constant contact with their customers and these tools, along with other types of social media, have become an integral part of most marketers' marketing communications programs. However, the increased use of the Internet and social media is only the latest in a number of fundamental changes that have been occurring in the way companies plan, develop, and execute their marketing communications programs.

For decades the advertising business was dominated by large, full-service Madison Avenue–type agencies. The advertising strategy for a national brand involved creating one or two commercials that could be run on network television, a few print ads that would run in general-interest magazines, and some sales promotion support such as coupons or premium offers. However, in today's world there are a myriad of media outlets—print, radio, cable and satellite TV, and the Internet—competing for consumers' attention. Marketers are looking beyond traditional media to find new and better ways to communicate with their customers because they no longer accept on faith the value of conventional advertising placed in traditional media. Major marketers are moving away from a reliance just on mass-media advertising and are spending more of their marketing communication budgets in specialized media that target specific markets. Companies are also spending more of their monies in other ways such as event marketing, sponsorships, cause-related promotions, and viral marketing. Advertising agencies are recognizing that they must change the way they do business.

In addition to redefining the role and nature of their advertising agencies, marketers are changing the way they communicate with consumers. They know they are operating in an environment where advertising messages are everywhere, consumers channel-surf past most commercials, and brands promoted in traditional ways often fail. New-age advertisers are redefining the notion of what an ad is and where it runs. Stealth messages are being woven into the culture and embedded into movies and TV shows or made into their own form of entertainment. Many experts argue that "branded content" is the wave of the future, and there is a growing movement to reinvent advertising and other forms of marketing communication to be more akin to entertainment. Companies are using branded entertainment as a way of reaching consumers by creating short films that can be viewed on their websites, arranging product placements, and integrating their brands into movies and television shows to promote their products and services.

A number of factors are impacting the way marketers communicate with consumers. The audiences that marketers seek, along with the media and methods for reaching them, have become increasingly fragmented. Advertising and promotional efforts have become more regionalized and targeted to specific audiences. Retailers have become larger and more powerful, forcing marketers to shift money from advertising budgets to sales promotion. Marketers often expect their promotional dollars to generate immediate sales and are demanding more accountability from their agencies. The Internet revolution is in full force, and new ways to communicate with consumers are constantly being developed. Many companies are coordinating all their communications efforts so that they can send cohesive messages to their customers. Some companies are building brands with little or no use of traditional media advertising, relying instead on digitial media. Many advertising agencies have acquired, started, or become affiliated with sales promotion, direct-marketing, interactive agencies, and public relations companies to better serve their clients' marketing communications needs. Their clients have become "media-neutral" and are asking that they consider whatever form of marketing communication works best to target market segments and build long-term reputations and short-term sales.

This text will introduce students to this fast-changing field of advertising and promotion. While advertising is its primary focus, it is more than just an introductory advertising text because there is more to most organizations' promotional programs than just advertising. The changes discussed above are leading marketers and their agencies to approach advertising and promotion from an integrated marketing communications (IMC) perspective, which calls for a "big picture" approach to planning marketing and promotion programs and coordinating the various communication functions. To understand the role of advertising and promotion in today's business world, one must recognize how a firm can use all the promotional tools to communicate with its customers.

# TO THE STUDENT: PREPARING YOU FOR THE NEW WORLD OF ADVERTISING AND PROMOTION

Some of you are taking this course to learn more about this fascinating field; many of you hope to work in advertising, digital media, or some other promotional area. The changes in the industry have profound implications for the way today's student is trained and educated. You will not be working for the same kind of communication agencies that existed a few years ago. If you work on the client side of the business, you will find that the way they approach advertising and promotion is changing dramatically.

Today's student is expected to understand all the major marketing communication tools: advertising, direct marketing, the Internet, interactive media, sales promotion, public relations, personal selling, as well as social and consumer-driven media. You will also be expected to know how to research and evaluate a company's marketing and promotional situation and how to use these various functions in developing effective communication strategies and programs. Marketers are also increasing their attention on the determination of return on investment (ROI) of various IMC tools as well as the problems companies face in attempting to make this evaluation. This book will help prepare you for these challenges.

As professors we were, of course, once students ourselves. In many ways we are perpetual students in that we are constantly striving to learn about and explain how advertising and promotion work. We share many of your interests and concerns and are often excited (and bored) by the same things. Having taught in the advertising and promotion area for a combined 50-plus years, we have developed an understanding of what makes a book in this field interesting to students. In writing this book, we have tried to remember how we felt about the various texts we used throughout the years and to incorporate the good things and minimize those we felt were of little use. We have tried not to overburden you with definitions, although we do call out those that are especially important to your understanding of the material.

We also remember that as students we were not really excited about theory. But to fully understand how integrated marketing communications works, it is necessary to establish some theoretical basis. The more you understand about how things are supposed to work, the easier it will be for you to understand why they do or do not turn out as planned.

Perhaps the question students ask most often is, How do I use this in the real world? In response we provide numerous examples of how the various theories and concepts in the text can be used in practice. A particular strength of this text is the integration of theory with practical application. Nearly every day an example of advertising and promotion in practice is reported in the media. We have used many sources, such as *Advertising Age, Adweek, The Wall Street Journal, Bloomberg Businessweek, The Economist, Fortune, Forbes, Sales & Marketing Management, Mediaweek, Promo,* and numerous online sites such as eMarketer, Mashable, MediaPost.com, and ClickZ News to find practical examples that are discussed throughout the text. We have spoken with marketing and agency personnel about the strategies and rationale behind the ads and other types of promotions we use as examples. Each chapter begins with a vignette that presents an example of an advertising or promotional campaign or other interesting insights. Every chapter also contains several **IMC Perspectives** that present in-depth discussions of particular issues related to the chapter material and show how companies are using integrated marketing communications. **Global Perspectives** are presented throughout the text in recognition of the increasing importance of international marketing and the challenges of advertising and promotion and the role they play in the marketing programs of multinational marketers. **Ethical Perspectives** focus attention on important social issues and show how advertisers must take ethical considerations into account when planning and implementing advertising and promotional programs. **Digital and Social Media Perspectives** focus on how changes and/or advances in the use of social media are impacting the field of integrated marketing communications.

Each chapter features beautiful four-color illustrations showing examples from many of the most current and best-integrated marketing communication campaigns being used around the world. We have included more than 350 advertisements and examples of numerous other types of promotion, all of which were carefully chosen to illustrate a particular idea, theory, or practical application. Please take time to read the opening vignettes to each chapter, the IMC, Global, Ethical, and Digital and Social Media Perspectives, and study the diverse ads and illustrations. We think they will stimulate your interest and relate to your daily life as a consumer and a target of advertising and promotion.

## TO THE INSTRUCTOR: A TEXT THAT REFLECTS THE CHANGES IN THE WORLD OF ADVERTISING AND PROMOTION

Our major goal in writing the tenth edition of *Advertising and Promotion* was to continue to provide you with the most comprehensive and current text on the market for teaching advertising and promotion from an IMC perspective. This new edition focuses on the many changes that are occurring in areas of marketing communications and how they influence advertising and promotional strategies and tactics. We have done this by continuing with the *integrated marketing communications perspective.* More and more companies are approaching advertising and promotion from an IMC perspective, coordinating the various promotional-mix elements with other marketing activities that communicate with a firm's customers. Many advertising agencies are also developing expertise in direct marketing, sales promotion, event sponsorship, the Internet, social media, and other areas so that they can meet all their clients' integrated marketing communication needs—and, of course, survive.

The text is built around an integrated marketing communications planning model and recognizes the importance of coordinating all of the promotional-mix elements to develop an effective communications program. Although media advertising is often the most visible part of a firm's promotional program, attention must also be given to direct marketing, sales promotion, public relations, interactive media, and personal selling.

This text integrates theory with planning, management, and strategy. To effectively plan, implement, and evaluate IMC programs, one must understand the overall marketing process, consumer behavior, and communications theory. We draw from the extensive research in advertising, consumer behavior, communications, marketing, sales promotion, and other fields to give students a basis for understanding the marketing communications process, how it influences consumer decision making, and how to develop promotional strategies.

While this is an introductory text, we do treat each topic in some depth. We believe the marketing and advertising student of today needs a text that provides more than just an introduction to terms and topics. The book is positioned primarily for the introductory advertising, marketing communications, or promotions course as taught in the business/marketing curriculum. It can also be used in journalism/communications courses that take an integrated marketing communications perspective. Many schools also use the text at the graduate level. In addition to its thorough coverage of advertising, this text has chapters on sales promotion, direct marketing, the Internet and social media, and publicity/public relations. These chapters stress the integration of advertising with other promotional mix elements and the need to understand their role in the overall marketing program.

## ORGANIZATION OF THIS TEXT

This book is divided into seven major parts. In Part One we examine the role of advertising and promotion in marketing and introduce the concept of integrated marketing communications. Chapter 1 provides an overview of advertising and promotion and its role in modern marketing. The concept of IMC and the factors that have led to its growth are discussed. Each of the promotional-mix elements is defined, and an IMC planning model shows the various steps in the promotional planning process. This model provides a framework for developing the integrated marketing communications program and is followed throughout the text. Chapter 2 examines the role of advertising and promotion in the overall marketing program, with attention to the various elements of the marketing mix and how they interact with advertising and promotional strategy. We have also included coverage of market segmentation and positioning in this chapter so that students can understand how these concepts fit into the overall marketing programs as well as their role in the development of an advertising and promotional program.

In Part Two we cover the promotional program situation analysis. Chapter 3 describes how firms organize for advertising and promotion and examines the role of ad agencies and other firms that provide marketing and promotional services. We discuss how ad agencies are selected, evaluated, and compensated as well as the changes occurring in the agency business. Attention is also given to other types of marketing communication organizations such as direct marketing, sales promotion, and digital interactive agencies as well as public relations firms. We also consider whether responsibility for integrating the various communication functions lies with the client or the agency. Chapter 4 covers the stages of the consumer decision-making process and both the internal psychological factors and the external factors that influence consumer behavior. The focus of this chapter is on how advertisers can use an understanding of buyer behavior to develop effective advertising and other forms of promotion.

Part Three analyzes the communication process. Chapter 5 examines various communication theories and models of how consumers respond to advertising messages and other forms of marketing communications. Chapter 6 provides a detailed discussion of source, message, and channel factors.

In Part Four we consider how firms develop goals and objectives for their integrated marketing communications programs and determine how much money to spend trying to achieve them. Chapter 7 stresses the importance of knowing what to expect from advertising and promotion, the differences between advertising and communication objectives, characteristics of good objectives, and problems in setting objectives. We have also integrated the discussion of various methods for determining and allocating the promotional budget into this chapter. These first four sections of the text provide students with a solid background in the areas of marketing, consumer behavior, communications, planning, objective setting, and budgeting. This background lays the foundation for

the next section, where we discuss the development of the integrated marketing communications program.

Part Five examines the various promotional-mix elements that form the basis of the integrated marketing communications program. Chapter 8 discusses the planning and development of the creative strategy and advertising campaign and examines the creative process. In Chapter 9 we turn our attention to ways to execute the creative strategy and some criteria for evaluating creative work. Chapters 10 through 13 cover media strategy and planning and the various advertising media. Chapter 10 introduces the key principles of media planning and strategy and examines how a media plan is developed. Chapter 11 discusses the advantages and disadvantages of the broadcast media (TV and radio) as well as issues regarding the purchase of radio and TV time and audience measurement. Chapter 12 considers the same issues for the print media (magazines and newspapers). Chapter 13 examines the role of traditional support media such as outdoor and transit advertising, advertising in movie theaters, and promotional products, as well as the tremendous increase in the use of nontraditional branded entertainment strategies such as product placements, product integration, and in-game advertising.

In Chapters 14 through 17 we continue the IMC emphasis by examining other promotional tools that are used in the integrated marketing communications process. Chapter 14 looks at direct marketing. This chapter examines the ways companies communicate directly with target customers through various media, including direct mail, infomercials, direct-response TV commercials, and e-commerce. Chapter 15 provides a detailed discussion of marketers' increasing use of digital media, including the Internet and wireless technologies, to market their products and services. We examine the increasing use of blogs, mobile, paid search, and other social and digital media strategies. We also give attention to how the Internet is used to implement various IMC activities including both Web 1.0 and 2.0 strategies, as well as mobile marketing. Chapter 16 examines the area of sales promotion, including both consumer-oriented promotions and programs targeted to the trade (retailers, wholesalers, and other intermediaries). Chapter 17 covers the role of publicity and public relations in IMC as well as corporate advertising and cause-related marketing. Basic issues regarding personal selling and its role in promotion strategy are presented in Chapter 22, which is available online in this edition.

Part Six of the text consists of Chapter 18, where we discuss ways to measure the effectiveness of various elements of the integrated marketing communications program, including methods for pretesting and posttesting advertising messages and campaigns, and examine some of the ways marketers attempt to measure the effects of social media. In Part Seven we turn our attention to special markets, topics, and perspectives that are becoming increasingly important in contemporary marketing. In Chapter 19 we examine the global marketplace and the role of advertising and other promotional-mix variables such as sales promotion, public relations, and the Internet in international marketing.

The text concludes with a discussion of the regulatory, social, and economic environments in which advertising and promotion operate. Chapter 20 examines industry self-regulation and regulation of advertising by governmental agencies such as the Federal Trade Commission, as well as rules and regulations governing sales promotion, direct marketing, and marketing on the Internet. Because advertising's role in society is constantly changing, our discussion would not be complete without a look at the criticisms frequently levied, so in Chapter 21 we consider the social, ethical, and economic aspects of advertising and promotion.

# CHAPTER FEATURES

The following features in each chapter enhance students' understanding of the material as well as their reading enjoyment.

## Learning Objectives

Learning objectives are provided at the beginning of each chapter to identify the major areas and points covered in the chapter and guide the learning effort. We also indicate where specific learning objectives are covered within the chapter and how the discussion questions are keyed to the objectives.

## Chapter Opening Vignettes

Each chapter begins with a vignette that shows the effective use of integrated marketing communications by a company or ad agency or discusses an interesting issue that is relevant to the chapter. These opening vignettes are designed to draw the students into the chapter by presenting an interesting example, development, or issue that relates to the material covered in the chapter. Companies, brands, and/or campaigns featured in the opening vignettes include social media campaigns for the Ford Fiesta automobile and the addition of a new flavor to the Mountain Dew soft drink product line; Gatorade, Volkswagen, Taco Bell, the Qatar 2022 FIFA World Cup, Tacori, and Tao Ti. Some of the chapter openers discuss current topics and issues impacting integrated marketing communications such as the rapid growth and popularity of social media; changes occurring in traditional media including television, magazines, and newspapers and how they are impacting their use by advertisers; the impact of television on college sports; public relations problems faced by companies such as Hoi Tin Tong, Abercrombie and Fitch, and the fines imposed by the FTC on several companies for the deceptive advertising of athletic toning shoes.

## IMC Perspectives

These boxed items feature in-depth discussions of interesting issues related to the chapter material and the practical application of integrated marketing communications. Each chapter contains several of these insights into the world of integrated marketing communications. Some of the companies/brands whose IMC programs are discussed in the IMC Perspectives include Nike, Siemens, Heinz, Ivory Soap, Under Armour, Facebook, and ESPN. Issues discussed in the IMC Perspectives include the changing role of account executives in advertising agencies; the role of neuroscience in studying the processing of advertising messages; changes in the measurement of viewing audiences for television commercials; how companies use the purchase funnel to manage and guide their IMC programs; the use of music to enhance the effectiveness of TV commercials; theories on why infomercials are effective; and the debate over the advertising practices of the food and beverage industries, including proposals to impose a tax on soft drinks.

## Global Perspectives

These boxed sidebars provide information similar to that in the IMC Perspectives, with a focus on international aspects of advertising and promotion. Some of the companies/brands whose international advertising programs are covered in the Global Perspectives include, Procter & Gamble, PepsiCo, and Facebook. The Global Perspectives also discuss topics such as the challenges of developing marketing communication programs in China, celebrities who appear in commercials in Japan while protecting their image in the United States, communication problems in international advertising, and developing IMC programs to reach consumers in third-world countries.

## Ethical Perspectives

These boxed items discuss the moral and/or ethical issues regarding practices engaged in by marketers and are also tied to the material presented in the particular chapter. Issues covered in the Ethical Perspectives include subliminal advertising, the battle between television networks and advertisers over tasteful advertising, issues related to native advertising, unethical practices by Internet marketers, controversies arising from the increase in advertising of hard liquor on television, and increased regulation of the marketing of tobacco products.

## Digital and Social Media Perspectives

These boxed items provide a detailed discussion of how changes and advances in digital and social media are impacting the practice of integrated marketing communications. Some of the topics and issues covered in the Digital and Social Media Perspectives include the various ways the digital revolution and developments in technology are impacting the practice of IMC; how many companies such as Nike, Procter & Gamble, and others are shifting the focus of their IMC programs away from traditional media and allocating more of their budgets to digital media; how technology and social media are changing the role of brand managers; how digital media are impacting traditional print media such as newspapers and magazines; how online magazines are using native advertising to respond to the digital disruption they are facing and attract more advertising; how many marketers are developing creative campaigns for their brands that can go viral through social media; how there is a need for a creative revolution in online marketing and advertising; how social media are being used in various areas of IMC such as sales promotion, public relations, and mobile marketing; how advertisers are using social media for developing IMC campaigns based on user-generated content; how social media are impacting the way we watch television; and how marketers are using various tools provided by companies such as Google, Facebook, Twitter, and other social media as part of their IMC programs.

## Key Terms

Important terms are highlighted in boldface throughout the text and listed at the end of each chapter with a page reference. These terms help call students' attention to important ideas, concepts, and definitions and help them review their learning progress.

## Chapter Summaries

These synopses serve as a quick review of important topics covered and a very helpful study guide.

## Discussion Questions

Questions at the end of each chapter give students an opportunity to test their understanding of the material and to apply it. These questions can also serve as a basis for class discussion or assignments. The discussion questions are also keyed to the learning objectives for the chapter.

## Four-Color Visuals

Print ads, photoboards, and other examples appear throughout the book. More than 400 ads, charts, graphs, and other types of illustrations are included in the text.

# CHANGES IN THE TENTH EDITION

We have made a number of changes in the tenth edition to make it as relevant and current as possible, as well as more interesting to students:

- **Updated Coverage of the Emerging Field of Integrated Marketing Communications** The tenth edition continues to place a strong emphasis on

studying advertising and promotion from an integrated marketing communications perspective. We examine contemporary perspectives of integrated marketing communications that have been developed by those doing research and theory development in the area. We also consider developments that are impacting the way marketers communicate with consumers, particularly through the use of digital and social media. Innovative social media–based campaigns for brands such as Old Spice, Mountain Dew, and the Ford Fiesta, which rely heavily on user-generated content, are featured, and attention is given throughout this edition to ways marketers are utilizing Facebook, Twitter, and other tools. Technologies such as the convergence of television, computers, mobile devices, and the Internet are changing the way companies are using advertising along with other marketing tools to communicate with their customers. In this new edition we examine how these cutting-edge developments are impacting the IMC program of marketers.

- **Updated Chapter on Digital and Social Media** The tenth edition includes up-to-date information on the Internet and other forms of interactive media and how they are being used by marketers. The Internet chapter has been revised to reflect the impact of developments related to Web 2.0 while updating information regarding Web 1.0 from the last edition. We discuss the use of various Web 2.0 tools that facilitate interactive information sharing and collaboration, including social media (Twitter, Facebook, Google+, and LinkedIn) and user-generated content, including videos (YouTube), blogs, and podcasts. Specific examples of how companies are using these tools in their IMC programs are provided. We discuss a number of Internet-based tools and strategies used by marketers, including paid search, behavioral targeting, RSS, and the use of mobile media. This chapter discusses the latest developments in areas such as audience measurement and methods for determining the effectiveness of Internet advertising. Discussion of the emerging role of digital and social media as an important integrated marketing communications tool and of the ways it is being used by marketers is integrated throughout the tenth edition.

- **Digital and Social Media Perspectives—New to This Edition** In this edition we are introducing a new feature called *Digital and Social Media Perspectives*. These boxed items are designed to focus attention on changes and advances in digital and social media and how they are impacting the practice of integrated marketing communications. There have been significant advances in technology over the past decade and most consumers now have a third screen in their lives either in the form of some type of mobile device such as a smartphone or a tablet such an iPad or

Android-based product. Mobile devices have become an integral part of the lives of many consumers, and traditional media such as magazines and newspapers are developing digital versions of their publications to retain readers as well as to survive. For most marketers, social media tools such as Facebook and Twitter have become a basic part of their IMC programs. Facebook now has over a billion registered users around the world while Twitter has more than 500 million. The purpose of the new digital and social media perspectives is to provide students with insight into how advances in digital technology are impacting the strategy and implementation of IMC programs. Many of these perspectives also discuss how companies and brands are using social media to communicate with consumers, often at the expense of traditional print media.

- **New Chapter Opening Vignettes** *All* of the chapter opening vignettes in the tenth edition are new and were chosen for their currency and relevance to students. They demonstrate how various companies and advertising agencies use advertising and other IMC tools. They also provide interesting insights into some of the current trends and developments that are taking place in the advertising world.
- **New and Updated IMC Perspectives** All of the boxed items focusing on specific examples of how companies and their communications agencies are using integrated marketing communications are new or updated, and they provide insight into many of the most current and popular advertising and promotional campaigns being used by marketers. The IMC Perspectives also address interesting issues related to advertising, sales promotion, direct marketing, marketing on the Internet, and personal selling.
- **New and Updated Global and Ethical Perspectives** Nearly all of the boxed items focusing on global and ethical issues of advertising and promotion are new; those retained from the nineth edition have been updated. The Global Perspectives examine the role of advertising and other promotional areas in international markets. The Ethical Perspectives discuss specific issues, developments, and problems that call into question the ethics of marketers and their decisions as they develop and implement their advertising and promotional programs.
- **Contemporary Examples** The field of advertising and promotion changes very rapidly, and we continue to keep pace with it. Wherever possible we updated the statistical information presented in tables, charts, and figures throughout the text. We reviewed the most current academic and trade literature to ensure that this text reflects the most current perspectives and theories on advertising, promotion, and the rapidly

evolving area of integrated marketing communications. We also updated most of the examples and ads throughout the book. *Advertising and Promotion* continues to be the most contemporary text on the market, offering students as timely a perspective as possible.

# SUPPORT MATERIAL

A high-quality package of instructional supplements supports the ninth edition. Nearly all of the supplements have been developed by the authors to ensure their coordination with the text. We offer instructors a support package that facilitates the use of our text and enhances the learning experience of the student.

## Instructor's Manual

The instructor's manual is a valuable teaching resource that includes learning objectives, chapter and lecture outlines, answers to all end-of-chapter discussion questions, and further insights and teaching suggestions. Additional discussion questions are also presented for each chapter. These questions can be used for class discussion or as short-answer essay questions for exams.

## Manual of Tests

A test bank of more than 1,500 multiple-choice questions has been developed to accompany the text. The questions provide thorough coverage of the chapter material, including opening vignettes and IMC, Global, and Ethical Perspectives.

## Computerized Test Bank

A computerized version of the test bank is available to adopters of the text.

## Home Page

 A home page on the Internet can be found at www.mheducation.asia/olc/belch It contains downloadable supplements for instructors and a wealth of study tools for students.

## YouTube Channel

A YouTube channel has been created for the tenth edition which can be accessed at youtube.com/user/belch&belch. The YouTube channel includes a playlist for each chapter that contains links to television commercials for the various companies and brands discussed as well as videos and other material relevant to the chapter. The YouTube channel provides instructors with easy access to numerous commercials and videos that can be shown during lectures and allows students to view them as well.

## Video Supplements

A video supplement package has been developed specifically for classroom use with this text. It includes six video cases that provide a detailed examination of the IMC strategies and programs for various companies and brands. All of the videos include interviews with key executives from the various companies and/or their advertising agencies and were produced in cooperation with each company. Three new video cases have been produced for the tenth edition. The first video focuses on Taco Bell's "LIVE MÁS" IMC campaign which is designed to make the brand attractive and relevant to young, hip, and cross-cultural consumers by focusing on food as an experience and lifestyle. This video also examines Taco Bell's introduction of the Doritos Locos Tacos (DLT) which emerged as a co-branding initiative with snack food giant Frito-Lay and has been one of the most successful new product introductions in the history of the fast-food industry. The IMC program used for the launch of the Nacho Cheese and Cool Ranch versions of the DLT is covered in the video. The second new video focuses on athletic shoe and apparel company Under Armour and the IMC program developed by the company to target women. The video examines the female-focused campaign developed by Under Armour, which relies heavily on social media such as Facebook, Twitter, Pinterest, and Tumblr in addition to traditional media. It also focuses on how the company used IMC to focus on specific segments of the athletic-shoe market such as running, training, and basketball. The third new video focuses on the IMC efforts used by the Middle Eastern country of Qatar to be chosen as the host nation for the 2022 FIFA World Cup football (soccer) tournament. The video examines the strategy used by the Qatar Supreme Committee to compete against other countries for the rights to host the World Cup and the IMC program that will be used over the next eight years to promote the event to soccer fans around the globe.

The video supplement package also includes three videos produced for the ninth edition which are still very relevant. These include a video that focuses on the PunchDub IMC campaign created by the Deutsch LA advertising agency for Volkswagen of America that was created to increase awareness of Volkswagen's product line in the U.S. market. The second video focuses on the innovative social media campaign called the "Fiesta Movement" which was used by the Ford Motor Co. to introduce the new Fiesta subcompact automobile to the U.S. market. The "Fiesta Movement" was very successful and a second generation of the social media campaign was used again in 2013. The third video is for PepsiCo's Mountain Dew soft-drink brand and examines the "Dewmocracy" campaign which is another social media–driven initiative that the company used to add a new flavor of the product line for the popular soft drink. The video focuses on how collective intelligence and user-generated content from loyal Mountain Dew drinkers was used to develop the flavor, packaging, and name as well as the advertising to launch the latest addition to the brand franchise.

# MCGRAW-HILL *CONNECT*™ *MARKETING*

## Less Managing. More Teaching. Greater Learning.

McGraw-Hill *Connect*™ *Marketing* is an online assignment and assessment solution that connects students with the tools and resources they'll need to achieve success. *Connect*™ *Marketing* helps prepare students for their future by enabling faster learning, more efficient studying, and higher retention of knowledge.

## McGraw-Hill *Connect*™ *Marketing* Features

*Connect*™ *Marketing* offers a number of powerful tools and features to make managing assignments easier, so faculty can spend more time teaching. With *Connect*™ *Marketing* students can engage with their coursework anytime and anywhere, making the learning process more accessible and efficient. *Connect*™ *Marketing* offers you the features described below.

### Online Interactives

Online Interactives are engaging tools that teach students to apply key concepts in practice. These Interactives provide students with immersive, experiential learning opportunities. Students will engage in a variety of interactive scenarios to deepen critical knowledge on key course topics. They receive immediate feedback at intermediate steps throughout each exercise, as well as comprehensive feedback at the end of the assignment. All Interactives are automatically scored and entered into the instructor's gradebook.

### Student Progress Tracking

*Connect*™ *Marketing* keeps instructors informed about how each student, section, and class is performing, allowing for more productive use of lecture and office hours. The progress-tracking function enables you to:

- View scored work immediately and track individual or group performances with assignment and grade reports.
- Access an instant view of student or class performances relative to learning objectives.
- Collect data and generate reports required by many accreditation organizations, such as AACSB.

## Smart Grading

When it comes to studying, time is precious. *Connect™ Marketing* helps students learn more efficiently by providing feedback and practice material when they need it, where they need it. When it comes to teaching, your time is also precious. The grading function enables you to:

- Have assignments scored automatically, giving students immediate feedback on their work and side-by-side comparisons with correct answers.
- Access and review each response; manually change grades or leave comments for students to review.
- Reinforce classroom concepts with practice tests and instant quizzes.

## Simple Assignment Management

With *Connect™ Marketing* creating assignments is easier than ever, so you can spend more time teaching and less time managing. The assignment management function enables you to:

- Create and deliver assignments easily with selectable end-of-chapter questions and test bank items.
- Streamline lesson planning, student progress reporting, and assignment grading to make classroom management more efficient than ever.
- Go paperless with eBooks and online submission and grading of student assignments.

## Instructor Library

The *Connect™ Marketing* Instructor Library is your repository for additional resources to improve student engagement in and out of class. You can select and use any asset that enhances your lecture. The *Connect™ Marketing* Instructor Library includes:

- Instructor's Manual
- PowerPoint files
- TestBank
- Videos
- eBook

## Student Study Center

The *Connect™ Marketing* Student Study Center is the place for students to access additional resources. This center:

- Offers students quick access to lectures, practice materials, eBooks, and more.
- Provides instant practice material and study questions, easily accessible on the go.
- Gives students access to the Personalized Learning Plan described below.

## Lecture Capture via Tegrity Campus

Increase the attention paid to lecture discussion by decreasing the attention paid to note taking. For an additional charge Lecture Capture offers new ways for students to focus on the in-class discussion, knowing they can revisit important topics later. See below for further information.

## McGraw-Hill *Connect™ Plus Marketing*

McGraw-Hill reinvents the textbook learning experience for the modern student with *Connect™ Plus Marketing*. A seamless integration of an eBook and *Connect™ Marketing*, *Connect™ Plus Marketing* provides all of the *Connect™ Marketing* features plus the following:

- An integrated eBook, allowing for anytime, anywhere access to the textbook.
- Dynamic links between the problems or questions you assign to your students and the location in the eBook where that problem or question is covered.
- A powerful search function to pinpoint and connect key concepts easily.

In short, *Connect™ Marketing* offers you and your students powerful tools and features that will optimize your time and energies, enabling you to focus on course content, teaching, and student learning. *Connect™ Marketing* also offers a wealth of content resources for both instructors and students. This state-of-the-art, thoroughly tested system will support you in preparing students for the world that awaits.

For more information about Connect, go to http://connect.mheducation.com, or contact your local McGraw-Hill sales representative.

# TEGRITY CAMPUS: LECTURES 24/7

Tegrity Campus is a service that makes classtime available 24/7 by automatically capturing every lecture in a searchable format for students to review when they study and complete assignments. With a simple one-click start-and-stop process, you capture all computer screens and corresponding audio. Students can replay any part of any class with easy-to-use browser-based viewing on a PC or Mac.

Educators know that the more students can see, hear, and experience class resources, the better they learn. In fact, studies prove it. With Tegrity Campus, students quickly recall key moments by using Tegrity Campus's unique search feature. This search helps students efficiently find what they need, when they need it, across an entire semester of class recordings. Help turn all your students' study time into learning moments immediately supported by your lecture.

Lecture Capture enables you to:

- Record and distribute your lecture with a click of a button.

- Record and index PowerPoint® presentations and anything shown on your computer so it is easily searchable, frame by frame.
- Offer access to lectures anytime and anywhere by computer, iPod, or mobile device.
- Increase intent listening and class participation by easing students' concerns about note taking. Lecture Capture will make it more likely you will see students' faces, not the tops of their heads.

To learn more about Tegrity watch a 2-minute Flash demo at http://tegritycampus.mhhe.com.

# ASSURANCE OF LEARNING READY

Many educational institutions today are focused on the notion of *assurance of learning,* an important element of some accreditation standards. *Advertising and Promotion: An Integrated Marketing Communications Perspective* is designed specifically to support your assurance of learning initiatives with a simple, yet powerful solution.

Each test bank question for *Advertising and Promotion: An Integrated Marketing Communications Perspective* maps to a specific chapter learning outcome/objective listed in the text. You can use our test bank software, EZ Test and EZ Test Online, or *Connect™ Marketing* to easily query for the learning outcomes/objectives that directly relate to the learning objectives for your course. You can then use the reporting features of EZ Test to aggregate student results in a similar fashion, making the collection and presentation of assurance of learning data simple and easy.

## AACSB Statement

The McGraw-Hill Companies is a proud corporate member of AACSB International. Understanding the importance and value of AACSB accreditation, *Advertising and Promotion: An Integrated Marketing Communications Perspective,* 10e, recognizes the curricula guidelines detailed in the AACSB standards for business accreditation by connecting selected questions (in the text and/or the test bank) to the six general knowledge and skill guidelines in the AACSB standards.

The statements contained in *Advertising and Promotion: An Integrated Marketing Communications Perspective,* 10e, are provided only as a guide for the users of this textbook. The AACSB leaves content coverage and assessment within the purview of individual schools, the mission of the school, and the faculty. While *Advertising and Promotion: An Integrated Marketing Communications Perspective,* 10e, and the teaching package make no claim of any specific AACSB qualification or evaluation, we have within *Advertising and Promotion: An Integrated Marketing Communications Perspective,*

10e, labeled selected questions according to the six general knowledge and skills areas.

## Create create™

Craft your teaching resources to match the way you teach! With McGraw-Hill Create, www.mcgrawhill-create.com, you can easily rearrange chapters, combine material from other content sources, and quickly upload content you have written like your course syllabus or teaching notes. Find the content you need in Create by searching through thousands of leading McGraw-Hill textbooks. Arrange your book to fit your teaching style. Create even allows you to personalize your book's appearance by selecting the cover and adding your name, school, and course information. Order a Create book and you'll receive a complimentary print review copy in three to five business days or a complimentary electronic review copy (eComp) via e-mail in about one hour. Go to www.mcgrawhillcreate.com today and register. Experience how McGraw-Hill Create empowers you to teach *your* students *your* way.

# MCGRAW-HILL HIGHER EDUCATION AND BLACKBOARD HAVE TEAMED UP. WHAT DOES THIS MEAN FOR YOU?

- **Your life, simplified.** Now you and your students can access McGraw-Hill's Connect™ and Create™ right from within your Blackboard course—all with one single sign-on. Say goodbye to the days of logging in to multiple applications.

- **Deep integration of content and tools.** Not only do you get single sign-on with Connect™ and Create™, you also get deep integration of McGraw-Hill content and content engines right in Blackboard. Whether you're choosing a book for your course or building Connect™ assignments, all the tools you need are right where you want them—inside of Blackboard.

- **Seamless Gradebooks.** Are you tired of keeping multiple gradebooks and manually synchronizing grades into Blackboard? We thought so. When a student completes an integrated Connect™ assignment, the grade for that assignment automatically (and instantly) feeds your Blackboard grade center.

- **A solution for everyone.** Whether your institution is already using Blackboard or you just want to try Blackboard on your own, we have a solution for you. McGraw-Hill and Blackboard can now offer you easy access to industry leading technology and content, whether your campus hosts it, or we do. Be sure to ask your local McGraw-Hill representative for details.

# ACKNOWLEDGMENTS

While this tenth edition represents a tremendous amount of work on our part, it would not have become a reality without the assistance and support of many other people. Authors tend to think they have the best ideas, approach, examples, and organization for writing a great book. But we quickly learned that there is always room for our ideas to be improved on by others. A number of colleagues provided detailed, thoughtful reviews that were immensely helpful in making this a better book. We are very grateful to the following individuals who worked with us on earlier editions. They include

David Allen, *St. Joseph's University*
Craig Andrews, *Marquette University*
Subir Bandyopadhyay, *University of Ottawa*
Michael Barone, *Iowa State University*
Jerri Beggs, *Illinois State University*
Mike Behan, *Western Technical College and Viterbo University*
John Bennet, *University of Missouri*
Elizabeth Blair, *Ohio University*
Janice Blankenburg, *University of Wisconsin–Milwaukee*
Karen Bowman, *University of California–Riverside*
Kathy Boyle, *University of Maryland*
Terry Bristol, *Oklahoma State University*
Beverly Brockman, *University of Alabama*
Lauranne Buchanan, *University of Illinois*
Jeffrey Buchman, *Fashion Institute of Technology*
Roy Busby, *University of North Texas*
Christopher Cakebread, *Boston University*
Margaret C. Campbell, *University of Colorado–Boulder*
Les Carlson, *Clemson University*
Lindell Chew, *University of Missouri–St. Louis*
Catherine Cole, *University of Iowa*
Sherry Cook, *Missouri State University*
Robert Cutter, *Cleveland State University*
Richard M. Daily, *University of Texas–Arlington*
Don Dickinson, *Portland State University*
Robert H. Ducoffe, *Baruch College*
Roberta Elins, *Fashion Institute of Technology*
Nancy Ellis, *Suffolk Community College*
Robert Erffmeyer, *University of Wisconsin–Eau Claire*
John Faier, *Miami University*
Raymond Fisk, *Oklahoma State University*
Alan Fletcher, *Louisiana State University*
Marty Flynn, *Suffolk Community College*
Judy Foxman, *Southern Methodist University*
Amy Frank, *Wingate University*
Jon B. Freiden, *Florida State University*

Stefanie Garcia, *University of Central Florida*
Geoff Gordon, *University of Kentucky*
Norman Govoni, *Babson College*
Donald Grambois, *Indiana University*
Stephen Grove, *Clemson University*
Robert Gulonsen, *Washington University*
Bill Hauser, *University of Akron*
Ron Hill, *Villanova University*
JoAnn Hopper, *Western Carolina University*
Paul Jackson, *Ferris State College*
Karen James, *Louisiana State University–Shreveport*
Patricia Kennedy, *University of Nebraska*
Robert Kent, *University of Delaware*
Don Kirchner, *California State University–Northridge*
Paul Klein, *St. Thomas University*
Susan Kleine, *Arizona State University*
Patricia Knowles, *Clemson University*
Dr. Barbara Lafferty, *University of South Florida*
Dana Lanham, *University of North Carolina–Charlotte*
Clark Leavitt, *Ohio State University*
Lauren Lev, *Fashion Institute of Technology*
Aron Levin, *Northern Kentucky University*
Tina Lowry, *Rider University*
Karen Machleit, *University of Cincinnati*
Scott Mackenzie, *Indiana University*
Elizabeth Moore, *Notre Dame*
Joe Msylivec, *Central Michigan University*
Darrel Muehling, *Washington State University*
Barbara Mueller, *San Diego State University*
John H. Murphy II, *University of Texas–Austin*
Peter Noble, *Southern Methodist University*
Mandy H. Ortiz, *University of Alabama–Tuscaloosa*
Carol Osborne, *USF Tampa*
Charles Overstreet, *Oklahoma State University*
Notis Pagiavlas, *University of Texas–Arlington*
Paul Prabhaker, *DePaul University, Chicago*
William Pride, *Texas A&M University*
Astrid Proboll, *San Francisco State University*
Sanjay Putrevu, *SUNY University at Albany*
Sekar Raju, *University at Buffalo*
Joel Reedy, *University of South Florida*
Glen Reicken, *East Tennessee State University*
Scott Roberts, *Old Dominion University*
Michelle Rodriques, *University of Central Florida*
Herbert Jack Rotfield, *Auburn University*
Judith Sayre, *University of North Florida*
Allen D. Schaefer, *Missouri State University*
Carol Schibi, *State Fair Community College*
Denise D. Schoenbachler, *Northern Illinois University*

Lisa Sciulli, *Indiana University of Pennsylvania*

Andrea Scott, *Pepperdine University*

Elaine Scott, *Bluefield State College*

Eugene Secunda, *New York University*

Tanuja Singh, *Northern Illinois University*

Lois Smith, *University of Wisconsin*

Harlan Spotts, *Northeastern University*

Monique Stampleman, *Fashion Institute of Technology*

Mary Ann Stutts, *Southwest Texas State University*

James Swartz, *California State Polytechnic University*

Ric Sweeney, *University of Cincinnati*

Janice Taylor, *Miami University*

Robert Taylor, *Radford University*

Brian Tietje, *Cal State Polytechnic*

Frank Tobolski, *DePaul University*

Mike Weigold, *University of Florida–Gainesville*

John Weitzel, *Western Michigan University*

Kenneth C. Wilbur, *University of Southern California*

Roy Winegar, *Grand Valley State University*

Richard Wingerson, *Florida Atlantic University*

Terrence Witkowski, *California State University–Long Beach*

Merv H. Yeagle, *University of Maryland–College Park*

Elaine Young, *Champlain College*

Robert Young, *Northeastern University*

We are particularly grateful to the individuals who provided constructive comments on how to make this edition better:

Lisa Abendroth, University of Saint Thomas; Natalie Adkins, Creighton University–Omaha; Bruce Alford, Louisiana Tech University; Neil Alperstein, Loyola University Maryland; Sheila Baiers, Kalamazoo Valley Community College; Allen Bargfrede, Berklee College of Music; Elizabeth Blair, Ohio University–Athens; Janice Blankenburg, University of Wisconsin, Milwaukee; Kendrick Brunson, Liberty University; Victoria Bush, University of Mississippi; Nathaniel Calloway, University of Maryland–University College; Oscar Chilabato, Johnson & Wales University; Bob Cline, University of Iowa–Iowa City; Mary Conran, Temple University–Philadelphia; Sherry Cook, Missouri State University; Kevin Cumiskey, Oklahoma State U–Stillwater; Andrew Czaplewski, University of Colorado, Colorado Springs; Terri Faraone, Mt. San Antonio College; Theresa Flaherty, James Madison University; Debora Grossman, Suny Buffalo; Charles Gulas, Wright State University–Dayton; Holly Hapke, University of Kentucky–Lexington; Diana Haytko, Florida Gulf Coast University; Yi He, California State University East Bay; Amanda Helm, University of Wisconsin, Whitewater; Christopher Joiner, George Mason University; Leslie Kendrick, Johns Hopkins University; David Koehler, University of Illinois–Chicago; Gary Kritz, Seton Hall University; Ivy Kutlu, Old Dominion University; Barbara Lafferty, University of South Florida–Tampa; Ron Lennon, Barry University; Aron Levin, Northern Kentucky University; Stacey Massey, Texas A & M University; George Meier, University of California–Irvine; Darrel Muehling, Washington State University–Pullman; Mark Neckes, Johnson & Wales University; Kathy O'Donnell, San Francisco State University; Kristen Regine, Johnson & Wales University; Herb Ritchell, DePaul University; Herb Rotfeld, Auburn University–Auburn; Hope Schau, University of Arizona; Eugene Secunda, New York University; James Swartz, California State Poly U–Pomona; Kevin Toomb, University North Carolina Charlotte; Mindy Treftz, Columbia College–Christian County; Lisa Troy, Texas A & M University; Deb Utter, Boston University; Jim Walker, Northwest Missouri State University; Donna Wertalik, Virginia Polytechnic Institute.

We would also like to acknowledge the cooperation we received from many people in the business, advertising, and media communities. This book contains several hundred ads, illustrations, charts, and tables that have been provided by advertisers and/or their agencies, various publications, and other advertising and industry organizations. Many individuals took time from their busy schedules to provide us with requested materials and gave us permission to use them. A special thanks to all of you.

A manuscript does not become a book without a great deal of work on the part of the publisher. Various individuals at McGraw-Hill have been involved with this project over the past several years. Our sponsoring editor on the tenth edition, Sankha Basu provided valuable guidance and was instrumental in making sure this was much more than just a token revision. A special thanks goes to Sean Pankuch, our developmental editor, for all of his efforts and for being so great to work with. Thanks also to Dana Pauley for doing a superb job of managing the production process. We also want to acknowledge the outstanding work of Jennifer Blankenship for obtaining permissions for most of the ads that appear throughout the book. Thanks to the other members of the product team, Srdj Savanovic, Jeremy Cheshareck, Janean Utley, and Debra Sylvester, for all their hard work on this edition. We also want to acknowledge Derek

Belch for his help with researching and writing many of the IMC and Digital and Social Media Perspectives boxes.

We would like to acknowledge the support we have received from the College of Business at San Diego State University. As always, a great deal of thanks goes to our families for putting up with us while we were revising this book. Once again we look forward to returning to what we think is normal. Finally, we would like to acknowledge each other for making it through this ordeal for the tenth time! Our families and friends will be happy to know that we still get along after all this—though it is definitely getting tougher and tougher and tougher. Our parents would be proud!

*George E. Belch*

*Michael A. Belch*

The publisher would like to thank the following contributors for the material they have provided for this Global Edition:

Fanny Cheung Sau Lan, *City University of Hong Kong*

Leung Wing Fai, *Chu Hai College of Higher Education*

# Your guide through the exciting world

## Why It's a Powerful Learning Tool

The tenth edition continues to provide you with the most comprehensive and current text on the market in the area of advertising and promotion from an integrated marketing communications perspective. The following features in each chapter enhance students' understanding of the material as well as their reading enjoyment.

## CHAPTER OPENERS

**Learning Objectives** are provided at the beginning of each chapter to identify the major areas and points covered in the chapter and guide the learning effort. Each chapter also begins with a **Chapter Opening Vignette** that shows the effective use of integrated marketing communications by a company or ad agency or discusses an interesting issue that is relevant to the chapter. Some of the companies and brands profiled in the opening vignettes include Volkswagen, Gatorade, Tacori, Taco Bell, Ford, Mountain Dew, and the Phoenix Coyotes.

# of advertising and promotion.

EXHIBIT 2-11
Nielsen Claritas provides
cluster profiles for marketers

## CHAPTER PEDAGOGY

**Four-Color Visuals** throughout the book consist of photoboards, commercial shots, charts, graphs, and over 400 print ads. **Key Terms** are highlighted in boldface throughout the text and listed at the end of each chapter with a page reference. **Chapter Summaries** serve as a quick review of important topics covered and as a study guide. **Discussion Questions** tagged to learning objectives at the end of each chapter give students an opportunity to test their understanding of the material and to apply it. These questions can also serve as a basis for class discussion or assignments.

# REAL-LIFE EXAMPLES

The authors have used many sources to find practical examples to use throughout the text. In addition to the integration of the strategy and rationale behind the ads and other types of promotion that are used for current examples of industry practice, there are special in-depth discussions highlighted in boxed sections. **IMC Perspectives** present in-depth discussion of particular issues related to the chapter material and show how companies are using integrated marketing communications. **Global Perspectives** are presented throughout the text in recognition of the increasing importance of international marketing and the challenges of advertising and promotion and the roles they play in the marketing programs of multinational marketers. **Ethical Perspectives** focus attention on important social issues and show how advertisers must take ethical considerations into account when planning and implementing advertising and promotional programs. **Digital and Social Media Perspectives** provide a detailed discussion of how changes and advances in technology the use of digital media are impacting the practice of integrated marketing communications.

# ONLINE LEARNING CENTER

# www.mheducation.asia/olc/belch

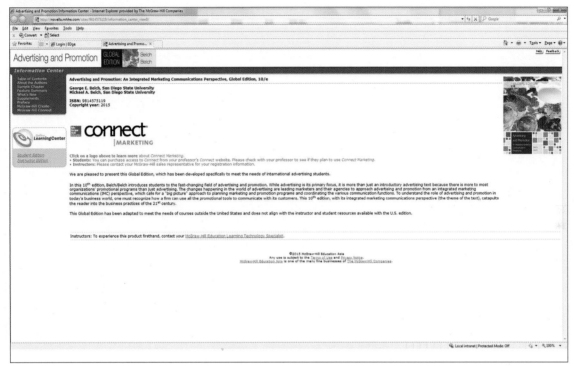

# FOR INSTRUCTORS

The resources available online for instructors include downloadable versions of the Instructor's Manual, Video Instructor's Manual, PowerPoint Presentations, Cases and case teaching notes. Instructors can access Advertising Target Practice, and the video clips through

http://connect.mheducation.com.

# FOR STUDENTS

A wealth of study tools is available for students at the site, including self-assessing quizzes, PowerPoint Presentations, and an online Campaign Planner.

# BRIEF CONTENTS

# DETAILED CONTENTS

**Part One**         Introduction to Integrated Marketing Communications

## Part Three

## Analyzing the Communication Process

Part Four Objectives and Budgeting for Integrated Marketing
Communications Programs

Part Five Developing the Integrated Marketing
Communications Program

## 17 PUBLIC RELATIONS, PUBLICITY, AND CORPORATE ADVERTISING 577

## Part Six          Monitoring, Evaluation, and Control

## 18 MEASURING THE EFFECTIVENESS OF THE PROMOTIONAL PROGRAM 607

## Part Seven      Special Topics and Perspectives

## LEARNING OBJECTIVES

**LO1** To examine the marketing communication function and the growing importance of advertising and other promotional elements in the marketing programs of domestic and foreign companies.

**LO2** To introduce the concept of integrated marketing communications (IMC) and consider how it has evolved.

**LO3** To examine reasons for the increasing importance of the IMC perspective in planning and executing advertising and promotional programs.

**LO4** To introduce the various elements of the promotional mix and consider their roles in an IMC program.

**LO5** To examine the various types of contact points through which marketers communicate with their target audiences.

**LO6** To introduce a model of the IMC planning process and examine the steps in developing a marketing communications program.

# 1 An Introduction to Integrated Marketing Communications

## GATORADE TRANSFORMS ITSELF

In the summer of 1965, the football coach at the University of Florida met with a group of university medical researchers and asked if they could determine why so many of his players were being affected by the heat and heat-related illnesses. The research team discovered two key factors that were causing the Gator football players to wilt in the heat: The fluids and electrolytes being lost through profuse sweating were not being replaced, and the carbohydrates the players' bodies used for energy were not being replenished. The researchers then took their findings into the lab and developed a new carbohydrate-electrolyte balanced beverage formulated to replace the key components lost during rigorous athletic competition or exercise. The name for the new product came from the university's athletic teams, "the Gators." The Florida football team credited the new beverage as playing an important role in its first Orange Bowl victory over Georgia Tech in 1967. The new drink generated even more buzz in the athletic community when the Yellow Jackets' coach, Bobby Dodd, when asked why his team lost, replied, "Because we didn't have Gatorade. That was the difference."

Shortly after the Orange Bowl victory, the university medical researchers entered into an agreement with Stokely–Van Camp, a canned-food packing company, to produce and market Gatorade. In 1983, the Gatorade brand was purchased by the Quaker Oats Company and soon thereafter became the official sports drink of the National Football League (NFL)—a sponsorship it holds to this day. Gatorade's proven success on the playing field made it very popular among college and professional athletes, and the brand became the official sports drink of a number of other professional sports leagues and teams, including Major League Baseball (MLB), Major League Soccer (MLS), the National Hockey League (NHL), the National Basketball Association (NBA), the Women's National Basketball Association (WNBA), and more

than 70 Division I college teams. Gatorade also became known for its creative advertising, including the famous "Be like Mike" ads featuring NBA star Michael Jordan of the Chicago Bulls, who won six championships during the 1990s. By the start of the new millennium, Gatorade had become a global brand with sales of more than $2 billion, and in 2001 multinational food and beverage giant PepsiCo purchased the Quaker Oats Company for $13 billion. Many analysts noted that a major reason for the acquisition was PepsiCo's desire to add Gatorade to its portfolio of beverage products that include Pepsi, Mountain Dew, Tropicana, Aquafina, and other popular brands.

During the first decade of the new millennium, Gatorade continued to grow as PepsiCo pushed the brand through its massive distribution system and introduced a myriad of new flavors and package variations. Gatorade also continued to add professional athletes to its stable of high-profile endorsers, including New York Yankee star Derek Jeter, NFL quarterbacks Peyton and Eli Manning, NBA stars Dwyane Wade and Kevin Durant, tennis star Serena Williams, and track star Usain Bolt. By 2007, the sports-drink market had grown to nearly $8 billion per year in the United States alone and Gatorade controlled almost 80 percent of it. Gatorade was spending nearly 90 percent of its marketing budget on mass market TV advertising that was being targeted primarily at men between the ages of 18 to 49, including high school athletes, weekend warrior types, and others who loved the brand. However, in 2008 the sports-drink market began to crash along with the U.S. economy, and after several decades of steady growth, Gatorade saw its sales and market share decline. During this time a number of emerging products continued to be introduced to the market, such as energy bars and beverages, vitamin fortified waters, protein powders, and other supplements, giving consumers more sports nutrition choices than ever before.

Gatorade's marketing team recognized that the iconic brand was being inundated by new competitors and had started losing its relevance among its target audience (athletes aged 13–17) as more and more choices flooded the market. The team also recognized a need and opportunity to provide athletic consumers with products that meet all of their fueling needs versus concentrating on hydration alone. To respond to these challenges and provide athletes with a spectrum of sports nutrition products designed to meet their fueling needs for all phases of activity, the brand launched Gatorade Prime and Gatorade Recover as part of the G Series in 2010.

With the launch of the new products, Gatorade implemented its new, broader strategy, to achieve a number of marketing communication objectives, including driving awareness, trial and scientific understanding of its new product line among the core performance target market as well as building scientific credibility and trust among key influencers. As part of this, the brand developed the Gatorade Mobile Locker Room, which traveled to nine high schools across the country, educating the target athlete about the new products through the lens of an elite athlete experience as well as the Gatorade Performance Lab, a mobile version of the Gatorade Sports Science Institute, where relevant media could test alongside Gatorade athletes and experience firsthand how the G Series drove sports fuel innovation.

During this time, Gatorade also positioned itself at the forefront of social media and redefined the way it interacted with athletes in the digital space with the launch of "Mission Control," a room in Chicago where employees of the company and its digital and social media agencies monitor mentions of the brand on social platforms. Mission Control became an engine for engaging and gathering insights from competitive athletes, as well as those who influence them, deepening their consumer relationships and furthering the brand's understanding of athletes. Since its inception in 2010, Mission Control has resulted in thousands of conversations on Gatorade's social media platforms and helped fuel Gatorade's rapid growth in the social media space.

Since the launch of the G Series, Gatorade has continued to use traditional media advertising but reduced its dependence on mass media and focused on fully integrated marketing campaigns that utilize a variety of tools to connect with consumers, including grassroots efforts, branded entertainment, sponsorships, and social media. Most recently, a web series called "Everything to Prove" featured sports science front and center by documenting the journeys of 14 top-rated NFL rookies as they worked with the Gatorade Sports Science Institute to help maximize their performance and succeed at the professional level.

As Gatorade has continued to evolve from a sports drink company to a sports performance innovator, it has covered the market with a full spectrum of products. Understanding that athletes have very specific fueling needs, the brand has recently rebranded a line of products called Gatorade Endurance to meet the very specific fueling needs of endurance athletes. Between the G Series and Gatorade Endurance, this brand has succeeded in providing athletes with multiple innovations designed to deliver the foods, fluids, and nutrients for all phases of athletic activity.

Gatorade's ultimate goal is to move from being a big fish in the sports-drink industry to an even bigger fish in the $20 billion sports nutrition market by establishing the brand as the hub of sports fueling knowledge. Gatorade's new strategy is already paying off and has the brand on the rebound as 2011 sales increased by 9 percent and were followed by mid-single-digit growth in 2012. Throughout its nearly 50-year history, Gatorade has continually been an innovator and reinforced its leadership position. As the company transitions from a beverage giant to a sports nutrition company, Gatorade continues to be living up to its advertising tagline: "Win From Within."

Sources: Duane Stanford, "Gatorade Goes Back to the Lab," *Bloomberg Businessweek*, December 4, 2011, pp. 83–88; Jason Feifer, "How to Redefine a Flagging Brand," *Fast Company*, June 2012, pp. 102–103; Natalie Zmuda, "Inside Gatorade's Social Media 'Mission Control,'" *Advertising Age*, September 28, 2010, p. 2; Gatorade Case Study, FleishmanHillard, Consumer Marketing, Chicago, 2010.

YTC 01–01
**Gatorade**
youtube.com/10ebelch

The opening vignette illustrates how Gatorade has adapted its marketing strategy to respond to changes in the market and to better position the brand for future growth. However, it also provides an excellent example of how the roles of advertising and other forms of marketing communication are changing in the modern world of marketing. In the past, advertising was a relatively simple process as most companies relied primarily on ads run in the mass media to deliver their marketing messages to large numbers of consumers who watched television, listened to radio, and read magazines and newspapers. However, today's marketers recognize that

**EXHIBIT 1–1**
Consumers can learn about the G Series product line on the Gatorade website

**YTC 01–02**

**Gatorade—Everything to Prove**

youtube.com/10ebelch

the rapidly changing media environment is making it increasingly difficult to reach their target audiences and communicate effectively with them. The mass media are losing their viewers, listeners, and readers to the highly fragmented but more narrowly targeted digital media that allow consumers to be more actively engaged in the communication process. Consumers are no longer passive message recipients who will sit back and receive unfiltered advertising messages dictated by marketers. They want to be in more control of the content they receive from the media, and they are seeking out information, as well as entertainment, from a myriad of sources.

The various marketing communication tools used by Gatorade show how companies are using *integrated marketing communications* (IMC) to reach their target audiences. Gatorade still use utilizes traditional mass-media advertising through TV, magazines, newspapers, and banner ads to drive awareness, communicate information, and build a brand image for the Gatorade product line. It also uses these off-line channels to influence online search behavior by driving consumers to its website (www.gatorade.com), which provides detailed information about the various Gatorade products such as the G Series (Exhibit 1–1). Gatorade is also using a variety of social media tools that have become an increasingly important part of the digital marketing campaigns of many companies. The commercials created for Gatorade's advertising campaigns, as well as other videos such as the "Everything to Prove" webisodes, can be viewed on the Gatorade YouTube channel. Consumers are also encouraged to connect with Gatorade through Facebook and Twitter. The Mission Control center monitors the online conversations surrounding Gatorade, its competitors, and broader topics like sports nutrition and hydration. Gatorade uses the agency FleishmanHillard to handle its public relations efforts as well as a variety of other agencies including TBWA\CHIAT\DAY for advertising creative, OMD for advertising planning, and VML for social and digital marketing. Publicity for Gatorade and its marketing communication campaigns is generated through media relations and other public relations activities that are designed to result in feature stories in magazines and newspapers as well as online news sources. Sponsorship of world-class athletes as well as professional sports leagues such as the NFL, MLB, NBA, and NHL along with individual teams is an important part of Gatorade's marketing program. The company's sponsor partnerships also include NASCAR and major sporting events from the Super Bowl to the ING New York City Marathon. Gatorade's familiar orange coolers have been on the sidelines of major events across all sports for decades and help send a strong message regarding how its products hydrate athletes and help fuel their performance. Promotional efforts for Gatorade are extended to retail stores where point-of-purchase displays and other materials are used to encourage retailers to stock and promote its products.

Gatorade, along with thousands of other companies, recognizes that the way it communicates with consumers and other relevant audiences to promote its products and services is changing rapidly and it must keep pace by integrating a variety of communication tools into its marketing programs.

The fragmentation of mass markets, the rapid growth of the Internet and other new digital media, the emergence of global markets, economic uncertainties, and changing lifestyles and media consumption habits of consumers are all changing the way companies develop their marketing programs—particularly advertising and promotion.[1] Developing marketing communication programs that are responsive to these changes is critical to the success of every company.

# THE GROWTH OF ADVERTISING AND PROMOTION

Advertising and promotion are an integral part of our social and economic systems. In our complex society, advertising has evolved into a vital communications system for both consumers and businesses. The ability of advertising and other promotional methods to deliver carefully prepared messages to target audiences has given them a major role in the marketing programs of most organizations. Companies ranging from large multinational corporations to small retailers increasingly rely on advertising and promotion to help them market products and services. In market-based economies, consumers have learned to rely on advertising and other forms of promotion for information they can use in making purchase decisions.

In 1980, advertising and sales promotion were the dominant forms of marketing communication used by most companies, and total expenditures in the United States across the two was just over $100 billion. Media advertising accounted for $53 billion while $49 billion was spent on sales promotion techniques such as product samples, coupons, contests, sweepstakes, premiums, rebates and trade allowances, and discounts to retailers. By 2013, total advertising and nonadvertising marketing communications expenditures in the United States were estimated to be $589 billion, with $198 billion being spent on media advertising, $303 billion for consumer and trade promotion, $41 billion going to direct mail and other forms of direct marketing such as e-mail marketing, and $33 billion spent on sponsorships and experiential/event marketing.[2]

It is particularly interesting to note the amount of marketing communications dollars spent on the Internet and other types of nontraditional media. For example, nearly $21 billion was expected to be spent for online and mobile search marketing advertising in 2013 and another $4.6 billion on online social marketing. When added to the $7.5 billion spent on online display advertising (the banner ads we have become accustomed to seeing on websites) and another $2 billion on online video ads, overall Internet advertising reached an estimated $35 billion in 2013. Another new form of advertising, mobile marketing, whereby ads and promotions are sent directly to various types of mobile devices such as cell phones and smartphones, also accounted for nearly $4 billion in expenditures. Thus, while the traditional media and sales promotion still account for the majority of companies' marketing communications expenditures, more monies are being allocated to nontraditional media and the amount is expected to continue to increase rapidly, particularly for digital-originated spending. Much of the growth in marketing communications investments will come from the shift of traditional "below-the-line" promotional spending in areas such as coupon distribution, contests and sweepstakes, public relations, loyalty programs, and trade-directed marketing to digital solutions that provide marketers with more efficiency.[3]

Global marketing communications expenditures have grown as well over the past several decades. Advertising expenditures outside North America increased from $55 billion in 1980 to an estimated $365 billion in 2013.[4] While the United States still accounts for nearly a third of the world's advertising expenditures, nearly half of global ad expenditures are now occurring in Western Europe and the Asia/Pacific region followed by Latin America. After the United States, the top countries in advertising spending are Japan, China, Germany, Brazil, and the United Kingdom. Both foreign and domestic companies spend billions more on sales promotion, direct marketing, event sponsorship, and public relations as well as various forms of nontraditional media, all of which have become important components of their marketing communication programs. As is the case in the United States, Internet ad spending—which includes mobile, social, display, and search ads—is growing rapidly around the globe and is expected to increase its share of the ad market to 21 percent by 2014.[5]

Advertising and promotion spending is expected to increase over the next few years as marketers around the world recognize the value and importance of advertising and other forms of marketing communication. Integrated marketing communications play an important role in the marketing programs of companies in their efforts to communicate with and sell their products and services to consumers. To understand the role integrated marketing communications play in the marketing process, let us first examine the marketing function.

# THE ROLE OF MARKETING

Marketing has never been more important or more pervasive than it is today. Organizations ranging from large multinational corporations to small entrepreneurial companies and local businesses recognize that marketing is an important business function and plays a critical role in their ability to compete in the marketplace. For nearly two decades, the American Marketing Association (AMA), the organization that represents marketing professionals in the United States and Canada, defined marketing as *the process of planning and executing the conception, pricing, promotion, and distribution of ideas, goods, and services to create exchanges that satisfy individual and organizational objectives.*[6] This definition of marketing focused on **exchange** as a central concept in marketing and the use of the basic marketing activities to create and sustain relationships with customers.[7] For exchange to occur there must be two or more parties with something of value to one another, a desire and ability to give up that something to the other party, and a way to communicate with each other. Advertising and promotion play an important role in the exchange process by informing customers of an organization's product or service and convincing them of its ability to satisfy their needs or wants.

Not all marketing transactions involve the exchange of money for a product or service. Nonprofit organizations such as various causes, charities, religious groups, the arts, and colleges and universities (probably including the one you are attending) receive millions of dollars in donations every year. Many nonprofit organizations used ads to solicit contributions from the public such as the one shown in Exhibit 1–2 which asks for contributions to help victims of Superstorm Sandy, which hit the Mid-Atlantic and Northeast regions of the United States in late October 2012. Donors generally do not receive any material benefits for their contributions; they donate in exchange for intangible social and psychological satisfactions such as feelings of goodwill and altruism.

**EXHIBIT 1–2**
Nonprofit organizations use advertising to solicit contributions and support

**Please donate to American Red Cross Disaster Relief**

Survivors of disasters urgently need your help. With your support, the American Red Cross is providing warm meals, shelter and hope to families when they need it most.

Donate today at redcross.org or call 1-800-RED CROSS

While many still view exchange as the core phenomenon or domain for study in marketing, there is also agreement among most academicians and practitioners that the discipline is rapidly changing. To reflect these changes, the AMA adopted a revised definition of **marketing** in 2007, which is as follows:

> Marketing is the activity, set of institutions, and processes for creating, communicating, delivering and exchanging offerings that have value for customers, clients, partners, and society at large.[8]

This revised definition is viewed as being more reflective of the role of nonmarketers to the marketing process. It also recognizes the important role marketing plays in the process of creating, communicating, and delivering value to customers, as well as society at large. Today, most markets are seeking more than just a one-time exchange or transaction with customers. The focus of market-driven companies is on developing and sustaining *relationships* with their customers. Successful companies recognize that creating, communicating, and delivering *value* to their customers is extremely important. **Value** is the customer's perception of all of the benefits of a product or service weighed against all the costs of acquiring and consuming it.[9] Benefits can be functional (the performance of the product), experiential (what it feels like to use the product), and/or psychological (feelings such as self-esteem or status that result from owning a particular brand). Costs include the money paid for the product or service as well as other factors such as acquiring information about the product/service, making the purchase, learning how to use it, maintaining the product, and disposing of it.

## The Marketing Mix

Marketing facilitates the exchange process and the development of relationships by carefully examining the needs and wants of consumers, developing a product or service that satisfies these needs, offering it at a certain price, making it available through a particular place or channel of distribution, and developing a program of promotion or communication to create awareness and interest. These four Ps—product, price, place (distribution), and promotion—are elements of the **marketing mix**. The basic task of marketing is combining these four elements into a marketing program to facilitate the potential for exchange with consumers in the marketplace.

The proper marketing mix does not just happen. Marketers must be knowledgeable about the issues and options involved in each element of the mix. They must also be aware of how these elements can be combined to form an effective marketing program that delivers value to consumers. The market must be analyzed through consumer research, and the resulting information must be used to develop an overall marketing strategy and mix.

The primary focus of this book is on one element of the marketing mix: the promotional variable. However, the promotional program must be part of a viable marketing strategy and be coordinated with other marketing activities. A firm can spend large sums on advertising, sales promotion, or other forms of marketing communication, but it stands little chance of success if the product is of poor quality, is priced improperly, or does not have adequate distribution to consumers. Marketers have long recognized the importance of combining the elements of the marketing mix into a cohesive marketing strategy. Many companies also recognize the need to integrate their various marketing communications efforts, such as media advertising, direct marketing, sales promotion, Internet marketing, social media, event sponsorships, and public relations, to achieve more effective marketing communications.

# INTEGRATED MARKETING COMMUNICATIONS

For many years, the promotional function in most companies was dominated by mass-media advertising. Companies relied primarily on their advertising agencies for guidance in nearly all areas of marketing communication. Most marketers did use additional promotional and marketing communication tools, but sales promotion and direct-marketing agencies as well as package design firms were generally viewed as auxiliary services and often used on a per-project basis. Public relations agencies were used to manage the organization's publicity, image, and affairs with relevant publics on an ongoing basis but were not viewed as integral participants in the marketing communications process.

Many marketers built strong barriers around the various marketing and promotional functions and planned and managed them as separate practices, with different budgets, different views of the market, and different goals and objectives. These companies failed to recognize that the wide range of marketing and promotional tools must be coordinated to communicate effectively and present a consistent image to target markets.

## The Evolution of IMC

During the 1980s, many companies began taking a broader perspective of marketing communication and recognizing the need for a more strategic integration of their promotional tools. The decade was characterized by the rapid development of areas such as sales promotion, direct marketing, and public relations, which began challenging advertising's role as the dominant form of marketing communication. These firms began moving toward the process of **integrated marketing communications (IMC)**, which involves coordinating the various promotional elements and other marketing activities that communicate with a firm's customers.[10] As marketers embraced the concept of integrated marketing communications, they began asking their ad agencies to coordinate the use of a variety of promotional tools rather than relying primarily on media advertising. A number of companies also began to look beyond traditional advertising agencies and use other types of promotional specialists to develop and implement various components of their promotional plans.

Many agencies responded to the call for synergy among the promotional tools by acquiring PR, sales promotion, and direct-marketing companies and touting themselves as IMC agencies that offer one-stop shopping for all their clients' promotional needs.[11] Some agencies became involved in these nonadvertising areas to gain control over their clients' promotional programs and budgets and struggled to offer any real value beyond creating advertising. However, the advertising industry soon recognized that IMC was more than just a fad. Terms such as *new advertising, orchestration,* and *seamless communication* were used to describe the concept of integration.[12] A task force from the American Association of Advertising Agencies (the "4As") developed one of the first definitions of integrated marketing communications:

> a concept of marketing communications planning that recognizes the added value of a comprehensive plan that evaluates the strategic roles of a variety of communication disciplines—for example, general advertising, direct response, sales promotion, and public relations—and combines these disciplines to provide clarity, consistency, and maximum communications impact.[13]

The 4As' definition focuses on the process of using all forms of promotion to achieve maximum communication impact. However, advocates of the IMC concept argued for an even broader perspective that considers *all sources of brand or company contact* that a customer or prospect has with a product or service.[14] They noted that the process of integrated marketing communications calls for a "big-picture" approach to planning marketing and promotion programs and coordinating the various communication functions. It requires that firms develop a total marketing communications strategy that recognizes how all of a firm's marketing activities, not just promotion, communicate with its customers.

Consumers' perceptions of a company and/or its various brands are a synthesis of the bundle of messages they receive or contacts they have, such as media advertisements, price, package design, direct-marketing efforts, publicity, sales promotions, websites, point-of-purchase displays, and even the type of store where a product or service is sold. The integrated marketing communications approach seeks to have all of a company's marketing and promotional activities project a consistent, unified image to the marketplace. It calls for a centralized messaging function so that everything a company says and does communicates a common theme and positioning. For example, Montblanc uses classic design and a distinctive brand name as well as high price to position its watches as high-quality, high-status products. This upscale image is enhanced by the company's strategy of distributing its products only through boutiques, jewelry stores, and other exclusive shops, including its own stores. Notice how this image is reflected in the ad shown in Exhibit 1–3.

Many companies have adopted this broader perspective of IMC. They see it as a way to coordinate and manage their marketing communication programs to ensure that they send customers a consistent

**EXHIBIT 1–3**

Montblanc uses a variety of marketing mix elements, including price, product design, brand name, and distribution strategy, to create a high-quality, upscale image for its watches

**Montblanc TimeWalker Chronograph Automatic**
Automatic chronograph movement, 43 mm stainless steel case, sapphire crystal case back, fine silver dial.
SWISS MADE BY MONTBLANC.

MONTBLANC BOUTIQUE
800-995-4810
WWW.MONTBLANC.COM

message about the company and/or its brands. For these companies, integration represents an improvement over the traditional method of treating the various marketing and promotion elements as virtually separate activities. However, this perspective of IMC has been challenged on the basis that it focuses primarily on the tactical coordination of various communication tools with the goal of making them look and sound alike.[15] It has been criticized as an "inside-out marketing" approach that is a relatively simple matter of bundling promotional mix elements together so they have one look and speak with one voice.[16] As IMC continued to evolve, both academicians as well as practitioners recognized that a broader perspective was needed that would view the discipline from a more strategic perspective.

## A Contemporary Perspective of IMC

As marketers become more sophisticated and develop a better understanding of IMC, they are recognizing that it involves more than just coordinating the various elements of their marketing and communications programs into a "one look, one voice" approach. IMC is now recognized as a business process that helps companies identify the most appropriate and effective methods for communicating and building relationships with customers and other stakeholders. Don Schultz of Northwestern University has developed what many think is a more appropriate definition of IMC, as follows:

> Integrated marketing communication is a strategic business process used to plan, develop, execute and evaluate coordinated, measurable, persuasive brand communications programs over time with consumers, customers, prospects, employees, associates and other targeted relevant external and internal audiences. The goal is to generate both short-term financial returns and build long-term brand and shareholder value.[17]

There are several important aspects of this definition of IMC. First, it views IMC as an ongoing strategic business process rather than just tactical integration of various communication activities. It also recognizes that there are a number of relevant audiences that are an important part of the process. Externally these include customers, prospects, suppliers, investors, interest groups, and the general public. It also views internal audiences such as employees as an important part of the IMC process. Schultz also notes that this definition reflects the increasing emphasis that is being placed on the demand for accountability and measurement of the *outcomes* of marketing communication programs as well as marketing in general.

Many companies are realizing that communicating effectively with customers and other stakeholders involves more than just the tactical use of the traditional marketing communication tools. These firms, along with many advertising agencies, are embracing IMC and incorporating it into their marketing and business practices. It is true, however, that not all companies have moved beyond the stage of simply bundling promotional mix elements together and made the organization changes and investment that are needed for true integration. Moreover, some academics and practitioners have questioned whether IMC is just another "management fashion" whose influence will be transitory.[18] Critics of IMC argue that it merely reinvents and renames existing ideas and concepts and question its significance for marketing and advertising thought and practice.[19]

While the debate over the value and relevance of IMC is likely to continue, proponents of the concept far outnumber the critics. IMC is proving to be a permanent change that offers significant value to marketers in the rapidly changing communications environment they are facing in the new millennium. IMC has been described as one of the "new-generation" marketing approaches being used by companies to better focus their efforts in acquiring, retaining, and developing relationships with customers and other stakeholders.[20] We will now discuss some of the reasons for the growing importance of IMC.

# Reasons for the Growing Importance of IMC

LO 01-3

The IMC approach to marketing communications planning and strategy is being adopted by both large and small companies and has become popular among firms marketing consumer products and services as well as business-to-business marketers. There are a number of reasons why marketers are adopting the IMC approach. A fundamental reason is that they understand the value of strategically integrating the various communications functions rather than having them operate autonomously. By coordinating their marketing communications efforts, companies can avoid duplication, take advantage of synergy among promotional tools, and develop more efficient and effective marketing communications programs. Advocates of IMC argue that it is one of the easiest ways for a company to maximize the return on its investment in marketing and promotion.[21]

The move to integrated marketing also reflects an adaptation by marketers to a changing environment, particularly with respect to consumers, technology, and media consumption behavior. For decades, reaching consumers was relatively easy as marketers could run their ads in mass media (so named because they reach mass audiences) such as television, radio, magazines, and newspapers. The formula was really very simple as the mass media had a symbiotic relationship with mass marketers such as automotive firms, consumer packaged goods companies, and many others. The media companies would develop and deliver expensive, but high-quality content that would in turn attract large audiences. The marketers would pay large amounts of money to the television and radio networks and stations and/or magazine and newspaper publishers for access to the mass audiences who would receive the advertising messages that encouraged them to purchase the marketers' products and services. The advertising revenue that the media companies received would be used to produce the high-quality content which in turn would allow the media to continue to deliver the viewers, listeners, and readers that the marketers coveted.

Over the past decade, however, there have been major changes in the media landscape that are impacting the traditional mass media and the economic model that has supported them. There has been an evolution to *micromarketing* as the mass audience assembled by network television and augmented by other mass media is fragmenting at an accelerating rate.[22] Viewing audiences are moving from the traditional broadcast networks (ABC, CBS, NBC, and Fox) to more narrowly targeted programs on cable networks such as ESPN, VH1, and MTV, as well as to other forms of entertainment such as DVDs, video on demand (VOD), the Internet, and videogames. The Internet is rapidly coming of age as an important advertising medium with online versions of nearly every television station, newspaper, and magazine in the country. The Web offers marketers tremendous opportunities for targeting based on numerous dimensions. The crude banners and pop-up ads that initially defined Internet advertising are giving way to more refined formats such as paid search, which is the fastest-growing form of online advertising.

Advertisers can use the Internet in a more targeted way than traditional media. They can run their ads on websites that are narrowly targeted to consumer interests or have their ads appear on search engines such as Google, Yahoo!, and Bing which are seen when people are seeking information about a product or service. For example, Google dominates as the online search advertising marketer with its keyword-targeted advertising program called AdWords (Exhibit 1–4). Social networking sites such as Facebook, Google+, Twitter, LinkedIn, and YouTube have become pervasive on the Internet and make it possible for people to share content, opinions, insights, and experiences as well as educate one another about companies, brands, and various issues.[23]

**EXHIBIT 1–4**
Google AdWords is the most popular program for online search advertising

To respond to the media fragmentation, marketers are increasing their spending on media that are more targeted and can reach specific market segments. Many marketers are shifting more of their advertising budgets to the Internet as online ad spending is expected to increase from 18 percent of total U.S. advertising expenditures in 2012 to 23 percent in 2015. Meanwhile, traditional print advertising is expected to shrink by 1 percent annually. At this rate, Internet advertising will surpass newspaper and magazine advertising combined by 2015.[24] There appears to be no stopping the fragmentation of the consumer market as well as the proliferation of media. The success of marketing communication programs will depend on how well companies make the transition from the fading age of mass marketing to the new era of micromarketing. Most marketers are learning that it no longer makes economic sense to send an advertising message to the many in hopes of persuading the few. Digital and Social Media Perspective 1–1 discusses how integrated marketing communications have been impacted by technology in the first decade of the new millennium.

In addition to the proliferation of media and fragmentation of audiences, marketers are also facing the challenge of consumers being less responsive to traditional advertising. Many consumers are turned off by advertising and other forms of marketing communication as they are tired of being bombarded with sales messages.[25] Many consumers in generation Y, the age cohort born between 1979 and 1994 (which includes most college students), are very skeptical of traditional advertising. Having grown up in an even more media-saturated and brand-conscious world than their parents did, they respond to advertising differently and prefer to encounter marketing messages in different places and from different sources. Marketers recognize that to penetrate the skepticism and to capture the attention of the gen Ys they have to bring their messages to these people in different ways. For example, when Gatorade launched its new product line, one of the major challenges the company was facing was educating its core target audience regarding how each product is designed to meet their nutrition needs. The G Series line is targeted at 13- to 17-year-old high school performance-focused athletes, while Gatorade Endurance products are designed for and marketed to endurance athletes who are focused on longer-duration activities like marathons and triathlons. Gatorade uses advertising, such as its "Win From Within" campaign, to encourage these athletes to recognize that what they put into their bodies is just as important as what they put on them, like high performance shoes, apparel, and equipment. However, Gatorade has communicated with its target audience in other ways, such as the Gatorade Mobile Locker Room, which was a traveling locker room that made its way to high schools across the country to help young athletes understand how the G Series can meet their nutritional needs and drive their performance (Exhibit 1–5). Gatorade also educates and engages its fans on its Facebook page, which now has nearly 6 million fans and has become a place where consumers can have online conversations about sports performance and nutrition.[26]

**EXHIBIT 1–5**
Gatorade engages consumers through its Mobile Locker Room

The integrated marketing communications movement is also being driven by fundamental changes in the way companies market their products and services and an ongoing marketing revolution that is changing the rules of marketing.[27] These changes and developments are affecting everyone involved in the marketing and promotional process. Companies are recognizing that they must change the ways they market and promote their products and services. They can no longer be tied to a specific communication tool (such as media advertising); rather, they should use whatever contact methods offer the best way of delivering the message to their target audiences. Ad agencies continue to reposition themselves as offering more than just advertising expertise; they strive to convince their clients that they can manage all or any part of clients' integrated communications needs. Most agencies recognize that their future success depends on their ability to understand all areas of promotion and help their clients develop and implement integrated marketing communications programs.

## The Role of IMC in Branding

One of the major reasons for the growing importance of integrated marketing communications over the past decade is that it plays a major role in the process of developing and sustaining brand identity and equity. As branding expert Kevin Keller notes, "Building and properly managing brand equity has become a priority for companies of all sizes, in all types of industries, in all types of markets."[28] With more and more products and services competing for consideration by customers who have less and less time to make choices, well-known brands have a major competitive advantage in today's marketplace. Building and maintaining brand identity and equity require the creation of well-known brands that have favorable, strong, and unique associations in the mind of the consumer.[29] Companies recognize that brand equity is as important an asset as factories, patents, and cash because strong brands have the power to command a premium price from consumers as well as investors. Figure 1–1 shows the world's most valuable brands, as measured by Interbrand, a leading brand consultancy company.

*Brand identity* is a combination of many factors, including the name, logo, symbols, design, packaging, and performance of a product or service as well as the image or type of associations that comes to mind when consumers think about a brand. It encompasses the entire spectrum of consumers' awareness, knowledge, and image of the brand as well as the company behind it. It is the sum of all points of encounter or contact that consumers have with the brand, and it extends beyond the experience or outcome of using it. These contacts can also result from various forms of integrated marketing communications activities used by a company, including mass-media advertising, sales promotion offers, sponsorship activities at sporting or entertainment events, websites on the Internet, and direct-mail pieces such as letters, brochures, catalogs, or videos. Consumers can also have contact with or receive information about a brand in stores at the point of sale; through articles or stories they see, hear, or read in the media; or through interactions with a company representative, such as a salesperson. For many companies, mass-media advertising has long been the cornerstone of their brand-building efforts. However, companies recognize that the way consumers relate to brands is changing and they

**YTC 01–03**

Interbrand

youtube.com/10ebelch

**FIGURE 1–1**

Best Global Brands 2013 Report

| Rank | Brand | Brand Value (billions) |
|------|-------|------------------------|
| 1 | Apple | $98,316 |
| 2 | Google | 93,291 |
| 3 | Coca-Cola | 79,213 |
| 4 | IBM | 78,808 |
| 5 | Microsoft | 59,546 |
| 6 | General Electric | 46,947 |
| 7 | McDonald's | 41,992 |
| 8 | Samsung | 39,610 |
| 9 | Intel | 37,257 |
| 10 | Toyota | 30,280 |

Source: "Interbrand's Best Global Brands 2013" report is a look at financial performance of the brand, role of brand in the purchase decision process, and the brand strength. Go to www.bestglobalbrands.com for more information.

# Digital and Social Media Perspective 1–1 > > >

## The Digital Revolution Hits IMC

When the new millennium began, technology was just beginning to impact the practice of integrated marketing communications. The Internet was still constrained by technological limitations such as bandwidth problems, and most consumers were accessing the web via dial-up telephone services such as AOL, NetZero, and EarthLink. Search engines such as Google, Yahoo, and MSN were in their infancy and products such as the BlackBerry and the iPod were just being launched. In 2000 the average consumer spent less than 30 minutes online each day versus nearly four hours today. When planning a new IMC campaign for a client, advertising agencies would conceive and develop advertising primarily for mass-media channels such as television, radio, and/or print. The online component would be an add-on that played a supportive role such as providing information about a company or brand, promotional offers, or a place to watch commercials or view print ads or brochures. Many experts were still pointing to the bursting of the dot-com bubble and failure of online companies as evidence that the web was overhyped, and it would be many years before its potential would be realized.

However, by the middle of the first decade of the new millennium, the transformation of the Internet was well under way as a new version of the World Wide Web was taking shape. The term "Web 2.0" is often used to describe the changes that have taken place with the Internet which include applications that facilitate interactive information sharing and collaboration and bilateral, as opposed to unilateral, communication. On Web 2.0 sites users are not limited to the passive viewing of information and can interact with one another as well as change website content. These applications gave rise to social networking sites, video sharing sites, wikis, blogs, and online communities that have experienced explosive growth.

At the beginning of 2005, Facebook, Twitter, YouTube, Hulu, and LinkedIn did not even exist and MySpace was only a year old. However, by 2010 Facebook had more than 500 million members and just two years later in September 2012, the social media network reached the milestone of 1 billion monthly active members. In 2012 Facebook purchased Instagram, which now has over 100 million users who upload more than 5 million photos each day. Twitter was launched in July 2006 and by the end of 2012 had more than 500 million registered users who sent nearly 350 million tweets each day. YouTube was launched in 2005 by three former PayPal employees and a little more than a year later the video sharing website was purchased by Google for $1.6 billion and quickly became the world's largest video sharing website. More than 4 billion videos are viewed on YouTube every day, making it one of the most visited sites on the Internet. Companies of all sizes recognize the value of YouTube as a marketing tool and have developed YouTube brand channels as a way of engaging consumers and delivering content to them.

The digital revolution is also impacting the other major screens in consumers' lives such as their televisions, smartphones, and tablets. The number of homes with digital video recorders has increased from 3.5 million in 2003 to more than 50 million in 2013, which represents nearly half of the 115 million U.S. television households. With the penetration of digital cable and direct broadcast satellite services, the average household can now receive 135 channels, versus 61 in 2000, which has led to fragmentation of television viewing audiences. The vast majority of households watching television are now doing so on large, flat-screen, high-definition televisions (HDTVs) which have been shown to positively impact how advertising and television programming are consumed. In many homes these HDTVs are now web enabled so consumers can have movies as well as television shows streamed to their sets on Netflix or Hulu Plus. The long-predicted convergence of television has become a reality, and videogaming consoles such as Sony PlayStations, Microsoft Xboxes, and Nintendo Wiis along with Apple TV and Roku streaming devices make it possible to deliver customer-tailored content that directly competes with television programs. Television viewers of the future are likely to be doing more fast-forwarding, pausing, and searching for content with the remote-control devices or computer mouse, which means they may be watching less live television and fewer commercials. Advertisers have recognized these threats and are working on ways to integrate their marketing messages into TV shows, movies, and other forms of entertainment.

Mobile phones have also become an important part of our lives as nearly 90 percent of Americans now own a cell phone and most of us find them indispensable, as evidenced by the more than 200 billion text messages

can no longer build and maintain brand equity merely by spending large sums of money on media advertising and other forms of marketing communication. The recent recession and its lingering effects have strongly impacted consumers, not only in terms of their purchase behavior but also with respect to how they perceive companies, which is changing the way firms market their products and services to them. IMC Perspective 1–1 discusses how marketing is entering the relationship era marketing programs that can deliver messages and promotion offers directly to consumers' mobile devices and can be targeted to specific locations and consumption situations.

As we navigate our way through the second decade of the new millennium, yet another screen is becoming an important part of the lives of many consumers—the tablet computer. Electronic readers (e-readers) were the predecessor to the tablet PC, with the first products being introduced by Amazon (the Kindle) and Sony (Reader), which introduced these devices as a way of storing and reading traditional books. However, this market quickly changed when Apple introduced the iPad tablet in April 2010, and over the past three years a number of other companies have launched tablet PC models, including the Samsung Galaxy, Google Nexus, Kindle Fire, and Microsoft Surface. Twenty-five percent of American adults now own a tablet PC and their global market penetration is projected to reach a similar level over the next few years. Many magazines and newspapers have developed digital versions of their publications for tablets, which include full-screen and full-color interactive ads as well as the capability to watch commercials and other videos.

The rapid pace of technological change that is impacting the daily lives of consumers presents a major challenge to marketers who must adapt their integrated marketing communications programs or risk having them become irrelevant. Marketing and advertising consultant Avi Dan has described the challenge very well by noting that "Ten years ago a marketer needed to know maybe 100 things to be effective: some aspects of positioning, some aspects of media, some media research, some pricing and some distribution. However, now that number is in the thousands. And whereas technology used to advance incrementally, it now evolves exponentially." It is likely that the advances in technology that occurred during the first decade of the new millennium will pale in comparison to those that will occur over the next 10 years. However, marketers will have little choice but to embrace these changes and view them as an opportunity rather than a threat.

sent every month. Americans between the ages of 18 and 29 send and receive an average of 88 text messages every day, and the telephone call is becoming a dying institution among young people. Nearly half of U.S. adults now own a smartphone, with ownership being particularly high among those aged 18 to 29 (66 percent) and in households earning $75,000 or more (68 percent). When the iPhone debuted in 2007, there were no software applications (apps) available, and Android phones (which are now the most popular by market share) were not available until late 2008 when the HTC Dream was launched. By the end of 2012 there were 700,000 apps available for the Google Android operating system, equaling the number available for Apple iPhones. Many of these apps deliver media such as magazines and newspapers as well as other online content directly to mobile phones. A number of these apps are designed to facilitate the purchase process and include applications for comparison shopping, product and service reviews, or coupon delivery directly to phones. Many marketers are developing mobile

Sources: Michael D. McNiven, Dean Krugman, and Spencer F. Tinkham, "The Big Picture for Large Screen Television Viewing," *Journal of Advertising Research*, December 2012, pp. 421–32; Geoffrey A. Fowler, "Facebook: One Billion and Counting," *The Wall Street Journal*, October 4, 2012, p. B1; David Car, "A TV Schedule in the Hands of Whoever Holds the Remote," *The New York Times*, May 14, 2012, p. B3; Avi Dan, "Why Brands Should Embrace Technological Change," *Advertising Age*, January 19, 2010, www.adage.com/print?artic_id=141478.

and the need for companies to connect with consumers based on trust, transparency, engagement, and authenticity.

Marketers recognize that in the modern world of marketing there are many different opportunities and methods for *contacting* current and prospective customers to provide them with information about a company and/or brands. The challenge is to understand how to use the various IMC tools to make such contacts and deliver the branding

# IMC Perspective 1–1 > > >

## Branding Enters the Relationship Era

Consider for a moment the important role brands play in the lives of consumers. Many of us feel a sense of pride and satisfaction from owning and using Apple products such as iPhones, iPods, iPads, or MacBook computers; wearing Nike, Under Armour, or lululemon apparel when we exercise; or the experience of enjoying a cup of coffee at Starbucks. Most companies recognize that brands are one of the most valuable assets their firm possesses. While competitors may be able to duplicate their product designs and manufacturing processes, it is very difficult to duplicate the beliefs, images, and impressions that are ingrained in the mind of consumers as well as the emotions brands evoke. However, companies recognize that the ways of building strong brands are changing. Brands are becoming less about the actual product and more about how people relate to them. Consumers today demand more than just product quality or performance as many view brands as a form of self-expression.

The relationship between brands and their customers has become much more complex. One reason for this is that today's consumer knows much more about brands and the companies that make them than ever before. The value chain of companies has become increasingly visible, and consumers often select brands based on the social, economic, and environmental records and policies of the companies that make them. Cynicism about corporations remains high following the Great Recession, and many companies must continue to work hard to gain consumer trust and confidence. Companies are also finding it more difficult to control

their brand image as the Internet provides consumers with a wealth of information about their products and services that can be easily accessed and shared. They can use the Internet to make price and quality comparisons or to learn what others think about various brands as well as learn about their experiences or satisfaction with them. The pervasiveness of social media has transformed traditional word-of-mouth into viral "word-of-mouse" messages that fly around Facebook, Twitter, YouTube, or Yelp at the speed of send.

Advertising and marketing consultants Bob Garfield and Doug Levy argue that until recently we were in the *consumer era* where marketers could connect with consumers by using marketing research to determine what they wanted, developing products and services to meet their needs, and creating and delivering advertising messages to seduce, impress, entertain, and/or flatter the target audience. In this era traditional marketing and advertising tools and ideas such as market segmentation, positioning, and unique selling propositions were used to win over consumers. However, the value of many of these universal marketing practices began to be challenged nearly a decade ago with the emergence of what Garfield referred to as the "Chaos Scenario" whereby the mass audiences assembled by the television networks and augmented by other mass media began fragmenting at an accelerating rate with the emergence of online media and other technologies such as digital video recorders, video on demand, and smartphones. In addition to the hyperfragmentation of markets and breakdown of mass media and mass

message effectively and efficiently. A successful IMC program requires that marketers find the right combination of communication tools and techniques, define their role and the extent to which they can or should be used, and coordinate their use. To accomplish this, the persons responsible for the company's communication efforts must have an understanding of the IMC tools that are available and the ways they can be used.

# THE PROMOTIONAL MIX: THE TOOLS FOR IMC

**Promotion** has been defined as the coordination of all seller-initiated efforts to set up channels of information and persuasion in order to sell goods and services or promote an idea.[30] While implicit communication occurs through the various elements of the marketing mix, most of an organization's communications with the marketplace take place as part of a carefully planned and controlled promotional program. The basic tools used to accomplish an organization's communication objectives are often referred to as the **promotional mix** (Figure 1–2).

Traditionally the promotional mix has included four elements: advertising, sales promotion, publicity/public relations, and personal selling. However, in this text we view direct marketing as well as the digital/Internet active media as major promotional-mix elements that modern-day marketers use to communicate with their target markets. Each element of the promotional mix is viewed as an integrated marketing communications tool that plays a distinctive role in an IMC program. Each may take on a variety of forms. And each has certain advantages.

marketing, the marketing environment was impacted by the Great Recession, which resulted in the collapse of the housing market and implosion of financial markets. While the U.S. economy has been slowly recovering from the recession, it led many consumers to distrust the companies that were seen as responsible for causing the financial crisis, such as banks and financial services firms, as well as business as a whole.

Garfield and Levy note that marketing is now entering the *relationship era* where trust and transparency are among the most important factors consumers use to judge companies and decide whether to purchase their products and services and to become loyal to their brands. They note that the big winners in this era will be companies that are able to build sustainable relationships with consumers based on trust, honesty, transparency, engagement, and authenticity rather than those that try to do so via a clever slogan or by spending more money on advertising. David Rodgers, executive director of Columbia Business School's Center on Global Brand Leadership, notes that traditional top of the purchase funnel metrics such as awareness, opinion, and consideration are being supplanted by bottom of the funnel measures such as loyalty and advocacy. He notes that the new imperative for marketers is to get loyal customers not only to buy your product but to post comments, links, and photos on social media such as Facebook and Twitter that can generate conversations and influence other customers who are in the process of forming impressions or considering purchasing a brand. Garfield and Levy note that companies such as Apple, Amazon, Costco, and USAA Insurance can spend less money on advertising and promotion because they have such strong relationships with their customers.

Consumers' passion for brands shows no sign of waning and in fact may be getting stronger. However, marketers must recognize that the ways they connect consumers to

| THE OLD WAY<br>CONSUMER ERA | ADVERTISING | THE WINNING WAY<br>RELATIONSHIP ERA |
|---|---|---|
| Sell more | OBJECTIVE | Build sustainable relationships (sell more and increase trust) |
| Interrupt and persuade people | STRATEGY | Engage people |
| What the brand does | STARTS WITH | Why the brand exists |
| Channels most conducive to influencing people | MEDIA | Channels most conducive to engaging people |
| Presents the brand positively | CONTENT | Presents the brand authentically |
| Impact on transactions | SUCCESS MEASURE | Impact on both transaction and trust |

them is changing. They must learn to rely less on the advertising and promotion tools rooted in the consumer era and focus more on activities that will help them build sustainable relationships. As Anindita Mukherjee, the chief marketing officer at Frito-Lay North America, notes: "the future of marketing isn't getting people to buy your brand, but to buy *into* your brand." The chart above shows some of the major differences Garfield and Levy highlight as differences between the old consumer era and the new relationship era.

Sources: Doug Levy and Bob Garfield, "The Dawn of the Relationship Era," *Advertising Age*, January 2, 2012, pp. 1, 8–11; "From Idea to Innovation, *Fast Company*, February 2013, p. 52; Bob Garfield and Doug Levy, "How to Venn Friends and Influence People," *Advertising Age*, January 2, 2012, p. 9; Bob Garfield, *The Chaos Scenario* (Nashville, TN: Stielsta Publishing, 2009).

YTC 01–04
**Relationship era**
youtube.com/10ebelch

## Advertising

**Advertising** is defined as any paid form of nonpersonal communication about an organization, product, service, or idea by an identified sponsor.[31] The *paid* aspect of this definition reflects the fact that the space or time for an advertising message generally must be bought. An occasional exception to this is the public service announcement (PSA), whose advertising space or time is donated by the media.

The *nonpersonal* component means that advertising involves mass media (e.g., TV, radio, magazines, newspapers) that can transmit a message to large groups of individuals, often at the same time. The nonpersonal nature of advertising means that there is generally no opportunity for immediate feedback from the message recipient

**FIGURE 1–2**

Elements of the Promotional Mix

**The Promotional Mix**

| Advertising | Direct marketing | Digital/ Internet marketing | Sales promotion | Publicity/ public relations | Personal selling |

FIGURE 1–3

25 Leading Advertisers in
the United States, 2012

| Rank | Advertiser | Ad Spending (Millions) |
| --- | --- | --- |
| 1 | Procter & Gamble | 4,830 |
| 2 | General Motors Co. | 3,067 |
| 3 | Comcast Corp. | 2,981 |
| 4 | AT&T | 2,910 |
| 5 | Verizon Communications | 2,381 |
| 6 | Ford Motor Co. | 2,277 |
| 7 | L'Oreal | 2,240 |
| 8 | JPMorgan Chase & Co. | 2,087 |
| 9 | American Express Co. | 2,071 |
| 10 | Toyota Motor Corp. | 2,008 |
| 11 | Fiat (Chrysler Corp.) | 1,947 |
| 12 | Walt Disney Co. | 1,879 |
| 13 | Walmart Stores | 1,820 |
| 14 | Time Warner | 1,715 |
| 15 | Target Corp. | 1,653 |
| 16 | Johnson & Johnson | 1,650 |
| 17 | Pfizer | 1,637 |
| 18 | Bank of America Corp. | 1,615 |
| 19 | Macy's | 1,603 |
| 20 | Berkshire Hathaway | 1,576 |
| 21 | Anheuser-Busch InBev | 1,514 |
| 22 | Sears Holdings Corp. | 1,427 |
| 23 | McDonald's Corp. | 1,424 |
| 24 | Sprint Nextel Corp. | 1.400 |
| 25 | Unilever | 1,328 |

Source: "100 Leading National Advertisers," *Advertising Age*, June 24, 2013, p. 16.
Copyright ©Crain Communications 2013

(except in direct-response advertising). Therefore, before the message is sent, the advertiser must consider how the audience will interpret and respond to it.

Advertising is the best-known and most widely discussed form of promotion, probably because of its pervasiveness. It is also a very important promotional tool, particularly for companies whose products and services are targeted at mass consumer markets such as automobile manufacturers and packaged goods and drug companies. More than 200 companies spend over $100 million on advertising and promotion in the United States each year. Figure 1–3 shows the advertising expenditures of the 25 leading national advertisers.

There are several reasons why advertising is such an important part of many marketers' IMC programs. First, media advertising is still the most cost-effective way to reach large numbers of consumers with an advertising message. Television in particular is an excellent way for marketers to reach mass markets. The average television program on the four major television networks during prime time

A secret formula revealed.

**Advertising.**
The way great brands
get to be great brands.

American Advertising Federation  aaf.org

**EXHIBIT 1–6**
The American Advertising Federation promotes the value of advertising

(8:00 p.m. to 11:00 p.m.) reaches nearly 5 million households. The cost per thousand households reached on network TV during prime time in 2013 was $25.06.[32] Popular shows such as *NCIS, American Idol,* and *The Big Bang Theory* can reach between 15 and 20 million viewers each week. And while the viewing audiences for cable networks such as ESPN, CNN, and MTV are smaller than those for the major networks, their programming appeals to more specific audiences that many marketers are trying to reach. Magazines such as *Time, Sports Illustrated,* and *People* have a weekly circulation of more than 3 million and can reach more than 10 million people since there are multiple readers of each issue. Thus, for marketers who want to build or maintain brand awareness and reach mass markets with their advertising message, media advertising remains an excellent way to do so.[33]

Advertising is also a valuable tool for building company or brand equity as it is a powerful way to provide consumers with information as well as to influence their perceptions. Advertising can be used to create favorable and unique images and associations for a brand which can be very important for companies selling products or services that are difficult to differentiate on the basis of functional attributes. Brand image plays an important role in the purchase of many products and services, and advertising is still recognized as one of the best ways to build a brand. Exhibit 1–6 shows an ad from a campaign run by the American Advertising Federation promoting the value of advertising.

The nature and purpose of advertising differ from one industry to another and/or across situations. Companies selling products and services to the consumer market generally rely heavily on advertising to communicate with their target audiences, as do retailers and other local merchants. However, advertising can also be done by an industry to stimulate demand for a product category such as beef or milk. Advertising is also used extensively by companies who compete in the business and professional markets to reach current and potential customers. For example, business-to-business marketers use advertising to perform important functions such as building awareness of the company and its products, generating leads for the sales force, reassuring customers about the purchase they have made, or helping create a favorable image of the company. Exhibit 1–7 shows an ad from the campaign for the General Electric Company's ecomagination sustainability initiative, which is a companywide commitment to address global challenges such as the need for cleaner, more efficient sources of energy, reduced emissions, and abundant sources of clean water.

**EXHIBIT 1–7**
Business-to-business advertisers such as General Electric use advertising to build awareness of the company and its programs

Business-to-business advertising is targeted primarily to the customers and prospects B-to-B marketers want to reach to sell their products and services and generally appears in business and trade magazines or on business-oriented cable networks such as CNBC. However, today many products such as personal computers, smartphones, and printers along with services such as wireless Internet, phone, and cable serve both business customers and consumers. Thus, marketers sometimes develop ad campaigns that serve both markets.[34] Figure 1–4 describes the most common types of advertising.

FIGURE 1–4

Classifications of
Advertising

## ADVERTISING TO CONSUMER MARKETS

**National Advertising**
Advertising done by large companies on a nationwide basis or in most regions of the country. Most of the ads for well-known companies and brands that are seen on prime-time TV or in other major national or regional media are examples of national advertising. The goals of national advertisers are to inform or remind consumers of the company or brand and its features, benefits, advantages, or uses and to create or reinforce its image so that consumers will be predisposed to purchase it.

**Retail/Local Advertising**
Advertising done by retailers or local merchants to encourage consumers to shop at a specific store, use a local service, or patronize a particular establishment. Retail or local advertising tends to emphasize specific patronage motives such as price, hours of operation, service, atmosphere, image, or merchandise assortment. Retailers are concerned with building store traffic, so their promotions often take the form of direct-action advertising designed to produce immediate store traffic and sales.

**Primary- versus Selective-Demand Advertising**
Primary-demand advertising is designed to stimulate demand for the general product class or entire industry. Selective-demand advertising focuses on creating demand for a specific company's brands. Most advertising for products and services is concerned with stimulating selective demand and emphasizes reasons for purchasing a particular brand.

An advertiser might concentrate on stimulating primary demand when, for example, its brand dominates a market and will benefit the most from overall market growth. Primary-demand advertising is often used as part of a promotional strategy to help a new product gain market acceptance, since the challenge is to sell customers on the product concept as much as to sell a particular brand. Industry trade associations also try to stimulate primary demand for their members' products, among them cotton, milk, orange juice, pork, and beef.

## ADVERTISING TO BUSINESS AND PROFESSIONAL MARKETS

**Business-to-Business Advertising**
Advertising targeted at individuals who buy or influence the purchase of industrial goods or services for their companies. Industrial goods are products that either become a physical part of another product (raw material or component parts), are used in manufacturing other goods (machinery), or are used to help a company conduct its business (e.g., office supplies, computers). Business services such as insurance, travel services, and health care are also included in this category.

**Professional Advertising**
Advertising targeted to professionals such as doctors, lawyers, dentists, engineers, or professors to encourage them to use a company's product in their business operations. It might also be used to encourage professionals to recommend or specify the use of a company's product by end-users.

**Trade Advertising**
Advertising targeted to marketing channel members such as wholesalers, distributors, and retailers. The goal is to encourage channel members to stock, promote, and resell the manufacturer's branded products to their customers.

## Direct Marketing

One of the fastest-growing sectors of the U.S. economy is **direct marketing**, in which organizations communicate directly with target customers to generate a response and/or a transaction. Traditionally, direct marketing has not been considered an element of the promotional mix. However, because it has become such an integral part of the IMC program of many organizations and often involves separate objectives, budgets, and strategies, we view direct marketing as a component of the promotional mix.

Direct marketing is much more than direct mail and mail-order catalogs. It involves a variety of activities, including database management, direct selling, telemarketing, and direct-response ads through direct mail, the Internet, and various broadcast and print media. Some companies, such as Tupperware, Discovery Toys, and Amway, do not use any other distribution channels, relying on independent contractors to sell their products directly to consumers. Companies such as L.L. Bean, Lands' End, and J. Crew have been very successful in using direct marketing to sell their clothing products. Dell became a market leader in the computer industry by selling a full line of personal computers through direct marketing.

One of the major tools of direct marketing is **direct-response advertising**, whereby a product is promoted through an ad that encourages the consumer to purchase directly from the manufacturer. Traditionally, direct mail has been the primary medium for direct-response advertising, although television, magazines, and the Internet have become increasingly important media. Direct-response advertising and other forms of direct marketing have become very popular over the past two decades, owing primarily to changing lifestyles, particularly the increase in two-income households. This has meant more discretionary income but less time for in-store shopping. The availability of credit cards and toll-free phone numbers has also facilitated the purchase of products from direct-response ads. More recently, the rapid growth of the Internet is fueling the growth of direct marketing. The convenience of shopping through catalogs or on a company's website and placing orders by phone or online has become very appealing to many consumers, and marketers recognize that this can be an effective way to augment their sales through traditional retail channels. For example, Under Armour, the leading company in the performance apparel market, generates a significant amount of sales through its website in addition to selling its products through sports retail stores (Exhibit 1–8).

Direct-marketing tools and techniques are also being used by companies that distribute their products through traditional distribution channels or have their own sales force. Direct marketing plays a big role in the integrated marketing communications programs of consumer-product companies and business-to-business marketers. They use telemarketing to call customers directly and attempt to sell them products and services or qualify them as sales leads. Marketers also send out direct-mail pieces ranging from simple letters and flyers to detailed brochures, catalogs, and DVDs to give potential customers information about their products or services. Direct-marketing techniques are also used to distribute product samples.

Many companies now have extensive databases containing customer names, mail and e-mail addresses; geographic, demographic, and psychographic profiles; purchase patterns, media preferences, credit, and other financial information; and other relevant customer characteristics. Marketers use this information to target their current and prospective customers through a variety of direct-marketing methods such as direct mail, e-mail marketing, telemarketing, and others. These databases are an integral part of companies' customer relationship management (CRM) programs, which involve the systematic tracking of customer preferences and behaviors and modifying a product or service to meet individual needs and wants.[35]

**EXHIBIT 1–8**

Under Armour sells its products online as well as through retail channels

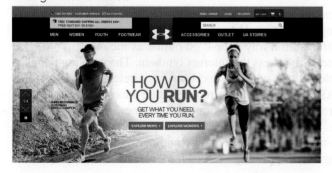

## Digital/Internet Marketing

Over the past decade or so we have been experiencing perhaps the most dynamic and revolutionary changes of an era in the history of marketing and integrated marketing communications in particular. These changes are being driven by advances in technology and developments that have led to the dramatic growth of communication through interactive, digital media, particularly via the Internet. **Interactive media** allow for a two-way flow of communication whereby users can participate in and modify the form and content of the information they receive in real time. Unlike other forms of marketing communication—such as traditional media advertising—that are one-way in nature, the new interactive media allow users to perform a variety of activities such as receive, alter, and share information and images; make inquiries; respond to questions; and even make purchases online. The rapid growth of the Internet and, more recently, social media is changing the nature of how companies do business and the ways they communicate and interact with consumers. Every day more consumers around the world are gaining access to the Internet's World Wide Web of information available to users. There are now more than 2.4 billion Internet users around the world, including 245 million in the United States, where 78 percent of the households are connected to the Internet and 85 percent of these homes have broadband access.[36] Nearly all marketers are making the Internet an integral part of their marketing communications, as well as overall business strategy.

The Internet is actually a multifaceted marketing communications tool. On one hand, it is an advertising medium as many marketers pay to run display or banner ads promoting their products and services on the websites of other companies, organizations, and web publishers. Advertisers also pay Internet search engines such as Google, Microsoft's Bing, and Yahoo! to place ads in or near relevant search results based on keywords. Paid search has become the most widely used form of Internet advertising. The Internet can also be used as a marketing communication tool in its own right because it is a medium that can be used to execute all of the elements of the promotional mix. In addition to advertising on the Web, marketers offer sales promotion incentives such as coupons, contests, and sweepstakes online, and they use the Internet to conduct direct marketing, personal selling, and public relations activities more effectively and efficiently.

We are well into the second phase of the Internet revolution (often referred to as "Web 2.0"), where the focus is on collaboration and sharing among Internet users. This has given rise to the development and growth of **social media**, which refers to online means of communication and interactions among people that are used to create, share, and exchange content such as information, insights, experiences, perspectives, and even media themselves. It is estimated that over 66 percent of Americans are connected to one or more social media platforms such as Facebook, Twitter, Google+, LinkedIn, and Pinterest, and usage of them has been increasing steadily. Social media have revolutionized how companies communicate with, listen to, and learn from their customers and have become a major marketing tool for most companies. Companies and organizations are using social media as well by creating Facebook pages or Twitter accounts, or by posting advertisements and videos on YouTube and other sites.[37]

For many years consumers accessed the Internet and social media primarily through their personal computers (PCs). However, with the growth of smartphones there has been a dramatic shift in the way people go online as the majority of those who own mobile devices prefer to access the Internet on them. The growing popularity of smartphones and tablets along with the decisions of wireless carriers such as Sprint, Verizon Wireless, AT&T, and T-Mobile to open their mobile phone services to advertising and other forms of promotion has opened up a new way for marketers to connect with consumers.[38] Advertising is already pervasive on the first two screens in most consumers' lives—televisions and personal computers—and more and more ads and promotional messages are appearing on the "third screen" of mobile phones.

**Shop smarter with RedLaser**
See how we can help you shop smarter and faster.

**Buy it!**
Easy to buy! Buy directly from your phone, and our partner retailers can have your items waiting for you at a nearby store.

**Find local prices**
RedLaser knows what's nearby. When you scan with us, we'll share prices from stores right down the road.

**Avoid allergens**
RedLaser can help identify allergens! Scan a food with RedLaser, and we'll let you know about many allergens.

**Price Comparison**
RedLaser can save you money! Scan a barcode or search by voice or image), and then compare prices between thousands of online and offline retailers.

**EXHIBIT 1–9**
The RedLaser app allows shoppers to make price comparisons before making a purchase

**YTC 01–05**

**RedLaser**
youtube.com/10ebelch

Although mobile marketing and advertising is still in its nascent stage, spending in the medium is expected to reach nearly $12 billion by 2016 and to increase from 1.35 percent of U.S. media ad spending in 2012 to more than 5 percent over this period.[39]

Marketers are extremely interested in mobile marketing as messages can be delivered that are specific to a consumer's location or consumption situation.[40] One of the major factors driving the growth of this medium is the development of mobile shopping services and apps that consumers can use to make shopping more economical, efficient, productive, and fun. Services are now available that provide consumers with mobile coupons sent directly to their cell phones that can be redeemed at the point of purchase. Other mobile apps that are now available include price comparison apps such as ShopSavvy or RedLaser which allow consumers to scan a barcode and compare prices at a given location against nearby competitors or online retailers and social sourcing apps such as Fashim or Bazaarvoice that provide consumers with outside opinions and feedback on their mobile devices while making a purchase (Exhibit 1–9). Marketers are finding a number of creative ways to connect with consumers through their mobile devices by developing their own brand-specific applications as well as games, videos, and ads. For example, Starbucks has developed apps for iPhones and Android mobile devices that allow customers to pay for purchases, find Starbucks locations, look up nutritional information, and manage their Starbucks Rewards accounts.

The interactive nature of the Internet and social media is one of their major advantages. This capability enables marketers to gather valuable personal information from customers and prospects and to adjust their offers accordingly, in some cases in real time. For example, a number of companies adjust prices and display different product offers to consumers based on a variety of characteristics such as their web browsing history and location, which includes proximity to rival stores.[41] Another advantage of the Internet is that it provides marketers with the capability to more closely and precisely measure the effects of their advertising and other forms of promotion. There a number of metrics that can be generated when consumers visit websites or spend time on social media, which allow marketers to determine how consumers are responding to their campaigns, how well they are engaging them, and the return on investment they are receiving from their promotional dollars.

Companies recognize the advantages of the Internet, and many are increasing the role various forms of digital and social media play in their IMC programs. They are developing campaigns that integrate their websites, social media, and mobile marketing with other aspects of their IMC programs such as media advertising. Digital and Social Media Perspective 1–2 discusses how Nike has reduced the amount of its marketing budget allocated to traditional media advertising and is devoting more of its marketing efforts to digital media.

## Sales Promotion

The next variable in the promotional mix is **sales promotion**, which is generally defined as those marketing activities that provide extra value or incentives to the sales force, the distributors, or the ultimate consumer and can stimulate immediate sales. Sales promotion is generally broken into two major categories: consumer-oriented and trade-oriented activities.

*Consumer-oriented sales promotion* is targeted to the ultimate user of a product or service and includes couponing, sampling, premiums, rebates, contests, sweepstakes,

## Nike Goes Digital

Over the past quarter century very few companies have been able to rival the advertising creativity of Nike. For more than 20 years nearly all of the advertising for Nike was handled by Wieden + Kennedy, which began as a small agency in Portland, Oregon, and grew with the success of its largest and best-known client. W + K became known for its outstanding creative work for Nike and created numerous memorable and iconic commercials and print ads. The Nike ethos of pure, brash performance was captured in the "Just do it" slogan which became a catchphrase for the sports world and was personified in ads featuring sports stars such as Michael Jordan, Bo Jackson, Tiger Woods, Maria Sharapova, and many other star athletes. W + K's outstanding creative work for Nike earned the agency a myriad of creative awards and also resulted in a number of the companies' campaigns being honored as among the best in the world.

Nike's creative advertising has played a major role in the success of the company as its sales reached $24 billion in 2012, making it the world's largest sports company, nearly 30 percent bigger than its closest rival adidas. And while Nike has established itself as the preeminent global sports brand through the innovation, design, and style of its products, the company continues to change the way it communicates with consumers. Although media advertising has been a critical component of its success over the past three decades, Nike has reduced its spending on traditional media such as television and print, even though its total marketing budget has increased. So why has Nike been abandoning the very media advertising that helped make the company what it is today? The reason is really simple: Nike is going where its

core customers—teenagers, who spend more on athletic shoes and apparel than their adult counterparts—can be reached more easily: online, rather than through traditional media. Nike is worried that by not promoting its product through social channels it risks becoming, in the words of its CEO Mark Parker, "not as cool, as interesting, as relevant, or as innovative" as other upstart, competing brands such as lululemon, Under Armour, and others.

Nike's annual spending on traditional media advertising—TV, print, and radio—in the U.S. market has steadily declined over the past decade from over $200 million in 2000 to just over $100 million a decade later. Nike's spending on TV and print advertising dropped by 40 percent in just three years even as its total marketing budget rose to a record $2.4 billion. Today Nike is allocating most of its marketing budget to "nontraditional" media such as direct marketing, Internet paid search advertising, and social media. The $800 million the company spent on nontraditional advertising represents a greater percentage of its U.S. advertising budget than any other top 100 U.S. advertiser.

Nike's increased focus on the digital world began in 2005, when the company introduced Nike iD, an online store where customers could design their own shoes; within only a few years, the website had produced over $100 million in sales. Shortly thereafter, the company partnered with Apple to create Nike + , a chip-enabled device that could be put in Nike running shoes and synchronized with an iPod to capture personal exercise data that could then be uploaded to a website. The Nike + website allows users to track their runs and challenge others in the brand

and various point-of-purchase materials (Exhibit 1–10). These promotional tools encourage consumers to make an immediate purchase and thus can stimulate short-term sales. *Trade-oriented sales promotion* is targeted toward marketing intermediaries such as wholesalers, distributors, and retailers. Promotional and merchandising allowances, price deals, sales contests, and trade shows are some of the promotional tools used to encourage the trade to stock and promote a company's products.

Among many consumer packaged-goods companies, sales promotion is often 60 to 70 percent of the promotional budget.[42] In recent years many companies have shifted the emphasis of their promotional strategy from advertising to sales promotion. Reasons for the increased emphasis on sales promotion include declining brand loyalty and increased consumer sensitivity to promotional deals. Another major reason is that retailers have become larger and more powerful and are demanding more trade promotion support from companies.

*Promotion* and *sales promotion* are two terms that often create confusion in the advertising and marketing fields. As noted, promotion is an element of marketing by which firms communicate with their customers; it includes all the promotional-mix elements we have just discussed. However, many marketing and advertising practitioners use the term more narrowly to refer to sales promotion activities to either consumers or the trade (retailers, wholesalers). In this book, *promotion* is used in the broader sense to refer to the various marketing communications activities of an organization.

community to distance and timed competitions. The Nike + community has grown tremendously over the past few years with the addition of new products like the Nike + GPS app, Nike + GPS Sportwatch, and Nike Fuel Band and now has more than 5 million members. Many of Nike's major digital campaigns are tied to major sporting events such as the World Cup soccer tournament or the Olympic Games. For example, W + K created the "Write the Future" campaign for the 2010 World Cup in South Africa which included an elaborately produced three-minute video that featured soccer stars such England's Wayne Rooney, Brazil's Ronaldinho, and Portugal's Ronaldo competing as alternative versions of their future flash before their eyes with every brilliant move or missed kick. Nike released the video on its Facebook page several weeks before the games began and it went viral, breaking the record for the largest audience in the first week of a campaign with 7.8 million views.

Today, Nike's digital marketing efforts include Internet ads, a YouTube channel, Facebook pages and campaigns, and Twitter-enabled billboards the size of 30-story office buildings. The shift has also changed the way in which Nike creates its marketing messages. Whereas Wieden + Kennedy used to handle the majority of Nike's U.S. marketing communications, the company's IMC efforts are now spread across multiple agencies as R/GA, AKQA, and Mindshare that specialize in social media and

new digital technologies. Nike has even created its own Nike Digital Sport division, whose goal is to develop chip-enabled customer loyalty devices and technologies similar to Nike + across all sports. The division is so secret that few Nike employees are even allowed inside the third-floor building in which it is housed on Nike's Beaverton, Oregon, campus.

Of course, Nike's new marketing efforts must translate to the bottom line and they clearly are doing so. Nike's revenues have more than doubled since 2001, including a 50 percent increase over the past five years while the stock has returned 120 percent over the same period and recently split for the sixth time since the company went public in 1980. Industry insiders agree that Nike's new approach is working because it has its finger on the pulse of what consumers are looking for and stays ahead of competitors such as adidas, Reebok, PUMA, and others. When Mark Parker took over as Nike's new CEO in 2007 he noted that the company's mass appeal, which was created through traditional media advertising, was no longer good enough. He noted the need for Nike to find new ways to forge closer and more meaningful connections to consumers through more customized, personal experiences. According to Parker, the formula for connecting with consumers used to be: "Here's some product, and here's some advertising. We hope you like it. Connecting today is a dialogue." For decades Nike's advertising message to the consumer was "Just do it." However, Nike appears to be moving on to a new world in which its consumers want to be told less and just do more.

Sources: Scott Cendrwoski, "Nike's New Marketing Mojo," *Fortune*, February 27, 2012, pp. 81–88; Michael Learmouth, "Nike Breaks Own Viral Record with World Cup Ad," *Advertising Age*, May 27, 2010, http://adage.com/print/144083; Erica Swallow, "How Nike Outruns the Social Media Competition," *Mashable*, September 22, 2011, http://mashable.com/2011/09/22/nike-social-media/; "Nike's 'Write The Future' Scores Cannes Film Grand Prix," *Advertising Age*, June 25, 2011, http://adage.com/print/228432.

YTC 01–06

**Nike**

youtube.com/10ebelch

## Publicity/Public Relations

Another important component of an organization's promotional mix is publicity/public relations.

**Publicity** **Publicity** refers to nonpersonal communications regarding an organization, product, service, or idea not directly paid for or run under identified sponsorship. It usually comes in the form of a news story, editorial, or announcement about an organization and/or its products and services. Like advertising, publicity involves nonpersonal communication to a mass audience, but unlike advertising, publicity is not directly paid for by the company. The company or organization attempts to get the media to cover or run a favorable story on a product, service, cause, or event to affect awareness, knowledge, opinions, and/or behavior. Techniques used to gain publicity include press releases, press conferences, feature articles, photographs, films, and video news releases.

An advantage of publicity over other forms of promotion is its credibility. Consumers generally tend to be less skeptical toward favorable information about a product or service when it comes from a source they perceive as unbiased. For example, the success (or failure) of a new movie is often determined by the reviews it receives from film critics, who are viewed by many moviegoers as objective

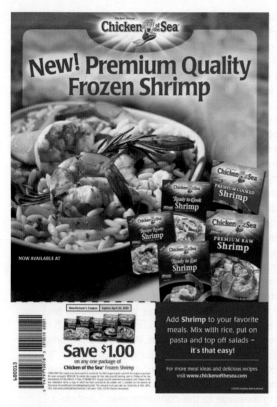

**EXHIBIT 1–10**
Coupons are a popular consumer-oriented sales promotion tool

**EXHIBIT 1–11**
Advertising is often used to enhance a company's corporate image

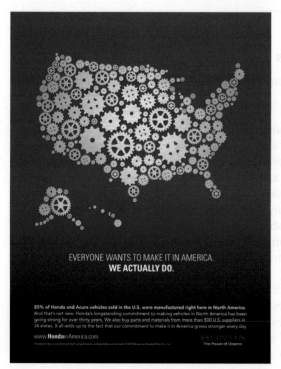

evaluators. Another advantage of publicity is its low cost, since the company is not paying for time or space in a mass medium such as TV, radio, or newspapers. While an organization may incur some costs in developing publicity items or maintaining a staff to do so, these expenses will be far less than those for the other promotional programs.

Publicity is not always under the control of an organization and is sometimes unfavorable. Negative stories about a company and/or its products can be very damaging. For example, recently the food and beverage industry has received a great deal of negative publicity regarding the nutritional value of their products as well as their marketing practices, particularly to young people. Companies such as Kraft Foods, General Mills, PepsiCo, Coca-Cola, and others have been the target of criticism by consumer activists who have argued that these companies contribute to the obesity problem in the United States by advertising unhealthy foods to children.[43] Toyota Motor Corp., the world's largest automobile manufacturer, had to deal with a tremendous amount of negative publicity in the U.S. market resulting from a problem with sticking gas pedals that were linked to a sudden-acceleration problem in some of its vehicles. The company issued a massive product recall and temporarily halted sales of eight of its top-selling vehicles.[44] Toyota had to spend a significant amount of money on advertising to address the issue and restore consumer confidence in its vehicles and also increased its sales incentives to car buyers to help regain its lost market share.[45]

**Public Relations**   It is important to recognize the distinction between publicity and public relations. When an organization systematically plans and distributes information in an attempt to control and manage its image and the nature of the publicity it receives, it is really engaging in a function known as public relations. **Public relations** is defined as "the management function which evaluates public attitudes, identifies the policies and procedures of an individual or organization with the public interest, and executes a program of action to earn public understanding and acceptance."[46] Public relations generally has a broader objective than publicity, as its purpose is to establish and maintain a positive image of the company among its various publics. Thus, it involves managing relationships with a number of important audiences, including investors, employees, suppliers, communities, and governments (federal, state, and local) as well as consumers.

Public relations uses publicity and a variety of other tools—including special publications, participation in community activities, fund-raising, sponsorship of special events, and various public affairs activities—to enhance an organization's image. Companies also use advertising as a public relations tool. For example, the ad shown in Exhibit 1–11 is part of the American Honda Motor Co.'s corporate social responsibility campaign which communicates the company's stance on important issues such as social values, human rights, working conditions, business ethics, diversity, environmental stewardship, and community involvement. The ad notes that 85 percent of Honda and Acura vehicles sold in the United States are manufactured in North America.

Traditionally, publicity and public relations have been considered more supportive than primary to the marketing and promotional process. However, many firms have begun making PR an integral part of their predetermined marketing and promotional strategies. PR firms are increasingly touting public relations as a communications tool that can take over many of the functions of conventional advertising and marketing.[47]

### Personal Selling

The final element of an organization's promotional mix is **personal selling**, a form of person-to-person communication in which a seller attempts to assist and/or persuade prospective buyers to purchase the company's product or service or to act on an idea. Unlike advertising, personal selling involves direct contact between buyer and seller, either face-to-face or through some form of telecommunications such as telephone sales. This interaction gives the marketer communication flexibility; the seller can see or hear the potential buyer's reactions and modify the message accordingly. The personal, individualized communication in personal selling allows the seller to tailor the message to the customer's specific needs or situation.

Personal selling also involves more immediate and precise feedback because the impact of the sales presentation can generally be assessed from the customer's reactions. If the feedback is unfavorable, the salesperson can modify the message. Personal-selling efforts can also be targeted to specific markets and customer types that are the best prospects for the company's product or service.

While personal selling is an important part of the promotional mix, it will not be covered in this text because it is not a direct part of the IMC program in most companies. Also, personal selling is managed separately in most organizations and is not under the control of the advertising or marketing communications manager. However, throughout the text we will address the many ways and situations in which various IMC tools such as media advertising and sales promotion must be coordinated with the personal-selling program.

# IMC INVOLVES AUDIENCE CONTACTS

The various promotional-mix elements are the major tools that marketers use to communicate with current and/or prospective customers as well as other relevant audiences. However, each of these promotional-mix tools is multifaceted as there are various types of media advertising (print, broadcast, outdoor) and sales promotion as well as ways by which marketers use the Internet (websites, social media, online advertising). Moreover, there are additional ways companies communicate with current and prospective customers that extend beyond the traditional promotional mix. Figure 1–5 provides a more extensive list of the ways by which marketers can communicate with their target audiences.

Many companies are taking an *audience contact* or *touch point* perspective in developing their IMC programs whereby they consider all of the potential ways of reaching their target audience and presenting the company or brand in a favorable manner. A **contact (or touch) point** refers to each and every opportunity the customer has to see or hear about the company and/or its brands or have an encounter or experience with it. These contacts can range from simply seeing or hearing an ad for a brand to actually having the opportunity to use or experience a brand in a retail store or interacting with the company during a sales transaction or service encounter. Tom Duncan notes that there are four basic categories of contact or touch points.[48] These are as follows:

- *Company created touch points* are planned marketing communication messages created by the company such as advertisements, websites, news/press releases, packaging, brochures and collateral material, sale promotions, and point-of-purchase displays along with other types of in-store décor. Company-created touch points account for a large part of an IMC program and have the advantage of being under the control of the marketer.

| Broadcast media (TV/radio) | Print media (newspapers, magazines) | Public relations/ publicity | Digital • Internet/ interactive • Social Media • Mobile |

| Out-of-home media | | Direct marketing |

| Personal selling | Target audience | Sales promotion |

| Point-of-purchase (displays, packaging) | Word of mouth | Events and sponsorships | • Product placements (TV and movies) • Branded entertainment |

**FIGURE 1–5**

IMC Audience Contact Tools

■ *Intrinsic touch points* are interactions that occur with a company or brand during the process of buying or using the product or service such as discussions with retail sales personnel or customer service representatives. Intrinsic touch points are often not under the direct control of the marketing department or IMC program. However, Duncan notes that marketers should make suggestions regarding ways to manage and improve these interactions with customers in order to send a positive message about the company or brand. There are also various types of intrinsic touch points that are controlled, or at least may be influenced by, the marketing or IMC manager. These include the design and functioning of the company and/or brand website, as well as the packaging, which can contain product information as well as impact the customers' experience of using a product. Marketers are also finding ways to communicate with consumers during the process of making a purchase by using some of the mobile marketing techniques discussed earlier.

■ *Unexpected touch points* are unanticipated references or information about a company or brand that a customer or prospect receives that is beyond the control of the organization. Probably the most influential type of unexpected contact is a word-of-mouth message which refers to a personal communication that comes from friends, associates, neighbors, co-workers, or family members. Unexpected messages may also come from other sources such as the media which may print or broadcast stories about a company and/or its brands, as well as experts who write about products and services. Another type of unexpected point that has become very influential is websites that provide reviews of products and services. Some of these sites provide expert reviews while others give reviews from other customers. For example, CNET is widely used by consumers looking for reviews of specific brands of consumer electronic products. TripAdvisor provides nearly 2 million travel-related reviews and opinions each year from travelers around the world. It is important to note that information received from unexpected touch points can be either positive or negative. Most of you have probably relied on reviews from Yelp for a variety of local businesses such as restaurants, bars, retail stores, and professional services. Yelp has nearly 100 million unique visitors each month, and the reviews provided on its website are a very important source of information for many consumers (Exhibit 1–12).

■ *Customer-initiated touch points* are interactions that occur whenever a customer or prospect contacts a company. Most of these contacts involve inquiries or

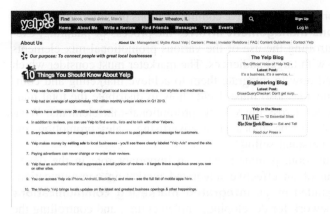

**EXHIBIT 1–12**
Reviews on Yelp are a very important source of information for consumers in selecting local businesses

complaints consumers might have regarding the use of a product or service and occur through calls made directly to the company, via e-mails, or through specific sections of websites to which customers are directed. Many of the customer-initiated contacts are handled through customer service departments, although a number of companies have in-bound telemarketing departments as part of their direct sales efforts. The manner in which marketers handle customer-initiated contacts has a major impact on their ability to attract and retain customers. Moreover, many companies try to differentiate themselves on the basis of customer service and promote their customer orientation in their advertising and other aspects of their IMC programs. They also encourage current or prospective customers to contact them by calling toll-free numbers or by putting their website addresses on packages, in ads, and in various promotional materials.

Marketers who take a contact or touch point perspective recognize that consumers' perceptions and opinions of a brand, as well as their purchase behavior, result from the information they receive and experiences and interactions they have with the company and its products or services. They also recognize that not all touch points are equally effective and they differ in regard to a company's ability to control or influence them. Figure 1–6 plots the four categories of touch points in terms of their relative impact and the marketer's ability to control them.

As can be seen in this figure, company-planned touch points are the easiest to control but are lowest in terms of impact. Marketers can control the nature and type of advertising and other forms of promotion that they send to their target audiences, but consumers often discount these messages since they receive so many of them and they recognize the persuasive intent that underlies them. At the other extreme, unexpected messages are often the most impactful but are the most difficult to control. Duncan notes than an unexpected message can be very powerful because it has the power of third-party credibility since the people who provide the information are often perceived as more believable than company sources because they have no vested interest in the success or failure of the company or brand.[49] Customer-initiated and intrinsic messages fall in between unexpected and company-created messages with respect to impact as well as the ability of the marketer to control them.

Marketers must determine how valuable each of these contact tools are for communicating with their current and prospective customers and how they can be combined to form an effective IMC program. This is generally done by starting with the target audience and determining which IMC tools will be most effective in reaching, informing, and persuading them and ultimately influencing their behavior. It is the responsibility of those involved in the marketing communications process to determine how the various contact tools will be used to reach the target audience and help achieve the company's marketing objectives. The IMC program is generally developed with specific goals and objectives in mind and is the end product of a detailed marketing and promotional planning process. We will now look at a model of the process that companies follow in developing and executing their IMC programs.

## THE IMC PLANNING PROCESS

In developing an integrated marketing communications strategy, a company combines the various promotional-mix elements, balancing the strengths

**FIGURE 1–6**

IMC Contact Points:
Control vs. Impact

LO 01-6

and weaknesses of each to produce an effective communications program. **Integrated marketing communications management** involves the process of planning, executing, evaluating, and controlling the use of the various promotional-mix elements to effectively communicate with target audiences. The marketer must consider which promotional tools to use and how to integrate them to achieve marketing and communication objectives. Companies also must decide how to distribute the total marketing communications budget across the various promotional-mix elements. What percentage of the budget should be allocated to advertising, sales promotion, the Internet, sponsorships, and personal selling?

As with any business function, planning plays an important role in the development and implementation of an effective integrated marketing communications program. This process is guided by an **integrated marketing communications plan** that provides the framework for developing, implementing, and controlling the organization's IMC program. Those involved with the IMC program must decide on the role and function of the specific elements of the promotional mix, develop strategies for each element, determine how they will be integrated, plan for their implementation, and consider how to evaluate the results achieved and make any necessary adjustments. Marketing communications is but one part of, and must be integrated into, the overall marketing plan and program.

A model of the IMC planning process is shown in Figure 1–7 on page 32. The remainder of this chapter presents a brief overview of the various steps involved in this process.

## Review of the Marketing Plan

The first step in the IMC planning process is to review the marketing plan and objectives. Before developing a promotional plan, marketers must understand where the company (or the brand) has been, its current position in the market, where it intends to go, and how it plans to get there. Most of this information should be contained in the **marketing plan**, a written document that describes the overall marketing strategy and programs developed for an organization, a particular product line, or a brand. Marketing plans can take several forms but generally include five basic elements:

1. A detailed situation analysis that consists of an internal marketing audit and review and an external analysis of the market competition and environmental factors.
2. Specific marketing objectives that provide direction, a time frame for marketing activities, and a mechanism for measuring performance.
3. A marketing strategy and program that include selection of target market(s) and decisions and plans for the four elements of the marketing mix.
4. A program for implementing the marketing strategy, including determining specific tasks to be performed and responsibilities.
5. A process for monitoring and evaluating performance and providing feedback so that proper control can be maintained and any necessary changes can be made in the overall marketing strategy or tactics.

For most firms, the promotional plan is an integral part of the marketing strategy. Thus, the promotional planners must know the roles advertising and other promotional-mix elements will play in the overall marketing program. The promotional plan is developed similarly to the marketing plan and often uses its detailed information. Promotional planners focus on information in the marketing plan that is relevant to the promotional strategy.

## Promotional Program Situation Analysis

After the overall marketing plan is reviewed, the next step in developing a promotional plan is to conduct the situation analysis. In the IMC program, the situation analysis focuses on the factors that influence or are relevant to the development of a promotional strategy. Like the overall marketing situation analysis, the promotional program situation analysis includes both an internal and an external analysis.

**Internal Analysis**   The **internal analysis** assesses relevant areas involving the product/service offering and the firm itself. The capabilities of the firm and its ability to develop and implement a successful promotional program, the organization of the promotional department, and the successes and failures of past programs should be reviewed. The analysis should study the relative advantages and disadvantages of performing the promotional functions in-house as opposed to hiring an external agency (or agencies). For example, the internal analysis may indicate the firm is not capable of planning, implementing, and managing certain areas of the promotional program. If this is the case, it would be wise to look for assistance from an advertising agency or some other promotional facilitator. If the organization is already using an ad agency, the focus will be on the quality of the agency's work and the results achieved by past and/or current campaigns.

In this text we will examine the functions ad agencies perform for their clients, the agency selection process, compensation, and considerations in evaluating agency performance. We will also discuss the role and function of other promotional facilitators such as sales promotion firms, direct-marketing companies, public relations agencies, digital/interactive agencies, and marketing and media research firms.

Another aspect of the internal analysis is assessing the strengths and weaknesses of the firm or the brand from an image perspective. Often the image a firm brings to the market will have a significant impact on the way the firm can advertise and promote itself as well as its various products and services. Companies or brands that are new to the market or those for whom perceptions are negative may have to concentrate on their images, not just the benefits or attributes of the specific product or service. On the other hand, a firm with a strong reputation and/or image is already a step ahead when it comes to marketing its products or services. For example, Starbucks has an outstanding image that is a result of the quality of its coffee and other products as well as its reputation as a socially responsible company. The company is recognized as a good citizen in its dealings with communities, employees, suppliers, and the environment. Starbucks recognizes that being recognized as a socially responsible company is an important part of its tremendous growth and success. The company publishes a Global Responsibility Annual Report each year that describes its social, environmental, and economic impacts on the communities in which it does business (Exhibit 1–13).

The internal analysis also assesses the relative strengths and weaknesses of the product or service; its advantages and disadvantages; any unique selling points or benefits it may have; its packaging, price, and design; and so on. This information is particularly important to the creative personnel who must develop the advertising message for the brand.

**YTC** 01–07

**Starbucks social responsiblity**

youtube.com/10ebelch

**EXHIBIT 1–13**

Starbucks has a very strong brand image and reputation as a socially responsible company

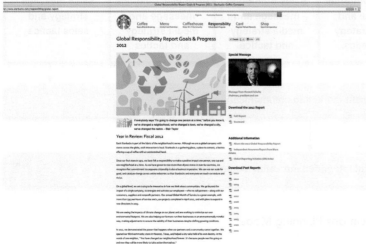

Figure 1–8 is a checklist of some of the areas one might consider when performing analyses for promotional planning purposes. Addressing internal areas may require information the company does not have available internally and must gather as part of the external analysis.

**External Analysis**   The **external analysis** focuses on factors such as characteristics of the firm's customers, market segments, positioning strategies, and competitors, as shown in Figure 1–8. An important part of the external analysis is a detailed consideration of customers' characteristics and buying patterns, their decision processes, and factors influencing their purchase decisions. Attention must also be given to consumers' perceptions and attitudes,

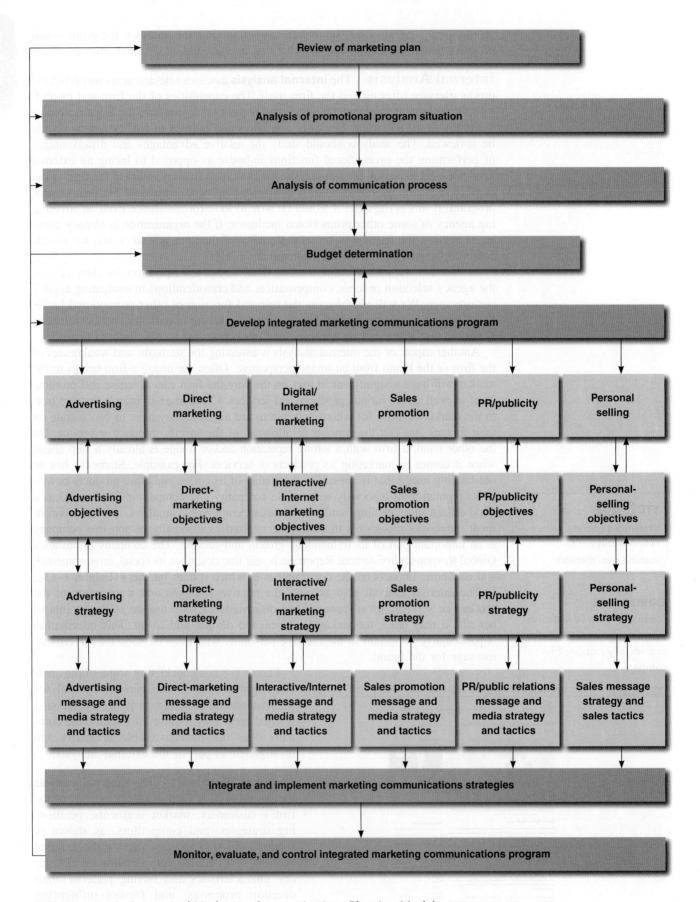

**FIGURE 1–7** An Integrated Marketing Communications Planning Model

FIGURE 1–7   (Continued)

**Review of Marketing Plan**
Examine overall marketing plan and objectives
Role of advertising and promotion
Competitive analysis
Assess environmental influences

**Analysis of Promotional Program Situation**

| Internal analysis | External analysis |
|---|---|
| Promotional department organization | Consumer behavior analysis |
| Firm's ability to implement promotional program | Market segmentation and target marketing |
| Agency evaluation and selection | Market positioning |
| Review of previous program results | |

**Analysis of Communication Process**
Analyze receiver's response processes
Analyze source, message, channel factors
Establish communication goals and objectives

**Budget Determination**
Set tentative marketing communications budget
Allocate tentative budget

**Develop Integrated Marketing Communications Program**

| Advertising | Sales promotion |
|---|---|
| Set advertising objectives | Set sales promotion objectives |
| Determine advertising budget | Determine sales promotion budget |
| Develop advertising message | Determine sales promotion tools and develop messages |
| Develop advertising media strategy | Develop sales promotion media strategy |
| Direct marketing | |
| Set direct-marketing objectives | Public relations/publicity |
| Determine direct-marketing budget | Set PR/publicity objectives |
| Develop direct-marketing message | Determine PR/publicity budget |
| Develop direct-marketing media strategy | Develop PR/publicity messages |
| | Develop PR/publicity media strategy |
| Digial/Internet marketing | Personal selling |
| Set interactive/Internet marketing objectives | Set personal-selling and sales objectives |
| Determine interactive/Internet marketing budget | Determine personal-selling/sales budget |
| Develop interactive/Internet message | Develop sales message |
| Develop interactive/Internet media strategy | Develop selling roles and responsibilities |

**Integrate and Implement Marketing Communications Strategies**
Integrate promotional-mix strategies
Create and produce ads
Purchase media time and space
Design and implement direct-marketing programs
Design and distribute sales promotion materials
Design and implement public relations/publicity programs
Design and implement digital/Internet marketing programs

**Monitor, Evaluate, and Control Integrated Marketing Communications Program**
Evaluate promotional program results/effectiveness
Take measures to control and adjust promotional strategies

| Internal Factors | External Factors |
|---|---|
| *Assessment of Firm's Promotional Organization and Capabilities* | *Customer Analysis* |
| Organization of promotional department | Who buys our product or service? |
| Capability of firm to develop and execute promotional programs | Who makes the decision to buy the product? |
| | Who influences the decision to buy the product? |
| Determination of role and function of ad agency and other promotional facilitators | How is the purchase decision made? Who assumes what role? |
| | What does the customer buy? What needs must be satisfied? |
| *Review of Firm's Previous Promotional Programs and Results* | Why do customers buy a particular brand? |
| Review previous promotional objectives | Where do they go or look to buy the product or service? |
| Review previous promotional budgets and allocations | When do they buy? Any seasonality factors? |
| | What are customers' attitudes toward our product or service? |
| Review previous promotional-mix strategies and programs | What social factors might influence the purchase decision? |
| | Do the customers' lifestyles influence their decisions? |
| Review results of previous promotional programs | How is our product or service perceived by customers? |
| *Assessment of Firm or Brand Image and Implications for Promotion* | How do demographic factors influence the purchase decision? |
| | *Competitive Analysis* |
| *Assessment of Relative Strengths and Weaknesses of Product or Service* | Who are our direct and indirect competitors? |
| | What key benefits and positioning are used by our competitors? |
| What are the strengths and weaknesses of product or service? | What is our position relative to the competition? |
| What are its key benefits? | How big are competitors' ad budgets? |
| Does it have any unique selling points? | What message and media strategies are competitors using? |
| Assessment of packaging, labeling, and brand image | *Environmental Analysis* |
| How does our product or service compare with competition? | Are there any current trends or developments that might affect the promotional program? |

**FIGURE 1–8**

Areas Covered in the Situation Analysis

lifestyles, and criteria for making purchase decisions. Often, marketing research studies are needed to answer some of these questions.

A key element of the external analysis is an assessment of the market. The attractiveness of various market segments must be evaluated and the segments to target must be identified. Once the target markets are chosen, the emphasis will be on determining how the product should be positioned. What image or place should it have in consumers' minds?

This part of the promotional program situation analysis also includes an in-depth examination of both direct and indirect competitors. While competitors were analyzed in the overall marketing situation analysis, even more attention is devoted to promotional aspects at this phase. Focus is on the firm's primary competitors: their specific strengths and weaknesses; their segmentation, targeting, and positioning strategies; and the promotional strategies they employ. The size and allocation of their promotional budgets, their media strategies, and the messages they are sending to the marketplace should all be considered.

The external phase also includes an analysis of the marketing environment and current trends or developments that might affect the promotional program. For example, one of the most significant developments impacting IMC is the explosive growth of social networking sites such as Facebook, which now has more than 1 billion users. Marketers recognize that it is essential not only to have a Facebook page, but to find creative ways to leverage the access they provide to consumers' lives, behavior, and communications with one another.[50] For example, Naked Juice, which makes a line

**EXHIBIT 1-14**
Naked Juice used a creative Facebook application to promote its new recyclable bottle

of all-natural fruit juices and smoothies, worked with its interactive agency to develop a Facebook application to promote how the company had become the first nationally distributed brand to move to a recyclable polyethylene bottle (the Naked reNEWabottle). The "Naked Message in a Bottle" campaign asked Facebook users to pass along virtual bottles and fun "Naked" messages to their friends.[51] For every bottle passed Naked Juice donated five cents to Keep America Beautiful and its recycling education initiatives (Exhibit 1-14).

## Analysis of the Communication Process

This stage of the promotional planning process examines how the company can effectively communicate with consumers in its target markets. The promotional planner must think about the process consumers will go through in responding to marketing communications. The response process for products or services for which consumer decision making is characterized by a high level of interest is often different from that for low-involvement or routine purchase decisions. These differences will influence the promotional strategy.

Communication decisions regarding the use of various source, message, and channel factors must also be considered. The promotional planner should recognize the different effects various types of advertising messages might have on consumers and whether they are appropriate for the product or brand. Issues such as whether a celebrity spokesperson should be used and at what cost may also be studied. Preliminary discussion of media-mix options (print, TV, radio, newspaper, direct marketing, Internet) and their cost implications might also occur at this stage.

An important part of this stage of the promotional planning process is establishing communication goals and objectives. In this text, we stress the importance of distinguishing between communication and marketing objectives. **Marketing objectives** refer to what is to be accomplished by the overall marketing program. They are often stated in terms of sales, market share, or profitability.

**Communication objectives** refer to what the firm seeks to accomplish with its promotional program. They are often stated in terms of the nature of the message to be communicated or what specific communication effects are to be achieved. Communication objectives may include creating awareness or knowledge about a product and its attributes or benefits; creating an image; or developing favorable attitudes, preferences, or purchase intentions. Communication objectives should be the guiding force for development of the overall marketing communications strategy and of objectives for each promotional-mix area.

## Budget Determination

After the communication objectives are determined, attention turns to the promotional budget. Two basic questions are asked at this point: What will the promotional program cost? How will the money be allocated? Ideally, the amount a firm needs to spend on promotion should be determined by what must be done to accomplish its communication objectives. In reality, promotional budgets are often determined using a more simplistic approach, such as how much money is available or a percentage of a company's or brand's sales revenue. At this stage, the budget is often tentative. It may not be finalized until specific promotional-mix strategies are developed.

## Developing the Integrated Marketing Communications Program

Developing the IMC program is generally the most involved and detailed step of the promotional planning process. As discussed earlier, each promotional-mix element has certain advantages and limitations. At this stage of the planning process, decisions have to be made regarding the role and importance of each element and their coordination with one another. As Figure 1–7 shows, each promotional-mix element has its own set of objectives and a budget and strategy for meeting them. Decisions must be made and activities performed to implement the promotional programs. Procedures must be developed for evaluating performance and making any necessary changes.

For example, the advertising program will have its own set of objectives, usually involving the communication of some message or appeal to a target audience. A budget will be determined, providing the advertising manager and the agency with some idea of how much money is available for developing the ad campaign and purchasing media to disseminate the ad message.

Two important aspects of the advertising program are development of the message and the media strategy. Message development, often referred to as *creative strategy*, involves determining the basic appeal and message the advertiser wishes to convey to the target audience. This process, along with the ads that result, is to many students the most fascinating aspect of promotion. *Media strategy* involves determining which communication channels will be used to deliver the advertising message to the target audience. Decisions must be made regarding which types of media will be used (e.g., newspapers, magazines, radio, TV, outdoor, digital) as well as specific media selections (e.g., a particular magazine or TV program). This task requires careful evaluation of the media options' advantages and limitations, costs, and ability to deliver the message effectively to the target market.

Once the message and media strategies have been determined, steps must be taken to implement them. Most large companies hire advertising agencies to plan and produce their messages and to evaluate and purchase the media that will carry their ads. However, most agencies work very closely with their clients as they develop the ads and select media, because it is the advertiser that ultimately approves (and pays for) the creative work and media plan.

A similar process takes place for the other elements of the IMC program as objectives are set, an overall strategy is developed, message and media strategies are determined, and steps are taken to implement them. While the marketer's advertising agencies may be used to perform some of the other IMC functions, they may also hire other communication specialists such as direct-marketing and interactive and/or sales promotion agencies, as well as public relations firms.

## Monitoring, Evaluation, and Control

The final stage of the IMC planning process is monitoring, evaluating, and controlling the promotional program. It is important to determine how well the IMC program is meeting communication objectives and helping the firm accomplish its overall marketing goals and objectives. The IMC planner wants to know not only how well the promotional program is doing but also why. For example, problems with the advertising program may lie in the nature of the message or in a media plan that does not reach the target market effectively. The manager must know the reasons for the results in order to take the right steps to correct the program.

This final stage of the process is designed to provide managers with continual feedback concerning the effectiveness of the IMC program, which in turn can be used as input into the planning process. As Figure 1–7 shows, information on the results achieved by the IMC program is used in subsequent promotional planning and strategy development.

# PERSPECTIVE AND ORGANIZATION OF THIS TEXT

Traditional approaches to teaching advertising, promotional strategy, or marketing communications courses have often treated the various elements of the promotional mix as separate functions. As a result, many people who work in advertising, sales promotion, direct marketing, interactive/Internet, or public relations tend to approach marketing communications problems from the perspective of their particular specialty. An advertising person may believe marketing communications objectives are best met through the use of media advertising; a promotional specialist argues for a sales promotion program to motivate consumer response; a public relations person advocates a PR campaign to tackle the problem. These orientations are not surprising, since each person has been trained to view marketing communications problems primarily from one perspective.

In the contemporary business world, however, individuals working in marketing, advertising, and other promotional areas are expected to understand and use a variety of marketing communications tools, not just the one in which they specialize. Ad agencies no longer confine their services to the advertising area. Many are involved in sales promotion, public relations, direct marketing, event sponsorship, Internet/interactive, and other marketing communications areas. Individuals working on the client or advertiser side of the business, such as brand, product, or promotional managers, are developing marketing programs that use a variety of marketing communications methods.

This text views advertising and promotion from an integrated marketing communications perspective. We will examine the promotional-mix elements and their roles in an organization's integrated marketing communications efforts. Although media advertising may be the most visible part of the communications program, understanding its role in contemporary marketing requires attention to other promotional areas such as the Internet and interactive marketing, direct marketing, sales promotion, and public relations. Not all the promotional-mix areas are under the direct control of the advertising or marketing communications manager. For example, as noted earlier, personal selling is typically a specialized marketing function outside the control of the advertising or promotional department. Likewise, publicity/public relations is often assigned to a separate department. All these departments should, however, communicate to coordinate all the organization's marketing communications tools.

The purpose of this book is to provide you with a thorough understanding of the field of advertising and other elements of a firm's promotional mix and show how they are combined to form an integrated marketing communications program. To plan, develop, and implement an effective IMC program, those involved must understand marketing, consumer behavior, and the communication process. The first part of this book is designed to provide this foundation by examining the roles of advertising and other forms of promotion in the marketing process. We examine the process of market segmentation and positioning and consider their part in developing an IMC strategy. We also discuss how firms organize for IMC and make decisions regarding ad agencies and other firms that provide marketing and promotional services.

We then focus on consumer behavior considerations and analyze the communication process. We discuss various communications models of value to promotional planners in developing strategies and establishing goals and objectives for advertising and other forms of promotion. We also consider how firms determine and allocate their marketing communications budget.

After laying the foundation for the development of a promotional program, this text will follow the integrated marketing communications planning model presented in Figure 1–7. We examine each of the promotional-mix variables, beginning with advertising. Our detailed examination of advertising includes a discussion of creative strategy and the process of developing the advertising message, an overview of media strategy, and an evaluation of the various media (print, broadcast, and support media). The discussion then turns to the other areas of the promotional mix: direct marketing, interactive/Internet marketing, sales promotion, and public relations/publicity. Our examination of the IMC planning process concludes with a discussion of how the program is monitored, evaluated, and controlled. Particular attention is given to measuring the effectiveness of advertising and other forms of promotion.

The final part of the text examines special topic areas and perspectives that have become increasingly important in contemporary marketing. We will examine the area of international advertising and promotion and the challenges companies face in developing IMC programs for global markets as well as various countries around the world. The text concludes with an examination of the environment in which integrated marketing communications operates, including the regulatory, social, and economic factors that influence, and in turn are influenced by, an organization's advertising and promotional program.

## Summary

Advertising and other forms of promotion are an integral part of the marketing process in most organizations. Over the past decade, the amount of money spent on advertising, sales promotion, direct marketing, and other forms of marketing communication has increased tremendously, both in the United States and in foreign markets. There has been a very large increase in the amount of monies spent on the Internet as well as various forms of nontraditional media, some of which did not exist at the beginning of the new millennium. To understand the role of advertising and promotion in a marketing program, one must understand the role and function of marketing in an organization. The basic task of marketing is to combine the four controllable elements, known as the marketing mix, into a comprehensive program that facilitates exchange with a target market. The elements of the marketing mix are the product or service, price, place (distribution), and promotion.

For many years, the promotional function in most companies was dominated by mass-media advertising. However, more and more companies are recognizing the importance of integrated marketing communications, coordinating the various marketing and promotional elements to achieve more efficient and effective communication programs. A number of factors underlie the move toward IMC by marketers as well as ad agencies and other promotional facilitators. Reasons for the growing importance of the integrated marketing communications perspective include a rapidly changing environment with respect to consumers, technology, and media. The IMC movement is also being driven by changes in the ways companies market their products and services. A shifting of marketing expenditures from traditional media advertising to other forms of promotion as well as nontraditional media, the rapid growth of the Internet and social media, a shift in marketplace power from manufacturers to

retailers, the growth and development of database marketing, the demand for greater accountability from advertising agencies and other marketing communication firms, and the fragmentation of media markets, as well as changing media consumption patterns, are among the key changes taking place.

Promotion is best viewed as the communication function of marketing. It is accomplished through a promotional mix that includes advertising, personal selling, publicity/public relations, sales promotion, direct marketing, and interactive/Internet marketing. The inherent advantages and disadvantages of each of these promotional-mix elements influence the roles they play in the overall marketing program. In developing the IMC program, the marketer must decide which tools to use and how to combine them to achieve the organization's marketing and communication objectives. Many companies are taking an audience contact or touch point perspective in developing their IMC programs whereby they consider all of the potential ways of reaching their target audience and presenting the company or brand in a favorable manner. The four primary categories of contact points include company planned, intrinsic, unexpected, and customer initiated. These contact points vary with respect to the impact they have on the customer and marketers' ability to control them.

Promotional management involves coordinating the promotional-mix elements to develop an integrated program of effective marketing communication. The model of the IMC planning process in Figure 1–7 contains a number of steps: a review of the marketing plan; promotional program situation analysis; analysis of the communication process; budget determination; development of an integrated marketing communications program; integration and implementation of marketing communications strategies; and monitoring, evaluation, and control of the promotional program.

## Key Terms

exchange p. 7
marketing p. 7
value p. 7
marketing mix p. 8
integrated marketing communications
  (IMC) p. 9
promotion p. 16
promotional mix p. 16
advertising p. 17

direct marketing p. 21
direct-response advertising p. 21
interactive media p. 22
social media p. 22
sales promotion p. 23
publicity p. 25
public relations p. 26
personal selling p. 27
contact (or touch) point p. 27

integrated marketing communications
  management p. 30
integrated marketing communications
  plan p. 30
marketing plan p. 30
internal analysis p. 31
external analysis p. 31
marketing objectives p. 35
communication objectives p. 35

## Discussion Questions

1. Discuss the role of integrated marketing communications in the marketing program of a product such as Gatorade. How can Gatorade use the various IMC tools to achieve its objective of expanding into the sports nutrition market? (LO2, 5)

2. Evaluate Gatorade's decision to launch the new G Series product line and the challenge this presents to the company from an integrated marketing communications perspective. (LO2, 5)

3. Discuss the role integrated marketing communications plays in the marketing program of companies and organizations. Discuss some of the reasons for the tremendous growth in advertising and other forms of marketing communication in the United States as well as in global markets. (LO1)

4. Discuss how integrated marketing communications differs from traditional advertising and promotion. What are some of the reasons marketers are taking an IMC perspective to their marketing communications programs? (LO2, 3)

5. Discuss how the digital revolution is impacting the ways marketers plan and implement their integrated marketing communications programs. Identify three specific technological developments and discuss how each is impacting the IMC program of companies. (LO3, 4)

6. Discuss how brand building is changing as marketing moves from the consumer era to the relationship era. Find an example of a company that has made the transition to the relationship era and discuss how it has done so. (LO3)

7. Discuss the opportunities and challenges facing marketers with regard to the use of mobile marketing. What are some of the ways marketers can use mobile marketing as part of their IMC program? (LO4, 5)

8. What is meant by a consumer contact or touch point? Choose a specific company or brand and discuss how it is using the four categories of contact points discussed in the chapter. (LO5)

9. Evaluate Nike's decision to move away from the use of traditional mass-media advertising and focus more of its marketing budget on digital media. Do you agree with this decision or do you think Nike should be allocating more of its IMC budget to traditional media advertising? (LO5, 6)

10. Why is it important for those who work in marketing to understand and appreciate all the various integrated marketing communication tools and how they can be used effectively? (LO6, 7)

## LEARNING OBJECTIVES

**LO1** To understand the marketing process and the role of advertising and promotion in an organization's integrated marketing program.

**LO2** To understand the concept of target marketing in an integrated marketing communications program.

**LO3** To recognize the role of market segmentation and its use in an integrated marketing communications program.

**LO4** To understand the use of positioning and repositioning strategies.

**LO5** To know the various decision areas under each element of the marketing mix and how they influence and interact with advertising and promotional strategy.

# 2 The Role of IMC in the Marketing Process

## REACHING MILLENNIALS—A TRUE MARKETING CHALLENGE

One would think that a cohort that consists of 80 million persons with a spending power of $172 billion would be the ideal target market for American companies. Yet the millennials generation—those born between 1982 and 2000 and also known as gen Y—is proving to be one of the most difficult of any segment for marketers to reach in decades. Marketers have referred to this group as "the cheapest ever," "stingy," and/or "disinterested"—among other not so endearing terms—when describing their buying behaviors. It seems they just don't want to buy. At the same time, the cohort is just too large in size and has too much buying power to ignore: They are expected to spend over $10 trillion in their lifetimes. As a result, a number of companies, rather than ignoring them, are attempting to better understand them in an attempt to develop marketing programs that might attract their interest.

Unfortunately, millennials are not that easily understood. Maybe they don't buy because much of their life has been spent in a bad economy. Jobs have been hard to come by, salaries are not increasing, and housing is expensive. As a result, many (even after graduating from college) live at home with their parents, take mass transit, carpool, or walk to work and don't have a lot of disposable income. Perhaps they suffer from information overload, as almost all of them are socially connected, the vast majority multitask frequently, and they are the most educated, mobile, and tech-savvy generation in history. Or maybe what they are interested in purchasing is different from previous generations—travel spending has increased over recent years, while new car purchases have been less than expected. Many would prefer to pay for enhanced cell phone services rather than make a car payment. There is no doubt that their media habits are more complex, making it easier to reach them but harder to get their attention. Or maybe

the media contribute to their consumer behaviors by making it easier to communicate with others, sharing many things such as product evaluations in their discussions.

Since World War II, the U.S. economy has been driven by automobile and home sales. Now it seems that millennials are not interested in either—at least when it comes to buying. Rather, they have become a "sharing economy" in which everything from clothing to homes to automobiles is shared rather than purchased. Companies like car2go and Zipcar—the world's largest car-sharing company with over 700,000 members—are growing at a rapid pace. So fast, in fact, that Avis (the car rental conglomerate) purchased Zipcar for $500 million in 2013. Also expanding is Airbnb, a place for travelers to share bedrooms and other household accommodations, and there has been a proliferation of websites for selling one's no longer used clothing.

One company trying to understand millennials is General Motors (GM). GM's research has shown that new vehicle purchases in the 21- to 34-year-old age group are down 35 percent from 1985. The percentage of teens and twenty-somethings with driver's licenses has also decreased. While some of this can be attributed to the economy, all of it cannot. Because of their high connectivity and educational status (higher-educated persons tend to have greater buying power) GM believes that millennials still provide strong market potential, but automakers just haven't figured them out yet. Rather than impose the values of the older generations, GM is trying to adapt by reaching them on their own terms. Chevrolet has partnered with RelayRides, a company that allows members to rent out their vehicles to other users. GM has also introduced a number of new "concept cars" designed specifically for millennials by emphasizing higher gas mileage and high-tech features, while downplaying horsepower and torque attributes. The key to capturing millennials according to 31-year-old John McFarland—GM's "youth emissary," is to "give them exactly what they want and nothing more." Dodge is trying exactly that with its new Dodge Dart. After poor introductory sales, Dodge has established an online promotion that "combines crowdsourcing and pizzazz with millennial appeal" in which one can register to buy a Dart and have friends sponsor the components they want in the car.

Another seeking to do business with gen Y is Wawanesa, an insurance company that has been around since 1896 but is far less known than competitors like State Farm, Allstate, and GEICO. Wawanesa recently discovered that millennials don't want to take the time to complete insurance forms the traditional way—on paper. (Allstate apparently found this out earlier, which led to the founding of Esurance.) To respond to this threat, Wawanesa increased its web presence, offering online quotes and allowing customers to pay bills and even file claims online. In addition, the company increased its marketing efforts targeted to this cohort. GEICO now advertises a mobile app to allow access to one's insurance account.

Offering a strong online presence is not the only strategy that must be undertaken to reach millennials, however. As noted by Erin Mulligan Nelson in *Advertising Age* magazine, if companies think all they have to do to reach this cohort is to employ social media, they are going to miss the mark. Nelson contends that to reach millennials, marketers must employ media that provide content about the brand—blogs, websites, and applications—even strangers providing testimonials. Millenials want to be informed, and want to be heard, often valuing their mobile phones over other tangible good items. If successful, companies will also find them to be highly loyal, and willing to tell others of their product and service experiences. Emma Bazilian, reporting on a study of 1,000 consumers between the ages of 18 and 34, agrees that social media may be the best way to reach millennials, but also believes that traditional media are still important. The study conducted by MPA and GfK MRI found that while Facebook is the most used social site, 93 percent of those surveyed said they read magazines and that contests and coupons are also a big influence on their purchase decisions, as is word of mouth—particularly from their friends.

So while millennials may be different, maybe the ways in which we reach them may not be as complicated as it seems to be. Only time will tell.

Sources: Dale Buss, "Dodge Dart Lowers Barrier to Entry for Millennials with Online Registry," www.BrandChannel.com, January 21, 2013; Andrew Martin, "Car Sharing Catches on as Zipcar Sells to Avis," www.nytimes.com, January 2, 2013, pp. 1–5; Sheila Shayon, "Campbell's Go Soup Targets Millennials, Still 'Mmm Mmm Good,'" www.brandchannel.com, August 29, 2012; Erin Mulligan Nelson, "Millennials Want to Party with Your Brand but on Their Own Terms," www.advertisingage.com, August 2, 2012; Emma Bazilian, "Study: Millennials Engage with Magazines via Social Media," www.adweek.com, August 23, 2012, p. 1; Jordan Weissmann, "How Do You Sell a Car to a Millennial?" www.theatlantic.com, April 4, 2012, pp. 1–10.

**YTC** `02–01`

**Marketing to Millennials**

youtube.com/10ebelch

Marketers know that to be successful they most understand their buyers and potential buyers and develop specific strategies to best reach them. These include the identification of market opportunities, market segmentation, target marketing and positioning, and marketing program development. As can be seen in the lead-in to this chapter, this is often a challenging task.

In this chapter, we take a closer look at how marketing strategies influence the role of promotion and how promotional decisions must be coordinated with other areas of the marketing mix. In turn, all elements of the marketing mix must be consistent in a strategic plan that results in an integrated marketing communications program. We use the model in Figure 2–1 as a framework for analyzing how promotion fits into an organization's marketing strategy and programs.

This model consists of four major components: the organization's marketing strategy and analysis, the target marketing process, the marketing planning program development (which includes the promotional mix), and the target market. As the model shows, the marketing process begins with the development of a marketing strategy and analysis in which the company decides the product or service areas and particular markets where it wants to compete. The company must then coordinate the various elements of the marketing mix into a cohesive marketing program that will reach the target market effectively. Note that a firm's promotion program is directed not only to the final buyer but also to the channel or "trade" members that distribute its products to the ultimate consumer. These channel members must be

**FIGURE 2–1**

Marketing and Promotions
Process Model

convinced there is a demand for the company's products so they will carry them and will aggressively merchandise and promote them to consumers. Promotions play an important role in the marketing program for building and maintaining demand not only among final consumers but among the trade as well.

As noted in Chapter 1, all elements of the marketing mix—price, product, distribution, and promotions—must be integrated to provide consistency and maximum communications impact. Development of a marketing plan is instrumental in achieving this goal.

As Figure 2–1 shows, development of a marketing program requires an in-depth analysis of the market. This analysis may make extensive use of marketing research as an input into the planning process. This input, in turn, provides the basis for the development of marketing strategies in regard to product, pricing, distribution, and promotion decisions. Each of these steps requires a detailed analysis, since this plan serves as the road map to follow in achieving marketing goals. Once the detailed market analysis has been completed and marketing objectives have been established, each element in the marketing mix must contribute to a comprehensive integrated marketing program. Of course, the promotional program element (the focus of this text) must be combined with all other program elements in such a way as to achieve maximum impact.

# MARKETING STRATEGY AND ANALYSIS

Any organization that wants to exchange its products or services in the marketplace successfully should have a **strategic marketing plan** to guide the allocation of its resources. A strategic marketing plan usually evolves from an organization's overall corporate strategy and serves as a guide for specific marketing programs and policies.

As we noted earlier, marketing strategy is based on a situation analysis—a detailed assessment of the current marketing conditions facing the company, its product lines, or its individual brands. From this situation analysis, a firm develops an understanding of the market and the various opportunities it offers, the competition, and the **market segments** or target markets the company wishes to pursue. We examine each step of the marketing strategy and *planning* in this chapter.

## Opportunity Analysis

A careful analysis of the marketplace should lead to alternative market opportunities for existing product lines in current or new markets, new products for current markets, or new products for new markets. **Market opportunities** are areas where there are favorable demand trends, where the company believes customer needs and opportunities are not being satisfied, and where it can compete effectively. The Manischewitz company—you may have heard the ad slogan "Man-O-Manischewitz! What a wine!"—a marketer of kosher foods, has revived its decades-old slogan to take advantage of a new marketing opportunity. Based on research that showed that four out of five buyers of kosher foods are not traditional Jewish consumers, Manischewitz has increased its marketing efforts in an attempt to capture more of the mainstream market. Knowing that there has been an increase in interest in ethnic foods and health consciousness and that, as a result of the recession, more consumers are eating meals at home, the company hopes to reach more consumers (Exhibit 2–1). The company's new IMC program includes a multimillion-dollar advertising budget, web programs, in-store promotions, a "Cook Off," and public relations activities designed to promote its kosher food line.[1]

A company usually identifies market opportunities by carefully examining the marketplace and noting demand trends and competition in various market segments. A market can rarely be viewed as one large homogeneous group of customers; rather, it consists of many heterogeneous groups, or segments. In recent years, many companies have recognized the importance of tailoring their marketing to meet the needs and demand trends of different market segments.

For example, different market segments in the personal computer (PC) industry include the home, government, education, science, and business markets. These segments can be even further divided. The business market consists of both small companies and large corporations; the education market can range from elementary schools to colleges and universities. A company that is marketing its products in the auto industry must decide in which particular market segment or segments it wishes to compete. This decision depends on the amount and nature of competition the brand will face in a particular market. Many auto companies are now competing in the hybrid car market, offering a variety of models (Exhibit 2–2). A competitive analysis is an important part of marketing strategy development and warrants further consideration.

## Competitive Analysis

In developing the firm's marketing strategies and plans for its products and services, the manager must carefully analyze the competition to be faced in the marketplace. This may range from direct brand competition (which can also include its own brands) to more indirect forms of competition, such as product substitutes. For example, growth in the bottled water market has led numerous

**EXHIBIT 2–1**

Manischewitz sees the mainstream market as an opportunity

**EXHIBIT 2–2**

Many car companies now compete in the hybrid market

companies to compete in this area and offer different product varieties (Exhibit 2–3).

At a more general level, marketers must recognize they are competing for the consumer's discretionary income, so they must understand the various ways potential customers choose to spend their money. The impact of the worldwide economic downturn has made manufacturers of luxury goods brands rethink their marketing strategies. Sales of luxury products fell in 2008 and again in 2009. However, by 2012 the market rebounded with growth expected to be in the 6 to 7 percent range.[2]

An important aspect of marketing strategy development is the search for a **competitive advantage,** something special a firm does or has that gives it an edge over competitors. Ways to achieve a competitive advantage include having quality products that command a premium price, providing superior customer service, having the lowest production costs and lower prices, and dominating channels of distribution. Competitive advantage can also be achieved through advertising that creates and maintains product differentiation and brand equity, an example of which was the long-running advertising campaign for Michelin tires, which stressed security as well as performance. The strong brand images of Apple, Campbell's Soup, Nike, BMW, and McDonald's give them a competitive advantage in their respective markets.

Recently, there has been concern that some marketers have not been spending enough money on advertising to allow leading brands to sustain their competitive edge. Advertising proponents have been calling for companies to protect their brand equity and franchises by investing more money in advertising instead of costly trade promotions. Some companies, recognizing the important competitive advantage strong brands provide, have been increasing their investments in them. Campbell Soup Company introduced a new advertising campaign in an attempt to revitalize its 80-year-old V8 vegetable juice brand. Replicating the highly successful campaign of the 1970s in which people got bopped on the head with the catchphrase "I could've had a V8," and stressing the brand's health aspects while extending the product line, Campbell's saw double-digit sales gains in 2011[3] (Exhibit 2–4).

Competitors' marketing programs have a major impact on a firm's marketing strategy, so they must be analyzed and monitored. The reactions of competitors to a company's marketing and promotional strategy are also very important. Competitors may cut price, increase promotional spending, develop new brands, or attack one another

**EXHIBIT 2–3**

Sobe offers a variety of enhanced waters

You've tried trickery.
You've tried bribery.
But have you tried strawberry?

Kids not eating
their veggies?
Try V8 V-Fusion.®
A full serving
of fruit with a
full serving of
vegetables!
(But they only
taste the fruit.)

**EXHIBIT 2-4**

V8 revitalizes its image

LO 02-2

**EXHIBIT 2-5**

Competitors sometimes
position themselves through
comparative ads

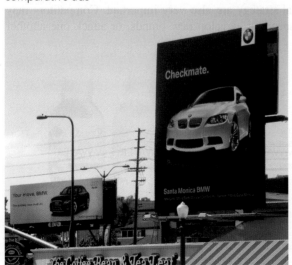

through comparative advertising (Exhibit 2–5). One of the more intense competitive rivalries is the battle between Coca-Cola and Pepsi. A number of other intense competitive rivalries exist in the marketplace, including Hertz and Avis, Ford and GM, and Apple and Samsung.

A final aspect of competition is the growing number of foreign companies penetrating the U.S. market and taking business from domestic firms. In products ranging from beer to cars to electronics, imports are becoming an increasingly strong form of competition with which U.S. firms must contend. As we now compete in a global economy, U.S. companies must not only defend their domestic markets but also learn how to compete effectively in the international marketplace.

## Target Market Selection

After evaluating the opportunities presented by various market segments, including a detailed competitive analysis, the company may select one, or more, as a target market. This target market becomes the focus of the firm's marketing effort, and goals and objectives are set according to where the company wants to be and what it hopes to accomplish in this market. As noted in Chapter 1, these goals and objectives are set in terms of specific performance variables such as sales, market share, and profitability. The selection of the target market (or markets) in which the firm will compete is an important part of its marketing strategy and has direct implications for its advertising and promotional efforts.

Recall from our discussion of the integrated marketing communications planning program that the situation analysis is conducted at the beginning of the promotional planning process. Specific objectives—both marketing and communications—are derived from the situation analysis, and the promotional-mix strategies are developed to achieve these objectives. Marketers rarely go after the entire market with one product, brand, or service offering. Rather, they pursue a number of different strategies, breaking the market into segments and targeting one or more of these segments for marketing and promotional efforts. This means different objectives may be established, different budgets may be used, and the promotional-mix strategies may vary, depending on the market approach used.

# THE TARGET MARKETING PROCESS

Because few, if any, products can satisfy the needs of all consumers, companies often develop different marketing strategies to satisfy different consumer needs. The process by which marketers do this (presented in Figure 2–2) is referred to as **target marketing** and involves four basic steps: identifying markets with unfulfilled needs, segmenting the market, targeting specific segments, and positioning one's product or service through marketing strategies.

## Identifying Markets

When employing a target marketing strategy, the marketer identifies the specific needs of groups of people (or segments), selects one or more of these segments as a target, and develops marketing programs directed to each. This approach has found increased applicability in marketing for a number of reasons, including changes in the market (consumers are becoming much more diverse in their needs, attitudes, and

| Identifying markets with unfulfilled needs | → | Determining market segmentation | → | Selecting a market to target | → | Positioning through marketing strategies |

**FIGURE 2–2**

The Target Marketing Process

lifestyles); increased use of segmentation by competitors; and the fact that more managers are trained in segmentation and realize the advantages associated with this strategy. Perhaps the best explanation, however, comes back to the basic premise that you must understand as much as possible about consumers to design marketing programs that meet their needs most effectively.

Target market identification isolates consumers with similar lifestyles, needs, and the like, and increases our knowledge of their specific requirements. The more marketers can establish this common ground with consumers, the more effective they will be in addressing these requirements in their communications programs and informing and/or persuading potential consumers that the product or service offering will meet their needs.

Let's use the beer industry as an example. Years ago, beer was just beer, with little differentiation, many local distributors, and few truly national brands. The industry began consolidating; many brands were assumed by the larger brewers or ceased to exist. As the number of competitors decreased, competition among the major brewers increased. To compete more effectively, brewers began to look at different tastes, lifestyles, and so on, of beer drinkers and used this information in their marketing strategies. This process resulted in the identification of many market segments, each of which corresponds to different customers' needs, lifestyles, and other characteristics.

As you can see in Figure 2–3, the beer market now consists of 10 segments with numerous offerings available to each.[4] Most large brewers have product offerings in each segment, competing with each other as well as smaller craft microbreweries (Exhibit 2–6). Each appeals to a different set of needs. Taste is certainly one; others include image, cost, and the size of one's waistline. A variety of other reasons for purchasing are also operating, including the consumer's social class, lifestyle, and economic status.

Marketers competing in nearly all product and service categories are constantly searching for ways to segment their markets in an attempt to better satisfy customers' needs. The remainder of this section discusses ways to approach this task.

## Market Segmentation

It is not possible to develop marketing strategies for every consumer. Rather, the marketer attempts to identify broad classes of buyers who have the same needs and

**FIGURE 2–3**

The U.S. Beer Market

| Imports |
| Domestic specialties/drafts |
| Super premium |
| Premium regular |
| Light |
| Ice |
| Malt alternatives |
| Malt liquor |
| Popular regular |
| All others |

Source: Ted Goldammer, *The Brewer's Handbook,* 2nd ed. Apex Publishers, 2012.

**EXHIBIT 2–6**

MillerCoors offers a variety of beers

will respond similarly to marketing actions. **Market segmentation** is dividing a market into distinct groups that (1) have common needs and (2) will respond similarly to a marketing action.

The more marketers segment the market, the more precise is their understanding of it. But the more the market becomes divided, the fewer consumers there are in each segment. Thus, a key decision is, How far should one go in the segmentation process? Where does the process stop? As you can see by the strategy taken in the beer industry, it can go far!

In planning the promotional effort, managers consider whether the target segment is substantial enough to support individualized strategies. More specifically, they consider whether this group is accessible. Can it be reached with a communications program? For example, you will see in Chapter 10 that in some instances there are no media that can efficiently be used to reach some targeted groups. Or the promotions manager may identify a number of segments but unable to develop the required programs to reach them. The firm may have insufficient funds to develop the required advertising campaign, inadequate sales staff to cover all areas, or other promotional deficiencies. After determining that a segmentation strategy is in order, the marketer must establish the basis on which it will address the market. The following section discusses some of the bases for segmenting markets and demonstrates examples of advertising and promotions applications.

**Bases for Segmentation**   As shown in Figure 2–4, several methods are available for segmenting markets. Marketers may use one of the segmentation variables or a combination of approaches. Consider the market segmentation strategy that might be employed to market snow skis. The consumer's lifestyle—active, fun-loving, enjoys outdoor sports—is certainly important. But so are other factors, such as age (participation in downhill skiing drops off significantly at about age 30) and income (have you seen the price of a lift ticket lately?), as well as marital status. Let us review the bases for segmentation and examine some promotional strategies employed in each.

**Geographic Segmentation** In the **geographic segmentation** approach, markets are divided into different geographic units. These units may include nations, states,

**FIGURE 2–4** Some Bases for Market Segmentation

| Main Dimension | Segmentation Variables | Typical Breakdowns |
|---|---|---|
| **Customer Characteristics** | | |
| Geographic | Region | Northeast; Midwest; South; West; etc. |
| | City size | Under 10,000; 10,000–24,999; 25,000–49,999; 50,000–99,999; 100,000–249,999; 250,000–499,999; 500,000–999,999; 1,000,000 or more |
| | Metropolitan area | Metropolitan statistical area (MSA) |
| | Density | Urban; suburban; small town; rural |
| Demographic | Gender | Male; female |
| | Age | Under 6 yrs; 6–11 yrs; 12–17 yrs; 18–24 yrs; 25–34 yrs; 35–44 yrs; 45–54 yrs; 55–64 yrs; 65–74 yrs; 75 yrs plus |
| | Race | African American; Asian; Hispanic; White/Caucasian; etc. |
| | Life stage | Infant; preschool; child; youth; collegiate; adult; senior |
| | Birth era | Baby boomer (1946–1964); generation X (1965–1976); baby boomlet/generation Y (1977–present) |
| | Household size | 1; 2; 3–4; 5 or more |
| | Residence tenure | Own home; rent home |
| | Marital status | Never married; married; separated; divorced; widowed |
| Socioeconomic | Income | <$15,000; $15,000–$24,999; $25,000–$34,999; $35,000–$49,999; $50,000–$74,999; $75,000–$99,999; $100,000 + |
| | Education | Some high school or less; high school graduate (or GED); etc. |
| | Occupation | Managerial and professional specialty; technical, sales and administrative support; service; farming, forestry, and fishing |
| Psychographic | Personality | Gregarious; compulsive; introverted; aggressive; ambitious |
| | Values (VALS) | Actualizers; fulfilleds; achievers; experiencers; believers; strivers; makers; strugglers |
| | Lifestyle (Claritas) | Settled in; white picket fence; and 46 other household segments |
| **Buying Situations** | | |
| Outlet type | In-store | Department; specialty; outlet; convenience; supermarket; superstore/mass merchandiser; catalog |
| | Direct | Mail order/catalog; door-to-door; direct response; Internet |
| Benefits sought | Product features | Situation specific; general |
| | Needs | Quality; service; price/value; financing; warranty; etc. |
| Usage | Usage rate | Light user; medium user; heavy user |
| | User status | Nonuser; ex-user; prospect; first-time user; regular user |
| Awareness and intentions | Product knowledge | Unaware; aware; informed; interested; intending to buy; purchaser; rejection |
| Behavior | Involvement | Minimum effort; comparison; special effort |

**EXHIBIT 2–7**

Cheerwine is more popular in
a specific geographic region

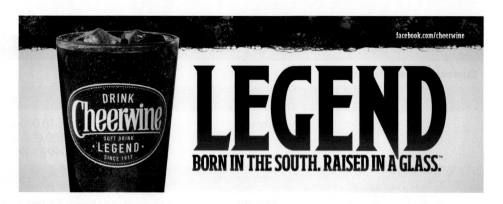

YTC **02–02**

**The Cheerwine story**

youtube.com/10ebelch

counties, or even neighborhoods. Consumers often have different buying habits
depending on where they reside. Regional differences may exist in regard to food,
drinks, attitudes toward foreign products, and the like. For example, many companies
consider California a very different market from the rest of the United States and
have developed specific marketing programs targeted to the consumers in that state.
Other companies have developed programs targeted at specific regions. Exhibit 2–7
shows an ad for Cheerwine, just one of the regional soft drink "cult brands"—
along with Jackson Hole Huckleberry (Wyoming), Vernors (Michigan), and Moxie
(New England)—that have found success by marketing in regional areas (in this case,
the South). One company—Olde Brooklyn Beverage Company—even went so far as
to promote a brand based on a specific section of New York City, differentiating it
from bigger brands by promoting the product's "Brooklyn Attitude."

**Demographic Segmentation** Dividing the market on the basis of demographic
variables such as age, sex, family size, education, income, and social class is called
**demographic segmentation.** Secret deodorant and the Lady Schick shaver are
products that have met with a great deal of success by using the demographic variable
of sex as a basis for segmentation. iVillage, a website targeting women, may be one of
the most successful websites on the Internet (Exhibit 2–8). It is interesting to note that
the top 10 websites for women are further segmented by age, lifestyle, and so forth.

   Although market segmentation on the basis of demographics may seem obvious,
companies discover that they need to focus more attention on a specific demographic group. For example, IKEA—noting that more than 70 percent of its shoppers are women—has enhanced its store environment to be more "women friendly,"
as have Home Depot and Walmart. Dell Computers and Verizon (among others)
have discovered that this may not be as easy as it seems, as recent efforts by both
companies have achieved less than favorable results.[5,6] As seen in the lead-in to this
chapter, companies are also finding it difficult to reach the millennial age segment.
A number of companies have begun to focus more attention on the baby boomer

**EXHIBIT 2–8**

iVillage's website is targeted
at women

**EXHIBIT 2–9**

*AARP* The Magazine targets the 50+ segment

YTC **02–03**

**AARP Life @50+**

youtube.com/10ebelch

market—those 76 million Americans born between 1946 and 1964. Given their huge spending power, this age segment has become more attractive to a number of companies including travel agencies and pharmaceutical companies among others. Recognizing their need for retirement planning, Wachovia has increased its marketing efforts to this segment.[7] *AARP, The Magazine,* is targeted to the 43 percent of the population who are 50+, and has over 37 million readers[8] (Exhibit 2–9). This number is expected to constitute 45 percent of the U.S. population by 2015.[9] IMC Perspective 2–1 shows how other companies have marketed to this segment.

Other products that have successfully employed demographic segmentation include Dove (sex), Doan's Pills (age), Coca-Cola (race), Mercedes-Benz, Lexus, and BMW cars (income), and Banquet prepackaged dinners (family size).

While demographics may still be the most common method of segmenting markets, it is important to recognize that other factors may be the underlying basis for homogeneity and/or consumer behavior. The astute marketer will identify additional bases for segmenting and will recognize the limitations of demographics. As noted by media strategist Jamie Beckland, many marketers are relying less on demographics and more on psychographic profiling.[10]

**Psychographic Segmentation** Dividing the market on the basis of personality, lifecycles, and/or lifestyles is referred to as **psychographic segmentation.** While there is some disagreement as to whether personality is a useful basis for segmentation, lifestyle factors have been used effectively. Many consider lifestyle the most effective criterion for segmentation.

The determination of lifestyles is usually based on an analysis of the activities, interests, and opinions (AIOs) of consumers. These lifestyles are then correlated with the consumers' product, brand, and/or media usage. For many products and/or services, lifestyles may be the best discriminator between use and nonuse, accounting for differences in food, clothing, and car selections, among numerous other consumer behaviors.[11]

Psychographic segmentation has been increasingly more popular with the advent of the values and lifestyles (VALS) program. Although marketers employed lifestyle segmentation long before VALS and although a number of alternatives—for example, PRIZM—are available, VALS remains one of the more popular options. VALS 2 divides Americans into eight lifestyle segments that exhibit distinctive attitudes, behaviors, and decision-making patterns. VALS is also available for the Japan and UK markets (both have six lifestyle segments).[12] The VALS 2 system is an excellent predictor of consumer behaviors, and a number of companies now employ lifestyle segmentation to position brands, determine value propositions, and select media.

Another form of psychographic analysis relies on the use of multiple databases including social profile data (available through almost all social networks), behavioral data (tracking users through their online behaviors), and lifecycle data (stage of the consumer's lifecycle, e.g., buying diapers, graduating high school, etc.). Amazon.com has successfully used this strategy for some time, and others are now starting to see the advantages offered over traditional demographic profiling.[13]

**Behavioristic Segmentation** Dividing consumers into groups according to their usage, loyalties, or buying responses to a product is **behavioristic segmentation.** For example, product or brand usage, degree of use (heavy vs. light), and/or brand loyalty are combined with demographic and/or psychographic criteria to develop profiles of market segments. In the case of usage, the marketer assumes that

# IMC Perspective 2–1 > > >

## As Hispanic Market Grows, So Do Problems for Marketers

How important is the U.S. Hispanic market to marketers? Consider these facts: (1) Hispanics constitute 17 percent of the U.S population, numbering over 50 million; (2) they control well over $1 trillion in buying power; (3) the Hispanic food market more than doubled between 2005 and 2010 and will constitute over 25 percent of the total retail food market by 2015; (4) by 2020 Hispanics will constitute 20 percent of the total U.S. population; and (5) they are younger than the rest of the U.S. general population. That's the good news. There is no doubt that Hispanics constitute an attractive market segment, and will for years to come.

Now for the bad news. Due to the diversity of this group, marketers are finding it extremely difficult to market to them. Their shopping behaviors differ markedly from the general population as they tend to be more careful, deliberate, and knowledgeable about products, spending more time considering the options. Latinos differ in other ways as well. Hispanics have a higher than average poverty level, are more likely to be bilingual, and are more likely to live in urban areas. At the same time they are considered to be more "tech savvy" than the general population, with 45 percent owning smartphones (versus 34 percent for the general market) and are more likely to compare prices via mobile devices—but less likely to download coupons or apps or use QR codes. Unlike their general market counterparts, Latinos rarely do one-stop shopping for convenience and to save time, preferring to shop until they feel they get the best deal. They also like to shop close to home, preferring to deal with friends, family, and peers when they buy. While they were once considered to be fiercely brand loyal, this is no longer the case. Most importantly, the value to the family is first and foremost in the Latino purchase decision.

Given this diversity (and there are more differences than discussed here), what does the marketer need to do to reach this lucrative segment of the population? Nestlé has found success by reaching out to Latina moms with an integrated bilingual strategy. The campaign "Echale Agua a Tu Vida" ("Put Water in Your Life") for its Pure Life brand of water underscores the importance of healthy hydration and active lifestyles for the moms and their families. Among other tactics, Nestlé has teamed up with the U.S. Soccer Foundation, offering free soccer instruction and interactive and educational clinics for kids 5 to 12 in a number of cities in the United States. (Soccer is clearly the sport of choice to Hispanics.) Nestlé has employed TV personality Cristina Saralegui to be its spokesperson and has devoted a website to inspire moms to be healthier by incorporating water into their daily routines.

Dunkin' Donuts has also launched a campaign targeted specifically to this segment. The theme of this campaign "Que estas tomando?" ("What are you drinking?") also uses an integrated strategy employing Hispanic television, radio, social media, public relations, and in-store promotions as well as a Spanish-language website. The primary goal of the campaign, says John Castello, chief global marketing and innovation officer at Dunkin' Brands, is to "reflect the importance and the loyalty of our Hispanic consumers." For the first time ever the longtime tagline "America Moves with Dunkin'" will also appear in Spanish ("America se Mueve con Dunkin'").

Old Navy has taken a different approach through its introduction of a six-part online mini-novela series emphasizing fashion. "Estilos Robados" ("Stolen Styles") was created and produced by Telemundo, which is also responsible for the marketing of the series. Each episode ends with a showing of a variety of Old Navy clothes with their price tags and a 25 percent coupon, though Old Navy is never mentioned in the script. Ads promoting the show appear on Telemundo's TV network, website, and mobile sites, as well as on Old Navy's Spanish YouTube channel and on outdoor billboards in heavily Hispanic areas. Thousands of flyers have been distributed to promote the series in Old Navy stores and ads appear in numerous print magazines that reach a large Hispanic audience. And, of course, there are postings on Facebook.

Companies have clearly discovered the value and importance of the Hispanic market. The companies here seem to have developed strategies to reach this market as well.

Sources: Laura Wood, "Marketing to US Hispanics—Social, Demographic, Economic and Cultural Intricacies," *Business Wire*, July 19, 2012; Terry Mangano, "As Hispanic Population Grows, So Too Do Challenges for Marketers—5 Insights," *Promo* (online), January 23, 2012; Karlene Lukovitz, "Dunkin' Launches Multi-Platform Hispanic Campaign," *Marketing Daily*, March 29, 2012; Allison Cerra, "Nestlé Pure Life Centers 'Echale Agua a Tu Vida' Campaign around Latina Moms," www.drugstorenews.com, August 16, 2011;———"In Hispanic Effort, Old Navy Backs Online Mini-Novela "Stolen Styles," www.adage.com, October 17, 2011.

nonpurchasers of a brand or product who have the same characteristics as purchasers hold greater potential for adoption than nonusers with different characteristics. As you will see in Chapter 15, many companies target consumers through social media like Facebook based on behavioristic segmentation.

Degree of use relates to the fact that a few consumers may buy a disproportionate amount of many products or brands. Industrial marketers refer to the **80–20 rule,** meaning 20 percent of their buyers account for 80 percent of their sales volume. Again, when the characteristics of these users are identified, targeting them allows for a much greater concentration of efforts and less wasted time and money. The same heavy-half strategy is possible in the consumer market as well. The majority of purchases of many products (e.g., soaps and detergents, shampoos, cake mixes, beer, dog food, colas, bourbon, and toilet tissue—yes, toilet tissue!) are accounted for by a small proportion of the population. Perhaps you can think of some additional examples.

**Benefit Segmentation** In purchasing products, consumers are generally trying to satisfy specific needs and/or wants. They are looking for products that provide specific benefits to satisfy these needs. The grouping of consumers on the basis of attributes sought in a product is known as **benefit segmentation** and is widely used (Exhibit 2–10).

Consider the purchase of a wristwatch. While you might buy a watch for particular benefits such as accuracy, water resistance, or stylishness, others may seek a different set of benefits. Watches are commonly given as gifts for birthdays, Christmas, and graduation. Certainly some of the same benefits are considered in the purchase of a gift, but the benefits the purchaser derives are different from those the user will obtain. Ads that portray watches as good gifts stress different criteria to consider in the purchase decision. The next time you see an ad or commercial for a watch, think about the basic appeal and the benefits it offers.

**The Process of Segmenting a Market** The segmentation process develops over time and is an integral part of the situation analysis. It is in this stage that marketers attempt to determine as much as they can about the market: What needs are not being fulfilled? What benefits are being sought? What characteristics distinguish among the various groups seeking these products and services? A number of alternative segmentation strategies may be used. Each time a specific segment is identified, additional information is gathered to help the marketer understand this group.

For example, once a specific segment is identified on the basis of benefits sought, the marketer will examine psychographic characteristics and demographics to help characterize this group and to further its understanding of this market. Behavioristic segmentation criteria will also be examined. In the purchase of ski boots, for example, specific benefits may be sought—flexibility or stiffness—depending on the type of skiing the buyer does. All this information will be combined to provide a complete profile of the skier.

A number of companies offer research services to help marketing managers define their markets and develop strategies targeting them. The VALS and PRIZM systems discussed earlier are just a few of the services offered; others use demographic, socioeconomic, and geographic data to cluster consumer households into distinct "microgeographic" segments. One of these companies, Nielsen Claritas, provides demographic and psychographic profiles of geographic areas as small as census track, block group, or zip code +4. Users of the system include Ace Hardware, Walmart, and numerous others. (See Exhibit 2–11.)

## Selecting a Target Market

The outcome of the segmentation analysis will reveal the market opportunities available. The next phase in the target marketing process involves

**EXHIBIT 2–10**

AT&T offers a benefit to those who wish to have worldwide coverage on their cell phones

| URBAN | SUBURBAN | SECOND CITY | TOWN AND COUNTRY |
|---|---|---|---|

HIGH ↑

| **U1**<br>**URBAN UPTOWN**<br><br>04 Young Digerati<br>07 Money & Brains<br>16 Bohemian Mix<br>26 The Cosmopolitans<br>29 American Dreams | **S1**<br>**ELITE SUBURBS**<br><br>01 Upper Crust<br>02 Blue Blood Estates<br>03 Movers & Shakers<br>06 Winner's Circle | **C1**<br>**SECOND CITY SOCIETY**<br><br>10 Second City Elite<br>12 Brite Lites, Li'l City<br>13 Upward Bound | **T1**<br>**LANDED GENTRY**<br><br>05 Country Squires<br>09 Big Fish, Small Pond<br>11 God's Country<br>20 Fast-Track Families<br>25 Country Casuals |
|---|---|---|---|
| **U2**<br>**MIDTOWN MIX**<br><br>31 Urban Achievers<br>40 Close-In Couples<br>54 Multi-Culti Mosaic | **S2**<br>**THE AFFLUENTIALS**<br>08 Executive Suites<br>14 New Empty Nests<br>15 Pools & Patios<br>17 Beltway Boomers<br>18 Kids & Cul-de-Sacs<br>19 Home Sweet Home<br><br>**S3**<br>**MIDDLEBURBS**<br>21 Gray Power<br>22 Young Influentials<br>30 Suburban Sprawl<br>36 Blue-Chip Blues<br>39 Domestic Duos | **C2**<br>**CITY CENTERS**<br><br>24 Up-and-Comers<br>27 Middleburg Managers<br>34 White Picket Fences<br>35 Boomtown Singles<br>41 Sunset City Blues | **T2**<br>**COUNTRY COMFORT**<br><br>23 Greenbelt Sports<br>28 Traditional Times<br>32 New Homesteaders<br>33 Big Sky Families<br>37 Mayberry-ville<br><br>**T3**<br>**MIDDLE AMERICA**<br>38 Simple Pleasures<br>42 Red, White & Blues<br>43 Heartlanders<br>45 Blue Highways<br>50 Kid Country, USA<br>51 Shotguns & Pickups |
| **U3**<br>**URBAN CORES**<br><br>59 Urban Elders<br>61 City Roots<br>65 Big City Blues<br>66 Low-Rise Living | **S4**<br>**INNER SUBURBS**<br><br>44 New Beginnings<br>46 Old Glories<br>49 American Classics<br>52 Suburban Pioneers | **C3**<br>**MICRO-CITY BLUES**<br><br>47 City Startups<br>53 Mobility Blues<br>60 Park Bench Seniors<br>62 Hometown Retired<br>63 Family Thrifts | **T4**<br>**RUSTIC LIVING**<br><br>48 Young & Rustic<br>55 Golden Ponds<br>56 Crossroads Villagers<br>57 Old Milltowns<br>58 Back Country Folks<br>64 Bedrock America |

$ (middle) LOW ↓

**EXHIBIT 2–11**

Nielsen Claritas provides cluster profiles for marketers

two steps: (1) determining how many segments to enter and (2) determining which segments offer the most potential.

**Determining How Many Segments to Enter** Three market coverage alternatives are available. **Undifferentiated marketing** involves ignoring segment differences and offering just one product or service to the entire market. For example, when Henry Ford brought out the first assembly-line automobile, all potential consumers were offered the same basic product: a black Ford. For many years, Coca-Cola offered only one product version. While this standardized strategy saves the company money, it does not allow the opportunity to offer different versions of the product to different markets.

**Differentiated marketing** involves marketing in a number of segments, developing separate marketing strategies for each. For example, the Marriott hotel chain offers a variety of customer services for different travelers, including vacation, business, long or short stay, and so forth.

The third alternative, **concentrated marketing,** is used when the firm selects one segment and attempts to capture a large share of this market. Volkswagen used this strategy in the 1950s when it was the only major automobile company competing in the economy-car segment in the United States. While Volkswagen has now assumed a more differentiated strategy, other companies have found the concentrated

**EXHIBIT 2–12**

Hilton uses positioning that focuses on the consumer

LO 02-4

**EXHIBIT 2–13**

Positioning that focuses on the competition

strategy effective. For example, Rolls-Royce has focused its automobile business exclusively on the high-income segment, while L'Oréal competes in the cosmetics and beauty segment.

**Determining Which Segments Offer Potential**  The second step in selecting a market involves determining the most attractive segment. The firm must examine the sales potential of the segment, the opportunities for growth, the competition, and its own ability to compete. Then it must decide whether it can market to this group. Stories abound of companies that have entered new markets only to find their lack of resources or expertise would not allow them to compete successfully. After selecting the segments to target and determining that it can compete, the firm proceeds to the final step in Figure 2–2: the market positioning phase.

## Market Positioning

**Positioning** has been defined as "the art and science of fitting the product or service to one or more segments of the broad market in such a way as to set it meaningfully apart from competition."[14] As you can see, the position of the product, service, or even store is the image that comes to mind and the attributes consumers perceive as related to it. This communication occurs through the message itself, which explains the benefits, as well as the media strategy employed to reach the target group. Take a few moments to think about how some products are positioned and how their positions are conveyed to you. For example, what comes to mind when you hear the name Mercedes, Dr Pepper, or Apple? What about department stores such as Neiman Marcus, Sears, and JCPenney? Now think of the ads for each of these products and companies. Are their approaches different from their competitors'? When and where are these ads shown? What is the message they are trying to communicate?

**Approaches to Positioning**  Positioning strategies generally focus on either the consumer or the competition. While both approaches involve the association of product benefits with consumer needs, the former does so by linking the product with the benefits the consumer will derive or creating a favorable brand image, as shown in Exhibit 2–12. The latter approach positions the product by comparing it and the benefit it offers versus the competition. Products like Scope Outlast mouthwash (positioning itself as five times longer lasting than competitors) and Burt's Bees (positioned as a better value than its competitors) have employed this strategy successfully (Exhibit 2–13).

Many advertising practitioners consider market positioning the most important factor in establishing a brand in the marketplace. David Aaker and John Myers note that the term *position* has been used to indicate the brand's or product's image in the marketplace.[15] Jack Trout and Al Ries suggest that this brand image must contrast with those of competitors. They say, "In today's marketplace, the competitors' image is just as important as your own. Sometimes more important."[16] Trout notes that a good branding strategy cannot exist without positioning. He further states that branding is about the process of building a brand, while positioning is about putting that brand in the mind of the consumer.[17] Thus, *positioning,* as used in this text, relates to the image of the product and/or brand relative to competing products or brands. The position of the product or brand is the key factor in communicating the benefits it offers and differentiating it from the competition. Let us now turn to strategies marketers use to position a product.

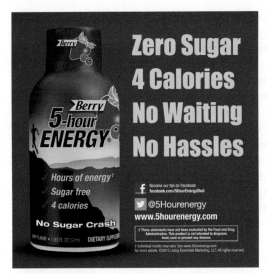

**EXHIBIT 2–14**

5–hour ENERGY positions the product as an energy shot

**EXHIBIT 2–15**

Kohl's positions its brand as having good value for the right price

# DEVELOPING A POSITIONING STRATEGY

A number of positioning strategies might be employed in developing a promotional program. David Aaker and J. Gary Shansby discuss six such strategies: positioning by product attributes, price/quality, use, product class, users, and competitor.[18] Aaker and Myers add one more approach, positioning by cultural symbols.[19]

**Positioning by Product Attributes and Benefits** A common approach to positioning is setting the brand apart from competitors on the basis of the specific characteristics or benefits offered. Sometimes a product may be positioned on more than one product benefit. Marketers attempt to identify **salient attributes** (those that are important to consumers and are the basis for making a purchase decision). For example, when Apple first introduced its computers, the key benefit stressed was ease of use—an effective strategy, given the complexity of computers in the market at that time. While Apple still maintains this position, it is innovative products that comes to mind as well. More recently, there have been a number of new water products that enhance hydration, help the body to exert physical power, increase immunities, and so on. 5-hour ENERGY positions itself as a sugar-free energy shot (Exhibit 2–14).

**Positioning by Price/Quality** Marketers often use price/quality characteristics to position their brands. One way they do this is with ads that reflect the image of a high-quality brand where cost, while not irrelevant, is considered secondary to the quality benefits derived from using the brand. Premium brands positioned at the high end of the market use this approach to positioning.

Another way to use price/quality characteristics for positioning is to focus on the quality or value offered by the brand at a very competitive price. For example, Kohl's takes the position of a family-oriented speciality store offering good value (Exhibit 2–15). Remember that although price is an important consideration, the product quality must be comparable to, or even better than, competing brands for the positioning strategy to be effective.

**Positioning by Use or Application** Another way to communicate a specific image or position for a brand is to associate it with a specific use or application. The Intuit ad shown in Exhibit 2–16 is specifically targeted to small business owners and/or entrepreneurs.

While this strategy is often used to enter a market on the basis of a particular use or application, it is also an effective way to expand the usage of a product. For example, Arm & Hammer baking soda has been promoted for everything from baking to relieving heartburn to eliminating odors in carpets and refrigerators (Exhibit 2–17).

**Positioning by Product Class** Often the competition for a product comes from outside the product class. For example, airlines know that while they compete with other airlines, trains and buses are also viable alternatives. Amtrak has positioned itself as an alternative to airplanes, citing cost savings, enjoyment, and other advantages. Dole fruit juices encourage consumers to "drink their fruits," claiming that 8 ounces of juice is the equivalent of two fruits. V8 promotes drinking one's vegetables (Exhibit 2–18).

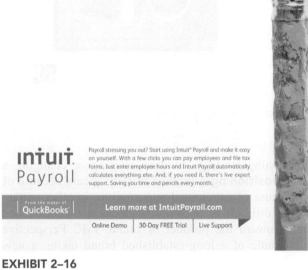

*Payroll doesn't have to be so frustrating. Unless you like the extra fiber in your diet.*

**Intuit** Payroll

From the maker of | QuickBooks

Payroll stressing you out? Start using Intuit® Payroll and make it easy on yourself. With a few clicks you can pay employees and file tax forms. Just enter employee hours and Intuit Payroll automatically calculates everything else. And, if you need it, there's live expert support. Saving you time and pencils every month.

Learn more at IntuitPayroll.com

Online Demo | 30-Day FREE Trial | Live Support

**EXHIBIT 2–16**

Intuit offers products specifically useful to small business owners

**EXHIBIT 2–17**

Arm & Hammer baking soda demonstrates numerous product uses

Rather than positioning against another brand, an alternative strategy is to position oneself against another product category. The California Avocado Information Bureau launched a major IMC campaign to more strongly position itself as a fruit (as opposed to a vegetable). The print, radio, outdoor, and online campaign took a humorous approach, positioning the avocado as a "fun fruit," while at the same time demonstrating the healthy advantages relative to other fruits and vegetables, and providing numerous products for which it might become an alternative, including cream cheese, butter, and dips. Copy points for the ads are provided by the bureau to retailers A Mountain High yogurt ad positions the product as a substitute for other baking ingredients.

**Positioning by Product User** Positioning a product by associating it with a particular user or group of users is yet another approach. An example would be the DC Shoes ad shown in Exhibit 2–19. This ad emphasizes identification or association with a specific group, in this case, skateboarders.

**Positioning by Competitor** Competitors may be as important to positioning strategy as a firm's own product or services. Advertisers used to think it was a cardinal sin to mention a competitor in their advertising. However, in today's market, an effective positioning strategy for a product or brand may focus on specific competitors. This approach is similar to positioning by product class, although in this case the competition is within the same product category. Perhaps the best-known example of this strategy was Avis, which positioned itself against the car-rental leader, Hertz, by stating, "We're number two, so we try harder." The billboard shown earlier (Exhibit 2–5) is an example of positioning a brand against the competition. When positioning by competitor, a marketer must often employ another positioning strategy as well to differentiate the brand.

**Positioning by Cultural Symbols** Aaker and Myers include an additional positioning strategy in which cultural symbols are used to differentiate brands. When it is associated with a meaningful symbol, the brand is easily identifiable and differentiated from others. Examples are the Jolly Green Giant, the Keebler elves, Speedy Alka-Seltzer, the Pillsbury Doughboy, the Wells Fargo stagecoach, Ronald McDonald, Chiquita Banana, and Mr. Peanut. Tony the Tiger (who has been used by Kellogg's for over 60 years—with a few minor facelifts) clearly qualifies as a cultural symbol (Exhibit 2–20). Each of these symbols has successfully differentiated the product it represents from competitors'.

WES KREMER HATES ON HEEL BRUISES.
THE TRUE S WITH VULCANIZED SOLE AND CUSHIONING.

**EXHIBIT 2–18**

V8 positions itself as a drink that substitutes for vegetables

**EXHIBIT 2–19**

DC positions by product user—in this case, skateboarders

**YTC 02–07**

**DC Shoes Channel**

youtube.com/10ebelch

**Repositioning** One final positioning strategy involves altering or changing a product's or brand's position. **Repositioning** a product usually occurs because of declining or stagnant sales or because of anticipated opportunities in other market positions. Repositioning is often difficult to accomplish because of entrenched perceptions about and attitudes toward the product or brand. IMC Perspective 2–2 discusses an interesting example of a long-established brand taking a new direction.

After a sales slump that began in 2008, Gatorade—once the world's most popular sports drink—changed its name to "G2," reduced the size of its lightning bolt trademark, and began to broaden its appeal to other markets (Exhibit 2–21). As noted by David Burwick, CEO of PepsiCo North America, "The functional difference is that we're going from a brand that speaks to really elite athletes to a brand that speaks for the athlete in everyone." While the repositioning originally had disappointing results, within a few years significant brand share gains were achieved.[20,21]

**EXHIBIT 2–20**

Tony the Tiger has become a cultural symbol

**EXHIBIT 2–21**

Gatorade has made changes to appeal to a broader market

# IMC Perspective 2–2 > > >

## Repositioning: Sometimes It Works, Sometimes Not

YTC 02–08
MTV Channel
youtube.com/10ebelch

What do MTV, JCPenney, and La-Z-Boy have in common? The answer? Each of these iconic brands has changed its image—or at least has attempted to change it—by repositioning.

*MTV* At the time there was nothing like it, and perhaps there never will be again. To some it is a shame that it's gone, to others it's a relief. Nevertheless, love it or hate it, one of the most powerful networks to ever hit cable television is now 30 years old. In the first week of February 2010, MTV formally changed its logo, dropping the part that said Music Television. In fact, the MTV of today is a reality TV channel, only occasionally airing something that has to do with music.

When MTV debuted in 1981, "the channel confirmed the concept of cable niche programming, reshaped music marketing, and became a symbol of youth culture," notes Bryan Reesman of *Billboard* magazine. Showing little more than music videos and DJs, music lovers tuned in in droves. By the end of its first year, MTV had over 2.1 million subscribing households. By its second year, the "I Want My MTV" ad campaign was in full force, featuring a number of rock stars, including Pete Townshend, Stevie Nicks, Mick Jagger, and David Bowie, among others. Michael Jackson premiered both "Beat It" and "Thriller" on MTV in 1983. MTV had taken off, and parents everywhere were becoming concerned with their children's "addiction" to music videos.

By the mid-80s things started to change. A British sitcom was added to the programming, as was support for young comedians such as Chris Rock, Ben Stiller, and Jon Stewart. The network also started to engage in philanthropic events by airing 17 hours of the Live Aid concert, running safe sex commercials, and showing "Just Say No" antidrug spots. Eventually, MTV started running its own "Rock Against Drugs"—the first of many attempts to engage viewers with social programming. One of MTV's most popular shows featuring new artists, *Unplugged*, debuted in the early 1990s. By the late 1990s numerous programs were added, with less time for rock videos. The number of antidrug and other social marketing programs also increased.

Throughout the early years of the 21st century, MTV continued to broaden both its programming and its social involvement, launched new channels (there were 64 in 2011), and expanded internationally. The network had clearly begun to reposition itself as something other than just a music channel. Music stars like Madonna, Michael Jackson, and Britney Spears have been replaced by "Snooki" Polizzi from the reality show *Jersey Shore* and Heidi Montag from *The Hills.* As noted by Scott Collins, "MTV has evolved into a reality channel that occasionally runs programs that have to do with music." But why?

David Howe, president of SyFy (which itself used to be the Sci-Fi Channel), says that MTV—like Sci-Fi—realized that being just music television was too limiting, and current viewers didn't relate to it as a music channel anymore. Instead, the programming has changed MTV, as it no longer competes with VH1 and Fuse but competes with other reality programs more, and the logo is important in communicating that fact.

*JCPenney* Once again—as it did in 2010 and 2011—JCPenney announced that it was repositioning the brand in 2012, hoping that the third time will be the charm. With a new pricing strategy, thousands fewer employees, and yet another new logo, the retailer's new president said that the store "is redefining the JCPenney brand to become a store for all Americans, by offering an experience they cannot get anywhere else." To do this, the number of sales promotions were drastically cut, replaced by an everyday low price policy. New partnerships were established, including a Martha Stewart line of clothing, as well as an exclusive line with fashion designer Nanette Lepore. Ellen DeGeneres (once a JCPenny employee) was the new brand ambassador, in hopes that she will inject new life and excitement to the brand. The logo also has been changed for the third time in three years. All of these strategies were designed to help JCPenney hold on to its existing customers, and hopefully attract even more. Unfortunately, the strategy did not work. At the time of this writing. Penneys removed its president and is seeking yet another positioning strategy.

*La-Z-Boy* JCPenney probably wishes it had La-Z-Boy's problem. As noted by trade publication *Brandweek,* the strong brand recognition enjoyed by the furniture company may actually be a liability. The problem is that while La-Z-Boy makes sofas, ottomans, love seats, and sectionals, the brand has become synonymous with recliners, and the other stationary products don't reap the benefits of the strong brand name. So La-Z-Boy hired Brooke Shields to be its new spokesperson, hoping that her celebrity status would gain attention for the new message that the company has an entire furniture line—not just recliners. A series of five new commercials to be shown on A&E, Animal Planet, Bravo, and CNN (among others) will be accompanied by print ads in magazines that include *Better Homes and Gardens, Good Housekeeping,* and *House Beautiful,* and a strong public relations effort.

Sometimes repositioning is desirable to maintain success. Sometimes it is a requirement to stay afloat. It is always a difficult strategy to implement.

Sources: Andrew Hampp, "Unplugged to Return to MTV, Courtesy Starburst," *Advertising Age,* March 4, 2010; Scott Collins, "The Network Name Game," *Los Angeles Times,* February 13, 2010, pp. D1,12; Bryan Reesman, "Timeline: Rewinding 25 Years of MTV History," *Billboard,* September 2, 2008, pp. 36–45; Mark J. Miller, "JC Penney Re-Refreshes Brand—Third Time's the Charm?" www.brandchannel.com, January 26, 2012, pp. 1–6; Stuart Elliott, "La-Z-Boy, Meet Brooke Shields," *The New York Times,* November 29, 2010, pp. 1–5.

Before leaving this section, you might stop to think for a moment about the positioning (and repositioning) strategies pursued by different companies. Any successful product that comes to mind probably occupies a distinct market position.

# DEVELOPING THE MARKETING PLANNING PROGRAM

The development of the marketing strategy and selection of a target market(s) tell the marketing department which customers to focus on and what needs to attempt to satisfy. The next stage of the marketing process involves combining the various elements of the marketing mix into a cohesive, effective marketing program. Each marketing-mix element is multidimensional and includes a number of decision areas. Likewise, each must consider and contribute to the overall IMC program. We now examine product, price, and distribution channels and how each influences and interacts with the promotional program.

## Product Decisions

An organization exists because it has some product, service, or idea to offer consumers, generally in exchange for money. This offering may come in the form of a physical product (such as a soft drink, pair of jeans, or car), a service (banking, airlines, or legal assistance), a cause (Special Olympics, American Cancer Society), or even a person (a political candidate). The product is anything that can be marketed and that, when used or supported, gives satisfaction to the individual.

A *product* is not just a physical object; it is a bundle of benefits or values that satisfies the needs of consumers. The needs may be purely functional, or they may include social and psychological benefits. For example, the campaign for Michelin tires stresses the quality built into Michelin tires (value) as well as their performance and durability (function). The term **product symbolism** refers to what a product or brand means to consumers and what they experience in purchasing and using it.[22] For many products, strong symbolic features and social and psychological meaning may be more important than functional utility.[23] For example, designer clothing such as Versace, Gucci, and Prada is often purchased on the basis of its symbolic meaning and image, particularly by teenagers and young adults. Advertising plays an important role in developing and maintaining the image of these brands.

Product planning involves decisions not only about the item itself, such as design and quality, but also about aspects such as service and warranties as well as brand name and package design. Consumers look beyond the reality of the product and its ingredients. The product's quality, branding, packaging, and even the company standing behind it all contribute to consumers' perceptions.[24] In an effective IMC program, advertising, branding, and packaging are all designed to portray the product as more than just a bundle of attributes. All are coordinated to present an image or positioning of the product that extends well beyond its physical attributes.

**Branding** Branding is about building and maintaining a favorable identity and image of the company and/or its products or services in the mind of the consumer. The goal of branding is to (1) build and maintain brand awareness and interest, (2) develop and enhance attitudes toward the company, product, or service, and (3) build and foster relationships between the consumer and the brand. The **brand identity** consists of the combination of the name, logo, symbols, design, packaging, and image of associations held by consumers. Think for a minute about the

THE SCIENTIST'S WATCH

THE MILGAUSS

ROLEX

**EXHIBIT 2–22**

Rolex creates strong brand equity through advertising

**EXHIBIT 2–23**

This ad for WD-40 shows just a few of the many uses for the product

REMOVES
insects from front grill
USE #67

STOPS
belt noise
USE #93

BUFFS OUT
scuff marks on bumpers
USE #35

REMOVES
grit from windshield wipers
USE #49

EASES
removal of stuck spark plugs
USE #24

STOPS
squeaks in car strut mounts
USE #111

FOR 2000+ USES ON OR OFF THE TRACK, VISIT WD40.COM.

WD-40
There's Always Another Use...

| DATE | JOB | TITLE | | PUBLICATION | ISSUE | CLOSE | REVISE |
|------|-----|-------|-|-------------|-------|-------|--------|
| 12/14/09 | WD-09-98 | ISC Racing Ad | | ISC Racing Program | Yearly | 12/18 | r0 |

| LIVE | TRIM | BLEED | COLORS | BUILT AT | LASER AT |
|------|------|-------|--------|----------|----------|
| 8.125" x 10.625" | 8.375" x 10.875" | 8.625" x 11.125" | CMYK | 100% | 100% |

| SA | SM | PM | TM | CW | AD | ECD | EAC | AE | AS/MS | ATD | EE | AGENCY |
|----|----|----|----|----|----|----|----|----|-------|-----|----|--------|
| | | | | | | | | | | | | o'leary |

NOTES / DELIVERY SPECIFICATIONS
outline fonts

ads for Nike; the product benefits and attributes are usually not even mentioned—yet information about the brand is communicated effectively.

One important role of advertising in respect to branding strategies is creating and maintaining **brand equity,** which can be thought of as an intangible asset of added value or goodwill that results from the favorable image, impressions of differentiation, and/or the strength of consumer attachment to a company name, brand name, or trademark. Brand equity allows a brand to earn greater sales volume and/or higher margins than it could without the name, providing the company with a competitive advantage. The strong equity position a company and/or its brand enjoys is often reinforced through advertising. For example, Rolex watches command a premium price because of their high quality as well as the strong brand equity they have developed through advertising (Exhibit 2–22).

**Packaging** Packaging is another aspect of product strategy that has become increasingly important. Traditionally, the package provided functional benefits such as economy, protection, and storage. However, the role and function of the package have changed because of the self-service emphasis of many stores and the fact that more and more buying decisions are made at the point of purchase. One study estimated that as many as two-thirds of all purchases made in the supermarket are unplanned. The package is often the consumer's first exposure to the product, so it must make a favorable first impression. A typical supermarket has more than 30,000 items competing for attention. Not only must a package attract and hold the consumer's attention, but it must also communicate information on how to use the product, divulge its composition and content, and satisfy any legal requirements regarding disclosure. Moreover, many firms design the package to carry a sales promotion message such as a contest, sweepstakes, or premium offer.

Many companies view the package as an important way to communicate with consumers and create an impression of the brand in their minds. In other instances packages can extend the brand by offering new uses (Exhibit 2–23). Design factors such as size, shape, color, and lettering all contribute to the appeal of a package and can be as important as a commercial in determining what goes from the store shelf to the consumer's shopping cart. Many companies use packaging to create a distinctive brand image and identity. The next time you walk by a perfume counter, stop to look at the many unique package designs (see Exhibit 2–24).

## Price Decisions

The *price variable* refers to what the consumer must give up to purchase a product or service. While price is discussed in terms of the dollar amount exchanged for an item, the cost of a product to the consumer includes time, mental activity, and behavioral effort.[25] The marketing manager is usually concerned with establishing a price level, developing pricing policies, and monitoring competitors' and consumers' reactions to prices in the marketplace. A firm must consider a number of factors in determining the price it charges for its product or service, including costs, demand factors, competition, and perceived value. From an IMC perspective, the price must be

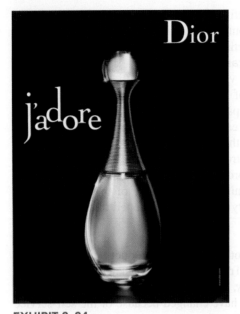

**EXHIBIT 2–24**

This packaging creates product image

consistent with the perceptions of the product, as well as the communications strategy. Higher prices, of course, will communicate a higher product quality, while lower prices reflect bargain or "value" perceptions. A product positioned as highest quality but carrying a lower price than competitors would only confuse consumers. In other words, the price, the advertising, and the distribution channels must present one unified voice speaking to the product's positioning.

**Relating Price to Advertising and Promotion** Factors such as product quality, competition, and advertising all interact in determining what price a firm can and should charge. Studies have shown that pricing and advertising strategies go together. High relative ad expenditures should accompany premium prices, and low relative ad expenditures should be tailored to low prices. These results obviously support the IMC perspective that one voice must be conveyed. In a recent and comprehensive study, it was shown that exposure to television ads reduces consumers' tendencies to react to price changes. The study further showed that heavy users of the product category were most likely to have their sensitivities reduced.[26]

## Distribution Channel Decisions

As consumers, we generally take for granted the role of marketing intermediaries or channel members. If we want a six-pack of soda or a box of detergent, we can buy it at a supermarket, a convenience store, or even a drugstore. Manufacturers understand the value and importance of these intermediaries.

One of a marketer's most important marketing decisions involves the way it makes its products and services available for purchase. A firm can have an excellent product at a great price, but it will be of little value unless it is available where the customer wants it, when the customer wants it, and with the proper support and service. **Marketing channels,** the place element of the marketing mix, are "sets of interdependent organizations involved in the process of making a product or service available for use or consumption."[27]

The distribution strategy should take into consideration the communication objectives and the impact that the channel strategy will have on the IMC program. Stewart and colleagues discuss the need for "integrated channel management," which "reflects the blurring of the boundaries of the communications and distribution functions."[28] Consistent with the product and pricing decisions, where the product is distributed will send a communications message. Does the fact that a product is sold at Neiman Marcus or Saks convey a different message regarding its image than if it were distributed at Kmart or Walmart? If you think about it for a moment, the mere fact that the product is distributed in these channels communicates an image about it in your mind. Stewart gives examples of how channel elements contribute to communication—for example, grocery store displays, point-of-purchase merchandising, and shelf footage. The distribution channel in a well-integrated marketing program serves as a form of reminder advertising. The consumer sees the brand name and recalls the advertising. (Think about the last time you passed a McDonald's. Did it remind you of any of McDonald's ads?)

A company can choose not to use any channel intermediaries but, rather, to sell to its customers through **direct channels.** This type of channel arrangement is sometimes used in the consumer market by firms using direct-selling programs, such as Avon, Tupperware, and Mary Kay, or firms that use direct-response advertising, telemarketing, or the Internet to sell their products. Direct channels are also frequently used by manufacturers of industrial products and services, which are often selling expensive and complex products that require extensive negotiations and sales efforts, as well as service and follow-up calls after the sale.

Chapter 15 provides a discussion of the role of the Internet in an IMC program. As will be seen, the Internet is relied upon by many companies as a direct channel of distribution, since they offer products and services for sale on their websites. Amazon.com and Barnesandnoble.com are just two of the many examples of such efforts.

Most consumer-product companies distribute through **indirect channels,** usually using a network of wholesalers (institutions that sell to other resellers) and/or retailers (which sell primarily to the final consumer).

### Developing Promotional Strategies: Push or Pull?

Most of you are aware of advertising and other forms of promotion directed toward ultimate consumers or business customers. We see these ads in the media and are often part of the target audience for the promotions. In addition to developing a consumer marketing mix, a company must have a program to motivate the channel members. Programs designed to persuade the trade to stock, merchandise, and promote a manufacturer's products are part of a **promotional push strategy.** The goal of this strategy is to push the product through the channels of distribution by aggressively selling and promoting the item to the resellers, or trade.

Promotion to the trade includes all the elements of the promotional mix. Company sales representatives call on resellers to explain the product, discuss the firm's plans for building demand among ultimate consumers, and describe special programs being offered to the trade, such as introductory discounts, promotional allowances, and cooperative ad programs. The company may use **trade advertising** to interest wholesalers and retailers and motivate them to purchase its products for resale to their customers. Trade advertising usually appears in publications that serve the particular industry.

A push strategy tries to convince resellers they can make a profit on a manufacturer's product and to encourage them to order the merchandise and push it through to their customers. An alternative strategy is a **promotional pull strategy,** spending money on advertising and sales promotion efforts directed toward the ultimate consumer. The goal of a pull strategy is to create demand among consumers and encourage them to request the product from the retailer. Seeing the consumer demand, retailers will order the product from wholesalers (if they are used), which in turn will request it from the manufacturer. Thus, stimulating demand at the end-user level pulls the product through the channels of distribution.

Whether to emphasize a push or a pull strategy depends on a number of factors, including the company's relations with the trade, its promotional budget, and demand for the firm's products. Companies that have favorable channel relationships may prefer to use a push strategy and work closely with channel members to encourage them to stock and promote their products. A firm with a limited promotional budget may not have the funds for advertising and sales promotion that a pull strategy requires and may find it more cost-effective to build distribution and demand by working closely with resellers. When the demand outlook for a product is favorable because it has unique benefits, is superior to competing brands, or is very popular among consumers, a pull strategy may be appropriate. Companies often use a combination of push and pull strategies, with the emphasis changing as the product moves through its life cycle.

# THE ROLE OF ADVERTISING AND PROMOTION

As shown in the marketing model in Figure 2–1, the marketing program includes promotion both to the trade (channel members) and to the company's ultimate customers. Marketers use the various promotional-mix elements—advertising, sales promotion, direct marketing, publicity/public relations, and personal selling—to inform consumers about their products, their prices, and places where the products are available. Each promotional-mix variable helps marketers achieve their promotional objectives, and all variables must work together to achieve an integrated marketing communications program.

To this point, we have discussed the various elements of the marketing plan that serves as the basis for the IMC program. The development and implementation of an IMC program is based on a strong foundation that includes market analysis, target marketing and positioning, and coordination of the various marketing-mix elements. Throughout the following chapters of this text, we will explore the role of various IMC elements in helping to achieve marketing objectives.

## Summary

Promotion plays an important role in an organization's efforts to market its product, service, or ideas to its customers. Figure 2–1 shows a model for analyzing how promotions fit into a company's marketing program. The model includes a marketing strategy and analysis, target marketing, program development, and the target market. The marketing process begins with a marketing strategy that is based on a detailed situation analysis and guides for target market selection and development of the firm's marketing program.

In the planning process, the situation analysis requires that the marketing strategy be assumed. The promotional program is developed with this strategy as a guide. One of the key decisions to be made pertains to the target marketing process, which

includes identifying, segmenting, targeting, and positioning to target markets. There are several bases for segmenting the market and various ways to position a product.

Once the target marketing process has been completed, marketing program decisions regarding product, price, distribution, and promotions must be made. All of these must be coordinated to provide an integrated marketing communications perspective, in which the positioning strategy is supported by one voice. Thus all product strategies, pricing strategies, and distribution choices must be made with the objective of contributing to the overall image of the product or brand. Advertising and promotion decisions, in turn, must be integrated with the other marketing-mix decisions to accomplish this goal.

## Key Terms

strategic marketing plan p. 43
market segments p. 44
market opportunities p. 44
competitive advantage p. 45
target marketing p. 46
market segmentation p. 48
geographic segmentation p. 48
demographic segmentation p. 50
psychographic segmentation p. 51
behavioristic segmentation p. 51

80–20 rule p. 53
benefit segmentation p. 53
undifferentiated marketing p. 54
differentiated marketing p. 54
concentrated marketing p. 54
positioning p. 55
salient attributes p. 56
repositioning p. 58
product symbolism p. 59
brand identity p. 59

brand equity p. 61
marketing channels p. 62
direct channels p. 62
indirect channels p. 63
promotional push strategy p. 63
trade advertising p. 63
promotional pull strategy p. 63

## Discussion Questions

**1.** The lead-in to this chapter discussed the millennial generation. Discuss some of the ways that this market segment is different from previous age cohorts. (LO3)

**2.** IMC Perspective 2–1 discusses the importance of the Hispanic market. What makes this subculture different, and what must marketers do to successfully target them? (LO2)

**3.** What is meant by repositioning? Discuss some companies that have successfully employed this strategy. (LO4)

**4.** Many companies have maintained their same brand identity for years by keeping the same logos, packaging, and so on, while others have made changes. Give examples of companies employing both of these strategies and discuss their results. (LO5)

**5.** Some marketers feel that grouping consumers into age cohorts like millennials, baby boomers, and so forth, results in unreliable generalizations and that such strategies might not be successful. Give the pros and cons of this argument. (LO2)

6. Discuss the role that integrated marketing communications plays in creating a brand image. How do media contribute to the development of these images? (LO1)

7. Choose a company and discuss how it communicates with its customers in different market segments. (LO4)

8. Discuss the strategy of market segmentation and some of the reasons marketers are employing such techniques.

Are there any ethical issues involved in this strategy? (LO4)

9. Marketing strategies are placing more and more effort on target marketing. What is target marketing? Give examples of companies currently employing this strategy. (LO3)

10. Discuss the difference between demographic and psychographic segmentation. Give examples of companies employing each. (LO4)

## LEARNING OBJECTIVES

**LO1** To understand how companies organize for advertising and other aspects of integrated marketing communications.

**LO2** To evaluate the advantages and disadvantages of the various ways companies organize for advertising and promotion.

**LO3** To understand the role of advertising agencies and the services they perform as well as the various types of agencies and media specialist companies.

**LO4** To examine methods for selecting, compensating, and evaluating advertising agencies.

**LO5** To explain the role and functions of specialized marketing communication organizations.

**LO6** To examine various perspectives on the use of integrated services and responsibilities of advertisers versus agencies.

# 3 Organizing for Advertising and Promotion: The Role of Ad Agencies and Other Marketing Communication Organizations

## DEUTSCH LA HAS VOLKSWAGEN ON A ROLL

In 2008, Volkswagen chief executive officer Martin Winterkorn announced that the German company was planning on moving past Toyota to become the world's largest automaker by 2018. Winterkorn's "Strategy 2018" goals also included making Volkswagen Group the world's most profitable automaker as well as the most fascinating and sustainable one. Volkswagen's growth strategy included going head-to-head with its major European competitors, including BMW, Mercedes, Renault, and Fiat, as well as pursuing the rapidly growing markets of China, Southeast Asia, and India. However, its most ambitious plans were in the U.S. market, where the goal was to double sales to more than 400,000 cars by 2012 and to 800,000 vehicles per year by 2018. Volkswagen, which is the largest automaker in Europe and number 2 in China, once was the largest foreign auto brand in the United States back in the days when the Beetle was a cultural icon and dominated the small-car market. However, over the past two decades Volkswagen fell behind Japanese competitors such as Toyota and Honda and then began facing new competition from Korean brands such as Hyundai and Kia. Adding to VW's problems was the fact that the strong euro made its German-built cars expensive in the U.S. market in recent years.

Volkswagen decided to invest in the American market and build a state-of-the-art plant dedicated to producing cars specifically for the North American market. The plant in Tennessee, which eventually opened in 2011, reduced production and shipping costs and kept the overall costs of the vehicle down. VW also plans to expand its product line over the next five years by introducing new compact and midsize sedans as part of its strategy and to sell American car buyers on German engineering and styling at affordable prices. However, when the automaker announced its aggressive growth plans for the U.S. market, it recognized that it faced a formidable marketing challenge as nearly 80 percent of Americans were aware of the VW brand but only 2 percent were buying its cars. Most Americans recognized the Beetle and Jetta but drew a blank on the company's other models, such as the Passat, Golf, GTI, Routan, Eos, Tiguan, and Touareg. Thus, to increase its sales volume in the U.S. market, Volkswagen had to become more relevant and the appeal of the brand had to move beyond the base of loyal enthusiasts and captivate consumers in the mainstream market.

Volkswagen of America took its first step toward changing the perceptions of Americans and showing them that it sells more than Beetles and Jettas, when it awarded its advertising and marketing communications business to a new advertising agency, Deutsch LA, in October 2009. Volkswagen chose Deutsch LA over a number of other agencies that were competing for the account. However, after a rigorous agency review process, Deutsch won the account by focusing on the bottom-line issue of selling vehicles and by impressing VW's management with its strategic thinking and its creative ideas, which included ways to extend the marketing campaign into the digital space and particularly into the fast-growing realm of social media. The agency team recognized that the initial challenges they faced were to make the Volkswagen brand relevant again, increase awareness of the VW product line, and gain consumers' interest and consideration by letting them know that the company has a vehicle that fits their needs.

To address these challenges, Deutsch LA developed a new campaign called "Punch Dub" which was an update on the classic Punch Buggy (or Slug Bug) game that kids used to play in the heyday of the original VW Beetle, where the first person to see a Beetle would yell "Punch Bug" and playfully slug his or her friend. The campaign was launched with a lighthearted 30-second commercial on the 2010 Super Bowl which featured a variety of people in different driving situations gently slugging each other in the arm every time they spotted a Volkswagen model, and included cameo appearances by actor-comedian Tracy Morgan and singing legend Stevie Wonder. An online version of "Punch Dub" also debuted on the popular Facebook social networking site on Super Bowl Sunday that encouraged people to dole out virtual "slugs" to friends and family for a chance to win a weekly prize (six-month leases on specific VW vehicles listed online) and the grand prize of a new Volkswagen CC sedan. Players could pick any 1 of 13 VW vehicles, customize their punch, and choose a Facebook friend to punch. The more friends they punched, the better the chances of winning a prize. The game was also available on the Volkswagen of America website, along with an online guide to the game that players could use to develop and hone their punching technique. The "Punch Dub" spot was one of the most popular commercials to air during the Super Bowl, and within a few days had received more than 1 million online views while the game had 5,000 registered users and nearly 30,000 punches were thrown.

As part of the campaign, Volkswagen revealed that it had found the creator of the original game—Charlie "Sluggy" Patterson—and made it possible for people to interact with him via a special blog and Twitter feed as well as through a series of videos on YouTube. Within a few weeks of the launch of the campaign the videos had generated more than 100,000 views on YouTube and thousands of Twitter followers. The two-month campaign included outdoor, radio, and newspaper advertising and was also extended to Volkswagen dealerships as special point-of-sale kits were developed to promote a national sales event called "Punch Dub Days," which included special offers on various VW models.

After a few months, Volkswagen transitioned into the second phase of the campaign that leveraged the theme "Das Auto," which is the global tagline for Volkswagen. Deutsch tweaked the tagline for the U.S. market to "That's Das Auto," and the campaign continued to showcase the company's product line and highlight how VW delivers German engineering at a great value in a playful yet direct tone. The ads in the second phase of the campaign promoted the innovative feature and benefits of the various Volkswagen models. As part of its strategy VW continued to develop new cars for the U.S. market, such as the new CC sedan, and new models of the Jetta and U.S.-built Passat, and Deutsch continued to find creative ways to promote them. The agency created a commercial for the 2011 Super Bowl called "The Force" which featured a little boy dressed as Darth Vader, the villain from the *Star Wars* movie. The ad was one of the most popular spots to air during the big game. The spot featured the boy unsuccessfully trying to use his imaginary powers to get a reaction from various items including an exercise bike, appliances, and a sleeping dog until he encounters a new 2012 Passat sedan in the driveway. This time the car appears to magically come to life when the boy raises his hands after his father secretly starts the engine using the remote start feature on the key fob. Deutsch LA carefully "leaked" the spot onto YouTube a few days prior to Super Bowl Sunday, and it had an incredible 12.4 million views and dominated pregame buzz on social media such as Twitter and Facebook. The spot went on to become a global cultural phenomenon as it has amassed more than 56 million views on YouTube, making it one of the top 10 viral ads of all time.

Deutsch LA has continued to deliver outstanding creative work across all areas of Volkswagen's advertising channels and is helping the company achieve its ambitious sales goal for the U.S. market. Volkswagen exceeded its sales goals in the United States in 2012, setting a record and topping the company's historical 1970 peak. Volkswagen's success is winning over onetime skeptics who questioned whether the company could ever again become a major player in the U.S. market. The automaker's success has also helped make Deutsch LA one of the hottest agencies in the business, as evidenced by its selection to the *Advertising Age* 2013 "A-List" which recognizes the shops whose creativity transcends ads and solves business problems with big ideas.

Sources: Maureen Morrison, "Ad Age Agency A-List," *Advertising Age*, January 28, 2013, p. 20; Christina Ross, "VW Gains Traction with Strong U.S. Push," *The Wall Street Journal*, January 22, 2013, p. B5; Stephen Williams, "Volkswagen Returns to Glory Road," *Advertising Age*, November 6, 2011, http://adage.com/print/230839; Jean Halliday, "Hits Keep Coming from VW's Super Bowl Ads," *Automotive News*, February 12, 2010, p. 2; Jean Halliday, "How Deutsch L.A. Snared Plum VW Account," *Advertising Age*, October 26, 2009, pp. 1, 56.

Developing and implementing an integrated marketing communications program is usually a complex and detailed process involving the efforts of many persons. As consumers, we generally give little thought to the individuals or organizations that create the clever advertisements that capture our attention, the websites we visit, or the contests and sweepstakes we hope to win. But for those involved in the marketing process, it is important to understand the nature of the industry and the structure and functions of the organizations involved. As discussed in the first two chapters, the advertising and promotions business is changing as marketers search for better ways to communicate with their customers. These changes are impacting the way marketers organize for marketing communications, as well as their relationships with advertising agencies and other communication specialists.

This chapter examines the various organizations that participate in the IMC process, their roles and responsibilities, and their relationship to one another. We discuss how companies organize internally for advertising and promotion. For most companies, advertising is planned and executed by an outside ad agency. Many large agencies offer a variety of other IMC capabilities, including public relations, digital/interactive, sales promotion, and direct marketing. Thus, we will devote particular attention to the ad agency's role and the overall relationship between company and agency.

Other participants in the promotional process (such as direct-marketing, sales promotion, and interactive agencies and public relations firms) are becoming increasingly important as more companies take an integrated marketing communications approach to promotion. We examine the role of these specialized marketing communication organizations in the promotional process as well. The chapter concludes with a discussion of whether marketers are best served by using the integrated services of one large agency or the separate services of a variety of communications specialists.

# PARTICIPANTS IN THE INTEGRATED MARKETING COMMUNICATIONS PROCESS: AN OVERVIEW

Before discussing the specifics of the industry, we'll provide an overview of the entire system and identify some of the players. As shown in Figure 3–1, participants in the integrated marketing communications process can be divided into five major groups: the advertiser (or client), advertising agencies, media organizations, specialized communication services, and collateral services. Each group has specific roles in the promotional process.

The advertisers, or **clients**, are the key participants in the process. They have the products, services, or causes to be marketed, and they provide the funds that pay for advertising and promotions. The advertisers also assume major responsibility for developing the marketing program and making the final decisions regarding the advertising and promotional program to be employed. The organization may perform most of these efforts itself either through its own advertising department or by setting up an in-house agency.

However, many organizations use an **advertising agency**, an outside firm that specializes in the creation, production, and/or placement of the communications message and that may provide other services to facilitate the marketing and promotions process. Many large advertisers retain the services of a number of agencies, particularly when they market a number of products. For example, Kraft Foods uses as many as eight advertising agencies for its various brands, while General Motors uses seven primary agencies for its various automotive divisions, which include Buick, Cadillac, Chevrolet, and GMC Truck, along with a major media buying service. GM also uses a public relations agency as well as several digital, promotional, and experiential marketing agencies; an entertainment marketing agency; a retail marketing agency; and an agency that specializes in sports marketing. Many large companies often use additional agencies that specialize in developing ads for multicultural markets. For example, in addition to its primary agency of record, Toyota Motor Corporation uses additional agencies in the United States to create ads for the African American, Hispanic, and Asian American markets. More and more, ad agencies are acting as partners with advertisers and assuming more responsibility for developing the marketing and promotional programs.

**Media organizations** are another major participant in the advertising and promotions process. The primary function of most media is to provide information or entertainment to their subscribers, viewers, or readers. But from the perspective of the promotional planner, the purpose of media is to provide an environment for the firm's marketing communications message. The media must have editorial or program content that attracts consumers so that advertisers and their agencies will want to buy time or space with them. Exhibit 3–1 shows an ad run in advertising trade publications promoting the value of *National Geographic* magazine and its family of media products as a way to reach consumers around the world. While the media perform many other functions that help advertisers understand their markets and their customers, a medium's primary objective is to sell itself as a way for companies to reach their target markets with their messages effectively.

The next group of participants are organizations that provide **specialized marketing communication services**. They include direct-marketing agencies, sales promotion agencies, digital/interactive agencies, and public relations firms. These organizations provide services in their areas of expertise. A direct-response agency develops and implements direct-marketing programs, while sales promotion agencies develop promotional programs such as contests and sweepstakes, premium offers, or sampling programs. Digital/interactive agencies are being retained to develop websites for the Internet and help marketers as they move deeper into the realm of interactive media. Public relations firms are used to generate and manage publicity for a company and its products and services as well as to focus on its relationships and communications with its relevant publics.

The final participants shown in the promotions process of Figure 3–1 are those that provide **collateral services**, the wide range of support functions used by advertisers, agencies, media organizations, and specialized marketing communication firms. These individuals and companies perform specialized functions the other participants use in planning and executing advertising and other promotional functions. We will now examine the role of each participant in more detail. (Media organizations will be examined in Chapters 10 through 14.)

# ORGANIZING FOR ADVERTISING AND PROMOTION IN THE FIRM: THE CLIENT'S ROLE

Virtually every business organization uses some form of marketing communication. However, the way a company organizes for these efforts depends on several factors, including its size, the number of products

**EXHIBIT 3–1**

*National Geographic* promotes its value to advertisers

What's so cool 👓 about National Geographic? It's checking out National Geographic interactive 🤚 magazine editions on your new iPad. It's going to the redesigned NationalGeographic.com ⌨ and finding an awe-inspiring 💡 photo from the other side of the world. It's tuning in to the new Nat Geo Wild Channel 📱 to see Casey Anderson and meet his best friend, Brutus, an 800-pound grizzly 🐾 bear. It's joining a conversation 💬 with one million other people on National Geographic's Facebook page. It's getting a Nat Geo tweet 🐦 while you're out with friends. It's checking in on 📍 Gowalla to complete a National Geographic 🔦 trip. It's all the different ways you can interact with the best content in the 🌐 world: through award-winning 📚 magazines, websites and TV networks, books, films and DVDs, games and apps, photos and maps, expeditions and events. 🎤

Reach a global audience of over 345 million consumers —wherever, whenever, and however you want— with the brand that rocks their world.

NATIONAL GEOGRAPHIC

*National Geographic and the yellow border design are trademarks of the National Geographic Society, used with permission.*

**FIGURE 3–1**

Participants in the
Integrated Marketing
Communications Process

LO 03-1

it markets, the role of advertising and promotion in its marketing mix, the advertising and promotion budget, and its marketing organization structure. Many individuals throughout the organization may be involved in the advertising and promotion decision-making process. Marketing personnel have the most direct relationship with advertising and are often involved in many aspects of the decision process, such as providing input to the campaign plan, agency selection, and evaluation of proposed programs. Top management is usually interested in how the advertising program represents the firm, and this may also mean being involved in advertising decisions even when the decisions are not part of its day-to-day responsibilities.

While many people both inside and outside the organization have some input into the advertising and promotion process, direct responsibility for administering the program must be assumed by someone within the firm. Many companies have an advertising department headed by an advertising or communications manager operating under a marketing director. An alternative used by many large multiproduct firms is a decentralized marketing (brand management) system. A third option is to form a separate agency within the firm, an in-house agency. Each of these alternatives is examined in more detail in the following sections.

## The Centralized System

LO 03-2

**FIGURE 3–2**

The Advertising
Department under a
Centralized System

In many organizations, marketing activities are divided along functional lines, with advertising placed alongside other marketing functions such as sales, marketing research, and product planning, as shown in Figure 3–2. The **advertising manager** is responsible for all promotions activities except sales (in some companies this individual has the title of marketing communications manager). In the most common

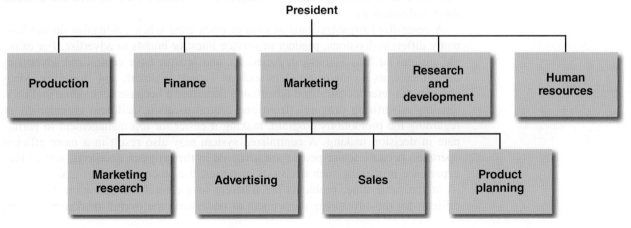

example of a **centralized system**, the advertising manager controls the entire promotions operation, including budgeting, coordinating creation and production of ads, planning media schedules, and monitoring and administering the sales promotions programs for all the company's products or services.

The specific duties of the advertising or marketing communications manager depend on the size of the firm and the importance it places on promotional programs. Basic functions the manager and staff perform include the following.

**Planning and Budgeting**   The advertising department is responsible for developing advertising and promotions plans that will be approved by management and recommending a promotions program based on the overall marketing plan, objectives, and budget. Formal plans are submitted annually or when a program is being changed significantly, as when a new campaign is developed. While the advertising department develops the promotional budget, the final decision on allocating funds is usually made by top management.

**Administration and Execution**   The manager must organize the advertising department and supervise and control its activities. The manager also supervises the execution of the plan by subordinates and/or the advertising agency. This requires working with such departments as production, media, art, copy, digital/interactive, and sales promotion. If an outside agency is used, the advertising department is relieved of much of the executional responsibility; however, it must review and approve the agency's plans.

**Coordination with Other Departments**   The manager must coordinate the advertising department's activities with those of other departments, particularly those involving other marketing functions. For example, the advertising department must communicate with marketing research and/or sales to determine which product features are important to customers and should be emphasized in the company's communications. Research may also provide profiles of product users and nonusers for the media department before it selects broadcast or print media. The advertising department may also be responsible for preparing material the sales force can use when calling on customers, such as sales promotion tools, advertising materials, and point-of-purchase displays.

**Coordination with Outside Agencies and Services**   Many companies have an advertising department but still use many outside services. For example, companies may develop their advertising programs in-house while employing media buying services to place their ads and/or use collateral services agencies to develop brochures, point-of-purchase materials, and so on. The department serves a liaison between the company and any outside service providers and also determines which ones to use. Once outside services are retained, the manager will work with other marketing managers to coordinate their efforts and evaluate their performances.

A centralized organizational system is often used when companies do not have many different divisions, product or service lines, or brands to advertise. For example, airlines such as Southwest, American, and JetBlue have centralized advertising departments, as do major retailers such as Target, Walmart, and Best Buy. Many companies prefer a centralized advertising department because developing and coordinating advertising programs from one central location facilitates communication regarding the promotions program, making it easier for top management to participate in decision making. A centralized system may also result in a more efficient operation because fewer people are involved in the program decisions, and as their experience in making such decisions increases, the process becomes easier.

At the same time, problems are inherent in a centralized operation. First, it is difficult for the advertising department to understand the overall marketing strategy

**EXHIBIT 3–2**

Many of Procter & Gamble's brands compete against each other

YTC **03–02**

**Procter & Gamble**

youtube.com/10ebelch

for the brand. The department may also be slow in responding to specific needs and problems of a product or brand. As companies become larger and develop or acquire new products, brands, or even divisions, the centralized system may become impractical.

## The Decentralized System

In large corporations with multiple divisions and many different products, it is very difficult to manage all the advertising, promotional, and other functions through a centralized department. These types of companies generally have a **decentralized system**, with separate manufacturing, research and development, sales, and marketing departments for various divisions, product lines, or businesses. Many companies that use a decentralized system, such as Procter & Gamble, Unilever, PepsiCo, and Nestlé, assign each product or brand to a **brand manager** who is responsible for the total management of the brand, including planning, budgeting, sales, and profit performance. (The term *product manager* is also used to describe this position.) The brand manager, who may have one or more assistant brand managers, is also responsible for the planning, implementation, and control of the marketing program.[1]

Under this system, the responsibilities and functions associated with advertising and promotions are transferred to the brand manager, who works closely with the outside advertising agency and other marketing communications specialists as they develop the promotional program.[2] In a multiproduct firm, each brand may have its own ad agency and may compete against other brands within the company, not just against outside competitors. For example, Exhibit 3–2 shows ads for Tide and Gain, which are both Procter & Gamble products that compete for a share of the laundry detergent market.

As shown in Figure 3–3, the advertising department is part of marketing services and provides support for the brand managers. The role of marketing services is to assist the brand managers in planning and coordinating the integrated marketing communications program. In some companies, the marketing services group may include sales promotion. The brand managers may work with sales promotion people to develop budgets, define strategies, and implement tactical executions for both trade and consumer promotions. Marketing services may also provide other types of support services, such as package design and merchandising.

Some companies may have an additional layer(s) of management above the brand managers to coordinate the efforts of all the brand managers handling a related group of products. This system—generally referred to as a **category management**

**FIGURE 3–3**

A Decentralized Brand
Management System

**system**—includes category managers as well as brand and advertising managers. The category manager oversees management of the entire product category and focuses on the strategic role of the various brands in order to build profits and market share.[3] Each category manager will have one or more brand managers reporting to him or her for each specific brand as well as an advertising manager.

The advertising manager may review and evaluate the various parts of the program and advise and consult with the brand managers. This person may have the authority to override the brand manager's decisions on advertising. In some multiproduct firms that spend a lot on advertising, the advertising manager may coordinate the work of the various agencies to obtain media discounts for the firm's large volume of media purchases. Category management is often used in large multiproduct or divisional companies. For example, Procter & Gamble's broad portfolio includes nearly 100 brands (25 of which generate more than a billion dollars in revenue each year) that are assigned to one of three major divisions: Beauty & Grooming, Health & Well Being, and Household Care (Exhibit 3–3). Each division includes multiple product categories to which individual brands are assigned for management purposes. For example, the North American Household Care Brands division contains eight product categories, including laundry and fabric care, household cleaners, baby and child care, batteries, paper, dishwashing, air fresheners, and paper.

**EXHIBIT 3–3**

P&G's broad portfolio of brands are assigned to various categories for management

An advantage of the decentralized system is that each brand receives concentrated managerial attention, resulting in faster response to both problems and opportunities. The brand managers have full responsibility for the marketing program, including the identification of target markets as well as the development of integrated marketing communications programs that will differentiate the brand.[4] The brand manager system is also more flexible and makes it easier to adjust various aspects of the advertising and promotional program, such as creative platforms and media and sales promotion schedules.[5]

There are some drawbacks to the decentralized approach. Brand managers often lack training and experience. The promotional strategy for a brand may be developed by a brand manager who does not really understand what advertising or sales promotion can and cannot do and how each should be used. Brand managers may focus too much on short-run planning and administrative tasks, neglecting the development of long-term programs.

Another problem is that individual brand managers often end up competing for management attention, marketing dollars, and other resources, which can lead to unproductive rivalries and potential misallocation of funds. The manager's persuasiveness may become a bigger factor in determining budgets than the long-run profit potential of the brands. These types of problems were key factors in Procter & Gamble's decision to switch to a category management system.

Finally, the brand management system has been criticized for failing to provide brand managers with authority over the functions needed to implement and control the plans they develop.[6] Some companies have dealt with this problem by expanding the roles and responsibilities of the advertising and sales promotion managers and their staff of specialists. The staff specialists counsel the individual brand managers, and advertising or sales promotion decision making involves the advertising and/or sales promotion manager, the brand manager, and the marketing director. For example, General Motors, which is one of the largest advertisers in the United States, decided to drop its brand management system and give division marketing directors more control of the advertising and promotion for its various models.[7] The traditional brand management system has come under attack recently as critics argue that brand managers spend too much time on internal issues such as planning and budgeting and do not devote enough effort to external matters or to creativity and problem solving.[8] It also has been argued that the brand management system must change in order for managers to keep abreast of the rapidly changing world of digital and social media, as is discussed in Digital and Social Media Perspective 3–1.[9]

## In-House Agencies

LO 03-2

Some companies, in an effort to reduce costs and maintain greater control over agency activities, have set up their own advertising agencies internally. An **in-house agency** is an advertising agency that is set up, owned, and operated by the advertiser. Some in-house agencies are little more than advertising departments, but in other companies they are given a separate identity and are responsible for the expenditure of large sums of advertising dollars. Large advertisers that use in-house agencies include Under Armour, Hyundai, Avon, Revlon, Fidelity Investments, and Benetton. Many companies use in-house agencies exclusively; others combine in-house efforts

## Ad Age Insights

**TREND REPORT**

# MANAGING YOUR BRAND'S SOCIAL LIFE

The brand management concept originated at Procter & Gamble over 80 years ago. A young employee working on an advertising campaign for the company's Camay soap brand became frustrated with having to compete against competing brands from Lever Bros. and Palmolive as well as P&G's own flagship Ivory soap brand. He sent a memo to P&G management that argued more focused attention should be paid to Camay, as well as to other P&G brands,

and suggested there should be an individual or team of people responsible for overseeing all aspects of marketing each product. The idea was that each brand would be managed as if it were its own company, which would result in more attention being given to it, particularly with respect to marketing. The brand management system was adopted by P&G and widely emulated in one form or another by companies throughout the world, particularly those with multiple brands competing in a product category. Marketers viewed brand management as a way to decentralize their decision making and give more autonomy to front-line managers while still maintaining some centralized control over all of the individual brands in their portfolio.

The brand management system has persisted and evolved throughout the 20th century and into the new millennium. For most of this time period brand managers have focused their efforts on areas such as planning, budgeting, target marketing, and looking for ways to differentiate the products they manage. They also have worked closely with the agencies that handle the advertising, promotion, and other elements of their IMC programs. However, some critics are arguing that the traditional brand management system is becoming increasingly out-of-date in today's world of digital media where brand meaning and identity is increasingly being determined by consumers rather than marketers. In 2009 Forrester Research, a leading technology and market research company, released a major report titled "Adaptive Brand Marketing: Rethinking Your Approach to Branding in the Digital Age" which notes that today's brand marketing organizations are ill equipped to handle the complex world of media fragmentation and "always on" marketing in the digital age. Forrester suggested that to remain relevant, marketing leaders needed to embrace what they term *adaptive brand marketing*, which they describe as a more consumer-centric approach that encourages rapid response to align consumer and brand needs.

with those of outside agencies. For example, retail giant Target has an internal creative department that handles the design of its weekly circulars, direct-mail pieces, in-store displays, promotions, and other marketing materials. However, the retailer uses outside agencies to develop most of its branding and image-oriented ads and for specific TV and print assignments. Other retailers such as Benetton and Banana Republic also have in-house advertising departments that work with outside agencies.

A major reason for using an in-house agency is to reduce advertising and promotion costs. Companies with very large advertising budgets pay a substantial amount to outside agencies in the form of media commissions or negotiated fees. With an internal structure, these commissions or fees go to the in-house agency. An in-house

The Forrester report also called for changes in the brand management system. The authors suggested that brand managers be renamed brand "advocates" and recommended restructuring their role to better accommodate the real-time digital world. They also advocated the elimination of the formal annual budgeting process which generally includes an up-front allocation of funds for specific media, in favor of more frequently updated and spontaneous plans that can be adapted as conditions change. Forrester also recommended that market research and analytics, which they called "consumer intelligence," be given a more prominent and central role and that brand advocates should shift their emphasis from long-term external partnerships with advertising agencies to alliances with media and other content creators that can shift more rapidly.

Some of the major marketers that utilize the brand management system argue that they are already doing much of what is recommended in the Forrester report. For example, Procter & Gamble is among the many companies that are relying more on digital and social media as part of their brand building strategies. P&G's Global Brand Building Officer Marc Pritchard says, "Our media strategy is pretty simple: follow the consumer. And the consumer is becoming more and more engaged in the digital world." He notes that online social media platforms are now a fundamental part of P&G's marketing programs, and adds: "Part of our jobs as brand builders is to create content that people want to share."

Chief marketing officers, brand managers, and others in charge of brand building in their companies recognize that the role of social media in their IMC programs is likely to increase. Consumers are spending a significant amount of their time on social media and are increasingly learning and sharing information about brands through social media platforms such as Facebook, YouTube, Twitter, and Pinterest, along with many other sites. However, Chris Perry, president of digital communications at the Weber Shandwick Global PR firm, argues that a crisis may be looming for brands in the new age of social media as they run the risk of losing their most precious asset, which is their *identity*. He notes that the rapid rise in the use of tweets, posts, blogs, and branded social network sites has created a far more fragmented and inconsistent online presence and voice for many brands, and what was once

a clearly defined brand identity can easily be lost in the effort to communicate with consumers through social media. Perry argues that "a pressing need is emerging: to communicate who you are as a brand and what you stand for through social media in a far more consistent, strategic and global way." He suggests that brands develop a social identity or "Social/ID" to coordinate communications across all of their social media platforms and touch points.

Others in the advertising and marketing industry have recognized the importance of managing the identity of a brand across social media platforms. For example, *Advertising Age* recently released an Ad Age Insights report, "Managing Your Brand's Social Life," which is designed to help brand managers decide which platforms should get the investment of limited staff and time, what to consider when creating internal social media guidelines, whether to handle social media in-house or outsource it, and metrics a brand should consider in evaluating return on investment. The report includes "Platform Playbooks" for social media sites such as Facebook, Google+, Pinterest, Tumblr, YouTube, and Foursquare.

Lisa Braner, the principal author of the Forrester report on adaptive brand marketing, notes that much of brand managers' time is subsumed by internal management issues and much of the creative process and planning is outsourced to agencies and other parties. She argues that "brand advocates really need to be in charge of the heart and soul of what the brand stands for." For many marketers, this means that they need to begin making changes in their brand management systems to prepare for the challenges their managers will face in the rapidly changing world of social media.

Sources: Jenna Schnuer, "How to Manage Your Brand's Social Life," *Advertising Age*, April 23, 2012, http://adage.com/print/234309; Chris Perry, "What's Your Brand's Social ID? Lost Amid the Tweets Posts, Streams and Feeds Is Your Brand's Social Identity," *Advertising Age*, September 8, 2010, http://adage.com/print/145795; Cotton Delo, "P&G Marketing Chief Touts Role of Facebook, Yahoo in 'Thank You, Mom' Campaign," *Advertising Age*, August 9, 2012, http://adage.com/print/236590; Jack Neff, "Why It's Time to Do Away with the Brand Manager," *Advertising Age*, October 12, 2009, http://adage.com/print/139593; Tom Hinkes, "Our Biggest Brands Can No Longer Be Managed by Nerds," *Advertising Age*, March 17, 2010, http://adage.com/print/142841.

agency can also provide related work such as production of collateral materials, digital media, package design, and public relations at a lower cost than outside agencies. In-house agencies are also preferred by some companies because they keep the marketing communications function more closely tied to top management. A study by Forrester Research found that nearly 60 percent of in-house agencies report directly to the company's CEO or chief marketing officer (CMO).[10] Another reason is the stability an in-house agency provides because external agencies have much higher turnover levels which can take a toll on the client–agency relationship. In contrast, in-house agencies are known for retaining their personnel and have a turnover rate of less than 5 percent.[11]

Saving money is not the only reason companies use in-house agencies. Time savings, bad experiences with outside agencies, and the increased knowledge and understanding of the market that come from working on advertising and promotion for the product or service day by day are also reasons. Companies can also maintain tighter control over the process and more easily coordinate promotions with the firm's overall marketing program.

YTC 03–03

Google Creative Lab

youtube.com/10ebelch

Some companies use an in-house agency simply because they believe it can do a better job than an outside agency could.[12] They may feel they have more knowledge about the market and competitors as well as a better understanding of the intricacies and complexities of their business. For example, Google launched an in-house agency in 2007 to handle its advertising. The company did very little advertising during its first 10 years in business because it relied primarily on the extensive publicity the company received and promotions done by other companies that would mention its search engine. However, as Google introduced more products and services, the company recognized the need to promote them to a broader audience and felt this could be done effectively using its own internal capabilities.[13] Thus, the company created a type of in-house agency known as the Google Creative Lab which develops much of its advertising and hired several former agency executives to run it. However, in recent years as Google has grown and expanded beyond online search and introduced new products and services such as its Chrome web browser, Nexus tablets, and Android operating system, it has begun to use outside agencies. Google has used large agencies such as Bartle Bogle Hagarty, which did promotion work for the Chrome browser, as well as a number of small independent agencies that fit well with the company's culture.[14]

Opponents of in-house agencies say they can give the advertiser neither the experience and objectivity of an outside agency nor the range of services. They argue that outside agencies have more highly skilled specialists and attract the best creative talent and that using an external firm gives a company a more varied perspective on its advertising problems and greater flexibility. Outside agencies also can provide greater strategic planning capabilities, outside perspectives on customers, and more creative experience with certain media such as television.[15] In-house personnel may become narrow or grow stale while working on the same product line, but outside agencies may have different people with a variety of backgrounds and ideas working on the account. Flexibility is greater because an outside agency can be dismissed if the company is not satisfied, whereas changes in an in-house agency could be slower and more disruptive.

The cost savings of an in-house agency must be evaluated against these considerations. For many companies, high-quality advertising is critical to their marketing success and should be the major criterion in determining whether to use in-house services. Companies like Rockport and Redken Laboratories have moved their in-house work to outside agencies in recent years. Redken cited the need for a "fresh look" and objectivity as the reason, noting that management gets too close to the product to come up with different creative ideas. Companies often hire outside agencies as they grow and their advertising budgets and needs increase. For example, Best Buy, the largest electronics retailer in the United States, handled all of its advertising through its in-house agency for nearly 20 years. However, in 2007 the company hired an outside agency to handle its advertising. The in-house shop was retained to work on the retailer's newspaper inserts, Hispanic, and direct and local marketing, as well as local store openings and advertising for some of the company's private-label brands. Best Buy management felt that an outside agency was needed to help achieve its aggressive growth goals and better position the company as a trusted retailer in the complex and competitive technology marketplace. Best Buy now uses the Crispin Porter + Bogusky agency to handle its brand-related advertising work as well as ads focusing on its Geek Squad customer-support unit.[16] However, Best Buy still maintains an in-house agency known as Yellow Tag Productions that works with agency partners like CP + B and also

| Organizational System | Advantages | Disadvantages |
|---|---|---|
| *Centralized* | ■ Facilitated communications<br>■ Fewer personnel required<br>■ Continuity in staff<br>■ Allows for more top-management involvement | ■ Less involvement with and understanding of overall marketing goals<br>■ Longer response time<br>■ Inability to handle multiple product lines |
| *Decentralized* | ■ Concentrated managerial attention<br>■ Rapid response to problems and opportunities<br>■ Increased flexibility | ■ Ineffective decision making<br>■ Internal conflicts<br>■ Misallocation of funds<br>■ Lack of authority<br>■ Internal rather than external focus |
| *In-house agencies* | ■ Cost savings<br>■ More control<br>■ Increased coordination<br>■ Stability<br>■ Access to top management | ■ Less experience<br>■ Less objectivity<br>■ Less flexibility<br>■ Less access to top creative talent |

**FIGURE 3–4**

Comparison of Advertising Organizational Systems

handles content for the retailer's media network, cooperative advertising, circulars, and other areas.[17]

The ultimate decision as to which type of advertising organization to use depends on which arrangement works best for the company. The advantages and disadvantages of the three systems are summarized in Figure 3–4. We now turn our attention to the functions of outside agencies and their roles in the promotional process.

# ADVERTISING AGENCIES

Many major companies use an advertising agency to assist them in developing, preparing, and executing their promotional programs. An ad agency is a service organization that specializes in planning and executing advertising programs for its clients. More than 15,000 U.S. and international agencies are listed in the *Standard Directory of Advertising Agencies* (the "Red Books"); however, most are individually owned small businesses employing fewer than five people. The U.S. ad agency business is highly concentrated. Nearly two-thirds of the domestic **billings** (the amount of client money agencies spend on media purchases and other equivalent activities) are handled by the top 500 agencies. In fact, just 10 U.S. agencies handle nearly 30 percent of the total volume of business done by the top 900 agencies in the United States. The top agencies also have foreign operations that generate substantial billings and income. The top 10 agencies, ranked by their U.S. gross revenue, are listed in Figure 3–5. The figure shows that the advertising business is also geographically concentrated, with 9 of the top 10 agencies headquartered in New York City. Nearly 40 percent of U.S. agency business is handled by New York–based agencies. Other leading advertising centers in the United States include Boston, Chicago, Los Angeles, the Detroit area, Dallas, and Minneapolis. New York City is clearly the center of the advertising industry in the United States as nearly half of the top 100 agencies are headquartered in the city or the surrounding area

FIGURE 3–5

Top 10 United States
Advertising Agencies, 2012

| Rank | Agency | Headquarters | U.S. Revenue (millions) |
|------|--------|--------------|-------------------------|
| 1 | BBDO Worldwide (Omnicom) | New York | $541 |
| 2 | McCann Erickson Worldwide (Interpublic) | New York | 427 |
| 3 | Y&R (WPP) | New York | 389 |
| 4 | JWT (WPP) | New York | 351 |
| 5 | TBWA Worldwide (Omnicom) | New York | 321 |
| 6 | Leo Burnett Worldwide/Arc (Publicis) | Chicago | 273 |
| 7 | DDB Worldwide (Omnicom) | New York | 264 |
| 8 | Publicis USA (Publicis) | New York | 260 |
| 9 | Grey (WPP) | New York | 252 |
| 10 | Saatchi & Saatchi (Publicis) | New York | 250 |

Source: *Advertising Age*, 2013 Agency Report, April 29, 2013, p. 37.

(Exhibit 3–4). In addition to advertising agencies, 9 of the top 10 media specialist companies are based in the Big Apple as are many of the direct-marketing, digital, promotion, and marketing services agencies.[18] There are several reasons why New York City is the hub of the IMC business in the United States. Many of the major companies with large advertising and promotion budgets are based in the city or the surrounding area. In 2013, 43 of the companies ranked in the *Fortune* 500 were headquartered in New York City while another 40 or so of the top firms were located nearby in suburbs or in cities in Connecticut or New Jersey. New York is also the world's leading media center as nearly all of the major television and radio networks are based in the city as well as many magazine and news organizations.[19]

During the late 1980s and into the 90s, the advertising industry underwent major changes as large agencies merged with or acquired other agencies and support organizations to form large advertising organizations, or superagencies. These **superagencies** were formed so that agencies could provide clients with integrated marketing communications services worldwide. Some advertisers became disenchanted with the superagencies and moved to smaller agencies that were flexible and more responsive.[20] However, during the mid-90s the agency business went through another wave of consolidation as a number of medium-size agencies were acquired

EXHIBIT 3–4

New York City is the center of
the advertising industry in the
United States

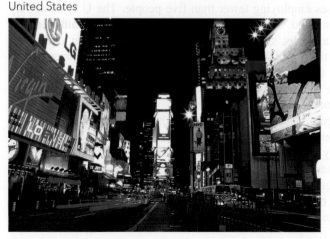

and became part of large advertising organizations such as Omnicom Group, WPP Group, and the Interpublic Group of Cos. Many of the midsize agencies were acquired by or forged alliances with larger agencies because their clients wanted an agency with international communications capabilities and their alignment with larger organizations gave them access to a network of agencies around the world. The consolidation of the agency business continued into the new millennium as large agencies such as Fallon Worldwide, Leo Burnett, Saatchi & Saatchi, and Kaplan Thaler were acquired by the giant French holding company Publicis Groupe. In 2012, the top four holding companies—WPP, Omnicom Group, Interpublic Group, and Publicis Groupe— accounted for a little move than half of U.S. agency

**EXHIBIT 3–5**

Primary holdings of the world's top four agency holding companies

**EXHIBIT 3–6**

Mentus specializes in creating ads for high-tech companies

revenue. Exhibit 3–5 shows the primary holdings of the top agency holding companies.

With the move toward IMC, agencies are now getting much of their revenue from more than just traditional advertising services which now account for just a third of the revenue for U.S. agencies. In 2012 agencies' revenue came from other areas such as media buying (8 percent), public relations (11 percent), digital (30 percent), CRM direct marketing (17 percent), and promotion (8 percent).[21] Many of the advertising organizations and major agencies have been acquiring companies specializing in areas such as digital/interactive communications, public relations, customer relationship management (CRM), direct marketing, and sales promotion so that they can offer their clients an ever-broader range of integrated marketing communication services. Particularly noteworthy in these numbers is the percentage of agency revenue that is being generated by digital media. Overall, U.S. agencies now generate over 30 percent of their revenue from digital media versus only 10 percent in 2010. About 60 percent of this revenue comes from digital-specialty agencies that focus on digital "pure-plays" such as search marketing, social media, and mobile marketing. The tremendous increase in digital is not limited to the United States. The major agency holding companies such as Publicis Groupe and WPP have noted that they now receive about 30 percent of their worldwide revenue from various forms of digital and interactive media.[22]

## The Ad Agency's Role

The functions performed by advertising agencies might be conducted by the clients themselves through one of the designs discussed earlier in this chapter, but most large companies use outside firms. This section discusses some reasons advertisers use external agencies.

**Reasons for Using an Agency**  Probably the main reason outside agencies are used is that they provide the client with the services of highly skilled individuals who are specialists in their chosen fields. An advertising agency staff may include artists, writers, media analysts, researchers, and others with specific skills, knowledge, and experience who can help market the client's products or services. Many agencies specialize in a particular type of business and use their knowledge of the industry to assist their clients. For example, Mentus Inc. is an agency that specializes in integrated marketing communications for the high-technology, e-commerce, and bioscience industries (Exhibit 3–6).

An outside agency can also provide an objective viewpoint of the market and its business that is not subject to internal company policies, biases, or other limitations. The agency can draw on the broad range of experience it has gained while working on a diverse set of marketing problems for various clients. For example, an ad agency that is handling a travel-related account may have individuals who have worked with airlines, cruise ship companies, travel agencies, hotels, and other travel-related industries. The agency may have experience in this area or may even have previously worked on the advertising account of one of the client's competitors. Thus, the agency can provide the client with insight into the industry (and, in some cases, the competition).

## Types of Ad Agencies

Since ad agencies can range in size from a one- or two-person operation to large organizations with over 1,000 employees, the services offered and functions performed will vary. This section examines the different types of agencies, the services they perform for their clients, and how they are organized.

**Full-Service Agencies** Many companies employ what is known as a **full-service agency**, which offers its clients a full range of marketing, communications, and promotions services, including planning, creating, and producing the advertising; performing research; and selecting media. A full-service agency may also offer nonadvertising services such as strategic market planning; sales promotions, direct marketing, and digital/interactive capabilities; package design; and public relations and publicity.

The full-service agency is made up of departments that provide the activities needed to perform the various advertising functions and serve the client, as shown in Figure 3–6.

**FIGURE 3–6**

Full-Service Agency
Organizational Chart

**Account Services**   Account services, or account management, is the link between the ad agency and its clients. Depending on the size of the client and its advertising budget, one or more account executives serve as liaison. The **account executive** is responsible for understanding the advertiser's marketing and promotions needs and interpreting them to agency personnel. He or she coordinates agency efforts in planning, creating, and producing ads. The account executive also presents agency recommendations and obtains client approval.

As the focal point of agency–client relationships, the account executive must know a great deal about the client's business and be able to communicate this to specialists in the agency working on the account.[23] The ideal account executive has a strong marketing background as well as a thorough understanding of all phases of the advertising process. College graduates with undergraduate and graduate degrees in marketing, advertising, and other disciplines are often hired for account executive positions and go on to have careers in account management. However, with the revolutionary changes sweeping the advertising business, the role of account reps is changing dramatically and they are struggling to remain relevant.[24] Cost-cutting by marketers has thinned the once-bloated ranks of account management personnel in agencies by as much as 30 percent in recent years. Moreover, for those who remain, the expectations and demands of the position are changing. Agencies want account executives who are good strategic thinkers and have broad-based business acumen, not just expertise in advertising. And as other integrated marketing communications tools such as direct, digital, and social media become more central, they want them to have an understanding of and be able to coordinate activities and relationships in these areas. They also want individuals whose skill set includes solving complex communication problems, communicating in a mature fashion, selling the agency and its capabilities, and knowing when to push back on a client.

Some agencies are developing client-services training programs for their account executives that are designed to educate them in a variety of areas, including basic agency business issues, strategic marketing, the procurement process, and relationship building. Agencies and clients often work together to address this problem by developing communication and indoctrination programs that provide agency personnel with an overview of their clients' business objectives and marketing strategy as well as their financial/budget situation. This allows them to understand the limits within which creative solutions have to be developed.[25] Account representatives will continue to serve an important role in managing the relationships between agencies and their clients. However, the days of the old-school account executive in the gray wool suit are long gone as agencies look for more from those who work most closely with their clients (Exhibit 3–7).

**Marketing Services**   Over the past two decades, use of marketing services has increased dramatically. One service gaining increased attention is research, as agencies realize that to communicate effectively with their clients' customers, they must have a good understanding of the target audience. As shown in Chapter 1, the advertising planning process begins with a thorough situation analysis, which is based on research and information about the target audience.

Most full-service agencies maintain a *research department* whose function is to gather, analyze, and interpret information that will be useful in developing advertising for their clients. This can be done through primary research—where a study is designed, executed, and interpreted by the research department—or through the use of secondary (previously published) sources of information. Sometimes the research department acquires studies conducted by independent syndicated research firms or consultants. The research staff then interprets these reports and passes on the information to other agency personnel working on that account. The research department

**EXHIBIT 3–7**

The role of account executives has changed

YTC 03-04
Account Managers
youtube.com/10ebelch

may also design and conduct research to pretest the effectiveness of advertising the agency is considering. For example, copy testing is often conducted to determine how messages developed by the creative specialists are likely to be interpreted by the receiving audience.

In many large agencies, the marketing services department may include **account planners** who are individuals that gather information that is relevant to the client's product or service and can be used in the development of the creative strategy as well as other aspects of the IMC campaign. Account planners work with the client as well as other agency personnel including the account executives, creative team members, media specialists, and research department personnel to collect information that can be helpful in gaining a better understanding of the client's target audience and the best ways to communicate with them. They gather and organize information about consumers as well as developments in the marketplace that can be used to prepare the *creative brief,* which is a document that the agency's creative department uses to guide the development of advertising ideas and concepts. Account planners may also be involved in assessing consumers' reactions to the advertising and other elements of the IMC program and providing the creative staff as well as other agency personnel with feedback regarding performance.

Account planning has become a very important function in many agencies because it provides the creative team, as well as other agency personnel, with more insight into consumers and how to use advertising and other IMC tools to communicate with them.[26] However, the account planning function has also become more demanding as the number of marketing communication channels and ways of contacting consumers increases. Account planners increasingly find themselves interacting with individuals from a variety of marketing communication disciplines and have to keep up with developments that are occurring in all of these areas. John Thorpe, the director of brand strategy for Goodby Silverstein & Partners, an agency that is known for its account planning, notes: "No longer can planners just be good at strategy. It's a cross-silo activity. They have to be good at a lot of things that run across advertising. Ambidexterity is required across the house."[27]

The *media department* of an agency analyzes, selects, and contracts for space or time in the media that will be used to deliver the client's advertising message. The media department is expected to develop a media plan that will reach the target market and effectively communicate the message. Since most of the client's ad budget is spent on media time and/or space, this department must develop a plan that both communicates with the right audience and is cost-effective.

Media specialists must know what audiences the media reach, their rates, and how well they match the client's target market. The media planning department reviews information on demographics, magazine and newspaper readership, radio listenership, and consumers' Internet and TV viewing patterns to develop an effective media plan. The media buyer implements the media plan by purchasing the actual time and space.

The media department is becoming an increasingly important part of the agency business. An agency's ability to negotiate prices and effectively use the vast array of media vehicles, as well as other sources of customer contact, is becoming as important as its ability to create ads. Some of the major agencies and/or their holding companies have formed independent media services companies to better serve their clients. For example, Starcom MediaVest Group is a subsidiary of the Publicis Groupe and has a network of over 100 offices in 67 countries, while McCann Erickson Worldwide formed Universal McCann, which is now known as UM and is one of the primary media specialist agencies for the Interpublic Group along with Initiative. Other large media specialist companies include Mindshare Worldwide, which is owned by the WPP Group, and OMD Worldwide, which is owned by the Omnicom Group. These media specialist firms serve the media needs of the agencies that are part of their parent holding companies but may also offer media services to other clients as well.

The research and media departments perform most of the functions that full-service agencies need to plan and execute their clients' advertising programs. Some agencies offer additional marketing services to their clients to assist in other promotional areas. An agency may have a sales promotion department, or merchandising department, that specializes in developing contests, premiums, promotions, point-of-sale materials, and other sales materials. It may have direct-marketing specialists and package designers, as well as a PR/publicity department. Many agencies have developed digital/interactive media departments to create websites for their clients. The growing popularity of integrated marketing communications has prompted many full-function agencies to develop capabilities and offer services in these other promotional areas. Traditional advertising agencies are recognizing that they must develop integrated marketing capabilities that extend beyond media advertising.

**Creative Services**   The creative services department is responsible for the creation and execution of advertisements. The individuals who conceive the ideas for the ads and write the headlines, subheads, and body copy (the words constituting the message) are known as **copywriters**. They may also be involved in determining the basic appeal or theme of the ad campaign and often prepare a rough initial visual layout of the print ad or television commercial.

While copywriters are responsible for what the message says, the *art department* is responsible for how the ad looks. For print ads, the art director and graphic designers prepare *layouts,* which are drawings that show what the ad will look like and from which the final artwork will be produced. For TV commercials, the layout is known as a *storyboard,* a sequence of frames or panels that depict the commercial in still form.

Members of the creative department work together to develop ads that will communicate the key points determined to be the basis of the creative strategy for the client's product or service. Writers and artists generally work under the direction of the agency's creative director, who oversees all the advertising produced by the organization. The director sets the creative philosophy of the department and may even become directly involved in creating ads for the agency's largest clients.

Once the copy, layout, illustrations, and mechanical specifications have been completed and approved, the ad is turned over to the *production department.* Most agencies do not actually produce finished ads; they hire printers, engravers, photographers, typographers, and other suppliers to complete the finished product. For broadcast production, the approved storyboard must be turned into a finished commercial. The production department may supervise the casting of people to appear in the ad and the setting for the scenes as well as choose an independent production studio. The department may hire an outside director to turn the creative concept into a commercial. For example, Nike has used film directors such as David Fincher and Spike Lee to direct some of its commercials; BMW has used well-known film directors such as Guy Ritchie, Ang Lee, and the late Tony Scott to direct some of its commercials and webisodes. Copywriters, art directors, account managers, people from research and planning, and representatives from the client side may all participate in production decisions, particularly when large sums of money are involved.

Creating an advertisement often involves many people and takes several months. In large agencies with many clients, coordinating the creative and production processes can be a major problem. A *traffic department* coordinates all phases of production to see that the ads are completed on time and that all deadlines for submitting the ads to the media are met. The traffic department may be located in the creative services area of the agency, or be part of media or account management, or be separate.

**Management and Finance**   Like any other business, an advertising agency must be managed and perform basic operating and administrative functions such as accounting, finance, and human resources. It must also attempt to generate new business. Large agencies employ administrative, managerial, and clerical people to perform these functions. The bulk of an agency's income (approximately 64 percent) goes to salary and benefits for its employees. Thus, an agency must manage its personnel carefully and get maximum productivity from them.

**Agency Organization and Structure** Full-function advertising agencies must develop an organizational structure that will meet their clients' needs and serve their own internal requirements. Most medium-size and large agencies are structured under either a departmental or a group system. Under the **departmental system**, each of the agency functions shown in Figure 3–6 is set up as a separate department and is called on as needed to perform its specialty and serve all of the agency's clients. Ad layout, writing, and production are done by the creative department; marketing services is responsible for any research or media selection and purchases; and the account services department handles client contact. Some agencies prefer the departmental system because it gives employees the opportunity to develop expertise in servicing a variety of accounts.

Many large agencies use the **group system**, in which individuals from each department work together in groups to service particular accounts. Each group is headed by an account executive or supervisor and has one or more media people, including media planners and buyers; a creative team, which includes copywriters, art directors, artists, and production personnel; and one or more account executives. The group may also include individuals from other departments such as marketing research, direct marketing, or sales promotion. The size and composition of the group vary depending on the client's billings and the importance of the account to the agency. For very important accounts, the group members may be assigned exclusively to one client. In some agencies, they may serve a number of smaller clients. Many agencies prefer the group system because employees become very knowledgeable about the client's business and there is continuity in servicing the account.

## Other Types of Agencies and Services

Not every agency is a large full-service agency. Many smaller agencies expect their employees to handle a variety of jobs. For example, account executives may do their own research, work out their own media schedule, and coordinate the production of ads written and designed by the creative department. Many advertisers, including some large companies, are not interested in paying for the services of a full-service agency but are interested in some of the specific services agencies have to offer. Over the past few decades, several alternatives to full-service agencies have evolved, including creative boutiques and media buying services.

**Creative Boutiques** **Creative boutiques** are small ad agencies that provide only creative services and have long been an important part of the advertising industry. These specialized agencies have creative personnel such as writers and artists on staff but do not have media, research, or account planning capabilities. Creative boutiques have developed in response to some companies' desires to use only the creative services of an outside agency while maintaining control of other marketing communication functions internally. While most creative boutiques work directly for companies, full-service agencies often subcontract work to them when they are very busy or want to avoid adding full-time employees to their payrolls. They are usually compensated on a project or hourly fee basis.

Many creative boutiques have been formed by members of the creative departments of full-service agencies who leave the firm and take with them clients who want to retain their creative talents. An advantage of these smaller agencies is their ability to turn out inventive creative work quickly and without the cumbersome bureaucracy and politics of larger agencies. Many companies also prefer working directly with a smaller creative boutique because they can get more attention and better access to creative talent than they would at a larger agency. An example of a successful independent

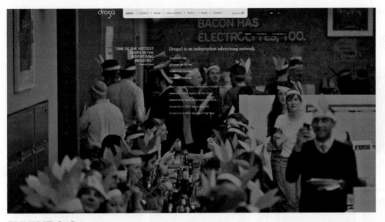

**EXHIBIT 3–8**

Droga5 is a very successful creative agency

YTC 03–05

**Droga5**

youtube.com/10ebelch

creative agency is New York–based Droga5, whose clients include Prudential, American Express, The Coca-Cola Company, Mondelez International, Spotify, PUMA, Kraft Foods Group, Hennessy, Unilever, and the United Nations, among others. Droga5 also created the popular "No Bollocks" campaign for New Castle Brown Ale, which pokes fun at some of the conventional ploys used to advertise beer. This hot agency was named one of *Fast Company* magazine's Most Innovative companies in 2013 and was *Adweek*'s 2012 Agency of the Year (Exhibit 3–8). Other independent agencies that have become well known for their creative work include San Francisco–based Pereira & O'Dell, whose clients include Intel, Toshiba, and Mattel, and Miami-based La Comunidad, which handles multicultural and digital advertising for clients such as Corona, Volvo, MTV, and Trident gum.[28]

Creative boutiques will continue to be an important part of the advertising industry. However, they face challenges as many find themselves competing against larger agencies for business, particularly when there are cutbacks in advertising spending. Moreover, many clients want the range of services that large agencies provide as they are often looking for strategic and business-building ideas rather than just creative work.[29]

**Media Specialist Companies**   **Media specialist companies** are companies that specialize in the buying of media, particularly radio and television time. The task of purchasing advertising media has grown more complex as specialized media proliferate, so media buying services have found a niche by specializing in the analysis and purchase of advertising time and space. Agencies and clients usually develop their own media strategies and hire the buying service to execute them. Some media buying services do help advertisers plan their media strategies. Because media buying services purchase such large amounts of time and space, they receive large discounts and can save the small agency or client money on media purchases. Media buying services are paid a fee or commission for their work.

Media buying services have been experiencing strong growth in recent years as clients seek alternatives to full-service agency relationships. Many companies have been unbundling agency services and consolidating media buying to get more clout from their advertising budgets. Nike, Revlon, and Hyundai/Kia are among those that have switched some or all of their media buying from full-service agencies to independent media buyers. As noted earlier, many of the major agencies have formed independent media services companies that handle the media planning and buying for their clients and also offer their services separately to companies interested in a more specialized or consolidated approach to media planning, research, and/or buying. A number of large advertisers have consolidated their media buying with these large media specialist companies to save money and improve media efficiency. For example, MillerCoors consolidated its $400 million U.S. media planning and buying with Initiative, which is part of the Interpublic Group, while Heineken moved its $500 million global media budget to Starcom MediaVest.[30] A number of companies such as PepsiCo and Campbell Soup Co. also use media specialist companies to handle all of their global media buying, which helps them achieve economies of scale and more uniform media strategies and implementation across various countries.

The rise of the independent media buying services, operating outside the structure of the traditional ad agency media department, and the divestment of these departments from the agency system are two of the most significant developments that have occurred in the advertising industry in recent years. A study conducted for the Association of National Advertisers found a small percentage of companies still use

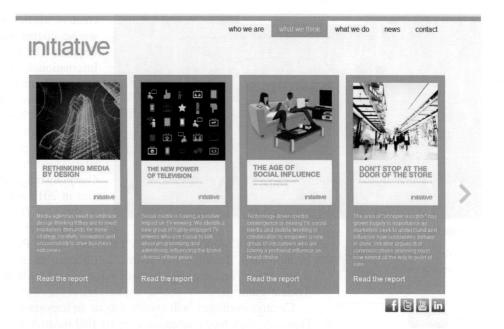

a "general" ad agency to handle their media planning and buying as the vast majority use a media agency specialist to handle these functions. These media specialists are often part of the same agency holding company as the primary agency that handles their creative work, particularly for large advertisers. However, about a third of the time the media specialist agency is not related to the primary agency.[31] Exhibit 3–9 shows how Initiative, which is one of the largest media specialist companies, promotes its services.

# AGENCY COMPENSATION

As you have seen, the type and amount of services an agency performs vary from one client to another. As a result, agencies use a variety of methods to get paid for their services. Agencies are typically compensated in three ways: commissions, some type of fee arrangement, or percentage charges.

## Commissions from Media

The traditional method of compensating agencies is through a **commission system**, where the agency receives a specified commission (usually 15 percent) from the media on any advertising time or space it purchases for its client. (For outdoor advertising, the commission is $16\,^2/_3$ percent.) This system provides a simple method of determining payments, as shown in the following example.

Assume an agency prepares a full-page magazine ad and arranges to place the ad on the back cover of a magazine at a cost of $100,000. The agency places the order for the space and delivers the ad to the magazine. Once the ad is run, the magazine will bill the agency for $100,000, less the 15 percent ($15,000) commission. The media will also offer a 2 percent cash discount for early payment, which the agency may pass along to the client. The agency will bill the client $100,000 less the 2 percent cash discount on the net amount, or a total of $98,300, as shown in Figure 3–7. The $15,000 commission represents the agency's compensation for its services.

**Appraisal of the Commission System** While the commission system was the primary agency compensation method for many years, it has always been controversial. Critics of the commission system have long argued that it encourages

**FIGURE 3–7**

Example of Commission
System Payment

| Media Bills Agency | | Agency Bills Advertiser | |
|---|---|---|---|
| Costs for magazine space | $100,000 | Costs for magazine space | $100,000 |
| Less 15% commission | −15,000 | Less 2% cash discount | −1,700 |
| Cost of media space | 85,000 | Advertiser pays agency | $ 98,300 |
| Less 2% cash discount | −1,700 | | |
| Agency pays media | $ 83,300 | Agency income | $ 15,000 |

agencies to recommend high-priced media to their clients to increase their commission level. The system has also been criticized on the grounds that it ties agency compensation to media costs, which have been skyrocketing over the past decade. Still others charge that the system encourages agencies to recommend mass-media advertising and avoid noncommissionable IMC tools such as direct mail, sales promotion, public relations, and event sponsorships unless they are requested by the clients.

Defenders of the commission system argue that it is easy to administer and keeps the emphasis in agency compensation on nonprice factors such as the quality of the advertising developed for clients. Proponents of the system argue that agency services are proportional to the size of the commission, since more time and effort are devoted to the large accounts that generate high revenue for the agency. They also note that the system is more flexible than it appears as agencies often perform other services for large clients at no extra charge as a way of justifying the large commission they receive.

Companies began moving away from the commission system during the 1990s, and most companies no longer use it as the basis for compensating their agencies. The most recent study of agency compensation conducted by the Association of National Advertisers (ANA) found that only 6 percent of major advertisers in the United States still paid commissions to their agencies, down from 16 percent in 2007.[32] Among those companies that do pay commissions, most do not pay the traditional 15 percent. Many advertisers have gone to a **negotiated commission** system whereby the commissions average from 8 to 10 percent or are based on a sliding scale that becomes lower as the clients' media expenditures increase. Agencies are also relying less on media commissions for their income as their clients expand their IMC programs to include other forms of promotion and cut back on mass-media advertising. The amount of agency income coming from media commissions is declining as many companies are now using other methods of agency compensation such as fees and performance-based incentives. The 2012 ANA survey was the first study of global ad agency compensation, and found that reliance on commissions is a more common practice outside the United States as more than a third of global marketers still use traditional media commissions to compensate their agencies. One reason for the higher use of commissions is that in some countries, such as Brazil and Japan, the use of commissions to compensate agencies is mandated by law or is a common practice.[33]

## Fee, Cost, and Incentive-Based Systems

Since many believe the commission system is not equitable to all parties, many agencies and their clients have developed some type of fee arrangement or cost-plus agreement for agency compensation. Some are using incentive-based compensation, which is a combination of a commission and a fee system.

**Fee Arrangement**   There are two basic types of fee arrangement systems. In the straight or **fixed-fee method**, the agency charges a basic monthly fee for all of its services and credits to the client any media commissions earned. Agency and client agree on the specific work to be done and the amount the agency will be paid for it. Sometimes agencies are compensated through a **fee–commission combination**, in which the media commissions received by the agency are credited against the fee. If the commissions are less than the agreed-on fee, the client must make up the difference. If the agency does much work for the client in non-commissionable media, the fee may be charged over and above the commissions received.

Both types of fee arrangements require that the agency carefully assess its costs of serving the client for the specified period, or for the project, plus its desired profit margin. To avoid any later disagreement, a fee arrangement should specify exactly what services the agency is expected to perform for the client. The 2012 ANA study found that a fee-based structure, whereby agencies are paid fixed or labor-based fees for services provided, is the dominant form of compensation, with 57 percent of global marketers using this type of plan. Blended compensation plans that use a combination of fees and commissions to compensate agencies were used by 37 percent of the companies surveyed.

**Cost-Plus Agreement** Under a **cost-plus system**, the client agrees to pay the agency a fee based on the costs of its work plus some agreed-on profit margin (often a percentage of total costs). This system requires that the agency keep detailed records of the costs it incurs in working on the client's account. Direct costs (personnel time and out-of-pocket expenses) plus an allocation for overhead and a markup for profits determine the amount the agency bills the client.

Fee agreements and cost-plus systems are commonly used in conjunction with a commission system. The fee-based system can be advantageous to both the client and the agency, depending on the size of the client, advertising budget, media used, and services required. Many clients prefer fee or cost-plus systems because they receive a detailed breakdown of where and how their advertising and promotion dollars are being spent. However, these arrangements can be difficult for the agency, as they require careful cost accounting and may be difficult to estimate when bidding for an advertiser's business. Agencies are also reluctant to let clients see their internal cost figures.

**FIGURE 3–8**

Performance Criteria Used for Incentive Plans

| Performance reviews | 82% |
|---|---|
| Sales goals | 53 |
| Brand/ad awareness | 51 |
| Achieve project objectives | 44 |
| Brand perceptions | 33 |
| Copy test results | 24 |
| Market share goals | 24 |
| Profit goals | 24 |
| Other criteria | 13 |
| *Basis for Incentives* | |
| Agency performance | 27% |
| Company performances | 13 |
| Both agency and company | 53 |

Source: Association of National Advertisers, *Trends in Agency Compensation*, 14th ed., 2007.

**Incentive-Based Compensation** Many clients are demanding more accountability from their agencies and tying agency compensation to performance through some type of **incentive-based system**. Recently a new variation of this system has emerged in the form of *value-based compensation* whereby agencies are compensated above their basic costs, if they achieve or exceed results as measured by agreed-upon metrics.[34] The costs are determined by the tasks that the agency is expected to perform, staffing required, and hourly rates. While there are many variations, the basic idea is that the agency's ultimate compensation level will depend on how well it meets predetermined performance goals. These goals often include objective measures such as sales or market share as well as more subjective measures such as evaluations of the quality of the agency's creative work. Companies using incentive-based systems determine agency compensation through media commissions, fees, bonuses, or some combination of these methods. The use of performance incentives varies by the size of the advertiser, with large advertisers the most likely to use them. Figure 3–8 shows the various performance criteria used along with the basis for the incentive.

Recognizing the movement toward incentive-based systems, some agencies have agreed to tie their compensation to performance. Agency executives note that pay for performance works best when the agency has complete control over a campaign. Thus, if a campaign fails to help sell a product or service, the agency is willing to assume complete responsibility and take a reduction in compensation. On the other hand, if sales increase, the agency can receive greater compensation for its work.

## Percentage Charges

Another way to compensate an agency is by adding a markup of **percentage charges** to various services the agency purchases from outside providers. These may include market research, artwork, printing, photography, and other services or materials. Markups usually range from 17.65 to 20 percent and are added to the client's overall bill. Since suppliers of these services do not allow the agency a commission, percentage charges cover administrative costs while allowing a reasonable profit for the agency's efforts. (A markup of 17.65 percent of costs added to the initial cost would yield a 15 percent commission. For example, research costs of $100,000 \times 17.65\% = $100,000 + $17,650 = $117,650. The $17,650 markup is about 15 percent of $117,650.)

## The Future of Agency Compensation

As you can see, there is no one method of agency compensation to which everyone subscribes. Companies have continued to make significant changes in their agency compensation plans over the past decade, including the use of incentive-based compensation systems. The 2012 ANA study found that 49 percent of the advertisers surveyed said they have a performance incentive component in their agency compensation agreements and a significant number are considering doing so.[35]

YTC 03–06

**Agency Compensation**

youtube.com/10ebelch

As more companies adopt IMC approaches, they are reducing their reliance on traditional media advertising, and this is leading to changes in the way they compensate their agencies. For example, Procter & Gamble (P&G), which is the world's largest advertiser, no longer uses the commission system to compensate its agencies. In 2000, P&G implemented a major change in its compensation structure by moving from a commission-based system to a sales-based incentive system. P&G made the change to encourage its agencies to focus less on expensive commissionable media such as television and magazines and to make use of other IMC tools such as direct mail, event marketing, public relations, and the Internet. P&G has been very satisfied with its incentive-based compensation system and has extended it to media agencies and other marketing services providers.[36] In 2009 the Coca-Cola Company began using a "value-based" compensation model whereby agencies are guaranteed only recouped costs, with any profit coming only if certain agreed-upon targets are met. The new model will encompass all of the company's advertising and media agency. Coke is also encouraging the advertising industry to adopt value-based models as a standard practice.[37]

Recently, undergarment manufacturer Jockey International implemented a value-based compensation model the company refers to as "Accountable Com" whereby the agency must earn its entire profit margin based on meeting company goals and is paid solely based on creative output rather than the number of hours or full-time employees assigned to the account. Also, a total dollar amount for what the agency can earn is determined in advance based on a mutually agreed-upon scope of work.[38] While value-based compensation models have received a great deal of attention in recent years, the number of companies using them is still very small as the 2012 ANA survey found that they are used by only 4 percent of the respondents.

The changes in agency compensation are also being driven by economic factors as most companies cut their advertising and promotion budgets during the recession as part of their efforts to save money across all areas of their marketing programs. Most marketers have not increased their marketing budgets and continue to be conservative with their spending for advertising and other forms of marketing communications. While clients recognize that their agencies must be able to make a profit, many are likely to continue to challenge them to reduce internal expenses, identify areas for cost reductions, and tightly manage their controllable spending.[39]

Companies are also making their agencies more accountable for the fees they charge them for services and are asking for more transparency in how agencies structure, determine, and present fee compensation.[40] One of the most significant findings from the ANA global agency compensation survey was the increased involvement of corporate procurement departments in the management and negotiation of agency compensation. Seventy-five percent of the global respondents indicated that their procurement departments are involved in the agency compensation negotiations, with nearly half reporting that the process is procurement led with marketing support and only 28 percent saying the process is marketing led. IMC Perspective 3–1 discusses how the involvement of procurement specialists is impacting agency compensation as well as concerns that this may be leading to a practice known as media rebates, whereby discounts from media buys are not passed on from the agency to the client.

# EVALUATING AGENCIES

Given the substantial amounts of money being spent on advertising and promotion, demand for accountability of the expenditures has increased. Regular reviews of the agency's performance are necessary. The agency evaluation process usually involves two types of assessments, one financial and operational and the other more qualitative. The **financial audit** focuses on how the agency conducts its business. It is designed to verify costs and expenses, the number of personnel hours charged to an account, and payments to media and outside suppliers. The **qualitative audit** focuses on the agency's efforts in planning, developing, and implementing the client's advertising programs and considers the results achieved.

The agency evaluation is often done on a subjective, informal basis, particularly in smaller companies where ad budgets are low or advertising is not seen as the most critical factor in the firm's marketing performance. However, some companies have developed formal, systematic evaluation systems, particularly when budgets are large and the advertising function receives much emphasis. The top management of these companies wants to be sure money is being spent efficiently and effectively. As the costs of advertising and other forms of promotion rise, more companies are adopting formal procedures for evaluating the performance of their agencies. For example, a survey conducted by the Association of National Advertisers found that 76 percent of marketers have a formal evaluation process for traditional creative agencies while 68 percent have one for traditional media agencies. The survey also found that qualitative performance is weighted more heavily than quantitative factors. Among the leading qualitative performance criteria identified in the survey were innovation, ideas, teamwork, meeting deadlines, strategy, and implementation. An interesting finding of the study was that formal reviews were much less likely to be conducted for digital, public relations, direct, and multicultural agencies.[41]

One example of a formal agency evaluation system is that used by Whirlpool, which markets a variety of consumer products. Whirlpool management meets once a year with the company's agencies to review their performance. Whirlpool managers complete an advertising agency performance evaluation, part of which is shown in Exhibit 3–10. These reports are compiled and reviewed with the agency at each annual meeting. Whirlpool's evaluation process covers six areas of performance. The company and the agency develop an action plan to correct areas of deficiency.

An important consideration in evaluating agencies is the *value* they provide to their client's business. The American Association of Advertising Agencies and Association of National Advertisers conducted a major study to understand how both agencies and clients define value and the agency activities that provide the most value to the client's business.[42] The top seven dimensions of agency activity that advertisers indicated add the most value to their business are shown in

**FIGURE 3–9**

How Agencies Add Value
to Client's Business

1. Developing and producing creative ideas that are fresh and appropriate.

2. Ensuring that agency disciplines and functions are integrated and that agency teams and divisions collaborate well on behalf of the client.

3. Working in a collaborative way with the client by creating an environment of low egos and high mutual respect.

4. Developing ideas and programs that can be integrated into multiple communication channels.

5. Assigning its best people to the client's business and making its top executives available when needed.

6. Evaluating brand drivers like awareness, consideration, and purchase intent.

7. Providing guidance and solutions in new media and technologies.

Source: "Report on the Agency–Advertiser Value Survey," American Association of Advertising Agencies and Association of National Advertisers, August 2007.

Figure 3–9. The study also considered how clients add value to the client–agency relationship and found that the key value drivers include understanding the brand's problems/opportunities, giving the agency the necessary time and resources to do its best work, articulating expected outcomes, giving clear direction, and providing constructive feedback.[43]

**EXHIBIT 3–10**

Whirlpool's Ad Agency
Performance Evaluation

### CREATIVE SERVICES

| Always 4 | Often 3 | Occasionally 2 | Seldom 1 | Never 0 | NA | Marks Scored |
|---|---|---|---|---|---|---|

1. Agency produces fresh ideas and original approaches

2. Agency accurately interprets facts, strategies and objectives into usable advertisements and plans

3. Creative group is knowledgeable about company's products, markets and strategies

4. Creative group is concerned with good advertising communications and develops campaigns and ads that exhibit this concern

5. Creative group produces on time

6. Creative group performs well under pressure

7. Creative group operates in a businesslike manner to control production costs and other creative charges

8. Agency presentations are well organized with sufficient examples of proposed executions

9. Creative group participates in major campaign presentations

10. Agency presents ideas and executions not requested but felt to be good opportunities

11. Agency willingly accepts ideas generated by other locations/agency offices vs. being over-protective of its own creative product

12. Other areas not mentioned

13. Agency demonstrates commitment to client's business

14. Agency creative proposals are relevant and properly fulfill creative brief

### ACCOUNT REPRESENTATION & SERVICE

| Always 4 | Often 3 | Occasionally 2 | Seldom 1 | Never 0 | NA | Marks Scored |
|---|---|---|---|---|---|---|

1. Account representatives act with personal initiative

2. Account representatives anticipate needs in advance of direction by client (ie: are proactive)

3. Account group takes direction well

4. Agency is able to demonstrate results of programs implemented

5. Account representatives function strategically rather than as creative advisors only

6. Account representatives are knowledgeable about competitive programs and share this information along with their recommendations in a timely manner

7. Account representatives respond to client requests in a timely fashion

8. Account group operates in a business-like manner to control costs

9. Agency recommendations are founded on sound reasoning and supported factually, and appropriately fit within budget constraints

10. Agency is able to advise the client on trends and developments in technology

11. Account representatives demonstrate a high degree of professionalism in both written and oral communication

12. Agency presents ideas and executions not requested but felt to be good opportunities

13. Agency makes reasoned recommendations on allocation of budgets

14. Agency demonstrates commitment to client's business

15. There is a positive social relationship between client and agency

Value—(marks)

| Rating: | | |
|---|---|---|
| Excellent | 90–100% | Total marks scored |
| Good | 80–89% | |
| Average | 70–79% | Total possible marks |
| Fair | 60–69% | |
| Poor | below 60% | Score |

Value—(marks)

| Rating: | | |
|---|---|---|
| Excellent | 90–100% | Total marks scored |
| Good | 80–89% | |
| Average | 70–79% | Total possible marks |
| Fair | 60–69% | |
| Poor | below 60% | Score |

# IMC Perspective 3–1 > > >

## Agencies Face Off with Procurement Specialists

For many years Madison Avenue was a world unto itself. Advertising agencies were compensated based on a 15 percent commission on the media purchases they made for their clients: Every time an ad appeared on television, played on radio, or was placed in a magazine, the cash registers rang on Madison Avenue. Agencies were dominated by "creatives" who came up with big ideas that could be translated into TV, print, radio, or billboard ads that would be run through these mass media to be seen or heard by the millions of consumers comprising the mass markets.

During the late 90s, the ad industry prospered, in large part due to the advertising frenzy driven by the Internet bubble, and many agencies were still able to get many of their clients to agree to pay them based on a percentage of their media billings. However, during the first decade of the new millennium, many major advertisers did away with commissions entirely. The vast majority of clients now compensate their agencies by paying fees based on the agency's labor costs. To make matters more complicated, some companies now have their procurement officers negotiate contracts with their advertising agencies rather than their marketing or advertising managers. Many agencies are finding the procurement people to be much more difficult to negotiate with on issues such as their allocation of labor costs, employee salaries, overhead, and reasonable profit. The agencies argue that procurement departments really do not understand the advertising business and the role they play in brand building. Some agencies have tried to take a stand against clients who view them as vendors rather than marketing partners. However, other agencies are often willing to accept lower margins to gain new business, which has resulted in a loss of pricing power for many agencies. The intervention of procurement departments into the advertising process is also receiving a cold reception from many marketing executives who argue that the advertising process is different from sourcing raw materials for manufacturing. They note that creating ideas is different from creating widgets and also express concern over procurement executives and chief financial officers (CFOs) trying to take over the agency selection process. They argue that too much emphasis is put on policing the financial aspects of the client–agency relationship and advertising, and agency fees are viewed as an expense rather than an investment. Many marketing executives and the majority of those on the agency side feel that it is difficult to judge the value of an agency's work on the basis of the number of hours they log on a client's account but recognize that this is becoming the new model under which they must operate.

There is also a shift in the balance of power occurring within agencies. Many of the holding companies have spun off their media divisions into freestanding firms that handle only media buying. These large media buying firms can use their size and clout to extract better media prices and cost savings for their clients.

However, a new issue has emerged from the increased emphasis on procurement-driven cost cutting: the practice of media rebates, which are loosely defined as an agency's

## Gaining and Losing Clients

The evaluation process described previously provides valuable feedback to both the agency and the client, such as indicating changes that need to be made by the agency and/or the client to improve performance and make the relationship more productive. Many agencies have had very long-lasting relationships with their clients. For example, General Electric has been with the BBDO Worldwide agency for over 80 years. Other well-known companies or brands that have had long-lasting relationships include Marlboro/Leo Burnett (56 years), McDonald's/DDB Worldwide (43 years), and Allstate/Leo Burnett (55 years).

While many successful agency–client relationships go on for years, loyalty to a single agency is becoming less common as marketers seek new ways of connecting with consumers.[44] In recent years, a number of long-standing client relationships have been terminated. For example, ExxonMobil ended one of the longest-running relationships ever when the energy giant moved its account from McCann Erickson to BBDO. McCann had been Exxon's agency for nearly 100 years as it first began working with the company after the breakup of the Standard Oil empire in 1911.[45] In 2012 Harley-Davidson parted ways with the Carmichael Lynch agency, citing differences in opinions over creativity, while Dr Pepper ended its 40-year relationship with Y&R.[46]

receipt of a volume discount or compensation from media buys that is not always passed on to the client. Media rebates are a reviled but tolerated practice outside the United States, and a survey conducted by the Association of National Advertisers (ANA) in 2012 revealed that they may be becoming more commonplace here as well. The ANA released a white paper report titled "Media Rebates/ Incentives Require Full Transparency" that noted that nearly a third of U.S. marketers are aware of rebates and incentives offered by media companies that may not be reimbursed to the advertiser. The report also noted that the vast majority of marketers surveyed by the ANA believed agencies should turn any rebates they receive over to their clients as keeping the payments could impair their objectivity in media choices. Marketers are concerned that media incentives and rebates might affect their agencies' media-purchasing decisions and result in less than optimal allocations of their marketing budgets.

Marketers and agencies agree that rebates are not a problem if they are disclosed and passed on to clients. However, a problem arises in defining exactly what constitutes a media rebate and what should be passed on to clients because rebates seldom take the form of a simple cash payment from the media seller to the agency for reaching a volume target. Industry experts note that they often take more creative forms such as discounts for early payment of invoices, payment from the media company to the agency for research or other services, or bonus inventory, which the media agency may then be able to sell to clients that do not require an invoice. Rebates can also flow into specialized agency holding-company entities, where they become very difficult to track.

The ANA white paper recommends that language used in agency contracts calling for rebates be fully disclosed and documented and require that any discounts be passed on to clients. However, even those in the industry who are critical of rebates argue that they are a natural result of marketers' efforts to squeeze agency costs and procurement procedures that have narrowed margins to the point where they are seeking these incentives.

While agency executives may not like the changes that are occurring in the world of advertising, most recognize that they have little choice but to adapt to the changes. The involvement of clients' procurement departments is here to stay and one former agency executive's response to those who complain about it is "Welcome to the real world." He notes that most of those on the client side have had to deal with a purchasing department or hard-nosed buyer almost from the day they started work.

Many persons working in the advertising industry argue that the two sides must find a way to work together. Marketers must recognize that a relationship in which the agency is barely making any money is not sustainable and respect the right of agencies to make a reasonable profit, while agencies will have to continue to find ways to reduce their costs and accept smaller profit margins. However, they note that clients who continue to tighten the vise on their agencies may be cutting off their nose to spite their face as the quality of service they receive may suffer when the agency caves in to their demands.

Sources: Avi Dan, "Agencies Must Wake Up to a Different Business Model," *Advertising Age*, September 24, 2007, p. 18; Chris Ingram, "Time for Ad World to Meet the Real World," *Advertising Age*, July 2, 2006, p. 14; Rupal Parekh, "Fed-Up Shops Pitch a Fit at Procurement," *Advertising Age*, October 26, 2009, pp. 1, 17; Bob Liodice, "Transparency Is the Only Way to Avoid Abuse of Media Rebates and Incentives," *Advertising Age*, October 1, 2012, p. 49; Jack Neff, "The Great Rebate Debate: Are Media Buyers Getting Cash Back?," *Advertising Age*, September 10, 2012, pp. 52–54.

---

**YTC 03–07**

**Hyundai USA**

youtube.com/10ebelch

Some companies switch agencies quite often in search of better creative work or for a variety of other reasons such as reorganizations that lead to changes in top management, changes in marketing or advertising strategy, or conflicts that might arise from mergers and acquisitions among both clients and agencies. A company may also switch agencies in order to consolidate all of its advertising and marketing efforts in one shop. A number of global marketers such as Samsung, IBM, Colgate, Microsoft, and others have reduced the number of agencies they work with in recent years as a way to gain more control over their marketing communications and create a consistent brand image worldwide.[47]

In 2009, Hyundai Motor America moved all of the creative work for its Hyundai automotive brand to Innocean Worldwide America. Innocean is the U.S. arm of its Seoul-based agency of the same name, which is a subsidiary of the Korean parent company Hyundai Motor Group. The move was partly due to Hyundai wanting a more cohesive and consistent brand image worldwide. Innocean has done excellent creative work that has helped make Hyundai one of the fastest-growing automotive brands in the U.S. market over the past five years.[48] The agency has developed advertising and digital campaigns for models such as the Elantra and Sonata and has also helped Hyundai move into the upscale luxury sedan market with ads for the Genesis and Equus (Exhibit 3–11).

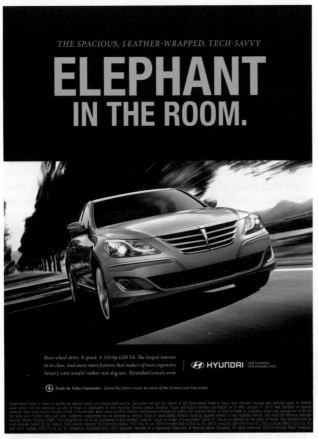

THE SPACIOUS, LEATHER-WRAPPED, TECH-SAVVY

# ELEPHANT
# IN THE ROOM.

*Rear-wheel drive. 8-speed. A 333-hp GDI V6. The largest interior in its class. And many more features that makers of more expensive luxury cars would rather not discuss. HyundaiGenesis.com*

HYUNDAI NEW THINKING. NEW POSSIBILITIES.

$ Trade-In Value Guarantee - Know the future trade-in value of the Genesis you buy today.

**EXHIBIT 3–11**

Ads created by Innocean have helped make Hyundai one of the fastest-growing automotive brands in the United States

There are a number of reasons clients switch agencies. Understanding these potential problems can help the agency avoid them.[49] In addition, it is important to understand the process agencies go through in trying to win new clients.

**Why Agencies Lose Clients**   Some of the more common reasons agencies lose clients follow:

- *Poor performance or service.* The client becomes dissatisfied with the quality of the advertising and/or the service provided by the agency.
- *Poor communication.* The client and agency personnel fail to develop or maintain the level of communication necessary to sustain a favorable working relationship.
- *Unrealistic demands by the client.* The client places demands on the agency that exceed the amount of compensation received and reduce the account's profitability.
- *Personality conflicts.* People working on the account on the client and agency sides do not have enough rapport to work well together.
- *Personnel changes.* A change in personnel at either the agency or the advertiser can create problems. New managers may wish to use an agency with which they have established ties. Agency personnel often take accounts with them when they switch agencies or start their own.
- *Changes in size of the client or agency.* The client may outgrow the agency or decide it needs a larger agency to handle its business. If the agency gets too large, the client may represent too small a percentage of its business to command attention.
- *Conflicts of interest.* A conflict may develop when an agency merges with another agency or when a client is part of an acquisition or merger. In the United States, an agency cannot handle two accounts that are in direct competition with each other. In some cases, even indirect competition will not be tolerated.
- *Changes in the client's corporate and/or marketing strategy.* A client may change its marketing strategy and decide that a new agency is needed to carry out the new program. As more companies adapt an integrated marketing communications approach, they are looking for agencies that have integrated capabilities and can handle more than just their media advertising.
- *Declining sales.* When sales of the client's product or service are stagnant or declining, advertising may be seen as contributing to the problem. A new agency may be sought for a new creative approach.
- *Conflicting compensation philosophies.* Disagreement may develop over the level or method of compensation. As more companies move toward incentive-based compensation systems, disagreement over compensation is becoming more commonplace.
- *Changes in policies.* Policy changes may result when either party reevaluates the importance of the relationship, the agency acquires a new (and larger) client, or either side undergoes a merger or acquisition.
- *Disagreements over marketing and/or creative strategy.* Agencies sometimes disagree with clients over the marketing strategy they want to pursue or the creative approach that might be best for the brand. For example, the Crispin Porter + Bogusky agency terminated relationships with several clients including Gateway and the Miller Brewing Co. over disagreements regarding marketing and creative strategy.

**TUMBLEWEEDS**      **by TOM K. RYAN**

- *Lack of integrated marketing capabilities.* Many clients are changing agencies in search of a shop with a broader range of capabilities across various integrated marketing communication areas or greater expertise in a particular area such as digital marketing. In some cases clients are looking for an agency that can provide more integrated marketing services under one roof. However, many marketers are moving toward an open source model whereby they hire agencies and other marketing communication partners on a project basis, based on their special talents and expertise.[50]

If the agency recognizes these warning signs, it can try to adapt its programs and policies to make sure the client is satisfied. Some of the situations discussed here are unavoidable, and others are beyond the agency's control. But to maintain the account, problems within the agency's control must be addressed.

The time may come when the agency decides it is no longer in its best interest to continue to work with the client. Personnel conflicts, changes in management philosophy, and/or insufficient financial incentives are just a few of the reasons for such a decision. An agency may also decide to leave for a better business opportunity that allows it to grow and make more money. When agencies become known for doing excellent work and developing effective IMC campaigns, they often have the opportunity to pursue larger clients, which may include a company in the same industry. Conflict of interest policies preclude an agency from working for more than one company in a product or service category.[51]

**How Agencies Gain Clients**    Competition for accounts in the agency business is intense, since most companies have already organized for the advertising function and only a limited number of new businesses require such services each year. While small agencies may be willing to work with a new company and grow along with it, larger agencies often do not become interested in these firms until they are able to spend at least $1 million per year on advertising. Many of the top agencies won't accept an account that spends less than $5 million per year. Once that expenditure level is reached, competition for the account intensifies.

In large agencies, most new business results from clients that already have an agency but decide to change their relationships. Thus, agencies must constantly search and compete for new clients. Some of the ways they do this follow.

**Referrals**   Many good agencies obtain new clients as a result of referrals from existing clients, media representatives, and even other agencies. These agencies maintain good working relationships with their clients, the media, and outside parties that might provide business to them.

**Solicitations**   One of the more common ways to gain new business is through direct solicitation. In smaller agencies, the president may solicit new accounts. In most large agencies, a new business development group seeks out and establishes contact with new clients. The group is responsible for writing solicitation letters, making cold calls, and following up on leads. The cutbacks in ad spending by many companies during the recent recession have resulted in many agencies pitching their services on an unsolicited basis to marketers who are satisfied with their agencies. Senior executives recognize that new business is the lifeblood of their agencies and are encouraging their business development teams to pursue advertisers who have not even put their accounts up for review.[52]

**Presentations** A basic goal of the new business development group is to receive an invitation from a company to make a presentation. This gives the agency the opportunity to sell itself—to describe its experience, personnel, capabilities, and operating procedures, as well as to demonstrate its previous work.

The agency may be asked to make a speculative presentation, in which it examines the client's marketing situation and proposes a tentative communications campaign that includes creative ideas. Because spec presentations require a great deal of time and preparation and may cost the agency a considerable amount of money without a guarantee of gaining the business, many firms refuse to participate in "creative shoot-outs." They argue that agencies should be selected on the basis of their experience and the services and programs they have provided for previous clients. Critics also note that in addition to the costs, which can be hundreds of thousands of dollars to pitch a major account, the creative work developed for speculative presentations is often not used and they do not always give a true indication of how the agency and client will work together.[53] However, many marketers still feel that spec presentations are an important part of the process of selecting a new agency and continue to use them. Thus, most agencies do participate in this form of solicitation, either by choice or because they must do so to gain accounts.

Due in part to the emphasis on speculative presentations, a very important role has developed for *ad agency review consultants,* who specialize in helping clients choose ad agencies. These consultants are often used to bring an objective perspective to the agency review process and to assist advertisers who may lack the resources, experience, or organizational consensus needed to successfully conduct a review. The use of search consultants is increasing as studies have shown that they are used in 30 to 40 percent of the agency reviews where the ad budget for the account is worth $10 million or more.[54] Because their opinions are respected by clients, the entire agency review process may be structured according to their guidelines. However, one study found that while many companies use search consultants to help them with their reviews, they do not always have a direct influence on the final decision regarding which agency they hire.[55]

**Public Relations** Agencies also seek business through publicity/public relations efforts. They often participate in civic and social groups and work with charitable organizations pro bono (at cost, without pay) to earn respect in the community. Participation in professional associations such as the American Association of Advertising Agencies and the Advertising Research Foundation can also lead to new contacts. Successful agencies often receive free publicity throughout the industry as well as in the mass media.

**Image and Reputation** Perhaps the most effective way an agency can gain new business is through its reputation for doing excellent work for the clients it serves. Word travels fast through the advertising and marketing industry regarding the agencies that are doing outstanding creative work in advertising as well as in other areas of IMC. There are many award competitions in which advertisers may enter their work and have it recognized, such as the Effie Awards, which are given each year to IMC campaigns based on the results they achieve as well as the strategy that goes into creating them. There are many other awards that recognize outstanding advertising creativity as well as work done in specific areas such as media planning and strategy, digital media, public relations, and sales promotion. For example, the Cannes Lions Awards are presented each year as

# Congrats on das A-list, Deutsch LA

Here's to the road ahead.

**Das Auto.**

**EXHIBIT 3–12**

Deutsch LA is recognized by Volkswagen for making the *Advertising Age* Agency A-List

**LO 03-5**

**EXHIBIT 3–13**

Anderson Direct-Marketing promotes its services

part of the Cannes International Advertising Festival and have become one of the most prestigious awards in the marketing communications industry. The CLIO Awards are also one of the world's most recognized international advertising, design, and communications competitions and reward creative excellence across a variety of categories and media types.

The major industry publications such as *Advertising Age* and *Adweek* also recognize the top agencies each year based on the quality of their creative work.[56] Being recognized by these publications, as well as other industry groups and associations, enhances the reputation and image of an agency. Exhibit 3–12 shows an ad Volkswagen ran to congratulate Deutsch LA for being named to the *Advertising Age* Agency A-List in 2013.

## SPECIALIZED SERVICES

Many companies assign the development and implementation of their promotional programs to an advertising agency. But several other types of organizations provide specialized services that complement the efforts of ad agencies. Direct-response agencies, sales promotion agencies, and public relations firms are important to marketers in developing and executing IMC programs in the United States as well as international markets. Let us examine the functions these organizations perform.

### Direct-Marketing Agencies

One of the fastest-growing areas of IMC is direct marketing, where companies communicate with consumers through telemarketing, direct mail, television, the Internet, and other forms of direct-response advertising. As this industry has grown, numerous direct-response agencies have evolved that offer companies their specialized skills in both consumer and business markets. Many of the top direct-marketing agencies such as Direct Partners, Wunderman, and OgilvyOne are subsidiaries of large agency holding companies. However, there are also a number of independent direct-marketing agencies including those that serve large companies as well as smaller firms that handle the needs of local companies (Exhibit 3–13).

**Direct-marketing agencies** provide a variety of services, including database analytics and management, direct mail, research, media services, and creative and production capabilities. While direct mail was traditionally their primary weapon, many direct-response agencies are expanding their services to include such areas as infomercial production, digital marketing, analytics, and database management. Database development and management is becoming one of the most important services provided by direct-response agencies. Many companies are using database marketing to pinpoint new customers and build relationships and loyalty among existing customers.

A typical direct-response agency is divided into three main departments: account management, creative, and media. Some agencies also have a department whose function is to develop and manage databases for their clients. The account managers work with their clients to plan direct-marketing programs and determine their role in the overall integrated marketing communications process. The creative department consists of copywriters, artists, and producers. Creative is responsible for developing the direct-response message, while the media department is concerned with its placement.

Like advertising agencies, direct-response agencies must solicit new business and have their performance reviewed by their existing clients, often through formal assessment programs. Most direct-response agencies are compensated on a fee basis.

## Sales Promotion Agencies

Developing and managing sales promotion programs such as contests, sweepstakes, refunds and rebates, premium and incentive offers, and sampling programs are very complex tasks. Most companies use a **sales promotion agency** to develop and administer these programs. Some large ad agencies have created their own sales promotion department or acquired a sales promotion firm. However, most sales promotion agencies are independent companies that specialize in providing the services needed to plan, develop, and execute a variety of sales promotion programs.

Sales promotion agencies often work in conjunction with the client's advertising and/or direct-response agencies to coordinate their efforts with the advertising and direct-marketing programs. Services provided by large sales promotion agencies include promotional planning, creative research, tie-in coordination, fulfillment, premium design and manufacturing, catalog production, and contest/sweepstakes management. Many sales promotion agencies are also developing direct/database marketing and telemarketing to expand their integrated marketing services capabilities. Sales promotion agencies are generally compensated on a fee basis. Exhibit 3–14 shows a page from the website of Don Jagoda Associates, one of the leading sales promotion agencies.

## Public Relations Firms

**EXHIBIT 3–14**

Don Jagoda Associates is one of the leading promotional agencies

Many large companies use both an advertising agency and a PR firm. The **public relations firm** develops and implements programs to manage the organization's publicity, image, and affairs with consumers and other relevant publics, including employees, suppliers, stockholders, government, labor groups, citizen action groups, and the general public. The PR firm analyzes the relationships between the client and these various publics, determines how the client's policies and actions relate to and affect these publics, develops PR strategies and programs, implements these programs using various public relations tools, and evaluates their effectiveness.

The activities of a public relations firm include planning the PR strategy and program, generating publicity, conducting lobbying and public affairs efforts, becoming involved in community activities and events, preparing news releases and other communications, conducting research, promoting and managing special events, and managing crises. As companies adopt an IMC approach to promotional planning, they are increasingly coordinating their PR activities with advertising and other promotional areas. Many companies are integrating public relations and publicity into the marketing communications mix to increase message credibility and save media costs.[57] Public relations firms are generally compensated by retainer. We will examine their role in more detail in Chapter 17.

## Digital/Interactive Agencies

With the rapid growth of the Internet and other forms of interactive media, a new type of specialized marketing communications organization has evolved—the interactive agency. Many marketers are using **digital/interactive agencies** that specialize in the development and strategic use of various digital marketing tools such as websites for the Internet, banner ads, search engine optimization, mobile marketing, and social media campaigns. They recognize that the development of successful interactive marketing programs requires expertise in digital technology as well as areas such as creative website design, database marketing, digital media, and customer relationship management. In addition to their advertising agencies, many marketers now choose to work with agencies that specialize in digital media. This has led many large agencies to develop their own digital shops that operate as separate entities within the agency such as Digital@Ogilvy and Leo Burnett/Worldwide Arc. Also, a number of other large digital agencies such as AKQA, Razorfish, Digitas, and R/GA are owned by major agency holding companies, which provides other agencies in their network with a digital resource. Many traditional advertising agencies have developed digital/interactive capabilities ranging from a few specialists within the agency to entire digital departments that work closely with other parts of the agency in developing integrated campaigns for their clients. For example, the digital arm of the Deutsch agency develops and manages the websites, social media, and online campaigns for clients such as Volkswagen, Taco Bell, and Snapple. Exhibit 3–15 shows an image from the Volkswagen website for an interactive game that Deutsch LA created as part of the "Punch Dub" campaign discussed in the chapter opener.

While many agencies have or are developing interactive capabilities, a number of marketers are turning to more specialized interactive agencies to develop websites and interactive media. They feel these companies have more expertise in designing and developing websites as well as managing and supporting them. Interactive agencies range from smaller companies that specialize in website design and creation to full-service interactive agencies that provide all the elements needed for a successful digital/interactive marketing program. These services include strategic consulting regarding the use of the Internet and online branding, technical knowledge, systems integration, and the development of electronic commerce capabilities.

YTC 03–08

Razorfish

youtube.com/10ebelch

**EXHIBIT 3–15**

Deutsch LA handles the digital/interactive part of Volkswagen's IMC program

Socially intelligent marketing with Google

Work across your enterprise to create social landing pages, posts, and ads that are integrated with the Google products that you're already using. Make the most of your ad dollars and measure revenues generated from social.

**EXHIBIT 3–16**

Wildfire provides social media software and solutions that are used by marketers

**YTC 03–09**

**Wildfire**

youtube.com/10ebelch

Full-service interactive agencies, such as AKQA, have created successful digital marketing programs for a number of companies and brands, including Nike, Audi, Budweiser, and Gap. As the Internet and social media become increasingly important marketing tools, more companies will be turning to digital agencies to help them develop successful interactive marketing programs. The growth of social media and mobile marketing is also giving rise to companies that specialize in developing applications and campaigns for Facebook, Twitter, Google+, and other social platforms. For example, there are a number of companies that help marketers build, monitor, manage, and measure their social media efforts across a variety of social and mobile platforms. These companies work with marketers to develop various ways to engage consumers, including promotions such as coupons and sweepstakes, as well as through user-generated photo, essay, and video contests. An example of a company that works with marketers as well as advertising and/or digital agencies to assist them in developing and implementing their social media programs is Wildfire, a division of Google that is one of the world's largest social media marketing software and solutions providers (Exhibit 3–16). Wildfire works with a number of the world's top companies and brands such as PUMA, Unilever, Cobra Golf, and Sony to help them develop and manage their social media programs. The number of digital agencies, as well as companies that specialize in the development of campaigns for social and mobile media, will continue to grow, as will their importance as marketers move more of their IMC efforts away from traditional media into the digital space.

## COLLATERAL SERVICES

The final participants in the promotional process are those that provide various collateral services. They include marketing research companies, package design firms, consultants, photographers, printers, video production houses, and event marketing services companies. One of the more widely used collateral service organizations is the marketing research firm. Companies are increasingly turning to marketing research to help them understand their target audiences and to gather information that will be of value in designing and evaluating their advertising and promotions programs. Even companies with their own marketing research departments often hire outside research agencies to perform some services. Marketing research companies offer specialized services and can gather objective information that is valuable to the advertiser's promotional programs. They conduct *qualitative* research such as in-depth interviews and focus groups, as well as *quantitative* studies such as market surveys.

## INTEGRATED MARKETING COMMUNICATIONS SERVICES

**LO 03-6**

You have seen that marketers can choose from a variety of specialized organizations to assist them in planning, developing, and implementing an integrated marketing communications program. But companies must decide whether to use a different organization for each marketing communications function or consolidate them with a large advertising agency that offers all of these services under one roof.

As noted previously in the chapter, during the 1980s and 90s, many of the large agencies realized that their clients were shifting their promotional dollars away from traditional advertising to other forms of promotion and began developing IMC capabilities. Some did this through mergers and acquisitions and became superagencies consisting of advertising, public relations, sales promotion, and direct-response agencies. Many large agencies are continuing to expand their IMC capabilities by acquiring specialists in various fields. All the major agency holding companies either own or have substantial investments in digital/interactive, sales promotion, and direct-marketing agencies as well as public relations firms.

## Pros and Cons of Integrated Services

It has been argued that the concept of integrated marketing is nothing new, particularly in smaller companies and communication agencies that have been coordinating a variety of promotional tools for years. And larger advertising agencies have been trying to gain more of their clients' promotional business for over 20 years. However, in the past, the various services were run as separate profit centers. Each was motivated to push its own expertise and pursue its own goals rather than develop truly integrated marketing programs. Moreover, the creative specialists in many agencies resisted becoming involved in sales promotion or direct marketing. They preferred to concentrate on developing magazine ads or television commercials rather than designing coupons or direct-mail pieces.

Proponents of integrated marketing services contend that past problems are being solved and the various individuals in the agencies and subsidiaries are learning to work together to deliver a consistent message to the client's customers. They argue that maintaining control of the entire promotional process achieves greater synergy among each of the communications program elements. They also note that it is more convenient for the client to coordinate all of its marketing efforts—media advertising, direct mail, special events, sales promotions, and public relations—through one agency. An agency with integrated marketing capabilities can create a single image for the product or service and address everyone, from wholesalers to consumers, with one voice.

But not everyone wants to turn the entire IMC program over to one agency. Opponents say the providers become involved in political wrangling over budgets, do not communicate with each other as well and as often as they should, and do not achieve synergy. They also claim that agencies' efforts to control all aspects of the promotional program are nothing more than an attempt to hold on to business that might otherwise be lost to independent providers. They note that synergy and economies of scale, while nice in theory, have been difficult to achieve and competition and conflict among agency subsidiaries have been a major problem.[58]

Many companies use a variety of vendors for communication functions, choosing the specialist they believe is best suited for each promotional task, be it advertising, sales promotion, or public relations. While many ad agencies are working to master integration and compete against one another, they still must compete against firms that offer specialized services. As marketing consultant Jack Trout notes, "As long as there are a lot of specialized players, integrating an agency will be tricky. Specialists walk in the door and say 'this is all we do and we're good at it,' which is a hell of an argument. An agency that has all marketing operations in-house will never be perceived as the best in breed."[59]

The already complex client–agency relationship is becoming even more challenging as a result of several other factors, such as the reduction in marketing budgets stemming from the recession and the accompanying desire of companies to reduce the cost of their IMC programs, and the rise of social media, mobile marketing, and other nontraditional forms of communication. A study by Forrester Research called "The Future of Agency Relationship" suggests that one of the biggest challenges facing marketers today is knowing who to turn to when they want to change their advertising and/or IMC strategies. The study notes that many of the major agencies are trying to bundle all of the traditional and nontraditional services together and position themselves as being able to offer all of them.[60] However, the more likely scenario is that marketers will have a number of agencies from different areas working on their business and it is important that they get them to work together. They also must decide who is going to be in charge of managing and coordinating the IMC program. Some companies, particularly those involved heavily in e-commerce or having major technology components to their business, are now opting to have digital agencies lead their IMC programs. For example, a number of companies including Travelocity, Intel, and Sheraton designated the Publicis Groupe's Razorfish as the lead agency on their accounts.[61]

## Responsibility for IMC: Agency versus Client

Surveys of advertisers and agency executives have shown that both groups believe integrated marketing is important to their organizations' success and that it will be even more important in the future.[62] However, marketers and agency executives have very different opinions regarding who should be in charge of the integrated marketing communications process. Many advertisers prefer to set strategy for and coordinate their own IMC campaigns, but some agency executives see this as their domain.

While agency executives believe their shops are capable of handling the various elements an integrated campaign requires, many marketers, particularly larger firms, disagree. Marketing executives say the biggest obstacle to implementing IMC is the lack of people with the broad perspective and skills to make it work. Internal turf battles, agency egos, and fear of budget reductions are also cited as major barriers to successful integrated marketing campaigns.[63] A study of agency and marketing executives regarding integrated marketing found that the most challenging aspect of integration is ensuring that the strategy is executed consistently in all forms along with measuring the success of different aspects of an IMC campaign. The survey also found that compensation of integrated programs is a problem as each communication discipline has a different cost structure.[64]

A study by the Corporate Executive Board's Advertising and Marketing Roundtable surveyed the heads of advertising and marketing communication departments at global companies as well as agency executives regarding the use of multiple agency partners. The study found that "the traditional, static model of a single ad agency or a fixed roster of agencies working on a brand is being supplanted by an open-source model for some marketers. Under this model, marketers hire numerous disparate marketing partners—sometimes on a project basis—to leverage their special talents and expertise as needed."[65] The CEB report notes that clients will increasingly be relegating their lead agencies to be brand stewards and coordinators of a network of specialists in various IMC areas.

Many advertising agencies do not accept the premise that they must accept a new role as stewards and coordinators of specialists. These agencies still view themselves as strategic and executional partners and are adding more resources to offer their clients a full line of services. They are expanding their agencies' capabilities in digital/interactive, multimedia advertising, database management, direct marketing, public relations, and sales promotion. However, many marketers still want to set the strategy for their IMC campaigns and seek specialized expertise, more quality and creativity, and greater control and cost efficiency by using multiple providers. Steven Center, the former chief marketing officer for Honda of America, takes a position that is probably shared by most top marketing executives. He notes that "Agencies are exposed to much more than us, and they have to bring in raw ideas, market reconnaissance, and intelligence. But they will not tell us how to organize our company to accomplish our marketing mission. That responsibility should always fall entirely with the owner of the brand."[66]

## Summary

The development, execution, and administration of an advertising and promotions program involve the efforts of many individuals, both within the company and outside it. Participants in the integrated marketing communications process include the advertiser or client, ad agencies, media organizations, specialized marketing communications firms, and providers of collateral services.

Companies use three basic systems to organize internally for advertising and promotion. Centralized systems offer the advantages of facilitated communications, lower personnel requirements, continuity in staff, and more top-management involvement. Disadvantages include a lower involvement with overall marketing goals, longer response times, and difficulties in handling multiple product lines.

Decentralized systems offer the advantages of concentrated managerial attention, more rapid responses to problems, and increased flexibility, though they may be limited by ineffective decision making, internal conflicts, misallocation of funds, and a lack of authority. In-house agencies, while offering the advantages of cost savings, control, and increased coordination, have the disadvantage of less experience, objectivity, and flexibility.

Many firms use advertising agencies to help develop and execute their programs. These agencies may take on a variety of forms, including full-service agencies, creative boutiques, and media buying services. The first offers the client a full range of services (including creative, account, marketing, and financial and management services); the other two specialize in creative services and media buying, respectively. Agencies are compensated through commission systems, percentage charges, and fee—and cost-based systems. Recently, the emphasis on agency accountability has increased. Agencies are being evaluated on both financial and qualitative aspects, and some clients are using incentive-based compensation systems that tie agency compensation to performance measures such as sales and market share.

In addition to using ad agencies, marketers use the services of other marketing communication specialists, including direct-marketing agencies, sales promotion agencies, public relations firms, and digital/interactive agencies. A marketer must decide whether to use a different specialist for each promotional function or have all of its integrated marketing communications done by an advertising agency that offers all of these services under one roof.

Recent studies have found that most marketers believe it is their responsibility, not the ad agency's, to set strategy for and coordinate IMC campaigns. The lack of a broad perspective and specialized skills in nonadvertising areas are seen as major barriers to agencies' increased involvement in integrated marketing communications.

## Key Terms

clients p. 69
advertising agency p. 69
media organizations p. 70
specialized marketing communication services p. 70
collateral services p. 70
advertising manager p. 71
centralized system p. 71
decentralized system p. 73
brand manager p. 73
category management system p. 73
in-house agency p. 75

billings p. 79
superagencies p. 80
full-service agency p. 82
account executive p. 83
account planners p. 84
copywriters p. 85
departmental system p. 86
group system p. 86
creative boutique p. 86
media specialist companies p. 87
commission system p. 88
negotiated commission p. 89

fixed-fee method p. 89
fee–commission combination p. 90
cost-plus system p. 90
incentive-based system p. 90
percentage charges p. 91
financial audit p. 92
qualitative audit p. 92
direct-marketing agencies p. 99
sales promotion agency p. 100
public relations firm p. 100
digital/interactive agencies p. 101

## Discussion Questions

1. The chapter opener discusses the success of Volkswagen in the U.S. market over the past five years. Evaluate the advertising the Deutsch LA agency has done for Volkswagen of America and the role it has played in helping to turn around the company in the U.S. market. How important is advertising for an automotive company such as Volkswagen? (LO3, 5)

2. Evaluate the "Punch Dub" campaign that the Deutsch LA agency developed when it took over the Volkswagen of America account. Discuss the pros and cons of the campaign. (LO3, 5)

3. Who are the various participants in the integrated marketing communications process? Briefly discuss the roles and responsibilities of each. (LO1)

4. Discuss the various challenges faced by companies that use the brand management system when organizing for advertising and promotion. What are some of the things that marketers can do to address these problems and ensure that their brand managers are keeping abreast of external changes occurring in the market? (LO2)

5. Discuss the pros and cons of using an in-house advertising agency. What are some of the reasons why

companies might change from using an in-house agency and hire an outside agency? (LO2)

6. Discuss the reasons companies such as Under Armour or Calvin Klein might use an in-house advertising agency rather that an external agency. Why might a company change from using an in-house agency and hire an outside agency? (LO2)

7. Discuss how technology and the emerging role of digital and social media are impacting the role of brand managers. What types of skills are needed to be a successful brand manager today? What can companies do to train brand managers so they can keep up with the changes occurring in digital and social media? (LO2)

8. What is an agency holding company? Discuss how the emergence of major holding companies is impacting the advertising industry as well as the entire field of integrated marketing communications. (LO3)

9. Discuss the role of media specialist companies. Why are marketers likely to use a media specialist company to handle their media buying and planning versus the media department of an agency? (LO3)

10. Discuss the challenges advertising agencies face in negotiating compensation structures with their clients when the procurement department becomes involved in the process. How might an agency respond to clients who demand to see their labor costs, overhead, and profit margins as part of the negotiation process? (LO4)

11. Discuss the various criteria that might be used by an automobile company such as Volkswagen in evaluating its advertising agencies. Which of these criteria do you think would receive the most weight and why? (LO4)

12. Discuss the reasons why advertising agencies lose accounts. Find an example of a company that changed advertising agencies and identify the factors that led them to switch to another agency. (LO4)

13. Discuss the pros and cons for a marketer having one company handle all of its integrated marketing communications needs versus using specialized marketing communications firms to handle the various components of the program. (LO5, 6)

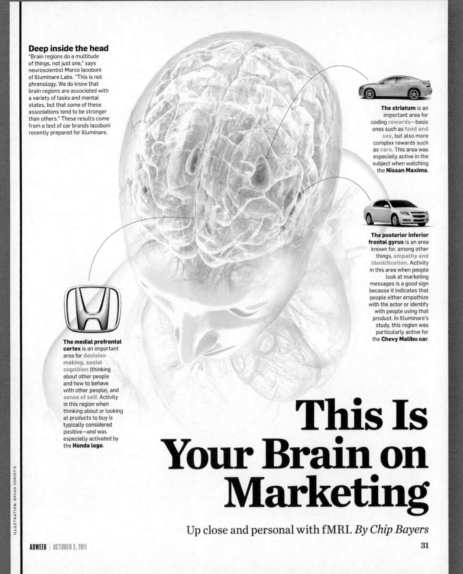

**Deep inside the head**
"Brain regions do a multitude of things, not just one," says neuroscientist Marco Iacoboni of Illuminare Labs. "This is not phrenology. We do know that brain regions are associated with a variety of tasks and mental states, but that some of these associations tend to be stronger than others." These results come from a test of car brands Iacoboni recently prepared for Illuminare.

**The striatum** is an important area for coding rewards—basic ones such as food and sex, but also more complex rewards such as cars. This area was especially active in the subject when watching the **Nissan Maxima.**

**The posterior inferior frontal gyrus** is an area known for, among other things, empathy and identification. Activity in this area when people look at marketing messages is a good sign because it indicates that people either empathize with the actor or identify with people using that product. In Illuminare's study, this region was particularly active for the **Chevy Malibu car.**

**The medial prefrontal cortex** is an important area for decision making, social cognition (thinking about other people and how to behave with other people), and sense of self. Activity in this region when thinking about or looking at products to buy is typically considered positive—and was especially activated by the **Honda logo.**

ILLUSTRATION: BRYAN CHRISTIE

# This Is Your Brain on Marketing

Up close and personal with fMRI. *By Chip Bayers*

ADWEEK | OCTOBER 3, 2011

31

## LEARNING OBJECTIVES

**LO1** To understand the role consumer behavior plays in the development and implementation of advertising and promotional programs.

**LO2** To understand the consumer decision-making process and how it varies for different types of purchases.

**LO3** To understand various internal psychological processes, their influence on consumer decision making, and implications for advertising and promotion.

**LO4** To recognize the various approaches to studying the consumer learning process and their implications for advertising and promotion.

**LO5** To recognize external factors such as culture, social class, group influences, and situational determinants and how they affect consumer behavior.

**LO6** To understand alternative approaches to studying consumer behavior.

# 4 Perspectives on Consumer Behavior

## MARKETERS EXPLORE THE SUBCONSCIOUS TO UNDERSTAND CONSUMER BEHAVIORS—HAVE WE COME FULL CIRCLE?

Decades ago when marketers first began to attempt to understand consumer behaviors, one of the first areas turned to in an attempt to gain insights was social psychology. Psychologists like Ernest Dichter and James Vicary researched the underlying motivations behind consumers' purchases, focusing on Freud's psychoanalytic theory and subconscious needs as the drivers of decisions. Numerous *Fortune* 500 companies employed their services, and the results were interesting to say the least.

For a variety of reasons, marketers moved away from trying to discover subconscious purchasing motives and moved on to other theories that examined consumers from a more conscious, information-processing, and problem-solving orientation. This approach has dominated marketing research ever since, with focus group and survey methodologies becoming the primary tools used to determine why consumers buy. (It is estimated that over $4.5 billion is spent yearly worldwide on qualitative research alone.)

But wait a minute. All of a sudden, the new "it" trend in marketing research has changed! Consumer research has once again (you guessed it!) begun to place more and more emphasis on the subconscious motives underlying consumer behaviors—albeit with a different research methodology. This new methodology, *neuroscience*, really isn't new at all. It has been adapted from the field of medicine, and already has archrival companies whose employees include neuroscientists, radiologists, and marketers who argue that their approach to understanding the relationships between brain functions and consumer behaviors is superior. The two most prevalent methodologies use functional magnetic resonance imaging (fMRI—scan of blood flow) and electroencephalography (EEG—electrical activity on the scalp) to, as one author said, "Hack into your brain." While the proponents of each method disagree as to which is better, both contend that

neuroscience is superior to the traditional research methods used, such as focus groups and surveys. It appears that some major corporations agree with them.

Procter & Gamble, McDonald's, Viacom, L'Oréal, and Starcom are just a few of the companies that have used fMRI. Marketing guru Martin Lindstrom praised the methodology in his *New York Times* best-seller *Buyology*, and filmmaker Morgan Spurlock appeared inside an fMRI in his documentary *POM Wonderful: The Greatest Movie Ever Sold*. On the EEG side are Frito-Lay, CBS, ESPN, Intel, eBay, and PayPal, among others. Apple used EEG to determine why people like the iPad. The research organization NeuroFocus earned a Grand Ogilvy award from the Advertising Research Foundation (its highest award for advertising research) for its work with Cheetos for "demonstrating the most successful use of research in the creation of superior advertising that achieves a critical business objective." Douglas Van Praet, in his book *Unconscious Branding: How Neuroscience Can Empower (and Inspire) Marketing*, notes that "While quantitative surveys have more robust, stable and projectable sample sizes, these tools, as currently structured, often fail to reach the deeper emotional unconscious" (p. 23). His book discusses the overall superiority of neuroscience research to traditional methods.

But not everyone is on the bandwagon. Researchers are quick to criticize neuroscience research due to the fact that it is a relatively new science, and that all of the research has been funded by private corporations. Ray Poynter, a social media consultant, believes that it is far more hype than science and that neuromarketers "massively overclaim" their success stories. Poynter, among others, wants to wait to see more results before he buys in.

So, has the discipline of consumer behavior, which started with seeking subconscious motives for purchasing, returned to its roots? Dr. Marco Iacoboni, founder of one of the neuromarketing research firms and professor of psychiatry and behavioral sciences at UCLA, seems to think so. Commenting on neuroscience research, Iacoboni said, "Well, this sounds like the same thing Freud said 100 years ago!"

Sources: Douglas Van Praet, *Unconscious Branding: How Neuroscience Can Empower (and Inspire) Marketing*, Palgtave Macmillan, 2012, New York; Adam Penenberg, "They Have Hacked Your Brain," *Fast Company*, September 2011, pp. 85–89, 123–124; Chip Bayers, "This Is Your Brain on Marketing," *Adweek*, October 3, 2011, pp. 31–33.

The introduction to this chapter demonstrates how much importance marketers place on consumer research to guide their marketing strategies and how the search for the best research methodology continues to change. Marketers know that many factors may directly or indirectly influence consumers' decision making. What is important for them to know is how and why consumers' needs develop, what they are, and who is likely to use the product or service. Specifically, marketers will study consumer behaviors in an attempt to understand the many factors that lead to and impact purchase decisions. Often, in an attempt to gain insights, marketers will employ techniques borrowed from other disciplines. Research methods used in psychology, anthropology, sociology, and neuroscience are becoming more popular in businesses as managers attempt to explore consumers' purchasing motives. These motives along with consumers' attitudes, lifestyles, and decision-making processes need to be understood before effective marketing strategies can be formulated.

These are just a few of the aspects of consumer behavior that promotional planners must consider in developing integrated marketing communications programs. As you will see, consumer choice is influenced by a variety of factors.

It is beyond the scope of this text to examine consumer behavior in depth. However, promotional planners need a basic understanding of consumer decision making, factors that influence it, and how this knowledge can be used in developing promotional strategies and programs. We begin with an overview of consumer behavior.

# AN OVERVIEW OF CONSUMER BEHAVIOR

A challenge faced by all marketers is how to influence the purchase behavior of consumers in favor of the product or service they offer. For companies like Visa, this means getting consumers to charge more purchases on their credit cards. For BMW, it means getting them to purchase or lease a car; for business-to-business marketers like Xerox or FedEx, it means getting organizational buyers to purchase more of their office products or use their services. While their ultimate goal is to influence consumers' purchase behavior, most marketers understand that the actual purchase is only part of an overall process.

**Consumer behavior** can be defined as the process and activities people engage in when searching for, selecting, purchasing, using, evaluating, and disposing of products and services so as to satisfy their needs and desires. For many products and services, purchase decisions are the result of a long, detailed process that may include an extensive information search, brand comparisons and evaluations, and other activities. Other purchase decisions are more incidental and may result from little more than seeing a product prominently displayed at a discount price in a store. Think of how many times you have made impulse purchases while in the store.

Marketers' success in influencing purchase behavior depends in large part on how well they understand consumer behavior. Marketers need to know the specific needs customers are attempting to satisfy and how they translate into purchase criteria. They need to understand how consumers gather information regarding various alternatives and use this information to select among competing brands, and how they make purchase decisions. Where do they prefer to buy a product? How are they influenced by marketing stimuli at the point of purchase? Marketers also need to understand how the consumer decision process and reasons for purchase vary among different types of customers. For example, purchase decisions may be influenced by the personality or

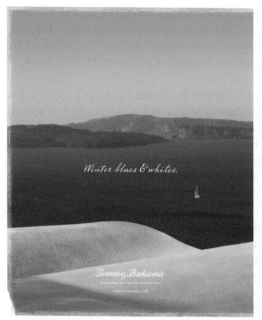

**EXHIBIT 4–1**

Tommy Bahama appeals to
the beach/island lifestyle

LO 04-2

**FIGURE 4–1**

A Basic Model of Consumer
Decision Making

lifestyle of the consumer. Notice how the ad shown in Exhibit 4–1 portrays a product for the beachgoer lifestyle.

The conceptual model in Figure 4–1 will be used as a framework for analyzing the consumer decision process. We will discuss what occurs at the various stages of this model and how advertising and promotion can be used to influence decision making. We will also examine the influence of various psychological concepts, such as motivation, perception, attitudes, and integration processes. Variations in the consumer decision-making process will be explored, as will perspectives regarding consumer learning and external influences on the consumer decision process. The chapter concludes with a consideration of alternative means of studying consumer behavior.

# THE CONSUMER DECISION-MAKING PROCESS

As shown in Figure 4–1, the consumer's purchase decision process is generally viewed as consisting of stages through which the buyer passes in purchasing a product or service. This model shows that decision making involves a number of internal psychological processes. Motivation, perception, attitude formation, integration, and learning are important to promotional planners, since they influence the general decision-making process of the consumer. We will examine each stage of the purchase decision model and discuss how the various subprocesses influence what occurs at this phase of the consumer behavior process. We will also discuss how promotional planners can influence this process.

## Problem Recognition

Figure 4–1 shows that the first stage in the consumer decision-making process is **problem recognition**, which occurs when the consumer perceives a need and becomes motivated to solve the problem. The problem recognition stage initiates the subsequent decision processes.

Problem recognition is caused by a difference between the consumer's *ideal state* and *actual state*. A discrepancy exists between what the consumer wants the situation to be like and what the situation is really like. (Note that *problem* does not always imply a negative state. A goal exists for the consumer, and this goal may be the attainment of a more positive situation.)

**Sources of Problem Recognition**   The causes of problem recognition may be very simple or very complex and may result from changes in the consumer's current and/or desired state. These causes may be influenced by both internal and external factors.

**A. Stages in the Consumer Decision-Making Process**

| Problem recognition | Information search | Alternative evaluation | Purchase decision | Postpurchase evaluation |

**B. Relevant Internal Psychological Processes**

| Motivation | Perception | Attitude formation | Integration | Learning |

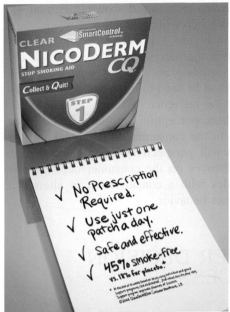

**EXHIBIT 4–2**

Nicoderm offers to help those who want to quit smoking

**EXHIBIT 4–3**

Splat encourages consumers to rebel by changing their hair color

**Out of Stock** Problem recognition occurs when consumers use their existing supply of a product and must replenish their stock. The purchase decision is usually simple and routine and is often resolved by choosing a familiar brand or one to which the consumer feels loyal.

**Dissatisfaction** Problem recognition is created by the consumer's dissatisfaction with the current state of affairs and/or the product or service being used. For example, a consumer may think her snow boots are no longer comfortable or stylish enough. Advertising may be used to help consumers recognize when they have a problem and/or need to make a purchase. The Nicoderm ad shown in Exhibit 4–2 offers assistance for those who may be dissatisfied with smoking and want to quit.

**New Needs/Wants** Changes in consumers' lives often result in new needs and wants. For example, changes in one's financial situation, employment status, or lifestyle may create new needs and trigger problem recognition. As you will see, when you graduate from college and begin your professional career, your new job may necessitate a change in your wardrobe. (Good-bye blue jeans and T-shirts, hello suits and ties.)

Not all product purchases are based on needs. Some products or services sought by consumers are not essential but are nonetheless desired. A **want** is a desire for something one does not have. Many products sold to consumers satisfy their wants rather than their basic needs.

**Related Products/Purchases** Problem recognition can also be stimulated by the purchase of a product. For example, the purchase of a new iPod may lead to the recognition of a need for accessories, such as a dock, an attachment for the car, or a carrying case. The purchase of an iPad may lead to buying a cover and screen cleaner. The purchase of a personal computer may prompt the need for software programs, upgrades, a printer, and so on.

**Marketer-Induced Problem Recognition** Another source of problem recognition is marketers' actions that encourage consumers not to be content with their current state or situation. Ads for personal hygiene products such as mouthwash, deodorant, and foot sprays may be designed to create insecurities that consumers can resolve through the use of these products. Marketers change fashions and clothing designs and create perceptions among consumers that their wardrobes are out of style. Exhibit 4–3 shows how splat encourages people to change their hair color.

Marketers also take advantage of consumers' tendency toward *novelty-seeking behavior*, which leads them to try different brands. Consumers often try new products or brands even when they are basically satisfied with their regular brand. Marketers encourage brand switching by introducing new brands into markets that are already saturated and by using advertising and sales promotion techniques such as free samples, introductory price offers, and coupons.

**New Products** Problem recognition can also occur when innovative products are introduced and brought to the attention of consumers. Marketers are constantly

**EXHIBIT 4–4**

Apps for smartphones now number in the hundreds of thousands

introducing new products and services and telling consumers about the types of problems they solve. For example, the cell phone has become much more than a telephone, as more and more apps are now available to do just about anything you can think of. Apple's applications (apps) store has over 300,000 free and for-purchase apps for their smartphones and iPads (Exhibit 4–4). As more apps are added, these products will become appealing to more consumers.

Marketers' attempts to create problem recognition among consumers are not always successful. Consumers may not see a problem or need for the product the marketer is selling. Using the cell phone example just provided, for some, all of the potential provided by apps may be considered unnecessary—they just want to be able to send and receive phone calls.

## Examining Consumer Motivations

LO 04-3

Marketers recognize that while problem recognition is often a basic, simple process, the way a consumer perceives a problem and becomes motivated to solve it will influence the remainder of the decision process. For example, one consumer may perceive the need to purchase a new watch from a functional perspective and focus on reliable, low-priced alternatives. Another consumer may see the purchase of a watch as more of a fashion statement and focus on the design and image of various brands. To better understand the reasons underlying consumer purchases, marketers devote considerable attention to examining **motives**—that is, those factors that compel a consumer to take a particular action.

**Hierarchy of Needs**   One of the most popular approaches to understanding consumer motivations is based on the classic theory of human motivation popularized many years ago by psychologist Abraham Maslow. His **hierarchy of needs** theory postulates five basic levels of human needs, arranged in a hierarchy based on their importance. As shown in Figure 4–2, the five needs are (1) *physiological*—the basic level of primary needs for things required to sustain life, such as food, shelter, clothing, and sex; (2) *safety*—the need for security and safety from physical harm;

**FIGURE 4–2**

Maslow's Hierarchy of Needs

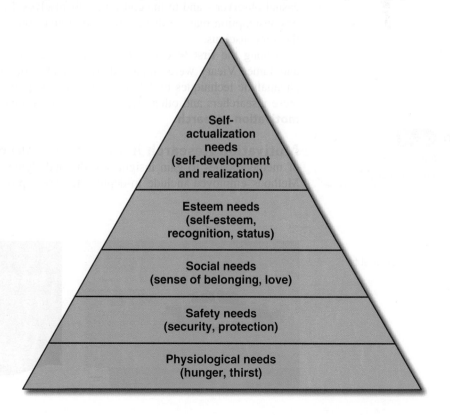

(3) *social/love and belonging*—the desire to have satisfying relationships with others and feel a sense of love, affection, belonging, and acceptance; (4) *esteem*—the need to feel a sense of accomplishment and gain recognition, status, and respect from others; and (5) *self-actualization*—the need for self-fulfillment and a desire to realize one's own potential.

According to Maslow's theory, the lower-level physiological and safety needs must be satisfied before the higher-order needs become meaningful. Once these basic needs are satisfied, the individual moves on to attempting to satisfy higher-order needs such as self-esteem. In reality, it is unlikely that people move through the needs hierarchy in a stairstep manner. Lower-level needs are an ongoing source of motivation for consumer purchase behavior. However, since basic physiological needs are met in most developed countries, marketers often sell products that fill basic physiological needs by appealing to consumers' higher-level needs.

While Maslow's need hierarchy has flaws, it offers a framework for marketers to use in determining what needs they want their products and services to be shown satisfying. Advertising campaigns can then be designed to show how a brand can fulfill these needs. Marketers also recognize that different market segments emphasize different need levels. For example, a young single person may be attempting to satisfy social or self-esteem needs in purchasing a car, while a family with children will focus more on safety needs. The Volvo ad in Exhibit 4–5 focuses on security needs of consumers, while the Jaguar ad addresses self-actualization.

**Psychoanalytic Theory**   A somewhat more controversial approach to the study of consumer motives is the **psychoanalytic theory** pioneered by Sigmund Freud. Although his work dealt with the structure and development of personality, Freud also studied the underlying motivations for human behavior. Psychoanalytic theory had a strong influence on the development of modern psychology and on explanations of motivation and personality. It has also been applied to the study of consumer behavior by marketers interested in probing deeply rooted motives that may underlie purchase decisions.

Those who attempt to relate psychoanalytic theory to consumer behavior believe consumers' motivations for purchasing are often very complex and unclear to the casual observer—and to the consumers themselves. Many motives for purchase and/or consumption may be driven by deep motives one can determine only by probing the subconscious.

Among the first to conduct this type of research in marketing, Ernest Dichter and James Vicary were employed by a number of major corporations to use psychoanalytic techniques to determine consumers' purchase motivations. The work of these researchers and others who continue to use this approach assumed the title of **motivation research**.

YTC 04–01
**Volvo and Jaguar**
youtube.com/10ebelch

**Motivation Research in Marketing**   Motivation researchers use a variety of methodologies to gain insight into the underlying causes of consumer behavior. Methods employed include in-depth interviews, projective techniques, association

**EXHIBIT 4–5**
Volvo uses an appeal to security needs

FIGURE 4–3

Some of the Marketing
Research Methods Used
to Probe the Mind of the
Consumer

**In-depth interviews**
Face-to-face situations in which an interviewer asks a consumer to talk
freely in an unstructured interview using specific questions designed to
obtain insights into his or her motives, ideas, or opinions.

**Projective techniques**
Efforts designed to gain insights into consumers' values, motives, attitudes,
or needs that are difficult to express or identify by having them project
these internal states upon some external object.

**Association tests**
A technique in which an individual is asked to respond with the first thing
that comes to mind when he or she is presented with a stimulus; the
stimulus may be a word, picture, ad, and so on.

**Focus groups**
A small number of people with similar backgrounds and/or interests who are
brought together to discuss a particular product, idea, or issue.

tests, and focus groups in which consumers are encouraged to bring out associations
related to products and brands (see Figure 4–3). As one might expect, such associations often lead to interesting insights as to why people purchase. For example:

- A man's purchase of a high-priced fur for his wife proves his potency.[1]
- Consumers prefer large cars because they believe such cars protect them from
  the "jungle" of everyday driving.[2]
- A man buys a convertible as a substitute mistress.
- Women like to bake cakes because they feel like they are giving birth to a baby.
- Women wear perfume to "attract a man" and "glorify their existence."
- Men like frankfurters better than women do because cooking them (frank-
  furters, not men!) makes women feel guilty. It's an admission of laziness.
- When people shower, their sins go down the drain with the soap as they rinse.[3]

As you can see from these examples, motivation research has led to some very
interesting, albeit controversial, findings and to much skepticism from marketing
managers. However, major corporations and advertising agencies continue to use
motivation research to help them market their products.

**Problems and Contributions of Psychoanalytic Theory and
Motivation Research** Psychoanalytic theory has been criticized as being
too vague, unresponsive to the external environment, and too reliant on the early
development of the individual. It also uses a small sample for drawing conclusions.
Because of the emphasis on the unconscious, results are difficult if not impossible to verify, leading motivation research to be criticized for both the conclusions
drawn and its lack of experimental validation. Since motivation research studies
typically use so few participants, there is also concern that it really discovers the
idiosyncrasies of a few individuals and its findings are not generalizable to the
whole population.

Still, it is difficult to ignore the psychoanalytic approach in furthering our understanding of consumer behavior. Its insights can often be used as a basis for advertising messages aimed at buyers' deeply rooted feelings, hopes, aspirations, and fears.
Such strategies are often more effective than rationally based appeals.

Some corporations and advertising agencies have used motivation research to gain further insights into how consumers think. Examples include the following:

- Chrysler had consumers sit on the floor, like children, and use scissors to cut words out of magazines to describe a car.[4]
- McCann Erickson asked women to draw and describe how they felt about roaches. The agency concluded that many women associated roaches with men who had abandoned them and that this was why women preferred roach killers that let them see the roaches die.
- Saatchi & Saatchi used psychological probes to conclude that Ronald McDonald created a more nurturing mood than did the Burger King (who was perceived as more aggressive and distant).
- Foote Cone & Belding gave consumers stacks of photographs of faces and asked them to associate the faces with the kinds of people who might use particular products.
- The advertising agency Marcus Thomas, LLC conducted in-depth one-on-one interviews and used projective techniques to determine underlying motivations for choosing one cardiovascular care facility over another.

While often criticized, motivation research has also contributed to the marketing discipline. The qualitative nature of the research is considered important in assessing how and why consumers buy. Focus groups and in-depth interviews are valuable methods for gaining insights into consumers' feelings, and projective techniques are often the only way to get around stereotypical or socially desirable responses. In addition, motivation research is the forerunner of psychographics (discussed in Chapter 2).

Finally, we know that buyers are sometimes motivated by symbolic as well as functional drives in their purchase decisions. Some believe that as competition for advertisers' dollars has increased, the amount and explicitness of sexual content on TV has increased as well as many programs and commerials now push the limits as to what is acceptable.[5] At the same time, some companies are using sex in advertising in less explicit ways. The Lexus ad in Exhibit 4–6 employs interactive technology and QR codes to send a sexy message. When the viewer scans the QR codes placed in the ad, *Sports Illustrated* swimsuit models appear in various scenes. While simply viewing the ad reveals no sexual content on the surface, when scanned, there is no doubt about the use of sex.

**YTC 04–02**

**Angie's List**
youtube.com/10ebelch

**EXHIBIT 4–6**
This Lexus ad employs interactive technology and QR codes to present a sexy. ad in the *Sports Illustrated* swimsuit edition

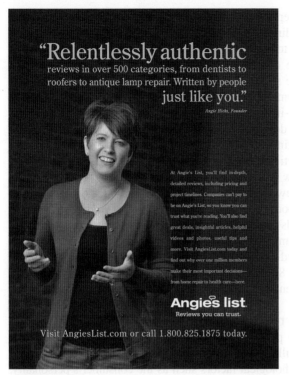

**EXHIBIT 4–7**

AnglesList.com is a valuable source of information for many consumers

YTC **04–03**

**Tropicana**

youtube.com/10ebelch

**EXHIBIT 4–8**

Tropicana uses color to focus attention on orange juice

Tropicana
pure premium

**Each drop comes
from the fruit**

## Information Search

The second stage in the consumer decision-making process is *information search.* Once consumers perceive a problem or need that can be satisfied by the purchase of a product or service, they begin to search for information needed to make a purchase decision. The initial search effort often consists of an attempt to scan information stored in memory to recall past experiences and/or knowledge regarding various purchase alternatives. This information retrieval is referred to as **internal search**. For many routine, repetitive purchases, previously acquired information that is stored in memory (such as past performance or outcomes from using a brand) is sufficient for comparing alternatives and making a choice.

If the internal search does not yield enough information, the consumer will seek additional information by engaging in **external search**. External sources of information include:

- *Internet sources,* such as organic and sponsored information available through companies' websites, consumers postings, and organizations like Angie's List, Yelp, and so on (Exhibit 4–7).
- *Personal sources,* such as friends, relatives, or co-workers.
- *Marketer-controlled (commercial) sources,* such as information from advertising, salespeople, or point-of-purchase displays and the Internet.
- *Public sources,* including articles in magazines or newspapers and reports on TV and so on.
- *Personal experience,* such as actually handling, examining, or testing the product.

Determining how much and which sources of external information to use involves several factors, including the importance of the purchase decision, the effort needed to acquire information, the amount of past experience relevant, the degree of perceived risk associated with the purchase, and the time available. For example, the selection of a movie to see on a Friday night might entail simply talking to a friend or checking the movie guide on the Internet. A more complex purchase such as a new car might use a number of information sources—perhaps a review of *Road & Track, Motortrend,* or *Consumer Reports;* discussion with family members and friends; conducting an online search; and test-driving of cars. At this point in the purchase decision, the information-providing aspects of advertising are extremely important.

## Perception

Knowledge of how consumers acquire and use information from external sources is important to marketers in formulating communication strategies. Marketers are particularly interested in (1) how consumers sense external information, (2) how they select and attend to various sources of information, and (3) how this information is interpreted and given meaning. These processes are all part of **perception**, the process by which an individual receives, selects, organizes, and interprets information to create a meaningful picture of the world. Perception is an individual process; it depends on internal factors such as a person's beliefs, experiences, needs, moods, and expectations. The perceptual process is also influenced by the characteristics of a stimulus (such as its size, color, and intensity) and the context in which it is seen or heard (Exhibit 4–8).

**ISN'T IT FUNNY HOW STEREO ADS ARE BORING UNTIL YOU WANT A STEREO?**

We admit it. There are times when advertising isn't especially interesting.

For instance, stereo ads when you're not looking for a new stereo. Or insurance ads when you're not looking for a new insurance company. Or detergent ads when you're not looking for a new detergent.

But suppose your stereo breaks down. Or your insurance rates go up. Or your laundry comes out gray.

All of a sudden, stereo ads, insurance ads and detergent ads start looking a lot more interesting.

It's one of the basic truths of advertising.

We try to be entertaining, but that's not really our job. Our job is to help you make the right choices

when you're in the market for any kind of product or service.

Of course, when you're not in the market, we recognize that advertising may seem beside the point. In that case, you're free to pretend it isn't there.

In fact, you're free to ignore advertising for as long as you choose.

Right up until your stereo breaks down.

**ADVERTISING.**
**ANOTHER WORD FOR FREEDOM OF CHOICE.**
American Association of Advertising Agencies

**EXHIBIT 4–9**

This ad reminds consumers of how advertising responds to their needs

**FIGURE 4–4**

The Selective Perception Process

**Sensation**   Perception involves three distinct processes. **Sensation** is the immediate, direct response of the senses (taste, smell, sight, touch, and hearing) to a stimulus such as an ad, package, brand name, or point-of-purchase display. Perception uses these senses to create a representation of the stimulus. Marketers recognize that it is important to understand consumers' physiological reactions to marketing stimuli as shown in the lead-in to this chapter. For example, the visual elements of an ad or package design must attract consumers' favorable attention.

Marketers sometimes try to increase the level of sensory input so that their advertising messages will get noticed. For example, Bloomingdales' New York store sprayed Donna Karan's new perfume DKNY onto the sidewalks outside the store to introduce the perfume to consumers. Kraft Foods promoted the new DiGiorno Garlic Bread Pizza with scent strip cards in stores, while Avon uses scent strips for many products from perfumes to bubble baths in its catalogs. Scent strips have long been used in magazines, and a study of *Allure* magazine readers showed that 86 percent of readers said they had tried the scent strips, with 72 percent saying they purchased the product as a result.[6]

**Selecting Information**   Sensory inputs are important but are only one part of the perceptual process. Other determinants of whether marketing stimuli will be attended to and how they will be interpreted include internal psychological factors such as the consumer's personality, needs, motives, expectations, and experiences. These psychological inputs explain why people focus attention on some things and ignore others. Two people may perceive the same stimuli in very different ways because they select, attend, and comprehend differently. An individual's perceptual processes usually focus on elements of the environment that are relevant to his or her needs and tune out irrelevant stimuli. Think about how much more attentive you are to advertising for personal computers, tires, or stereos when you are in the market for one of these products (a point that is made by the message from the American Association of Advertising Agencies in Exhibit 4–9).

**Interpreting the Information**   Once a consumer selects and attends to a stimulus, the perceptual process focuses on organizing, categorizing, and interpreting the incoming information. This stage of the perceptual process is very individualized and is influenced by internal psychological factors. The interpretation and meaning an individual assigns to an incoming stimulus also depend in part on the nature of the stimulus. For example, many ads are objective, and their message is clear and straightforward. Other ads are more ambiguous, and their meaning is strongly influenced by the consumer's individual interpretation.

Selectivity occurs throughout the various stages of the consumer's perceptual process. Perception may be viewed as a filtering process in which internal and external factors influence what is received and how it is processed and interpreted. The sheer number and complexity of the marketing stimuli a person is exposed to in any given day require that this filtering occur. **Selective perception** may occur at the exposure, attention, comprehension, or retention stage of perception, as shown in Figure 4–4.

**Selective Perception**   **Selective exposure** occurs as consumers choose whether or not to make themselves available to information. For example, a viewer of a television show may change channels or leave the room during commercial breaks.

**Selective attention** occurs when the consumer chooses to focus attention on certain stimuli while excluding others. One study of selective attention estimated that

| Selective exposure | → | Selective attention | → | Selective comprehension | → | Selective retention |

**EXHIBIT 4–10**
Color is used to attract attention to VO5

the typical consumer is exposed to nearly 1,500 ads per day yet perceives only 76 of these messages.[7] Other estimates range as high as 4,000 exposures per day. This means advertisers must make considerable effort to get their messages noticed. Advertisers often use the creative aspects of their ads to gain consumers' attention. For example, some advertisers set their ads off from others by showing their products in color against a black-and-white background. This creative tactic has been used in advertising for many products, among them Cherry 7UP, Nuprin, Pepto-Bismol, and Tropicana. Notice how the color red is used in the ad for VO5 to attract attention while also focusing on the product line, packaging, and brand identity in Exhibit 4–10.

Even if the consumer does notice the advertiser's message, there is no guarantee it will be interpreted in the intended manner. Consumers may engage in **selective comprehension**, interpreting information on the basis of their own attitudes, beliefs, motives, and experiences. They often interpret information in a manner that supports their own position. For example, an ad that disparages a consumer's favorite brand may be seen as biased or untruthful, and its claims may not be accepted.

The final screening process shown in Figure 4–4 is **selective retention**, which means consumers do not remember all the information they see, hear, or read even after attending to and comprehending it. Advertisers attempt to make sure information will be retained in the consumer's memory so that it will be available when it is time to make a purchase. **Mnemonics** such as symbols, rhymes, associations, and images that assist in the learning and memory process are helpful. Many advertisers use telephone numbers that spell out the company name and are easy to remember (for example, 1-800-GOFEDEX).

**Subliminal Perception**   Advertisers know consumers use selective perception to filter out irrelevant or unwanted advertising messages, so they employ various creative tactics to get their messages noticed. One controversial tactic advertisers have been accused of using is appealing to consumers' subconscious. **Subliminal perception** refers to the ability to perceive a stimulus that is below the level of conscious awareness. Psychologists generally agree it is possible to perceive things without being consciously aware of them.

As you might imagine, the possibility of using hidden persuaders such as subliminal audio messages or visual cues to influence consumers might be intriguing to advertisers but would not be welcomed by consumers. The idea of marketers influencing consumers at a subconscious level has strong ethical implications. IMC Perspective 4–1 discusses researchers' mixed opinions as to whether motivation research and subliminal advertising are likely to be effective in influencing consumer behavior.

## Alternative Evaluation

After acquiring information during the information search stage of the decision process, the consumer moves to alternative evaluation. In this stage, the consumer compares the various brands or products and services he or she has identified as being capable of solving the consumption problem and satisfying the needs or motives that initiated the decision process. The various brands identified as purchase options to be considered during the alternative evaluation process are referred to as the consumer's *evoked set.*

## Subliminal Advertising—50 Years Old and Still Going Strong!

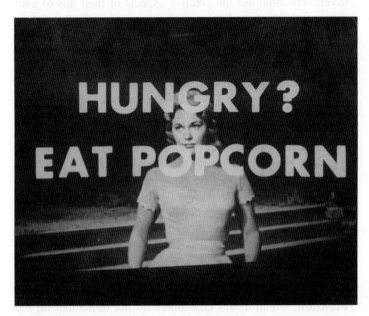

HUNGRY? EAT POPCORN

It has been more than half a century since Vance Packard's famous book *The Hidden Persuaders* shocked the world. In his book, Packard accused advertisers of using research techniques like "depth interviews" and "motivation research" to develop messages that appealed to consumers' subconscious. These appeals led consumers to be persuaded to make purchases without consciously being aware why they made their choices. At about the same time, James Vicary, a motivational researcher, introduced the concept of subliminal advertising, reporting that he had increased the sales of popcorn and Coke by subliminally flashing the messages "eat popcorn" and "drink Coca-Cola" across the screen. (2012 marked the 50th anniversary of Vicary's confession that his research study was a hoax.) Wilson Bryant Key further fueled the fires with his books claiming that subliminal advertising was, indeed, manipulating consumer behaviors.

A rash of research studies, articles, and books designed to explore motivation research and subliminal advertising soon followed in an attempt to determine the veracity of these techniques. In a series of extensive reviews on the topic (1982, 1988), Timothy Moore concluded that there was no evidence to support the fact that subliminal messages can affect consumers' motivations, perceptions, or attitudes. For a long period of time subliminal advertising, motivation research, and the application of psychoanalytic theory to consumer behaviors seemed to go away, with members of society and academia apparently losing interest. But while the studies went away, they never really disappeared.

In the 1990s a number of studies surfaced arguing that subliminal advertising could work. Then in the 2000 Bush–Gore presidential campaign, the Republicans were accused of subliminally implanting the word *rats* into ads to attach the meaning to Al Gore. They ran the ad about 4,000 times before it was discovered and pulled due to protests. Eight years later political scientist Joel Weinberger, inspired by the controversy surrounding the ad, ran an experiment in which he found that flashing the word *RAT* in a TV commercial could increase the negative evaluations of a politician. Once again, motivation research was back in the spotlight.

More recently, scientists at the University College of London in the UK claimed that they proved conclusively that people can perceive the emotional value of subliminal messages. Another researcher also claimed that his series of research studies proved that music, country of origin, and even product weight have subliminal influences on consumers. Still another showed that in an experiment when viewers had the words *Lipton Iced Tea* flashed subliminally before them, when offered a drink after the experiment, 85 percent of them selected that drink out of a choice of three drinks, while only 20 percent did so without the exposure.

This time, however, no one seems to be getting alarmed, though Leonard Mlodinow—a best-selling author who teaches at California Institute of Technology, thinks they ought to be. Mlodinow believes that one of the more effective ways of using subliminal messages may be through product placements. He cites examples of product placements by Dr Pepper in the movie *Spider Man* and Pepsi in the movie *Home Alone* to support his position that subliminal placements work and are being used. After 50 years, consumers and researchers don't seem to be concerned that they need to worry about subliminal advertising. But they certainly haven't lost interest.

Sources: Martin Lindstrom, "How Subliminal Advertising Works," www.parade.com, January 4, 2009; "Hypnosis Reveals Ad Effects," *Adweek Asia*, January 29, 1999, p. 4; "Breaking French Connection," *Advertising Age*, March 22, 1999, p. 52; Kathryn Theus, "Subliminal Advertising and the Psychology of Processing Unconscious Stimuli: A Review of Research," *Psychology & Marketing* 11, no. 3 (1994), pp. 271–90; Timothy Moore, "Subliminal Advertising: What You See Is What You Get," *Journal of Marketing* 46, no. 2 (Spring 1982), pp. 38–47; Timothy Moore, "The Case against Subliminal Manipulation," *Psychology and Marketing* 5, no. 4 (Winter 1988), pp. 297–316; Kalpana Srinivasan, "FCC Ends Probe on Republican Ad," www.individual.com, March 12, 2001, pp. 1–2; George E. Condon Jr. and Toby Eckert, "Flap over 'RATS' Latest to Plague Bush's Drive," *San Diego Tribune*, September 13, 2000, p. A1; Richard Alleyne, "Subliminal Advertising Really Does Work, Claim Scientists," www.telegraph.co.uk, September 2009.

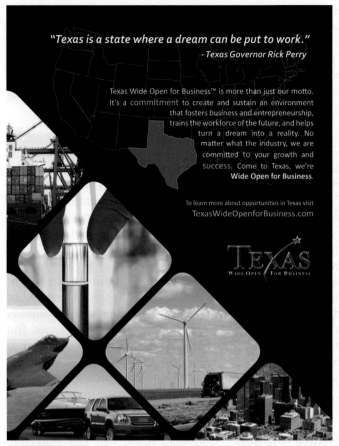

"Texas is a state where a dream can be put to work."
- Texas Governor Rick Perry

Texas Wide Open for Business™ is more than just our motto. It's a commitment to create and sustain an environment that fosters business and entrepreneurship, trains the workforce of the future, and helps turn a dream into a reality. No matter what the industry, we are committed to your growth and success. Come to Texas, we're **Wide Open for Business.**

To learn more about opportunities in Texas visit
TexasWideOpenforBusiness.com

**EXHIBIT 4–11**

Texas wants to be in the evoked set of business locations

**The Evoked Set** The evoked set is generally only a subset of all the brands of which the consumer is aware. The consumer reduces the number of brands to be reviewed during the alternative evaluation stage to a manageable level. The exact size of the evoked set (sometimes referred to as the consideration threat) varies from one consumer to another and depends on such factors as the importance of the purchase and the amount of time and energy the consumer wants to spend comparing alternatives.

The goal of most advertising and promotional strategies is to increase the likelihood that a brand will be included in the consumer's evoked set and considered during alternative evaluation. Marketers use advertising to create *top-of-mind awareness* among consumers so that their brands are part of the evoked set of their target audiences. Popular brands with large advertising budgets use *reminder advertising* to maintain high awareness levels and increase the likelihood they will be considered by consumers in the market for the product. Marketers of new brands or those with a low market share need to gain awareness among consumers and break into their evoked sets. The ad promoting Texas as a better place to live and do business (Exhibit 4–11) shows this strategy being used in a different context from products and brands. The ad presents the many benefits of Texas and encourages prospective businesses to consider it in their evoked set of places to locate or relocate.

Advertising is a valuable promotional tool for creating and maintaining brand awareness and making sure a brand is included in the evoked set. However, marketers also work to promote their brands in the actual environment where purchase decisions are made. Point-of-purchase materials and promotional techniques such as in-store sampling, end-aisle displays, and shelf tags touting special prices encourage consumers to consider brands that may not have initially been in their evoked set.

**Evaluative Criteria and Consequences** Once consumers have identified an evoked set and have a list of alternatives, they must evaluate the various brands. This involves comparing the choice alternatives on specific criteria important to the consumer. **Evaluative criteria** are the dimensions or attributes of a product or service that are used to compare different alternatives. Evaluative criteria can be objective or subjective. For example, in buying an automobile, consumers use objective attributes such as price, warranty, and fuel economy as well as subjective factors such as image, styling, and performance.

Evaluative criteria are usually viewed as product or service attributes. Many marketers view their products or services as *bundles of attributes,* but consumers tend to think about products or services in terms of their *consequences* or *outcomes* instead. They distinguish between two broad types of consequences. **Functional consequences** are concrete outcomes of product or service usage that are tangible and directly experienced by consumers. The taste of a soft drink or a potato chip, the acceleration of a car, and the speed of the Internet service provider are examples of functional consequences. **Psychosocial consequences** are abstract outcomes that are more intangible, subjective, and personal, such as how a product makes you feel or how you think others will view you for purchasing or using it.

Product/service attributes and the consequences or outcomes consumers think they will experience from a particular brand are very important, for they are often the basis on which consumers form attitudes and purchase intentions and decide among various choice alternatives. Two subprocesses are very important during the alternative evaluation stage: (1) the process by which consumer attitudes are created, reinforced, and changed and (2) the decision rules or integration strategies consumers use to compare brands and make purchase decisions. We will examine each of these processes in more detail.

## Attitudes

Attitudes are learned predispositions to respond to an object and are some of the most heavily studied concepts in consumer behavior.[8] More recent perspectives view an attitude as a summary construct that represents an individual's overall feelings toward or evaluation of an object.[9] Consumers hold attitudes toward a variety of objects that are important to marketers, including individuals (celebrity endorsers such as Novak Djokovic or Danica Patrick), brands (Cheerios, Special K), companies (AT&T and Bank of America), product categories (beef, pork, tuna), retail stores (Walmart, Sears), or even advertisements (Nike).

Attitudes are important to marketers because they theoretically summarize a consumer's evaluation of an object (or brand or company) and represent positive or negative feelings and behavioral tendencies. Marketers' keen interest in attitudes is based on the assumption that they are related to consumers' purchase behavior. But attitudes are very important to marketers. Advertising and promotion are used to create favorable attitudes toward new products/services or brands, reinforce existing favorable attitudes, and/or change negative attitudes. An approach to studying and measuring attitudes that is particularly relevant to advertising is multiattribute attitude models.

**Multiattribute Attitude Models**  Consumer researchers and marketing practitioners have been using multiattribute attitude models to study consumer attitudes for two decades. A **multiattribute attitude model** views an attitude object, such as a product or brand, as possessing a number of attributes that provide the basis on which consumers form their attitudes. According to this model, consumers have beliefs about specific brand attributes and attach different levels of importance to these attributes. Using this approach, an attitude toward a particular brand can be represented as

$$A_B = \sum_{i=1}^{n} B_i \times E_i$$

where $A_B$ = attitude toward a brand

$B_i$ = beliefs about the brand's performance on attribute $i$

$E_i$ = importance attached to attribute $i$

$n$ = number of attributes considered

For example, a consumer may have beliefs ($B_i$) about various brands of toothpaste on certain attributes. One brand may be perceived as having fluoride and thus preventing cavities, tasting good, and helping control tartar buildup. Another brand may not be perceived as having these attributes, but consumers may believe it performs well on other attributes such as freshening breath and whitening teeth.

To predict attitudes, one must know how much importance consumers attach to each of these attributes ($E_i$). For example, parents purchasing toothpaste for their children may prefer a brand that performs well on cavity prevention, a preference that leads to a more favorable attitude toward the first brand. Teenagers and young adults may prefer a brand that freshens their breath and makes their teeth white and thus prefer the second brand.

Consumers may hold a number of different beliefs about brands in any product or service category. However, not all of these beliefs are activated in forming an attitude. Beliefs concerning specific attributes or consequences that are activated and form the basis of an attitude are referred to as **salient beliefs**. Marketers should identify and understand these salient beliefs and recognize that the saliency of beliefs varies among different market segments, over time, and across different consumption situations.

**Attitude Change Strategies**   Multiattribute models help marketers understand and diagnose the underlying basis of consumers' attitudes. By understanding the beliefs that underlie consumers' evaluations of a brand and the importance of various attributes or consequences, the marketer is better able to develop communication strategies for creating, changing, or reinforcing brand attitudes. The multiattribute model provides insight into several ways marketers can influence consumer attitudes, including:

- Increasing or changing the strength or belief rating of a brand on an important attribute (Colgate Optic White toothpaste has the best whitening power).
- Changing consumers' perceptions of the importance or value of an attribute (Michelin tires emphasizing higher gas mileage and safety).
- Adding a new attribute to the attitude formation process (the fact that the product is environmentally friendly [Clorox Green]).
- Changing perceptions of belief ratings for a competing brand (GM showing its cars can compete with anyone's).

The first strategy is commonly used by advertisers. They identify an attribute or consequence that is important and remind consumers how well their brand performs on this attribute. In situations where consumers do not perceive the marketer's brand as possessing an important attribute or the belief strength is low, advertising strategies may be targeted at changing the belief rating. Even when belief strength is high, advertising may be used to increase the rating of a brand on an important attribute. BMW's "The Ultimate Driving Machine" campaign is a good example of a strategy designed to create a belief and reinforce it through advertising.

Marketers often attempt to influence consumer attitudes by changing the relative importance of a particular attribute. This second strategy involves getting consumers to attach more importance to the attribute in forming their attitude toward the brand. Marketers using this strategy want to increase the importance an attribute has to solve a problem (Exhibit 4–12).

The third strategy for influencing consumer attitudes is to add or emphasize a new attribute that consumers can use in evaluating a brand. Marketers often do this by improving their products or focusing on additional benefits or consequences associated with using the brand. For example, Tom's Shoes donates one pair of shoes for each pair sold to an impoverished person. The company does the same for each pair of eyeglasses sold.

A final strategy marketers use is to change consumer beliefs about the attributes of competing brands or product categories. This strategy has become much more common with the increase in comparative advertising, where marketers compare their brands to competitors' on specific product attributes.

## Integration Processes and Decision Rules

Another important aspect of the alternative evaluation stage is the way consumers combine information about the characteristics of brands to arrive at a purchase decision. **Integration processes** are the way product knowledge, meanings, and beliefs are combined to evaluate two or more alternatives.[10] Analysis of the integration process focuses

**YTC 04–04**
**Michelin**
youtube.com/10ebelch

**EXHIBIT 4–12**
This Michelin ad stresses that "the right tire changes everything"

The MICHELIN® DEFENDER® tire allows you to stop up to 31 feet shorter¹ and drive up to 21,000 miles longer² than a leading competitor², and is backed by our 90,000-mile limited warranty.⁴ Find out more at **michelinman.com/defender**

1 – Based on internal wet braking test results versus Goodyear® Assurance® ComforTred® Touring tire size 185/65R15. 2 – Based on commissioned third-party wear test results versus Continental® ProContact™ with EcoPlus Technology tire size 215/60R16. 4 – 90,000-mile limited warranty for H- and T-rated tires; 80,000-mile limited warranty for V-rated tires. See michelinman.com for warranty details.

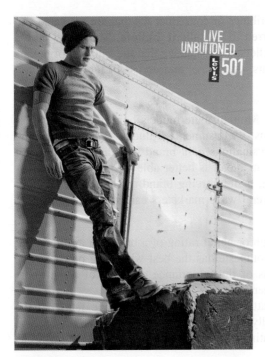

**EXHIBIT 4–13**
Market leaders such as Levi's can appeal to consumer affect

on the different types of *decision rules* or strategies consumers use to decide among purchase alternatives.

Consumers often make purchase selections by using formal integration strategies or decision rules that require examination and comparison of alternatives on specific attributes. This process involves a very deliberate evaluation of the alternatives, attribute by attribute. When consumers apply such formal decision rules, marketers need to know which attributes are being considered so as to provide the information the consumers require.

Sometimes consumers make their purchase decisions using more simplified decision rules known as **heuristics**. For familiar products that are purchased frequently, consumers may use price-based heuristics (buy the least expensive brand) or promotion-based heuristics (choose the brand for which I can get a price reduction through a coupon, rebate, or special deal).

One type of heuristic is the **affect referral decision rule**, in which consumers make a selection on the basis of an overall impression or summary evaluation of the various alternatives under consideration. This decision rule suggests that consumers have affective impressions of brands stored in memory that can be accessed at the time of purchase.

Marketers selling familiar and popular brands may appeal to an affect referral rule by stressing overall affective feelings or impressions about their products. Market leaders, whose products enjoy strong overall brand images, often use ads that promote the brand by appealing to affect. Allstate's "You're in Good Hands," Gillette's "The Best a Man Can Get," and Nationwide's "Nationwide is on your side" are all examples of this strategy (Exhibit 4–13).

## Purchase Decision

At some point in the buying process, the consumer must stop searching for and evaluating information about alternative brands in the evoked set and make a *purchase decision.* As an outcome of the alternative evaluation stage, the consumer may develop a **purchase intention** or predisposition to buy a certain brand. Purchase intentions are generally based on a matching of purchase motives with attributes or characteristics of brands under consideration. Their formation involves many of the personal subprocesses discussed in this chapter, including motivation, perception, attitude formation, and integration.

A purchase decision is not the same as an actual purchase. Once a consumer chooses which brand to buy, he or she must still implement the decision and make the actual purchase. Additional decisions may be needed, such as when to buy, where to buy, and how much money to spend. Often, there is a time delay between the formation of a purchase intention or decision and the actual purchase, particularly for highly involved and complex purchases such as automobiles, personal computers, and consumer durables.

For nondurable products, which include many low-involvement items such as consumer package goods, the time between the decision and the actual purchase may be short. Before leaving home, the consumer may make a shopping list that includes specific brand names because they have developed **brand loyalty**—a preference for a particular brand that results in its repeated purchase; of course, brand loyalty is not limited to nondurables. Consumers develop loyalties to many types of products and services. Marketers strive to develop and maintain brand loyalty among consumers. They use reminder advertising to keep their brand names in front of consumers, maintain prominent shelf positions and displays in stores, and run periodic promotions to deter consumers from switching brands.

Gaining and maintaining consumers' brand loyalty is not easy. Bank of America saw its loyalty go from number 1 to the bottom of the bank list in just one year. Competitors use many techniques to encourage consumers to try their brands, among them new product introductions and free samples. Figure 4–5 shows some of the brands that have achieved this goal. Marketers must continually battle to maintain their loyal consumers while replacing those who switch brands.

As seen, purchase decisions for nondurable, convenience items sometimes take place in the store, almost simultaneous with the purchase. Marketers must ensure that consumers have top-of-mind awareness of their brands so that they are quickly recognized and considered. Packaging, shelf displays, point-of-purchase materials, and promotional tools such as on-package coupons or premium offers can influence decisions made through constructive processes at the time of purchase.

## Postpurchase Evaluation

The consumer decision process does not end with the purchase. After using the product or service, the consumer compares the level of performance with expectations and is either satisfied or dissatisfied. *Satisfaction* occurs when the consumer's expectations are either met or exceeded; *dissatisfaction* results when performance is below expectations. The postpurchase evaluation process is important because the feedback acquired from actual use of a product will influence the likelihood of future purchases. Positive performance means the brand is likely to be retained in

**FIGURE 4–5**

Brands That Have the Most Brand Loyalty

| Category | Winner[a] |
|---|---|
| Airlines | US Airways |
| Athletic footwear | Skechers (tie) |
| Automobiles | Ford/Hyundai (tie) |
| Bank | JPMorgan Chase |
| Car rental | Avis |
| Coffee | Dunkin' Donuts |
| Computers (laptop) | Samsung/Apple (tie) |
| Credit cards | Discover |
| E-reader | Kindle |
| Evening news show | ABC |
| Flat-screen TV | Samsung |
| Hotels (luxury) | InterContinental |
| Insurance | New York Life |
| Online travel site | Expedia |
| Soft drinks (reg/diet) | Pepsi/Diet Pepsi Coke/Diet Coke |
| Toothpaste | Colgate |
| Vodka | Grey Goose |
| Wireless phone service | AT&T Wireless |

[a] Brands listed have highest loyalty ranking in Brand Keys 2013 Customer Loyalty Engagement Index.

Source: www.brandkeys.com/awards, 2013.

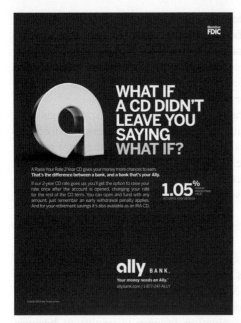

**EXHIBIT 4–14**

Ally Bank attempts to capitalize on consumers' dissatisfaction with banks

WHAT IF A CD DIDN'T LEAVE YOU SAYING WHAT IF?

A Raise Your Rate 2-Year CD gives your money more chances to earn. That's the difference between a bank, and a bank that's your Ally.

If our 2-year CD rate goes up, you'll get the option to raise your rate once after the account is opened, changing your rate for the rest of the CD term. You can open and fund with any amount, just remember an early withdrawal penalty applies. And for your retirement savings it's also available as an IRA CD.

1.05%

ally BANK.
Your money needs an Ally.™
allybank.com | 1-877-247-ALLY

Member FDIC

the evoked set and increases the likelihood it will be purchased again. Unfavorable outcomes may lead the consumer to form negative attitudes toward the brand, lessening the likelihood it will be purchased again or even eliminating it from the evoked set.

Another possible outcome of a purchase is **cognitive dissonance**, a feeling of psychological tension or postpurchase doubt that a consumer experiences after making a difficult purchase choice. Dissonance is more likely to occur in important decisions where the consumer must choose among close alternatives (especially if the unchosen alternative has unique or desirable features that the selected alternative does not have).

Consumers experiencing cognitive dissonance may use a number of strategies to attempt to reduce it. They may seek out reassurance and opinions from others to confirm the wisdom of their purchase decision, lower their attitudes or opinions of the unchosen alternative, deny or distort any information that does not support the choice they made, or look for information that does support their choice. An important source of supportive information is advertising as consumers tend to be more attentive to advertising for the brand they have chosen.[11] Thus, it may be important for companies to advertise to reinforce consumer decisions to purchase their brands.

Marketers have come to realize that postpurchase communication is also important. Some companies send follow-up letters and brochures to reassure buyers and reinforce the wisdom of their decision. Many companies have set up toll-free numbers or e-mail addresses for consumers to call if they need information or have a question or complaint regarding a product. Some marketers also offer liberalized return and refund policies and extended warranties and guarantees to ensure customer satisfaction. Some have used customers' postpurchase dissatisfaction as an opportunity for gaining new business, as is reflected in Exhibit 4–14.

## Variations in Consumer Decision Making

The preceding pages describe a general model of consumer decision making. But consumers do not always engage in all five steps of the purchase decision process or proceed in the sequence presented. They may minimize or even skip one or more stages if they have previous experience in purchasing the product or service or if the decision is of low personal, social, or economic significance. To develop effective promotional strategies and programs, marketers need some understanding of the problem-solving processes their target consumers use to make purchase decisions.

Many of the purchase decisions we make as consumers are based on a habitual or routine choice process. For many low-priced, frequently purchased products, the decision process consists of little more than recognizing the problem, engaging in a quick internal search, and making the purchase. The consumer spends little or no effort engaging in external search or alternative evaluation.

Marketers of products characterized by a routine response purchase process need to get and/or keep their brands in the consumer's evoked set and avoid anything that may result in their removal from consideration. Established brands that have strong market share position are likely to be in the evoked set of most consumers. Marketers of these brands want consumers to follow a routine choice process and continue to purchase their products. This means maintaining high levels of brand awareness through reminder advertising, periodic promotions, and prominent shelf positions in retail stores.

Marketers of new brands or those with a low market share face a different challenge. They must find ways to disrupt consumers' routine choice process and get them to consider different alternatives. High levels of advertising may be used to encourage trial or brand switching, along with sales promotion efforts in the form of free samples, special price offers, high-value coupons, and the like.

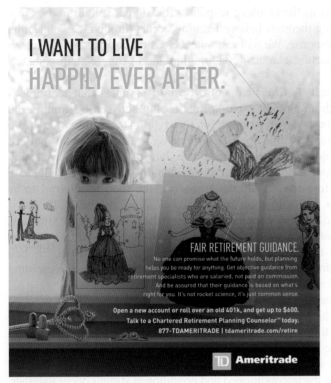

**EXHIBIT 4–15**
This ad for Ameritrade shows how marketers can appeal to consumers engaging in extended problem solving

LO 04-4

YTC 04–05
**Ameritrade**
youtube.com/10ebelch

A more complicated decision-making process may occur when consumers have limited experience in purchasing a particular product or service and little or no knowledge of the brands available and/or the criteria to use in making a purchase decision. They may have to learn what attributes or criteria should be used in making a purchase decision and how the various alternatives perform on these dimensions. For products or services characterized by problem solving, whether limited or extensive, marketers should make information available that will help consumers decide. Advertising that provides consumers with detailed information about a brand and how it can satisfy their purchase motives and goals is important. Distribution channels should have knowledgeable salespeople available to explain the features and benefits of the company's product or service and why it is superior to competing products.

The Ameritrade ad in Exhibit 4–15 is a good example of how advertising can appeal to consumers who may be engaging in extended problem solving when considering financial planning. Notice how the ad communicates with consumers who may be concerned about achieving their dreams. The ad helps the consumer by offering expert advice and planning a variety of options.

# THE CONSUMER LEARNING PROCESS

The discussion of the decision process shows that the way consumers make a purchase varies depending on a number of factors, including the nature of the product or service, the amount of experience they have with the product, and the importance of the purchase. One factor in the level of problem solving to be employed is the consumer's *involvement* with the product or brand. Chapter 5 examines the meaning of involvement, the difference between low- and high-involvement decision making, and the implications of involvement for developing advertising and promotional strategies.

Our examination of consumer behavior thus far has looked at the decision-making process from a *cognitive orientation*. The five-stage decision process model views the consumer as a problem solver and information processor who engages in a variety of mental processes to evaluate various alternatives and determine the degree to which they might satisfy needs or purchase motives. There are, however, other perspectives regarding how consumers acquire the knowledge and experience they use in making purchase decisions. To understand these perspectives, we examine various approaches to learning and their implications for advertising and promotion.

Consumer learning has been defined as "the process by which individuals acquire the purchase and consumption knowledge and experience they apply to future related behavior."[12] Two basic approaches to learning are the behavioral approach and cognitive learning theory.

## Behavioral Learning Theory

Behavioral learning theories emphasize the role of external, environmental stimuli in causing behavior; they minimize the significance of internal psychological processes. Behavioral learning theories are based on the *stimulus–response orientation* (S–R), the premise that learning occurs as the result of responses to external stimuli in the environment. Behavioral learning theorists believe learning occurs through the connection between a stimulus and a response. We will examine the basic principles of two behavioral learning theory approaches: classical conditioning and operant conditioning.

**Classical Conditioning**  **Classical conditioning** assumes that learning is an *associative process* with an already existing relationship between a stimulus and a response. Probably the best-known example of this type of learning comes from the studies done with animals by the Russian psychologist Pavlov. Pavlov noticed that at feeding times, his dogs would salivate at the sight of food. The connection between food and salivation is not taught; it is an innate reflex reaction. Because this relationship exists before the conditioning process, the food is referred to as an *unconditioned stimulus* and salivation is an *unconditioned response*. To see if salivation could be conditioned to occur in response to another neutral stimulus, Pavlov paired the ringing of a bell with the presentation of the food. After a number of trials, the dogs learned to salivate at the sound of the bell alone. Thus, the bell became a **conditioned stimulus** that elicited a **conditioned response** resembling the original unconditioned reaction.

Two factors are important for learning to occur through the associative process. The first is contiguity, which means the unconditioned stimulus and conditioned stimulus must be close in time and space. In Pavlov's experiment, the dog learns to associate the ringing of the bell with food because of the contiguous presentation of the two stimuli. The other important principle is *repetition,* or the frequency of the association. The more often the unconditioned and conditioned stimuli occur together, the stronger the association between them will be.

**Applying Classical Conditioning**  Learning through classical conditioning plays an important role in marketing. Buyers can be conditioned to form favorable impressions and images of various brands through the associative process. Advertisers strive to associate their products and services with perceptions, images, and emotions known to evoke positive reactions from consumers. Many products are promoted through image advertising, in which the brand is shown with an unconditioned stimulus that elicits pleasant feelings. When the brand is presented simultaneously with this unconditioned stimulus, the brand itself becomes a conditioned stimulus that elicits the same favorable response.

Figure 4–6 provides a diagram of this process, and the ad for Lollipop Bling in Exhibit 4–16 shows an application of this strategy. Notice how this ad associates the product with the look and sweetness of a lollipop. The brand's positioning plays off this association.

Classical conditioning can also associate a product or service with a favorable emotional state. A study by Gerald Gorn used this approach to examine how background music in ads influences product choice.[13] He found that subjects were more likely to choose a product when it was presented against a background of music they liked rather than music they disliked. These results suggest the emotions generated by a commercial are important because they may become associated with

**FIGURE 4–6**

The Classical Conditioning Process

**EXHIBIT 4–16**
Mariah Carey's new perfume associates its product with the looks and sweetness of lollipops

the advertised product through classical conditioning. Other studies have shown that music that was congruent with the message enhanced both ad recall and recognition[14] and that music can be used effectively as a mnemonic device to enhance the recall of advertising slogans. Advertisers often attempt to pair a neutral product or service stimulus with an event or situation that arouses positive feelings, such as humor, an exciting sports event, or popular music.

**Operant Conditioning**   Classical conditioning views the individual as a passive participant in the learning process who simply receives stimuli. Conditioning occurs as a result of exposure to a stimulus that occurs before the response. In the **operant conditioning** approach, the individual must actively *operate* or act on some aspect of the environment for learning to occur. Operant conditioning is sometimes referred to as *instrumental conditioning* because the individual's response is instrumental in getting a positive reinforcement (reward) or negative reinforcement (a form of reward that occurs when a negative outcome is removed when the desired behavior is performed).

**Reinforcement,** the reward or favorable consequence associated with a particular response, is an important element of instrumental conditioning. Behavior that is reinforced strengthens the bond between a stimulus and a response. Thus, if a consumer buys a product in response to an ad and experiences a positive outcome, the likelihood that the consumer will use this product again increases. If the outcome is not favorable, the likelihood of buying the product again decreases.

The principles of operant conditioning can be applied to marketing, as shown in Figure 4–7. Companies attempt to provide their customers with products and services that satisfy their needs and reward them to reinforce the probability of repeat purchase. Reinforcement can also be implied in advertising; many ads emphasize the benefits or rewards a consumer will receive from using a product or service. Reinforcement also occurs when an ad encourages consumers to use a particular product or brand to avoid unpleasant consequences. For example, the ad for Kyocera printers in Exhibit 4–17 shows how using this product will help avoid negative consequences—that is, the high cost of printing.

Two concepts that are particularly relevant to marketers in their use of reinforcement through promotional strategies are schedules of reinforcement and shaping.

**FIGURE 4–7**

Instrumental Conditioning in Marketing

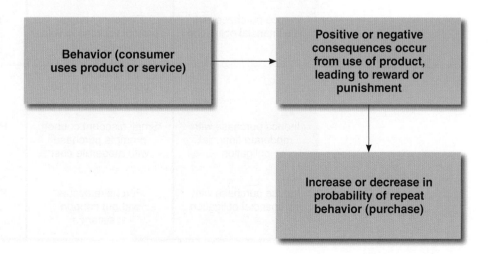

Behavior (consumer uses product or service)

Positive or negative consequences occur from use of product, leading to reward or punishment

Increase or decrease in probability of repeat behavior (purchase)

**Chapter 4** PERSPECTIVES ON CONSUMER BEHAVIOR   129

**Afraid to look at what your printers really cost? Make the wise choice.**

ECO-nomical. ECO-logical.
**ECOSYS Printers from Kyocera.**

How much did your company spend on printing last month? How about last year? If your company is like most companies, it's probably too much. Switching to ECOSYS Printers from Kyocera could save your company hundreds, even thousands of dollars per year. That's because Kyocera's durable long-life consumables mean less waste, reducing costs—and lowering impact on the environment. Brilliant color, crisp black and white, low Total Cost of Ownership, and environmentally friendly. Now that's a wise choice.

Visit our *TCO Tracker* at www.kyoceramita.com.
Calculate your cost today. Save tomorrow.

**KYOCERA**

**EXHIBIT 4–17**

Kyocera shows how to avoid negative consequences

Different **schedules of reinforcement** result in varying patterns of learning and behavior. Learning occurs most rapidly under a *continuous reinforcement schedule,* in which every response is rewarded—but the behavior is likely to cease when the reinforcement stops. Marketers must provide continuous reinforcement to consumers or risk their switching to brands that do.

Learning occurs more slowly but lasts longer when a *partial* or *intermittent reinforcement schedule* is used and only some of the individual's responses are rewarded. Promotional programs have partial reinforcement schedules. A firm may offer consumers an incentive to use the company's product. The firm does not want to offer the incentive every time (continuous reinforcement), because consumers might become dependent on it and stop buying the brand when the incentive is withdrawn. A study that examined the effect of reinforcement on bus ridership found that discount coupons given as rewards for riding the bus were as effective when given on a partial schedule as when given on a continuous schedule.[15] The cost of giving the discount coupons under the partial schedule, however, was considerably less.

Reinforcement schedules can also be used to influence consumer learning and behavior through a process known as **shaping**, the reinforcement of successive acts that lead to a desired behavior pattern or response.

In a promotional context, shaping procedures are used as part of the introductory program for new products. Figure 4–8 provides an example of how samples and discount coupons can be used to introduce a new product and take a consumer from trial to repeat purchase. Marketers must be careful in their use of shaping procedures: If they drop the incentives too soon, the consumer

**FIGURE 4–8**

Application of Shaping Procedures in Marketing

**Terminal Goal: Repeat Purchase Behavior**

| Approximation Sequence | Shaping Procedure | Reinforcement Applied |
|---|---|---|
| Induce product trial | Free samples distributed; large discount coupon | Product performance; coupon |
| Induce purchase with little financial obligation | Discount coupon prompts purchase with little cost; coupon good for small discount on next purchase enclosed | Product performance; coupon |
| Induce purchase with moderate financial obligation | Small discount coupon prompts purchase with moderate cost | Product performance |
| Induce purchase with full financial obligation | Purchase occurs without coupon assistance | Product performance |

**FIGURE 4–9**

The Cognitive Learning Process

may not establish the desired behavior; but if they overuse them, the consumer's purchase may become contingent on the incentive rather than the product or service.

### Cognitive Learning Theory

Behavioral learning theories have been criticized for assuming a mechanistic view of the consumer that puts too much emphasis on external stimulus factors. They ignore internal psychological processes such as motivation, thinking, and perception; they assume that the external stimulus environment will elicit fairly predictable responses. Many consumer researchers and marketers disagree with the simplified explanations of behavioral learning theories and are more interested in the complex mental processes that underlie consumer decision making. The cognitive approach to studying learning and decision making has dominated the field of consumer behavior in recent years. Figure 4–9 shows how cognitive theorists view the learning process.

Since consumer behavior typically involves choices and decision making, the cognitive perspective has particular appeal to marketers, especially those whose product/ service calls for important and involved purchase decisions. Cognitive processes such as perception, formation of beliefs about brands, attitude development and change, and integration are important to understanding the decision-making process for many types of purchases. The subprocesses examined during our discussion of the five-stage decision process model are all relevant to a cognitive learning approach to consumer behavior.

# ENVIRONMENTAL INFLUENCES ON CONSUMER BEHAVIOR

The consumer does not make purchase decisions in isolation. A number of external factors have been identified that may influence consumer decision making. They are shown in Figure 4–10 and examined in more detail in the next sections.

**FIGURE 4–10**

External Influences on Consumer Behavior

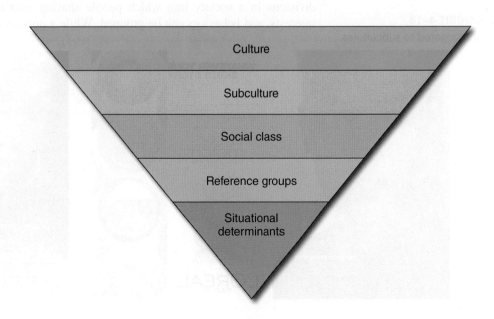

## Culture

The broadest and most abstract of the external factors that influence consumer behavior is **culture,** or the complexity of learned meanings, values, norms, and customs shared by members of a society. Cultural norms and values offer direction and guidance to members of a society in all aspects of their lives, including their consumption behavior. It is becoming increasingly important to study the impact of culture on consumer behavior as marketers expand their international marketing efforts. Each country has certain cultural traditions, customs, and values that marketers must understand as they develop marketing programs.

Marketers must also be aware of changes that may be occurring in a particular culture and the implications of these changes for their advertising and promotional strategies and programs. American culture continually goes through many changes that have direct implications for advertising. Marketing researchers monitor these changes and their impact on the ways companies market their products and services.

While marketers recognize that culture exerts a demonstrable influence on consumers, they often find it difficult to respond to cultural differences in different markets. The subtleties of various cultures are often difficult to understand and appreciate, but marketers must understand the cultural context in which consumer purchase decisions are made and adapt their advertising and promotional programs accordingly.

## Subcultures

Within a given culture are generally found smaller groups or segments whose beliefs, values, norms, and patterns of behavior set them apart from the larger cultural mainstream. These **subcultures** may be based on age, geographic, religious, racial, and/or ethnic differences. A number of subcultures exist within the United States. The three largest racial/ethnic subcultures are African Americans, Hispanics, and various Asian groups. These racial/ethnic subcultures are important to marketers because of their size, growth, purchasing power, and distinct purchasing patterns. Marketers develop specific marketing programs for various products and services for these target markets. The ads in Exhibit 4–18 are just two of the many specifically designed to appeal to U.S. subcultures—in these cases, Ethiopians and Hispanics. Many others can easily be found that target teens, generations X and Y, older adults, and so on. Figure 4–11 demonstrates how one's generation may influence purchases.

**Social Class**   Virtually all societies exhibit some form of stratification whereby individuals can be assigned to a specific social category on the basis of criteria important to members of that society. **Social class** refers to relatively homogeneous divisions in a society into which people sharing similar lifestyles, values, norms, interests, and behaviors can be grouped. While a number of methods for determining

**EXHIBIT 4–18**
Ads targeted to subcultures

FIGURE 4–11

Generational Differences
in Shopping Behaviors

A generation is a group of contemporaries, all born during the same period, having shared interests and attitudes. Of interest to marketers, of course, are their shopping behaviors, some of which are shown below. While there are some variations in how different generations are defined, in general the following age groups are pretty much agreed upon:

*Greatest Generation: Born prior to 1946*

With much of their behavior influenced by the Great Depression and World War II, they are frequent shoppers though they often claim they dislike shopping; heavily deal prone; use print cookbooks; spend more than other groups on ice cream, vitamins, also a lot on wine. Like to shop at smaller stores.

*Baby Boomers: Born 1946–1964*

Have the highest annual spending of all groups; spend more than all other groups on wine, pet food, and carbonated beverages; deal prone; comfortable with e-mail and online shopping. Like to shop at local groceries and drugstores.

*Gen X: Born 1965–1976*

Feel pressure for time; like indulgences such as lattes and coffee; spend more than other groups on hair care, cereal, and baby food; like to shop at merchandisers; love to shop at Target.

*Gen Y (Millennials): Born 1977–1994*

More likely to make impulse purchases; prefer mass merchandisers and supercenters; use online coupons and shop online; will tweet and text others about products, brands, and deals; love shopping at Target.

*Gen Z: Born after 1994*

We know least about this group's shopping behaviors to date—may be the hardest to reach; the most connected generation; love electronics; have videogames and TVs in their rooms; use their cell phones as cameras, videorecorders, and MP3 players; most technologically advanced; concerned about the environment; multitasking marvels. They tend to stay indoors more than other generations; and 80 percent of those ages 12–17 use social networks—most daily. Communications travel quickly.

*Tweens: Born 1996–2004*

While all do not agree on the exact age range, tweens are those who are somewhere between being a child and a teenager (approximately 10 years old). They reject child-like images and aspire to act more like teens. While they often know what they want, their buying power is still controlled by adults, often through gifts, allowances, etc. Much money is spent purchasing for them through gifts, etc. Segment is inundated with media attention, including direct mail, television shows, and the Internet. Companies like Girls Intelligence Agency and the "Best Friends Network" are examples of companies that provide tween girls with products to discuss (and promote) to their peers.

social class exist, class structures in the United States are usually based on occupational status, educational attainment, and income. Sociologists generally agree there are three broad levels of social classes in the United States: the upper (14 percent), middle (70 percent), and lower (16 percent) classes.

Social class is an important concept to marketers, since consumers within each social stratum often have similar values, lifestyles, and buying behavior. Thus, the various social class groups provide a natural basis for market segmentation. Consumers in the different social classes differ in the degree to which they use various products and services and in their leisure activities, shopping patterns, and media habits. Marketers respond to these differences through the positioning of their products and services, the media strategies they use to reach different social classes, and the types of advertising appeals they develop. The ad in Exhibit 4–19 shows how a product attempts to appeal to the upper classes in both copy and illustration.

## Reference Groups

Think about the last time you attended a party. As you dressed for the party, you probably asked yourself (or someone else) what others would be wearing. Your selection of attire may have been influenced by those likely to be present. This simple example reflects one form of impact that groups may exert on your behavior.

A group has been defined as "two or more individuals who share a set of norms, values, or beliefs and have certain implicitly or explicitly defined relationships to one another such that their behavior is interdependent."[16] Groups are one of the primary factors influencing learning and socialization, and group situations constitute many of our purchase decisions.

A **reference group** is "a group whose presumed perspectives or values are being used by an individual as the basis for his or her judgments, opinions, and actions." Consumers use three types of reference groups (associative, aspirational, and disassociative) as a guide to specific behaviors, even when the groups are not present. In the party example, your peers—although not present—provided a standard of dress that you referred to in your clothing selection. Likewise, your college classmates, family, and co-workers, or even a group to which you aspire, may serve as referents, and your consumption patterns will typically conform to the expectations of the groups that are most important to you.

Marketers use reference group influences in developing advertisements and promotional strategies. The ads in Exhibit 4–20 are examples of *aspirational* reference groups (to which we might like to belong) and *disassociative* groups (to which we do not wish to belong), respectively.

**Family Decision Making: An Example of Group Influences** In some instances, the group may be involved more directly than just as a referent. Family members may serve as referents to each other, or they may actually be

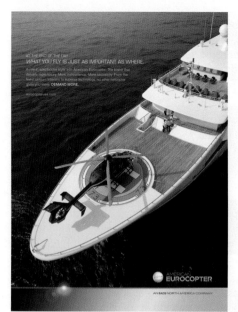

**EXHIBIT 4–19**
This American Eurocopter ad attempts to appeal to the upper classes

**YTC 04–06**
**Marketing Luxury**
youtube.com/10ebelch

**EXHIBIT 4–20**
The ad on the left shows an aspirational reference group; the one on the right stresses a disassociative reference group

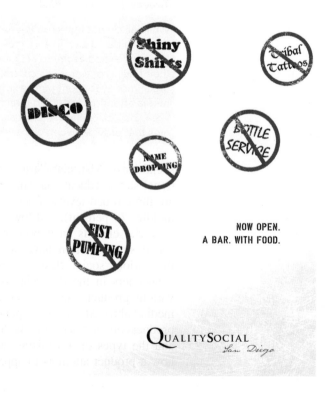

FIGURE 4–12

Roles in the Family
Decision–Making Process

| |
|---|
| **The initiator.** The person responsible for initiating the purchase decision process—for example, the mother who determines she needs a new car. |
| **The information provider.** The individual responsible for gathering information to be used in making the decision—for example, the teenage car buff who knows where to find product information in specific magazines or collects it from dealers. |
| **The influencer.** The person who exerts influence as to what criteria will be used in the selection process. All members of the family may be involved. The mother may have her criteria, whereas others may each have their own input. |
| **The decision maker(s).** That person (or persons) who actually makes the decision. In our example, it may be the mother alone or in combination with another family member. |
| **The purchasing agent.** The individual who performs the physical act of making the purchase. In the case of a car, a husband and wife may decide to choose it together and sign the purchase agreement. |
| **The consumer.** The actual user of the product. In the case of a family car, all family members are consumers. For a private car, only the mother might be the consumer. |

**YTC 04–07**

**The U.S. Army**

youtube.com/10ebelch

involved in the purchase decision process—acting as an individual buying unit. As shown in Figure 4–12, family members may assume a variety of roles in the decision-making process. Each role has implications for marketers.

First, the advertiser must determine who is responsible for the various roles in the decision-making process so messages can be targeted at that person (or those people). These roles will also dictate media strategies, since the appropriate magazines, newspapers, or TV or radio stations must be used. Second, understanding the decision-making process and the use of information by individual family members is critical to the design of messages and choice of promotional program elements. In sum, to create an effective promotional program, a marketer must have an overall understanding of how the decision process works and the role that each family member plays.

## Situational Determinants

The final external factor is the purchase and usage situation. The specific situation in which consumers plan to use the product or brand directly affects their perceptions, preferences, and purchasing behaviors. Three types of **situational determinants** may have an effect: the specific usage situation, the purchase situation, and the communications situation.

*Usage* refers to the circumstance in which the product will be used. For example, purchases made for private consumption may be thought of differently from those that will be obvious to the public. The *purchase* situation more directly involves the environment operating at the time of the purchase. Time constraints, store environments, and other factors may all have an impact. The *communications* situation is the condition in which an advertising exposure occurs (in a car listening to the radio, with friends, etc.). This may be most relevant to the development of promotional strategies, because the impact on the consumer will vary according to the particular situation. For example, a consumer may pay more attention to a commercial that is heard alone at home than to one heard in the presence of friends, at work, or anywhere distractions may be present. If advertisers can isolate a particular time when the listener is likely to be attentive, they will probably earn his or her undivided attention.

In sum, situational determinants may either enhance or detract from the potential success of a message. To the degree that advertisers can assess situational influences that may be operating, they will increase the likelihood of successfully communicating with their target audiences.

# Ethical Perspective 4–1 > > >

## When Does Consumer Research Become an Invasion of Privacy?

Research designed to learn more about consumers has been used to guide marketers for decades—if not forever. A variety of methods have been employed to gather data, including observational techniques, focus groups, in-depth interviews, surveys, and even physiological studies. Most of us understand the reason for such information gathering, and may even welcome it so long as it helps marketers provide us with better goods and services and provides more marketing efficiencies. No one has seemed to mind, so long as we could opt out if we so choose. We could refuse the offer to participate in a focus group, not complete a survey, or not volunteer to participate in a lab experiment.

But over the past few years there has been a rising tide of current against some marketers' efforts to learn more about us as consumers. Most of this discontent has been directed at practices used on the Internet and through social media. Consider some of the following: (1) Facebook's changes in privacy settings since 2005 have now made your information regarding photos, wall posts, pictures, likes, and other data potentially available not only to your friends but to all Facebook users and the entire Internet; (2) Google's Street View has brought on an array of privacy concerns, including security and privacy invasion issues; (3) Google has expanded the limits as to what it can do with information obtained from your visits to Gmail, Google+, YouTube, search, and more. And these are just a sampling of the information collected not only by these companies but many others as well.

And while these practices may be offensive to some, there is yet another online research tool that may have even more consumers upset. *Behavioral targeting* uses information collected on an individual's web-browsing behavior such as searches made, pages visited, products purchased, and so on to more specifically target ads, suggest products to buy, books to read, friends to contact, and more. For example, Amazon will suggest items you might like based on your previous purchases. Linkedin, Twitter, and Facebook may suggest people whom you know, and advertisers can direct ads to you if you have searched for a product in the category in which they compete.

Proponents of behavioral targeting offer a number of advantages to this form of data gathering. They say that it allows them to (1) know their customers better, offering them products and services that they want; (2) anticipate customers' future needs as well as those of potential new customers; (3) be more efficient and effective in their marketing by reducing wasted time and effort on noninterested customers while better meeting the needs of potential ones; and (4) offering a new way to do research on why customers buy. Overall, proponents say, behavioral targeting is a win–win for both customers and advertisers.

Opponents, on the other hand, say "not so fast!" Their primary concern is with the privacy issues involved. Of most concern is the use of the information being extracted for data mining purposes—very often without the knowledge or permission of the customer. Others feel that marketers should not be able to gather information unless granted permission, as those data have value and using them should require compensation. For many others, they just don't want anyone having that much insight into what they do, read, or buy or where they go when on the Internet. Some experts argue that the marketers' claims of cost efficiencies are exaggerated or untrue, and that while targeting may work for some products it is much less effective for others. They seem to imply that those collecting this information may have other motives in mind.

Oh, by the way, it's not just your computer that is tracking you. When you use your iPhone and or iPad, data are being logged into a file at Apple, Inc. This information includes any searches you do, photos you take, or sites you visit. Even when you aren't using it, information is being transmitted from your iPhone as to where you are, with a record kept at Apple, Inc. Television is quickly developing technologies to collect data on what you watch, when, how long, and so forth.

Many of those collecting the data ask what the big deal is. They say we have been collecting consumer data and studying consumer behaviors for years. So why are consumers so concerned now? Maybe it's because in the past consumers knew you were collecting their information, maybe even paid them for it. Or maybe they just want to be able to opt in or out when it comes to their personal behaviors. Or maybe they feel that it is just too Orwellian!

Sources: "Do You Know Who's Watching You?" www.wordstreaminc.com, February 15, 2013; "Behavioral Targeting Pros and cons," www.behavior-altargeting.biz, May 17, 2012; Jaci Russo, "Behavoral Targeting—Privacy Invasion or Brand Building?" www.therussogroup.com, May 4, 2011; David Sarno, "Watching a Screen? It Watches You Too," *LA Times*, October 2, 2011, pp. A18–A19.

# ALTERNATIVE APPROACHES TO CONSUMER BEHAVIOR

In addition to the perspectives discussed, consumer researchers complement these psychological approaches with perspectives driven from other scientific disciplines, such as economics, sociology, anthropology, philosophy, semiotics, neuroscience, and history. These cross-disciplinary perspectives have broadened the realm of methodologies used to study consumers and have provided additional insights into consumer decision processes. In addition new technologies have provided new means for exploring consumers' behaviors. As shown in Ethical Perspective 4–1, sometimes these methods make consumers worry that they may be going too far.

## New Methodologies

Whereas psychologists often study consumer responses to advertising and other forms of communication in controlled settings, where environmental variables can be kept constant, sociologists and anthropologists study behavior in context. For this reason, they often employ qualitative methodologies such as individual interviews, participant observation studies, and/or ethnographies. These methods help capture the social, cultural, and environmental influences that may affect consumer behavior.

The humanities have also been a source of new methodologies for consumer research. Historians and semioticians focus their analyses on the advertising messages and other forms of communications themselves. These researchers examine the significance of communications from a linguistic or historical perspective. Research methods such as semiotic and structural analyses examine the symbolic meanings of advertising and different facets of consumption.

## New Insights

These alternative perspectives and methodologies provide additional insights and expand our knowledge of consumers. For example, the cultural significance of advertising messages in shaping cultures and triggering communities is now better understood. Likewise, marketers now have a better understanding of how advertising campaigns become popular and help shape our culture. Thanks to the many interpretive analyses of advertisements over recent years, we are also more aware of the influence of advertising images on society.

Some consumer researchers believe that cross-disciplinary research is better suited for the study of consumers because it takes into account their complexity and multidimensionality. When considered along with psychological research, these alternative approaches help us better understand the impact of communications.

## Summary

This chapter introduced you to the field of consumer behavior and examined its relevance to promotional strategy. Consumer behavior is best viewed as the process and activities that people engage in when searching for, selecting, purchasing, using, evaluating, and disposing of products and services to satisfy their needs and desires. A five-stage model of the consumer decision-making process consists of problem recognition, information search, alternative evaluation, purchase, and postpurchase evaluation. Internal psychological processes that influence the consumer decision-making process include motivation, perception, attitude formation and change, and integration processes.

The decision process model views consumer behavior primarily from a cognitive orientation. The chapter considered other perspectives by examining various approaches to consumer learning

and their implications for advertising and promotion. Behavioral learning theories such as classical conditioning and operant (instrumental) conditioning were discussed. Problems with behavioral learning theories were noted, and the alternative perspective of cognitive learning was discussed. New techniques, such as the use of neuroscience to determine what you buy and why you buy it.

The chapter also examined relevant external factors that influence consumer decision making. Culture, subculture, social class, reference groups, and situational determinants were discussed, along with their implications for the development of promotional strategies and programs. The chapter concluded with an introduction to alternative perspectives on the study of consumer behavior (also called interpretive, postmodern, or postpositivist perspectives).

## Key Terms

**consumer behavior** p. 110
**problem recognition** p. 111
**want** p. 112

**motives** p. 113
**hierarchy of needs** p. 113
**psychoanalytic theory** p. 114

**motivation research** p. 114
**internal search** p. 117
**external search** p. 117

## Discussion Questions

**1.** Hispanics are one of the fastest-growing market segments in the United States. Yet it would be a mistake for marketers to generalize that all Hispanics are the same. Discuss how there may be multiple subsets of Hispanics and the marketing implications of this fact. (LO5)

**2.** The chapter discusses a variety of research methodologies to examine consumers' behaviors. Discuss some of these, focusing on the advantages and disadvantages of each. (LO1)

**3.** What are some of the problems inherent with the use of psychoanalytic theory to understand consumer behaviors? Are there any positive benefits to taking this approach to studying consumer behavior? (LO3)

**4.** Behavioral targeting has been attacked by many as an invasion of privacy. Describe what behavioral targeting is and the pros and cons of this ethical argument. (LO4)

**5.** Marketers recognize that subcultures have an influence on consumer behaviors. Give examples of how various subcultures may impact one's buying decision. (LO5)

**6.** Consumers experience different forms of problem recognition. Explain each type of problem recognition and give an example of a purchase of this type. (LO2)

**7.** The chapter discusses the role of neuroscience in understanding consumer behavior. Discuss what is meant by neuroscience and provide examples of how this field of study may be useful to consumer behavior. (LO3)

**8.** How might one's social class influence his or her consumer behaviors? Give examples of products and/or services that might be influenced by social class standing. (LO5)

**9.** There has been controversy over the existence and impact of subliminal advertising for quite some time. Explain why. Why do you think this topic continues to hold so much interest? (LO3)

**10.** Explain the process of selective perception and the various ways in which consumers may filter information. What is the relevance of this for consumer behavior? (LO3)

We're looking for the most vibrant voices and talented storytellers to be agents in the Fiesta Movement. Do you have what it takes to become one of them?

## LEARNING OBJECTIVES

**LO1** To understand the basic elements of the communication process and the role of communications in IMC.

**LO2** To examine various models of the communication process.

**LO3** To understand the important role of word-of-mouth influence and viral marketing.

**LO4** To analyze the response processes of receivers of marketing communications, including alternative response hierarchies and their implications for promotional planning and strategy.

**LO5** To understand how the consumer decision process is influenced by social media.

**LO6** To examine the nature of consumers' cognitive processing of marketing communications.

# 5 The Communication Process

## FORD RETURNS TO SOCIAL MEDIA TO MARKET THE FIESTA

The past few years have been very difficult for the automobile industry, as auto sales around the world have been impacted by the global recession and are still struggling to recover in some markets. However, unlike some of its competitors, the Ford Motor Company managed to make it through the recession without any government help and has positioned itself well for growth. A major part of Ford's strategy has been to focus on smaller, greener, more fuel-efficient "global" cars that are built on a single platform, which reduces costs and, with some minor modifications, can be sold in markets around world. One of the cars Ford has relied on to fuel its growth is the Fiesta, a global subcompact that has was introduced in Europe in 1976 and has sold more than 13 million units since then.

The most recent generation of the Fiesta was launched in Europe in 2008 followed by China in 2009 before coming to the United States in mid-2010. However, the company recognized that it would face some challenges in marketing the Fiesta here, because unlike drivers in Europe and Asia, most American don't like small cars. Moreover, among those who buy small cars, Ford is generally not among the brands they consider as the company had not offered a vehicle in this segment for nearly 30 years. Another challenge Ford faced in launching the Fiesta was that its primary target market—millennials between the ages of 21 and 34—do not drive as much as previous generations of young people and are buying fewer new cars.

Traditionally automotive marketers launched a new car such as the Fiesta with a heavy rotation of television commercials, four-color ads in magazines, billboards, and flashy websites. However, rather than use a traditional marketing campaign, Ford took a much different and riskier approach that utilized an aggressive social media program. To gear up for its small-car revolution, Ford launched the "Fiesta Movement," which involved enlisting a team of 100 special agents to drive the new vehicles and participate in monthly challenges that would allow them to share interesting content with their friends through various forms of social media.

The idea behind the Fiesta Movement was born in the summer of 2008 when Ford's Vice President of Global Marketing, Jim Farley, asked the Fiesta brand manager what the company could do if 1,000 Fiestas were shipped from Europe to the United States. Ford's marketing team recognized that the market it was targeting for the Fiesta was changing as the baby boomers and gen Xers were being supplanted by the 20-something millennials who are more comfortable with social media such as blogs, Facebook, Twitter, and YouTube rather than traditional media advertising. Ford calls these new buyers "lifestreamers" because they like to constantly update their status on Facebook and text or tweet about things going on in their life such as a song they like, things they are doing, or something that just happened, such as a cool car that just drove by. Given this target audience, Ford worked with its advertising agency, Team Detroit, to brainstorm how to best put the Fiestas in the hands of consumers. The agency and Ford marketing group worked together to develop the idea of the Fiesta Movement and embarked on what could have been just a 100-person test drive.

The 100 Fiesta agents were chosen from more than 4,000 consumers who applied by creating a YouTube video answering one simple question: Why do you want to drive a Ford Fiesta for six months? Participants were selected based on their entrepreneurial spirit, number of social network followers or friends, social vibrancy, and creative vision and were spread among major markets across the United States. The social media trendsetters were given a new Fiesta, insurance, and gas cards, and in the spring of 2009 began driving the cars. Ford had just one requirement of the Fiesta agents—they had to complete one "mission" or task each month, such as "drive until you run out of gas," and document their experiences behind the wheel by posting videos and updating their friends and followers on Facebook, YouTube, Twitter, and other social media. The first chapter of the Fiesta Movement was about building awareness of the car and was very successful as by the end of 2009, the program generated more than 6.2 million YouTube views, more than 750,000 Flickr views, and nearly 4 million Twitter impressions.

In March 2010 chapter two of the Fiesta Movement began, with the goal being to show more features of the new car. For the second phase of the campaign 40 people were selected from more than 1,000 applicants, and 20 teams composed of 2 agents each were formed to spread the word about the Fiesta in 16 markets across the country where small cars sell well. The agent teams were given a series of missions asking them to complete challenges that were tied to people and activities in their local community, allowing them to open the discussion about the Fiesta through social media and at the events they hosted. After completing a mission, the agents produced and placed the creative content online at a special Fiesta Movement website where followers could also keep up with their favorite agents.

The Fiesta Movement went far beyond what any automotive marketer had done in the past to launch a new product and was very risky given that Ford put no restrictions on what its agents could say about the car. And while Ford was very confident about the quality of the Fiesta, Scott Monty, Ford's director of social media, noted that "faith in a product or no, trusting it enough to unleash 100 to regular consumers and ask them to offer honest thoughts and reviews is a leap for most marketers." Ford's big leap paid off; by the time the Fiesta hit the dealer showrooms in the summer of 2010, more than 6,000 consumers had made reservations for the Fiesta and more than 100,000 "handraisers" were showing interest in the new car and requesting more information about it. The Fiesta Movement created an awareness level of nearly 60 percent before Ford even began advertising for the new car. Vice President Jim Farley estimated that it would have taken $60 million in traditional media advertising to achieve what was done for less than $10 million. More importantly, the Fiesta Movement helped jump-start sales of the new vehicle as Ford sold more than 23,000 cars in the first six months. Fiesta sales skyrocketed to nearly 70,000 units in 2011, making it the most popular subcompact car in America, outselling other brands in the segment such as the Honda Fit, Nissan Versa, and Toyota Yaris.

Fiesta sales declined in 2012, however, in large part due to the fact that it was at the end of its three-year design cycle and many small car buyers were gravitating toward another popular Ford model, the completely overhauled Focus. In 2013 the Fiesta received its own updating, and Ford once again returned to social media to generate buzz about the redesigned 2014 model. In the spring of 2013 Ford launched the "Fiesta Movement: A Social Remix" campaign by once again giving 100 new Fiestas to social media savvy consumers to use for up to eight months. A small percentage of the cars were also reserved for celebrities, current Fiesta owners, and alumni of the original Fiesta Movement campaign. As with the original Fiesta Movement, the agents were again asked to complete monthly missions, each of which had a specific theme and included promotional events tied to the popular television show *American Idol,* as well as the Bonaroo Music and Arts Festival and the X-Games. As part of Ford's partnership, Fiesta agents were given inside access to the events, including a behind-the-scenes look at *American Idol.*

One of the major changes for the new campaign was the use of user-generated content for all of the TV, print, and digital advertising used for the Fiesta launch. Ford distributed the content through paid media, social media, and experiential events that were held as part of the Fiesta Movement. The reason for having the content crowdsourced was to extend the Fiesta Movement beyond social media platforms and feature material created exclusively by social influencers. Ford's advertising manager noted that: "Millenials like being part of the brands they feel represent them and are accustomed to creating content about their lives, so it just makes sense to give their creativity a bigger platform with greater scale. It's all part of the democratization of media." And hopefully part of a successful social media campaign for the Fiesta.

Sources: Melanie White, "Social Media Week: Ford Embraces Relationships with Relaunch of Fiesta Movement Campaign," February 22, 2013, *ClickZ,* www.clickz.com/clickz/news/2250163/; "Power to the People! Fiesta Movement: A Social Remix Gives Control of New Ford Fiesta Ad Campaign to the People." *PR Newswire,* February 19, 2013; "New Set of Agents Team Up to Bring Ford Fiesta Local with Fiesta Movement Chapter 2," *PR Newswire,* March 1, 2010; Mark Rechtin, "Fiesta Viral Marketing: Chapter 2," *Automotive News,* 84 (6390), December 14, 2009, p. 6; Michael Learmonth, "Ford's Fiesta to Party on—without the Fiesta," *Advertising Age,* September 14, 2009, http:adage.com/print?article_id5138979; Eric Tegler, "Ford is Counting on Army of 100 Bloggers to Launch New Fiesta," *Advertising Age,* April 20 2009, p. 17.

YTC **05-01**

**Fiesta Movement**

youtube.com/10ebelch

The function of all elements of the integrated marketing communications program is to communicate. An organization's IMC strategy is implemented through the various communications it sends to current or prospective customers as well as other relevant publics. Organizations send communications and messages in a variety of ways, such as through advertisements, brand names, logos and graphic systems, websites, press releases, package designs, promotions, and visual images. As was discussed in the chapter opener, companies such as Ford are developing more innovative ways to communicate with consumers and deliver their marketing messages as it is becoming increasingly difficult to do so through traditional media.

The way marketers communicate with their target audiences depends on many factors, including how much current and/or potential customers know and what they think about a company or brand and the image it hopes to create. Those involved in the planning and implementation of an IMC program need to understand the communication process and what it means in terms of how they create, deliver, manage, and evaluate messages about a company or brand. Developing an effective marketing communications program is far more complicated than just choosing a product feature or attribute to emphasize. Marketers must understand how consumers will perceive and interpret their messages and how these reactions will shape consumers' responses to the company and/or its product or service. And as the use of social media becomes more prevalent, it is important that marketers understand how consumers communicate with one another and how they can participate in and even influence these conversations.

This chapter reviews the fundamentals of communication and examines various perspectives and models regarding how consumers respond to advertising and promotional messages. Our goal is to demonstrate how valuable an understanding of the communication process can be in planning, implementing, and evaluating the marketing communications program.

# THE NATURE OF COMMUNICATION

**Communication** has been variously defined as the passing of information, the exchange of ideas, or the process of establishing a commonness or oneness of thought between a sender and a receiver.[1] These definitions suggest that for communication to occur, there must be some common thinking between two parties and information must be passed from one person to another (or from one group to another). As you will see in this chapter, establishing this commonality in thinking is not always as easy as it might seem; many attempts to communicate are unsuccessful.

The communication process is often very complex. Success depends on such factors as the nature of the message, the audience's interpretation of it, and the environment in which it is received. The receiver's perception of the source and the medium used to transmit the message may also affect the ability to communicate, as do many other factors. Words, pictures, sounds, and colors may have different meanings to different audiences, and people's perceptions and interpretations of them vary. For example, if you ask for a soda on the East Coast or West Coast, you'll receive a soft drink such as Coke or Pepsi. However, in parts of the Midwest and South, a soft drink is referred to as pop. If you ask for a soda, you may get a glass of pop with ice cream in it. Marketers must understand the meanings that words and symbols take on and how they influence consumers' interpretation of products and messages.

Language is one of the major barriers to effective communication, as there are different languages in different countries, different languages or dialects within a single country, and more subtle problems of linguistic nuance and vernacular. This can be particularly challenging to companies marketing their products in foreign countries, as discussed in Global Perspective 5–1. The growth of bilingual, multicultural ethnic markets in the United States is also creating challenges for domestic

# Global Perspective 5–1 > > >

## Communication Problems in International Marketing

Communication is a major problem facing companies that market their products and services in foreign countries. Language is one of the main barriers to effective communication, as there can be different languages or dialects within a single country, and more subtle problems of linguistic nuance and vernacular. For example, China has many languages and dialects, with differences great enough that people from different regions of the country often cannot understand each other. As another example, about 40 percent of the Canadian population does not use English as its preferred language. Of the non-English speakers, about 60 percent speak French, with the balance spread among a dozen or so other languages.

Mistranslations and faulty word choices have often created problems for companies in foreign markets, as well as for companies that are marketing their products and services to increasingly diverse and multicultural audiences in their domestic markets. International marketers must also be aware of the connotation of the words, signs, symbols, and expressions they use as brand names or logos or in various forms of promotion. Also, advertising copy, slogans, and symbols do not always transfer well into other languages. This not only impedes communication but also sometimes results in embarrassing blunders that can damage a company's or a brand's credibility or image and thereby cost it customers.

There are several widely cited examples of translation problems. For example, when Coca-Cola introduced its brand into China, the Chinese characters sounded like *Coca-Cola* but meant "bite the wax tadpole." With the help of a language specialist, the company substituted four Mandarin characters that retained the Coca-Cola sound but mean "can happy, mouth happy." KFC also encountered translation problems when the company first entered China in 1986 as its classic "Finger-lickin good" tagline was wrongly translated in Chinese to "Eat your fingers off." Then there is the classic story of when General Motors (GM) and Chevrolet introduced its Nova to Latin America: The car did not do well because "no va" means "won't go" in Spanish. However, GM denied that the name was a problem, noting that the brand did pretty well in these markets and that in grammatical terms, "no va" is *not* how a Spanish speaker would describe a dead car. However, the company did change the name of the car to the Caribe in Spanish-speaking markets.

Global marketers sometimes try to internationalize various components of their marketing programs such as packaging, logos, and advertising messages to eliminate the time, effort, and costs required to adapt, or localize, a product or brand for international markets. One way of doing so is to rely on images rather than text or copy, which can be more susceptible to mistranslation. However, the use of images can present problems as well and can be subject to misinterpretation. For example, the Swedish company Cederroth reportedly ran an ad for its Samarin brand of antacid in an Arabic newspaper using only a series of three images and the product name. The images were designed to tell the story: The first image showed a man looking as if he were ill, the second showed him drinking a glass of Samarin, and in the third image he appears happy and well. However, the ad did not account for the fact that Arabic speakers read from right to left and often process advertising images the same way, and thus left consumers with the impression that the man became ill after consuming the product.

Another company that ran into problems in international markets over an advertising message is Burger King. A campaign created for BK's Texican Whopper that ran in the United Kingdom and Spain featured ads showing a short Mexican wrestler draped in a cape resembling his country's flag standing next to a lanky American cowboy and

**EXHIBIT 5–1**

This outdoor ad for milk targets Hispanic consumers by appealing to love for family

marketers. For example, while many marketers are recognizing the importance of appealing to the Hispanic market, they find that communicating with this fast-growing segment can be very challenging. They have to decide whether to use ads with a Hispanic-focused creative, dub or remake general market campaigns into Spanish, or run English-language ads and hope that they will be picked up by bilingual Hispanics. Many companies are creating ads specifically for the Hispanic market. Exhibit 5–1 shows an outdoor ad the California Milk Processor Board developed to target Hispanic consumers. Notice how the message in the ad (Family, Love and Milk) addresses commitment to family, which is a strong traditional Latino value.

the tagline "the taste of Texas with a little spicy Mexican." Mexico's ambassador to Spain said the ad inappropriately displayed the Mexican flag, whose image is protected under national law, and requested that the ads be discontinued. Many Mexicans as well as Hispanic consumers in the United States were also critical of the ads, arguing that they were offensive. Burger King said that the ads were meant to show how influences from the southwestern United States and Mexico can mix, and were not meant to poke fun at Mexican culture. However, the company issued an apology and changed the advertising.

Global marketers can also encounter barriers with regard to culture and language when trying to describe characteristics of new products, such as their attributes and benefits or the way they perform, in terms that consumers in other countries can understand. The Chicago-based market research firm Synovate uses a technique for its clients called vocabulary elicitation to identify a list of attributes that consumers use to describe various product qualities in terms that are relevant to their language and culture. One of the company's clients, a large multinational beverage company, planned to introduce a new product in Japan that had recently been introduced in North America. However, the description of some of the product attributes used in ads run in the United States and Canada lacked meaning in Japanese culture. To address the problem, Synovate conducted a vocabulary elicitation study to identify characteristics that Japanese consumers could use to evaluate the new product. For example, one of the beverage attributes was understood by consumers in North America to mean "creaminess in the mouth" but Japanese consumers lacked a corresponding descriptor for the trait. Synovate's research found that the term "milk feel" could be used to describe the product characteristic so that it would be understood by Japanese consumers in advertising as well as other marketing communications.

Many multinational companies are trying to develop global brands that can be marketed internationally using the same brand name and advertising campaigns. However, they must be careful that brand names, advertising slogans, signs, symbols, and other forms of marketing communication don't lose something in the translation. There are several things international marketers can do to avoid joining the top 10 list of language blunders. The first line of defense is to hire a translation service to review the material and make sure there are no problems. However, experts note that relying on translators alone may not be foolproof as they may not be steeped in current slang or the subtleties of a language. The experts recommend that translated materials be read by a linguistically mixed staff as well as by contacts in the local market who know dialects and slang. For example, at the international branding consulting firm Landor Associates, new brand names or ad slogans trigger native-speaker checks in eight languages.

While the use of translators and native-speaker checks can help to identify language problems, they do not solve the problem of how well an ad campaign translates into another culture. The vice president of marketing for the direct marketing agency Infocore notes that ad campaign concepts will never translate perfectly into another culture, which is a problem that many marketers do not want to acknowledge. He cites two basic problems, including multinational ad agencies being constrained by managers who do not want to surrender power to strangers in foreign markets and the "don't mess with the creative" mantra of marketers who assume that the magic of a campaign that works in one culture can be grafted onto another.

Time and again, problems with brand names, ad slogans, and visual signs and symbols have come back to haunt even the best of marketers. As Simon Anholt, a British marketing and branding expert, notes: "Language is in many respects such a silly little thing, but it has the power to bring marketing directors to their knees. That's where the terror lies."

Sources: Mark Laswell, "Lost in Translation," *Business 2.0*, August 2004, pp. 68–70; Deborah L. Venice, "Proper Message, Design in Global Markets Requires Tests," *Marketing News*, September 1, 2006, pp. 18, 24–25; Emily Maltby, "Expanding Abroad? Avoid Cultural Gaffes," *The Wall Street Journal*, January 19, 2010, p. B5; Adam Wooten, "International Business: The Wrong Marketing Picture Can Be a Thousand Words Lost in Translation," *Desert News*, March 26, 2011, www.deseretnews.com/article/705369323; Rupal Parekh and Emily Bryson York, "B K to Revise Ad after Complaints from Mexican Official," *Advertising Age*, April 14, 2009, http://adage.com/print/135989.

# A BASIC MODEL OF COMMUNICATION

LO 05-2

Over the years, a basic model of the various elements of the communication process has evolved, as shown in Figure 5–1 on page 146.[2] Two elements represent the major participants in the communication process, the sender and the receiver. Another two are the major communication tools, message and channel. Four others are the major communication functions and processes: encoding, decoding, response, and feedback. The last element, noise, refers to any extraneous factors in the system that can interfere with the process and work against effective communication.

**YTC 05–02**

**Communication Problems**

youtube.com/10ebelch

## Source Encoding

The sender, or **source**, of a communication is the person or organization that has information to share with another person or group of people. The source may be an

FIGURE 5–1

A Model of the
Communication Process

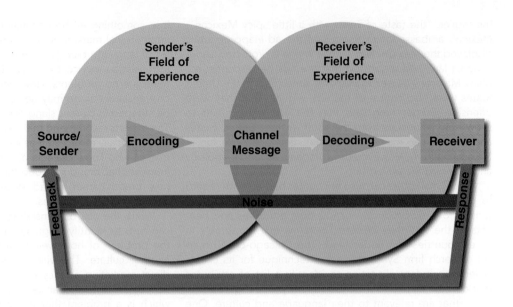

**EXHIBIT 5–2**

Professional golfer Paula
Creamer is a source in this ad
for Citizen Eco-Drive watches

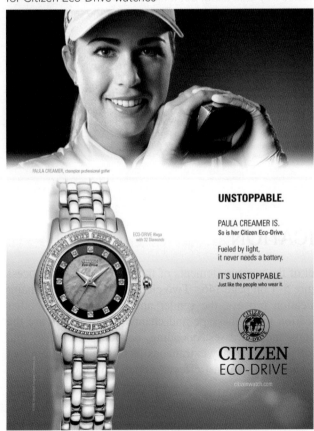

individual (say, a salesperson or hired spokesperson, such as a celebrity, who appears in a company's advertisements) or a nonpersonal entity (such as the corporation or organization itself). For example, the source of many ads is the company, since no specific spokesperson or source is shown. However, many companies use a spokesperson to appear in their ads and to deliver their advertising messages. In some cases, a popular spokesperson can play a very important role in attracting attention to a company's advertising and delivering the message, as well as influencing how well it is received by the target audience. For example, the Citizen Watch Company has featured a variety of rising sports stars as spokespersons in the "Unstoppable" campaign for its Eco-Drive watches. Exhibit 5–2 shows one of the ads from the campaign featuring professional golfer Paula Creamer.

Because the receiver's perceptions of the source influence how the communication is received, marketers must be careful to select a communicator the receiver believes is knowledgeable and trustworthy or with whom the receiver can identify or relate in some manner. (How these characteristics influence the receiver's responses is discussed further in Chapter 6.)

The communication process begins when the source selects words, symbols, pictures, and the like, to represent the message that will be delivered to the receiver(s). This process, known as **encoding**, involves putting thoughts, ideas, or information into a symbolic form. The sender's goal is to encode the message in such a way that it will be understood by the receiver. This means using words, signs, or symbols that are familiar to the target audience. Many symbols have universal meaning, such as the familiar circle with a line through it to denote no parking, no smoking, and so forth. Many companies also have highly recognizable symbols—such as McDonald's golden arches, Nike's swoosh, or the Coca-Cola trademark—that are known to consumers around the world. Marketers must pay very close attention to the symbols associated with their company or brand such as logos as they often become a shorthand way for consumers to identify them. In some cases marketers may change their logos as way of sending a different message to consumers. For example, in 2011 Starbucks changed its logo and dropped the green ring with the text "Starbucks Coffee" to more prominently display its iconic siren. The change was made to help consumers "think beyond coffee" when they see the Starbucks logo because the company is broadening its strategic focus to include other product categories.[3] In some cases consumers may become very attached to a company's logo and react negatively when they change it. The Gap experienced this a few years ago when the retail chain introduced a redesigned logo that it felt was more contemporary. Responses to the new logo on social media were very negative and the Gap returned to its old design after just four days.[4]

**EXHIBIT 5–3**
The image projected by an ad often communicates more than words

## Message

The encoding process leads to development of a **message** that contains the information or meaning the source hopes to convey. The message may be verbal or nonverbal, oral or written, or symbolic. Messages must be put into a transmittable form that is appropriate for the channel of communication being used. In advertising, this may range from simply writing some words or copy that will be read as a radio message to producing an expensive television commercial. For many products, it is not the actual words of the message that determine its communication effectiveness but rather the impression or image the ad creates. Notice how the Coach ad shown in Exhibit 5–3 uses only a picture to deliver its message. However, the use of the brand name and picture is an effective way to communicate Coach's intended message of the eloquent simplicity as well as classic design and American style of its handbags.

Marketers must make decisions regarding the *content* of the messages they send to consumers as well as the *structure* and *design* of these messages. Content refers to the information and/or meaning contained in the message while structure and design refer to the way the message is put together in order to deliver the information or intended meaning. More attention will be given to issues regarding message appeal and structure in the next chapter while message design is discussed in the chapters on creative strategy (Chapters 8 and 9).

## Channel

The **channel** is the method by which the communication travels from the source or sender to the receiver. At the broadest level, channels of communication are of two types, nonpersonal and personal. *Nonpersonal channels* of communication are those that carry a message without direct, interpersonal contact between the sender and receiver. Nonpersonal channels are generally referred to as the **mass media** or mass communications, since the message they contain is directed to more than one person and is often sent to many individuals at one time. For example, a TV commercial broadcast on a prime-time show may be seen by 10 million people in a given evening while a print ad appearing in a popular magazine may be seen by millions of readers over the course of a week or month.

Nonpersonal channels of communication consist of two major types, print and broadcast. Print media include newspapers, magazines, direct mail, and billboards; broadcast media include radio and television. The Internet has characteristics of both nonpersonal as well as personal forms of communication. It has become a mass-media vehicle as it is now an important source of information for most consumers and many advertising messages are delivered through various forms of online advertising including banner ads, paid search, and ads on social media sites. In many ways the Internet is nonpersonal in nature as consumers are often just consuming the information or content provided online and there is no personal contact between them and the companies that disseminate this information on their website or through online advertising. However, the Internet is increasingly becoming a form of personal communication as consumers can interact with marketers online as well as communicate and share information with one another through the use of various forms of social media.

*Personal channels* involve direct communication between two or more persons and can occur through interpersonal contact (face-to-face) or via other methods such as e-mail or through social media. Salespeople serve as personal channels of communication when they deliver a selling message or presentation to a buyer or potential customer. A major advantage of personal channels of communication is that the message or presentation can be tailored to the individual or audience and the sender receives direct feedback from them. Members of one's social networks such as friends, neighbors, associates, co-workers, or family members are also personal channels of communication. They often represent **word-of-mouth (WOM)** influence that involves informal communication among consumers about products and services and is a very powerful source of information.[5]

Many companies work hard to generate positive word-of-mouth discussion for their companies or brands using various buzz marketing techniques. **Buzz marketing** is just one of the new names for what used to be known simply as word-of-mouth communication while terms such as *consumer-generated marketing* and *viral marketing* are also used to describe the process.[6] The use of word-of-mouth marketing is really nothing new as marketers have long been handing out product samples and providing products to influential people and encouraging them to recommend the brand to others. For example, alcoholic beverage marketers have long understood the value of getting bartenders and servers to hype their brands while pharmaceutical companies have always worked to encourage influential physicians to talk up their products to their peers.

What makes buzz marketing different from traditional word-of-mouth communication is that it includes systematic and organized efforts to encourage people to speak favorably about a company, brand, organization, or issue and often to recommend it to others in their social network. What is also new is the number of companies that are now using buzz marketing, and the sophisticated ways they are going about it. Marketers often use techniques such as contests that encourage consumers to create user-generated content—such as photographs, videos, recipes, and product usage ideas—and then use social media as a way to disseminate it, which helps spread the word about their brands. In some cases consumers may be asked to vote on the user-generated content and also to share it with their friends and associates and encourage them to vote as well. For example, Frito-Lay has sponsored the "Crash the Super Bowl" online commercial production competition since 2007 whereby consumers are invited to create 30-second commercials for its Doritos brand.[7] The company's advertising agency and marketing team select the five finalists that traditionally are posted to a micro website for a monthlong public vote, with the two spots receiving the most votes airing during the big game (Exhibit 5–4). Frito-Lay moved the contest to Facebook in 2013 and received nearly

CHAPTER 5

3,500 video entries. The five finalist videos drew nearly 100 million views as the social media site helped the videos go viral.[8]

**Viral Marketing**   The "Crash the Super Bowl" contest is an excellent example of the use of **viral marketing**, which refers to the act of propagating marketing-relevant messages through the help and cooperation of individual consumers.[9] Many marketers along with their advertising and/or digital agencies now use a variety of tools and techniques to generate viral buzz about their brands, many of which take advantage of the emergence and growth of online communities and social media such as Facebook, Google+, Twitter, Pinterest, Instagram, and YouTube. However, successful viral marketing can be very difficult to achieve as the outcomes are affected by many factors that are often beyond a marketer's control.

Researchers have identified three major factors that affect the success of a viral marketing program, including message characteristics, individual sender or receiver characteristics, and social network characteristics.[10] Message characteristics relate to the content and creative design of a viral message and include factors such as whether the information is entertaining, engaging, novel, humorous, and/or informative. For example, many videos and commercials have a strong viral component that make them popular and encourage consumers to watch as well share them. The top 10 viral ad campaigns and commercials in 2012 included the Red Bull "Stratos" video, which captured the record-breaking free fall of Felix Baumgartner from the stratosphere (171 million views); a commercial for the Samsung Galaxy S III smartphone, which poked fun at people waiting in line for new iPhones (72 million views); and Procter & Gamble's "Proud Sponsor of Mom" commercial, which paid tribute to the hard work and dedication of the mothers of Olympic athletes (47 million views).

In addition to the message, characteristics of the individual consumer also play an important role in the viral marketing process. Factors such as demographics, personality traits, and motivation for sharing content and messages as well as receiving them impact the effectiveness of viral campaigns.[11] For example, female and younger consumers tend to exert more influence on their target recipients and be more susceptible to viral influences than male and older consumers, while traits such as extroversion, innovativeness, and altruism are related to tendencies to share messages.[12] With regard to social network characteristics, the structure of networks

YTC **05–04**

**Top Viral Videos**
youtube.com/10ebelch

**EXHIBIT 5–5**

Seeding is an agency that specializes in developing social marketing campaigns

through which a message spreads as well as the consumers' position in the social network, as defined by relationships with others, can influence the diffusion of a viral message. Many marketers try to identify individuals who are very influential in various social media domains, such as bloggers and persons with a large number of Facebook fans or Twitter followers; then they work hard to get their messages to them in hopes that they pass them on to others in their social network.

Another important aspect of viral marketing is what is often referred to as **seeding**, which involves identifying and choosing the initial group of consumers who will be used to start the diffusion or spreading of a message.[13] Companies that utilize viral marketing must develop a *seeding strategy* which involves determining how many initial consumers or "seeds" are needed and selecting the right consumers to start the viral process. For example, Glacéau Vitaminwater uses an "influencer seeding model" as part of its strategy to expand the brand into international markets that focuses on trendsetting consumers who are highly creative and closely connected to culture. During the 2012 Summer Olympics the Glacéau Tasting Vehicle made its way through the streets of London and set up games such as oversize Jenga and Twister. Consumers were provided with samples of the product as well as information that could be passed on to others through social media and word of mouth.[14] There are also companies that specialize in working with clients to develop viral marketing programs and seeding strategies. Exhibit 5–5 shows how Seeding, a digital strategy and social marketing agency, promotes its services.

Some companies are also building Web communities so consumers can chat about their product experiences online. For example, in 2005 Procter & Gamble, which ironically is the world's largest advertiser, initiated a new word-of-mouth program brand community called Vocalpoint to reach the most influential group of shoppers in America: moms. Recently P&G has broadened the focus of Vocalpoint to include women age 28 to 45 and now has more than 670,000 members. These women are very involved with their social networks through social media such as Facebook, Twitter, and various blogs and speak or interact with a number of other women during a typical day. P&G has also used the success of Vocalpoint to develop a new brand community called Orgullosa that targets Spanish-speaking women in the United States. Vocalpoint and Orgullosa are the flagship brand communities for P&G and are likely to be used as models for reaching other target audiences in the future. (Exhibit 5–6)

**EXHIBIT 5–6**

Vocalpoint and Orgullosa are online communities where women can share information about products and various issues

**Integrating Word-of-Mouth with IMC**  While viral techniques have become a popular way to generate buzz about a brand, research conducted by the Keller Fay Group—a market research company that focuses on word-of-mouth marketing—has shown that some 90 percent of conversations about products, services, and brands take place off-line.[15] Face-to-face interaction accounts for the vast majority of word-of-mouth communications (75 percent) about a brand while phone conversations rank second (15 percent). Only 10 percent of word of mouth takes place through online channels such as e-mail/instant messages, blogs, and chat rooms. Their research also shows that nearly half the word-of-mouth conversations included references to the various IMC tools used for a brand, including print and television ads, websites, and other marketing tools such as point-of-sale displays and promotions.

Another important finding was that advertising influenced by word-of-mouth conversations is significantly more likely to involve recommendations to buy or try a brand when compared to other WOM-induced discussions about brands. Moreover, these WOM discussions are very powerful as consumers ascribe a high credibility to the information they hear from others; 50 percent say they are very likely to buy as a result of these conversations.[16]

Subsequent research by Keller Fay has found that the role of advertising in WOM is even stronger, as a quarter of all consumer conversations about brands involve discussions about advertising. And of the brand conversations in which consumers talk about advertising, television advertising is the most prevalent form, which is not surprising given that more money is spent on TV ads than any other medium. However, collectively, other forms of advertising including magazine, newspaper, the Internet, radio, and outdoor are about equal with respect to generating conversations about advertising, which suggests that a variety of IMC tools can be used to drive word of mouth.[17]

These findings are very important from an integrated marketing communications perspective in several respects. First, they show that that there can be powerful "pass-along" benefits from consumers talking favorably about a brand and referencing various elements of its IMC program. However, with consumers being bombarded by so many irrelevant marketing messages each day, it is very difficult to get them to talk about them. Thus, marketers must develop creative advertisements and other forms of communication that can trigger conversations and are worthy of sharing. They also reinforce the importance of marketers recognizing that all of the IMC elements work in unison to impact how consumers perceive a brand and the word-of-mouth discussion that is generated by it. The fact that consumers appear to be influenced the most by their conversations with other people shows that marketers need to finds ways to favorably influence these interactions. However, as Keller and Fay note, since most WOM discussions take place off-line, marketers cannot rely only on social media to drive these conversations; they need to deploy a more robust set of IMC tools to drive brand advocacy.[18]

Marketers must be careful about the assumptions they make when using buzz marketing techniques. For example, a study conducted by David Godes and Diane Mayzlin on the effects of a word-of-mouth campaign for a chain store examined the characteristics of the most successful "agents" so that firms could better understand at whom they should target their buzz marketing efforts.[19] They found that agents who were not loyal customers of the store were more effective at generating sales through word of mouth than were loyal customers. The explanation offered for these somewhat counterintuitive findings is that loyal customers have already told their friends and acquaintances about a product and are already generating positive word of mouth. On the other hand, nonloyal customers may be more responsive to buzz marketing campaigns designed to encourage them to spread the word about a product. However, marketers still have to identify the best generators of buzz among both loyal and nonloyal customers such as those who are considered opinion leaders by their peers and "social butterflies" who have a high propensity to meet new people and connect with friends.

While the use of buzz and viral marketing campaigns is becoming more prevalent, concern has been expressed over its use and whether the person spreading the product message should disclose his or her affiliation. The Word of Mouth Marketing Association, was formed in 2004 to promote and improve the use of word-of-mouth marketing and protect consumers and the industry by providing ethical guidelines for its use. The WOMMA has developed a set of rules and guidelines that mandate that marketers must make sure that people recommending products or services disclose whom they are working for. Gary Ruskin, the former executive director of Commercial Alert, a nonprofit organization dedicated to protecting consumers from commercial exploitation, notes that without such disclosures there is "a danger of the basic commercialization of human relations, where friends treat one another as advertising pawns, undercutting social trust."[20]

Experts note that buzz marketing techniques are very resistant to manipulation and marketers must be careful about how they use them. Several companies have had buzz marketing campaigns backfire when consumers recognized that the companies were artificially trying to promote buzz for their brands. Some argue that the growing popularity of buzz marketing could well spell its downfall, because when consumers recognize that everyone is trying to create a buzz for their brand, they are likely to be turned off to the technique.[21] However, with the growth of social media and consumers becoming less attentive to and interested in traditional media advertising, it is likely that marketers will continue to seek ways to develop and deliver branded content and messages that consumers will share with one another. This will extend the reach and impact of their marketing messages and may add an implicit consumer endorsement as well.

The effective use of buzz marketing requires that marketers take a strategic approach in the development and implementation of campaigns that are designed to have strong WOM and viral components. For example, Keller and Fay note that marketers should think in terms of social consumers rather than just social media and focus on the stories that consumers share with one another about a brand or a product or service category to ensure that there is a good fit between the consumer story and the brand story. They also suggest that it is the job of brand strategists to identify the people who are most likely to talk about their brand or category and seek to understand when, where, and why people talk.[22] For example, when

YTC 05-05
**Word-of-Mouth Marketing**
youtube.com/10ebelch

Ford developed the "Fiesta Movement" social media campaign, the agency and brand team selected the agents based on their social vibrancy and how active they are across various social media platforms. They then encouraged them to record and share their personal experiences with the Fiesta and share them with others on social media.

## Receiver/Decoding

The **receiver** is the person(s) with whom the sender shares thoughts or information. Generally, receivers are the consumers in the target market or audience who read, hear, and/or see the marketer's message and decode it. **Decoding** is the process of transforming the sender's message back into thought. This process is heavily influenced by the receiver's frame of reference or **field of experience**, which refers to the experiences, perceptions, attitudes, and values he or she brings to the communication situation.

For effective communication to occur, the message decoding process of the receiver must match the encoding of the sender. Simply put, this means the receiver understands and correctly interprets what the source is trying to communicate. As Figure 5–1 showed, the source and the receiver each have a frame of reference (the circle around each) that they bring to the communication situation. Effective communication is more likely when there is some *common ground* between the two parties. (This is represented by the overlapping of the two circles.) The more knowledge the sender has about the receivers, the better the sender can understand their needs, empathize with them, and communicate effectively. Exhibit 5–7 shows an ad for the Pew Environmental Group's Campaign for America's Wilderness that uses the concept of common ground by noting how both Republicans and Democrats agree on the importance of protecting the American wilderness by passing legislation to give permanent protection to wilderness land in thirteen states.

While this notion of common ground between sender and receiver may sound basic, it often causes great difficulty in the advertising communications process. Marketing and advertising people often have very different fields of experience from the consumers who constitute the mass markets with whom they must communicate. Most advertising and marketing people are college-educated and work and/or reside in large urban areas such as New York, Chicago, or Los Angeles. Yet they are attempting to develop commercials that will effectively communicate with millions of consumers who have never attended college, work in blue-collar occupations, and live in rural areas or small towns. The executive creative director of a large advertising agency described how advertising executives become isolated from the cultural mainstream: "We pull them in and work them to death. And then they begin moving in sushi circles and lose touch with Velveeta and the people who eat it."[23]

Another factor that can lead to problems in establishing common ground between senders and receivers is age. As the population of the United States and many other countries grows older, concern has been expressed over the potential problems that might arise because of age differences between advertising agency personnel and older consumers. A study conducted for the Association of Advertising Agencies International found that professionals who work in advertising agencies are much younger than the general population. Nearly 40 percent of agency personnel staff is between the ages of 30 to 39 while only 20 percent of the U.S. adult population is in their 30s.[24] The youth bias is particularly evident in the creative departments as many of those who work in this area are under the age of 40. The age gap has become very prevalent in the digital/interactive area as well because these departments are dominated by younger people. Digital and Social Media Perspective 5–1 discusses how digital media is creating a new

**EXHIBIT 5–7**

This ad uses the concept of common ground

## Digital Media Create a New Type of Ageism in IMC

It has long been argued that there is a youth bias in the advertising industry. The claim is that marketers are fixated with reaching younger consumers while paying less attention to those over the age of 50, despite the fact that older consumers control half of the wealth, spend trillions of dollars on products and services each year, and comprise a large percentage of the population in most countries. Madison Avenue has been focused on the younger adult market (generally aged 18 to 49) for decades, and the media are obsessed with the under 50 demographic as well; most of the broadcast and cable networks have been filling their schedules with shows and programming aimed at people in their 20s, 30s, and 40s. Another area where advertising and marketing communications are often seen as having a youth bias is among agency personnel. Studies have shown that professionals who work in advertising agencies in the United States as well as other countries are much younger than the adult population. The youth bias is particularly evident in creative departments, where agency employment drops like a rock after age 40, particularly among those involved in creating the ads. It should be noted that the youth movement for those working in advertising is not limited to the United States. For example, in the United Kingdom the average age of advertising employees in 2012 was 34, with more than 40 percent under age 30 and only 5 percent over age 50.

There are a number of reasons why agencies seem to be focusing their hiring toward young people. One reason is basic economics: Younger means cheaper, and in an industry notorious for taking every opportunity to cut costs, a 20-year veteran copywriter is much more expensive than a college graduate. (That younger, less experienced employees are paid less is, of course, true in most industries, not just advertising.) A second reason is creativity as agencies tend to think that younger employees are better suited to creative thinking, especially under tight deadlines and high pressure to perform. A third reason is the shift toward the use of digital media. Many agencies, as well as

their clients, view the tried-and-true advertising methods used for decades—print, direct mail, and telemarketing—as suddenly being a thing of the past. They are focusing their attention on new methods of reaching and engaging consumers as the use of social media such as Twitter, Google+, Facebook, LinkedIn, and YouTube has become more prevalent and assumed to be better understood by the younger generation.

With the growth of the Internet and new forms of digital and social media, a new type of ageism is taking place in the world of advertising, both in agencies and among companies that market their products and services to younger consumers. As technology continues to change and grow at an ever-expanding pace, ad agencies and marketing departments assume that young people are those best equipped to navigate the digital world. Whereas gray hair and work experience were once viewed as assets for marketing and advertising executives, Madison Avenue agencies are increasingly turning to freshly minted college grads who are (presumably) more in touch with the digital platforms that have become so vital for customer engagement.

Of course, industry veterans in the 55-and-over club—both employed and unemployed—will contend the industry has it all wrong, arguing that they too know the intricacies of the digital world and recognize that social media are more than a passing fad and have taken the time to learn about them. In fact, many creatives and account managers saw the writing on the wall years ago and have subsequently taken it upon themselves to learn how to use the various social media platforms, such as Facebook and Twitter, along with search engine optimization and web analytics. Thus, this "ageism" is frustrating for "gray-haired" members of the work force who feel that they should be looked at as even *more* valuable to their companies and agencies as they can combine their new digital knowledge with significant work experience. Unfortunately, Madison Avenue firms, as well as most companies, do not seem to be budging as they delegate social media strategy and tasks to junior employees

type of ageism in the marketing communications industry as many companies, as well as agencies, prefer to hire younger workers whom they view as more digital savvy than older people.

Critics argue that most advertising is really about the people who create it, not about the consumers who actually buy the products and services being advertised. It is important that marketers and their agencies understand the frame of reference and perspectives of the consumers in the target markets that are receiving their messages. Many companies spend a considerable amount of time and money pretesting messages to make sure consumers understand them and decode them in the manner the advertiser intended.

whom they assume know the platforms much better and will enjoy spending time in the space.

So what can older advertising and marketing professionals do to distinguish themselves as capable employees in the digital age? Most experts recommend first taking a long look in the mirror to determine exactly where the deficiencies in their digital skills may exist. Advertising professionals who grew up with a different generation of traditional media advertising must get up to speed on the most current trends in the digital world and be able to demonstrate their new knowledge. A "digital presence" is also essential through either a personal website or an extensive public profile on LinkedIn, Facebook, and Twitter. They also should consider many of the online tutorials that are available to educate themselves and stay current in various aspects of digital and social media. For example, Google offers online courses and training modules where one can learn how to use Google advertising and web marketing tools. It also offers Google certification tests for Google Analytics, AdWords, and other online tools. Facebook also provides in-depth explanation for how to use its advertising and analytics platforms, and entire sections on its website are dedicated to helping a business develop a Facebook ad campaign. Twitter also offers a best practices guide for those interested in using the popular social media tool.

Many marketers are recognizing the importance of training their middle-aged managers and executives in the use of social media rather than look for younger replacements. For example, Procter & Gamble, Unilever, and The Home Depot have all dedicated significant time and money over the past several years to increase customer engagement through digital media and have taken steps to accelerate social media learning in their companies. Unilever recently implemented a "reverse mentoring" program that pairs young employees with senior executives. The goal of the program was to educate the executives about the digital world so that they could then incorporate social media into the company's overall strategy. Procter & Gamble has done employee swaps with Google whereby the two companies traded two dozen employees for several weeks and held digital nights pairing digital media and agency executives with P&G marketing directors so they could learn more about the opportunities and limitations of social media.

With every passing year, older people who work in advertising and marketing are likely to find it harder to gain employment in an industry that is getting younger by the day. Thus, it is important that middle-aged managers and executives immerse themselves in digital media in order to stay relevant and, perhaps more importantly, gainfully employed.

Sources: Rupel Parekh, "Aging in Adland: The Gray-Hair Phobia That's Hindering Older Execs," *Advertising Age*, January 30, 2012, pp. 1, 8–9; Nancee Martin, "Six Tips for Older Job Hunters TBWA Talent Director's Do's and Don'ts to Get the Agency Gig You're Looking For," *Advertising Age*, January 29, 2012, http://adage.com/print/232402; Ellen Byron, "A New Odd Couple: Google, P&G Sway Workers to Spur Innovation," *The Wall Street Journal*, November 19, 2008, http://online.wsj.com/article/SB122705787917439625.html; Meg James, "Over 50 and Out of Favor," *Los Angeles Times*, May 10, 2005, pp. A1,10.

YTC 05–06

**Digital Media Tutorials**

youtube.com/10ebelch

Advertisers spend millions of dollars every year to understand the frames of reference of the target markets who receive their messages. They also spend much time and money pretesting messages to make sure consumers understand and decode them in the manner the advertiser intended.

## Noise

Throughout the communication process, the message is subject to extraneous factors that can distort or interfere with its reception. This unplanned distortion or interference is known as **noise**. Errors or problems that occur in the encoding of the message, distortion in a radio or television signal, and distractions at the point of reception are examples of noise. When you are watching your favorite commercial on TV and a problem occurs in the signal transmission, it will obviously interfere with your reception, lessening the impact of the commercial.

Noise may also occur because the fields of experience of the sender and receiver don't overlap. Lack of common ground may result in improper encoding of the message—using a sign, symbol, or words that are unfamiliar or have different meaning to the receiver. The more common ground there is between the sender and the receiver, the less likely it is this type of noise will occur.

### Response/Feedback

The receiver's set of reactions after seeing, hearing, or reading the message is known as a **response**. Receivers' responses can range from nonobservable actions such as storing information in memory to immediate action such as dialing a toll-free number to order a product advertised on television. Marketers are very interested in **feedback**, that part of the receiver's response that is communicated back to the sender. Feedback, which may take a variety of forms, closes the loop in the communications flow and lets the sender monitor how the intended message is being decoded and received.

For example, in a personal-selling situation, customers may pose questions, comments, or objections or indicate their reactions through nonverbal responses such as gestures and frowns.[25] The salesperson has the advantage of receiving instant feedback through the customer's reactions. But this is generally not the case when mass media are used. Because advertisers are not in direct contact with the customers, they must use other means to determine how their messages have been received. While the ultimate form of feedback occurs through sales, it is often hard to show a direct relationship between advertising and purchase behavior. So marketers use other methods to obtain feedback, among them customer inquiries, store visits, coupon redemptions, and reply cards. Research-based feedback analyzes readership and recall of ads, message comprehension, attitude change, and other forms of response. With this information, the advertiser can determine reasons for success or failure in the communication process and make adjustments.

Successful communication is accomplished when the marketer selects an appropriate source, develops an effective message or appeal that is encoded properly, and then selects the channels or media that will best reach the target audience so that the message can be effectively decoded and delivered. In Chapter 6, we will examine the source, message, and channel decisions and see how promotional planners work with these controllable variables to develop communication strategies. Since these decisions must consider how the target audience will respond to the promotional message, the remainder of this chapter examines the receiver and the process by which consumers respond to advertising and other forms of marketing communications.

## ANALYZING THE RECEIVER

To communicate effectively with their customers, marketers must understand who the target audience is, what (if anything) it knows or feels about the company's product or service, and how to communicate with the audience to influence its decision-making process. Marketers must also know how the market is likely to respond to various sources of communication or different types of messages. Before they make decisions regarding source, message, and channel variables, promotional planners must understand the potential effects associated with each of these factors. This section focuses on the receiver of the marketing communication. It examines how the audience is identified and the process it may go through in responding to a promotional message. This information serves as a foundation for evaluating the controllable communication variable decisions in the next chapter.

## Identifying the Target Audience

The marketing communication process really begins with identifying the audience that will be the focus of the firm's advertising and promotional efforts. The target audience may consist of individuals, groups, niche markets, market segments, or a general public or mass audience (Figure 5–2). Marketers approach each of these audiences differently.

The target market may consist of *individuals* who have specific needs and for whom the communication must be specifically tailored. This often requires person-to-person communication and is generally accomplished through personal selling. Other forms of communication, such as advertising, may be used to attract the audience's attention to the firm, but the detailed message is carried by a salesperson who can respond to the specific needs of the individual customer. Life insurance, financial services, and real estate are examples of products and services promoted this way.

A second level of audience aggregation is represented by the *group.* Marketers often must communicate with a group of people who make or influence the purchase decision. For example, organizational purchasing often involves buying centers or committees that vary in size and composition. Companies marketing their products and services to other businesses or organizations must understand who is on the purchase committee, what aspect of the decision each individual influences, and the criteria each member uses to evaluate a product. Advertising may be directed at each member of the buying center, and multilevel personal selling may be necessary to reach those individuals who influence or actually make decisions.

Marketers look for customers who have similar needs and wants and thus represent some type of market segment that can be reached with the same basic communication strategy. Very small, well-defined groups of customers are often referred to as *market niches.* They can usually be reached through personal-selling efforts or highly targeted media such as direct mail. The next level of audience aggregation is *market segments,* broader classes of buyers who have similar needs and can be reached with similar messages. As we saw in Chapter 2, there are various ways of segmenting markets and reaching the customers in these segments. As market segments get larger, marketers usually turn to broader-based media such as newspapers, magazines, and TV to reach them.

Marketers of most consumer products attempt to attract the attention of large numbers of present or potential customers (*mass markets*) through mass communication such as advertising or publicity. Mass communication is a one-way flow of

**FIGURE 5–2**

Levels of Audience Aggregation

information from the marketer to the consumer. Feedback on the audience's reactions to the message is generally indirect and difficult to measure.

TV advertising, for example, lets the marketer send a message to millions of consumers at the same time. But this does not mean effective communication has occurred. This may be only one of several hundred messages the consumer is exposed to that day. There is no guarantee the information will be attended to, processed, comprehended, or stored in memory for later retrieval. Even if the advertising message is processed, it may not interest consumers or may be misinterpreted by them. Studies by Jacob Jacoby and Wayne D. Hoyer have shown that nearly 20 percent of all print ads and even more TV commercials are miscomprehended by readers.[26]

Unlike personal or face-to-face communications, mass communications do not offer the marketer an opportunity to explain or clarify the message to make it more effective. The marketer must enter the communication situation with knowledge of the target audience and how it is likely to react to the message. This means the receiver's response process must be understood, along with its implications for promotional planning and strategy.

# THE RESPONSE PROCESS

Perhaps the most important aspect of developing effective communication programs involves understanding the *response process* the receiver may go through in moving toward a specific behavior (like purchasing a product) and how the promotional efforts of the marketer influence consumer responses. In many instances, the marketer's only objective may be to create awareness of the company or brand name, which may trigger interest in the product. In other situations, the marketer may want to convey detailed information to change consumers' knowledge of and attitudes toward the brand and ultimately change their behavior.

## Traditional Response Hierarchy Models

A number of models have been developed to depict the stages a consumer may pass through in moving from a state of not being aware of a company, product, or brand to actual purchase behavior. Figure 5–3 shows four of the best-known response hierarchy models. While these response models may appear similar, they were developed for different reasons.

The **AIDA model** was developed to represent the stages a salesperson must take a customer through in the personal-selling process.[27] This model depicts the buyer as passing successively through attention, interest, desire, and action. The salesperson must first get the customer's attention and then arouse some interest in the company's product or service. Strong levels of interest should create desire to own or use the product. The action stage in the AIDA model involves getting the customer to make a purchase commitment and closing the sale. To the marketer, this is the most important stage in the selling process, but it can also be the most difficult. Companies train their sales reps in closing techniques to help them complete the selling process. More detailed models of the personal-selling process have been developed over the years that go beyond the basic steps of the AIDA model and focus on approaches such as "solution selling" and "insight selling."[28]

Perhaps the best known of these response hierarchies is the model developed by Robert Lavidge and Gary Steiner as a paradigm for setting and measuring advertising objectives.[29] Their **hierarchy of effects model** shows the process by which advertising works; it assumes a consumer passes through a series of steps in sequential order from initial awareness of a product or service to actual purchase. A basic premise of this model is that advertising effects occur over a period of time. Advertising communication may not lead to immediate behavioral response or purchase; rather,

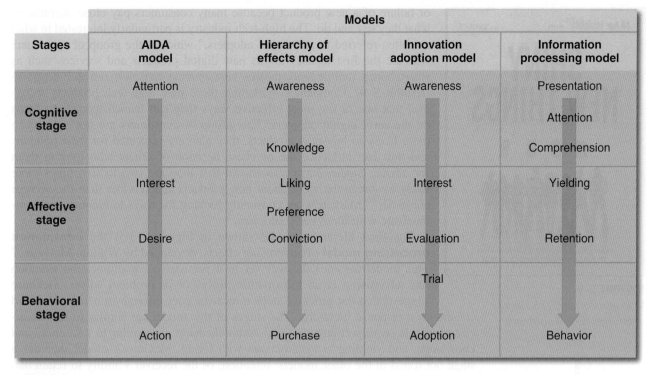

| | Models | | | |
|---|---|---|---|---|
| **Stages** | **AIDA model** | **Hierarchy of effects model** | **Innovation adoption model** | **Information processing model** |
| **Cognitive stage** | Attention | Awareness | Awareness | Presentation |
| | | | | Attention |
| | | Knowledge | | Comprehension |
| **Affective stage** | Interest | Liking | Interest | Yielding |
| | | Preference | | |
| | Desire | Conviction | Evaluation | Retention |
| **Behavioral stage** | | | Trial | |
| | Action | Purchase | Adoption | Behavior |

**FIGURE 5–3**

Models of the Response Process

**EXHIBIT 5–8**

Sampling or demonstration programs encourage trial of new products such as disposable contact lenses

a series of effects must occur, with each step fulfilled before the consumer can move to the next stage in the hierarchy. This model is also the basis for the classic *purchase funnel* metaphor that is often used to depict the decision process consumers go through. The consumer starts at the top of funnel with a number of brands in mind, methodically reduces that number as he or she becomes familiar with and evaluates these alternatives, and then emerges with the brand he or she chooses to purchase.[30] As we will see in Chapter 7, the hierarchy of effects model as well as the purchase funnel have become the foundation for setting objectives and measuring the effectiveness of advertising and other IMC tools in many companies.

The **innovation adoption model** evolved from work on the diffusion of innovations.[31] This model represents the stages a consumer passes through in adopting a new product or service. Like the other models, it says potential adopters must be moved through a series of steps before taking some action (in this case, deciding to adopt a new product). The steps preceding adoption are awareness, interest, evaluation, and trial. The challenge facing companies introducing new products is to create awareness and interest among consumers and then get them to evaluate the product favorably. The best way to evaluate a new product is through actual use so that performance can be judged. Marketers often encourage trial by using demonstration or sampling programs or allowing consumers to use a product with minimal commitment (Exhibit 5–8). After trial, consumers either adopt the product or reject it.

The innovation adoption model is especially important to companies who are using IMC tools to introduce new products to the market. These marketers recognize that there are certain types of consumers who are of particular interest to them because of their interest in new products and their ability to influence others.[32] This influential group is commonly referred to as "early adopters," and they play a critical role in determining the success

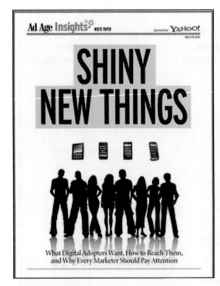

**EXHIBIT 5–9**
Marketers often try to identify and target digital adopters

or failure of a new product because many consumers pay close attention to what they say and do. The high-tech industry is particularly interested in what are often referred to as "digital adopters," which is the group of consumers who are the first to use various new digital products and services such as smartphones, mobile apps, tablets, videogaming consoles, and web browsers (Exhibit 5–9). Companies marketing these new high-tech products recognize that one of the most effective ways they can launch them is to focus on the early digital adopters. This group of consumers are not only much more likely to buy new products, they also are respected for their opinions and thus can influence the purchase decision of others who look to them for advice. Studies have also shown that they are two to five times more likely to spread the word about new products and services than the average consumer.[33] Marketers are constantly looking for ways to identify and communicate with these early adopters.

The final hierarchy model shown in Figure 5–3 is the **information processing model** of advertising effects, developed by William McGuire.[34] This model assumes the receiver in a persuasive communication situation like advertising is an information processor or problem solver. McGuire suggests that the series of steps a receiver goes through in being persuaded constitutes a response hierarchy. The stages of this model are similar to the hierarchy of effects sequence; attention and comprehension are similar to awareness and knowledge, and yielding is synonymous with liking. McGuire's model includes a stage not found in the other models: retention, or the receiver's ability to retain that portion of the comprehended information that he or she accepts as valid or relevant. This stage is important since most promotional campaigns are designed not to motivate consumers to take immediate action but rather to provide information they will use later when making a purchase decision.

Each stage of the response hierarchy is a dependent variable that must be attained and that may serve as an objective of the communication process. As shown in Figure 5–4,

**FIGURE 5–4**

Methods of Obtaining Feedback in the Response Hierarchy

| Steps in persuasion process | Effectiveness tests |
| --- | --- |
| Exposure/presentation | Viewer/listener audience size web page views |
| Attention | Listener, reader, viewer recognition |
| Comprehension | Recall, checklists |
| Message acceptance/yielding | Brand attitudes, purchase intent |
| Retention | Recall over time |
| Purchase behavior | Inventory, point-of-purchase consumer panel Scanner data |

**EXHIBIT 5–10**

Microsoft's Surface tablet is an innovative new product

each stage can be measured, providing the advertiser with feedback regarding the effectiveness of various strategies designed to move the consumer to purchase. The information processing model may be an effective framework for planning and evaluating the effects of a promotional campaign.

**Implications of the Traditional Hierarchy Models** The hierarchy models of communication response are useful to promotional planners from several perspectives. First, they delineate the series of steps potential purchasers must be taken through to move them from unawareness of a product or service to readiness to purchase it. Second, potential buyers may be at different stages in the hierarchy, so the advertiser will face different sets of communication problems. For example, a company introducing an innovative product like the Microsoft Surface tablet may use media advertising to make people aware of the product along with its features and benefits (Exhibit 5–10). Microsoft provides product information in its ads but also encourages consumers to visit retail stores as well as its website to learn more about the Surface. Consumers who visit the website store or go to a retail store for a product demonstration will progress through the response hierarchy and move closer to purchase than those who only see an ad. Marketers of a mature brand that enjoys customer loyalty may need only supportive or reminder advertising to reinforce positive perceptions and maintain the awareness level for the brand.

The hierarchy models can also be useful as intermediate measures of communication effectiveness. The marketer needs to know where audience members are on the response hierarchy. For example, research may reveal that one target segment has low awareness of the advertiser's brand, whereas another is aware of the brand and its various attributes but has a low level of liking or brand preference.

For the first segment of the market, the communication task involves increasing the awareness level for the brand. The number of ads may be increased, or a product sampling program may be used. For the second segment, where awareness is already high but liking and preference are low, the advertiser must determine the reason for the negative feelings and then attempt to address this problem in future advertising.

When research or other evidence reveals a company is perceived favorably on a particular attribute or performance criterion, the company may want to take advantage of this in its advertising.

**Evaluating Traditional Response Hierarchy Models** As you saw in Figure 5–3, the four models presented all view the response process as consisting of movement through a sequence of three basic stages. The *cognitive stage* represents what the receiver knows or perceives about the particular product or brand. This stage includes awareness that the brand exists and knowledge, information, or comprehension about its attributes, characteristics, or benefits. The *affective stage* refers to the receiver's feelings or affect level (like or dislike) for the particular brand. This stage also includes stronger levels of affect such as desire, preference, or conviction. The *conative* or *behavioral stage* refers to the consumer's action toward the brand: trial, purchase, adoption, or rejection.

All four models assume a similar ordering of these three stages. Cognitive development precedes affective reactions, which precede behavior. One might assume that consumers become aware of and knowledgeable about a brand, develop feelings toward it, form a desire or preference, and then make a purchase. While this logical progression is often accurate, the response sequence does not always operate this way.

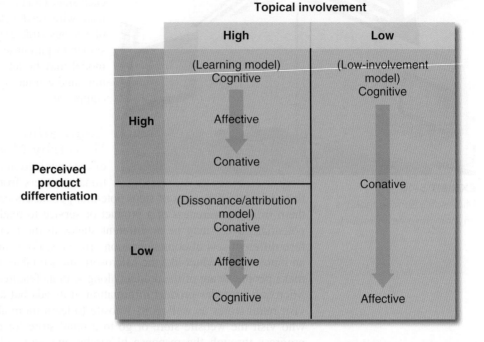

Over the past two decades, considerable research in marketing, social psychology, and communications has led to questioning of the traditional cognitive → affective → behavioral sequence of response. Several other configurations of the response hierarchy have been theorized.

## Alternative Response Hierarchies

Michael Ray has developed a model of information processing that identifies three alternative orderings of the three stages based on perceived product differentiation and product involvement.[35] These alternative response hierarchies are the standard learning, dissonance/attribution, and low-involvement models (Figure 5–5).

**The Standard Learning Hierarchy** In many purchase situations, the consumer will go through the response process in the sequence depicted by the traditional communication models. Ray terms this a **standard learning model**, which consists of a learn → feel → do sequence. Information and knowledge acquired or *learned* about the various brands are the basis for developing affect, or *feelings*, that guide what the consumer will *do* (e.g., actual trial or purchase). In this hierarchy, the consumer is viewed as an active participant in the communication process who gathers information through active learning.

Ray suggests the standard learning hierarchy is likely when the consumer is highly involved in the purchase process and there is much differentiation among competing brands. High-involvement purchase decisions such as those for industrial products and services and consumer durables like personal computers, printers, cameras, appliances, and cars are areas where a standard learning hierarchy response process is likely. Ads for products and services in these areas are usually very detailed and provide customers with information that can be used to evaluate brands and help them make a purchase decision. Notice how the ad for the new Honda Civic shown in Exhibit 5–11 appeals to the cognitive and affective steps in the standard learning hierarchy.

**The Dissonance/Attribution Hierarchy** A second response hierarchy proposed by Ray involves situations where consumers first behave, then develop attitudes or feelings as a result of that behavior, and then learn or process

**EXHIBIT 5–11**
This Honda Civic ad addresses the various stages in the standard learning hierarchy

We made the best Civic even better.

Introducing a funner, smarter, techier Honda Civic. Funner, with Pandora® compatibility. Smarter, with a customizable multi-informational display and SMS texting functionality. Techier, with standard features like Bluetooth® USB integration and rearview camera. Basically, it's everything…er.

CIVIC

**EXHIBIT 5–12**
This ad reinforces the wisdom of the decision to use a Discover credit card

Nothing like it.

GET it AT DISCOVER.COM

information that supports the behavior. This **dissonance/attribution model**, or do → feel → learn, occurs in situations where consumers must choose between two alternatives that are similar in quality but are complex and may have hidden or unknown attributes. The consumer may purchase the product on the basis of a recommendation by some nonmedia source and then attempt to support the decision by developing a positive attitude toward the brand and perhaps even developing negative feelings toward the rejected alternative(s). This reduces any *postpurchase dissonance* or anxiety the consumer may experience resulting from doubt over the purchase (as discussed in Chapter 4). Dissonance reduction involves *selective learning,* whereby the consumer seeks information that supports the choice made and avoids information that would raise doubts about the decision.

According to this model, marketers need to recognize that in some situations, attitudes develop *after* purchase, as does learning from the mass media. Ray suggests that in these situations the main effect of the mass media is not the promotion of original choice behavior and attitude change but rather the reduction of dissonance by reinforcing the wisdom of the purchase or providing supportive information. For example, the ad shown in Exhibit 5–12 reinforces consumers' decision to use a Discover Credit Card by noting that there is "nothing like it."

As with the standard learning model, this response hierarchy is likely to occur when the consumer is involved in the purchase situation; it is particularly relevant for postpurchase situations. For example, a consumer may purchase tires recommended by a friend and then develop a favorable attitude toward the company and pay close attention to its ads to reduce dissonance.

Some marketers resist this view of the response hierarchy because they can't accept the notion that the mass media have no effect on the consumer's initial purchase decision. But the model doesn't claim the mass media have no effect—just that their major impact occurs after the purchase has been made. Marketing communications planners must be aware of the need for advertising and promotion efforts not just to encourage brand selection but to reinforce choices and ensure that a purchase pattern will continue.

**The Low-Involvement Hierarchy** Perhaps the most intriguing of the three response hierarchies proposed by Ray is the **low-involvement hierarchy**, in which the receiver is viewed as passing from cognition to behavior to attitude change. This learn → do → feel sequence is thought to characterize situations of low consumer involvement in the purchase process. Ray suggests this hierarchy tends to occur when involvement in the purchase decision is low, there are minimal differences among brand alternatives, and mass-media (especially broadcast) advertising is important.

The notion of a low-involvement hierarchy is based in large part on Herbert Krugman's theory explaining the effects of television advertising.[36] Krugman wanted to find out why TV advertising produced a strong effect on brand awareness and recall but little change in consumers' attitudes toward the product. He hypothesized that TV is basically a low-involvement medium and the viewer's perceptual defenses are reduced or even absent during commercials. In a low-involvement situation, the consumer does not compare the message with previously acquired beliefs, needs, or past experiences. The commercial results in subtle changes in the consumer's knowledge structure, particularly with repeated exposure. This change in the consumer's knowledge does not result in attitude change but is related to learning something about the advertised brand, such as a brand name, ad theme, or slogan. According to Krugman, when the consumer enters a purchase situation, this information may be sufficient to trigger a purchase. The consumer will then form an attitude toward the purchased brand as a result of experience with it. Thus, in the low-involvement situation the response sequence is as follows:

Message exposure under low involvement →

Shift in cognitive structure → Purchase →

Positive or negative experience → Attitude formation

In the low-involvement hierarchy, the consumer engages in *passive learning* and *random information catching* rather than active information seeking. The advertiser must recognize that a passive, uninterested consumer may focus more on nonmessage elements such as music, characters, symbols, and slogans or jingles than actual message content. The advertiser might capitalize on this situation by developing a catchy jingle that is stored in the consumer's mind without any active cognitive processing and becomes salient when he or she enters the actual purchase situation.

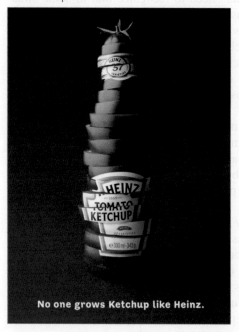

**EXHIBIT 5–13**
Heinz has been the leader in the ketchup market

No one grows Ketchup like Heinz.

Advertisers of low-involvement products also repeat simple product claims such as a key copy point or distinctive product benefit. A study by Scott Hawkins and Stephen Hoch found that under low-involvement conditions, repetition of simple product claims increased consumers' memory of and belief in those claims.[37] They concluded that advertisers of low-involvement products might find it more profitable to pursue a heavy repetition strategy than to reach larger audiences with lengthy, more detailed messages. For example, Heinz has dominated the ketchup market for over 30 years by repeatedly telling consumers that its brand is the thickest and richest. Heinz has used a variety of advertising campaigns over the years. However, they all have communicated the same basic message that Heinz is the best and most preferred brand of ketchup (Exhibit 5–13).

Low-involvement advertising appeals prevail in much of the advertising we see for frequently purchased consumer products: Wrigley's Doublemint gum invites consumers to "Double your pleasure." Bounty paper towels claim to be the "quicker picker-upper." Oscar Mayer uses the catchy jingle, "I wish I were an Oscar Mayer wiener." Each of these appeals is designed to help consumers make an association without really attempting to formulate or change an attitude.

Another popular creative strategy used by advertisers of low-involvement products is what advertising analyst Harry McMahan calls *VIP,* or *visual image personality.*[38] Advertisers often use symbols like the Pillsbury doughboy, Morris the cat, Tony the tiger, and Mr. Clean to develop visual images that will lead consumers to identify and retain ads. Eveready began using the pink bunny in ads for its Energizer batteries in 1989, and he has helped sales of the brand keep going and going for nearly 25 years. As can be seen in Exhibit 5–14, the Energizer Bunny even has his own Facebook page which has more than 265,000 fans.

## Implications of the Alternative Response Models

Advertising and consumer researchers recognize that not all response sequences and behaviors are explained adequately by either the traditional or the alternative response hierarchies. Advertising is just one source of information consumers use in learning about products, forming attitudes, and/or making purchase decisions. Consumers are likely to integrate information from advertising and other forms of

**EXHIBIT 5–14**
The Energizer Bunny is still a popular personality symbol for the brand

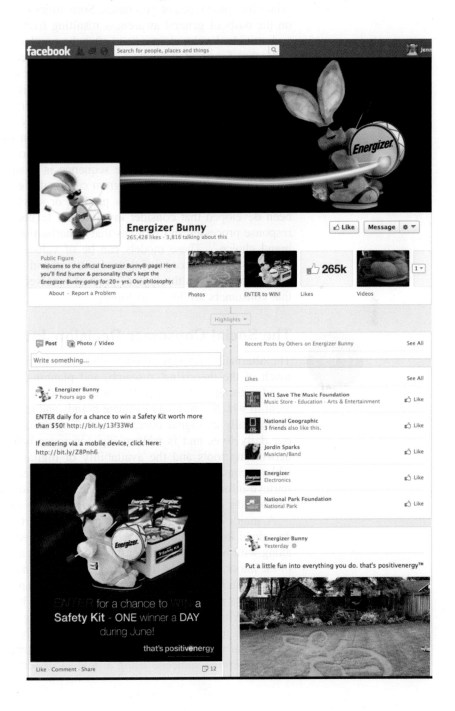

marketing communication as well as direct experience in forming judgments about a brand. For example, a study by Robert Smith found that advertising can lessen the negative effects of an unfavorable trial experience on brand evaluations when the ad is processed before the trial. However, when a negative trial experience precedes exposure to an ad, cognitive evaluations of the ad are more negative.[39] More recent research has also shown that advertising can affect consumers' objective sensory interpretation of their experiences with a brand and what they remember about it.[40]

The various response models offer an interesting perspective on the ways consumers respond to advertising and other forms of marketing communication. They also provide insight into promotional strategies marketers might pursue in different situations. A review of these alternative models of the response process shows that the traditional standard learning model does not always apply. The notion of a highly involved consumer who engages in active information processing and learning and acts on the basis of higher-order beliefs and a well-formed attitude may be inappropriate for some types of purchases. Sometimes consumers make a purchase decision on the basis of general awareness resulting from repetitive exposure to advertising, and attitude development occurs after the purchase, if at all. The role of advertising and other forms of promotion may be to induce trial, so consumers can develop brand preferences primarily on the basis of their direct experience with the product.

From a promotional planning perspective, it is important that marketers examine the communication situation for their product or service and determine which type of response process is most likely to occur. They should analyze involvement levels and product/service differentiation as well as consumers' use of various information sources and their levels of experience with the product or service. Once the manager has determined which response sequence is most likely to operate, the integrated marketing communications program can be designed to influence the response process in favor of the company's product or service. Several planning models have been developed that consider involvement levels as well as other factors including response processes and motives that underlie the attitude formation and subsequent brand choice.[41] These models can be of value to marketers as they develop IMC strategies as they recognize that advertising and other promotional tools work differently depending on the type of product involved and the decision process sequence that consumers are likely to follow.

## The Social Consumer Decision Journey

**LO 05-5**

The alternative response models discussed in the previous section have dominated much of the theorizing, research, and planning regarding how consumers respond to advertising and other IMC tools. However, over the past decade the environment in which consumers evaluate brands and make purchase decisions has changed dramatically as digital content—including social media—has become pervasive in our daily lives and is influencing consumer behavior. With the advent of social networking tools and the availability of digital devices such as smartphones and tablets, consumers are more empowered than ever before as they can access and retrieve information, connect with one another to share it, discuss products/services and brands, and interact with marketers quickly and easily.

A major study commissioned by the Advertising Research Foundation (ARF) examined how digital and social media are used in the purchase-decision process along with how and when consumers turn to them to help manage this process. One of the major findings of this study is that "consumers, in effect, are always on as they are constantly considering potential purchases and evaluating the various providers of products and service" and that they can be in both an active and passive shopping mode.[42] When they are in a "passive" shopping mode, the information and advice consumers need to make a purchase comes to them unsolicited, such as a comment on a social media site; an ad seen on a TV show, in a magazine, or on a website; or by observing someone using a product or service. At other times consumers are in an "active" shopping mode whereby they are purposefully seeking information and/or assistance so they can make informed purchase decisions with confidence. Consumers in an active shopping mode may visit the website of a company or brand, go to a search engine such as Google or Bing, go to a retail store, or have a conversation with a friend or associate (either online or in person).

Another important conclusion from this study, as well as research conducted by the McKinsey & Company's Global Digital Marketing Strategy practice group, is that consumers do not make purchase decisions in the linear manner depicted by the traditional hierarchy of effects and purchase funnel models whereby they start at the wide part of the funnel with many brands in mind and narrow them down to a final choice.[43] The research conducted by McKinsey as well as the ARF study show that consumers go through a much more iterative and less reductive process and that they can enter a purchase path at various points, depending on whether they first engage with a brand, research a product or service, or hear about a product through their social networks. Based on these findings, David Edelman and his associates at McKinsey proposed a "consumer decision journey" framework for understanding how consumers interact with companies and brands during the purchase decision process. The decision journey has four basic stages: *consider, evaluate, buy,* and *enjoy-advocate-bond.*[44] This framework views the consumer decision-making process as a winding journey with multiple feedback loops rather than a linear, single uniform path to purchase based on active shopping and influenced by marketer dominated and controlled touch points such as media advertising.

Recognizing the increasing importance and influence of social media on consumer behavior, Edelman and his colleagues expanded the consumer decision journey framework to include social media, as shown in Figure 5–6. The social consumer decision journey framework recognizes that consumers connect with large numbers of brands through digital and social media channels that are often beyond the marketers' or retailers' control, evaluate a shifting array of them, and often expand the pool before narrowing it. After a purchase, consumers may remain very engaged and publicly promote or disparage the products or services they have purchased, often through digital and social media.[45] The McKinsey group note that "social media is a unique component of the consumer decision journey: it's the only form of marketing that can touch consumers at each and every stage, from when they're pondering brands and products right through the period after a purchase, as their experience influences the brands they prefer and their potential advocacy influences others."[46] As can be seen in Figure 5–6, there are a number of ways various digital and social media tools such as YouTube, Pinterest, Twitter, Facebook, Google+, and foursquare can influence consumers at various stages of the decision journey.

The consumer decision journey framework has a number of implications for marketers as they develop their IMC programs. Edelman notes that instead of determining how to allocate spending across the various IMC tools such as various forms of media advertising, marketers should target stages in the decision journey. Marketers often spend a large percentage of their IMC budgets on advertising and sales promotion which are designed to influence consumers at the consider and buy stages. However, consumers may often be influenced more during the evaluate and enjoy-advocate-bond stages. For many consumers the most important incentive to buy may be another person's advocacy or recommendation. He notes that it is also important for marketers to focus on the portion of their budget allocated to paid media—or what is sometimes referred to as "working media spend"—and consider *owned* media that a brand controls (such as websites and Facebook fan pages) as well as *earned media* (customer-created content on blogs, forums, and social media platforms).

Some of the findings from the ARF-commissioned study also are relevant to the role of social and digital media on the consumer decision journey. This study found that consumers like to tout their effectiveness and prowess as shoppers to others, which means that marketers can leverage this desire by providing forums for consumers to share their stories and experiences with others. The study also found that

YTC 05–07

**Consumer Decision Journey**

youtube.com/10ebelch

**2 Consumer evaluates brand**
Watches YouTube video posted
by enthusiastic owner showing
the product's innovative uses

**3 Consumer buys
product**
Photographs the product
in store, posts it for
others to comment on,
and receives personal
message with coupon
from the brand

**1 Consumer considers
purchase**
Views your brand
on retailer site and
is impressed by
enthusiastic user
reviews

**6 Consumer bonds**
"Tips" friends on foursquare
after revisiting your store
to purchase again

**5 Consumer advocates
for brand**
Comments on your
representative's helpful advice
in a user forum, then "likes"
your Facebook page

**4 Consumer interacts
with brand after purchase**
"Follows" your expert on
Twitter to receive product
updates; retweets to friends

**FIGURE 5–6**

The Social Consumer
Decision Journey

much online activity occurs after products are purchased, which points to an opportunity for marketers to develop a dialogue with consumers, engage them in discussions, and deepen their loyalty and affinity for their brands. The ARF study noted that the purchase journey of consumers varies by product or service category as high-risk/involvement products having longer cycles than lower-risk/involvement products. It is also important to note that the ARF research indicates that brand perceptions and offline advertising are still important in driving consideration throughout the cycle. Thus it is important for marketers to build and maintain strong brands and be visible and pervasive throughout the decision journey. Digital and Social Media Perspective 5–2 discusses whether low-involvement products such as consumer packaged goods can be marketed through digital media.

# COGNITIVE PROCESSING OF COMMUNICATIONS

The hierarchical response models were for many years the primary focus of approaches for studying the receivers' responses to marketing communications. Attention centered on identifying relationships between specific controllable variables (such as source and message factors) and outcome or response variables (such as attention, comprehension, attitudes, and purchase intentions). This approach has been criticized on a number of fronts, including its black-box nature, since it can't explain what is causing these reactions.[47] In response to these concerns, researchers began trying to understand the nature of cognitive reactions to persuasive messages. Several approaches have been developed to examine the nature of consumers' cognitive processing of advertising messages.

| Cognitive responses | Attitudes | Purchase intent |
|---|---|---|

Exposure to advertisement → Product/message thoughts, Source-oriented thoughts, Ad execution thoughts

Brand attitudes, Attitude toward the advertisement → Purchase intention

**FIGURE 5–7**

A Model of Cognitive Response

## The Cognitive Response Approach

One of the most widely used methods for examining consumers' cognitive processing of advertising messages is assessment of their **cognitive responses**, the thoughts that occur to them while reading, viewing, and/or hearing a communication.[48] These thoughts are generally measured by having consumers write down or verbally report their reactions to a message. The assumption is that these thoughts reflect the recipient's cognitive processes or reactions and help shape ultimate acceptance or rejection of the message.

The cognitive response approach has been widely used in research by both academicians and advertising practitioners. Its focus has been to determine the types of responses evoked by an advertising message and how these responses relate to attitudes toward the ad, brand attitudes, and purchase intentions. Figure 5–7 depicts the three basic categories of cognitive responses researchers have identified—product/message, source-oriented, and ad execution thoughts—and how they may relate to attitudes and intentions.

**EXHIBIT 5–15**

Consumers often generate support arguments in response to ads for quality products

**DEEP DISASTER:**

Cherry Pie Packed Pleats.

**DEEP CLEAN:**

WHEN STAINS GET DEEP IN ULTRA TIDE GETS THEM CLEAN OUT.

**Product/Message Thoughts** The first category of thoughts comprises those directed at the product or service and/or the claims being made in the communication. Much attention has focused on two particular types of responses, counterarguments and support arguments.

**Counterarguments** are thoughts the recipient has that are opposed to the position taken in the message. For example, consider the ad for Ultra Tide shown in Exhibit 5–15. A consumer may express disbelief or disapproval of a claim made in an ad. ("I don't believe that any detergent could get that stain out!") Other consumers who see this ad may generate **support arguments**, or thoughts that affirm the claims made in the message. ("Ultra Tide looks like a really good product—I think I'll try it.")

The likelihood of counterarguing is greater when the message makes claims that oppose the receiver's beliefs. For example, a consumer viewing a commercial that attacks a favorite brand is likely to engage in counterarguing. Counterarguments relate negatively to message acceptance; the more the receiver counterargues, the less likely he or she is to accept the position advocated in the message.[49] Support arguments, on the other hand, relate positively to message acceptance. Thus, the marketer should develop ads or other promotional messages that minimize counterarguing and encourage support arguments.

**Source-Oriented Thoughts** A second category of cognitive responses is directed at the source of the communication. One of the most

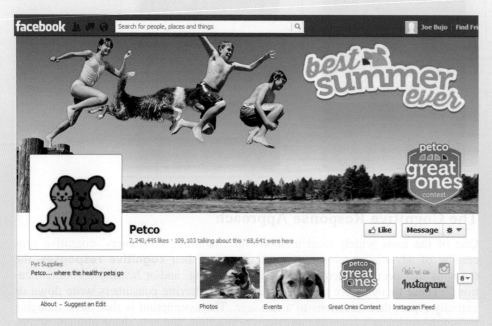

Consumer packaged goods (CPG) companies such as Unilever, Procter & Gamble, Reckitt Benckiser, Kraft Foods, and others have traditionally relied on mass-media advertising such as television, magazines, and newspapers to market their products. CPGs marketers account for about 13 percent of measured advertising spending in the United States and represent 45 of the top 100 global advertisers and 35 of the top 100 U.S. advertisers. The reliance on media advertising is not surprising, as many packaged goods are low-risk/reward types of products that are characterized by shorter purchase cycles and lower levels of involvement and in the decision-making process. CPG marketers spend a large percentage of their IMC budgets on TV and print to build and maintain brand awareness, as well as on consumer and trade promotions that provide consumers with coupons, discounts, or some other type of extra incentive to buy.

The Interactive Advertising Bureau estimates that CPG companies spent only about 5 percent of their marketing budgets on digital advertising in 2012. This low percentage is somewhat surprising as it was nearly 20 years ago that Ed Arzt, who was then CEO of Procter & Gamble, which is one of the world's largest advertising spenders, gave a speech to the American Association of Advertising Agencies warning of the disruptive potential of interactive advertising and calling for ad agencies to climb on board the train or be left behind. And while digital spending now accounts for about 10 percent of P&G's marketing spending, a similar share to that of its global rivals such as Unilever, it still lags behind traditional media such as

important types of responses in this category is **source derogations**, or negative thoughts about the spokesperson or organization making the claims. Such thoughts generally lead to a reduction in message acceptance. If consumers find a particular spokesperson annoying or untrustworthy, they are less likely to accept what this source has to say.

Of course, source-related thoughts are not always negative. Receivers who react favorably to the source generate favorable thoughts, or **source bolsters**. As you would expect, most advertisers attempt to hire spokespeople their target audience likes so as to carry this effect over to the message. Considerations involved in choosing an appropriate source or spokesperson will be discussed in Chapter 6.

**Ad Execution Thoughts** The third category of cognitive responses shown in Figure 5–7 consists of the individual's thoughts about the ad itself. Many of the thoughts receivers have when reading or viewing an ad do not concern the product and/or message claims directly. Rather, they are affective reactions representing the consumer's feelings toward the ad. These thoughts may include reactions to ad

TV and print. However, a number of industry experts predict that digital spending by CPG firms is likely to increase as they recognize that the return on investment for digital and social media may be just as good as television or print.

There are several reasons why CPG firms are beginning to embrace digital media and make them a significant part of their IMC programs. First, companies such as Nielsen and ComScore are developing measurement systems for digital display and video viewing audiences using some the same metrics that are available for television and which CPG marketers and their agencies are accustomed to using. A second reason is the advanced analytics that are now available from digital media that allow CPG marketers, many of whom are highly data-driven, to identify target audiences based on their purchase or other behavior. For example, in 2012 Facebook introduced a "Customer Audiences" program aimed at CPG marketers that allows them to upload their customer relationship management (CRM) databases and better target messages to their consumers on the social media site. In early 2013 Facebook entered into a partnership with several data mining firms to target ads to users based on their off-line shopping habits and recent in-store purchases.

CPG markets are also recognizing the value of using digital and social media to build brand advocacy and as valuable tools for reaching consumers when they are at the consideration stage of the purchase process rather than just as a way of building brand awareness. Marketers are also realizing that the value of social media goes beyond their role as media vehicles; they also can be used as market research tools to gain insights from social monitoring, listening, and analysis of conversations about products and brands. You might recall from Chapter 1 how Gatorade has set up its Mission Control center to monitor comments and conversations about the brand on social media.

CPG marketers are also recognizing the value of integrating digital media with traditional media. While many marketers view the use of digital media as a way to extend the reach and frequency of their off-line advertising, others recognize that the two can be complementary, not just in terms of reaching additional consumers but as a way to engage consumers in different ways. Social media in particular are a way for CPG marketers to get consumers to endorse their brands to their friends and associates.

Another reason why CPG marketers are paying more attention to digital media is that they are conduits for price promotions. The average CPG company spends around two-thirds of its marketing budget on sales promotion, with much of this money going to trade promotions. Traditionally print has been the medium of choice for communicating price and promotional messages through freestanding inserts (FSIs) in newspapers as well as circulars. However, with the decline in newspaper readership, CPG marketers are looking for other ways to deliver promotional offers to bargain-minded consumers. Many are using social media sites such as Facebook and Twitter as a platform to offer promotional incentives to consumers and also as a way to engage consumers through contests and other types of promotions.

Traditional media advertising is likely to continue to be the key component of the IMC program for most packaged goods marketers. However, CPG marketing and brand managers are learning from their counterparts in automotive, retail, telecom, travel, and other industries, with whom they often share best practices, about the value and return on investment (ROI) potential of digital and social media. Thus, it is very likely that the role of digital will become an increasingly important part of the IMC program for companies selling brands across the various CPG categories.

Sources: Cotton Delo, "Facebook Inks Deal with Acxiom, Epsilon, and Others to Show Ads Based on Shopping Habits," *Advertising Age*, February 27, 2013, http://adage.com/print/240054; Jack Neff, "Can Facebook Crack the CPG Market? With CPG Summit, Social Network Seeks to Prove It Speaks the Language," *Advertising Age*, January 29, 2013, http://adage.com/print/239477; Jack Neff, "Does Digital Sell Soap?," *Advertising Age*, June 18, 2012, pp. 120–21.

execution factors such as the creativity of the ad, the quality of the visual effects, colors, and voice tones. **Ad execution–related thoughts** can be either favorable or unfavorable. They are important because of their effect on attitudes toward the advertisement as well as the brand.

Much attention has focused on consumers' affective reactions to ads, especially TV commercials.[50] **Attitude toward the ad** (A → ad) represents the receivers' feelings of favorability or unfavorability toward the ad. Advertisers are interested in consumers' reactions to the ad because they know that affective reactions are an important determinant of advertising effectiveness, since these reactions may be transferred to the brand itself or directly influence purchase intentions. One study found that people who enjoy a commercial are twice as likely as those who are neutral toward it to be convinced that the brand is the best.[51]

Consumers' feelings about the ad may be just as important as their attitudes toward the brand (if not more so) in determining an ad's effectiveness.[52] The importance of affective reactions and feelings generated by the ad depends on several factors, among them the nature of the ad and the type of processing engaged in by the receiver.[53] Many advertisers now use emotional ads designed to evoke feelings

# IMC Perspective 5-1 > > >

## Do Men and Women Process Sexy Ads Differently?

Advertisers are always looking for ways to break through the clutter of competing messages in various media such as television and magazines and draw attention to their ads. One technique sometimes used by marketers to attract consumers' attention and interest is to utilize sexually themed ads. The use of sexual appeals is quite common in the United States as well as many other countries where the societies are more liberal and accepting of them. In fact, social critic John Lahr notes that "Society drives people crazy with lust and calls it advertising."

Sexual appeals can vary in terms of their nature, content, and purpose. At one end of the spectrum are ads using decorative models whose primary role is to adorn the visual portion of the message and help attract the attention of the viewer or reader. These types of ads use physically attractive models as well as nudity or partial nudity and the model really serves no functional purpose other than to attract attention and interest. These types of appeals are often used in ads for automobiles, beer, and liquor although they are prevalent for other types of products and services as well. Of course they are also used for products where the sexual attractiveness of the model is relevant as the ad is being used to help sell a product that may have sexual connotations such as clothing, fragrances, and lingerie. At the other end of the spectrum are ads that use overt sexuality and are sexually provocative or suggestive. A number of marketers use ads that are sexually explicit and very risqué based on an assumption that these messages will attract the attention and interest of consumers and can create an image that may help sell their brands.

There is considerable debate as to whether sexual appeals, whether subtle or overt, are effective and can help sell a product. Numerous studies have been conducted by academicians as well as advertising practitioners regarding the impact of sexual messages. The findings from these studies generally show that the use of sex and nudity does increase attention to the ad but may distract consumers from attending to the brand name or advertising message. Most of these studies show consumers ads using sexual appeals and then measure their reactions by having them provide various types of cognitive and affective responses. However, a recent study conducted by an advertising research company, MediaAnalyzer Software & Research, used a different and very interesting approach to explore how men and women visually process sexually themed ads and what effect this processing might have on the ads' effectiveness.

MediaAnalyzer used its AttentionTracking software to follow the visual pattern of consumers as they looked at print ads, one sexual and one nonsexual, from each of five product categories, including cigarettes, credit cards, jeans, shoes, and liquor. The software has a user move his or her computer mouse over the ad to indicate the part of the ad where he or she is looking. The company used data from the visual test to determine respondents' viewing patterns (shown by the arrows) and the percentage of time spent viewing each part of the ad.

The results of the visual tests found, as might be expected, that men tend to focus on an ad's sexual imagery (breast, legs, skin), which draws their attention away from

and affective reactions as the basis of their creative strategy. The success of this strategy depends in part on the consumers' involvement with the brand and their likelihood of attending to and processing the message. Another way marketers try to get consumers to attend to their advertising is by using sexual imagery in the visual portion of the ad. IMC Perspective 5-1 discusses the results of an interesting study that compared visual processing of ads using sexual imagery for men versus women.

We end our analysis of the receiver by examining a model that integrates some of the factors that may account for different types and levels of cognitive processing of a message.

## The Elaboration Likelihood Model

Differences in the ways consumers process and respond to persuasive messages are addressed in the **elaboration likelihood model (ELM)** of persuasion, shown in Figure 5–8.[54] The ELM was devised by Richard Petty and John Cacioppo to explain the process by which persuasive communications (such as ads) lead to persuasion by influencing *attitudes*. According to this model, the attitude formation or change process depends on the amount and nature of *elaboration*, or processing, of relevant information that occurs in response to a persuasive message. High elaboration means the receiver engages in careful consideration, thinking, and evaluation of the other elements of the ad such as the logo, product shot, or headline. This visual pattern may explain why men's brand recall was lower for sexual ads than for the nonsexual ones. An average of 19.8 percent recalled the correct brand/product for the nonsexual ads versus only 9.8 percent for the sexual ads. MediaAnalyzer researchers call this the "vampire effect" as strong sexual imagery sucks up a lot of the attention that would have otherwise been spent on the product-related components of the advertisement. A somewhat different pattern of results was found for women

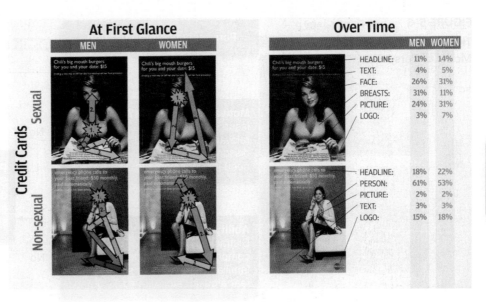

| At First Glance | | | Over Time | | |
|---|---|---|---|---|---|
| | MEN | WOMEN | | MEN | WOMEN |
| Sexual | | | HEADLINE: | 11% | 14% |
| | | | TEXT: | 4% | 5% |
| | | | FACE: | 26% | 31% |
| | | | BREASTS: | 31% | 11% |
| | | | PICTURE: | 24% | 31% |
| | | | LOGO: | 3% | 7% |
| Non-sexual | | | HEADLINE: | 18% | 22% |
| | | | PERSON: | 61% | 53% |
| | | | PICTURE: | 2% | 2% |
| | | | TEXT: | 3% | 3% |
| | | | LOGO: | 15% | 18% |

as they tend to avoid looking at the sexual imagery, although their brand recall was also lower for the sexual (10.8 percent) versus the nonsexual ads (22.8 percent). MediaAnalyzer researchers hypothesized that this might be the result of a general numbing effect that sexual stimuli have on the brain.

An example of the visual processing differences between men and women can be seen in the result found for the MasterCard ads shown above. Men devoted a lot of their processing time on the sexual imagery elements of the ad, starting with the model's breasts, then moving either to her face above or the hamburger below, largely ignoring any of the text copy in the ad. Women, however, mostly avoided the sexual imagery in the ad. The differences in visual processing were not as great for the nonsexual ad, although the viewing paths did diverge. Men explored the model's body first, including her legs, before eventually reaching the logo

while women almost immediately focused on the text elements of the ads.

MediaAnalyzer also measured the effectiveness of the sexual versus nonsexual ads using criteria such as liking the ad, product liking, and purchase intentions. Men indicated that they liked the sexual ads more and would be more likely to buy these products while women rated the sexual ads lower on all three criteria. Marketers are likely to continue to use sexual appeals in their advertisements. However, the results of the MediaAnalyzer study suggest that these ads may be providing men in particular with eye candy rather than an effective advertising message.

Source: Tim Nudd, "Does Sex Really Sell?" *Adweek*, October 17, 2005, pp. 14–17; Tom Reichart, "Sex in Advertising Research: A Review of Content, Effects, and Functions of Sexual Information in Consumer Advertising," *Annual Review of Sex Research* 13 (2002), pp. 242–74.

information or arguments contained in the message. Low elaboration occurs when the receiver does not engage in active information processing or thinking but rather makes inferences about the position being advocated in the message on the basis of simple positive or negative cues.

The ELM shows that elaboration likelihood is a function of two elements, motivation and ability to process the message. *Motivation* to process the message depends on such factors as involvement, personal relevance, and individuals' needs and arousal levels. *Ability* depends on the individual's knowledge, intellectual capacity, and opportunity to process the message. For example, an individual viewing a humorous commercial or one containing an attractive model may be distracted from processing the information about the product.

According to the ELM, there are two basic routes to persuasion or attitude change. Under the **central route to persuasion**, the receiver is viewed as a very active, involved participant in the communication process whose ability and motivation to attend, comprehend, and evaluate messages are high. When central processing of an advertising message occurs, the consumer pays close attention to message content and scrutinizes the message arguments. A high level of cognitive response activity or processing occurs, and the ad's ability to persuade the receiver depends primarily on the receiver's evaluation of the quality of the arguments presented. Predominantly

**FIGURE 5–8**

The Elaboration Likelihood
Model of Persuasion

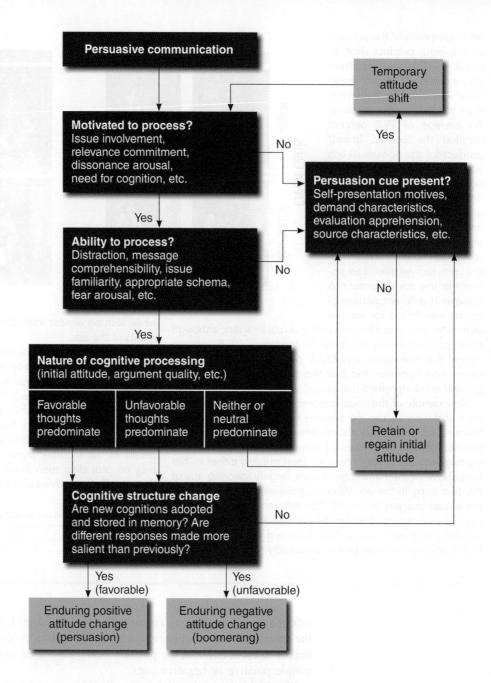

favorable cognitive responses (support arguments and source bolsters) lead to favorable changes in cognitive structure, which lead to positive attitude change, or persuasion.

Conversely, if the cognitive processing is predominantly unfavorable and results in counterarguments and/or source derogations, the changes in cognitive structure are unfavorable and *boomerang,* or result in negative attitude change. Attitude change that occurs through central processing is relatively enduring and should resist subsequent efforts to change it.

Under the **peripheral route to persuasion,** shown on the right side of Figure 5–8, the receiver is viewed as lacking the motivation or ability to process information and is not likely to engage in detailed cognitive processing. Rather than evaluating the information presented in the message, the receiver relies on peripheral cues that may be incidental to the main arguments. The receiver's reaction to the message depends on how he or she evaluates these peripheral cues.

**EXHIBIT 5–16**

This ad contains peripheral cues, most notably a celebrity endorser

**YTC 05–08**

**Peak**

youtube.com/10ebelch

The consumer may use several types of peripheral cues or cognitive shortcuts rather than carefully evaluating the message arguments presented in an advertisement.[55] Favorable attitudes may be formed if the endorser in the ad is viewed as an expert or is attractive and/or likable or if the consumer likes certain executional aspects of the ad such as the way it is made, the music, or the imagery. Notice how the ad in Exhibit 5–16 for Peak Long Life antifreeze contains several positive peripheral cues, including an attractive and highly relevant celebrity endorser (race car driver Danica Patrick) and appealing visual imagery that is consistent with the brand positioning. These cues might help consumers form a positive attitude toward the brand even if they do not process the message portion of the ad.

Peripheral cues can also lead to rejection of a message. For example, ads that advocate extreme positions, use endorsers who are not well liked or have credibility problems, or are not executed well (such as low-budget ads for local retailers) may be rejected without any consideration of their information or message arguments. As shown in Figure 5–8, the ELM views attitudes resulting from peripheral processing as temporary. So favorable attitudes must be maintained by continual exposure to the peripheral cues, such as through repetitive advertising.

**Implications of the ELM** The elaboration likelihood model has important implications for marketing communications, particularly with respect to involvement. For example, if the involvement level of consumers in the target audience is high, an ad or sales presentation should contain strong arguments that are difficult for the message recipient to refute or counterargue. If the involvement level of the target audience is low, peripheral cues may be more important than detailed message arguments.

An interesting test of the ELM showed that the effectiveness of a celebrity endorser in an ad depends on the receiver's involvement level.[56] When involvement was low, a celebrity endorser had a significant effect on attitudes. When the receiver's involvement was high, however, the use of a celebrity had no effect on brand attitudes; the quality of the arguments used in the ad was more important.

The explanation given for these findings was that a celebrity may serve as a peripheral cue in the low-involvement situation, allowing the receiver to develop favorable attitudes based on feelings toward the source rather than engaging in extensive processing of the message. A highly involved consumer, however, engages in more detailed central processing of the message content. The quality of the message becomes more important than the identity of the endorser.

The ELM suggests that the most effective type of message depends on the route to persuasion the consumer follows. Many marketers recognize that involvement levels are low for their product categories and consumers are not motivated to process advertising messages in any detail. That's why marketers of low-involvement products often rely on creative tactics that emphasize peripheral cues and use repetitive advertising to create and maintain favorable attitudes toward their brand.

# SUMMARIZING THE RESPONSE PROCESS AND THE EFFECTS OF ADVERTISING

As you have seen from our analysis of the receiver, the process consumers go through in responding to marketing communications can be viewed from a number of perspectives. Vakratsas and Ambler recently reviewed more than 250 journal articles and books in an effort to better understand how advertising works and affects the consumer.[57] On the basis of their review of these studies, they concluded that

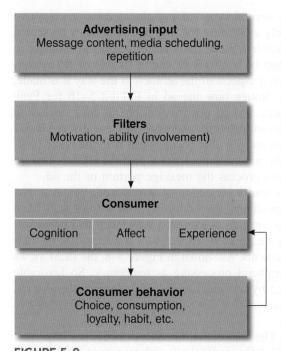

**Advertising input**
Message content, media scheduling,
repetition

**Filters**
Motivation, ability (involvement)

**Consumer**

| Cognition | Affect | Experience |
|-----------|--------|------------|

**Consumer behavior**
Choice, consumption,
loyalty, habit, etc.

**FIGURE 5–9**

A Framework for Studying
How Advertising Works

although effects hierarchies have been actively employed for nearly 100 years, there is little support for the concept of a hierarchy of effects in the sense of temporal sequence. They note that in trying to understand the response process and the manner in which advertising works, there are three critical intermediate effects between advertising and purchase (Figure 5–9). These include *cognition,* the "thinking" dimension of a person's response; *affect,* the "feeling" dimension; and *experience,* which is a feedback dimension based on the outcomes of product purchasing and usage. They conclude that individual responses to advertising are mediated or filtered by factors such as motivation and ability to process information, which can radically alter or change the individual's response to advertising. They suggest that the effects of advertising should be evaluated using these three dimensions, with some intermediate variables being more important than others, depending on factors such as the product category, stage of the product life cycle, target audience, competition, and impact of other marketing-mix components.

Other researchers have been critical of the hierarchy models as well. For example, Hall argues that advertisers need to move away from explicit and implicit reliance on hierarchical models of advertising effects and develop models that place affect and experience at the center of the advertising process.[58] The implication of these criticisms is that marketers should focus on cognition, affect, and experience as critical variables that advertising may affect. However, they should not assume a particular sequence of responses but, rather, engage in research and analysis to better understand how advertising and other forms of promotion may affect these intermediate variables in various product/market situations.

While a number of issues and concerns regarding hierarchy of effects models have been noted, many believe that they are of value to advertising practice and research. For example, Thomas Barry contends that despite their limitations, hierarchical models do help predict behavior. He notes that these models also provide insight into whether advertising strategies need to focus on impacting cognition, affect, and/or behavior based on audience or segmentation experiences and they provide valuable planning, training, and conceptual frameworks.[59]

Those responsible for planning the IMC program need to learn as much as possible about their target audience and how it may respond to advertising, along with other forms of marketing communication. For example, William Weilbacher has noted that marketing communications programs include more than just advertising.[60] Consumers are continually immersed in brand-sponsored communications that also include public relations, a broad range of sales promotion activities, social media, direct marketing, event sponsorships, movie and TV show product placements, and other forms of marketing communication. He argues that hierarchy models must move beyond just explaining the effects of advertising and consider how, and with what effects, consumers synthesize information from all the various integrated marketing communications activities for a brand. As we have seen from the discussion of the social consumer decision journey, information from the numerous forms of social media and other digital sources is adding to the number of factors that influence the consumer response process and decision making.

The various models discussed in this chapter are important as they present the basic elements of communication and provide insight into how consumers process and respond to advertising and other IMC tools. It is vital to understand the communication process as it provides a foundation for studying and evaluating integrated marketing communications. Those involved in various aspects of IMC find that understanding the communication process helps them make better decisions in planning, implementing, and evaluating their marketing communication programs.

## Summary

The function of all elements of the IMC program is to communicate, so promotional planners must understand the communication process. This process can be very complex; successful marketing communications depend on a number of factors, including the nature of the message, the audience's interpretation of it, and the environment in which it is received. For effective communication to occur, the sender must encode a message in such a way that it will be decoded by the receiver in the intended manner. Feedback from the receiver helps the sender determine whether proper decoding has occurred or whether noise has interfered with the communication process.

Nonpersonal channels of communication are those that carry a message without direct, interpersonal contact between the sender and receiver and are generally referred to as the mass media. Personal channels involve direct communication between two or more persons and can occur through interpersonal contact (face-to-face) or via other methods such as e-mail or through social media. Members of one's social networks such as friends, neighbors, associates, co-workers, or family members are also personal channels of communication and represent word-of-mouth (WOM) influence, which can be a very powerful source of information. Marketers often try to generate WOM through viral marketing, which refers to the act of propagating marketing-relevant messages through the help and cooperation of individual consumers.

Promotional planning begins with the receiver or target audience, as marketers must understand how the audience is likely to respond to various sources of communication or types of messages. For promotional planning, the receiver can be analyzed with respect to both its composition (i.e., individual, group, or mass audiences) and the response process it goes through. A number of models of the response process have been developed, including the AIDA, hierarchy of effects, innovation adoption, and information processing model. Different orderings of the traditional response hierarchy include the standard learning, dissonance/attribution, and low-involvement models.

The environment in which consumers evaluate brands and make purchase decisions has changed dramatically as digital content—including social media—has become pervasive in our daily lives and is influencing consumer behavior. The social consumer decision journey framework recognized that consumers can enter the purchase path at various points, depending on whether they first engage with a brand, research a product or service, or hear about it through their social networks.

The cognitive response approach examines the thoughts evoked by a message and how they shape the receiver's ultimate acceptance or rejection of the communication. The elaboration likelihood model of attitude formation and change recognizes two forms of message processing, the central and peripheral routes to persuasion, which are a function of the receiver's motivation and ability to process a message. There are three critical intermediate effects between advertising and purchase, including cognition, affect, and experience. Those responsible for planning the IMC program should learn as much as possible about their target audience and how it may respond to advertising and other forms of marketing communications.

## Key Terms

communication p. 143
source p. 145
encoding p. 146
message p. 147
channel p. 147
mass media p. 147
word-of-mouth (WOM) p. 148
buzz marketing p. 148
viral marketing p. 149
seeding p. 150
receiver p. 153
decoding p. 153

field of experience p. 153
noise p. 155
response p. 156
feedback p. 156
AIDA model p. 158
hierarchy of effects model p. 158
innovation adoption model p. 159
information processing model p. 160
standard learning model p. 162
dissonance/attribution model p. 163
low-involvement hierarchy p. 164
cognitive responses p. 169

counterarguments p. 169
support arguments p. 169
source derogations p. 170
source bolsters p. 170
ad execution–related thoughts p. 171
attitude toward the ad p. 171
elaboration likelihood model (ELM) p. 172
central route to persuasion p. 173
peripheral route to persuasion p. 174

## Discussion Questions

**1.** The chapter opener discussed the Fiesta Movement social media campaign used by Ford to launch its new Fiesta subcompact car in the U.S. market. Discuss the pros and cons of this program and assess the amount of risk Ford took in allowing the agents to use social media to communicate with their friends about the car. (LO1, 2)

**2.** Do you think it was a good strategy for Ford to use the Fiesta Movement again in 2013 as part of its IMC program for the redesigned Fiesta? Why or why not? (LO1, 2)

**3.** Global Perspective 5–1 discusses the problems marketers can encounter when developing advertising messages in different languages and for different cultures.

Discuss some of the ways marketers can deal with this problem and avoid mistranslations. (LO1)

4. What is meant by encoding? Discuss how encoding differs for radio versus television commercials as well as for print ads. (LO2)

5. Explain the concept of viral marketing and how it relates to word-of-mouth communication. Find an example of a company that used viral marketing successfully and one that encountered problems when using this technique. (LO3)

6. Do you think a company that recruits consumers to participate in an online brand community such as Procter & Gamble's Vocalpoint programs should encourage participants to disclose their association with the organization when discussing a product with others? Why or why not? (LO2)

7. Discuss the characteristics of early digital adopters and the role they play in the introduction of a new high-technology product. Find an example of an ad or blog for a new high-tech product that is targeting early adopters and analyze its effort to do so. (LO4)

8. Digital and Social Media Perspective 5–1 discusses the age bias that exists in advertising and digital agencies against older people, who may not be as digitally savvy as the younger generation. Do you think it is acceptable for agencies to favor younger people in the hiring process? How might an older person address the age bias problem? (LO1, 3)

9. Discuss how the implications of the social consumer decision journey framework might differ for a marketer of a high-involvement product such as a tablet computer versus a company marketing a low-involvement product such as soft drinks or paper towels. (LO5)

10. IMC Perspective 5–1 discusses the results of a study showing how men and women differ in their visual processing of sexual imagery in print ads. On the basis of these findings, what suggestions would you make to a marketer of hard liquor who is considering using a revealing photo of an attractive model in a print ad for the company's product? Would your answer differ for the marketer of a personal computer? (LO6)

11. Explain what is meant by a central versus peripheral route to persuasion and the factors that might determine when each might be used by consumers in response to an advertisement or other form of marketing communication. (LO6)

Nike stood by Woods as surveys showed that attitudes toward him remained favorable among its target demographic of male golfers.

Three years later, Nike faced another major problem when seven-time Tour de France winner Lance Armstrong finally admitted to the use of performance-enhancing drugs. While the company stood by Armstrong throughout a decade of allegations that the cyclist used PEDs throughout his career, the evidence eventually became too overwhelming and Nike finally recognized that it could no longer afford to be associated with him. Armstrong also lost an estimated $70 million in endorsement deals with other companies, including Oakley, UPS, Anheuser-Busch InBev, Trek, Honey Stinger, 24 Hour Fitness, RadioShack, Giro, and FRS.

While the storm surrounding Lance Armstrong was still playing out in the media, Nike ran into another problem in early 2013 when South African Paralympian Oscar Pistorius was charged with shooting to death his girlfriend. Nicknamed the "Blade Runner" for racing on carbon-fiber artificial legs, Pistorius had made history a few months earlier at the 2012 London Olympics by becoming the first double-leg amputee to participate in the games. Media coverage of the tragedy included mentions of the fact that Nike had been running an ad with photos showing Pistorius coming out of the starting blocks and copy that read "I am the bullet in the chamber." Adding to the controversy was the dispute over gun control raging in the United States and debate over how far advertisers should go when using weaponry-related language or images in their ads.

Some marketing experts noted that the problems Nike has encountered with endorsers is not surprising given that they have so many athletes under contract around the globe, including the superstars in most sports. They also note that Nike has a policy of standing by its athlete endorsers—except in the most extreme cases—and the brand is strong enough to withstand these setbacks. While problems with endorsers may not do too much damage to larger companies that have a stable of celebrities endorsing their products, the effects can be very damaging to smaller companies whose brand is closely tied to, and often defined by, an athlete endorser.

In an age when athletes and other celebrities have a myriad of platforms on which to speak such as Facebook and Twitter and the media are dedicating more resources than ever toward uncovering their transgressions, what can companies do to protect themselves? Aside from language in the contract barring such behavior, the simplest answer is—very little. No matter how much money a company pays endorsers, it cannot monitor them around the clock. Instead, brands must be very selective in selecting endorsers and in how much they pay them. Or as one agency executive suggests, marketers can go back to basics and hire real, credible experts and let the product be the star rather the athletes. It is an interesting suggestion, but it is very unlikely that Nike or other companies will just do it.

Sources: Gabriel Beltrone, "Nike's Scandal Woes Just a Numbers Game," *Adweek*, February 17, 2013, www.adweek.com/news/advertising-branding/nikes-scandal-woes-just-numbers-game-147359; Noreen O'Leary, "Other Lance Armstrong Sponsors Follow Nike," *Adweek*, October 17, 2012, www.adweek.com/news/144522; Jeremy Mullman, "For Nike, the Tiger Woods Brand Was Too Big to Fail," *Advertising Age*, April 12, 2010, pp. 1, 21; Jack Neff, "Tiger Woods' Pitchman Days Are Far from Over, Study Says," *Advertising Age*, March 17, 2010, http://adage.com/print?article_id=142835; Emily Bryson, "Subway Puts Phelps Back in Its Advertising Pool," *Advertising Age*, July 2, 2009, http://adage.com/print/137736.

**YTC** 06–01

**Athletes as Endorsers**

youtube.com/10ebelch

In this chapter, we analyze the major variables in the communication system: the source, the message, and the channel. We examine the characteristics of sources, how they influence reactions to promotional messages, and why one type of communicator is more effective than another. We then focus on the message itself and how structure and type of appeal influence its effectiveness. Finally, we consider how factors related to the channel or medium affect the communication process.

# PROMOTIONAL PLANNING THROUGH THE PERSUASION MATRIX

LO 06-1

To develop an effective advertising and promotional campaign, a firm must select the right spokesperson to deliver a compelling message through appropriate channels or media. Source, message, and channel factors are controllable elements in the communications model. The **persuasion matrix** (Figure 6–1) helps marketers see

# 6 Source, Message, and Channel Factors

## ARE ATHLETE ENDORSERS WORTH THE RISK?

Companies have been using popular athletes to endorse their products and services and serve as advertising pitchmen for years. Marketers realize the value of using athletes who are recognized and often admired by their target audience as a way to draw attention to their advertising messages. While sports stars are also frequently used to promote athletic products such as shoes, apparel, and sports equipment, the popularity of high-profile athletes often transcends sports and they are used to endorse a variety of other products and services, including cars, fast food, soft drinks, clothing, airlines, watches, and consumer electronics. For example, watch companies such as Rolex, Omega, and TAG Heuer use high-profile athletes such as Tiger Woods, Maria Sharapova, Lindsey Vonn, Roger Federer, and other sports icons as brand ambassadors while Samsung has used NBA star LeBron James in ads for its Galaxy smartphones.

There are a number of reasons why marketers use athletes to pitch their products. Consumers are likely to see athletes as experts who can reassure them about the quality of an athletic product or brand, particularly when it is perceived as being related to the athlete's performance level. Another reason is that many athletes achieve celebrity status because of their popularity and sports fans admire, and often idolize, them and view the use of a brand they endorse as a way of identifying with them. Avid sports fans often engage in a psychological process known as BIRGing, or "basking in reflective glory," whereby they associate themselves with successful others such that another's success becomes their own.

But what happens when a controversy arises regarding an athlete and how might it affect companies or brands he or she is endorsing and closely aligned with? Over the past decade there have been numerous examples of athletes running into problems in their personal lives, which creates problems for the companies whose brands they are endorsing. For example, superstar swimmer Michael Phelps, who won seven gold medals in the 2008 Olympic Games, lost a lucrative endorsement deal with cereal company Kellogg after a few months when a British tabloid published photos of him inhaling from a bong at a party. However, several companies decided to stand by him including sandwich chain Subway, Visa, and Speedo. Subway had just signed Phelps to a multiyear endorsement deal and delayed its campaign a few months, but its decision to retain him paid off. Phelps became the most decorated Olympic athlete ever with his performance at the 2012 Olympic Games in London, and he has been an integral part of Subway's IMC campaign which positions the chain as the "official training restaurant of athletes everywhere."

One company that has had a string of controversies surrounding its endorsers is Nike, which pays out an estimated $500 million in endorsement fees each year. In 2003 NBA superstar Kobe Bryant was charged with sexual assault, and even though the charges against him were dropped, his image as an endorser was damaged. In 2007 NFL quarterback Michael Vick was charged with sponsoring and participating in dogfighting and Nike subsequently dropped him (along with every other sponsor Vick had amassed to that point in his career) and canceled the release of the Air Zoom Vick V football shoe. Vick had become the face of Nike's football division and was also paid $100 million to sign with the company just a few years earlier. In late 2009 the company ran into another problem when professional golfer Tiger Woods was involved in a car accident outside his home following an argument with his wife. The intense media scrutiny of his personal life that followed led to revelations that the superstar, who was married with two young children, had been involved in numerous extramarital affairs. Nike had built the company's golf division around Woods and he single-handedly helped make Nike one of the fastest-growing brands in the industry.

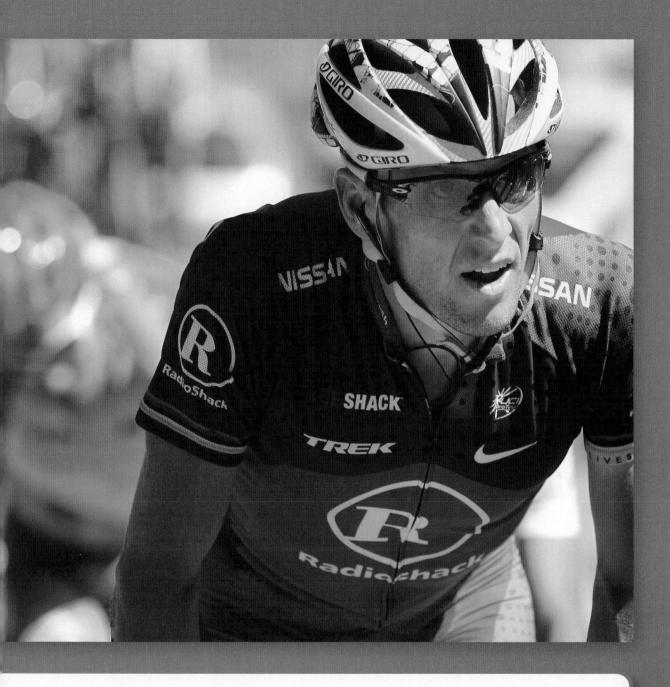

## LEARNING OBJECTIVES

**LO1** To study the major variables in the communication system and how they influence consumers' processing of promotional messages.

**LO2** To examine the considerations involved in selecting a source or communicator of a promotional message.

**LO3** To examine different types of message structures and appeals that can be used to develop a promotional message.

**LO4** To consider how the channel or medium used to deliver a promotional message influences the communication process.

| Dependent variables: Steps in being persuaded | Independent variables: The communication components | | | | |
|---|---|---|---|---|---|
| | Source | Message | Channel | Receiver | Destination |
| Message presentation | | | (2) | | |
| Attention | (4) | | | | |
| Comprehension | | | | (1) | |
| Yielding | | (3) | | | |
| Retention | | | | | |
| Behavior | | | | | |

**FIGURE 6–1**

The Persuasion Matrix

how each controllable element interacts with the consumer's response process.[1] The matrix has two sets of variables. *Independent variables* are the controllable components of the communication process, outlined in Chapter 5; *dependent variables* are the steps a receiver goes through in being persuaded. Marketers can choose the person or source who delivers the message, the type of message appeal used, and the channel or medium. And although they can't control the receiver, they can select their target audience. The destination variable is included because the initial message recipient may pass on information to others, such as friends or associates, through word of mouth.

Promotional planners need to know how decisions about each independent variable influence the stages of the response hierarchy so that they don't enhance one stage at the expense of another. A humorous message may gain attention but result in decreased comprehension if consumers fail to process its content. Many ads that use humor, sexual appeals, or celebrities capture consumers' attention but result in poor recall of the brand name or message. The following examples, which correspond to the numbers in Figure 6–1, illustrate decisions that can be evaluated with the persuasion matrix.

1. *Receiver/comprehension: Can the receiver comprehend the ad?* Marketers must know their target market to make their messages clear and understandable. A less educated person may have more difficulty interpreting a complicated message. Jargon may be unfamiliar to some receivers. The more marketers know about the target market, the more they see which words, symbols, and expressions their customers understand.

2. *Channel/presentation: Which media will increase presentation?* A popular prime-time-TV show such as *The Big Bang Theory* is seen by as many as 18 million people each week while magazines such as *Time* and *People* reach over 4 million readers with each weekly publication and millions more through their digital editions. But the important point is how well a media vehicle reaches the marketer's target audience. A show such *as Keeping Up With the Kardashians,* which appears on the E! cable network, reaches around 3 million viewers each week and its audience primarily consists of young men and women

between the ages of 18 and 24 who are very fashion conscious and technically savvy—a group that is highly coveted by many advertisers as they are prime prospects for clothing fashion, consumer electronics, and many other products.[2]

3. *Message/yielding: What type of message will create favorable attitudes or feelings?* Marketers generally try to create agreeable messages that lead to positive feelings toward the product or service. Humorous messages often put consumers in a good mood and evoke positive feelings that may become associated with the brand being advertised. Music adds emotion that makes consumers more receptive to the message. Many advertisers use explicit sexual appeals designed to arouse consumers or suggest they can enhance their attractiveness to the opposite sex. Some marketers compare their brands to the competition.

4. *Source/attention: Who will be effective in getting consumers' attention?* The large number of ads we are bombarded with every day makes it difficult for advertisers to break through the clutter. Marketers deal with this problem by using sources who will attract the target audience's attention—actors, athletes, rock stars, or attractive models.

# SOURCE FACTORS

LO 06-2

The source component is a multifaceted concept. When Tiger Woods appears in a commercial for Nike, is the source Woods himself, the company, or some combination of the two? And, of course, consumers get information from friends, relatives, and neighbors; in fact, personal sources may be the most influential factor in a purchase decision. Word-of-mouth information transmitted from one individual to another is often perceived as more reliable and trustworthy than that received through more formal marketing channels such as advertising. As was discussed in Chapter 5, marketers are using buzz and stealth marketing methods to generate favorable word-of-mouth discussion and recommendations for their products and services.[3]

We use the term **source** to mean the person involved in communicating a marketing message, either directly or indirectly. A *direct source* is a spokesperson who delivers a message and/or endorses a product or service, like country music star Miranda Lambert who appears in an ad that is part of the breakfast project campaign sponsored by the Milk Processor Education Program that encourages people to eat a nutritious breakfast that includes milk (Exhibit 6–1). An *indirect source,* say, a model, doesn't actually deliver a message but draws attention to and/or enhances the appearance of the ad. Some ads use neither a direct nor an indirect source; the source is the organization with the message to communicate. Since most research focuses on individuals as a message source, our examination of source factors follows this approach.

**EXHIBIT 6–1**

Singer Miranda Lambert endorses milk as part of "The Breakfast Project" campaign.

Companies are very careful when selecting individuals to deliver their selling messages. Many firms spend huge sums of money for a specific person to endorse their product or company. They also spend millions recruiting, selecting, and training salespeople to represent the company and deliver sales presentations. They recognize that the characteristics of the source affect the sales and advertising message.

Marketers try to select individuals whose traits will maximize message influence. The source may be knowledgeable, popular, and/or physically attractive; typify the target audience; or have the power to reward or punish the receiver in some manner. Herbert Kelman developed three basic categories of source attributes: credibility, attractiveness, and power.[4] Each influences the recipient's attitude or behavior through a different process (see Figure 6–2).

FIGURE 6–2

Source Attributes and
Receiver Processing Modes

| Source attribute | Process |
|---|---|
| Credibility | Internalization |
| Attractiveness | Identification |
| Power | Compliance |

## Source Credibility

**Credibility** is the extent to which the recipient sees the source as having relevant knowledge, skill, or experience and trusts the source to give unbiased, objective information. There are two important dimensions to credibility, expertise and trustworthiness.

A communicator seen as knowledgeable—someone with expertise—is more persuasive than one with less expertise. But the source also has to be trustworthy—honest, ethical, and believable. The influence of a knowledgeable source will be lessened if audience members think he or she is biased or has underlying personal motives for advocating a position (such as being paid to endorse a product).

One of the most reliable effects found in communications research is that expert and/or trustworthy sources are more persuasive than sources who are less expert or trustworthy.[5] Information from a credible source influences beliefs, opinions, attitudes, and/or behavior through a process known as **internalization**, which occurs when the receiver adopts the opinion of the credible communicator since he or she believes information from this source is accurate. Once the receiver internalizes an opinion or attitude, it becomes integrated into his or her belief system and may be maintained even after the source of the message is forgotten.

A highly credible communicator is particularly important when message recipients have a negative position toward the product, service, company, or issue being promoted, because the credible source is likely to inhibit counterarguments. As discussed in Chapter 5, reduced counterarguing should result in greater message acceptance and persuasion.

**Applying Expertise** Because attitudes and opinions developed through an internalization process become part of the individual's belief system, marketers want to use communicators with high credibility. Companies use a variety of techniques to convey source expertise. Sales personnel are trained in the product line, which increases customers' perceptions of their expertise. Marketers of highly technical products recruit sales reps with specialized technical backgrounds in engineering, computer science, and other areas to ensure their expertise.

Spokespeople are often chosen because of their knowledge, experience, and expertise in a particular product or service area. Endorsements from individuals or groups recognized as experts, such as doctors or dentists, are also common in advertising (Exhibit 6–2). The importance of using expert sources was shown in a study by Roobina Ohanian, who found that the perceived expertise of celebrity endorsers was more important in explaining purchase intentions than their attractiveness or trustworthiness. She suggests that celebrity spokespeople are most effective when they are knowledgeable, experienced, and qualified to talk about the product they are endorsing.[6] A number of other studies have shown that celebrities perceived as having expertise with a product or service can lend persuasive power to an advertising message.[7]

EXHIBIT 6–2

Dove promotes the fact that
it is recommended by experts
in skin care

Dermatologists
have put
something
unusually strong
in this
skin cleanser.

*Dove*

Their trust.

# Global Perspective 6–1 > > >

## Celebrities Sell Out—But Only Abroad

While many celebrities make huge sums of money endorsing products and serving as advertising spokespeople, some big stars won't appear in ads in the United States as they don't want fans to think they've sold out. There has also long been a feeling among actors that appearing in commercials might devalue their image among the powerful Hollywood producers and directors. However, this has been changing in recent years as even some of the biggest names in entertainment have decided to cash in on their celebrity and appear in commercials. For example, Catherine Zeta-Jones received an estimated $20 million for four years to be the spokesperson for wireless service provider T-Mobile, while Nicole Kidman was paid $8 million to appear in commercials for the Chanel No. 5 fragrance line. In 2012 Chanel hired Brad Pitt as its first male spokesperson for its signature fragrance, which may not have been a wise decision as the TV spot, which featured him rambling on about journeys and fate, was widely criticized and parodied on YouTube and shows such as *Saturday Night Live*.

While some of the A-list celebrities still resist the temptation to cash in on their fame in the United States, they are only too happy to appear in ads in foreign countries. And nowhere are ads starring American celebrities more prevalent than in Japan. Even the rich and famous have trouble saying no to Japanese advertisers who will pay them between $1 million and $3 million for a few hours' work to make 10-second spots that their Western fans across the Pacific will never see. In Japan, celebrities make more money for less work and because the commercials will never air in the United States, they think they can make the money without looking like they are selling their artistic souls.

Actor Leonardo DiCaprio, who is arguably one of the most famous actors in the world, recently appeared in a 15-second spot for the Jim Beam bourbon brand in which the only words he says are "cool bourbon, Jim Beam." The company said the ad would be used only in Japan but it made its way to the United States and other countries via YouTube as soon as it was aired there.

Megastars such as Charlize Theron, Brad Pitt, Sean Connery, Kiefer Sutherland, Kevin Costner, and Harrison Ford have been paid millions for appearing in Japanese commercials. Theron has appeared in an ad for Honda and for Lux bath products, while Ford received several million dollars for appearing sweaty and bare-chested in Kirin beer commercials and print ads. Pitt has appeared in ads for canned coffee and blue jeans. Actor Tommy Lee Jones endorses Boss canned coffee and is a very effective endorser for the brand because the primary drinkers of canned coffee

**Applying Trustworthiness** While expertise is important, the target audience must also find the source believable. Finding celebrities or other figures with a trustworthy image is often difficult. Many trustworthy public figures hesitate to endorse products because of the potential impact on their reputation and image. E-Poll Market Research conducts ongoing consumer surveys to gauge the popularity and marketability of celebrities by measuring attributes such as trustworthy, sincere, trendsetter, and influential. The company publishes its E-Score Celebrity Report each year which includes a spokesperson index score that reflects a celebrity's perceived credibility and authority and suggests his or her potential as a spokesperson.[8] The highest scoring celebrity on its most recent list was actor Betty White followed by Tom Hanks, Robin Williams, Sandra Bullock, Michael J. Fox, Will Smith, Johnny Depp, Jennifer Aniston, Harrison Ford, and Leonardo DiCaprio. Talk-show host and entertainment producer Oprah Winfrey has also been a very trusted source through the years, and her "Favorite Things" list has served as trusted source for product recommendations for many consumers. While nearly all of these top celebrities could command large sums of money as endorsers and spokespersons, very few of them do, often out of concern for how their image might be impacted. Global Perspective 6–1 discusses how some American celebrities protect their image by endorsing products in Japan and other countries rather than in the United States.

Advertisers use various techniques to increase the perception that their sources are trustworthy. Hidden cameras are used to show that the consumer is not a paid are middle-aged men who view him as representing ruggedness, depth, character, worldliness, and strength. Sometimes celebrities are forced to change their images or personalities to suit the advertising style of Japanese companies and the tastes of audiences in Japan. Japanese commercials have a totally different feel than those in the United States and Europe and have often been described as "tacky" or "cheesy" by Western standards. For example, a commercial for Takara sake featured a kimono-clad Madonna wielding a sword and declaring "I'm pure," while another actor, Sean Connery, was shown carrying a ham into a room accompanied by the theme music from the James Bond movies. The late actor Dennis Hopper appeared in an unusual ad that showed him sitting in a tub with a rubber ducky to promote a line of Japanese bath products. Hopper acknowledged that he did the ad for the money, noting that "if I could do one of these every year, I could retire."

There are several reasons why Japanese companies are willing to shell out huge sums of money for these stars. Many Japanese are fascinated by American culture and its celebrities, and endorsement of a brand by a star gives it a certain international cachet. Also, Japanese advertising emphasizes style and mood rather than substance; consumers expect to be entertained rather than bored by product information or testimonials. And more than 80 percent of Japanese commercials are 10- or 15-second spots and around 85 percent use celebrities to capture viewers' attention.

Japan is not the only country where the Hollywood celebrities are hawking products. George Clooney appears in ads overseas for the Nespresso coffee system and defended his right to do so at the 2012 Newsweek Oscar Roundtable, noting that he did not care if people viewed him as selling out by doing commercials. Actor Penelope Cruz appears in Nespresso ads that air in the United States and Canada.

Richard Gere has appeared in ads for Fiat in Europe, including a spot showing him driving a Lancia Delta from Hollywood to Tibet. Even though the ad aired in Italy, it created an uproar in China, where Gere is disliked for being an outspoken supporter of the Dalai Lama.

Some celebrities cashing in on endorsement deals abroad still try to protect their image at home and not be seen as selling out for money. Many stars have nondisclosure clauses in their contracts, specifying that the ads cannot be shown, or sometimes even discussed (oops!), outside Japan. They still see their appearance in TV ads as being potentially harmful to their reputations back home. However, with the growth of the Internet, it is difficult to limit the viewing of the ads to one country as many of the commercials can now be found online on popular websites such as YouTube. Linda Thaler, the chief executive officer of the Kaplan Thaler Group advertising agency, notes that "the days of Brad Pitt doing a commercial in Japan that he thought no one was going to see are gone." However, she also notes that the stigma that celebrities are selling out by doing a commercial has also gone by the wayside as Hollywood snobbery toward appearing in commercials declines.

Celebrities are used to getting their way, and most would probably still prefer that the knowledge of their overseas endorsements stay there. Sorry about that.

Sources: James Parsons, "Japan's Ads Are Far from Being Lost in Translation," *Campaign*, September 14, 2007, p. 21; Dave McCaughan, "The Fine Art of Matching a Celebrity with a Brand," *Advertising Age*, April 16, 2007, p. 34; Louise Story, "Seeing Stars," *The New York Times*, October 12, 2006, p. C1; Jeff Labrecque, "Leonardo DiCaprio and the easy money of foreign commercials," *EW.com*, February 19, 2013, http://popwatch .ew.com/2013/02/19/leonardo-dicaprio-celebrity-foreign-commercials/; Rupal Parekh, "Brad Pitt Endorsing Chanel No. 5? Just Another Pretty Face," *Advertising Age*, May 9, 2012, http://adage.com/article/adages/ brad-pitt-endorsing-chanel-5-pretty-face/234653/.

**YTC** 06–02

**Celebrities in Foreign Ads**

youtube.com/10ebelch

spokesperson and is making an objective evaluation of the product. Disguised brands are compared. (Of course, the sponsor's brand always performs better than the consumer's regular brand, and he or she is always surprised.) Advertisers also use the overheard-conversation technique to enhance trustworthiness. This involves creating a situation in a commercial where a person is shown overhearing a conversation in which favorable claims are made about a product or service. Most consumers are skeptical of these techniques, so they may have limited value in enhancing perceptions of an advertiser's credibility.

Marketers can also deal with the source-trustworthiness issue by using other IMC tools such as publicity. Information received from sources such as newscasters is often very influential because these individuals are perceived as unbiased and thus more credible, even though they are often presenting stories that stem from press releases. In some situations celebrities may appear on news programs or talk shows and promote an upcoming cause or event such as the release of a new movie or music CD. With the increase in stealth marketing techniques, many consumers are becoming wary of endorsements made by celebrities on news programs and talk shows. For example, a *New York Times* article revealed that drug companies were making payments to celebrities or their favorite charities in return for the celebrities' touting the companies' pharmaceutical products on news and talk shows. As a result of the controversy from the article, CNN and the major broadcast networks announced that they would disclose any such financial deals during an interview.[9]

Concerns over potential bias in touting a product or service can involve more than celebrities. Several so-called consumer advocates and product experts have been criticized for giving favorable reviews and/or promoting specific products on local and national TV news programs and other shows without disclosing that they were being paid by the companies to mention their brands. Concern has been expressed over the practice as most television shows present the information presented by trend and fashion gurus or individuals with expertise in areas such as consumer electronics as unbiased and based solely on their expertise. However, the presentation is misleading to consumers if the experts have been paid to mention the products.[10]

With the growth of social media another area of concern has arisen regarding the trustworthiness of sources that endorse companies and brands and make recommendations on sites such as Facebook and Twitter as well as through online reviews or on blogs. In 2009 the Federal Trade Commission passed a set of guidelines requiring online endorsers and bloggers to disclose any material connection they might have to a company. However, studies have shown that as many as 30 percent of online reviews are fake and may be coming from someone who has been paid to write them or fails to reveal their association with a company or brand.[11]

**Using Corporate Leaders as Spokespeople**  Another way of enhancing source credibility is to use the company president or chief executive officer as a spokesperson in the firm's advertising. Many companies believe the use of their president or CEO is the ultimate expression of the company's commitment to quality and customer service. For some firms, the use of a president or CEO in their ads can help create an identity and personality for the company and/or brand. For example, Richard Branson's irreverence and zeal for life have helped personify the image of Virgin's empire of megastores, airlines, mobile phones, and soft drinks. Branson has been used occasionally in ads for various Virgin brands. As the executive director of global brand consulting firm Enterprise IG notes: "The CEO is the absolute bottom line for a company. There's a lot of power in that."[12] There have been cases where ad campaigns featuring CEOs have not only increased sales but also helped turn the company leaders into celebrities.[13] One of the most popular corporate spokespersons ever was Dave Thomas, the founder of Wendy's fast-food restaurants. Thomas appeared in more than 800 ads for Wendy's between 1989 and early 2002, when he passed away.[14] A recent study by the research firm Ace Metrix found that the most effective CEO spokespersons currently are John Schnatter of the Papa John's pizza chain and Jim Koch, who is the head of the Boston Beer Company, which markets the popular Samuel Adams brands.[15] Schnatter has appeared in more than 50 ads for Papa John's and is perceived to be authentic and genuine, which are two important traits for the effective use of CEOs in ads for their companies (Exhibit 6–3). The practice of using company founders, owners, and presidents as advertising spokespersons is particularly prevalent among small and midsize companies such as retailers and auto dealers serving local markets.

Many marketing and advertising experts question the strategy of using company presidents or owners in ads and note that it is often ego rather than logic that is the reason for their use.[16] The experts suggest that businesspeople should get in front of the camera only if they exude credibility and possess the intangible quality of provoking a warm, fuzzy feeling in viewers. For example, Microsoft chair Bill Gates appeared in several TV commercials that were designed to help build a stronger image for the company. Gates was paired with comedian Jerry Seinfeld in the spots, which attempted to use quirky humor to get consumers to think about Microsoft in a different way. However, the ads aired

YTC 06–03
CEO Endorsers
youtube.com/10ebelch

**EXHIBIT 6–3**
John Schnatter is one of the most effective CEO spokespersons

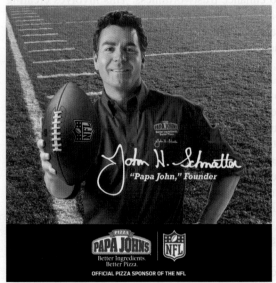

for only a short time and many ad critics noted that Gates did not come across well in the ads.[17]

Another concern is that creating an image or culture around the CEO can make the corporate brand image more vulnerable if the individual becomes involved in any type of controversy such as a labor dispute, political issue, or personal problem. Critics of the practice also note that CEO spokespeople who become very popular may get more attention than their company's product/service or advertising message. And if a firm's image becomes too closely tied to a popular leader, there can be problems if that person leaves the company. For example, Wendy's had a difficult time replacing Dave Thomas, who had become an advertising icon and was the voice and personality of the company.[18] It has also been argued that the recent financial crisis and scandals involving top executives in some companies has eroded confidence in executives, which affects their ability to come across as trustworthy as they would have a few years ago. Moreover, in the new era of social media it is very easy to criticize corporate leaders who do not come across as trustworthy and believable.[19]

Major corporations are likely to continue to use their top executives in their advertising, particularly when they have celebrity value that helps enhance the firm's image. Some research suggests the use of a company president or CEO can improve attitudes and increase the likelihood that consumers will inquire about a company's product or service.[20] Defenders of the practice argue that the use of top executives or business owners in ads is an effective way of projecting an image of trust and honesty and, more important, the idea that the company isn't run by some faceless corporate monolith. As one expert notes: "These guys come into people's living rooms every night and, over the course of weeks and years, become like members of the family. It gets to the point that when you think of a certain product category, you think of the guy you see all the time on TV."[21]

**Limitations of Credible Sources**  Several studies have shown that a high-credibility source is not always an asset, nor is a low-credibility source always a liability. High- and low-credibility sources are equally effective when they are arguing for a position opposing their own best interest.[22] A very credible source is more effective when message recipients are not in favor of the position advocated in the message.[23] However, a very credible source is less important when the audience has a neutral position, and such a source may even be less effective than a moderately credible source when the receiver's initial attitude is favorable.[24]

Another reason a low-credibility source may be as effective as a high-credibility source is the **sleeper effect**, whereby the persuasiveness of a message increases with the passage of time. The immediate impact of a persuasive message may be inhibited because of its association with a low-credibility source. But with time, the association of the message with the source diminishes and the receiver's attention focuses more on favorable information in the message, resulting in more support. However, many studies have failed to demonstrate the presence of a sleeper effect.[25] Many advertisers hesitate to count on the sleeper effect, since exposure to a credible source is a more reliable strategy.[26]

## Source Attractiveness

A source characteristic frequently used by advertisers is **attractiveness**, which encompasses similarity, familiarity, and likability.[27] *Similarity* is a supposed resemblance between the source and the receiver of the message, while *familiarity* refers to knowledge of the source through exposure. *Likability* is an affection for the source as a result of physical appearance, behavior, or other personal traits. Even when the sources are not athletes or movie stars, consumers often admire their physical appearance, talent, and/or personality.

Source attractiveness leads to persuasion through a process of **identification**, whereby the receiver is motivated to seek some type of relationship with the source and thus adopts similar beliefs, attitudes, preferences, or behavior. Maintaining this position depends on the source's continued support for the position as well as the receiver's continued identification with the source. If the source changes position, the receiver may also change. Unlike internalization, identification does not usually integrate information from an attractive source into the receiver's belief system. The receiver may maintain the attitudinal position or behavior only as long as it is supported by the source or the source remains attractive.

Marketers recognize that receivers of persuasive communications are more likely to attend to and identify with people they find likable or similar to themselves. Similarity and likability are the two source characteristics marketers seek when choosing a communicator.

**Applying Similarity** Marketers recognize that people are more likely to be influenced by a message coming from someone with whom they feel a sense of similarity.[28] If the communicator and receiver have similar needs, goals, interests, and lifestyles, the position advocated by the source is better understood and received. Similarity is used in various ways in marketing communications. Companies select salespeople whose characteristics match well with their customers'. A sales position for a particular region may be staffed by someone local who has background and interests in common with the customers. Global marketers often hire foreign nationals as salespeople so customers can relate more easily to them.

Companies may also try to recruit former athletes to sell sporting goods or beer, since their customers usually have a strong interest in sports. Several studies have shown that customers who perceive a salesperson as similar to themselves are more likely to be influenced by his or her message.[29]

Similarity is also used to create a situation where the consumer feels empathy for the person shown in the commercial. In a slice-of-life commercial, the advertiser usually starts by presenting a predicament with the hope of getting the consumer to think, "I can see myself in that situation." This can help establish a bond of similarity between the communicator and the receiver, increasing the source's level of persuasiveness. Many companies feel that the best way to connect with consumers is by using regular-looking, everyday people with whom the average person can easily identify. For example, some of the most popular commercials for many years were those from the "Whassup?" campaign for Budweiser beer. In these ads the agency cast a group of real-life friends from Philadelphia, rather than actors, who greet each other with an exaggerated "Whassup?" when they speak with one another or get together to watch a game and enjoy a Bud.[30]

Marketers like to cast actors in their commercials whom consumers will notice, recognize, identify with, and remember, as well as help differentiate their products and services. In some cases they try to create a personality figure for the company or brand that consumers will find likable such as Flo, the enthusiastic sales agent for Progressive insurance. Casting directors consider these factors when looking for talent to use in commercials. However, as discussed in IMC Perspective 6–1, being cast in a certain role or as a specific character for a commercial can be risky for actors as they often become typecast, which may limit their opportunities to appear in ads for other brands and even damage their acting career.

**Applying Likability: Using Celebrities** Advertisers recognize the value of using spokespeople who are admired: TV and movie stars, athletes, musicians, and other popular public figures. Estimates of the percentage of all television commercials in the United States that feature a celebrity range from 14 to 20 percent, although an analysis of prime-time shows found only 9 percent.[31] The prevalence of celebrities in magazine ads is similar to television; a content analysis study of advertising appearing in 38 different magazines found that celebrities were used in only 10 percent of the ads. The use of celebrities was the highest for fashion, sports, and teen magazines and lowest for general news and business publications. With regard

YTC 06–04
**Budweiser Whassup**
youtube.com/10ebelch

**EXHIBIT 6–4**
Maria Sharapova has endorsement contracts with a number of companies, including Nike, Tiffany, Porsche, and Cole Haan

to product category, the use of celebrities was highest for athletic products, fashion/apparel, and cosmetics.[32] The use of celebrities in TV commercials is much higher in other countries such as South Korea and Japan.[33]

The top celebrity endorser for many year was golfer Tiger Woods, who at one point was making more than $100 million per year from his various endorsement deals. Woods lost a number of endorsements after his infidelity issues surfaced in 2009 as a number of companies terminated their relationships with him including Accenture, AT&T, Gatorade, and Gillette. The top American endorser in 2012 was golfer Phil Mickelson, who made an estimated $57 million, followed by Woods at $55 million. Other top American athlete endorsers include NBA stars LeBron James, Kobe Bryant, and Derrick Rose as well as NASCAR drivers Dale Earnhardt Jr. and Jeff Gordon. The top international endorsers include Swiss tennis player Roger Federer, followed by soccer stars David Beckham, Cristiano Ronaldo, and Lionel Messi.[34]

For women, the top endorser is tennis star Maria Sharapova, who makes an estimated $22 million per year from her deals with Nike, Tiffany, Evian, Samsung, Head, TAG Heuer, and Cole Haan (Exhibit 6–4). Other top female endorsers include tennis stars Venus and Serena Williams, actor-singer Jennifer Lopez, singer Beyoncé, and race car driver Danica Patrick.

Why do companies spend huge sums to have celebrities appear in their ads and endorse their products? They think celebrities have *stopping power*. That is, they draw attention to advertising messages in a very cluttered media environment. Marketers think a popular celebrity will favorably influence consumers' feelings, attitudes, and purchase behavior. And they believe celebrities can enhance the target audience's perceptions of the product in terms of image and/or performance. For example, a well-known athlete may convince potential buyers that the product will enhance their own performance.

A number of factors must be considered when a company decides to use a celebrity spokesperson, including the dangers of overshadowing the product and being overexposed, the target audience's receptivity, and risks to the advertiser.

**Overshadowing the Product** How will the celebrity affect the target audience's processing of the advertising message? Consumers may focus their attention on the celebrity and fail to notice the brand. Advertisers should select a celebrity spokesperson who will attract attention and enhance the sales message, yet not overshadow the brand. For example, high-end clothing brand St. John decided that it was best to drop actor Angelina Jolie from its advertising after a few years. The company felt that she was overshadowing the brand. Jolie was viewed as a very good fit for St. John, including her role as the voice of its children's charity—a cause she is well known for supporting. However, the company felt that she was simply too famous and decided to use a top British fashion model in its ads.[35] Automaker Chrysler ran into a similar problem when it launched a major campaign featuring singer Celine Dion as part of its "Drive & Love" campaign, which was designed to give the brand a more upscale image. However, the campaign was not successful as Chrysler's marketing team felt that her celebrity persona overshadowed the products and was more effective at promoting her than the cars.[36]

# IMC Perspective 6–1 > > >

## Actors in Commercials Often Get Typecast

Imagine being a struggling actor, attending audition after audition hoping to land a part in a TV commercial but going months without getting a callback. Then one day your agent calls with excellent news. The producer of a commercial you tried out for two weeks ago wants *you* to be the face of an ad campaign for a new brand of toothpaste. You're thrilled, and of course accept immediately. Over the next few years, things couldn't be going any better. You've shot six different versions of the ad, your face is everywhere, and you've made hundreds of thousands of dollars. Thirty-six months ago you were eating Top Ramen and macaroni and cheese for every meal and sleeping on your friend's couch. Now you're dining out five nights a week while living in a cool apartment in Manhattan or West Hollywood. As they say in the business, you've made it. Then something strange happens. Over the next year, you're back on the rejection train. Television shows, movies, commercials—you've nailed each audition, but once again can't get a bite. The toothpaste campaign is still running, but you're worried it may be over soon. You need to make a steady income and you also want to continue to advance in your acting career. The toothpaste commercial was fun and lucrative, but you have bigger plans. Now if that phone would just ring . . .

This example is not unlike the experience of many actors who have achieved success doing TV commercials for major companies and brands. In fact, accomplished TV actors are often less likely to gain future employment *because* of their success. Why so? you may ask. Remember that advertising is all about standing out, drawing the attention of viewers,

and creating a certain image for a company or brand. Good actors are usually cast in roles because they can help an advertiser do these things and get consumers to remember, identify, and differentiate their products. However, when an actor gets labeled as "the toothpaste girl," "the computer dude," or "the male enhancement pill guy," it is difficult for viewers to erase those images from their minds and think of them in other ways. Look no further than Stephanie Courtney, who has starred as Flo, the chipper sales clerk, in dozens of Progressive commercials and helped the company become a leader in auto and home insurance. If you saw Flo in a commercial for McDonald's, would you really be thinking about a Big Mac during the ad? Or would your mind naturally wander to Progressive, Flo's signature white clothing, and car insurance? If you're McDonald's pouring tens of millions of dollars into a TV campaign, you certainly don't want the latter.

So what is an aspiring actor to do? As in the fictitious example just presented, a TV spot in the ultracompetitive acting profession is a great resume builder, a source of immediate income, and can prove incredibly lucrative if the spot turns into a multiyear campaign. There are probably very few actors who tell their agents, "Turn it down . . . I don't want to pigeonhole myself a few years down the road." However, marketers often do not want to use actors who are identified with a specific company or brand or are appearing in too many different commercials because that may confuse consumers about which brand is being advertised. And in some cases, companies may want the actors in their commercials

---

**Overexposure** Consumers are often skeptical of endorsements because they know the celebrities are being paid.[37] This problem is particularly pronounced when a celebrity endorses too many products or companies and becomes overexposed. For example, at one time cyclist Lance Armstrong had endorsement contracts with nearly 20 different companies, including Nike, PowerBar, General Mills, Oakley, and many others, and had to limit his endorsements so he did not become overexposed.[38] Soccer star David Beckham has endorsement contracts with a number of companies/brands including Gillette, Pepsi, Samsung, adidas, Armani, H&M, and Breitling watches (Exhibit 6–5). Advertisers can protect themselves against overexposure with an exclusivity clause limiting the number of products a celebrity can endorse. However, such clauses are usually expensive, and most celebrities agree not to endorse similar products anyway. Many celebrities, knowing their fame is fleeting, try to earn as much endorsement money as possible, yet they must be careful not to damage their credibility by endorsing too many products. For example, singer-actor Cher damaged her credibility as an advertising spokesperson by appearing in too many infomercials. When she realized that appearing in so many infomercials was devastating to her acting career as well, she ceased doing them.[39]

**Target Audiences' Receptivity** One of the most important considerations in choosing a celebrity endorser is how well the individual matches with and is received by the advertiser's target audience. Many former athletes such as to keep a low profile and appear only in ads for their company or brand. For example, Paul Marcarelli was the Test Man for Verizon wireless in the "Can you hear me now?" campaign which ran from 2002 until 2011. Marcarelli never gave interviews or made appearances related to his role and in an *Atlantic* magazine interview revealed that his contract with the company prohibited him from appearing in other commercials and from speaking about his role as the Verizon Test Man.

Money aside, being the face of a major company or brand can have its drawbacks and make it difficult to get future work. For example, Ben Curtis starred as Steven the Dell Dude in a campaign for Dell computers for several years and became known for his classic line—"Dude, you're getting a Dell." However, in early 2003 Curtis was arrested while trying to buy a bag of marijuana in Manhattan just as he was about to sign a lucrative contract extension with Dell. Although the charges were dropped, a decade after his stint as a promoter for Dell ended Curtis has not been able to advance his acting career past a few low-profile theater and independent film gigs. According to Curtis, "I'm just not the new, hot guy anymore . . . a lot of people feel like they've seen my best work." Curtis contends that that's not the case, but good luck convincing casting directors.

Of course, there are success stories in ad land of actors who do appear in commercials for more than one company or brand. Allyn Rachel is one of them; the quirky actor has done commercials for the Toyota Venza, McDonald's, AT&T, IHOP, MetLife, Dish Network, Kotex, and Nokia throughout

her career. In an interview with *Advertising Age*, Rachel acknowledged how fortunate she has been to work with the same director on several different spots. "You never know, it's not like a regular TV job where you can be in 4,000 things and everybody is great with that," she said. "No one necessarily wants to see all the same people all the time. I feel lucky they've kept me around." To her credit, Rachel is preparing for the day when she may get shunned by the TV commercial community. For now, however, she is riding the wave of success while she still can. "As of now, I'm not associated too strongly with one brand, or one specific product, so it hasn't been a problem. At a certain point, [however], I'd consider maybe stepping away from commercials if they seem to be preventing other opportunities."

The creative director at one of the agencies that has used Rachel says that great talent is hard to find for commercials, which is good news for many aspiring actors. Also, the longer a commercial runs the more money an actor makes, which means that being part of a long-running campaign can be very lucrative. However, the overexposure can lead to a stereotypical image which can be very difficult to overcome and can result in someone acting himself or herself right out of acting.

Sources: Shareen Pathak, "Can an Actor Be in Too Many Ads?" *Advertising Age*, October 22, 2012, p. 14; Felix Gillette, "Branded for Life," *Bloomberg Businessweek*, September 27, 2012, ww.businessweek.com/articles/2012-09-27/branded-for-life; Thomas Pardee, "Meet Allyn Rachel: The Woman in More Spots Than Sofia Vergara," *Advertising Age*, April 13, 2012, http://adage.com/article/news/allyn-rachel-woman-commercials/234115/.

**YTC 06–05**

**Actors in Commercials**
youtube.com/10ebelch

Arnold Palmer and Michael Jordan are still effective endorsers because they have very favorable images among aging baby boomers and seniors. NBA star LeBron James has been an effective spokesperson for several companies since turning professional, including Nike, Samsung, and Coca-Cola because he has tremendous name recognition and is very popular among younger consumers who are the primary target market for athletic shoes and soft drinks. McDonald's signed James to a multiyear endorsement deal, noting that his personal qualities make him a good fit for the company and that he is popular among young males who are heavy users of fast food.[40]

Consumers who are particularly knowledgeable about a product or service or have strongly established attitudes may be less influenced by a celebrity than those with little knowledge or neutral attitudes. One study found that college-age students were more likely to have a positive attitude toward a product endorsed by a celebrity than were older consumers.[41] The teenage market has generally been very receptive to celebrity endorsers, as evidenced by the frequent use of entertainers and athletes in ads targeted to this group for products such as apparel, cosmetics, and beverages. However, many marketers are finding that teenage consumers are more skeptical and cynical toward the use of celebrity endorsers and respond better to ads using humor, irony, and unvarnished truth. Some marketers targeting teenagers have responded to this by no longer using celebrities in their campaigns or by poking fun at their use.

Some companies avoid the use of celebrities entirely as they have determined that the market they are targeting is really not influenced by their endorsements. For example, New Balance became the number 2 athletic footwear company behind

**EXHIBIT 6–6**
Yes! Golf promotes that it
does not pay pro golfers to
use its putters

Nike without the aid of celebrity endorsers. Its core customers are between the ages of 25 and 49 and are older and more mature than the youth and teen market that most athletic shoe companies target. Until recently, the company had an across-the-board policy against hiring athletes to endorse its products and ran several ad campaigns through the years that poked fun at its competitors for paying exorbitant amounts of money to athletes to wear their shoes. Small companies that do not have the marketing budget to pay professionals to use their products or are opposed to doing so sometimes use this to their advantage. For example, Exhibit 6–6 shows an ad that Yes! Golf used when the company was first started. The ad explains how Yes! competes on the quality of its putters rather than by paying endorsement fees to pro golfers.

**Risk to the Advertiser** A celebrity's behavior may pose a risk to a company.[42] A number of entertainers and athletes have been involved in activities that could embarrass the companies whose products they endorsed. Several companies including McDonald's, Coca-Cola, Spalding, and Nutella terminated endorsement deals with NBA superstar Kobe Bryant when he was charged with sexual assault in 2003. Other companies such as Nike and Upper Deck had long-term contracts with Bryant but limited their use of him as an endorser for a number of years. Even though the charges against Bryant were dropped, it took him years to repair his image and become a marketable endorser once again. However, Bryant has been able to recover most of his status as a viable endorser by winning the NBA's Most Valuable Player award in 2008, leading the Los Angeles Lakers to world championships in 2009 and 2010, and, of course, avoiding any further controversies both on and off the court. Over the past few years several companies/brands have signed Bryant to endorsement deals including Sony, the Guitar Hero World Tour music videogame, and Vitaminwater (which ironically is now owned by the Coca-Cola Company). Bryant also signed a lucrative endorsement deal with Turkish Airlines to serve as a "global ambassador" for the international carrier. He appears in print ads as well as TV commercials for the airline alongside of soccer star Lionel Messi.[43]

Marketers are recognizing that the use of celebrity endorsers can be a very expensive and high-risk strategy because what the celebrities do in their personal lives can impact their image and the way they are viewed by the public. Some companies may face a dilemma in selecting celebrity endorsers: While they prefer them to be upright, they still want them to have an edge or be somewhat irreverent to be able to connect with consumers. This may be particularly true for companies marketing their products to younger consumers.

To avoid problems, companies often research a celebrity's personal life and background. Many endorsement contracts include a morals clause allowing the company to terminate the contract if a controversy arises. Several companies, including luxury brands Burberry and Chanel as well as fashion retailer H&M, canceled their contracts with supermodel Kate Moss in the wake of a British tabloid photo that showed her using cocaine.[44] However, marketers should remember that adding morals clauses to their endorsement contracts only gets them out of a problem; it does not prevent it from happening. Thus, it is important that they carefully consider the character of a celebrity as well as the potential risk associated with using him or her as a spokesperson or endorser for the company or one of its brands.[45]

**Return on Investment** Perhaps the most important factor a company must consider regarding the use of celebrity endorsers is the return on investment from using them. Marketers use celebrities to increase awareness of and attention to their company and/or brands, as well as their advertisements, and to develop strong associations between the celebrity and the brand that will result in higher purchase intentions. However, all of these factors must translate into higher sales in order for the company to get a positive return on the investment from an endorsement deal, which often does not occur. For example, General Motors used Tiger Woods as a spokesperson for its Buick brand from 1999 until the end of 2008. However, during that time period Buick sales declined from around 400,000 cars per year to under 200,000 units.[46] GM stated that Woods did help change the image of Buick as an older person's car and attract a younger demographic to the brand.[47] However, many experts questioned GM's use of Woods and argued that he was not a good fit with Buick and might have been more effectively used for another model such as Cadillac.

Many companies do not reveal the increases in sales and/or market share that result from the use of celebrity endorsers. However, an interesting study was conducted by Anita Elberse and Jeroen Verleun that examined the economic impact of a sample of 347 endorsement deals for 180 athletes across six packaged-goods product categories. The results of their study found that sales did increase significantly over the first six months that the athlete endorsers were used—about 4 percent. However, subsequent major achievements by the athletes did not improve the sales of the brands studied relative to their competitors which calls into question the long-term value of endorsement deals.[48]

It should be noted that there are many examples of companies that have seen sales increase, and there can be other factors that marketers consider in determining the value gained from using a celebrity endorser. Thus it is likely that many marketers will continue to use them, despite some of the drawbacks associated with their use that have been discussed. Some companies are changing their relationships with celebrity endorsers and having them become more involved with their companies and brands rather than just appearing in advertisements (Exhibit 6–7). A number of high-profile celebrities have become involved in areas such as product design and development as well as the advertising creative process. For example, Anheuser-Busch recently hired Justin Timberlake as the creative and musical curator for its Bud Light Platinum brand while BlackBerry retained singer Alicia Keys as a global creative director.[49] PepsiCo hired Beyoncé as a "brand ambassador" as part of a long-term $50 million endorsement deal that includes having her help create content and develop new ways to engage consumers and fans.[50] Some marketing experts argue that these celebrity deals are little more than window dressing while others argue that they can be valuable.

Marketers are also becoming more creative in the way they pay celebrities and even giving them a stake in the company. For example, rapper 50 Cent (Curtis Jackson) received a minority stake in Glacéau Vitaminwater which increased his involvement with the company. He developed a flavor, appeared in ads, and even mentioned the brand in some of this songs. When the company was acquired by Coca-Cola, Jackson made an estimated $400 million.[51] When Rihanna released the hit single "Umbrella" in 2007, Totes Isotoner, which had been manufacturing umbrellas for over 30 years, approached the pop singer about branding the company's umbrellas side-by-side with her and the song. What followed was an entirely new offering from Totes that allowed customers to design their own (sparkly, glittery) umbrellas that were consistent with Rihanna's image. Rihanna, in exchange for her commitment to the company and the use of her image and song, received a percentage of umbrella sales and other perks.[52] And when Under Armour signed New England Patriots quarterback Tom Brady to an endorsement deal a few years ago, he received an equity stake in the company. According to Under Armour CEO Kevin Plank, this is an ideal arrangement for the firm as it makes Brady fully invested in the company's success.[53]

YTC 06–06

**Celebrities as Brand Ambassadors**

youtube.com/10ebelch

**EXHIBIT 6–7**

Marketers are using celebrities for more than just appearing in ads

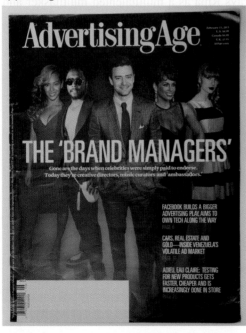

**Understanding the Meaning of Celebrity Endorsers** Advertisers must try to match the product or company's image, the characteristics of the target market, and the personality of the celebrity.[54] The image celebrities project to consumers can be just as important as their ability to attract attention. An interesting perspective on celebrity endorsement was developed by Grant McCracken.[55] He argues that credibility and attractiveness don't sufficiently explain how and why celebrity endorsements work and offers a model based on meaning transfer (Figure 6–3).

According to this model, a celebrity's effectiveness as an endorser depends on the culturally acquired meanings he or she brings to the endorsement process. Each celebrity contains many meanings, including status, class, gender, and age as well as personality and lifestyle. In explaining stage 1 of the meaning transfer process, McCracken notes:

> Celebrities draw these powerful meanings from the roles they assume in their television, movie, military, athletic, and other careers. Each new dramatic role brings the celebrity into contact with a range of objects, persons, and contexts. Out of these objects, persons, and contexts are transferred meanings that then reside in the celebrity.[56]

Examples of celebrities who have acquired cultural meaning that they bring to endorsements include actor Zooey Deschanel (from her role as the cute, quirky, and offbeat but loveable roommate on the sitcom *New Girl*) and Charlie Sheen (from his role as the free-spirited, bachelor/playboy on the hit show *Two and a Half Men*). Deschanel's character image has been used in commercials for the Apple iPhone, while she also appears in ads for Rimmel cosmetics and Pantene shampoo which capitalize on her attractiveness. Sheen's bad-boy image was utilized in a commercial for the Fiat Abarth which featured him driving the car around the inside of an opulent mansion as a group of attractive women cheer him on. The spot also poked fun at his personal problems as it showed him stepping out of the car and saying, "I love being under house arrest."[57] Kelly Ripa, who serves as the cohost of the popular daytime show *Live with Kelly and Michael* and has also costarred in several television shows including *All My Children* and *Hope & Faith,* has developed a very favorable image as a multitalented "do-it-all woman" who can balance a demanding career with her personal life.

McCracken suggests celebrity endorsers bring their meanings and image into the ad and transfer them to the product they are endorsing (stage 2 of the model in Figure 6–3). For example, Electrolux has been using Ripa in an integrated marketing campaign for its premium line of stylish, high-performance appliances that capitalizes on her image.[58] The campaign portrays Ripa as a multitalented multitasker and

YTC 06–07
**Celebrity Meaning Transfer**
youtube.com/10ebelch

**FIGURE 6–3**

Meaning Movement and the Endorsement Process

Key:  ⟶ = Path of meaning movement

▨ = Stage of meaning movement

## EXHIBIT 6–8
Kelly Ripa helps create the impression that Electrolux appliances are designed for the "do-it-all" woman

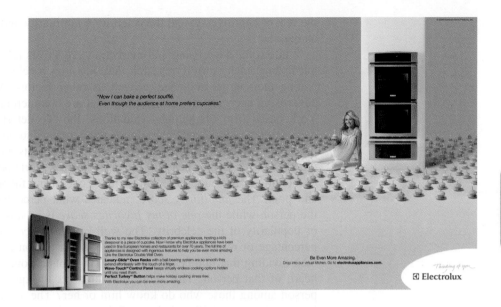

shows her in various roles in her busy life including scenes at work, entertaining at home, and interacting with her daughters (Exhibit 6–8). She is an effective endorser for the brand since she represents the quintessential do-it-all woman with an endless things-to-do list but who gets it all done.

In the final stage of McCracken's model, the meanings the celebrity has given to the product are transferred to the consumer. By using Ripa in its ads, Electrolux can deliver a powerful brand idea that its appliances are designed to help women who are already doing amazing things in their lives to be even more amazing. To help deliver this message Electrolux uses Ripa in TV and print ads and has also created an entertaining short film on its website starring her that women can watch and share with their friends. McCracken notes that this final stage is complicated and difficult to achieve. The way consumers take possession of the meaning the celebrity has transferred to a product is probably the least understood part of the process.

The meaning transfer model has some important implications for companies using celebrity endorsers. Marketers must first decide on the image or symbolic meanings important to the target audience for the particular product, service, or company. They must then determine which celebrity best represents the meaning or image to be projected. An advertising campaign must be designed that captures that meaning in the product and moves it to the consumer. Marketing and advertising personnel often rely on intuition in choosing celebrity endorsers for their companies or products, but some companies conduct research studies to determine consumers' perceptions of celebrities' meaning.

Marketers may also pretest ads to determine whether they transfer the proper meaning to the product. When celebrity endorsers are used, the marketer should track the campaign's effectiveness. Does the celebrity continue to be effective in communicating the proper meaning to the target audience? Celebrities who are no longer in the limelight may lose their ability to transfer any significant meanings to the product.

# CHOOSING A CELEBRITY ENDORSER

As we have seen, marketers must consider many factors when choosing a celebrity to serve as an advertising spokesperson for the company or a particular brand. Studies have shown that advertising and marketing managers take these various factors into account when choosing a celebrity endorser.[59] Among the most important factors are the celebrity's match with the target audience and the product/service or brand, the overall image of the celebrity, the cost of acquiring the celebrity, trustworthiness, the risk of controversy, and the celebrity's familiarity and likability among the target audience.

While some advertising and marketing executives rely on their own intuition and gut feeling, many turn to research that measures a celebrity's familiarity and appeal among their target audience as well as other factors. Many companies and their advertising agencies rely on Q-scores that are commercially available from the New York–based firm Marketing Evaluations, Inc. To determine its Q-scores for sport personalities, actors, and entertainers, the company surveys a representative national panel of consumers several times a year. Respondents are asked to indicate whether they have ever seen or heard of the performer or sports personality and, if they have, to rate him or her on a scale that includes one of my favorites, very good, good, fair, and poor. The *familiarity score* indicates what percentage of people has heard of the person while the *one of my favorites score* is an absolute measure of the appeal or popularity of the celebrity. The well-known *Q-score* is calculated by taking the percentage of respondents who indicate that a person is "one of my favorites" and then dividing that number by the percentage of respondents who indicate they have heard of that person. This score thus answers the question, How appealing is the person among those who do know him or her? The average Q-score for performers is generally around 18 and about 17 for sports personalities. Marketing Evaluation's Q-scores are also broken down on the basis of various demographic criteria such as a respondent's age, income, occupation, education, and race so that marketers have some idea of how a celebrity's popularity varies among different groups of consumers. Marketing Evaluations also now reports a negative Q-score which is the percentage of respondents who rate the personality as fair or poor divided by only those who are familiar with the person. Exhibit 6–9 shows a sample page from the Performer Q study. In addition to Q-scores, marketers use information provided by a number of other research firms that provide them with data on the popularity of various celebrities and insight into how well their image might fit with their company or brand.

YTC 06–08

Q-Scores

youtube.com/10ebelch

**Applying Likability: Decorative Models**   Advertisers often draw attention to their ads by featuring a physically attractive person who serves as a passive or decorative model rather than as an active communicator. Research suggests that physically attractive communicators generally have a positive impact and generate more favorable evaluations of both ads and products than less attractive models.[60] The gender appropriateness of the model for the product being advertised and his or her relevance to the product are also important considerations.[61] Products such as cosmetics or fashionable clothing are likely to benefit from the use of an attractive model, since physical appearance is very relevant in marketing these items.

Some models draw attention to the ad but not to the product or message. Studies show that an attractive model facilitates recognition of the ad but does not enhance copy readership or message recall. Thus, advertisers must ensure that the consumer's attention will go beyond the model to the product and advertising message.[62] Marketers must also consider whether the use of highly attractive models might negatively impact advertising effectiveness. Several recent studies have shown that some women experience negative feelings when comparing themselves with beautiful models used in ads and the images of physical perfection they represent.[63]

Some companies have developed marketing campaigns that undermine the traditional approach to beauty care advertising by telling women, as well as young girls, that they're beautiful just the way they are. For example, Unilever's Dove brand has long eschewed the use of supermodels in its ads and uses everyday women and girls who resemble its typical consumers. Since 2004 the company has been running an interesting global integrated marketing campaign designed to appeal to everyday women.[64] The "Campaign for Real Beauty" includes magazine ads, extensive public relations, and a website (www.campaignforrealbeauty.com) where women can discuss beauty-related issues (Exhibit 6–10). Dove has taken a social advocacy

| | PERSONALITY NAME | | | | | | |
| | ONE OF MY FAVORITES | VERY GOOD | GOOD | FAIR/ POOR | TOTAL FAMILIAR | POSITIVE Q SCORE | NEGATIVE Q SCORE |
|---|---|---|---|---|---|---|---|
| TOTAL SAMPLE | 9 | 18 | 30 | 25 | 83 | 11 | 31 |
| 6 - 11 YEARS | 16 | 12 | 18 | 9 | 56 | 29 | 17 |
| 12 - 17 YEARS | 11 | 21 | 30 | 23 | 86 | 13 | 27 |
| 18 - 34 YEARS | 11 | 22 | 33 | 29 | 95 | 11 | 31 |
| 35 - 49 YEARS | 11 | 20 | 34 | 26 | 90 | 12 | 29 |
| 50 AND OVER | 4 | 13 | 28 | 27 | 72 | 6 | 37 |
| 18 - 49 YEARS | 11 | 21 | 34 | 28 | 93 | 11 | 30 |
| 18 YEARS AND OVER | 8 | 18 | 32 | 27 | 85 | 10 | 32 |
| 25 - 54 YEARS | 11 | 20 | 32 | 28 | 91 | 12 | 31 |
| | | | | | | | |
| TOTAL MALES | | | | | | | |
| 6 AND OVER | 9 | 16 | 31 | 25 | 81 | 11 | 31 |
| 18 - 34 YEARS | 10 | 21 | 33 | 29 | 94 | 10 | 31 |
| 35 - 49 YEARS | 13 | 18 | 33 | 25 | 89 | 15 | 28 |
| 50 AND OVER | 4 | 11 | 28 | 25 | 67 | 5 | 36 |
| 18 - 49 YEARS | 11 | 20 | 33 | 27 | 91 | 13 | 30 |
| 18 YEARS AND OVER | 9 | 17 | 31 | 26 | 83 | 11 | 32 |
| 25 - 54 YEARS | 12 | 21 | 30 | 27 | 90 | 13 | 30 |
| | | | | | | | |
| TOTAL FEMALES | | | | | | | |
| 6 AND OVER | 10 | 19 | 30 | 26 | 84 | 12 | 31 |
| 18 - 34 YEARS | 12 | 22 | 33 | 30 | 97 | 12 | 31 |
| 35 - 49 YEARS | 8 | 21 | 35 | 27 | 91 | 9 | 30 |
| 50 AND OVER | 5 | 15 | 28 | 29 | 76 | 7 | 38 |
| 18 - 49 YEARS | 10 | 22 | 34 | 28 | 94 | 10 | 30 |
| 18 YEARS AND OVER | 8 | 19 | 32 | 29 | 87 | 9 | 33 |
| 25 - 54 YEARS | 10 | 20 | 34 | 29 | 92 | 11 | 31 |
| HOUSEHOLD INCOME | | | | | | | |
| UNDER $20,000 | 8 | 13 | 30 | 20 | 71 | 11 | 28 |
| $20,000 - $39,999 | 9 | 18 | 31 | 26 | 85 | 11 | 31 |
| $40,000 - $59,999 | 11 | 14 | 34 | 27 | 86 | 13 | 31 |
| $60,000 AND OVER | 9 | 21 | 28 | 27 | 85 | 11 | 31 |
| $75,000 AND OVER | 9 | 19 | 29 | 28 | 85 | 11 | 32 |
| EDUCATION (ADULT) | | | | | | | |
| HIGH SCHOOL GRADUATE/LESS | 10 | 19 | 30 | 23 | 80 | 12 | 28 |
| SOME COLLEGE/DEGREE | 7 | 17 | 34 | 32 | 90 | 8 | 36 |
| OCCUPATION (ADULT) | | | | | | | |
| WHITE COLLAR | 7 | 21 | 35 | 29 | 91 | 7 | 32 |
| BLUE COLLAR | 10 | 16 | 32 | 28 | 85 | 12 | 32 |
| RACE | | | | | | | |
| NON BLACK | 7 | 17 | 31 | 27 | 81 | 9 | 33 |
| BLACK | 26 | 25 | 23 | 16 | 90 | 29 | 17 |
| ETHNICITY | | | | | | | |
| HISPANIC | 12 | 17 | 37 | 23 | 89 | 13 | 26 |
| NIELSEN COUNTY SIZE | | | | | | | |
| A | 11 | 18 | 32 | 26 | 87 | 12 | 30 |
| B | 9 | 19 | 30 | 25 | 83 | 11 | 30 |
| C & D | 8 | 16 | 28 | 24 | 75 | 10 | 32 |
| REGION | | | | | | | |
| NORTHEAST | 10 | 21 | 25 | 30 | 85 | 12 | 35 |
| NORTH CENTRAL | 9 | 19 | 32 | 24 | 83 | 11 | 28 |
| SOUTH | 11 | 18 | 32 | 21 | 82 | 13 | 26 |
| WEST | 7 | 13 | 30 | 30 | 80 | 9 | 38 |

**EXHIBIT 6-9**

Sample page from Marketing Evaluations, Inc. Performer Q Study

approach in the campaign, which it proclaims "aims to change the status quo and offer in its place a broader, healthier, more democratic view of beauty."[65]

## Source Power

The final characteristic in Kelman's classification scheme is **source power**. A source has power when he or she can actually administer rewards and punishments to the receiver. As a result of this power, the source may be able to induce another person(s) to respond to the request or position he or she is advocating. The power of the source depends on several factors. The source must be perceived as being able to administer positive or negative sanctions to the receiver *(perceived control)* and the receiver must think the source cares about whether or not the receiver conforms

Let's face it, firming the thighs of a size 2 supermodel is no challenge. Real women have real curves. And according to women who tried new Dove® Firming, it left their skin feeling firmer in just one week. What better way to celebrate the curves you were born with? New Dove Firming. Lotion, Cream and Body Wash. For beautifully firm skin.

**EXHIBIT 6–10**

Dove's "Campaign for Real Beauty" uses everyday women rather than supermodels in its ads

*(perceived concern).* The receiver's estimate of the source's ability to observe conformity is also important *(perceived scrutiny).*

When a receiver perceives a source as having power, the influence process occurs through a process known as **compliance**. The receiver accepts the persuasive influence of the source and acquiesces to his or her position in hopes of obtaining a favorable reaction or avoiding punishment. The receiver may show public agreement with the source's position but not have an internal or private commitment to this position. Persuasion induced through compliance may be superficial and last only as long as the receiver perceives that the source can administer some reward or punishment.

Power as a source characteristic is very difficult to apply in a nonpersonal influence situation such as advertising. A communicator in an ad generally cannot apply any sanctions to the receiver or determine whether compliance actually occurs. An indirect way of using power is by using an individual with an authoritative personality as a spokesperson. For example, Take Pride in America uses actor-director Clint Eastwood, whose movie roles earned him an image as a rugged tough guy, in public service campaigns commanding people not to pollute or damage public lands (Exhibit 6–11). Eastwood has used his imposing image in TV commercials calling for people who abuse public lands "to clean up their act or get out of town."

The use of source power applies more in situations involving personal communication and influence. For example, in a personal-selling situation, the sales rep may have some power over a buyer if the latter anticipates receiving special rewards or favors for complying with the salesperson. Some companies provide their sales reps with large expense accounts to spend on customers for this very purpose. Representatives of companies whose product demand exceeds supply are often in a position of power; buyers may comply with their requests to ensure an adequate supply of the product. Sales reps must be very careful in their use of a power position, since abusing a power base to maximize short-term gains can damage long-term relationships with customers.

# MESSAGE FACTORS

**LO 06-3**

The way marketing communications are presented is very important in determining their effectiveness. Marketers must consider not only the content of their persuasive messages but also how this information will be structured for presentation and what type of message appeal will be used. Advertising, in all media except radio, relies heavily on visual as well as verbal information. Many options are available with respect to the design and presentation of a message. This section examines the structure of messages and considers the effects of different types of appeals used in advertising.

## Message Structure

Marketing communications usually consist of a number of message points that the communicator wants to get across. An important aspect of message strategy is knowing the best way to communicate these points and overcome any opposing viewpoints audience members may hold. Extensive research has been conducted on how the structure of a persuasive message can influence its effectiveness, including order

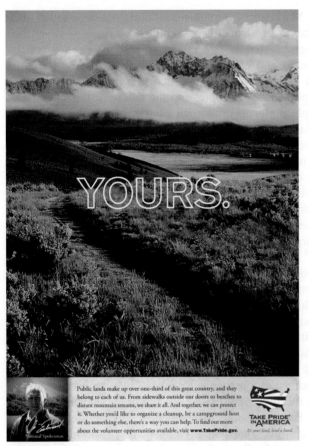

**EXHIBIT 6–11**

Actor Clint Eastwood's authoritative image makes him an effective source

of presentation, conclusion drawing, message sidedness, refutation, and verbal versus visual message characteristics.

**Order of Presentation**   A basic consideration in the design of a persuasive message is the arguments' order of presentation. Should the most important message points be placed at the beginning of the message, in the middle, or at the end? Research on learning and memory generally indicates that items presented first and last are remembered better than those presented in the middle (see Figure 6–4).[66] This suggests that a communicator's strongest arguments should be presented early or late in the message but never in the middle.

Presenting the strongest arguments at the beginning of the message assumes a **primacy effect** is operating, whereby information presented first is most effective. Putting the strong points at the end assumes a **recency effect**, whereby the last arguments presented are most persuasive.

Whether to place the strongest selling points at the beginning or the end of the message depends on several factors. If the target audience is opposed to the communicator's position, presenting strong points first can reduce the level of counterarguing. Putting weak arguments first might lead to such a high level of counterarguing that strong arguments that followed would not be believed. Strong arguments work best at the beginning of the message if the audience is not interested in the topic, so they can arouse interest in the message. When the target audience is predisposed toward the communicator's position or is highly interested in the issue or product, strong arguments can be saved for the end of the message. This may result in a more favorable opinion as well as better retention of the information.

The order of presentation can be critical when a long, detailed message with many arguments is being presented. Most effective sales presentations open and close with strong selling points and bury weaker arguments in the middle. For short communications, such as a 15- or 30-second TV or radio commercial, the order may be less critical. However, many product and service messages are received by consumers with low involvement and minimal interest. Thus, an advertiser may want to present the brand name and key selling points early in the message and repeat them at the end to enhance recall and retention. Order of presentation is also an important consideration in other forms of marketing communication. For example, many press releases use the "pyramid style" of writing, whereby most of the important information is presented up front to ensure that it is read since editors often cut from the end of articles.

**FIGURE 6–4**

Ad Message Recall as a Function of Order of Presentation

**Conclusion Drawing** Marketing communicators must decide whether their messages should explicitly draw a firm conclusion or allow receivers to draw their own conclusions. Research suggests that, in general, messages with explicit conclusions are more easily understood and effective in influencing attitudes. However, other studies have shown that the effectiveness of conclusion drawing may depend on the target audience, the type of issue or topic, and the nature of the situation.[67]

More highly educated people prefer to draw their own conclusions and may be annoyed at an attempt to explain the obvious or to draw an inference for them. But stating the conclusion may be necessary for a less educated audience, who may not draw any conclusion or may make an incorrect inference from the message. Marketers must also consider the audience's level of involvement in the topic. For highly personal or ego-involving issues, message recipients may want to make up their own minds and resent any attempts by the communicator to draw a conclusion. One study found that open-ended ads (without explicit conclusions) were more effective than closed-ended arguments that did include a specific conclusion—but only for involved audiences.[68]

Whether to draw a conclusion for the audience also depends on the complexity of the topic. Even a highly educated audience may need assistance if its knowledge level in a particular area is low. Does the marketer want the message to trigger immediate action or a more long-term effect? If immediate action is an objective, the message should draw a definite conclusion. This is a common strategy in political advertising, particularly for ads run close to election day. When immediate impact is not the objective and repeated exposure will give the audience members opportunities to draw their own conclusions, an open-ended message may be used.

Drawing a conclusion in a message may make sure the target audience gets the point the marketer intended. But many advertisers believe that letting customers draw their own conclusions reinforces the points being made in the message. For example, a health services agency in Kentucky found that open-ended ads were more memorable and more effective in getting consumers to use health services than were ads stating a conclusion. Ads that posed questions about alcohol and drug abuse and left them unanswered resulted in more calls by teenagers to a help line for information than did a message offering a resolution to the problem.[69] The ad shown in Exhibit 6–12, which is from the Montana Meth Project (MMP) drug prevention messaging campaign, is a good example of this strategy. The ad challenges teens to consider what they know about methamphetamine and prompts them to learn more by visiting the MMP website.

**Message Sidedness** Another message structure decision facing the marketer involves message sidedness. A **one-sided message** mentions only positive attributes or benefits. A **two-sided message** presents both good and bad points. One-sided messages are most effective when the target audience already holds a favorable opinion about the topic. They also work better with a less educated audience.[70]

Two-sided messages are more effective when the target audience holds an opposing opinion or is highly educated. Two-sided messages may enhance the credibility of the source.[71] A better-educated audience usually knows there are opposing arguments, so a communicator who presents both sides of an issue is likely to be seen as less biased and more objective. Martin Eisend conducted a meta-analysis of the research conducted on the effects of one- versus two-sided advertising messages. The results of his analysis showed that the persuasive impact of message sidedness depends on a number of factors including the amount and importance of negative information in the ad, attribute quality, placement of the negative information, the correlation between negative and positive attributes, and whether the advertiser discloses negative information voluntarily or because it is required to do so.[72]

**EXHIBIT 6–12**
This ad for is a good example of the use of open-ended messaging

WILL METH
CHANGE WHO I AM?
METHPROJECT.ORG

Most advertisers use one-sided messages. They are concerned about the negative effects of acknowledging a weakness in their brand or don't want to say anything positive about their competitors. There are exceptions, however. Sometimes advertisers compare brands on several attributes and do not show their product as being the best on every one. There also may be situations in which a company feels that is best to acknowledge its shortcomings and let its customers know that it has addressed them.

An example of a company that used a two-sided message very effectively is the Domino's Pizza chain, which took the strategy to a whole new level in an integrated marketing campaign used to introduce its new, reformulated pizza in 2010. Domino's recognized that changes were needed after conducting research that revealed many consumers had issues with the taste of its pizza; after 18 months of research and development and consumer testing, the chain was ready to roll out its reformulated product. However, Domino's and its advertising agency, Crispin Porter + Bogusky, deliberated over how to acknowledge that there were problems with the taste of the old pizza while telling consumers that they would like the taste of the new formulation. CP + B argued that credibility was the key and the best way to achieve it was for Domino's to acknowledge that its pizza could have been better. As part of its "Pizza Turnaround" campaign Domino's used commercials showing the chain's new CEO in front of the camera admitting that he had heard what the focus groups had to say and that it took it to heart. The spots then pointed viewers to a special website (www.pizzaturnaround.com) that featured a four-minute documentary chronicling Domino's employees' reactions to the negative comments coming from the focus groups and telling about the company's quest to make a better pizza (Exhibit 6–13). The website also showed both positive and negative viewer comments, as well as tweets that were linked in from Twitter.

Many marketing and advertising experts argued that Domino's took a big risk with the campaign as it could have easily backfired. While Domino's and its agency knew the campaign might be risky, they moved forward with it and the results were very favorable: They received a great deal of publicity regarding the ads, much of which praised the company for conceding the shortcomings of its product and explaining what it was doing about it. The two-sided message strategy also had a very positive impact on sales as the chain generated a record increase in same-store sales in 2010 despite overall pizza sales remaining flat due to the weak economy.[73]

**Refutation**   In a special type of two-sided message known as a **refutational appeal**, the communicator presents both sides of an issue and then refutes the opposing viewpoint. Since refutational appeals tend to "inoculate" the target audience against a competitor's counterclaims, they are more effective than one-sided

YTC **06–09**

**Domino's**

youtube.com/10ebelch

**EXHIBIT 6–13**

Domino's two-sided message strategy was a very effective way to introduce its reformulated pizza

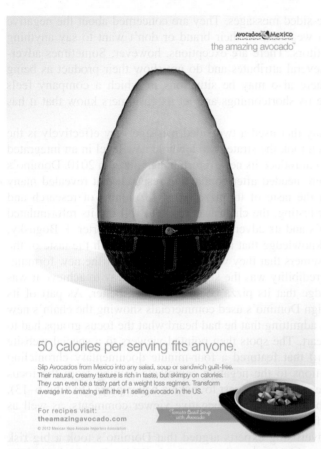

Avocados from Mexico
the amazing avocado

50 calories per serving fits anyone.

Slip Avocados from Mexico into any salad, soup or sandwich guilt-free.
Their natural, creamy texture is rich in taste, but skimpy on calories.
They can even be a tasty part of a weight loss regimen. Transform
average into amazing with the #1 selling avocado in the US.

For recipes visit:
theamazingavocado.com

© 2012 Mexican Hass Avocado Importers Association

Tomato Basil Soup
with Avocado

**EXHIBIT 6–14**

A refutational appeal is used
to address concerns that
avocados are high in calories

messages in making consumers resistant to an opposing message.[74]

Refutational messages may be useful when marketers wish to build attitudes that resist change and must defend against attacks or criticism of their products or the company. For example, Exhibit 6–14 shows a clever ad used by the Mexican Hass Avocado Importers Association to refute concerns that avocados are high in calories and state they can be part of a weight-loss regimen. Market leaders, who are often the target of comparative messages, may find that acknowledging competitors' claims and then refuting them can help build resistant attitudes and customer loyalty.

**Verbal versus Visual Messages**  Thus far our discussion has focused on the information, or verbal, portion of the message. However, the nonverbal, visual elements of an ad are also very important. Many ads provide minimal amounts of information and rely on visual elements to communicate. Pictures are commonly used in advertising to convey information or reinforce copy or message claims.

Both the verbal and visual portions of an ad influence the way the advertising message is processed.[75] Consumers may develop images or impressions based on visual elements such as an illustration in an ad or the scenes in a TV commercial. In some cases, the visual portion of an ad may reduce its persuasiveness, since the processing stimulated by the picture may be less controlled and consequently less favorable than that stimulated by words.[76]

Pictures affect the way consumers process accompanying copy. A study showed that when verbal information was low in imagery value, the use of pictures providing examples increased both immediate and delayed recall of product attributes.[77] However, when the verbal information was already high in imagery value, the addition of pictures did not increase recall. Advertisers often design ads where the visual image supports the verbal appeal to create a compelling impression in the consumer's mind. Notice how the ad for Arrowhead Mountain Spring Water shown in Exhibit 6–15 uses a beautiful visual image of the mountains to communicate the key product attribute of purity.

Sometimes advertisers use a different strategy; they design ads in which the visual portion is incongruent with or contradicts the verbal information presented. The logic behind this strategy is that the use of an unexpected picture or visual image will grab consumers' attention and get them to engage in more effortful or elaborative processing.[78] A number of studies have shown that the use of a visual that is inconsistent with the verbal content leads to more recall and greater processing of the information presented.[79] The ad for Gain dishwashing liquid shown in Exhibit 6–16 is a good example of this technique. The visual image showing people happily washing dishes is not consistent with the ad copy stating that "dishwashing may never feel this great."

## Message Appeals

One of the advertiser's most important creative strategy decisions involves the choice of an appropriate appeal. Some ads are designed to appeal to the rational, logical aspect of the consumer's decision-making process; others appeal to feelings in an attempt to evoke some emotional reaction. Many believe that effective advertising combines the practical reasons for purchasing a product with emotional values. In this section we will examine several common types of message appeals, including comparative advertising, fear, and humor.

### Comparative Advertising

**Comparative advertising** is the practice of either directly or indirectly naming competitors in an ad and comparing one or more specific attributes.[80] This form of advertising became popular after the Federal Trade Commission (FTC) began advocating its use in 1972. The FTC reasoned that direct comparison of brands would provide better product information, giving consumers a more rational basis for making purchase decisions. Television networks cooperated with the FTC by lifting their ban on comparative ads, and the result was a flurry of comparative commercials.

Initially, the novelty of comparative ads resulted in greater attention. But since they have become so common, their attention-getting value has probably declined. Some studies show that recall is higher for comparative than noncomparative messages, but comparative ads are generally not more effective for other response variables, such as brand attitudes or purchase intentions.[81] Advertisers must also consider how comparative messages affect credibility. Users of the brand being attacked in a comparative message may be especially skeptical about the advertiser's claims.

Comparative advertising may be particularly useful for new brands, since it allows a new market entrant to position itself directly against the more established brands and to promote its distinctive advantages. Direct comparisons can help position a new brand in the evoked, or choice, set of brands the customer may be considering. Comparative advertising is often used for brands with a small market share. They compare themselves to an established market leader in hopes of creating an association and tapping into the leader's market.

The use of comparative advertising is not limited to new brands or those with a small market share; a number of high-profile marketers have been using comparative appeals to differentiate their brands in a competitive marketplace.[82] For example, Apple ran its comparative "Get a Mac" campaign, which poked fun at Microsoft's Windows operating system while promoting the user friendliness of Mac computers for over three years. The campaign included 66 TV spots that portrayed actor Justin Long as the hip, unflappable Mac and *New York Times Magazine* writer John Hodgman as the uptight and somewhat nerdy PC who is frustrated by the Mac's capabilities (Exhibit 6–17). The campaign was credited with helping increase Apple's share of the PC market in the United States from 2 to 8 percent and was named the best advertising campaign of the first decade of the new century by industry trade publication *Adweek*.[83]

A number of other companies and brands have been using comparative advertising effectively in recent years including AT&T, Miller Lite, and Samsung. Ironically, Samsung has used comparative ads to gain market share in the smartphone market by comparing its Samsung Galaxy phone to Apple's iPhone. For example, shortly after Apple launched the iPhone 5, Samsung ran a commercial for its Galaxy S III that mocked iPhone loyalists for waiting in line to get the new smartphone. The ad was one of several spots in Samsung's "The Next Best Thing Is Already Here" campaign that were very popular with consumers and led to Samsung being named the most viral brand of 2012.[84] Exhibit 6–18 shows one of the ads used by Samsung to compare the Galaxy S III to the iPhone.

**EXHIBIT 6–15**

Visual images are an effective way to communicate an important product attribute

YTC **06-10**

**Comparative Ads**

youtube.com/10ebelch

**EXHIBIT 6–16**

This ad uses a visual image that may encourage more elaborative processing

**EXHIBIT 6–17**

Apple used comparative advertising in its "Get a Mac" campaign

Market leaders often hesitate to use comparison ads, as most believe they have little to gain by featuring competitors' products in their ads. There are exceptions, of course; Coca-Cola resorted to comparative advertising in response to challenges made by Pepsi that were reducing Coke's market share. Anheuser-Busch also responded to the comparative ads used by the Miller Brewing Company when its rival started gaining market share at the expense of Bud Light and other brands. Microsoft has responded to Apple's comparative campaign by running a series of ads that defended PC users and was critical of Apple for stereotyping them. Microsoft also ran a "Laptop Hunters" campaign showing consumers comparing prices of Macs versus PCs and learning that Apple's products were often priced higher.[85]

Another area where comparative messages are quite commonly used is political advertising. Political advertising is viewed as an important component of political speech and thus enjoys more First Amendment protection than commercial speech and less regulation by either government or self-policing agencies. Thus, it has become quite common for political ads to contain negative, one-sided attacks on an opposing candidate's weaknesses such as character flaws, voting record, public misstatements, broken promises, and the like.[86] The goal of these ads is to discredit the character, record, or position of an opponent and create doubt in voters' minds about his or her ability to govern effectively. A major reason why negative political ads are used successfully is that voters often tend to weight negative information more heavily than positive information when forming impressions of political candidates.[87] However, studies have shown that the use of "attack advertising" by politicians can result in negative perceptions of both candidates.[88] IMC Perspective 6–2 discusses how the use of attack ads has become very common in presidential elections in the United States and why they are often very effective.

**Fear Appeals**   Fear is an emotional response to a threat that expresses, or at least implies, some sort of danger. Ads sometimes use **fear appeals** to evoke this emotional response and arouse individuals to take steps to remove the threat. Some, like the antidrug ads used by the Partnership for a Drug-Free America, stress physical danger that can occur if behaviors are not altered. Others—like those for deodorant, mouthwash, or dandruff shampoos—threaten disapproval or social rejection.

**How Fear Operates**   Before deciding to use a fear appeal–based message strategy, the advertiser should consider how fear operates, what level to use, and how different target audiences may respond. One theory suggests that the relationship between the level of fear in a message and acceptance or persuasion is curvilinear, as shown in Figure 6–5.[89] This means that message acceptance increases as the amount of fear used rises—to a point. Beyond that point, acceptance decreases as the level of fear rises.

**EXHIBIT 6–18**

Samsung's comparative ads position the Galaxy S III against the iPhone 5

This relationship between fear and persuasion can be explained by the fact that fear appeals have both facilitating and inhibiting effects.[90] A low level of fear can have facilitating effects; it attracts attention and interest in the message and may motivate the receiver to act to resolve the threat. Thus, increasing the level of fear in a message from low to moderate can result in increased persuasion. High levels of fear, however, can produce inhibiting effects; the receiver may emotionally block the message by tuning it out, perceiving it selectively, or denying its

**FIGURE 6–5**

Relationship between
Fear Levels and Message
Acceptance

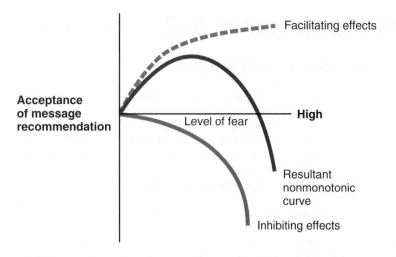

arguments outright. Figure 6–5 illustrates how these two countereffects operate to produce the curvilinear relationship between fear and persuasion.

A study by Anand-Keller and Block provides support for this perspective on how fear operates.[91] They examined the conditions under which low- and high-fear appeals urging people to stop smoking are likely to be effective. Their study indicated that a communication using a low level of fear may be ineffective because it results in insufficient motivation to elaborate on the harmful consequences of engaging in the destructive behavior (smoking). However, an appeal arousing high levels of fear was ineffective because it resulted in too much elaboration on the harmful consequences. This led to defensive tendencies such as message avoidance and interfered with processing of recommended solutions to the problem.

Another approach to the curvilinear explanation of fear is the protection motivation model.[92] According to this theory, four cognitive appraisal processes mediate the individual's response to the threat: appraising (1) the information available regarding the severity of the perceived threat, (2) the perceived probability that the threat will occur, (3) the perceived ability of a coping behavior to remove the threat, and (4) the individual's perceived ability to carry out the coping behavior.

This model suggests that both the cognitive appraisal of the information in a fear appeal message and the emotional response mediate persuasion. An audience is more likely to continue processing threat-related information, thereby increasing the likelihood that a coping behavior will occur.

The protection motivation model suggests that ads using fear appeals should give the target audience information about the severity of the threat, the probability of its occurrence, the effectiveness of a coping response, and the ease with which the response can be implemented.[93] For example, the ad shown in Exhibit 6–19 uses a mild fear appeal for Seagate Technology's Replica product, which is used to back up computer hard drives. The ad uses playful illustrations in a graphic style to communicate the message of what can happen if your computer crashes and all of the files are lost. Notice how the ad also offers a solution to the threat by showing the ease of using the Replica product and the resulting peace of mind.

It is also important to consider how the target audience may respond. Fear appeals are more effective when the message recipient is self-confident and prefers to cope

**EXHIBIT 6–19**

Seagate uses a mild fear
appeal that alerts consumers
to a problem and offers a
solution

State 1

State 2

State 3

State 4

State 5

State 6

# IMC Perspective 6–2 > > >

## Attack Ads Become Pervasive

If you watch TV on any sort of regular basis, you've probably noticed that every two years the airwaves experience a huge influx of political advertising. Depending on the campaign cycle, the number of ads airing to promote candidates running for either local, state, or national political office will increase. Political ads generally fall into one of two categories. The first type is self-promoting, positive ads that highlight all of the great things the candidate has done throughout his or her career; the second type is negative or "attack ads" that target an opponent's platform, record, background, or character. These negative ads have become commonplace in political campaigns over the past decade and far outweigh the number of positive messages. And if you are like most voters, you are very annoyed by these ads and tired of seeing and/or hearing them.

While negative advertising in politics is indeed pervasive, the commonly held perception that negative ads are shown more often than their positive counterparts was not always the case. The 2004 presidential election between George W. Bush and John Kerry, for example, was viewed as the "most negative" presidential race since the 1950s, but only a little over 50 percent of all ads that aired were negative. However, it did feature the infamous Swift Boat ad in which former veterans claimed that Kerry lied to get one of his two decorations for bravery and two of his three purple hearts from the Vietnam War. Although the accusations were contradicted by Kerry's former crew members and by Navy records, the ad played an important role in helping Bush defeat Kerry. And if you think negative political advertising is a recent phenomenon, think again. The 1988 election between Bush's father, George H. W., and democratic candidate Michael Dukakis, for example, brought viewers the famous "Willie Horton" and

"tank" ads that all but doomed Dukakis's chances. Lyndon Johnson's "Daisy" attack ad, against Barry Goldwater in the 1964 presidential election, that suggested that the Republican candidate would draw the United States into a nuclear war is often cited as the most negative and powerful political ads of all time. In the early 1800s, Andrew Jackson was portrayed as a murderer and Abraham Lincoln called "stupid" and an "ape" by his opponent in the 1860 election. When viewing attack ads in this light, one might argue that political candidates have actually become somewhat soft in recent years!

Of course the question most people ask when they become annoyed by all of the negative advertising that takes place during political campaigns is, does it work? Unfortunately for the voters who have to watch them, the answer appears to be yes. Studies have shown that negative ads are more powerful, memorable, and much more likely to discuss real issues in an election than positive ads. Positive ads can get away with flowery language and hyperbole to try to "prop up" a candidate, while negative ads must work hard to achieve credibility and provide evidence to support his or her claims. If a negative ad makes an assertion that is untrue, the candidate who created it may experience a backlash far worse than anything an opposing ad could provide. When negative ads do attack an opponent on a personal level, they usually highlight inexperience or dishonesty, two attributes that are very important when electing someone to public office. And attack ads may seem to be everywhere because they are having the intended effect whereby you may recall them long after seeing them.

Critics of negative political ads argue that they distract voters from the real issues by getting them to focus on meaningless personal attacks, encourage deception and

**YTC** 06–11

**Political Attack Ads**

youtube.com/10ebelch

with dangers rather than avoid them.[94] They are also more effective among nonusers of a product than among users. Thus, a fear appeal may be better at keeping nonsmokers from starting than persuading smokers to stop.

In reviewing research on fear appeals, Herbert Rotfeld has argued that some of the studies may be confusing different types of threats and the level of potential harm portrayed in the message with fear, which is an emotional response.[95] He concludes that the relationship between the emotional responses of fear or arousal and persuasion is not curvilinear but rather is monotonic and positive, meaning that higher levels of fear do result in greater persuasion. However, Rotfeld notes that not all fear messages are equally effective, because different people fear different things. Thus they will respond differently to the same threat, so the strongest threats are not always the most persuasive. This suggests that marketers using fear appeals must consider the emotional responses generated by the message and how they will affect reactions to the message.

While research suggests that message recipients might tune out a message that uses too much fear, there are examples of advertising campaigns where high levels of fear have been effective at changing behavior. For example, the Montana Meth Project (MMP) is a large-scale prevention program aimed at reducing methamphetamine use, particularly among teenagers, through public service messaging, policy, and community outreach. The integrated campaign uses hard-hitting TV, radio, print,

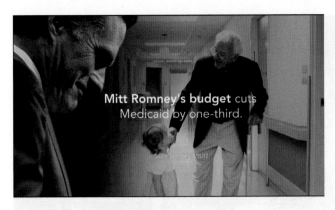

Mitt Romney's budget cuts
Medicaid by one-third.

Source: Bloomberg, 3/15/12

incivility, and end up disillusioning voters. However, many political analysts are still very much in favor of them, arguing that if negativity were to disappear from our electoral battles so would the democratic system in which we take so much pride. While a significant number of studies show that people are skeptical of and irritated by negative ads, political consultants point to studies showing that despite the public's feelings toward the moral or ethical nature of them, attack ads are often successful in shifting voters' perceptions of a candidate. In fact, the effects of attack ads are so strong that many marketers wonder why more marketers don't advertise their products and services the same way. While comparative ads have become very common in the United States and many other countries, we rarely see companies disparaging and attacking one another the way politicians do in nearly every campaign.

One final reason why attack ads seem so ubiquitous is because networks are obligated to show all forms of political advertising. Legal requirements state that if a candidate requests ad time, the station must provide it at the lowest possible market rate. That means that even if another advertiser booked airtime months in advance, the station can replace it with a political spot for no other reason other than

it has to do so. This has several effects for both political and nonpolitical ads as the rates for airtime often rise considerably during an election year and particularly during presidential elections, where the amount of money available for media advertising is very high. While one might argue that corporations could simply pull their ads to avoid paying the inflated costs for media time, they would be running the risk of having their awareness levels decline and possibly losing market share to competitors.

Politicians and their campaign managers realize that it is very difficult to win an election today without attacking their opponent. Candidates for public office often start a campaign by taking the high ground, but then waste little time turning to attack ads when they fall behind in the polls or feel they have to respond to an accusation made in one of their opponents' ads. The 2012 presidential election between Barrack Obama and Mitt Romney set a record for most negative campaign ads in history, according to the Wesleyan Media Project, which tracks political advertising; 86 percent of Obama's TV ads and 79 percent of Romney's were negative. Political analysts noted that the campaign was very negative because both campaigns recognized that anything that moved even 1 percent of the voters could make a difference in the seven or eight key battleground states. It clearly looks like attack ads will remain the norm, and the question now is whether we will ever see a positive political ad again.

Sources: Donovan Slack, "RIP Positive Ads in 2012," *Politico*, November 4, 2012, www.politico.com/news/stories/1112/83262.html; Rance Crain, "Marketers Could Learn from Negative Political Ads: Keep It Simple," *Advertising Age*, February 20, 2012, http://adage.com/article/rance-crain/marketers-learn-political-ads-simple/232797/; Brian Steinberg, "Surviving the Political Ad Deluge in Swing States Such as Virginia, TV Stations Are Swamped with Campaign Cash—But Some Local Advertisers Are Getting Boxed Out," *Advertising Age*, October 14, 2012, http://age.com/article/media/surviving-political-ad-deluge/237726/; Tom Denari, "Why Attack Ads and Disney Movies Are So Darned Effective," *Advertising Age*, October 19 2010, http://adage.com/article/146579/.

YTC 06–12

**Montana Meth Project**
youtube.com/10ebelch

digital, and social media messaging to communicate the risks of meth use.[96] Many of the ads used in the campaign use a high level of fear to communicate the risks of meth use and addiction such as the one shown in Exhibit 6–20. The MMP has been very successful: meth use in Montana has declined significantly and the campaign

**EXHIBIT 6–20**
The Montana Meth Project uses ads with a high level of fear

NO ONE EVER THINKS THEY'LL WAKE UP HERE. METH WILL CHANGE THAT.

THE METH PROJECT

METH
not even once.

MethProject.org

EXHIBIT 6–21
This clever ad is an example
of how humor can be
executed in print media

BEWARE
OF CARS WITH
LESS THAN
4 STARS
★★★★★
ancap.com.au

ANCAP

YTC 06–13

**Humorous Commercials**

youtube.com/10ebelch

has been expanded to a number of other states. A recent study of fear appeals by Andrea Morales, Eugenia Wu, and Gavan Fitzsimons suggests that ads such as those used in the MMP campaign may be effective because they activate disgust as well as fear through some of the disturbing images they contain.[97]

**Humor Appeals** Humorous ads are often the best known and best remembered of all advertising messages. Many advertisers, including FedEx, GEICO, AT&T, and Bud Light, use humor appeals effectively. Humor is usually presented through radio and TV commercials as these media lend themselves to the execution of humorous messages. However, humor is occasionally used in print ads as well. The clever ad shown in Exhibit 6–21 is a good example of how humor can be used effectively in print. The ad is used by the Australasian New Car Assessment Program (ANCAP) which provides consumers in Australia and New Zealand with information on the level of occupant protection provided by vehicles in front and side crashes.

Advertisers use humor for many reasons. Humorous messages attract and hold consumers' attention. They enhance effectiveness by putting consumers in a positive mood, increasing their liking of the ad itself and their feeling toward the product or service. And humor can distract the receiver from counterarguing against the message.[98]

Critics argue that funny ads draw people to the humorous situation but distract them from the brand and its attributes. Also, effective humor can be difficult to produce and some attempts are too subtle for mass audiences. And, there is concern that humorous ads may wear out faster than serious appeals. **Wearout** refers to the tendency of a television or radio commercial to lose its effectiveness when it is seen and/or heard repeatedly.[99] Wearout may occur if consumers no longer pay attention to a commercial after several exposures or become annoyed at seeing or hearing an ad multiple times. Some experts argue that humorous ads wear out faster than other formats because once the consumer gets the joke, the ad becomes boring. However, advocates of humor argue that funny ads are effective longer as consumers will respond more favorably to a well-executed humorous ad than a serious message.[100] IMC Perspective 6–3 discusses why marketers often run the same ads repeatedly and how humor and other techniques may be used to deal with the problem of wearout.

Clearly, there are valid reasons both for and against the use of humor in advertising. Not every product or service lends itself to a humorous approach. A number of studies have found that the effectiveness of humor depends on several factors, including the type of product and audience characteristics.[101] For example, humor has been more prevalent and more effective with low-involvement, feeling products than high-involvement, thinking products.[102] A recent study examined how audience involvement moderates the effects of humorous ads. The researchers found that for products that are not intrinsically humorous, the use of humor in an advertising message is more effective when involvement is relatively low rather than high. These findings support the idea that high-involvement products may not be as well suited for advertising humor as low-involvement products.[103] An interesting study surveyed the research and creative directors of the top 150 advertising agencies.[104] They were asked to name which communications objectives are facilitated through the appropriate situational use of humor in terms of media, product, and audience factors. The general conclusions of this study are shown in Figure 6–6.

# CHANNEL FACTORS

LO 06-4

The final controllable variable of the communication process is the channel, or medium, used to deliver the message to the target audience. While a variety of methods are available to transmit marketing communications, as noted in Chapter 5, they can be classified into two broad categories, personal and nonpersonal media.

## Personal versus Nonpersonal Channels

There are a number of basic differences between personal and nonpersonal communications channels. Information received from personal influence channels is generally more persuasive than information received via the mass media. Reasons

**FIGURE 6–6**

Summary of Top Ad Agency Research and Creative Directors' Opinions Regarding Humor

- Humor does aid awareness and attention, which are the objectives best achieved by its use.
    - Humor may harm recall and comprehension in general.
    - Humor may aid name and simple copy registration.
    - Humor may harm complex copy registration.
    - Humor may aid retention.
- Humor does not aid persuasion in general.
    - Humor may aid persuasion to switch brands.
    - Humor creates a positive mood that enhances persuasion.
- Humor does not aid source credibility.
- Humor is generally not very effective in bringing about action/sales.
- Creatives are more positive on the use of humor to fulfill all the above objectives than research directors are.
- Radio and TV are the best media in which to use humor; direct mail and newspapers are least suited.
- Consumer nondurables and business services are best suited to humor; corporate advertising and industrial products are least suited.
- Humor should be related to the product.
- Humor should not be used with sensitive goods or services.
- Audiences that are younger, better educated, upscale, male, and professional are best suited to humor; older, less educated, and downscale groups are least suited to humor appeals.

# IMC Perspective 6–3 > > >

## Why Do We Have to Watch Some Ads So Many Times?

If you watch television regularly, or even on a limited basis, at some point it is likely that you have become annoyed at seeing the same commercial being shown over and over. An issue that is always of concern to advertisers is the problem of commercial wearout, or the tendency of a message to lose its effectiveness when it is seen or heard repeatedly. Wearout may occur for several reasons. One is inattention as consumers may no longer pay attention to a TV or radio commercial after watching or listening to it several times, because it no longer is novel and/or interesting. Another reason is when the same ad airs too often, consumers become bored, annoyed, or even irate as advertisers can drive them crazy by subjecting them to the same spot over and over. Having to endure the same ad multiple times can be particularly annoying during sporting events such as football, baseball, and basketball games which last for several hours. The problem can also be compounded when multiple games or events are shown during a concentrated period, such as the summer and winter Olympics, the NCAA "March Madness" college basketball tournament, the college football bowl games, or the playoffs for various professional sports. Some marketers will air the same ad multiple times during a single game and hundreds of times over the duration of a major event or playoffs, which can be very irritating to people who are heavy viewers.

The problem of advertising wearout has intrigued advertising practitioners as well as academic researchers for decades. Studies suggest that TV commercials can be viewed anywhere from 4 to 25 times before losing their effectiveness, although a study by the Publicis Groupe's Starcom MediaVest Group found that ads with storylines wore out more slowly than hard sell ads with an aggressive call to action. The study also found that pairing humor and music together helped reduce wearout, and ads that went off the air for at least 12 weeks could start up again and retain their effectiveness. However, Kate Sirkin, who is the global research director at Starcom, recently noted that consumers have become much more sensitive to multiple showings of the same commercial and

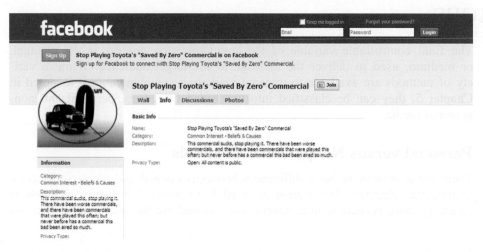

for the differences are summarized in the following comparison of advertising and personal selling:

> From the standpoint of persuasion, a sales message is far more flexible, personal, and powerful than an advertisement. An advertisement is normally prepared by persons having minimal personal contact with customers. The message is designed to appeal to a large number of persons. By contrast, the message in a good sales presentation is not determined in advance. The salesman has a tremendous store of knowledge about his product or service and selects appropriate items as the interview progresses. Thus, the salesman can adapt this to the thinking and needs of the customer or prospect at the time of the sales call. Furthermore, as objections arise and are voiced by the buyer, the salesman can treat the objections in an appropriate manner. This is not possible in advertising.[105]

Personal channels are used in several ways in an IMC program. As was discussed in Chapter 5, many marketers are recognizing the importance of word-of-mouth communications which is becoming more prevalent with the growth of social media. The more traditional use of personal communications is through sales programs which are implemented through a company's sales force as well as at the point of purchase through retail sales personnel. However, the advertising and promotion programs for that a TV ad can reach a wearout point after only 8 showings, versus the 15 to 20 found in the 2003 study. She notes that consumers are more aware of a greater range of entertainment options and are "all multitasking, less patient, and don't like to have their time wasted."

There are several ways that marketers can deal with the wearout problem. One of the ways is to develop multiple executions that can be rotated. Large advertisers often create "pool-outs" or multiple executions around a commercial theme that can be rotated so no one ad airs incessantly. Advertisers can also use certain creative techniques that may make a commercial tolerable for a longer time such as appeals that tap into consumer emotions rather than hard sell approaches. As noted above, the original Starcom study found that utilizing humor or popular music can be helpful in staving off viewer fatigue. However, some industry experts argue that humorous ads can wear out at the same rate as other types of ads because once consumers see the ad a few times, the hilarity loses its impact.

While marketers, agency executives, and media buyers recognize that wearout is a problem, many companies still bombard their target audiences repeatedly with the same commercial, which begs the question of why they continue to do so. One reason is that companies do not have large budgets to create multiple ads for a campaign and often may rely on only one or two executions. The average production costs for a high-quality TV commercial is nearly $400,000 and many ads cost much more to produce. Smaller advertisers such as local retailers, automobile dealers, banks, and other companies are particularly likely to have a limited budget for their TV creative work and often end up producing one TV spot that airs repeatedly. Another reason is that television has become a much more complex medium to buy. The fragmentation of the media market has resulted in the top shows delivering much smaller audiences than in the past, which means that marketers must run the same ad more often to reach the millions of people they want to attract. Also

contributing to the problem is the increasing penetration of DVRs which allow consumers to fast-forward through commercials when they play back recorded shows and thus make it difficult for marketers to achieve their desired levels of reach and frequency. Finally, many marketers are turning to the use of 15-second commercials rather than 30-second spots. They argue that consumers' attention spans are getting shorter, and research shows that the shorter ads hold on to more eyeballs longer than the longer format. Moreover, 15-second spots cost about the same per second as longer ads and can be run twice as often for the same budget.

In some cases it is likely that marketers know that they are saturating the airways with their ads and actually do so intentionally. For example, in late 2008 and early 2009, Toyota created an ad based on the 1983 hit song "Saved by Zero" by the group Fixx that promoted the company's no-interest payment option that was run so often that it resulted in the creation of a Facebook group with nearly 9,000 fans who organized to try to get the company to stop running the ad. However, a company spokesperson noted that Toyota intentionally ran the ad repeatedly to counter all the media reports that credit was not available for new car buyers. Advertisers can also get better rates on TV advertising time when they purchase large numbers of spots, which leads to media efficiencies.

It is unlikely that many of the advertisers whose media plans include heavy repetition of their commercials are going to change any time soon. However, the more astute marketers may want to consider whether they are doing more harm than good by bombarding consumers with the same commercial over and over and over.

Sources: Brian Steinberg, "Ad Nauseam: Repetition of TV Spots Risks Driving Consumers Away," *Advertising Age*, December 1, 2008, http://adage.com/print?article_id=132884; George Anders, "Marketers Get Creative to Stave Off Ad Fatigue," *The Wall Street Journal*, October 1, 2007, p B5; Emily Fredrix, "Shorter TV Spots Prove to Be More Effective," *San Diego Union-Tribune*, October 28, 2010, pp. C1, 4.

most marketers rely heavily on media advertising as well as the Internet. Thus, we will discuss some of the important factors that marketers must consider with respect to the mass media.

## Effects of Alternative Mass Media

The various mass media that advertisers use to transmit their messages differ in many ways, including the number and type of people they reach, costs, information processing requirements, and qualitative factors. The mass media's costs and efficiency in exposing a target audience to a communication will be evaluated in Chapters 10 through 12. However, we should recognize differences in how information is processed and how communications are influenced by context or environment.

**Differences in Information Processing**    There are basic differences in the manner and rate at which information from various forms of media is transmitted and can be processed. Information from ads in print media, such as newspapers, magazines, or direct mail, as well as the Internet is *self-paced*; readers process the ad at their own rate and can study it as long as they desire. In contrast, information from the broadcast media of radio and television is *externally paced;* the transmission rate is controlled by the medium.

The difference in the processing rate for print and broadcast media has some obvious implications for advertisers. Self-paced print media make it easier for the message recipient to process a long, complex message. Advertisers often use print ads when they want to present a detailed message with a lot of information. Broadcast media are more effective for transmitting shorter messages or, in the case of TV, presenting pictorial information along with words.

While there are limits to the length and complexity of broadcast messages, advertisers can deal with this problem. One strategy is to use a radio or TV ad to get consumers' attention and direct them to specific print media for a more detailed message. For example, home builders use radio ads to draw attention to new developments and direct listeners to the real estate section of the newspaper for more details. Some advertisers develop broadcast and print versions of the same message. The copy portion is similar in both media, but the print ad can be processed at a rate comfortable to the receiver.

## Effects of Context and Environment

Interpretation of an advertising message can be influenced by the context or environment in which the ad appears. Communication theorist Marshall McLuhan's thesis, "The medium is the message," implies that the medium communicates an image that is independent of any message it contains.[106] A **qualitative media effect** is the influence the medium has on a message. The image of the media vehicle can affect reactions to the message. For example, an ad for a high-quality men's clothing line might have more of an impact in a fashion magazine like *GQ* than in *Sports Afield.* Airlines, destination resorts, and travel-related services advertise in publications such as *Travel & Leisure* partly because the articles, pictures, and other ads help to excite readers about travel (Exhibit 6–22).

**EXHIBIT 6–22**
*Travel & Leisure* magazine creates an excellent reception environment for travel-related ads

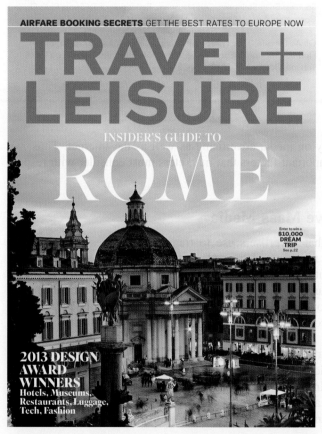

AIRFARE BOOKING SECRETS GET THE BEST RATES TO EUROPE NOW

TRAVEL+
LEISURE

INSIDER'S GUIDE TO
ROME

Enter to win a
$10,000
DREAM
TRIP
See p. 22

2013 DESIGN
AWARD
WINNERS
Hotels, Museums,
Restaurants, Luggage,
Tech, Fashion

A media environment can also be created by the nature of the program in which a commercial appears. One study found that consumers reacted more positively to commercials seen during a happy TV program than a sad one.[107] Advertisers pay premium dollars to advertise on popular programs that create positive moods, like sitcoms, the Olympic Games, and Christmas specials. Conversely, advertisers tend to avoid programs that create a negative mood among viewers or may be detrimental to the company or its products. Many companies won't advertise on programs with excessive violence or sexual content. Coca-Cola never advertises on TV news programs because it thinks bad news is inconsistent with Coke's image as an upbeat, fun product. A study by Andrew Aylesworth and Scott MacKenzie found that commercials placed in programs that induce negative moods are processed less systematically than ads placed in programs that put viewers in positive moods.[108] They suggest that media buyers might be well advised to follow the conventional wisdom of placing their ads during "feel-good" programming, especially if the message is intended to work through a central route to persuasion. However, messages intended to operate through a peripheral route to persuasion might be more effective if they are shown during more negative programs, where presumably viewers will not analyze the ad in detail because of their negative mood state.

## Clutter

Another aspect of the media environment which is important to advertisers is the problem of **clutter**, which has been defined as the amount of advertising in a medium.[109] However, for television, clutter is often viewed as including all the nonprogram material that appears in the broadcast environment—commercials, promotional messages for shows, public service announcements (PSAs), and the like. Clutter is of increasing concern to advertisers since there are so many messages in various media competing for the consumer's attention. Half of the average magazine's pages contain ads, and in some publications the ratio of ads to editorial content is even higher. On average, around a quarter of a broadcast hour on TV is devoted to commercials, while most radio stations carry an average of 10 to 12 minutes of commercial time per hour. The high level of advertising often annoys consumers and makes it difficult for ads to communicate effectively.

Clutter has become a major concern among television advertisers as a result of increases in nonprogram time and the trend toward shorter commercials. While the 30-second commercial replaced 60-second spots as the industry standard in the 1970s, many advertisers are now using 15-second spots. The advertising industry continues to express concern over the highly cluttered viewing environment on TV, as the amount of clutter increased as much as 30 percent during the 1990s and another 8 percent since 2000. However, the four major networks have kept their clutter levels relatively flat in recent years but are still running an average of around 15 minutes of nonprogram time per hour in prime time.[110] A study found that the average length of a commercial break during prime time on the major networks is just over three minutes. Thus, a viewer watching three hours of prime-time programs on the major networks would be subjected to as many as 100 commercials, programming promotions, and public service announcements (PSAs).[111] Clutter levels are even higher on many cable networks and during daytime programs. The problem is also greater during popular shows, to which the networks add more commercials because they can charge more. And, of course, advertisers and their agencies perpetuate the problem by pressuring the networks to squeeze their ads into top-rated shows with the largest audiences.

Advertisers and agencies want the networks to commit to a minimum amount of program time and then manage the nonprogram portion however they see fit. If the networks wanted to add more commercials, it would come out of their promos, PSAs, or program credit time. The problem is not likely to go away, however, and advertisers will continue to search for ways to break through the clutter, such as using humor, celebrity spokespeople, or novel, creative approaches.[112]

## Summary

This chapter focused on the controllable variables that are part of the communication process—source, message, and channel factors. Decisions regarding each of these variables should consider their impact on the various steps of the response hierarchy the message receiver passes through. The persuasion matrix helps assess the effect of controllable communication decisions on the consumer's response process.

Selection of the appropriate source or communicator to deliver a message is an important aspect of communications strategy. Three important attributes are source credibility, attractiveness, and power. Marketers enhance message effectiveness by hiring communicators who are experts in a particular area and/or have a trustworthy image. The use of celebrities to deliver advertising messages has become very popular; advertisers hope they will catch the receivers' attention and influence their attitudes or behavior through an identification process. The chapter discusses the meaning a celebrity brings to the endorsement process and the importance of matching the image of the celebrity with that of the company or brand.

The design of the advertising message is a critical part of the communication process. There are various options regarding message structure, including order of presentation of message arguments, conclusion drawing, message sidedness, refutation, and verbal versus visual traits. The advantages and disadvantages of different message appeal strategies were considered, including comparative messages and emotional appeals such as fear and humor.

Finally, the channel or medium used to deliver the message was considered. Differences between personal and nonpersonal channels of communication were discussed. Alternative mass media can have an effect on the communication process as a result of information processing and qualitative factors. The context in which an ad appears and the reception environment are important factors to consider in the selection of mass media. Clutter has become a serious problem for advertisers, particularly on TV, where commercials have become shorter and more numerous.

## Key Terms

persuasion matrix  p. 182
source  p. 184
credibility  p. 185
internalization  p. 185
sleeper effect  p. 189
attractiveness  p. 189
identification  p. 189

source power  p. 199
compliance  p. 200
primacy effect  p. 201
recency effect  p. 201
one-sided message  p. 202
two-sided message  p. 202
refutational appeal  p. 203

comparative advertising  p. 205
fear appeals  p. 206
wearout  p. 210
qualitative media effect  p. 214
clutter  p. 215

## Discussion Questions

1.   The chapter opener discusses the series of problems Nike has had with some of its endorsers because of controversies that have arisen in their personal lives. Discuss how the problems surrounding these endorsers might impact the image and reputation of Nike. How long do you think Nike should stand by endorsers when they run into personal problems? (LO2)

2.   Discuss how marketers can use the persuasion matrix shown in Figure 6–1 to plan their integrated marketing communications programs. Choose a TV commercial or print ad and use the persuasion matrix to evaluate how it might influence consumers' response process. (LO1)

3.   Discuss the three primary source attributes noted by Herbert Kelman and the different processes by which they can influence attitude and/or behavior change. Find an example of an advertisement or other type of promotional message that utilizes each attribute. (LO2)

4.   The recent study by Ace Metrix found Papa John's John Schnatter and Boston Beer Company's Jim Koch to be the most effective CEO endorsers. Find examples of an advertising message in which each appears and analyze it. Why do you think Schnatter and Koch are such effective endorsers? (LO2)

5.   NBA star Kobe Bryant has been able to rebuild his image after being charged with sexual assault a number of years ago. Do you agree with the decision by companies and brands such as Turkish Airlines and Vitaminwater to use Bryant as an endorser? Why or why not? (LO2)

6.   Find a celebrity who is currently appearing in an ad for a particular company or brand and use McCracken's meaning transfer model (shown in Figure 6–4) to analyze the use of this individual as a spokesperson. (LO2)

7.   Evaluate Domino's decision to run an advertising campaign acknowledging the problems with the taste of its pizza as a way to promote its new recipe. Do you think this strategy was an effective way to promote its reformulated product? (LO3)

8.   Visit the website for the Montana Meth Project (www.methproject.org) and choose three ads that use various levels of fear in the message. Discuss why each ad may or may not be effective. (LO3)

9.   Discuss the factors that lead to commercial wearout, giving attention to some of the reasons marketers often run the same ad repeatedly. What are some strategies for delaying or even avoiding wearout? (LO4)

10.   What is meant by a qualitative media effect? Select a television program and discuss the nature of the media reception environment created by the show. What type of companies or brands might be attracted to advertising on this program? (LO4)

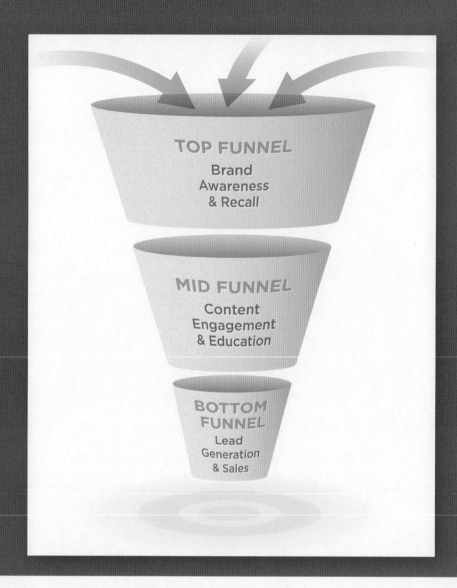

## LEARNING OBJECTIVES

**LO1** To recognize the importance and value of setting specific objectives for advertising and promotion.

**LO2** To understand the role objectives play in the IMC planning process and the relationship of promotional objectives to marketing objectives.

**LO3** To know the differences between sales and communications objectives and the issues regarding the use of each.

**LO4** To recognize some problems marketers encounter in setting objectives for their IMC programs.

**LO5** To understand the process of budgeting for IMC.

**LO6** To understand theoretical issues involved in budget setting.

**LO7** To know various methods of budget setting.

# 7 Establishing Objectives and Budgeting for the Promotional Program

## ARE SOCIAL AND DIGITAL MEDIA CHANGING THE WAY CONSUMERS MAKE PURCHASE DECISIONS?

Discussions of consumer response hierarchies have appeared in the marketing literature for over a half century and have had probably as many opponents as proponents regarding their usefulness in developing marketing and communications strategies. Nevertheless, a number of large companies including Sprint, Honda, and General Motors have employed their own hierarchies, typically referring to them as purchase funnels. These purchase funnels have been used as a planning guide to move consumers from awareness to final purchase. They are referred to as funnels, as the number of consumers who continue through the stages of the funnel decreases, with fewer actually making a purchase than are actually aware of the product or brand. While consumer purchase funnels have their advocates, there are still some nonbelievers out there.

For example, a study published in the *McKinsey Quarterly* proclaimed the purchase funnel dead, arguing that consumers do not make decisions in a linear fashion and have changed the way they go about making purchase decisions. Relying on a study of five industries on three continents, the report states that decision making has become more complex and dynamic, and the stages have become interdependent; consumers can be influenced at any time during the process. The study also concludes that because of these changes, marketers must focus more attention on reaching consumers at the precise moment that most influences their decision—something marketers have failed to do. According to McKinsey, marketers must employ touch points including advertising, news reports, product experiences, and so on, throughout the buying process to have maximum impact.

Sue Unerman, chief strategy officer at MediaCom, claims that the purchasing funnel is not dead but alive and pregnant. She contends that the traditional model is being threatened by new media and that marketers must understand the impact of these media and adopt these strategies accordingly. Unerman notes that the traditional funnel shape is being replaced by one that shows the traditional narrowing at the consideration stage but then bulges when the known and trusted brands are joined by new ones found on Internet searches, blogs, Facebook, and other new media. Like the McKinsey report, she argues that media planners must focus on touch points, switching much of their focus to reaching consumers throughout the process.

Like Unerman, Joseph Jaffe, president of Crayon, doesn't think the purchase funnel is dead either. He thinks it needs to be flipped! According to Jaffe, the traditional funnel is outmoded, as marketers spend too much money trying to funnel the consumer universe (many of whom don't care about the product or service) down to a handful. He says monies should be spent on this handful to get more out of them, resulting in a more efficient, effective, and profitable strategy. By focusing on establishing a strong relationship with customers after the sale, companies can take advantage of the new viral world as consumers interact with and influence many other consumers, each of whom may make multiple transactions.

However, not everyone is convinced that we need to bury the funnel, impregnate it, or flip it. In a study designed to determine if the purchase funnel works or not, the Television Bureau of Advertising (TVB) was more interested in how media impacts consumers in the decision-making process. Yankelovich (a research company) and TVB took a slightly different approach to studying the purchase funnel. Instead of looking at how consumers move through the funnel, this study examined the effect of various media at each stage, and how these media interact to influence the purchase decision process across 15 product categories. The study examined how 3,002 consumers employed traditional and new media at each step in the process. The results indicated that media had an influence on 80 percent of the consumers at the awareness phase, declining to 53 percent at the transaction stage, and that the impact varied depending upon the product category. Television (the traditional medium) was considered to be the most impactful at the awareness, consideration, preference, and purchase levels, with the Internet second at each. Interestingly, the survey dispelled popular thinking that traditional media (particularly TV) would have the most impact at the top of the funnel, with interactive media being more effective near the bottom, as both TV and the Internet showed the most impact *throughout* the process.

One of the latest examinations of how the consumer decision process works comes from an extensive three-phase study commissioned by the Advertising Research Foundation (ARF), which examines many of the issues addressed in the earlier studies while adding valuable new insights. This new study (which was noted in Chapter 5 under the social consumer decision journey framework) provides valuable insight into the important questions many marketers are asking such as, Have social and digital media altered the way in which consumers make purchase decisions? The study both supports and refutes some of the earlier findings. First, it agrees with some of the conclusions of the McKinsey report that the traditional linear model should be reconsidered, and that consumers may enter the response hierarchies at any level. It also supports the conclusions of the previous studies that consumers use multiple media sources (both traditional and online) throughout the process and that touch points must be available in as many places where consumers might seek information as is possible. The ARF study also supports the findings from previous studies that the decision-making process will vary by product type.

The new study does not consider the traditional decision-making models to be dead or even of limited value. Rather, the study was based on the assumption that the models have value, but need to be examined in a new light given the impact of social and digital media. As was noted in Chapter 5, the ARF study contends that consumers are constantly considering potential purchases and evaluating brands, but at some times are in a more active shopping mode and purposefully seeking assistance so they can make a purchase decision with confidence. While various media may have an impact in the more passive state, it is the active state where consumers rely more heavily on social media to gain information from websites, friends, product experts, and so on. Interestingly, the goal may be more of a confirmation process, as in most cases the brand or product has already been decided upon by this stage. Thus, no single source is driving the purchase decision, but all can make a contribution in different ways. Another key finding is that trust is important, as social media expand the range of people consumers feel they can trust, including family, friends, colleagues, and others. Feeling comfortable that they are making the right decision is critical. The ability to rely on these sources increases the confidence that consumers are making the right decision.

Overall, the ARF study concludes that purchase decisions may be more emotional than logical, and that consumers do not distinguish between information they receive from various media. Their primary goal is to feel comfortable and relaxed with the purchase, and digital and social media help them achieve this. In other words, they don't just go to social media for the "fuzzy stuff," but for assistance in decision making as well. No wonder so many advertisers believe these media impact our purchase decisions!

Sources: Sue Unerman, "The Year Ahead for . . . Media Planning," *Campaign*, January 8, 2010, p. 19; Martin Bihl, "Marketing to the Masses? Here's Why You Shouldn't," www.adage.com, March 23, 2010; Jon Lafayette, "Study Shows TV's Impact on Consumer Purchasing Behavior," www.tvweek.com, April 15, 2009; David Court, Dave Elzinga, Susan Mulder, and Ole Jorgen Vetvik, "The Consumer Decision Journey," *The McKinsey Quarterly*, 2009, p. 96; Todd Powers, Dorothy Advincula, Manila Austin, Stacy Graiko, and Jasper Snyder, "Digital and Social Media in the Purchase Decision Process," *Journal of Advertising Research*, December 2012, pp. 479–489.

The lead-in to this chapter discusses the value of using a consumer purchase funnel to set communications objectives. As you can see, while many large companies have been using these purchase decision models for a number of years, and continue to do so, not everyone agrees with their use or their validity, arguing that the models are either outdated or should never have been used in the first place. As the media environment continues to change, marketers continue to examine these models. As this chapter will demonstrate, the success of a program can and should be measured by both marketing and communications objectives. This chapter will examine how the goals for the integrated marketing communications program follow the company's overall marketing strategy and how these goals determine and are determined by the promotional budget.

Unfortunately, many companies have difficulty with the most critical step in the promotional planning process—setting realistic objectives that will guide the development of the IMC program. Complex marketing situations, conflicting perspectives regarding what advertising and other promotional mix elements are expected to accomplish, and uncertainty over resources make the setting of marketing communications objectives "a job of creating order out of chaos." While the task of setting objectives can be complex and difficult, it must be done properly because specific goals and objectives are the foundation on which all other promotional decisions are made. Budgeting for advertising and other promotional areas, as well as creative and media strategies and tactics, evolves from these objectives. They also provide a standard against which performance can be measured.

Setting specific objectives should be an integral part of the planning process. However, many companies either fail to use specific marketing communications objectives or set ones that are inadequate for guiding the development of the promotional plan or measuring its effectiveness. Many marketers are uncertain as to what integrated marketing communications should be expected to contribute to the marketing program. The goal of their company's advertising and promotional program is simple: to generate sales. They fail to recognize the specific tasks that advertising and other promotional-mix variables must perform in preparing customers to buy a particular product or service.

As we know, advertising and promotion are not the only marketing activities involved in generating sales. Moreover, it is not always possible or necessary to measure the effects of advertising in terms of sales. For example, the Standard Bank ad shown in Exhibit 7–1 has a goal beyond just supporting its bank. The ad appeared in a special advertising section of *Fortune* magazine supporting the All for Africa Organization.

Consider the Qatar Foundation ad shown in Exhibit 7–2. What objectives might the company have for this ad? How might its effectiveness be measured?

This chapter examines the nature and purpose of objectives and the role they play in guiding the development, implementation, and evaluation of an IMC program. Attention is given to the various types of objectives appropriate for different situations. We will also examine the budget-setting process and the interdependence of objective setting and budgeting.

# THE VALUE OF OBJECTIVES

Perhaps one reason many companies fail to set specific objectives for their integrated marketing communications programs is that they don't recognize the value of doing so. Another may be disagreement as to what the specific objectives should be. Advertising and promotional objectives are needed for several reasons, including the functions they serve in communications, planning and decision making, and measurement and evaluation.

## Communications

Specific objectives for the IMC program facilitate coordination of the various groups working on the campaign. Many people are involved in the planning and development of an integrated marketing communications program on the client side as well as in the various promotional agencies. The advertising and promotional program must be coordinated within the company, inside the ad agency, and between the two. Any other parties involved in the promotional campaign, such as public relations and/or sales promotion firms, research specialists, and media buying services, must

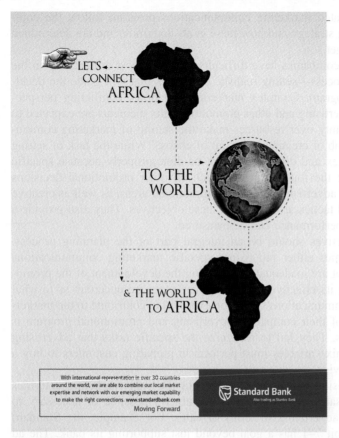

EXHIBIT 7–1
The objective of this ad is to demonstrate the Standard Bank's support for Africa

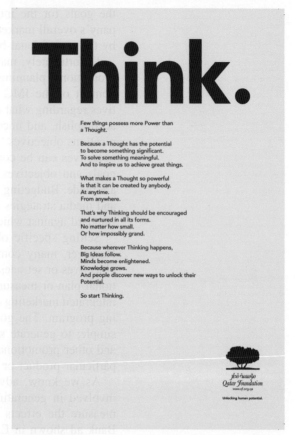

EXHIBIT 7–2
The Qatar Foundation's objectives for this ad may be other than generating sales

**YTC 07–01**

**Qatar and Standard Bank**
youtube.com/10ebelch

also know what the company hopes to accomplish through its marketing communications program. Many problems can be avoided if all parties have written, approved objectives to guide their actions and serve as a common base for discussing issues related to the promotional program.

## Planning and Decision Making

Specific promotional objectives also guide development of the integrated marketing communications plan. All phases of a firm's promotional strategy should be based on the established objectives, including budgeting, creative, and media decisions as well as direct marketing, public relations/publicity, sales promotion, and/or reseller support programs.

Meaningful objectives can also be a useful guide for decision making. Promotional planners are often faced with a number of strategic and tactical options in terms of choosing creative options, selecting media, and allocating the budget among various elements of the promotional mix. Choices should be made based on how well a particular strategy matches the firm's promotional objectives.

## Measurement and Evaluation of Results

An important reason for setting specific objectives is that they provide a benchmark against which the success or failure of the promotional campaign can be measured. Without specific objectives, it is extremely difficult to determine what the firm's advertising and promotion efforts accomplished. One characteristic of good objectives is that they are *measurable;* they specify a method and criteria for determining how well the promotional program is working. By setting specific and meaningful objectives, the promotional planner provides a measure(s) that can be used to evaluate the effectiveness of the marketing communications program. Most organizations are concerned about the return on their promotional investment, and comparing actual performance against measurable objectives is the best way to determine if the return justifies the expense.

# DETERMINING INTEGRATED MARKETING COMMUNICATIONS OBJECTIVES

Integrated marketing communications objectives should be based on a thorough situation analysis that identifies the marketing and promotional issues facing the company or a brand. The situation analysis is the foundation on which marketing objectives are determined and the marketing plan is developed. IMC objectives evolve from the company's overall marketing plan and are rooted in its marketing objectives. Advertising and promotion objectives are not the same as marketing objectives (although many firms tend to treat them as synonymous).

## Marketing versus Communications Objectives

**Marketing objectives** are generally stated in the firm's marketing plan and are statements of what is to be accomplished by the overall marketing program within a given time period. Marketing objectives are usually defined in terms of specific, measurable outcomes such as sales volume, market share, profits, or return on investment. Good marketing objectives are *quantifiable;* they delineate the target market and note the time frame for accomplishing the goal (often one year). For example, a copy machine company may have as its marketing objective "to increase sales by 10 percent in the small-business segment of the market during the next 12 months." To be effective, objectives must also be *realistic* and *attainable.*

A company with a very high market share may seek to increase its sales volume by stimulating growth in the product category. It might accomplish this by increasing consumption by current users or encouraging nonusers to use the product. Some firms have as their marketing objectives expanding distribution and sales of their product in certain market areas. Companies often have secondary marketing objectives that are related to actions they must take to solve specific problems and thus achieve their primary objectives.

Once the marketing communications manager has reviewed the marketing plan, he or she should understand where the company hopes to go with its marketing program, how it intends to get there, and the role advertising and promotion will play. Marketing goals defined in terms of sales, profit, or market share increases are usually not appropriate promotional objectives. They are objectives for the entire marketing program, and achieving them depends on the proper coordination and execution of all the marketing-mix elements, including not just promotion but product planning and production, pricing, and distribution. For example, a company may be very successful in its promotional program, creating interest and/or trial for a product. But what if the product is unavailable when the consumer goes to buy it, or what if, once in the store, the consumer feels the product is overpriced and decides not to buy? Should the promotional program be blamed when the product's poor performance is due to other marketing strategies or tactics?

**Integrated marketing communications objectives** are statements of what various aspects of the IMC program will accomplish. They should be based on the particular communications tasks required to deliver the appropriate messages to the target audience. Managers must be able to translate general marketing goals into communications goals and specific promotional objectives.

LO 07-2

Sometimes companies do not have a formal marketing plan, and the information needed may not be readily available. In this case, the promotional planner must attempt to gather as much information as possible about the product and its markets from sources both inside and outside the company.

After reviewing all the information, the promotional planner should see how integrated marketing communications fits into the marketing program and what the firm hopes to achieve through advertising and other promotional elements. The next step is to set objectives in terms of specific communications goals or tasks.

Many planners approach promotion from a communications perspective and believe the objective of advertising and other promotional-mix elements is usually to communicate information or a selling message about a product or service. Other managers argue that sales or some related measure, such as market share, is the only meaningful goal for advertising and promotion and should be the basis for setting objectives. These two perspectives have been the topic of considerable debate and are worth examining further.

# SALES VERSUS COMMUNICATIONS OBJECTIVES

### Sales-Oriented Objectives

To many managers, the only meaningful objective for their promotional program is sales. They take the position that the basic reason a firm spends money on advertising and promotion is to sell its product or service. Promotional spending represents an investment of a firm's resources that requires an economic justification. Managers generally compare investment options on a common financial basis, such as return on investment (ROI). However, determining the specific return on advertising and promotional dollars is often quite a difficult task. At the same time, many managers believe that monies spent on advertising and other forms of promotion should produce measurable results, such as increasing sales volume by a certain percentage or dollar amount or increasing the brand's market share. They believe objectives (as well as the success or failure of the campaign) should be based on the achievement of sales results.

As a result, many managers have increased their efforts to make agencies more accountable for their performances. In turn, some agencies have developed their own tools to attempt to provide more ROI information in regard to how their integrated communications programs are performing. These agencies often attempt to differentiate themselves from others on this premise.

**YTC 07–02**

**GEICO**

youtube.com/10ebelch

Some managers prefer sales-oriented objectives to make the individuals involved in advertising and promotion think in terms of how the promotional program will influence sales. For example, GEICO, once ranked fourth behind State Farm, Allstate, and Progressive insurance companies, increased its advertising budget by 75 percent—nearly double that of its competitors, and broadened its media placements. As a result, GEICO is now the number 1 insurance company in new customer acquisitions.[1] Likewise, Heinz doubled its IMC budget, resulting in a 19 percent sales increase.[2] The success of these advertising and promotional campaigns was judged by attainment of these goals.

**Problems with Sales Objectives**  It appears that increases in advertising expenditures seemed to work for GEICO and Heinz as both experienced sales increases. Does this mean that these results can be attributed directly to the increased advertising budgets? Not necessarily. It might help to compare this situation to a football game and think of advertising as a quarterback. The quarterback is one of the most important players on the team but can be effective only with support from the other players. If the team loses, is it fair to blame the loss entirely on the quarterback? Of course not. Just as the quarterback is but one of the players on the football team, promotion is but one element of the marketing program, and there are many other reasons why the targeted sales level was not reached. The quarterback can lead his team to victory only if the linemen block, the receivers catch his passes, and the running backs help the offense establish a balanced attack of running and passing. Even if the quarterback plays an outstanding game, the team can still lose if the defense gives up too many points.

In the business world, sales results can be due to any of the other marketing-mix variables, including product design or quality, packaging, distribution, or pricing. Advertising can make consumers aware of and interested in the brand, but it can't make them buy it, particularly if it is not readily available or is priced higher than a competing brand. As shown in Figure 7–1, sales are a function of many factors, not just advertising and promotion. There is an adage in marketing that states, "Nothing will kill a poor product faster than good advertising." Taken with the other factors shown in Figure 7–1, this adage demonstrates that all the marketing elements must work together if a successful plan is to be implemented.

Another problem with sales objectives is that the effects of advertising often occur over an extended period. Many experts recognize that advertising has a lagged or **carryover effect**; monies spent on advertising do not necessarily have an immediate impact on sales.[3] Advertising may create awareness, interest, and/or favorable attitudes toward a brand, but these feelings will not result in an actual purchase until the consumer enters the market for the product, which may occur later. A review of econometric studies that examined the duration of cumulative advertising effects found that for mature, frequently purchased, low-priced products, advertising's effect on sales lasts up to nine months.[4] Models have been developed to account for the carryover effect of advertising and to help determine the long-term effect of advertising on sales.[5] The carryover effect adds to the difficulty of determining the precise relationship between advertising and sales.

Another problem with sales objectives is that they offer little guidance to those responsible for planning and developing the promotional program. The creative and media people working on the account need some direction as to the nature of the advertising message the company hopes to communicate, the intended audience, and the particular effect or response sought. As you will see shortly, communications

**FIGURE 7–1**

Factors Influencing Sales

**EXHIBIT 7–3**

Kayem Foods's marketing strategy led to sales increases

YTC 07-03

**Kayem**

youtube.com/10ebelch

YTC 07-04

**Domino's Pizza**

youtube.com/10ebelch

**EXHIBIT 7–4**

Mercury Insurance Group uses direct-response advertising to sell products and services

objectives are recommended because they provide operational guidelines for those involved in planning, developing, and executing the advertising and promotional program.

**Where Sales Objectives Are Appropriate**   While there can be many problems in attempting to use sales as objectives for a promotional campaign, there are situations where sales objectives are appropriate. Certain types of promotion efforts are direct action in nature; they attempt to induce an immediate behavioral response from the prospective customer. A major objective of most sales promotion programs is to generate short-term increases in sales. At the same time, short-term strategies hopefully will lead to longer-term gains as well. A good example is that of Kayem Foods of Chelsea, Massachusetts. To celebrate its 100th anniversary, Kayem changed the design of its frankfurter package. After consumer research suggested changing the copy and label on the package, the product was reintroduced. In the first 12 weeks Kayem saw sales rise by 15.7 percent (Exhibit 7–3), and the regional company planned for a national rollout.[6]

Direct-response advertising is one type of advertising that evaluates its effectiveness on the basis of sales. Merchandise is advertised in material mailed to customers, in newspapers and magazines, through the Internet, or on television. The consumer purchases the merchandise by mail, on the Internet, or by calling a toll-free number. The direct-response advertiser generally sets objectives and measures success in terms of the sales response generated by the ad. For example, objectives for and the evaluation of a direct-response ad on TV are based on the number of orders received each time a station broadcasts the commercial. Because advertising is really the only form of communication and promotion used in this situation and response is generally immediate, setting objectives in terms of sales is appropriate. The Mercury Insurance Group ad shown in Exhibit 7–4 is an example of a product sold through direct-response advertising.

Retail advertising, which accounts for a significant percentage of all advertising expenditures, is another area where the advertiser often seeks an immediate response, particularly when sales or special events are being promoted. The ad for JCPenney's 60 percent off sale shown in Exhibit 7–5 is designed to attract consumers to stores during the sales period (and to generate sales volume). JCPenney's management can determine the effectiveness of its promotional effort by analyzing store traffic and sales volume during the sale and comparing them to figures for nonsale days. But retailers may also allocate advertising and promotional dollars to image-building campaigns designed to create and enhance favorable perceptions of their stores. For example, after a period of declining sales, Domino's Pizza made significant changes to its product. To announce these changes, Domino's introduced a new advertising campaign that included television commercials showing participants from the focus groups denigrating the pizza and then being delivered the new product formulation. The campaign was clearly a risky strategy for a company that has been in the pizza business since the 1960s with over 8,000 stores worldwide. In this case using sales-oriented objectives alone would not be appropriate; the effectiveness of the campaign would be based on its ability to create or change consumers' image of the brand, as well.

Sales-oriented objectives are also used when advertising plays a dominant role in a

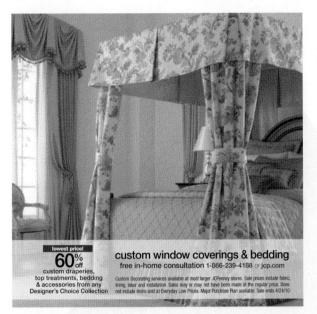

**EXHIBIT 7–5**

JCPenney seeks sales from this ad

**EXHIBIT 7–6**

Consolidated Edison creates an image of its company

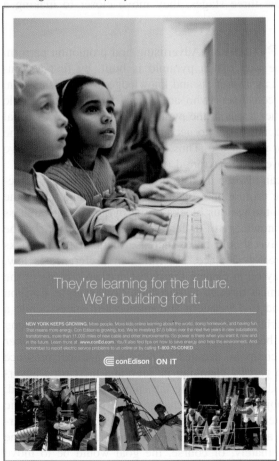

firm's marketing program and other factors are relatively stable. For example, many packaged-goods companies compete in mature markets with established channels of distribution, stable competitive prices and promotional budgets, and products of similar quality. They view advertising and sales promotion as the key determinants of a brand's sales or market share, so it may be possible to isolate the effects of these promotional mix variables. Many companies have accumulated enough market knowledge with their advertising, sales promotion, and direct-marketing programs to have considerable insight into the sales levels that should result from their promotional efforts. Mark Baynes, vice president of Kellogg's Morning Foods Division, attributed a turnabout in sales to effective advertising, brand repositioning, and more emotional appeals that generate interest.[7] Thus, many companies believe it is reasonable to set objectives and evaluate the success of their promotional efforts in terms of sales results.

Advertising and promotional programs tend to be evaluated in terms of sales, particularly when expectations are not being met. Marketing and brand managers under pressure to show sales results often take a short-term perspective in evaluating advertising and sales promotion programs. They are often looking for a quick fix for declining sales or loss of market share. They ignore the pitfalls of making direct links between advertising and sales, and campaigns, as well as ad agencies, may be changed if sales expectations are not being met. As discussed in Chapter 3, many companies want their agencies to accept incentive-based compensation systems tied to sales performance. Thus, while sales may not be an appropriate objective in many advertising and promotional situations, managers are inclined to keep a close eye on sales and market share figures and make changes in the promotional program when these numbers become stagnant or decline.

## Communications Objectives

Some marketers do recognize the problems associated with sales-oriented objectives. They recognize that the primary role of an IMC program is to communicate and that planning should be based on communications objectives. Advertising and other promotional efforts are designed to achieve such communications as brand knowledge and interest, favorable attitudes and image, and purchase intentions. Consumers are not expected to respond immediately; rather, advertisers realize they must provide relevant information and create favorable predispositions toward the brand before purchase behavior will occur.

For example, the ad in Exhibit 7–6 is designed to inform consumers of the company's focus on building for the future. While there is no call for immediate action, the ad creates favorable impressions about the company by using pictures of children alongside Con Ed workers in action to create a distinct image of the company. Viewers will consider this image when they think about Consolidated Edison.

Advocates of communications-based objectives generally use some form of the hierarchical models discussed in Chapter 5 and the opening vignette when setting advertising

**FIGURE 7–2**

Communications Effects
Pyramid

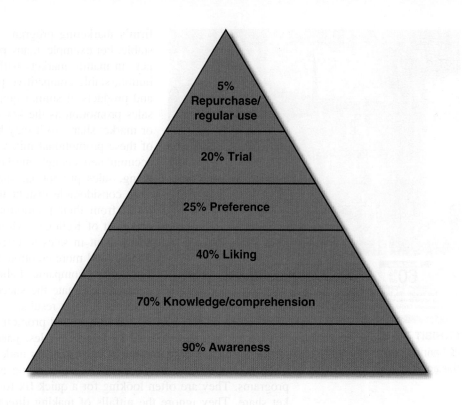

and promotion objectives. In all these models, consumers pass through three successive stages: cognitive (thinking), affective (feeling), and conative (behavioral). As consumers proceed through the three stages, they move closer to making a purchase.

YTC 07–05

**Caribou**

youtube.com/10ebelch

**Communications Effects Pyramid** Advertising and promotion perform communications tasks in the same way that a pyramid is built, by first accomplishing lower-level objectives such as awareness and knowledge or comprehension. Subsequent tasks involve moving consumers who are aware of or knowledgeable about the product or service to higher levels in the pyramid (Figure 7–2). The initial stages, at the base of the pyramid, are easier to accomplish than those toward the top, such as trial and repurchase or regular use. Thus, the percentage of prospective customers will decline as they move up the pyramid (or down the funnel).

The communications pyramid can also be used to determine promotional objectives for an established brand. The promotional planner must determine where the target audience lies with respect to the various blocks in the pyramid. If awareness

**EXHIBIT 7–7**

Caribou Coffee must set different objectives for different target markets

levels for a brand and knowledge of its features and benefits are low, the communications objective should be to increase them. If these blocks of the pyramid are already in place, but liking or preference is low, the advertising goal may be to change the target markets' image of the brand and move consumers through to purchase. For example, Caribou Coffee, a regional brand in 15 eastern and midwestern states, while a distant number 2 to Starbucks, has a very favorable brand image among its customers, and has been ranked number 1 in quality by *Consumer Reports*. In 2010, the company decided to pursue a national presence and rebranded itself, in part by changing its logo and increasing advertising expenditures[8] (Exhibit 7–7). Using the communications pyramid, you can see that the objectives would change for different geographic areas, with a focus on creating awareness and knowledge in new markets, while reinforcing and maintaining the current brand image in the East and Midwest. Ultimately, of course, the goal would be to move everyone in the target market to trial and purchase.

**Problems with Communications Objectives**   Not all marketing and advertising managers accept communications objectives; some say it is too difficult to translate a sales goal into a specific communications objective. But at some point a sales goal must be transformed into a communications objective. If the marketing plan for an established brand has an objective of increasing sales by 10 percent, the promotional planner will eventually have to think in terms of the message that will be communicated to the target audience to achieve this. Possible objectives include the following:

■ Increasing the percentage of consumers in the target market who associate specific features, benefits, or advantages with our brand.
■ Increasing the number of consumers in the target audience who prefer our product over the competition's.
■ Encouraging current users of the product to use it more frequently or in more situations.
■ Encouraging consumers who have never used our brand to try it.

In some situations, promotional planners may gain insight into communications objectives' relationship to sales from industry research. Figure 7–3 provides an example of the GfK International purchase funnel used by many in the automobile industry as a diagnostic model of consumer decision making.

In attempting to translate sales goals into specific communications objectives, promotional planners often are not sure what constitutes adequate levels of awareness, knowledge, liking, preference, or conviction. There are no formulas to provide this information. The promotional manager will have to use his or her personal experience and that of the brand or product managers, as well as the marketing history of this and similar brands. Average scores on various communications measures for this and similar products should be considered, along with the levels achieved by competitors' products. This information can be related to the amount of money and time spent building these levels as well as the resulting sales or market share figures. However, at some point, sales-oriented objectives must be translated into what the company hopes to communicate and to whom it hopes to communicate it.

**FIGURE 7–3**
GfK Purchase Funnel

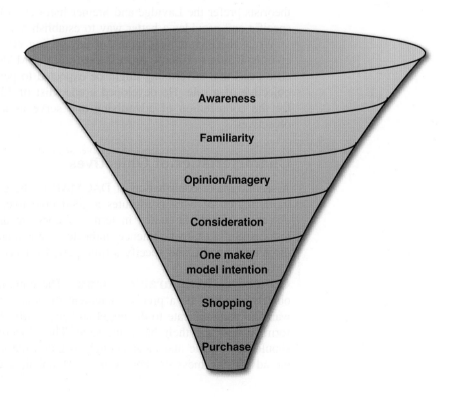

Many marketing and promotional managers recognize the value of setting specific communications objectives and their important role as operational guidelines to the planning, execution, and evaluation of the promotional program. Communications objectives are the criteria used in the DAGMAR approach to setting advertising goals and objectives, which has become one of the most influential approaches to the advertising planning process.

# DAGMAR: AN APPROACH TO SETTING OBJECTIVES

In 1961, Russell Colley prepared a report for the Association of National Advertisers titled *Defining Advertising Goals for Measured Advertising Results* (DAGMAR).[9] In it, Colley developed a model for setting advertising objectives and measuring the results of an ad campaign. The major thesis of the **DAGMAR** model is that communications effects are the logical basis for advertising goals and objectives against which success or failure should be measured.

Under the DAGMAR approach, an advertising goal involves a **communications task** that is specific and measurable. A communications task, as opposed to a marketing task, can be performed by, and attributed to, advertising rather than to a combination of several marketing factors. Colley proposed that the communications task be based on a hierarchical model of the communication process with four stages:

- *Awareness*—making the consumer aware of the existence of the brand or company.
- *Comprehension*—developing an understanding of what the product is and what it will do for the consumer.
- *Conviction*—developing a mental disposition in the consumer to buy the product.
- *Action*—getting the consumer to purchase the product.

As discussed earlier, other hierarchical models of advertising effects can be used as a basis for analyzing the communications response process. Some advertising theorists prefer the Lavidge and Steiner hierarchy of effects model, since it is more specific and provides a better way to establish and measure results.[10]

While the hierarchical model of advertising effects was the basic model of the communications response process used in DAGMAR, Colley also studied other specific tasks that advertising might be expected to perform in leading to the ultimate objective of a sale. He developed a checklist of 52 advertising tasks to characterize the contribution of advertising and serve as a starting point for establishing objectives.

## Characteristics of Objectives

A second major contribution of DAGMAR to the advertising planning process was its definition of what constitutes a good objective. Colley argued that advertising objectives should be stated in terms of concrete and measurable communications tasks, specify a target audience, indicate a benchmark starting point and the degree of change sought, and specify a time period for accomplishing the objective(s).

### Concrete, Measurable Tasks
The communications task specified in the objective should be a precise statement of what appeal or message the advertiser wants to communicate to the target audience. Advertisers generally use a copy platform to describe their basic message. The objective or copy platform statement should be specific and clear enough to guide the creative specialists who develop the advertising message. For example, Hyundai, after years of being at or near the

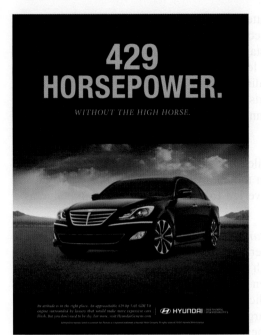

**429 HORSEPOWER.**

*WITHOUT THE HIGH HORSE.*

*Its attitude is in the right place. An approachable 429 hp 5.0L GDI V8 engine surrounded by luxury that would make more expensive cars blush. But you don't need to be shy. For more, visit HyundaiGenesis.com*

@ HYUNDAI | NEW THINKING. NEW POSSIBILITIES.

**EXHIBIT 7–8**

Hyundai has moved to the top of the list in customer satisfaction

YTC 07–06

**Hyundai**

youtube.com/10ebelch

bottom of the list of automobiles in customer satisfaction ratings, focused its attention on increasing the quality, as well as improving consumers' perceptions, of its cars. The result is that Hyundai is now at the very top of the list in customer satisfaction (Exhibit 7–8). According to DAGMAR, the objective must also be measurable. As can be seen in Exhibit 7–8, the various awards won along the way provided a measure of Hyundai's success.

**Target Audience**  Another important characteristic of good objectives is a well-defined target audience. The primary target audience for a company's product or service is described in the situation analysis. It may be based on descriptive variables such as geography, demographics, and psychographics (on which advertising media selection decisions are based) as well as on behavioral variables such as usage rate or benefits sought.

**Benchmark and Degree of Change Sought**  To set objectives, one must know the target audience's present status concerning response hierarchy variables such as awareness, knowledge, image, attitudes, and intentions and then determine the degree to which consumers must be changed by the campaign. Determining the target market's present position regarding the various response stages requires **benchmark measures**. Often a marketing research study must be conducted to determine prevailing levels of the response hierarchy. In the case of a new product or service, the starting conditions are generally at or near zero for all the variables, so no initial research is needed.

Establishing benchmark measures gives the promotional planner a basis for determining what communications tasks need to be accomplished and for specifying particular objectives. For example, a preliminary study for a brand may reveal that awareness is high but consumer perceptions and attitudes are negative. The objective for the campaign must then be to change the target audience's perceptions of and attitudes toward the brand.

Quantitative benchmarks are not only valuable in establishing communications goals and objectives but essential for determining whether the campaign was successful. Objectives provide the standard against which the success or failure of a campaign is measured. An ad campaign that results in a 90 percent awareness level for a brand among its target audience cannot really be judged effective unless one knows what percentage of the consumers were aware of the brand before the campaign began. A 70 percent precampaign awareness level would lead to a different interpretation of the campaign's success than would a 30 percent level.

**Specified Time Period**  A final consideration in setting advertising objectives is specifying the time period in which they must be accomplished. Appropriate time periods can range from a few days to a year or more. Most ad campaigns specify time periods from a few months to a year, depending on the situation facing the advertiser and the type of response being sought. For example, awareness levels for a brand can be created or increased fairly quickly through an intensive media schedule of widespread, repetitive advertising to the target audience. Repositioning of a product requires a change in consumers' perceptions and takes much more time.

## Assessment of DAGMAR

The DAGMAR approach to setting objectives has had considerable influence on the advertising planning process. Many promotional planners use this model as a basis for setting objectives and assessing the effectiveness of their promotional campaigns.

DAGMAR also focused advertisers' attention on the value of using communications-based rather than sales-based objectives to measure advertising effectiveness and encouraged the measurement of stages in the response hierarchy to assess a campaign's impact. Colley's work has led to improvements in the advertising and promotional planning process by providing a better understanding of the goals and objectives toward which planners' efforts should be directed. This usually results in less subjectivity and leads to better communication and relationships between client and agency.

**Criticisms of DAGMAR**   While DAGMAR has contributed to the advertising planning process, it has not been totally accepted by everyone in the advertising field. A number of problems have led to questions regarding its value as a planning tool:[11]

■ *Problems with the response hierarchy.* A major criticism of the DAGMAR approach is its reliance on the hierarchy of effects model. The fact that consumers do not always go through this sequence of communications effects before making a purchase has been recognized, and alternative response models have been developed. As indicated in the lead-in to this chapter, much of the criticism stems from the argument that digital and social media have significantly changed the consumer's decision-making process from a linear one to one in which consumers can enter or leave at any stage, resulting in a more circular process (Exhibit 7–9). DAGMAR MOD II recognizes that the appropriate response model depends on the situation and emphasizes identifying the sequence of decision-making steps that apply in a buying situation.[12]

■ *Sales objectives.* Another objection to DAGMAR comes from those who argue that the only relevant measure of advertising objectives is sales. They have little tolerance for ad campaigns that achieve communications objectives but fail to increase sales. Advertising is seen as effective only if it induces consumers to make a purchase. The problems with this logic were addressed in our discussion of communications objectives.

■ *Practicality and costs.* Another criticism of DAGMAR concerns the difficulties involved in implementing it. Money must be spent on research to establish quantitative benchmarks and measure changes in the response hierarchy. This is costly and time-consuming and can lead to considerable disagreement over method, criteria, measures, and so forth. Many critics argue that DAGMAR is practical only for large companies with big advertising and research budgets. Many firms do not want to spend the money needed to use DAGMAR effectively.

■ *Inhibition of creativity.* A final criticism of DAGMAR is that it inhibits advertising creativity by imposing too much structure on the people responsible for developing the advertising. Many creative personnel think the DAGMAR approach is too concerned with quantitative assessment of a campaign's impact on awareness, brand-name recall, or specific persuasion measures. The emphasis is on passing the numbers test rather than developing a message that is truly creative and contributes to brand equity.

**EXHIBIT 7–9**
Performics suggests that consumers go through a marketing spiral

# PROBLEMS IN SETTING OBJECTIVES

Although the DAGMAR model suggests a logical process for advertising and promotion planning, most advertisers and their agencies fail to follow these basic principles. They fail to set specific objectives for their campaigns and/or do not have the proper evidence to determine the success of their promotional programs. Many advertising agencies do not state appropriate objectives for determining success and thus can't demonstrate whether a supposedly successful campaign was really a success. Even though these campaigns may be doing something right, they generally did not know what it is.

One study examined the advertising practices of business-to-business marketers to determine whether their ads used advertising objectives that met Colley's four DAGMAR criteria.[13] Entries from the annual Business/Professional Advertising Association Gold Key Awards competition, which solicits the best marketing communications efforts from business-to-business advertisers, were evaluated with respect to their campaigns' objectives and summaries of results. Most of these advertisers did not set concrete advertising objectives, specify objective tasks, measure results in terms of stages of a hierarchy of effects, or match objectives to evaluation measures.

## Improving Promotional Planners' Use of Objectives

As we have seen, it is important that advertisers and their agencies pay close attention to the objectives they set for their campaigns. They should strive to set specific and measurable objectives that not only guide promotional planning and decision making but also can be used as a standard for evaluating performance. Unfortunately, many companies do not set appropriate objectives for their integrated marketing communications programs.

Many companies fail to set appropriate objectives because top management has only an abstract idea of what the firm's IMC program is supposed to be doing. In a study by the American Business Press that measured the attitudes of chairs, presidents, and other senior managers of business-to-business advertising companies, more than half of the 427 respondents said they did not know whether their advertising was working and less than 10 percent thought it was working well.[14] This study showed overwhelmingly that top management did not even know what the company's advertising was supposed to do, much less how to measure it.

Few firms will set objectives that meet all the criteria set forth in DAGMAR. However, promotional planners should set objectives that are specific and measurable and go beyond basic sales goals. Even if specific communications response elements are not always measured, meeting the other criteria will sharpen the focus and improve the quality of the IMC planning process.

## Setting Objectives for the IMC Program

One reason so much attention is given to advertising objectives is that for many companies advertising has traditionally been the major way of communicating with target audiences. Other promotional-mix elements such as sales promotion, direct marketing, and publicity are used intermittently to support and complement the advertising program.

Another reason is that traditional advertising-based views of marketing communications planning, such as DAGMAR, have dominated the field for so long. These approaches are based on a hierarchical response model and consider how marketers can develop and disseminate advertising messages to move consumers along an effects path. This approach, shown in Figure 7–4, is what professor Don Schultz calls *inside-out planning*. He says, "It focuses on what the marketer wants to say, when the marketer wants to say it, about things the marketer believes are important about his or her brand, and in the media forms the marketer wants to use."[15]

Schultz advocates an *outside-in planning* process for IMC that starts with the customer and builds backward to the brand. This means that promotional planners

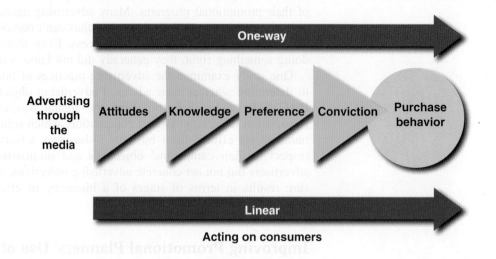

study the various media customers and prospects use, when the marketer's messages might be most relevant to customers, and when they are likely to be most receptive to the message.

A similar approach is suggested by Professor Tom Duncan, who argues that IMC should use **zero-based communications planning**, which involves determining what tasks need to be done and which marketing communications functions should be used and to what extent.[16] This approach focuses on the task to be done and searches for the best ideas and media to accomplish it. Duncan suggests that an effective IMC program should lead with the marketing communications function that most effectively addresses the company's main problem or opportunity and should use a promotional mix that draws on the strengths of whichever communications functions relate best to the particular situation.

While Schultz and Duncan discuss strategies for setting objectives based on traditional response hierarchies, attention should also be given to competing models. As seen in Chapter 5, considering decision making as a "social consumer decision journey" necessitates the establishment of communications objectives as viewed from a different perspective. The rows in Figure 7–5 show the steps in the consumer decision journey ranging from consideration to bonding. The columns depict the objectives that marketers need to accomplish at each stage, while the 10 marketing responses necessary to achieve these objectives are listed within the matrix. In this perspective, the marketer must *monitor*—that is, know what is being said online about the product or brand to gain insights as to how it is being perceived in the marketplace and then respond accordingly. This process—according to the model—must take place continuously. Second, marketers must *respond* to specific issues at a personal level. Responses may be positive in nature (customer service or sales leads) or (more likely) be part of crisis management, dealing with negative issues regarding the product or brand. *Amplification* deals with designing the communications program—particularly as it relates to social media—to foster engagement and sharing, as well as loyalty. The objective of amplifying is to get consumers more involved in the brand, extending the experience the brand has to offer, and have them communicate their positive experiences to others in the social network. The final objective, *lead,* is designed to take the consumer to long-term behavioral changes. At the early stages of the process it may simply include creating more brand awareness. Later in the process, lead may be designed to create buzz or promote time-sensitive issues like sales or promotions. The model also advocates the solicitation of consumer input upon completion of the purchase for the purpose of creating continuous inputs.

While the social consumer decision journey may differ from traditional response hierarchies, it is also similar in that it envisions going through stages in the purchase

Source: Expert interviews; McKinsey analysis

decision. Like traditional model, marketers need to take specific marketing actions to help the consumer along through the process.

Many of the considerations for determining advertising objectives are relevant to setting goals for other elements of the integrated marketing communications program. The promotional planner should determine what role various sales promotion techniques, publicity and public relations, direct marketing, the Internet, and personal selling will play in the overall marketing program and how they will interact with advertising as well as with one another.

For example, the marketing communications program for the San Diego Zoo Global has a number of objectives. First, it must provide funding for the zoo's programs and maintain a large and powerful base of supporters for financial strength. The communications must educate the public about the zoo's various programs and maintain a favorable image on a local, regional, and even international level. A major objective of the IMC program is drawing visitors to the zoo and its affiliated Safari Park (Exhibit 7–10).

Like the San Diego Zoo Global, other zoos may establish similar objectives. As can be seen in Figure 7–6 these programs may employ a variety of integrated marketing communications tools. When setting objectives for these promotional elements, planners must consider what the firm hopes to communicate through the use of this element, among what target audience, and during what time period. As with advertising, results should be measured and evaluated against the original objectives, and attempts should be made to isolate the effects of each promotional element. Objectives for marketing communications elements other than advertising are discussed more thoroughly in Part Five of the text.

**YTC 07–07**

**San Diego Zoo**
youtube.com/10ebelch

# ESTABLISHING AND ALLOCATING
# THE PROMOTIONAL BUDGET

LO 07-5

If you take a minute to look back at the IMC planning model in Chapter 1, you will see that while the arrows from the review of the marketing plan and the promotional situation analysis to analysis of the communications process are *unidirectional,* the

**EXHIBIT 7–10**
The San Diego Zoo Global
attempts to attract visitors
through a variety of media

flow between the communications analysis and budget determination is a *two-way interaction.* What this means is that while establishing objectives is an important part of the planning process, the limitations of the budget are important too. No organization has an unlimited budget, so objectives must be set with the budget in mind.

Often when we think of promotional expenditures of firms, we think only about the huge amounts being spent. We don't usually take the time to think about how these monies are being allocated and about the recipients of these dollars. The budgeting decisions have a significant impact not only on the firm itself but also on numerous others involved either directly or indirectly. The remainder of this chapter provides insight into some underlying theory with respect to budget setting, discusses how companies budget for promotional efforts, and demonstrates the inherent strengths and weaknesses associated with these approaches. Essentially, we focus on two primary budgeting decisions: establishing a budget amount and allocating the budget.

## Establishing the Budget

The size of a firm's advertising and promotions budget can vary from a few thousand dollars to more than a billion. When companies like AT & T and Verizon spend more than $2 billion per year to promote their products, they expect such expenditures to accomplish their stated objectives. The budget decision is no less critical to a firm spending only a few thousand dollars; its ultimate success or failure may depend on the monies spent. One of the most critical decisions facing the marketing manager is how much to spend on the promotional effort.

Unfortunately, many managers fail to realize the value of advertising and promotion. They treat the communications budget as an expense rather than an investment. Instead of viewing the dollars spent as contributing to additional sales and market share, they see budget expenses as cutting into profits. As a result, when times get tough, the advertising and promotional budget is the first to be cut—even though there is strong evidence that exactly the opposite should occur, as Exhibit 7–11 argues. Figure 7–7 shows the results of an extensive review of research involving advertising during a recession. The review covers 40 studies in the United States from 1926 to 2009. As can be seen, the argument for continuing to advertise during an economic

**Advertising**

**Objectives:** Drive attendance to Zoo. Uphold image and educate target audience and inform them of new attractions and special events and promotions.

**Audience:** Members and nonmembers of Zoological Society. Households in primary and secondary geographic markets consisting of Allegheny Country and 5 other countries in the tri-state regional area. Tertiary markets of 7 states. Tourist and group sales markets.

**Timing:** As allowed and determined by budget. Mostly timed to coincide with promotional efforts.

**Tools/media:** Television, radio, newspaper, magazines, direct mail, outdoor, tourist media (television and magazine).

**Sales Promotions**

**Objectives:** Use price, product, and other variables to drive attendance when it might not otherwise come.

**Audience:** Targeted, depending on co-op partner, mostly to Western Pennsylvania market.

**Timing:** To fit needs of Zoo and co-sponsoring partner.

**Tools/media:** Coupons, sweepstakes, tours, broadcast tradeouts, direct mail: statement stuffers, fliers, postcards, online ticket discounts.

**Public Relations**

**Objectives:** Inform, educate, create, and maintain image for Zoological Society and major attractions; reinforce advertising message.

**Audience:** From local to international, depending on subject, scope, and timing.

**Timing:** Ongoing, although often timed to coincide with promotions and other special events. Spur-of-the-moment animal news and information such as acquisitions, births, etc.

**Tools/media:** Coverage by major news media, articles in local, regional, national and international newspapers, magazines and other publications such as visitors' guides, tour books and guides, appearances by Zoo spokepersons on talk shows (such as *The David Letterman Show*), zoo newsletter, adopt an animal program, support conservation program.

**Cause Marketing/Corporate Sponsorships/Events Underwriting**

**Objectives:** To provide funding for Zoological Society programs and promote special programs and events done in cooperation with corporate sponsor. Must be win-win business partnership for Society and partner.

**Audience:** Supporters of both the Zoological Society and the corporate or product/service partner.

**Timing:** Coincides with needs of both partners, and seasonal attendance generation needs of Zoo.

**Tools:** May involve advertising, publicity, discount co-op promotions, ticket trades, hospitality centers. Exposure is directly proportional to amount of underwriting by corporate sponsor, both in scope and duration, education programs.

**Direct Marketing**

**Objectives:** Maintain large powerful base of supporters for financial and political strength.

**Audience:** Local, regional, national and international. Includes children's program, seniors (60+), couples, single memberships, and incremental donor levels.

**Timing:** Ongoing, year-round promotion of memberships.

**Tools:** Direct mail and on-grounds visibility.

**Group Sales**

**Objectives:** Maximize group traffic and revenue by selling group tours to Zoo.

**Audience:** Conventions, incentive groups, bus tours, associations, youth, scouts, schools, camps, seniors, clubs, military, organizations, domestic and foreign travel groups.

**Timing:** Targeted to drive attendance in peak seasons or at most probable times such as convention season.

**Tools:** Travel and tourism trade shows, telemarketing, direct mail, trade publication advertising.

**Internet**

**Objectives:** Provide information regarding the Zoo, programs, memberships and public relations activities.

**Audience:** All audiences interested in acquiring more information about the Zoo.

**Timing:** Ongoing, updated frequently over time.

**Tools:** Website, blog, including videos, Facebook, Twitter, and other social media.

**FIGURE 7–6** An Example of a Zoo's Objectives for Various Promotional Elements

## IN A RECESSION, THE BEST DEFENSE IS A GOOD OFFENSE.

It's a recession. Your instincts demand that you cut the ad budget. But, as the McGraw-Hill Research' analysis of business-to-business advertising expenditures during the 1981-82 recession shows, it's those with the courage to maintain or increase advertising in a recession who reap a major sales advantage over their competitors who panic and fall back into a defensive posture.

**Effects of Advertising in a Recession on Sales (Indices)**

Companies that Maintained or Increased Advertising in Both 1981 and 1982

Companies that Eliminated or Decreased Advertising in Both 1981 and 1982

| 1980 | 1981 | 1982 | 1983 | 1984 | 1985 |
|------|------|------|------|------|------|
| 100 100 | 137 / 96 | 159 / 88 | 195 / 89 | 283 / 106 | 375 / 119 |

McGraw-Hill Research, 1986.

And this advantage continues to expand long after the recession is over. Recessions last an average of 11 months, but any advertising decision made during one can have permanent repercussions. The McGraw-Hill study demonstrates that nervous advertisers lose ground to the brave and can't gain it back. In 1980, according to the chart seen here, sales indices were identical, but by 1985 the brave had racked up a 3.2 to 1 sales advantage. A similar study done by McGraw-Hill during the 1974-75 recession corroborates the 1980's research.

A recession is the single greatest period in which to make short- and long-term gains. And, surprisingly, increasing advertising modestly during one has much the same effect on your profits as cutting advertising does. According to The Center for Research & Development's October 1990 study of consumer advertising during a recession, advertisers who yield "to the natural inclination to cut spending in an effort to increase profits in a recession find that it doesn't work." This study, relying on the PIMS' database, also uncovered that aggressive recessionary advertisers picked up 4.5 times as much market share gain as their overcautious competitors, leaving them in a far better position to exploit the inevitable recovery and expansion.

Chevrolet countered its competitors during the 1974-75 recession by aggressively beefing up its ad spending and attained a two percent market share increase. Today, two share points in the automotive industry are worth over $4 billion. Delta Airlines and Revlon also boosted ad spending in the 1974-75 recession and achieved similar results.

Continuous advertising sustains market leadership. And it's far easier to sustain momentum than it is to start it up again. Consider this list of market category leaders: Campbell's, Coca-Cola, Ivory, Kellogg, Kodak, Lipton and Wrigley. This is the leadership list for 1925. And 1990. These marketers have maintained a relentless commitment to their brands in both good times and bad. Kellogg had the guts to pump up its ad spending during the Great Depression and cemented a market leadership it has yet to relinquish.

These are the success stories. Space and diplomacy don't allow the mention of the names of those who lacked gusto and chose to cut their ad spending in recessionary times.

But if you would like to learn more about how advertising can help make the worst of times the best of times, please write to Department C, American Association of Advertising Agencies, 666 Third Avenue, New York, New York 10017, enclosing a check for five dollars. You will receive a booklet covering the pertinent research done on all the U.S. recessions since 1923. Please allow 4 to 6 weeks for delivery.

McGraw-Hill Research, 1986. ' The Center for Research and Development ©1990.
' Profit Impact of Market Strategies. The Strategic Planning Institute, Cambridge, MA.

**AAAA**

**EXHIBIT 7–11**

The American Association of Advertising Agencies (AAAA) promotes the continued use of advertising in a recession

LO 7.6

**FIGURE 7–7**

Conclusions on Research of Advertising in a Recession

- Advertising is strongly related to economic cycles across major world economies.
- The single most compelling reason for cutting back advertising during a recession is that sales during a recession are likely to be lower than they would be during an expansion.
- There is strong, consistent evidence that cutting back on advertising can hurt sales during and after a recesssion.
- Not cutting back on advertising during a recession could increase sales during and after the recession.
- Firms that increased advertising during a recession experienced higher sales, market share, or earnings during or after the recession.
- Most firms tend to cut back on advertising during a recession, reducing noise and increasing the effectiveness of advertising of the firm that advertises.

Source: G. Tellis and K. Tellis, "Research on Advertising in a Recession," *Journal of Advertising Research* 49, no.3 (2009), pp. 304–27.

downturn outweighs that of decreasing ad expenditures.[17] As shown in IMC Perspective 7–1, a number of successful companies agree, as indicated by their ad expenditures. Moreover, the decision is not a one-time responsibility. A new budget is formulated every year, each time a new product is introduced, or when either internal or external factors necessitate a change to maintain competitiveness.

While it is one of the most critical decisions, budgeting has perhaps been the most resistant to change. A comparison of advertising and promotional texts over the past 10 years would reveal the same methods for establishing budgets. The theoretical basis for this process remains rooted in economic theory and marginal analysis. (Advertisers also use an approach based on **contribution margin**—the difference between the total revenue generated by a brand and its total variable costs. But, as Robert Steiner says, *marginal analysis* and *contribution margin* are essentially synonymous terms.)[18] We begin our discussion of budgeting with an examination of these theoretical approaches.

**Theoretical Issues in Budget Setting** Most of the models used to establish advertising budgets can be categorized as taking an economic or a sales response perspective.

**Marginal Analysis** Figure 7–8 graphically represents the concept of **marginal analysis**. As advertising/promotional expenditures increase, sales and gross margins also increase to a point, but then they level off. Profits are shown to be a result of the gross margin minus advertising expenditures. Using this theory to establish its budget, a firm would continue to spend advertising/promotional dollars as long as the marginal revenues created by these expenditures exceeded the incremental advertising/promotional costs. As shown on the graph, the optimal expenditure level is the point where marginal costs equal the marginal revenues they generate (point A). If the sum of the advertising/promotional expenditures exceeded the revenues they generated, one would conclude the appropriations were too high and scale down the budget. If revenues were higher, a higher budget might be in order. (We will see later in this chapter that this approach can also be applied to the allocation decision.)

**FIGURE 7–8**

Marginal Analysis

While marginal analysis seems logical intuitively, certain weaknesses limit its usefulness. These weaknesses include the assumptions that (1) sales are a direct result of advertising and promotional expenditures and this effect can be measured and (2) advertising and promotion are solely responsible for sales. Let us examine each of these assumptions in more detail.

1. *Assumption that sales are a direct measure of advertising and promotion efforts.* Earlier in this chapter we discussed the fact that the advertiser needs to set communications objectives that contribute to accomplishing overall marketing objectives but at the same time are separate. One reason for this strategy is that it is often difficult, if not impossible, to demonstrate the effects of advertising and promotions on sales. In studies using sales as a direct measure, it has been almost impossible to establish the contribution of advertising and promotion. In the words of David Aaker and James Carman, "Looking for the relationship between advertising and sales is somewhat worse than looking for a needle in a haystack."[19] Thus, to try to show that the size of the budget will directly affect sales of the product is misleading. A more logical approach would be to examine the impact of various budgets on the attainment of communications objectives.

   As we saw in the discussion of communications objectives, sales are not the only goal of the promotional effort. Awareness, interest, attitude change, and other communications objectives are often sought, and while the bottom line may be to sell the product, these objectives may serve as the basis on which the promotional program is developed.

2. *Assumption that sales are determined solely by advertising and promotion.* This assumption ignores the remaining elements of the marketing mix—price, product, and distribution—which do contribute to a company's success. Environmental factors may also affect the promotional program, leading the marketing manager to assume the advertising was or was not effective when some other factor may have helped or hindered the accomplishment of the desired objectives.

Overall, you can see that while the economic approach to the budgeting process is a logical one, the difficulties associated with determining the effects of the promotional effort on sales and revenues limit its applicability. Marginal analysis is seldom used as a basis for budgeting (except for direct-response advertising).

**Sales Response Models** You may have wondered why the sales curve in Figure 7–8 shows sales leveling off even though advertising and promotions efforts continue to increase. The relationship between advertising and sales has been the topic of much research and discussion designed to determine the shape of the response curve.

Almost all advertisers subscribe to one of two models of the advertising/sales response function: the concave-downward function or the S-shaped response curve.

# IMC Perspective 7-1 > > >

## Companies Look for Edge in a Recession by Spending More

For most companies, a downturn in the economy leads to spending cutbacks. Unfortunately, one of the first areas to feel the pain of these cutbacks is marketing—particularly advertising. Indeed, in a survey conducted by the Association of National Advertisers in 2009, a staggering 77 percent of marketers indicated that they had plans to reduce their advertising media budgets in the upcoming months. Seventy-two percent planned to reduce their production budgets, 48 percent were considering reducing agency compensation, and 68 percent said they would challenge their agencies to find ways to cut costs. Clearly, these companies were looking at ways to save money. But were they doing the right thing? It appears that some of the leading advertisers don't agree with this strategy.

Two of the most successful consumer packaged goods companies in the United States do not subscribe to this strategy. During what might be considered the height of the recession in 2010, P&G increased its advertising spending by $1 billion in an attempt to grow sales and market share. Most of the increase went to campaigns for Gillette Fusion ProGlide razors, Pantene shampoo, and the launch of

Fix that thirst but good...here's your
**real thirst-quencher!**

*Nothing does it like Seven-Up!* You like it... it likes you!

Pampers Dry Max diapers. The result was an increase of 4 share points in men's shaving and 0.5 point in shampoo. Pampers also rose by 1.5 share points in all marketing channels. When questioned about the wisdom of increasing ad spending in the midst of a recession, CFO Jon Moeller said, "Put simply, we would have been crazy to do anything else."

Like P&G, Kraft Foods agrees with the strategy of increasing expenditures when others are cutting. Kraft also increased its advertising spending in the latter half of 2010, noting that the company "would not tolerate the widespread use of promotions to enhance its position." Irene Rosenfeld, Kraft's CEO, stated that along with the increase in ad spending, the emphasis on aggressive promotional pricing and discounts would be reduced significantly. Rosenfeld believes that aggressive brand building would pay significant benefits going forward. The numbers seem to support her strategy as Tang and Oreo both saw 30 to 40 percent growth due to effectrive advertising and communications initiatives. Other Kraft brands also benefited from increased expenditures, including Capri-Sun, Kool-Aid, and Maxwell House Coffee.

■ *The concave-downward function.* After reviewing more than 100 studies of the effects of advertising on sales, Julian Simon and Johan Arndt concluded that the effects of advertising budgets follow the microeconomic law of diminishing returns.[20] That is, as the amount of advertising increases, its incremental value decreases. The logic is that those with the greatest potential to buy will likely act on the first (or earliest) exposures, while those less likely to buy are not likely to change as a result of the advertising. For those who may be potential buyers, each additional ad will supply little or no new information that will affect their decision. Thus, according to the **concave-downward function model**, the effects of advertising quickly begin to diminish, as shown in Figure 7–9A. Budgeting under this model suggests that fewer advertising dollars may be needed to create the optimal influence on sales.

■ *The S-shaped response function.* Many advertising managers assume the **S-shaped response curve** (Figure 7–9B), which projects an S-shaped response function to the budget outlay (again measured in sales). Initial outlays of the advertising budget have little impact (as indicated by the essentially flat sales curve in range A). After a certain budget level has been reached (the beginning of range B), advertising and promotional efforts begin to have an effect, as additional increments of expenditures result in increased sales. This incremental gain continues only to a point, however, because at the beginning of range C additional expenditures begin to return little or nothing in the way

Yet another successful brand, 7UP, also agrees with the P&G and Kraft strategy. The soft-drink brand now owned by Dr Pepper Snapple Group has never fully recovered from its elimination from the soft-drink line of PepsiCo and being replaced by Sierra Mist. Sales in 2008 were off by 8.1 percent, and in the first six months of 2009, they declined by another 7.7 percent. To make things worse, the overall soft-drink category was in a decline, with lemon-lime flavors among the hardest hit. 7-UP's plans for 2010 were pretty ambitious, including the first new advertising campaign in three years, new positioning, product line extensions, and an in-store facelift. The new budget was significantly increased over the $21 million (not including online) spent the year before. When asked "Why spend now?" David Falk, director of 7UP and flavors at the Dr Pepper Snapple Group, had a simple response: "Brands that advertise during economic lulls come out of those times a lot stronger."

Similar thinking is apparent at Burger King. The fast-food company announced a double-digit (20–25 percent) increase in ad spending over its $294 million in 2008, beginning in late 2009, with a big boost in the summer of 2010, the biggest season for fast-food sales. Interestingly, not only is Burger King going against the grain in spending, but the largest increases were targeted for television ads as opposed to those in digital media. As noted by Russ Klein, Burger King's chief marketing officer, "There is no way to replace television," underscoring the medium's broad reach. Klein also noted, "With the economic downturn, it's important for us to be front and center with value messaging, innovation and strategy. . . . There is strong historical evidence about companies that step up with their innovation and advertising and their ability to move through economic downturns and then emerge with stronger brands on the other end."

Another reason for increased ad spending comes from General Mills. As the recession lingered on, General Mills's research indicated that more Americans were eating at home due to uncertainty about their fortunes in the years ahead. After a 25 percent increase in ad spending in the first quarter, the cereal company announced another high single-digit increase later in the year, believing that "the reinvestment is fueling net sales growth." (General Mills's retail sales increased 12 percent and operating profits were up 30 percent even with the increased ad spending.)

A number of other retailers also bucked the cutback trend in an attempt to increase Christmas holiday sales. Kmart, Walmart, and JCPenney all doubled their advertising spending from the previous year, while Home Depot and Lowe's were up by 50 percent. Gap increased its spending by $25 million in the third quarter and by $45 million in the fourth. Gap also went back to television advertising for the first time in two years. According to a Walmart spokesperson, the world's number 1 retailer has always believed in maintaining spending even during a recession, noting that it benefits from media cost deflation.

Looking at the names on this list of companies that are not cutting—and actually increasing—advertising expenditures during a downturn, one wonders if maybe they know something the other 77 percent don't know.

Sources: Kenneth Hein, "To Counter Downward Sales Trend, 7UP Ups Ad Spend," *Brandweek*, October 12, 2009, p. 5; Suzanne Vranica, "Retailers Boost Spending on Holiday Advertising," www.wsj.com, Nov. 9, 2009; Emily Bryson York, "Burger King to Boost Ad Spending," www.adage.com, April 17, 2009; David Goetzl, "General Mills to Increase Ad Spending," www.mediapost.com, July 6, 2009; David Goetzl, "Coca-Cola, P&G to Keep Spending," www.warc.com, April 23, 2009; Jack Neff, "P&G Hikes Ad Spending by $1 Billion to Gow Share Sales," www.adage.com, August 3, 2010; Seeking Alpha, "Kraft Boosts AdSpend, CHTS Back on Promotions," www.warc.com, August 9, 2010.

of sales. This model suggests a small advertising budget is likely to have no impact beyond the sales that may have been generated through other means (for example, word of mouth). At the other extreme, more does not necessarily mean better: Additional dollars spent beyond range B have no additional impact on sales and for the most part can be considered wasted. As with marginal analysis, one would attempt to operate at that point on the curve in area B where the maximum return for the money is attained.

Weaknesses in these sales response models render them of limited use to practitioners for direct applications. Many of the problems seen earlier—the use of sales as a dependent variable, measurement problems, and so on—limit the usefulness of these models. At the same time, keep in mind the purpose of discussing such models. Even though marginal analysis and the sales response curves may not apply directly, they give managers some insight into a theoretical basis of how the budgeting process should work. There's some empirical evidence indicating the models may have validity.

The studies discussed in earlier chapters on learning and the hierarchy of effects also demonstrate the importance of repetition for gaining awareness and for subsequent higher-order objectives such as adoption. Thus, while these models may not provide a tool for setting the advertising and promotional budget directly, we can use them to guide our appropriations strategy from a theoretical basis. As you will see later in this chapter, such a theoretical basis has advantages over many of the methods currently being used for budget setting and allocation.

**A. The Concave-Downward Response Curve**

Incremental sales

Advertising expenditures

**B. The S-Shaped Response Function**

Incremental sales

Range A    Range B    Range C

Advertising expenditures

**FIGURE 7–9**

Advertising Sales/Response Functions

**FIGURE 7–10**

Factors Influencing Advertising Budgets

**Additional Factors in Budget Setting**   While the theoretical bases just discussed should be considered in establishing the budget appropriation, a number of other issues must also be considered. A weakness in attempting to use sales as a *direct* measure of response to advertising is that various situational factors may have an effect. Some of the factors that have been shown to affect the advertising/sales ratio are shown in Figure 7–10. For a product characterized by emotional buying motives, hidden product qualities, and/or a strong basis for differentiation, advertising would have a noticeable impact on sales. Products characterized as large-dollar purchases and those in the maturity or decline stages of the product would be less likely to benefit.

| Factor | Relationship of Advertising/Sales | Factor | Relationship of Advertising/Sales |
|---|---|---|---|
| **Product Factors** | | Competition: | |
| Basis for differentiation | + | Active | + |
| Hidden product qualities | + | Concentrated | + |
| Emotional buying motives | + | **Customer Factors** | |
| | − | Concentration of users | + |
| | − | **Strategy Factors** | |
| Purchase frequency | Curvilinear | Early stage of brand life cycle | + |
| **Market Factors** | | Long channels of distribution | + |
| Stage of product life cycle: | | High prices | + |
| Introductory | + | High quality | + |
| Growth | + | Media strategy | + |
| Maturity | − | Creative strategy | + |
| Decline | − | Promotional strategy | + |
| Inelastic demand | + | **Cost Factors** | |
| Market share | − | High profit margins | + |

Note: + relationship means the factor leads to a positive effect of advertising on sales; − relationship indicates little or no effect of advertising on sales.

As we will see later in this chapter, the percentage-of-sales method of budgeting has inherent weaknesses in that the advertising and sales effects may be reversed. So we cannot be sure whether the situation actually led to the advertising/sales relationship or vice versa. Thus, while these factors should be considered in the budget appropriation decision, they should not be the sole determinants of where and when to increase or decrease expenditures.

The *Advertising Age* Editorial Sounding Board consists of 92 executives of the top 200 advertising companies in the United States (representing the client side) and 130 executives of the 200 largest advertising agencies and 11 advertising consultants (representing the agency side). A survey of the board yielded the factors shown in Figure 7–11 that are important in budget setting.

Overall, the responses of these two groups reflect in part their perceptions as to factors of importance in how budgets are set. To understand the differences in the relative importance of these factors, it is important to understand the approaches currently employed in budget setting. The next section examines these approaches.

## Budgeting Approaches

LO 7-7

The theoretical approaches to establishing the promotional budget are seldom employed. In smaller firms, they may never be used. Instead, a number of methods developed through practice and experience are implemented. This section reviews some of the more traditional methods of setting budgets and the relative advantages and disadvantages of each. First, you must understand two things: (1) Many firms employ more than one method, and (2) budgeting approaches vary according to the size and sophistication of the firm.

**Top-Down Approaches**   The approaches discussed in this section may be referred to as **top-down approaches** because a budgetary amount is established (usually at an executive level) and then the monies are passed down to the various departments (as shown in Figure 7–12). These budgets are essentially predetermined and have no true theoretical basis. Top-down methods include the affordable method, arbitrary allocation, percentage of sales, competitive parity, and return on investment (ROI).

**The Affordable Method**   In the **affordable method** (often referred to as the "all-you-can-afford method"), the firm determines the amount to be spent in various areas such as production and operations. Then it allocates what's left to advertising and promotion, considering this to be the amount it can afford. The task to be performed by the advertising/promotions function is not considered, and the likelihood of under- or overspending is high, as no guidelines for measuring the effects of various budgets are established.

Strange as it may seem, this approach is common among small firms. Unfortunately, it is also used in large firms, particularly those that are not marketing-driven and do not understand the role of advertising and promotion. For example, many high-tech

**FIGURE 7–11**

Factors Considered in Budget Setting

| | |
|---|---|
| Changes in advertising strategy and/or creative approach | 51% |
| Competitive activity and/or spending levels | 47 |
| Profit contribution goal or other financial target | 43 |
| Level of previous year's spending, with adjustment | 17 |
| Senior management dollar allocation or set limit | 11 |
| Volume share projections | 8 |
| Projections/assumptions on media cost increases | 25 |
| Modifications in media strategy and/or buying techniques | 17 |

**FIGURE 7–12**

Top-Down versus
Bottom-Up Approaches to
Budget Setting

firms focus on new product development and engineering and assume that the product, if good enough, will sell itself. In these companies, little money may be left for performing the advertising and promotions tasks.

The logic for this approach stems from "We can't be hurt with this method" thinking. That is, if we know what we can afford and we do not exceed it, we will not get into financial problems. While this may be true in a strictly accounting sense, it does not reflect sound managerial decision making from a marketing perspective. Often this method does not allocate enough money to get the product off the ground and into the market. In terms of the S-shaped sales response model, the firm is operating in range A. Or the firm may be spending more than necessary, operating in range C. When the market gets tough and sales and/or profits begin to fall, this method is likely to lead to budget cuts at a time when the budget should be increased.

**Arbitrary Allocation** Perhaps an even weaker method than the affordable method for establishing a budget is **arbitrary allocation**, in which virtually no theoretical basis is considered and the budgetary amount is often set by fiat. That is, the budget is determined by management solely on the basis of what is felt to be necessary. In a discussion of how managers set advertising budgets, Melvin Salveson reported that these decisions may reflect "as much upon the managers' psychological profile as they do economic criteria."[21] While Salveson was referring to larger corporations, the approach is no less common in small firms and nonprofit organizations.

The arbitrary allocation approach has no obvious advantages. No systematic thinking has occurred, no objectives have been budgeted for, and the concept and purpose of advertising and promotion have been largely ignored. Other than the fact that the manager believes some monies must be spent on advertising and promotion and then picks a number, there is no good explanation why this approach continues to be used. Yet budgets continue to be set this way, and our purpose in discussing this method is to point out only that it is used—not recommended.

**Percentage of Sales** Perhaps the most commonly used method for budget setting (particularly in large firms) is the **percentage-of-sales method,** in which the advertising and promotions budget is based on sales of the product. Management determines the amount by either (1) taking a percentage of the sales dollars or (2) assigning a fixed amount of the unit product cost to promotion and multiplying this amount by the number of units sold. These two methods are shown in Figure 7–13.

FIGURE 7–13

Alternative Methods for
Computing Percentage of
Sales

| METHOD 1: STRAIGHT PERCENTAGE OF SALES | | |
|---|---|---|
| 2014 | Total dollar sales | $1,000,000 |
| | Straight % of sales at 10% | $100,000 |
| 2015 | Advertising budget | $100,000 |
| **METHOD 2: PERCENTAGE OF UNIT COST** | | |
| 2014 | Cost per product to manufacturer | $4.00 |
| | Unit cost allocated to advertising | 1.00 |
| 2015 | Forecasted sales, 100,000 units | |
| 2015 | Advertising budget (100,000 × $1) | $100,000 |

A variation on the percentage-of-sales method uses a percentage of projected future sales as a base. This method also uses either a straight percentage of projected sales or a unit cost projection. In the straight-percentage method, sales are projected for the coming year based on the marketing manager's estimates. The budget is a percentage of these sales, often an industry standard percentage like those presented in Figure 7–14.

One advantage of using future sales as a base is that the budget is not based on last year's sales. As the market changes, management must factor the effect of these changes on sales into next year's forecast rather than relying on past data. The resulting budget is more likely to reflect current conditions and be more appropriate.

Figure 7–14 reveals that the percentage allocated varies from one industry to the next. Some firms budget a very small percentage (for example, 0.5 percent in bakery products), and others spend a much higher proportional amount (14.3 percent in distilled and blended liquors; 10.4 percent in dolls and stuffed toys). Actual dollar amounts spent vary markedly according to the company's total sales figure. Thus, a smaller percentage of sales in the construction machinery industry may actually result in significantly more advertising dollars being spent.

Proponents of the percentage-of-sales method cite a number of advantages. It is financially safe and keeps ad spending within reasonable limits, as it bases spending on the past year's sales or what the firm expects to sell in the upcoming year. Thus, there will be sufficient monies to cover this budget, with increases in sales leading to budget increases and sales decreases resulting in advertising decreases. The percentage-of-sales method is simple, straightforward, and easy to implement. Regardless of which basis—past or future sales—is employed, the calculations used to arrive at a budget are not difficult. Finally, this budgeting approach is generally stable. While the budget may vary with increases and decreases in sales, as long as these changes are not drastic the manager will have a reasonable idea of the parameters of the budget.

At the same time, the percentage-of-sales method has some serious disadvantages, including the basic premise on which the budget is established: sales. Letting the level of sales determine the amount of advertising and promotions dollars to be spent reverses the cause-and-effect relationship between advertising and sales. It treats advertising as an expense associated with making a sale rather than an investment. As shown in Figure 7–15, companies that consider promotional expenditures an investment reap the rewards (as was shown in IMC Perspective 7–1).

A second problem with this approach was actually cited as an advantage earlier: stability. Proponents say that if all firms use a similar percentage, that will bring stability to the marketplace. But what happens if someone varies from this standard percentage? The problem is that this method does not allow for changes in strategy either internally or from competitors. An aggressive firm may wish to allocate more monies to the advertising and promotions budget, a strategy that is not possible with a percentage-of-sales method unless the manager is willing to deviate from industry standards.

FIGURE 7–14  Advertising-to-Sales Ratios by Industry Sector

| | | 2012 AD-TO-SALES RATIOS | | | | | |
|---|---|---|---|---|---|---|---|
| Industry Name | SIC Code No. | 2011 Ad Spending ($000) | 2012 Ad Spending ($000) | Annual Ad Growth Rate (%) | Annual Sales Growth Rate | 2011 Ad $ as % of Sales | 2011 Ad $ as % of Margin |
| ABRASIVE, ASBESTOS, MISC MINRL | 3290 | 19.974 | 20.919 | 4.6 | 5.6 | 0.3 | 0 |
| ACCIDENT & HEALTH INSURANCE | 6321 | 562.646 | 560.981 | –5.1 | 2.4 | 1.3 | 5.2 |
| ADHESIVES AND SEALANTS | 2891 | 0.002 | 0 | –100 | 11.6 | 0 | 0 |
| ADVERTISING | 7310 | 197.107 | 197.941 | 3.9 | 3.2 | 1.8 | 0 |
| ADVERTISING AGENCIES | 7311 | 0.119 | 0 | –100 | 6.5 | 0 | 0 |
| AGRIC PROD-LVSTK, ANIMAL SPEC | 200 | 7.927 | 9.277 | 15.8 | 5.8 | 0.4 | –4.5 |
| AGRICULTURAL CHEMICALS | 2870 | 3285.057 | 3924.558 | 18.2 | 13.6 | 5.9 | 0 |
| AGRICULTURAL SERVICES | 700 | 155.1 | 156.407 | 0.7 | 2.5 | 4.8 | 10.2 |
| AGRICULTURE PRODUCTION-CROPS | 100 | 289.196 | 295.01 | 2.7 | 1.6 | 1 | 0 |
| AIR COURIER SERVICES | 4513 | 454.77 | 446.815 | –1.8 | 4 | 0.6 | 3.1 |
| AIR TRANSPORT, NONSCHEDULED | 4522 | 0.008 | 0.007 | –14.6 | 9 | 0 | 0.1 |
| AIR TRANSPORT, SCHEDULED | 4512 | 2454.034 | 2666.457 | 8.3 | 12.6 | 0.7 | 0 |
| AIR-COND, HEATING, REFRIG EQ | 3585 | 102.216 | 95.55 | –6.8 | 7.2 | 1.1 | 0.8 |
| AIRCRAFT | 3721 | 205.894 | 211.871 | 2.7 | –1.6 | 0.2 | –6 |
| AIRCRAFT AND PARTS | 3720 | 0.009 | 0.01 | 11.9 | 3.6 | 0 | 0.3 |
| AIRPORTS & TERMINAL SERVICES | 4581 | 2.245 | 2.335 | 3.9 | 13.6 | 1.5 | 4.8 |
| AMUSEMENT & RECREATION SVCS | 7900 | 267.936 | 292.044 | 8 | 10.5 | 3.9 | –41 |
| AMUSEMENT PARKS | 7996 | 115.5 | 107.108 | –7.5 | 5.2 | 5 | 6.3 |
| APPAREL & OTHER FINISHED PDS | 2300 | 1970.392 | 2170.307 | 10.5 | 12.9 | 4.8 | 0 |
| APPAREL AND ACCESSORY STORES | 5600 | 390.804 | 415.16 | 5.9 | 6.6 | 3.5 | 1.3 |
| APPAREL, PIECE GDS, NOTNS-WHSL | 5130 | 18.386 | 20.007 | 8.5 | 9.8 | 2.1 | 3 |
| ARRANGE TRANS-FREIGHT, CARGO | 4731 | 2.913 | 3.261 | 11.3 | 14.1 | 0.1 | 0.2 |
| AUTO AND HOME SUPPLY STORES | 5531 | 312.774 | 326.786 | 4.4 | 6.9 | 1.4 | 2.1 |
| AUTO DEALERS, GAS STATIONS | 5500 | 621.795 | 673.193 | 8 | 13.2 | 0.6 | 0 |
| AUTO RENT & LEASE, NO DRIVERS | 7510 | 384.301 | 402.152 | 5.3 | 6.8 | 1.5 | 0 |
| AUTO REPAIR, SERVICES, PARKING | 7500 | 5.751 | 0.706 | –70.2 | 5.8 | 0 | 0 |
| AUTOMATIC REGULATNG CONTROLS | 3822 | 3.675 | 3.949 | 7.2 | 13.1 | 2.5 | 5.7 |
| BAKERY PRODUCTS | 2050 | 16.467 | 16.986 | 3.2 | 3.5 | 0.5 | 0.8 |
| BALL AND ROLLER BEARINGS | 3562 | 88.463 | 105.251 | 16.7 | 12 | 0.6 | 0.6 |
| BEVERAGES | 2080 | 5156 | 5735.703 | 10.8 | 16.2 | 4.3 | 4.5 |
| BIOLOGICAL PDS, EX DIAGNSTICS | 2836 | 846.552 | 912.853 | 7 | 7.6 | 1.4 | –97.6 |
| BITUMINOUS COAL, LIGNITE MNG | 1220 | 62.28 | 73.012 | 17 | 21 | 0.2 | 0.3 |
| BLANKBOOKS, BINDERS, BOOKBIND | 2780 | 201.109 | 194.729 | –2.9 | 2.4 | 6.9 | 9.1 |
| BLDG MATL, HARDWR, GARDEN-RETL | 5200 | 81.268 | 89.371 | 9.5 | 11.3 | 1 | 0.3 |
| BOOKS: PUBG, PUBG & PRINTING | 2731 | 265.127 | 271.735 | 2.7 | 1 | 1.6 | 0.9 |
| BRDWOVEN FABRIC MILL, COTTON | 2211 | 0.4 | 0.262 | –38.2 | 1.5 | 0 | 0.3 |
| BTLD & CAN SOFT DRINKS, WATER | 2086 | 2005.46 | 2123.299 | 5 | 2.5 | 4.4 | 0 |
| BUSINESS SERVICES, NEC | 7389 | 429.799 | 452.117 | 5.6 | 9.8 | 1.5 | –85.2 |
| CABLE AND OTHER PAY TV SVCS | 4841 | 3754.593 | 3899.777 | 3.6 | 8.4 | 1.7 | 0 |
| CALCULATE, ACCT MACH, EX COMP | 3578 | 61.719 | 67.007 | 8.5 | 8.9 | 0.5 | 0.1 |
| CAN FRUIT, VEG, PRESRV, JAM, JEL | 2033 | 165.318 | 186.379 | 12 | 7.5 | 2.3 | 1.8 |
| CAN, FROZN, PRESRV FRUIT & VEG | 2030 | 792.446 | 821.287 | 3.5 | 4.4 | 3.1 | 0 |
| CARPETS AND RUGS | 2273 | 35.847 | 30.074 | –17 | 3.9 | 0.5 | 1.3 |
| CATALOG, MAIL-ORDER HOUSES | 5961 | 2464.015 | 2846.827 | 15.1 | 17.4 | 3.2 | 0 |
| CEMENT, HYDRAULIC | 3241 | 3.136 | 3.745 | 18.3 | –4.4 | 0.9 | 1.2 |
| CHEMICALS & ALLIED PDS-WHSL | 5160 | 0.01 | 0.012 | 21.3 | 10.2 | 1 | –24.4 |
| CHEMICALS & ALLIED PRODUCTS | 2800 | 2371.061 | 2447.883 | 3 | 10.1 | 5 | 8.7 |
| CIGARETTES | 2111 | 537.099 | 563.446 | 4.5 | 5.5 | 0.5 | 0 |
| CMP AND CMP SOFTWARE STORES | 5734 | 74.041 | 78.571 | 5.9 | 2.4 | 0.8 | 1.1 |
| CMP INTEGRATED SYS DESIGN | 7373 | 1285.919 | 1395.001 | 8.8 | 4.6 | 0.8 | –4.8 |
| CMP PROCESSING, DATA PREP SVC | 7374 | 328.502 | 333.977 | 1.8 | 9 | 0.7 | 0 |
| CMP PROGRAMMING, DATA PROCESS | 7370 | 11351.946 | 12710.266 | 11.4 | 9.9 | 4.8 | –84.5 |
| COGENERATN-SM POWER PRODUCER | 4991 | 118.035 | 132.283 | 12.1 | 4.7 | 0.3 | 0.7 |
| COML PHYSICAL, BIOLOGCL RESH | 8731 | 11.618 | 8.46 | –21.8 | 5.7 | 0.1 | –0.9 |
| COMMERCIAL PRINTING | 2750 | 19.522 | 17.662 | –8.5 | 13.2 | 0.1 | 0.2 |

| | | 2012 AD-TO-SALES RATIOS | | | | | |
|---|---|---|---|---|---|---|---|
| Industry Name | SIC Code No. | 2011 Ad Spending ($000) | 2012 Ad Spending ($000) | Annual Ad Growth Rate (%) | Annual Sales Growth Rate | 2011 Ad $ as % of Sales | 2011 Ad $ as % of Margin |
| COMMUNICATIONS EQUIP, NEC | 3669 | 47.735 | 47.232 | 1.6 | 7.3 | 2.9 | 0 |
| COMMUNICATIONS SERVICES, NEC | 4899 | 1559.535 | 1736.466 | 10.8 | 5.6 | 4.5 | −28.4 |
| COMPUTER & OFFICE EQUIPMENT | 3570 | 1576.471 | 1640.732 | 4 | 4.7 | 0.6 | 0.8 |
| COMPUTER COMMUNICATION EQUIP | 3576 | 445.991 | 488.91 | 9.2 | 9.1 | 0.8 | −33.1 |
| COMPUTER PERIPHERAL EQ, NEC | 3577 | 1801.835 | 2031.169 | 10.8 | 13.8 | 2.2 | 0 |
| COMPUTER PROGRAMMING SERVICE | 7371 | 1.247 | 1.38 | 8.2 | 12.5 | 0 | 0 |
| COMPUTER STORAGE DEVICES | 3572 | 121.644 | 124.205 | 7.6 | 11.7 | 0.2 | 0 |
| COMPUTERS & SOFTWARE-WHSL | 5045 | 471.987 | 527.903 | 10.9 | 9.1 | 0.5 | 0 |
| CONCRETE PDS, EX BLOCK, BRICK | 3272 | 0.346 | 0.343 | −1 | −3.1 | 1.3 | 3.1 |
| CONCRETE, GYPSUM, PLASTER PDS | 3270 | 70.886 | 64.475 | −9.5 | −11.4 | 0.3 | −3.3 |
| CONGLOMERATE | 9997 | 569.993 | 561.455 | −1.4 | 4.4 | 0.3 | −9.6 |
| CONSTR, MINING, MATL HANDLE EQ | 3530 | 3.599 | 3.613 | 0.4 | 9.5 | 0.5 | 1.7 |
| CONSTRUCTION MACHINERY & EQ | 3531 | 141.55 | 164.367 | 15.1 | 16.1 | 0.2 | 0.2 |
| CONSTRUCTION-SPECIAL TRADE | 1700 | 1.116 | 0.888 | −12.2 | 18.4 | 0 | −0.1 |
| CONVENIENCE STORES | 5412 | 0.105 | 0.116 | 9.8 | 7.3 | 0.4 | 0.4 |
| CONVRT PAPR, PAPRBRD, EX BOXES | 2670 | 618.96 | 695.974 | 11.8 | 12.3 | 0.8 | 0 |
| COOKIES AND CRACKERS | 2052 | 20.1 | 24.549 | 21.6 | 19.3 | 1.2 | 0.3 |
| CREDIT REPORTING AGENCIES | 7320 | 209.856 | 212.719 | 1.7 | 6.2 | 2.1 | 1 |
| CRUDE PETROLEUM & NATURAL GS | 1311 | 0.051 | 0.055 | 8.6 | 18.3 | 0 | 0 |
| CUT STONE AND STONE PRODUCTS | 3281 | 13.49 | 21.03 | 45.5 | 21.2 | 6.6 | 0 |
| CUTLERY, HANDTOOLS, GEN HRDWR | 3420 | 418.197 | 548.617 | 25.8 | 22.8 | 2.7 | 0.1 |
| DAIRY PRODUCTS | 2020 | 858.269 | 944.665 | 9.5 | 8.2 | 2.9 | −75.4 |
| DEEP SEA FRN TRANS-FREIGHT | 4412 | 5.498 | 6.64 | 20.7 | 4.1 | 0 | 1 |
| DENTAL EQUIPMENT & SUPPLIES | 3843 | 118.19 | 125.634 | 6.2 | 8.7 | 2.8 | 1.2 |
| DEPARTMENT STORES | 5311 | 3660.817 | 3643.711 | −0.5 | 3.1 | 4.1 | 0.7 |
| DISTILLED AND BLENDED LIQUOR | 2085 | 2728.67 | 2798.199 | 2.5 | 1.7 | 14.3 | 6.2 |
| DIVERSIFIED MULTI-MEDIA | 4888 | 11471.764 | 11860.445 | 2.8 | 4.2 | 8.6 | 1.3 |
| DOLLS AND STUFFED TOYS | 3942 | 714.747 | 757.563 | 5.8 | 5 | 10.4 | 4.3 |

Source: Schonfeld and Associates, Inc.–2012 Advertising Ratios and Budgets

**FIGURE 7–15**

Investments Pay Off in
Later Years

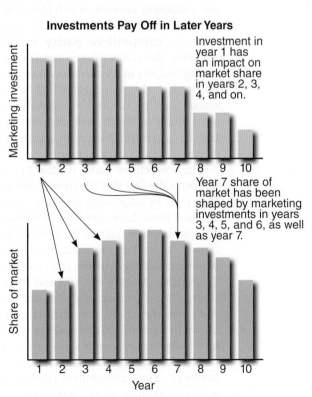

Investments Pay Off in Later Years

Investment in year 1 has an impact on market share in years 2, 3, 4, and on.

Year 7 share of market has been shaped by marketing investments in years 3, 4, 5, and 6, as well as year 7.

The percentage-of-sales method of budgeting may result in severe misappropriation of funds. If advertising and promotion have a role to perform in marketing a product, then allocating more monies to advertising will, as shown in the S-shaped curve, generate incremental sales (to a point). If products with low sales have smaller promotion budgets, this will hinder sales progress. At the other extreme, very successful products may have excess budgets, some of which may be better appropriated elsewhere.

The percentage-of-sales method is also difficult to employ for new product introductions. If no sales histories are available, there is no basis for establishing the budget. Projections of future sales may be difficult, particularly if the product is highly innovative and/or has fluctuating sales patterns.

Finally, if the budget is contingent on sales, decreases in sales will lead to decreases in budgets when they most need to be increased. Continuing to cut the advertising and promotion budgets may just add impetus to the downward sales trend. On the other hand, some of the more successful companies have allocated additional funds during hard times or downturns in the cycle of sales as shown earlier. Companies that maintain or increase their ad expenditures during recessions achieve increased visibility and higher growth in both sales and market share (compared to those that reduce advertising outlays).

While the percentage-of-future-sales method has been proposed as a remedy for some of the problems discussed here, the reality is that problems with forecasting, cyclical growth, and uncontrollable factors limit its effectiveness.

**Competitive Parity** If you asked marketing managers if they ever set their advertising and promotions budgets on the basis of what their competitors allocate, they would probably deny it. Yet if you examined the advertising expenditures of these companies, both as a percentage of sales and in respect to the media where they are allocated, you would see little variation in the percentage-of-sales figures for firms within a given industry. Such results do not happen by chance alone. Companies that provide competitive advertising information, trade associations, and other advertising industry periodicals are sources for competitors' expenditures. Larger corporations often subscribe to services such as Competitive Media Reporting, which estimates the top 1,000 companies' advertising in 10 media and in total. Smaller companies often use a **clipping service**, which clips competitors' ads from local print media, allowing the company to work backward to determine the cumulative costs of the ads placed.

In the **competitive parity method**, managers establish budget amounts by matching the competition's percentage-of-sales expenditures. The argument is that setting budgets in this fashion takes advantage of the collective wisdom of the industry. It also takes the competition into consideration, which leads to stability in the marketplace by minimizing marketing warfare. If companies know that competitors are unlikely to match their increases in promotional spending, they are less likely to take an aggressive posture to attempt to gain market share. This minimizes unusual or unrealistic ad expenditures.

The competitive parity method has a number of disadvantages, however. For one, it ignores the fact that advertising and promotions are designed to accomplish specific objectives by addressing certain problems and opportunities. Second, it assumes that because firms have similar expenditures, their programs will be equally effective. This assumption ignores the contributions of creative executions and/or media allocations, as well as the success or failure of various promotions. Further, it ignores possible advantages of the firm itself; some companies simply make better products than others. A study by Yoo and Mandhachitara indicates that a competitive parity strategy must consider the fact that a competitor's advertising can actually benefit one's own firm, and that one competitor's gain is not always the other's loss. As shown in Figure 7–16 there are four different situations to determine how the competitive budgets may impact sales—only one of which involved the zero-sum scenario.[22]

Also, there is no guarantee that competitors will continue to pursue their existing strategies. Since competitive parity figures are determined by examination of competitors' previous years' promotional expenditures (short of corporate espionage),

**FIGURE 7–16**

Competitors' Advertising Outlays Do Not Always Hurt

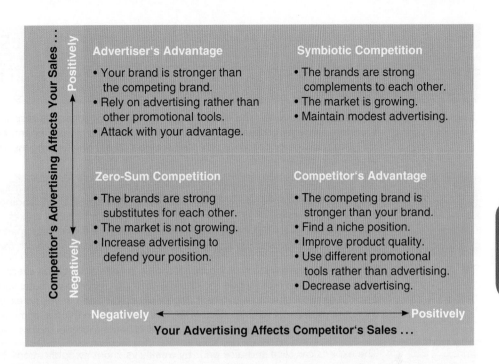

changes in market emphasis and/or spending may not be recognized until the competition has already established an advantage. Further, there is no guarantee that a competitor will not increase or decrease its own expenditures, regardless of what other companies do. Finally, competitive parity may not avoid promotional wars. Coke versus Pepsi and AT&T versus Verizon have been notorious for their spending wars, each responding to the other's increased outlays.

In summary, few firms employ the competitive parity method as a sole means of establishing the promotional budget. This method is typically used in conjunction with the percentage-of-sales or other methods. It is never wise to ignore the competition; managers must always be aware of what competitors are doing. But they should not just emulate them in setting goals and developing strategies.

**Return on Investment (ROI)** In the percentage-of-sales method, sales dictate the level of advertising appropriations. But advertising causes sales. In the marginal analysis and S-shaped curve approaches, incremental investments in advertising and promotions lead to increases in sales. The keyword here is *investment*. In the **ROI budgeting method**, advertising and promotions are considered investments, like plant and equipment. Thus, the budgetary appropriation (investment) leads to certain returns. Like other aspects of the firm's efforts, advertising and promotion are expected to earn a certain return. ROI has received a great deal of attention by practitioners over the past few years, with many still disagreeing as to how it should be measured. Figure 7–17 reports the results of *Advertising Age*'s report of the Aegis Group rating of how various media perform under this criterion (5 = best).

While the ROI method looks good on paper, the reality is that it is rarely possible to assess the returns provided by the promotional effort—at least as long as sales continue to be the basis for evaluation. Thus, while managers are certain to ask how much return they are getting for such expenditures, the question remains unanswered and, as shown in the chapter introduction, depends on the criteria used to determine effectiveness. ROI remains a difficult method to employ.

**Summary of Top-Down Budgeting Methods** You are probably asking yourself why we even discussed these budgeting methods if they are not recommended for use or have severe disadvantages that limit their effectiveness. But you must understand the various methods used in order to recognize their limitations, especially since these flawed methods are commonly employed by marketers. Research conducted

| Medium | The Measurement Challenge | ROI Measurability |
|---|---|---|
| Direct Response | Direct mail, telemarketing, and other forms are the most measurable of media listed here. Direct can have a synergistic effect, especially for pharma, telecom, and financial services. | 5 |
| Sales Promotion | Offers such as coupons and discounts generate a lot of consumer response and therefore a bounty of data. The data lend themselves to measurement, especially for package goods via syndicated scanner data. Freestanding inserts generate much valuable data. | 5 |
| Internet | The Internet can be influential for big-ticket purchases like cars. Very measurable, with the cautionary note that "Internet is a very broad net," ranging from search engines to ads in content to websites such as in the auto market, where such marques as Saab get lots of hits, and all should be looked at separately. The goal is to understand how the consumer is interacting online with the brand. | 5 |
| TV | While promotions have very pronounced, short-term effects that allow precise measurement, TV has a more subtle and gradual effect that may show greater variability. But ROI can be measured with a high degree of accuracy, and there's no excuse for TV not to show a measurable effect. MMA clients have been using a lot more analysis to create a better mix between :15s and :30s, and better allocation across dayparts. | 4.5 |
| Print | The experts can slice and dice print by weekly vs. monthly publications, by targeted vs. general market, by promotional ads vs. equity-building. Print promotional materials, like freestanding inserts, are a separate—and much more measurable—matter. As with all other media, accuracy and timing of the data are crucial in determining how measurable the medium is. Print can play a strong role in expanding the reach of the media mix. | 4.5 |
| Public Relations | There are companies that specialize in the measurement of PR campaigns' quality; they can measure the number of impressions delivered—via positive or negative PR—for a brand name or category. PR can have a measurable impact on sales (think trans fats in food). The problem: Many marketers aren't buying these PR data. | 4 |
| Videogames | Whether the game is played online or off-line is crucial. An ad embedded in a game cartridge is very hard to measure because there's no way to know how often it's played, though there's no denying "True Crime's" Nick Kang is a big hit. With online games, there are great data available through the Internet. | Online Off-line |

**SCALE: 5 = BEST**

**FIGURE 7–17**

Aegis Rated ROI of Various Media

over a number of years by various researchers indicates that the affordable, competitive parity, percentage of sales, and objective and task methods are the most commonly employed budgeting methods. As noted, the emphasis on ROI has dramatically increased over the past few years.[23–27] Tradition and top management's desire for control are probably the major reasons why top-down methods continue to be popular.

**Build-Up Approaches**   The major flaw associated with the top-down methods is that these judgmental approaches lead to predetermined budget appropriations often not linked to objectives and the strategies designed to accomplish them. A more effective budgeting strategy would be to consider the firm's communications objectives and budget what is deemed necessary to attain these goals. As noted earlier, the promotional planning model shows the budget decision as an interactive process, with the communications objectives on one hand and the promotional-mix alternatives on the other. The idea is to budget so these promotional-mix strategies can be implemented to achieve the stated objectives.

**Objective and Task Method**   It is important that objective setting and budgeting go hand in hand rather than sequentially. It is difficult to establish a budget without specific objectives in mind, and setting objectives without regard to how much

| Medium | The Measurement Challenge | ROI Measurability |
|---|---|---|
| Radio | The available data typically aren't as strong as those for its traditional-media colleagues of TV and print, and this hampers radio. | 3 |
| Cinema | Movie advertising can be measured by the number of impressions delivered, much like outdoor or kiosk advertising would be measured. | 3 |
| Sponsored Events | Measurability depends on whether sponsorship is likely to spark short-term effect. A major recurring event like the Olympics is very measurable. Others can be difficult to measure short term. Measurement can be complex because events have so many pieces, including how the event is advertised, the PR buzz, signage, and the recollection of the event itself. | 3 |
| Product Placement | There are companies that measure quality of placement as well as the quantity of exposures. Treated much like TV advertising, with the caveat that not every product placement is the same. Fox's *American Idol* is a great example: AT&T Wireless's tie-in, which involves voting by text message, is interactive—even part of the entertainment—while the judges drinking from a Coke cup is not. (P.S. AT&T Wireless, now owned by Cingular, isn't an MMA client.) So the question becomes: How do you score the quality of placement? | 3 |
| Outdoor | Available data are limited due to the nature of outdoor advertising; there's no syndicated vendor that sells the needed data on outdoor. And outdoor lacks "variance"—the billboard is up X number of months and seen by an unchanging X number of people each day. | 2 |
| Guerrilla Marketing | Hard to measure if the variable you're using is sales. If 10,000 people at an event get free T-shirts, it's difficult to measure the effect on the 400,000 people living in that market. Because guerrilla can encompass so many different kinds of tactics, getting useful data can be a problem—it depends on how measurable the response is. Marketers' ROI expectations for guerrilla are lower than for other media, so the urgency to measure is less. Not to mention they spend a lot less on guerrilla than on traditional media like TV. | 1 |
| | **SCALE: 5 = BEST** | |

**FIGURE 7–17**

(Concluded)

money is available makes no sense. For example, a company may wish to create awareness among *X* percent of its target market. A minimal budget amount will be required to accomplish this goal, and the firm must be willing to spend this amount.

The **objective and task method** of budget setting uses a **buildup approach** consisting of three steps: (1) defining the communications objectives to be accomplished, (2) determining the specific strategies and tasks needed to attain them, and (3) estimating the costs associated with performance of these strategies and tasks. The total budget is based on the accumulation of these costs.

Implementing the objective and task approach is somewhat more involved. The manager must monitor this process throughout and change strategies depending on how well objectives are attained. As shown in Figure 7–18, this process involves several steps:

1. *Isolate objectives.* When the promotional planning model is presented, a company will have two sets of objectives to accomplish—the marketing objectives for the product and the communications objectives. After the former are established, the task involves determining what specific communications objectives will be designed to accomplish these goals. Communications objectives must be specific, attainable, and measurable, as well as time limited.

2. *Determine tasks required.* A number of elements are involved in the strategic plan designed to attain the objectives established. (These strategies constitute the remaining chapters in this text.) These tasks may include advertising in various media, sales promotions, and/or other elements of the promotional mix, each with its own role to perform.

**FIGURE 7–18**

The Objective and Task
Method

Establish objectives
(create awareness of new product
among 20 percent of target market)

Determine specific tasks
(advertise on market area
television and radio stations
and in major newspapers)

Estimate costs associated with tasks
(television advertising, $575,000;
radio advertising, $225,000;
newspaper advertising, $175,000)

3. *Estimate required expenditures.* Buildup analysis requires determining the estimated costs associated with the tasks developed in the previous step. For example, it involves costs for developing awareness through advertising, trial through sampling, and so forth.
4. *Monitor.* As you will see in Chapter 18 on measuring effectiveness, there are ways to determine how well one is attaining established objectives. Performance should be monitored and evaluated in light of the budget appropriated.
5. *Reevaluate objectives.* Once specific objectives have been attained, monies may be better spent on new goals. Thus, if one has achieved the level of consumer awareness sought, the budget should be altered to stress a higher-order objective such as evaluation or trial.

The major advantage of the objective and task method is that the budget is driven by the objectives to be attained. The managers closest to the marketing effort will have specific strategies and input into the budget-setting process.

The major disadvantage of this method is the difficulty of determining which tasks will be required and the costs associated with each. For example, specifically what tasks are needed to attain awareness among 50 percent of the target market? How much will it cost to perform these tasks? While these decisions are easier to determine for certain objectives—for example, estimating the costs of sampling required to stimulate trial in a defined market area—it is not always possible to know exactly what is required and/or how much it will cost to complete the job. This process is easier if there is past experience to use as a guide, with either the existing product or a similar one in the same product category. But it is especially difficult for new product introductions. As a result, budget setting using this method is not as easy to perform or as stable as some of the methods discussed earlier. Given this disadvantage, many marketing managers have stayed with those top-down approaches for setting the total expenditure amount.

The objective and task method offers advantages over methods discussed earlier but is more difficult to implement when there is no track record for the product. The following section addresses the problem of budgeting for new product introductions.

**Payout Planning** The first months of a new product's introduction typically require heavier-than-normal advertising and promotion appropriations to stimulate higher levels of awareness and subsequent trial. After studying more than 40 years of Nielsen figures, James O. Peckham estimated that the average share of advertising to sales ratio necessary to launch a new product successfully is approximately 1.5:2.0.[28] This means that a new entry should be spending at approximately twice the desired market share, as shown in the two examples in Figure 7–19. For example, in the

**FIGURE 7–19**

Share of Advertising Sales Relationship (Two-Year Summary)

### A. New Brands of Food Products

| Brand | Average share of advertising | Attained share of sales | Ratio of share of advertising to share of sales |
|---|---|---|---|
| 101 | 34% | 12.6% | 2.7 |
| 102 | 16 | 10.0 | 1.6 |
| 103 | 8 | 7.6 | 1.1 |
| 104 | 4 | 2.6 | 1.5 |
| 105 | 3 | 2.1 | 1.4 |

### B. New Brands of Toiletry Products

| Brand | Average share of advertising | Attained share of sales | Ratio of share of advertising to share of sales |
|---|---|---|---|
| 401 | 30% | 19.5% | 1.5 |
| 402 | 25 | 16.5 | 1.5 |
| 403 | 20 | 16.2 | 1.2 |
| 404 | 12 | 9.4 | 1.3 |
| 405 | 16 | 8.7 | 1.8 |
| 406 | 19 | 7.3 | 2.6 |
| 407 | 14 | 7.2 | 1.9 |
| 408 | 10 | 6.0 | 1.7 |
| 409 | 7 | 6.0 | 1.2 |
| 410 | 6 | 5.9 | 1.0 |
| 411 | 10 | 5.9 | 1.7 |
| 412 | 6 | 5.2 | 1.2 |

food industry, brand 101 gained a 12.6 percent market share by spending 34 percent of the total advertising dollars in this category. Likewise, brand 401 in the toiletry industry had a 30 percent share of advertising dollars to gain 19.5 percent of sales.

To determine how much to spend, marketers often develop a **payout plan** that determines the investment value of the advertising and promotion appropriation. The basic idea is to project the revenues the product will generate, as well as the costs it will incur, over two to three years. Based on an expected rate of return, the payout plan will assist in determining how much advertising and promotions expenditure will be necessary and when the return might be expected. A three-year payout plan is shown in Figure 7–20. The product would lose money in year 1, almost break even in year 2, and finally begin to show substantial profits by the end of year 3.

The advertising and promotion figures are highest in year 1 and decline in years 2 and 3. This appropriation is consistent with Peckham's findings and reflects the additional outlays needed to make as rapid an impact as possible. (Keep in mind that shelf space is limited, and store owners are not likely to wait around for a product to become successful.) The budget also reflects the firm's guidelines for new product expenditures, since companies generally have established deadlines by which the product must begin to show a profit. Finally, keep in mind that building market share may be more difficult than maintaining it—thus the substantial dropoff in expenditures in later years.

**FIGURE 7–20**

Example of Three-Year
Payout Plan ($ Millions)

|  | Year 1 | Year 2 | Year 3 |
|---|---|---|---|
| Product sales | 15.0 | 35.50 | 60.75 |
| Profit contribution (@ $0.50/case) | 7.5 | 17.75 | 30.38 |
| Advertising/promotions | 15.0 | 10.50 | 8.50 |
| Profit (loss) | (7.5) | 7.25 | 21.88 |
| Cumulative profit (loss) | (7.5) | (0.25) | 21.63 |

While the payout plan is not always perfect, it does guide the manager in establishing the budget. When used in conjunction with the objective and task method, it provides a much more logical approach to budget setting than the top-down approaches previously discussed. Yet on the basis of the studies reported on earlier, payout planning does not seem to be a widely employed method.

**Quantitative Models** Attempts to apply *quantitative models* to budgeting have met with limited success. For the most part, these methods employ **computer simulation models** involving statistical techniques such as multiple regression analysis to determine the relative contribution of the advertising budget to sales. Because of problems associated with these methods, their acceptance has been limited, and quantitative models have yet to reach their potential. As requirements for accountability continue to increase, more sophisticated models may be forthcoming. Specific discussion of these models is beyond the scope of this text, however. Such methods do have merit but may need more refinement before achieving widespread success.

**Summary of Budgeting Methods** There is no universally accepted method of setting a budget figure. Weaknesses in each method may make it unfeasible or inappropriate. As earlier studies have shown, the use of the objective and task method continues to stay high, whereas less sophisticated methods vary in their rates of adoption. More advertisers are also employing the payout planning approach.

In a study of how managers make decisions regarding advertising and promotion budgeting decisions, George Low and Jakki Mohr interviewed 21 managers in eight consumer-product firms. Their research focused on the decision processes and procedures used to set spending levels on the factors that influence the allocation of advertising and promotion dollars.

On the basis of their results (shown in Figure 7–21), the authors concluded that the budget-setting process is still a perplexing issue to many managers and that institutional pressures led to a greater proportion of dollars being spent on sales promotions than managers would have preferred. In addition, the authors concluded that to successfully develop and implement the budget, managers must (1) employ a comprehensive strategy to guide the process, avoiding the piecemeal approach often employed, (2) develop a strategic planning framework that employs an integrated marketing communications philosophy, (3) build in contingency plans, (4) focus on long-term objectives, and (5) consistently evaluate the effectiveness of programs.[29]

By using these approaches in combination with the percentage-of-sales methods, these advertisers are likely to arrive at a more useful, accurate budget. For example, many firms now start the budgeting process by establishing the objectives they need to accomplish and then limit the budget by applying a percentage-of-sales or another method to decide whether or not it is affordable. Competitors' budgets may also influence this decision.

FIGURE 7–21

How Advertising and
Promotions Budgets Are
Set

**The Nature of the Decision Process**

- Managers develop overall marketing objectives for the brand.
- Financial projections are made on the basis of the objectives and forecasts.
- Advertising and promotions budgets are set on the basis of quantitative models and managerial judgment.
- The budget is presented to senior management, which approves and adjusts the budgets.
- The plan is implemented (changes are often made during implementation).
- The plan is evaluated by comparing the achieved results with objectives.

**Factors Affecting Budget Allocations**

- The extent to which risk taking is encouraged and/or tolerated.
- Sophistication regarding the use of marketing information.
- Managerial judgment.
- Use of quantitative tools.
- Brand differentiation strategies.
- Brand equity.
- The strength of the creative message.
- Retailer power.
- Short- versus long-term focus.
- Top-down influences.
- Political sales force influences.
- Historical inertia.
- Ad hoc changes.

## Allocating the Budget

Once the budget has been appropriated, the next step is to allocate it. The allocation decision involves determining which markets, products, and/or promotional elements will receive which amounts of the funds appropriated.

**Allocating to IMC Elements**   As noted earlier, many advertisers are shifting some of their budget dollars away from traditional advertising media and into digital and social media. Figure 7–22 shows that most traditional media advertisers expect to decrease their expenditures in these media into the future as well. Digital and Social Media Perspective 7–1 discusses some of the changes taking place in more detail.

Some marketers have also used the allocation decision to stretch their advertising dollar and get more impact from the same amount of money. Companies have taken a number of steps, including consolidating and cutting division expenditures, reducing agency fees, producing fewer campaigns, and relying more on targeted media. As noted earlier, P&G has made efforts to become more innovative and efficient by allocating significant portions of their budget from traditional to nontraditional media. Others have also shifted allocations, and this trend is likely to continue. A study conducted by Digiday (Figure 7–23) indicates that 64% of advertisers planned to increase their paid social media budgets in 2013.

**Client–Agency Policies**   Another factor that may influence budget allocation is the individual policy of the company or the advertising agency. The agency may discourage the allocation of monies to sales promotion, preferring to spend them on the advertising area. The agency may take the position that these monies are harder to track in terms of effectiveness and may be used improperly if not under its control. (In many cases commissions are not made on this area, and this fact may contribute to the agency's reluctance.)

The orientation of the agency or the firm may also directly influence where monies are spent. Many ad agencies are managed by officers who have ascended through the

# Digital and Social Media Perspective 7-1 > > >

## Traditional Media Budgets Continue to Feel the Digital and Social Impact in Both *B-to-B* and *B-to-C* Markets

The year 2012 was not the best year for traditional media, particularly for print media. That's because 2012 marked the first year in which online ad spending surpassed ad spending for newspapers and magazines. In fact, online spending surpassed the *combined* ad spend for the two print mediums. While this doesn't mean newspapers and magazines will disappear anytime soon, it does confirm a fundamental shift in the way in which advertisers view the value of media. Since 2000, ad spending has decreased across most forms of traditional advertising—magazines, newspapers, and radio—while continuing to grow for television. At the same time, in the past few years online spending has increased substanially: a robust 23 percent between 2011 and 2012 to now nearly $40 billion. During this same period, print advertising billings fell from $36 billion to just under $34 billion. Clearly, times have changed when it comes to the monies allocated to mediums through which companies market products and services.

But the decline in print ad revenues is only part of the story. There has also been a fundamental shift throughout the IMC budget landscape with dollars being shifted around, leading to a different future for all media catgories. Specifically, "unmeasured" media are experiencing rapid growth as companies pour more and more money into social media and other channels that they feel directly connect them with target customers. In 2012 *eMarketer* estimated that nearly 90 percent of all U.S. companies with 100 or more employees were using social media tools for marketing purposes. And, unlike companies' experimentation with social media just five years ago (often at very little expense to the company other than time), today's social media campaigns have become an integral part of their IMC programs, constituting a significant portion of the communications budget. Instead of developing social campaigns in-house, many companies now outsource the tasks to ad agencies they are already using for traditional media development or to companies that specialize in digital and social media marketing. In either case, it means more of the budget allocated for new media spending and shifted away from traditional channels. As of this writing, it is estimated

**FIGURE 7–22**

U.S. Media Expenditures, 2013

Marketing Strategies US Marketing Professionals Expect to Decrease Their Focus on in 2013

*% of respondents*

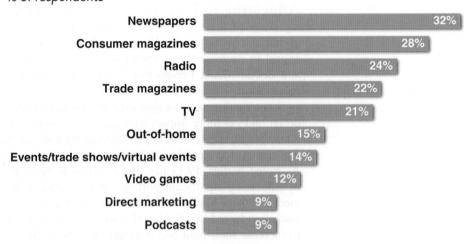

Newspapers — 32%
Consumer magazines — 28%
Radio — 24%
Trade magazines — 22%
TV — 21%
Out-of-home — 15%
Events/trade shows/virtual events — 14%
Video games — 12%
Direct marketing — 9%
Podcasts — 9%

*Source: Aquent and American Marketing Association (AMA), "Marketing Salaries" conducted by Inavero, Jan 24, 2013*

creative ranks and are inclined to emphasize the creative budget. Others may have preferences for specific media. For example, some agencies position themselves as experts in nontraditional media and often spend more client money in this medium. Both the agency and the client may favor certain aspects of the promotional program, perhaps on the basis of past successes, that will substantially influence where dollars are spent.

that social media spending at major companies across the United States accounts for 4 to 11 percent of the marketing budget.

In addition to increased spending in social media, digital spending (typically composed of paid search, online video, and mobile ads) is estimated to constitute a combined 75 percent of Internet spending as a whole. Within that group, online video expenditures is growing the fastest, with marketers pulling dollars from traditional TV ads, non-video display (banner) ads, and other online advertising in favor of ads that precede, follow, or interrupt streaming videos online.

The same trends hold true for business-to-business (B-to-B) advertisers. In 2012 the top 50 B-to-B advertisers increased spending by 6.5 percent overall, again with much of this going to nontraditional media. Internet display advertising saw the largest gains (19.2 percent), while magazines (−9.6 percent), newspapers (−9.5 percent), and business magazines (−1.7 percent) experienced the deepest cuts. A study by BtoB magazine found that 47 percent of business-to-business marketers claim they are "very involved" or "fully integrated" with social marketing, while fully 96 percent say they use social media in some fashion.

So while it doesn't look good for print, let's not bury traditional media just quite yet. Television still remains at the top of the advertising spending pyramid for both business-to-consumer (B-to-C) and B-to-B advertisers and has continued to experience increased expenditures over the past decade. Despite the increses in online spending and the allocation losses to digital, TV grew its share of total ad spending from 43 percent in 2001 to nearly 51 percent in 2010, and increased 6.8 percent in 2012 to a record $64.8 billion in the consumer market. In the B-to-B market, TV advertising constituted up to 55.9 percent of the budget—clearly the leading medium. While this number may be somewhat inflated due to the Summer Olympics and presidential election in the same year, it doesn't change the fact that TV ad spending is still greater than spending on all other media combined. Both radio and outdoor also experienced gains in expenditures in the B-to-B market. Thus, while many marketers continue to restructure their budgets to give online spending more attention, it is still clear that advertisers still recognize the value of traditional media—particularly television, the long-standing leader in media expenditures.

Sources: Kate Maddox, "Top 50 b2b Advertisers Increase Spending 6.5%," www.btobonline.com, March 4, 2013: Christopher Hosford, "Social Media Marketing Reaches Maturity," www.btobonline.com March 4, 2013; Daisy Whitney, "Marketers selling from TV Budgets for Online Video in 2012," www.mediapost.com, December 15, 2011; Dack Loechner, "Television Still the Big Bucks Leader in Ad Spend their 2013," www.mediapost.com, October 10, 2012.

**Market Size**  While the budget should be allocated according to the specific promotional tools needed to accomplish the stated objectives, the *size* of the market will affect the decision. In smaller markets, it is often easier and less expensive to reach the target market. Too much of an expenditure in these markets will lead to saturation and a lack of effective spending. In larger markets, the target group may be more dispersed and thus more expensive to reach. Think about the cost of purchasing media in Chicago or New York City versus a smaller market like Columbus, Ohio, or Birmingham, Alabama. The former would be much more costly and would require a higher budget appropriation.

**FIGURE 7–23**

Change in Paid Social Media Ad Budgets in 2013 According to U.S. Advertisers (% of respondents)

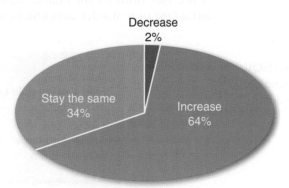

Source: Vizu, "Paid Social Media Advertising" conducted by Digiday, Jan 29, 2013

**Market Potential**   For a variety of reasons, some markets hold more potential than others. Marketers of snow skis would find greater returns on their expenditures in Denver, Colorado, than in Fort Lauderdale, Florida. Imported Mexican beers sell better in the border states (Texas, Arizona, California) than in the Midwest. A disproportionate number of imported cars are sold in California and New England. When particular markets hold higher potential, the marketing manager may decide to allocate additional monies to them. (Keep in mind that just because a market does not have high sales does not mean it should be ignored. The key is *potential*—and a market with low sales but high potential may be a candidate for additional appropriations.)

**Market Share Goals**   Two studies in the *Harvard Business Review* discussed advertising spending with the goal of maintaining and increasing market share.[30] John Jones compared the brand's share of market with its share of advertising voice (the total value of the main media exposure in the product category). Jones classified the brands as "profit taking brands, or underspenders" and "investment brands, those whose share of voice is clearly above their share of market." His study indicated that for those brands with small market shares, profit takers are in the minority; however, as the brands increase their market share, nearly three out of five have a proportionately smaller share of voice.

Jones noted that three factors can be cited to explain this change. First, new brands generally receive higher-than-average advertising support. Second, older, more mature brands are often "milked"—that is, when they reach the maturity stage, advertising support is reduced. Third, there's an advertising economy of scale whereby advertising works harder for well-established brands, so a lower expenditure is required. Jones concluded that for larger brands, it may be possible to reduce advertising expenditures and still maintain market share. Smaller brands, on the other hand, have to continue to maintain a large share of voice.

James Schroer addressed the advertising budget in a situation where the marketer wishes to increase market share. His analysis suggests that marketers should:

- Segment markets, focusing on those markets where competition is weak and/or underspending instead on a national advertising effort.
- Determine their competitors' cost positions (how long the competition can continue to spend at the current or increased rate).
- Resist the lure of short-term profits that result from ad budget cuts.
- Consider niching strategies as opposed to long-term wars.

Figure 7–24 shows Schroer's suggestions for spending priorities in various markets.

**Economies of Scale in Advertising**   Some studies have presented evidence that firms and/or brands maintaining a large share of the market have an advantage over smaller competitors and thus can spend less money on advertising

**FIGURE 7–24**

The Share of Voice (SOV) Effect and Ad Spending: Priorities in Individual Markets and realize a better return.[31] Larger advertisers can maintain advertising shares that are smaller than their market shares because they get better advertising rates, have declining average costs of production, and accrue the advantages of advertising several products jointly. In addition, they are likely to enjoy more favorable time and space positions, cooperation of middlepeople, and favorable publicity. These advantages are known as **economies of scale**.

Reviewing the studies in support of this position and then conducting research over a variety of small package products, Kent Lancaster found that this situation did not hold true and that in fact larger brand share products might actually be at a disadvantage.[32] His results indicated that leading brands spend an average of 2.5 percentage points more than their brand share on advertising. More specifically, his study concluded:

1. There is no evidence that larger firms can support their brands with lower relative advertising costs than smaller firms.
2. There is no evidence that the leading brand in a product group enjoys lower advertising costs per sales dollar than do other brands.
3. There is no evidence of a static relationship between advertising costs per dollar of sales and the size of the advertiser.

The results of this and other studies suggest there really are no economies of scale to be accrued from the size of the firm or the market share of the brand.[33]

**Organizational Characteristics**   In a review of the literature on how allocation decisions are made between advertising and sales promotion, George Low and Jakki Mohr concluded that organizational factors play an important role in determining how communications dollars are spent.[34] The authors note that the following factors influence the allocation decision. These factors vary from one organization to another, and each influences the relative amounts assigned to advertising and promotion:

- The organization's structure—centralized versus decentralized, formalization, and complexity.
- Power and politics in the organizational hierarchy.
- The use of expert opinions (for example, consultants).
- Characteristics of the decision maker (preferences and experience).
- Approval and negotiation channels.
- Pressure on senior managers to arrive at the optimal budget.

One example of how these factors might influence allocations relates to the level of interaction between marketing and other functional departments, such as accounting and operations. The authors note that the relative importance of advertising versus sales promotion might vary from department to department. Accountants, being dollars-and-cents minded, would argue for the sales impact of promotions, while operations would argue against sales promotions because the sudden surges in demand that might result would throw off production schedules. The marketing department might be influenced by the thinking of either of these groups in making its decision.

The use of outside consultants to provide expert opinions might also affect the allocation decision. Trade journals, academic journals, and even books might also be valuable inputs into the decision maker's thinking. In sum, it seems obvious that many factors must be taken into account in the budget allocation decision. Market size and potential, specific objectives sought, and previous company and/or agency policies and preferences all influence this decision.

# Summary

This chapter has examined the role of objectives in the planning and evaluation of the IMC program and how firms budget in an attempt to achieve these objectives. Specific objectives are needed to guide the development of the promotional program, as well as to provide a benchmark against which performance can be measured and evaluated. Objectives serve important functions as communications devices, as a guide to planning the IMC program and deciding on various alternatives, and for measurement and evaluation.

Objectives for IMC evolve from the organization's overall marketing plan and are based on the roles various promotional-mix elements play in the marketing program. Many managers use sales or a related measure such as market share as the basis for setting objectives. However, many promotional planners believe the role of advertising and other promotional-mix elements is to communicate because of the various problems associated with sales-based objectives. They use communications-based objectives like those in the response hierarchy as the basis for setting goals.

Much of the emphasis in setting objectives has been on traditional advertising-based views of marketing communications. However, many companies are moving toward zero-based communications planning, which focuses on what tasks need to be done, which marketing communications functions should be used, and to what extent. Many of the principles used in setting advertising objectives can be applied to other elements in the promotional mix.

As you have probably concluded, the budget decision is not typically based on supporting experiences or strong theoretical foundations. Nor is it one of the more soundly established elements of the promotional program. The budgeting methods used now have some major problems. Economic models are limited, often try to demonstrate the effects on sales directly, and ignore other elements of the marketing mix. Some of the methods discussed have no theoretical basis and ignore the roles advertising and promotion are meant to perform.

One possible way to improve the budget appropriation is to tie the measures of effectiveness to communications objectives rather than to the broader-based marketing objectives. Using the objective and task approach with communications objectives may not be the ultimate solution to the budgeting problem, but it is an improvement over the top-down methods. Marketers often find it advantageous to employ a combination of methods.

As with determining the budget, managers must consider a number of factors when allocating advertising and promotions dollars. Market size and potential, agency policies, and the preferences of management itself may influence the allocation decision.

# Key Terms

marketing objectives p. 223
integrated marketing communications objectives p. 223
carryover effect p. 225
DAGMAR p. 230
communications task p. 230
benchmark measures p. 231
zero-based communications planning p. 234

contribution margin p. 238
marginal analysis p. 238
concave-downward function model p. 240
S-shaped response curve p. 240
top-down approaches p. 243
affordable method p. 243
arbitrary allocation p. 244
percentage-of-sales method p. 244

clipping service p. 248
competitive parity method p. 248
ROI budgeting method p. 249
objective and task method p. 251
buildup approach p. 251
payout plan p. 253
computer simulation models p. 254
economies of scale p. 259

# Discussion Questions

1. Companies like P&G and Kraft Foods have found success by increasing their IMC budgets while other companies reduce theirs during a recession. Explain why they have likely achieved this success. (LO7)

2. Some marketers feel that the hierarchy of effects models may no longer reflect the characteristics of the consumer decision-making process. Discuss the pros and cons of these arguments. (LO4)

3. Some economists believe that the impact of advertising on sales follows an S-shaped curve, while others argue for a concave-downward curve. Discuss the differences in these perspectives. Is it possible for both to be correct? (LO6)

4. Explain why it is so difficult to directly measure the impact of advertising on sales. What factors may inhibit this determination? (LO3)

5. Explain some of the reasons marketers are shifting their budget allocations from traditional to digital and social media. What are some of the advantages and disadvantages with this reallocation? (LO5)

6. Why is it important for marketers to set specific objectives for advertising and promotion: What criteria must these objectives meet to be valid? (LO1)

7. What are some of the problems associated with setting communications objectives? How can marketers overcome these problems? Cite examples. (LO4)

8. What are the values associated with setting objectives for IMC? How can marketers improve their communications programs by establishing specific objectives? (LO1)

9. What are the two key issues that marketers must make in regard to budgeting? Explain the differences, and give examples of each. (LO5)

10. Explain the S-shaped response curve and the concave-downward curve as they relate to budget setting. What are the differences in these two curves? Give examples of how each might be more appropriate for different products. (LO6)

## LEARNING OBJECTIVES

**LO1** To discuss what is meant by advertising creativity and examine the role of creative strategy in advertising.

**LO2** To consider the process that guides the creation of advertising messages and the research inputs into the stages of the creative process.

**LO3** To examine creative strategy development and the roles of various client and agency personnel involved in it.

**LO4** To examine various approaches used for determining major selling ideas that form the basis of an advertising campaign.

# 8 Creative Strategy: Planning and Development

## CREATING ICONIC PASSION FOR TACORI

Tacori Enterprises is widely recognized as an innovator in the design, creation, and marketing of fine jewelry. The Tacori story began when family patriarch Haig Tacorian left Europe in 1969 to start a new life in the United States. Haig settled in California, and he and his wife, Gilda, devoted themselves to creating fine jewelry with a unique and distinctive European flair. Over the next four decades Tacori built a reputation as one of the premier jewelers by creating some of the world's most highly regarded diamonds and precious stone collections. The Tacorian family's proud tradition of passion is expressed in everything they create, and Tacori designs have fused classic elegance with modern inspiration, creating beautiful and intricately crafted artisan jewelry.

When the Lambesis agency began working with Tacori in 2007, the family-run business was known primarily for engagement rings, offering exquisite artisanship in each detailed piece. Although Tacori rings were known for their beauty and intricacy, the brand had generated little awareness among consumers, which was limiting the company's ability to expand its product mix as well as growth. The market for fine jewelry is highly competitive, and few brands, other than Tiffany, have been able to develop and sustain a distinct brand image. For many years Tacori was competing in the mid-tier market for engagement rings and other types of fine jewelry, a market space saturated with forgettable ads featuring product shots and lifestyle images. The company also was facing challenges at the point of sale in jewelry stores where most brands were doing very little to create a recognizable and distinctive brand image or a memorable retail experience. Lambesis recognized these issues as an opportunity to create an image that Tacori could own and that was centered on the brand's inherent passion and special jewelry-giving moments, such as marriage proposals.

In developing an integrated marketing program that would be used to build the brand, Lambesis's strategy was to fuse Tacori's handcrafted elegance with a clean, modern style. To execute the strategy, the agency developed "Iconic Passion," an IMC and branding platform that extended across all consumer touch points—from television and print to retail, digital/social media, and out-of-home. The IMC campaign was targeted to both male and female consumers with the goal of reaching both sexes during the jewelry shopping process. During the course of developing the campaign, Lambesis conducted extensive research on how couples become engaged and used these insights in developing an integrated point-of-sale campaign. The agency helped Tacori develop store-within-a-store boutiques at the retail level as well as retailer and consumer incentive programs.

An integral part of the IMC campaign Lambesis created for Tacori is the print ads that capture the brand's exquisite artisanship and stunning designs through dramatic still-life photos. The print ads—which are run in upscale women's fashion magazines such as *InStyle, Elle,* and *Allure*—communicate aspirational yet attainable luxury and showcase the range of jewelry offered by Tacori including necklaces and bracelets, as well as rings. The ads often juxtapose Tacori jewelry with objects signifying passion such as a Cupid's arrow which symbolizes romance, ornate ebony and bone chess pieces which are a metaphor for the passion of conquest, luscious red apples with a bite taken out of them to capture the essence of temptation, and a tilted martini glass that serves as a toast to glamour and sophistication. The striking images seamlessly translate to out-of-home media such as billboards and transit ads that are placed in strategic locations in major cities around the country and help communicate the glamour and elegance of the Tacori brand.

The "Iconic Passion" theme is also communicated on the Tacori website, which is designed to give consumers an engaging, informative, and interactive online experience. One of the unique features of the site is a short film produced by Lambesis called *Par Chance* which plays off the idea that love at first sight can happen at any given moment and around every corner. Renowned director and screenwriter Steven Antin, best known for his film *Burlesque*, directed the heartfelt and light-hearted story about a chance meeting between two strangers, who must reconnect with each other by following a series of sexy and romantic clues. Many beautiful Tacori jewelry pieces are highlighted during the three-minute webisode, which was filmed in a Parision setting and blossoms into a passionate fairy-tale romance that leads to a marriage proposal and the handsome young man surprising her with an engagement ring. In February 2013, Tacori launched a "By Chance" Valentine's Day campaign on its website and Facebook page that was inspired by the short film. To enter the contest, fans of Tacori were asked to share a photo and the story of how they found love "by chance" in 10 words or less and could win up to $5,000 in Tacori jewelry.

The "Iconic Passion" campaign is now in its sixth year and not only has contributed to the company's sales growth but has focused the industry's eye on Tacori as the brand to watch. Sales have shown double- and triple-digit increases annually, even during the difficult recession years of 2008 and 2009, and *Design Magazine* named Tacori one of the three most visible jewelry brands and the number 1 brand that jewelers are adding to their product offerings. Tacori is expanding into international markets and also extending its retail footprint into department stores and boutiques while expanding its product line to include men's wedding bands; diamond earrings, necklaces, and bracelets; and fashion jewelry. The campaign has also been successful in expanding Tacori's online fan base, including both actual and aspirational purchasers. Tacori's president and head of sales and marketing, Paul Tacorian, notes that the Lambesis agency has been a quintessential partner in helping build the Tacori brand. Fusing both creative and business thinking, they have created a branding platform that has catapulted Tacori into one of the most sought after jewelry brands in America and one that, unlike the theme of the short film, appears to leave little to chance.

Sources: "25 Years of Building Strong Brands," Lambesis Agency 2013 Brand Book; "Tacori Launches 'By Chance' Valentine's Day Campaign," *PR Newswire*, February 13, 2013, http://buyersteps.ulitzer.com/node/2539284.

---

YTC 08–01

**Tacori**

youtube.com/10ebelch

One of the most important components of an integrated marketing communications program is the advertising message. While the fundamental role of an advertising message is to communicate information, it does much more. The commercials we watch on TV or hear on radio, the print ads we see in magazines and newspapers, and the banner ads and other forms of advertising on the Internet are a source of entertainment, motivation, fascination, fantasy, and sometimes irritation as well as information. Ads and commercials appeal to, and often create or shape, consumers' problems, desires, and goals. From the marketer's perspective, the advertising message is a way to tell consumers how the product or service can solve a problem or help satisfy desires or achieve goals. Advertising can also be used to create images or associations and position a brand in the consumer's mind as well as transform the experience of buying and/or using a product or service. Many consumers who have never driven or even ridden in a BMW perceive it as "the ultimate driving machine" (Exhibit 8–1). Many people feel good about sending Hallmark greeting cards because they have internalized the company's advertising theme, "when you care enough to send the very best."

One need only watch an evening of commercials or peruse a few magazines to realize there are a myriad of ways to convey an advertising message. Underlying all of these messages, however, are a **creative strategy** that determines what the advertising message will say or communicate and **creative tactics** for how the message strategy will be executed. In this chapter, we focus on advertising creative strategy. We consider what is meant by creativity, particularly as it relates to advertising, and examine a well-known approach to creativity in advertising.

We also examine the creative strategy development process and various approaches to determining the *big idea* that will be used as the central theme of the advertising campaign and translated into attention-getting, distinctive, and memorable messages.

**EXHIBIT 8–1**
Excellent advertising helps create an image for BMW automobiles as "the ultimate driving machine"

Creative specialists are finding it more and more difficult to come up with big ideas that will break through the clutter and still satisfy the concerns of their risk-averse clients. Yet their clients are continually challenging them to find the creative message that will strike a responsive chord with their target audience.

Some of you may not be directly involved in the design and creation of ads; you may choose to work in another agency department or on the client side of the business. However, because creative strategy is often so crucial to the success of the firm's IMC effort, everyone involved in the promotional process should understand the creative strategy and tactics that underlie the development of advertising campaigns and messages, as well as the creative options available to the advertiser. Also, individuals on the client side as well as agency people outside the creative department must work with the creative specialists in developing the advertising campaign, implementing it, and evaluating its effectiveness. Thus, marketing and product managers, account representatives, researchers, and media personnel must appreciate the creative process and develop a productive relationship with creative personnel.

# THE IMPORTANCE OF CREATIVITY IN ADVERTISING

For many students, as well as many advertising and marketing practitioners, the most interesting aspect of advertising is the creative side. We have all at one time or another been intrigued by an ad and admired the creative insight that went into it. A great ad is a joy to behold and often an epic to create, as the cost of producing a TV commercial can exceed $1 million. Many companies see this as money well spent. They realize that the manner in which the advertising message is developed and executed is often critical to the success of the promotional program, which in turn can influence the effectiveness of the entire marketing program. Major advertisers such as Procter & Gamble, Verizon, AT&T, Unilever, Ford Motor Co., Nike, McDonald's, Coca-Cola, and many other companies spend millions of dollars each year to develop advertising messages that will win the hearts and minds of consumers. They also spend hundreds of millions of dollars more to purchase media time and space to run these messages. While these companies make excellent products, they realize creative advertising is also an important part of their marketing success.

For generations, young men would bathe or shower using a bar of soap such as Ivory, Safeguard, Zest, Irish Spring, Coast, or one of many other brands. However, over the past decade the body cleansing category has been changing dramatically, as males who were heavy users of bar soap have been converting to body washes. Procter & Gamble was one of the first major U.S. companies to enter the body-wash market when it launched its Old Spice Hair & Body Wash products in 2003. P&G launched a number of new products under the Old Spice brand that became market leaders such as its men's deodorant line. However, the company began facing stiff competition from Unilever's Axe brand, which had been a market leader in Europe and Latin America before entering the U.S. market in 2003. Over a span of several years, Axe launched a number of grooming and body-wash products that were supported with irreverent and often risqué ads filled with suggestive taglines and attractive young women throwing themselves at average-looking Axe users.

In 2006 P&G decided to switch advertising agencies and named Wieden + Kennedy as its global agency for the Old Spice brand. After taking over the Old Spice account, W + K conducted focus groups and market research studies that revealed that the target market of 13- to 34-year-old males were confused by the array of body cleansing products on the store shelves and were hesitant to spend much time sorting through the options, most of which they described as too complicated, overly feminine, or just "not for me." The research also revealed that most young men were not aware of the Old Spice brand. Armed with this information, W + K set out to position Old Spice as a simple, manly choice for no-nonsense guys in the increasingly complicated body product category.

One of the first campaigns W + K developed for Old Spice Hair & Body Wash used humor to celebrate the diversity of men and their ability to grow hair in strange and wondrous places. Dozens of "hair archetypes," each highlighting a different hair and body combination, were created and a print and digital campaign was developed to illustrate them and encourage young men to visit a website (oshairbodymetrics.com). Once there, they could use an interactive, pseudo-scientific tool to depict their current hair situation and analyze their hair/body profile. The TV spots spoofed pharmaceutical ads such as those for male enhancement drugs and used humor to deliver the message that Old Spice Hair & Body Wash works for all types of men, with all types of hair. The campaign launched in early 2008 and helped increase sales by 70 percent from the previous year in the first few months.

In early 2010 W + K developed another highly popular creative campaign for its Old Spice After Hours brand. The tongue-in-cheek ads developed for the "Smell Like a Man, Man" campaign featured a bare-chested, Casanova-like character (played by Isaiah Mustafa, a former NFL wide receiver and obscure actor with a magnetic presence to go along with his six-pack abs) who tells female viewers that Old Spice body wash will make their male partners smell like him. The most popular spot in the series, "The Man Your Man Could Smell Like," opens with him stepping out of the shower with a towel around his waist brandishing a bottle of Old Spice body wash and saying: "Hello ladies, look at your man. Now back to me. Now back at your man. Now back to me. Sadly it isn't me. But if he stopped using lady-scented body wash and switched to Old Spice, he could smell like me." The spot goes on to show him on a boat wielding an oyster filled with "tickets to that thing you love" as it changes to a handful of diamonds

Good creative strategy and execution can often be central to determining the success of a product or service or reversing the fortunes of a struggling brand. For example, Digital and Social Media Perspective 8–1 discusses how creative advertising was able to revive Procter & Gamble's Old Spice brand and make it the market leader in the body wash category. The commercials and online videos developed for the campaign have made Old Spice one of the most viewed brands online over the past few years. The popular "The Man Your Man Could Smell Like" spot alone has been viewed nearly 45 million times on YouTube over the past three years. Conversely, an advertising campaign that is poorly conceived or executed can be a liability. Many companies have solid marketing and promotional plans and spend substantial amounts of money on advertising yet have difficulty coming up with a creative campaign that will differentiate them from their competitors. However, just because an ad or commercial is creative or popular does not mean it will increase sales or revive a declining brand. Many ads have won awards for creativity but failed to increase sales. In some instances, the failure to generate sales has cost the agency the account. For example, the Leo Burnett agency handled the advertising for Altoids breath mints for 13 years, and the "Curiously Strong" and ends with the camera pulling back, revealing the shirtless Mustafa on horseback as he redundantly says what has become the signature line from the spot: "I'm on a horse."

The ad ran in theaters on Valentine's Day and was also released on Old Spice's Facebook page, where a quarter of the fans were female. The spot became a viral sensation on the Internet; it logged more than 20 million hits on YouTube within a few months and also generated over 7,000 comments on Old Spice's Facebook page. A follow-up spot in June garnered another 15 million views. Around this time W + K had hired a new global head of digital creative who came up with an idea for leveraging the popularity of the ads by soliciting questions for the "Old Spice Guy" via Twitter and Facebook and having him answer them in short video clips online. Thousands of questions and comments poured in from fans and W + K shot nearly 200 video clips with Mustafa's responses, including one in which he proposed to a man's girlfriend for him. Within a week, online views of the new videos soon eclipsed the original TV spots and Google searches for "Old Spice" increased by 2,000 percent. Old Spice became the most-viewed brand in online videos in 2010 and kept the momentum going in 2011 by unleashing a new ad and set of viral videos featuring former romance-novel cover model Fabio. This was followed by a video in which Mustafa challenges Fabio to a duel for the heart and minds of women and asks viewers to vote, via link buttons on the video, to support him or "long hair," as the brand's spokesperson. The duel between the two helped Old Spice continue its domination of the viral video charts for a second consecutive year in 2011.

The wildly popular ads did more than top the video charts; they also resulted in double-digit sales increases for the Old Spice brand and helped make it the market leader in the body-wash category. The ad "The Man Your Man Could Smell

SMELL LIKE A MAN, MAN.
Old Spice

Like" also won the Grand Prix award as the best commercial in the world at the 2010 Cannes Lions International Advertising Festival, while the "Responses" online campaign was named a Grand Prix winner in 2011. David Hallerman, a senior analyst at *eMarketer*, notes that the Old Spice campaign is an excellent example of the integration of paid, owned, and earned media. The campaign started with paid media consisting of television commercials supplemented by cinema ads, then migrated to an interactive mix of owned media that included Facebook, Twitter, and a branded micro website. It continued its momentum in earned media through viral interaction on social media sites such as YouTube.

Wieden + Kennedy and P&G have continued to develop humorous ads for Old Spice that introduce new characters such as the "Muscle Music" spot which features another former NFL player, Terry Crews, playing the drums with his muscular legs and biceps. In 2013 they took the campaign in a new direction to launch a new premium line of Old Spice scents by creating videos featuring a wolf that poses as the brand's new marketing director. In the spots Mr. Wolfdog keeps a host of cliché businessman decorations at hand and brags about how he makes a million dollars by essentially doing nothing. It appears that W + K found a way to crack the viral video code with its creative advertising for Old Spice and sell a lot of body wash in the process.

Sources: "Old Spice Has a Wolfish New Marketing Director," *Advertising Age*, March 11, 2013, http://adage.com/article/creativity-pick-of-the-day/spice-a-wolfish-marketing-director/240267/; Jack Neff, "Meet the Man Your Man Could Smell Like," *Advertising Age*, March 29, 2010, pp. 2, 3; David Hallerman, "What Marketers Can Learn from the Old Spice 'Your Man' Campaign," *Advertising Age*, August 26, 2010, http://adage.com/article/digitalnext/marketers-learn-spice-man-campaign/145603/; Cotton Delo, "Online Video: Old Spice the Most Viral Brand of the Year—Again," *Advertising Age*, December 28, 2011, http://adage.com/article/the-viral-video-chart/spice-viral-brand-year-video/231780/; Barbara Lippert, "Man, This Man Can Sell," *Adweek*, March 1, 2010, p. 9.

YTC 08-02
Old Spice
youtube.com/10ebelch

campaign they created for the brand won numerous creative awards (Exhibit 8–2). However, Altoids lost its position as the market leader in the breath-freshener category.[1] More recently, Anheuser-Busch InBev terminated its 30-year relationship with the DDB agency, which had created a number of award-winning campaigns for its Bud Light brand such as the Spuds McKenzie mascot, "Whassup?", and "Real Men of Genius" radio campaign as well as a number of award-winning commercials featuring the iconic Clydesdales for Budweiser. Sales of both Budweiser and Bud Light had declined over the past several years and AB InBev felt that a change was needed in creative strategy for the brands.[2]

Many advertising and marketing people have become ambivalent toward, and in some cases even critical of, advertising awards.[3] They argue that agency creative people are often more concerned with creating ads that win awards than ones that sell their clients' products. Other advertising people believe awards are a good way to recognize creativity that often does result in effective advertising. As we saw in Chapter 7, the success of an ad campaign cannot always be judged in terms of sales. However, many advertising and marketing personnel, particularly those on the client side, believe advertising must ultimately lead the consumer to purchase the product

**EXHIBIT 8–2**

Advertising for Altoids won creative awards but the brand lost its position as market leader

LO 08-1

YTC 08–03

**Creativity**

youtube.com/10ebelch

or service. Finding a balance between creative advertising and effective advertising is difficult. To better understand this dilemma, we turn to the issue of creativity and its role in advertising.

# ADVERTISING CREATIVITY

## What Is Creativity?

*Creativity* is probably one of the most commonly used terms in advertising. Ads are often called creative. The people who develop ads and commercials are known as creative types. And advertising agencies develop reputations for their creativity. Perhaps so much attention is focused on the concept of creativity because many people view the specific challenge given to those who develop an advertising message as being creative. It is their job to turn all of the information regarding product features and benefits, marketing plans, consumer research, and communication objectives into a creative concept that will bring the advertising message to life. This begs the question: What is meant by *creativity* in advertising?

## Different Perspectives on Advertising Creativity

Perspectives on what constitutes creativity in advertising differ. At one extreme are people who argue that advertising is creative only if it sells the product. An advertising message's or campaign's impact on sales counts more than whether it is innovative or wins awards. At the other end of the continuum are those who judge the creativity of an ad in terms of its artistic or aesthetic value and originality. They contend creative ads can break through the competitive clutter, grab the consumer's attention, and have some impact.

As you might expect, perspectives on advertising creativity often depend on one's role. A study by Elizabeth Hirschman examined the perceptions of various individuals involved in the creation and production of TV commercials, including management types (brand managers and account executives) and creatives (art director, copywriter, commercial director, and producer).[4] She found that product managers and account executives view ads as promotional tools whose primary purpose is to communicate favorable impressions to the marketplace. They believe a commercial should be evaluated in terms of whether it fulfills the client's marketing and communicative objectives. The perspective of those on the creative side was much more self-serving, as Hirschman noted:

> In direct contrast to this client orientation, the art director, copywriter, and commercial director viewed the advertisement as a communication vehicle for promoting their own aesthetic viewpoints and personal career objectives. Both the copywriter and art director made this point explicitly, noting that a desirable commercial from their standpoint was one which communicated their unique creative talents and thereby permitted them to obtain "better" jobs at an increased salary.[5]

In her interviews, Hirschman also found that brand managers were much more risk-averse and wanted a more conservative commercial than the creative people, who wanted to maximize the impact of the message.

What constitutes creativity in advertising is probably somewhere between the two extremes. To break through the clutter and make an impression on the target audience, an ad often must be unique and entertaining. As noted in Chapter 5, research has shown that a major determinant of whether a commercial will be successful in changing brand preferences is its "likability," or the viewer's overall reaction.[6] TV commercials and print ads that are well designed and executed and generate emotional responses can create positive feelings that are transferred to the product or service being advertised.

Many creative people believe this type of advertising can come about only if they are given considerable latitude in developing advertising messages. But ads that are creative only for the sake of being creative often fail to communicate a relevant or meaningful message that will lead consumers to purchase the product or service.

Everyone involved in planning and developing an advertising campaign must understand the importance of balancing the "it's not creative unless it sells" perspective with the novelty/uniqueness and impact position. Marketing and brand managers or account executives must recognize that imposing too many sales- and marketing-oriented communications objectives on the creative team can result in mediocre advertising, which is often ineffective in today's competitive, cluttered media environment. At the same time, the creative specialists must recognize that the goal of advertising is to assist in selling the product or service and good advertising must communicate in a manner that helps the client achieve this goal.

## Determinants of Creativity

**Advertising creativity** is the ability to generate fresh, unique, and appropriate or relevant ideas that can be used as solutions to communication problems. Those who study as well as work in advertising generally agree on these two central determinants of creativity, which are often viewed in terms of divergence and relevance.[7] **Divergence** refers to the extent to which an ad contains elements that are novel, different, or unusual. Robert Smith and his colleagues have identified five major factors that could account for the ways divergence can be achieved in advertising, which they describe as follows:[8]

1. *Originality* Ads that contain elements that are rare, surprising, or move away from the obvious and commonplace.
2. *Flexibility* Ads that contain different ideas or switch from one perspective to another.
3. *Elaboration* Ads that contain unexpected details or finish and extend basic ideas so they become more intricate, complicated, or sophisticated.
4. *Synthesis* Ads that combine, connect, or blend normally unrelated objects or ideas.
5. *Artistic value* Ads that contain artistic verbal impressions or attractive shapes and colors.

There are other ways divergence can be achieved in developing creative advertising such as through the use of humor, fantasy, emotion, and imagery, which are discussed in Chapter 9 as the basis for advertising execution techniques. In some cases the focus of the creative strategy may be to achieve *fluency* which refers to the ability to generate a large number of ideas around a creative idea. For example, the popular "Got Milk?" campaign developed by the California Milk Processor Board has been running for nearly two decades. A myriad of humorous TV commercials, print ads, and even interactive games have been developed around the basic creative idea of showing people in uncomfortable situations because they have run out of milk, encouraging them to keep an ample supply on hand (Exhibit 8–3).

The second major determinant of creativity is **relevance**, which reflects the degree to which the various elements of the ad are meaningful, useful, or valuable to the consumer.[9] Smith et al. suggest that relevance can be achieved in two ways. *Ad-to-consumer relevance* refers to

YTC 08–04
"Got Milk?"
youtube.com/10ebelch

**EXHIBIT 8–3**

Many humorous ads have been created around the "Got Milk?" creative idea

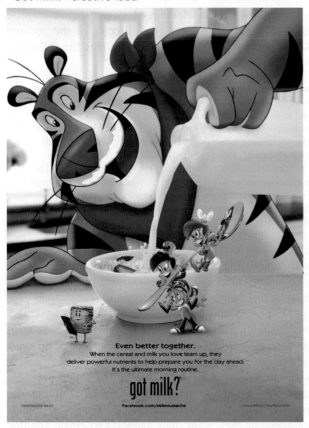

Even better together.
When the cereal and milk you love team up, they deliver powerful nutrients to help prepare you for the day ahead. It's the ultimate morning routine.

got milk?

Facebook.com/MilkMustache

**EXHIBIT 8–4**

The Volkswagen Beetle ski-mask commercial uses divergence based on originality and surprise

YTC 08–05

**Volkswagen**

youtube.com/10ebelch

situations where the ad contains execution elements that are meaningful to consumers. For example, advertisers may use celebrities with whom consumers identify, music that they like, or visual images and other execution techniques that capture their interest and attention. *Brand-to-consumer relevance* refers to situations where the advertised brand of a product or service is of personal interest to consumers. Relevance or appropriateness can also be viewed in terms of the degree to which an advertisement provides information or an image that is pertinent to the brand. Ads for many products such as fashionable clothing, jewelry, cosmetics, and liquor often rely on visual images to deliver their message rather than providing specific product information. However, these images are important to consumers in forming impressions and attitudes toward these brands and deciding whether to select one brand over another.

The ad for the Volkswagen Beetle convertible shown in Exhibit 8–4 is a good example of creative advertising that relies on the divergence criterion of originality. The humorous spot shows a man entering a convenience store wearing a ski mask and stocking up on chips and candy, totally unaware that he is terrifying everyone else in the store as they think he is committing a robbery. As the 60-second spot unfolds, the other shoppers cringe while the man at the counter becomes increasingly tense. And when the masked man goes to pay for his items, the cashier says, "I don't want any trouble," to which he innocently responds: "I don't want any trouble either." The masked man then goes outside to join his friends in the VW convertible with its top down and the driver says to him: "You know you forgot to take your mask off, right?" As police siren wails in the background, one of the other men notes that they should probably get out of there. The spot ends with the men driving through a winter wonderland as the voiceover says: "Introducing the new Beetle convertible, now every day is a top-down day." The spot is a creative way to grab and hold the attention of the viewer and has an element of suspense and surprise to it with the unexpected ending. Douglas Van Praet, the director of the account planning team at Deutsch LA, the agency for Volkswagen, provides the following perspective on the commercial:[10]

> "Launching a convertible in the middle of winter can be a challenge. But for Volkswagen, it was an opportunity to tell a simple, human story in a clever way. The Beetle is the soul of Volkswagen—the original and iconic car everyone knows. And in 'Mask', Deutsch and Volkswagen married those elements into a clever and relatable story. 'Mask' follows a young man perusing a mini-mart, grabbing a few items for a road trip with his friends. Only, they are road tripping in the middle of winter, in the Beetle Convertible wearing ski masks. Our shopper forgot to take his mask off, frightening everyone in the store. The unexpected misdirect, which leaves viewers wondering if they're watching a robbery until the end of the spot—when the car is revealed driving through a snowy mountain scene— is classic Volkswagen advertising. A clever surprise and a unique approach to play up the launch of the Beetle Convertible during winter."

A number of studies have been conducted showing that advertising creativity impacts consumers' responses to advertising messages across various stages of the response hierarchy, including cognitive, affective, and behavioral responses.[11] For example, advertising that is more novel has been shown to require consumer processing time, resulting in longer exposure and greater attention. Studies have also shown that creative ads draw more attention to the advertised brand, higher levels of recall, greater motivation to process the information, and deeper levels of processing.[12] In addition to these cognitive outcomes, studies have also shown that creative advertising positively impacts emotional reactions including attitudes and purchase intentions.[13] Several of these studies have shown that novelty in terms of divergence is a particularly important component of advertising creativity. However, clients often favor relevance over divergence as they want their agencies to create ads that communicate pertinent information such as specific product features and benefits. Smith and his colleagues suggest that clients should be less resistant to divergent approaches and note that there is a fundamental need for divergent thinkers in the ad development process.[14] Considering that most advertising messages are seen and/ or heard in a very cluttered media environment where marketers must compete for the attention of consumers, it is important that attention be given to creating ads that are novel and divergent as well as relevant and meaningful.

Those who work in agencies, particularly in the creative departments, recognize the importance of developing advertising messages that are novel and unique but still communicate relevant information to the target audience. Figure 8–1 shows the guidelines for developing creative advertising that the former D'Arcy Masius Benton & Bowles agency developed to guide its creative efforts and help achieve superior creative work. The agency views a creative advertising message as one that is built around a core or power idea (which will be discussed later in this chapter) and uses excellent design and execution to communicate information that is relevant to the target audience. The agency used these principles to develop outstanding creative work for clients such as Procter & Gamble's Charmin and Pampers brands, Norelco, Budweiser, and many other popular brands. The agency was integrated into the Publicis Groupe in 2002, but these Universal Advertising Standards are still used by the various agencies that are part of the Publicis's agency family.

# PLANNING CREATIVE STRATEGY

## The Creative Challenge

Those who work on the creative side of advertising often face a real challenge. They must take all the research, creative briefs, strategy statements, communications objectives, and other input and transform them into an advertising message. Their job is to write copy, design layouts and illustrations, or produce commercials that effectively communicate the central theme on which the campaign is based. Rather than simply stating the features or benefits of a product or service, they must put the advertising message into a form that will engage the audience's interest and make the ads memorable.[15]

The job of the creative team is challenging because every marketing situation is different and each campaign or advertisement may require a different creative approach. Numerous guidelines have been developed for creating effective advertising,[16] but there is no magic formula. As copywriter Hank Sneiden notes in his book *Advertising Pure and Simple:*

> Rules lead to dull stereotyped advertising, and they stifle creativity, inspiration, initiative, and progress. The only hard and fast rule that I know of in advertising is that there are no rules. No formulas. No right way. Given the same problem, a dozen creative talents would solve it a dozen different ways. If there were a sure-fire formula for successful advertising, everyone would use it. Then there'd be no need for creative people. We would simply program robots to create our ads and commercials and they'd sell loads of product—to other robots.[17]

## Taking Creative Risks

Many creative people follow proven formulas when creating ads because they are safe. Clients often feel uncomfortable with advertising that is too different. Bill Tragos, former chair of TBWA, the advertising agency noted for its excellent creative work for Absolut vodka, Evian, and many other clients, says, "Very few clients realize that the reason that their work is so bad is that they are the ones who commandeered it and directed it to be that way. I think that at least 50 percent of an agency's successful work resides in the client."[18]

**FIGURE 8–1**

## D'Arcy Masius Benton & Bowles's Universal Advertising Standards

Source: Reprinted with permission.

1. *Does this advertising position the product simply and with unmistakable clarity?*

   The target audience for the advertised product or service must be able to see and sense in a flash *what* the product is for, *whom* it is for, and *why* they should be interested in it.

   Creating this clear vision of how the product or service fits into their lives is the first job of advertising. Without a simple, clear, focused positioning, no creative work can begin.

2. *Does this advertising bolt the brand to a clinching benefit?*

   Our advertising should be built on the most compelling and persuasive consumer benefit—not some unique-but-insignificant peripheral feature.

   Before you worry about how to say it, you must be sure you are saying *the right thing*. If you don't know what the most compelling benefit is, you've got to find out before you do anything else.

3. *Does this advertising contain a Power Idea?*

   The Power Idea is the vehicle that transforms the strategy into a dynamic, creative communications concept. It is the core creative idea that sets the stage for brilliant executions to come. The ideal Power Idea should:

   - Be describable in a simple word, phrase, or sentence without reference to any final execution.
   - Be likely to attract the prospect's attention.
   - Revolve around the clinching benefit.
   - Allow you to brand the advertising.
   - Make it easy for the prospect to vividly experience our client's product or service.

4. *Does this advertising design in Brand Personality?*

   The great brands tend to have something in common: the extra edge of having a Brand Personality. This is something beyond merely identifying what the brand does for the consumer; all brands *do* something, but the great brands also *are* something.

   A brand can be whatever its designers want it to be—and it can be so from day one.

5. *Is this advertising unexpected?*

   Why should our clients pay good money to wind up with advertising that looks and sounds like everybody else's in the category? They shouldn't.

   We must dare to be different, because sameness is suicide. We can't be outstanding unless we first stand out.

   The thing is not to *emulate* the competition but to *annihilate* them.

6. *Is this advertising single-minded?*

   If you have determined the right thing to say and have created a way to say it uncommonly well, why waste time saying anything else?

   If we want people to remember one big thing from a given piece of advertising, let's not make it more difficult than it already is in an overcommunicated world.

   The advertising should be all about that one big thing.

7. *Does this advertising reward the prospect?*

   Let's give our audience something that makes it easy—even pleasurable—for our message to penetrate: a tear, a smile, a laugh. An emotional stimulus is that special something that makes them want to see the advertising again and again.

8. *Is this advertising visually arresting?*

   Great advertising you remember—and can play back in your mind—is unusual to look at: compelling, riveting, a nourishing feast for the eyes. If you need a reason to strive for arresting work, go no further than Webster: "Catching or holding the attention, thought, or feelings. Gripping. Striking. Interesting."

9. *Does this advertising exhibit painstaking craftsmanship?*

   You want writing that is really written. Visuals that are designed. Music that is composed.

   Lighting, casting, wardrobe, direction—all the components of the art of advertising are every bit as important as the science of it. It is a sin to nickel-and-dime a great advertising idea to death.

   Why settle for good, when there's great? We should go for the absolute best in concept, design, and execution. This is our craft—the work should sparkle.

   "Our creative standards are not a gimmick. They're not even revolutionary. Instead, they are an explicit articulation of a fundamental refocusing on our company's only reason for being.

   "D'Arcy's universal advertising standards are the operating link between our vision today—and its coming reality."

WE ARE ALL WITNESSES.

Believe at nikebasketball.com

It's not a room. It's a Residence.™

Many creative people say it is important for clients to take some risks if they want breakthrough advertising that gets noticed. One agency that has been successful in getting its clients to take risks is Wieden + Kennedy, best known for its excellent creative work for companies such as Nike, Microsoft, and ESPN (see Exhibit 8–5). The agency's founders believe a key element in its success has been a steadfast belief in taking risks when most agencies and their clients have been retrenching and becoming more conservative.[19] The agency can develop great advertising partly because clients like Nike are willing to take risks and go along with the agency's priority system, which places the creative work first and the client–agency relationship second. The agency has even terminated relationships with large clients like Gallo when they interfered too much with the creative process. Several major advertisers including Procter & Gamble and Coca-Cola have added Wieden + Kennedy to their agency roster in efforts to increase the creativity of their advertising.[20] The Old Spice campaign discussed earlier in the chapter is an example of the excellent creative work being done by W + K.

An example of a company that has been taking more of a creative risk with its advertising in recent years is Residence Inn by Marriott, the brand that originated the extended-stay category in the hospitality industry. A new campaign for the brand—themed "It's Not a Room. It's a Residence"—was developed to illustrate how Residence Inn is positioned to meet the needs of today's long-term-stay guests. The ads spotlight Residence Inn's focus on providing ample room to work, relax, and maintain balance by creatively using a cast of animals including an elephant, giraffe, and family of penguins. Using both actual shots and computer-generated images, the spots featuring the elephant and giraffe demonstrate the spaciousness of the Residence Inn rooms by showing them going through the same routine that a guest might follow and taking advantage of in-room amenities desired by most travelers such as free Internet, spacious suites, fully equipped kitchens, luxury bedding, and more. One of the particularly endearing ads in the campaign features a family of penguins marching into a Residence Inn suite and relaxing in the room by playing on the desk chairs, swimming in the bathtub, chilling out with frozen desserts, and unwinding by watching a movie about penguins on the television (Exhibit 8–6). The television spots are part of an integrated campaign that includes print, online, and mobile ads. The use of the animals in the ads is a creative way to showcase the features of the Residence Inn suites and is a deviation from the conventional approach of showing people relaxing in a hotel room. The campaign has been very effective; it has helped Residence Inn maintain an occupancy rate that is 18 percent higher than the industry average.[21]

Not all companies or agencies agree that advertising has to be risky to be effective, however. Many marketing managers are more comfortable with advertising that simply communicates product or service features and benefits and gives the consumer a reason to buy. They see their ad campaigns as multimillion-dollar investments whose goal is to sell the product rather than finance the whims of their agency's creative staff. They argue that some creative people have lost sight of advertising's bottom line: Does it sell? There has been an ongoing debate over the artsy, image-oriented approach to advertising taken by many creative types versus the more hard-sell approach that many clients prefer.

## The Perpetual Debate: Creative versus Hard-Sell Advertising

For decades there has been a perpetual battle over the role of advertising in the marketing process. The war for the soul of advertising has been endlessly fought between those who believe ads should move people and those who just want to move product. On one side are the "suits" or "rationalists" who argue that advertising must sell the product or service, and that the more selling points or information in an ad, the better its chance of moving the consumer to purchase. On the other side are the "poets" or proponents of creativity who argue that advertising has to build an emotional bond between consumers and brands or companies that goes beyond product advertising. The debate over the effectiveness of creative or artsy advertising is not new. The rationalists have taken great delight in pointing to long lists of creative and award-winning campaigns over the years that have failed in the marketplace. Some note that even legendary advertising executive David Ogilvy, whom many consider the greatest copywriter of all time, once said: "If it doesn't sell, it's not creative."[22]

The "poets" argue that the most important thing good advertising does is make an emotional connection with consumers. They note that consumers do not want to be bombarded by ads; they want to be entertained and inspired. Indeed a recent survey of regular TV viewers found that 64 percent look for ways to avoid commercials rather than watch them.[23] Thus, advertising has to be creative and enjoyable enough that consumers will not zap it, yet still be able to help sell a product or service. It is the second part of this mandate that causes concern among the "suits." They note that there are many examples of creative campaigns that moved consumers' emotions but were terminated because they did not increase sales and/or market share and put accounts and reputations on the line. A number of major advertisers have dismissed agencies that earned critical acclaim and awards for their creative work but failed to move the sales needle, including Levi Strauss, PepsiCo, MillerCoors, Gateway, and many others.[24]

Most of the "poets" who support advertising that connects on an emotional level insist that selling product is as much a priority for them as it is for those on the rational side of the debate. One top agency executive notes that "we've proven that this kind of advertising works, otherwise we wouldn't be in business, us or the agencies that practice the craft at this level." However, Brent Bouchez, former executive creative director at the Bozzell agency, argues the poets are losing sight of the fact that advertising is about selling things and being really creative in advertising means solving problems and building interesting brands that people want to buy. He notes, "It's time we stopped teaching young creative people to consider it a victory if the logo in an ad is hard to find, or if the product doesn't appear in the commercial at all. It's time we stopped using 'break through the clutter' as an excuse to say nothing about what it is we're selling or why you should buy it."[25]

The issue of how much latitude creative people should be given and how much risk the client should be willing to take is open to considerable debate. However, clients and agency personnel generally agree that the ability to develop novel yet appropriate approaches to communicating with the customer makes the creative specialist valuable—and often hard to find.

## Creative Personnel

The image of the creative advertising person perpetuated in novels, movies, and TV shows is often one of a freewheeling, freethinking, eccentric personality. The educational background of creative personnel is often in nonbusiness areas such as art, literature, music, humanities, or journalism, so their interests and perspectives

## MORE PEOPLE

▶ WATCH

🔊 LISTEN

📖 READ

⤴ CLICK

👍 LIKE

📌 PIN

# TWEET US

### THANKS TO YOU.

## Congratulations, PHD!

Adweek Global Media Agency of the Year.

SAFEWAY
Ingredients for life.®

**EXHIBIT 8–7**

Awards for creativity are given for media planning as well as other components of an IMC program

tend to differ from those of managers with a business education or background. Creative people tend to be more abstract and less structured, organized, or conventional in their approach to a problem, relying on intuition more often than logic. For example, Arthur Kover conducted a study of advertising copywriters and found that they work without guidance from any formal theories of communication. However, those interviewed in his study did have similar informal, implicit theories that guide them in creating ads. These theories are based on finding ways to break through the ad clutter, open the consciousness of consumers, and connect with them to deliver the message.[26]

Advertising creatives are sometimes stereotyped as odd, perhaps because they dress differently and do not always work the conventional 9-to-5 schedule. Of course, from the perspective of the creatives, it is the marketing or brand managers and account executives (the "suits") who are strange. In many agencies, you can't tell the creative personnel from the executives by their dress or demeanor. Yet the differences between creative and managerial personalities and perspectives must be recognized and tolerated so that creative people can do their best work and all those involved in the advertising process can cooperate.

It is important to note that creativity is not the exclusive domain of those who work in the creative department of ad agencies. Integrated marketing communications requires creative thinking from everyone involved in the planning and execution of IMC programs. Personnel from other parts of the agency such as account services and planning, media planners, digital media specialists and researchers, as well as those on the client side, such as marketing and brand managers, must all seek creative solutions to challenges faced in planning developing, and executing an IMC campaign. For example, awards are given each year for creativity in areas such as media planning, sales promotion, and digital and interactive media. Exhibit 8–7 shows an ad run by the Safeway grocery store chain congratulating PHD, an agency that is part of the Omnicom Media Group, for winning *Adweek*'s Global Media Agency of the Year award in 2012. PHD was honored for its creativity and media planning for companies such as Safeway as well as Unilever, Foot Locker, and Sony.

It is also important that those working on the client side do not create a relationship with their agencies that inhibits the creative processes required to produce good advertising. Shelia Sasser and Scott Koslow point out that the most highly skilled creatives aspire to work with open-minded clients who are receptive to new ideas. They also note some of the best creative work developed by agencies does not get used because clients are resistant to taking creative risks, unless they are under pressure to perform.[27] Advertising agencies, as well as other IMC specialist organizations thrive on creativity as it is at the heart of what they do. Thus, agencies, as well as clients, must create an environment that fosters the development of creative thinking and creative advertising. Clients must also understand the differences between the perspectives of the creative personnel and marketing and product managers. While the client has ultimate approval of the advertising, the opinions of creative specialists must be respected when advertising ideas and content are evaluated. (Evaluation of the creatives' ideas and work is discussed in more detail in Chapter 9.)

# THE CREATIVE PROCESS

LO 08-2

Some advertising people say creativity in advertising is best viewed as a process and creative success is most likely when some organized approach is followed. This does not mean there is an infallible blueprint to follow to create effective advertising; as we saw earlier, many advertising people reject attempts to standardize creativity or develop rules. However, most do follow a process when developing an ad.

One of the most popular approaches to creativity in advertising was developed by James Webb Young, a former creative vice president at the J. Walter Thompson agency. Young said, "The production of ideas is just as definite a process as the production of Fords; the production of ideas, too, runs an assembly line; in this production the mind follows an operative technique which can be learned and controlled; and that its effective use is just as much a matter of practice in the technique as in the effective use of any tool."[28] Young's model of the creative process contains five steps:

1. *Immersion.* Gathering raw material and information through background research and immersing yourself in the problem.
2. *Digestion.* Taking the information, working it over, and wrestling with it in the mind.
3. *Incubation.* Putting the problems out of your conscious mind and turning the information over to the subconscious to do the work.
4. *Illumination.* The birth of an idea—the "Eureka! I have it!" phenomenon.
5. *Reality or verification.* Studying the idea to see if it still looks good or solves the problem; then shaping the idea to practical usefulness.

Young's process of creativity is similar to a four-step approach outlined much earlier by English sociologist Graham Wallas in his classic book *The Art of Thought.*[29]

1. *Preparation.* Gathering background information needed to solve the problem through research and study.
2. *Incubation.* Getting away and letting ideas develop.
3. *Illumination.* Seeing the light or solution.
4. *Verification.* Refining and polishing the idea and seeing if it is an appropriate solution.

Models of the creative process are valuable to those working in the creative area of advertising, since they offer an organized way to approach an advertising problem. Preparation or gathering of background information is the first step in the creative process. As we saw in earlier chapters, the advertiser and agency start by developing a thorough understanding of the product or service, the target market, and the competition. They also focus on the role of advertising in the marketing and promotional program.

These models do not say much about how this information will be synthesized and used by the creative specialist because this part of the process is unique to the individual. In many ways, it's what sets apart the great creative minds and strategists in advertising. However, many agencies are now using a process called *account planning* to gather information and help creative specialists as they go through the creative process of developing advertising.

## Account Planning

To facilitate the creative process, many agencies now use **account planning**, which is a process that involves conducting research and gathering all relevant information about a client's product or service, brand, and consumers in the target audience. Account planning began in Great Britain during the 1960s and 70s and has spread to agencies in the United States as well as throughout Europe and Asia. The concept has become very popular in recent years as many agencies have seen the successful campaigns developed by agencies that are strong advocates of account planning.[30] One such agency is Goodby, Silverstein & Partners, which has used account planning to develop highly successful campaigns for clients such as E-Trade, Hewlett-Packard, Sega, and Nike, as well as the popular "Got Milk?" ads for the California Milk Processor Board.

Jon Steel, a former vice president and director of account planning at the agency's San Francisco office, has written an excellent book on the process titled *Truth, Lies & Advertising: The Art of Account Planning.*[31] He notes that the account planner's job is to provide the key decision makers with all the information they require to make an intelligent decision. According to Steel, "Planners may have to work very hard to influence the way that the advertising turns out, carefully laying out a strategic foundation with the client, handing over tidbits of information to creative people when, in their judgment, that information will have the greatest impact, giving feedback on ideas, and hopefully adding some ideas of their own."

Account planning plays an important role during creative strategy development by driving the process from the customers' point of view. Planners will work with the client as well as other agency personnel, such as the creative team and media specialists. They discuss how the knowledge and information they have gathered can be used in the development of the creative strategy as well as other aspects of the advertising campaign. Account planners are usually responsible for all the research (both qualitative and quantitative) conducted during the creative strategy development process. In the following section we examine how various types of research and information can provide input to the creative process of advertising. This information can be gathered by account planners or others whose job it is to provide input to the process.

## Inputs to the Creative Process: Preparation, Incubation, Illumination

**Background Research**   Only the most foolish creative person or team would approach an assignment without first learning as much as possible about the client's product or service, the target market, the competition, and any other relevant background information. The creative specialist should also be knowledgeable about general trends, conditions, and developments in the marketplace, as well as research on specific advertising approaches or techniques that might be effective. The creative specialist can acquire background information in numerous ways. Some informal fact-finding techniques have been noted by Sandra Moriarty:

- Reading anything related to the product or market—books, trade publications, general interest articles, research reports, and the like.
- Asking everyone involved with the product for information—designers, engineers, salespeople, and consumers.
- Listening to what people are talking about. Visits to stores, malls, restaurants, and even the agency cafeteria can be informative. Listening to the client can be particularly valuable, since he or she often knows the product and market best.
- Using the product or service and becoming familiar with it. The more you use a product, the more you know and can say about it.
- Working in and learning about the client's business to understand better the people you're trying to reach.[32]

To assist in the preparation, incubation, and illumination stages, many agencies provide creative people with both general and product-specific preplanning input. **General preplanning input** can include books, periodicals, trade publications, websites, scholarly journals, pictures, and clipping services, which gather and organize magazine, newspaper, and online articles on the product, the market, and the competition, including the latter's ads. This input can also come from research studies conducted by the client, the agency, the media, or other sources.

YTC 08-08

**Brands**

youtube.com/10ebelch

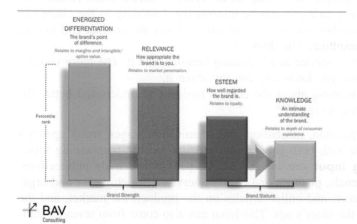

Essential Brand Dimensions: The Four Pillars

Another useful general preplanning input concerns trends, developments, and happenings in the marketplace. Information is available from a variety of sources, including local, state, and federal governments, secondary research suppliers, and various industry trade associations, as well as advertising and media organizations. For example, advertising industry groups like the American Advertising Federation (AAF), American Association of Advertising Agencies, and media organizations like the Television Advertising Bureau and the Association of Magazine Media publish research reports and newsletters that provide information on market trends and developments and how they might affect consumers. Those involved in developing creative strategy can also gather relevant and timely information by reading publications like *Adweek, Advertising Age, Marketing News,* and *The Wall Street Journal* (see Exhibit 8–8).

**Product- or Service-Specific Research**   In addition to getting general background research and preplanning input, creative people receive **product- or service-specific preplanning input**. This information generally comes in the form of specific studies conducted on the product or service, the target audience, or a combination of the two. Quantitative and qualitative consumer research such as attitude studies, market structure, and positioning studies such as perceptual mapping and lifestyle research, focus group interviews, and demographic and psychographic profiles of users of a particular product, service, or brand are examples of product-specific preplanning input.

Many product- or service-specific studies helpful to the creative team are conducted by the client or the agency. A number of years ago, the BBDO ad agency developed an approach called **problem detection** for finding ideas around which creative strategies could be based.[33] This research technique involves asking consumers familiar with a product (or service) to generate an exhaustive list of things that bother them or problems they encounter when using it. The consumers rate these problems in order of importance and evaluate various brands in terms of their association with each problem. A problem detection study can provide valuable input for product improvements, reformulations, or new products. It can also give the creative people ideas regarding attributes or features to emphasize and guidelines for positioning new or existing brands.

Some agencies conduct psychographic studies annually and construct detailed psychographic or lifestyle profiles of product or service users. DDB Worldwide conducts a large-scale psychographic study each year that taps into the minds of 4,000 consumers to measure their activities, interests, opinions, and attitudes as well as their usage of a wide range of products and services. The information is used to construct a psychographic profile of the target audiences for whom they are developing ads as well as to gain insight into general consumer trends.

A number of advertising agencies conduct branding research to help better identify clients' customers and how they connect to their brands. For example, the Y&R Group developed a proprietary tool, BAV™, for building and managing a brand. The model uses four pillars: energized differentiation, relevance, esteem, and knowledge. These pillars identify cores issues for the brand and evaluate current and future financial performance and potential (Exhibit 8–9). The Leo Burnett Institute of Behaviour includes a Brand Consulting division to guide its global brand building philosophy and practice. LBIB focuses on brand purpose, design, and internal alignment int this approach to brand building.

Nearly all of the major agencies are conducting branding research and/or developing models or systems that they can use to gain better insight into consumers and develop more effective campaigns for their clients. The importance of building and maintaining strong brands is likely to become even greater in the future. This will put even more pressure on agencies to develop new and better tools and techniques that can be used to guide their clients' advertising campaigns.

**Qualitative Research Input**  Many agencies, particularly larger ones with strong research departments, have their own research programs and specific techniques they use to assist in the development of creative strategy and provide input to the creative process. In addition to the various quantitative research studies, qualitative research techniques such as in-depth interviews or focus groups can provide the creative team with valuable insight at the early stages of the creative process. **Focus groups** are a research method whereby consumers (usually 10 to 12 people) from the target market are led through a discussion regarding a particular topic. Focus groups give insight as to why and how consumers use a product or service, what is important to them in choosing a particular brand, what they like and don't like about various products or services, and any special needs they might have that aren't being satisfied. A focus group session might also include a discussion of types of ad appeals to use or evaluation of the advertising of various companies.

Focus group interviews bring the creative people and others involved in creative strategy development into contact with the customers. Listening to a focus group gives copywriters, art directors, and other creative specialists a better sense of who the target audience is, what the audience is like, and who the creatives need to write, design, or direct to in creating an advertising message. Focus groups can also be used to evaluate the viability of different creative approaches under consideration and suggest the best direction to pursue.[34] Many marketers are now conducting focus groups online using groups of consumers who are part of an online community, as well as Internet research panels of 80 to 100 consumers organized by research firms such as Greenfield Online and Invoke Solutions. Concepts can be presented to these panels using instant-message and chatroom styles, and detailed feedback can be gathered and processed in a few hours versus several weeks that are needed to get comparable results from traditional focus groups.[35]

Agency creative personnel have long expressed concern over the idea of having their ideas and work critiqued by consumers. Many creatives insist that good ideas don't need to be tested and that testing can often weaken a creative execution. Moreover, they argue that it interferes with the creative process and limits their ability to develop innovative and breakthrough advertising messages.[36] Those critical of focus groups note that highly successful campaigns such as the one featuring the Aflac duck would never have made it on the air if the company had heeded the responses of focus group participants. While many participants found the duck funny, others found it insulting. The duck survived only after executives from the Kaplan Thaler Group convinced the company to allow the Ipso-ASI research firm to test the ad along with four others it created and four spots from other agencies competing for the account.[37] The recall score of the spot featuring the duck was the highest score Ipsos-ASI had seen in the insurance category at the time. Kaplan Thaler won the account, and the award-winning campaign featuring the duck debuted in late 1999 and has been running ever since (Exhibit 8–10). It also has helped increase raise awareness of Aflac and led to significant increases in sales for the supplemental insurance provider.

While many creative personnel may be opposed to having their ideas scrutinized in a focus group, there are, of course, numerous examples of situations where input from focus groups has proved to be very valuable and insightful. Creative personnel

YTC **08–09**

Aflac

youtube.com/10ebelch

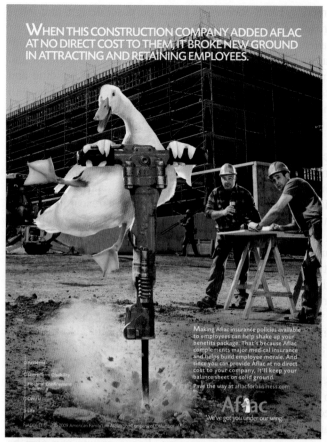

**EXHIBIT 8–10**

The Aflac duck did not test well in focus groups but has been the basis for a very successful campaign

must recognize that companies want to ensure that the ads that are being developed for their brands have the best possible chance of evoking favorable reactions from consumers and encouraging them to purchase their product and/or services. Joe Plummer, the former chief research officer of the Advertising Research Foundation, explains their position pretty well by noting that "Any creative director worth his salt who really thinks a client is going to lay down $100 million without a high level of confidence of success is naïve."[38]

Another form of qualitative input that has become popular among advertising agencies is **ethnographic research**, which involves observing consumers in their natural environment.[39] Some agencies send anthropologists or trained researchers into the field to study and observe consumers in their homes, at work, or at play. For example, the Ogilvy & Mather agency has a research unit called the Discovery Group, which moves into consumers' homes, follows consumers in their leisure pursuits, or trails them as they move through their daily lives. For Ogilvy client MillerCoors, Discovery staffers traveled around the country filming Miller drinkers, as well as those drinking competitive brands. They used the tapes to study group dynamics and how the dynamics changed while people were drinking. The agency used the insights gained from the study to help develop a new advertising campaign for Miller Lite beer.

The Goodby, Silverstein & Partners agency conducted ethnographic research in developing an ad campaign for the Chevrolet Silverado truck that was used to differentiate it from the popular Ford F-150. The ethnographic study began with a nine-day, 1,500-mile road trip across five states from Texas to Iowa to explore the truck culture firsthand. The insights uncovered by the ethnographers revealed several key findings, including the migration of the truck culture from its rural hunting and farming roots to the fabric of suburban men's social lives. The research also revealed that trucks and truck culture served to open up new, meaningful experiences with friends and family that helped them connect to one another, in addition to allowing truck owners to get their work independently by being a "do-it-yourselfer." The ethnographic insights were used to develop the "There's Life to Be Done" campaign, which focused on reinforcing the Silverado's strengths (most dependable, long lasting) while adding a differentiating emotional layer that connected these core strengths to the part of the truck buyers' personal lives they are most focused on: providing financial and emotional support for their families.[40]

Many marketing and agency researchers prefer ethnographic research over the use of focus groups, as the latter technique has a number of limitations. Strong personalities can often wield undue influence in focus groups, and participants often will not admit, or may not even recognize, their behavior patterns and motivations. However, ethnographic studies can cost more to conduct and are more difficult to administer.

Generally, creative people are open to any research or information that will help them understand the client's target market better and assist in generating creative ideas. The advertising industry is recognizing the importance of using research to guide the creative process. The Advertising Research Foundation initiated the David Ogilvy Awards, named after the advertising legend who founded Ogilvy & Mather. These awards are presented to teams of advertising agencies, client companies, and

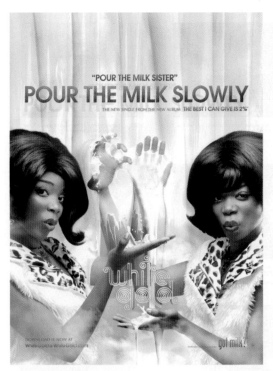

"POUR THE MILK SISTER"

POUR THE MILK SLOWLY

THE NEW SINGLE FROM THE NEW ALBUM THE BEST I CAN GIVE IS 2%

white gold

got milk?

DOWNLOAD IT NOW AT
WhiteGoldisWhiteGold.com

**EXHIBIT 8–11**

Research played an important role in the development of this Ogilvy award-winning campaign

**EXHIBIT 8–12**

This ad campaign for Vicks Cold Products won the Grand Ogilvy Award for an IMC campaign based on market research

DREW BREES

WHEN YOU'RE AN NFL QUARTERBACK,
**THERE ARE NO SICK DAYS...OR NIGHTS.**

research companies in recognition of research that has been used successfully to determine the strategy and effectiveness of ad campaigns.

The Goodby, Silverstein & Partners agency won an Ogilvy award for a research-driven campaign created for the California Milk Processor Board to target teens and increase their milk consumption. Research showed that freshly liberated teens living away from home (such as college students) were drinking less milk, particularly when they were around their friends, as they preferred beverages with a cooler image such as Red Bull, VitaminWater, or Starbucks's teas and coffee. The agency used both qualitative and quantitative research as the basis for a social media–based campaign that repositioned milk to teens as a *vessel of health and hotness.* The agency invented a fictitious band called White Gold that was named after its lead singer and guitarist and backed up by the Calcium Twins Wholena and Skimberly (Exhibit 8–11). The agency wrote and recorded humorous songs about milk and its transformative superpowers and even produced full-length music videos of some of the songs. To give the band a social media networking presence band pages were created for MySpace and Facebook and a special website was created for the campaign. Television and rock-poster-style print ads were used to tell the story of the band and drive teens to the website and social media pages. The campaign has been very successful in changing teens' perceptions of milk on its key image attributes, elevating its social acceptability, and increasing consumption among teens in California.[41]

The Grand Ogilvy Award winner in 2012 was a campaign developed for the Vicks® NyQuil® and DayQuil® brands whose goal was to increase the exposure to consumers of the cold and flu remedy products. The Vicks® team and its agency, Publicis, used market segmentation research to identify its primary prospect, which they referred to as the Performance Consumer who is characterized by his desire to knock out a cold as soon as he senses its onset, as it is viewed as an uninvited intrusion that affects his ability to accomplish everything he needs to do. This individual also wants to get rid of the cold so he can get back to his busy day. The research led to the idea of an integrated campaign that included having the Vicks® brands become an Official Sponsor of the National Football League (NFL), a sport synonymous with power that aligned perfectly with the cold and flu season. The theme for the advertising centered around the idea of "In the NFL there are no Sick Days … or Nights." The television commercial and print ads created for the campaign feature NFL star quarterback Drew Brees and focus on the brands' ability to provide cold and flu relief to allow him to perform at a high level when facing the most rigorous test—Game Day in the NFL (Exhibit 8–12). The campaign was very effective at increasing awareness, as well as sales, of both the DayQuil® and NyQuil® brands.[42]

## Inputs to the Creative Process: Verification, Revision

The verification and revision stage of the creative process evaluates ideas generated during the illumination stage, rejects inappropriate ones, refines and polishes those that remain, and gives them final expression. Techniques used at this stage include directed focus groups to evaluate creative concepts, ideas, or themes; message communication studies; portfolio tests; and evaluation measures such as viewer reaction profiles.

VIDEO:   A private Lear jet takes off during sunset as heat vapors rise from runway.
AUDIO:   Sound of muffled cocktail music.

VIDEO:   Close up of jet racing out of city as night falls over skyline.
AUDIO:   Sound of jet engines.

VIDEO:   Camera zooms in window to inside of plane. Close up of girl opening bottle of SKYY Blue and blowing mist from bottle.
AUDIO:   Refreshing sound of bottle opening.

VIDEO:   Camera pans down to woman sitting on modern jet refrigerator as she opens the door and man pulls out two bottles of SKYY Blue.
AUDIO:   Sounds of bottles clinking.

VIDEO:   Pan continues past couple as they put on a record on jet's high-tech turntable.
AUDIO:   Classic cocktail music plays.

VIDEO:   Pan continues past woman as she has straw inserted into her bottle.
AUDIO:   Cocktail music plays.

VIDEO:   Pan continues to close up of man wearing mirrored sunglasses looking out cabin window as clouds and a glimpse of sunlight reflect off sunglasses.
AUDIO:   Cocktail music plays.

VIDEO:   Man responds by opening another shade to let sunlight in as girl dances in aisle with SKYY Blue.
AUDIO:   Cocktail music plays.

VIDEO:   Jet zooms over a new city skyline with sun rising in background.
AUDIO:   Muffled cocktail music. Jet engines.

At this stage of the creative process, members of the target audience may be asked to evaluate rough creative layouts and to indicate what meaning they get from the ad, what they think of its execution, or how they react to a slogan or theme. The creative team can gain insight into how a TV commercial might communicate its message by having members of the target market evaluate the ad in storyboard form. A **storyboard** is a series of drawings used to present the visual plan or layout of a proposed commercial. It contains a series of sketches of key frames or scenes along with the copy or audio portion for each scene (see Exhibit 8–13).

Testing a commercial in storyboard form can be difficult because storyboards are too abstract for many consumers to understand. To make the creative layout more realistic and easier to evaluate, the agency may produce an **animatic**, a videotape of the storyboard along with an audio soundtrack. Storyboards and animatics are useful for research purposes as well as for presenting the creative idea to other agency personnel or to the client for discussion and approval.

At this stage of the process, the creative team is attempting to find the best creative approach or execution style before moving ahead with the campaign themes and going into actual production of the ad. The verification/revision process may include more formal, extensive pretesting of the ad before a final decision is made. Pretesting and related procedures are examined in detail in Chapter 19.

YTC 08-10
animatics
youtube.com/10ebelch

# CREATIVE STRATEGY DEVELOPMENT

LO 08-3

## Advertising Campaigns

Most ads are part of a series of messages that make up an IMC or **advertising campaign**, which is a set of interrelated and coordinated marketing communications activities that center on a single theme or idea that appears in different media across a specified time period. Determining the unifying theme around which the campaign will be built is a critical part of the creative process, as it sets the tone for the individual ads and other forms of marketing communications that will be used. A **campaign theme** should be a strong idea, as it is the central message that will be communicated in all the advertising and other promotional activities. The theme for the advertising campaign is usually expressed through a **slogan** or **tagline** that reduces the key idea into a few words or a brief statement. The advertising slogan should serve as a summation line that succinctly expresses the company or brand's positioning, as well as the message it is trying to deliver to the target audience.[43] The slogan usually appears in every advertisement and is often used in other forms of marketing communications to serve as a reminder of, and to reinforce, the marketer's branding message. Kohli, Leuthesser, and Suri note that slogans are a key element of a brand's identity as they can enhance a brand's image, aid in its recognition and recall, and help differentiate it in the minds of consumers, thus contributing to brand equity.[44] They note that while a brand name and/or logo cannot say much in a literal sense, slogans can bridge this gap and say something about the image of the product or service. They can also serve as a "hook" or "handle" that helps capture the meaning of a brand and help relay what makes it special.[45]

Advertising campaign plans are short term in nature and, like marketing and IMC plans, are done on an annual basis. However, the campaign themes are usually developed with the intention of being used for a longer time period. Unfortunately, many campaign themes last only a short time, usually because they are ineffective or market conditions and/or competitive developments in the marketplace change. IMC Perspective 8–1 discusses some of the reasons why many advertising slogans do a poor job of communicating a distinctive identity for a company or brand and offers some guidelines for developing more effective taglines.

While some marketers change their campaign themes often, a successful campaign theme may last for decades. Philip Morris has been using the "Marlboro country" campaign for over 50 years, General Mills has positioned Wheaties cereal as the "Breakfast of Champions" for decades, and BMW has used the "ultimate driving machine" theme since 1974. Even though BMW has changed agencies several times over the past three decades, the classic tagline has been retained. Figure 8–2 lists some of the advertising slogans currently being used by marketers that are recognized as being very effective because they are memorable and communicate a unique message for the company or brand.

Like any other area of the marketing and promotional process, the creative aspect of advertising and the development of the campaign theme is guided by specific

**FIGURE 8–2**

Examples of Effective Advertising Slogans

| Company or brand | Slogan |
| --- | --- |
| 1. Nike | Just do it |
| 2. Home Depot | More saving. More doing. |
| 3. Gillette | The Best a Man Can Get |
| 4. McDonald's | I'm Lovin' It! |
| 5. De Beers | A Diamond Is Forever |
| 6. Coca-Cola | Open Happiness |
| 7. Bounty | The Quicker Picker-Upper |
| 8. Gatorade | Win From Within |
| 9. Under Armour | We Must Protect This House. I Will. |
| 10. Macy's | The Magic of Macy's |

# IMC Perspective 8–1 > > >

## Creating More Effective Ad Slogans

We as consumers are exposed to hundreds of advertising messages as we go through our daily media consumption routines of reading newspapers and magazines, listening to radio, watching television, and surfing the Internet. And nearly every advertisement that we see and/or hear contains a slogan or tagline that is designed to serve as a summation line that quickly and succinctly expresses the company or brand's positioning as well as the message it is trying to deliver to the target audience. Stop and think for a moment about Nike's "Just do it" tagline, which has been used in its advertising for more than two decades and is recognized by nearly everyone. The tagline is designed to encourage personal athletic achievement, whether through playing a sport or engaging in some type of exercise or workout routine such as running, biking, aerobics, or even walking. Of course Nike wants us all to do it while wearing its shoes or exercise apparel, which millions of consumers around the world proudly do. Even when we see a Nike ad that does not contain the slogan, the famous "swoosh" trademark often prompts consumers to rehearse the "Just do it" line in their minds.

Nike's tagline was chosen as one of the top five ad slogans of all time and has even been enshrined in the Smithsonian Institution. Some of the other top taglines that effectively communicate the benefits or unique feature of a company or brand include "M&M's: Melts in your mouth, not in your hands," McDonald's "I'm Lovin' It," Allstate Insurance's "You're in Good Hands with Allstate," and Kay Jewelers's "Every kiss begins with Kay." And while there are many other examples of good taglines, there are probably many more examples of very poor slogans that are vague and mean absolutely nothing. Communication professor Stephen

Winzenburg notes that many major companies do a poor job of communicating their identities by using meaningless phrases in their taglines. Examples of slogans that he cites as generic and bland include JCPenney's "Every day matters," Sears's "Where it begins," Kohl's "Expect great things," and Radio Shack's "Do stuff." Winzenburg argues these slogans are meaningless and fail to give the consumer a sense of what these companies are about. He also notes that these slogans are interchangeable and do little, if anything, to differentiate these companies from their competitors.

Marketing experts note that a good tagline must break through the advertising clutter, differentiate the company or brand, and be memorable. John Mathes, director of brand services at Bancography, a bank branding and positioning consulting company, notes that "The tagline is a hardworking collection of words that should give you that 'aha' moment every time you see or hear it." He reminds marketers that a tagline is your brand's sound bite and is often all you can expect consumers to remember. Mathes suggests that a good tagline starts with the brand positioning statement, which should be well articulated and truly differentiating, and he offers a helpful guideline: A brand's positioning can be expressed verbatim as a tagline (think BMW and "ultimate driving machine"), but a tagline is not usually the brand positioning unless it is a direct lift from the positioning statement.

Long-time marketing executive Steve Cone argues that creating strong slogans is a marketer's most important job but today is a forgotten part of marketing planning. He suggests that advertising messages should contain "power-lines," or powerful taglines, which he describes as "words that are well chosen and have the power to awe, inspire,

---

goals and objectives. A creative strategy that focuses on what must be communicated will guide the selection of the campaign theme and the development of all messages used in the ad campaign. The creative strategy is based on several factors, including identification of the target audience; the basic problem, issue, or opportunity the advertising must address; the major selling idea or key benefit the message needs to communicate; and any supportive information that needs to be included in the ad. Once these factors are determined, a creative strategy statement should describe the message appeal and execution style that will be used. Many ad agencies outline these elements in a document known as the copy or creative platform.

### Creative Brief

The written **creative brief** specifies the basic elements of the creative strategy. Different agencies may call this document a *creative platform* or *work plan, creative blueprint,* or *creative contract.* The account representative or manager assigned to the account usually prepares the creative brief. In larger agencies, an individual from research or the strategic account planning department may write it. People from the agency team or group assigned to the account, including creative personnel as well

Steve Cone offers four basic guidelines for creating a compelling tagline that will get noticed and stand the test of time. He suggests that a good tagline should say why the company or brand is different and not use common words; it should have real attitude and bypass wishy-washy phrases; appear at all customer touch points and ideally be the headline of every marketing promotion; and marketers should recognize that creating good taglines is an art, as the best ones come from flashes of inspirations by great copywriters who see clear and compelling brand promises and make them come to life.

The importance of slogans in the branding process is also noted by digital marketing manager Kumail Hemani, who notes that they often play an important strategic role in influencing the minds of consumers. His guidelines for creating effective slogans, which are shown in the chart, include recognizing that a slogan is a shadow for a brand as it is used everywhere along with it and thus has a key role in communicating the essence of a brand. He also notes that slogans should be simple, catchy, and predictable as well as connect with the consumer on an emotional level.

The next time you see an ad, pay attention to the tagline and evaluate it against these guidelines. If Cone is correct, 98 percent of the time the tagline will fail to communicate anything unique or relevant, nor will it contribute to the image of the company or brand. However, those that have a powerline can help make a company or brand's marketing message more memorable and effective and give it a leg up on the competition.

Sources: Steve Cone, "Help Taglines Regain Lost Glory," *Advertising Age*, April 14, 2008, http://adage.com/print?article_id=126290; Stephen Winzenburg, "Your Advertising Slogans Are Crummy. Can't You Do Better?" *Advertising Age*, January 14, 2008, p.15; John Mathes, "Taglines That Stick; Here's How to Create an Effective Brand Summation Line. How Long Should It Be? Is It the Same as Your Brand Positioning? How Often Do You Need to Refresh It?," *ABA Bank Marketing*, December 1, 2008, pp. 22–25; Kumail Hemani, "Impact of Slogans on Branding," *SocialMedia Today*, March 26, 2012, http://socialmediatoday.com/node/475582.

motivate, alienate, subjugate, and in a marketing context, change the buying habits of consumers." He argues that since we are bombarded by so many advertising messages, a powerline can do the heavy lifting and break through all of the sensory overload.

One factor marketers must consider is how long they can use a tagline before it becomes wallpaper to the target audience. Mathes suggests that taglines should be reviewed every two to three years and that ongoing brand awareness and attribute-tracking studies can provide the benchmarks needed to determine whether a slogan is doing its job or is wearing out. Cone cautions against changing advertising slogans too often and argues that the more things change, the more taglines should not, particularly if they are a special promise or claim that a competitor cannot easily duplicate.

YTC **08–11**
ad slogans
youtube.com/10ebelch

as representatives from media and research, have input. The advertising manager and/or the marketing and brand managers from the client side ultimately approve the creative brief. Figure 8–3 shows a sample copy platform outline that can be used to guide the creative process. Just as there are different names for the creative brief, there are variations in the outline and format used and in the level of detail included.

Several components of the creative brief were discussed in previous chapters. For example, Chapter 7 examined the DAGMAR model and showed how the setting of advertising objectives requires specifying a well-defined target audience and developing a communication task statement that spells out what message must be communicated to this audience. Determining what problem the product or service will solve or what issue must be addressed in the ad helps in establishing communication objectives for the campaign to accomplish. Two critical components of the brief are the development of the major selling idea and creative strategy development. These two steps are often the responsibility of the creative team or specialist and form the basis of the advertising campaign theme.

Many creative briefs also include supporting information and requirements (brand identifications, disclaimers, and the like) that should appear in any advertising message. This information may be important in ensuring uniformity across various

**FIGURE 8–3**

Creative Brief Outline

1. Basic problem or issue the advertising must address.

2. Advertising and communications objectives.

3. Target audience.

4. Major selling idea or key benefits to communicate.

5. Creative strategy statement (campaign theme, appeal, and execution technique to be used).

6. Supporting information and requirements.

executions of the ads used in a campaign or in meeting any legal requirements. Exhibits 8–14A and B show an example of a creative brief used by the Lambesis agency to create a print campaign for Tacori and an ad that was created based on the brief. As noted in the brief, the primary objective of the advertising for Tacori is to establish the Tacori collection as a more accessible fashion jewelry line.

Obtaining information regarding customers, the product or service, and the market that can be used in developing the creative brief is an important part of the creative planning process. While it is important that this basic information is provided to agency creatives, this may not always occur due to breakdowns in communication on the client as well as the agency side or between the two. John Sutherland, Lisa Duke, and Avery Abernethy developed a model of the flow of marketing information from clients to the agency creative staff, shown in Figure 8–4.[46] The model shows that there are five major communication interfaces and decision points where gatekeepers can impede the flow of information to agency creatives.

A great deal of attention has been paid to the client–agency communication interface that occurs between the brand manager and/or advertising manager on the client side and the account manager on the agency side. Communication problems can occur between clients and their agencies, which can make the job of the creative staff

**EXHIBIT 8–14A**

Creative brief for Tacori jewelry

**Lambesis**

2800 Roosevelt Street, Carlsbad California, 92008 Main 760.547.2333 Fax 760.547.2331 lambesis.com

**Creative Brief**

Client:     Tacori

**Assignment**
Develop new print concepts for the launch of the 18K925 line by Tacori

**Objectives**
• Support the long-term goal of growing 18K925 to become 50% of Tacori's business by clearly establishing the new Tacori collection as a more accessible, fashion jewelry line

**Target**
• Women, Age 25-49, HHI $75K+, Urban dwellers, Brand driven consumers, in market for fashion jewelry for self or as a gift for someone special.

• *What do they currently think?*
I know and love Tacori as a high-end jewelry brand that's gifted for special occasions (=expressions of love)

• *What do we want them to think?*
Tacori is also a brand with bold, statement-making, accessible designs that still have that distinctly artisanal Tacori touch (=expressions of style)

**Product positioning**
Tacori's 18K925 designer jewelry line is the ultimate expression of passion, with modern, accessible style and lasting quality.

**Reasons to believe**
• Accessible price points between $400 - $3000
• Bold, fun, wearable designs fuse colorful gemstones and gold+silver metals, with classic Tacori design cues
• Distinct Tacori brand name and image

**Tonality**
Modern meets heirloom, bold, aspirational, unique

**Creative considerations**
• Develop concepts within the Iconic Passion campaign
• Creative requirements:
    • Demonstrate aspirational, yet attainable luxury
    • Accommodate a variety of product imagery including necklaces, bracelets and/or rings to showcase the range of jewelry
    • Use the Tacori logo
• Other considerations that need be addressed:
    • Concepts must be able to work for print and horizontal OOH and B&W newspaper
    • Concepts need to ensure that retailer tags added to the bottom of the ad are legible

**EXHIBIT 8–14B**

Print ad created based on creative brief to establish Tacori as an accessible fashion jewelry line

TACORI

**FIGURE 8–4**

Model of Marketing
Information Flow from the
Marketing Manager to the
Creative Staff

Source: John Sutherland, Lisa Duke,
and Avery Abernethy, "A Model of
Marketing Information Flow," *Journal
of Advertising* 33, no. 4 (Winter
2004), p. 42. Copyright © 2004 by
American Academy of Advertising.
Reprinted with permission of M. E.
Sharpe, Inc. All rights reserved. Not
for reproduction.

much more difficult. However, this model shows that there are four other potential communication interface failure points, including (1) the client or client gatekeeper lacking knowledge of some or all of the information needed for effective advertising; (2) the client deciding not to share with the agency all of the available information that is relevant to creating effective advertising; (3) the agency gatekeeper(s) deciding not to share with creative staffers all of the client information received; and (4) internal agency communication failures that may result in the creative staff not receiving all of the relevant information received from the client.

Sutherland, Duke, and Abernethy conducted an extensive survey of agency creative directors, copywriters, and art directors on the specific types of marketing information that is made available to them for use in developing and executing a creative strategy. They identified six specific types of marketing information, including the demographic profile of the target audience, customer product usage information, client's product performance information, competitors' product performance information, marketing strategy information, and the main selling point supplied by the client. Their study showed that agency creative personnel often lack the information needed to effectively design and execute creative strategies. They found that information in these specific categories was provided to creatives only around one-half to two-thirds of the time. Even the most basic target demographic profile was not provided 30 percent of the time. This study indicates that there is a gap in the information that creative personnel need to develop effective advertising and what they are being provided and points to the need for better communication between clients and agencies.

The information contained in the copy platform provides the creative staff with important background information and the basic elements of the overall advertising strategy. The next step in the creative process is the development of the message strategy and begins with the search for the *big idea* that will build on the strategy and bring it to life. One of the major challenges for the creative team is determining the major selling idea that will be used as the basis of the campaign. We will examine some approaches often used for determining the major selling idea and campaign theme.

## The Search for the Major Selling Idea

LO 08-4

An important part of creative strategy is determining the central theme that will become the **major selling idea** of the ad campaign. As A. Jerome Jeweler states in his book *Creative Strategy in Advertising:*

> The major selling idea should emerge as the strongest singular thing you can say about your product or service. This should be the claim with the broadest and most meaningful appeal to your target audience. Once you determine this message, be certain you can live with it; be sure it stands strong enough to remain the central issue in every ad and commercial in the campaign.[47]

Some advertising experts argue that for an ad campaign to be effective it must contain a big idea that attracts the consumer's attention, gets a reaction, and sets the advertiser's product or service apart from the competition's. Well-known ad executive John O'Toole describes the *big idea* as "that flash of insight that synthesizes the purpose of the strategy, joins the product benefit with consumer desire in a fresh, involving way, brings the subject to life, and makes the reader or audience stop, look, and listen."[48]

Of course, the real challenge to the creative team is coming up with the big idea to use in the ad. Many products and services offer virtually nothing unique, and it can be difficult to find something interesting to say about them. The late David Ogilvy, generally considered one of the most creative advertising copywriters ever to work in the business, has stated:

YTC 08-12

**Big Ideas**

youtube.com/10ebelch

> I doubt if more than one campaign in a hundred contains a big idea. I am supposed to be one of the more fertile inventors of big ideas, but in my long career as a copywriter I have not had more than 20, if that.[49]

While really great ideas in advertising are difficult to come by, there are many big ideas that became the basis of very creative, successful advertising campaigns. Classic examples include "We Try Harder," which positioned Avis as the underdog car-rental company that provided better service than Hertz; the "Pepsi Generation" theme and subsequent variations like "The Taste of a New Generation" and "GenerationNext"; the "Be All You Can Be" theme used in recruitment ads for the U.S. Army; the "Intel Inside" campaign for Intel microprocessors that go in personal computers; Nike's "Just Do It"; the "Got Milk?" and milk moustache themes used to promote milk consumption; and Apple's "Think Different" campaign.

More recent big ideas that have resulted in effective advertising campaigns include the "I'm Lovin' It!" theme for McDonald's, the "We Love Logistics" idea for UPS, and Chrysler Corporation's "Imported from Detroit" campaign. Chrysler has used its big idea to position the company against import brands and tout the revival of U.S. automakers (Exhibit 8–15). The company has developed a number of high-profile TV commercials around the theme, including several critically acclaimed Super Bowl ads such as one featuring rapper Eminem and another spot that aired on the 2012 game called "Half Time in America" that featured actor Clint Eastwood delivering an inspirational message about job growth and the spirit of America in recovering from the economic crisis. The campaign has helped increase Chrysler sales over the past three years; the company's market share has gone from 8.9 to 11.5 percent and the Chrysler Group was named 2012 Marketer of the Year by *Advertising Age.*[50]

**EXHIBIT 8–15**

Chrysler's "Imported from Detroit" advertising theme is an example of an effective major selling idea

IMPORTED FROM DETROIT

Big ideas are important in business-to-business advertising, and B-to-B marketers are recognizing the importance of building awareness as well as a clear brand identity for their companies. B-to-B marketers such as General Electric, IBM, Xerox, and many others also face the challenge of communicating how their products and services can be used to solve complex business problems and help other companies run their businesses and achieve their goals.[51] IMC Perspective 8–2 discusses how Siemens, the German-based electronics and engineering company, developed the "Answers" campaign to build awareness, as well as a brand identity for the company in the U.S. market.

## Developing the Major Selling Idea

It is difficult to pinpoint the inspiration for a big idea or teach advertising creatives an easy way to find one. As noted earlier, Arthur Kover conducted a study of advertising copywriters to understand how they approach the creative process and search for big ideas. He found that they view the purpose of a big idea as breaking through the advertising clutter and delivering a message.[52] Advertising professor John Rossiter argues most copywriters focus on communicating the *key benefit claim,* which refers to the benefit thought by the copywriter to be the key to selling the advertised product. He notes that most creative ideas are based on finding ways to dramatically and effectively convey the key benefit claim.[53] As noted earlier, the key benefit claim is often explicit in the tagline that is used as the basis for the advertising campaign such as the "I'm Lovin It!" theme for McDonald's. However, the creative team must still work to develop effective ways to communicate this message in the executions of the advertising and other components of the IMC program.

There are myriad ways that creative personnel can approach the search for big ideas and how to execute them. However, over the years several dominant approaches have emerged that can guide the creative team's search for a major selling idea and the development of effective advertising. Among the four best-known approaches are the following:

- Using a unique selling proposition.
- Creating a brand image.
- Finding the inherent drama.
- Positioning.

EXHIBIT 8–16

This Colgate Total ad uses a unique selling proposition

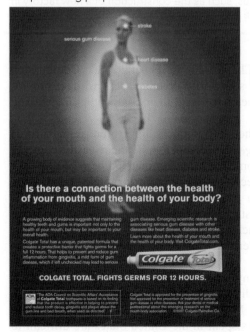

**Unique Selling Proposition**  The concept of the **unique selling proposition (USP)** was developed by Rosser Reeves, former chair of the Ted Bates agency, and is described in his influential book *Reality in Advertising.* Reeves noted three characteristics of unique selling propositions:

1.  Each advertisement must make a proposition to the consumer. Not just words, not just product puffery, not just show-window advertising. Each advertisement must say to each reader: "Buy this product and you will get this benefit."
2.  The proposition must be one that the competition either cannot or does not offer. It must be unique either in the brand or in the claim.
3.  The proposition must be strong enough to move the mass millions, that is, pull over new customers to your brand.[54]

Reeves said the attribute claim or benefit that forms the basis of the USP should dominate the ad and be emphasized through repetitive advertising. An example of advertising based on a USP is the campaign for Colgate's Total toothpaste (Exhibit 8–16). The brand has a unique, patented formula that creates a protective barrier that fights germs for 12 hours which helps reduce and prevent gum disease.

For Reeves's approach to work, there must be a truly unique product or service attribute, benefit, or inherent advantage that can be used in the claim. The approach may require considerable research on the product and consumers, not only to determine the USP but also to

# IMC Perspective 8–2 > > >

## Siemens Finds the Right Answer

Four years before Klaus Kleinfeld became the CEO of Siemens Corp, the global behemoth based in Munich, Germany, he was passing through customs at JFK International Airport in New York when he had a troubling experience. When asked who he worked for in the United States, Kleinfeld proudly answered Siemens, assuming that the agent would recognize the German company that is a powerhouse in electronics and engineering and operates in the industry, energy, health care, and Infrastructure/cities sectors. The agent responded by saying: "That's a great company; I buy their furniture all the time" as he mistook the 164-year-old Siemens for *Seaman's*, a New York–based furniture store founded in 1933. Kleinfeld, who was moving to the United States to become COO at the company's U.S. headquarters, was beside himself that one of the largest companies in the world with more than $100 billion in revenue (including $20 billion in the United States) was clearly not a household name in the United States as it was in Germany. Making matters worse was the fact that the lack of awareness of Siemens or confusion with the furniture brand was very common in the United States. However, there was a positive outcome from Kleinfeld's distressing exchange with the customs agent: It would become the catalyst for the company to renew its focus on marketing and lead to a multifaceted branding campaign just a few years later.

In 2007, Siemens launched a comprehensive, global advertising campaign called "Answers" that sought to unify the company's diverse business units into one brand identity. The campaign was similar in size and scope to IBM's "Smarter" and General Electric's "Imagination," both of which resonated strongly with consumers and business executives and helped brand the companies as more than just computer and appliance manufacturers, respectively. The "Answers" campaign took an informative, solutions-focused angle to its print and television ads, opting for emotional imagery and words that tied Siemens' B-to-B offerings to the everyday lives of the American people. For example, one of the print ads posed the question: "How can disease be detected before it strikes?" The Siemens answer was "early detection and prevention" as the ad copy went on to explain how Siemens was combining state-of-the-art laboratory diagnostics with imaging technologies to enable early disease detection. The initial results, according to internal research conducted by Siemens, was an increase in brand awareness in the U.S. market over the previous year. But despite the success "Answers" had achieved in a short period of time, further research suggested there was still some confusion about Siemens' business offerings. As such, Siemens' advertising agency, Ogilvy & Mather, which created the branding template, recognized that more work was needed to shape the company's identity as well as communicate its advertising agency, Ogilvy & Mather, which created the branding template, recognized that more work was needed to shape the company's identity as well as communicate its product and service offerings. The agency spent 18 months interviewing 50 Siemens executives and over 100 Siemens customers and prospects.

In 2009, during a recessionary period in which rivals such as General Electric were slashing marketing spending, Siemens *increased* its marketing budget for the "Answers" campaign, working with Ogilvy to implement new advertisements that emphasized Siemens' impact on local economies across America. This second phase of the campaign was called "Somewhere in America" and was designed to assure prospects that doing business with Siemens would help the U.S. economy during the recession. It included webisode documentaries that appeared on the company's website and on its YouTube channel that emphasized Siemens' impact on local economies, such as the construction of a new factory in

document the claim. As we will see in Chapter 20, the Federal Trade Commission objects to advertisers' making claims of superiority or uniqueness without providing supporting data. Also, some companies have sued their competitors for making unsubstantiated uniqueness claims.[55]

Advertisers must also consider whether the unique selling proposition affords them a *sustainable competitive advantage* that competitors cannot easily copy. In the packaged-goods field in particular, companies quickly match a brand feature for feature, so advertising based on USPs becomes obsolete. For example, a few years ago MillerCoors introduced MGD 64, a 64-calorie version of its Miller Genuine Draft brand and the lowest-calorie domestic beer on the market. However, within a year its major rival Anheuser-Busch launched Bud Select 55, which contained only 55 calories, after noting the success Miller had with its ultra-low-calorie beer.[56]

**Creating a Brand Image** In many product and service categories, competing brands are so similar that it is very difficult to find or create a unique attribute or benefit to use as the major selling idea. Many of the packaged-goods products that account for most of the advertising dollars spent in the United States are difficult to a rural Kansas town and the expansion of a manufacturing plant in Ohio. This localized marketing approach was so effective that Siemens ran similar campaigns in other markets such as China and South America.

Siemens has evidence that the Answers campaign has indeed been the answer to the company's identity problem in the U.S. market with brand awareness increasing as well as Google search referrals and page views on Siemens' website, which went from 200,000 views in 2010 to more than 700,000 per month a year later. The company feels that it now has a clear brand identity going forward to help in overall future revenue growth. Siemens continues to use the "Answers" campaign, which is constantly evolving to keep the messaging fresh and to focus on important issues such as sustainability, manufacturing, and IT. In 2012, Siemens launched a new phase of the campaign called "Answers for America" that focuses on the tangible impact the company is having in America today and features customer and community examples. The TV commercials, print and digital ads, and web documentaries show the impact of Siemens' technologies in areas such as health care, energy, and American cities.

Siemens' experience with the "Answers" campaign underscores the challenges many B-to-B marketers around the world face as they feel that their company is misunderstood or there is a lack of recognition of what they do. These companies often struggle in communicating the myriad of products and services they offer to other businesses or to consumers who may only indirectly use their products or not even realize when they are doing so on a daily basis. For example, Xerox is predominantly known as a copier company, even

Energizing our grids and our economy.

siemens.com/answers

though 50 percent of its revenues come from other types of business services. In 2010, however, the company tried to shed that label by launching its "Ready for Business" campaign that highlighted Xerox's B-to-B offerings for major clients such as Marriott and Virgin America. According to Xerox vice president of global advertising Barbara Basney, the goal of the "Ready for Business" campaign was to "reposition the brand where we're not just a technology company, but a business services company, and help people better understand what we do for other companies and brands behind the scenes."

General Electric has taken a similar approach in educating consumers about what the company does and how it helps other high-profile companies conduct business and achieve their goals. In 2012, as part of its "GE Works" campaign, the company ran a commercial on the Super Bowl, the goal of which was to "humanize" the tech giant. The spot featured GE employees talking about how turbines they build provide power to Anheuser-Busch's InBev plants that keep Budweiser beer cold during the brewing process. This spot, and subsequent ads in the campaign, were very powerful and helped GE achieve its goal of making the brand easier to understand for the consumers, many of whom are businesspeople. "The average person isn't buying a turbine," said GE director of creative content Andrew Goldberg, but the average person is turning on their light and possibly reaching into their cold fridge and grabbing a beer."

Sources: "New Siemens Campaign from Ogilvy Features 'Answers,'" *PR Newswire*, February 7, 2012, www.prnewswire.com/news-releases/new-siemens-campaign-from-ogilvy-features-answers-138860189.html; Christine Birkner, "Success by Association," *Marketing News*, April 30, 2013, pp. 14–18; Piet Levy, "The Right Answer," *Marketing News*, September 15, 2011, pp. 19–22.

YTC 08–13

Siemens Answers

youtube.com/10ebelch

differentiate on a functional or performance basis. The creative strategy used to sell these products is based on the development of a strong, memorable identity for the brand through **image advertising**.

David Ogilvy popularized the idea of brand image in his famous book *Confessions of an Advertising Man*. Ogilvy said that with image advertising, "every advertisement should be thought of as a contribution to the complex symbol which is the brand image." He argued that the image or personality of the brand is particularly important when brands are similar:

> The greater the similarity between brands, the less part reason plays in brand selection. There isn't any significant difference between the various brands of whiskey, or cigarettes, or beer. They are all about the same. And so are the cake mixes and the detergents and the margarines. The manufacturer who dedicates his advertising to building the most sharply defined personality for his brand will get the largest share of the market at the highest profit. By the same token, the manufacturers who will find themselves up the creek are those shortsighted opportunists who siphon off their advertising funds for promotions.[57]

Image advertising has become increasingly popular and is used as the main selling idea for a variety of products and services, including soft drinks, liquor, cigarettes,

**EXHIBIT 8–17**
bebe uses advertising to build an image as a sexy and stylish brand

**EXHIBIT 8–18**
Advertising for Hallmark often uses inherent drama

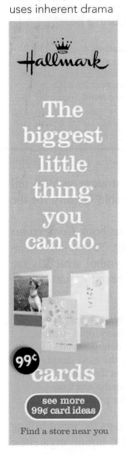

cars, airlines, financial services, perfume/colognes, and clothing. Many consumers wear designer jeans or Ralph Lauren polo shirts or drink certain brands of beer or soft drinks because of the image of these brands. The key to successful image advertising is developing an image that will appeal to product users. This is often done by associating a brand with certain symbols or artifacts that have cultural meaning. For example, Marlboro became the leading brand of cigarettes by using advertising that associates the brand with the cowboy, who is perceived as rugged, individualistic, and a symbol of freedom and independence. Many fashion brands build an image by using ads that feature attractive models and visual appeals that convey psychosocial associations and feelings such as sexy, stylish, glamorous, and sophisticated. Advertising for bebe embodies many of these image characteristics as a way of building an emotional connection with young women who are interested in style and fashion (Exhibit 8–17).

**Finding the Inherent Drama**  Another approach to determining the major selling idea is finding the **inherent drama** or characteristic of the product that makes the consumer purchase it. The inherent drama approach expresses the advertising philosophy of Leo Burnett, founder of the Leo Burnett agency in Chicago. Burnett said inherent drama "is often hard to find but it is always there, and once found it is the most interesting and believable of all advertising appeals."[58] He believed advertising should be based on a foundation of consumer benefits with an emphasis on the dramatic element in expressing those benefits.

Burnett advocated a down-home type of advertising that presents the message in a warm and realistic way. Some of the more famous ads developed by his agency using the inherent-drama approach are for McDonald's, Maytag appliances, Kellogg cereals, and Hallmark cards. For example, during the recent recession Burnett developed an emotion-based campaign for Hallmark, touting a greeting card as "The biggest little thing you can do." The ads emphasized the gratitude and appreciation that can come from a small gesture such as sending a card and promoted the 99-cent line of cards Hallmark had been selling for many years. The campaign featured a series of 15-second TV commercials that showed how spouses, children, and mentors respond to unexpected cards and used John Mayer's "Say What You Need to Say" as a musical backdrop for the message. The campaign also used rich media Internet banner ads such as the one shown in Exhibit 8–18 that, when clicked on and opened, allowed the consumer to choose the card that is given to the person in the ad and then sit back and view the different reactions by the person who receives it.[59]

**Positioning**  The concept of *positioning* as a basis for advertising strategy was introduced by Jack Trout and Al Ries in the early 1970s and has become a popular basis of creative development.[60] The basic idea is that advertising is used to establish or "position" the product or service in a particular place in the consumer's mind. Positioning is done for companies as well as for brands. Many of the top brands in various product and service categories have retained their market leadership because they have established and maintained a strong position or identity in the minds of consumers.[61] For example, Crest has built and maintained the success of its toothpaste based on the position of cavity prevention, while BMW's positioning of its car as the "ultimate driving machine" transcends and helps differentiate its entire product line.

Positioning is also done for entire companies as well as various divisions of large corporations. For example, General Electric positions itself as an innovative and imaginative company that is making a difference in the world by building the energy, health, transportation, and technology infrastructure for the new millennium. Exhibit 8–19 shows an ad from GE's Healthyimagination campaign which focuses on how the company is changing health care delivery in more than 100 countries by focusing on early diagnosis, intervention, and prevention of illness.

PORTABLE ECG TECHNOLOGY THAT FITS IN A BACKPACK

IS HELPING ENSURE THAT PEOPLE IN REMOTE AREAS

ARE NEVER FAR FROM QUALITY HEALTHCARE.

IT'S WHAT WE CALL HEALTHYMAGINATION,

AND IT'S HAPPENING RIGHT

NOW.

*GE* imagination at work          healthy**magination**.com

**EXHIBIT 8–19**
General Electric positions itself as an innovative company in areas such as health care

**EXHIBIT 8–20**
Advertising for Pennzoil and Quaker State positions the brands differently

Trout and Ries originally described positioning as the image consumers had of the brand in relation to competing brands in the product or service category, but the concept has been expanded beyond direct competitive positioning. As discussed in Chapter 2, products can be positioned on the basis of product attributes, price/quality, usage or application, product users, or product class. Any of these can spark a major selling idea that becomes the basis of the creative strategy and results in the brand's occupying a particular place in the minds of the target audience. Since positioning can be done on the basis of a distinctive attribute, the positioning and unique selling proposition approaches can overlap. Positioning approaches have been used as the foundation for a number of successful creative strategies. In some situations marketers recognize that they must adapt their positioning strategy for different market segments. For example, athletic apparel company Under Armour has been expanding beyond its traditional male-dominated market and generates a significant percentage of its sales from women. IMC Perspective 8–3 discusses how Under Armour has changed its positioning and approach to advertising as well as other parts of its IMC program such as its social media strategy to better connect with women.

Positioning is often the basis of a firm's creative strategy when it has multiple brands competing in the same market. For example, the two top-selling brands of motor oil, Pennzoil and Quaker State, became part of the same company following a merger a few years ago and are now owned by the Shell Oil Company. The company creates separate identities for the two brands by positioning them differently and targeting a slightly different group of motor oil consumers for each.[62] Pennzoil is positioned as a brand that stands for protection and is targeted at the "Active Specifier" or person who will most likely pay to have their oil changed. Quaker State/Q uses a performance positioning and targets the "Enthusiast" segment that is involved in maintaining their car and will most likely purchase their own oil and install it themselves. Exhibit 8–20 shows ads for each brand reflecting these positioning themes.

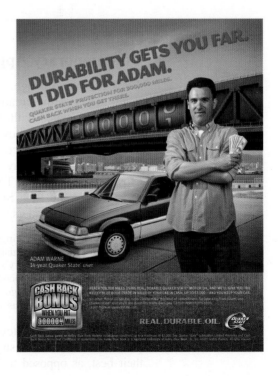

# IMC Perspective 8–3 > > >

## Under Armour Changes Its Positioning Strategy for Women

For many years, companies that sell athletic shoes, equipment, and apparel such as Nike, adidas, Reebok, and Under Armour were focused primarily on the male market. The positioning strategy used by these companies for their products often involved choosing a "side" when it came to gender and most of their advertising and promotion efforts were oriented to males. However, these companies recognize that gender lines are blurring in the sports and fitness markets; women are just as physically active as men and make up a high percentage of the fan base for many sports such as football, basketball, tennis, and golf. Sports companies and brands that were historically male dominated are now trying to connect with female consumers as well as recognizing that women represent a tremendous growth opportunity.

Such is the case for athletic apparel manufacturer Under Armour (UA), which was founded in 1996 by Kevin Plank, a former college football player at the University of Maryland. Plank began by selling compression clothing that could "wick" sweat away from an athlete's body to college sports teams out of the trunk of his car. UA achieved great success and grew very quickly in its early years by forming a brand identity that was associated with the raw emotion and muscle-filled world of football and other predominantly male team sports. As UA continued to grow and began moving beyond male-dominated sports such as football and baseball, the company made a conscious effort to bring more women to the brand. However, its initial strategy for attracting female customers was pretty simple: "shrink it and pink it" by creating smaller and more colorful versions of its men's apparel to fit the female form and expanding its product line to include items such as shorts, tops, and sport bras. While this strategy helped

generate incremental sales from female customers, the company recognized that in order to truly establish itself as a major player in women's athletic apparel, it would have to revamp its entire approach to this market. The company's first move in this direction came in 2008 when it hired an accomplished female marketer, Adrienne Lofton Shaw, to run its women's division. Immediately, Lofton Shaw challenged the management UA team to identify its core female customer. Unlike competitors such as Nike, Reebok, and lululemon, which market women's products in specific sports such as running, tennis, and yoga, UA realized that its sweet spot was young female athletes who, similar to their male counterparts, participated in team sports. As such, UA's first woman-focused marketing campaign featured young female athletes competing alongside men in 60-second TV spots that appeared primarily on teen-oriented programs airing on networks such as MTV and the CW.

While this was a good first step for UA's effort to target women, there was one major problem: only a small percentage of girls who participate in a team sport go on to play in college, and very few play an organized sport after graduation. Focus group research conducted with more than 250 women revealed that they viewed UA as a brand for serious and elite athletes, potentially alienating the "real women" who work out at fitness classes, in boot camps, or alone at the gym. Lofton Shaw observed that while UA's first campaign was successful in branding UA to girls who participated in team sports, the company was losing those same women to competing brands as they transitioned out of the world of organized sports. As such, UA's marketing team recognized that it would have to expand its product offerings and messaging to reach these women.

## Contemporary Approaches to the Big Idea

The USP, brand image, inherent-drama, and positioning approaches are often used as the basis of the creative strategy for ad campaigns. These creative styles have become associated with some of the most successful creative minds in advertising and their agencies.[63] However, many other creative approaches are available.

Some of the more contemporary advertising visionaries who have had a major influence on modern-day advertising include Hal Riney of Hal Riney & Partners, Lee Clow and Jay Chiat of TBWA/Chiat/Day, Dan Wieden of Wieden + Kennedy, and Jeff Goodby and Rich Silverstein of Goodby, Silverstein & Partners. In describing today's creative leaders, Anthony Vagnoni of *Advertising Age* writes:

> The modern creative kings don't write books, rarely give interviews or lay out their theories on advertising. They've endorsed no set of rules, professed no simple maxims like Mr. Ogilvy's famous "When you don't have anything to say, sing it." If pronouncements and books are out the window, what's replaced them is a conscious desire to lift the intelligence level of advertising. Today's leaders see advertising as an uplifting social force, as a way to inspire and entertain.[64]

Goodby and Silverstein note: "Advertising works best when it sneaks into people's lives, when it doesn't look or feel like advertising. It's about treating people at their best, as opposed to dealing with them at their lowest common denominator."

Insights gained from UA's consumer research revealed that social media would be the best way to connect with women who indicated that they spent a lot of time on Facebook as well as sites such as Pinterest, Twitter, and Tumblr. In April 2012, UA launched its first female-focused social media campaign titled "What's Beautiful." The campaign featured the creation of an online community in which it sought to juxtapose beauty and femininity alongside the effort and sweat that come with yoga, exercise classes, and gym sessions. Instead of inundating users with product placements and sales pitches, the company made the site largely user-generated. Women could create profiles, set workout goals, and encourage each other using traditional social features such as "likes" and comments. Users were also encouraged to post photos of themselves working out and submit inspirational stories. After a few months, UA selected the 10 most inspirational stories and invited those users to attend "Camp Sweat," an inaugural event held at a UA-branded athletic training facility in Florida that featured some of UA's professional athlete endorsers and trainers.

When the "What's Beautiful" campaign was launched the UA Facebook page had 100,000 followers. After just three months, that number grew to over 500,000 as UA was beginning to change the perception that it was only a brand for elite male athletes. The next step was to keep the momentum going. Following "What's Beautiful," UA created TV and digital spots that included modified versions of the iconic "We Must Protect This House. I Will." tagline used in Under Armour's male-oriented advertising. The new TV spots used the altered tagline, "No Matter What Sweat Every Day. I Will." and featured women working out very intensely in Under Armour gear in training settings that usually would be associated with male athletes. The 30- and 45-second spots aired on cable TV networks such as ESPN and MTV as well as nonsports websites like Gilt Group and DailyCandy. UA was now casting its net wider and moving beyond its core market of competitive, serious athletes.

When Under Armour hired Lofton Shaw in 2008, she was the only member of the women's team. Today, the UA women's division is UA's fastest-growing part of the company with over 30 members (10 in marketing and another 20 in product design) and women's apparel accounts for roughly 30 percent of the company's revenues. While Under Armour has expanded its offerings into the women's high-fashion market, it still is not losing sight of its roots. "There are stats that say in a few years there will be more girls participating in sports than boys," Lofton Shaw noted in an interview with *Advertising Age*. "From a generational level, young kids are being groomed to participate. We need to be part of the conversation early in a young girls' life. We've built the right product, we're dialed in, and we've got the right message. We just need to introduce our brand to more women, more often." Under Amour as well as other companies that are expanding their marketing efforts toward women recognize that they face a challenging balancing act: They must make women feel appreciated and empowered while not patronizing them. They also must be careful not to alienate their core male consumer as they market more to female customers. However, one thing for certain is that the old days of just "shrinking and pinking" are gone.

Sources: Molly Soat, "Moving Beyond Shrink It & Pink It," *Marketing News*, February 2013, pp. 32–36; Natalie Zmuda, "No More 'Shrinking It and Pinking It' at Under Armour," *Advertising Age*, September 23, 2012, http://adage.com/article/cmo-interviews/shrinking-pinking-armour/237375/.

YTC 08–15
**Under Armour**
youtube.com/10ebelch

They describe their creative formula as doing intelligent work that the public likes to see and that, at the same time, has a sales pitch.[65] Lee Clow says, "No rule book will tell you how to target the masses anymore. The best of us understand the sociocultural realities of people and how they interact with the media. If we didn't, we couldn't make the kinds of messages that people would be able to connect with."[66]

Specific agencies are by no means limited to any one creative approach. For example, the famous "Marlboro Country" campaign, a classic example of image advertising, was developed by Leo Burnett Co. Many different agencies have followed the unique selling proposition approach advocated by Rosser Reeves at Ted Bates. The challenge to the creative specialist or team is to find a major selling idea—whether it is based on a unique selling proposition, brand image, inherent drama, position in the market, or some other approach—and use it as a guide in developing an effective creative strategy.

Advertisers are facing major challenges in their search for the big idea in the new world of integrated marketing communications. They are faced with the challenge of developing creative ideas that can differentiate their brands and extend beyond traditional mass media. Most marketers and their agencies recognize that they must come up with big ideas that can be used across a variety of media and can engage consumers and enter into a dialogue with them.[67] The problem facing advertisers was noted recently by Jeff Goodby, co-chair of Goodby, Silverstein & Partners,

San Francisco, which was selected as Agency of the Year by the trade publication *Adweek* for its excellent creative work for clients such as Hyundai, Sprint, and Hewlett-Packard. In explaining the success of the agency and its ability to adapt, Goodby stated that "the company has changed more in the last two years than it did in the first 23. It's a necessary change and the whole business is going to have to change to exist. Nobody knows what advertising is anymore and the change in our company is a reaction to that."[68]

The challenge of developing creative advertising that captures the attention of consumers and impacts them has become even greater with the proliferation of new media. Lee Clow, now the chairman of TBWA/Media Arts Lab, which is Apple's lead creative agency and the 2013 honoree of the prestigious Lion of St. Mark award given to an individual for his or her contribution to creativity in advertising, was asked to comment on how advertising has changed over the past several decades and the creative challenge facing agencies. Clow responded as follows: "Brands have the ability to connect with people in all kinds of ways and have an ongoing dialogue and relationship with them as opposed to the monologue, how it used to be. We haven't come close to figuring out how to use all these new-media opportunities and most clients are very conflicted about what media they should use and why. They keep thinking there's some new silver bullet in the new media world that will allow them save money or find a new way to twist consumers' arms."[69] Clow summarizes the challenge facing those who work on the creative side in the new world of advertising quite well. However, marketers will continue to challenge their agencies to find innovative ideas and creative solutions for advertising and other forms of marketing communications.

## Summary

The creative development and execution of the advertising message are crucial parts of a firm's integrated marketing communications program and are often the key to the success of a marketing campaign. Marketers generally turn to ad agencies to develop, prepare, and implement their creative strategy since these agencies are specialists in the creative function of advertising. The creative specialist or team is responsible for developing an effective way to communicate the marketer's message to the customer. Other individuals on both the client and the agency sides work with the creative specialists to develop the creative strategy, implement it, and evaluate its effectiveness.

The challenge facing the writers, artists, and others who develop ads is to be creative and come up with fresh, unique, and appropriate ideas that can be used as solutions to communications problems. Creativity in advertising is a process of several stages, including preparation, incubation, illumination, verification, and revision. Various sources of information are available to help the creative specialists determine the best campaign theme, appeal, or execution style.

Creative strategy development is guided by specific goals and objectives and is based on a number of factors, including the target audience, the basic problem the advertising must address, the objectives the message seeks to accomplish, and the major selling idea or key benefit the advertiser wants to communicate. These factors are generally stated in a copy platform, which is a work plan used to guide development of the ad campaign. An important part of creative strategy is determining the major selling idea that will become the central theme of the campaign. There are several approaches to doing this, including using a unique selling proposition, creating a brand image, looking for inherent drama in the brand, and positioning.

## Key Terms

creative strategy p. 264
creative tactics p. 264
advertising creativity p. 269
divergence p. 269
relevance p. 269
account planning p. 276
general preplanning input p. 277

product- or service-specific
  preplanning input p. 278
problem detection p. 278
focus groups p. 279
ethnographic research p. 280
storyboard p. 282
animatic p. 282
advertising campaign p. 282

campaign theme p. 283
slogan (tagline) p. 283
creative brief p. 284
major selling idea p. 288
unique selling proposition (USP)
  p. 289
image advertising p. 291
inherent drama p. 292

## Discussion Questions

1. Evaluate the "Iconic Passion" branding platform and IMC campaign that the Lambesis agency created for Tacori. Why do you think this campaign has been so successful in creating a brand identity for Tacori and increasing sales of its jewelry products? (LO1, 3)

2. Digital and Social Media Perspective 8–1 discusses how the Wieden + Kennedy agency has created an effective advertising campaign for Old Spice Hair and Body Wash with popular ads such as "The Man Your Man Could Smell Like" commercial. Analyze this commercial from an advertising creativity perspective and discuss some of the reasons it has gone viral and generated nearly 45 million views on YouTube. Do you think this campaign is an effective way to sell a product such as body wash? Why or why not? (LO1)

3. The chapter discusses how the DDB agency was recently fired by Anheuser-Busch InBev even though the agency had created a number of award-winning advertisements for brands such as Budweiser and Bud Light. Evaluate the decision by AB InBev to dismiss DDB and hire a new agency given the excellent creative work it did for these brands through the years. (LO1)

4. Advertising creativity is viewed as the ability to generate unique and appropriate ideas that can be used as solutions to communication problems. This definition suggests that a creative ad is one that is novel but also relevant or appropriate. Find an example of an advertisement (either a print ad or TV commercial) that is novel but not necessarily relevant to the product or service. Discuss why the client would have approved this ad. (LO1)

5. Discuss the various factors that account for the way divergence can be achieved in advertising creativity. Find an example of an advertisement that reflects these various characteristics and explain how it does so. (LO1)

6. What is meant by ethnographic research? Discuss how this type of qualitative research might be used by an advertising agency during the preparation, illumination, and incubation stages of the creative process. Find an example of an advertising campaign that has used ethnographic research as input to the creative process. (LO2, 3)

7. Many advertising creative personnel are opposed to focus group research as they argue that it may inhibit the creative process. Discuss the problems, as well as the value, of using focus groups to evaluate advertising creative work. (LO2)

8. Assume that you have been hired as an account planner by an advertising agency and assigned to work on the advertising campaign for a new brand of bottled water. Describe the various types of general and product-specific preplanning input you might provide to the creative team. (LO2)

9. Discuss the role an advertising slogan plays in the development of an advertising campaign as well as some of the factors that should be considered in developing an effective tagline. Find an example of a good tagline as well as one that does not communicate effectively. Discuss the reasons why you view these as either good or bad examples of advertising slogans. (LO3)

10. IMC Perspective 8–2 discusses how Siemens developed the "Answers" campaign to increase awareness of the company and create a stronger brand identity. Evaluate the big idea used for the "Answers" campaign and discuss what other business-to-business marketers might learn from analyzing this campaign. (LO4)

11. Discuss the challenges Under Armour faces in the female market for exercise apparel. Evaluate the strategy behind the "What's Beautiful" campaign. Do you think this IMC campaign will be an effective way to position Under Armour as a brand for women? Why or why not? (LO4)

12. Find an example of an ad or campaign that you think reflects one of the approaches used to develop a major selling idea such as unique selling proposition, brand image, inherent drama, or positioning. Discuss how the major selling idea is reflected in this ad or campaign. (LO4)

## LEARNING OBJECTIVES

**LO1** To analyze various types of appeals that can be used in the development and implementation of an advertising message.

**LO2** To analyze the various creative execution styles that advertisers can use and the advertising situations where they are most appropriate.

**LO3** To analyze various tactical issues involved in the creation of print advertising and TV commercials.

**LO4** To consider how clients evaluate the creative work of their agencies and discuss guidelines for the evaluation and approval process.

# 9 Creative Strategy: Implementation and Evaluation

## TACO BELL GETS CONSUMERS TO "LIVE MÁS"

Taco Bell Corp. is a subsidiary of Yum! Brands, Inc., the world's largest restaurant company with nearly 40,000 restaurants in more than 125 countries. The Yum! brands, which also include KFC and Pizza Hut, are the global leaders in the chicken, pizza, and Mexican-style food categories. Taco Bell is the leading Mexican-inspired quick-service restaurant in the United States with nearly 6,000 locations across the country that serve more than 36 million customers every week. Taco Bell has had a number of creative advertising campaigns over the years, including the popular "Yo Quiero Taco Bell" campaign that featured a Chihuahua with an attitude who became a pop-culture and advertising icon. The ads featuring the dog helped generate the highest advertising awareness ever for the chain as well as burnish Taco Bell's image as a hip place to eat. Over the past decade Taco Bell ran a number of other successful advertising campaigns, including those using the "Run for the Border" and "Think Outside the Bun" themes.

While Taco Bell was able to weather the recent recession, in 2011, the company's sales stagnated as same store sales declined by 1 percent, which was in part attributed to some negative publicity resulting from a lawsuit regarding the composition of its ground beef. Taco Bell responded to the false claims quickly and aggressively with a national print and web campaign countering the unfounded charges, and it was withdrawn. Taco Bell is the largest and most profitable Yum! Brands chain in the United States and the company was looking for ideas to grow its store traffic and tweak its positioning. The company's marketing and agency teams decided it was time to move beyond the "Think Outside the Bun" campaign that had been running for a number of years and make the brand more vital and exciting to its core target market of cross-cultural millennials. In early 2012 Taco Bell introduced a new

campaign slogan, "LIVE MÁS" (*más* is Spanish for "more"), which it views as a bilingual phrase that sums up why the brand is attractive and relevant to young, hip, and cross-cultural consumers. The tagline also represents a movement of the brand from the idea of "food as fuel" to food as an experience and lifestyle. The senior vice president of strategic planning at DraftFCB, the agency that created the new campaign theme, explained the thinking behind it: "The brand has moved past the point of the idea of 'food as fuel.' Young people in our new multicultural landscape don't see it that way. They look at food as an experience. That's what the new Taco Bell will provide. And that's the story we're telling." Taco Bell's CEO, Greg Creed, concurred with the new strategy and positioning, noting that "our customers told us they want a more relevant Taco Bell, and we've taken numerous steps focusing on our food and improving the customer experience. 'Live Más' connects us back to our explorer roots and speaks to people with a genuine voice that feels much more true to who we are and what we believe in." Taco Bell has also been an innovator in the fast-food industry as they were the first to introduce the crunchy taco to the U.S. market, the first to offer free refills on beverages, and the first to team with another company to make a flavored taco shell from chips.

As part of its new strategy, Taco Bell rolled out a slate of new products and a new upscale menu called Cantina Bell, featuring higher-quality ingredients. The chain enlisted celebrity chef Lorena Garcia, a judge from NBC's *America's Next Great Restaurant* and a contestant on Bravo's *Top Chef Masters*, to create the menu and establish credibility behind the effort. However, Taco Bell sales really took off in the spring of 2012 when a new product line was introduced called Doritos Locos Tacos (DLTs), which was the product of a co-branding effort with snack food giant Frito-Lay. The idea for the DLTs came from a visit by CEO Greg Creed with Frito-Lay executives to discuss how to celebrate Taco Bell's upcoming 50th anniversary in 2012. A variety of flavors were tested before deciding on Nacho Cheese for the initial launch. The taco has a shell made from Nacho Cheese Doritos Chips and is served in custom packaging to prevent cheese dust from getting on consumers' fingers.

There was tremendous buzz prior to the launch of the new tacos, and Taco Bell took advantage of the excitement surrounding the introduction. A clock on Taco Bell's website ticked down the Doritos Locos Tacos launch and the winner of a Twitter contest was sent a truck loaded with the tacos. Consumers went "loco" for the new tacos; as more than 10 million were sold in just 10 days and within a year DLTs were accounting for nearly a quarter of all the taco sales at Taco Bell. In early 2013 Taco Bell launched the second flavor of the new tacos, Cool Ranch Doritos Locos Tacos, with its largest integrated marketing and consumer engagement effort ever. The campaign used television, radio, outdoor, digital, and cinema advertising, including a 3-D spot aired in movie theaters that featured a Doritos chip spinning and exploding with pieces of chip and seasoning flying out as it morphs in the Cool Ranch DLT Supreme.

A number of the TV spots used consumer-generated ideas that were tied to buzz about the new product as the marketing team at Taco Bell searched social media for user experiences and reactions to the Doritos Locos Tacos. For example, one of the commercials was based on a YouTube video showing a consumer who drove 900 miles to find a DLT while another featured a series of Instagram posts strung together showing consumers taking their first bite of the Cool Ranch DLT. To build awareness and buzz prior to the launch of the Cool Ranch DLT, social media sites such as YouTube, Twitter, and Facebook were used to provide sneak peeks of the new flavor as fans identified as social media influencers were invited to sample the product early by giving them a secret passcode. Once the passcode was unlocked, the fans were prompted to spread the word via social media so others could try the product as well at password-only "speakeasy" events in New York, Dallas, and Los Angeles.

The launch was also supported by a robust television campaign that was inspired by consumer responses to the original Nacho Cheese DLT and subsequent demand for a Cool Ranch version, which is the second most popular Doritos flavor. The launch spot, "World's Most Obvious Idea,"

capitalized on the group swell of consumers wondering when Taco Bell would make a Cool Ranch verison. Fifteen-second spots were also created that featured the reaction of consumers and celebrities as they try the new taco for the first time. The campaign also invited fans to post to Instagram or tweet their best #wow or #duh face—using those specific hash tags, followed by #CoolRanchDLT—for a chance to see their photo reactions on a giant billboard in Times Square. The invitations also appeared on DLT packages as well as beverage cups as part of the integrated campaign. To take advantage of the popularity of the DLTs, Frito-Lay rolled out a new line of Doritos in a "Taco Bell flavor" as a limited-time product.

The tremendous success of Doritos Locos Tacos has not been the only thing generating excitement and buzz for Taco Bell; a commercial created for the 2013 Super Bowl based on the "LIVE MÁS" theme was also a big hit. The 60-second spot called "Viva Young" features a group of senior citizens sneaking out of their retirement home late at night and embarking on an epic night of partying that includes dancing, getting tattoos, sneaking into neighbors' swimming pools, and other escapades. They eventually end up, of course, at a Taco Bell for a "Fourthmeal" before returning to the home as the sun comes up. A Spanish version of Fun's hit song "We Are Young" was used as the music in the commercial, which was one of the most popular spots in the Super Bowl and also the ad receiving the most buzz on social media. While some ad critics questioned how Taco Bell's core audience of millennials might respond to a commercial featuring a posse of older adults behaving badly, surveys showed that young people loved the spot and the message it sent that you are never too old to LIVE MÁS. Taco Bell appears to be well on its way to getting consumers of all ages to experience more and LIVE MÁS.

Sources: "Taco Bell Implements Its Largest Marketing Campaign Ever, QSRweb.com, March 7, 2013, www.qsrweb .com/article/209459/Taco-Bell-implements-its-largest-marketing-campaign-ever; Emma Bazilian, "Taco Bell, Doritos Dominated Super Bowl Social Media," Adweek, February 4, 2013, www.adweek.com/news/advertising-branding/taco-bell-doritos-dominated-super-bowl-social-media-147029; Candace Choi, "Doritos to Roll Out Chips in 'Taco Bell' Flavor," Bloomberg Businessweek, January 31, 2013, http://businessweek.com/ap/2013-01-31/doritos-to-roll-out-chips-in-taco-bell-flavor; Mike Hammer, "Taco Bell Gets a More Relevant Attitude," Adweek, March 11, 2012, www.adweek.com/sa-article/taco-bell-gets-more-relevant-attitude-138823; Maureen Morrison, "Taco Bell to Exchange 'Think Outside the Bun' for 'Live Mas,'" Advertising Age, February 21, 2012, http://adage.com/article/news/taco-bell-exchange-bun-live-mas/232849/.

YTC 09-01
Taco Bell
youtube.com/10ebelch

In Chapter 8, we discussed the importance of advertising creativity and examined the various steps in the creative process. We focused on determining what the advertising message should communicate. This chapter focuses on *how* the message will be executed. It examines various appeals and execution styles that can be used to develop the ad and tactical issues involved in the design and production of effective advertising messages. We conclude by presenting some guidelines clients can use to evaluate the creative work of their agencies.

# APPEALS AND EXECUTION STYLES

The **advertising appeal** refers to the approach used to attract the attention of consumers and/or to influence their feelings toward the product, service, or cause. An advertising appeal can also be viewed as "something that moves people, speaks to their wants or needs, and excites their interest."[1] The **creative execution style** is the way a particular appeal is turned into an advertising message presented to the consumer. According to William Weilbacher:

> The appeal can be said to form the underlying content of the advertisement, and the execution the way in which that content is presented. Advertising appeals and executions are usually independent of each other; that is, a particular appeal can be executed in a variety of ways and a particular means of execution can be applied to a variety of advertising appeals. Advertising appeals tend to adapt themselves to all media, whereas some kinds of executional devices are more adaptable to some media than others.[2]

## Advertising Appeals

LO 09-1

Many different appeals can be used as the basis for advertising messages. At the broadest level, these approaches are generally broken into two categories: informational/rational appeals and emotional appeals. In this section, we focus on ways to use rational and emotional appeals as part of a creative strategy. We also consider how rational and emotional appeals can be combined in developing the advertising message.

**Informational/Rational Appeals**   **Informational/rational appeals** focus on the consumer's practical, functional, or utilitarian need for the product or service and emphasize features of a product or service and/or the benefits or reasons for owning or using a particular brand. The content of these messages emphasizes facts, learning, and the logic of persuasion.[3] Rational-based appeals tend to be informative, and advertisers using them generally attempt to convince consumers that their product or service has a particular attribute(s) or provides a specific benefit that satisfies their needs. Their objective is to persuade the target audience to buy the brand because it is the best available or does a better job of meeting consumers' needs. For example, Exhibit 9–1 shows an ad featuring professional golfer Fred Couples that uses a rational appeal by focusing on the various features and benefits of Bridgestone tires.

Many rational motives can be used as the basis for advertising appeals, including comfort, convenience, economy, health, and sensory benefits such as touch, taste, and smell. Other rational motives or purchase criteria commonly used in advertising include quality, dependability, durability, efficiency, efficacy, and performance. The particular features, benefits, or evaluative criteria that are important to consumers and can serve as the basis of an informational/rational appeal vary from one product or service category to another as well as among various market segments.

Weilbacher identified several types of advertising appeals that fall under the category of rational approaches, among them feature, competitive advantage, favorable price, news, and product/service popularity appeals.

Ads that use a *feature appeal* focus on the dominant traits of the product or service. These ads tend to be highly informative and present the customer with a

CHAPTER 9

**EXHIBIT 9–1**

A rational appeal is used to promote the features and benefits of Bridgestone tires

**EXHIBIT 9–2**

Red Bull uses a feature appeal to promote its product benefits to students

number of important product attributes or features that will lead to favorable attitudes and can be used as the basis for a rational purchase decision. Technical and high-involvement products such as automobiles often use this type of advertising appeal. However, a feature appeal can be used for a variety of products and services. These types of appeals often show how product attributes can result in specific benefits for consumers. For example, Exhibit 9–2 shows an ad for Red Bull that focuses on the various ingredients contained in the energy drink and the benefits they provide such as enhanced performance, endurance, and concentration. This particular ad is targeted to students, who are an important target market for energy drinks, and suggests that Red Bull can help you stay awake and alert when studying for exams.

When a *competitive advantage appeal* is used, the advertiser makes either a direct or an indirect comparison to another brand (or brands) and usually claims superiority on one or more attributes. This type of appeal was discussed in Chapter 6 under Comparative Advertising.

A *favorable price appeal* makes the price offer the dominant point of the message. Price appeal advertising is used most often by retailers to announce sales, special offers, or low everyday prices. Price appeal ads are often used by national advertisers during recessionary times. Many fast-food chains have made price an important part of their marketing strategy through promotional deals and "value menus" or lower overall prices, and their advertising strategy is designed to communicate this. Many other types of advertisers use price appeals as well, such as airlines and car-rental companies. Price-based appeals are also often used by business-to-business marketers to advertise products and/or services and promote their value or affordability. For example, the Hewlett-Packard advertisement shown in Exhibit 9–3 promotes the affordability of the HP Officejet Pro printer for business use. The ad copy explains how it can print in color at a cost that is up to 50 percent less per page than a laser printer and consumes less energy. The visual portion of the ad also uses very vivid colors to represent the number 50 and deliver a message regarding the quality of the color printing capabilities of the Officejet Pro.

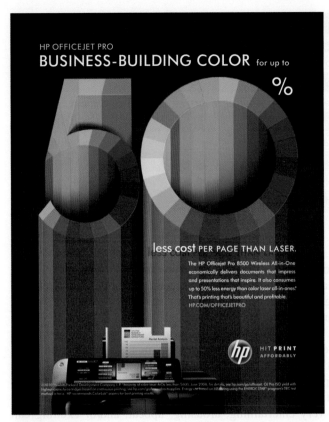

**EXHIBIT 9–3**
HP advertises the affordability of color printing to businesses that use the Officejet Pro

*News appeals* are those in which some type of news or announcement about the product, service, or company dominates the ad. This type of appeal can be used for a new product or service or to inform consumers of significant modifications or improvements. This appeal works best when a company has important news it wants to communicate to its target market. For example, airlines sometimes use news appeals when they begin offering service to new cities or opening new routes as a way of informing consumers as well as generating media interest that can result in publicity for them.

*Product/service popularity appeals* stress the popularity of a product or service by pointing out the number of consumers who use the brand, the number who have switched to it, the number of experts who recommend it, or its leadership position in the market. The main point of this advertising appeal is that the wide use of the brand proves its quality or value and other customers should consider using it. The ad shown in Exhibit 9–4 uses a popularity appeal by noting how the TaylorMade R1 is the number 1 driver on the PGA tour. Ads such as this are used to implement TaylorMade's marketing strategy, which focuses on innovation, the technological superiority of its golf equipment, and the popularity and use of its clubs by tour professionals who exert a strong influence on the purchase decisions of amateur golfers.

**Emotional Appeals** **Emotional appeals** relate to the customers' social and/or psychological needs for purchasing a product or service. Many consumers' motives for their purchase decisions are emotional, and their feelings about a brand can be more important than knowledge of its features or attributes. Advertisers for many products and services view rational, information-based appeals as dull. Many advertisers believe appeals to consumers' emotions work better at selling brands that do not differ markedly from competing brands, since rational differentiation of them is difficult.[4]

Many feelings or needs can serve as the basis for advertising appeals designed to influence consumers on an emotional level, as shown in Figure 9–1. These appeals are based on the psychological states or feelings directed to the self (such as pleasure or excitement), as well as those with a more social orientation (such as status

**EXHIBIT 9–4**
TaylorMade promotes the popularity of its drivers among professional golfers

## FIGURE 9–1

Bases for Emotional Appeals

| Personal States or Feelings | | Social-Based Feelings |
|---|---|---|
| Safety | Arousal/stimulation | Recognition |
| Security | Sorrow/grief | Status |
| Fear | Pride | Respect |
| Love | Achievement/accomplishment | Involvement |
| Affection | Self-esteem | Embarrassment |
| Happiness | Actualization | Affiliation/belonging |
| Joy | Pleasure | Rejection |
| Nostalgia | Ambition | Acceptance |
| Sentiment | Comfort | Approval |
| Excitement | | |

or recognition). The ad shown in Exhibit 9–5, featuring actor actor/singer Victoria Justice appeals to emotional motives such as self-esteem and pride and is part of the "Body by Milk" integrated marketing campaign created by America's Milk Processors. The ads are targeted at teens and designed to educate them about the nutritional benefits of milk and how it can help them look their best.

Advertisers can use emotional appeals in many ways in their creative strategy. Kamp and Macinnis note that commercials often rely on the concept of *emotional integration,* whereby they portray the characters in the ad as experiencing an emotional benefit or outcome from using a product or service.[5] Ads using humor, sex, and other appeals that are very entertaining, arousing, upbeat, and/or exciting can affect the emotions of consumers and put them in a favorable frame of mind. Many TV advertisers use poignant ads that bring a lump to viewers' throats. Hallmark, Campbell's Soup, Nike, and McDonald's often create commercials that evoke feelings of warmth, nostalgia, and/or sentiment. Marketers use emotional appeals in hopes that the positive feeling they evoke will transfer to the brand and/or company. Research shows that positive mood states and feelings created by advertising can have a favorable effect on consumers' evaluations of a brand.[6] Studies also show that emotional advertising is better remembered than nonemotional messages.[7]

The effectiveness of emotion-based appeals has also been documented in research conducted by Hamish Pringle and Peter Field and is discussed in their new book *Brand Immortality.*[8] Pringle and Field analyzed 880 case studies of successful advertising campaigns submitted for the United Kingdom–based Institute of Practitioners in Advertising Effectiveness Award competition over the past three decades and included campaigns from the UK as well as international competitions. Their analysis compared advertising campaigns that relied primarily on emotional appeals versus those that used rational persuasion and information. A key finding from their study is that advertising campaigns with purely emotional content are nearly twice as likely to generate large profit gains than campaigns using only rational content. The emotional-only campaigns were also more effective than those that used a combination of emotional and rational content. Their research also showed that one of the reasons why emotional campaigns work so well is that they reduce price sensitivity and strengthen the ability of brands to charge a price premium which contributes to profitability. They also found that emotional campaigns continue to work well during economic downturns such as the recent global recession.[9]

Many marketers rely on emotional appeals as the basis for their advertising campaigns. For example, retailer JCPenney recently

**EXHIBIT 9–5**

This milk ad appeals to emotional motives such as self-esteem and pride

Look good. Feel victorious. got milk?

**EXHIBIT 9–6**
JCPenney uses emotional advertising to connect with consumers

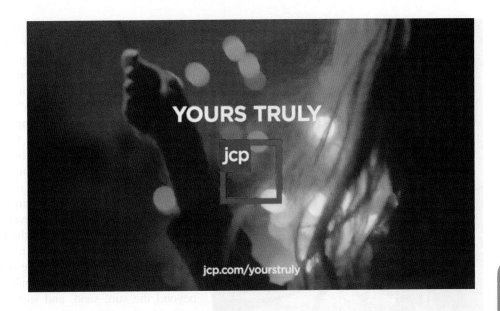

YOURS TRULY.

jcp

jcp.com/yourstruly

YTC 09–02

JCP

youtube.com/10ebelch

introduced an emotional-based campaign themed around the tagline "Yours Truly, JCP." The initial ad in the campaign was a poignant 90-second spot that took the form of a love letter from JCP to America and was addressed to more than 20 types of people, from dreamers to the faithful, arrayed against heartfelt scenes of daily life. The message in the ads was: "You deserve to look better. You deserve to live better. That's what we've believed for 100 years. And we will believe for 100 more."[10] A number of shorter commercials that carry the same theme but promote individual brands available at JCPenney—such as Levi's, Cosabella, Pearl by Georgina Chapman, and Joe Fresh—are also part of the campaign. The integrated campaign has a micro website (jcp/yourstruly) as well that promotes the "you deserve to look better and live better" theme and various brands (Exhibit 9–6).

Another reason for using emotional appeals is to influence consumers' interpretations of their product usage experience. One way of doing this is through what is known as transformational advertising. A **transformational ad** is defined as "one which associates the experience of using (consuming) the advertised brand with a unique set of psychological characteristics which would not typically be associated with the brand experience to the same degree without exposure to the advertisement."[11]

Transformational ads create feelings, images, meanings, and beliefs about the product or service that may be activated when consumers use it, transforming their interpretation of the usage experience. Christopher Puto and William Wells note that a transformational ad has two characteristics:

1. It must make the experience of using the product richer, warmer, more exciting, and/or more enjoyable than that obtained solely from an objective description of the advertised brand.
2. It must connect the experience of the advertisement so tightly with the experience of using the brand that consumers cannot remember the brand without recalling the experience generated by the advertisement.[12]

Transformational advertising can help differentiate a product or service by making the consumption experience more enjoyable by suggesting the type of experiences consumers might have when they consume the product or service. This type of advertising is often used by companies in the travel industry to help consumers envision the experience or feeling they might have when they take a trip such as a cruise or visit a particular destination.

**EXHIBIT 9–7**

Corona's "Find Your Beach" campaign is an excellent example of transformational advertising

**EXHIBIT 9–8**

Advertising for American Airlines often appeals to emotional as well as rational motives

Image advertising, which is designed to give a company or brand a unique association or personality, is often transformational in nature. It is designed to create a certain feeling or mood that is activated when a consumer uses a particular product or service. An excellent example of this type of advertising is the "Find Your Beach" campaign for the import beer brand Corona Extra. Advertising for Corona over the years has helped establish the brand as the beer to drink when relaxing on a white-sand tropical beach. The "Find Your Beach" campaign extends this theme to other consumption situations by showing people enjoying Corona on a city rooftop, during a break from skiing, on an airplane, or in a bar in the city with a group of friends. However, the final scene in all of the spots takes the viewer back to the familiar tropical-beach scene and concludes with an onscreen super that instructs viewers to "Find your beach." The ads are designed to preserve Corona's iconic beach image while extending the Corona state of mind beyond the sun, sand, and surf. The campaign also includes print ads that help position the brand as a little more urban, and are designed to appeal to consumers in major markets[13] (Exhibit 9–7).

**Combining Rational and Emotional Appeals**   In many advertising situations, the decision facing the creative specialist is not whether to choose an emotional or a rational appeal but, rather, determining how to combine the two approaches. As noted copywriters David Ogilvy and Joel Raphaelson have stated:

> Few purchases of any kind are made for entirely rational reasons. Even a purely functional product such as laundry detergent may offer what is now called an emotional benefit—say, the satisfaction of seeing one's children in bright, clean clothes. In some product categories the rational element is small. These include soft drinks, beer, cosmetics, certain personal care products, and most old-fashioned products. And who hasn't experienced the surge of joy that accompanies the purchase of a new car?[14]

Consumer purchase decisions are often made on the basis of both emotional and rational motives, and attention must be given to both elements in developing effective advertising. Purchase decisions regarding services can also be based on both rational and emotional motives. For example, many consumers choose an airline based on factors such as price, availability, arrival and/or departure time, and the ability to earn miles or points for their travel. However, airlines recognize that it is also important to appeal to emotional factors in competing for passengers. Frequent flyers in particular often become loyal to one airline based on emotional as well as rational motives, and some airlines use ads that are designed to connect to these travelers on an emotional level. For example, American Airlines has been running its "We Know Why You Fly" campaign since 2004, which was created to demonstrate that American has a genuine understanding of the frequent flyers with respect to how and why they fly. The TV commercials and print ads used in the campaign are designed to illustrate how American can better help flyers navigate through their entire travel experience (Exhibit 9–8). The award-winning campaign has helped American connect emotionally with its most valuable customers and increase their brand loyalty.[15]

Advertising researchers and agencies have given considerable thought to the relationship between rational and emotional motives in consumer decision making and how advertising influences both. McCann Erickson Worldwide, in conjunction with advertising professor

**FIGURE 9–2**

Levels of Relationships with Brands

Michael Ray, developed a proprietary research technique known as *emotional bonding*. This technique evaluates how consumers feel about brands and the nature of any emotional rapport they have with a brand compared to the ideal emotional state they associate with the product category.[16]

The basic concept of emotional bonding is that consumers develop three levels of relationships with brands, as shown in Figure 9–2. The most basic relationship indicates how consumers *think* about brands in respect to product benefits. This occurs, for the most part, through a rational learning process and can be measured by how well advertising communicates product information. Consumers at this stage are not very brand loyal, and brand switching is common.

At the next stage, the consumer assigns a *personality* to a brand. For example, a brand may be thought of as self-assured, aggressive, and adventurous, as opposed to compliant and timid. The consumer's judgment of the brand has moved beyond its attributes or delivery of product/service benefits. In most instances, consumers judge the personality of a brand on the basis of an assessment of overt or covert cues found in its advertising.

McCann Erickson researchers believe the strongest relationship that develops between a brand and the consumer is based on feelings or emotional attachments to the brand. Consumers develop *emotional bonds* with certain brands, which result in positive psychological movement toward them. The marketer's goal is to develop the greatest emotional linkage between its brand and the consumer. McCann Erickson believes advertising can develop and enrich emotional bonding between consumers and brands. McCann and its subsidiary agencies use emotional bonding research to provide strategic input into the creative process and determine how well advertising is communicating with consumers. McCann Erickson used emotional bonding research as the basis for the "Priceless" campaign for MasterCard International, which has been extremely successful. When the agency took over the account in the late 90s, MasterCard had become the third card in the consumer's wallet behind Visa and American Express. The challenge was to reposition the brand and create an emotional bond between consumers and MasterCard while retaining the brand's functional appeal. The idea behind the campaign is that good spenders use credit cards to acquire things that are important to them and enrich their daily lives. The creative execution involves showing a shopping list of items that could be purchased for a certain dollar amount and one key item that could not and thus was deemed "Priceless." The tagline "There are some things money can't buy. For everything else there's MasterCard" positions the card as the way to pay for everything that matters. An entire integrated marketing campaign has been built around the "Priceless" campaign theme that includes sponsorships with Major League Baseball, the National Hockey League, and the PGA golf tour. Contests and sweepstakes have also been part of the campaign. The campaign now runs in 112 countries and 53 languages and has won numerous creative awards. MasterCard and McCann made a slight modification

**YTC** 09–04

**MasterCard**

youtube.com/10ebelch

The Duchess of Cambridge

Her Royal Highness Princess William

The Countess of Strathearn

George's Mum: Priceless®

Congratulations Kate on
your most important title yet.

MasterCard

to the campaign recently by changing the focus from observing priceless moments to *enabling* priceless moments.[17] Exhibit 9–9 shows a clever ad for MasterCard that was run following the birth of Kate Middleton and Prince William's son Prince George.

**Additional Types of Appeals**  Not every ad fits neatly into the categories of rational or emotional appeals. For example, ads for some brands can be classified as **reminder advertising**, which has the objective of building brand awareness and/or keeping the brand name in front of consumers. Well-known brands and market leaders often use reminder advertising to maintain top-of-mind awareness among consumers in their target markets. For example, Nature Valley runs clever ads such as the one shown in Exhibit 9–10 in golf magazines to remind golfers to carry its granola bars in their bags. Many golfers consume granola and energy bars during a round, and this ad uses a golf metaphor (What do you carry?) to encourage them to add Nature Valley bars to the clubs and other accessories in their bags. Products and services that have a seasonal pattern to their consumption also use reminder advertising, particularly around the appropriate period. For example, marketers of candy products often increase their media budgets and run reminder advertising around Halloween, Valentine's Day, Christmas, and Easter.

Online ads often serve as a form of reminder advertising. Many of the banner ads that are pervasive on Internet websites have very low click-through rates but still can be effective and serve a valuable function by fostering familiarity, even though most consumers may never click through to the source of the ads. Research into the psychology of online advertising has shown that repeated exposure to banner advertising can enhance familiarity with and generate positive feelings toward a brand.[18] These favorable feelings often occur through what psychologists have identified as the *mere exposure effect,* whereby repeated exposure to a stimulus (such as a brand name) can result in favorable feelings toward it.[19] While digital advertising may have positive effects through the incidental exposure that takes place when consumers visit a website, many advertising experts argue that consumers tune out most of the banner ads, as well as other

**EXHIBIT 9–11**

Under Armour often uses teaser ads prior to the launch of new products

YTC 09–05

**UGC ads**

youtube.com/10ebelch

LO 09-2

**EXHIBIT 9–12**

Ford relied entirely on user-generated content in the "Fiesta Movement: A Social Remix" campaign

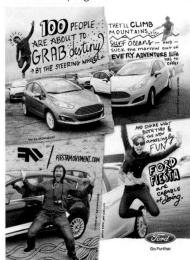

forms of Internet advertising. They note that it is becoming increasingly difficult to get people visiting a website to attend to, let alone engage with, digital ads.[20] Digital and Social Media Perspective 9–1 discusses how many in the advertising industry have noted the need for a creative revolution in digital advertising.

Advertisers introducing a new product often use **teaser advertising**, which is designed to build curiosity, interest, and/or excitement about a product or brand by talking about it but not actually showing it. Teasers, or *mystery ads* as they are sometimes called, are also used by marketers to draw attention to upcoming product launches and/or advertising campaigns and generate interest and publicity for them. For example, Under Armour has used teaser ads to create interest and excitement around new product introductions such as running and basketball shoes. The company recently used teaser ads as part of its prelaunch campaign for its Armour39™ performance monitoring system, as shown in Exhibit 9–11.

Teaser ads also are often used for new movies or TV shows and for major product launches. They are especially popular among automotive advertisers for introducing a new model or announcing significant changes in a vehicle. Teaser campaigns can generate interest in a new product, but advertisers must be careful not to extend them too long or they will lose their effectiveness. As one advertising executive says, "Contrary to what we think, consumers don't hold seminars about advertising. You have to give consumers enough information about the product in teaser ads to make them feel they're in on the joke."[21]

Another form of advertising that is becoming increasingly popular is **user-generated content (UGC)**, whereby ads are created by consumers rather than by the company and/or its agency.[22] A number of marketers have developed contests that involve having consumers create ads and submit them for consideration. As discussed in Chapter 5, Frito-Lay was one of the first marketers to use UGC on a major level when it sponsored a "Crash the Super Bowl" creative competition and ran a user-generated ad that was entirely conceived and produced by amateurs rather than advertising professionals. A number of other marketers have made UGC part of their advertising campaigns by using TV commercial or print ads that have been crowd-sourced. However, Ford took the use of UGC to an entirely new level by making all of the TV, print, and digital advertising used to launch its 2014 Fiesta model crowd-sourced.[23] The reason for having the campaign entirely based on UGC was to extend the rekindling of the "Fiesta Movement," which was discussed in Chapter 5, beyond social media platforms and make it a totally integrated campaign. Exhibit 9–12 shows one of the UGC ads for the Fiesta that was created as part of the campaign. The increasing use of interactive and social media such as YouTube and Facebook is likely to result in greater use of UGC by marketers as a way of getting consumers more involved with their brands.[24]

Many ads are not designed to sell a product or service but rather to enhance the image of the company or meet other corporate goals such as soliciting investment or recruiting employees. These are generally referred to as corporate image advertising and are discussed in detail in Chapter 17.

## Advertising Execution

Once the specific advertising appeal that will be used as the basis for the advertising message has been determined, the creative specialist or team begins its execution. *Creative execution* is the way an advertising appeal is presented. While it is obviously important for an ad to have a meaningful appeal or message to communicate to the consumer, the manner in which the ad is executed is also important.

Before reading this page, take a moment to click on the home page of a popular website such as YouTube.com, ESPN.com, or MSN.com, spend a minute or so on the site as you might normally do, and then close the site. Now answer this simple question: Do you recall the name of any company or brand that was advertised in a banner ad on the site or through some other type of message such as a commercial video? Chances are that few, if any, of the products or services being advertised on this website caught your attention and it is extremely unlikely that you clicked on a banner ad or watched an entire commercial video. While a great deal of attention has been given to advertising creativity over the years, much of the focus has been on traditional forms of advertising such as print, television, or outdoor. However, as marketers move large amounts of their media budgets to the online space, more attention needs to be given to creativity for Internet advertising as well.

It has been noted that those creating digital advertising need to step up their creative game. Getting consumers to pay attention to, not to mention engage with, a digital ad is very difficult since doing so takes them away from the content on the website. Television and radio ads air during commercial breaks and do not compete for viewers' attention during a program, while print ads often appear on separate pages of a magazine or newspaper and can easily be attended to or ignored by simply turning the page. However, online ads often interrupt our viewing sessions, and unless they are providing relevant information that gives consumers something they really need, it is likely they will be ignored.

Critics argue that one of the major problems with Internet advertising is that it has been too focused on ubiquitous banner ads as well as the targeting and measurement of them in terms of click-through rates. A great deal of effort focuses on optimizing media placement and measuring the effects of digital advertising campaigns, but less attention is given to creative considerations. Randall Rothenberg, CEO of the Interactive Advertising Bureau, argues that advertising on the Internet has been "an unthinking hostage to a direct-marketing culture and tradition that devalues creativity and its long-term effect on brands" and has called for a "creative renaissance" for digital advertising. Rothenberg is not alone in his criticism of digital advertising. Shaw Riegsecker, founder and CEO of Centro, a company that facilitates the buying and selling of digital media, notes that too many marketers are trying to build a favorable brand identity by simply buying massive amounts of banner ads across a myriad of websites. He argues that marketers have been enticed by the idea of cheap banner impressions and spend most of their resources on quantitative analysis, predictive measurement, and audience targeting while ignoring the fundamentals of great advertising.

Creativity for Internet advertising is beginning to receive more attention. One of the firms that is leading the way in this effort is Dynamic Logic, a digital advertising research group that is owned by Millward Brown, a leading marketing and advertising research company. Dynamic Logic conducted an extensive study of Internet advertising and factors that determine its effectiveness by analyzing the highest and lowest performers from its database of more than 170,000 digital ads. The study found that creative factors such as persistent branding, strong calls to action, and the use of human faces result in better ad recall, brand awareness, and purchase intentions rather than highly targeted or high-profile online ad placements. The results of the study support past research conducted by the company which has shown that creative quality accounts for 50 to 75 percent of the success or failure of online advertising while factors such as ad size, technology, and targeting make up the remainder.

One of the best-known advocates of the importance of creative execution in advertising was William Bernbach, founder of the Doyle Dane Bernbach agency. In his famous book on the advertising industry, *Madison Avenue*, Martin Mayer notes Bernbach's reply to David Ogilvy's rule for copywriters that "what you say in advertising is more important than how you say it." Bernbach replied, "Execution can become content, it can be just as important as what you say. A sick guy can utter some words and nothing happens; a healthy vital guy says them and they rock the world."[25] Bernbach was one of the revolutionaries of his time who changed advertising creativity on a fundamental level by redefining how headlines and visuals were used, how art directors and copywriters worked together, and how advertising could be used to arouse feelings and emotions.

An advertising message can be presented or executed in numerous ways:

- Straight-sell or factual message
- Scientific/technical evidence

Dynamic Logic's research manager for custom solutions notes that while the finding that good creative makes for better advertising borders on the obvious, the firm still sees a "shockingly large percentage of creative that falls short of its potential." This, of course, leads to the question of why there are so many problems with the creative quality of online advertising. Rei Inamoto, chief creative officer at digital agency AKQA, feels that creative quality suffers because publisher-determined digital ad formats are limiting, while the myriad of banner sizes requires creative that has to be constantly reformatted to fit into ad constraints that vary from one website to another. He notes that "unlike TV or, to some extent print, where formats are fairly consistent, online ads suffer from numerous formats. Agencies have to create so many of the same things. Thus the creative becomes somewhat generic and standards are all over the place."

Another problem that impacts online advertising is the overreliance on large-size ad formats such as horizontally oriented leaderboards (a 728 × 90 pixel ad unit that stretches across a web page) or skyscrapers (120 × 600 or 160 × 600 pixel–wide version) that are vertically oriented and give advertisers the ability to place an ad adjacent to the website content. The Dynamic Logic study analyzed results from 4,800 online campaigns and found that the best-performing ad unit in terms of metrics such as brand awareness, recall, and purchase intent was the traditional 180 × 150 pixel rectangular banner ad. Ken Mallon, a senior vice president for the company, notes that ads surrounding content, such as well-worn skyscraper and leaderboard units, are the least effective, as people have developed "banner blindness." Mallon says: "It's like going into an art gallery—if I found you later and asked what color the frame on such-and-such a painting was, you'll have no clue because you're trained to block out the frame. But you could probably answer questions about the painting."

Traditional rectangular banner ads are thought to be more effective because they are often closer to and interrupt the content, which means that as you read the information on the site, your eye naturally has to roll over the ad. However, ads that cover content are also among the most annoying online advertising formats. Dynamic Logic suggests that digital ads should never cover the content a user is trying to find and should not be so busy that they are annoying. A study conducted in a Harris Interactive Poll reinforces these points as the survey found that ads that cover content or do not have a "skip" or "close" button are the most annoying online advertising formats.

Those involved in creating digital advertising are, of course, facing new challenges as more consumers access the web through mobile devices such as smartphones and tablets rather than through desktops or laptops with larger screens. Moreover, many mobile users have spent time personalizing devices with wallpapers, games, and apps and don't like the intrusion of advertising that disrupts their user experience. While some advertisers view mobile devices as being too small to deliver effective advertising messages, others view them as a way to achieve microtargeting and deliver brand experiences that are fun and engaging for consumers by using extensive interactive banners, full-page interstitials, and a range of image-laden video formats to provide rich media engagement.

Marketers are likely to continue to move more of their advertising to the Internet as they know that their target audiences are spending more time online. Moreover, many marketers feel that the targeting and measurement capabilities of the Internet and digital devices more than make up for the creative limitations of online advertising. However, it is also important for marketers to challenge their agencies to develop digital ads that are entertaining and engaging rather than continuing to bombard consumers with more leaderboards, skyscrapers, banner ads, and/or video buttons to click. Most industry experts agree that digital advertising will work even better if there is an interactive creative revolution.

Sources: "Online Advertising Needs a Different Kind of Creativity," editorial—*Advertising Age*, October 26, 2009, http://adage.com/print?article_id=139931; Kunur Patel, "Online Ads Not Working for You? Blame the Creative," *Advertising Age*, October 20, 2009, http://adage.com/print?article_id=139795; Hernan Lopez, "Why Interactive Advertising Needs a Creative Revolution," *Advertising Age*, June 15, 2009, http://adage.com/print?article_id=137246; Rob Thurner, "Effective Mobile Advertising," *Smart Insights*, December 4, 2012, www.smartinsights.com/mobile-marketing/mobile-advertising/mobile-advertising-examples/.

- Demonstration
- Comparison
- Testimonial
- Slice of life
- Animation
- Personality symbol
- Imagery
- Dramatization
- Humor
- Combinations

We now examine these formats and considerations involved in their use.

**Straight-Sell or Factual Message**   One of the most basic types of creative executions is the straight-sell or factual message. This type of ad relies on

**EXHIBIT 9–13**
This ad for the Mach3 Sensitive razor uses a creative straight-sell execution

a straightforward presentation of information concerning the product or service. The execution is often used with informational/rational appeals, where the focus of the message is the product or service and its specific attributes and/or benefits.

Straight-sell executions are commonly used in print ads. A picture of the product or service occupies part of the ad, and the factual copy takes up the rest of the space. They are also used in TV advertising, with an announcer generally delivering the sales message while the product/service is shown on the screen. Ads for high-involvement consumer products as well as industrial and other business-to-business products generally use this format. Straight-sell advertising executions are often used for various types of consumer products and services as well and can be very effective when done creatively. For example, the ad for the Gillette Mach3 Sensitive razor shown in Exhibit 9–13 uses a very clever and creative execution to communicate the product's features and benefits. The Mach3 Sensitive was launched by Gillette in 2013 in response to a market research study that found a high percentage of men don't shave every day because they have sensitive skin that can be aggravated by shaving and leave their faces raw and irritated.[26] Notice how the ad copy addresses these issues while using a little hyperbole by suggesting that using the Mach3 will make your lady love your face even more.

**Scientific/Technical Evidence**   In a variation of the straight sell, scientific or technical evidence is presented in the ad. Advertisers often cite technical information, results of scientific or laboratory studies, or endorsements by scientific bodies or agencies to support their advertising claims. For example, an endorsement from the American Council on Dental Therapeutics on how fluoride helps prevent cavities was the basis of the campaign that made Crest the leading brand of toothpaste. The ad for Kinerase anti-aging skin care treatment shown in Exhibit 9–14 uses this execution style by noting how the product has been clinically proven to reduce signs of aging.

**Demonstration**   Demonstration advertising is designed to illustrate the key advantages of the product/service by showing it in actual use or in some staged situation. Demonstration executions can be very effective in convincing consumers of a product's utility or quality and of the benefits of owning or using the brand. TV is particularly well suited for demonstration executions, since the benefits or advantages of the product can be shown right on the screen. Although perhaps a little less dramatic than TV, demonstration ads can also work in print. The ad for Samsung's new LED 9000 high-definition TV shown in Exhibit 9–15 is an excellent example of the use of this technique. The image showing a side view of the television being held between two fingers is a very effective way to demonstrate the ultra-thin feature of the TV as well as its elegant design.

**EXHIBIT 9–14**
Kinerase promotes how clinical test results support the product performance claim

**Comparison**   Brand comparisons can also be the basis for the advertising execution. The comparison execution approach is increasingly popular among advertisers,

**EXHIBIT 9–15**

This ad is an effective way to demonstrate the ultra thin feature of Samsung's LED TV

YTC **09–06**

**Testimonials**

youtube.com/10ebelch

**EXHIBIT 9–16**

Jenny Craig uses testimonials to advertise its weight-loss program

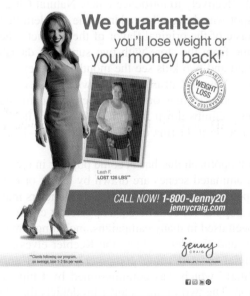

since it offers a direct way of communicating a brand's particular advantage over its competitors or positioning a new or lesser-known brand with industry leaders. Comparison executions are often used to execute competitive advantage appeals, as discussed earlier.

**Testimonial**   Many advertisers prefer to have their messages presented by way of a testimonial, where a person praises the product or service on the basis of his or her personal experience with it. Testimonial executions can have ordinary satisfied customers discuss their own experiences with the brand and the benefits of using it. This approach can be very effective when the person delivering the testimonial is someone with whom the target audience can identify or who has an interesting story to tell. The testimonial must be based on actual use of the product or service to avoid legal problems, and the spokesperson must be credible.

A number of marketers, such as weight-loss companies, use testimonials to advertise their products, services, and programs. For example, Jenny Craig uses television commercials and print ads featuring ordinary consumers as well as celebrities discussing how they have been able to lose weight by following the company's programs. Exhibit 9–16 shows an ad showing a person who lost weight using the Jenny Craig program.

A related execution technique is the *endorsement,* where a well-known or respected individual such as a celebrity or expert in the product or service area speaks on behalf of the company or the brand. When endorsers promote a company or its products or services, the message is not necessarily based on their personal experiences.

**Slice of Life**   A widely used advertising format, particularly for packaged-goods products, is the slice-of-life execution, which is generally based on a problem/solution approach. This type of ad portrays a problem or conflict that consumers might face in their daily lives. The ad then shows how the advertiser's product or service can resolve the problem.

Slice-of-life executions are often criticized for being unrealistic and irritating to watch because they are often used to remind consumers of problems of a personal nature, such as dandruff, bad breath, body odor, and laundry problems. Often these ads come across as contrived, silly, phony, or even offensive to consumers. However, many advertisers still prefer this style because they believe it is effective at presenting a situation to which most consumers can relate and at registering the product feature or benefit that helps sell the brand. For many years, Procter & Gamble was known for its reliance on slice-of-life advertising executions as many of the company's commercials used either the slice-of-life or testimonial format. However, P&G has begun using humor, animation, and other less traditional execution styles and now relies less on slice of life or testimonials.[27]

Slice-of-life or problem/solution execution approaches are not limited to consumer-product advertising. Many business-to-business marketers use this type of advertising to demonstrate how their products and services can be used to solve business problems.[28] Some business-to-business marketers use a variation of the problem/solution execution that is sometimes referred to as *slice-of-death advertising.*[29] This execution style is used in conjunction with a fear appeal, as the focus is on the negative consequences that result when businesspeople make the wrong decision in choosing a supplier or service provider. For example, FedEx has used this type of advertising for

**EXHIBIT 9–17**
Listerine uses a slice-of-life
execution to introduce
a new flavor

nearly three decades through humorous but to-the-point commercials that show what might happen when important packages and documents aren't received on time.

Execution is critical in using the technique effectively as these ads are designed to be dramatizations of a supposedly real-life situation that consumers might encounter. Getting viewers to identify with the situation and/or characters depicted in the ad can be very challenging. Since the success of slice-of-life ads often depends on how well the actors come across and execute their roles, professional actors are often used to achieve credibility and to ensure that the commercial is of high quality. Smaller companies and local advertisers often do not have ad budgets large enough to hire the talent or to pay for the production quality needed to effectively create slice-of-life spots. Thus, this execution technique is more likely to be used by companies with ad budgets that are large enough to fund the use of professional talent and production of quality commercials.

Many marketers like to use the slice-of-life genre as they believe it can be an effective way of addressing a problem or issue and offering a solution. For example, Listerine used a slice-of-life commercial effectively to introduce a new Natural Citrus flavor of the popular mouthwash. The spot was designed to address the problem that some consumers have with the intense taste of the original flavor of the product. The spot opens with a mother returning home from the store with two surprises: danish and Listerine. However, when her husband and two kids see the mouthwash they run and hide. The mother then tells them it is Natural Citrus Listerine, which tastes less intense. The humorous spot ends with the father coming out of a kitchen cupboard and pots and pans dangling as one of the boys climbs down from the top of the kitchen island as the voiceover says, "You can handle it. Germs can't" (see Exhibit 9–17).

**Animation** An advertising execution approach that has become popular in recent years is animation. With this technique, animated scenes are drawn by artists or created on the computer, and cartoons, puppets, or other types of fictional characters may be used. Cartoon animation is especially popular for commercials targeted at children. Animated cartoon characters have also been used in many campaigns, including Green Giant vegetables (the Jolly Green Giant) and Keebler cookies (the Keebler elves).

An excellent example of a commercial created using computer-generated animation is a spot called "Back to the Start" which was commissioned by Chipotle Mexican Grill for its Cultivate Foundation. The two-minute short film depicts the life of a farmer as he slowly turns his family farm into an industrial animal factory before

**EXHIBIT 9–18**
This "Back to the Start" Cannes Lions Film Grand Prix Winner 2012 for the Chipotle Cultivate Foundation uses computer-generated animation

seeing the errors of his ways and realizes the benefits of sustainable farming and turns it back (Exhibit 9–18). The film has a specially commissioned track of Coldplay's "The Scientist" sung by Willie Nelson; Chipotle encouraged viewers to download the song on iTunes, with proceeds going to the Cultivate Foundation. The spot ran online, in movie theaters, and as Chipotle's first national TV ad and won the Grand Prix and Gold Lion awards at the 2012 Cannes International Advertising Festival. The use of animation as an execution style may increase as creative specialists find more ways to use computer-generated graphics and other technological innovations.[30]

**Personality Symbol**  Another type of advertising execution involves developing a central character or personality symbol that can deliver the advertising message and with which the product or service can be identified. This character can be a person, like Mr. Whipple, who asked shoppers, "Please don't squeeze the Charmin," or the Maytag repairman, who sits anxiously by the phone but is never needed because the company's appliances are so reliable.

Personality figures can also be built around animated characters and animals. As discussed in Chapter 5, personality symbols such as Morris the cat, Tony the tiger, and Charlie the tuna have been used for decades to promote 9-Lives cat food, Kellogg's Frosted Flakes, and Star-Kist tuna, respectively. Other popular personality symbols that have been used more recently include the Energizer bunny, GEICO insurance's gecko, and the Burger King character.

One of the most popular and effective advertising personality symbols has been the Aflac duck which has been very successful in raising awareness, as well as sales, for the supplemental insurance company over the past five years.[31] Aflac has even integrated the duck into the company's redesigned corporate logo to take advantage of the tremendous equity that has resulted from the ads featuring the character.

Another example of the effective use of an advertising personality symbol for brand is "The Most Interesting Man in the World" campaign created by Havas Worldwide for the Dos Equis beer brand. Research conducted by the agency with import beer drinkers revealed that they were annoyed by much of the beer advertising, which used images of sexy women, sophomoric humor, and tired clichés. The research also revealed that they felt misrepresented and misunderstood and, more than anything, wanted to be perceived as interesting and conversely, not boring. Based on these insights, the agency creative team came up with a big idea of creating a personality symbol for brand that they labeled "The Most Interesting Man in the World." The agency created a fictitious character played by veteran actor Jonathan Goldsmith, who is portrayed in the ads as a suave and debonair gentleman with an exotic accent, silver beard,

**EXHIBIT 9-19**

"The Most Interesting Man in the World" personality character has been very effective for Dos Equis

YTC 09-09

**Dos Equis**

youtube.com/10ebelch

and no-nonsense attitude (Exhibit 9–19). The James Bond meets Ernest Hemmingway character is always impeccably dressed and the commercials show him in highly exotic and intriguing situations and locales such as leading mysterious expeditions, running with the bulls in Pamplona, or arm wrestling with Fidel Castro. At the end of every ad he acknowledges that he does not always drink beer, but when he does, he prefers Dos Equis and then delivers the signature line "Stay thirsty my friends." The implied message from the ads is that all beer drinkers could and should be living a more interesting life and, of course, can vicariously do so by drinking Dos Equis. The campaign launched in 2007 and over the past six years has helped make Dos Equis, which was once a low-profile brand sold mostly in Texas and California, the sixth largest imported beer in the United States.[32]

A number of insurance companies have also created advertising campaigns based around personality symbols for their brands such as the GEICO gecko lizard character and Flo, the white-clad, perky sales clerk character who appears in ads for Progressive. IMC Perspective 9–1 discusses the various creative strategies used by insurance companies and whether they are effective.

**Imagery** You have probably noticed that some ads contain little or no information about the brand or company and are almost totally visual. These advertisements use imagery executions whereby the ad consists primarily of visual elements such as pictures, illustrations, and/ or symbols rather than information. An imagery execution is used when the goal is to encourage consumers to associate the brand with the symbols, characters, and/or situation shown in the ad. Imagery ads are often the basis for emotional appeals that are used to advertise products or services where differentiation based on physical characteristics is difficult, such as soft drinks, liquor, designer clothing, and cosmetics. However, image is important for all types of products and services as marketers want the target audience to hold a favorable set of psychosocial associations for their company or brand.

An imagery execution may be based on *usage imagery* by showing how a brand is used or performs and the situation in which it is used. For example, advertising for trucks and SUVs often shows the vehicles navigating tough terrain or in challenging situations such as towing a heavy load. Usage imagery executions are also often used in the marketing of services to show favorable images related to the use of a company's service offering. An excellent example of this is the ad shown in Exhibit 9–20 for Singapore Airlines all-business class service between the United States and Asia. The visual image used in the ad is a very effective way for Singapore Airlines to promote this service by communicating the message that it has the most spacious business class seats of any airline. This type of execution can also be based on *user imagery* where the focus is on the type of person who uses the brand. Ads for cosmetics, jewelry, and designer clothing brands often use very attractive models in the hope of getting consumers to associate his or her physical attractiveness with the brand (see Exhibit 9–21). Image executions rely heavily on visual elements such as photography, color, tonality, and design to communicate the desired image to the consumer. Marketers who rely on image executions have to be sure that the usage or user imagery with which they associate their brand evokes the right feelings and reactions from the target audience.

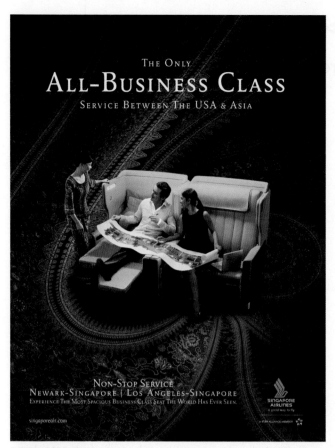

**EXHIBIT 9–20**

Singapore Airlines utilizes usage imagery by communicating the spaciousness of its business class seats

**EXHIBIT 9–21**

This bebe ad uses an attractive model to create a favorable image for the brand

**Dramatization**   Another execution technique particularly well suited to television is dramatization, where the focus is on telling a short story with the product or service as the star. Dramatization is somewhat akin to slice-of-life execution in that it often relies on the problem–solution approach, but it uses more excitement and suspense in telling the story. The purpose of using drama is to draw the viewer into the action it portrays. Advocates of drama note that when it is successful, the audience becomes lost in the story and experiences the concerns and feelings of the characters.[33] According to Sandra Moriarty, there are five basic steps in a dramatic commercial:

> First is exposition, where the stage is set for the upcoming action. Next comes conflict, which is a technique for identifying the problem. The middle of the dramatic form is a period of rising action where the story builds, the conflict intensifies, the suspense thickens. The fourth step is the climax, where the problem is solved. The last part of a drama is the resolution, where the wrap-up is presented. In advertising that includes product identification and call to action.[34]

In his excellent book *Creative Advertising,* Mario Pricken lists several relevant questions that should be considered when telling a story through a dramatic execution: What everyday situations could you develop around the product to show its advantages in the best light? What sort of story could involve the product as best friend or partner? In what everyday situation could it attract attention in a provocative way? In what situation could it become a star, a lifesaver, or a helper? In what everyday story could it make people laugh? He also notes that there are a number of dramatic styles that might be best suited for telling the story. These include, but are not limited to, genres such as thriller, adventure, comedy, slapstick, love story, and documentary.[35]

# IMC Perspective 9–1 > > >

## Auto Insurance Companies Use Different Creative Strategies, but Do They Work?

Automobile insurance companies face a unique marketing opportunity because regardless of age, gender, or socioeconomic status, all drivers need insurance. In fact, liability coverage is required by law in 47 states. However, this opportunity also presents a challenge as auto insurers must market their services to a wide range of consumers who represent a broad spectrum of characteristics, including age, education, and income, as well as purchase motives. As a result, in recent years we have seen auto insurance companies create a diverse range of advertisements designed to appeal to many different types of consumers. The goal of these campaigns, of course, is to attract as many customers as possible by encouraging consumers to switch from one insurance company to another. However, this is no easy feat in an industry that is becoming increasingly consumer-independent; buyers are purchasing insurance more frequently on their own (predominantly online) rather than relying on agents to sell them a policy.

For some auto insurers, their advertising strategy is to use a big-budget, multipronged advertising approach with several creative campaigns running simultaneously. GEICO, for example, which has an advertising budget nearly twice as large as most of its competitors, at any given time has as many as six different ad campaigns running, each with its own unique style, flavor, and taglines. The company first began using its popular gecko character in 1999, and the lizard with the Cockney English accent still appears in many of the company's print and TV ads. GEICO has also used a variety of other characters including the metrosexual cavemen who are insulted by the tagline, "So easy, a caveman can do it." The company's approach runs against conventional advertising wisdom but has been very effective; GEICO's market share has grown 20 percent over the past five years compared to 10 percent for the industry's

second-best performer, Progressive. GEICO spends nearly $1 billion per year on various forms of advertising, including television, print, outdoor, and the Internet, and its heavy investment has been paying off as it is now the third largest automotive insurance company behind State Farm and Allstate.

But not all auto insurers have been so fortunate. In an effort to keep pace with GEICO's aggressive spending and humor-based, multipronged ad campaigns, other insurers have increased their advertising spending and created ad campaigns based on humor (or at least *attempted* humor). In most cases, the results of these efforts haven't been nearly as strong as GEICO's. Nationwide Insurance launched the humorous "World's Greatest Spokesperson" campaign and although brand awareness increased for the first time in over a decade, the company's market share declined by 9 percent compared to precampaign levels and continues to fall. Even State Farm's clever and popular "Discount Double-Check" campaign featuring

---

The challenge facing the creative team when using a dramatic execution is how to encompass the various elements and tell the story effectively in 30 seconds, which is the length of the typical commercial.

An example of the effective use of a dramatization execution in a commercial is a recent spot for the Buick Enclave sport utility vehicle created by Leo Burnett Detroit (Exhibit 9–22). The commercial opens with an aura of tension as it shows a family on an airplane landing in a snowstorm; the pilot announces that the wind chill outside is 10 below and the flight attendant tells the passengers "there are record lows out there so bundle up." As the plane touches down on the snowy runway, the man takes out his smartphone and uses the MyBuick remote start feature to start the Enclave, which is sitting in the airport parking lot, and sets the temperature to 82 degrees and activates the heated seats. The tone of the commercial then turns upbeat as the song "Not a Care" begins to play and the voiceover says: "With MyBuick remote start the new Buick Enclave makes sure you're ready for anything." The commercial ends with the family getting off the parking bus and into their warm and comfortable car.

YTC 09–10

**Buick Enclave**

youtube.com/10ebelch

the Green Bay Packers' MVP quarterback Aaron Rodgers has not been enough to increase the company's market share, which has remained flat for three consecutive years. Progressive still uses its popular Flo character who has been featured in its ads since 2008, and was recently named a top 10 female advertising icon. However, the company has been introducing some new characters into some of its more hard-sell-focused direct-response advertising such as a character called "The Messenger"—a mustachioed, leather-jacket-wearing man who sneaks up on customers and pitches them on discounts. While Flo is used to reach consumers who are already in the market for insurance, The Messenger is meant to get more people thinking about insurance. The company also recently introduced commercials featuring a talking Progressive "box" character which is voiced by comic actor Chris Parnell. As many as nine messages are packed into the 60-second spots such as telling viewers that they do not have to wait for their current policy to expire to switch companies.

In some cases, *not* following the industry trend toward humorous campaigns has been a recipe for success. USAA Group, for example—which caters to military personnel, veterans, and their families—launched its first-ever national marketing campaign in 2011 using emotion and a serious tone instead of humor. The results were very positive, as USAA experienced an 8 percent jump in market share since the campaign began. Another example is Allstate's "Mayhem" campaign, which was first launched in 2010 and features actor Dean Winters, who has a reputation for playing dark characters in TV series such as *Rescue Me* and *30 Rock*. Winters plays a villainous character in the spots who wreaks havoc on other cars and property as a way of showing that many accidents involve more than your average fender bender. The campaign utilizes both dry humor and the serious consequences that can result from an auto accident, and, according to Allstate CMO Mark LaNeve, are intended to be "disruptive" in an industry whose primary focus is on price. The "Mayhem" campaign was well received among young people, which was one of the LaNeve's goals. The campaign has also been an effective counter to GEICO and Progressive's discount-focused advertising as it encourages

consumers to recognize that you get what you pay for when purchasing insurance.

Given the varying levels of success across the industry, there is significant debate by industry analysts as to whether the approaches used by car insurance companies are working at all. A study commissioned by *Advertising Age*, for example, found that while it is clear consumers are very fond of characters such as GEICO's gecko and Progressive's Flo, it is not clear whether their *message* is sticking with consumers. One respondent in the study recalled GEICO's tagline to be "50 minutes can save you 50%," vastly overstating the "15 minutes" and "15%" tagline the company has used for over a decade. Additionally, industry analysts are increasingly skeptical as to whether the humorous ads are resulting in sales conversions. The Insurance Information Institute estimates that over the past decade only about 1 in 10 drivers actually switch policies despite the industry's advertising barrage. Instead of taking the time and effort to switch, many consumers raise their deductibles or drop coverage on other vehicles to save money.

Of course, the one thing that matters most in the debate on whether or not car insurance ads are working is the bottom line. The goal of many of these ads is to encourage consumers to call a toll-free number, visit the advertiser's website, or call one of their agents to compare rates and coverage and consider switching carriers. However, one could certainly argue that given the reluctance of consumers to switch companies, many auto insurance ads may be doing little more than providing them with a good laugh during a commercial break.

Sources: Leslie Scism and Erik Holm, "Bombarded by Ads, Few Drivers Switch Car Insurer," *The Wall Street Journal*, January 30, 2013, http://search.proquest.com/docview/1282579635?accountid=13758; E. J. Schultz, "Flo Gets More Company as Progressive Rolls Out 'The Box,'" *Advertising Age*," December 5, 2012, http://adage.com/article/news/flo-company-progressive-rolls-box/238621/; Gary Strauss, "Except for Discounters, Insurers' Funny Ads Not Paying Off," *USA Today*, July 25, 2012, pp. C1,C2; Leslie Scism and Erik Holm, "Geico Spends Nearly $1 Billion on Ads as Car Insurers Battle," *The Wall Street Journal*, June 25, 2012, pp. B1,B7; Judann Pollack, "In the Insurance Ad War, Consumers Ask: Who's Who? Study Respondents Find Difficulty Matching Spots with Providers," *Advertising Age*, February 21, 2011, http://adage.com/article/news/insurance-ad-war-consumers/148994/.

YTC 09–11

**Insurance ads**

youtube.com/10ebelch

**Humor** Like comparisons, humor was discussed in Chapter 6 as a type of advertising appeal, but this technique can also be used as a way of presenting other advertising appeals. Humorous executions are particularly well suited to television or radio, although some print ads attempt to use this style. The pros and cons of using humor as an executional technique are similar to those associated with its use as an advertising appeal.

**Combinations** Many of the execution techniques can be combined to present the advertising message. For example, animation is often used to create personality symbols or present a fantasy. Slice-of-life ads are often used to demonstrate a product or service. Comparisons are sometimes made using a humorous approach. FedEx uses humorous executions of the slice-of-death genre depicting businesspeople experiencing dire consequences when they use another delivery service and an important document doesn't arrive on time. It is the responsibility of the creative specialist(s) to determine whether more than one execution style should be used in creating the ad.

# CREATIVE TACTICS

Our discussion thus far has focused on the development of creative strategy and various appeals and execution styles that can be used for the advertising message. Once the creative approach, type of appeal, and execution style have been determined, attention turns to creating the actual advertisement. The design and production of advertising messages involve a number of activities, among them writing copy, developing illustrations and other visual elements of the ad, and bringing all of the pieces together to create an effective message. In this section, we examine the verbal and visual elements of an ad and discuss tactical considerations in creating print ads and TV commercials.

## Creative Tactics for Print Advertising

The basic components of a print ad are the headline, the body copy, the visual or illustrations, and the layout (the way they all fit together). The headline and body copy portions of the ad are the responsibility of the copywriters; artists, often working under the direction of an art director, are responsible for the visual presentation. Art directors also work with the copywriters to develop a layout, or arrangement of the various components of the ad: headlines, subheads, body copy, illustrations, captions, logos, and the like. We briefly examine the three components of a print ad and how they are coordinated.

**Headlines**   The **headline** is the words in the leading position of the ad—the words that will be read first or are positioned to draw the most attention. Headlines are usually set in larger type and are often set apart from the body copy or text portion of the ad to give them prominence. Most advertising people consider the headline the most important part of a print ad.

The most important function of a headline is attracting readers' attention and interesting them in the rest of the message. While the visual portion of an ad is obviously important, the headline often shoulders most of the responsibility of attracting readers' attention. Research has shown the headline is generally the first thing people look at in a print ad, followed by the illustration. Only 20 percent of readers go beyond the

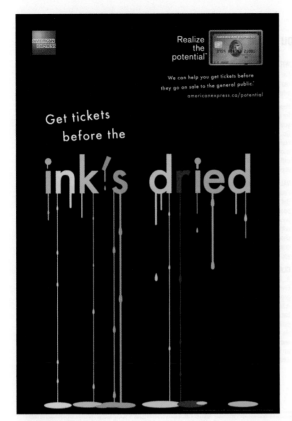

**EXHIBIT 9–23**

The headline of this ad attracts attention by noting how American Express Card Members can get products before the general public.

headline and read the body copy.[36] So in addition to attracting attention, the headline must give the reader good reason to read the copy portion of the ad, which contains more detailed and persuasive information about the product or service. To do this, the headline must put forth the main theme, appeal, or proposition of the ad in a few words. Some print ads contain little if any body copy, so the headline must work with the illustration to communicate the entire advertising message.

Headlines also perform a segmentation function by engaging the attention and interest of consumers who are most likely to buy a particular product or service. Advertisers begin the segmentation process by choosing to advertise in certain types of publications (e.g., a travel or fashion magazine). An effective headline goes even further in selecting good prospects by addressing their specific needs, wants, or interests. For example, the headline in the ad shown in Exhibit 9–23 attracts attention by noting that one of the benefits of using an American Express credit card is being able to get tickets before the general public or, as the ad states, "before the ink's dried."

**Types of Headlines** There are numerous headline possibilities. The type used depends on several factors, including the creative strategy, the particular advertising situation (e.g., product type, media vehicle[s] being used, timeliness), and its relationship to other components of the ad, such as the illustration or body copy. Headlines can be categorized as direct and indirect. **Direct headlines** are straightforward and informative in terms of the message they are presenting and the target audience they are directed toward. Common types of direct headlines include those offering a specific benefit, making a promise, or announcing a reason the reader should be interested in the product or service.

**Indirect headlines** are not straightforward about identifying the product or service or getting to the point. But they are often more effective at attracting readers' attention and interest because they provoke curiosity and lure readers into the body copy to learn an answer or get an explanation. Techniques for writing indirect headlines include using questions, provocations, how-to statements, and challenges.

Indirect headlines rely on their ability to generate curiosity or intrigue so as to motivate readers to become involved with the ad and read the body copy to find out the point of the message. This can be risky if the headline is not provocative enough to get the readers' interest. Advertisers deal with this problem by using indirect headlines that are interesting enough to generate interest or curiosity as well as employing a strong visual appeal that will attract attention and offer a reason for reading more of the message. For example, the ad for the American Indian College Fund shown in Exhibit 9–24 uses an indirect headline (25,000 People Are Counting on Me To Save One Language) that might create curiosity among magazine readers and encourage them to read the copy below for an explanation of what is meant by it. The body copy at the bottom of the ad explains how this student learned the Lakota language at home and plans to teach it when he graduates from college. It also notes how only 5 percent of American Indians can afford college without assistance and encourages people to support the American Indian College Fund.

**Subheads** While many ads have only one headline, it is also common to see print ads containing the main head and one or more secondary heads, or **subheads**. Subheads are usually smaller than the main headline but larger than the body copy. Subheads are often used to enhance the readability of the message by breaking up large amounts of body copy and highlighting key sales points. Their content reinforces the headline and advertising slogan or theme. The ad for GEICO auto insurance shown in

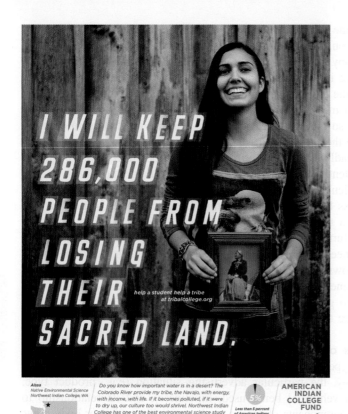

I WILL KEEP 286,000 PEOPLE FROM LOSING THEIR SACRED LAND.

help a student help a tribe
at tribalcollege.org

Alisa
Native Environmental Science
Northwest Indian College, WA

Do you know how important water is in a desert? The Colorado River provide my tribe, the Navajo, with energy, with income, with life. If it becomes polluted, if it were to dry up, our culture too would shrivel. Northwest Indian College has one of the best environmental science study programs in the country, giving me knowledge I can take home to help my tribe thrive.

5%
Less than 5 percent of American Indians can afford college without assistance.

AMERICAN INDIAN COLLEGE FUND

**EXHIBIT 9–24**
This ad for the American Indian College Fund uses an indirect headline that encourages people to read the body copy

**"You could save hundreds by switching to GEICO."**

**WITH GEICO, IT'S EASY TO SAVE.**
I'm here to save you money. Well…not really here in your kitchen, but you know what I mean.

People say to me, I don't have time to shop for car insurance. And I say to them, have you ever made $500 in 15 minutes? Go to **geico.com**. Answer some quick questions and you get an accurate rate quote. You buy right then, or if you want, call **1-800-947-AUTO** to buy over the phone. Either way, you could save $500.

**VALUE. IT'S SAVINGS AND SERVICE.**
People know they could save hundreds. But what about GEICO's service? I tell people, GEICO isn't just about saving hundreds. There's also the 24/7 service with real live people. They're on the phones at all hours answering your questions. And you can also get the help you need at **geico.com**.

**CLAIMS MADE EASY.**
A friend gets into a small accident. Everyone is OK. When he gets home he goes to **geico.com**, reports the claim and schedules an appointment. Later he goes back to the website, prints out his estimate and views photos of the damage. He then goes to a GEICO-approved shop and his claim repairs are guaranteed for as long as he owns his car. Now that's what I call service.

**DEPENDABILITY. IT'S THE GEICO WAY.**
I get asked, how dependable is GEICO? They've been consistently protecting drivers and delivering great value for more than 70 years. That sounds dependable to me.

**PROTECT LOTS OF THINGS WITH GEICO.**
Sure, GEICO does cars. Everyone knows that. But, you could also save big when GEICO insures your motorcycle or ATV. Homeowner's and renter's insurance? GEICO can help you with those, and boats and PWCs, too.

**LOOK, IT ALL MAKES A LOT OF SENSE.**
It's easy to switch, so contact GEICO. You'll get the value and claim service all my mates love.

15 minutes could save you 15%.

**GEICO.**
geico.com
**1-800-947-AUTO**
or call your local office.

Average savings based on GEICO New Policyholder Survey Data through February 2007. Some discounts, coverages, payment plans, and features are not available in all states or in all GEICO companies. Government Employees Insurance Co. • GEICO General Insurance Co. • GEICO Indemnity Co. • GEICO Casualty Co. These companies are subsidiaries of Berkshire Hathaway Inc. GEICO auto insurance is not available in MA. Homeowner's, motorcycle and ATV insurance are currently not available in some states. Homeowner's, renter's, boat, and PWC coverages are written through non-affiliated insurance companies and are secured through Insurance Counselors Inc., the GEICO Property Agency. The GEICO gecko image © GEICO 1999 – 2007. GEICO: Washington, DC 20076. © 2006-2007 GEICO

GEN

**EXHIBIT 9–25**
This GEICO ad uses subheads to make the copy easier to read as well as to highlight features and benefits

Exhibit 9–25 is a good example of the effective use of subheads to present a large amount of advertising copy and highlight the major points of the message.

**Body Copy**   The main text portion of a print ad is referred to as the **body copy** (or sometimes just *copy*). While the body copy is usually the heart of the advertising message, getting the target audience to read it is often difficult. The copywriter faces a dilemma: The body copy must be long enough to communicate the advertiser's message yet short enough to hold readers' interest.

Body copy content often flows from the points made in the headline or various subheads, but the specific content depends on the type of advertising appeal and/ or execution style being used. For example, straight-sell copy that presents relevant information, product features and benefits, or competitive advantages is often used with the various types of rational appeals discussed earlier in the chapter. Emotional appeals often use narrative copy that tells a story or provides an interesting account of a problem or situation involving the product.

Advertising body copy can be written to go along with various types of creative appeals and executions—comparisons, price appeals, demonstrations, humor, dramatizations, and the like. Copywriters choose a copy style that is appropriate for the type of appeal being used and effective for executing the creative strategy and communicating the advertiser's message to the target audience.

**Visual Elements**   The third major component of a print ad is the visual element. The illustration is often a dominant part of a print ad and plays an important role in

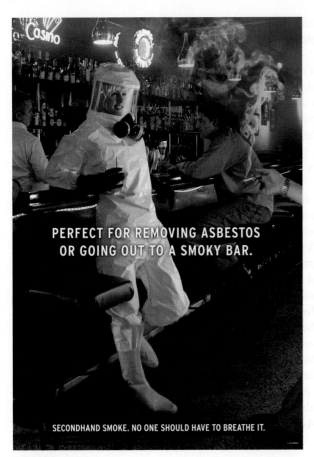

**EXHIBIT 9–26**
This ad uses a clever visual image to deliver a message about the dangers of secondhand smoke

**EXHIBIT 9–27**
This creative print ad was used to launch DASANI's new PlantBottle™ packaging

determining its effectiveness. The visual portion of an ad must attract attention, communicate an idea or image, and work in a synergistic fashion with the headline and body copy to produce an effective message. In some print ads, the visual portion of the ad is essentially the message and thus must convey a strong and meaningful image. For example, the antismoking ad shown in Exhibit 9–26 uses a clever visual image showing a woman in a bar wearing the type of protective suit used by workers who remove asbestos from buildings to protect herself from secondhand smoke. The simple line of copy at the bottom reinforces the message presented by the visual image.

Many decisions have to be made regarding the visual portion of the ad: what identification marks should be included (brand name, company or trade name, trademarks, logos); whether to use photos or hand-drawn or painted illustrations; what colors to use (or even perhaps black and white or just a splash of color); and what the focus of the visual should be.

**Layout** While each individual component of a print ad is important, the key factor is how these elements are blended into a finished advertisement. A **layout** is the physical arrangement of the various parts of the ad, including the headline, subheads, body copy, illustrations, and any identifying marks. The layout shows where each part of the ad will be placed and gives guidelines to the people working on the ad. The layout helps the copywriter determine how much space he or she has to work with and how much copy should be written. It can also guide the art director in determining the size and type of photos.

While the layout of a print ad is often straightforward, some creative executions can be challenging but also provide marketers with a very effective way to deliver a branding message. For example, the Lambesis agency created a unique print ad for DASANI® Purified water that was part of an integrated campaign designed to communicate the Earth-inspired design for the brand's new bottle. The advertising used to launch the new PlantBottle™ packaging included a print ad with a peel-off plantable seeded paper leaf insert (Exhibit 9–27). The campaign helped enhance consumer perceptions of DASANI® as being innovative and environmentally conscious. Layouts are often done in rough form and presented to the client so that the advertiser can visualize what the ad will look like before giving preliminary approval. The agency should get client approval of the layout before moving on to the more costly stages of print production.

## Creative Tactics for Television

As consumers, we see so many TV commercials that it's easy to take for granted the time, effort, and money that go into making them. Creating and producing commercials that break through the clutter on TV and communicate effectively is a detailed, expensive process. On a cost-per-minute basis, commercials are the most expensive productions seen on television.

TV is a unique and powerful advertising medium because it contains the elements of sight, sound, and motion, which can be combined to create a variety of advertising appeals and executions. Unlike print, the viewer does not control the rate at which the message is presented, so there is no opportunity to review points of interest or reread things that are not communicated clearly. As with any form of advertising, one of the first goals in creating TV commercials is to get the viewers' attention and then maintain it. This can be particularly challenging because of the clutter and because people often view TV commercials while doing other things (reading a book or magazine, talking).

Like print ads, TV commercials have several components. The video and audio must work together to create the right impact and communicate the advertiser's message.

**Video**  The video elements of a commercial are what is seen on the TV screen. The visual portion generally dominates the commercial, so it must attract viewers' attention and communicate an idea, message, and/or image. A number of visual elements may have to be coordinated to produce a successful ad. Decisions have to be made regarding the product, the presenter, action sequences, demonstrations, and the like, as well as the setting(s), the talent or characters who will appear in the commercial, and such other factors as lighting, graphics, color, and identifying symbols.

**Audio**  The audio portion of a commercial includes voices, music, and sound effects. Voices are used in different ways in commercials. They may be heard through the direct presentation of a spokesperson or as a conversation among various people appearing in the commercial. A common method for presenting the audio portion of a commercial is through a **voiceover**, where the message is delivered or action on the screen is narrated or described by an announcer who is not visible. A trend among major advertisers is to have celebrities with distinctive voices do the voiceovers for their commercials.[37] Actor Morgan Freeman does the voiceover commercials for Visa, Patrick Dempsey does State Farm Insurance, and Verizon Wireless has used actor Demi Moore's voice in some of its TV spots. Other celebrities who have been paid large sums of money to do voiceovers for commercials include George Clooney for Budweiser, Julia Roberts for Nationwide Insurance, and Lisa Kudrow for Yoplait.

Music is also an important part of many TV commercials and can play a variety of roles.[38] In many commercials, the music provides a pleasant background or helps create the appropriate mood. Advertisers often use **needledrop**, which Linda Scott describes as follows:

> Needledrop is an occupational term common to advertising agencies and the music industry. It refers to music that is prefabricated, multipurpose, and highly conventional. It is, in that sense, the musical equivalent of stock photos, clip art, or canned copy. Needledrop is an inexpensive substitute for original music; paid for on a one-time basis, it is dropped into a commercial or film when a particular normative effect is desired.[39]

In some commercials, music is much more central to the advertising message. It can be used to get attention, break through the advertising clutter, communicate a key selling point, help establish an image or position, or add feeling.[40] For example, the David & Goliath agency has used music very effectively in commercials it has created for the Kia Soul subcompact car which feature the animated hamster characters shown driving the car and wearing hip-hop gear (Exhibit 9–28). Advertising for the Kia Soul is targeted at millennials and four pillars of their lifestyle: music, sports, pop culture, and "connected life" which includes a connection to technology and close ties to friends and family.[41] A number of hit songs have been used in the commercials, including hip-hop duo Black Sheep's song "This or That" and LMFAO's hit song "Party Rock Anthem." The "Share Some Soul" commercial that uses "Party Rock Anthem" shows the hamsters rolling up to a robot warzone in a Kia Soul. The robots hear the music playing inside the car and stop shooting and stare at the bright green vehicle. As the hamsters step out, decked out in fluorescent hipster gear, they break into their famous dance shuffle to the song and the robots follow suit. Eventually everyone is dancing and the hamsters hop back in the car and drive off after completing their mission to make, as the song lyrics state, "everybody just have a good time."

YTC **09–12**

**Celebrity Voiceovers**

youtube.com/10ebelch

**EXHIBIT 9–28**

Music is an integral part of the TV commercials for the Kia Soul that feature the hip-hop hamsters

Another example of the effective use of music is advertising for various NicoDerm nicotine replacement products that are used by many smokers who are trying to quit the habit. Classic songs such as Rare Earth's "I Just Want to Celebrate" and Marvin Gaye and Tammi Terrell's hit "Ain't No Mountain High Enough" are used in its commercials to reinforce the message that every time someone trying to stop smoking says no to a cigarette, it is cause for celebration as he or she is moving closer to achieving the goal.

Steve Oakes conducted a review and analysis of research on consumers' cognitive and affective responses to music in advertising.[42] He found that increased congruity between the music and advertising with respect to variables such as mood, genre, score, image, and tempo contributes to the communication effectiveness of an advertisement by enhancing recall, brand attitude, affective response, and purchase intention. Research has also shown that music can work through a classical conditioning process to create a positive mood that makes consumers more receptive to an advertising message.[43] These studies underscore the importance of considering the mood induced by music and how it might influence responses to ads.

Because music can play such an important role in the creative strategy, many companies have paid large sums for the rights to use popular songs in their commercials. There are two kinds of works to which companies negotiate rights when licensing music for use in commercials. The *musical composition* includes the music notes and the words, while the *master recording* includes the voice(s) of the original artist.[44] The latter is usually much more expensive to buy, so advertisers will often negotiate for the rights to use the music and have it performed by someone with a similar voice. Rights to music can be held by various parties, such as the original artist, the artist's estate, or a music publishing company. For example, the rights to songs done by the late reggae star Bob Marley are held by his estate, while the rights to songs by the Beatles are controlled by a music publishing company. While it is less expensive to rerecord the music, some advertisers are willing to pay millions of dollars to use the voices of the original artists in their commercials. IMC Perspective 9–2 discusses how marketers also have made songs an important part of their commercials in recent years.

Another important musical element in both TV and radio commercials is **jingles**, catchy songs about a product or service that usually carry the advertising theme and a simple message. For example, Doublemint gum has used the well-known "Double your pleasure, double your fun with Doublemint, Doublemint gum" for years. The jingle is very memorable and serves as a good reminder of the product's minty flavor. Subway Restaurants' "Five-dollar foot-long" jingle has been an integral part of one of the most effective promotional campaigns ever developed in the fast-food industry. The catchy jingle ("Five. Five. Five dollar. Five dollar foot-long") repeats the word *five* several times to help register the price of the product and help promote the value of the large sandwiches.[45] Oscar Mayer has used the popular jingles for some of its products, such as the bologna song ("My bologna has a first name/ It's O-S-C-A-R") and the Oscar Mayer wiener song ("I'd love to be an Oscar Mayer wiener"), as the basis of integrated marketing programs. The company's fleet of wienermobiles travel the country as part of the Oscar Mayer Talent Search, where local auditions are held in search of children who will continue the 30-year tradition of singing the catchy bologna and wiener jingles.[46] Other popular jingles include those for retailer Toys "Я" Us ("I don't wanna grow up, I'm a ToysЯ Us kid"), Folgers coffee ("The best part of waking up is Folgers in your cup"), and Kay Jewelers ("Every kiss begins with Kay").

YTC 09–13

Jingles

youtube.com/10ebelch

In some commercials, jingles are used more as a form of product identification and appear at the end of the message. Jingles are often composed by companies that specialize in writing commercial music for advertising. These jingle houses work with the creative team to determine the role music will play in the commercial and the message that needs to be communicated.

While the use of jingles dates back to the 1950s, they are used less frequently today than in the past as many advertisers are using current and classic pop songs in their ads. The director of music at the Leo Burnett agency notes that companies using jingles must be careful, noting that "we are living in a world of iPods, MTV, and video and jingles sound corny."[47] However, despite these concerns, many marketers

# IMC Perspective 9-2 > > >

## Advertisers Recognize the Value of Music in Their Commercials

While music has always been an important part of television commercials, more and more advertisers are using popular songs in their ads that resonate with consumers and help keep their brands top-of-mind. Songs from artists such as Madonna, Beyoncé, Jay-Z, the Black Eyed Peas, Lil Wayne, the Rolling Stones, and the Beatles serve as the backdrop in commercials for just about everything including cars, beer, fast food, soft drinks, athletic shoes, and insurance. There are a number of reasons why companies pay large amounts of money to use popular songs in their commercials. Marketers know that music can draw attention to a commercial that might otherwise be ignored, and it can help create the mood they desire by tapping into consumer emotions such as nostalgia, excitement, or sentiment. When advertisers marry the right song with the right product, they can strike a responsive chord with consumers, which gets them to attend to the ad and can help differentiate the company or brand.

Nike pioneered the commercial use of music from major artists in 1987 when it featured the original recording of the class Beatles song "Revolution" in ads for its shoes. Since then a number of major companies have paid large sums of money to use the music and lyrics of hit songs to deliver their advertising messages. Some of the largest deals between companies and artists have included Cadillac paying Led Zeppelin several million dollars to use the legendary band's rock song "Rock and Roll" for its "Break Through" ad campaign. Microsoft reportedly paid $12 million to the Rolling Stones for use of its hit song "Start Me Up," which was featured in ads for its Windows 95 operating system. Six years later Microsoft entered into another multimillion-dollar deal to use Madonna's hit song "Ray of Light" to introduce its new XP software.

A number of other artists also have recently struck major deals to have their music used in commercials such as Lady Gaga, whose song "Edge of Glory" is in a 90-second spot for the Google Chrome web browser; Jay-Z, whose music is used in a spot for Duracell's Powermat; and Alicia Keys, whose hit song "Girl on Fire" can be heard in Citibank commercials.

For many years, popular singers and rock groups would not allow their songs to be used in commercials, and some are still unwilling to do so. There is a scene in the movie *The Doors* that shows Jim Morrison going on a tirade when he learns his bandmates sold the group's hit song "Light My Fire" for use in a car commercial. Rumor has it that Cadillac originally wanted to use the classic Doors song "Break on Through (to the Other Side)" as the music in its commercials, but the surviving members of the group turned down the deal. However, many artists have learned that the benefits, exposure, and money often far outweigh an outdated concern over selling out to the advertising world. The lines that once separated artists from the dreaded perception of commercialism have become intertwined as many now write songs specifically for ads. Jack White does work for Coca-Cola, the Black Eyed Peas wrote music for Snickers commercials, and even the legendary Bob Dylan and rock group U2 have had their music used in Apple ads.

There are a number of reasons for the shift in artists' attitudes toward having their music used in advertising. It has become increasingly difficult to get on the playlists of many radio stations because many play established hits rather than try to discover new ones. Eric Hirshberg, the former president and chief creative officer of Deutsch LA, notes that there are several other factors that have changed the game regarding

still use jingles. In fact, jingles have made somewhat of a comeback in recent years as many marketers want to include original music as part of their advertising messages.[48] A number of companies have been reinventing their own jingles for a new generation of consumers such as State Farm, which did a hip-hop version of its classic "Like a good neighbor, State Farm is there" jingle and Meow Mix cat food, which recently had artist Cee Lo Green do a remix of the iconic Meow Mix jingle.[49]

Jingles are also still commonplace in the television and radio commercials used by local advertisers; these companies view them as an effective way to keep their company name and/or slogan in the minds of their customers and prospects. The position of many advertisers regarding the use of jingles is perhaps best summed up by a Procter & Gamble brand manager who stated that the company believes jingles still work, noting that "if they are humming it, they are buying it."[50]

### Planning and Production of TV Commercials
One of the first decisions that has to be made in planning a TV commercial is the type of appeal and execution style that will be used. Television is well suited to both rational and emotional advertising appeals or combinations of the two. Various execution styles used with rational appeals, such as a straight sell or announcement, demonstration, testimonial, or comparison, work well on TV. Television is particularly well suited

the use of music in commercials. He points to the great creative work done for advertisers such as Mitsubishi, Apple, Gap, Target, and Volkswagen that has used the work of relatively unknown bands. For example, "Start the Commotion" by the Wiseguys didn't hit Billboard's top-40 list until it was featured in a commercial for the Mitsubishi Eclipse two years later. The song "Jerk It Out" by The Caesars did not generate significant sales until it was featured in an iPod ad two years after its release. Another artist who benefited by having her music used in an Apple ad is Feist as downloads of the song "1234" skyrocketed when the catchy tune was used in an iPod Nano commercial. Thus, many musicians are finding that landing a song in the right commercial can do more for their careers than securing a recording contract.

While advertisers know that music plays an important role in commercials, they also recognize that using music effectively has become more challenging today because the Internet has created such varied and sophisticated musical tastes. Music has become totally decentralized and diffuse, which means it can come from anywhere and marketers often find clever ways to use it. For example, Wonder Pistachios developed an entertaining 30-second spot featuring South Korean musician Psy singing his hit song "Gangnam Style" and doing his signature horse dance. The spot capitalized on the popularity of the song and dance, which became the first YouTube video to reach a billion hits in late 2012. Absolut vodka created a music video and TV spot for its Greyhound cocktail featuring the music of Swedish House Mafia, the popular electronic dance trio from Stockholm. Watching TV commercials these days is almost like turning the radio dial as more songs from every kind of era and every kind of artist can be heard.

Some advertising creative people argue that music can account for as much as 50 percent of the effectiveness of a commercial and are pushing their clients to put more money into great music tracks. Film and commercial editor Livio Sanchez notes that using celebrities, artists, and athletes in ads is nothing new, but finding new ways to incorporate them into ads is possible by using great music. He cites the example of a spot he edited for soft drink Mountain Dew where the challenge was to reach a young and diverse demographic by using hip-hop artists such as Lil Wayne and Mac Miller, country-music singer Jason Aldean, NASCAR driver Dale Earnhardt Jr., and several action sports stars. To integrate all of them into one ad, the creative team incorporated a statement recorded live at a Lil Wayne concert and used a montage of visuals with the tagline, "This is how we Dew."

Many major advertising agencies and companies have been giving more attention to associating themselves with original music and the development of artists by acquiring independent music labels. For example, PepsiCo's Mountain Dew brand formed Green Label Sound, which has released new songs from indie bands such as Matt & Kim and The Cool Kids, while the Interpublic Group of Cos. McCann Erikson agency formed an in-house record label StayU Music on behalf of client Holiday Inn. The label's first single, "You Always Make Me Smile," by Kyle Andrews was featured in a global advertising campaign for Holiday Inn a few years ago.

There was a time when artists felt having their music used in commercials or creating songs for ads was "selling out." However, more artists now recognize that it is more beneficial and lucrative to "sell in" and become open to having their music used in commercials. This means it is likely we will hear even more of our favorite songs as part of the pitch for a variety of products and services.

Sources: Rance Crain, "Music Might Be the Most Crucial Element in Your Commercial Mix," *Advertising Age*, February 3, 2013, www.adage.com/article/rance-crain/music-crucial-element-commercial-mix/239500/; Andrew Hampp, "A Reprise for Jingles on Madison Avenue: Brands, Agencies Rediscovering Power of Original Tunes in Ad Campaigns," *Advertising Age*, September 6, 2010, Eric Hirshberg, "Music in Advertising: Once Selling Out, Now Buying In," *Billboard*, September 30, 2006, p. 4; Domenic Priore, "The Band Play On: When Marketing Gives Music a Lift," *Brandweek*, July 25, 2005, pp. 26, 27; Dawn Sutter Madell, "Only You Can Prevent Music-Licensing Disasters," *Advertising Age*, May 18, 2009, http://adage.com/print?article_id=136686.

**YTC 09–14**

**Music in Commercials**

youtube.com/10ebelch

to emotional appeals such as humor, fear, romance, and fantasies, which are often executed using dramatizations and slice-of-life commercials.

Advertisers recognize that they need to do more than talk about, demonstrate, or compare their products or services. Their commercials have to break through the clutter and grab viewers' attention; they must often appeal to emotional, as well as rational, buying motives. Television is essentially an entertainment medium, and many advertisers recognize that their commercials are most successful when they entertain as well as inform. Many of the most popular advertising campaigns are characterized by commercials with strong entertainment value, like the musical spots for Apple and the Gap, the many engaging Nike ads, and humorous ads for companies/brands such as GEICO, FedEx, and Bud Light.

Television commercials are an integral part of the IMC program for most marketers, particularly larger companies that are advertising their products and services to mass markets. However, the costs of planning and producing a TV commercial can be very high and must be considered as part of the budget for an advertising campaign. While it is possible to produce a commercial for a few thousand dollars (such as many spots that air for local retailers and businesses), marketers recognize that a poorly produced TV ad will not be effective and may have a negative impact on the company and/or brand's image. Thus, large amounts of money are often required to

FIGURE 9–3

Production Costs for a
30-Second Television
Commercial

**Big Time Productions**
1234 Production Place
Santa Monica, CA 90404

| Bid Date 3/25/10 | | Firm Bid (x)   Cost Plus Fixed Fee ( ) | |
|---|---|---|---|
| Production Co: | Big Time Productions | Agency: | Awesome Ads |
| Address: | 1234 Production Place | Address: | 1234 Advertising Way |
| | Santa Monica, CA 90404 | | Santa Monica, CA 90404 |
| Telephone: | (310)555-5555 | Telephone: | (310)555-5555 |
| Fax: | (310)444-4444 | Fax: | (310)444-4444 |
| Job #: | M10-340 | Agency Prod: | Ashley Producer |
| Director: | | Agency Art Dir: | Brian Artist |
| Executive Producer: | | Agency Writer: | Deborah Writer |
| Production Contact: | | Agency Bus Mgr: | Alan Business |
| DP: | | Client: | FAST FOOD CHAIN |
| Art Director: | | Product: | Sandwich, Burger, |
| Editor: | Fine Edits | Bid Name: | |
| Pre-Production | | | |
| Days: | | | |
| Build & Strike Days: | | Commercial Title: | Length: |
| Pre-Light Days: | One | 1) "Delicious Sandwich" | :30 |
| Studio Shoot Days: | | 2) "Yummy Burger" | :30 |
| Location Days: | Two       Hours: 10 & 14 | | |
| Locations(s) | Los Angeles | | |

| SUMMARY OF PRODUCTION COSTS | TOTAL |
|---|---|
| PRE-PRODUCTION & WRAP | $76,676 |
| SHOOTING LABOR | $93,901 |
| LOCATIONS & TRAVEL | $65,690 |
| PROPS, WARDROBE & ANIMALS | $18,670 |
| STUDIO & SET CONSTRUCTION | $88,056 |
| EQUIPMENT | $42,750 |
| FILMSTOCK DEVELOP & PRINT | $22,920 |
| DIRECTOR/CREATIVE FEES | $32,400 |
| INSURANCE | $12,288 |
| PRODUCTION MARK UP | $92,153 |
| NEEDLEDROP MUSIC | $2,000 |
| EDITING | $66,504 |
| TALENT | $33,905 |
| | |
| GRAND TOTAL | $647,913 |

produce high-quality TV commercials. The most recent Television Production Cost Survey by the American Association of Advertising Agencies (4As) revealed that the average cost for producing a 30-second commercial for a national brand was $354,000.[51] Figure 9–3 shows an example of the production costs for a commercial that was produced for a major fast-food chain.

There are many factors that contribute to the costs of producing a TV commercial, including production personnel, equipment, location fees, video editing, sound recording and mixing, music fees, and talent. Increases in television commercial production costs are a major concern among marketers, and many companies are looking for ways to reduce them. For example, a large expense item is talent costs as actors and actresses who appear in commercials receive *residuals* that are based primarily on how many times a commercial airs. However, the Joint Policy Committee on Broadcast Relations, an advertising industry group that represents advertisers and agencies in bargaining with talent unions, has proposed a new compensation system that will base pay for commercial actors on gross ratings points that are calculated by determining the size of the audience the spot reaches as well as the number of times it is run. However, this new compensation system is still in the pilot testing stage.[52]

**Planning the Commercial** The various elements of a TV commercial are brought together in a **script**, a written version of a commercial that provides a detailed description of its video and audio content. The script shows the various audio components of the commercial—the copy to be spoken by voices, the music, and sound effects. The video portion of the script provides the visual plan of the commercial—camera actions and angles, scenes, transitions, and other important descriptions. The script also shows how the video corresponds to the audio portion of the commercial.

| Preproduction | Production | Postproduction |
|---|---|---|
| • Selection of a director<br>• Selection of a production company<br>• Bidding<br>• Cost estimation and timing<br>• Production timetable<br>    Set construction<br>    Location<br>    Agency and client approvals<br>    Casting<br>    Wardrobes<br>• Preproduction meeting | • Location versus set shoots<br>• Night/weekend shoots<br>• Talent arrangements | • Editing<br>• Processing<br>• Recording of sound effects<br>• Audio/video mixing<br>• Opticals<br>• Client–agency approval<br>• Duplicating<br>• Release/shipping |

**FIGURE 9–4**

The Three Phases of
Production for Commercials

Once the basic script has been conceived, the writer and art director get together to produce a storyboard, a series of drawings used to present the visual plan or layout of a proposed commercial. The storyboard contains still drawings of the video scenes and descriptions of the audio that accompanies each scene. Like layouts for print ads, storyboards provide those involved in the production and approval of the commercial with a good approximation of what the final commercial will look like. In some cases an animatic (a videotape of the storyboard along with the soundtrack) may be produced if a more finished form of the commercial is needed for client presentations or pretesting.

**Production** Once the storyboard or animatic of the commercial is approved, it is ready to move to the production phase, which involves three stages:

1. *Preproduction*—all the work and activities that occur before the actual shooting/recording of the commercial.
2. *Production*—the period during which the commercial is filmed or videotaped and recorded.
3. *Postproduction*—activities and work that occur after the commercial has been filmed and recorded.

The various activities of each phase are shown in Figure 9–4. Before the final production process begins, the client must usually review and approve the creative strategy and the various tactics that will be used in creating the advertising message.

# CLIENT EVALUATION AND APPROVAL OF CREATIVE WORK

While the creative specialists have much responsibility for determining the advertising appeal and execution style to be used in a campaign, the client must evaluate and approve the creative approach before any ads are produced. A number of people on the client side may be involved in evaluating the creative work of the agency, including the advertising or communications manager, product or brand managers, marketing director or vice president, representatives from the legal department, and sometimes even the president or chief executive officer (CEO) of the company or the board of directors.

The amount of input each of these individuals has in the creative evaluation and approval process varies depending on the company's policies, the importance of the product to the company, the role of advertising in the marketing program, and the advertising approach being recommended. For example, the Chiat/Day agency had to convince Apple's board of directors to air the famous "1984" commercial used to introduce the Macintosh personal computer, as discussed in IMC Perspective 9–3.

# IMC Perspective 9–3 > > >

## Apple's "1984" Commercial: A Tribute to the Legendary Ad and Steve Jobs

If you asked many marketing and advertising executives to name the best and/or most influential television commercial ever, it is very likely they would answer Apple's "1984" spot. If asked why they chose this ad, many would mention how it aired only one time during the 1984 Super Bowl, helped make the big game the advertising showcase it has become, and was the beginning of the new era of integrated marketing communications. It is also likely they would link the spot to Steve Jobs, Apple's visionary leader who two decades later would bring the world revolutionary products such as the iPod, iPhone, and iPad before passing away in 2011. And they might mention how the "1984" spot almost never aired because Apple's board of directors absolutely hated it. All of this still might lead you to wonder why a commercial that is now over three decades old is still talked about and held in such high regard. Before reading further you might want to go on YouTube to watch the "1984" commercial, which will help frame this discussion of it.

To understand why the "1984" spot has become legendary, it is important to understand what led to its creation and purpose. In 1983 Apple Computer was planning the introduction of its new line of Macintosh personal computers. Apple had just lost its lead in the PC market to IBM, and its previous product introduction, the $10,000 Lisa, had not been very successful. Some analysts suggested that the survival of Apple might depend on the market's response to the Mac. Apple's marketing strategy called for the launch of the Macintosh to be a major event that would bring immediate attention to the product and generate support for it. Apple's advertising agency, Chiat/Day, was given the creative challenge of coming up with a blockbuster idea that would result in a dramatic commercial to introduce the Mac. Steve Hayden, who was the senior vice president and creative director at the agency at the time, notes that Steve Jobs's creative brief for the commercial was simple: "I want to stop the world in its tracks."

Chiat/Day's creative team developed a commercial based on the concept of Big Brother from George Orwell's classis novel *1984*. The ad used stark images of Orwell's dystopia, including zombie-like citizens marching into a room and staring at a huge screen where Big Brother is on a rant speaking about Orwellian concepts such as "information purification, unprincipled dissemination of facts, and unification of thought." Against this ominous backdrop a young woman, dressed in athletic gear and being chased by helmeted militia, runs into the theater and hurls a sledgehammer into the screen, causing an explosion that shatters Big Brother. A message then flashes on the screen accompanied by a voiceover that says: "On January 24th, Apple Computer will introduce Macintosh and you'll see why 1984 will not be like 1984." More than $500,000 was spent to produce the commercial, which was filmed in London by well-known film director Ridley Scott and contained a cast of more than 200.

When the "1984" spot was first shown at Apple's annual sales meeting in 1983, there was stunned silence followed by a standing ovation. And although when Steve Jobs introduced the spot at the meeting he cast IBM in the role of Big Brother, Hayden notes that that was never the intention. He says that "the real villain was our collective fear of technology, not a corporation either real or imagined. We wanted to democratize technology, telling people that the power was now literally in their hands." While Steve Jobs and the Apple sales team loved the "1984" spot, the sentiment was not shared by Apple's board of directors. When Jobs and Apple's marketing director Michael Murray played the commercial for the board, Murray reported that most of the board members were holding their heads in their hands, shaking them ruefully, and the board chair asked for a motion to fire the ad agency. The board thought the commercial was too controversial and might be detrimental to Apple's image, particularly in the business segment of the market. They also thought the Super Bowl ad rates were too expensive and directed the agency to sell the two minutes of ad time they had purchased. The agency began working to sell the media time while simultaneously lobbying Apple not to cancel the spot. Jobs and Apple's co-founder, Steve Wozniak, even offered to pay half the cost of running it out of their own personal accounts. The agency did manage to sell one of the 60-second time slots (30 seconds to Hertz

Earlier in this chapter, we noted that Procter & Gamble has been moving away from testimonials and slice-of-life advertising executions to somewhat riskier and more lively forms of advertising. But the company remains conservative and has been slow to adopt the avant-garde ads used by many of its competitors. Agencies that do the advertising for various P&G brands recognize that quirky executions that challenge the company's subdued corporate culture are not likely to be approved.[53]

In many cases, top management is involved in selecting an ad agency and must approve the theme and creative strategy for the campaign. Evaluation and approval of the individual ads proposed by the agency often rest with the advertising and product managers who are primarily responsible for the brand. The account executive

On January 24th,
Apple Computer will introduce
Macintosh.
And you'll see why 1984
won't be like "1984"

and another 30 seconds to Heinz) but could not attract a reasonable offer for the other. Two days before the game the board left it up to Jobs and Apple CEO John Sculley whether to run the controversial commercial. The "1984" commercial did end up running and the rest, as they say, is history.

The impact of the "1984" commercial was tremendous as it quickly became the focus of attention in the media and the talk of the advertising and marketing industries. It earned an estimated additional $150 million in media value by being replayed as the subject of stories and commentary on all of the major networks and local news shows. However, there are some interesting additional aspects to the "1984" spot that are often overlooked when discussing or writing about it. For example, one myth surrounding the spot is that the 1984 Super Bowl was the only time the spot aired on television. In an *Adweek* article paying tribute to the spot, Hayden notes that the agency ran a 30-second version of "1984" in the top 10 U.S. markets and in an 11th market, Boca Raton, Florida, which is where IBM's PC division was headquartered. Hayden notes that the fact that only the Super Bowl version is remembered is testimony to the importance of the right media buy (the Super Bowl) and the power of a 60- versus 30-second spot. It is also interesting to note that "1984" was originally scheduled to air on New Year's Day college football games but was pushed back to the Super Bowl to be closer to the Macintosh's official introduction at the annual board and shareholder's meeting. Ironically, Steve Jobs questioned

the idea of running the ad on the Super Bowl as he did not know anyone who watched the game and had to be convinced that computer buyers even watched football. While the "1984" commercial achieved Jobs's goal of stopping everyone in their tracks, it also helped Apple reach its very ambitious sales goal of selling 50,000 Macs in the first 100 days as actual sales surpassed 72,000 units. However, the sales were not due only to the power of the "1984" spot; Jobs and Sculley both realized that the commercial would create an information vacuum. To address this problem they ordered a 20-page insert for *Time* and *Newsweek* magazines, as well as a series of product-focused TV spots highlighting the features of the Mac and what made it "the computer for the rest of us."

Many articles and stories have been written about the "1984" spot, and it has accumulated numerous accolades over the years. In 1999 *TV Guide* named the spot the greatest TV commercial of all time and *Advertising Age* recognized it as the best commercial of the 20th century. It is interesting to note that a few years after the Macintosh was launched, Apple struggled to compete in the personal computer industry, as PCs with the Microsoft Windows operating systems dominated the market, and Jobs was ousted as the company's chair. Apple also moved its advertising from Chiat/Day to BBDO, which handled the account for 10 years. However, when Jobs returned to Apple in 1996, the first thing he did was rehire Chiat/Day and had the agency produce another great Super Bowl commercial called "Here's to the Crazy Ones," which was part of the critically acclaimed "Think Different" campaign. There is little doubt that Jobs always thought different, and the succession of hit products he created over the past two decades are testimony to his brilliance. So the next time you listen to music on your iPod, make a call on your iPhone, or read something on your iPad, think back to the "1984" spot and how it contributed to the genesis of the computer revolution. And also think about the genius of Steve Jobs.

Sources: Michael Learmonth, "He Thought Different," *Advertising Age*, October 10, 2011, pp. 1–3; Steve Hayden, "'1984': As Good As It Gets," *AdweekMedia*, January 31, 2011, pp. 14, 15; Bob Garfield, "The Central Genius of Apple's Advertising under Jobs: It Was True," *Advertising Age*, October 6, 2011, http://adage.com/article/bob-garfield/central-genius-apple-s-advertising-jobs/230239/; Dottie Enrico, "The Best Ads Keep Going and . . . Going," *TV Guide*, July 2–9, 1999, pp. 2–6; Bradley Johnson, "Ten Years after Apple's '1984': The Commercial and the Product That Changed Advertising," *Advertising Age*, January 10, 1994, www.adage.com/article/news/ten-years-apple-s-1984-commercial-product-changed-advertising/88772/.

**YTC 09–15**
Apple "1984"
youtube.com/10ebelch

and a member of the creative team present the creative concept to the client's advertising and product and/or marketing managers for their approval before beginning production. A careful evaluation should be made before the ad actually enters production, since this stage requires considerable time and money as suppliers are hired to perform the various functions required to produce the actual ad.

The client's evaluation of the print layout or commercial storyboard can be difficult, since the advertising or brand manager is generally not a creative expert and must be careful not to reject viable creative approaches or accept ideas that will result in inferior advertising. However, personnel on the client side can use the guidelines discussed next to judge the efficacy of creative approaches suggested by the agency.

## Guidelines for Evaluating Creative Output

Advertisers use numerous criteria to evaluate the creative approach suggested by the ad agency. In some instances, the client may want to have the rough layout storyboard or animatic pretested to get quantitative information to assist in the evaluation. (Various methods for pretesting print ads and TV commercials will be discussed in Chapter 18.) However, the evaluation process is usually more subjective; the advertising or brand manager relies on qualitative considerations. Basic criteria for evaluating creative approaches are discussed next:

- *Is the creative approach consistent with the brand's marketing and advertising objectives?* One of the most important factors the client must consider is whether the creative appeal and execution style recommended by the agency are consistent with the marketing strategy for the brand and the role advertising and promotion have been assigned in the overall marketing program. This means the creative approach must be compatible with the image of the brand and the way it is positioned in the marketplace and should contribute to the marketing and advertising objectives. For example, SKYY Spirits recently extended

**EXHIBIT 9–29**
Advertising for SKYY Infusions builds off the core brand equity base and is consistent with marketing objectives

its product line by introducing an all natural, infused super-premium vodka to capitalize on the growth in the flavored segment of the vodka market. Advertising for the new SKYY Infusions line uses bold creative featuring strong visual images that communicate the natural flavor ingredients, as well as the brand's distinctive cobalt blue bottle (Exhibit 9–29). These ads are consistent with the core brand equity base of SKYY, from which several new product lines have been launched. The SKYY Infusions line extension also contributes to the equity of the core SKYY brand, which helps build the strength and value of the overall brand franchise.

- *Is the creative approach consistent with the creative strategy and objectives? Does it communicate what it is supposed to?* The advertising appeal and execution must meet the communications objectives laid out in the copy platform, and the ad must say what the advertising strategy calls for it to say. Creative specialists can lose sight of what the advertising message is supposed to be and come up with an approach that fails to execute the advertising strategy. Individuals responsible for approving the ad should ask the creative specialists to explain how the appeal or execution style adheres to the creative strategy and helps meet communications objectives.

- *Is the creative approach appropriate for the target audience?* Generally, much time has been spent defining, locating, and attempting to understand the target audience for the advertiser's product or service. Careful consideration should be given to whether the ad appeal or execution recommended will appeal to, be understood by, and communicate effectively with the target audience. This involves studying all elements of the ad and how the audience will respond to them. Advertisers do not want to approve advertising that they believe will receive a negative reaction from the target audience. For example, it has been suggested that advertising targeted to older consumers should use models who are 10 years younger than the average age of the target audience, since most people feel younger than their chronological age.[54] Advertisers also face a considerable challenge developing ads for the teen market because teenagers' styles, fashions, language, and values change so rapidly. They may find they are using an advertising approach, a spokesperson, or even an expression that is no longer popular among teens.

■ *Does the creative approach communicate a clear and convincing message to the customer?* Most ads are supposed to communicate a message that will help sell the brand. Many ads fail to communicate a clear and convincing message that motivates consumers to use a brand. While creativity is important in advertising, it is also important that the advertising communicate information attributes, features and benefits, and/or images that give consumers a reason to buy the brand.

■ *Does the creative execution keep from overwhelming the message?* A common criticism of advertising, and TV commercials in particular, is that so much emphasis is placed on creative execution that the advertiser's message gets overshadowed. Many creative, entertaining commercials have failed to register the brand name and/or selling points effectively. For example, Aflac had to modify the commercials using its iconic duck character after several research studies showed that many consumers were not exactly sure what Aflac insurance was. Consumers indicated that the advertising didn't explain what supplemental insurance is and what Aflac does, so recent ads focus more attention on explaining the product and the company.[55]

With the increasing amount of clutter in most advertising media, it may be necessary to use a novel creative approach to gain the viewer's or reader's attention. However, the creative execution cannot overwhelm the message. Clients must walk a fine line: Make sure the sales message is not lost, but be careful not to stifle the efforts of the creative specialists and force them into producing dull, boring advertising.

■ *Is the creative approach appropriate for the media environment in which it is likely to be seen?* Each media vehicle has its own specific climate that results from the nature of its editorial content, the type of reader or viewer it attracts, and the nature of the ads it contains. Consideration should be given to how well the ad fits into the media environment in which it will be shown. For example, the Super Bowl has become a showcase for commercials. People who care very little about advertising know how much a 30-second commercial costs and pay as much attention to the ads as to the game itself, so many advertisers feel compelled to develop new ads for the Super Bowl or to save new commercials for the game. In some cases marketers may develop ads specifically for certain media vehicles such as magazines. For example, many of the ads run in the popular *Sports Illustrated Swimsuit Issue* that is published each February are adapted to fit with the theme of the magazine. Exhibit 9–30 shows an example of a clever ad done by TaylorMade Golf for the annual *SI* swimsuit edition.

■ *Is the ad truthful and tasteful?* Marketers also have to consider whether an ad is truthful, as well as whether it might offend consumers. For example, household cleaner marketer Method recently had to pull the "Shiny Suds" online commercial for its organic bathroom tile cleaning product. The video began by showing a woman appearing in a commercial featuring the friendly bubble creatures who are similar to those shown in the ads for rival SC Johnson's Scrubbing Bubbles brand. However, when the woman takes

**EXHIBIT 9–30**

This clever ad was created specifically for the special swimsuit edition of *Sports Illustrated*

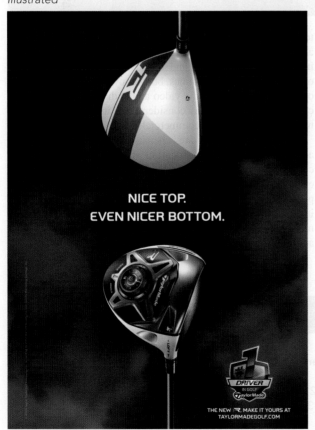

NICE TOP.
EVEN NICER BOTTOM.

THE NEW ℝ, MAKE IT YOURS AT
TAYLORMADEGOLF.COM

a shower the next day, the bubble creatures are still there and turn into leering perverts who make sexually suggestive comments while the woman is cleansing her body. The commercial was intended to be a parody of advertising for traditional household cleaner advertising and support the Household Product Labeling Acts, which would require disclosure of ingredients in household cleaners. However, the spot evoked negative reactions from some consumers who felt that the spot was degrading to women and threatened to boycott Method products. Although Method indicated that most of the comments it received about the spot were positive, it removed the spot from its website.[56]

The ultimate responsibility for determining whether an ad deceives or offends the target audience lies with the client. It is the job of the advertising or brand manager to evaluate the approach suggested by the creative specialists against company standards. The firm's legal department may be asked to review the ad to determine whether the creative appeal, message content, or execution could cause any problems for the company. It is much better to catch any potential legal problems before the ad is shown to the public.

The advertising manager, brand manager, or other personnel on the client side can use these basic guidelines in reviewing, evaluating, and approving the ideas offered by the creative specialists. There may be other factors specific to the firm's advertising and marketing situation. Also, there may be situations where it is acceptable to deviate from the standards the firm usually uses in judging creative output. As we will see in Chapter 18, the client may want to move beyond these subjective criteria and use more sophisticated pretesting methods to determine the effectiveness of a particular approach suggested by the creative specialist or team.

## Summary

In this chapter, we examined how the advertising message is implemented and executed. Once the creative strategy that will guide the ad campaign has been determined, attention turns to the specific type of advertising appeal and execution format to carry out the creative plan. The appeal is the central message used in the ad to elicit some response from consumers or influence their feelings. Appeals can be broken into two broad categories, rational and emotional. Rational appeals focus on consumers' practical, functional, or utilitarian need for the product or service; emotional appeals relate to social and/ or psychological reasons for purchasing a product or service. Numerous types of appeals are available to advertisers within each category.

The creative execution style is the way the advertising appeal is presented in the message. A number of common execution techniques were examined in the chapter, along with considerations for their use. Attention was also given to tactical issues involved in creating print and TV advertising. The components of a print ad include headlines, body copy, illustrations, and layout. We also examined the video and audio components of TV commercials and various considerations involved in the planning and production of commercials.

Creative specialists are responsible for determining the advertising appeal and execution style as well as the tactical aspects of creating ads. However, the client must review, evaluate, and approve the creative approach before any ads are produced or run. A number of criteria can be used by advertising, product, or brand managers and others involved in the promotional process to evaluate the advertising messages before approving final production.

## Key Terms

advertising appeal p. 301
creative execution style p. 301
informational/rational appeals p. 301
emotional appeals p. 303
transformational ad p. 305
reminder advertising p. 308

teaser advertising p. 309
user-generated content (UGC) p. 309
headline p. 320
direct headlines p. 321
indirect headlines p. 321
subheads p. 321

body copy p. 322
layout p. 323
voiceover p. 324
needledrop p. 324
jingles p. 325
script p. 328

1. The chapter opener discusses the new "Live Más" campaign for Taco Bell. Analyze the creative strategy used for this campaign, giving attention to the type of creative appeals used as well as the advertising execution. (LO1,2)

2. Discuss some of the reasons why emotion-based advertising appeals are effective. Find an example of a company or brand that is using an advertising campaign based on emotional appeals and analyze its effectiveness. (LO1)

3. Explain the concept of transformational advertising. Find an example of a company that is using transformational ads and discuss how the ads might enhance the experience of using the product or service. (LO1)

4. Discuss the reasons marketers might use user-generated content (UGC) for an advertising campaign. Do you agree with the decision by Ford to rely entirely on UGC for the advertising done to support the "Fiesta Movement: A Social Remix" campaign? Why or why not? (LO1,2)

5. What is meant by the mere exposure effect? Discuss how the banner ads that appear on various websites might take advantage of the mere exposure effect. (LO1,2)

6. Choose three of the advertising execution techniques discussed in the chapter and find examples of advertisements that are using them. Discuss why the marketers might be using these particular ad execution techniques. (LO2)

7. Discuss some of the reasons a marketer might choose to create a personality symbol or character to represent the company or brand. Analyze the strategy behind Dos Equis's use of "The Most Interesting Man in the World" campaign. Why has this campaign been so effective? (LO2)

8. Discuss the role of headlines in a print advertisement. What is the difference between a direct headline and an indirect headline and when might each type be used? (LO3)

9. Discuss the role of music in advertising. Find an example of a television commercial that is using a song and discuss the role the music plays in delivering the message. (LO3)

10. Choose a current advertising campaign and analyze it with respect to the creative guidelines discussed in the last section of the chapter. Identify any areas where you feel the campaign does not meet the guidelines and discuss why this is so. (LO4)

11. IMC Perspective 9–3 discusses the legendary "1984" commercial used to introduce the Apple Macintosh personal computer. Why do you think Apple chose to never run this ad again after the Super Bowl, given its popularity and impact? Do you think the "1984" spot would be as effective today as it was 30 years ago? Why or why not? (LO3,4)

## LEARNING OBJECTIVES

(LO1) To understand the key terminology used in media planning.

(LO2) To know how a media plan is developed.

(LO3) To know what constitutes media objectives.

(LO4) To know the process of developing and implementing media strategies.

(LO5) To be familiar with various characteristics of media.

# 10 Media Planning and Strategy

## THE BEST MEDIA PLANS FOCUS ON INTEGRATION

One of the most respected periodicals in the advertising industry is *Adweek*. Founded in 1978, the original purpose of the magazine was to provide a regional focus on the advertising industry's creative process, account changes, and decision makers. As reflected in its name, *Adweek*'s focus was specifically on the advertising industry. As the industry has changed, *Adweek* has kept pace, maintaining its leadership role. Each year the magazine awards companies with the prestigious Media Plan of the Year award in different categories based on media expenditures. What is different about the awards now is that rather than overall advertising media awards, the winners are based on their integrated approach. Following are the top integrated winners:

*Lexus*—While Lexus has always been a respected and well-selling automobile, the company wanted to infuse some excitement into the launch of its revamped 2013 Lexus GS sedan. The primary target market: "forty something men who embrace technology." Using a combination of traditional media—Lexus's first-ever Super Bowl spot; a spread in the *Sports Illustrated Swimsuit Issue* which featured a racetrack hugging the curves of swimsuit model Tori Praver; commercials on NCAA March Madness; and ads in *The Wall Street Journal* and *Motor Trend*—Lexus's agency Team One also employed a variety of new approaches. Consumers could download a branded game using their iPhones, place an NFC-enabled phone over an ad in *Wired* to see how the GS sedan's new dashboard works or use their mobile apps to access information. Branded content included a Speed Channel show *Shut Up and Drive,* and involvement with NBC Universal programs including E!'s *The Soup.* Clearly the $25 million plus plan worked. Within a month of the launch, Lexus's share of sales in the luxury sedan market jumped from 2 to 17 percent and were on pace to reach 24,000 units by the end of the year—four times the norm. Within two months, Lexus's Facebook likes soared by 39 percent, reaching 1.2 million!

*Sony Pictures*—In the $10 to $25 million expenditure category, Sony Pictures may have accomplished the impossible—getting men to want to see a movie based on dating advice for women (who would have ever thunk it?). To promote the movie *Think Like a Man,* a romantic comedy, agency Universal McCann created a battle of the sexes media blitz using content integrations in telecasts on BET's *Let's Stay Together,* VH1's *Basketball Wives,* and TNT's *Inside the NBA* to reach their target audience of African Americans. A heavy exposure on prime-time TV programs and cable as well as "lots of sports" constituted most of the traditional TV expenditures. Print ads in magazines like *Complex* and "Tweetstakes" raffles on online publications were used to drive awareness. The campaign helped the film achieve a $33.6 opening and a two-week run as number 1 at the box office. Talk about a powerful campaign!

*Samsung*—The agency for Samsung—Starcom MediaVest Group—proved that you don't have to spend multimillions of dollars to be successful. Their media challenge was to support the launch of Samsung's Galaxy SII smartphone and Galaxy Tab 10.1 tablet with a global message across multiple languages and cultures. Linking up with ESPN International, the pitch include a 12-part digital branded content series titled "Project Teamwork," following athletes in five countries on four continents by using the new products in a variety of ways and engaging in the universal language—sports. The Dutch beach volleyball team used the tablet to analyze its training regimen. Parkour runners in Morocco used the phone to review their adventures and a flash soccer game guerrilla event in London's Victoria Station were just some of the examples of the content posted on Samsung Mobile's YouTube page and the ESPN microsite to engage online/digital and offline elements in one overall campaign. The videos were viewed by more than 10 million visitors. More important, in a before and after survey, nearly 40 percent of consumers said they preferred Samsung after the campaign versus before, while more than 25 percent said they'd be more likely to purchase one of the Samsung products.

Sources: "Media Plan of the Year," *Adweek*, July 23, 2012, pp. 20–24; "Project Teamwork," www.youtube.com, October 11, 2011.

**YTC 10–01**

**Project Teamwork**

youtube.com/10ebelch

The discussion in this chapter's opening vignette provides a few examples of award-winning media plans. As noted, these plans involve an integrated approach to media planning employing multiple media to reach the target audiences. As a result, media planning has become more complex than ever before. As you will see in the following chapters, these changes offer the marketer opportunities not previously available, but they also require in-depth knowledge of all the media alternatives. Integrated marketing communications programs are no longer a luxury; they are a necessity. Media planners must now consider multiple new options as well as recognize the changes that are occurring in traditional sources. New and evolving media contribute to the already difficult task of media planning. Planning when, where, and how the message will be delivered is a complex and involved process that is constantly evolving. The primary objective of the media plan is to develop a framework that will deliver the message to the target audience in the most efficient, cost-effective manner possible—that will communicate what the product, brand, and/or service can do.

This chapter presents the various methods of message delivery available to marketers, examines some key considerations in making media decisions, and discusses the development of media strategies and plans. Later chapters will explore the relative advantages and disadvantages of the various media and examine each in more detail.

It should be noted that while new media often use their own terms and concepts, many also use the more traditional metrics as well. Much of the focus in this chapter will be on traditional concepts, with subsequent chapters dealing with media-specific terminology. For example, in social media, a medium would be user-generated video, YouTube as a platform, and a channel would be www.60secondmarketer.com.[1] Nevertheless, the value and necessity of a planning framework still exists across media.

# AN OVERVIEW OF MEDIA PLANNING

The media planning process is not an easy one. Options include mass media such as television, newspapers, radio, and magazines (and the choices available within each of these categories) as well as out-of-the-home media such as outdoor advertising, transit advertising, and electronic billboards. A variety of other media such as direct marketing, the Internet, promotional products, and others such as sales promotions and in-store point-of-purchase options must also be considered. A proliferation of new media, including branded entertainment, social media, and interactive media, has also provided the marketer with many options to consider.

While at first glance the choices among these alternatives might seem relatively straightforward, this is rarely the case. Part of the reason media selection becomes so involved is the nature of the media themselves. TV combines both sight and sound, an advantage not offered by most other media. Magazines can convey more information and may keep the message available to the potential buyer for a much longer time. Newspapers also offer their own advantages, as do outdoor, direct media, and each of the others. The Internet offers many of the advantages of other media but is also limited in its capabilities. The characteristics of each alternative must be considered, along with many other factors. This process becomes even more complicated when the manager has to choose between alternatives within the same medium—for example, between *Time* and *The Week* or between *The Good Wife* and *NCIS*, or Facebook and Google+.

Many companies, large and small, have come to realize the importance of a sound media strategy. They are focusing additional attention on the integration of creative work and media as well as the use of multiple media vehicles to achieve the optimal impact. For example, ads that have been shown on TV now appear for viewing on the company's Internet site. Many of the commercials that were on the 2013 Super Bowl were first released on YouTube. Some commercials now feature the television program's actors and actresses in commercials shown during the program. Target and Neiman Marcus partnered to purchase all of the commercials in the TV hit *Revenge* for an evening. The long-form commercials were approximately two minutes in length and featured different actors from the show receiving Christmas presents. Target and Neiman Marcus hoped that by integrating the show's characters, viewers would be more likely to pay attention to the commercials. (Exhibit 10–1).

The product and/or service being advertised affects the media planning process. As demonstrated in Figure 10–1, firms have found some media more useful than others in conveying their messages to specific target audiences. For example, Verizon, AT&T, and Procter & Gamble spend heavily on broadcast media, whereas others like American Express and Bank of America, while still spending on TV, allocate higher percentages of the budget to the Internet. The result is placement of advertising dollars in these preferred media—and significantly different media strategies.

YTC **10–02**

**Target and Neiman Marcus**

youtube.com/10ebelch

## Some Basic Terms and Concepts

LO 10-1

Before beginning our discussion of media planning, we review some basic terms and concepts used in the media planning and strategy process.

**Media planning** is the series of decisions involved in delivering the promotional message to the prospective purchasers and/or users of the product or brand. Media planning is a process, which means a number of decisions are made, each of which may be altered or abandoned as the plan develops.

The media plan is the guide for media selection. It requires development of specific **media objectives** and specific **media strategies** (plans of action) designed to attain these objectives. Once the decisions have been made and the objectives and strategies formulated, this information is organized into the media plan.

The **medium** is the general category of available delivery systems, which includes broadcast media (like TV and radio), print media (like newspapers and magazines), direct marketing, outdoor advertising, and other support media. The **media vehicle** is the specific carrier within a medium category. For example, *Vanity Fair* and *In Style* are print vehicles; *The Good Wife* and *60 Minutes* are broadcast vehicles. As you will see in later chapters, each vehicle has its own characteristics as well as its own relative advantages and disadvantages. Specific decisions must be made as to the value of each in delivering the message.

**Reach** is a measure of the number of different audience members exposed at least once to a media vehicle in a given period of time. **Coverage** refers to the potential audience that might receive the message through a vehicle. Coverage relates to potential audience; reach refers to the actual audience delivered. (The importance of this distinction will become clearer later in this chapter.) Finally, **frequency** refers to the number of times the receiver is exposed to the media vehicle in a specified period. While there are numerous more media planning terms that are important and commonly used (for a useful reference see *Media Planning & Buying in the 21st Century*),[2] we will begin our discussion with these as they are critical to your understanding of the planning process.

**EXHIBIT 10–1**

*Revenge* cast members appeared in commercials during the show

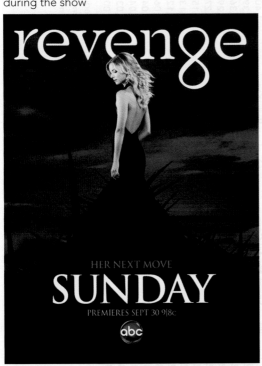

FIGURE 10–1 Leading National Advertisers, Ranked by Total U.S. Advertising Spending, 2011—$ Millions

| RANK 2011 | RANK 2010 | MARKETER | HEADQUARTERS | TOTAL U.S. SPENDING 2011 | % CHG | ESTIMATED UNMEASURED | MEASURED MEDIA | U.S. MEASURED-MEDIA SPENDING BREAKOUT IN 2011 MAGAZINE | NEWSPAPER | OUTDOOR | TV | RADIO | INTERNET |
|---|---|---|---|---|---|---|---|---|---|---|---|---|---|
| 1 | 1 | Procter & Gamble Co. | Cincinnati | $4,971.5 | 5.6 | $1,837.1 | $3,134.4 | $1,050.1 | $182.2 | $2.6 | $1,719.2 | $7.3 | $172.9 |
| 2 | 3 | General Motors Co. | Detroit | 3,055.7 | 11.3 | 1,281.5 | 1,774.2 | 223.9 | 152.0 | 6.9 | 1,114.9 | 34.7 | 241.8 |
| 3 | 4 | Verizon Communications | New York | 2,523.0 | 2.9 | 859.8 | 1,663.2 | 34.9 | 164.2 | 60.2 | 1,062.0 | 100.1 | 241.7 |
| 4 | 6 | Comcast Corp.¹ | Philadelphia | 2,465.4 | 14.3 | 880.8 | 1,584.6 | 114.8 | 123.5 | 66.9 | 834.8 | 233.5 | 211.1 |
| 5 | 2 | AT&T | Dallas | 2,359.0 | −21.1 | 505.2 | 1,853.8 | 52.1 | 193.6 | 35.0 | 1,325.3 | 92.5 | 155.3 |
| 6 | 13 | JPMorgan Chase & Co. | New York | 2,351.8 | 22.3 | 1,699.1 | 652.7 | 63.8 | 60.0 | 58.7 | 352.8 | 44.6 | 72.9 |
| 7 | 14 | Ford Motor Co. | Dearborn, Mich. | 2,141.3 | 11.8 | 1,081.0 | 1,060.3 | 144.9 | 11.5 | 2.3 | 779.9 | 31.6 | 90.2 |
| 8 | 5 | American Express Co. | New York | 2,125.3 | −6.0 | 1,719.8 | 405.4 | 64.8 | 74.1 | 17.5 | 105.3 | 23.5 | 120.2 |
| 9 | 11 | L'Oréal | Clichy, France | 2,124.6 | 7.4 | 744.2 | 1,380.4 | 709.4 | 41.2 | 1.8 | 602.6 | 0.5 | 24.8 |
| 10 | 12 | Walt Disney Co. | Burbank, Calif. | 2,112.2 | 9.3 | 1,121.1 | 991.1 | 175.1 | 55.1 | 38.6 | 546.8 | 60.2 | 115.3 |
| 11 | 7 | Pfizer | New York | 2,071.7 | −3.5 | 728.2 | 1,343.5 | 406.8 | 30.4 | 0.2 | 849.2 | 17.1 | 40.0 |
| 12 | 9 | Time Warner | New York | 2,050.9 | 0.3 | 770.8 | 1,280.1 | 281.2 | 63.5 | 76.2 | 766.8 | 21.2 | 71.2 |
| 13 | 10 | Johnson & Johnson | New Brunswick, N.J. | 1,939.6 | −4.3 | 898.9 | 1,040.8 | 247.7 | 48.2 | 0.9 | 699.1 | 2.8 | 42.0 |
| 14 | 8 | Walmart Stores | Bentonville, Ark. | 1,890.9 | −8.0 | 1,217.6 | 673.3 | 69.4 | 58.5 | 5.4 | 419.0 | 86.4 | 34.5 |
| 15 | 27 | Fiat (Chrysler Group) | Turin, Italy/Auburn Hills, Mich. | 1,770.9 | 52.1 | 484.5 | 1,286.4 | 164.2 | 41.7 | 8.9 | 957.3 | 29.6 | 84.8 |
| 16 | 16 | Toyota Motor Corp. | Toyota City, Japan | 1,727.6 | 0.3 | 639.2 | 1,088.4 | 139.1 | 12.4 | 18.3 | 767.0 | 13.6 | 137.9 |
| 17 | 17 | Bank of America Corp. | Charlotte, N.C. | 1,704.6 | 9.8 | 1,291.4 | 413.2 | 25.3 | 60.8 | 10.7 | 191.3 | 15.7 | 109.6 |
| 18 | 15 | Sears Holdings Corp. | Hoffman Estates, Ill. | 1,688.2 | −6.5 | 1,011.0 | 677.3 | 35.2 | 146.2 | 1.6 | 408.5 | 63.4 | 22.2 |
| 19 | 18 | Target Corp. | Minneapolis | 1,616.0 | 7.2 | 922.1 | 693.9 | 96.1 | 127.3 | 12.9 | 378.7 | 34.5 | 44.4 |
| 20 | 19 | Macy's | Cincinnati | 1,507.0 | 6.4 | 672.2 | 834.8 | 77.7 | 428.8 | 6.3 | 263.7 | 35.8 | 22.6 |
| 21 | 22 | Anheuser-Busch InBev | Leuven, Belgium/St. Louis | 1,423.0 | 4.8 | 907.1 | 515.9 | 30.8 | 3.0 | 30.4 | 409.4 | 26.5 | 15.8 |
| 22 | 20 | Sprint Nextel Corp. | Overland Park, Kan. | 1,400.0 | 0.0 | 519.2 | 880.8 | 89.1 | 69.3 | 10.5 | 584.5 | 13.1 | 114.4 |
| 23 | 23 | Berkshire Hathaway | Omaha, Neb. | 1,393.7 | 3.2 | 390.2 | 1,003.4 | 158.5 | 20.1 | 27.2 | 680.3 | 99.2 | 18.1 |
| 24 | 26 | McDonald's Corp. | Oak Brook, Ill. | 1,366.9 | 5.5 | 403.5 | 963.4 | 48.7 | 4.2 | 71.6 | 741.4 | 70.1 | 27.3 |
| 25 | 21 | Unilever | Rotterdam/London | 1,297.4 | −5.9 | 603.6 | 693.8 | 137.3 | 33.6 | 1.2 | 477.6 | 4.5 | 39.5 |
| 26 | 24 | New Corp. | New York | 1,274.8 | −3.4 | 492.1 | 782.7 | 48.8 | 158.7 | 37.0 | 387.3 | 81.7 | 69.3 |
| 27 | 25 | J.C. Penny Co. | Plano, Texas | 1,157.0 | −11.9 | 713.4 | 443.6 | 53.6 | 70.9 | 1.5 | 289.1 | 12.6 | 15.8 |
| 28 | 29 | Honda Motor Co. | Tokyo | 1,139.9 | 4.8 | 433.2 | 706.7 | 101.9 | 9.7 | 3.4 | 510.5 | 7.6 | 73.6 |
| 29 | 31 | Kohl's Corp. | Menomonee Falls, Wis. | 1,123.0 | 10.4 | 791.7 | 331.3 | 10.6 | 98.6 | 0.3 | 172.6 | 37.0 | 12.2 |
| 30 | 37 | Viacom | New York | 1,060.8 | 9.4 | 402.0 | 658.8 | 30.7 | 33.1 | 29.2 | 497.4 | 28.2 | 40.2 |
| 31 | 41 | Capital One Financial Corp. | McLean, Va. | 1,043.0 | 18.8 | 534.1 | 508.9 | 6.3 | 58.5 | 14.8 | 280.4 | 15.5 | 133.5 |
| 32 | 32 | Sony Corp. | Tokyo | 1,040.8 | 3.1 | 241.1 | 799.7 | 36.0 | 85.0 | 28.0 | 564.0 | 26.2 | 60.4 |
| 33 | 39 | Microsoft Corp. | Redmond, Wash. | 1,032.5 | 11.5 | 575.7 | 456.8 | 51.7 | 5.6 | 6.4 | 330.8 | 10.3 | 52.0 |
| 34 | 61 | Google² | Mountain View, Calif. | 1,004.9 | 60.9 | 746.9 | 258.0 | 12.6 | 8.2 | 2.7 | 102.3 | 3.4 | 128.8 |

Source: Ad Age DataCenter. Measured media from WPP's Kantar Media (kantarmediana.com). See notes on p. 18.
1. Estimated 2011 pro forma U.S. ad spending (and pro forma percent change from 2010) for Comcast Corp., including NBC Universal. Comcast bought 51% stake in NBC Universal in January 2011.
2. Estimated 2011 pro forma U.S. ad spending (and pro forma percent change from 2010) for Google, including Motorola Mobility. Google bought Motorola Mobility in May 2012.

## The Media Plan

The media plan determines the best way to get the advertiser's message to the market. In a basic sense, the goal of the media plan is to find that combination of media that enables the marketer to communicate the message in the most effective manner to the largest number of potential customers at the lowest cost.

The activities involved in developing the media plan and the purposes of each are presented in Figure 10–2. As you can see, a number of decisions must be made throughout this process. As the plan evolves, events may occur that necessitate changes. Many advertisers find it necessary to alter and update their objectives and strategies frequently.

## Problems in Media Planning

Unfortunately, the media strategy decision has not become a standardized task. A number of problems contribute to the difficulty of establishing the plan and reduce its effectiveness. These problems include insufficient information, inconsistent terminologies, time pressures, and difficulty measuring effectiveness.

**Insufficient Information** While a great deal of information about markets and the media exists, media planners often require more than is available. Some data are just not measured, either because they cannot be or because measuring them would be too expensive. For example, continuous measures of radio listenership exist, but only periodic listenership studies are reported due to sample size and cost constraints. There are problems with some measures of audience size in other media as well.

The timing of measurements is also a problem; some audience measures are taken only at specific times of the year. (For example, **sweeps periods** in February, May, July, and November are used for measuring TV audiences and setting advertising rates.) This information is then generalized to succeeding months, so future planning decisions must be made on past data that may not reflect current behaviors. (In the largest 56 TV markets meters are used to provide information.) Think about planning for TV advertising for the fall season. There are no data on the audiences of new shows, and audience information taken on existing programs during the summer may not indicate how these programs will do in the fall because summer viewership is generally much lower. While the advertisers can review these programs before they air, all markets do not have actual audience figures.

The lack of information is even more of a problem for small advertisers, or smaller markets, who may not be able to afford to purchase the information they require. As a result, their decisions are based on limited or out-of-date data that were provided by the media themselves, or no data at all.

**Inconsistent Terminologies** Problems arise because the cost bases used by different media often vary and the standards of measurement used to establish these costs are not always consistent. For example, print media may present cost data in terms of the cost to reach a thousand people (cost per thousand, or CPM), broadcast media use the cost per ratings point (CPRP), and outdoor media use the number of showings. The advent of the Internet brought about a whole new lexicon of terminologies. Audience information that is used as a basis for these costs has also been collected by different methods. Finally, terms that actually mean something different (such as *reach* and *coverage*) may be used synonymously by some, adding to the confusion.

In 2006, a joint task force composed of members of the of ANA, AAAA, DMA, ARF, and IAB and the Advertising Research Foundation (ARF) launched an initiative to determine a better way to measure consumer exposure to an advertisement. The group unveiled an initiative that would significantly change the way exposure was measured, essentially replacing the use of frequency (the number of exposures to an ad) with engagement, a measure they said would better reflect the growing number of media choices available to consumers. Although the committee agreed on backing the

## The situation analysis

Purpose: To understand the marketing problem. An analysis is made of a company and its competitors on the basis of:

1. Size and share of the total market.
2. Sales history, costs, and profits.
3. Distribution practices.
4. Methods of selling.
5. Use of advertising.
6. Identification of prospects.
7. Nature of the product.

## The marketing strategy plan

Purpose: To plan activities that will solve one or more of the marketing problems. Includes the determination of:

1. Marketing objectives.
2. Product and spending strategy.
3. Distribution strategy.
4. Which elements of the marketing mix are to be used.
5. Identification of "best" market segments.

## The creative strategy plan

Purpose: To determine what to communicate through advertisements. Includes the determination of:

1. How product can meet consumer needs.
2. How product will be positioned in advertisements.
3. Copy themes.
4. Specific objectives of each advertisement.
5. Number and sizes of advertisements.

## Setting media objectives

Purpose: To translate marketing objectives and strategies into goals that media can accomplish.

## Determining media strategy

Purpose: To translate media goals into general guidelines that will control the planner's selection and use of media. The best strategy alternatives should be selected.

## Selecting broad media classes

Purpose: To determine which broad class of media best fulfills the criteria. Involves comparison and selection of broad media classes such as newspapers, magazines, radio, television, social, digital, and others. The analysis is called intermedia comparisons. Audience size is one of the major factors used in comparing the various media classes.

## Selecting media within classes

Purpose: To compare and select the best media within broad classes, again using predetermined criteria. Involves making decisions about the following:

1. If magazines were recommended, then which magazines?
2. If television was recommended, then
   a. Broadcast or cable television?
   b. Network or spot television?
   c. If network, which programs?
   d. If spot, which markets?
3. If radio or newspapers were recommended, then
   a. Which markets will be used?
   b. What criteria will buyers use in making purchases of local media?
4. If Internet, what sites to be on?
5. If social media, which to use?

## Media use decisions—broadcast

1. What kind of sponsorship (sole, shared, participating, or other)?
2. What levels of reach and frequency will be required?
3. Scheduling: On which days and months are commercials to appear?
4. Placement of spots: In programs or between programs?

## Media use decisions—print

1. Number of ads to appear and on which days and months?
2. Placements of ads: Any preferred position within media?
3. Special treatment: Gatefolds, bleeds, color, etc.?
4. Desired reach or frequency levels?

## Media use decisions—other media

1. Billboards
   a. Location of markets and plan of distribution?
   b. Kinds of outdoor boards to be used?
2. Other media: Decisions peculiar to those media. (see subsequent chapters)

**FIGURE 10–2**

Activities Involved in Developing the Media Plan

**FIGURE 10–3**

Most Engaging TV Genres

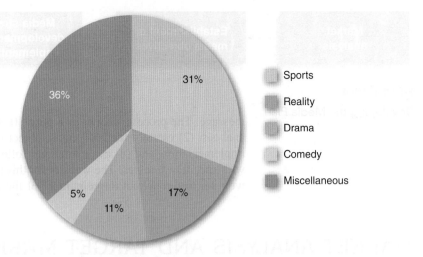

Source: Trendrr.TV, "Most Socially-Engaging TV Genres, January–November 2012," http://trends.e-strategyblog.com/2012/12/26/most-socially-engaging-tv-genres/6753, December 26, 2012.

new term, others were not so willing, asking for a more precise definition of *engagement*. The committee agreed to further examine and validate the concept.[3] However, even today there is no concensus as to the meaning of the term.

At the same time, the importance of engagement has been recognized by marketers. The Nielsen Company, which provides ratings data, recently purchased IAG Research—one of many firms now providing engagement data, while Toyota struck a deal with NBC that guaranteed that its ads would appear only in shows with high audience engagement.[4] Other companies also provide engagement data (Figure 10–3).

**Time Pressures** It seems that advertisers are always in a hurry—sometimes because they need to be, other times because they think they need to be. Actions by a competitor—for example, the cutting of airfares by one carrier—require immediate response. But sometimes a false sense of urgency dictates time pressures. In either situation, media selection decisions may be made without proper planning and analysis of the markets and/or media.

**Difficulty Measuring Effectiveness** Because it is so hard to measure the effectiveness of advertising and promotions in general, it is also difficult to determine the relative effectiveness of various media or media vehicles. (Recall the discussion of ROI from Chapter 7.) While progress is being made in this regard, the media planner may have little more than an estimate of or a good guess at the impact of these alternatives.

Because of these problems, not all media decisions are quantitatively determined. Sometimes managers have to assume the image of a medium in a market with which they are not familiar, anticipate the impact of recent events, or make judgments without full knowledge of all the available alternatives.

While these problems complicate the media decision process, they do not render it an entirely subjective exercise. The remainder of this chapter explores in more detail how media strategies are developed and ways to increase their effectiveness.

# DEVELOPING THE MEDIA PLAN

The promotional planning model in Chapter 1 discussed the process of identifying target markets, establishing objectives, and formulating strategies for attaining them. The development of the media plan and strategies follows a similar path, except that the focus is more specifically keyed to determining the best way to deliver the

**FIGURE 10-4**

Developing the Media Plan

message. The process, shown in Figure 10–4, involves a series of stages: (1) market analysis, (2) establishment of media objectives, (3) media strategy development and implementation, and (4) evaluation and follow-up. Each of these is discussed in turn, with specific examples. The website for this text contains an actual media plan, which we refer to throughout the remainder of the chapter to exemplify each phase further.

# MARKET ANALYSIS AND TARGET MARKET IDENTIFICATION

The situation analysis stage of the overall promotional planning process involves a complete review of internal and external factors, competitive strategies, and the like. In the development of a media strategy, a market analysis is again performed, although this time the focus is on the media and delivering the message. The key questions at this stage are these: To whom will we advertise (who is the target market)? What internal and external factors may influence the media plan? Where (geographically) and when should we focus our efforts?

## To Whom Will We Advertise?

While a number of target markets might be derived from the situation analysis, to decide which specific groups to go after, the media planner may work with the client, account representative, marketing department, and creative directors. A variety of factors can assist media planners in this decision. Some will require primary research, whereas others will be available from published (secondary) sources.

Experian Simmons, formerly the Simmons Market Research Bureau (SMRB), provides information through its annual *Experian National Consumer Study*. The study provides information regarding traditional media usage (English and Spanish languages), product, brands and services used, and demographic and psychographic characteristics. Experian also provides a *New Media Study* providing insights into Americans' use of mobile phones, social networking, and dozens of other new emerging technologies. The company's competitor GfK-Mediamark Research, Inc. (GfK MRI), also provides consumer information and media usage characteristics of the population.

Media planners are often more concerned with the percentage figures and index numbers than with the raw numbers. This is largely due to the fact that they may have their own data from other sources, both primary and secondary; the numbers provided may not be specific enough for their needs; or they question the numbers provided because of the methods by which they were collected. The total (raw) numbers provided by Experian and GfK MRI are used in combination with the media planner's own figures.

On the other hand, the **index number** is considered a good indicator of the potential of the market. This number is derived from the formula

$$\text{Index} = \frac{\text{Percentage of users in a demographic segment}}{\text{Percentage of population in the same segment}} \times 100$$

An index number over 100 means use of the product is proportionately greater in that segment than in one that is average (100) or less than 100. For example, the GfK MRI data in Figure 10–5 show that people in the age groups 35–44 and 25–34, respectively, are more likely to engage in snowboarding, while those who did not

| | Total '000 | Proj '000 | Pct Across | Pct Down | Index |
|---|---|---|---|---|---|
| Total | 232469 | 29288 | 12.6 | 100 | 100 |
| Men | 112618 | 15402 | 13.7 | 52.6 | 109 |
| Women | 119851 | 13886 | 11.6 | 47.4 | 92 |
| Educ: graduated college plus | 64519 | 10422 | 16.2 | 35.6 | 128 |
| Educ: attended college | 44597 | 6022 | 13.5 | 20.6 | 107 |
| Educ: graduated high school | 70692 | 8218 | 11.6 | 28.1 | 92 |
| Educ: did not graduate HS | 30354 | 1785 | 5.9 | 6.1 | 47 |
| Educ: post graduate | 25596 | 4121 | 16.1 | 14.1 | 128 |
| Educ: no college | 101629 | 9900 | 9.7 | 33.8 | 77 |
| Age 18–24 | 29802 | 4275 | 14.3 | 14.6 | 114 |
| Age 25–34 | 41810 | 6529 | 15.6 | 22.3 | 124 |
| Age 35–44 | 40059 | 6856 | 17.1 | 23.4 | 136 |
| Age 45–54 | 44215 | 6396 | 14.5 | 21.8 | 115 |
| Age 55–64 | 37176 | 3294 | 8.9 | 11.2 | 70 |
| Age 65+ | 39407 | 1938 | 4.9 | 6.6 | 39 |
| Adults 18–34 | 71612 | 10803 | 15.1 | 36.9 | 120 |
| Adults 18–49 | 133798 | 21064 | 15.7 | 71.9 | 125 |
| Adults 25–54 | 126083 | 19781 | 15.7 | 67.5 | 125 |
| Men 18–34 | 36167 | 5349 | 14.8 | 18.3 | 117 |
| Men 18–49 | 66772 | 10868 | 16.3 | 37.1 | 129 |
| Men 25–54 | 62378 | 10418 | 16.7 | 35.6 | 133 |
| Women 18–34 | 35445 | 5454 | 15.4 | 18.6 | 122 |
| Women 18–49 | 67025 | 10196 | 15.2 | 34.8 | 121 |
| Women 25–54 | 63706 | 9363 | 14.7 | 32 | 117 |
| Occupation: Professional and Related Occupations | 30719 | 5521 | 18 | 18.9 | 143 |
| Occupation: Management, Business and Financial Opera | 22354 | 3733 | 16.7 | 12.7 | 133 |
| Occupation: Sales and Office Occupations | 32228 | 4495 | 13.9 | 15.3 | 111 |
| Occupation: Natural Resources, Construction and Mainte | 12610 | 2056 | 16.3 | 7 | 129 |
| Occupation: Other employed | 41417 | 5490 | 13.3 | 18.7 | 105 |
| HHI: $150,000+ | 24133 | 3849 | 15.9 | 13.1 | 127 |
| HHI: $75,000–$149,999 | 65415 | 10898 | 16.7 | 37.2 | 132 |
| HHI: $60,000–$74,999 | 25027 | 3891 | 15.5 | 13.3 | 123 |
| HHI: $50,000–$59,999 | 18933 | 2613 | 13.8 | 8.9 | 110 |
| HHI: $40,000–$49,999 | 20303 | 2375 | 11.7 | 8.1 | 93 |
| HHI: $30,000–$39,999 | 21989 | 2244 | 10.2 | 7.7 | 81 |
| HHI: $20,000–$29,999 | 23291 | 1614 | 6.9 | 5.5 | 55 |
| HHI: <$20,000 | 33378 | 1804 | 5.4 | 6.2 | 43 |
| Census Region: North East | 42554 | 4209 | 9.9 | 14.4 | 79 |
| Census Region: South | 86542 | 7165 | 8.3 | 24.5 | 66 |
| Census Region: Midwest | 50653 | 7335 | 14.5 | 25 | 115 |
| Census Region: West | 52720 | 10579 | 20.1 | 36.1 | 159 |

FIGURE 10–5

GfK MRI Report on Snowboarders

Source: Mediamark Research, GfK MRI. Reprinted with permission.

YTC 10–03

MRI + Tutorial

youtube.com/10ebelch

graduate high school, lower-income groups, and older adults are the least likely to snowboard. Geographically, those living in the West and the Midwest are more likely to snowboard than those in the South. Depending on their overall strategy, marketers may wish to use this information to determine which groups are now using the product and target them or to identify a group that is currently using the product less and attempt to develop that segment. Figure 10–6 provides more instruction on how to read a GfK MRI report. (There is also an instructional video on YouTube—Google GfK MRI-PLUS.)

While the index is helpful, it should not be used alone. Percentages and product usage figures are also needed to get an accurate picture of the market. Just because

CHAPTER 10

# How to Read an Internet Reporter Report

Below is a screen capture of a Reporter Report, complete with explanations of key numbers. Please note that the numbers are based on the 2002 Fall MRI study and that the projected numbers (000) are expressed in thousands.

Base counts: in the MRI Fall 2002 study weighted to Total '000, there were 64,715,000 Adults 18-34 in the 48 contiguous United States

Projected Count (000): projected to the full population, 46,006,000 Adults 18-34 have drank a Regular Cola Drink, Not Diet in the Last 6 Months.

Percent Across: out of Adults 18-34, 71.1% drank Regular Cola Drinks, Not Diet in Last 6 months.

Percent Down: out of all the people who drank Regular Cola Drinks, Not Diet, 38.6% are Adults 18-34.

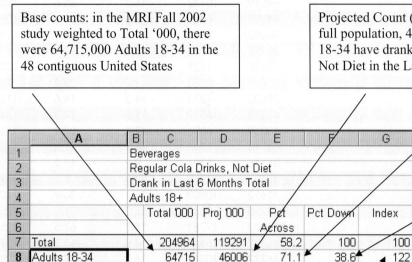

| | A | B | C | D | E | F | G |
|---|---|---|---|---|---|---|---|
| 1 | | Beverages | | | | | |
| 2 | | Regular Cola Drinks, Not Diet | | | | | |
| 3 | | Drank in Last 6 Months Total | | | | | |
| 4 | | Adults 18+ | | | | | |
| 5 | | | Total '000 | Proj '000 | Pct Across | Pct Down | Index |
| 6 | | | | | | | |
| 7 | Total | | 204964 | 119291 | 58.2 | 100 | 100 |
| 8 | Adults 18-34 | | 64715 | 46006 | 71.1 | 38.6 | 122 |
| 9 | Adults 18-49 | | 130165 | 84623 | 65 | 70.9 | 112 |
| 10 | Adults 25-54 | | 120777 | 74669 | 61.8 | 62.6 | 106 |

" * " Sign: If there is an asterisk sign, that means the sample size is less than 50 respondents and the numbers are unstable and should not be used.

Index: people who drank Regular Cola Drinks, Not Diet, are (122-100=) 22% more likely than the general population to be Adults 18-34; also, Adults 18-34 are 22% more likely than the general population to drink Regular Cola Drinks, Not Diet.

| How the Numbers are Derived | |
|---|---|
| Pct. Across= 71.1 | The percent calculated by dividing the Proj '000 value in the row by the Total '000 value in the base column=46006/64715=71.1%. |
| Pct. Down= 38.6 | The percent calculated by dividing the Proj' 000 value in the row by the Proj. '000 value in the base row=46006/119291=38.6%. |
| Index=122 | The percent calculated by dividing the Pct. Across in the row by the Pct. Across in the base row (71.1/58.2). |

**FIGURE 10–6**

How to Read an Internet
Reporter Report

Source: Mediamark Research
& Intelligence, LLC (GfK MRI).
Reprinted with permission.

the index for a particular segment of the population is very high, that doesn't always mean it is an attractive segment to target. The high index may be a result of a low denominator (a very small proportion of the population in this segment). In Figure 10–7, the 18- to 24-year-old age segment has the highest index, but it also has both the lowest product usage and the lowest population percentage. A marketer who relied solely on the index would be ignoring a full 82 percent of product users.

Keep in mind that while Experian and GfK MRI provide demographic, geographic, and some psychographic information, other factors may also be useful in defining specific markets and media usage. IMC Perspective 10–1 on page 350 shows how other factors may have an impact.

FIGURE 10–7

How High Indexes Can Be Misleading

| Age Segment | Population in Segment (%) | Product Use in Segment (%) | Index |
|---|---|---|---|
| 18–24 | 15.1 | 18.0 | 119 |
| 25–34 | 25.1 | 25.0 | 100 |
| 35–44 | 20.6 | 21.0 | 102 |
| 45 + | 39.3 | 36.0 | 91 |

## What Internal and External Factors Are Operating?

Media strategies are influenced by both internal and external factors operating at any given time. *Internal factors* may involve the size of the media budget, managerial and administrative capabilities, or the organization of the agency. *External factors* may include the economy (the rising costs of media), changes in technology (the availability of new media), competitive factors, and the like. While some of this information may require primary research, much information is available through secondary sources, including magazines, syndicated services, and even the daily newspaper.

One service's competitive information was shown in Figure 10–1. The Competitive Media Reporting Service provides media spending figures for various brands competing in the same market. Competitive information is also available from many other sources.

## Where to Promote?

The question of where to promote relates to geographic considerations. As noted in Chapter 7, companies often find that sales are stronger in one area of the country or the world than another and may allocate advertising expenditures according to the market potential of an area. For example, the Mexican beer Pacifico has a much greater brand share of the beer market in the Pacific census region than in the Midwest census region. The question is, where will the ad dollars be more wisely spent? Should Pacifico allocate additional promotional monies to those markets where the brand is already among the leaders to maintain market share, or does more potential exist in those markets where the firm is not doing as well and there is more room to grow? Perhaps the best answer is that the firm should spend advertising and promotion dollars where they will be the most effective—that is, in those markets where they will achieve the desired objectives. Unfortunately, as we have seen so often, it is not always possible to measure directly the impact of promotional efforts. At the same time, certain tactics can assist the planner in making this determination.

**Using Indexes to Determine Where to Promote**  In addition to the indexes from Simmons and GfK MRI, three other indexes may also be useful:

1. The **survey of buying power index** is conducted for every major metropolitan market in the United States and is based on a number of factors, including population, effective buying income, and total retail sales in the area. Each of these factors is individually weighted to drive a buying power index that charts the potential of a particular metro area, county, or city relative to the United States as a whole. The resulting index gives media planners insight into the relative value of that market, as shown in Figure 10–8. When used in combination with other market information, the survey of buying power index helps the marketer determine which geographic areas to target.
2. The **brand development index (BDI)** helps marketers factor the rate of product usage by geographic area into the decision process.

| DMA | Total Population | Households | Asian / Pacific Islander | African-American Pop. | Hispanic Pop. | 2 - 11 | 12 - 17 | 18 - 24 | 25 - 34 | 35 - 49 | 50+ |
|---|---|---|---|---|---|---|---|---|---|---|---|
| | | | | | | Population by Age Group | | | | | |

Population by Age Group

| DMA | Total Population | Households | Asian / Pacific Islander | African-American Pop. | Hispanic Pop. | 2 - 11 | 12 - 17 | 18 - 24 | 25 - 34 | 35 - 49 | 50+ |
|---|---|---|---|---|---|---|---|---|---|---|---|
| Ft. Myers-Naples, FL | 1,217,708 | 508,145 | 15,343 | 84,084 | 247,548 | 141,863 | 80,224 | 85,712 | 149,848 | 222,580 | 508,015 |
| Gainesville, FL | 322,150 | 129,627 | 12,118 | 55,007 | 22,018 | 34,805 | 22,127 | 59,388 | 47,021 | 57,414 | 93,993 |
| Jacksonville, FL | 1,758,602 | 680,711 | 44,550 | 384,062 | 99,011 | 240,379 | 142,160 | 158,680 | 235,808 | 379,557 | 552,285 |
| Miami-Ft. Lauderdale, FL | 4,300,579 | 1,561,568 | 90,165 | 886,325 | 1,979,958 | 542,344 | 334,111 | 384,710 | 502,057 | 984,256 | 1,443,731 |
| Orlando-Daytona Beach-Melbourne, FL | 3,723,526 | 1,464,418 | 105,286 | 488,912 | 640,945 | 457,847 | 276,477 | 323,235 | 493,413 | 775,064 | 1,304,938 |
| Panama City, FL | 368,863 | 148,310 | 4,522 | 50,011 | 12,953 | 43,900 | 26,555 | 31,351 | 51,089 | 76,883 | 129,719 |
| Tallahassee-Thomasville, FL-GA | 725,699 | 281,591 | 10,361 | 230,056 | 36,005 | 92,149 | 54,215 | 95,867 | 106,825 | 142,844 | 213,904 |
| Tampa-St.Petersburg (Sarasota), FL | 4,368,468 | 1,821,660 | 98,189 | 464,796 | 620,598 | 519,526 | 310,946 | 343,185 | 531,163 | 867,935 | 1,691,454 |
| West Palm Beach-Ft. Pierce, FL | 1,905,978 | 786,561 | 37,615 | 272,071 | 318,530 | 223,654 | 134,638 | 144,177 | 218,045 | 372,294 | 768,673 |

| DMA | Total EBI | Retail Sales | Buying Power Index |
|---|---|---|---|
| Ft. Myers-Naples, FL | 31,562,042,500 | 21,286,463,216 | 0.4633 |
| Gainesville, FL | 5,844,027,500 | 4,651,926,011 | 0.0968 |
| Jacksonville, FL | 37,164,647,500 | 28,725,730,663 | 0.5906 |
| Miami-Ft. Lauderdale, FL | 89,188,970,000 | 75,015,224,126 | 1.4625 |
| Orlando-Daytona Beach-Melbourne, FL | 77,523,552,500 | 59,556,677,892 | 1.2333 |
| Panama City, FL | 7,087,285,000 | 5,238,076,874 | 0.1133 |
| Tallahassee-Thomasville, FL-GA | 12,952,682,500 | 10,535,214,913 | 0.2166 |
| Tampa-St.Petersburg (Sarasota), FL | 96,233,265,000 | 65,492,720,766 | 1.4595 |
| West Palm Beach-Ft. Pierce, FL | 51,014,940,000 | 35,632,927,152 | 0.7529 |

**FIGURE 10–8**

Survey of Buying Power Index

FIGURE 10–9

Calculating BDI

$$BDI = \frac{\text{Percentage of brand sales in South Atlantic region}}{\text{Percentage of U.S. population in South Atlantic region}} \times 100$$

$$= \frac{50\%}{16\%} \times 100$$

$$= 312$$

$$BDI = \frac{\text{Percentage of brand to total U.S. sales in the market}}{\text{Percentage of total U.S. population in the market}} \times 100$$

The BDI compares the percentage of the brand's total U.S. sales in a given market area with the percentage of the total population in the market to determine the sales potential for that brand in that market area. An example of this calculation is shown in Figure 10–9. The higher the index number, the more market potential exists. In this case, the index number indicates this market has high potential for brand development.

3. The **category development index (CDI)** is computed in the same manner as the BDI, except it uses information regarding the product category (as opposed to the brand) in the numerator:

$$CDI = \frac{\text{Percentage of product category total sales in market}}{\text{Percentage of total U.S. population in market}} \times 100$$

The CDI provides information on the potential for development of the total product category rather than specific brands. When this information is combined with the BDI, a much more insightful promotional strategy may be developed. For example, consider the market potential for coffee in the United States. One might first look at how well the product category does in a specific market area. In Utah and Idaho, for example, the category potential is low (see Figure 10–10). The marketer analyzes the BDI to find how the brand is doing relative to other brands in this area. This information can then be used in determining how well a particular product category and a particular brand are performing and figuring what media weight (or quantity of advertising) would be required to gain additional market share, as shown in Figure 10–11.

While these indexes provide important insights into the market potential for the firm's products and/or brands, this information is supplemental to the

FIGURE 10–10

Using CDI and BDI to Determine Market Potential

$$CDI = \frac{\text{Percentage of product category sales in Utah/Idaho}}{\text{Percentage of total U.S. population in Utah/Idaho}} \times 100$$

$$= \frac{1\%}{1\%} \times 100$$

$$= 100$$

$$BDI = \frac{\text{Percentage of total brand sales in Utah/Idaho}}{\text{Percentage of total U.S. population in Utah/Idaho}} \times 100$$

$$= \frac{2\%}{1\%} \times 100$$

$$= 200$$

# IMC Perspective 10–1 > > >

## What Your Personality Says about Your Media Use and Vice Versa

For as long as anyone can remember, media purchasing has relied heavily on demographics. For example, the most sought after age group for buyers of TV time is the 18- to 49-year-old female (which, in itself, is a little scary in assuming that there are no differences between 18- and 49-year-old females!). GfK MRI and Experian (SMRB) focus attention on demographics, as does virtually every media kit. Over the years, numerous articles have appeared in the literature espousing the position that demographics may not be the optimal way to make media purchase decisions, but little (if anything) has changed. But now more evidence has been found to support the fact that other factors may be responsible for one's media usage beyond age, income, and gender.

A study conducted by the Entertainment Technology Center at the University of Southern California, the Hallmark Channel, and E-Poll Market Research concludes that a better predictor of media usage is the user's lifestyle. Identifying nine lifestyle groups (teens, college students, recent graduates, single, no kids, new nesters, established families, married couples with no children, and empty nesters), the researchers concluded that while cohorts of these groups may have similar demographic profiles, they may have different attitudes and media usage habits. For example, new nesters rate the importance of family relationships as more important than do childless couples (70 versus 56 percent). New nesters also watch more TV than other groups, and place high value on devices that filter content, like DVRs, video on demand services, and DVD players, to display family-appropriate programming. Childless couples, on the other hand, tend to be engaged more outside the home,

---

**FIGURE 10–11**

Using BDI and CDI Indexes

|  | High BDI | Low BDI |
|---|---|---|
| **High CDI** | High market share<br>Good market potential | Low market share<br>Good market potential |
| **Low CDI** | High market share<br>Monitor for sales decline | Low market share<br>Poor market potential |

| | |
|---|---|
| High BDI and high CDI | This market usually represents good sales potential for both the product category and the brand. |
| High BDI and low CDI | The category is not selling well, but the brand is; probably a good market to advertise in but should be monitored for declining sales. |
| Low BDI and high CDI | The product category shows high potential but the brand is not doing well; the reasons should be determined. |
| Low BDI and low CDI | Both the product category and the brand are doing poorly; not likely to be a good place for advertising. |

relying less on TV, and when they do watch TV, they prefer drama to family programming. Differences also exist in regard to other media, for example, social networking. New nesters use social networks to stay in touch with friends and family, and are the most satisfied with the technology. Childless couples are less satisfied, primarily using the networking sites for professional purposes. The conclusion of the study is that there are clear and distinct differences between these groups that offer media buyers an advantage over demographics.

Another study, conducted by the psychographic research company Mindset Media, provided similar findings. Examining both demographic data and personalities, this study concluded that younger people use new media more than their elders; older generations prefer print; and women read magazines more than men. Not much new there. But the study also concluded that the more exciting findings are related to the influence of one's personality on media usage. For example, while almost everyone uses the Internet for a variety of reasons, the heaviest users tend to be high in openness and bravado, while low-level users are high in dogmatism, socially conservative, and religious. Liberals are most likely to have the Internet as their most consumed medium. Newspaper readers are more likely to be optimists, recycle, purchase a luxury car, and are dynamic and leaders. Magazine readers are also dynamic, but are more open than newspaper readers. They are comfortable with their emotions, like the movies, and have music collections. Introverts and those low in self-motivation are less likely to read magazines. On the other hand, dynamic people don't watch TV, nor do those who exhibit high openness and leadership. Those high in bravado and risk takers are TV watchers, as are those who score low on openness and leadership, and are less likely to plan. Finally, there are the radio listeners. The most dynamic of media users, they watch very little TV and always have the radio on in the car or at home. Introverts use almost no radio, are most likely to watch TV for five or more hours a day, and rarely plan. They also discourage their children from using the Internet. Overall, the study concludes, personality may be a better predictor of media usage than are age, gender, and income, and researchers may be better off using a personality test rather than focus groups and demographic data to determine media usage.

Looking at it from the other side, a recent study of Facebook users also yielded some interesting findings. Researchers from the University of Cambridge examined data from Facebook members who agreed to take online personality and intelligence tests, and were able to determine that what they "liked" on the popular media website told a lot about them and their personalities. Besides easily predicting one's gender and ethnicity, political and religious affiliations could be determined as well. In addition, the researchers were able to find personality traits that correlated with the endorsements. For example, those who "liked" NASCAR and *The Bachelor* tended to be more conservative and less open to new ideas. If you "like" the *Colbert Report* you are more likely to have a high IQ and like curly fries. Curly fries? Another study conducted by Pew Internet and American Life Project researchers concluded that social network users are more trusting and more willing to share information than those not on a social network, and less concerned with privacy issues. The same holds true for Internet users who check into Facebook more than once a day than for those who don't. As noted by Fred Wolens, a public policy manager for Pew, "No matter the vehicle for information—a bumper sticker, yard sign, logos on clothing or other data found online—it has already been proven that it is possible for social scientists to draw conclusions about personal attributes based on these characteristics." Yikes!

Sources: Geoffrey Mohan, "On Facebook, You Are What You 'Like,' Researchers Say," *Los Angeles Times,* March 12, 2013, p. A8; Steve McClellan, "Are Demographics Dead?" www.adweek.com, February 23, 2010, pp. 1–2; Beth Snyder Bulik, "How Personality Can Predict Media Usage," www.adage.com, May 4, 2009, pp. 1–4.

overall strategy determined earlier in the promotional decision-making process. In fact, much of this information may have already been provided to the media planner. Since it may be used more specifically to determine the media weights to assign to each area, this decision ultimately affects the budget allocated to each area as well as other factors such as reach, frequency, and scheduling.

# ESTABLISHING MEDIA OBJECTIVES

Just as the situation analysis leads to establishment of marketing and communications objectives, the media situation analysis should lead to determination of specific media objectives. The media objectives are not ends in themselves. Rather, they are designed to lead to the attainment of communications and marketing objectives. Media objectives are the goals for the media program and should be limited to those that can be accomplished through media strategies. An example of media objectives is this: Create awareness in the target market through the following:

■ Use broadcast media to provide coverage of 80 percent of the target market over a six-month period.

- Reach 60 percent of the target audience at least three times over the same six-month period.
- Create a positive brand image through mood and creativity.

# DEVELOPING AND IMPLEMENTING MEDIA STRATEGIES

Having determined what is to be accomplished, media planners consider how to achieve these objectives. That is, they develop and implement media strategies, which evolve directly from the actions required to meet objectives and involve the criteria in Figure 10–12.

## The Media Mix

A wide variety of media and media vehicles are available to advertisers. While it is possible that only one medium and/or vehicle might be employed, it is much more likely that a number of alternatives will be used. The objectives sought, the characteristics of the product or service, the size of the budget, and individual preferences are just some of the factors that determine what combination of media will be used.

As an example, consider a promotional situation in which a product requires a visual demonstration to be communicated effectively. In this case, TV or the Internet may be the most effective medium. If the promotional strategy calls for coupons to stimulate trial, print media may be necessary. (Some companies also provide the capability to print coupons from their websites.) For in-depth information, the Internet may be best, while for spreading the word among friends it may be social media.

By employing a media mix, advertisers can add more versatility to their media strategies, since each medium contributes its own distinct advantages (as demonstrated in later chapters). By combining media, marketers can increase coverage, reach, and frequency levels while improving the likelihood of achieving overall communications and marketing goals.

## Target Market Coverage

The media planner determines which target markets should receive the most media emphasis. Developing media strategies involves matching the most appropriate media to this market by asking, "Through which media and media vehicles can I best get my message to prospective buyers?" The issue here is to get coverage of the market, as shown in Figure 10–13. The optimal goal is full market coverage, shown in the second pie chart. But this is a very optimistic scenario. More realistically, conditions shown in the third and fourth charts are most likely to occur. In the third chart, the coverage of the media does not allow for coverage of the entire market, leaving some potential customers without exposure to the message. In the fourth chart, the marketer is faced with a problem of overexposure (also called **waste coverage**), in which the media coverage exceeds the targeted audience. If media coverage reaches people who are not sought as buyers and are not potential users, then it is wasted. (This term is used for coverage that reaches people who are not potential buyers and/or users. Consumers may not be part of the intended target market but may still be considered as potential—for example, those who buy the product as a gift for someone else.)

The goal of the media planner is to extend media coverage to as many of the members of the target audience as possible while minimizing the amount of waste coverage. The situation usually involves trade-offs. Sometimes one has to live with less coverage than desired; other times, the most effective media expose people not sought. In this instance, waste coverage is justified because the media

**FIGURE 10–12**

Criteria Considered in the Development of Media Plans

- The media mix
- Target market coverage
- Geographic coverage
- Scheduling
- Reach and frequency
- Recency
- Creative aspects and mood
- Flexibility
- Budget considerations

## FIGURE 10–13

Marketing Coverage Possibilities

| | Full Market Coverage | Partial Market Coverage | Coverage Exceeding Target Market |

- Population excluding target market
- Target market (18- to 35-year-old males and females)
- Media coverage
- Media overexposure

employed are likely to be the most effective means of delivery available and the cost of the waste coverage is exceeded by the value gained from their use.

When watching football games on TV, you may have noticed commercials for stock brokerage firms such as Charles Schwab, Ameritrade, and E*Trade. Not all viewers are candidates for stock market services, but a very high percentage of potential customers can be reached with this strategy. So football programs are considered a good media buy because the ability to generate market coverage outweighs the disadvantages of high waste coverage.

Figure 10–14 shows how information provided by GfK MRI can be used to match media to target markets. This excerpt is from the report that profiles magazines

## FIGURE 10–14

GfK MRI Provides Media Usage of Snowboarders

FALL 2012 PRODUCT: LEISURE/SPORTS—Snowboarding: Participated in Last 12 Months—TOTAL ADULTS

| | | | | | |
|---|---|---|---|---|---|
| TV Show Types: Skating - Specials | * | 12883 | 78 | 0.6 | 2.5 | 45 |
| TV Show Types : Soccer | * | 9686 | 267 | 2.8 | 8.5 | 204 |
| TV Show Types: Sports Anthologies - Weeke | * | 14415 | 217 | 1.5 | 6.9 | 112 |
| TV Show Types: Sunday News/Interview | * | 6491 | 61 | 0.9 | 1.9 | 69 |
| TV Show Types: Syndicated Adult General | * | 5312 | 73 | 1.4 | 2.3 | 101 |
| TV Show Types: Tennis | * | 9008 | 178 | 2 | 5.7 | 146 |
| TV Show Types: Track & Field Games | * | 5546 | 100 | 1.8 | 3.2 | 134 |
| Web Sites: AOL Mail | * | 17817 | 310 | 1.7 | 9.9 | 129 |
| Web Sites: Gmail.com | | 58833 | 1487 | 2.5 | 47.3 | 187 |
| Web Sites: Windows Live Hotmail | * | 23947 | 523 | 2.2 | 16.6 | 161 |
| Web Sites: Yahool Mail | | 66124 | 1042 | 1.6 | 33.2 | 117 |
| Web Sites: abc.com | * | 9899 | 158 | 1.6 | 5 | 118 |
| Web Sites: cbs.com | * | 7779 | 116 | 1.5 | 3.7 | 111 |
| Web Sites: disney .com | * | 5351 | 136 | 2.5 | 4.3 | 188 |
| Web Sites: #Fandango | * | 4483 | 102 | 2.3 | 3.2 | 168 |
| Web Sites: FarmVille | * | 2857 | 2 | 0.1 | 0.1 | 5 |
| Web Sites: fox.com | * | 9704 | 210 | 2.2 | 6.7 | 160 |
| Web Sites: Hulu.com | * | 12554 | 426 | 3.4 | 13.6 | 251 |
| Web Sites: IMDb.com | * | 13714 | 493 | 3.6 | 15.7 | 266 |
| Web Sites: iTunes.com | | 31143 | 866 | 2.8 | 27.6 | 206 |
| Web Sites: iVillage.com | * | 586 | 5 | 0.9 | 0.2 | 67 |
| Web Sites: Moviefone.com | * | 3329 | 83 | 2.5 | 2.6 | 184 |
| Web Sites: MSN Movies | * | 1578 | 0 | 0 | 0 | 0 |
| Web Sites: MTV.com | * | 3975 | 150 | 3.8 | 4.8 | 279 |
| Web Sites: nbc.com | * | 7538 | 150 | 2 | 4.8 | 148 |
| Web Sites: Pandora.com | | 33423 | 913 | 2.7 | 29.1 | 202 |
| Web Sites: pbs.org | * | 5807 | 112 | 1.9 | 3.6 | 143 |

Source: Mediamark Research, GfK MRI. Reprinted with permission.

read, cable TV show types watched, and websites visited, etc., by the snowboarders identified in Figure 10–5. (You can practice using index numbers here.) From Figure 10–14, you can see that Pandora.com and MTV.com would likely be wise selections, whereas FarmVille and TV skating specials would be less likely to lead to the desired exposures.

## Geographic Coverage

Snow skiing is much more popular in some areas of the country than in others. It would not be the wisest of strategies to promote skis in those areas where interest is not high, unless you could generate an increase in interest. It may be possible to promote an interest in skiing in the Southeast, but a notable increase in sales of ski equipment is not very likely, given the market's distance from snow. The objective of weighting certain geographic areas more than others makes sense, and the strategy of exerting more promotional efforts and dollars in those areas follows naturally.

## Scheduling

Obviously, companies would like to keep their advertising in front of consumers at all times as a constant reminder of the product and/or brand name. In reality, this is not possible for a variety of reasons (not the least of which is the budget). Nor is it necessary. The primary objective of *scheduling* is to time promotional efforts so that they will coincide with the highest potential buying times. For some products these times are not easy to identify; for others they are very obvious. Three scheduling methods available to the media planner—continuity, flighting, and pulsing—are shown in Figure 10–15. Appendix A shows how running shoe brand ASICS uses scheduling in their media plan.

**Continuity** refers to a continuous pattern of advertising, which may mean every day, every week, or every month. The key is that a regular (continuous) pattern is developed without gaps or nonadvertising periods. Such strategies might be used for advertising for food products, laundry detergents, or other products consumed on an ongoing basis without regard for seasonality.

A second method, **flighting**, employs a less regular schedule, with intermittent periods of advertising and nonadvertising. At some time periods there are heavier promotional expenditures, and at others there may be no advertising. Many banks, for example, spend no money on advertising in the summer but maintain advertising throughout the rest of the year. Snow skis are advertised heavily between October and April; less in May, August, and September; and not at all in June and July.

**Pulsing** is actually a combination of the first two methods. In a pulsing strategy, continuity is maintained, but at certain times promotional efforts are stepped up. In the beer industry, advertising continues throughout the year but may increase at holiday periods such as Memorial Day, Labor Day, or the Fourth of July. The scheduling strategy depends on the objectives, buying cycles, and budget, among other factors. There are certain advantages and disadvantages to each scheduling method, as shown in Figure 10–16. One recent and comprehensive study (acclaimed

**FIGURE 10–15**

Three Methods of
Promotional Scheduling

FIGURE 10–16

Characteristics of
Scheduling Methods

| Continuity | |
|---|---|
| Advantages | Serves as a constant reminder to the consumer |
| | Covers the entire buying cycle |
| | Allows for media priorities (quantity discounts, preferred locations, etc.) |
| Disadvantages | Higher costs |
| | Potential for overexposure |
| | Limited media allocation possible |

| Flighting | |
|---|---|
| Advantages | Cost efficiency of advertising only during purchase cycles |
| | May allow for inclusion of more than one medium or vehicle with limited budgets |
| Disadvantages | Weighting may offer more exposure and advantage over competitors |
| | Increased likelihood of wearout |
| | Lack of awareness, interest, retention of promotional message during nonscheduled times |
| | Vulnerability to competitive efforts during nonscheduled periods |

| Pulsing | |
|---|---|
| Advantages | All of the same as the previous two methods |
| Disadvantages | Not required for seasonal products (or other cyclical products) |

by many in the TV research community as "the most comprehensive study ever to shed light on scheduling") indicates that continuity is more effective than flighting. On the basis of the idea that it is important to get exposure to the message as close as possible to when the consumer is going to make the purchase, the study concludes that advertisers should continue weekly schedules as long as possible.[5] The key here may be the "as long as possible" qualification. Given a significant budget, continuity may be more of an option than it is for those with more limited budgets.

## Reach versus Frequency

Since advertisers have a variety of objectives and face budget constraints, they usually must trade off reach and frequency. They must decide whether to have the message be seen or heard by more people (reach) or by fewer people more often (frequency).

**How Much Reach Is Necessary?**   Thinking back to the hierarchies discussed in Chapter 5, you will recall that the first stage of each model requires awareness of the product and/or brand. The more people are aware, the more they are likely to move to each subsequent stage. Achieving awareness requires reach—that is, exposing potential buyers to the message. New brands or products need a very high level of reach, since the objective is to make all potential buyers aware of the new entry. High reach is also desired at later stages of the hierarchy. For example, at the trial stage of the adoption hierarchy, a promotional strategy might use cents-off coupons or free samples. An objective of the marketer is to reach a larger number of people with these samples in an attempt to make them learn of the product, try it, and develop favorable attitudes toward it. (In turn, these attitudes may lead to purchase.)

The problem arises because there is no known way of determining how much reach is required to achieve levels of awareness, attitude change, or buying intentions, nor

How many viewers actually watch a commercial? R. D. Percy & Co. reports that its advanced people meters, equipped with heat sensors that detect viewers present, indicate that spots retain, on average, 82 percent of the average-minute ratings for the quarter hour. During early morning news programs, "commercial efficiency" (as Percy calls it) is lower because so many people are bustling about, out of the room (blue), but the rate rises at night.

**A. Efficiency of Spots during News Programming**

6–9 a.m. Mon.–Fri.

| 60 | 35 | 5 |

5–7 p.m. Mon.–Fri.

| 86 | 9 | 5 |

7–8 p.m. Mon.–Fri.

| 84 | 9 | 7 |

11–11:30 p.m. Mon.–Fri.

| 88 | 10 | 2 |

**B. Efficiency of Spots during Sports Programming**

Noon–3 p.m. Sat.–Sun.

| 80 | 6 | 14 |

3–5 p.m. Sat.–Sun.

| 79 | 10 | 11 |

5–7 p.m. Sat.–Sun.

| 84 | 6 | 10 |

8–11 p.m. Mon.–Fri.

| 88 | 1 | 11 |

Percentage of program audience retained by spot (commercial efficiency)

Percentage of audience lost: out of the room

Percentage of audience lost: changing channels

**FIGURE 10–17**

Who's Still There to Watch the Ads?

can we be sure an ad placed in a vehicle will actually reach the intended audience. (There has been some research on the first problem, which will be discussed in the following section on effective reach.)

If you buy advertising time on *60 Minutes,* will everyone who is tuned to the program see the ad? No. Many viewers will leave the room, be distracted during the commercial, and so on, as shown in Figure 10–17 (which also provides a good example of the difference between reach and coverage). If I expose everyone in my target group to the message once, will this be sufficient to create a 100 percent level of awareness? The answer again is no. This leads to the next question: What frequency of exposure is necessary for the ad to be seen and to have an impact?

**What Frequency Level Is Needed?**   With respect to media planning, *frequency* carries a slightly different meaning. (Remember when we said one of the problems in media planning is that terms often take on different meanings?) Here frequency is the number of times one is exposed to the media vehicle in a specified time period (usually 13 weeks), not necessarily to the ad itself. Figure 10–17 demonstrates that depending on the program, this number may range from 12 to 40 percent. Marketers have always known that everyone who is watching a program is not going to stay in the room to watch the commercials. Given the rise in the number of people able to skip ads, one can be sure the number of those not exposed to the ad is on the increase. As noted, marketers continue to seek ways to increase engagement, hoping to reduce the number leaving the room during commercial breaks.

Most advertisers do agree that a 1:1 exposure ratio does not exist. So while your ad may be placed in a certain vehicle, the fact that a consumer has been exposed to that vehicle does not ensure that your ad has been seen. As a result, the frequency level expressed in the media plan overstates the actual level of exposure to the ad. This overstatement has led some media buyers to refer to the reach of the media vehicle as "opportunities to see" an ad rather than actual exposure to it.

Because the advertiser has no sure way of knowing whether exposure to a vehicle results in exposure to the ad, the media and advertisers have adopted a compromise: One exposure to the vehicle constitutes reach, given that this exposure must occur for the viewer even to have an opportunity to see the ad. Thus, the exposure figure is used to calculate reach and frequency levels. But this compromise does not help determine the frequency required to make an impact. The creativity of the ad, the involvement of the receiver, noise, and many other intervening factors confound any attempts to make a precise determination.

At this point, you may be thinking, "If nobody knows this stuff, how do they make these decisions?" That's a good question, and the truth is that the decisions are not always made on hard data. Says Joseph Ostrow, executive vice president/director of communications services with Young and Rubicam, "Establishing frequency goals for an advertising campaign is a mix of art and science but with a definite bias toward art."[6] Let us first examine the process involved in setting reach and frequency objectives and then discuss the logic of each.

**Establishing Reach and Frequency Objectives**   It is possible to be exposed to more than one media vehicle with an ad, resulting in repetition (frequency). If one ad is placed on one TV show one time, the number of people exposed is the reach. If the ad is placed on two shows, the total number exposed once is **unduplicated reach**. Some people will see the ad twice. The reach of the two shows, as depicted in Figure 10–18, includes a number of people who were reached by both shows (C). This overlap is referred to as **duplicated reach**.

Both unduplicated and duplicated reach figures are important. Unduplicated reach indicates potential new exposures, while duplicated reach provides an estimate of frequency. Most media buys include both forms of reach. Let us consider an example.

A measure of potential reach in the broadcast industry is the TV (or radio) **program rating**. This number is expressed as a percentage. For an estimate of the total number of homes reached, multiply this percentage times the number of homes with TV sets. For example, if there are 114.2 million homes with TV sets in the United States and the program has a rating of 30, then the calculation is 0.30 times 114.2, or 34.2 million homes. (We go into much more detail on ratings and other broadcast terms in Chapter 11.)

**Using Gross Ratings Points**   To determine how much advertising volume or weight is necessary to accomplish advertiser's objectives, marketers rely on ratings (the number of people reached) and frequency (the average number of times exposed) figures. A summary measure that combines the program rating and the

**FIGURE 10–18**

Representation of Reach and Frequency

**A. Reach of One TV Program**

Total market audience reached

**B. Reach of Two Programs**

Total market audience reached

**C. Duplicated Reach**

Total market reached
with both shows

**D. Unduplicated Reach**

Total reach less
duplicated reach

average number of times the home is reached during this period (frequency of exposure) is a commonly used reference point known as **gross ratings points (GRPs)**:

$$GRP = Reach \times Frequency$$

GRPs are based on the total audience the media schedule may reach using a duplicated reach estimate. **Target ratings points (TRPs)** refer to the number of people in the primary target audience the media buy will reach—and the number of times. Unlike GRP, TRP does not include waste coverage.

Given that GRPs do not measure actual reach, the advertiser must ask: How many GRPs are needed to attain a certain reach? How do these GRPs translate into effective reach? For example, how many GRPs must one purchase to attain an unduplicated reach of 50 percent, and what frequency of exposure will this schedule deliver? The following example may help you to understand how this process works.

First you must know what these ratings points represent. A purchase of 100 GRPs could mean 100 percent of the market is exposed once or 50 percent of the market is exposed twice or 25 percent of the market is exposed four times, and so on. As you can see, this information must be more specific for the marketer to use it effectively. To know how many GRPs are necessary, the manager needs to know how many members of the intended audience the schedule actually reaches. The graph in Figure 10–19 helps make this determination.

In Figure 10–19, a purchase of 100 TRPs on one network would yield an estimated reach of 32 percent of the total households in the target market. This figure would climb to 37.2 percent if two networks were used and 44.5 percent with three. Working backward through the formula for GRPs, the estimate of frequency of exposure—3.125, 2.688, and 2.247, respectively—demonstrates the trade-off between reach and frequency.

An interesting example of the use of GRPs is provided by a recent race to be the Republican candidate for California governor. With the election to be held in June, the advertising schedule for March for the leading candidate Meg Whitman consisted of 1,000 GRPs per week in 11 California media markets. This buy was expected to yield a frequency of approximately 10 exposures per week to the average TV watcher in the largest markets, and approximately 6 per week in the smaller ones. The opposing candidate spent an estimated 15 to 50 percent of this amount, depending on the specific market.[7] Whitman won the race.

The overriding question is, how many GRPs are necessary to achieve our objectives? According to Scott Walker, most advertisers prefer to get 500 to 700 GRPs to be sure their message is seen and seen often.[8] A number of researchers have explored this issue. David Berger, vice president and director of research at Foote Cone & Belding, has determined that 2,500 GRPs are likely to lead to roughly a 70 percent probability of high awareness, 1,000 to 2,500 would yield about a 33 percent

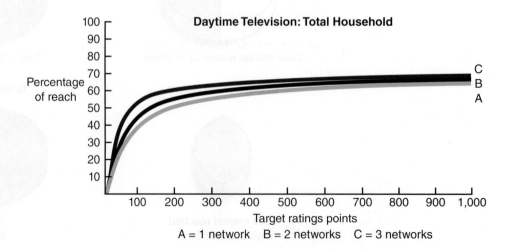

**FIGURE 10–19**

Estimates of Reach for Network TRPs

FIGURE 10–20

The Effects of Reach and Frequency

1. One exposure of an ad to a target group within a purchase cycle has little or no effect in most circumstances.
2. Since one exposure is usually ineffective, the central goal of productive media planning should be to enhance frequency rather than reach.
3. The evidence suggests strongly that an exposure frequency of two within a purchase cycle is an effective level.
4. Beyond three exposures within a brand purchase cycle or over a period of four or even eight weeks, increasing frequency continues to build advertising effectiveness at a decreasing rate but with no evidence of decline.
5. Although there are general principles with respect to frequency of exposure and its relationship to advertising effectiveness, differential effects by brand are equally important.
6. Nothing we have seen suggests that frequency response principles or generalizations vary by medium.
7. The data strongly suggest that wearout is not a function of too much frequency; it is more of a creative or copy problem.

probability, and less than 1,000 would probably result in almost no awareness.[9] David Olson obtained similar results and further showed that as awareness increased, trial of the product would also increase, although at a significantly slower rate.[10] In both cases, it was evident that high numbers of GRPs were required to make an impact.

Figure 10–20 summarizes the effects that can be expected at different levels of exposure, on the basis of research in this area. A number of factors may be operating, and direct relationships may be difficult to establish. In addition to the results shown in Figure 10–20, Joseph Ostrow has shown that while the number of repetitions increases awareness rapidly, it has much less impact on attitudinal and behavioral responses.[11]

You can imagine how expensive it was for the candidate mentioned earlier to purchase 1,000 GRPs per week in 11 markets well before the election. To spend at that level for an extended period of time could result in overexposure (not to mention a major hit on the pocketbook), as viewers might get tired of the ads.

**Determining Effective Reach**   Since marketers have budget constraints, they must decide whether to increase reach at the expense of frequency or increase the frequency of exposure but to a smaller audience. A number of factors influence this decision. For example, a new product or brand introduction will attempt to maximize reach, particularly unduplicated reach, to create awareness in as many people as possible as quickly as possible. At the same time, for a high-involvement product or one whose benefits are not obvious, a certain level of frequency is needed to achieve effective reach.

**Effective reach** represents the percentage of a vehicle's audience reached at each effective frequency increment. This concept is based on the assumption that one exposure to an ad may not be enough to convey the desired message. As we saw earlier, no one knows the exact number of exposures necessary for an ad to make an impact, although advertisers have settled on three as the minimum. Effective reach (exposure) is shown in the shaded area in Figure 10–21 in the range of 3 to 10 exposures. Fewer than 3 exposures is considered insufficient reach, while more than 10 is considered overexposure and thus ineffective reach. This exposure level is no guarantee of effective communication; different messages may require more or fewer exposures. For example, Jack Myers, president of Myers Reports, argues that the three-exposure theory was valid in the 1970s when consumers were exposed to approximately 1,000 ads per day. Now that they are exposed to 3,000 to 5,000 per day, three exposures may not be enough. Adding in the fragmentation of television, the proliferation of magazines, and the advent of a variety of alternative media leads Myers to believe that 12 exposures may be the *minimum* level of frequency required. Also, Jim Surmanek, president/CEO of Media Analysis Plus, contends

**Total Exposure versus Effective Exposure
of a Prime-Time Television Schedule**

No exposure

Ineffective exposure

Threshold of effectiveness

Reinforcement of effectiveness

Effective exposure

Excessive exposure

Negative exposure

Total exposure = 400 GRPs
Effective exposure = 221 ERPs

GRPs = Gross ratings points
ERPs = Effective rating points

Percentage of reach

Number of exposures

**FIGURE 10–21**

Graph of Effective Reach

that the complexity of the message, message length, and recency of exposure also impact this figure.[12]

Since they do not know how many times the viewer will actually be exposed, advertisers typically purchase GRPs that lead to more than three exposures to increase the likelihood of effective reach and frequency. Surmanek also argues that effective reach can be as low as one exposure, if the exposure is very recent or close to the purchase occasion (thus, recency is more important than frequency). He contends that more exposures are necessary when the message is complex and requires several exposures to be understood.[13]

Erwin Ephron, an expert in media planning, disagrees. Ephron notes that while increasing reach at minimum frequency was popular in the 1990s, it is no longer a viable strategy as changes in the marketplace (commercial avoidance, multitasking, and technological innovations like the DVR) have made it more difficult to get exposure to an ad. As a result, it is important to create plans that value both reach and frequency to ensure that the ad gets seen and has an impact. In other words, higher frequency results in higher reach.[14] Determining effective reach is further complicated by the fact that when calculating GRPs, advertisers use a figure that they call **average frequency**, or the average number of times the target audience reached by a media schedule is exposed to the vehicle over a specified period. The problem with this figure is revealed in the following scenario:

Consider a media buy in which:
50 percent of audience is reached 1 time.
30 percent of audience is reached 5 times.
20 percent of audience is reached 10 times.
Average frequency = 4

In this media buy, the average frequency is 4, which is slightly more than the number established as effective. Yet a full 50 percent of the audience receives only one exposure. Thus, the average frequency number can be misleading, and using it to calculate GRPs might result in underexposing the audience.

Although GRPs have their problems, they can provide useful information to the marketer. A certain level of GRPs is necessary to achieve awareness, and increases in GRPs are likely to lead to more exposures and/or more repetitions—both of which are necessary to have an effect on higher-order objectives. Perhaps the best advice for purchasing GRPs is offered by Ostrow, who recommends the following strategies:[15]

**1.** Instead of using average frequency, the marketer should decide what minimum frequency goal is needed to reach the advertising objectives effectively and then maximize reach at that frequency level.

FIGURE 10–22

Factors Important in
Determining Frequency
Levels

## Marketing Factors

- *Brand history.* Is the brand new or established? New brands generally require higher frequency levels.
- *Brand share.* An inverse relationship exists between brand share and frequency. The higher the brand share, the lower the frequency level required.
- *Brand loyalty.* An inverse relationship exists between loyalty and frequency. The higher the loyalty, the lower the frequency level required.
- *Purchase cycles.* Shorter purchasing cycles require higher frequency levels to maintain top-of-mind awareness.
- *Usage cycle.* Products used daily or more often need to be replaced quickly, so a higher level of frequency is desired.
- *Competitive share of voice.* Higher frequency levels are required when a lot of competitive noise exists and when the goal is to meet or beat competitors.
- *Target group.* The ability of the target group to learn and to retain messages has a direct effect on frequency.

## Message or Creative Factors

- *Message complexity.* The simpler the message, the less frequency required.
- *Message uniqueness.* The more unique the message, the lower the frequency level required.
- *New versus continuing campaigns.* New campaigns require higher levels of frequency to register the message.
- *Image versus product sell.* Creating an image requires higher levels of frequency than does a specific product sell.
- *Message variation.* A single message requires less frequency; a variety of messages requires more.
- *Wearout.* Higher frequency may lead to wearout. This effect must be tracked and used to evaluate frequency levels.
- *Advertising units.* Larger units of advertising require less frequency than smaller ones to get the message across.

## Media Factors

- *Clutter.* The more advertising that appears in the media used, the more frequency is needed to break through the clutter.
- *Editorial environment.* The more consistent the ad is with the editorial environment, the less frequency is needed.
- *Attentiveness.* The higher the level of attention achieved by the media vehicle, the less frequency is required. Low-attention-getting media require more repetitions.
- *Scheduling.* Continuous scheduling requires less frequency than does flighting or pulsing.
- *Number of media used.* The fewer media used, the lower the level of frequency required.
- *Repeat exposures.* Media that allow for more repeat exposures (for example, monthly magazines) require less frequency.

**2.** To determine effective frequency, one must consider marketing factors, message factors, and media factors. (See Figure 10–22.)

In summary, the reach-versus-frequency decision, while critical, is very difficult to make. A number of factors must be considered, and concrete rules do not always apply. The decision is often more of an art than a science.

**Recency**   As noted by Ephron, the idea that one exposure to an ad had a greater impact than additional exposures did if it was shown in the week preceding a purchase led many advertisers to focus more attention on reach, less on frequency, and an emphasis on **recency**. Campaigns employed **recency planning**—focusing on short interval reach at minimum frequency levels as close to the purchase decision as possible. Rather than focusing on a four-week planning period for reach, recency planning calls for a continuous schedule over a one week period, and less targeting to gain exposure to reach as many potential consumers as possible.[16] While one might argue that many of the exposures are then wasted, Ephron would disagree, noting that people are in the market at different times and that awareness and image building also can benefit by the exposures.[17] Both Ephron and Krugman suggest that advertising needs to act like a brand and that "Advertising needs to be like a product sitting on the shelf, because you never know when the consumer is going to be looking for you, so advertising has to rent the shelf-space all the time."

## Creative Aspects and Mood

The context of the medium in which the ad is placed may also affect viewers' perceptions. A specific creative strategy may require certain media. Because TV provides both sight and sound, it may be more effective in generating emotions than other media; magazines may create different perceptions from newspapers. In developing a media strategy, marketers must consider both creativity and mood factors. Let us examine each in more detail.

**Creative Aspects**   It is possible to increase the success of a product significantly through a strong creative campaign. But to implement this creativity, you must employ a medium that will support such a strategy. For example, the campaign for Lollipop Bling shown in Chapter 4 used print media to communicate the message effectively. Hallmark, among many others, has effectively used TV to create emotional appeals. In some situations, the media strategy to be pursued may be the driving force behind the creative strategy, as the media and creative departments work closely together to achieve the greatest impact with the audience of the specific media.

**Mood**   Certain media enhance the creativity of a message because they create a mood that carries over to the communication. For example, think about the moods created by the following magazines: *Gourmet, Skiing, Travel and Leisure,* and *House Beautiful.* Each of these special-interest vehicles puts the reader in a particular mood. The promotion of fine wines, ski boots, luggage, and home products is enhanced by this mood. What different images might be created for your product if you advertised it in the following media?

> *The New York Times* versus the *National Enquirer*
> *Architectural Digest* versus *Reader's Digest*
> A highly rated prime-time TV show versus an old rerun
> Television versus the Internet

The message may require a specific medium and a certain media vehicle to achieve its objectives. Likewise, certain media and vehicles have images that may carry over to the perceptions of messages placed within them.

## Flexibility

An effective media strategy requires a degree of flexibility. Because of the rapidly changing marketing environment, strategies may need to be modified. If the plan has not built in some flexibility, opportunities may be lost and/or the company may not be able to address new threats. Flexibility may be needed to address the following:

1. *Market opportunities.* Sometimes a market opportunity arises that the advertiser wishes to take advantage of. For example, wine companies have attempted to capitalize on the increasing interest in this drink created by changing trends in the U.S. marketplace. The development of a new advertising medium may offer an opportunity that was not previously available.

2. *Market threats.* Internal or external factors may pose a threat to the firm, and a change in media strategy is dictated. For example, a competitor may alter its media strategy to gain an edge. Failure to respond to this challenge could create problems for the firm.

3. *Availability of media.* Sometimes a desired medium (or vehicle) is not available to the marketer. Perhaps the medium does not reach a particular target segment or has no time or space available. There are still some geographic areas that certain media do not reach. Even when the media are available, limited advertising time or space may have already been sold or cutoff dates for entry may have passed. Alternative vehicles or media must then be considered.

4. *Changes in media or media vehicles.* A change in the medium or in a particular vehicle may require a change in the media strategy. For example, the advent of cable TV opened up new opportunities for message delivery, as will the introduction of interactive media. The Internet has led many consumer companies to adopt this medium while a number of new technologies have provided additional options. New special-interest magazines, mobile phones, social networks, and videogame ads are just a few. Likewise, a drop in ratings or a change in editorial format may lead the advertiser to use different alternatives.

Fluctuations in these factors mean the media strategy must be developed with enough flexibility to allow the manager to adapt to specific market situations.

## Budget Considerations

One of the more important decisions in the development of media strategy is cost estimating. The value of any strategy can be determined by how well it delivers the message to the audience with the lowest cost and the least waste. We have already explored a number of factors, such as reach, frequency, and availability, that affect this decision. The marketer tries to arrive at the optimal delivery by balancing cost with each of these. As the following discussion shows, understanding cost figures may not be as easy as it seems.

Advertising and promotional costs can be categorized in two ways. The **absolute cost** of the medium or vehicle is the actual total cost required to place the message. For example, a full-page ad in *The Week* magazine costs about $72,800. **Relative cost** refers to the relationship between the price paid for advertising time or space and the size of the audience delivered; it is used to compare media vehicles. Relative costs are important because the manager must try to optimize audience delivery within budget constraints. Since a number of alternatives are available for delivering the message, the advertiser must evaluate the relative costs associated with these choices. The way media costs are provided and problems in comparing these costs across media often make such evaluations difficult.

**Determining Relative Costs of Media**   To evaluate alternatives, advertisers must compare the relative costs of media as well as vehicles within these media. Unfortunately, the broadcast, print, and out-of-home media do not always provide the same cost breakdowns, nor necessarily do vehicles within the print media. Following are the cost bases used:

1. **Cost per thousand (CPM).** For years the magazine industry has provided cost breakdowns on the basis of cost per thousand people reached. The formula for this computation is

$$\text{CPM} = \frac{\text{Cost of ad space (absolute cost)}}{\text{Circulation}} \quad \text{Cost of ad space} \times 1{,}000$$

Figure 10–23 provides an example of this computation for two vehicles in the same medium—*Time* and *The Week*—and shows that (all other things being equal) *Time* is a more cost-effective buy, even though its absolute cost is higher. (We will come back to "all other things being equal" in a moment.)

FIGURE 10–23

Cost per Thousand
Computations: *Time* versus
*The Week*

| | Time | The Week |
|---|---|---|
| Cost per page | $366,380 | $72,800 |
| Circulation | 4.07 million | 535,000 |
| Calculation of CPM | 366,380 × 1,000 | $72,800 × 1,000 |
| | 4,007,000 | 535,000 |
| CPM | $91.44 | $136.08 |

2. **Cost per ratings point (CPRP).** The broadcast media provide a different comparative cost figure, referred to as cost per ratings point or *cost per point (CPP),* based on the following formula:

$$\text{CPRP} = \frac{\text{Cost of commercial time}}{\text{Program rating}}$$

An example of this calculation for a spot ad in a local TV market is shown in Figure 10–24. It indicates that *Survivor* would be more cost-effective than *American Idol.*

3. **Daily inch rate.** For newspapers, cost-effectiveness is based on the daily inch rate, which is the cost per column inch of the paper. Like magazines, newspapers now use the cost-per-thousand formula discussed earlier to determine relative costs. As shown in Figure 10–25, the *Pittsburgh Post Gazette* costs significantly less to advertise in than does the *Cleveland Plain Dealer* (again, all other things being equal).

As you can see, it is difficult to make comparisons across various media. What is the broadcast equivalent of cost per thousand or the column inch rate? In an attempt

| | American Idol | Survivor |
|---|---|---|
| Cost per ad | $467,617 | $153,636 |
| Rating | 3.8 | 2.67 |
| Reach (Millions HH) | 12.84 | 9.58 |
| Calculation | $467,617/3.8 | $153,636/2.67 |
| CPRP (CPP) | $123,057 | $57,541 |

FIGURE 10–25

Comparative Costs in
Newspaper Advertising

| | Pittsburgh Post Gazette | Cleveland Plain Dealer |
|---|---|---|
| Cost per page | $20,969 | $59,598 |
| Cost per inch | 303.90 | 473 |
| Circulation | 184,234 | 271,180 |
| Calculation | $CPM = \dfrac{\text{Page cost} \times 1,000}{\text{Circulation}}$ | |
| | $\dfrac{\$20,969 \times 1,000}{184,234}$ | $\dfrac{\$59,598 \times 1,000}{271,180}$ |
| | $113.81 | $219.77 |

to standardize relative costing procedures, the broadcast and newspaper media have begun to provide costs per thousand, using the following formulas:

$$\text{Television:} \frac{\text{Cost of 1 unit of time} \times 1,000}{\text{Program rating}} \quad \text{Newspapers:} \frac{\text{Cost of ad space} \times 1,000}{\text{Circulation}}$$

While the comparison of media on a cost-per-thousand basis is important, intermedia comparisons can be misleading. The ability of TV to provide both sight and sound, the longevity of magazines, and other characteristics of each medium make direct comparisons difficult. The media planner should use the cost-per-thousand numbers but must also consider the specific characteristics of each medium and each media vehicle in the decision.

The cost per thousand may overestimate or underestimate the actual cost-effectiveness. Consider a situation where some waste coverage is inevitable. The circulation (using the *Time* magazine figures to demonstrate our point) exceeds the target market. If the people reached by this message are not potential buyers of the product, then having to pay to reach them results in too low a cost per thousand, as shown in scenario A of Figure 10–26. We must use the potential reach to the target market—the destination sought—rather than the overall circulation figure. A medium with a much higher cost per thousand may be a wiser buy if it is reaching more potential receivers. (Most media buyers rely on **target CPM**, or **TCPM**, which calculates CPMs based on the target audience, not the overall audience.)

CPM may also underestimate cost efficiency. Magazine advertising space sellers have argued for years that because more than one person may read an issue, the actual reach is underestimated. They want to use the number of **readers per copy** as the true circulation. This would include a **pass-along rate**, estimating the number of people who read the magazine without buying it. Scenario B in Figure 10–26

**FIGURE 10–26**

Cost-per-Thousand Estimates

| Scenario A: Overestimation of Efficiency | |
|---|---|
| Target market | 18–49 |
| Magazine circulation | 3,250,000 |
| Circulation to target market | 65% (2,112,500) |
| Cost per page | $287,440 |

$$\text{CPM} = \frac{\$287,480}{3,250.00} = \frac{\$88.40}{\$287,480}$$

$$\text{CPM (actual target audience)} = \frac{\$287,440 \times 1,000}{2,112,500} = \$136.07$$

| Scenario B: Underestimation of efficiency | |
|---|---|
| Target market | All age groups, male and female |
| Magazine circulation | 3,250,000 |
| Cost per page | $287,440 |
| Pass-along rate | 3* (33% of households) |

$$\text{CPM (based on readers per copy)} = \frac{\text{Page cost} \times 1,000}{\text{Circulation} + 3(1,072,500)} = \frac{(287,440 \times 1,000)}{4,322,500}$$
$$= \$66.50$$

*Assuming pass-along was valid.

shows how this underestimates cost efficiency. Consider a family in which a father, mother, and two teenagers read each issue of *Time*. Assume such families constitute 33 percent of *Time*'s circulation base. While the circulation figure includes only one magazine, in reality there are four potential exposures in these households, increasing the total reach to 4.32 million.

While the number of readers per copy makes intuitive sense, it has the potential to be extremely inaccurate. The actual number of times the magazine changes hands is difficult to determine. How many people in a fraternity read each issue of *Sports Illustrated* or *Maxim* that is delivered? How many people in a sorority or on a dorm floor read each issue of *Cosmopolitan* or *Vanity Fair*? How many of either group read each issue of *Bloomberg Businessweek*? While research is conducted to make these determinations, pass-along estimates are very subjective and using them to estimate reach is speculative. These figures are regularly provided by the media, but managers are selective about using them. At the same time, the art of media buying enters, for many magazines' managers have a good idea how much greater the reach is than their circulation figures provided.

In addition to the potential for over- or underestimation of cost efficiencies, CPMs are limited in that they make only *quantitative* estimates of the value of media. Although they may be good for comparing very similar vehicles (such as *Time* and *The Week*), they are less valuable in making intermedia comparisons, for example, CPM for magazines versus Internet banner ads. We have already noted some differences among media that preclude direct comparisons.

You can see that the development of a media strategy involves many factors. Ostrow may be right when he calls this process an art rather than a science, as so much of it requires going beyond the numbers.

# EVALUATION AND FOLLOW-UP

All plans require some evaluation to assess their performance. The media plan is no exception.

In outlining the planning process, we stated that objectives are established and strategies developed for them. Having implemented these strategies, marketers need to know whether or not they were successful. Measures of effectiveness must consider two factors: (1) How well did these strategies achieve the media objectives? (2) How well did this media plan contribute to attaining the overall marketing and communications objectives? If the strategies were successful, they should be used in future plans. If not, their flaws should be analyzed.

The problem with measuring the effectiveness of media strategies is probably obvious to you at this point. At the outset of this chapter, we suggested the planning process was limited by problems with measurements and lack of consistent terminology (among others). While these problems limit the degree to which we can assess the relative effectiveness of various strategies, it is not impossible to make such determinations. Sometimes it is possible to show that a plan has worked. Even if the evaluation procedure is not foolproof, it is better than no attempt. We will discuss more about measuring effectiveness in Chapter 18.

# CHARACTERISTICS OF MEDIA

To this point, we have discussed the elements involved in the development of media strategy. One of the most basic elements in this process is the matching of media to markets. In the following chapters, you will see that each medium has its own

FIGURE 10–27

Media Characteristics

| Media | Advantages | Disadvantages |
|---|---|---|
| **Television** | Mass coverage<br>High reach<br>Impact of sight, sound, and motion<br>High prestige<br>Low cost per exposure<br>Attention getting<br>Favorable image | Low selectivity<br>Short message life<br>High absolute cost<br>High production costs<br>Clutter |
| **Radio** | Local coverage<br>Low cost<br>High frequency<br>Flexible<br>Low production costs<br>Well-segmented audiences | Audio only<br>Clutter<br>Low attention getting<br>Fleeting message |
| **Magazines** | Segmentation potential<br>Quality reproduction<br>High information content<br>Longevity<br>Multiple readers | Long lead time for ad placement<br>Visual only<br>Lack of flexibility |
| **Newspapers** | High coverage<br>Low cost<br>Short lead time for placing ads<br>Ads can be placed in interest sections<br>Timely (current ads)<br>Reader controls exposure<br>Can be used for coupons | Short life<br>Clutter<br>Low attention-getting capabilities<br>Poor reproduction quality<br>Selective reader exposure |
| **Outdoor** | Location specific<br>High repetition<br>Easily noticed | Short exposure time requires short ad<br>Poor image<br>Local restrictions |
| **Direct mail** | High selectivity<br>Reader controls exposure<br>High information content<br>Opportunities for repeat exposures | High cost/contact<br>Poor image (junk mail)<br>Clutter |
| **Digital/ interactive** | User selects product information<br>User attention and involvement<br>Interactive relationship<br>Direct selling potential<br>Flexible message platform | Privacy concerns<br>Potential for deception<br>Clutter<br>Few valid measurement techniques |

characteristics that make it better or worse for attaining specific objectives. First, Figure 10–27 provides an overall comparison of media and some of the characteristics by which they are evaluated. This is a very general comparison, and the various media options must be analyzed for each situation. Nevertheless, it is a good starting point and serves as a lead-in to subsequent chapters.

# Summary

This chapter has presented an overview of the determination of media objectives, development of the media strategy, and formalization of objectives and strategy in the form of a media plan. Sources of media information, characteristics of media, and key media decisions were also discussed.

The media strategy must be designed to supplement and support the overall marketing and communications objectives. The objectives of this plan are designed to deliver the message the program has developed.

The basic task involved in the development of media strategy is to determine the best matching of media to the target market, given the constraints of the budget. The media planner attempts to balance reach and frequency and to deliver the message to the intended audience with a minimum of waste coverage. At the same time, a number of additional factors affect the media decision. Media strategy development has been called more of an art than a science because while many quantitative data are available, the planner also relies on creativity and nonquantifiable factors.

This chapter discussed many factors, including developing a proper media mix, determining target market and geographic coverage, scheduling, and balancing reach and frequency. Creative aspects, budget considerations, the need for flexibility in the schedule, and the use of computers in the media planning process were also considered.

The chapter also introduced a number of resources available to the media planner. A summary chart of advantages and disadvantages of various media was provided.

# Key Terms

media planning p. 339
media objectives p. 339
media strategies p. 339
medium p. 339
media vehicle p. 339
reach p. 339
coverage p. 339
frequency p. 339
sweeps periods p. 341
index number p. 344
survey of buying power index p. 347
brand development index (BDI) p. 347

category development index (CDI) p. 349
waste coverage p. 352
continuity p. 354
flighting p. 354
pulsing p. 354
unduplicated reach p. 357
duplicated reach p. 357
program rating p. 357
gross ratings points (GRPs) p. 358
target ratings points (TRPs) p. 358
effective reach p. 359

average frequency p. 360
recency p. 361
recency planning p. 361
absolute cost p. 363
relative cost p. 363
cost per thousand (CPM) p. 363
cost per ratings point (CPRP) p. 364
daily inch rate p. 364
target CPM (TCPM) p. 365
readers per copy p. 365
pass-along rate p. 365

# Discussion Questions

1. Research has indicated that the number of exposures to reach optimal frequency to a commercial is three. However, this research was conducted decades ago, and many marketers believe that this number may be too low. Discuss the concept of optimal frequency and some of the factors that support or refute this number. (LO3)

2. Figure 10–27 discusses the advantages and disadvantages of media. Describe any factors that may be taking place that might change the disadvantages or advantages of various media. (LO5).

3. One of the more popular metrics now being used in nontraditional media (Internet, social media, etc.) is *engagement*. This term has also been used in evaluating traditional media. Explain what is meant by engagement. Is this term being used the same in referring to both traditional and nontraditional media way? (LO1)

4. Discuss the differences between CDI and BDI. When would an advertiser use these indexes? (LO2)

5. A number of studies have examined the role that personality and/or other personal characteristics may have on consumers' media usage. Discuss some of these studies. Do you think that these characteristics may have an impact, or should marketers rely primarily on demographic characteristics? (LO2)

6. One well-known media planner has noted that media buying is a combination of art and science with a definite bias toward art. Explain what this means and give examples of circumstances or situations in which this might be the case. (LO4)

7. GfK MRI and Experian Simmons both provide indexes to describe profiles of product users. Using the index provided in Figure 10–5, describe the profile of

the snowboarders. Who is least likely to engage in snow-boarding? (LO2)

8. What does it mean for a company when it discovers that its product has a high BDI but low CDI? What about a low CDI and low BDI? (LO2)

9. As the media landscape continues to change, and advertisers shift more and more of their monies into new media, there are those who predict that some traditional media like TV and newspapers may not survive—at least in their present forms. Discuss whether you think this is an accurate statement and why or why not. (LO5)

10. Some media claim that advertisers should focus more attention on readers per dollar than CPM as a relative cost figure. Explain why they feel this way, and discuss some of the advantages and disadvantages with the use of both of these measures. (LO2)

# A ASICS AMERICA SUMMARY FLOWCHART

| | January | | | | February | | | | March | | | | | April | | | | May | | | | June | | |
|---|---|---|---|---|---|---|---|---|---|---|---|---|---|---|---|---|---|---|---|---|---|---|---|---|
| | 29 | 5 | 12 | 19 | 26 | 2 | 9 | 16 | 23 | 2 | 9 | 16 | 23 | 30 | 6 | 13 | 20 | 27 | 4 | 11 | 18 | 25 | 1 | 8 |
| **Global/Branding** | | | | | | | | | | | | | | | | | | | | | | | | |
| TV | | | | | | | | | | | | | | | | | | | | | | | | |
| Hulu-online TV | | | | | | | | | | | | | | | | | | | | | | | | |
| **Performance Running** | | | | | | | | | | | | | | | | | | | | | | | | |
| Print | | | | | | | | | | | | | | | | | | | | | | | | |
| Online | | | | | | | | | | | | | | | | | | | | | | | | |
| **Onitsuka Tiger** | | | | | | | | | | | | | | | | | | | | | | | | |
| Print | | | | | | | | | | | | | | | | | | | | | | | | |
| Online | | | | | | | | | | | | | | | | | | | | | | | | |
| **NYC Marathon** | | | | | | | | | | | | | | | | | | | | | | | | |
| Outdoor/Online/TV | | | | | | | | | | | | | | | | | | | | | | | | |
| **Trade** | | | | | | | | | | | | | | | | | | | | | | | | |
| Print | | | | | | | | | | | | | | | | | | | | | | | | |

## LEARNING OBJECTIVES

**LO1**  To examine the structure of the television and radio industries and the role of each medium in the advertising program.

**LO2**  To consider the advantages and limitations of TV and radio as advertising media.

**LO3**  To explain how advertising time is purchased for the broadcast media, how audiences are measured, and how rates are determined.

**LO4**  To consider future trends in TV and radio and how they will influence the use of these media in advertising.

# 11 Evaluation of Media: Television and Radio

## TELEVISION PAYS THE WAY FOR COLLEGE SPORTS

Collegiate sports have long been an important part of the college experience; many students love football weekends at their schools or going to a basketball game and often stay connected to their alma maters by cheering for their sports teams. Despite their popularity, these are challenging times for intercollegiate sports as only a fraction of college athletic departments support themselves. Most rely on student fees and support from the school's general fund. The economic situation for colleges, particularly public schools, has changed dramatically in recent years. Most states have been facing budget deficits and have reduced funding for higher education. The percentage of per-student funding that comes from state or local sources has fallen from 79 percent in 1980 to only about 57 percent in 2013. Adding to the problem is the fact that various groups in many states are challenging the use of student fees to fund collegiate sports. The National Collegiate Athletic Association (NCAA), the organization that governs all of college sports, realizes that college sports may not survive unless additional revenue sources can be found.

Only about 20 percent of the 120 athletic departments in college football's top division, the Division 1 NCAA Football Bowl Subdivision (FBS), make a profit each year. However, the schools that do make a profit all have one thing in common: a big-time, high-profile football program. And as colleges scramble to cover the budget shortfalls in their athletic departments, they have recognized that the best opportunity to do so is by leveraging college football, which is their most marketable asset. The good news for athletic directors is that the television networks are welcoming them with open arms as they know that college football is one of the best ways for them to reach the most important segment of their target audience—the millions of viewers who want to watch live sports.

College football, like most sporting events, is nearly always watched live on TV, which reduces the number of people who record the games and fast-forward through commercials. Advertisers are willing to pay more for broadcast rights for sporting events such as college football games because they are a good way to reach young men who are a valuable and elusive target audience for marketers. The television networks have agreed to pay about $25 billion in rights fees to college conferences and their member schools over the next 15 years, including a deal whereby ESPN is paying an estimated $7 billion over the next 12 years to televise major college football's first FBS playoff, a four-team tournament that began in 2014. To accommodate the networks' golden goose, college football teams are doing whatever they can to maximize television revenue including adding conference championship games, jumping to new conferences, abandoning long-standing rivalries, and dismantling the old system of postseason bowl games. Over the past few years a number of conferences including the Big Ten and Pac-12 have expanded and added new teams from major media markets. For example, Maryland and Rutgers were invited to join the Big Ten Conference while the universities of Colorado and Utah joined the Pac-12, largely for the TV markets they brought with them.

The major television networks are willing to pay the NCAA as well as the conferences large sums of money for rights fees to televise games because as an advertising category, college football is more popular than ever. Marketers are now spending more than a billion dollars per season to air national ads on college football games and several hundred million more for local ad time. A number of companies such as AT&T, General Motors, and Aflac have increased their spending on college football over the past several years. For example, GM, which is the second largest advertiser in the category behind AT&T, has increased its spending on college football despite cutting its overall U.S. media budget.

There are a number of reasons why marketers are advertising on college football games and making them a major part of their IMC programs. While college football games are a way to reach young males (and often females), they also provide marketers with a way of connecting with affluent males through live sports programming but at a lower price than National Football League games. About 16 percent of homes that watch college football regularly make more than $75,000 per year, while 28 percent earn over $100,000. Another reason why college football is popular among marketers is the integrated marketing opportunities it offers them. For example, supplemental insurance company Aflac has increased its spending on college football by nearly 50 percent over the past three years and has also become the sponsor of the Heisman Trophy, which is the award given to the best player each year. The company takes the trophy to college games around the country and hosts corporate clients in box suites at games. Aflac, like other marketers, likes the fact that the NCAA offers more flexibility than the NFL in allowing integration of sponsors into the broadcast of college football games. In addition to running ads, Aflac shows images of its duck mascot running across the screen during games, and an Aflac-branded trivia question about the Heisman Trophy appears as part of many broadcasts.

A number of other companies and brands are using football games as a way to connect with students on college campuses, including AllState, Home Depot, Vizio, and Chevrolet. Home Depot sponsors ESPN's popular "College Game Day" which airs from the campus where one of the biggest games of the week is being played and televised. Chevrolet sets up kiosks at the event where students can learn more about its cars, offers tailgaters rides to the stadium, and sponsors college football themed sweepstakes.

Football is not the only collegiate sport that is generating revenue for colleges. In 2010 the NCAA signed a 14-year deal with CBS and Turner broadcasting to televise the men's basketball tournament that has become known as "March Madness." The deal will funnel at least $740 million annually to NCAA member colleges, which is much needed revenue for athletic programs that have been experiencing major budget cuts. Revenue from TV broadcast rights helps fund collegiate athletic programs, including women's sports programs as well as many minor sports that generate little revenue.

College sports programs have become very dependent on the monies the networks are willing to pay to broadcast their football and basketball games. However, the future success of the relationship between college sports, advertisers, and the TV networks will depend on several factors, including viewers' willingness to pay higher monthly bills as cable operators pass on the rights fees to subscribers, many of whom do not watch sports. It will also depend on whether the networks raise their advertising rates and make it prohibitive for companies to advertise during the games. There is also concern that the airways will become oversaturated with football and basketball games and the colleges themselves will slay the goose that is laying the golden egg.

Sources: Michael McCarthy, "How Much Longer Can Sports Prices Defy Gravity—While Still Delivering ROI?" *Advertising Age*, April 8, 2013, p. 10; Rachel Bachman and Matthew Futterman, "College Football's Big-Money, Big-Risk Business Model," *The Wall Street Journal*, December 10, 2012, pp. B1, B4; Suzanne Vranica, "Gridiron Telecasts Become Magnet for Ad Dollars," *The Wall Street Journal*, December 10, 2012, pp. B1, B4; Thomas O'Toole, "NCAA Reaches 14-Year Deal with CBS/Turner for Men's Basketball Tournament, Which Expands to 68 Teams for Now," *USA Today*, April 22, 2010, pp. B1, B2.

Television has been the dominant form of entertainment in most households for more than half a century. Advertising has been the lifeblood of the industry for nearly as long. Ever since Bulova ran the first TV ad in 1941 at a cost of ten dollars, the commercial has been considered the quintessential form of advertising for many marketers. Television advertising has gone through many changes over the past 70 years. For decades it was dominated by three major broadcast networks (ABC, CBS, and NBC), which could deliver more than 90 percent of the prime-time viewing audience on any given evening. However, with the growth of cable and direct broadcast satellite services, most television households can receive more than 100 channels that offer various types of shows, news, sports, music, information, and other entertainment genres. The device that delivers all of this into our homes has evolved, as well as the squat cubes that are rapidly being replaced by larger, flat-panel, high-definition televisions (HDTVs) that offer sharper and brighter digital images along with high-quality sound. Moreover, these HDTVs in our living rooms are being joined by other devices including digital video recorders (DVRs), gaming consoles, and computers, while the cable and satellite companies that deliver the signals also offer access to movies, sports, and other forms of entertainment through their on-demand services. And many experts argue that it is only a matter of time before all of this content is delivered to TV sets online via the Internet.

The changes that are occurring in the television industry are important as they are having a profound impact on the largest advertising medium. TV has virtually saturated households throughout the United States and most other countries and has become a mainstay in the lives of most people. The average American household watches nearly five hours of TV a day, and the tube has become the predominant source of news and entertainment for many people. Over 90 percent of TV households in the United States have a DVD player, 43 percent have digital video recorders (DVRs), and an estimated 75 percent have HDTVs on which they can watch their favorite television programs and movies. On any given evening during the prime-time hours of 8 to 11 P.M., more than 100 million people are watching TV. Popular shows like *Modern Family, NCIS,* and *The Big Bang Theory* can draw close to 20 million viewers. The large numbers of people who watch television are important to the TV networks and stations because they can sell time on these programs to marketers who want to reach that audience with their advertising messages. Moreover, the qualities that make TV a great medium for news and entertainment also encourage creative ads that can have a strong impact on customers.

Radio is also an integral part of our lives. Many of us wake up to clock radios and rely on radio programs to inform and/or entertain us while we drive to work or school. For many people, radio is a constant companion in their cars, at home, even at work. The average American listens to the radio nearly three hours each day.[1] Like TV viewers, radio listeners are an important audience for marketers.

In this chapter, we examine the broadcast media of TV and radio, including the general characteristics of each as well as their specific advantages and disadvantages. We examine how advertisers use TV and radio as part of their advertising and media strategies, how they buy TV and radio time, and how audiences are measured and evaluated for each medium. We also examine the factors that are changing the role of TV and radio as advertising media.

# TELEVISION

It has often been said that television is the ideal advertising medium. Its ability to combine visual images, sound, motion, and color presents the advertiser with the opportunity to develop the most creative and imaginative appeals of any medium. However, TV does have certain problems that limit or even prevent its use by many advertisers.

## Advantages of Television

TV has numerous advantages over other media, including creativity and impact, coverage and cost-effectiveness, captivity and attention, and selectivity and flexibility.

**Creativity and Impact**   Perhaps the greatest advantage of TV is the opportunity it provides for presenting the advertising message. The interaction of sight and sound offers tremendous creative flexibility and makes possible dramatic, lifelike representations of products and services. TV commercials can be used to convey a mood or image for a brand as well as to develop emotional or entertaining appeals that help make a dull product appear interesting.

Television is also an excellent medium for demonstrating a product or service as well as telling a story about a brand to highlight its features and benefits or create

**EXHIBIT 11–1**

Subaru uses television commercials to create an emotional attachment to its cars

YTC **11–01**

**Subaru**

youtube.com/10ebelch

an emotional attachment. For example, the Carmichael Lynch agency created a very poignant commercial for Subaru called "Cut the Cord," which shows a father putting his daughter on the school bus for the first time and then driving alongside it to make sure she's OK (Exhibit 11–1). As he drives the dad says, "I'm overprotective. That's why I got a Subaru," while the voiceover at the end of the spot says, "Love. It's what makes a Subaru, a Subaru." Television commercials such as this that rely on slice-of-life stories revolving around themes such as longevity, safety, versatility, and adventure have helped Subaru double its sales in the U.S. market over the past five years.[2]

**Coverage and Cost-Effectiveness**    Television advertising makes it possible to reach large audiences. Nearly everyone, regardless of age, sex, income, or educational level, watches at least some TV. Most people do so on a regular basis. According to Nielsen Media Research estimates, nearly 280 million people aged 2 or older live in the nation's 114.7 million TV households, close to 77 percent of whom are 18 or older.

Marketers selling products and services that appeal to broad target audiences find that TV lets them reach mass markets, often very cost-efficiently. The average prime-time TV show reaches 4.6 million homes; a top-rated show like *The Big Bang Theory* may reach nearly 10 million homes and almost twice that many viewers. In 2012, the average cost per thousand (CPM) homes reached was nearly $24 for network evening shows and $7.01 for daytime weekly shows.[3]

Because of its ability to reach large audiences in a cost-efficient manner, TV is a popular medium among companies selling mass-consumption products. Companies with widespread distribution and availability of their products and services use TV to reach the mass market and deliver their advertising messages at a very low cost per thousand. Television has become indispensable to large consumer packaged-goods marketers, telecommunication companies, carmakers, and major retailers. Telecommunication companies like Verizon, AT&T, and Sprint Nextel spend around two-thirds of their measured media budgets on various forms of television advertising—network, spot, cable, and syndicated programs—while major retailers such as JCPenney, Sears, and Walmart allocate nearly 60 percent. Figure 11–1 shows the top 10 network and cable TV advertisers and their expenditures. Digital and Social Media Perspective 11–1 discusses the Super Bowl, the television program that delivers the largest viewing audience each year. We discuss how many advertisers are turning their involvement with the Super Bowl into an integrated marketing opportunity by using social media to generate additional exposure and buzz for their ads, both before and after the game.

**Captivity and Attention**    Television is basically intrusive in that commercials impose themselves on viewers as they watch their favorite programs. Unless we make a special effort to avoid commercials, most of us are exposed to thousands of them each year. The increase in viewing options and the penetration of DVDs, DVRs, remote controls, and other automatic devices have made it easier for TV viewers to avoid commercial messages.[4] However, the remaining viewers are likely to devote some attention to many advertising messages. As discussed in Chapter 5,

FIGURE 11–1

Top 10 Network and Cable
Network Advertisers, 2012

| NETWORK TV | | |
|---|---|---|
| Rank | Company | Measured Broadcast (Millions) |
| 1 | Procter & Gamble Co. | $726.3 |
| 2 | AT&T | 674.6 |
| 3 | General Motors Co. | 652.7 |
| 4 | Verizon Communications | 609.6 |
| 5 | Ford Motor Co. | 550.8 |
| 6 | Apple | 476.4 |
| 7 | Toyota Motor Corp. | 418.6 |
| 8 | McDonald's Corp. | 406.7 |
| 9 | Sprint Nextel Corp | 374.6 |
| 10 | Microsoft Corp. | 353.0 |
| CABLE TV NETWORKS | | |
| 1 | Procter & Gamble Co. | $728.3 |
| 2 | Berkshire Hathaway | 349.6 |
| 3 | General Mills | 319.6 |
| 4 | General Motors Co. | 316.2 |
| 5 | AT&T | 295.6 |
| 6 | Yum Brands | 290.4 |
| 7 | PepsiCo | 271.7 |
| 8 | Toyota Motor Corp. | 263.3 |
| 9 | Comcast Corp. | 261.1 |
| 10 | Hershey Co. | 251.8 |

Source: "100 Leading National Advertisers," *Advertising Age*, June 24, 2013, p. 20. Copyright © 2013 Crain Communications.

the low-involvement nature of consumer learning and response processes may mean TV ads have an effect on consumers simply through heavy repetition and exposure to catchy slogans and jingles.

**Selectivity and Flexibility**   Television has often been criticized for being a nonselective medium, since it is difficult to reach a precisely defined market segment through the use of TV advertising. But some selectivity is possible due to variations in the composition of audiences as a result of program content, broadcast time, and geographic coverage. For example, Saturday morning TV caters to children; Saturday and Sunday afternoon programs are geared to the sports-oriented male; and weekday daytime shows appeal heavily to homemakers.

With the growth of cable TV, advertisers refine their coverage further by appealing to groups with specific interests such as sports, news, history, the arts, or music, as well as specific demographic groups. Exhibit 11–2 shows an ad promoting the Oxygen cable network and how it reaches young, upscale women who like to try new products, as well as recommend them to others.

## Marketers Use Social Media to Expand Their Super Bowl Playbook

America loves its football, and Super Bowl Sunday has become an unofficial national holiday. The game always draws the largest TV viewing audience of the year, and its appeal spans various age groups, sexes, and regions of the country. The game has even developed a global appeal; it is now seen in more than 200 countries. While most consumers think about the Super Bowl as the biggest football game of the year, many marketers view it as the premier marketing event as well. The Super Bowl has become the most important advertising showcase of the year, particularly for marketers willing to spend nearly $4 million for a 30-second commercial. Despite the high costs of advertising on the Super Bowl, many companies think it is well worth the money. They point out that the big game is usually the most-watched program of the year and delivers more than 100 million viewers in the United States and millions more abroad. Advertisers also note that the Super Bowl is one occasion when as much attention is paid to the commercials as to the program. Many

consumers actually wait to see the new ads that often debut during the telecast, and the spots often receive a considerable amount of hype and publicity prior to, as well as after, the game.

While the large and attentive viewing audience is a major reason why companies advertise on the Super Bowl, many also view their involvement with the game as an excellent integrated marketing opportunity. Marketers use a variety of other IMC tools to accompany the ads they run on Super Bowl Sunday, including user-generated ad contests, sweepstakes, video-sharing sites, blogs, mobile advertising, and webisodes. They also use pre- and post-game public relations efforts to maximize the value of their multimillion-dollar ad buys as many tout their Super Bowl ads with leaks to the press and partial reviews of their spots.

The goal of many marketers in hyping their Super Bowl ads is to generate buzz about them leading up to the big game and to prolong the shelf life of the ad well beyond the game. Nearly all of the companies or brands that advertise on the Super Bowl post their commercials on YouTube as well as their websites and Facebook pages and use social media to drive comments and conversations about them. Companies also use paid search ads on engines such as Google, Bing, and Yahoo! to draw more attention to their ads online. Marketers' efforts to extend the exposure to their ads are also facilitated by the numerous websites and video-sharing sites that have been developed around the Super Bowl commercials. YouTube, in conjunction with the trade publication *Adweek*, hosts all of the Super Bowl ads on its AdBlitz site and promotes it as a place where consumers can go to vote for their favorite

Advertisers can also adjust their media strategies to take advantage of different geographic markets through local or spot ads in specific market areas. Ads can be scheduled to run repeatedly or to take advantage of special occasions. For example, companies such as MillerCoors, Anheuser-Busch, and Gillette are often major sponsors during sporting events such as Major League Baseball or NFL games, which allows them to advertise heavily to men who constitute the primary market for their products.

### Limitations of Television

Although television is unsurpassed from a creative perspective, the medium has several disadvantages that limit or preclude its use by many advertisers. These problems include high costs, the lack of selectivity, the fleeting nature of a television message, commercial clutter, limited viewer attention, and distrust of TV ads.

commercials and share them with others. Various media such as *Advertising Age, Forbes*, and *USA Today*, as well as the major TV networks that host the game each year, also have microsites that host all of the Super Bowl spots. The national newspaper *USA Today* conducts its popular Ad Meter contest each year utilizing a panel of more than 7,000 consumers who log in and rate the ads during the game. The Ad Meter results are still widely recognized as determining which commercials were the most popular among consumers.

Marketers recognize that many consumers, as well as the media, want a sneak peak preview of their Super Bowl commercials and will post them online. In recent years the number of companies that make their commercials available prior to Super Bowl Sunday has been increasing; some marketers feel that unveiling the ads in the week or so before the game provides more opportunity for consumers to see them online and to generate media attention and exposure. Companies are also looking for ways to engage consumers and get them involved with their commercials. For example, Audi created a commercial for the 2013 Super Bowl that showed a shy, discouraged teenager with no date driving his father's new Audi S6 to his prom. The excitement of driving gives him the confidence to walk into the dance and kiss the prom queen. What happened next was left up to the viewers; they could go to YouTube to watch three alternative endings and vote for their favorite. When the spot aired on Super Bowl Sunday it used the fan's favorite ending called "Worth it" which showed the boy driving home with a black eye and a big smile on his face after being punched by her boyfriend. An Audi marketing executive noted that chatter about Super Bowl ads begins to fade a day or two after the game and unveiling the ad a week or so before gave them the opportunity to have a much longer conversation with consumers.

While as many as a quarter of all Super Bowl ads are now released prior to the game, some advertising experts question the strategy because it takes away the surprise element that has become such a big part of the experience. Marketing professor Charles Taylor notes that many advertisers who prerelease their spots or

run visual teasers of them lose the element of surprise, and its absence can lessen the effectiveness of ads that would have had more of an impact if not previewed. A number of companies still adhere to the traditional strategy of keeping their ads under wraps until they air during the game. For example, Mars Chocolate North America, which often advertises brands such M&M's and Snickers on the Super Bowl, still believes in the power of the "anticipation bubble" and plans to continue with its surprise-and-delight approach where everyone gets to see the ads at once.

The Super Bowl remains the showcase for advertising, but many companies balk at the idea of paying nearly $4 million to run a 30-second ad on the big game and prefer to use the money to buy multiple ads that will give them weeks or even months of exposure. Some experts question the wisdom of spending so much money for a single ad, particularly for smaller companies. Despite these concerns, the Super Bowl is likely to continue to be a popular media buy among companies that can afford it and for good reason. In terms of cost per thousand, the Super Bowl is a very efficient medium and is still the only time advertisers can reach so many people at one time. Also, the results of an econometric modeling study by research firm Millward Brown found that most brands experience an average sales lift of 12 percent the week following the game, and this impact is sustained much longer for large, established brands. Add to this the opportunities for additional exposure and buzz both before and after the game and it becomes pretty clear why the Super Bowl is likely to remain advertising's premier event.

Sources: Abbey Klassen, "How to Boost Your Super Bowl ROI," *Advertising Age*, December 7, 2009, http://adage.com/print?article_id=140896; Brian Steinberg, "Is Social Media Spoiling the Super Bowl Ad Surprise?" *Advertising Age*, January 13, 2013, http://adage.com/article/special-report-super-bowl/social-media-spoiling-super-bowl-ad-surprise/239147/; E. J. Schultz, "Why Mars Won't Be Releasing Its Super Bowl Ad Early," *Advertising Age*, January 11, 2013, http://adage.com/article/media/mars-releasing-super-bowl-ad-early/239145/; Philip Herr, "In the Era of 'Like,' How Much Does Liking a Super Bowl Ad Affect ROI?," *Advertising Age*, January 28, 2011, http://adage.com/article/special-report-super-bowl/super-bowl-ad-meter-rankings-equate-sales-boost/148546/.

YTC **11–02**

**Super Bowl**

youtube.com/10ebelch

**Costs** Despite the efficiency of TV in reaching large audiences, it is an expensive medium in which to advertise. The high cost of TV stems not only from the expense of buying airtime but also from the costs of producing a quality commercial. Production costs for a national brand 30-second spot average more than $350,000 and can reach over $1 million for more elaborate commercials.[5] Many advertisers also develop commercials specifically for certain ethnic markets such as African Americans and Hispanics.[6] More advertisers are using media-driven creative strategies that require production of a variety of commercials, which drive up their costs. Even local ads can be expensive to produce and often are not of high quality. The high costs of producing and airing commercials often price small and medium-size advertisers out of the market.

**Lack of Selectivity** Some selectivity is available in television through variations in programs and cable TV. But advertisers who are seeking a very specific,

**EXHIBIT 11–2**

Oxygen promotes its ability to reach young, upscale women

often small, target audience find the coverage of TV often extends beyond their market, reducing its cost effectiveness (as discussed in Chapter 10). Geographic selectivity can be a problem for local advertisers such as retailers, since a station bases its rates on the total market area it reaches. For example, stations in Pittsburgh, Pennsylvania, reach viewers in western and central Pennsylvania, eastern Ohio, northern West Virginia, and even parts of Maryland. The small company whose market is limited to the immediate Pittsburgh area may find TV an inefficient media buy, since the stations cover a larger geographic area than the merchant's trade area.

Audience selectivity is improving as advertisers target certain groups of consumers through the type of program or day and/or time when they choose to advertise. However, TV still does not offer as much audience selectivity as radio, magazines, newspapers, or direct mail for reaching precise segments of the market.

**Fleeting Message**   TV commercials usually last only 30 seconds or less and leave nothing tangible for the viewer to examine or consider. Commercials have become shorter and shorter as the demand for a limited amount of broadcast time has intensified and advertisers try to get more impressions from their media budgets. Thirty-second commercials became the norm in the mid-1970s, and in September 1986, the three major networks began accepting 15-second spots across their full schedules (except during children's viewing time). Since 1987, these shorter spots have been accounting for a little more than a third of all network commercials and up to 14 percent of nonnetwork commercial activity. Thirty-second spots remain the dominant commercial length, accounting for 51 percent of network spots and nearly 70 percent of nonnetwork ads.[7]

An important factor in the decline in commercial length has been the spiraling inflation in media costs over the past decade. With the average cost of a prime-time spot now exceeding $100,000, many advertisers see shorter commercials as the only way to keep their media costs in line. A 15-second spot typically sells for half the price of a 30-second spot. By using 15- or even 10-second commercials, advertisers think they can run additional spots to reinforce the message or reach a larger audience. Many advertisers believe shorter commercials can deliver a message just as effectively as longer spots for much less money.

Several years ago, many advertising people predicted 15-second spots would become the dominant commercial unit. However, the use of 15-second commercials on the major networks has settled at around 38 percent since 2003. This may be due to several factors, including creative considerations, lower prices for network time, and a desire by the networks to restrict clutter.[8] Their use on nonnetwork local stations is much lower, however, as it is around 20 percent.

**Clutter**   The problems of fleeting messages and shorter commercials are compounded by the fact that the advertiser's message is only one of many spots and other nonprogramming material seen during a commercial break, so it may have trouble being noticed. One of advertisers' greatest concerns with TV advertising is the potential decline in effectiveness because of such *clutter.*

The next time you watch TV, count the number of commercials, promotions for the news or upcoming programs, or public service announcements that appear during a station break and you will appreciate why clutter is a major concern. With all of these messages competing for our attention, it is easy to understand why the viewer comes away confused or even annoyed and unable to remember or properly identify the product or service advertised.

While the use of shorter commercials by advertisers has contributed to the problem, clutter also increases when the networks and individual stations run promotional announcements for their shows, make more time available for commercials, and redistribute time to popular programs. For many years, the amount of time available for commercials was restricted by the Code Authority of the National Association of Broadcasters to 9.5 minutes per hour during prime time and 12 minutes during nonprime time. The Justice Department suspended the code in 1982 on the grounds that it violated antitrust law. At first the networks did not alter their time standards, but over the past two decades they have increased the number of commercial minutes in their schedules. The networks argue that they must increase commercial inventory or raise their already steep rates. Advertisers and agencies have been pressuring the networks to cut back on the commercials and other sources of clutter.

**Limited Viewer Attention**   When advertisers buy time on a TV program, they are not purchasing guaranteed exposure but rather the opportunity to communicate a message to large numbers of consumers. But there is increasing evidence that the size of the viewing audience shrinks during a commercial break. People leave the room to go to the bathroom or to get something to eat or drink, or they are distracted in some other way during commercials.

Getting consumers to pay attention to commercials has become an even greater challenge in recent years as many homes have the ability to record programs with a DVR. Moreover, most households have either cable or satellite service and receive an average of more than 100 channels, which means there are more viewing options available. These factors have contributed to the problems of zipping and zapping. **Zipping** occurs when viewers fast-forward through commercials as they play back a previously recorded program. With the increased penetration of DVRs, more people are watching recorded shows and fast-forwarding through the commercials. The problem is being compounded by the fact that many of the networks schedule their most popular shows against one another on the same nights (usually Wednesday and Thursday) and in the same time slots. Thus, the most popular shows also end up being the most recorded. Moreover, the audience for these shows is composed of upscale viewers in the 18-to-49 age group that are highly coveted by many advertisers.[9]

TiVo, the company that is the leading provider of digital video recorders, sells advertisers second-by-second ratings of programs and commercials based on the viewing habits of its subscribers. The service is called Stop/Watch, and in addition to the commercial ratings data, it includes demographic information as well as the opportunity for marketers to survey a panel of 350,000 TiVo subscribers to better understand their viewing habits and why they might skip ads (Exhibit 11–3). Nielsen Media Research also has conducted studies of those who fast-forward through ads and have found that men and women between the ages of 18 and 34 skip more commercials and older women tend to skip fewer ads than younger women.[10]

**Zapping** refers to changing channels to avoid commercials. Nearly all televisions come with remote controls, which enable viewers to switch channels easily. An observational study conducted by John Cronin found as much as a third of program audiences may be lost to electronic zapping when commercials appear.[11] A Nielsen study found that most commercial zapping occurs at the beginning and, to a lesser extent, the end of a program. Zapping at these points is likely to occur because commercial breaks are so long and predictable. Zapping has also been fueled by the 24-hour continuous-format programming on cable channels such as CNN, MTV2, and ESPN. Viewers can switch over for a few news headlines, sports scores, or a music video and then switch back to the program. Research shows that young adults zap more than older adults and that men are more likely to zap than women.[12]

Studies conducted on zapping behavior among television viewers have found that people stop viewing TV during a commercial

**EXHIBIT 11–3**

TiVo tracks the viewing patterns of its subscribers

**EXHIBIT 11–4**

GSN promotes the engagement level of its viewers

break because they have a reason to stop watching television altogether or they want to find out what is being shown on other channels. The number of people zapping in and out was not related to the type of product being advertised or specific characteristics of the commercials.[13] Research has also shown that zappers recalled fewer of the brands advertised than nonzappers and that most of the brands that were recalled by zappers were placed near the end of the commercial break, which is when viewers would be likely to return to a program.[14]

As more consumers become turned off by advertising and the number of channels available to them increases, the level of zapping is likely to increase. Thus, the challenge facing the networks, as well as advertisers, is how to discourage viewers from changing channels during commercial breaks and be more receptive to the advertising. Exhibit 11-4 shows an ad for Game Show Network (GSN) promoting how higher engagement with its programming increases the engagement level of its viewers, which in turn leads to greater receptivity to advertising messages and higher purchase intentions. Some advertisers believe that producing different executions of a campaign theme is one way to maintain viewers' attention. Others think the ultimate way to zap-proof commercials is to produce creative advertising messages that will attract and hold viewers' attention. However, this is easier said than done, as many consumers just do not want to watch commercials.

Advances in technology are likely to continue to lead to changes in television viewing habits, which will impact the number of consumers who watch TV commercials. DVRs are becoming a major threat to the television industry. As noted earlier, 43 percent of TV households have DVRs, although research conducted by Nielsen shows that these homes spend only about three to four hours per week watching recorded programs and nearly half of them say they do not fast-forward through the commercials.[15] However, DVRs are expected to continue to present a problem for advertisers, particularly if devices such as the Dish Network's Hopper, which allows viewers to automatically skip ads on all TV programs they record, become more prevalent.[16] Also of concern to the television industry is how TV viewing patterns are being impacted by another time-shifting technology—video on demand (VOD)—that is offered by cable operators as well as satellite services. It is estimated that VOD services will be used in 57 percent of homes by 2016. VOD services allow users to select and watch programs interactively, and pause, fast-forward, or rewind the program just as they might do with a DVR player.

DVR penetration in U.S. homes appears to have plateaued and is being surpassed by VOD use, particularly as program offerings from the cable and satellite operators as well as the television networks expand. The major networks are now making current episodes of programs available on demand which means that viewers no longer need a DVR to watch their favorite shows. For a number of years, TV shows available through VOD did not contain any ads and the networks made a limited number of shows available as they were reluctant to allow viewers access to shows without commercials since they were concerned they would become accustomed to that type of viewing experience. However, the networks have begun to make their programs available with commercials and the cable operators and other distributors have, in some cases, agreed to disable a viewer's ability to fast-forward through them. Some of the networks have also begun to include VOD viewership in the advertising packages they make available to advertisers along with viewership on their websites as well as other devices such as tablets and smartphones.[17]

It is likely that viewers' interest in watching TV shows in alternative ways and on their own time schedule will increase as more homes acquire DVRs and VOD services. More people are also watching TV shows online through video-streaming subscription services including Netflix, Amazon, and Hulu Plus while the networks and local TV stations are making more shows available on their websites. The challenge facing the TV industry is how to accommodate the demand for these alternative viewing methods and capture revenue from them while protecting their traditional advertising business model. They also must consider that the way many people watch television is changing as viewers are using their laptops, tablets, and smartphones to multitask when watching TV. Digital and Social Media Perspective 11–2 discusses how multitasking and social media are changing the way we watch television and the implications for advertisers.

**Distrust and Negative Evaluation**  To many critics of advertising, TV commercials personify everything that is wrong with the industry. Critics often single out TV commercials because of their pervasiveness and the intrusive nature of the medium. Consumers are seen as defenseless against the barrage of TV ads, since they cannot control the transmission of the message and what appears on their screens. Viewers dislike TV advertising when they believe it is offensive, uninformative, or shown too frequently or when they do not like its content.[18] Studies have shown that of the various forms of advertising, distrust is generally the highest for TV commercials.[19] Also, concern has been raised about the effects of TV advertising on specific groups, such as children or older adults.[20]

The results from Nielsen's Global Trust in Advertising Survey of more than 28,000 people in 56 countries found that 47 percent of consumers around the world say they trust television advertising and print. The survey also found that trust in TV ads declined by 24 percent between 2009 and 2012.[21]

# BUYING TELEVISION TIME

A number of options are available to advertisers that choose to use TV as part of their media mix. They can purchase time in a variety of program formats that appeal to various types and sizes of audiences. They can purchase time on a national, regional, or local basis. Or they can sponsor an entire program, participate in the sponsorship, or use spot announcements during or between programs.

The purchase of TV advertising time is a highly specialized phase of the advertising business, particularly for large companies spending huge sums of money. Large advertisers that do a lot of TV advertising generally use agency media specialists or specialized media buying services to arrange the media schedule and purchase TV time. Decisions have to be made regarding national or network versus local or spot purchases, selection of specific stations, sponsorship versus participation, different classes of time, and appropriate programs. Local advertisers may not have to deal with the first decision, but they do face all the others.

## Network versus Spot

A basic decision for all advertisers is allocating their TV media budgets to network versus local or spot announcements. Most national advertisers use network schedules to provide national coverage and supplement this with regional or local spot purchases to reach markets where additional coverage is desired.

**Network Advertising**  A common way advertisers disseminate their messages is by purchasing airtime from a **television network**. A network assembles a series of affiliated local TV stations, or **affiliates**, to which it supplies programming and services. These affiliates, most of which are independently owned, contractually agree to preempt time during specified hours for programming provided by the networks and to carry the national advertising within the program. The networks share the advertising revenue they receive during these time periods with the affiliates. The affiliates are also free to sell commercial time in nonnetwork periods and during station breaks in the preempted periods to both national and local advertisers.

Television has long been the medium of choice for marketers who want to reach large audiences and deliver an impactful message. However, developments in digital technology over the past decade or so have had a profound impact on the way people watch TV and are challenging its role as the quintessential advertising medium. For nearly 60 years consumers watched TV on huge, boxlike tube sets with screen sizes that slowly evolved from 19 to 36 inches in size. However, today nearly 90 percent of homes have high-resolution, pixel-perfect HDTVs and as the prices decline, the size of the television in many homes gets larger. Most homes also have wireless Internet connectivity along with devices such as a PlayStation, Xbox, Apple TV, Roku box, or Google TV that help them stream video content to their televisions.

While HDTVs get larger and various devices are making TV viewing like surfing the Internet, not everyone is opting for "bigger is better" when it comes to watching television. Many people are going the opposite direction and are turning to their laptops, tablets, and even cell phones to watch their favorite movies, shows, and sports programs. In some cases, an iPad owner will stare at a 10-inch screen for hours when there is a 42-inch HDTV in the same room. He or she may be viewing the smaller screen because a spouse or roommate is watching another program or because the Internet connection is better through a computer or tablet than a video-streaming device. However, a growing number of people have become tired of paying $100-plus monthly bills for cable or satellite TV service and don't even use an antenna to get free signals over the air. The Nielsen Co. estimates that there are now around 5 million of these "Zero-TV" households that watch TV shows and movies on the Internet, often via mobile phone connections.

There are other ways in which TV viewing is being transformed by computers, tablets, and other mobile devices.

In fact, it's a similar concept to what you're probably doing while reading this book: multitasking. When is the last time you watched TV without surfing the Internet, texting friends, tweeting, going on Facebook, or playing games such as Words with Friends or Angry Birds? You probably can't remember, meaning you're among the 86 percent of TV watchers whom a recent Nielsen and Yahoo study found watch TV while multitasking on your computer or mobile device. Within that group, 40 percent use their mobile devices for social networking, 33 percent utilize various apps, and over half text family and friends.

The widespread multitasking and social media consumption during TV viewing is having a major effect on the television industry. One way is by bringing eyeballs to shows that otherwise would not be there. A 2012 Nielsen study showed that 46 percent of TV watchers started watching a show as a result of hearing about it through Facebook while Twitter came in second at 14 percent, websites of TV shows at 9 percent, and online discussion boards at 8 percent. Additionally, of those who took the survey, 70 percent indicated that they talked about a show through social media while it was on the air. The total number of comments about TV shows posted on social media platforms reached 75.5 million in July 2012, up from just 8.8 million a year before.

These are very powerful numbers that are getting the television industry to take note. The CW network's *Vampire Diaries*, for example, was flooded with questions and comments via Twitter when its season two finale included a scene in which a vampire entered a human's house uninvited (according to vampire lore, a vampire can't enter a human's home without an invitation). The writers of the show ignored the feedback for a while, but eventually so many of the season three comments—57,000 per episode, among the highest of any scripted TV show—were about the breach of "vampire etiquette" that the writers

---

The three traditional major networks are NBC, ABC, and CBS. The Fox Broadcasting Co. broadcasts its programs over a group of affiliated independent stations and has become the fourth major network. A number of Fox's prime-time programs, such as *Family Guy, American Idol, The X Factor,* and *Glee,* have become very popular, particularly among the 18-to-49 age group that is often targeted by advertisers. Fox has also become a major player in sports programming with its contracts to broadcast sporting events such as NFL football and Major League Baseball.[22]

The other television network in the United States is CW, which was formed in 2006 when two 11-year-old networks, WB and UPN, decided to merge.[23] The CW Network is co-owned by CBS/Viacom and Warner Bros., which is part of the Time Warner media conglomerate. Both WB and UPN targeted younger viewers with their shows and CBS and Warner Bros. hope that by combining the two networks' programming and affiliates they can eventually make CW the fifth major broadcast network. The CW Network still targets the 18-to-49 demographic but does not offer a full prime-time schedule. It airs 15 hours of prime-time programming over consumers who multitask while watching TV are beginning to pop up everywhere. MTV, for example, released a multiplatform ad service in 2012 that seeks to capture the attention of consumers who watch television while surfing the Internet or tweeting. The product, called Reverb, allows marketers to run an ad on the MTV cable channel, MTV website, and MTV mobile app all at the same time. The goal of the service is to give advertisers exposure to consumers no matter what they are doing at the moment the commercial runs. While MTV has developed a proprietary application for simultaneous advertising, it is not the first network to run ads on multiple platforms. During the 2012 Summer Olympics in London, NBC would not sell ad space to companies unless they signed up for both TV and digital spots. NBC Universal's executive VP of digital media sales cited the fact that "broadcast and social work better together" and said it was in the marketers' best interest to be using both despite higher costs. While this may simply have been a way to drive more revenue for NBC, social media usage patterns among TV viewers clearly support his position.

Finally, let's not forget the TV manufacturers themselves who are doing their best to adapt to changing times within their industry. Many HDTVs now offer "smart" capabilities, making them Internet-enabled and capable of connecting to Facebook, YouTube, and streaming services such as Hulu Plus and Netflix at the push of a button. While hardcore social TV viewers will contend that these features are not nearly as efficient as the content-browsing capabilities of today's tablets and mobile phones, companies such as Samsung, Sony, and Vizio recognize they must find ways to accommodate viewers as the ever-increasing number of multitaskers moves back and forth between screens.

Sources: Ryan Nakashima, "Broadcasters Worry about 'Zero TV' Homes," April 7, 2013, http://techland.time.com/2013/04/08/broadcasters-worry-about-zero-tv-homes/; Kevin Sintumuang, "Is a Tablet the Only TV You Need?" *The Wall Street Journal*, September 28, 2012, pp. D1, D2; John Jannarone, "When Twitter Fans Steer TV," *The Wall Street Journal*, September 17, 2012, p. B6; Suzanne Vranica, "MTV Aims for Multi-tasker," *The Wall Street Journal*, September 5, 2012, p. B4; Kunur Patel, "Is Social Media Killing TV?," *Advertising Age*, April 18, 2011, p. 4.

had no choice but to work something into the script to address why it happened. Twitter remains among the most powerful social media platforms for driving traffic to a TV show or a marketer's website. While hashtags are hardly "new" to the average Twitter user, the last few years have witnessed their being used more strategically by marketers and TV producers to promote discussion and drive eyeballs to shows and websites. When Comedy Central aired a show featuring a roast of Donald Trump, it included the hashtag #TrumpRoast in its Twitter promotions and received its highest ratings for a Tuesday night show in the network's history.

While some writers and producers might argue that fans shouldn't "steer" the direction and content of a show, others will contend that TV has become no different from politics in that it is critical to pay attention to your core base of followers. Viewers who are active in social media have become grass-roots organizers for the shows they watch and their social chatter often attracts new viewers to a show. Social media discussions can bring new viewers up to speed quickly so they feel as if they have been watching from day one.

Of course, advertisers are paying attention to the changes in TV consumption as well, as new methods of reaching

six days, with only a morning cartoon block on Saturdays. The new network has a number of popular programs, including *America's Next Top Model*, *Supernatural*, and *The Vampire Diaries* (Exhibit 11–5). In addition to CW and the four major networks, there are also several Spanish-language networks in the United States.[24] Spanish-language television networks such as Univision and Telemundo are becoming increasingly popular and provide advertisers a way to reach the fast-growing Hispanic market (Exhibit 11–6). Univision has become the nation's leading Hispanic media company and now challenges the four major broadcast TV networks with respect to size of its viewing audience. Hispanics now account for more than 52 million, or nearly 17 percent, of the U.S. population and advertising spending on Hispanic television continues to grow. The Hispanic population is also younger and is having a greater influence on the direction of pop culture, which makes them an important market for advertisers.[25]

The networks have affiliates throughout the nation for almost complete national coverage. When an advertiser purchases airtime from one of these four national

**EXHIBIT 11–5**

The CW Network has a number of popular shows such as *America's Next Top Model*

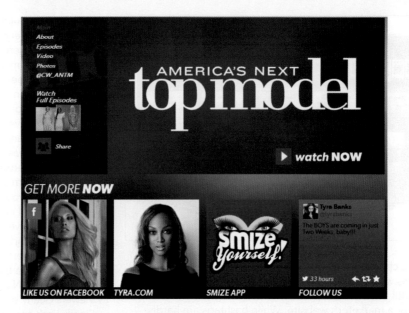

networks, the commercial is transmitted across the nation through the affiliate station network. Network advertising truly represents a mass medium, as the advertiser can broadcast its message simultaneously throughout the country.

A major advantage of network advertising is the simplification of the purchase process. The advertiser has to deal with only one party or media representative to air a commercial nationwide. The networks also offer many of the most popular and widely watched programs, particularly during prime time. Advertisers interested in reaching large national audiences generally buy commercials on shows that air during the prime-time viewing hours of 8 to 11 P.M. (7 to 10 P.M. in the Central and Mountain time zones).

**YTC 11–03**

**Up-Front Market**

youtube.com/10ebelch

**EXHIBIT 11–6**

Univision is the leading Spanish-language network

**Número Uno is the New #1.**

Univision swept ABC, CBS, NBC and FOX. For the first time ever, the Network's no-repeat lineup of **primetime novelas, variety** and **sports** made Univision **America's New #1 Network** among both adults 18-34 and 18-49, including men and women. In any language.

**Thank you, viewers, for making history with us.**

  UNIVISION

#UnivisionMakesHistory
univision.net

Source: Nielsen, NPM, 6/27/13-7/13/13, Mon-Sat 8-11pm/Sun 7-11pm, AA (000) A/W/M 18-34/ A/W/M 18-49, Live+SD.

While network advertising is an effective way to reach large audiences, the cost of advertising on prime-time shows is much higher because of the number of viewers they reach. Many of the popular prime-time shows such as *The Big Bang Theory, Modern Family,* and *Family Guy* can charge well over $200,000 for a 30-second spot. TV shows that do well among viewers in the 18-to-49 age group can often charge a premium since this demographic segment is very important to many advertisers. The most expensive TV program for the past several television seasons has been *NBC's Sunday Night Football,* which airs during the fall and charged an estimated $545,000 for a 30-second commercial during the 2012–2013 TV season. *American Idol,* which airs from January to May, has seen its ratings decline over the past few years but remains one of the most expensive shows on television along with *The Simpsons* and *The Big Bang Theory.* Many of the most popular shows on television are comedies, which are very popular among the coveted 18-to-49 audience.[26]

Availability of time can also be a problem as more advertisers turn to network advertising to reach mass markets. Traditionally, most prime-time commercial spots, particularly on the popular shows, are sold during the **up-front market**, a buying period that occurs before the TV season begins. Advertisers hoping to use prime-time network advertising must plan their media schedules and often purchase TV time as much as a year in advance. Demands from large clients who are heavy TV advertisers force the biggest agencies to participate in the up-front market. However, TV time is also purchased during the **scatter market** that runs through the TV season. Some key incentives for buying up front, such as cancellation options and lower prices, are becoming more available in the quarterly scatter market. Network TV can also be purchased on a regional basis, so an advertiser's message can be aired in certain sections of the country with one media purchase.

Recently the major networks as well as their cable counterparts have been reserving at least 10 percent or more of their inventory of advertising time rather than offering all of it for sale during the up-front market. This is done when sales during the up-front buying period are weak in hopes of being able to sell the advertising time at higher prices on the scatter market.[27] Networks can also get higher prices for commercial time on the scatter market for new shows that end up attracting large audiences over the course of the television season. Fluctuations in supply and demand for network time can also work to the benefit of advertisers as often they can take advantage of weak demand for ad time on certain programs and purchase it at lower rates on the scatter market.

**Spot and Local Advertising** **Spot advertising** refers to commercials shown on local TV stations, with time negotiated and purchased directly from the individual stations. All nonnetwork advertising done by a national advertiser is known as **national spot advertising**; airtime sold to local firms such as retailers, restaurants, banks, and auto dealers is known as **local advertising**. Local advertisers want media whose coverage is limited to the geographic markets in which they do business. This may be difficult to accomplish with TV, but many local businesses are large enough to make efficient use of TV advertising.

Spot advertising offers the national advertiser flexibility in adjusting to local market conditions. The advertiser can concentrate commercials in areas where market potential is greatest or where additional support is needed. This appeals to advertisers with uneven distribution or limited advertising budgets, as well as those interested in test marketing or introducing a product in limited market areas. National advertisers often use spot television advertising through local retailers or dealers as part of their cooperative advertising programs and to provide local dealer support.

A major problem for national advertisers is that spot advertising can be more difficult to acquire, since the time must be purchased from a number of local stations. Moreover, there are more variations in the pricing policies and discount structure of individual stations than of the networks. However, this problem has been reduced somewhat by the use of **station reps**, individuals who act as sales representatives for a number of local stations in dealings with national advertisers.

Spot ads are subject to more commercial clutter, since local stations can sell time on network-originated shows only during station breaks between programs, except when network advertisers have not purchased all the available time. Viewership generally declines during station breaks, as people may leave the room, zap to another channel, attend to other tasks, or stop watching TV.

While spot advertising is mostly confined to station breaks between programs on network-originated shows, local stations sell time on their own programs, which consist of news, movies, syndicated shows, or locally originated programs. Most cities have independent stations that spot advertisers use. Local advertisers find the independent stations attractive because they generally have lower rates than the major network affiliates.

The decision facing most national advertisers is how to combine network and spot advertising to make effective use of their TV advertising budget. Another factor that makes spot advertising attractive to national advertisers is the growth in syndication.

**Syndication** Advertisers may also reach TV viewers by advertising on **syndicated programs**, shows that are sold or distributed on a station-by-station, market-by-market basis. A syndicator seeks to sell its program to one station in every market. There are several types of syndicated programming. *Off-network syndication* refers to reruns of network shows that are bought by individual stations. Shows that are popular in off-network syndication include *The Big Bang Theory, Two and a Half*

*Men,* and *Family Guy.* The FCC prime-time access rule forbids large-market network affiliates from carrying these shows from 7 to 8 P.M., but independent stations are not affected by this restriction. A show must have a minimum number of episodes before it is eligible for syndication, and there are limits on network involvement in the financing or production of syndicated shows.

Off-network syndication shows are very important to local stations because they provide quality programming with an established audience. The syndication market is also very important to the studios that produce programs and sell them to the networks. Most prime-time network shows initially lose money for the studios, since the licensing fee paid by the networks does not cover production costs. Over four years (the time it takes to produce the number of episodes needed to break into syndication), half-hour situation comedies often run up a deficit of millions, and losses on a one-hour drama show are even higher. However, the producers recoup their money when they sell the show to syndication.

*First-run syndication* refers to shows produced specifically for the syndication market. The first-run syndication market is made up of a variety of shows, including some that did not make it as network shows. Examples of popular first-run syndication shows include talk shows such as *Live with Kelly & Michael* and *The Dr. Phil Show,* entertainment shows such as *Inside Edition* and *Entertainment Tonight,* and court shows such as *Judge Judy.*

*Advertiser-supported* or *barter syndication* is the practice of selling shows to stations in return for a portion of the commercial time in the show, rather than (or in addition to) cash. The commercial time from all stations carrying the show is packaged into national units and sold to national advertisers. The station sells the remaining time to local and spot advertisers. Both off-network and first-run syndicated programs are offered through barter syndication. Usually, more than half of the advertising time is presold, and the remainder is available for sale by the local advertiser. Barter syndication allows national advertisers to participate in the syndication market with the convenience of a network-type media buy, while local stations get free programming and can sell the remainder of the time to local or spot advertisers. Recently, the straight barter deal has given way to more barter/cash arrangements, where the station pays for a program at a reduced rate and accepts a number of preplaced bartered ads. Top-rated barter syndicated programs include *Wheel of Fortune* and *Jeopardy.*

Syndication now accounts for more than a third of the national broadcast audience and has become a very big business, generating ad revenue comparable to any of the big-four networks. Syndicated shows have become more popular than network shows in certain dayparts, such as daytime, early prime time, and late fringe. In some markets, syndicated shows like *Wheel of Fortune* draw a larger audience than the network news.

Many national advertisers use syndicated shows to broaden their reach, save money, and target certain audiences. For example, off-network syndication shows such as *The Big Bang Theory, Family Guy,* and *Modern Family* are popular with advertisers because they reach the highly sought after, and often difficult to reach, young-adult audience (ages 18 to 34) and are lower on a cost-per-thousand basis than network shows. Figure 11–2 shows the top 10 syndicated programs in 2012–2013. Syndication continues to gain in popularity, and more advertisers are making syndicated shows part of their television media schedules. Exhibit 11–7 shows how the Syndicated Network Television Association (SNTA) promotes the advantages of syndication for reaching adults during the summer.

**EXHIBIT 11–7**

The SNTA promotes the advantages of syndication for reaching adults

| Rank | Program | Household Rating |
|------|---------|------------------|
| 1 | *The Big Bang Theory* (AT) | 3.88 |
| 2 | *Wheel of Fortune* | 3.58 |
| 3 | *Judge Judy* | 3.33 |
| 4 | *Jeopardy* | 3.22 |
| 5 | *The Big Bang Theory* (weekend) B | 2.95 |
| 6 | *The Big Bang Theory* (weekend) A | 2.67 |
| 7 | *Two and a Half Men* | 2.54 |
| 8 | *Family Feud* | 2.39 |
| 9 | *Weekend Adventure* | 2.32 |
| 10 | *Made in Hollywood* | 2.19 |

Source: The Nielsen Company.

Syndication has certain disadvantages. The audience for some syndicated shows is often older and more rural, and syndicators do not supply as much research information as the networks do. Syndication also creates more problems for media buyers, since a syndicated show may not be seen in a particular market or may be aired during an undesirable time period. Thus, media buyers have to look at each market and check airtimes and other factors to put together a syndication schedule.

## Methods of Buying Time

In addition to deciding whether to use network versus spot advertising, advertisers must decide whether to sponsor an entire program, participate in a program, or use spot announcements between programs. Sponsorship of a program and participations are available on either a network or a local market basis, whereas spot announcements are available only from local stations.

**Sponsorship** Under a **sponsorship** arrangement, an advertiser assumes responsibility for the production and usually the content of the program as well as the advertising that appears within it. In the early days of TV, most programs were produced and sponsored by corporations and were identified by their name, for example, *Texaco Star Theater* and *The Colgate Comedy Hour.* Today most shows are produced by either the networks or independent production companies that sell them to a network.

Some companies are still involved in the production business. For example, Procter & Gamble, which has been producing soap operas since 1950, entered into an agreement with Paramount Television Groups to develop shows for network TV and first-run syndication. Several major companies have been sponsoring special programs for many years, such as the *Kraft Theater* and *Hallmark Hall of Fame* dramatic series. Sole sponsorship of programs is usually limited to specials and has been declining. However, some companies, including Ford, AT&T, General Electric, and IBM, do still use program sponsorships occasionally.

A company might choose to sponsor a program for several reasons. Sponsorship allows the firm to capitalize on the prestige of a high-quality program, enhancing the image of the company and its products. Traditionally, commercial-free sponsorships have been rare, particularly on the major networks, as sponsoring an entire show can be very costly; it requires buying out all of the national time as well as the local minutes from network affiliates. However, recently a number of companies have paid for shows to run commercial free as part of a larger package involving placements of their products in the program. For example, the Ford Motor Company sponsored commercial-free season premieres of the drama show *24* on Fox for several seasons in exchange for having its vehicles featured in the program.

Companies also sponsor programs to gain more control over the shows carrying their commercials including the number, placement, and content of commercials. Commercials can be of any length as long as the total amount of commercial time does not exceed network or station regulations. Advertisers introducing new products or brands sometimes sponsor a program and run commercials that are several minutes long to launch them. While these factors make sponsorship attractive to some companies, the high costs of sole sponsorship limit this option to large firms. Most commercial time is purchased through other methods, such as participations.

**Participations**  Most advertisers either cannot afford the costs of sponsorship or want greater flexibility than sole sponsorship permits. Nearly 90 percent of network advertising time is sold as **participations**, with several advertisers buying commercial time or spots on a particular program. An advertiser can participate in a certain program once or several times on a regular or irregular basis. Participating advertisers have no financial responsibility for production of the program; this is assumed by the network or individual station that sells and controls the commercial time.

There are several advantages to participations. First, the advertiser has no long-term commitment to a program, and expenditures can be adjusted to buy whatever number of participation spots fits within the budget. This is particularly important to small advertisers with a limited budget. The second advantage is that the TV budget can be spread over a number of programs, thereby providing for greater reach in the media schedule.

The disadvantage of participations is that the advertiser has little control over the placement of ads, and there may also be problems with availability. Preference is given to advertisers willing to commit to numerous spots, and the firm trying to buy single spots in more than one program may find that time is unavailable in certain shows, especially during prime time.

**Spot Announcements**  As discussed previously, spot announcements are bought from the local stations and generally appear during time periods adjacent to network programs (hence the term **adjacencies**), rather than within them. Spot announcements are most often used by purely local advertisers but are also bought by companies with no network schedule (because of spotty or limited distribution) and by large advertisers that use both network and spot advertising.

## Selecting Time Periods and Programs

Another consideration in buying TV time is selecting the right period and program for the advertiser's commercial messages. The cost of TV advertising time varies depending on the time of day and the particular program, since audience size varies as a function of these two factors. TV time periods are divided into **dayparts**, which are specific segments of a broadcast day.

The time segments that make up the programming day vary from station to station. However, a typical classification of dayparts for a weekday is shown in Figure 11–3. The various daypart segments attract different audiences in both size and nature, so advertising rates vary accordingly. Prime time draws the largest audiences, with 8:30 to 9 P.M. being the most watched half-hour time period and Sunday the most popular night for television. Since firms that advertise during prime time must pay premium rates, this daypart is dominated by the large national advertisers.

The various dayparts are important to advertisers since they attract different demographic groups. For example, daytime TV generally attracts women; early morning

**FIGURE 11–3**

Common Television
Dayparts

| Early morning | 5:00 A.M.–9:00 A.M. | Monday through Friday |
|---|---|---|
| Daytime | 9:00 A.M.–3:00 P.M. | Monday through Friday |
| Early fringe | 3:00 P.M.–5:00 P.M. | Monday through Friday |
| Early news | 5:00 P.M.–7:00 P.M. | Monday through Saturday |
| Prime access | 7:00 P.M.–8:00 P.M. | Monday through Saturday |
| Prime | 8:00 P.M.–11:00 P.M.<br>7:00 P.M.–11:00 P.M. | Monday through Saturday and Sunday |
| Late news | 11:00 P.M.–11:30 P.M. | Sunday through Saturday |
| Late fringe | 11:30 P.M.–2:00 A.M. | Monday through Friday |
| Overnight | 2:00 A.M.–5:00 A.M. | Monday through Friday |

Note: Times shown are for Eastern and Pacific time zones. Times may vary by market and station.

attracts women and children. The late-fringe (late-night) daypart period has become popular among advertisers trying to reach young adults who tune in to *The Late Show with David Letterman* on CBS, *Jimmy Kimmel Live!* on ABC, and NBC's *The Tonight Show with Jimmy Fallon.* Audience size and demographic composition also vary depending on the type of program.

## Cable Television

**The Growth of Cable**   Perhaps the most significant development in the television industry has been the expansion of **cable television**. Cable, or CATV (community antenna television), which delivers TV signals through fiber or coaxial wire rather than the airways, was developed to provide reception to remote areas that couldn't receive broadcast signals. Cable then expanded to metropolitan areas and grew rapidly due to the improved reception and wider selection of stations it offered subscribers. Cable has experienced substantial growth during the past two decades. In 1975, only 13 percent of TV households had cable. By 2013, cable penetration reached 91 percent of the nation's 114.7 million households either through wired cable or through alternative delivery systems such as direct broadcast satellite (DBS).

Cable subscribers pay a monthly fee for which they receive an average of more than 100 channels, including the local network affiliates and independent stations, various cable networks, superstations, and local cable system channels. Cable networks and channels have a dual revenue stream; they are supported by both subscriber fees and ad revenue. Cable operators also offer programming that is not supported by commercial sponsorship and is available only to households willing to pay a fee beyond the monthly subscription charge. These premium channels include HBO, Showtime, and The Movie Channel.

Cable TV broadens the program options available to the viewer as well as the advertiser by offering specialty channels, including all-news, pop music, country music, sports, weather, educational, and cultural channels as well as children's programming. Figure 11–4 shows the most popular cable channels along with the types of programming they carry. Many cable systems also carry **superstations**, independent local stations that send their signals nationally via satellite to cable operators to make their programs available to subscribers. Programming on superstations such as TBS and WGN generally consists of sports, movies, and reruns of network shows. The superstations do carry national advertising and are a relatively inexpensive option for cable households across the country.

**FIGURE 11–4**

Major Cable Networks

| Network | Type of Programming | Network | Type of Programming |
|---|---|---|---|
| ABC Family | Family/general/original | Hallmark Channel | Original movies/miniseries |
| A&E Network | Biographies/dramas/movies/documentaries | Headline News | News/information |
| | | HGTV | Decorating/gardening |
| Adult Swim | Young adult entertainment/programs | History Channel | Historical documentaries/movies |
| AMC | Movies/documentaries | History En Espanol | Historical programming/documentaries (Spanish language) |
| Animal Planet | Wildlife and nature documentaries/adventure/children's entertainment | Lifetime Networks | News/information/women's interests |
| | | Logo TV | Movies/documentaries/gay-themed programming |
| BBC America | Drama/comedy/news/arts | Military Channel | Military-focused programming/drama/aviation/technology |
| BET | Entertainment/information for African Americans | | |
| Big 10 Network | College Sports | MLB Network | Major League Baseball |
| BIO | Biographies, drama | MSNBC | News/information |
| Bloomberg Television | Business and financial news | MTV | Music/reality shows/drama |
| Bravo | Drama/movies/reality shows | MTV 2 | Music/videos/popular culture |
| Cartoon Network | Cartoons | mun2 Television | Bilingual programming for Hispanics/Latino youth culture |
| CBS College Sports | College sports/events | | |
| Centric | Entertainment/information for African Americans | NBC Sports | Sports |
| | | NGC (National Geographic Channel) | Adventure/exploration/science/culture |
| CMT Country | Country music video/concert/specials | | |
| | | NFL Network | NFL football |
| CNBC | Financial and business news/interviews and discussions | Nickelodeon/Nick at Nite | Youth interest/cartoons/comedy/game shows |
| CNN | News/information | OWN (Ophrah Winfrey Netwok) | Entertainment/movies/talk/specials |
| CNN Espanol | News/information (Spanish language) | | |
| | | Oxygen | Movies/news/comedy/women's interests |
| Comcast Sports Net | Regional sports | | |
| Comedy Central | Comedy programs/original | Pac-12 Network | Colleges sports/Pac-12 Conference |
| Cooking Channel | Food/cooking | | |
| Court TV | Court/legal | SOAPnet | Soap operas/drama |
| Discovery Channel | Family/health/technology/science | Syfy Channel | Science fiction |
| Disney XD | Children's programming/entertainment | Speed | Motor sports/automotive |
| | | Spike TV | Original programming/sports/entertainment for men |
| DIY Network | Home improvement/projects/crafts | | |
| | | Superstation WGN | Movies/dramas/sports/sitcoms/reality-based programs |
| E! Entertainment Television | Entertainment/celebrities/pop culture | | |
| | | TBS | Entertainment/movies/sports |
| ESPN | Sports/specials/events | Telemundo | Entertainment/news/sports (Spanish language) |
| ESPN 2 | Sports | | |
| ESPN Sports Classics | Sports history/biographies | Tennis Channel | Tennis/health and fitness/lifestyle |
| ESPN Deportes | Sports (Spanish language) | TLC (Learning Channel) | Science/history/adventure/behavior |
| ESPNEWS | Sports news | | |
| Food Network | Food/cooking/entertainment | TNT | Movies/general entertainment/sports |
| Fox Business Network | Business news | | |
| Fox News Channel | News/information | tru TV | Real-life stories/drama |
| Fox Soccer Channel | Soccer/sports | Travel Channel | Travel information |
| Fox Sports1 | Sports | TV Guide Channel | Television entertainment information |
| FSN | Sports | | |
| Fuse | Music/concerts | USA Network | Entertainment/movies/sports/drama |
| FX | Entertainment/original programs | | |
| GAC: Great American Country | Country music/concerts | VH1 | Music videos/movies/concerts/documentaries |
| Galavision | Programming/entertainment for Hispanics | Versus | Sports/outdoor/nature |
| | | Weather Channel | Weather |
| GSN: Game Show Network (GSN) | Game shows | WGN | Entertainment/sports/movies |
| | | WE tv | Women's entertainment/fashion/health |
| Golf Channel | Golf | | |

Cable has had a considerable influence on the nature of television as an advertising medium. First, the expanded viewing options have led to considerable audience fragmentation. Much of the growth in cable audiences has come at the expense of the four major networks. Cable channels now have more of the prime-time viewing audience than the major networks. Many cable stations have become very popular among consumers, leading advertisers to reevaluate their media plans and the prices they are willing to pay for network and spot commercials on network affiliate stations.

**Advertising on Cable** Cable advertising revenues have increased steadily since the mid-1980s and exceeded $25 billion in 2013. Much of this growth has come from advertising on the national cable networks such as ESPN, USA, TNT, MTV, and VH1. However, many national advertisers have been shifting some of their advertising budgets to spot cable and purchasing through local operators as well as the national cable networks. Over the past four years, spot cable revenues have also grown, exceeding $6 billion in 2013.

Like broadcast TV, cable time can be purchased on a national, regional, or local (spot) level. Many large marketers advertise on cable networks to reach large numbers of viewers across the country with a single media buy. Regional advertising on cable is available primarily through sports and news channels that cover a certain geographic area.

Many national advertisers are turning to spot advertising on local cable systems to reach specific geographic markets. Spot cable affords them more precision in reaching specific markets, and they can save money by using a number of small, targeted media purchases rather than making one network buy. The growth in spot cable advertising is also being facilitated by the use of **interconnects,** where a number of cable systems and networks in a geographic area are joined for advertising purposes. These interconnects increase the size of the audience an advertiser can reach with a spot cable buy. For example, the Comcast Spotlight interconnect in Chicago reaches more than 2.3 million cable TV households in the greater Chicago metropolitan area; the ADLINK Digital Interconnect delivers 3 million cable subscribers in Los Angeles and four surrounding counties (Exhibit 11–8). New York Interconnect reaches 3.7 million households in the largest market area in the country and offers advertisers targeting capabilities on 60 different networks.

**EXHIBIT 11–8**

Adlink Interconnect promotes its targeting potential to advertisers

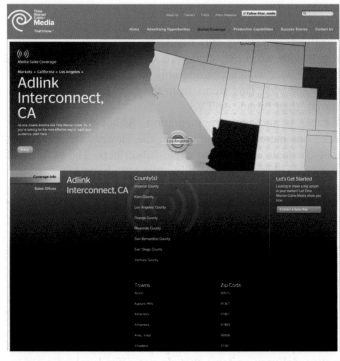

More sophisticated interconnect systems are developing that will pool large numbers of cable systems and allow spot advertisers to reach more viewers. These new systems will also allow local advertisers to make more selective cable buys, since they can purchase the entire interconnect or one of several zones within the system.

While spot cable is becoming very popular among national advertisers, it has some of the same problems as spot advertising on broadcast TV. The purchasing process is very complicated and time-consuming; media buyers must contact hundreds of cable systems to put together a media schedule consisting of spot cable buys. Local cable systems also do not provide advertisers with strong support or much information on demographics, lifestyle, or viewership patterns.

**Advantages of Cable** Cable TV has experienced tremendous growth as an advertising medium because it has some important advantages. A primary one is selectivity. Cable subscribers tend to be younger, more affluent, and better educated than nonsubscribers and have greater purchasing power.

**EXHIBIT 11–9**

The Travel Channel promotes its ability to deliver a very influential audience

Moreover, the specialized programming on the various cable networks reaches very specific target markets.

Many advertisers have turned to cable because of the opportunities it offers for **narrowcasting**, or reaching very specialized markets. For example, MTV is used by advertisers in the United States and many other countries to reach teenagers and young adults. CNBC is now the worldwide leader in business news and reaches a highly educated and affluent audience. The Travel Channel reaches an upscale and very influential audience that likes to explore and try new things and recommend them to others, including various products and services, as shown in Exhibit 11–9. ESPN has become synonymous with sports and is very popular among advertisers who want to target men of all ages. As discussed in IMC Perspective 11–1, ESPN has become more than just a 24-hour sports network as it has changed the way sports are covered and played a major role in making sports programming very popular and lucrative.

Advertisers are also interested in cable because of its low cost and flexibility. Advertising rates on cable programs are much lower than those for the shows on the major networks. Advertising time on network shows can cost two to three times as much on a cost-per-thousand basis in some time periods. Spot advertising is also considerably cheaper on most cable stations, while local cable is the most affordable television advertising vehicle available. This makes TV a much more viable media option for smaller advertisers with limited budgets and those interested in targeting their commercials to a well-defined target audience. Also, cable advertisers generally do not have to make the large up-front commitments, which may be as much as a year in advance, the networks require.

The low costs of cable make it a very popular advertising medium among local advertisers. Car dealers, furniture stores, restaurants, and many other merchants are switching advertising spending from traditional media such as radio, newspapers, and even magazines to take advantage of the low rates of local cable channels. Local cable advertising is one of the fastest-growing segments of the advertising market, and cable systems are increasing the percentage of revenue they earn from local advertising.

**Limitations of Cable** While cable has become increasingly popular among national, regional, and local advertisers, it still has some drawbacks. One major problem is that cable is still somewhat overshadowed by the major networks, as households with basic cable service watch considerably more network and syndicated programming than cable shows. This stems from the fact that cable generally has less popular programming than broadcast TV.

Another drawback of cable is audience fragmentation. Although cable's share of the TV viewing audience has increased significantly, the viewers are spread out among the large number of channels available to cable subscribers. The number of viewers who watch any one cable channel is generally quite low. Even MTV, ESPN, and CNN have prime-time ratings of only about 1 or 2 for their regular programming. The large number of cable stations has fragmented audiences and made buying procedures more difficult, since numerous stations must be contacted to reach the majority of the cable audience in a market. There are also problems with the quality and availability of local ratings for cable stations as well as research on audience characteristics.

Cable also still lacks total penetration, especially in some major markets. In 2013, overall cable penetration from both wired and alternative delivery systems such as satellite was 88 percent in the Los Angeles–designated market area (DMA), 82 percent in Houston, and 84 percent in the Dallas–Fort Worth DMA. In some designated market areas, wired cable penetration is low as many households receive cable programming from alternative delivery systems that do not offer local advertising.

For example, penetration of wired cable is under 60 percent in some major DMAs such as Los Angeles, Denver, and Dallas–Fort Worth. Thus, local advertisers in these markets would not be able to reach a significant number of households by advertising on local cable networks.

**The Future of Cable**  Cable TV should continue to experience strong growth as its audience share increases and advertisers spend more money to reach cable viewers. However, the cable industry faces several challenges: increases in the number of channels, leading to fragmentation of the audience, changes in government regulations, and competition in the programming distribution business from other telecommunications companies and direct broadcast satellite services. Advances in technology such as digital video compression and fiber optics, coupled with massive investments in system upgrades, are making it possible for cable operators to offer more channels and thus subject existing cable channels to greater competition. Increases in the number of channels available lead to further fragmentation of the cable audience and make it more difficult for cable networks to charge the ad rates needed to finance original programming. Some of the growth in cable channels will come from **multiplexing**, or transmitting multiple channels from one network. Several major cable networks, including A&E Television Networks, MTV ESPN, and Discovery Communications, own several channels.

The future of cable as an advertising medium will ultimately depend on the size and quality of the audiences cable stations can reach with their programs. This in turn will depend on cable's ability to offer programs that attract viewers and subscribers. Cable's image as a stepchild in program development and acquisition has changed. Cable networks such as VH1, E!, TBS, ESPN, and others have been creating original films, documentaries, and other programs that draw significant ratings. Networks like A&E, the Discovery Channel, the National Geographic Channel, and the History Channel provide outstanding cultural and educational programming.

Many advertising and media experts note that many people, and particularly children and young adults under the age of 35, really do not differentiate between cable and traditional broadcast television.[28] Cable programs generally cannot deliver the broad reach and mass audiences of popular network shows. However, cable networks have been developing high-quality and critically acclaimed programs such as

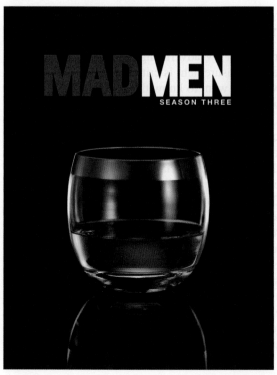

**EXHIBIT 11–10**

*Mad Men* is an example of the high-quality programs now shown on cable networks

AMC's *Mad Men,* a drama show that follows the lives of highly competitive men and women working on Madison Avenue during the glory days of advertising in the 1960s (Exhibit 11–10). The show has won numerous awards, including an Emmy for Outstanding Drama Series and two Golden Globe Awards for Best Television Drama Series. Other quality shows on cable networks include AMC's *Breaking Bad,* ABC Family's *Pretty Little Liars,* and Lifetime's *Army Wives.*

Cable TV will continue to be a popular source of sports programming and is very important to advertisers interested in reaching the male market. There are a number of regional sports networks (RSNs) that provide sports programming to local markets. The most important programming on these RSNs is live broadcasts of professional and college sports, events such as football, basketball, and baseball. Many of these regional networks are associated with Fox Sports, Time Warner Cable SportsNet, and Comcast SportsNet. Thus, advertisers purchase ads in multiple regions with one media buy.

As cable penetration increases, its programming improves, and more advertisers discover its efficiency and ability to reach targeted market segments, cable's popularity as an advertising medium should continue to grow. Many agencies and media specialist companies have developed specialists to examine the use of cable in their clients' media schedules.

# IMC Perspective 11–1 > > >

## ESPN—Television's Most Powerful Network

For many years, TV sports programming consisted primarily of football, baseball, and, to a lesser extent, basketball, shown primarily on weekends on network television. Hard-core sports fans had to wait until the weekend to see major sporting events such as NFL or college football games, and sports news coverage was limited to five-minute sportscasts on the 11 P.M. news on the local network affiliate. However, on September 7, 1979, a small cable network called ESPN began broadcasting from a trailer in a swampy industrial park in Bristol, Connecticut, showing Hartford Whalers ice-hockey games. The network was the idea of Bill Rasmussen, a former sportscaster whose original

concept was for it to be a sports network for Connecticut but who discovered that it would cost no more to offer the first cable network devoted entirely to sports.

When ESPN was launched, the critics declared that "All the good sports are already on the three networks" and ridiculed the network for broadcasting such sports as stock car racing, which was described as "two hours of left turns." To help fill 24 hours a day of programming, ESPN aired sports that the major broadcast networks did not cover such as Australian rules football, professional wrestling, boxing, and replays of college football and basketball games. However, no one is laughing at ESPN today, as the cable network that markets itself as "The Worldwide Leader in Sports" has become the world's largest sports media brand. In addition to reaching more than 100 million homes in the United States, ESPN has grown to include ESPN2, ESPN News, ESPNU, ESPN Deportes, and 47 international channels. Its media franchise also includes ESPN.com which is the most popular sports site on the Internet with over 50 million unique visitors a month, the largest sports-radio network in America, and *ESPN The Magazine*.

One of the reasons for the tremendous success and growth of ESPN is that it makes money from selling

## Measuring the TV Audience

One of the most important considerations in TV advertising is the size and composition of the viewing audience. Audience measurement is critical to advertisers as well as to the networks and stations. Advertisers want to know the size and characteristics of the audience they are reaching when they purchase time on a particular program. And since the rates they pay are a function of audience size, advertisers want to be sure audience measurements are accurate.

Audience size and composition are also important to the network or station, since they determine the amount it can charge for commercial time. Shows are frequently canceled because they fail to attract enough viewers to make their commercial time attractive to potential advertisers. Determining audience size is not an exact science and has been the subject of considerable controversy through the years. In this section, we examine how audiences are measured and how advertisers use this information in planning their media schedules.

**Audience Measures**    The size and composition of television audiences are measured by ratings services. The sole source of network TV and local audience information is Nielsen Media Research. For many years local audience information was also available from the Arbitron Co., but Arbitron exited the local TV ratings business at the end of 1993 due to steep financial losses.[29] Nielsen gathers viewership information from a sample of TV homes and then projects this information to the advertising time as well as cable subscriber fees which average nearly $5.00 per household per month for the flagship channel. By comparison the next highest national network, TNT, charges around $1.20 per month while other popular cable channels such as CNN and TBS can charge only around $0.60. ESPN uses the money it receives from its dual revenue stream to acquire the rights to the most popular sports programming. In 2012 it renewed its contract with the National Football League (NFL) for *Monday Night Football,* increasing payments by 70 percent, to $1.9 billion per season through 2021. A few months later ESPN signed a new eight-year deal for $700 million per year with Major League Baseball that includes TV, radio, digital, and international rights. The network also has major deals with the NBA as well as the rights to air college football and basketball games. In addition to its live sports programming, ESPN's signature show, *SportsCenter*—a one-hour sports news show that is aired numerous time throughout the day and night—is emblematic of the entire network and has helped position ESPN as the network for the ultimate sports fan.

While hardcore sports fans may feel they are in sports heaven when watching football, baseball, and basketball games or *SportsCenter* on ESPN, not everyone is in love with the sports network. Cable operators complain that ESPN has become too expensive and coercive in its terms and is a major reason for the increase in cable bills. The CEO of Liberty Media has called ESPN's rights fees "a tax on every American household." Cable channels are bundled in packages and ESPN has used its popularity and power to require its service as part of the lowest-level subscription offered by cable operators, which means that millions of homes that never watch sports end up paying for it anyway. Critics argue that cable subscribers should be able to pick and choose the channels they want to watch.

ESPN argues that it is not the only one driving up sports programing costs; the major broadcast networks also pay large sums of money for sports programming. For example, Fox, CBS, and NBC paid a combined $27 million for broadcast rights for NFL games through 2022. ESPN also notes that regional sports networks that are owned by cable operators such as Time Warner and Comcast, as well as networks such as Fox, also command high monthly fees. ESPN also defends its fees by noting that it is consistently ranked by cable operators as the most compelling driver of their businesses and its license fees reflect the value it provides to its distributors.

Some experts argue that the television is becoming oversaturated with sports, and the networks and cable channels must be careful not to overpay for the rights to sports programming. However, ESPN turns over more than $6 billion in revenue each year to Disney, which owns 80 percent of the company. Moreover, CBS, NBC, and Fox have all started their own national cable sports networks to compete with ESPN, which has led to more competition for rights fees for both professional and collegiate sports. It seems that no amount of sports on TV is too much, particularly when everyone is helping pay for it.

Sources: Andrew Hampp, "How ESPN Became the World's Biggest Sports-Media Brand," *Advertising Age,* August 31, 2009, http://adagec.com/print?article_id=13871111; Richard Sandomir and Amy Chozick, "Seeing Riches in Sports TV, Fox Will Create New Network," *The New York Times,* March 4, 2013, p. B10; Nick Summers, "Big. Bigger. Biggest.," *Newsweek,* January 23, 2012, pp. 36–41.

YTC **11–04**

**ESPN**

youtube.com/10ebelch

total viewing area. The techniques used to gather audience measurement information include diaries, electronic meters or recorders, and personal interviews. Nielsen provides various types of information that can be used to measure and evaluate a station's audience. These measures are important to media planners as they weigh the value of buying commercial time on a program.

**Television Households** An important metric needed to measure the size of a viewing audience is an estimate of the number of households in a market that own a television or a computer that can be used to watch TV shows. Nielsen now defines a **television household** as a home with at least one operable TV or monitor with the ability to deliver video via traditional means of antenna, cable set-top-box, or satellite receiver and/or with a broadband connection. This updated definition accounts for households that do not have antenna, cable, or satellite access but can still watch video over the Internet. Since more than 98 percent of U.S. households own a TV and have access to TV shows, television households generally correspond to the number of households in a given market. Nielsen estimates that the number of television households in the United States as of the 2102–2013 TV season was 114.7 million.

**Program Rating** Probably the best known of all audience measurement figures is the **program rating**, the percentage of TV households in an area that are tuned to a specific program during a specific time period. The program rating is calculated by dividing the number of households tuned to a particular show by the total number of households in the area. For example, if 10 million households (HH) watched *The Big Bang Theory*, the national rating would be 8.7, calculated as follows:

$$\text{Rating} = \frac{\text{HH tuned to show}}{\text{Total U.S. HH}} = \frac{10,000,000}{114,700,000} = 8.7$$

A **ratings point** represents 1 percent of all the television households in a particular area tuned to a specific program. On a national level, 1 ratings point represents 1,147,000 households. Thus, if a top-rated program like *The Big Bang Theory* averages a rating of 9, it would reach 10.3 million households each week (9 × 1,147,000).

The program rating is the key number to the stations, since the amount of money they can charge for commercial time is based on it. Ratings points are very important to the networks as well as to individual stations. A 1 percent change in a program's ratings over the course of a viewing season can gain or lose millions of dollars in advertising revenue. Advertisers also follow ratings closely, since they are the key measure for audience size and commercial rates.

**Households Using Television** The percentage of homes in a given area where TV is being watched during a specific time period is called **households using television (HUT)**. This figure, sometimes referred to as *sets in use,* is always expressed as a percentage. For example, if 70 million of the U.S. TV households have their sets turned on at 9 P.M. on a Thursday night, the HUT figure is 61 percent (70 million out of 114.7 million). Television usage varies widely depending on the time of day and season of the year.

**Share of Audience** Another important audience measurement figure is the **share of audience**, which is the percentage of households using TV in a specified time period that are tuned to a specific program. This figure considers variations in the number of sets in use and the total size of the potential audience, since it is based only on those households that have their sets turned on. Audience share is calculated by dividing the number of households (HH) tuned to a show by the number of households using television (HUT). Thus, if 70 million U.S. households had their sets turned on during the 8 P.M. time slot when *The Big Bang Theory* is shown, the share of audience would be 14.3, calculated as follows:

$$\text{Share} = \frac{\text{HH tuned to show}}{\text{U.S. households using TV}} = \frac{10,000,000}{70,000,000} = 14.3$$

Audience share is always higher than the program rating unless all the households have their sets turned on (in which case they would be equal). Share figures are important since they reveal how well a program does with the available viewing audience. For example, late at night the size of the viewing audience drops substantially, so the best way to assess the popularity of a late-night program is to examine the share of the available audience it attracts relative to competing programs.

Ratings services also provide an audience statistic known as **total audience**, the total number of homes viewing any five-minute part of a telecast. This number can be broken down to provide audience composition figures that are based on the distribution of the audience into demographic categories.

**YTC 11–05**

Nielsen

youtube.com/10ebelch

**National Audience Information** Nielsen Media Research has a national TV ratings service known as the **Nielsen Television Index** that provides daily and weekly estimates of the size and composition of the national viewing audiences for programs aired on the broadcast and major cable networks. To measure the viewing audience, Nielsen uses a national sample of approximately 10,000 homes carefully selected to be representative of the population of U.S. households. The widely cited Nielsen ratings are based on the viewing patterns of this cross section of homes, which are measured using an electronic metering technology. The **people meter**

**EXHIBIT 11–11**

Nielsen uses the people meter to measure national TV audiences

is an electronic measuring device that incorporates the technology of the old-style audimeter in a system that records not only what is being watched but also by whom in 10,000 households. The actual device is a small box with eight buttons—six for the family and two for visitors—that can be placed on the top of the TV (Exhibit 11–11). A remote-control unit permits electronic entries from anywhere in the room. Each member of the sample household is assigned a button that indicates his or her presence as a viewer. The device is also equipped with a sonar sensor to remind viewers entering or leaving the room to log in or out on the meter.

The viewership information the people meter collects from the household is stored in the home system until it is retrieved by Nielsen's computers. Data collected include when the TV is turned on, which channel is viewed, when the channel is changed, and when the TV is off, in addition to who is viewing. The demographic characteristics of the viewers are also in the system, and viewership can be matched to these traits. Nielsen's operation center processes all this information each week for release to the TV and advertising industries. Nielsen uses a sample of metered households in 55 markets across the country to provide overnight viewing results.

**Local Audience Information** Information on local audiences is important to both local advertisers and firms making national spot buys. Nielsen Media Research's local market measurement service is called Nielsen Station Index (NSI), which measures viewing audiences in 210 local markets known as **designated market areas (DMAs)**. DMAs are nonoverlapping areas used for planning, buying, and evaluating TV audiences and are generally a group of counties in which stations located in a metropolitan or central area achieve the largest audience share. NSI reports information on viewing by time periods and programs and includes audience size and estimates of viewing over a range of demographic categories for each DMA.

In addition to the national audience measurement, Nielsen also measures the largest local markets using electronic Local People Meter (LPM) technology. Local People Meters are used in the top 56 markets. In large to midsize local markets, viewing information is gathered from 400 to 500 households using electronic meters that capture only the channel to which the TV is tuned. This information is augmented at least four times a year with demographic data that are collected from separate samples of households that fill out seven-day paper viewing diaries (or eight-day diaries in homes with DVRs). Smaller markets (DMAs ranked over 60) are currently measured using paper diaries only, although Nielsen plans to extend electronic measurement to these markets as well.

Nielsen measures viewing audiences in every local television market at least four times a year during rating periods known as **sweeps**. The term dates back to the 1950s, when Nielsen began mailing diaries to households and reporting the results, beginning with the East Coast markets before *sweeping* across the country. Sweeps rating periods are held in November, February, May, and July. In some of the larger markets, diaries provide viewer information for up to three additional sweeps months. The viewing information gathered during the sweeps periods is used for program scheduling decisions by local television stations and cable systems and is a basis for pricing and selling advertising time. Exhibit 11–12 shows how WJZ, the CBS affiliate in Baltimore, promotes its dominance of the sweeps ratings in various categories.

Many advertising executives and media buyers are skeptical of the local audience estimates gathered during the sweeps periods. They argue that special programming and promotion efforts are often used by the networks and their local affiliates to bolster their ratings during

**EXHIBIT 11–12**

WJZ promotes its dominance of the sweeps rating period for local news the sweeps and that the numbers gathered during these periods are not indicative of audience size for the remaining weeks of the year.[30]

Much of the concern over the measurement system used by Nielsen involves the use of the paper diaries to measure viewing in local markets. The system requires households in the sample to keep a tally of what is being watched and by whom. With so many channels now available, along with the increase in viewing through DVRs and video on demand, it has become very challenging for the Nielsen panelists to accurately record all of their television viewing in the diaries. Many homes do not return completed diaries and many of those that are returned are often not filled out. Nielsen has acknowledged the problems with its measurement system for local markets and is working to correct them.[31] It is expanding the use of Local People Meters and hopes to extend full electronic measurement to more markets.

**Developments in Audience Measurement**   For years the advertising industry has been calling for changes in the way TV viewing audiences are measured at both the local and national levels. They have argued that new digital technologies are leading to major changes with regard to when, where, and how people watch television. They also argue that the Nielsen measurement system is being overwhelmed by the explosion in the number of TVs, delivery systems, and program options available. Advertisers and media planners note that these developments must be carefully monitored as they are having a major impact on audience size and composition and on the way advertisers use and should pay for TV as an advertising medium.

One of the major concerns of advertisers has been the need to measure ratings for television commercials, not just for programs. In 2007 Nielsen began providing **commercial ratings** data, known as "C3," which includes measures of the average viewership of the commercials both live and up to three days after the ads are played back on a DVR.[32] The new ratings do not track individual ads or specific time slots, but rather offer an average viewership of all the national commercial minutes in a program. Many advertisers now pay for advertising time on network shows based on Nielsen measures of how many viewers watched commercials live and on DVR-recorded playback within three days of the airing of the show, rather than simply on the traditional program ratings.

While Nielsen's current C3 ratings are seen as an improvement over the old measurement system, many are still dissatisfied with them since they are based on an average of all national commercial minutes in a program. Marketers argue that payment should be based on the viewership of each commercial rather than on an average across all commercial minutes. They note that there is a substantial amount of research data available showing that viewership of commercials during a break depends on the position, as the first or second commercial may have more viewers than spots aired during the middle of a two- or three-minute pod.[33] While marketers are clamoring for more precise commercial ratings, Nielsen has questioned whether they are willing to pay for it as encoding each ad so it can be tracked requires a substantial investment in technology.[34]

Another issue emerging as a result of time-shifted viewing through DVRs and video on demand is whether audience measures for viewership of commercials should be expanded to seven days rather than three. Many television network executives are pushing for "C7" or the inclusion of viewership of programs and commercials as many as seven days after the airing of a TV show. Viewership of some programs, including comedies such as *Modern Family,* has been shown to increase significantly over a seven-day period.[35] Although Nielsen currently provides C7 viewership numbers, advertisers and media buyers argue that better measurement of viewership across multiple platforms including tablets and mobile devices is needed to give marketers a better picture of total viewership of a program. It is likely that the industry will move to the use of C7 ratings in the next few years.[36]

While advertisers view the availability of commercial ratings as a significant improvement over program ratings, there is still concern over how viewing audiences are measured. Expanded use of the people meter is seen as an improvement over the use of paper diaries, but critics note that these devices still require cooperation on an ongoing basis from people in the metered homes. Panelists in the Nielsen households, including children, must enter a preassigned number on the remote-control device every time they start or stop watching. Media researchers argue that children in particular often forget and adults tire of the task over the two years they are in the Nielsen sample. There has been a call for the use of more passive measurement systems that require less involvement by people in the metered homes and can produce more accurate measures of the program, as well as commercial, viewing audiences.[37]

Nielsen is continually working to address the ongoing challenges of audience measurement. In 2006 the company began a major initiative known as *Anytime Anywhere Media Measurement* (A2/M2), which includes a number of improvements designed to respond to changes in the way people watch television. The initiative included the introduction of electronic measurement in all local markets and the addition of Internet and out-of-home measurement in Nielsen's People Meter sample, as well as the development of passive measurement devices.[38] As part of the initiative, Nielsen has begun measuring the television viewing patterns of college students. In 2007, for the first time ever, Nielsen Media Research's national ratings included information on the TV viewing patterns of students who live in households that are part of its national sample but live away at college. Nielsen's Extended Home study used people meters installed in dormitories and common areas, sorority and fraternity houses, and off-campus houses at college across the country to track the viewing patterns of students.

One of the more interesting findings from the Extended Home study was that college students watch as much television as other 18- to 24-year-olds. Students watch the tube up to 30 hours per week and they also watch a lot of late-night TV (after 11 P.M.). As might be expected, MTV ranked first among the networks watched by college students, followed by Turners Adult Swim, TBS, ESPN, and Comedy Central. The ratings showed that Comedy Central's *South Park* was the number 1 cable program among male college students between the ages of 18 and 24 (Exhibit 11–13). The results also showed that animated TV programming is very popular among college students and that the number of women watching sports is higher than media experts expected.[39] A recent study of college students by Nielsen based on the 2011–2012 school year found that 96 percent of students living away at school had access to cable but less than 10 percent had a DVR. About half of the students had a videogame console at school but only 15 percent owned a tablet. Most of the time spent by college students watching television is devoted to traditional TV, although they do spend about an hour and a half each week streaming video on the Internet.[40] As part of the A2/M2 initiative, Nielsen also now measures away-from-home viewing for a number of networks at places like health clubs, hotels, bars and restaurants, and transit locations.[41]

In 2013 Nielsen introduced its **Cross-Platform Campaign Ratings** which measures the number of people who watch an ad only on television, the number who view it online, and the overlap between the two. The cross-platform ratings build on Nielsen's online measurement system that measures consumer viewing of TV programs that are watched through a broadband connection in a home. Nielsen has also begun recognizing what it refers to as Zero-TV households, which are homes that have stopped paying for cable and satellite TV service and do not even use an antenna to get free signals over the airways. Nielsen estimates that there were just over 5 million of these households, which rely on the Internet to watch TV on

**EXHIBIT 11–13**

*South Park* is one of the most widely watched TV shows by male college students their computers or mobile devices, in the United States in 2013 and the amount has doubled since 2007.[42] Nielsen has begun incorporating video viewing in these homes in their audience measures. The networks welcome Nielsen's expanded definition of a television household, noting that it more accurately reflects changing media consumption patterns and technology advancements. Television executives have been concerned over the declines in viewership among audiences over the past few years and have argued that it important to consider cross-platform as well as time-shifted viewing to get an accurate estimate of the total audience that watches a show and is exposed to the commercials.[43]

# RADIO

LO 11-1

Television has often been referred to as the ideal advertising medium, and to many people it personifies the glamour and excitement of the industry. Radio, on the other hand, has been called the Rodney Dangerfield of media because it gets no respect from many advertisers. Dominated by network programming and national advertisers before the growth of TV, radio has evolved into a primarily local advertising medium. Network advertising generally accounts for less than 5 percent of radio's revenue. Radio has also become a medium characterized by highly specialized programming appealing to very narrow segments of the population.

The importance of radio to advertisers is best demonstrated by the numbers, as it is a pervasive medium. There are more than 11,300 commercial radio stations in the United States, including 4,700 AM and 6,600 FM stations. There are over 576 million radios in use, which is an average of 5.6 per household. Radio reaches 71 percent of all Americans over the age of 12 each day and has grown into a ubiquitous background to many activities, among them reading, driving, running, working, and socializing. The average American listens to radio over 2 hours every weekday and 3 hours every weekend.[44] Commercial radio dominates the time spent listening to some form of news or entertainment in a car, as nearly two-thirds of in-car listening time is on AM/FM radio. People are spending more time listening to the radio on computers and/or mobile devices; the online radio audience has doubled in the past six years and now exceeds more than 103 million monthly listeners. Online listening to radio is expected to continue to grow, and this audience complements rather than substitutes for broadcast radio.[45] The pervasiveness of this medium has not gone unnoticed by advertisers; radio advertising revenue grew from $8.8 billion in 1990 to over $16 billion in 2012.

Radio plays an integral role in the lifestyle of consumers and has the power to reach and influence their purchase behavior. It has survived and flourished as an advertising medium because it has a number of advantages that make it an effective way for marketers to communicate with consumers. The radio industry promotes these advantages to advertisers to encourage use of the medium (Exhibit 11–14).

**YTC 11–06**

**Radio Advertising Bureau**

youtube.com/10ebelch

**EXHIBIT 11–14**

The Radio Advertising Bureau promotes the value of radio to advertisers

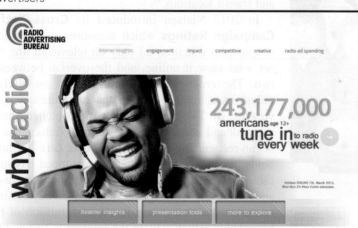

## Advantages of Radio

Radio has many advantages over other media, including cost and efficiency, receptivity, selectivity, flexibility, mental imagery, and integrated marketing opportunities.

**Cost and Efficiency** One of the main strengths of radio as an advertising medium is its low cost. Radio commercials are very inexpensive to produce.

LO 11-2

They require only a script of the commercial to be read by the radio announcer or a copy of a prerecorded message that can be broadcast by the station. The cost for radio time is also low. A minute on network radio may cost only $5,000, which translates into a cost per thousand of only $3 to $4. Local advertising on radio is lower on a cost-per-thousand basis, compared to local TV advertising. The low relative costs of radio make it one of the most efficient of all advertising media, and the low absolute cost means the budget needed for an effective radio campaign is often lower than that for other media.

The low cost of radio means advertisers can build more reach and frequency into their media schedule within a certain budget. They can use different stations to broaden the reach of their messages and multiple spots to ensure adequate frequency. Advertisers can use radio as a fast and relatively inexpensive way to get their names known. Radio commercials can be produced more quickly than TV spots, and the companies can run them more often. Many national advertisers also recognize the cost-efficiency of radio and use it as part of their media strategy.

**Receptivity**  Radio often provides advertisers with a very receptive environment for their advertising messages. The Radio Advertising Bureau has conducted studies in conjunction with the research firm Harris Interactive that show that consumers perceive radio advertising to be more personally relevant to them than ads on television or the Internet.[46] The study found that radio listeners have a unique relationship with radio as a medium because they often are more emotionally connected to the radio stations to which they listen. This emotional connection can make consumers more receptive to radio ads when the message is designed and placed properly. Figure 11–5 shows how consumers rate their emotional connection with radio versus other media. The study also found that consumers perceive radio advertising as being more personally relevant to them. This may be due to the nature of radio ads usually being targeted to the demographics and psychographic characteristics of the listeners of particular stations as discussed below.

**FIGURE 11–5**

Rating of Emotional Attributes for Radio

**Chapter 11** EVALUATION OF MEDIA: TELEVISION AND RADIO  403

**Selectivity** Another major advantage of radio is the high degree of audience selectivity available through the various program formats and geographic coverage of the numerous stations. Radio lets companies focus their advertising on specialized audiences such as certain demographic and lifestyle groups. Most areas have radio stations with formats such as adult contemporary, easy listening, classical music, country, news/talk shows, jazz, and all news, to name a few. Figure 11–6 shows the percentage of the radio listening audience captured by radio formats for various age groups. As can be seen in these numbers the Rock, CHR/Top 40, Rhythmic, and Alternative formats get a high percentage of their listeners from the 18-to-24 and 24-to-34 age groups while news/talk and Adult Standards formats get most of their listeners from adults over age 45. Elusive consumers like teenagers, college students, and working adults can be reached more easily through radio than most other media.

Radio can reach consumers other media can't. Light television viewers spend considerably more time with radio than with TV and are generally an upscale market in terms of income and education level. Light readers of magazines and newspapers also spend more time listening to radio. Radio has become a popular way to reach specific non-English-speaking ethnic markets. Los Angeles, New York City, Dallas, and Miami have several radio stations that broadcast in Spanish and reach these areas' large Hispanic markets. As mass marketing gives way to market segmentation and regional marketing, radio will continue to grow in importance.

**Flexibility** Radio is probably the most flexible of all the advertising media because it has a very short closing period, which means advertisers can change their message almost up to the time it goes on the air. Radio commercials can usually be produced and scheduled on very short notice. Radio advertisers can easily adjust their messages to local market conditions and marketing situations.

**Mental Imagery** A potential advantage of radio that is often overlooked is that it encourages listeners to use their imagination when processing a commercial message. While the creative options of radio are limited, many advertisers take advantage of the absence of a visual element to let consumers create their own picture of what is happening in a radio message.

Radio may also reinforce television messages through a technique called **image transfer**, where the images of a TV commercial are implanted into a radio spot.[47] First the marketer establishes the video image of a TV commercial. Then it uses a similar, or even the same, audio portion (spoken words and/or jingle) as the basis for the radio counterpart. The idea is that when consumers hear the radio message, they will make the connection to the TV commercial, reinforcing its video images. Image transfer offers advertisers a way to make radio and TV ads work together synergistically. This promotional piece put out by the Radio Advertising Bureau shows how the image transfer process works (Exhibit 11–15).

**Integrated Marketing Opportunities** Radio provides marketers with a variety of integrated marketing opportunities. It can be used in combination with other media, including television, magazines, newspapers, the Internet, and social media, to provide advertisers with synergistic effects in generating awareness and communicating their message. The radio industry has sponsored research studies to determine how radio works in combination with other media. These studies have shown that the synergistic use of radio, television, newspapers, and the Internet has a positive impact on various measures such as brand awareness, brand consideration, emotional connections, purchase intentions, and website visitation.[48] Marketers can also use radio in conjunction with digital and social media as applications such as Facebook and Twitter to allow listeners to publish audio content as well as receive song and station updates. Radio station websites as

FIGURE 11-6

Radio Format Profiles By
Age Group

| Format | 18–24 | 25–34 | 35–44 | 45–54 | 55–64 | 65+ |
|---|---|---|---|---|---|---|
| Adult Contemporary | 14.7% | 21.6% | 23.9% | 21.5% | 12.1% | 6.2% |
| Adult Hits ("Jack") | 10.5% | 22.4% | 26.4% | 30.4% | 7.6% | 2.8 |
| Adult Standards | 3.9% | 3.9% | 6.2% | 14.1% | 26.0% | 45.9 |
| All News | 4.6% | 10.6% | 16.7% | 22.6% | 22.6% | 22.8 |
| All Sports | 6.4% | 19.7% | 22.7% | 22.5% | 17.9% | 10.9 |
| All Talk | 3.5% | 13.1% | 19.3% | 22.0% | 20.9% | 21.3 |
| Alternative | 22.5% | 28.6% | 21.4% | 17.6% | 7.9% | 2.0 |
| CHR/Top 40 | 30.0% | 30.4% | 20.6% | 12.8% | 4.6% | 1.7 |
| Classic Hits | 12.4% | 15.1% | 17.8% | 28.1% | 19.5% | 7.3 |
| Classic Rock | 13.5% | 18.3% | 21.2% | 30.0% | 13.6% | 2.5 |
| Classical | 6.2% | 10.8% | 13.4% | 18.3% | 21.7% | 29.6 |
| Country | 14.5% | 19.7% | 17.8% | 19.4% | 15.6% | 13.0 |
| Easy Listening | 0.8% | 2.5% | 6.1% | 21.2% | 19.0% | 59.6 |
| Ethnic | 7.3% | 16.9% | 16.8% | 23.4% | 20.4% | 15.3 |
| Gospel | 6.6% | 13.2% | 17.3% | 20.7% | 19.7% | 22.6 |
| Hispanic (All Genres) | 16.8% | 24.7% | 24.2% | 17.6% | 9.0% | 7.7 |
| Jazz | 8.6% | 10.8% | 14.6% | 23.1% | 25.5% | 17.5 |
| Mexican/Tejano/Ranchera (subset of Hispanic) | 17.7% | 29.8% | 27.3% | 14.0% | 6.8% | 4.4 |
| News/Talk | 3.9% | 10.6% | 16.1% | 22.4% | 22.0% | 24.9 |
| Oldies | 9.2% | 11.3% | 14.6% | 23.9% | 26.0% | 15.0 |
| Public/Non-Commercial | 5.5% | 14.7% | 20.7% | 21.1% | 23.0% | 15.1 |
| Religious | 8.4% | 18.6% | 21.2% | 24.7% | 16.4% | 10.8 |
| Rhythmic | 35.9% | 30.2% | 19.6% | 9.6% | 3.9% | 0.8 |
| Rock | 21.7% | 27.3% | 24.2% | 19.2% | 6.3% | 1.4 |
| Soft AC/Lite Rock | 10.2% | 17.6% | 17.9% | 24.1% | 17.7% | 12.6 |
| Spanish AC (subset of Hispanic) | 19.1% | 23.2% | 27.5% | 18.5% | 7.0% | 4.7 |
| Tropical (subset of Hispanic) | 15.8% | 26.9% | 19.5% | 19.8% | 10.9% | 7.1 |
| Urban | 29.3% | 26.4% | 17.5% | 14.7% | 7.8% | 4.4 |
| Variety/Other | 11.2% | 21.0% | 20.8% | 19.7% | 16.7% | 10.6 |

Note: Numbers based on: *GfK MRI, 2012 Doublebase—Audience Composition based on Total Week Cume, Adults 18+ (may not add to 100% due to rounding).*

Source: Radio Format Profiles, Radio Fact Sheet, Radio Advertising Bureau, 2013.

- Local content and promotions that strengthen local community connections
- Audience engagement with sites that offer local music talent and playlist interactivity between listeners and station
- Community events driven by stations prove local radio's connection

**EXHIBIT 11–16**

Radio stations are often involved in local community events

well as their Facebook and Twitter sites can be used to create listener databases and engage them by offering promotions and deals.

Radio can also be used in conjunction with a variety of other IMC tools such as sales promotion, event marketing, and cause-related marketing. Radio stations are an integral part of many communities and the deejays and program hosts are often popular and influential figures. Advertisers often use radio stations and personalities to enhance their involvement with a local market and to gain influence with local retailers. Radio also works very effectively in conjunction with place-based/point-of-purchase promotions. Retailers often use on-site radio broadcasts combined with special sales or promotions to attract consumers to their stores and get them to make a purchase. Live radio broadcasts are also used in conjunction with event marketing. Marketers often sponsor live broadcast promotions at beaches, sporting events, and festivals, setting up product booths for sampling and giveaways. Exhibit 11–16 shows how the Radio Advertising Bureau promotes the value of radio by showing how it can be used to strengthen local community connections.

## Limitations of Radio

Several factors limit the effectiveness of radio as an advertising medium, among them creative limitations, fragmentation, chaotic buying procedures, limited research data, limited listener attention, and clutter. The media planner must consider them in determining the role the medium will play in the advertising program.

**Creative Limitations**   A major drawback of radio as an advertising medium is the absence of a visual image. The radio advertiser cannot show the product, demonstrate it, or use any type of visual appeal or information. A radio commercial is, like a TV ad, a short-lived and fleeting message that is externally paced and does not allow the receiver to control the rate at which it is processed. Because of these creative limitations many companies tend to ignore radio, and agencies often assign junior people to the development of radio commercials.

**Fragmentation**   Another problem with radio is the high level of audience fragmentation due to the large number of stations. The percentage of the market tuned to any particular station is usually very small. The top-rated radio station in many major metropolitan areas with a number of AM and FM stations may attract less than 10 percent of the total listening audience. Advertisers that want a broad reach in their radio advertising media schedule have to buy time on a number of stations to cover even a local market.

LO 11-2

**Chaotic Buying Procedures**   It should be readily apparent how chaotic the media planning and purchasing process can become for the advertiser that wants to use radio on a nationwide spot basis. Acquiring information and evaluating and contracting for time with even a fraction of the 11,300 commercial stations that operate across the country can be very difficult and time-consuming. This problem has diminished somewhat in recent years as the number of radio networks and of syndicated programs offering a package of several hundred stations increases.

**Limited Research Data**   Audience research data on radio are often limited, particularly compared with TV, magazines, or newspapers. Most radio stations

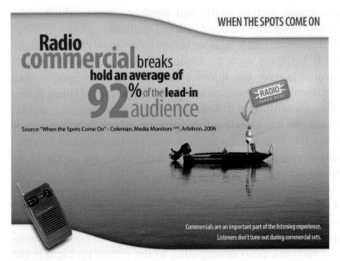

**EXHIBIT 11–17**

Radio promotes audience retention during commercial breaks

are small operations and lack the revenue to support detailed studies of their audiences. And most users of radio are local companies that cannot support research on radio listenership in their markets. Thus, media planners do not have as much audience information available to guide them in their purchase of radio time as they do with other media.

**Limited Listener Attention**   Another problem that plagues radio is that it is difficult to retain listener attention to commercials. Radio programming, particularly music, is often the background to some other activity and may not receive the listeners' full attention. Thus they may miss all or some of the commercials. One environment where radio has a more captive audience is in cars. But getting listeners to pay attention to commercials can still be difficult. Most people preprogram their car radio and change stations during commercial breaks. A study by Avery Abernethy found large differences between exposure to radio programs versus advertising for listeners in cars. They were exposed to only half of the advertising broadcast and changed stations frequently to avoid commercials.[49] However, a study by the companies Arbitron Inc. and Coleman Research analyzed the audience retained during commercial breaks by comparing the audience level for each minute of a commercial break to the audience for the minute before the commercials began.[50] The study found that on average 92 percent of the lead-in audience was retained during commercial breaks. Nearly the entire audience was retained during one-minute commercial pods (Exhibit 11–17). Another factor that is detracting from radio listening in motor vehicles is the rapid growth of mobile phones. A recent study found that half of commuters surveyed who own a cell phone reported listening to less radio than they did a year earlier.[51]

**Competition from Digital Media**   Radio is also facing threats from several digital-based technologies that are impacting the listening audience for commercial radio. A major source of competition for conventional broadcast radio is the growth of satellite radio, which bounces signals off satellites stationed over the East and West Coasts and back down to receivers that encode the signals digitally. The major satellite radio company is SiriusXM which was formed by the merger of the major two satellite radio companies (Sirius and XM Radio) in 2008 and now has around 24 million subscribers.[52] The market for satellite radio is vehicle owners who choose it as an option when purchasing a new car or who purchase a receiver for about $100 and pay a monthly subscription fee of around $13 for the digital quality radio service that includes 140+ channels of music, news, talk, sports, and children's programming. However, SiriusXM also targets other markets for its service, including homes, businesses, Internet/mobile devices, portable radios, boats, and planes (Exhibit 11–18). The music stations on SiriusXM are commercial free, while talk channels have approximately six minutes of commercials. Programming on SiriusXM features big-name entertainers and personalities such as shock jock Howard Stern, Martha Stewart, and Oprah Winfrey. Prior to their merger, both XM and Sirius spent large amounts of money to acquire the broadcast rights for professional and college sports as well as NASCAR. SiriusXM

**EXHIBIT 11–18**

SiriusXM's satellite radio service competes against traditional broadcast stations for listeners more locally tailored programming such as traffic and weather reports, which make them more competitive against terrestrial stations in local markets.

In addition to satellite, terrestrial radio is also being significantly impacted by the growing popularity of MP3 players such as Apple's iPod as well as music services that are becoming available over the Internet such as Pandora, Spotify, and Yahoo! Music. Apple recently entered the online radio market with its iTunes Radio streaming service, as has Google with its All Access service.[53] Another such digital technology that threatens radio is the growth of podcasting, which is a method of distributing audio content via the Internet. Podcasting enables independent producers to create their own radio shows and bypass the traditional entry barriers such as licenses, airwave frequencies, and transmission.

**Clutter**  Clutter is just as much a problem with radio as with other advertising media. Most radio stations carry an average of nearly 10 minutes of commercials every hour. During the popular morning and evening rush hours, the amount of commercial time may exceed 12 minutes. Also contributing to the clutter problem is the practice of some stations to offer "commercial-free" blocks of music to attract listeners. This practice results in more commercials being aired in a short time period and may also result in listeners switching to another station rather than listening through a long block of ads. Advertisers must create commercials that break through the clutter or use heavy repetition to make sure their messages reach consumers. In a study of radio listeners conducted by Edison Research, perceptions of increased ad clutter were cited by participants as a reason for spending less time listening to radio.[54]

A number of radio stations have begun to address the clutter problem by reducing the number of commercials. Clear Channel Communications, which owns more than 1,200 radio stations across 300 markets in the United States, cut back on the number of minutes of commercials its stations run per hour to entice both listeners and advertisers. Other large companies that own radio stations including Viacom and Entercom Communications have also reduced the frequency of commercials as have some individual stations in many markets.[55]

The radio industry is looking for other ways to make radio advertising more valuable to marketers. In 2010 Clear Channel began offering advertisers a new service known as contextual radio ads that can automatically insert radio commercials immediately after specific programming or certain kinds of content, including other ads.[56] A number of companies have been using the service to better target their radio advertising messages. For example, Walmart ran ads for AC/DC's *Black Ice* album, which was sold exclusively at its stores, on various rock stations owned by Clear Channel immediately after songs by the group were played. GEICO also used the service to air commercials with its "Save 15 percent on insurance" after ads for cars, motorcycles, or RVs aired.

## Buying Radio Time

The purchase of radio time is similar to that of television, as advertisers can make either network, spot, or local buys. Since these options were reviewed in the section on buying TV time, they are discussed here only briefly.

**Network Radio**  Advertising time on radio can be purchased on a network basis using one of the national networks. There are currently seven major national radio networks such as Westwood One, Citadel Media, and Premiere. There are also more than 100 regional radio networks across the country. Using networks minimizes the amount of negotiation and administrative work needed to get national or regional coverage, and the costs are lower than those for individual stations. However, the number of affiliated stations on the network roster and the types of audiences they reach can vary considerably, so the use of network radio reduces advertisers' flexibility in selecting stations.

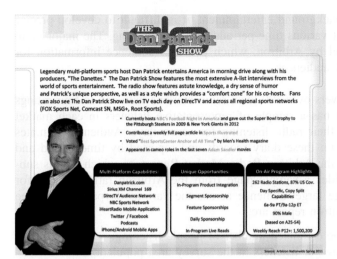

**EXHIBIT 11–19**

*The Dan Patrick Show* is syndicated nationally

An important trend in radio is the increasing number of radio networks and syndicated programs that offer advertisers a package of several hundred stations. For example, *The Dan Patrick Show* is a syndicated radio and television sports talk show hosted by former ESPN personality Dan Patrick. It is syndicated nationally by Premiere Radio Networks and carried by more than 250 stations reaching 1.3 million people weekly (Exhibit 11–19). The show is particularly popular among the 18-to-49 male audience. Syndication reduces audience fragmentation and purchasing problems and increases radio's appeal to national advertisers.

**Spot Radio**  National advertisers can also use spot radio to purchase airtime on individual stations in various markets. The purchase of spot radio provides greater flexibility in selecting markets, individual stations, and airtime and adjusting the message for local market conditions. Spot radio accounts for about 20 percent of radio time sold.

**Local Radio**  By far the heaviest users of radio are local advertisers; nearly 79 percent of radio advertising time is purchased from individual stations by local companies. Auto dealers, retailers, restaurants, and financial institutions are among the heaviest users of local radio advertising. But a number of radio advertisers are switching to local cable TV because the rates are comparable and there is the added advantage of TV's visual impact.

## Time Classifications

As with television, the broadcast day for radio is divided into various time periods or dayparts, as shown in Figure 11–7. The size of the radio listening audience varies widely across the dayparts, and advertising rates follow accordingly. The largest radio audiences (and thus the highest rates) occur during the early morning and late afternoon drive times. Radio rates also vary according to the number of spots or type of audience plan purchased, the supply and demand of time available in the local market, and the ratings of the individual station. Rate information is available directly from the stations and is summarized in SRDS's Radio Advertising Source, which provides spot radio rates and data for both local stations and radio networks. Some stations issue rate cards showing their ad rates across various dayparts. However, many stations do not adhere strictly to rate cards and the rates published in SRDS. Their rates are negotiable and depend on factors such as availability, time period, and number of spots purchased.

## Audience Information

One problem with radio is the lack of audience information. Because there are so many radio stations and thus many small, fragmented audiences, the stations cannot support the expense of detailed audience measurement. Also, owing to the nature

**FIGURE 11–7**

Dayparts for Radio

| | |
|---|---|
| Morning drive time | 6:00–10:00 A.M. |
| Daytime | 10:00 A.M.–3:00 P.M. |
| Afternoon/evening drive time | 3:00–7:00 P.M. |
| Nighttime | 7:00 P.M.–12:00 A.M. |
| All night | 12:00–6:00 A.M. |

of radio as incidental or background entertainment, it is difficult to develop precise measures of who listens at various time periods and for how long. The major radio ratings services are owned by Arbitron, which provides audience information for local stations and network audiences.

YTC 11-07

**Arbitron**

youtube.com/10ebelch

**Arbitron**   Arbitron covers over 300 local radio markets with one to four ratings reports per year. Arbitron has a sample of representative listeners in each market who maintain a diary of their radio listening for seven days. Audience estimates for the market are based on these diary records and reported by time period and selected demographics in the Arbitron Radio Market Report, to which clients subscribe. Figure 11–8 provides a sample page from the Arbitron ratings report for people in the 18-to-49 age target audience across the various dayparts. The three basic estimates in the Arbitron report are

- Person estimates—the estimated number of people listening.
- Rating—the percentage of listeners in the survey area population.
- Share—the percentage of the total estimated listening audience.

These three estimates are further defined by using quarter-hour and cume figures. The **average quarter-hour (AQH) figure** expresses the average number of people estimated to have listened to a station for a minimum of five minutes during any quarter-hour in a time period. For example, station KCBQ has an average quarter-hour listenership of 2,500 during the weekday 6 to 10 A.M. daypart. This means that any weekday, for any 15-minute period during this time period, an average of 2,500 people between the ages of 18 and 49 are tuned to this station. This figure helps determine the audience and cost of a spot schedule within a particular time period.

**Cume** stands for "cumulative audience," the estimated total number of different people who listened to a station for at least five minutes in a quarter-hour period within a reported daypart. In Figure 11–8, the cumulative audience of people 18 to 49 for station KCBQ during the weekday morning daypart is 26,300. Cume estimates the reach potential of a radio station.

**FIGURE 11–8**

Partial Sample Page from Arbitron Radio Ratings Report

| | MONDAY–FRIDAY 6–10 A.M. | | | | MONDAY–FRIDAY 10 A.M.–3 P.M. | | | |
|---|---|---|---|---|---|---|---|---|
| **TARGET AUDIENCE, PERSONS 18–49** | | | | | | | | |
| | AQH (00) | CUME (00) | AQH RTG | AQH SHR | AQH (00) | CUME (00) | AQH RTG | AQH SHR |
| KCBQ | | | | | | | | |
| METRO | 25 | 263 | .2 | .8 | 40 | 365 | .3 | 1.3 |
| TSA | 25 | 263 | | | 40 | 365 | | |
| KCBQ-FM | | | | | | | | |
| METRO | 101 | 684 | .7 | 3.1 | 117 | 768 | .9 | 3.7 |
| TSA | 101 | 684 | | | 117 | 768 | | |
| KCEO | | | | | | | | |
| METRO | 11 | 110 | .1 | .3 | 8 | 81 | .1 | .3 |
| TSA | 11 | 110 | | | 8 | 81 | | |
| KFMB | | | | | | | | |
| METRO | 171 | 790 | 1.3 | 5.3 | 106 | 678 | .8 | 3.3 |
| TSA | 171 | 790 | | | 106 | 678 | | |

The Arbitron Portable People Meter: An Introduction

The Arbitron Portable People Meter™ is the biggest development in radio audience measurement in the past 40 years. Indeed, PPM is the next generation of electronic ratings. Are you working on 2008 media plans? If so, know that PPM is scheduled to be in use in several Top 10 radio markets by the end of 2008. Adjustments to TRPs and CPPs will be needed.

Why the PPM?

Here are but a few reasons why the PPM offers new opportunities for advertisers:

1. **Enhanced credibility.** The PPM automatically detects the stations that panelists are exposed to, stores the information and sends it back to Arbitron each night.

2. **More stable survey-to-survey trends.**

3. **Faster data make radio more relevant.** PPM results are available within weeks following a broadcast.

4. **The PPM will measure 6- to 11-year-olds.**

5. **The PPM will measure** HD Radio® multicasts, online streaming, podcasts and other time-shifted content.

6. **Radio commercial audiences are much larger than suspected.** On average, radio holds more than 92% of its lead-in audience during commercial breaks.

7. **Working persons drive radio listening.** The PPM shows that working persons are the core of radio's listening base.

8. **Stations with younger formats skew older than prior measurement indicated,** and stations with older formats skew younger.

9. **Clearer understanding of the impact of play-by-play sports and special events for stations and advertisers.**

10. **Nights and weekends are stronger dayparts.** You now have additional avenues to reach consumers.

How Does PPM Compare to Diary?

| The Diary | The Portable People Meter |
|---|---|
| Person records listening for 1 week. | A household remains in the PPM panel for an average of 9 months. |
| 4 reports a year. | 13 reports a year. |
| Diary records listening recall. | PPM tracks actual station exposure. |
| Average Diary reports listening to 3.2 stations per week. | Average PPM records exposure to 6 stations per week. |

You Can't Spell RADIO Without R.O.I.

**EXHIBIT 11–20**

Arbitron promotes its Portable People Meter

The **average quarter-hour rating (AQH RTG)** expresses the estimated number of listeners as a percentage of the survey area population. The **average quarter-hour share (AQH SHR)** is the percentage of the total listening audience tuned to each station. It shows the share of listeners each station captures out of the total listening audience in the survey area. The average quarter-hour rating of station KCBQ during the weekday 6 to 10 A.M. daypart is 0.2, while the average quarter-hour share is 0.8.

In 2008 Arbitron introduced the **Portable People Meter (PPM),** which is a wearable, page-size device that electronically tracks what consumers listen to on the radio by detecting inaudible identification codes that are embedded in the programming. The PPM was developed in response to calls from the radio and advertising industries for Arbitron to provide more detailed measures of radio audiences.[57] The radio industry feels that the PPM system will show that more people are listening to radio, which in turn will encourage advertisers to buy more commercial time. Advertisers are welcoming the use of PPMs as they provide more detailed demographic information on radio listeners. Arbitron now uses the PPM to measure radio audiences in the top 50 markets and is expected to continue to expand its use to other markets over the next several years.[58] Exhibit 11–20 shows an ad from Arbitron promoting the value of the Portable People Meter.

Arbitron also recently began measuring listenership to webcasts. Arbitron Cross-Platform Service is an audience measurement service that measures Internet audio and video tuning across all webcasting sources. Arbitron's research has found that online listening to Internet radio stations continues to grow. This will make the measurement of radio listening over the Internet a very important area in the future. In late 2012 Nielsen acquired Arbitron for $1.26 billion and the deal was approved by the Federal Trade Commission in September 2013. The acquisition of Arbitron gives Nielsen nearly total control of the television and radio measurement industry.[59]

**RADAR** Another rating service that is now owned by Arbitron is RADAR (Radio's All Dimension Audience Research), which is supported by radio networks, media services companies, and advertisers. RADAR measurements are based on information collected throughout the year by means of diary interviews from a probability sample of 200,000 respondents age 12 and older who live in telephone households. Respondents are instructed to record all radio listening as well as the day of the week, time of day, and location for a one-week period. Demographic information is also collected in the diaries.

RADAR reports are issued four times a year and provide network audience measures, along with estimates of audience and various segments. The audience estimates are time-period measurements for the various dayparts. RADAR also provides estimates of network audiences for all commercials and commercials within various programs.

As with TV, media planners must use the audience measurement information to evaluate the value of various radio stations in reaching the advertiser's target audience and their relative cost. The media buyer responsible for the purchase of radio time works with information on target audience coverage, rates, time schedules, and availability to optimize the advertiser's radio media budget.

# Summary

Television and radio, or the broadcast media, are the most pervasive media in most consumers' daily lives and offer advertisers the opportunity to reach vast audiences. Both broadcast media are time- rather than space-oriented and organized similarly in that they use a system of affiliated stations belonging to a network, as well as individual stations, to broadcast their programs and commercial messages. Advertising on radio or TV can be done on national or regional network programs or purchased in spots from local stations.

TV has grown faster than any other advertising medium in history and has become the leading medium for national advertisers. No other medium offers its creative capabilities; the combination of sight, sound, and movement gives the advertiser a vast number of options for presenting a commercial message with high impact. Television also offers advertisers mass coverage at a low relative cost. Variations in programming and audience composition, along with the growth of cable, are helping TV offer more audience selectivity to advertisers. While television is often viewed as the ultimate advertising medium, it has several limitations, including the high cost of producing and airing commercials, a lack of selectivity relative to other media, the fleeting nature of the message, and the problem of commercial clutter. The latter two problems have been compounded in recent years by the trend toward shorter commercials. Television viewing is being impacted by the Internet as more television programs are now available online and consumers are watching television on personal computers, tablets, and smartphones. Social media are also changing the way people watch television and how they interact with TV programs.

Information regarding the size and composition of national and local TV audiences is provided by Nielsen Media Research.

The amount of money networks or stations can charge for commercial time on their programs is based on its audience measurement figures. This information is also important to media planners, as it is used to determine the combination of shows needed to attain specific levels of reach and frequency with the advertiser's target market.

Future trends in television include the continued growth of cable, competition to local cable operators from direct broadcast satellite systems, and a resulting increase in channels available to television households. Changes are also likely to occur in the measurement of viewing audiences—such as the change to C3 ratings which includes measures of viewing audiences both live and up to three days after a program airs on television.

The role of radio as an entertainment and advertising medium has changed with the rapid growth of television. Radio has evolved into a primarily local advertising medium that offers highly specialized programming appealing to narrow segments of the market. Radio offers advertisers the opportunity to build high reach and frequency into their media schedules and to reach selective audiences at a very efficient cost. It also offers opportunities for integrated marketing programs such as place-based promotions and event sponsorships.

The major drawback of radio is its creative limitations owing to the absence of a visual image. The short and fleeting nature of the radio commercial, the highly fragmented nature of the radio audience, and clutter are also problems. Radio stations are facing increased competition from online music services such as Pandora, Spotify, iTunes Radio, and Google All Access.

As with TV, the rate structure for radio advertising time varies with the size of the audience delivered. The primary sources of audience information are Arbitron for local radio and its RADAR studies for network audiences.

# Key Terms

## Discussion Questions

1. The chapter opener discusses how intercollegiate athletic programs have become very dependent on revenue from broadcast rights to football and basketball games. Discuss the impact this is having on colleges and their athletic programs in particular. What are some of the negative implications of this situation? (LO1)

2. Discuss the major developments that are impacting the television industry and TV's role as a major advertising medium. How might these factors impact the way marketers use television as part of their IMC programs? (LO1, 2, 4)

3. Discuss how companies advertising on the Super Bowl are using it as an integrated marketing opportunity and leveraging their involvement with the game. Evaluate the pros and cons of releasing a Super Bowl ad prior to the day it is shown on the big game. (LO2)

4. Discuss the advantages and limitations of television as an advertising medium and how these factors affect its use by both major national advertisers as well as smaller local companies. (LO2)

5. The most popular form of television commercials is the 30-second spot. Discuss why 30-second spots are so popular among advertisers. When might a marketer be able to effectively use a 10- or 15-second commercial? (LO2)

6. What are the various options available to advertisers for purchasing advertising time on television? How does the use of these options differ for national versus local advertisers? (LO3)

7. Discuss the reasons behind the growing popularity of sports programming on television and why television networks are willing to pay such large sums of money for the rights to televise college and professional sports. (LO2)

8. IMC Perspective 11–1 discusses the popularity of ESPN and the high rights fees cable operators must pay for the network as part of their basic cable package. Do you think it is fair for households that are not interested in sports programming to have to pay higher cable bills that include ESPN as part of the basic cable package? (LO2)

9. Evaluate the use of sweeps rating periods as a method for measuring local television viewing audiences. Do you think sweeps ratings provide reliable and valid estimates of local television viewing audiences? How might they be improved? (LO3)

10. Discuss recent developments in the measurement of television viewing audiences and their implications for advertisers. Do you think advertisers should have to pay for viewers who watch TV shows on a time-shifted basis on their DVRs or video on demand? (LO3)

11. What is a commercial rating, and how does this measure differ from a program rating? Discuss why advertisers and media planners prefer commercial ratings rather than program ratings. (LO3)

12. Discuss the advantages and disadvantages of advertising on radio. Discuss how radio advertising can be used by national versus local advertisers. (LO2)

13. Discuss how radio stations, as well as advertisers, can deal with the clutter problem on radio and draw attention to their commercials. Provide an example of an advertiser who might be able to benefit from the contextual programming service offered by Clear Channel. (LO3, 4)

## LEARNING OBJECTIVES

(LO1) To examine the various types of magazines and newspapers and the value of each as an advertising medium.

(LO2) To analyze the advantages and limitations of magazines and newspapers as advertising media.

(LO3) To discuss how advertising space is purchased in magazines and newspapers, how readership is measured, and how rates are determined.

(LO4) To consider future developments in magazines and newspapers and how these trends will influence their use as advertising media.

# 12 Evaluation of Media: Magazines and Newspapers

## NEWSPAPERS IN THE DIGITAL AGE

The past few years have not been kind to the traditional media of magazines and newspapers as they have been facing major challenges on a number of fronts. Both of these print media were impacted by the weak economy that has led many companies to reduce their advertising budgets and/or shift more of the monies they are spending to nontraditional media and the Internet in particular. Advertising revenue for magazines declined from nearly $25 billion in 2007 to $17 billion in 2013, while the total number of advertising pages has dropped by nearly 25 percent over the past five years. Total advertising spending in newspapers declined by more than 50 percent from $42 billion in 2007 to $23 billion in 2013. Revenue from advertising is the primary source of income for both magazines and newspapers, so the impact on publishers is obvious. However, advertising revenue is dependent on the number of readers that magazines and newspapers can deliver to advertising, and both mediums have been struggling to retain readers.

As you have likely noticed, newspapers are not what they used to be as the industry has undergone major changes in recent years. The rise of the Internet along with the increasing use of mobile devices, such as tablets and smartphones, to access content has had a dramatic impact on the newspaper industry. This digital disruption has changed the nature of the newspaper as a vehicle for information as well as its value as an advertising medium. Traditionally newspapers bundled together an array of content that is offered in various sections such as national, international, and local news; business; sports; entertainment; local stories, editorials and opinions; comics; and classified advertising for automobiles, real estate, rental, employment, and other products and services. Display advertising is interspersed throughout the paper and along with classified ads generates more than half of the revenue used to cover the costs of printing and distributing a physical paper.

However, digital technology has led to the unbundling of the content provided by newspapers with the explosion of the news and information sources available on the Internet. Moreover, aggregation sites such as the Huffington Post, Google News, and Reddit consolidate news and information from a myriad of websites that are constantly updated, which means the news delivered by newspapers is "old news" when it is delivered a day later. There are also aggregation sites for specific topics such as sports, business, entertainment, and most other areas of interest to readers.

Newspapers have also been impacted by the growth of online sites that have taken away much of their revenue from classified advertising. For example, employment sites such as Monster, CareerBuilder, theLadders, and many others are now used for recruiting employees; sites such as AutoTrader and Cars.com are used to buy and sell cars; while Craigslist has classified sections for virtually every product and service category. Newspapers have experienced a 70 percent decline in their revenue from classified advertising over the past decade; it has dropped from nearly $17 billion in 2003 to $4.7 billion in 2012. Revenue from display advertising has also been declining as many local retailers as well as national advertisers have been shifting their ad spending from newspapers to an array of digital alternatives.

The newspaper industry's initial response to the digital disruption was to put their content online for free, which resulted in a tremendous growth in the number of online readers. Most newspapers began offering online versions of their publications and selling display advertising on their sites, primarily in the form of banner ads, to generate revenue. However, revenue from online advertising has not been able to compensate for the decline in monies received for print advertising as online ad rates are significantly lower than those for print ads. Marketers are not willing to pay as much for online newspaper ads because there is an enormous number of advertising options on the Internet, driving down prices, and the click-through rates on most of the banner ads are minuscule. Moreover, they must compete against search advertising sites such as Google, Yahoo!, and Bing as well as social media sites such as Facebook that offer advertisers very sophisticated ad-targeting techniques. In essence, newspapers have been trading traditional print advertising dollars for digital pennies.

The challenges facing newspaper publishers have forced them to undergo significant cost-cutting measures while continuing to look for new sources of revenue. By 2013, more than a third of the nearly 1,400 daily newspapers had adopted digital pay plans or "paywalls" that require readers to pay for a digital subscription or lose access. These digital pay plans may allow a certain number of free articles each month and free access to articles found through search, links, and social media references. However, users must pay for full access to the newspaper, which provides newspaper publishers with an additional source of revenue and helps stabilize their print circulation as digital access is typically offered free or at a reduced rate to print subscribers. Many major newspapers have been successful in implementing digital pay plans. For example, *The New York Times* implemented a paywall in 2011 and had over 640,000 digital subscribers by 2013.

Newspapers are responding in other ways to the digital disruption they have faced over the past decade and will continue to face in the future. Many newspaper publishers are transforming their business model to generate revenue from a variety of new offerings such as providing digital agency and marketing services, helping businesses connect directly with consumers through e-commerce transactions, and expanding their integrated marketing capabilities to include areas such as event marketing and promotional services. Experts still question how long traditional print newspapers can survive in many markets. However, the president of the Newspaper Association of America is optimistic as she notes: "In virtually every community they serve, newspapers have the biggest newsrooms, the best-known brand, and significant audience market share. Now they are building on those to find new ways to serve audiences and local businesses." And hopefully to generate the revenue needed to survive in the new digital world.

Sources: Rick Edmonds, Emily Guskin, Amy Mitchell, and Mark Jurkowitz, "The State of the News Media 2013," *The Pew Research Center's Project for Excellence in Journalism,* March 18, 2013, http://stateofthemedia.org/; Newspaper Association of America, "The American Newspaper Media Industry Revenue Profile," www.naa.org/Trends-and-Numbers/Newspaper-Revenue/Newspaper-Media-Industry-Revenue-Profile-2012.aspx; Joe Pompeo, "A Year into the 'Times' Digital Subscription Program, Analysts and Insiders See Surprising Success, and More Challenges to Come," Capitalnewyork.com, March 19, 2012, www.capitalnewyork.com/article/media/2012/03/5509293/.

YTC 12–01

**Newspaper Association of America**

youtube.com/10ebelch

Magazines and newspapers have been advertising media for more than two centuries; for many years, they were the only major media available to advertisers. With the growth of the broadcast media, particularly television, reading habits declined. More consumers turned to TV viewing not only as their primary source of entertainment but also for news and information. But despite the competition from the broadcast media, newspapers and magazines remained important media vehicles to both consumers and advertisers.

Thousands of magazines are published in the United States and throughout the world. They appeal to nearly every specific consumer interest and lifestyle, as well as to thousands of businesses and occupations. By becoming a highly specialized medium that reaches specific target audiences, the magazine industry has prospered. Newspapers are still the primary advertising medium in terms of both ad revenue and number of advertisers. Newspapers are particularly important as a local advertising medium for hundreds of thousands of retail businesses and are often used by large national advertisers as well.

Magazines and newspapers are an important part of our lives. For many consumers, newspapers are their primary source of product information. They would not think of going shopping without checking to see who is having a sale or clipping coupons from the weekly food section or Sunday inserts. Many people read a number of different magazines each week or month to become better informed or simply entertained. Individuals employed in various occupations rely on business magazines to keep them current about trends and developments in their industries as well as in business in general.

While most of us are very involved with the print media, it is important to keep in mind that few newspapers or magazines could survive without the support of advertising revenue. Consumer magazines generate an average of 54 percent of their revenues from advertising; business publications receive nearly 73 percent. Newspapers generate nearly two-thirds 70 percent of their total revenue from advertising. In many cities, the number of daily newspapers has declined because they could not attract enough advertising revenue to support their operations. The print media must be able to attract large numbers of readers or a very specialized audience to be of interest to advertisers.

As discussed in the chapter opener and in Digital and Social Media Perspective 12–1, both magazines and newspapers are facing significant challenges from the Internet, which is impacting the number of people who read the traditional print version of each medium and is also attracting an increasingly larger amount of marketers' advertising budget each year. Many magazines and newspapers are struggling to get consumers to pay for their online editions and continue to look for ways to monetize them. While they can sell banners and other forms of online advertising to marketers, the ad rates they can charge on the web cannot match those in print and generate enough revenue to make up for the losses they are incurring from the decline in the sale of print ads. While e-readers and tablet PCs may be the publishing industry's digital life preserver, the costs of these devices are still high and it will take time for them to cross the technology chasm and achieve mass-market adoption. Thus, in the short-term magazines and newspapers have to continue to search for ways to attract and retain readers as well as the advertising pages and revenue that accompanies them. Despite the challenges they face, magazines and newspapers are still very important media vehicles for most advertisers.[1]

# THE ROLE OF MAGAZINES AND NEWSPAPERS

The role of magazines and newspapers in the advertiser's media plan differs from that of the broadcast media because they allow the presentation of detailed information that can be processed at the reader's own pace. The print media are not intrusive like radio and TV, and they generally require some effort on the part of the reader for the advertising message to have an impact. For this reason, newspapers and magazines are often referred to as *high-involvement media.*[2] Magazine readership has remained strong despite the growth of new media options as over 90 percent of adults 18+ read magazines and they read an average of 7 issues per month.[3]

The vast majority of U.S. adults read a newspaper each week across a variety of technology platforms. In a typical week nearly 70 percent of adults read newspapers in print or online, whereas 59 percent of young adults aged 18 to 24 read newspaper content. Major newspapers still reach a very broad target audience while specialized papers reach narrower or more specialized markets. Magazines are different from newspapers because the majority of them reach a very selective audience and can be valuable in reaching specific types of consumers and market segments. While magazines and newspapers are the major forms of print media and online editions of most publications are now available, the two are quite different as are the types of advertising each attracts. This chapter focuses on these two major forms of print media (including their online versions) and examines the specific advantages and limitations of each, along with factors that are important in determining their role in the media plan, as well as the overall IMC program.

# MAGAZINES

Over the past several decades, magazines have grown rapidly to serve the educational, informational, and entertainment needs of a wide range of readers in both the consumer and business markets. Magazines are the most specialized of all advertising media. While some magazines—such as *Reader's Digest, Time,* and *The Economist*—are general mass-appeal publications, most are targeted to a very specific audience. There is a magazine designed to appeal to nearly every type of

The chapter opener discussed how digital disruption has impacted the newspaper industry and the transition of readership from traditional print to online publications has resulted in declining circulation and lower advertising revenue. Magazines, which are the other major category of print media, are facing many of the same challenges as newspapers. As stated in the opener, advertising revenue for print magazines declined from nearly $25 billion in 2007 to $17 billion in 2013, reflecting the drop in the total number of advertising pages published in magazines. Like newspapers, magazines have been experiencing declines in readership, with single-copy sales that occur at newsstands particularly hard hit, as they declined by nearly 10 percent in each of the past four years. While single-copy sales account for a small percentage of circulation for most magazines, it is considered the best measure of a magazine's appeal to consumers since, unlike subscriptions, they cannot be artificially inflated by deep discounts or the distribution of free copies.

Newsweeklies and business magazines have been experiencing particularly large declines in newsstand sales as well as circulation; publications such as *Time, The Economist, Bloomberg Businessweek,* and *Fortune* experienced major drops in single-copy sales. *Newsweek,* which was one of the oldest and most widely read weekly news magazines, could not survive the decline in readership and advertising revenue. In 2012, a year and a half after it was sold by *The Washington Post,* the new owner announced plans to merge *Newsweek* with *the Daily Beast* and make it an online publication. The last print issue of the 79-year-old magazine was published in December 2012. Just a few months after *Newsweek* became an online publication, Time Warner Inc. announced that it would spin off its entire Time Inc. magazine group into a

separate subsidiary that includes flagship titles such as *Time, People, Fortune, Money,* and *Sports Illustrated.* While the move did not mean the magazines would discontinue print operations, the decision to remove the titles from Time Warner's business portfolio was viewed as yet another sign of the challenges facing the magazine industry.

While many reasons were cited for the moves by both *Newsweek* and Time Inc., chief among them were declining advertising revenue and huge drops in circulation. *Newsweek,* for example, had lost roughly half of its customers since 2005, and advertising revenue was down more than 80 percent during that same period. Similarly, ad revenue at Time Inc. had declined 38 percent over a 10-year period while overall revenue had dropped 50 percent. Time Inc. also noted a sharp drop in newsstand sales of *People* magazine, which had long accounted for a large percentage of its profits. Interestingly, in the days following Time Warner's announcement that it would shed its entire magazine division, its shares hit a 52-week high on Wall Street.

One of the major problems facing magazines, just like newspapers, is that more people are now going online to get their news as well as to read the magazines and newspapers that they are no longer willing to purchase. Nearly all of the major magazines and newspapers now offer online versions of their publications, but the problem is that consumers are used to getting this content for free and are not willing to pay for it. And, as is the case with newspapers, most magazines are not generating enough revenue from digital advertising to make up for the loss in traditional print ads. However, magazine publishers recognize that consumers are becoming very comfortable reading magazines on their mobile devices. Studies conducted by the

consumer in terms of demographics, lifestyle, activities, interests, or fascination. Numerous magazines are targeted toward specific businesses and industries as well as toward individuals engaged in various professions (Exhibit 12–1).

The wide variety makes magazines an appealing medium to a vast number of advertisers. Although TV accounts for the largest dollar amount of advertising expenditures among national advertisers, more companies advertise in magazines than in any other medium. Users of magazine ads range from large consumer-product companies such as Procter & Gamble and L'Oréal, which spend over $700 million a year on magazine advertising, to a small company advertising scuba equipment in the online edition of *Skin Diver* magazine.

## Classifications of Magazines

To gain some perspective on the various types of magazines available and the advertisers that use them, consider the way magazines are generally classified. The media research company SRDS, the primary reference source on periodicals for media planners, divides magazines into three broad categories based on the audience to which they are directed: consumer (which include farm), health care, and business

In these [ ] times of ours, you might think that [ ] don't read magazines. That the overwhelming [ ] of the online world has swept them right out of [ ]. But it's not true at all. From [ ] through their [ ] years, folks are reading magazines [MORE] than they were just a few years ago. Sure, there's a [ ] being spent online. But there's also a lot of [ ] being spent on magazines, with nearly 300 million paid subscriptions.

MAGAZINEs
The Power of Print®

Pew Research Center have found that nearly 80 percent of tablet owners read in-depth articles on their devices. Major magazines have also begun offering digital "app" versions of their publications for the iPad as well as tablets that use the Android operating system. The digital versions of these publications can offer full-screen ads that can deliver the best of the old world and the new: They can offer the same impact as magazine spreads or TV commercials, while also offering the same analytics as the Internet to measure viewership and other metrics.

Although the magazine industry recognizes that it must embrace its digital future, most publishers are not ready to abandon their traditional print publications. They still feel that there are inherent advantages of magazines to advertisers and have gone on the offensive to promote them. For example, five leading magazine publishers including Conde Nast, Hearst Magazines, Meredith Corporation, Time Inc., and Wenner Media joined forces and launched one of the largest print campaigns ever created to promote the value of magazines as an advertising medium. The tagline for the campaign, "Magazines, The Power of Print," was created by Y&R New York and is supported by the Association of Magazine Media, the industry association that represents consumer magazines and works closely with them to

represent their interests. The primary goal of the campaign was to promote the vitality of magazines and the idea that they remain an effective advertising medium in the age of the Internet because of the depth and lasting quality of print compared with the fleeting nature of much of the web's content. The campaign was also designed to remind people that many of the popular digital brands are rooted in print publications that have tremendous cultural and commercial influence.

Jann Wenner of Wenner Media, whose publications include *Rolling Stone*, *Us Weekly*, and *Men's Journal*, continues to argue that there is still a place for traditional print magazines. Wenner has noted that just as TV did not kill magazines, the Internet is a threat only to publications that lost focus on what makes magazines unique. He argues, "Magazines have enduring value for readers and advertisers that have gotten a little neglected and misunderstood in the era of Internet instant buzz and chatter. Magazines are beloved and powerful in people's lives for very good reasons that need to be remembered and reinforced." He also predicts that it will take a decade or more before there is a decisive shift from magazines to tablets and calls the rush to iPad and tablet editions of magazines the result of "sheer insanity, insecurity and fear." Many in the magazine industry probably hope that Wenner is correct in his assessment. However, it is likely that they will be hedging their bets and continuing to embrace their digital future.

Sources: Jane Sasseen, Katerina-Eva Matsa, and Amy Mitchell, "News Magazine: Embracing Their Digital Future," *The Pew Center's Project for Excellence in Journalism: The State of the News Media 2013*, http://stateofthemedia.org/2013/news-magazines-embracing-their-digital-future/; Katerina-Eva Matsa, Jane Sasseen, and Amy Mitchell, "Magazines: Are Hope for Tablets Overdone?" *The Pew Center's Project for Excellence in Journalism: The State of the News Media, 2012*, http://stateofthemedia.org/2012/magazines-are-hopes-for-tablets-overdone/; Nat Ives, "Jann Wenner: Magazines' Rush to iPad Is 'Sheer Insanity and Insecurity and Fear,'" *Advertising Age*, May 29, 2011, http://adage.com/article/media/jann-wenner-magazines-tablet-migration-decades/227827/.

YTC 12-02

**Association of Magazine Media Power of Print**

youtube.com/10ebelch

publications. Each category is then further classified according to the magazine's editorial content and audience appeal.

**Consumer Magazines**   Consumer magazines are bought by the general public for information and/or entertainment. SRDS divides 3,000 domestic consumer magazines into 80 classifications, among them news, men's, sports, travel, and women's. Another way of classifying consumer magazines is by distribution: They can be sold through subscription or circulation, store distribution, or both. *Time* and *InStyle* are sold both through subscription and in stores; *Woman's World* is sold primarily through stores. Figure 12–1 shows the top 10 magazines in terms of subscriptions and single-copy sales, respectively. Magazines can also be classified by frequency; weekly, monthly, and bimonthly are the most common.

Consumer magazines represent the major portion of the magazine industry, accounting for nearly two-thirds of all advertising dollars spent in magazines. Consumer magazines are best suited to marketers interested in reaching general consumers of products and services as well as to companies trying to reach a specific target market. The most frequently advertised categories in consumer magazines are toiletries and cosmetics; drugs and remedies; food and food products; apparel and

**EXHIBIT 12–1**

Magazines targeted to a specific industry or profession

accessories; retail; and automotive.[4] Marketers of tobacco products spend most of their media budget in magazines, since they are prohibited from advertising in the broadcast media.

While large national advertisers tend to dominate consumer magazine advertising in terms of expenditures, the 3,000 consumer magazines are also important to smaller companies selling products that appeal to specialized markets. Special-interest magazines assemble consumers with similar lifestyles or interests and offer marketers an efficient way to reach these people with little wasted coverage or circulation. For example, companies marketing women's apparel, such as J.Crew, Abercrombie & Fitch, Ralph Lauren, and Jones New York, that want to target young adult females might find magazines such as *Seventeen, Elle, Allure,* or *Cosmopolitan* effective media vehicles for advertising to them.

Not only are these specialty magazines of value to firms interested in reaching a specific market segment, but their editorial content often creates a very favorable advertising environment for relevant products and services. For example, avid skiers and snowboarders cannot wait for the first snowfall after reading the season's first issues of *Transworld Snowboarding* or *Skiing* magazine and may be quite receptive to the ads they carry for skiing and snowboarding products and destination ski resorts (Exhibit 12–2).

**Farm Publications**  The consumer SRDS category also consists of all the magazines directed to farmers and their families. About 300 publications are tailored to nearly every possible type of farming or agricultural interest. SRDS breaks farm publications into nine classifications, ranging from general-interest magazines aimed at all types of farmers (e.g., *Farm Journal, Successful Farming, Progressive Farmer*) to those in specialized agricultural areas such as poultry (*Gobbles*), hog farming (*National Hog Farmer*), or cattle raising (*Beef*—see Exhibit 12–3). A number of farm publications are directed at farmers in specific states or regions, such as *Nebraska Farmer* or *Montana Farmer Stockman*. Farm publications are not classified with business publications because historically farms were not perceived as businesses.

**FIGURE 12–1**

Top 10 Magazines By Subscriptions and Single Copy Sales

| Subscriptions | | Single Copy Sales | |
|---|---|---|---|
| 1. AARP the Magazine* | 22,721,661 | 1. Cosmopolitan | 1,190,669 |
| 2. AARP Bulletin* | 22,403,427 | 2. Woman's World | 1,143,985 |
| 3. Game Informer Magazine | 7,864,326 | 3. First for Women | 989,144 |
| 4. Better Homes and Gardens | 7,621,456 | 4. People | 971,668 |
| 5. Reader's Digest | 5,527,183 | 5. Family Circle | 636,363 |
| 6. Good Housekeeping | 4,354,740 | 6. Lindy's Football Annuals | 609,557 |
| 7. Family Circle | 4,143,942 | 7. In Touch Weekly | 536,030 |
| 8. National Geographic | 4,125,152 | 8. In Style | 528,418 |
| 9. People | 3,637,633 | 9. US Weekly | 528,027 |
| 10. Woman's Day | 3,374,479 | 10. Food Network Magazine | 483,773 |

*High proportion of title' circulation attributed to membership benefits.

Source: Alliance for Audited Media, Snapshot Report, February 2013, www.auditedmedia.com.

**EXHIBIT 12–2**

*Transworld Snowboarding* magazine is an excellent medium for reaching the serious snowboarder

**YTC 12–03**

**New Magazines**

youtube.com/10ebelch

**LO 12-2**

**EXHIBIT 12–3**

*Beef* magazine is read by many cattle ranchers

**Business Publications** Business publications are those magazines or trade journals published for specific businesses, industries, or occupations. Standard Rate and Data Service breaks down over 5,000 print and 5,000 digital U.S. magazines and trade journals into nearly 200 market classifications. The major classifications include:

1. Magazines directed at specific professional groups, such as *National Law Review* for lawyers and *Architectural Forum* for architects.
2. Industrial magazines directed at businesspeople in various manufacturing and production industries—for example, *Iron and Steelmaker, Chemical Week,* and *Industrial Engineering.*
3. Trade magazines targeted to wholesalers, dealers, distributors, and retailers, among them *Progressive Grocer, Drug Store News, Women's Wear Daily,* and *Restaurant Business.*
4. General business magazines aimed at executives in all areas of business, such as *Forbes, Fortune,* and *Bloomberg Businessweek.* (General business publications are also included in SRDS's consumer publications edition.)
5. Health care publications targeted to various areas, including dental, medical and surgical, nursing, biotechnological sciences, and hospital administration.

The numerous business publications reach specific types of professional people with particular interests and give them important information relevant to their industry, occupation, and/or careers. Business publications are important to advertisers because they provide an efficient way of reaching the specific types of individuals who constitute their target market. Much marketing occurs at the trade and business-to-business level, where one company sells its products or services directly to another.

## Advantages of Magazines

Magazines have a number of characteristics that make them attractive as an advertising medium. Strengths of magazines include their selectivity, excellent reproduction quality, creative flexibility, permanence, prestige, readers' high receptivity and involvement, and services they offer to advertisers.

**Selectivity** One of the main advantages of using magazines as an advertising medium is their **selectivity**, or ability to reach a specific target audience. Magazines are the most selective of all media except direct mail. Most magazines are published for special-interest groups. The thousands of magazines published in the United States reach all types of consumers and businesses and allow advertisers to target their advertising to segments of the population who buy their products. For example, *PC Magazine* is targeted toward computer buffs, *Rolling Stone* reaches those with an avid interest in music, and *Ebony* focuses on the upscale African American market. Many new magazines are introduced each year targeting new interests and trends. According to Dr. Sami Husni, who has been tracking magazine launches since 1985, 870 new publications were launched in 2012 (Exhibit 12–4).[5] New consumer magazines are continually being introduced to meet the changing needs, interests, and passions of the public in areas such as sports/recreation, entertainment/celebrity, travel, fashion/apparel, and beauty/grooming. New business publications are also frequently launched to respond to developments in business and industry.

**CHAPTER 12**

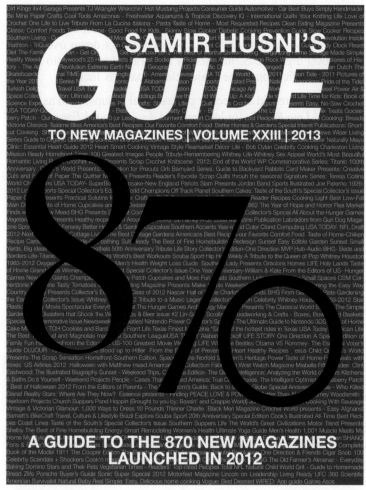

**EXHIBIT 12-4**

Magazine expert Sami Husni tracks the launch of new magazines each year

In addition to providing selectivity based on interests, magazines can provide advertisers with high demographic and geographic selectivity. *Demographic selectivity,* or the ability to reach specific demographic groups, is available in two ways. First, most magazines are, as a result of editorial content, aimed at fairly well-defined demographic segments. *Ladies' Home Journal, Ms., Self,* and *Cosmopolitan* are read predominantly by women; *Esquire, Maxim,* and *Sports Illustrated* are read mostly by men. Older consumers can be reached through publications like *Modern Maturity.* Celebrity-focused magazines, which are read primarily by women, have become extremely popular in recent years.

A second way magazines offer demographic selectivity is through special editions. Even magazines that appeal to broader audiences, such as *Reader's Digest, Time,* and *Good Housekeeping*, can provide a high degree of demographic selectivity through their special demographic editions. Most of the top consumer magazines publish different editions targeted at different demographic markets.

*Geographic selectivity* lets an advertiser focus ads in certain cities or regions. One way to achieve geographic selectivity is by using a magazine that is targeted toward a particular area. Magazines devoted to regional interests include *Yankee* (New England), *Southern Living* (South), *Sunset* (West), and *Texas Monthly* (guess where?), among many others. One of the more successful media developments of recent years has been the growth of city magazines in most major American cities. *Los Angeles Magazine, Philadelphia,* and *Boston,* to name a few, provide residents of these areas with articles concerning lifestyle, events, and the like, in these cities and their surrounding metropolitan areas. City and regional magazines make it possible for advertisers to focus on specific local markets that may be of interest to them. They also have a readership profile that appeals to marketers of upscale brands: high income, college educated, loyal, and influential in their communities. Most of these publications belong to the City and Regional Magazine Association, which represents magazines in 64 different markets (Exhibit 12–5). An advertiser can run an ad in all of the magazines that belong to the association with one media buy.

Another way to achieve geographic selectivity in magazines is through purchasing ad space in specific geographic editions of national or regional magazines. A number of publications divide their circulation into groupings based on regions or major metropolitan areas and offer advertisers the option of concentrating their ads in these editions. A magazine may break the United States into geographic areas and offer regional editions for each and/or offer advertisers their choice of editions directed to specific states or metropolitan areas. Many magazines allow advertisers to combine regional or metropolitan editions to best match the geographic market of interest to them.

SRDS lists more than 350 consumer magazines offering geographic and/or demographic editions. Regional advertisers can purchase space in editions that reach only areas where they have distribution, yet still enjoy the prestige of advertising in a

EXHIBIT 12–5
City magazines offer
advertisers high geographic
selectivity

major national magazine. National advertisers can use the geographic editions to focus their advertising on areas with the greatest potential or those needing more promotional support. They can also use regional editions to test-market products or alternative promotional campaigns in various regions of the country.

Ads in regional editions can also list the names of retailers or distributors in various markets, thus encouraging greater local support from the trade. The trend toward regional marketing is increasing the importance of having regional media available to marketers. The availability of regional and demographic editions can also reduce the cost per thousand for reaching desired audiences.

**Reproduction Quality** One of the most valued attributes of magazine advertising is the reproduction quality of the ads. Magazines are generally printed on high-quality paper stock and use printing processes that provide excellent reproduction in black and white or color. Since magazines are a visual medium where illustrations are often a dominant part of an ad, this is a very important property. The reproduction quality of most magazines is far superior to that offered by the other major print medium of newspapers, particularly when color is needed. The use of color has become a virtual necessity in most product categories, and more than two-thirds of all magazine ads now use color. The excellent reproduction quality of magazines provides the opportunity for innovative creative work by agencies. Many marketers are now integrating digital technology with print advertising. For example, the Team One agency developed a very creative ad for Lexus that becomes animated—the engine revs, the headlights flash, the wheels spin, and the background pulses with color, all to a musical soundtrack—when placed over an iPad that has a Lexus

**EXHIBIT 12–6**

This creative Lexus ad becomes animated when placed over an iPad with a microsite loaded

microsite loaded (Exhibit 12–6). Lexus and Team One developed a special technology called "CinePrint" that was used to create the dynamic ad.[6]

**Creative Flexibility** In addition to their excellent reproduction capabilities, magazines also offer advertisers a great deal of flexibility in terms of the type, size, and placement of the advertising material. Some magazines offer (often at extra charge) a variety of special options that can enhance the creative appeal of the ad and increase attention and readership. Examples include gatefolds, bleed pages, inserts, and creative space buys.

**Gatefolds** enable an advertiser to make a striking presentation by using a third page that folds out and gives the ad an extra-large spread. Gatefolds are often found at the inside cover of large consumer magazines or on some inside pages. Advertisers use gatefolds to make a very strong impression, especially on special occasions such as the introduction of a new product or brand. For example, automobile advertisers often use gatefolds to introduce new versions of their cars each model year. Not all magazines offer gatefolds, however, and they must be reserved well in advance and are sold at a premium.

**Bleed pages** are those where the advertisement extends all the way to the end of the page, with no margin of white space around the ad. Bleeds give the ad an impression of being larger and make a more dramatic impact. Many magazines charge an extra 10 to 20 percent for bleeds.

In addition to gatefolds and bleed pages, creative options available through magazines include unusual page sizes and shapes. Some advertisers have grabbed readers' attention by developing three-dimensional pop-up ads that jump off the page. Various other *inserts* are used in many magazines. These include return cards, recipe booklets, coupons, records, and even product samples. Cosmetic companies use scratch-and-sniff inserts to introduce new fragrances, and some companies use them to promote deodorants, laundry detergents, or other products whose scent is important. Inserts are also used in conjunction with direct-response ads and as part of sales promotion strategies.

Scented ads, pop-ups, singing ads, heavy card stock, stickers, and digital devices are among the types of inserts used by advertisers in magazines. Advertisers sometimes use special inserts to break through the clutter in magazines and to capture readers' attention. Marketers are becoming very strategic with regard to the type of inserts they are using in magazines and also continue to take advantage of technological advances in developing them. For example, the agency for Volkswagen South Africa, Ogilvy Cape Town, developed a very creative insert that embodies a green message for the automaker's eco-friendly BlueMotion technology by including a prepaid mailing label that could be used to send the magazine to a recycling plant. The ad copy simply said, "reduce your impact wherever you can," and the insert resulted in a response rate that was nearly double what was expected.[7] The CW Television Network developed a unique magazine insert designed to use Twitter to promote its new television shows for the 2012–2013 season.[8] The first-of-its-kind print insert was put inside an October issue of *Entertainment Weekly* magazine and featured a small LCD screen that displayed a video preview of new shows and a live Twitter feed of the last six tweets from the @CW Network account (Exhibit 12–7).

Many magazine publishers are willing to work with advertisers who want to use creative inserts because they are eager to show that magazines can compete

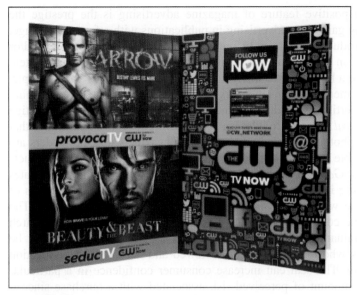

**EXHIBIT 12–7**

The CW network used a creative insert to promote its new television shows

**EXHIBIT 12–8**

WD-40 uses quarter-page ads to get greater impact from its media budget

USE #437

Painter takes artistic license with WD-40®. Van Fabel, an art teacher in North Carolina, says a shot of WD-40® and a little elbow grease are all he needs to clean his palette. It's great at removing crayon and scuff marks from walls and floors, too. Just spray, wait and wipe.

WD-40. THERE'S ALWAYS ANOTHER USE.

USE #973

Some fish story. Several letters from avid fishermen across the country praise the benefits of WD-40®. And not just for cleaning their rods and reels and protecting fish hooks from rust and corrosion. They swear it actually attracts fish when sprayed on lures.

WD-40. THERE'S ALWAYS ANOTHER USE.

USE #519

Cycling fanatic finally loses his grip. After struggling to remove his old handlebar grips, Gene Upshaw of Seattle found that a squirt of WD-40® was all he needed. It's great for cleaning and lubricating chains and protecting metal parts from corrosion, too.

WD-40. THERE'S ALWAYS ANOTHER USE.

USE #722

WD-40® gets kids out of sticky situation. A relieved mom (and son) from Athens, Georgia discovered that WD-40 is as good on stuck fingers as it is on stuck drawers. It's great for lubricating sliding glass doors, windows and anything else that sticks or squeaks.

WD-40. THERE'S ALWAYS ANOTHER USE.

with new media as a way to showcase products. While the inserts pose challenges to production staff and printers, these costs along with any extra postage fees are generally passed on to the advertisers. The total cost of manufacturing inserts varies depending on the complexity, weight, assembly requirements, and other factors. Some of the very elaborate inserts can cost advertisers as much as several million dollars.[9]

There has been some backlash against various types of *printaculars.* Critics argue that they alter the appearance and feel of a magazine and the reader's relationship to it. Advertisers do not want to run regular ads that have to compete against heavy inserts, pop-ups, talking ads, or other distractions. Some advertisers and agencies are even asking publishers to notify them when they plan to run any spectacular inserts so that they can decide whether to pull their regular ads from the issue.[10]

*Creative space buys* are another option of magazines. Some magazines let advertisers purchase space units in certain combinations to increase the impact of their media budget. For example, WD-40, an all-purpose lubrication product, uses half- or quarter-page ads on consecutive pages of several magazines, mentioning a different use for the product on each page, as shown in Exhibit 12–8. This strategy gives the company greater impact for its media dollars and is helpful in promoting the product's variety of uses.

**Permanence** Another distinctive advantage offered by magazines is their long life span. TV and radio are characterized by fleeting messages that have a very short life span; newspapers are generally discarded soon after being read. Magazines, however, are generally read over several days and are often kept for reference. They are retained in the home longer than any other medium and are generally referred to on several occasions. A study of magazine audiences found that readers devote nearly an hour over a period of two or three days to reading an average magazine.[11] Studies have also found that nearly 75 percent of consumers retain magazines for future reference.[12] One benefit of the longer life of magazines is that reading occurs at a less hurried pace and there is more opportunity to examine ads in considerable detail. This means ads can use longer and more detailed copy, which can be very important for high-involvement and complex products or services. The permanence of magazines also means readers can be exposed to ads on multiple occasions and can pass magazines along to other readers.

**Prestige**    Another positive feature of magazine advertising is the prestige the product or service may gain from advertising in publications with a favorable image. Companies whose products rely heavily on perceived quality, reputation, and/or image often buy space in prestigious publications with high-quality editorial content whose consumers have a high level of interest in the advertising pages. For example, *Esquire* and *GQ* cover men's fashions in a very favorable environment, and a clothing manufacturer may advertise its products in these magazines to enhance the prestige of its lines. *Architectural Digest* provides an impressive editorial environment that includes high-quality photography and artwork. The magazine's upscale readers are likely to have a favorable image of the publication that may transfer to the products advertised on its pages. *Good Housekeeping* has a unique consumer policy that states that if a product bearing its famous seal proves to be defective within two years of purchase, the magazine will replace the product or refund the purchase price. The research division of the company, now known as the Good Housekeeping Research Institute, has been evaluating products for more than a century. The seal may be used only by products whose ads have been reviewed and accepted for publication in *Good Housekeeping*. The seal can increase consumer confidence in a particular brand and reduce the amount of perceived risk associated with a purchase since it really is a money-back guarantee (Exhibit 12–9).[13]

While brands may enhance their prestige by advertising in magazines with a favorable image and high-quality editorial content, the type of ads that appear in a magazine may also influence readers' perceptions of a publication. The results of a study by Sara Rosengren and Micael Dahlén found that advertising content influences the perceptions of a magazine. Advertising for high-reputation brands or ads that were high in execution quality was beneficial to the evaluations of a magazine, while ads for brands with a poor reputation or that were low in execution quality were detrimental to the image of the publication.[14] These findings suggest that it is important for publishers to manage the advertising content of their magazines in both print and online editions. Some publishers have design guidelines stating that advertising should be treated as content and note that relevant, attractive advertising is an important part of the magazine experience as editorial content for readers.

While most media planners recognize that the environment created by a publication is important, it can be difficult to determine the image a magazine provides. Subjective estimates based on media planners' experience are often used to assess a magazine's prestige, as are objective measures such as reader opinion surveys.[15]

**Consumer Receptivity and Engagement**    With the exception of newspapers, consumers are more receptive to advertising in magazines than in any other

**EXHIBIT 12–9**
The *Good Housekeeping* seal gives consumers confidence in products advertised in the magazine

**59% of readers took action or plan to take action** as a result of exposure to specific print magazine ads.

actions include:

have a more favorable opinion about the advertiser

consider purchasing the advertised product or service

gather more information about advertised product or service

recommend the product or service

visit the advertiser's website

purchase product or service

clip or save the ad

visit or plan to visit dealership

Source: GfK MRI Starch, January-December 2012

magazine.org/factbook

**Advertising effectiveness by position**

| | noted | action taken |
|---|---|---|
| **first** quarter of book | 55% | 58% |
| **second** quarter of book | 50 | 58 |
| **third** quarter of book | 49 | 60 |
| **fourth** quarter of book | 50 | 59 |

Note: Includes all ads, size/color and cover positions
Source: GfK MRI Starch, January-December 2012

engagement    15

**EXHIBIT 12–10**

Actions taken by consumers after exposure to magazine advertising

medium. Magazines are generally purchased because the information they contain interests the reader, and ads provide additional information that may be of value in making a purchase decision. Studies have shown that magazines are consumers' primary source of information for a variety of products and services, including automobiles, beauty and grooming, clothing and fashion, financial planning, and personal and business travel.[16]

Media planners recognize that one of the major advantages of advertising in magazines is the ability of the medium to engage readers and hold their attention. Numerous studies have shown that consumers become involved with magazines when they read them and are also more likely to find ads acceptable, enjoyable, and even a valuable part of a publication. Intrusive media such as television, radio, and the Internet struggle with problems such as inattention and consumers trying to avoid advertising messages. And as advertisers try harder to get their commercials seen and heard in these media, the more consumers search for ways to tune them out. However, magazine readers recognize that they control the rate and duration of their exposure to editorial content as well as advertisements and view ads as less disruptive to their media consumption experience.

Research has shown that engagement with an advertising medium is important because it is directly related to increased advertising recall and specific actions taken such as searching for additional information about an advertiser's brand, visiting its website, saving an ad for future reference, and purchasing a product or service, as well as recommending it to others. Exhibit 12–10 shows the various actions magazine readers take or plan as a result of exposure to specific magazine ads based on research by GfK MRI Starch, which is the leading producer of media and consumer research in the United States.

**Services**   A final advantage of magazines is the special services some publications offer advertisers. Some magazines have merchandising staffs that call on trade intermediaries like retailers to let them know a product is being advertised in their publication and to encourage them to display or promote the item. Another service offered by magazines (usually the larger ones) is research studies that they conduct on consumers. These studies may deal with general consumer trends, changing purchase patterns, and media usage or may be relevant to a specific product or industry.

An important service offered by some magazines is **split runs**, where two or more versions of an ad are printed in alternate copies of a particular issue of a magazine. This service is used to conduct a split-run test, which allows the advertiser to determine which ad generates the most responses or inquiries, providing some evidence as to their effectiveness. Technological developments have also made it possible for magazines to offer advertisers the opportunity to deliver personalized messages to tightly targeted audiences through selective binding and ink-jet imaging. **Selective binding** is a computerized production process that allows the creation of hundreds of copies of a magazine in one continuous sequence. Selective binding enables magazines to target and address specific groups within a magazine's circulation base. The magazine publishers can then send different editorial or advertising messages to various groups of subscribers within the same issue of a publication. **Ink-jet imaging** reproduces a message by projecting ink onto paper rather than using mechanical plates. This process makes it possible to personalize an advertising message. Many publishers believe selective binding and ink-jet imaging will let advertisers target their messages more finely and let magazines compete more effectively with direct mail and other direct-marketing vehicles.

# Disadvantages of Magazines

Although the advantages offered by magazines are considerable, they have certain drawbacks too. These include the costs of advertising, their limited reach and frequency, the long lead time required in placing an ad, and the problem of clutter and heavy advertising competition.

**Costs**   The costs of advertising in magazines vary according to the size of the audience they reach and their selectivity. Advertising in large mass-circulation magazines like *Time, Reader's Digest,* and *Better Homes and Gardens* can be very expensive. For example, a full-page, four-color ad in *Time* magazine's national edition (circulation 3.3 million) cost $339,000 in 2013. Popular positions such as the back cover cost nearly $500,000.

Like any medium, magazines must be considered not only from an absolute cost perspective but also in terms of relative costs. Most magazines emphasize their effectiveness in reaching specific target audiences at a low cost per thousand. Also, an increasing number of magazines are offering demographic and geographic editions, which helps lower their costs. Media planners generally focus on the relative costs of a publication in reaching their target audience. However, they may recommend a magazine with a high cost per thousand because of its ability to reach a small, specialized market segment. Of course, advertisers with limited budgets will be interested in the absolute costs of space in a magazine and the costs of producing quality ads for these publications.

**Limited Reach and Frequency**   Magazines are generally not as effective as other media in offering reach and frequency. While nearly 90 percent of adults in the United States read one or more consumer magazines each month, the percentage of adults reading any individual publication tends to be much smaller, so magazines have a thin penetration of households. For example, *Reader's Digest* has the third-highest circulation of any magazine, at 5.5 million, but this represents only 5 percent of the 115 million households in the United States.

The top 25 consumer magazines based on total paid and verified circulation are shown in Figure 12–2. (It should be noted that publications such as *AARP Magazine* and *AARP Bulletin* have a high circulation because they are included as part of the benefits package to members of the organization.) As can be seen in Figure 12–2, even the most popular consumer magazines have a circulation of under 5 million, which means that they reach only about 2 to 4 percent of the households in the United States. While total readership of these magazines may be higher since there will be multiple readers of the publication, marketers seeking broad reach must run ads in a number of different magazines, which adds to the complexity of the media buying process. Marketers whose media plan calls for broad reach will often use magazines in conjunction with other media such as television as well the Internet and social media. Since most magazines are monthly or at best weekly publications, the opportunity for building frequency through the use of the same publication is limited. Using multiple ads in the same issue of a publication is an inefficient way to build frequency. Most advertisers try to achieve frequency by adding other magazines with similar audiences to the media schedule.

**Long Lead Time**   Another drawback of magazines is the long lead time needed to place an ad. Most major publications have a 30- to 60-day lead time, which means space must be purchased and the ad must be prepared well in advance of the actual publication date. No changes in the art or copy of the ad can be made after the closing date. This long lead time means magazine ads cannot be as timely as other media, such as radio or newspapers, in responding to current events or changing market conditions. However, as magazines face declines in ad pages and advertising revenue, many are shortening the lead times required to run ads in their publications. Advances in digital publishing and the use of computer-based production methods is also reducing the amount of lead time required to run an ad in a publication.

| | |
|---|---|
| AARP The Magazine | 22,721,661 |
| AARP Bulletin | 22,403,427 |
| Game Informer Magazine | 7,864,326 |
| Better Homes and Gardens | 7,621,456 |
| Reader's Digest | 5,527,183 |
| Good Housekeeping | 4,354,740 |
| Family Circle | 4,143,942 |
| National Geographic | 4,125,152 |
| People | 3,637,633 |
| Woman's Day | 3,374,479 |
| Time | 3,281,175 |
| Taste of Home | 3,268,549 |
| Ladies' Home Journal | 3,230,450 |
| Sports Illustrated | 3,174,888 |
| Cosmopolitan | 3,023,884 |
| Prevention | 2,921,618 |
| Southern Living | 2,867,235 |
| Maxim | 2,543,563 |
| AAA Living | 2,455,280 |
| O, The Oprah Magazine | 2,439,747 |
| Glamour | 2,324,170 |
| American Legion Magazine | 2,268,015 |
| Parenting | 2,232,707 |
| Redbook | 2,214,603 |
| ESPN The Magazine | 2,142,937 |

Note: Figures are averages for total paid and verified circulation for December 2012
based on Alliance for Audited Media Snapshot reports. www.auditedmedia.com.

**Clutter and Competition** While the problem of advertising clutter is
generally discussed in reference to the broadcast media, magazines also have this
drawback. The clutter problem for magazines is something of a paradox: The more
successful a magazine becomes, the more advertising pages it attracts, and this leads
to greater clutter. In fact, magazines generally gauge their success in terms of the
number of advertising pages they sell.

Magazine publishers do attempt to control the clutter problem by maintaining a
reasonable balance of editorial pages to advertising. According to the Association
of Magazine Media, the average consumer magazine contains 45 percent advertising and 55 percent editorial.[17] However, many magazines contain ads on more
than half of their pages. This clutter makes it difficult for an advertiser to gain
readers' attention and draw them into the ad. Thus, many print ads use strong
visual images, catchy headlines, or some of the creative techniques discussed

**EXHIBIT 12-11**

*Home Made Simple* is a custom magazine published by Procter & Gamble

earlier to grab the interest of magazine readers. Some advertisers create their own custom magazines to sidestep the advertising clutter problem as well as to have control over editorial content. A number of companies have also been publishing their own magazines to build relationships with their customers. For example, Farmers Insurance sends its customers a magazine called *The Friendly Review* that contains useful articles on a variety of topics. Custom-published magazines have also become very popular among tobacco companies, such as Philip Morris, which direct-mail them to their customer base.[18] Some companies have begun offering online versions of their custom magazines. For example, Procter & Gamble began publishing *Home Made Simple* several years ago and the custom publication branched into a program on the OWN Network and shopper marketing programs (Exhibit 12-11). Kraft Foods also publishes an online magazine called *Kraft Food & Family,* and the success of the online version led the company to begin offering a print version, which is sent to more than 3 million consumers.[19]

Clutter is not as serious an issue for the print media as for radio or TV, since consumers tend to be more receptive and tolerant of print advertising. They can also control their exposure to a magazine ad simply by turning the page.

## Magazine Circulation and Readership

Two of the most important considerations in deciding whether to use a magazine in the advertising media plan are the size and characteristics of the audience it reaches. Media buyers evaluate magazines on the basis of their ability to deliver the advertiser's message to as many people as possible in the target audience. To do this, they must consider the circulation of the publication as well as its total readership and match these figures against the audience they are attempting to reach.

**Circulation** Circulation figures represent the number of individuals who receive a publication through either subscription or store purchase. The number of copies distributed to these original subscribers or purchasers is known as *primary circulation* and is the basis for the magazine's rate structure. Circulation fluctuates from issue to issue, particularly for magazines that rely heavily on retail or newsstand sales. Many publications base their rates on *guaranteed circulation* and give advertisers a rebate if the number of delivered magazines falls below the guarantee. To minimize rebating, most guaranteed circulation figures are conservative; that is, they are set safely below the average actual delivered circulation. Advertisers are not charged for any excess circulation.

Many publishers became unhappy with the guaranteed circulation concept, since it requires them to provide refunds if guarantees are not met but results in a bonus for advertisers when circulation exceeds the guarantee. Thus, many publications have gone to a circulation rate base system. Rates are based on a set average circulation that is nearly always below the actual circulation delivered by a given issue but carries no guarantee. However, circulation is unlikely to fall below the rate base, since this would reflect negatively on the publication and make it difficult to attract advertisers at prevailing rates.

**Circulation Verification** Given that circulation figures are the basis for a magazine's advertising rates and one of the primary considerations in selecting a publication, the credibility of circulation figures is important. Most major publications are audited by one of the circulation verification services. Consumer magazines and farm publications are audited by the Alliance for Audited Media (AAM, formerly

**YTC 12-04**

**Alliance for Audited Media**

youtube.com/10ebelch

known as Audit Bureau of Circulations) which is a membership organization consisting of North America's leading advertisers, advertising agencies, and content providers. AAM provides independently verified data and information critical to evaluating and purchasing media including consumer magazines and has also begun auditing digital replica editions of magazines that are available for tablets such as the iPad. A digital replica edition must include the print edition's full editorial content, including photography. In addition, any advertiser appearing in the print edition must have the opportunity to appear in the digital replica edition.

AAM collects and evaluates information regarding the subscriptions and sales of magazines and newspapers to verify their circulation figures. Only publications with 70 percent or more paid circulation are eligible for verification audits by AAM. In 2002 the former ABC approved new guidelines for counting magazine circulation and sales. The changes did away with the long-standing "50 percent rule," in which copies that sold for less than half of the basic price of a magazine could not be counted as paid circulation. Under the new rules copies sold at any price may be counted, but the magazine must disclose sales and prices in its circulation statements.[20] More than 2,000 business publications are audited by the Business Publications Audit (BPA) of Circulation. Many of these are published on a **controlled-circulation basis**, meaning copies are sent (usually free) to individuals the publisher believes can influence the company's purchases.

Circulation verification services provide media planners with reliable figures regarding the size and distribution of a magazine's circulation that help them evaluate its worth as a media vehicle. The AAM statement also provides other important information. It shows how a magazine is distributed by state and size, as well as percentage of the circulation sold at less than full value and percentage arrears (how many subscriptions are being given away). Many advertisers believe that subscribers who pay for a magazine are more likely to read it than are those who get it at a discount or for free.

Media buyers are generally skeptical about publications whose circulation figures are not audited by one of the verification services, and some companies will not advertise in unaudited publications. Circulation data, along with the auditing source, are available from SRDS or from the publication itself. Exhibit 12–12 shows two pages of a sample publisher's statement from the Alliance for Audited Media for both print and digital editions. The publisher's statement includes information such as number of print and digital subscriptions as well as single-copy sales; circulation by issues, regions, and demographic editions; a trend analysis; and subscriptions and sales by state and county size.

**Readership and Total Audience**  Advertisers are often interested in the number of people a publication reaches as a result of secondary, or pass-along, readership. **Pass-along readership** can occur when the primary subscriber or purchaser gives a magazine to another person or when the publication is read in doctors' waiting rooms or beauty salons, on airplanes, and so forth.

Advertisers generally attach greater value to the primary in-home reader than the pass-along reader or out-of-home reader, as the former generally spends more time with the publication, picks it up more often, and receives greater satisfaction from it. Thus, this reader is more likely to be attentive and responsive to ads. However, the value of pass-along readers should not be discounted. They can greatly expand a magazine's readership. *People* magazine commissioned a media research study to determine that its out-of-home audience spends as much time reading the publication as do its primary in-home readers.

You can calculate the **total audience**, or **readership**, of a magazine by multiplying the readers per copy (the total number of primary and pass-along readers) by the circulation of an average issue. For example, a magazine such as *Time* may have a circulation base of 3.3 million but an audience of over 19 million readers since it has a high pass-along rate that yields up to six readers per copy. However, rate

## Prototype Magazine

Alliance for Audited Media
The New Audit Bureau of Circulations

MAGAZINE PUBLICATION
Publisher's Statement
Six months ended June 30, 2013
Subject to Audit

Field Served: Health.

Published by XYZ Publications
Frequency: 10 times/year

### 1. TOTAL AVERAGE PAID & VERIFIED CIRCULATION

| | Average for the Statement Period | % | Rate Base | Above (Below) | % Above (Below) |
|---|---|---|---|---|---|
| **Paid & Verified Circulation: (See Par. 6)** | | | | | |
| **Subscriptions:** | | | | | |
| Paid | | | | | |
| Print | 630,209 | 78.2 | | | |
| Digital (Replica) | 70,000 | 8.7 | | | |
| Total Paid Subscriptions | 700,209 | 86.9 | | | |
| Verified | | | | | |
| Print | 57,000 | 7.1 | | | |
| Digital (Replica) | 1,000 | 0.1 | | | |
| Total Verified Subscriptions | 58,000 | 7.2 | | | |
| **Total Paid & Verified Subscriptions** | 758,209 | 94.1 | | | |
| Single Copy Sales | | | | | |
| Print | 46,028 | 5.7 | | | |
| Digital (Replica) | 2,000 | 0.2 | | | |
| Total Single Copy Sales | 48,028 | 5.9 | | | |
| **Total Paid & Verified Circulation** | 806,237 | 100.0 | 800,000 | 6,237 | 0.8 |

### 2. PRICES

| | Suggested Retail Prices (1) | Average Price (2) Net | Average Price (2) Gross (Optional) |
|---|---|---|---|
| Average Single Copy | $3.95 | | |
| Subscription | $24.95 | | |
| Average Subscription Price Annualized (10 issue frequency) | | $15.80 | $21.00 |
| Average Subscription Price per Copy | | $1.58 | $2.10 |

(1) For the Statement period
(2) Represents subscriptions for the 12 months ended December 31, 2012

### 3. PAID & VERIFIED CIRCULATION BY ISSUE OF PRINT AND DIGITAL REPLICA

| Issue | Paid Subscriptions Print | Digital (Replica) | Total Paid Subscriptions | Verified Subscriptions Print | Digital (Replica) | Total Verified Subscriptions | Total Paid & Verified Subscriptions | Single Copy Sales Print | Digital (Replica) | Total Single Copy Sales | Total Paid & Verified Circulation Print | Total Paid & Verified Circulation Digital (Replica) | Total Paid & Verified Circulation |
|---|---|---|---|---|---|---|---|---|---|---|---|---|---|
| Jan. | 632,381 | 70,000 | 702,381 | 57,000 | 1,000 | 58,000 | 760,381 | 44,228 | 2,000 | 46,228 | 733,609 | 73,000 | 806,609 |
| Feb. | 631,848 | 70,000 | 701,848 | 57,000 | 1,000 | 58,000 | 759,848 | 44,601 | 2,000 | 46,601 | 733,449 | 73,000 | 806,449 |
| Mar. | 629,100 | 70,000 | 699,100 | 57,000 | 1,000 | 58,000 | 757,100 | 46,436 | 2,000 | 48,436 | 732,536 | 73,000 | 805,536 |
| Apr. | 626,899 | 70,000 | 696,899 | 57,000 | 1,000 | 58,000 | 754,899 | 49,602 | 2,000 | 51,602 | 733,501 | 73,000 | 806,501 |
| May/June | 630,818 | 70,000 | 700,818 | 57,000 | 1,000 | 58,000 | 758,818 | 45,273 | 2,000 | 47,273 | 733,091 | 73,000 | 806,091 |

### 4. AVERAGE CIRCULATION BY REGIONAL, METRO & DEMOGRAPHIC EDITIONS

| Edition | Number of Issues | Paid Subscriptions Print | Total Paid Subscriptions | Verified Subscriptions Print | Total Paid & Verified Subscriptions | Single Copy Sales Print | Total Paid & Verified Circulation (Print) | Total Paid & Verified Circulation | Rate Base |
|---|---|---|---|---|---|---|---|---|---|
| South | 5 | 130,200 | 130,200 | | 130,200 | | 130,200 | 130,200 | * |
| Northeast | 5 | 170,100 | 170,100 | | 170,100 | | 170,100 | 170,100 | * |

*None Claimed

### 5. TREND ANALYSIS

| | 2008 | % | 2009 | % | 2010 | % | 2011 | % | 2012 | % |
|---|---|---|---|---|---|---|---|---|---|---|
| **Subscriptions:** | | | | | | | | | | |
| Paid | 750,211 | 94.9 | 755,025 | 95.0 | 755,312 | 94.9 | 750,105 | 93.7 | 698,312 | 86.7 |
| Verified | | | | | | | | | 58,900 | 7.3 |
| **Total Paid & Verified Subscriptions** | 750,211 | 94.9 | 755,025 | 95.0 | 755,312 | 94.9 | 750,105 | 93.7 | 757,212 | 94.0 |
| Single Copy Sales | 40,101 | 5.1 | 40,210 | 5.0 | 45,311 | 5.1 | 50,101 | 6.3 | 48,211 | 6.0 |
| **Total Paid & Verified Circulation** | 790,312 | 100.0 | 795,235 | 100.0 | 800,623 | 100.0 | 800,206 | 100.0 | 805,423 | 100.0 |
| Year Over Year Percent of Change | | | | 0.5 | | 0.6 | | 0.7 | | 0.0 | | 0.7 |
| Avg. Annualized Subscription Price | $15.90 | | $15.40 | | $15.75 | | $15.23 | | $15.80 | |

48 W. Seegers Road • Arlington Heights, IL 60005-3913 • T: 224.366.6939 • F: 224.366.6949 • www.auditedmedia.com
04-00

Page 2 of 6 • 04-0000-0
Alliance for Audited Media

**EXHIBIT 12–12**

Example of an Alliance for Audited Media publisher's statement

Source: Reprinted with permission of Alliance for Audited Media.

structures are generally based on the more verifiable primary circulation figures, and many media planners devalue pass-along readers by as much as 50 percent. Total readership estimates are reported by major syndicated magazine research services (discussed next), but media buyers view these numbers with suspicion.

## Audience Information and Research for Magazines

A very valuable source for information on magazines is SRDS, whose print and online service provides complete planning information on domestic and international consumer magazines as well as business and health care trade publications. The SRDS Media Solutions proprietary database contains standardized ad rates, circulation figures, dates, general requirements, contact information, and links to online media kits, websites, and audit statements that provide additional information on readership and positioning.

While circulation and total audience size are important in selecting a media vehicle, the media planner is also interested in the match between the magazine's readers and the advertiser's target audience. Information on readers is available from several sources, including the publication's own research and syndicated studies. Most magazines now have online media kits that provide basic information such as reader demographics, circulation, editorial calendars, rates, specifications, contact information, and other valuable data for advertisers. Exhibit 12–13 shows the homepage of the online media kit for *Rolling Stone* magazine. Magazines generally provide media planners with even more detail than is available in online media kits. SRDS compiles these detailed media kits from most magazines and makes them available to advertisers and their agencies. Most magazines provide media planners with reports detailing readers' demographics, financial profile, lifestyle, and product usage characteristics. The larger the publication, the

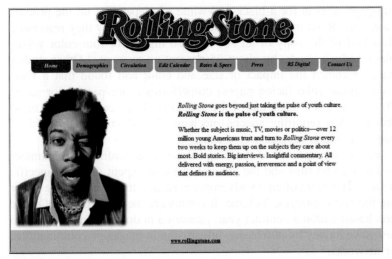

**EXHIBIT 12–13**

*Rolling Stone's* online media kit contains useful information for advertisers

more detailed and comprehensive the information it usually can supply about its readers.

Syndicated research studies are also available. For consumer magazines, primary sources of information are Experian Simmons and the studies of GfK, which was discussed in Chapter 10. These studies provide a broad range of information on the audiences of major national and regional magazines, including demographics, lifestyle characteristics, and product purchase and usage data. Most large ad agencies and media buying services also conduct ongoing research on the media habits of consumers. All this information helps determine the value of various magazines in reaching particular types of product users.

Audience information is generally more limited for business publications than for consumer magazines. The widely dispersed readership and nature of business publication readers make audience research more difficult. Media planners generally rely on information provided by the publication or by sources such as Business Publication Audits, which provide the titles of individuals who receive the publication and the type of industry in which they work. This information can be of value in understanding the audiences reached by various business magazines.

## Purchasing Magazine Advertising Space

**Cost Elements**   Magazine rates are primarily a function of circulation. Other variables include the size of the ad, its position in the publication, the particular editions (geographic, demographic) chosen, any special mechanical or production requirements, and the number and frequency of insertions.

An important consideration for advertisers when buying space in a magazine is whether they want some type of preferred placement or pay for a run-of-book ad that can appear anywhere in the magazine, at the discretion of the publisher. Most of the various preferred positions that magazines make available to advertisers are **first cover** (outside front), **second cover** (inside front), **third cover** (inside back), and **fourth cover** (outside back). These are considered to be very desirable positions in the magazine—particularly the fourth or back cover, for which there is often a waiting list. Because a cover ad position is a preferred position, it is almost always sold at a higher rate than any position inside the magazine. Very few publishers sell advertising space on the front cover of their magazines as the American Society of Magazine Editors guidelines discourage the practice. The front cover has always been considered editorial space and off limits to advertisers.[21]

Advertising space is generally sold on the basis of space units such as full page, half page, and quarter page, although some publications quote rates on the basis of column inches. The larger the ad, the greater the cost. However, many advertisers use full-page ads since they result in more attention and readership. Studies have found that full-page ads generated 30 percent more readership than half-page ads.[22]

Ads can be produced or run using black and white, black and white plus one color, or four colors. The more color used in the ad, the greater the expense because of the increased printing costs. On average, a four-color ad costs 30 percent more than a black-and-white ad. Advertisers generally prefer color ads because they have greater visual impact and are superior for attracting and holding attention.[23] Roper Starch Worldwide analyzed the effect of various factors on the readership of magazine ads. The "noted" scores (the percentage of readers who remember seeing the ad in a publication they read) are anywhere from 6 to 59 percent higher for a four-color

Ivy League Magazine Network

**EXHIBIT 12–14**

Advertisers can reach alumni of Ivy League schools through the Ivy League Network

full-page ad than for a black-and-white ad, depending on the product category. "Read-most" scores (the percentage who say they read more than half of the copy of an ad) are also higher for four-color versus black-and-white ads, by about 25 percent on average.[24] Other studies have examined the impact of size and color and found that a four-color spread (two facing pages) outperforms a one-page color ad by 30 percent and a black-and-white spread by 35 percent in terms of ad recall.[25] Ads requiring special mechanical production such as bleed pages or inserts may also cost extra.

Rates for magazine ad space can also vary according to the number of times an ad runs and the amount of money spent during a specific period. The more often an advertiser contracts to run an ad, the lower are the space charges. Volume discounts are based on the total space purchased within a contract year, measured in dollars. Advertisers can also save money by purchasing advertising in magazine combinations, or networks.

**Magazine networks** offer the advertiser the opportunity to buy space in a group of publications as a package deal. The publisher usually has a variety of magazines that reach audiences with similar characteristics. Networks can also be publishers of a group of magazines with diversified audiences or independent networks that sell space in groups of magazines published by different companies. For example, the Ivy League Magazine Network is a consortium of alumni magazines of Ivy League schools and two non-Ivies, Stanford University and the University of Chicago. Advertisers can purchase ad space and reach the well-educated, affluent alumni of all nine schools with one media purchase through the network (Exhibit 12–14).

## The Future for Magazines

LO 12-4

The past few years have been very difficult for the magazine industry; many publications are experiencing reductions in revenue as advertisers shift more of their spending to digital media and other IMC tools and have been slow to increase their ad spending following the recession. Many publications have seen their number of advertising pages decline and have found it difficult to raise rates to offset the reduction in ad pages.[26] And while advertising revenue has been decreasing, publishers' other major revenue stream, circulation, has also been declining for most magazines. Many magazines have gone out of business in recent years including some that were published for decades such as *Gourmet, Metropolitan,* and *Vibe,* whereas a number of magazines have ceased publishing their print editions and are now available only online, including *Teen People* and *PC Magazine.* Other well-known magazines that have shuttered their print editions recently and gone online are *Newsweek* and the *Sporting News.*[27]

While the health of the economy has a major impact on the magazine industry, there are a number of other important issues facing the industry. The costs of paper and ink continue to rise, and the industry has had to weather several significant increases in postal rates in recent years, which have had a major impact on their cost structure.[28] Magazines are also facing strong competition from other media such as television, the Internet, social media, and direct mail. Publishers are looking at a number of ways to improve their position—including stronger editorial platforms, better circulation management, cross-magazine and media deals, database marketing, technological advances, and electronic delivery methods—to make advertising in magazines more appealing to marketers.

**Stronger Editorial Platforms** Magazines with strong editorial platforms that appeal to the interests, lifestyles, and changing demographics of consumers as well as business and market trends are in the best position to attract readers and advertisers. For example, broadly focused magazines such as *Time, People,* and *Reader's*

**EXHIBIT 12–15**

*Men's Journal* and *Men's Health* magazines have been very successful in attracting the male audience

*Digest* have experienced declines in circulation as well as advertising pages. However, fashion and lifestyle magazines targeted to women such as *Allure, Marie Claire, InStyle,* and *Vogue* have done well as have publications such as *Food Network Magazine* and *Bon Appetit.*[29] Several publications with strong editorial platforms that appeal to younger male readers have also done very well, including *ESPN The Magazine, Men's Journal,* and *Men's Health* (Exhibit 12–15).

**Circulation Management**    One of the major challenges facing magazine publishers is trying to increase or even maintain their circulation bases. Circulation is the second major source of revenue for most publications, and publishers must carefully manage the costs of attracting and maintaining additional readers or subscribers. The cost of acquiring subscribers has increased dramatically over the past decade. However, publishers have not been able to pass on these increased costs because the prices consumers pay for subscriptions as well as single copies of magazines have increased only slightly. Thus, publishers have to pay more to maintain their rate bases (the circulation level guaranteed to advertisers), but they make less money on each subscription sold.

Publishers are also facing a drop in sweepstakes-generated circulation as a result of the controversy that developed over consumer confidence in the sweepstakes-related subscription offers. Agents such as Publishers Clearing House have been going through changes, both self-imposed and externally dictated, that have greatly reduced the number of subscriptions they generate for publishers. To compensate for losses from sweepstakes agents, publishers are looking to other methods of generating subscribers, such as making subscriptions available through websites, offering free trial copies online, conducting special promotions, and using other agents such as school-related subscription services.[30] Some publications such as *InStyle* have begun selling magazine subscriptions on Facebook by allowing users of the social media site to expand blurbs of magazine content that are common in news feeds into full articles that contain ads as well as options to subscribe.[31] Publishers have also been turning to daily-deal sites such as Groupon, Living Social, and Fab.com as publications such as *Esquire, Us Weekly, Reader's Digest, Allure, Men's Health,* and others have found them useful for attracting new subscribers. However, a major challenge publishers will face is getting subscribers to renew at higher rates once the discounted deals expire.[32]

Many magazines are also focusing more attention on managing their circulation bases. For many years, magazines focused on increasing their circulation under the assumption that higher circulation meant higher advertising rates. However, publishers are now realizing that the cost of attracting and maintaining the last 10 to 15 percent of their circulation base is often greater than the additional revenue generated, since these subscribers require numerous direct-mail solicitations, premium offers, or discount subscriptions.

A number of magazines have reduced their circulation base in recent years. Many publishers believe they can pass on price increases more easily to their core readers or subscribers and offer advertisers a more loyal and focused audience. Many advertisers welcome the improvement in circulation management. They would rather reach a few hundred thousand fewer subscribers than pay for inefficient circulation and be hit with advertising rate increases each year. Many magazines are also using the monies saved on the circulation side to improve the editorial content of their publications, which should attract more readers—and advertisers.

**Online Delivery Methods**    Many magazines are keeping pace with the digital revolution and the continuing consumer interest in technology by making their publications available online. According to the Association of Magazine Media, there are more than 15,000 magazines with websites, including nearly 7,500 consumer magazine websites.[33] The number of consumer and business magazine websites has nearly doubled over the past five years. Online versions of magazines offer the many advantages of the Internet to publishers as well as advertisers. They provide advertisers with the opportunity for sponsorships as well as running video and banner ads and promotions on the online versions of the magazines. More and more people are becoming comfortable with reading magazines online rather than in traditional print form, which is leading many publications to expand beyond their basic print publications. A number of publishers are extending their magazine brands to include online, social networking, mobile, and user-generated content, which provides increasing readership as well as advertising reach opportunities. Marketers are also recognizing that there are opportunities to integrate their advertising in online publications with the environment and editorial content. Digital and Social Media Perspective 12–2 discusses the concept of **native advertising**, which takes on the look and feel of the surrounding content, and how some critics argue that it is challenging the traditional church-and-state divide between editorial and advertising.

Another form of online delivery is digital editions of magazines developed specifically for tablets such as the iPad and devices using the Android operating system. By 2013 there were more than 1,200 iPad apps for magazines in the United States. The number of digital app editions of magazines will continue to grow as more consumers become comfortable with reading them on their tablets and advances in technology make the reading experience similar to that of a print publication. Digital editions of many magazines are now able to offer ads that can deliver the impact of full-page magazine ads, include video and TV commercials, and link directly to an advertiser's website.

# NEWSPAPERS

Newspapers, the second major form of print media, are the largest of all advertising media in terms of total dollar volume. In 2013, nearly $23 billion was spent on newspaper advertising, or about 14 percent of the total advertising expenditures in the United States. Newspapers are an especially important advertising medium to local advertisers, particularly retailers. However, newspapers are also valuable to national advertisers. Many of the advertising dollars spent by local retailers are actually provided by national advertisers through cooperative advertising programs (discussed in Chapter 16). Newspapers vary in terms of their characteristics and their role as an advertising medium.

## Types of Newspapers

The traditional role of newspapers has been to deliver prompt, detailed coverage of news as well as to supply other information and features that appeal to readers. The vast majority of newspapers are daily publications serving a local community. However, weekly, national, and special-audience newspapers have special characteristics that can be valuable to advertisers.

**Daily Newspapers** Daily newspapers, which are published each weekday, are found in cities and larger towns across the country. Many areas have more than one daily paper. Daily newspapers are read by approximately 42 percent of adults each weekday and by 43 percent on Sundays.[34] They provide detailed coverage of news, events, and issues concerning the local area as well as business, sports, and other relevant information and entertainment. Daily newspapers can further be classified as morning, evening, or Sunday publications. In 2013 there were nearly 1,400 daily newspapers in the United States; of these, 33 percent were evening papers and 67 percent morning. There were also 900 Sunday newspapers, most of which were published by daily newspapers.

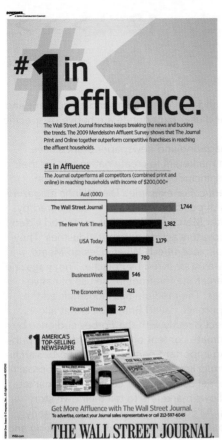

**EXHIBIT 12–16**

*The Wall Street Journal* is the leading national newspaper and reaches a very affluent audience

**Weekly Newspapers**   Most weekly newspapers originate in small towns or suburbs where the volume of news and advertising cannot support a daily newspaper. These papers focus primarily on news, sports, and events relevant to the local area and usually ignore national and world news, sports, and financial and business news. There are approximately 6,700 weekly newspapers published in the United States, and they have an average circulation of close to 7,500. Weeklies appeal primarily to local advertisers because of their geographic focus and lower absolute cost. Most national advertisers avoid weekly newspapers because of their duplicate circulation with daily or Sunday papers in the large metropolitan areas and problems in contracting for and placing ads in these publications. However, the contracting and scheduling problems associated with these papers have been reduced by the emergence of syndicates that publish them in a number of areas and sell ad space in all of their local newspapers through one office.

**National Newspapers**   Newspapers in the United States with national circulation include *USA Today, The Wall Street Journal,* and *The New York Times.* All three are daily publications and have editorial content with a nationwide appeal. *The Wall Street Journal* has the largest circulation of any newspaper in the country with just over 2 million readers and has recently passed *USA Today* to become the nation's leading paper. The *Journal* includes online readers in its circulation figures as it charges them a subscription fee to read its online edition, while most newspapers have not been successful at doing so and only count print subscriptions and newsstand sales. *The Wall Street Journal* is an excellent media vehicle for reaching businesspeople and also has a very affluent readership base as shown in the ad in Exhibit 12–16. The second most popular national newspaper is *USA Today,* which positions itself as "the nation's newspaper." *USA Today* has become a very popular daily newspaper, particularly among business and leisure travelers, with its coverage of national news as well as its money, sports, lifestyle, and entertainment sections. National newspapers appeal primarily to large national advertisers and to regional advertisers that use specific geographic editions of these publications. For example, *The Wall Street Journal* has three geographic editions covering 18 regions in which ads can be placed, while *USA Today* offers advertisers the opportunity to run ads in its national edition or any of 25 regionals.

In 1999, *The New York Times* was classified as a national newspaper rather than a regional publication by Competitive Media Reporting, which has developed a new policy on how it defines national newspapers.[35] This policy states that a paper must publish at least five times a week and have no more than 67 percent of its distribution in any one area. More than 33 percent of its display advertising must come from national advertising categories, and more than 50 percent of its advertising must come from national advertisers. Designation as a national newspaper is important to major newspapers in attracting national advertisers.[36]

*The Christian Science Monitor* is also considered a national newspaper although in 2008 the publication, which was founded in 1908, dropped its daily print edition to focus on publishing online. The paper now offers a print edition only on weekends.

**Special-Audience Newspapers**   A variety of papers offer specialized editorial content and are published for particular groups, including labor unions, professional organizations, industries, and hobbyists. Many people working in advertising read *Advertising Age,* while those in the marketing area read *Marketing News.* Specialized newspapers are also published in areas with large foreign-language-speaking ethnic groups, among them Polish, Chinese, Hispanics,

## Online Magazines Turn to Native Advertising

As it becomes increasingly difficult to reach consumers with traditional advertising messages, many marketers have been turning to alternative ways to promote their products and services. Product placement is very common in movies and TV shows and brands have seeped into videogames, songs, and even the plots of novels. Marketers also have been finding ways to more effectively integrate advertising messages and content in magazines such as by running ads next to magazine stories about the same product or service, getting products mentioned in stories, and creating contests linked to magazines. Another vehicle often used by marketers to enhance the credibility of their messages is *advertorials*, which are advertising messages or sections that look like editorial content.

While advertorials in magazines and newspapers have been around for decades, their use has been gaining popularity in the realm of digital advertising under the concept of what is being called "native advertising." There has been considerable debate over what the advertising industry means by native advertising; many argue that it is just a digital version of an editorial that might appear in a magazine or newspaper. However, some industry experts describe them as digital advertising formats that integrate more seamlessly into the aesthetics of a website or online publication as well as the editorial content to provide more value to both advertisers and readers. What this means basically is that an online ad takes on the look and feel of the surrounding content and its visual design and user experience are native or specific to the online site.

A number of magazine and newspaper brands have been working with marketers to create native ads for their online publications, including *Forbes*, the *Washington Post*, and *The Atlantic*. For example, *The Atlantic* magazine promoted a series of posts on Atlantic.com sponsored by automotive marketer Mercedes-Benz that contained video interviews with innovators across different industries. They also ran an editorial piece titled "Where Design Meets Technology" that was sponsored by Porsche. The magazine brand that has been at the forefront in the use of native advertising is *Forbes*. The medium has industrialized the concept with an approach called BrandVoice that allows marketers to connect directly with the *Forbes* audience by enabling them to create content on the *Forbes* digital publishing platform. An important part of the new *Forbes* architecture is a platform called ADVOICE which is an approach to integrating editorial content, user content, and marketers' content and allows marketers to tell their own story in their own words. All content on the platform is clearly labeled and transparent so readers know who is talking and the perspective from which they speak.

There are a number of reasons why online publishers are turning to native advertising models. One of the reasons is that online readers of a publication are more likely

Vietnamese, and Filipinos. In the United States, there are newspapers printed in more than 40 languages.

Newspapers targeted at various religious groups compose another large class of special-interest papers. For example, more than 140 Catholic newspapers are published across the United States. Another type of special-audience newspaper is one most of you probably read regularly during the school year, the college newspaper. More than 1,300 colleges and universities publish newspapers and offer advertisers an excellent medium for reaching college students, who are a difficult target audience for marketers to reach.

**Newspaper Supplements**   Although not a category of newspapers per se, many papers include magazine-type supplements, primarily in their Sunday editions. Sunday supplements have been part of most newspapers for many years and come in various forms. One type is the syndicated Sunday magazine, such as *Parade* or *USA Weekend*, distributed in hundreds of papers throughout the country. *Parade* is distributed through more than 500 newspapers and reaches 62 million readers (Exhibit 12–17); *USA Weekend* is carried by more than 800 newspapers and is seen by 22 million readers every weekend. These publications are similar to national magazines and carry both national and regional advertising.

Some large newspapers publish local Sunday supplements distributed by the parent paper. These supplements contain stories of local interest, and both local and national advertisers buy ad space. *The New York Times Sunday Magazine* is the to respond favorably to something that does not look like advertising but rather takes the form of the surrounding content on the web page. Publishers also recognize that they must move beyond traditional advertising formats such as various types of banner ads and offer advertisers something new and different to help their brands stand out. They also can charge more for various forms of native advertising as ads that appear next to custom or sponsored content have been shown to be more effective in terms of metrics such as awareness, engagement, measurable clicks, and sharing with others. These effectiveness measures are very enticing to marketers who view these types of ads as a way to get a greater ROI on their advertising budgets.

While native advertising offers many benefits to both online publishers as well as marketers, some concerns have been noted over the practice as critics argue that they are threatening one of the most important assets of a magazine—its relationship with readers. The church-and-state divide of editorial versus advertising has always been important; magazine and newspaper publishers regard the separation as essential to their independence and credibility. For years the American Society of Magazine Editors (ASME) has maintained guidelines upholding that separation. ASME guidelines state that ad pages should not be related to editorial material in a manner that implies editorial endorsement. The guidelines also state that advertiser-provided content should be clearly labeled as advertising, and the source of the content and the affiliation of the authors should be clearly acknowledged.

Some critics believe that native advertising is a way to get around the traditional church-and-state wall between advertising and editorial content. For example, in January 2013 *The Atlantic* came under criticism for running what many felt was a subtly sponsored post promoting the Church of Scientology, which reported that the controversial religion of Scientology had a milestone year and was expanding at a record pace under ecclesiastical leader David Miscavige. Opponents of the Church argued that the native ad resembled an *Atlantic* article while supporters defended its by noting that it was labeled as sponsored content. However, *The Atlantic* took down the native ad following an eruption of criticism and issued a statement indicating that it would review its policies as it explores new forms of digital advertising.

The pressure on magazines to respond to the demands of marketers to allow a mixing of advertising with content is getting greater, particularly since many publications are facing declines in circulation. Industry executives argue that magazines will have to adapt to remain competitive and need more flexibility to compete with other media. Critics will continue to argue that the church-and-state division lies at the heart of what magazines and newspapers sell to their readers, as well as the advertisers themselves. However, what the advertisers really want is for magazine readers to notice their ads, and native advertising may be a way of ensuring they will do so.

Sources: Frederic Filloux, "What's the Fuss about Native Ads?" Mondaynote.com, April 21, 2013, www.mondaynote.com/2013/04/21/whats-the-fuss-about-native-ads/; Mitch Joel, "We Need a Better Definition of 'Native Advertising,'" *Harvard Business Review Blog Network*, February 13, 2013, http://blogs.hbr.org/cs/2013/02/we_need_a_better_definition_of.html; Nat Ives, "The Atlantic Apologizes for 'Screw Up' on Scientology Advertorial," *Advertising Age*, January 15, 2013, http://adage.com/article/media/atlantic-pulls-advertorial-promoting-scientology/239185/; Jason Del Rey, "Native Advertising: Media Savior or Just the New Custom Campaign?" *Advertising Age*, October 29, 2012, pp. 12–13.

**YTC 12–05**

**Native Advertising**

youtube.com/10ebelch

best-known local supplement. The *Washington Post, San Francisco Examiner,* and *Los Angeles Times* have their own Sunday magazines.

In some areas, papers have begun carrying regional supplements as well as specialized weekday supplements that cover specific topics such as food, sports, or entertainment. Supplements are valuable to advertisers that want to use the newspaper yet get four-color reproduction quality in their ads.

## Types of Newspaper Advertising

LO 12-1

The ads appearing in newspapers can also be divided into different categories. The major types of newspaper advertising are display and classified. Other special types of ads and preprinted inserts also appear in newspapers.

**Display Advertising** **Display advertising** is found throughout the newspaper and generally uses illustrations, headlines, white space, and other visual devices in addition to the copy text. The two types of display advertising in newspapers are local and national (general).

*Local advertising* refers to ads placed by local organizations, businesses, and individuals who want to communicate with consumers in the market area served by the newspaper. Supermarkets and department stores are among the leading local display advertisers, along with numerous other retailers and service operations such as banks and travel agents. Local advertising is sometimes referred to as retail advertising because retailers account for 85 percent of local display ads.

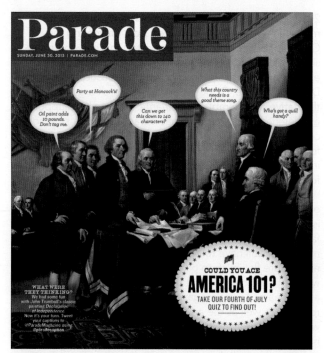

**EXHIBIT 12–17**
*Parade* is a popular Sunday
supplement

LO 12-2

**EXHIBIT 12–18**
Newspaper inserts are used
to reach target markets

*National* or *general advertising* refers to newspaper display advertising done by marketers of branded products or services that are sold on a national or regional level. These ads are designed to create and maintain demand for a company's product or service and to complement the efforts of local retailers that stock and promote the advertiser's products. Major retail chains, automakers, and airlines are heavy users of newspaper advertising.

**Classified Advertising**   **Classified advertising** also provides newspapers with a substantial amount of revenue. These ads are arranged under subheads according to the product, service, or offering being advertised. Employment, real estate, and automotive are the three major categories of classified advertising. While most classified ads are just text set in small type, some newspapers also accept classified display advertising. These ads are run in the classified section of the paper but use illustrations, larger type sizes, white space, borders, and even color to stand out.

**Special Ads and Inserts**   Special advertisements in newspapers include a variety of government and financial reports and notices and public notices of changes in business and personal relationships. Other types of advertising in newspapers include political or special-interest ads promoting a particular candidate, issue, or cause. **Preprinted inserts** are another type of advertising distributed through newspapers. These ads do not appear in the paper itself; they are printed by the advertiser and then taken to the newspaper to be inserted before delivery. Many retailers use inserts such as circulars, catalogs, or brochures in specific circulation zones to reach shoppers in their particular trade areas. Exhibit 12–18 shows how the *San Diego Union-Tribune* promotes its insert distribution service to advertisers.

## Advantages of Newspapers

Newspapers have a number of characteristics that make them popular among both local and national advertisers. These include their extensive penetration of local markets, flexibility, geographic selectivity, reader involvement, and special services.

**Market Penetration**   One of the primary advantages of newspapers is the high market coverage or penetration, they offer an advertiser. In most areas, 40 percent or more of households read a daily newspaper, and the reach figure may exceed 60 percent among households with higher incomes and education levels. Most areas are served by one or two daily newspapers, and often the same company owns both, publishing a morning and an evening edition. By making one space buy, the advertiser can achieve a high level of overall reach in a particular market.

The extensive penetration of newspapers makes them a mass medium and provides advertisers with an excellent opportunity for reaching all segments of the population with their message. Also, since many newspapers are published and read daily, the advertiser can build a high level of frequency into the media schedule.

**Flexibility**   Another advantage of newspapers is the flexibility they offer advertisers. First, they are flexible in terms of requirements

## CONGRATULATIONS

San Diego's Own Callaway Golf Company
Congratulates San Diego's Own Phil Mickelson.
**Champion Golfer of the Year.**
#BRINGIT

**EXHIBIT 12–19**
Callaway Golf used a
newspaper ad for a timely
ad congratulating golfer Phil
Mickelson

for producing and running the ads. Newspaper ads can be written, laid out, and prepared in a matter of hours. For most dailies, the closing time by which the ad must be received is usually only 24 hours before publication (although closing dates for special ads, such as those using color, and Sunday supplements are longer). The short production time and closing dates make newspapers an excellent medium for responding to current events or presenting timely information to readers. For, example, the Callaway Golf Company ran a newspaper ad congratulating professional golfer Phil Mickelson for winning the 2013 British Open golf tournament the day following the final round of the prestigious event. Mickelson is a member of the Callaway Golf team, and the ad was a very timely way to acknowledge his accomplishment and promote his use of Callaway golf equipment (Exhibit 12–19).

A second dimension of newspapers' flexibility stems from the creative options they make available to advertisers. Newspaper ads can be produced and run in various sizes, shapes, and formats; they can use color or special inserts to gain the interest of readers. Ads can be run in Sunday magazines or other supplements, and a variety of scheduling options are possible, depending on the advertiser's purpose.

**Geographic Selectivity**  Newspapers generally offer advertisers more geographic or territorial selectivity than any other medium except direct mail. Advertisers can vary their coverage by choosing a paper—or combination of papers—that reaches the areas with the greatest sales potential. National advertisers take advantage of the geographic selectivity of newspapers to concentrate their advertising in specific areas they can't reach with other media or to take advantage of strong sales potential in a particular area. For example, BMW, Mercedes, and Land Rover use heavy newspaper media schedules in California and New York/New Jersey to capitalize on the high sales potential for luxury import cars in these markets.

A number of companies use newspapers in their regional marketing strategies. Newspaper advertising lets them feature products on a market-by-market basis, respond and adapt campaigns to local market conditions, and tie into more retailer promotions, fostering more support from the trade.

Local advertisers like retailers are interested in geographic selectivity or flexibility within a specific market or trade area. Their media goal is to concentrate their advertising on the areas where most of their customers are. Many newspapers now offer advertisers various geographic areas or zones for this purpose. For example, the *Chicago Tribune* offers advertisers five different circulation area zones, as shown in Exhibit 12–20.

**Reader Involvement and Acceptance**  Another important feature of newspapers is consumers' level of acceptance and involvement with papers and the ads they contain. The typical daily newspaper reader spends time each day reading the weekday newspaper and even more time reading the Sunday paper. Most consumers rely heavily on newspapers not only for news, information, and entertainment but also for assistance with consumption decisions.

Many consumers actually purchase a newspaper *because* of the advertising it contains. Consumers use retail ads to determine product prices and availability and to see who is having a sale. One aspect of newspapers that is helpful to advertisers is readers' knowledge about particular sections of the paper. Most of us know that ads for automotive products and sporting goods are generally found in the sports section, while ads for financial services are found in the business section. The weekly food section in many newspapers is popular for recipe and menu ideas as well as for the grocery store ads and coupons offered by many stores and companies.

The value of newspaper advertising as a source of information has been shown in several studies. One study found that consumers look forward to ads in newspapers more than in other media. In another study, 80 percent of consumers said newspaper

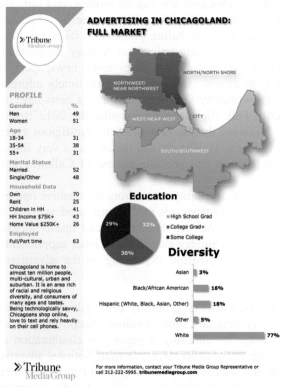

ADVERTISING IN CHICAGOLAND:
FULL MARKET

**PROFILE**

Gender | %
Men | 49
Women | 51

Age
18-34 | 31
35-54 | 38
55+ | 31

Marital Status
Married | 52
Single/Other | 48

Household Data
Own | 70
Rent | 25
Children in HH | 41
HH Income $75K+ | 43
Home Value $250K+ | 26

Employed
Full/Part time | 63

Chicagoland is home to almost ten million people, multi-cultural, urban and suburban. It is an area rich of racial and religious diversity, and consumers of many ages and tastes. Being technologically savvy, Chicagoans shop online, love to text and rely heavily on their cell phones.

**Education**

29% ■ High School Grad
32% ■ College Grad+
30% ■ Some College

**Diversity**

Asian | 3%
Black/African American | 16%
Hispanic (White, Black, Asian, Other) | 18%
Other | 5%
White | 77%

Source: Scarborough Research 2011 R2, Base 7,230,326 Adults 18+ in Chicagoland

» Tribune
MediaGroup

For more information, contact your Tribune Media Group Representative or call 312-222-5995. tribunemediagroup.com

**EXHIBIT 12–20**
The *Chicago Tribune* offers advertisers combinations of different circulation area zones

LO 12-2

**EXHIBIT 12–21**
Newspaper publishers are often an excellent source for information on local markets

ads were most helpful to them in doing their weekly shopping. Newspaper advertising has also been rated the most believable form of advertising in numerous studies.

**Services Offered**   The special services newspapers offer can be valuable to advertisers. For example, many newspapers offer merchandising services and programs to manufacturers that make the trade aware of ads being run for the company's product and help convince local retailers they should stock, display, and promote the item.

Many newspapers are also excellent sources of local market information through their knowledge of market conditions and research like readership studies and consumer surveys. For example, the publisher of the *San Diego Union-Tribune,* the major daily newspaper in San Diego, provides information on the local market through various reports and market studies (Exhibit 12–21).

Newspapers can also assist small companies through free copywriting and art services. Small advertisers without an agency or advertising department often rely on the newspaper to help them write and produce their ads.

## Limitations of Newspapers

While newspapers have many advantages, like all media they also have disadvantages that media planners must consider. The limitations of newspapers include their reproduction problems, short life span, lack of selectivity, and clutter.

**Poor Reproduction**   One of the greatest limitations of newspapers as an advertising medium is their poor reproduction quality. The coarse paper stock used for newspapers, the absence of color, and the lack of time papers have available to achieve high-quality reproduction limit the quality of most newspaper ads. Newspapers have improved their reproduction quality in recent years, and color reproduction has become more available. Also, advertisers desiring high-quality color in newspaper ads can turn to such alternatives as freestanding inserts or Sunday supplements. However, these are more costly and may not be desirable to many advertisers. As a general rule, if the visual appearance of the product is important, the advertiser will not rely on newspaper ads. Ads for food products and fashions generally use magazines to capitalize on their superior reproduction quality and color.

**Short Life Span**   Unlike magazines, which may be retained around the house for several weeks, a daily newspaper is generally kept less than a day. So an ad is unlikely to have any impact beyond the day of publication, and repeat exposure is very unlikely. Compounding this problem are the short amount of time many consumers spend with the newspaper and the possibility they may not even open certain sections of the paper. Media planners can offset these problems somewhat by using high frequency in the newspaper schedule and advertising in a section where consumers who are in the market for a particular product or service are likely to look. Figure 12–3 on page 443 shows readership figures for various sections of newspapers by gender, income, and education level.

FIGURE 12-3

Daily Newspaper Section Readership

| | BASE READERS | | | HOUSEHOLD INCOME | | | EDUCATION | | |
|---|---|---|---|---|---|---|---|---|---|
| | Mon.–Fri. | Men | Women | Less than $50K | $50K–$99K | $100,000 or More | High School Graduate or Less | Any College | College Grad + |
| Base Total | 100.0% | 100.0% | 100.0% | 100.0% | 100.0% | 100.0% | 100.0% | 100.0% | 100.0% |
| **Newspaper sections generally looked at/read Mon.–Fri.** | | | | | | | | | |
| Main news/front-page section | 79.9% | 79.2% | 80.6% | 78.1% | 81.2% | 81.7% | 77.6% | 81.5% | 82.5% |
| Local news section | 74.6 | 73.4 | 75.7 | 74.0 | 75.8 | 74.1 | 74.1 | 75.0 | 75.4 |
| Sports pages/section | 55.7 | 67.3 | 44.3 | 53.4 | 57.5 | 57.6 | 55.3 | 55.9 | 57.2 |
| Entertainment/lifestyle pages/section | 54.5 | 50.3 | 58.5 | 53.3 | 55.8 | 54.9 | 52.4 | 55.9 | 57.2 |
| International/national news | 53.2 | 55.9 | 50.6 | 52.0 | 53.7 | 54.8 | 51.2 | 54.6 | 56.8 |
| Comics | 53.0 | 53.9 | 52.1 | 54.7 | 52.7 | 50.0 | 53.4 | 52.7 | 52.2 |
| Advertising circulars/inserts/flyers | 51.4 | 48.4 | 54.4 | 51.8 | 52.7 | 48.8 | 52.1 | 51.0 | 50.2 |
| Food/cooking pages/section | 51.0 | 45.4 | 56.4 | 50.9 | 51.4 | 50.4 | 50.3 | 51.4 | 51.7 |
| Editorial/opinion pages | 49.8 | 50.9 | 48.8 | 48.8 | 50.6 | 50.8 | 48.0 | 51.1 | 53.0 |
| Classified advertising | 49.7 | 50.0 | 49.4 | 53.2 | 49.0 | 43.9 | 53.0 | 47.4 | 45.1 |
| Business/finance pages/section | 48.9 | 53.3 | 44.5 | 45.2 | 50.3 | 53.9 | 45.8 | 50.9 | 54.0 |
| Movie listings and reviews | 47.2 | 46.4 | 47.9 | 47.6 | 47.5 | 45.7 | 46.7 | 47.4 | 47.6 |
| Home and garden pages/section | 47.1 | 43.9 | 50.4 | 46.5 | 47.8 | 47.3 | 46.6 | 47.5 | 48.0 |
| TV or radio listings | 45.0 | 44.7 | 45.3 | 46.8 | 44.7 | 41.8 | 46.2 | 44.2 | 43.9 |
| Science and technology pages/section | 43.9 | 47.1 | 40.7 | 43.0 | 44.4 | 44.8 | 42.6 | 44.7 | 46.3 |
| Fashion pages/section | 42.3 | 39.6 | 45.0 | 42.3 | 42.7 | 41.6 | 42.5 | 42.2 | 42.6 |

Source: prepared by the Newspaper Association of America www.naa.org.

CHAPTER 12

**Lack of Selectivity** While newspapers can offer advertisers geographic selectivity, they are not a selective medium in terms of demographics or lifestyle characteristics. Most newspapers reach broad and very diverse groups of consumers, which makes it difficult for marketers to focus on narrowly defined market segments. For example, manufacturers of fishing rods and reels will find newspapers very inefficient because of the wasted coverage that results from reaching all the newspaper readers who don't fish. Thus, they are more likely to use special-interest magazines such as *Field & Stream* and *Fishing World*. Any newspaper ads for their products will be done through cooperative plans whereby retailers share the costs or spread them over a number of sporting goods featured in the ad.

**Clutter** Newspapers, like most other advertising media, suffer from clutter as the advertiser's message must compete with numerous other ads for consumers' attention and interest. Moreover, the creative options in newspapers are limited by the fact that most ads are black and white. Thus, it can be difficult for a newspaper advertiser to break through the clutter without using costly measures such as large space buys or color.

Many newspapers are now offering advertisers the opportunity to use innovative shape-based ads that utilize unconventional sizes and formats such as stairsteps, bookends, U-shapes, island ads, spadea ads, and half-page spreads. Many newspapers are also now accepting ads on the front page of their publications as well as on the first page of various sections of the paper. The use of these innovative formats makes it possible for advertisers to more easily attract the attention of readers and increase recall of their advertising message. Exhibit 12–22 shows a page from the media kit for the *Los Angeles Times* promoting several of the innovative ad forms that the paper now offers advertisers.

## The Newspaper Audience

As with any medium, the media planner must understand the nature and size of the audience reached by a newspaper in considering its value in the media plan. Since newspapers as a class of media do an excellent job of penetrating their market, the typical daily newspaper gives advertisers the opportunity to reach most of the households in a market. But, while local advertisers aim to cover a particular market or trade area, national advertisers want to reach broad regions or even the entire country. They must purchase space in a number of papers to achieve the desired level of coverage.

The basic sources of information concerning the audience size of newspapers come from the circulation figures available through rate cards, publishers' statements, or SRDS's *Newspaper Advertising Source*. Circulation figures for many newspapers are verified by the Alliance for Audited Media (AAM), which was discussed earlier. Advertisers that use a number of papers in their media plan generally find SRDS the most convenient source.

Newspaper circulation figures are generally broken down into three categories: the city zone, the retail trading zone, and all other areas. The **city zone** is a market area composed of the city where the paper is published and contiguous areas similar in character to the city. The **retail trading zone** is the market outside the city zone whose residents regularly trade with merchants within the city zone. The "all other" category covers all circulation not included in the city or retail trade zone.

Sometimes circulation figures are provided only for the primary market, which is the city and retail trade zones combined, and the other area. Both local

**LO 12-3**

**EXHIBIT 12–22**
The *Los Angeles Times* promotes the innovative advertising shapes it now offers

**Innovative Advertising**

Bookend          Stairstep

14

and national advertisers consider the circulation patterns across the various categories in evaluating and selecting newspapers.

National advertisers often buy newspaper space on the basis of the size of the market area they cover. For example, General Motors might decide to purchase advertising in the top 10 markets, the top 50 markets, the top 100 markets, and so on. A national advertiser gets different levels of market coverage depending on the number of market areas purchased.

**Audience Information**   Circulation figures provide the media planner with the basic data for assessing the value of newspapers and their ability to cover various market areas. However, the media planner also wants to match the characteristics of a newspaper's readers with those of the advertiser's target audience. Data on newspaper audience size and characteristics are available from studies conducted by the papers as well as from commercial research services. As for magazines, a very valuable source for information on newspapers is the SRDS, whose print and online service provides complete planning information on daily papers, newspaper groups, ethnic newspapers, college newspapers, comics, and newspaper-distributed magazines. The SRDS *Newspaper Advertising Source* data contain standardized ad rates, circulation figures, dates, general requirements, contact information, and other valuable information for media.

Companies such as Experian Simmons and GfK MRI provide syndicated research studies on lifestyles, media behavior, and product/brand preferences that include information on newspapers. These studies can be valuable for comparing newspapers with other media vehicles.

Many newspapers commission their own audience studies to provide current and potential advertisers with information on readership and characteristics of readers such as demographics, shopping habits, and lifestyles. These studies are often designed to promote the effectiveness of the newspaper in reaching various types of consumers. Since they are sponsored by the paper itself, many advertisers are skeptical of their results. Careful attention must be given to the research methods used and conclusions drawn by these studies.

## Purchasing Newspaper Space

Advertisers are faced with a number of options and pricing structures when purchasing newspaper space. The cost of advertising space depends not only on the newspaper's circulation but also on factors such as premium charges for color or special sections as well as discounts available. The purchase process and the rates paid for newspaper space differ for general and local advertisers.

**General versus Local Rates**   Newspapers have different rate structures for general or national advertisers and local or retail advertisers. **General advertising rates** apply to display advertisers outside the newspaper's designated market area (DMA) and to any classification deemed by the publisher to be "general" in nature. This includes ads run by national advertisers such as automotive, tobacco, packaged-goods, and pharmaceutical companies. **Retail** or **local advertising rates** apply to advertisers that conduct business or sell goods or services within the DMA. The rates paid by general advertisers are, on average, 75 percent higher than those paid by local advertisers. Newspaper publishers claim the rate differential is justified for several reasons. First, they argue it costs more to handle general advertising since ad agencies get a 15 percent commission and commissions must also be paid to the independent sales reps who solicit nonlocal advertising. Second, they note that general advertising is less dependable than local advertising; general advertisers usually don't use newspapers on a continual basis the way local advertisers do. Finally, newspaper publishers contend that demand for general advertising is inelastic—it will not increase if rates are lowered or decrease if rates are raised. This means there is no incentive to lower the national advertisers' rates.

**EXHIBIT 12–23**

The Newspaper National Network helps advertisers run ads across multiple markets

National advertisers do not view these arguments as valid justification for the rate differential. They argue that the costs are not greater for handling national advertising than for local business and that many national advertisers use newspapers on a regular basis. Since they use an agency to prepare their ads, national advertisers are less likely to request special services. The large and costly staff maintained by many newspapers to assist in the design and preparation of advertising is used mostly by local advertisers.

The differential rate structure for national versus local advertising has been the source of considerable controversy. Some newspapers are making efforts to narrow the rate differential, as is the Newspaper Association of America (NAA). In 1993, the NAA created the Newspaper National Network (NNN) to target national advertisers in six low-use categories: automotive, cosmetics and toiletries, food, household products, liquor and beverages, and drugs and remedies.[37] The network's goal is to attract more advertising dollars from national advertisers in these categories by promoting the strategic use of newspapers and facilitating the purchase of newspaper space with their one order–one bill model. Exhibit 12–23 shows how the NNN promotes its geotargeting service through which it works with advertisers and their agencies to help them run multimarket advertising campaigns in various cities across the country.

Many marketers sidestep the national advertiser label and the higher rates by channeling their newspaper ads through special category plans, cooperative advertising deals with retailers, and local dealers and distributors that pay local rates. However, the rate differential does keep many national advertisers from making newspapers a larger part of their media mix.

## Newspaper Rates

Traditionally, newspaper space for national advertisers has been sold by the agate line. The problem is that newspapers use columns of varying width. Some have six columns per page, while others have eight or nine, which affects the size, shape, and costs of an ad. This results in a complicated production and buying process for national advertisers purchasing space in a number of newspapers.

To address this problem and make newspapers more comparable to other media that sell space and time in standard units, the newspaper industry switched to **standard advertising units (SAUs)** in 1984. All newspapers under this system use column widths 2-1/16 inches wide, with tabloid-size papers five columns wide and standard or broadcast papers six columns. The column inch is the unit of measurement to create the standard broadsheet or tabloid ad size.

A national advertiser can prepare one ad in a particular SAU, and it will fit every newspaper in the country that uses that format size. Rates are quoted on that basis. Since most daily newspapers use the SAU system, the purchase and production process has been simplified tremendously for national advertisers.

Newspaper rates for local advertisers continue to be based on the column inch, which is 1 inch deep by 1 column wide. Advertising rates for local advertisers are quoted per column inch, and media planners calculate total space costs by multiplying the ad's number of column inches by the cost per inch.

**Rate Structures**   While the column inch and SAU are used to determine basic newspaper advertising rates, the media planner must consider other options and factors. Many newspapers charge **flat rates**, which means they offer no discount for quantity or repeated space buys. Others have an **open-rate structure**, which means various discounts are available. These discounts are generally based on frequency or bulk purchases of space and depend on the number of column inches purchased in a year.

Newspaper space rates also vary with an advertiser's special requests, such as preferred position or color. The basic rates quoted by a newspaper are **run of paper**

**(ROP)**, which means the paper can place the ad on any page or in any position it desires. While most newspapers try to place an ad in a requested position, the advertiser can ensure a specific section and/or position on a page by paying a higher **preferred position rate**. Color advertising is also available in many newspapers on an ROP basis or through preprinted inserts or Sunday supplements.

Advertisers can also buy newspaper space based on **combination rates**, where they get a discount for using several newspapers as a group. Typically, a combination rate occurs when a publisher owns both a morning and an evening newspaper in a market and offers a reduced single rate for running the same ad in both newspapers, generally within a 24-hour period. Combination discounts are also available when the advertiser buys space in several newspapers owned by the publisher in a number of markets or in multiple newspapers affiliated in a syndicate or newspaper group.

## The Future for Newspapers

Newspapers remain an important advertising medium, but as noted at the beginning of the chapter, advertising revenue for traditional print papers has declined dramatically over the past several years. Newspapers generate most of their advertising revenue from local advertisers, particularly retailers who use display ads to advertise their products and services and inform consumers of sales and other types of promotions. Newspapers account for less than 5 percent of advertising expenditures for national advertisers, so they are very dependent on regional and local marketers for their advertising revenue.

Newspapers' major strength lies in their role as a medium that can be used effectively by local advertisers on a continual basis. It is unlikely that newspapers' importance to local advertisers will change in the near future. However, there are a number of problems and issues newspapers must address to maintain their strong position as a dominant local advertising medium and to gain more national advertising. These include competition from other advertising media, maintaining and managing circulation, cross-media opportunities, and declining readership.

**Competition from Other Media**   The newspaper industry's battle to increase its share of national advertising volume has been difficult. In addition to the problems of reproduction quality and rate differentials, newspapers face competition from other media for both national and local advertisers' budgets.

The intermedia battle that newspapers find themselves involved in is no longer limited to national advertising. Many companies are using the Internet as a marketing tool and a place to invest advertising dollars that might otherwise go to newspapers. Local radio and TV stations (particularly cable stations), as well as the expanding number of Yellow Pages publishers, are aggressively pursuing local advertisers. Newspapers will have to fight harder to retain those advertisers.

Newspapers are also facing new competition from various online sites for classified and employment advertising, which have long been important major profit centers. Classified advertising revenue for U.S. newspapers has declined steadily since

**FIGURE 12–4**

Decline in Newspaper Classified Advertising Revenue 2000 to 2012

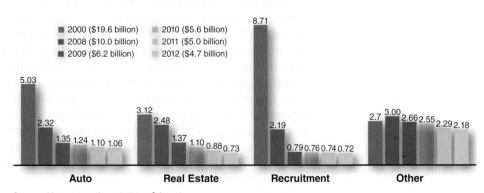

Source: Newspaper Association of America

2000, declining from nearly $20 billion to just $4.7 billion in 2012. As shown in Figure 12–4, reductions in classified advertising have occurred across all three of the major categories, including automotive, real estate, and recruitment ads. Newspapers must now compete against online employment sites such as Monster and Job.com for job listings. Websites such as eBay and Craigslist have become very popular ways for selling a variety of merchandise that traditionally was sold through classified ads in local newspapers. Craigslist, which began as a type of counterculture message board for young people in the San Francisco area, has now expanded to most major cities and has become popular among people of all ages. The online site includes sections for selling merchandise, apartment rentals, services, personals, and job listings. Some newspapers are recognizing that it is very difficult to compete against online sites for classified ads and are responding by offering free classified ads for merchandise under certain price points as a way to grow readership.

Newspapers are doing a number of other things to respond to the challenges from other media. Many papers have expanded their marketing capabilities and are making efforts to develop and sustain relationships with their advertisers. Some have created sophisticated databases and direct-mail capabilities, which they offer as value-added services. Others are increasing their marketing research departments, preparing comprehensive market studies for major customers, and, in some cases, serving as media advisors and marketing partners.

**Circulation**   The newspaper industry has been struggling for years to reverse declining circulation.[38] Most of the major newspapers in the United States have been experiencing a decline in circulation and are seeking ways to respond to the problem, such as by emphasizing readership measures and developing online versions of their papers. Like magazines, many newspapers are taking a closer look at their circulation and analyzing whether the cost of getting additional circulation is justified by the advertising revenue it generates. Many papers are raising newsstand and home delivery rates, and circulation revenue is accounting for more of their total revenue.

Several major metropolitan newspapers have found that advertisers use newspapers to reach consumers within specific geographic areas and do not want to pay for readers in outlying areas. Thus, some papers are eliminating what has been called "ego circulation" and focusing more on regional editions in their immediate trade area.

Newspapers have found that it is more cost-effective to focus on retaining subscribers rather than spending large sums of money to acquire new ones. The cancellation rate for newspaper subscribers has leveled off according to statistics from the Newspaper Association of America. These numbers reflect the fact that many newspapers are focusing more on retention of their core readers and offering programs such as discounts for automatic renewal payment plans.[39]

**Attracting and Retaining Readers**   The growth of newspapers as an advertising medium may be limited by the reduced popularity of the medium itself. Newspaper readership has been on a steady decline over the past decade. The percentage of the adult population reading a newspaper on the average weekday has declined from 78 percent in 1970 to 42 percent more recently. The percentage of Americans who say they regularly read a daily newspaper has declined from 54 percent in 2004 to 38 percent in 2012, while the percentage reading a print newspaper is even lower.[40] Moreover, many of those who do read newspapers now read them digitally. Readership of newspapers is somewhat higher across a typical week as print readership increases to 60 percent and print plus digital increases to 66 percent. However, the fact remains that the percentage of households receiving a print newspaper and reading it on a daily basis has declined dramatically over the past several decades.[41] The decline in newspaper readership can be attributed to several factors, including the fast-paced, time-poor lifestyle of the modern dual-income household and the increase in viewing options of TV, and of course, competition from the Internet.

**EXHIBIT 12–24**

The "Smart is the new sexy" campaign promotes the value of newspapers

A number of newspapers have been redesigned to be more interesting and easier and faster to read. Changes include the increased use of color and graphics as well as expanded coverage of sports and entertainment. Some papers have begun providing short summaries of articles in each section of the paper so readers can skim them and decide what they want to read.

Of particular concern to publishers is the decline in newspaper readership among important market segments such as women and young adults. Surveys show that the percentage of women who read a newspaper on a typical day declined from 67 percent in 1981 to 39 percent recently.[42] Newspapers and advertisers are concerned because women are far more likely than men to make buying decisions. Many newspapers are introducing new women's sections and revising old ones to make them more appealing to modern women. This means including articles on such issues as health, parenting, and careers—for example, how women with children and jobs manage their time.

Newspapers are also concerned about where their future readers will come from, since many young people are heavy TV viewers and also are spending more and more time surfing the Internet and on social media.

The newspaper industry is taking steps to address the problem of declining readership and to promote the value of newspapers. For example, the Newspaper Association of America recently sponsored the "Smart is the new sexy" ad campaign to reinforce the value of newspapers to existing and prospective readers (Exhibit 12–24). The campaign uses a series of ads with engaging illustrations to point out the distinctive editorial, advertising, and community attributes delivered by newspapers. The integrated campaign also uses digital and social media to promote online dialogue around newspapers and to highlight the multiplatform experience provided by newspapers. QR codes and digital prompts link audiences to the website for the campaign (www.naa.org/smartsexy), where they can read more about the "Smart–Sexy" newspaper connection. They are also encouraged to share their own connection with newspapers by tweeting with the #smartsexy hashtag or by posting comments or video clips to the NAA's Facebook page.[43]

## Online Delivery and Multiple Platforms

The digital transformation of media has hit the newspaper industry particularly hard and resulted in newspaper publishers broadening their portfolios well beyond the tradition printed page. Nearly every major newspaper now has a website, and most make their papers available online. The number of daily and weekly U.S. newspapers available online increased from less than 100 in 1995 to more than 3,000 in 2013. The digital newspaper audience increased from 70 million unique users per month in 2007 to nearly 114 million in 2013, while the average number of daily visitors to newspaper websites was nearly 23 million.[44] Publishers recognize that they must offer online versions of their newspapers as this has become the preferred mode of reading for many people, particularly younger consumers. Studies have shown that people who use online newspapers are highly engaged and are an upscale audience—they spend more time online, are better educated, and have higher incomes than online audiences in general. They are also more likely to make purchases online and to use the Internet to help them decide what to buy.[45]

Many newspapers are working to attract advertising dollars from both local and national advertisers. Networks are also forming to help local newspapers sell online ads on their websites to national advertisers. For example, the National Newspaper Network provides national advertisers with access to newspaper websites across the country and facilitates the purchase of online ads in the same way it does with traditional print ads. While newspaper publishers are focusing more attention on the sale of online advertising, they are also facing strong competition from the major Internet search players such as Google, Yahoo! Bing, and Local.com because these companies have made it inexpensive and easy for local companies to run ads with them. Many newspapers are forming alliances with these Internet search competitors whereby they can use their technology to sell more sophisticated ad offerings, such as behaviorally targeted ads.[46]

Most newspaper publishers are transforming themselves into *media* companies with products that include print and online newspapers, apps for those who read newspapers on mobile devices, and websites that include multiple products and services. By creating a variety of products and engaging consumers across multiple platforms, these companies can capitalize on new revenue opportunities that will undoubtedly present themselves in the future.

## Summary

Magazines and newspapers, the two major forms of print media, play an important role in the media plans and strategy of many advertisers. Magazines are a very selective medium and are very valuable for reaching specific types of customers and market segments. The three broad categories of magazines are consumer, farm, and business publications. Each of these categories can be further classified according to the publication's editorial content and audience appeal.

In addition to their selectivity, the advantages of magazines include their excellent reproduction quality, creative flexibility, long life, prestige, and readers' high receptivity to magazine advertising, as well as the services they offer to advertisers. Disadvantages of magazines include their high cost, limited reach and frequency, long lead time, and the advertising clutter in most publications.

Advertising space rates in magazines vary according to a number of factors, among them the size of the ad, position in the publication, particular editions purchased, use of color, and number and frequency of insertions. Rates for magazines are compared on the basis of the cost per thousand, although other factors such as the editorial content of the publication and its ability to reach specific target audiences must also be considered.

Newspapers are a very important medium to local advertisers, especially retailers. They are also used by national advertisers, although the differential rate structure for national versus local advertisers is a source of controversy. Newspapers are a broad-based medium that reaches a large percentage of households in a particular area. Newspapers' other advantages include flexibility, geographic selectivity, reader involvement, and special services. Drawbacks of newspapers include their lack of high-quality ad reproduction, short life span, lack of audience selectivity, and clutter.

Trends toward market segmentation and regional marketing are prompting many advertisers to make more use of newspapers and magazines. However, both magazines and newspapers face increasing competition from such other media as radio, cable TV, direct marketing, and the Internet. Both magazines and newspapers are working to improve the quality of their circulation bases, offer database marketing services, and initiate cross-media deals. Rising costs and declining readership are problems for many magazines and newspapers. Both magazines and newspapers are making their publications available across multiple platforms, as a way to retain readers and grow advertising revenue.

## Key Terms

selectivity p. 421
gatefolds p. 424
bleed pages p. 424
split runs p. 427
selective binding p. 427
ink-jet imaging p. 427
controlled-circulation basis p. 431
pass-along readership p. 431
total audience/readership p. 431
first cover p. 433

second cover p. 433
third cover p. 433
fourth cover p. 433
magazine networks p. 434
native advertising p. 436
display advertising p. 439
classified advertising p. 440
preprinted inserts p. 440
city zone p. 444
retail trading zone p. 444

general advertising rates p. 445
retail or local advertising rates p. 445
standard advertising units (SAUs) p. 446
flat rates p. 446
open-rate structure p. 446
run of paper (ROP) p. 446
preferred position rate p. 447
combination rates p. 447

1.  Discuss the digital disruption that is impacting the traditional print media of newspapers and magazines. What are some of the ways publishers can respond to these changes and attract and retain advertisers? (LO1)

2.  Discuss how mobile devices such as the iPad and other types of tablet computers are impacting magazines and newspapers as advertising media vehicles. Do you agree with Jann Wenner, publisher of *Rolling Stone* and other magazines, that it will take a decade or more before there is a shift from print magazines to digital editions? (LO1, 2)

3.  Discuss the role of magazines as part of an advertiser's media strategy. What are the advantages and limitations of magazines? (LO1, 2)

4.  What is meant by selectivity with regard to the purchase of advertising media? Discuss the various ways magazines offer selectivity to advertisers. (LO2)

5.  What is meant by native advertising? Do you think it is appropriate for advertisers to run native ads that appear to be editorial content rather than sponsored advertising? Why or why not? (LO4)

6.  If you were purchasing print advertising space for a manufacturer of golf clubs such as Callaway or TaylorMade, what factors would you consider? Would your selection of magazines be limited to golf publications? Why or why not? (LO3)

7.  Discuss some of the reasons why marketers would want to advertise in a college newspaper. Analyze the types of companies that advertise in the newspaper published by your university. (LO1, 3)

8.  What are the major challenges facing the newspaper industry and the use of newspapers as an advertising medium? How can newspapers respond to these challenges? (LO4)

9.  What are some of the reasons there has been such as dramatic decline in the readership of newspapers? What might newspaper publishers do to address this problem? (LO3, 4)

10.  What are some of the advantages online newspapers have for advertisers? Find the online media kit of a newspaper and analyze how the publisher is promoting the digital edition to prospective advertisers. (LO4)

## LEARNING OBJECTIVES

**LO1** To examine the role of support media in the IMC program.

**LO2** To recognize the various traditional and nontraditional support media available to the marketer in developing an IMC program.

**LO3** To develop an understanding of the advantages and disadvantages of support media.

**LO4** To know how audiences for support media are measured.

# 13 Support Media

## PRODUCT PLACEMENTS, REVERSE PRODUCT PLACEMENTS, AND MISUSED BRANDED ENTERTAINMENT

As consumers seem to be avoiding commercials at an increasing rate due to oversaturation and the fact that new technologies make it easier to skip ads, many marketers have turned to product placements and integrations—getting the product into the program (or movie or book)—as part of the context rather than as a separate communication. The growth in this industry has shown constant increases over the past decade both in the United States and internationally and, according to PQ Media's *Global Product Placement Spending Forecast,* will continue do so in the foreseeable future, leading PQ Media to refer to product placement as a "strategic must-have" in a company's consumer marketing mix.

Indeed, for some companies product placements are very much an integral part of their IMC strategy. Take Apple, for example. One of the most ubiquitous users of placements, Apple once again won the 2012 overall award in Brandchannel.com's Brand Cameo Product Placement Awards as its products appeared in over 40 percent of the top 40 films shown in 2011—twice that of the nearest brand. Interestingly, none of the placements were paid for as the company will not pay for placements. Coca-Cola, *USA Today*, POM Wonderful, and LouisVuitton among others also won awards.

In fact, so many companies are now doing product placements, they appear to be running out of places to put them, as the programs are able to pick and choose from among many "wannabees." One such TV show is *Modern Family*, whose producers say they turn down as many as 90 percent of advertisers trying to get placements. While Toyota, Target, and Audi have made appearances, other brands have been rejected for not being relevant to the plot and the characters, and were thought to be detracting from the realism of the story line. If the brand does not fit the character in the show,

it is also rejected. Nevertheless, companies are still lined up trying to get on the program, even though it is one of the most expensive for product placements. Other shows like *The Good Wife* and *American Idol* are also considered desirable venues for placements, in addition to a number of movies.

Sometimes, a fictional product portrayed in a show actually becomes a reverse product placement. While obviously not as common as placing a branded product, licensing agreements result either because of the popularity of the brand on the show, or as a designed strategy. For example, NBC recently signed a licensing arrangement with Staples to bring out a Dunder Mifflin brand from the show *The Office*. The Bubba Gump Shrimp Company restaurant chain was a spin-off from the movie *Forrest Gump*. The Wonka Candy Company is a real-life company launched from the book *Charlie and the Chocolate Factory*. And you can now buy an energy drink or alcohol called Duff—the very popular beer brand from *The Simpsons*.

While it is usually the case that companies are trying to get their brands placed in TV shows or movies, sometimes they don't want them placed and take steps to stop them or have them removed. Brands like Slip 'N Slide, Pepsi, and InSinkErator have brought suit against depictions of their products in movies, and more recently, so has Budweiser. In the movie *Flight*, Denzel Washington is portrayed as an airline pilot who is a functioning alcoholic—often drinking Bud, even while behind the wheel. As one might expect, Anheuser-Busch was not happy with the association and asked Paramount Pictures Corporation to obscure or remove the Budweiser logo from the film. So far, Paramount has refused, and there doesn't appear to be much Anheuser-Busch can do about it. Unfortunately for them, movie studios are not obligated to get permission before featuring a product in a movie. Stolichnaya vodka also was unhappy with the use of its brand in the movie without permission. Not exactly the kind of placement companies strive for.

As advertisers strive to get product placements in an attempt to get their brand shown, sometimes it works out, sometimes it doesn't. In some cases, you have to be careful what you wish for!

Sources: "Budweiser Seeks Removal from 'Flight,'" www. movies.msn.com, November 5, 2012; "Global Product Placement Spending Up 10% to $7.4 Billion in 2011, Pacing for 11% Growth in 2012," www.pqmedia.com, December 4, 2012; Abe Sauer, "Announcing the 2012 Brandcameo Product Placement Award Winners," www.brandchannel. com, February 13, 2012; Abe Sauer, "At the Movies: The Greatest Reverse Product Placements of All Time," www. brandchannel.com, December 2, 2011.

The lead-in to this chapter demonstrates how pervasive product placements have become, appearing everywhere from movies to television to videos and videogames. Given the increasing concern with consumers' abilities to avoid advertising, advertisers have turned to other ways to get their messages in front of prospective buyers. The result of this is increased attention to getting exposure, which, in turn, has led to significant changes in the media industry. Over the past few years there has been significant growth in the use of support media—both traditional and new media forms. In many ways, the consumers' efforts to avoid commercial exposure may have had an opposite effect, as it seems ads now appear in many places not previously home to such messages.

Ads have appeared on manhole covers, inside restroom stalls, on bus shelters, in grocery stores, on hubcaps, on cell phones, and even on people's bodies. In this chapter, we review a number of support media, some that are new to the marketplace and others that have been around a while. We discuss the relative advantages and disadvantages, how they are used, and audience measurement of each. We refer to them as **support media** because the media described in the previous chapters dominate the media strategies of large advertisers, particularly national advertisers. Support media are used to reach those people in the target market the primary media may not have effectively reached and to reinforce, or support, their messages. It is important to remember that some of these media are not used only for support, but for some companies may be the primary or sole medium used.

You may be surprised at how many different ways there are to deliver the messages and how often you are exposed to them. Let's begin by examining the scope of the support media industry and some of the many alternatives available to marketers.

# THE SCOPE OF THE SUPPORT MEDIA INDUSTRY

Support media are referred to by several titles, among them **alternative media**, **below-the-line media**, **nonmeasured media**, and **nontraditional media**. These terms describe a vast variety of channels used to deliver communications and to promote products and services. In this chapter we will discuss many of these media (though, as you might imagine, it would be impossible for us to discuss them all).

Many advertisers, as well as the top 100 advertising agencies, have increased their use of support media, and as new alternatives are developed, this use will continue to grow. Given the rapid emergence of a variety of new media, we will further divide support media into *traditional* and *nontraditional* support media categories. There is no particular necessity for this further distinction other than to demonstrate that many of the various forms of support media have been around for quite some time, while others have surfaced only recently. Let us examine some of these in more detail.

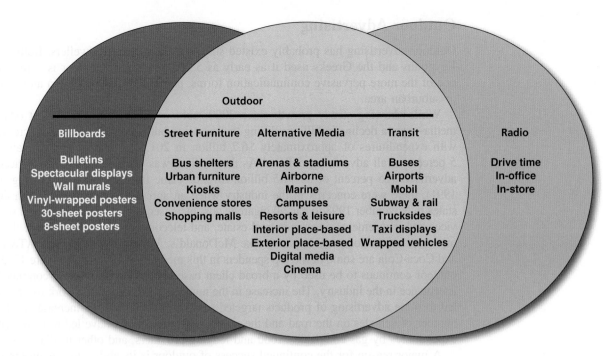

**FIGURE 13–1**

Out-of-Home Media: A Diverse Cross Section of Formats Comprise Outdoor Advertising Today

Source: Reprinted with permission of Outdoor Advertising Association of America, Inc.

# TRADITIONAL SUPPORT MEDIA

**Out-of-home advertising** media encompass many advertising forms (see Figure13–1). As can be seen, the Outdoor Advertising Association of America, Inc. (OAAA) categorizes these media as outdoor—including billboards, street furniture, alternative media, and transit—as well as specific forms of radio. As shown in Figure 13–2, billboards and street furniture together constitute 72 percent of the outdoor billings. Given the similarity of these forms, we will discuss them together while addressing transit and alternative media subsequently.

**FIGURE 13–2**

Four Major Product Categories, 2012 Total OOH Revenue: $6,700 Billion

Notes: Figures in millions.

Source: Outdoor Advertising Association of America, Inc.

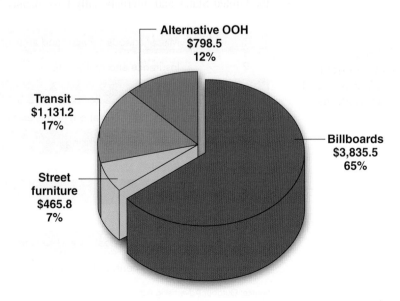

Alternative OOH
$798.5
12%

Transit
$1,131.2
17%

Street
furniture
$465.8
7%

Billboards
$3,835.5
65%

## Outdoor Advertising

Outdoor advertising has probably existed since the days of cave dwellers. Both the Egyptians and the Greeks used it as early as 5,000 years ago. Outdoor is certainly one of the more pervasive communication forms, particularly if you live in an urban or suburban area.

While showing steady growth since 2000, outdoor advertising—like most other media—saw a decline in billings during the recession but is now again on the increase with expenditures of approximately $6.7 billion in 2012—a total of approximately 5 percent of all advertising dollars.[1] As the medium was once dominated by tobacco advertisers (25 percent of its $1.5 billion revenue came from cigarette advertising in 1991), there were concerns in the industry when an agreement was reached with 46 states in November 1998 to ban all cigarette ads. Increased expenditures from local services and amusements, insurance, real estate, and telecom companies have more than made up for the losses. Companies like McDonald's, Verizon, Walt Disney, AT&T, and Coca-Cola are some of the top spenders in this medium. As shown in Figure 13–3, outdoor continues to be used by a broad client base, a demonstration of its continued acceptance in the industry. The increase in the number of women in the work force has led to more advertising of products targeted to this segment, and the increases in the number of vehicles on the road and the number of miles driven have led to increased expenditures by gas companies, food and lodging providers, and other media.

A major reason for the continued success of outdoor is its ability to remain innovative through technology. As Exhibit 13–1 shows, billboards are no longer limited to standard sizes and two dimensions; 3-D forms and extensions are now used to attract attention. Digital outdoor media have also contributed to the success. Digital messages on billboards, transit signs, and in stores have allowed more advertisers to participate as messages can be changed quickly and often. In addition, it allows outdoor advertising to appear in places previously unavailable, and in a timely fashion (Exhibit 13–2). You probably have been exposed to either signboards or electronic billboards at sports stadiums, in supermarkets, in the campus bookstores and dining halls, in shopping malls, on the freeways, or on the sides of buildings, from neon signs on skyscrapers in New York City to Mail Pouch Tobacco signs painted on the sides of barns in the Midwest. This is truly a pervasive medium.

Outdoor advertising, particularly billboards, does have its critics. Ever since Lady Bird Johnson tried to rid the interstate highways of billboard advertising during her husband's presidency with the Highway Beautification Act of 1965, there has been controversy regarding its use. As previously noted, legislation has passed in 46 states banning the advertising of cigarettes on billboards. In addition, a number of cities and states in the United States and internationally have banned or restricted the use of billboards.

YTC 13–01

Tesco

youtube.com/10ebelch

**FIGURE 13–3**

Top 10 Outdoor Advertising Categories (based on 2012 year-end outdoor expenditures)

| 1 | Miscellaneous services and amusements |
|---|---|
| 2 | Insurance and real estate |
| 3 | Communications |
| 4 | Public transportation, hotels and resorts |
| 5 | Media and advertising |
| 6 | Retail |
| 7 | Restaurants |
| 8 | Financial |
| 9 | Automotive dealers and services |
| 10 | Government, politics, and organizations |

Source: Outdoor Advertising Association of America, 2012.

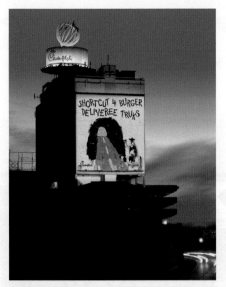

**EXHIBIT 13–1**
Billboards can be attention-getting

**EXHIBIT 13–2**
*PR Newswire* promotes through a billboard on Times Square

**Digital Outdoor**   One of the fastest-growing outdoor industries is that of **digital out-of-home media**. Digital outdoor media take three forms: (1) video advertising networks, which include digital video screens that appear in offices, stores, theaters, inside transit networks, and entertainment venues such as health clubs, sporting arenas, bars, and restaurants; and (2) digital billboards, or screens that transmit in LED (light emitting diodes) or LCD (liquid crystal display) technologies. Digital billboards include large boards found at sports and entertainment venues, retail locations (like malls), in transit locations (terminals, etc.), and at roadsides or large traffic locations. Ambient advertising, which is not a purely digital out-of-home medium, often uses digital technology to send its messages. These typically include smaller signs that appear in restrooms, stairs, personal vehicles, and on specialty items. The digital out-of-home media segment now accounts for over $2.06 billion in advertising revenues and is projected to reach $4.5 billion by 2016 due to its ability to be creative, attract attention, and engage the consumer (see Digital and Social Media Perspective 13–1).

**EXHIBIT 13–3**

A variety of companies use blimps as an advertising medium

## Alternative Out-of-Home Media

Several other forms of outdoor advertising are also available, including aerial advertising, place-based, mobile boards, and more. The OAAA classifies these as alternative media. Let's examine a few of these.

**Aerial Advertising**   Airplanes pulling banners, skywriting (in letters as high as 1,200 feet), and blimps all constitute another form of outdoor advertising available to the marketer: **aerial advertising**. Generally these media are not expensive in absolute terms and can be useful for reaching specific target markets. For example, Coppertone has often used skywriting over beach areas to promote its tanning lotions, beer companies (among others) commonly employ aerial advertising at sporting events, and local advertisers promote special events, sales, and the like. Exhibit 13–3 shows one of the many products, services, and/or events that have used this medium.

# Digital and Social Media Perspective 13–1 > > >

## Digital Out-of-Home Media Is Changing the Way We Look at Signs, and How They Look at Us

It has always been hard to ignore billboards, whether you want to or not, which is part of the reason the industry has not been as hard-hit as some other media during the economic downturn. Now due to technology, it may be even harder to ignore them. The growth of digital billboards (and other out-of-home advertising vehicles) may actually lead to consumers wanting to see—and even to interact with—a medium that many would like to see go away. Digital billboards are attracting attention around the world, for a variety of products, services, and causes.

To increase awareness of its international travel services, Delta Air Lines combined digital advertising with other traditional media. Working with a data aggregation company, Delta was able to identify where and when specific demographic consumers would see the outdoor ads, and placed its messages along the routes they traveled. The campaign resulted in more than a 28 percent increase in awareness of Delta as an international carrier. Among business travelers, the number who considered Delta as having flights to where they wanted to go internationally rose to 26 percent, and those who said they were likely to

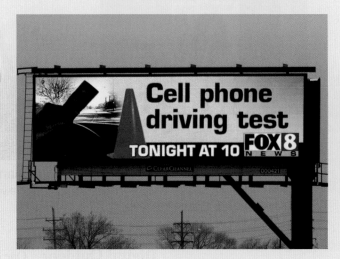

recommend Delta for international travel to others rose 61 percent.

Digital signs are used in a variety of settings as well as for a variety of purposes. The Dallas Cowboys football

---

**Mobile Billboards**  Another outdoor medium is **mobile billboards**. Some companies paint their cars with ads; others paint trucks and vans. Still others put ads on small billboards, mount them on trailers, and drive around and/or park in the geographic areas being targeted (Exhibit 13–4). Costs depend on the area and the mobile board company's fees, though even small and large organizations have found the medium affordable. A number of studies have shown that mobile billboards can lead to a high number of impressions, while a study conducted by the Product

**EXHIBIT 13–4**

An interesting and unusual example of a mobile billboard in an international setting

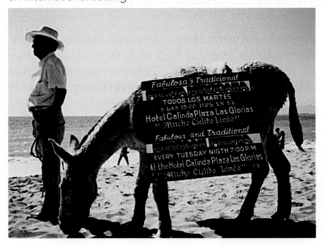

Trucks often serve as mobile billboards

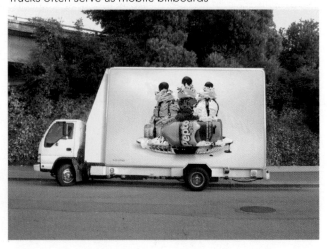

team uses digital signage to post the scores of the game as fans leave (at least when they win!), and the Tampa Bay Performing Arts Center uses them to enhance the visitors' experiences as they enter. LG, Verizon, Bank of America (BOA), and General Motors have used indoor digital signage to advertise for years, and BOA has used facial recognition to identify customers to target for specific services.

Digital signage companies have recently become integrated with social media like Flickr, Facebook, and Twitter. For example, a number of bars now have social media–enabled screens that they use to stage interactive games that allow customers to text answers to the displays, as well as send tweets or text messages to others in the bar (so long as they are appropriate content-wise). Tweets of specific menu or drink recommendations pop up on the indoor screens instantaneously. The Independent Coffee Network has also used Twitter and Flickr to catch the attention of customers in its stores, finding that it is effective in increasing engagement among the customers.

The FBI has also used the new billboard technology. As a result of a free public service provided by Clear Channel Outdoor, a 30 × 40 digital billboard in Times Square displays fugitives wanted for crimes in the New York area, resulting in thousands of exposures. The billboard—announced on the *Today Show* and seen by millions of viewers—can also be used to help rescue kidnap victims and provide high-security messages. Unlike traditional billboards, the messages can be posted or changed at a moment's notice—often right after the event occurs. Three other organizations have joined the effort, resulting in now over 1,500 billboards in 40 states that have already led to the solving of at least 30 cases.

Both Intel and NEC have developed digital billboards with a camera inside that can identify shoppers' age and gender as they walk by or stand in front of the display. The Venetian Resort in Las Vegas uses the technology to tailor suggestions for restaurants, entertainment, clubs, and so on. Kraft Foods and adidas have also experimented with facial recognition capabilities.

But not everyone is happy with this new technology. Privacy advocates are concerned that companies will collect data from persons without their knowledge or permission. The Electronic Privacy Information Center claims that the technology has the potential to violate one's civil liberties and violates the First Amendment. Both Facebook and Google have facial recognition capabilities but claim they don't use them. Or do they?

Sources: Steve Arel, "The Emergence of Social Media in Digital Signage," www.digitalsignagetoday.com, March 29, 2013; Shan Li and David Sarno, "New High-Tech Ads Look You in the Face," *Los Angeles Times*, August 21, 2011, pp. A1, A16; Andrew Hough, "'Minority Report' Digital Billboard Watches Consumers Shop," www.telegraph.co.uk, March 10, 2010; Andrew Hough, "Big Apple Joins National Initiative," www.fbi.gov, Jan. 15, 2010.

Acceptance and Research Organization indicates that mobile ads lead to high levels of recall and readership, and were likely to have an impact on sales.[2]

A number of companies including Walmart, Home Depot, and State Farm are frequent users of mobile ads.

## In-Store Media

YTC **13–02**

**Tesco in Store**

youtube.com/10ebelch

Advertisers use **in-store media** such as in-store ads, aisle displays, store leaflets, shopping cart signage, and in-store TV to reach shoppers at the place where they buy. A study by MEC Sensor and BMRB International revealed that one-third of shoppers say in-store ads influence them to make a purchase decision, 44 percent say they notice such ads, and 75 percent of those who noticed the ads said they are likely to purchase the advertised brand.[3]

Much of the attraction of point-of-purchase media is based on figures from the Point of Purchase Advertising International (POPAI) that states that approximately two-thirds of consumers' purchase decisions are made in the store; some impulse categories demonstrate an 80 percent rate.[4] Many advertisers are spending more of their dollars where decisions are made now that they can reach consumers at the point of purchase, providing additional product information while reducing their overall marketing efforts.

## Miscellaneous Outdoor Media

As shown in Figure 13–4, there are numerous outdoor media available, adding to the pervasiveness of this medium. The next time you are out, take a few moments to observe how many different forms of outdoor advertising you are exposed to.

| NUMBER OF OUT-OF-HOME DISPLAYS (2013) | | | |
|---|---|---|---|
| **Billboards** | **Street Furniture** | **Transit** | **Alternative** |
| Bulletins 158,868 faces | Bus Shelters 49,082 displays | Buses 205,426 faces | Cinema 17,800 |
| Digital Billboards 4,000 faces | Urban Furniture, i.e. Phone Kiosks Newsracks | Airports 68,560 faces | Digital Place-Based 300 Networks |
| Posters 165,606 faces | Shopping Malls 30,532 displays | Subway & Rail 184,078 faces | Arena & Stadiums 1,352 |
| Junior Posters 33,336 faces | | Truckside/Mobile 10,593 vehicles | Interior Place-Based, i.e. Convenience Stores Health Clubs Restaurants/Bars |
| Walls/Spectaculars 4,029 faces | | Taxis/Wrapped Vehicles 46,194 vehicles | Exterior Place-Based, i.e. Airborne Marine Resorts & Leisures |

**FIGURE 13-4**

Out-of-Home Displays

Source: Outdoor Advertising Association of America (OAAA), 2013.

## Transit Advertising

Another form of out-of-home advertising is **transit advertising**. Transit is targeted at the millions of people who are exposed to commercial transportation facilities, including buses, taxis, commuter trains, trolleys, airplanes, and subways.

Transit advertising has been around for a long time, but recent years have seen a renewed interest in this medium. Due in part to the increased number of women in the work force (they can be reached on their way to work more easily than at home), audience segmentation, and the fact that many people spend more time outside of the home than inside, transit continues to be a popular medium. McDonald's, Sprint, Frito-Lay, the United Way, numerous state lotteries, and others like transit's lower costs, frequency of exposures, flexibility, and point-of-sale presence. Kellogg's has found transit to be an effective medium for marketing Nutri-Grain, while the California Beef Council found that 42 percent of rail commuters in Northern California saw its beef ads inside terminals in just one month and as a result developed more positive attitudes toward beef.[5]

**Types of Transit Advertising** There are actually three forms of transit advertising: (1) inside cards, (2) outside posters, and (3) station, platform, or terminal posters.

**Inside Cards** If you have ever ridden a commuter bus, you have probably noticed the **inside cards** placed above the seats and luggage area advertising restaurants, TV or radio stations, or a myriad of other products and services. As noted earlier, companies now advertise on digital screens in transit vehicles, which deliver news, video ads, restaurant information, and so forth. The ability to change the message and the visibility provide the advertiser with a more attention-getting medium.

Transit cards can be controversial. For example, in the New York subway system, many of the ads for chewing gum, soup, and Smokey the Bear have given way to public service announcements about AIDS, unwanted pregnancies, rape, and infant mortality. While subway riders may agree that such issues are important, many of them complain that the ads are depressing and intrusive.

**Outside Posters** Advertisers use various forms of outdoor transit posters to promote products and services. These **outside posters** may appear on the sides, backs, and/or roofs of buses, taxis, trains, and subway and trolley cars.

EXHIBIT 13–5

Electronic outside posters
often appear on taxicabs

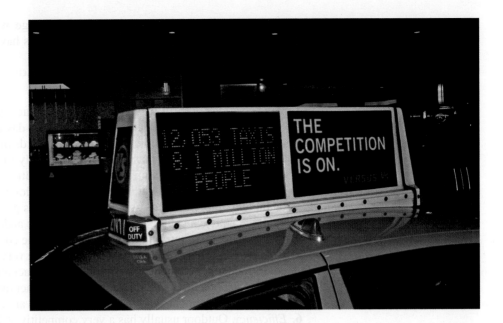

The increasing sophistication of this medium is demonstrated by a technology, developed by Vert, Inc. (a division of Clear Channel), that transforms ads on top of taxicabs into real-time animated electronic billboards. A web server that communicates with a global positioning satellite (GPS) is built into the taxi-top screen. The GPS determines the taxi's location and sends it to the local server, which then delivers the relevant ads for a particular area. A taxi traveling through a Hispanic community can have a message in Spanish, stock quotes could appear in the financial district, and so on. The message can also be changed by time of day—for example, to advertise coffee in the mornings and dinner specials later in the day. The ads appear in color in a format similar to banner ads, at 10 times the brightness of a TV screen (see Exhibit 13–5).

**Station, Platform, and Terminal Posters** Floor displays, island showcases, electronic signs, and other forms of advertising that appear in train or subway stations, airline terminals, and the like are all forms of transit advertising. As Exhibit 13–6 shows, **terminal posters** can be very attractive and attention-getting. Bus shelters

EXHIBIT 13–6

Terminal posters can be used
to attract attention

often provide the advertiser with expanded coverage where other outdoor boards may be restricted. Digital signs on subway platforms have become a common sight.

**Advantages and Disadvantages of Outdoor Advertising**   Outdoor advertising offers a number of advantages:

1. *Wide coverage of local markets.* With proper placement, a broad base of exposure is possible in local markets, with both day and night presence. Think about the millions of people exposed to billboards in Times Square!
2. *Frequency.* Because purchase cycles are typically for 30-day periods, consumers are usually exposed a number of times, resulting in high levels of frequency.
3. *Geographic flexibility.* Outdoor can be placed along highways, near stores, or on mobile billboards, almost anywhere that laws permit. For local advertisers, outdoor can reach people in specific geographic and/or demographic areas. Local, regional, or even national markets may be covered.
4. *Creativity.* As shown earlier, outdoor ads can be very creative. Large print, colors, and other elements like digital signs attract attention.
5. *Ability to create awareness.* Because of its impact (and the need for a simple message), outdoor can lead to a high level of awareness.
6. *Efficiency.* Outdoor usually has a very competitive CPM when compared to other media. The average CPM of outdoor is often one-half of radio and far less than that of TV, magazines, and newspapers. Transit is one of the least expensive media in both relative and absolute costs.
7. *Effectiveness.* Outdoor advertising can be effective, as demonstrated by the California Beef example. In a study reported by BBDO advertising, 35 percent of consumers surveyed said they had called a phone number they saw on an out-of-home ad.[6] A study reported by Mukesh Bhargava and Naveen Donthu showed that outdoor advertising can have a significant effect on sales, particularly when combined with a promotion.[7]
8. *Production capabilities.* Modern technologies have reduced production times for outdoor advertising to allow for rapid turnaround time, and digital messages can be changed in minutes.
9. *Timeliness.* Many outdoor ads appear in or near shopping areas or on or in the vehicles taking customers there, thus resulting in timely exposures.

At the same time, however, there are limitations to outdoor, many of them related to its advantages:

1. *Waste coverage.* While it is possible to reach very specific audiences, in many cases the purchase of outdoor results in a high degree of waste coverage. It is not likely that everyone driving past a billboard is part of the target market.
2. *Limited message capabilities.* Because of the speed with which most people pass by outdoor ads, exposure time is short, so messages are limited to a few words and/or an illustration. Lengthy appeals are not likely to be effective. Some transit forms are not conducive to creative messages.
3. *Wearout.* Because of the high frequency of exposures, outdoor may lead to a quick wearout. People are likely to get tired of seeing the same ad every day.
4. *Cost.* Because of the decreasing signage available and the higher cost associated with inflatables, outdoor advertising can be expensive in both an absolute and a relative sense.
5. *Measurement problems.* One of the more difficult problems of outdoor advertising lies in the accuracy of measuring reach, frequency, and other effects. (As you will see in the measurement discussion, this problem is currently being addressed, though it has not been resolved.)
6. *Image problems.* Outdoor advertising has suffered some image problems as well as some disregard among consumers.

In sum, outdoor advertising has both advantages and disadvantages for marketers. Some of these problems can be avoided with other forms of out-of-home advertising.

**Advantages and Disadvantages of Transit Advertising**  In addition to sharing some of the advantages and disadvantages of other outdoor media, transit has a few more specific to this medium. Advantages of using transit advertising include the following:

1. *Exposure.* Long length of exposure to an ad is one major advantage of indoor transit forms. The average ride on mass transit is 45 minutes, allowing for plenty of exposure time. As with airline tickets, the audience is essentially a captive one, with nowhere else to go and nothing much to do. As a result, riders are likely to read the ads—more than once. A second form of exposure transit advertising provides is the absolute number of people exposed. About 9 million people ride mass transit every week, and over 10.5 billion rides were taken in 2012, providing a substantial number of potential viewers.[8]
2. *Frequency.* Because our daily routines are standard, those who ride buses, subways, and the like are exposed to the ads repeatedly. If you rode the same subway to work and back every day, in one month you would have the opportunity to see the ad 20 to 40 times. The locations of station and shelter signs also afford high frequency of exposure.
3. *Cost.* The CPM for transit advertising is low on a relative cost basis.

Some disadvantages are also associated with transit:

1. *Reach.* While an advantage of transit advertising is the ability to provide exposure to a large number of people, this audience may have certain lifestyles and/or behavioral characteristics that are not true of the target market as a whole. For example, in rural or suburban areas, mass transit is limited or nonexistent, so the medium is not very effective for reaching these people.
2. *Mood of the audience.* Sitting or standing on a crowded subway may not be conducive to reading advertising, let alone experiencing the mood the advertiser would like to create. Controversial ad messages may contribute to this less than positive feeling. Likewise, hurrying through an airport may create anxieties that limit the effectiveness of the ads placed there.

## Measurement in Out-of-Home Media

In 2010 the OAAA announced a new audience measurement system that had been in development for the previous five years. Eyes On is considered to be an improvement over the traditional measure of opportunity to see, with a "likely to see" metric that can also provide demographic and ethnographic data. The new data include a combination of eye tracking, circulation, and travel survey data all combined into one rating by a coalition of research companies.[9]

A number of other sources of audience measurement and information are available:

- Competitive Media Reports provides information on expenditures on outdoor media by major advertisers.
- Experian Simmons Market Research Bureau conducts research annually for the Institute of Outdoor Advertising, providing demographic data, exposures, and the like. GfK, Mediamark Research & Intelligence (MRI) provides similar data.
- Point of Purchase Advertising International is a trade organization of point-of-purchase advertisers collecting statistical and other market information on POP advertising.
- The Outdoor Advertising Association of America (OAAA) is the primary trade association of the industry. It assists members with research, creative ideas, and more effective use of the medium and has a website at www.oaa.org.
- The Traffic Audit Bureau (TAB) is the auditing arm of the transit industry. TAB conducts traffic counts on which the published rates are based.
- The American Public Transportation Association (APTA) provides ridership statistics, studies, and other transit usage information.

# PROMOTIONAL PRODUCTS MARKETING

LO 13-2

According to the Promotional Products Association International (PPAI), **promotional products marketing** is "the advertising or promotional medium or method that uses promotional products, such as ad specialties, premiums, business gifts, awards, prizes, or commemoratives." Promotional products marketing is the more up-to-date name for what used to be called specialty advertising. **Specialty advertising** has now been provided with a new definition:

> A medium of advertising, sales promotion, and motivational communication employing imprinted, useful, or decorative products called advertising specialties, a subset of promotional products.
>
> Unlike premiums, with which they are sometimes confused (called advertising specialties), these articles are always distributed free—recipients don't have to earn the specialty by making a purchase or contribution.[10]

As you can see from these descriptions, specialty advertising is often considered both an advertising and a sales promotion medium. In our discussion, we treat it as a supportive advertising medium in the IMC program.

There are thousands of *advertising specialty* items, including ballpoint pens, coffee mugs, key rings, calendars, T-shirts, and matchbooks. Unconventional specialties such as plant holders, wall plaques, and gloves with the advertiser's name printed on them are also used to promote a company or its product; so are glassware, trophies, awards, and vinyl products. In fact, advertisers spend over $18.1 billion per year on specialty advertising items (Figure 13–5).[11]

If you stop reading for a moment and look around your desk (or bed or beach blanket), you'll probably find some specialty advertising item nearby. It may be the pen you are using, a scratch pad, or even a book cover with the campus bookstore name on it. Specialty items are used for many promotional purposes: to thank a customer for patronage, keep the name of the company in front of consumers, introduce new products, or reinforce the name of an existing company, product, or service. Advertising specialties are often used to support other forms of product promotions.

## Advantages and Disadvantages of Promotional Products Marketing

Like any other advertising medium, promotional products marketing offers the marketer both advantages and disadvantages. Advantages include the following:

1. *Selectivity.* Because specialty advertising items are generally distributed directly to target customers, the medium offers a high degree of selectivity. The communication is distributed to the desired recipient, reducing waste coverage.
2. *Flexibility.* As the variety of specialty items in Figure 13–5 demonstrates, this medium offers a high degree of flexibility. A message as simple as a logo or as long as is necessary can be distributed through a number of means. Both small and large companies can employ this medium for a variety of objectives limited only by their own creativity.
3. *Frequency.* Most forms of specialty advertising are designed for retention. Key chains, calendars, and pens remain with the potential customer for a long time, providing repeat exposures to the advertising message at no additional cost.
4. *Cost.* Some specialty items are rather expensive (for example, leather goods), but most are affordable to almost any size organization. While they are costly on a CPM basis when compared with other media, the high number of repeat exposures drives down the relative cost per exposure of this advertising medium.
5. *Goodwill.* Promotional products are perhaps the only medium that generates goodwill in the receiver. Because people like to receive gifts and many of the products are functional (key chains, calendars, etc.), consumers are grateful to receive them. The products also lead to a favorable impression of the advertiser.
6. *High recall.* Specialties lead to high recall of both the advertisers' name and message.

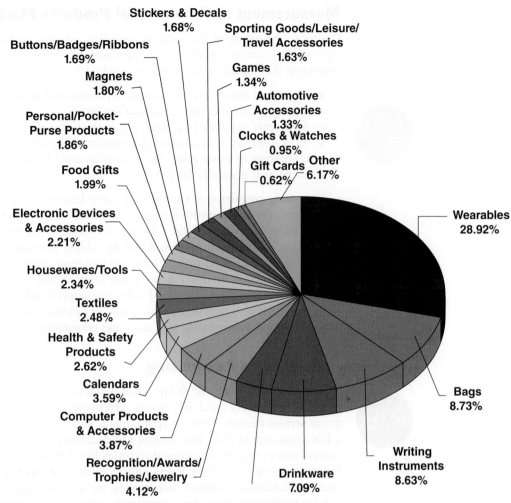

**Stickers & Decals**
1.68%

**Sporting Goods/Leisure/**
**Travel Accessories**
1.63%

**Buttons/Badges/Ribbons**
1.69%

**Games**
1.34%

**Magnets**
1.80%

**Automotive**
**Accessories**
1.33%

**Personal/Pocket-**
**Purse Products**
1.86%

**Clocks & Watches**
0.95%

**Food Gifts**
1.99%

**Gift Cards** **Other**
0.62% 6.17%

**Electronic Devices**
**& Accessories**
2.21%

**Wearables**
28.92%

**Housewares/Tools**
2.34%

**Textiles**
2.48%

**Health & Safety**
**Products**
2.62%

**Calendars**
3.59%

**Bags**
8.73%

**Computer Products**
**& Accessories**
3.87%

**Recognition/Awards/**
**Trophies/Jewelry**
4.12%

**Writing**
**Instruments**
8.63%

**Drinkware**
7.09%

**Desk/Office/Business**
**Accessories**
4.35%

**FIGURE 13–5**

2012 Sales by Product
Category (2011 figures in
parentheses)

7. *Supplementing other media.* A major advantage of promotional products marketing is its ability to supplement other media. Because of its low cost and repeat exposures, the simplest message can reinforce the appeal or information provided through other forms.

Promotional products have also been used to support trade shows, motivate dealers, recognize employees, and promote consumer and sales force contests.

Disadvantages of promotional products marketing include the following:

1. *Image.* While most forms of specialty advertising are received as friendly reminders of the store or company name, the firm must be careful choosing the specialty item. The company image may be cheapened by a chintzy or poorly designed advertising form.

2. *Saturation.* With so many organizations now using this advertising medium, the marketplace may become saturated. While you can always use another ballpoint pen or scratch pad, the value to the receiver declines if replacement is too easy, and the likelihood that you will retain the item or even notice the message is reduced. The more unusual the specialty, the more value it is likely to have to the receiver.

3. *Lead time.* The lead time required to put together a promotional products message is significantly longer than that for most other media.

4. *Reach.* Use of other media—such as television—leads to greater reach.

Even with its disadvantages, promotional products marketing can be an effective medium.

## Measurement in Promotional Products Marketing

Owing to the nature of the industry, specialty advertising has no established ongoing audience measurement system. Research has been conducted in an attempt to determine the impact of this medium, leading to the following results:

- 94 percent report having received a promotional product in the last 12 months.
- 89 percent recalled the advertiser's name.
- 83 percent say they like receiving promotional products.
- 38 percent say it is a constant reminder of the advertiser.
- 60 percent of those using the promotion used it once a week.
- 69 percent generally keep it.[12]

In a study conducted at Georgia Southern University, it was shown that promotional products had a positive impact on brand image, leading to a more positive perception of the business and a higher likelihood of recommending the business.[13] In addition, another study showed that by adding promotional products to an integrated media mix, brand impressions and purchase intent could be increased.[14]

The Promotional Products Association International (www.ppai.org) is the trade organization of the field. The PPAI helps marketers develop and use specialty advertising forms. It also provides promotional and public relations support for specialty advertising and disseminates statistical and educational information.

## Yellow Pages Advertising

How times have changed! While once a staple in almost everyone's home and a required medium for local advertisers, advertising expenditures in the **Yellow Pages** are in serious decline. From an approximate $13 billion per year in expenditures just a few years ago, in 2011 that amount had declined to $6.9 billion.[15] As younger consumers turn to search and online directories like Yelp to seek information, fewer and fewer are using the Yellow Pages either online or in print. Leisure-related searches such as restaurant locations and movies, as well as many of those for retail and service businesses, have gone completely online, to the detriment of the hard-copy YP books.

The opportunity for the Yellow Pages does still exist, as local media advertising is still expected to reach $148 billion by 2017—an increase of 2.3 percent from 2012.[16] In addition, at least one study has shown that calls to businesses advertising in phone directories actually increased by 17 percent from 2010 to 2011.[17] However, this opportunity seems to lie with the baby boomers segment, who have grown up with the Yellow Pages and remain heavy users even today (Figure 13–6). While the

**FIGURE 13–6**

Baby Boomers and Seniors

Source: CRM Associates, *Baby Boomers and Seniors: The Most Important Segments for Yellow Pages*, January 2012.

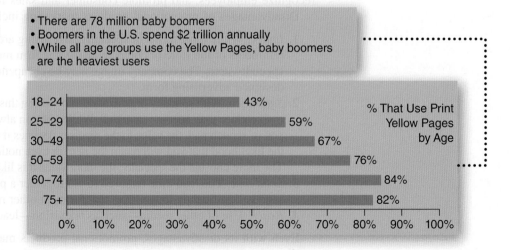

- There are 78 million baby boomers
- Boomers in the U.S. spend $2 trillion annually
- While all age groups use the Yellow Pages, baby boomers are the heaviest users

% That Use Print Yellow Pages by Age

| Age | % |
|---|---|
| 18–24 | 43% |
| 25–29 | 59% |
| 30–49 | 67% |
| 50–59 | 76% |
| 60–74 | 84% |
| 75+ | 82% |

**EXHIBIT 13–7**
The Yellow Pages are the final link in the buying cycle

boomer market is an attractive and lucrative one, nevertheless, the long-range forecast for the Yellow Pages—particularly the print edition—is not promising.

The Yellow Pages are often referred to as a **directional medium** because the ads do not create awareness or demand for products or services; rather, once consumers have decided to buy, the Yellow Pages point them in the direction where their purchases can be made (Exhibit 13–7). Seventy-five percent of all people who referenced the Yellow Pages (print or online) either made a purchase or said they were likely to do so. In addition, 33 percent of people who referenced the Yellow Pages were new customers to the business they chose.[18] The Yellow Pages are thus considered the final link in the buying cycle.

# OTHER TRADITIONAL SUPPORT MEDIA

There are numerous other traditional ways to promote products. Some are reviewed here.

LO 13-2

## Advertising in Movie Theaters

Another method of delivering a message that is increasing quickly (to the dismay of many) is the use of movie theaters to promote products and/or services. Commercials shown before the film and previews, with both local and national sponsorships, are now regularly shown in movie theaters. In addition, ads in theater lobbies, at kiosks, and on popcorn tubs and drink cups are used. Automotive, food, and package-goods companies and regional and local companies are just some of the product categories that find this medium attractive. The growth rate of the number of theaters showing a commercial before the movie has increased steadily since the 1980s.

Consumer reaction to ads in movie theaters is mixed. A number of earlier studies have shown that most people think these ads are annoying or very annoying, although now people may be becoming more used to them. The Cinema Advertising Council (CAC) reported that 63 percent of moviegoers say they do not mind ads before the movie starts.[19] On the other hand, many consumers complain that having paid for a ticket, they shouldn't have to sit through ads and/or commercials. A Portland, Oregon, group called Captive Motion Picture Audiences of America (CMPAA) recruited over 3,000 people to sign a petition against the ads.[20]

Nevertheless, a number of products and brands have used this advertising medium, including Allstate, BMW, Cadillac, Kmart, Old Navy, and Taco Bell, among others. Numerous brands have developed commercials specifically for the purpose of being shown before movies. In addition, a research study commissioned by one in-theater advertising broker showed that the ads were three times more likely to be remembered than TV ads.[21]

**Advantages of Movie Theater Advertising** Movies provide a number of advantages to advertisers, including the following:

1. *Exposure.* The number of people attending movies is substantial and continues to increase. Ticket sales were over $10.83 billion per year in 2012, up 6.5 percent from 2011.[22]

YTC **13-03**
**Carlsberg**
youtube.com/10ebelch

CHAPTER 13

2. *Emotional attachment.* A 2010 report found that 41.5 percent of moviegoers say they become emotionally attached to cinema ads and brands—more than the ads on the broadcasts of the *Super Bowl, Summer Olympics, World Series,* or the *Oscars.*[23] One neuromarketing research study showed movie-ad viewers to be much more engaged than those watching TV spots.[24]

3. *Cost.* The cost of advertising in a theater varies from one setting to the next. However, it is low in terms of both absolute and relative costs per exposure.

4. *Attention.* Movie watchers pay attention to the ads shown in theaters, as research indicates that cinema ads reach many consumers who say they are usually ad avoiders. These consumers are 157 percent more likely to see an ad in a movie than any other medium.[25]

5. *Clutter.* Lack of clutter is another advantage offered by advertising in movie theaters. Most theaters limit the number of ads.

6. *Proximity.* Since many theaters are located in or adjacent to shopping malls, potential customers are "right next door." (Of moviegoers, 74 percent combine the activity with dining out.[26])

7. *Segmentation.* A key advantage of movie advertising is the ability to target specific demographic segments. The profile of the moviegoer is above-average in education and affluence. The movie titles and ratings enable advertisements to reach specific groups.

8. *Integration.* Those who download movies online are actually more likely to attend a movie than is the typical adult.[27]

**Disadvantages of Movie Theater Advertising**   Some of the disadvantages associated with movie theaters as advertising media follow:

1. *Irritation.* Perhaps the major disadvantage is that many people do not wish to see advertising in these media. A number of studies suggest these ads may create a high degree of annoyance. If true, this dissatisfaction may carry over to the product itself, to the movies, or to the theaters.

2. *Cost.* While the cost of advertising in local theaters has been cited as an advantage because of the low rates charged, ads exposed nationally are often as much as 20 percent higher than an equal exposure on television. CPMs also tend to be higher than in other media.

While viewers seemingly either like or dislike cinema ads, it seems they are here to stay.

# NONTRADITIONAL SUPPORT MEDIA

## Branded Entertainment

One of the major changes (along with the growth of social and mobile media) that has occurred in the area of integrated marketing communications over the past few years is the enormous growth associated with **branded entertainment**. Branded entertainment is a form of advertising that blends marketing and entertainment through television, film, music talent, and technology. Essentially, the goal is to use entertainment media to gain consumers' attention and exposure to products and/or brands. It is extremely difficult to place a dollar amount on branded entertainment, but there is no doubt that its use continues to increase yearly.

Let's take a look at the ways companies use branded entertainment.

**Product Placements**   While **product placements** account for only a small portion of major advertisers' budgets, the use of this medium has increased tremendously in recent years, as shown in the lead-in to this chapter. Estimates are that in

LO 13-2

2011 paid global product placements spending reached $7.4 billion—$4.2 billion in the United States—and was expected to increase in double-digit percentages in 2012.[28] It should be noted, however, that it is difficult to assess the accuracy of these figures, as many product placements are free or provided in exchange for trade. Product placement agencies contend that as much as 70 to 95 percent of their placements are for trade.[29] An in-depth study of the product placement industry by Russell and Belch supports this contention.[30] Industry analysts expect this trend to continue as placements move from traditional media to alternative media, as personal video recorder growth sales continue (allowing for increased avoidance of commercials), and as consumers' lifestyles change. Placements have caught on in Europe, as the UK has now approved product placements on television, imposing more restrictions than in the United States.[31]

Interestingly, product placements are not a new phenomenon; placements are known to have existed as early as the 1930s and were commonly employed via soap operas in the 1950s. However, it was not until the turn of the century that the number of placements skyrocketed. Today, product placements are used to gain exposure by numerous companies large and small (Exhibit 13–8) and are a very important part of the IMC strategy for companies like BMW, Apple, PepsiCo, and Anheuser-Busch (just to name a few). Much of the logic behind product placement is that since the placement is embedded in the script or program setting, it cannot be avoided, thereby increasing exposure. Given the lack of intrusiveness of the placement, consumers may not have the same negative reactions to it as they may to a commercial. Further, research has demonstrated that association with a program or movie—or particularly with a celebrity—may enhance the image of the product and, in some instances, lead to increased sales.[32,33]

Given the intense growth in the number of product placements, some marketers are concerned that placements may be becoming too common. It is very rare to watch a movie or TV show without being exposed to one or more placements. Given the obvious attempt to gain exposure in many of these, placements may be becoming more obvious; consumers may perceive them more like ads and, as a result, they may have less impact on the viewer.[34] Some industry watchdogs have called for more regulation of placements, contending that they blur the lines between advertising and programming and therefore may be deceptive. The FCC is currently considering this possibility.

As of this time, however, product placements continue to increase both in number and in dollar amounts. In addition, placements are appearing in media and situations never before imagined, including music videos, videogames and books. Lady Gaga's

YTC 13–04

**Product Placements**

youtube.com/10ebelch

CHAPTER 13

**EXHIBIT 13–8**

Audi's Spyder was a hit in *Ironman 2*

videos—*Bad Romance* and *Telephone*—had a number of placements for brands such as Wonder Bread, Miracle Whip, Diet Coke, and Heart Beats earphones, to name just a few. Some of these were paid placements; others were not.

**Product Integration**   A more involved form of product placements actually leads to the placement being integrated throughout the program content and/or script. In **product integrations** the product is woven throughout the program or becomes the program itself. Like product placements, product integrations are on the increase as the networks continue to search for new program content, and the proliferation of cable media channels affords marketers with numerous integration opportunities. For example, on an episode of *Modern Family,* much of the show was devoted to the family's bumbling of the father's request for an Apple iPad for his birthday and their frantic efforts to find one. When the family actually obtained one, the program ended with the father sitting on the couch with the iPad in his lap, enjoying the product.[35] In another instance, GEICO was able to get TNT's NBA All-Star Game's classic "shoot out" changed from h-o-r-s-e to G-E-I-C-O. *America's Next Top Model* (Cover Girl) has also successfully employed integrations, as have others. *Dancing with the Stars* 2013 integrated one of the dancers into a commercial where she falls over a Sears appliance at the end. Likewise, in the movie *The Heat*, Denny's and SPANX were both integrated into scenes.

**Advertainment**   The creation of video and/or music content by an advertiser in an attempt to entertain viewers while advertising their products is known as **advertainment**. For example, Coca-Cola developed a long-form advertisement to reach TiVo viewers. The program included 25 minutes of interviews, music videos, behind-the-scenes footage, and live performances with recording artists Sting, Mary J. Blige, Ashanti, and Leona Ness. Coca-Cola ads were tagged so that TiVo users could see them and then click on an icon to download the program. Nike and SKYY Vodka have also produced ad films, as has BMW. The automaker had one of the first series of such films called *The Hire,* and later developed a new set of episodes. While initially shown only on the Internet, the advertisements have now made their way to a few cable and satellite channels.

**YTC 13–05**

**Advertainment Dior**

youtube.com/10ebelch

Another form of advertainment is that of **advergames**. A number of companies including Perrier, Audi, and Swatch have developed online games designed to promote their products. For example, the Audi game is a three-minute driving game demonstrating the handling of the A4. Perrier's advergame allows players to experience one hour and 20 minutes of happenings in a hidden place in Paris with 60 other guests. Expedia has a very popular geo-tagging game where participants pick up clues at various travel destinations.

**Content Sponsorship**   Rather than developing their own content, some advertisers agree to sponsor specific programs, receiving product placements, integration, and promotions in return. HGTV offers sponsorships to companies built around remodeling, gardening, home decorating, and more. Heineken has collaborated with the FIFA, and Rolex with the ATP World Tennis Tour. North Face had a significant content sponsorship in the Masters of Snowboarding webcast, and The Food Network and Travel Channel offer a variety of sponsorship opportunities. Turner Broadcasting offers content sponsorship opportunities on the Cartoon Network and Boomerang as well as some of its other channels. Content sponsorships are also common on the Internet; Calvin Klein and *Vanity Fair* and One a Day and *Eating Well* are just a few examples of collaborations.

**Ad-Supported Video on Demand (VOD)**   VODs are specialized content programs offered through cable TV networks that are developed by advertisers and provided to the cable operators for free. For example, General Motors produced a short feature on the history of the Corvette to be shown on CNN through Time Warner and Comcast's VOD channels. MTV launched a series called the *How to*

*Show* in which musicians, athletes, and celebrities offer the "tricks of their trades" (the U.S. Air Force was the first advertiser). ESPN and ABC have offered VODs of college football games 12 hours after they were played. A number of TV shows have been made available as well; the San Diego Zoo provides a video tour to San Diego cable subscribers.

**YTC 13–06**
Visa VOD
youtube.com/10ebelch

**Others**   While other forms of branded entertainment continue to develop through wireless, mobile, and "branded locations," space does not allow us to discuss each in detail. Suffice it to say that the use of branded entertainment continues to increase and will continue to do so as more and more technological innovations provide opportunities.

**Advantages of Branded Entertainment**   A number of advantages of branded entertainment have been suggested:

LO 13-3

1.  *Exposure.* In regard to product placements, a large number of people see movies each year (close to 2 billion admissions per year). The average film is estimated to have a life span of three and one-half years (with 75 million exposures), and most moviegoers are very attentive audience members. When this is combined with the home video market and network and cable TV (including HBO, Showtime, and the Movie Channel), the potential exposure for a product placed in a movie and on television is enormous. And this form of exposure is not subject to zapping, at least not in the theater.

    High exposure numbers are also offered for TV placements, based on the ratings and the possibility to direct the ad to a defined target market.

2.  *Frequency.* Depending on how the product is used in the movie (or program), there may be ample opportunity for repeated exposures (many, for those who like to watch a program or movie more than once). For example, if you are a regular watcher of the programs containing placements and/or integrations, you will be exposed to the products placed therein a number of times (think *American Idol* and Coke). Syndication will result in additional exposures.

3.  *Support for other media.* Branded entertainment supports other promotional tools. A trend is to have the client that is placing the product cross-promote the product and movie tie-in in multiple media venues. As noted, the tie-ins reinforce and are reinforced by ads and commercials.

4.  *Source association.* In Chapter 6 we discussed the advantages of source identification. When consumers see their favorite TV celebrities or movie stars using certain brands, the association may lead to a favorable product image or even to sales. In one study of 524 8- to 14-year-olds, 75 percent stated that they notice when brands are placed on their favorite shows, and 72 percent said that seeing a favorite character using a brand makes them want to purchase that brand.[36] Another study among adults showed that one-third of viewers said they try a product after seeing it on a TV show or movie.[37]

5.  *Cost.* While the cost of branded entertainment may range from free samples to millions, the latter is an extreme. The CPM for this form of advertising can be very low, owing to the high volume of exposures it generates. For many products, like the Apple iPad in the *Modern Family* episode, the placements may be free, except for the cost of the products.

6.  *Recall.* A number of firms have measured the impact of product placements on next-day recall. Results ranged, but most show recall is higher than for TV commercials.

7.  *Bypassing regulations.* In the United States as well as many foreign countries, some products are not permitted to advertise on television or to specific market segments. Product placements and integrations have allowed the cigarette and liquor industries to have their products exposed, circumventing these restrictions. In the fourth season of *Jersey Shore,* in one scene a sack of Marlboro cigarettes washed up onto the beach, raising the specter of a placement. Philip Morris disclaimed any involvement.[38] Recently there have been attempts to

control the bypassing of regulations. The Marin Institute, an alcohol industry watchdog group, filed suit against Budweiser for their tie-ins to the movie *The Wedding Crasher,* arguing that the movie encouraged underage drinking. Spirits manufacturers Diageo, Bacardi USA, and Brown-Forman have also been named in lawsuits for similar reasons.[39] Other companies have been accused of advertising junk foods to kids through placements.[40]

8. *Acceptance.* Studies have shown that viewers are accepting of product placements and in general evaluate them positively, though some products (alcohol, guns, cigarettes) are perceived as less acceptable. Other studies report similar results, with one showing that as many as 80 percent of consumers say they have a positive attitude toward placements.[41] In a study conducted with tweens, 43 percent said they found placements to be funny, 39 percent found them to be informative, and 35 percent found them entertaining and interesting.[42] A study by eMarketer reported similar results.[43]

9. *Targeting.* Content sponsorships and VOD may effectively reach potential customers with a strong interest in the subject matter (i.e., fashion, football).

### Disadvantages of Branded Entertainment
Some disadvantages are also associated with branded entertainment:

1. *High absolute cost.* While the CPM may be very low for various forms of branded entertainment, the absolute costs may be very high, pricing some advertisers out of the market. The increased demand branded entertainment, coupled with the rising emphasis by the studios on cross-promotions, drives costs up considerably. A study conducted by the National Association of Advertisers indicated that 79 percent of advertisers believe that the costs of branded entertainment deals are too high.[44] Some companies have ceased using this form of promotion citing the rising costs.

2. *Time of exposure.* While the way some products are exposed to the audience has an impact, there is no guarantee viewers will notice the product. Some product placements are more conspicuous than others. When the product is not featured prominently, the advertiser runs the risk of not being seen (although, of course, the same risk is present in all forms of media advertising).

3. *Limited appeal.* The appeal that can be made in some of these media forms is limited. There is no potential for discussing product benefits or providing detailed information. Rather, appeals are limited to source association, use, and enjoyment. The endorsement of the product is indirect, and the flexibility for product demonstration is subject to its use in the medium.

4. *Lack of control.* In many movies, the advertiser has no say over when and how often the product will be shown. Many companies have found that their placements in movies did not work as well as expected. Fabergé developed an entire Christmas campaign around its Brut cologne and its movie placement, only to find the movie was delayed until February. Others have had their placements cut from the script.

5. *Public reaction.* Many TV viewers and moviegoers are incensed at the idea of placing ads in programs or movies. These viewers want to maintain the barrier between program content and commercials. If the placement is too intrusive, they may develop negative attitudes toward the brand. The increased use of placements and integrations has led many consumers to be annoyed by what they consider to be crass commercialization. The FTC has explored options for limiting placements without consumer notification, though they have not sought increased regulation to date. Still others are upset about programs such as *Undercover Boss* in which a CEO goes undercover in his or her own company to see how his employees work. Critics contend that these shows are nothing more than public relations disguised as programming.

6. *Competition.* The appeal of branded entertainment has led to increased competition to get one's product placed, increasing demand and costs.

7. *Negative placements.* Some products may appear in movie scenes that are disliked by the audience or create a less than favorable mood or reflect poorly on the brand. For example, in the movie *Missing,* a very good, loyal father takes comfort in a bottle of Coke, while a Pepsi machine appears in a stadium where torturing and murders take place—not a good placement for Pepsi. Emerson—the manufacturer of the garbage disposal brand In-Sink-Erator—has sued NBC for showing a cheerleader getting her hand mangled in the program *Heroes.* NBC never received permission from Emerson to show their brand.

8. *Clutter.* The rapid growth of branded entertainment tie-ins has led to an overwhelming number of placements and integrations as noted previously. Like other forms of advertising, too many placements and integrations will eventually lead to clutter and loss of effectiveness.

**Measurement in Branded Entertainment** With the rapid growth in branded entertainment have come a number of research studies and companies attempting to monitor and measure the impact of this media form. At this time, there is no one accepted standard used by advertisers or industry members.[45] However, a number of high-profile companies now offer services in this area, including those listed below.

- *Nielsen Media Research.* The TV ratings company currently tracks product placements on network television. The company has plans to track cable programs in the near future.
- *Nielsen-IAG Research.* IAG maintains a panel where an average of 5,000 daily viewers take an online quiz about the previous night's prime-time programs, the commercials, and product placements therein. The information is used to determine which ads work best; what shows, spots, and placements are being remembered; and viewers' attitudes toward the same.
- *Deutsch/iTVX.* The advertising agency and product integration valuation company have combined efforts to measure Results-Oriented-Integration. The method values the quality of each hundredth of a second of an integration, and then translates them into a Product Placement/Commercial Cost Ratio to value the integration by comparing it to the value of a commercial.
- *Brand Advisors.* The company attempts to value brand integration in feature films. A number of other companies have begun to offer various services, including NextMedium, Delivery Agent, IEG, Image Impact, and others. As noted, however, none of these has received universal acceptance in the industry or among advertisers.

In addition to the studies reported earlier, research has provided evidence that an aura of glamour is added to products associated with celebrities.

## Guerrilla Marketing

In addition to branded entertainment another nontraditional way that advertisers are now attempting to reach consumers is referred to by a variety of names, including guerrilla marketing, stealth, street, buzz, ambush, or viral marketing. Whatever it is called, there seems to be no end in sight to where advertisers will attempt to reach you. While previously targeted primarily to college students and others of the same age group, these efforts have now been expanded to reach additional audiences as well.[46] In addition, larger portions of the communications budgets (while still small) are being allocated to this media form, and the size of the various projects is also getting larger.[47] Guerrilla marketing has benefited by technology in that they can be even more creative, as well as the fact that cell phones now have cameras, allowing viewers to send their pictures to others.

A variety of other well-known companies have used guerrilla tactics. Target rented an entire hotel during Fashion Week in New York, throwing open the curtains of exterior room windows to reveal 66 dancers clad in Day-Glo skeleton suits to catch the attention of eventgoers. Panasonic built a 9-foot-tall pigeon to promote the launch of a new camera, and Coke rigged a soda machine to dispense sunflowers, a doggie balloon, and a hot pepperoni pizza.

Some marketers wonder if the guerrilla tactics are being taken too far. To promote the movie *Dead Man Down,* a viral agency tagged a scene with two men fighting on the floor of an elevator to the shock and chagrin of unsuspecting onlookers. In another, the floor seemingly falls out of an elevator while riders are in it (of course, there was a glass bottom). To promote Carlsberg beer, an unsuspecting man is aroused from his sleep by a friend who says he is desperate for money and asks him to bring $400 to a seedy bar. When the friend delivers, everyone raises a glass to salute friendship while it is all being caught on tape.

While the stunts often go viral, they are often very expensive to produce, risky, and sometimes even dangerous. Robert Thompson, a professor of popular culture at Syracuse University, thinks that the pranks may have gone "over the top."[48] Many others agree.

## Miscellaneous Other Media

The variety of options for placing ads appears endless. Obviously, we have reported on only a few of these. Chapter 15 will discuss a few more, specifically online vehicles. Before leaving this chapter, however, we would like to mention a few of the faster-growing and more widely used options.

- *Videogame ads.* As the number of videogamers and the time they spend playing these games continues to increase, advertising in this medium is expected to grow right along with it. Companies such as Orbitz and T-Mobile have found videogame ads to be successful, as have Nike, Coca-Cola, Nokia, Levi Strauss & Company, and others. A Barack Obama ad appeared in an Xbox game promoting his campaign website, www.voteforchange.com. An estimated 68 percent of American households play computer games or videogames, 40 percent of whom are female.[49]

- *Parking lot ads.* An out-of-home medium showing increased growth is that of parking lot signage. From signs on cart docks to painting the walls of indoor parking garages, more companies are finding this medium attractive—particularly for point-of-purchase items. The ads reach a variety of demographics, depending on where they are placed. PepsiCo is just one of a number of companies employing this medium.

- *Gas station pump ads.* Screens appearing on gas pumps now reach an estimated 150 consumers monthly in over 125 markets. A study conducted by Nielsen shows that the ads have high recall and engagement rates; consumers enjoy them and find them entertaining and say that they would watch them again on their next visit.[50]

**YTC** 13–07
**Place Based**
youtube.com/10ebelch

- *Place-based media.* The idea of bringing the advertising medium to the consumers wherever they may be underlies the strategy behind place-based media. TV monitors and magazine racks have appeared in classrooms, doctors' offices, and health clubs, among a variety of other locations. PRN (the Premiere Retail Network) has TV channels in more than 10,000 locations, including Walmart, Costco, Best Buy, and Sam's Clubs in the United States, reaching an estimated 237 million consumers a month.[51] Place-based media have become a profitable venture and an attractive alternative for media buyers. Many advertisers, particularly pharmaceutical companies, have found place-based media an effective way to reach their markets, McDonald's now has a McDonald's TV Channel" in its stores. Nielsen now provides quarterly audience reports.

- *Others.* Just a few other examples of the use of support media: Coca-Cola installed 1,000 feet of light boxes in the Atlanta subway to show motion picture ads for Dasani; Muzak, a provider of background music, has teamed with Tyme ATMs to broadcast ads at bank ATM sites; ads now appear on luggage conveyors at some airports, on MetroCards, on hubcaps, in elevators, on bowling balls,

**EXHIBIT 13–9**

Advertising on people's bodies is becoming more common

LO 13-3

bike wheels, and in people's homes, and on fruit. People are even allowing ads to be placed on their bodies, including their heads, necks, and thighs (Exhibit 13–9). There are many other examples, as is well demonstrated in Exhibit 13–10 (at least he earned something from the fight!). Ethical Perspective 13–1 shows that ads are now appearing in unexpected places to serve other purposes.

## Advantages and Disadvantages of Miscellaneous Alternative Media
Advantages of alternative media include the following:

- *Awareness and attention.* Perhaps the major advantage of these tactics is their ability to attract attention. Given their novelty and the nontraditional locations in which they appear, they are likely to create awareness and gain attention.
- *Cost efficiencies.* Because of the nontraditional nature of alternative media, many advertisers are using media not previously used for advertising, or that, in general, do not require high expenditures. As such, the absolute and relative costs are not yet that high.
- *Targeting.* Depending on the tactic used, the campaign can be very targeted. It can be exposed only to a specific event, location, age, or interest group.

Disadvantages of alternative media include the following:

- *Irritation.* Unless the advertiser is careful, advertising placed in the wrong medium may have a negative impact, resulting in irritation, negative attitudes toward the advertiser, or even opportunities for the competitor. When Microsoft logos were painted on sidewalks, the city and consumers were not impressed and Microsoft was fined. One of its competitors gained significant public relations benefits when the company announced it would be happy to remove the paintings. The City of New York was not very happy with Snapple when the company's giant popsicle started to melt and created a flood in Union Square.
- *Wearout.* For now, many of these campaigns are novel and unique and are attracting consumer interest. As the number of efforts increases, however, there is the potential to lose the uniqueness associated with them.

**EXHIBIT 13–10**

Ads often appear in the strangest places

# Ethical Perspective 13-1 > > >

## The Uncomfortable Tie between Advertising and the Public Sector Motivates Concerned Organizations to Fight Back

While there are many critics of the increasing amounts of advertising we see, as well as the increasing intrusiveness, there are many in the public sector that are seeking even more. As the economic downturn dragged on, budgets for a variety of services continued to decrease, leaving managers to seek out alternative means of financing. One of these is to find advertisers to help allay the costs of a number of services. Consider some of the following:

After his school cut its materials and supplies budget by 30 percent to save jobs, a high school teacher in San Diego, California, started offering an opportunity to advertise on his students' quizzes and exams. Quizzes cost $10, chapter tests $20, and a semester final $30, with the ads appearing on the first page only. Most of the ads have come from small store owners, parents, and well wishers, and most students are receptive, knowing the financial situation. So far, the idea raised enough money to cover the teacher's deficit, with some extra left over for others in the math department.

Also in California, the state has considered offering advertisers the opportunity to place messages on digital signs on freeways that were installed for Amber Alerts and other emergencies. The ads would be allowed to appear when the signs are not in use, with the monies going to the state highway fund. While proponents argue that the money is sorely needed and that the signage would be improved, opponents say that's not what the 674 signs are intended for and that it would create an environmental blight while distracting motorists.

A high school in Houston, near the George Bush Intercontinental Airport, is offering its roof, parking lot, stadium, and even the bottom of its swimming pool to advertisers to raise money. Chicago is taking offers from advertisers to allow them to name individual station stops on its "L" line. Brooklyn, New York, has proposed selling ads on city trash cans and on construction scaffolding. A number of states (Texas, Utah, and Arizona, among others) allow advertising on the outside of school buses, while a number of others are considering the same (California, Florida, and New York). In Los Angeles, New York, and Philadelphia, 200 Domino's logos have been stenciled into ecofriendly images into the street grime to promote its American Legends pizza while also helping clean the streets. KFC is helping tackle the pothole problem in Louisville, Kentucky. KFC fills the potholes in exchange for the permission to stamp "Refreshed by KFC" on each one repaired. (The chalky stencils will fade away with the next rainstorm.) Toyota has donated 17 new four-wheel-drive vehicles to the city of Huntington Beach, California, for lifeguards to use while patrolling the beaches, while Toyota claims the moniker "The Official Vehicle of Huntington Beach." More public sector–advertiser deals are in the works.

While municipalities desperately need the money and other contributions (the Toyota deal saved Huntington Beach $500,000), not everyone thinks this type of advertising is such a good idea. The organization Campaign for Commercial Free Childhood (CCFC) has taken on the fight against school bus ads. It has also initiated legislation to prohibit the place-based News Channel 1 from showing 2 minutes of commercials in the 12 minutes of classroom news, and was successful in getting *Scholastic Magazine* to sever ties with the American Coal Foundation, which sponsored the fourth-grade "United States of Energy" program while promoting the merits of coal. CCFC has been joined by other organizations, including Rethinking Schools, Friends of the Earth, and the Center for Biological Diversity, among others, to fight similar causes. Others argue that the reason they pay taxes is for public services, and towns should not have to rely on private citizens. Still others contend the ads everywhere idea will contribute to visual pollution. It is the equivalent of selling our souls, they say.

For now, it seems everything is for sale.

Sources: Josh Golin, "Scholastic Severs Ties with the Coal Industry; Controversial Elementary School Materials Withdrawn after Protests," www.commercialfreechildhood.org, May 14, 2011; "2012 School Bus Ad Action Center," www.commercialfreechildhood.org, April 26, 2012; Emily Bryson York, "Need a Pothole Filled in Your City? Call KFC," www.adage.com, March 25, 2009; Elana Glowatz, "Domino's Ads Pop Up on City Sidewalks," www.brandweek.com, July 10, 2009; Linda Lou, "Funds Sliced, Teacher Sells Ads on Tests," *San Diego Union-Tribune*, November 22, 2008, pp. NC1–NC3; Patrick McGreevy, "Ads between Amber Alerts?" *Los Angeles Times*, September 24, 2008, pp. B1, B5; Robert Klara, "Cities for Sale," *Adweek Media*, March 9, 2009, pp. 6–8.

## Summary

This chapter introduced you to the vast number of support media available to marketers. These media, also referred to as nontraditional or alternative media, are just a few of the many ways advertisers attempt to reach their target markets. We have barely scratched the surface here. Support media include out-of-home advertising (outdoor, in-store, and transit), promotional products, and movie theater advertising, among many others. The fastest-growing area is that of branded entertainment, including product placements, product integrations, and others.

Support media offer a variety of advantages. Cost, ability to reach the target market, and flexibility are just a few of those cited in this chapter. In addition, many of the media discussed here have effectively demonstrated the power of their specific medium to get results.

But each of these support media has disadvantages. Perhaps the major weakness with most is the lack of audience measurement and verification. Unlike many of the media discussed earlier in this text, most nontraditional media do not provide audience measurement figures. So the advertiser is forced to make decisions without hard data or based on information provided by the media.

As the number and variety of support media continue to grow, it is likely the major weaknesses will be overcome. When that occurs, these media may no longer be considered nontraditional or alternative.

## Key Terms

support media p. 454
alternative media p. 454
below-the-line media p. 454
nonmeasured media p. 454
nontraditional media p. 454
out-of-home advertising p. 455
digital out-of-home media p. 457
aerial advertising p. 457

mobile billboards p. 458
in-store media p. 459
transit advertising p. 460
inside cards p. 460
outside posters p. 460
terminal posters p. 461
promotional products
  marketing p. 464

specialty advertising p. 464
Yellow Pages p. 466
directional medium p. 467
branded entertainment p. 468
product placements p. 468
product integrations p. 470
advertainment p. 470
advergames p. 470

## Discussion Questions

1. Content sponsorship has been on the increase in a variety of mediums. Give examples of sponsorships in different media and explain why their use is increasing. (LO3)

2. Explain why marketers have increased their use of product placements and integrations. Do you think that product placements and integrations are effective? Explain your answer. (LO2)

3. Digital advertising media seem to be more and more effective, but at the same time, more and more controversial. Explain why both of these situations have arisen. (LO2)

4. Why has the use of guerrilla marketing been on the increase? Take a position as to whether or not this form of marketing has become controversial, and explain whether or not this criticism is warranted. (LO2)

5. What are some of the advantages and disadvantages of promotional products? What are some of the situations in which promotional products may be most valuable to marketers? (LO2)

6. Digital out-of-home media have been experiencing rapid growth. Give examples of some of these new media forms and why they have an advantage over existing traditional out-of-home media. (LO2)

7. Promotional products, often referred to as advertising specialties, constitute a multibillion-dollar industry. Explain some of the various forms of promotional products, and how they might be used. (LO2)

8. Traditional out-of-home advertising such as billboards, transit, and so on have recently experienced growth in years when other media forms have seen their business decline. Why is this so? Give examples as to when outdoor may be more attractive to advertisers than other media. (LO3)

9. Discuss some of the advantages and disadvantages of branded entertainment. Do you see business in this area increasing or decreasing in the future? Explain your answer. (LO3)

10. Discuss some recent examples of product placements and/or integrations. Describe the context in which they were used, and how they intended to reach their target markets. Do you think these placements/integrations were successful? Why or why not? (LO4)

PHOENIX COYOTES

GOALden TICKET

## LEARNING OBJECTIVES

**LO1** To recognize the area of direct marketing as a communications tool.

**LO2** To know the strategies and tactics involved in direct marketing.

**LO3** To demonstrate the use of direct-marketing media.

**LO4** To determine the scope and effectiveness of direct marketing.

# 14 Direct Marketing

## SPORTS TEAMS AT ALL LEVELS USE DIRECT MARKETING TO SELL SEATS

What do the New York Jets, Phoenix Coyotes, and 59.2 percent of all colleges with sports teams have in common? The answer: they all use direct mail to help sell seats.

A 2013 study conducted by Research and Markets collected detailed data from over 100 colleges regarding their spending patterns, practices, and plans for sports marketing, including baseball, basketball, football, lacrosse, and other sports. The research examined spending habits on a variety of media, including outdoor, print, and digital as well as other marketing vehicles. The study showed that for colleges with an enrollment of 20,000 or more, over 81 percent advertise in newspapers, while only 34 percent of those in schools of less than 20,000 students do. Regardless of size, more than 65 percent of Division I schools employed opt-in e-mail to promote their team. Most of these schools found their efforts to be successful; almost 37 percent report increases in basketball attendance, even though their teams may not have played better.

Borrowing an idea from the University of Minnesota, the Phoenix Coyotes professional hockey team ran a promotion designed to incentivize fans to attend their final 10 home games. The promotion used a GOALden ticket, in which fans purchased tickets based on the number of goals they expected the home team to allow in those games. Once the goals were reached (for example, 5 games for 5 goals) the tickets were void. Fans could purchase up to as many as 25 goals, at a greatly reduced price. At the game the fans swiped a Personal Identification Card letting them in and indicating how many goals they had left. The Coyotes would also send an e-mail after each game reminding the fans how many goals remained on their cards. To advertise the promotion, the Coyotes relied on only two media—an e-mail campaign geared to past package and season ticket holders and a direct-mail campaign to season ticket holders going back to five or six years prior.

It worked! The promotion led to the sales of 200 packages and an incremental $35,000 in revenue. In addition, there was a substantial increase in cross-selling sales for other packages and future games, and an unmeasurable amount of buzz!

The New York Jets football team has never had a home of their own. Even though the franchise has been around for 50 years, they have never had their own stadium. Starting as the New York Titans in the original American Football League in 1960, the team played their first game in the Polo Grounds. In 1964 they moved to Shea Stadium—a venue built for baseball and the home of the New York Mets. After 20 years, the Jets moved to the Meadowlands in New Jersey—as a tenant. To make matters worse, the team shared the stadium with their crosstown rival New York Giants in—of all things—Giants Stadium. In the 1970s, 80s, and 90s the Jets were not very competitive and had troubles drawing fans. But by the turn of the century, the Jets once again began to compete for the division title and fill the stadium for almost every home game. Season tickets could not be bought for years, and it got so bad, fans gave up on trying to do so. So the Jets built a new facility—for the first time ever—their own stadium!

Good news, bad news! With the new Jets stadium set to open in fall 2010, marketing of season tickets started in 2008—right in the middle of the recession. While new season tickets had not been available for decades, the new stadium would hold 82,500 people, many of whom were unaware of ticket availability. The Jets hired a Manhattan advertising agency to coordinate the IMC campaign, which included advertising, an interactive microwebsite, support media, public relations, and a heavy emphasis on direct marketing. The campaign was called "Opportunity Knocks," and the initial theme line was "Finally, we're the home team." A three-pronged approach was taken with phase 1 focusing on branding and awareness and accompanied with call-to-action direct-response media. Existing ticket holders were invited to tour the new stadium when completed and received glossy brochures to encourage them to buy seats in the new venue. Finally, follow-up phone calls, e-mails, and direct-mail pieces were used to close the deal. Existing ticket holders were offered the best seating options based on their seniority, but good seats were still available.

While the season ticket holders responded well, seats remained. After the existing ticket holders had their chance, the unsold seats (including club seats) were made available to the general public—with a "Ticket for everybody" program that included a wide variety of price options and a 15-year financing program for the more expensive seats. All of the media efforts including the TV spot, a print campaign, direct mail, web advertising, and e-mails again included a specific call to action.

While all of the seats were not sold, the Jets considered the two-year campaign a success and believe that without it, many more tickets would have gone unsold. By 2013 the Jets were again playing in front of a full house. Now it's time for the Jets to do their part, and keep them there!

Sources: Dylan Bohanan, "Coyotes Create a Goalden Promotion," www.sportsforum.com, April 3, 2013; Laura Wood, "The 2013 Survey of College Sports Marketing Practices: 59.62% of Schools Used Direct Mail in the Past Year to Market Sporting Events," *Sports Techy*, April 17, 2013, p. 1; Thomas Haire, "Jets Audible into Direct Response," *Response*, January 2010, pp. 26–32; Thomas Haire, "New York Jets Engage Ad Agency Fly Communications to Help Market New Jets Stadium Scheduled to Open in August 2010," *Business Wire*, September 3, 2008, pp. 1–3.

The discussion of the Phoenix Coyotes' and New York Jets' marketing programs in this chapter's opener demonstrates just one of the means of effectively utilizing direct marketing. The team's use of various direct-response media, when combined with other IMC elements, led to successful marketing to put fans in seats. It is important to realize that there are numerous direct-marketing tools that can be used to reach one's target market. This chapter will discuss these direct media.

# DIRECT MARKETING

While many companies rely on a variety of promotional-mix elements to move their products and services through intermediaries, an increasing number are going directly to the consumer. These companies believe that while promotional-mix tools such as advertising, sales promotion, support media, and personal selling are effective in creating brand image, conveying information, and/or creating awareness, going direct can generate an immediate behavioral response. Direct marketing is a valuable tool in the integrated communications program, though it usually seeks somewhat different objectives.

In this chapter, we discuss direct marketing and its role as a communications tool. For many companies and organizations, direct marketing is a key element in their IMC program, and for some marketers it has become the medium of choice for reaching consumers. We begin by defining direct marketing and then examine direct-marketing media and their use in the overall communications strategy. The section concludes with a basis for evaluating the direct-marketing program and a discussion of the advantages and disadvantages of this marketing tool.

## Defining Direct Marketing

As noted in Chapter 1, **direct marketing** is a system of marketing by which organizations communicate directly with target customers to generate a response or transaction. This response may take the form of an inquiry, a purchase, or even a vote. The Direct Marketing Association (DMA) defines direct marketing as

> an interactive system of marketing which uses one or more advertising media to effect a measurable response and/or transaction at any location.[1]

First we must distinguish between direct marketing and direct-marketing media. As you can see in Figure 14–1, direct marketing is an aspect of total marketing—that is, it

FIGURE 14-1 U.S. Direct-Marketing Expenditures by Medium and Market (in Billions of Dollars)

| Channel | Market | 2006 | 2010 | 2011 | 2012 | 2016 | Compound Annual Growth Rate 2006–2011 | 2011–2016 |
|---|---|---|---|---|---|---|---|---|
| Commercial E-Mail | | $0.8 | $1.4 | $1.6 | $1.7 | $2.3 | 13.8% | 8.6% |
| | Business | 0.5 | 0.8 | 0.9 | 0.9 | 1.3 | 13.7 | 8.3 |
| | Consumer | 0.4 | 0.6 | 0.7 | 0.8 | 1.1 | 13.9 | 8.8 |
| Direct Mail (catalog) | | 20.1 | 16.4 | 17.3 | 17.7 | 20.5 | −3.0 | 3.5 |
| | Business | 7.7 | 6.4 | 6.8 | 7.0 | 8.2 | −2.5 | 3.9 |
| | Consumer | 12.4 | 9.9 | 10.4 | 10.7 | 12.3 | −3.3 | 3.3 |
| Direct Mail (noncatalog) | | 33.0 | 31.5 | 32.8 | 33.4 | 37.1 | −0.1 | 2.5 |
| | Business | 12.6 | 12.0 | 12.5 | 12.7 | 14.2 | −0.1 | 2.5 |
| | Consumer | 20.5 | 19.5 | 20.3 | 20.7 | 22.9 | −0.2 | 2.5 |
| Insert Media | | 1.9 | 2.1 | 2.1 | 2.2 | 2.3 | 2.4 | 1.7 |
| | Business | 0.7 | 0.8 | 0.8 | 0.8 | 0.9 | 2.7 | 1.8 |
| | Consumer | 1.2 | 1.3 | 1.4 | 1.4 | 1.5 | 2.2 | 1.6 |
| Internet Display | | 5.0 | 7.2 | 8.5 | 9.5 | 14.1 | 11.3 | 10.6 |
| | Business | 2.8 | 4.0 | 4.7 | 5.2 | 7.7 | 11.1 | 10.3 |
| | Consumer | 2.2 | 3.2 | 3.8 | 4.3 | 6.4 | 11.4 | 10.9 |
| Internet Other | | 1.9 | 3.2 | 3.9 | 4.4 | 5.9 | 15.7 | 8.8 |
| | Business | 1.0 | 1.8 | 2.1 | 2.4 | 3.2 | 15.6 | 8.6 |
| | Consumer | 0.8 | 1.4 | 1.7 | 2.0 | 2.7 | 15.8 | 9.1 |
| Internet Search | | 8.4 | 11.8 | 13.9 | 15.6 | 22.4 | 10.6 | 9.9 |
| | Business | 4.7 | 6.5 | 7.7 | 8.6 | 12.2 | 10.5 | 9.7 |
| | Consumer | 3.8 | 5.3 | 6.2 | 7.1 | 10.2 | 10.7 | 10.2 |
| Internet Social Networking | | 0.6 | 2.0 | 2.5 | 3.0 | 6.1 | 34.4 | 19.4 |
| | Business | 0.3 | 0.9 | 1.1 | 1.4 | 2.8 | 34.5 | 19.7 |
| | Consumer | 0.3 | 1.1 | 1.4 | 1.6 | 3.3 | 34.2 | 19.1 |
| DR Magazine | | 8.4 | 6.9 | 7.0 | 6.9 | 7.2 | −3.7 | 0.6 |
| | Business | 4.3 | 3.6 | 3.7 | 3.7 | 3.9 | −3.1 | 1.1 |
| | Consumer | 4.1 | 3.2 | 3.3 | 3.2 | 3.3 | −4.4 | 0.0 |
| Mobile | | 0.1 | 0.6 | 0.9 | 1.2 | 3.1 | 75.2 | 28.7 |
| | Business | 0.0 | 0.2 | 0.3 | 0.4 | 0.9 | 69.2 | 25.2 |
| | Consumer | 0.0 | 0.4 | 0.6 | 0.8 | 2.2 | 78.8 | 30.3 |
| DR Newspaper | | 16.1 | 8.4 | 7.8 | 7.0 | 4.9 | −13.6 | −9.0 |
| | Business | 6.1 | 3.2 | 3.0 | 2.7 | 1.9 | −13.1 | −8.7 |
| | Consumer | 10.0 | 5.2 | 4.8 | 4.3 | 3.0 | −13.9 | −9.1 |

| Channel | Market | 2006 | 2010 | 2011 | 2012 | 2016 | Compound Annual Growth Rate | |
|---|---|---|---|---|---|---|---|---|
| | | | | | | | 2006–2011 | 2011–2016 |
| DR Radio | | 4.9 | 3.9 | 3.9 | 3.8 | 3.9 | −4.4 | −0.2 |
| | Business | 2.4 | 2.0 | 2.0 | 2.0 | 2.0 | −3.7 | 0.1 |
| | Consumer | 2.5 | 1.9 | 1.9 | 1.9 | 1.9 | −5.2 | −0.5 |
| Telephone Marketing | | 44.8 | 36.3 | 36.6 | 36.9 | 38.1 | −3.9 | 0.8 |
| | Business | 26.8 | 22.0 | 22.2 | 22.4 | 23.2 | −3.7 | 0.9 |
| | Consumer | 17.9 | 14.4 | 14.4 | 14.5 | 14.9 | −4.3 | 0.6 |
| DR Television | | 22.0 | 20.8 | 22.1 | 22.9 | 25.9 | 0.1 | 3.2 |
| | Business | 9.7 | 9.5 | 10.2 | 10.6 | 12.2 | 0.9 | 3.7 |
| | Consumer | 12.3 | 11.3 | 11.9 | 12.3 | 13.7 | −0.7 | 2.9 |
| Other | | 2.8 | 2.0 | 2.1 | 2.1 | 2.3 | −5.2 | 1.4 |
| | Business | 1.2 | 0.9 | 1.0 | 1.0 | 1.0 | −4.5 | 1.9 |
| | Consumer | 1.6 | 1.1 | 1.2 | 1.2 | 1.2 | −5.6 | 1.0 |
| Total | | $170.8 | $154.4 | $163.0 | $168.5 | $196.0 | −0.9% | 3.8% |
| | Business | 80.8 | 74.6 | 79.1 | 81.8 | 95.6 | −0.4 | 3.9 |
| | Consumer | 90.0 | 79.8 | 83.9 | 86.7 | 100.4 | −1.4 | 3.6 |

Source: From the Direct Marketing Association, *The Power of Direct Marketing*, 2012.

involves marketing research, segmentation, evaluation, and the like, just as our planning model in Chapter 1 did. Direct marketing uses a set of **direct-response media**, including direct mail, telemarketing, interactive TV, print, the Internet, and other media. These media are the tools by which direct marketers implement the communication process.

The purchases of products and services through direct-response advertising currently exceed $2.05 trillion and are projected to reach $2.49 trillion by the year 2016.[2] Firms that use this marketing method range from major retailers such as the Gap, Restoration Hardware, and Victoria's Secret to airline companies to financial services and local companies. Business-to-business and industrial marketers have also significantly increased their direct-marketing efforts, with an estimated $1.09 trillion in sales forecast by 2016.[3]

## The Growth of Direct Marketing

Direct marketing has been around since the invention of the printing press in the 15th century. Ben Franklin was a very successful direct marketer in the early 1700s, and Warren Sears and Montgomery Ward were using this medium in the 1880s.

The major impetus behind the growth of direct marketing may have been the development and expansion of the U.S. Postal Service, which made catalogs available to both urban and rural dwellers. Catalogs revolutionized America's buying habits; consumers could now shop without ever leaving their homes.

But catalogs alone do not account for the rapid growth of direct marketing. A number of factors in American society have led to the increased attractiveness of this medium for both buyer and seller:

- *Consumer credit cards.* There are now more than 1 billion credit cards—bank, oil company, retail, and so on—in circulation in the United States. This makes it feasible for consumers to purchase both low- and high-ticket items through direct-response channels and assures sellers that they will be paid. It is estimated that over $2.09 trillion is charged on credit cards each year.[4] Of course, not all of this was through direct marketing, but a high percentage of direct purchases do use this method of payment, and companies such as American Express, Diners Club, MasterCard, and Visa are among the heaviest direct advertisers.

- *The changing structure of American society and the market.* One of the major factors contributing to the success of direct marketing is that so many Americans are now "money-rich and time-poor." The rapid increase in dual-income families has meant more income. (It is estimated that in 2012 women made up about 46.9 percent of the labor force.)[5] At the same time, the increased popularity of physical fitness, do-it-yourself crafts and repairs, and home entertainment has reduced the time available for shopping and has increased the attractiveness of direct purchases.

- *Technological advances.* The rapid technological advancement of the electronic media and the Internet has made it easier for consumers to shop and for marketers to be successful in reaching the desired target markets. Well over 110 million television homes receive home shopping programs. Virtually 100 percent of those homes are connected to cable and satellite.

- *Miscellaneous factors.* A number of other factors have contributed to the increased effectiveness of direct marketing, including changing values and lifestyles, more sophisticated marketing techniques, and the industry's improved image. These factors will also ensure the success of direct marketing in the future. The variety of companies employing direct marketing demonstrates its potential.

LO 14-2

While some organizations rely on direct marketing solely to generate a behavioral response, for many others direct marketing is an integral part of the IMC program. They use direct marketing to achieve other than sales goals and integrate it with other program elements. We first examine the role of direct marketing in the IMC program and then consider its more *traditional* role.

**EXHIBIT 14–1**

Bose uses multiple methods to promote its products

Bose® SoundDock® Portable digital music system

**Compare it to any other sound system for the iPod. Portable or not.**

1-XXX-XXX-XXXX, ext. xxxxx | Bose.com/SoundDock

**BOSE**
Better sound through research.

# The Role of Direct Marketing in the IMC Program

Long the stepchild of the promotional mix, direct marketing has now become an important component in the integrated marketing programs of many organizations. In fact, direct-marketing activities support and are supported by other elements of the promotional mix.

## Combining Direct Marketing with Advertising

Obviously, direct marketing is in itself a form of advertising. Whether through mail, print, or TV, the direct-response offer is an ad. It usually contains a toll-free number or a form that requests mailing information. Sometimes the ad supports the direct-selling effort. For example, Victoria's Secret runs image ads and commercials to support its store and catalog sales. Bose Audio also markets through stores and online, supporting its efforts through advertising (Exhibit 14–1). Direct-response ads or infomercials are also referred to in retail outlet displays. Sometimes an advertisement will be sent through direct mail.

## Combining Direct Marketing with Public Relations

As you will see later in this text, public relations activities often employ direct-response techniques. Private companies may use telemarketing activities to solicit funds for charities or co-sponsor charities that use these and other direct-response techniques to solicit funds. Likewise, corporations and organizations engaging in public relations activities may include toll-free numbers or website URLs in their ads or promotional materials. The DMA Nonprofit Federation has worked with numerous organizations and small and large companies in support of environmental issues.

**Combining Direct Marketing with Personal Selling**   Telemarketing and direct selling are two methods of personal selling used to generate sales. Nonprofit organizations like charities often use telemarketing to solicit funds. As you will see, for-profit companies are also using telemarketing with much greater frequency to screen and qualify prospects (which reduces selling costs) and to generate leads. Direct-mail pieces are often used to invite prospective customers to visit auto showrooms to test-drive new cars; the salesperson then assumes responsibility for the selling effort. Automobile manufacturers and their dealers have both made effective use of this approach.

**Combining Direct Marketing with Sales Promotions**   How many times have you received a direct-mail piece notifying you of a sales promotion or event or inviting you to participate in a contest or sweepstakes? Ski shops regularly mail announcements of special end-of-season sales. Airlines send out mailers or e-mails announcing promotional airfares. Nordstrom and other retail outlets call their existing customers to notify them of special sales promotions. Each of these is an example of a company using direct-marketing tools to inform customers of sales promotions (Exhibit 14–2). In turn, the sales promotion event may support the direct-marketing effort. A study conducted by Vertis indicated that marketers could increase the effectiveness of their direct-mail campaigns by offering exclusive deals and/or coupons. Seventy-two percent of adults surveyed said they had responded to a direct-mail offering of a buy-one-get-one-free offer, and 63 percent said they had responded to an offer of a percentage discount on merchandise. Both of these numbers had increased since a previous study conducted in 2005.[6] Databases are often built from the names and addresses acquired from a promotion, and direct mail and/or telemarketing calls follow.

**Combining Direct Marketing with Support Media**   Adding a promotional product to a direct mailer has proven to increase response rates. One company included a promotional product in half of its 10,000 mailers and not in the other half. The former generated 65 percent more orders. 3M used a promotional product as an incentive for people responding to a direct-mail offer. The incentive generated a 23 percent response rate versus only 9 percent for the regular mailer.

To successfully implement direct-marketing programs, companies must make a number of decisions. As in other marketing programs, they must determine (1) what the program's objectives will be, (2) which markets to target (through the use of a list or marketing database), (3) what direct-marketing strategies will be employed, and (4) how to evaluate the effectiveness of the program.

**EXHIBIT 14–2**
Costco sends promotional offers through the mail

## Direct-Marketing Objectives

The direct marketer usually seeks a direct response. The objectives of the program are normally behaviors—for example, test drives, votes, contributions, and/or sales. A typical objective is defined through a set response, perhaps a 2 to 3 percent response rate.

Not all direct marketing seeks a behavioral response, however. Many organizations use direct marketing to build an image, maintain customer satisfaction,

484   **Chapter 14**  DIRECT MARKETING

and inform and/or educate customers in an attempt to lead to future actions. When President Obama kicked off his presidential campaign in 2012, he did so with direct-response TV ads. The ads asked viewers to call an 888 phone number or visit JoinObama.com and enter their e-mail addresses and zip codes and to get more involved in his reelection efforts. The success of the president's reelection campaign was attributed to these types of grass-roots efforts. Exhibit 14–3 provides an example of how Acura and Pinehurst Golf Resort partnered to offer consumers a special three-hour use of an Acura—the "Preferred Vehicle of Pinehurst"—and a special package price for their vacation getaway. The two companies believe that they share a common target market profile and similar business philosophies of offering only the highest-quality product.

**YTC 14–01**

**Obama**

youtube.com/10ebelch

**LO 14-3**

## Direct-Marketing Strategies and Media

As with all other communications programs discussed in this text, marketers must decide the message to be conveyed, the size of the budget, and so on. Perhaps the major difference between direct-marketing programs and other promotional-mix programs regards the use of media.

As shown in Figure 14–1, direct marketing employs a number of media, including direct mail, telemarketing, direct-response broadcasting, the Internet, and print. Each medium is used to perform specific functions, although they all generally follow a one- or two-step approach.

In the **one-step approach**, the medium is used directly to obtain an order. You've probably seen TV commercials for products like wrench sets, workout equipment, or magazine subscriptions in which the viewer is urged to phone a toll-free number to place an order immediately. Their goal is to generate an immediate sale when the ad is shown.

The **two-step approach** may involve the use of more than one medium. The first effort is designed to screen, or qualify, potential buyers. The second effort generates the response (e.g., the order). For example, many companies use telemarketing to screen on the basis of interest and then follow up to interested parties with more information designed to achieve an order or use personal selling to close the sale.

**EXHIBIT 14–3**

Acura and Pinehurst Golf Resort partner on a direct-mail program

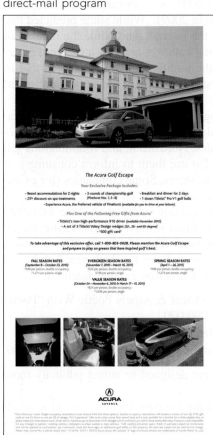

**Direct Mail** Direct mail is often called "junk mail"—the unsolicited mail you receive. More advertising dollars continue to be spent in direct mail than in almost any other advertising medium—an estimated $57.6 billion in 2016.[7] Direct mail is not restricted to small companies seeking our business. Respected large companies and organizations in the retail, financial services, and fund-raising sectors (among others) commonly employ this medium. In 2011, the average household in the United States received 21 direct-mail pieces per week.[8]

Many advertisers shied away from direct mail in the past, fearful of the image it might create or harboring the belief that direct mail was useful only for low-cost products. But this is no longer the case. For example, Porsche Cars North America, Inc. uses direct mail to target high-income, upscale consumers who are most likely to purchase its expensive sports cars. In one example, Porsche developed a direct-mail piece that was sent to a precisely defined target market: physicians in specialties with the highest income levels. This list was screened to match the demographics of Porsche buyers and narrowed further to specific geographic areas. The direct-mail piece was an X-ray of a Porsche 911 Carrera 4 written in the language of the medical audience. This creative campaign generated one of the highest response rates of any mailing Porsche has done in recent years. The piece shown in Exhibit 14–4 is just one sent by Maserati to market its new Quattroporte automobile. Exhibit 14–5 shows how direct mail can be used throughout the purchase funnel.

DRIVE, FEEL, DISCOVER.

MASERATI
QUATTROPORTE

Foreign Cars Italia invites you to test drive the 2014 Maserati Quattroporte.

**EXHIBIT 14–4**

Maserati used direct mail to introduce its new Quattroporte

Keys to the success of direct mail are the **mailing list**, which constitutes the database from which names are generated, and the ability to segment markets and, of course the offer. Lists have become more current and more selective, eliminating waste coverage. Segmentation on the basis of geography (usually through zip codes), demographics, and lifestyles has led to increased effectiveness. The most commonly used lists are of individuals who have already purchased direct-mail products.

The importance of the list has led to a business of its own. It has been estimated that there are over 38 billion names on lists, and many companies have found it profitable to sell the names of purchasers of their products and/or services to list firms. Companies like A. B. Zeller, Experian, and Nielsen Business Media (Exhibit 14–6) provide such lists on a national level, and in most metropolitan areas there are firms providing the same service locally.

While direct mail continues to be a favorite medium of many advertisers, and projections are that the market will grow, this medium has been seriously threatened by the Internet. The lower cost of e-mail and the convenience of the Internet have raised concerns among traditional direct-mail marketers. Interestingly, the Internet is both a threat and an opportunity, as Internet companies have increased their expenditures in direct mail to drive potential customers to their sites. Nevertheless, the traditional direct-mail business has experienced lower response rates from many consumers who see the offer first through direct mail and then go online to order. Many companies, have shifted from print to online catalogs, saving money and keeping more current.

**Catalogs**   Major participants in the direct-marketing business include retailers and other catalog companies. The number of catalogs mailed and the number of traditional catalog shoppers has decreased each year since 2007, with an estimated 11.8 billion catalogs mailed in 2012 (down from 13.5 billion in 2009).[9] While some predicted that catalogs would cease to exist with more use of the Internet, and while the number of catalogs mailed continues to decrease, traditional catalogs are still an effective way to reach consumers. The emotional appeal of the traditional catalog exceeds that of online catalogs and ultimately is one of the best ways to drive consumers online, as shown in Digital and Social Media Perspective 14–1.

**EXHIBIT 14–5**

Direct mail can be used to move consumers through the purchase funnel

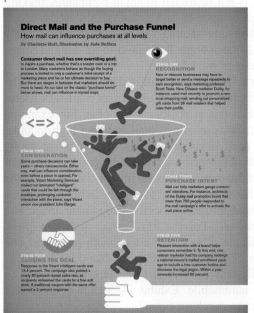

**Direct Mail and the Purchase Funnel**
How mail can influence purchases at all levels
By Charlotte Huff, Illustration by Jude Buffum

Many companies use catalogs in conjunction with their more traditional sales and promotional strategies. For example, companies like Pottery Barn, Bloomingdales, Nordstrom, and Illuminations sell directly through catalogs but also use them to inform consumers of product offerings available in the stores. Some companies (for example, Oriental Trading Company) rely solely on catalog sales. Others that started out exclusively as catalog companies have branched into retail outlets, among them Road Runner Sports, Eddie Bauer, Banana Republic, and Illuminations (Exhibit 14–7). The products being offered through this medium have reached new heights as well. The 2012 Neiman Marcus Christmas catalog featured:

■ His & Hers gift package, Van Cleef & Arpels Poetic Wish "Poetic Wish" watches and trip: $1,090,000.
■ Jetler R200, a water-propelled jet pack: $99,500.
■ A 2013 Neiman Marcus Edition McLaren 12C Spider: $354,000.

Of course, these products were designed to attract publicity more than anything else!

In addition to the traditional hard copies, catalogs are now available on the Internet for both consumer and business-to-business customers. In some instances in the consumer market the catalog

# Digital and Social Media Perspective 14–1 > > >

## Is Digital Killing the Catalog Store?

Years ago there was a song titled "Video Killed the Radio Star" by the Buggles that commiserated with the fact that the new technology was changing the music business and essentially killing radio. Right now, the catalog business may be asking itself a similar question—"Is digital technology killing the catalog store?"

For years, catalogs have come through the mail. Montgomery Ward published his first catalog (one page) in 1875, and eight years later his "Wish Book" contained over 10,000 items and was over 240 pages long. The Sears & Roebuck Company (Sears) published its first catalog in 1894, and by the next year it contained over 300 pages. As noted by Charles Nicholls, the print catalog has "interruptive value" because it arrives in the mailbox. It also is convenient, as it can be read in front of the TV, in bed, or wherever and whenever one pleases. Because it often lies on the table or is kept nearby on a shelf for an extended time, it is revisited and is an instant source of information. Research has demonstrated the success of the print catalog over the years, indicating that consumers who receive a catalog in the mail buy twice as often as those who don't.

But print catalogs have become quite expensive to produce, mailing costs have risen, and technology is beginning to replace the traditional catalog, just as it is the print newspaper and magazines. Is the print catalog dead or dying?

Recent studies by Adobe and Harris Interactive have shown that mobile shopping apps are beginning to take on the role of the catalog, with as many as 40 percent of tablet and smartphone users stating that they have retail apps. And, not only do they have them, but they like them and use them in much the same way print catalogs are used. The apps are used to see what new products the retailer is offering, to look for deals, to seek additional information about products, and to save time. Many of those surveyed said the shopping apps created a stronger connection to the retailer, and that if the retailer did not offer this service they would consider the store to be "old-fashioned."

Retailers are listening. IKEA—another well-known catalog purveyor—announced that the print catalog released every August will now be prereleased as a digital version in July. In addition the IKEA catalog app will be relaunched with a digital twist—augmented reality. Consumers will now be able to scan selected images in the print catalog to access extended content, including 3-D models, behind-the-scenes videos, and interactive features (adding furniture to a room). IKEA's 2013 print catalog will be its 63rd edition, available in 27 languages and 40 countries worldwide. Consumers can now request either a print or digital version (or both). Numerous other companies are offering digital versions of their print editions as well, including The Gap and Kawasaki, among others.

So, is the catalog as we knew it a relic of the past? Not quite yet. While digital catalogs offer some distinct advantages over print, the traditional versions still have their value. Remember what we said earlier, that receiving a catalog in the mail has a pleasurable "interruptive value" and that it is often revisited and enjoyable to read. And, while retailers have found that digital catalog sales are on the increase, they have also found that it is more difficult to cross-sell products or get add-on sales than it is through print versions. After a decline in catalog sales from 2006 to 2011, the Direct Marketing Association projects a 3.1 percent growth through 2016, to almost $147 billion. That's a long way from being dead!

Perhaps the two can live in harmony. Sears apparently thinks so, as it also now offers a digital version of its catalog. Think about it—Sears?

Sources: "Are Shopping Apps Taking on the Role of Catalogs," www.eMarketer, January 23, 2013; Sheila Shayon, "IKEA's 2013 Catalog Adds Ineractivity, Tears Down Walls," www.brandchannel.com, July 19, 2012; Charles Nicholls, "Do Digital Catalogs Drive Conversions?" www.practicalecommerce.com, March 26, 2012.

**YTC** 14–02

**IKEA Online Catalog**

youtube.com/10ebelch

merchandise is available in retail stores as well. In others, the catalog and retail divisions are treated as separate entities. For example, if you purchase through the Eddie Bauer catalog, you can exchange or return the merchandise to the retail stores. Victoria's Secret products must be returned to the catalog department. At the Gap, the catalog is used to supplement the inventory in stock, and phone orders for different sizes and so on can be made from the store and shipped for free.

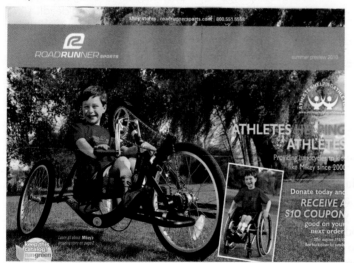

nielsen business media
················ **LIST** Reference Guide: Volume 8 ················

Reach
Over 3
Million
Decision
Makers

Postal

Email

Telemarketing

Co-Reg

Multi-Channel

EDITH
ROMAN

800-223-2194

**EXHIBIT 14–6**
Nielsen Business Media provides lists for purchase

**EXHIBIT 14–7**
Road Runner Sports is one of many successful catalog companies now in retail

**E-mail**   Direct mail on the Internet (**e-mail**) is essentially an electronic version of regular mail. Like regular mail it is highly targeted, relies heavily on lists, and attempts to reach consumers with specific needs through targeted messages. The use of e-mail marketing by both business-to-business and business-to-consumer marketers continues to grow, as both the low cost and the higher effectiveness than traditional direct mail appeal to marketers. A study conducted by the Harvard Business School showed that e-mail campaigns were as much as 95 times more effective than traditional direct-marketing campaigns when return on investment (ROI) was used as the effectiveness measure.[10]

Sometimes users may also receive less-targeted and unwanted e-mails. The electronic equivalent of junk mail, these messages are referred to as **spam**. Because of the high volumes of spam and the fact that many consumers consider it a nuisance, the U.S. government has passed laws regulating its use. In addition, anti-spam software has become effective in blocking most of the unwanted messages. Nevertheless, all indications are that the end of this form of advertising is not in sight.

**Broadcast Media**   The success of direct marketing in the broadcast industry has been truly remarkable; as far back as 1996 over 77 percent of the U.S. population reported that they had viewed a direct-response appeal on TV.[11] Direct-response TV is estimated to generate more than $13.73 billion in advertising billings in 2016.[12]

Two broadcast media are available to direct marketers: television and radio. While radio was used quite extensively in the 1950s, its use and effectiveness have dwindled substantially in recent years. Thus, the majority of direct-marketing broadcast advertising now occurs on TV, which receives the bulk of our attention here. It should be pointed out, however, that the two-step approach is still very common on the radio, particularly with local companies.

Direct marketing in the broadcast industry involves both direct-response advertising and support advertising. In **direct-response advertising**, the product or service is offered and a sales response is solicited, through either the one- or two-step approach previously discussed. Examples include ads for apparel, exercise equipment, collectables, and so on. Toll-free phone numbers are included so that the receiver can immediately call to order. **Support advertising** is designed to do exactly that—support other forms of advertising. Ads for Publishers Clearing House or *Reader's Digest* or other companies telling you to look in your mailbox for a sweepstakes entry are examples of support advertising.

Direct-response TV encompasses a number of media, including direct-response TV spots like those just mentioned, infomercials, and home shopping shows (teleshopping). And as noted in Chapter 10, Internet TV has recently been introduced.

**TV Spots**   Referred to in the direct-marketing industry as *short-form programs,* these spots include

Arnage T

BENTLEY

The Ultimate Driver's Bentley

**EXHIBIT 14–8**
Bentley has successfully used an infomercial to attract buyers

direct-response commercials commonly seen on television for products such as drugs and toiletries, audio and video supplies, household products, and more.

**Infomercials** The lower cost of commercials on cable and satellite channels has led advertisers to a new form of advertising. An **infomercial** is a long commercial that is designed to fit into a 30-minute or 1-hour time slot. Many infomercials are produced by the advertisers and are designed to be viewed as regular TV shows. Today's infomercials use both one- and two-step approaches. Programs such as "Liquid Luster," "Amazing Discoveries," and "Stainerator" (the so-called miracle-product shows) were the most common form of infomercial in the 1980s. While this form of show is still popular, the infomercial industry has been adopted by many large, mainstream marketers, including Coca-Cola, Braun, Disney, Nissan, Apple, and Microsoft. (See Exhibit 14–8.)

As to their effectiveness, IMC Perspective 14–1 proves that infomercials are watched and sell products. The demographics of the infomercial shopper reflect a married female, mean age of 45, Caucasian, working full time with a household income of $55,000+ per year.[13] This advertising medium is indeed effective with a broad demographic base, not significantly different from the infomercial nonshopper in age, education, income, or gender. Retail stores are benefiting from infomercials as well, as brand awareness leads to increased in-store purchases. For example, a $500,000 print campaign combined with an infomercial for the George Foreman grill led to more sales at retail stores than through direct TV.[14]

The popularity of the infomercial has led companies to expand into the more frequently watched daytime TV market and the creation of infomercial networks. GM's OnStar system has offered a daytime version of the infomercial called "Tales from the Road" it refers to as a "documercial," and an infomercial network called ExpoTV has been lanched and claims to reach 25 million households.[15,16]

However, some people are not sold on the idea of ads disguised as programs. For example, infomercials disguised as "ultrahip" TV shows have been targeted at teenagers, raising fears that kids under the age of 13 will be susceptible to their lure. Consumer complaints are on the rise, and the FTC has already levied fines for deceptive endorsements against infomercial sponsors, and has taken legal action against those engaging in deceptive practices. Well-known infomercial promoter Kevin Trudeau was fined $37.6 million by the FTC for making false claims in his infomercials. Four consumer groups (the Consumer Federation of America, Center for the Study of Commercialism, Center for Media Education, and Telecommunications Research and Action Center) have asked the FCC to require all infomercials to display a symbol that indicates a "paid ad" or "sponsored by" so that viewers won't confuse them with regular programming.

**Home Shopping** The development of toll-free telephone numbers, combined with the widespread use of credit cards, has led to a dramatic increase in the number of people who shop via their TV sets through home shopping channels. Jewelry, kitchenware, fitness products, insurance, household products, and a variety of items are now promoted (and sold) this way. The major shopping channel in the United States (QVC) broadcasts on TV 24 hours a day and online. While Internet e-commerce sales have hurt the TV home shopping channels, they have succeeded through adaptation: Both QVC and Home Shopping Network (HSN) have upgraded their product lines to include designer brand names and luxury goods at a lower price point.[17] The success of home shopping networks has led to a proliferation of shopping channels, including Shop@homeTV, Shop NBC, and the Liquidation

# IMC Perspective 14–1 > > >

## Infomercials: We May Not Like Them, but We Buy Anyway!

If you ever asked someone what they thought about info-mercials, you would likely get a negative response. While most people say they don't like this form of advertising, the fact is that research shows that as many as one-third of us have purchased something from an infomercial. The mere fact that you see them on TV is evidence that they work—otherwise they wouldn't be there. Successful long-form ads, as they are often called, have successfully marketed a variety of product lines including weight-loss products, personal care items, exercise equipment, and even churches, doctors, and pet-bird stores. Following is a sampling of some of the most effective infomercials of 2012.

*The Foodsaver Food Vacuum Packaging Machine* This handy little vacuum sealer gadget will suck the air out of your food to increase its shelf life fivefold. The makers say that by removing the air, freezer burn and dehydration are reduced and the flavors remain longer. According to the ad, by purchasing the machine for $129, consumers can save themselves over $2,000 in food loss.

*The Ped Egg* This product is designed to remove calluses and dead skin from one's feet. It looks like a cheese grater, but there is no mess, and your feet feel better and healthier. Studies conducted by *Consumer Reports* show that it does work!

*Snuggies* One of the more popular and enduring products of recent infomercial years, the Snuggie doubles as a robe and blanket. While laughed at by many when they were first introduced, the Snuggie has been a phenomenal success and is now available in hundreds of colors and designs. You can even get one for your dog!

*Bowflex* Another household name among infomercial viewers, the Bowflex home gym has been sold through infomercials for years, raking in millions of dollars. Buy one of these machines and you can become muscular and fit in just weeks (well, you do have to use it!). Bowflex offers testimonials from numerous users who claim to have gone from overweight to "uber-hot" in almost no time with their new perfect bodies.

*Proactiv* Perhaps the champion of all infomercials, the *Proactiv solution* anti-acne facial cleanser has used a variety of celebrities to promote the product, spending over $15 million a year in the process. Justin Bieber, P. Diddy, Jessica Simpson, Kelly Clarkson, Lindsey Lohan, and Vanessa Williams are just a few who have endorsed the product over the years. The ads have become so popular they have gone viral; Proactiv now has a YouTube page that has had over 1.5 million hits!

And these are just a few of the many successful infomercials. Whopper Choppers, George Foreman grills, Slap-Chops, and ShamWows can also be included in this list.

Numerous others have used infomercials as well. In Atlantic City, new Jersey, an independent television station WMCN has sold the long-form ads to churches, auto dealers, doctors, and pet-bird stores, charging them $75 to $500 to reach over 2.5 million homes in the South Jersey and Philadelphia markets. One plastic surgeon advertiser has become so popular he has his own following on Wednesday nights.

"But why?" you might ask. How can some of these messages be so irritating but so successful? Numerous explanations have been offered over the years. One is that the high-volume, high-action scripts increase viewers' dopamine levels by creating (or at least making us recognize) problems we never new we had, and then offer a solution. There is also the potential impact of the celebrities. Look at the Proactiv list mentioned earlier, then add in Chuck Norris, Susan Lucci, and George Foreman (among others)—all of whom have been successful infomercial product endorsers. Add in these factors and the ability to create and measure effective infomercials, and you have a remedy for success.

Maybe it is just possible that these products do what they say, and are worth the money!

Sources: Charles Klein, "Top 10 Most Popular Infomercial Products," www .toptenz.com, April 20, 2012; Bob Fernandez, "Atlantic City TV Station Looking Beyond Infomercials," McClatchy-Tribune Business News, May 29, 2011, p. 1.

Channel, to name just a few. As the demographics of shopping channel buyers continue to move upscale, the products offered on these channels continue to move upscale as well.

**Print Media** Magazines and newspapers are difficult media to use for direct marketing. Because these ads have to compete with the clutter of other ads and

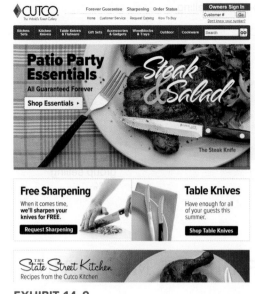

**EXHIBIT 14–9**

Cutco is one of many companies using direct selling

because the space is relatively expensive, response rates and profits may be lower than in other media. Print direct-response ads can still be found in specific interest areas like financial newspapers or sports, sex, or hobby magazines.

**Telemarketing**  If you have a telephone, you probably do not have to be told about **telemarketing**, or sales by telephone. Both profit and charitable organizations have employed this medium effectively in both one- and two-step approaches. Combined telemarketing sales (consumer and business-to-business), continuing to decrease since 2004, totaled over $305 billion in 2012.[18] Telemarketing is still a very big industry.

In recent years, the telemarketing industry has suffered from a decline due to a number of factors. Problems associated with telemarketing include its potential for fraud and deception and its potential for annoyance. These developments have led to the development of a Do Not Call list for both landline and cell phones.

Those in the telemarketing and telemedia industry have responded to public criticisms, while Dial-a-Porn and its ilk hold a diminishing share of 800, 900, and 976 offerings.

# DIRECT SELLING

**YTC 14–04**

**Direct Selling**

youtube.com/10ebelch

An additional element of the direct-marketing program is **direct selling**, the direct, personal presentation, demonstration, and sales of products and services to consumers in their homes. Amway, Avon, Cutco, Mary Kay, *Inc.*, and Tupperware are some of the best-known direct-selling companies in the United States and have now extended these programs overseas (Exhibit 14–9). A fairly recent entrant to the direct-selling market is jewelry company Stella & Dot. In 2013, Stella & Dot's sales were expected to exceed $200 million, and the company was number 57 in the Inc. 500 list of the 5,000 Fastest Growing Private Companies. Approximately 15.6 million people engage in direct selling throughout the United States, and 99 percent of them are independent contractors (not employees of the firm they represent). Direct selling generates over $29.87 billion in sales.[19]

The three forms of direct selling are

1. *Repetitive person-to-person selling.* The salesperson visits the buyer's home, job site, or other location to sell frequently purchased products or services (for example, Amway). Mary Kay has given away over 100,000 Cadillacs—the company's symbol of sales success.
2. *Nonrepetitive person-to-person selling.* The salesperson visits the buyer's home, job site, or other location to sell infrequently purchased products or services (for example, *World Book Encyclopedia*).
3. *Party plans.* The salesperson offers products or services to groups of people through home or office parties and demonstrations (for example, Tupperware and PartyLite Gifts).

While a number of products and services are sold through direct selling, home and family durables, weight-loss and wellness products, and personal services are the most popular. The "typical" direct-selling representative is female (over 80 percent), married (77 percent), and works part time (88 percent). For most of the representatives, direct selling is not a full-time job but an opportunity to earn additional income and a way to get the product at a discount for themselves. Over half of those in this industry spend fewer than 10 hours a week selling, and the vast majority spend less than 30 hours a week selling. Figure 14–2 reflects the means by which they sell.

CHAPTER 14

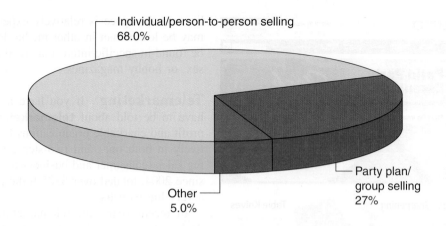

Individual/person-to-person selling
68.0%

Party plan/
group selling
27%

Other
5.0%

# EVALUATING THE EFFECTIVENESS OF DIRECT MARKETING

Because they generate a direct response, measuring the effectiveness of direct-marketing programs is not difficult. Using the **cost per order (CPO)**, advertisers can evaluate the relative effectiveness of an ad in only a few minutes based on the number of calls generated. By running the same ad on different stations, a direct marketer can determine the relative effectiveness of the medium itself. For example, if the advertiser targets a $5 return per order and a broadcast commercial (production and print) costs $2,500, the ad is considered effective if it generates more than 500 orders. Similar measures have been developed for print and direct-mail ads.

Another commonly employed measure of effectiveness is **Customer Lifetime Value (CLTV)**. CLTV is a simple formula that is used to assist marketers in determining the dollar value associated with a long-term relationship with a customer, thus evaluating his or her worth. The value is used to determine whether or not a customer should be acquired, as well as to optimize service levels to existing customers. Companies use CLTV to assist them in assessing future revenues and profit streams from the customer, so that they can focus more on the satisfaction and retention of their more profitable customers. Thus, the company can focus more attention on profitable customers while spending less marketing effort on those with a low CLTV score.

For direct-marketing programs that do not have an objective of generating a behavioral response, traditional measures of effectiveness can be applied. (We discuss these measures in Chapter 18.)

## Advantages and Disadvantages of Direct Marketing

Many of the advantages of direct marketing have already been presented. A review of these and some additions follow:

1. *Selective reach.* Direct marketing lets the advertiser reach a large number of people and reduces or eliminates waste coverage. Intensive coverage may be obtained through broadcast advertising or through the mail. While not everyone drives on highways where there are billboards or pays attention to TV commercials, virtually everyone receives mail. A good list allows for minimal waste, as only those consumers with the highest potential are targeted. For example, a political candidate can direct a message at a very select group of people (those living in a certain zip code or members of the Sierra Club, say); a book club can target recent purchasers or avid readers.

2. *Segmentation capabilities.* Marketers can rent lists of recent product purchasers, car buyers, bank-card holders, and so on. These lists may allow segmentation

on the basis of geographic area, occupation, demographics, and job title, to mention a few. Combining this information with the geocoding capabilities of Prizm or VALS (discussed in Chapter 2), marketers can develop effective segmentation strategies.

3. *Frequency.* Depending on the medium used, it may be possible to build frequency levels. The program vehicles used for direct-response TV advertising are usually the most inexpensive available, so the marketer can afford to purchase repeat times. Frequency may not be so easily accomplished through the mail, since consumers may be annoyed to receive the same mail repeatedly.

4. *Testing.* Direct marketing allows for a strong ability to test the effectiveness of the overall program as well as specific elements.

5. *Timing.* While many media require long-range planning and have long closing dates, direct-response advertising can be much more timely. Direct mail and e-mail, for example, can be put together very quickly and distributed to the target population. TV programs typically used for direct-response advertising are older, less sought programs that are likely to appear on the station's list of available spots. Another common strategy is to purchase available time at the last possible moment to get the best price.

6. *Personalization.* No other advertising medium can personalize the message as well as direct media. Parents with children at different age levels can be approached, with their child's name included in the appeal. Car owners are mailed letters congratulating them on their new purchase and offering accessories. Computer purchasers are sent software solicitations. College students receive very personalized information that recognizes their specific needs and offers solutions, as well as college loan offers.

7. *Costs.* While the CPM for direct mail may be very high on an absolute and a relative basis, its ability to specifically target the audience and eliminate waste coverage reduces the actual CPM. Costs may be higher than in other media, but direct methods may be more profitable. The ads used on TV are often among the lowest-priced available. E-mail is extremely inexpensive.

   A second factor contributing to the cost-effectiveness of direct-response advertising is the cost per customer purchasing. Because of the low cost of media, each sale generated is very inexpensive.

8. *Measures of effectiveness.* No other medium can measure the effectiveness of its efforts as well as direct response. Feedback is often immediate and always accurate.

Disadvantages of direct marketing include the following:

1. *Image factors.* As we noted earlier, the mail segment of this industry is often referred to as junk mail. Many people believe unsolicited mail promotes junk products, and others dislike being solicited. Even some senders of direct mail, including Motorola, GM, and Air Products & Chemicals, say they throw out most of the junk mail they receive. This problem is particularly relevant given the increased volume of mail being sent through e-mail. The Direct Marketing Association estimates that the typical household received almost 21 pieces of direct mail a week in 2012.[20]

   Likewise, direct-response ads on TV are often low-budget ads for lower-priced products, which contributes to the image that something less than the best products are marketed in this way. (Some of this image is being overcome by the home shopping channels, which promote some very expensive products.) Telemarketing is found to be irritating to many consumers, as is "spam" or Internet junk mail. Other factors have also created image problems for the direct-marketing industry.

2. *Accuracy.* One of the advantages cited for direct mail and telemarketing was targeting potential customers specifically. But the effectiveness of these methods depends on the accuracy of the lists used. People move, change

occupations, and so on, and if the lists are not kept current, selectivity will decrease. Computerization has greatly improved the currency of lists and reduced the incidence of bad names; however, the ability to generate lists is becoming a problem. The cost of generating a lead can range from a few dollars to as much as hundreds depending on its quality.

3. *Content support.* In our discussion of media strategy objectives in Chapter 10, we said the ability of magazines to create mood contributes to the overall effectiveness of the ads they carry. In direct-response advertising, mood creation is limited to the surrounding program and/or editorial content. Direct-mail and online services are unlikely to create a desirable mood.

4. *Rising costs.* As postal rates increase, direct-mail profits are immediately and directly impacted. The same is true for print costs, which drives up the costs of mailers and catalogs. The low cost of e-mail has led many companies to switch to this medium.

5. *Do Not Contact lists.* Do Not Call lists now exist for both landline and cell phones. A "Do Not Contact" list in which consumers can choose not to receive "junk mail" is under consideration by the FTC.

## Summary

This chapter introduced you to the rapidly growing field of direct marketing, which involves a variety of methods and media beyond direct mail and telemarketing. The versatility of direct marketing offers many different types of companies and organizations a powerful promotional and selling tool.

Direct-marketing continues to outpace other advertising and promotional areas in growth; many of the *Fortune* 500 companies now use sophisticated direct-marketing strategies. Database marketing has become a critical component of many marketing programs.

Advantages of direct marketing include its selective reach, segmentation, frequency, flexibility, and timing. Personalized and custom messages, low costs, and the ability to measure program effectiveness are also advantages of direct-marketing programs.

At the same time, a number of disadvantages are associated with the use of direct marketing. Image problems, deception, and the intrusive nature of the medium make some marketers hesitant to use direct-marketing tools. However, self-policing of the industry and involvement by large, sophisticated companies have led to significant improvements. As a result, the use of direct marketing will continue to increase.

## Key Terms

direct marketing p. 480
direct-response media p. 482
one-step approach p. 485
two-step approach p. 485
mailing list p. 486

e-mail p. 488
spam p. 488
direct-response advertising p. 488
support advertising p. 488
infomercial p. 489

telemarketing p. 491
direct selling p. 491
cost per order (CPO) p. 492
Customer Lifetime Value (CLTV) p. 492

## Discussion Questions

1. Explain what is meant by Customer Lifetime Value. How does this formula benefit the direct marketer? (LO4)

2. A study by the Harvard Business School has shown that e-mail marketing is much more effective than traditional direct mail in that it provides a much greater return on investment (ROI). Explain some of the reasons why this would be. (LO4).

3. Direct marketing has been an effective tool for marketers for a long time. Provide some reasons why direct marketing has been so effective. Do you think this trend will continue? (LO1)

4. Explain why digital catalogs will not drive the traditional catalog into extinction. Cite some of the advantages of maintaining a traditional print catalog. (LO3)

5. While a very effective medium, direct marketing also has a number of distinct disadvantages. Discuss some of these, and what marketers could do to decrease them. (LO4)

6. As noted in the text, a number of home shopping channels now offer a variety of upscale products. Discuss reasons why you think this will work to their advantage. Are there any disadvantages to this strategy? (LO1)

7. What is customer relationship management? Discuss how direct marketing can be employed to improve customer relationship management. (LO1)

8. What is an infomercial? What are some of the reasons that infomercials have been so successful? Which types of products and services do you think are likely to be candidates for successful infomercials? (LO3)

9. Direct marketers are very good at determining the effectiveness of their programs. Many direct marketers now measure the impact of the program on the consumer funnel. Explain how direct marketers measure effectiveness, and how they now use the consumer funnel for this purpose. (LO4)

10. As the Internet continues to grow in popularity, some marketers predict that the print catalogs will cease to exist, replaced by Internet catalogs. Others disagree. Explain some of the reasons why this situation may or may not occur. (LO1, 2)

**DEWmocracy 2** Media Hub

Explore the various stages of the DEWmocracy 2 campaign; from grassroots truck tour to advertising, by clicking through the various stages.

Stage **1** Truck Stop — TASTE THE FLAVORS

Stage **2** Make Your Voice Heard — FLAVOR NATIONS

Stage **3** Shoot Your Shade — COLOR SELECTION

Stage **4** Name Game — NAME THE PRODUCT
#231 LIME BLASTED DEW
#493 SMOOTH CITRUS DEW
#508 DEW

Stage **5** DEW Art — DESIGN YOUR CAN

Stage **6** Creative Juices — ADVERTISING

Stage **7** Vote in the Flavor Battle

## LEARNING OBJECTIVES

**LO1** To understand the role of the Internet and digital and social media in an IMC program.

**LO2** To understand the use of Web 1.0 and Web 2.0 media platforms in the IMC process.

**LO3** To understand how to evaluate the effectiveness of communications through the Internet and digital and social media.

**LO4** To know the advantages and disadvantages of the Internet and digital and social media.

**LO5** To examine the social and ethical issues associated with the Internet and digital and social media.

# 15 The Internet: Digital and Social Media

## MOUNTAIN DEW USES SOCIAL MEDIA AND DEWMOCRACY TO CREATE NEW BRANDS

From its initial creation by the Hartman Beverage Company in Tennessee in the late 1940s, Mountain Dew has always been known as the soft drink that provides a little extra. The drink was initially used as a mixer for liquor, and the founders named the product after an old-time Appalachian folk song that told of the pleasure of "mountain dew" moonshine whiskey. The bright yellow-green citrus-flavored drink came in a green bottle and contained more sugar and caffeine and less carbonation so it could be chugged quickly and provide the drinker with a rush. Mountain Dew evolved into a stand-alone soft drink with a renegade attitude as the initial advertising featured a comic hillbilly character named Willy. Over the next two decades the popularity of Mountain Dew spread beyond the Appalachian region and became a favorite along the Eastern Seaboard and into the Midwest.

PepsiCo noticed the growing popularity of Mountain Dew and purchased the brand in 1964 to add a non-cola-flavored soft drink to its product line. The hillbilly character was renamed Clem and was put in animated ads linked to the brand's backwoods heritage that used the tagline "Yahoo! Mountain Dew!" and proclaimed that "Thar's a bang in ever' bottle." In 1973 PepsiCo began working with BBDO on the advertising for Mountain Dew, and over the next two decades various campaigns were used to create a national identity for the brand that went beyond rural areas and into the major metropolitan markets as well. The advertising toned down the energizing effects of the extra sugar and caffeine and began positioning Mountain Dew as a refreshing part of an active, country lifestyle while expanding the target market to include suburban teenagers. A new campaign called "Country Cool" ran for a few years but soon gave way to a new creative approach built around daredevil athletic stunts involving alternative sports such as skateboarding, snowboarding, windsurfing, rollerblading, and BMX biking, which were becoming increasingly popular among urban teens.

By 1992 Mountain Dew had become a national brand, but distribution of the diet version of the product was still limited to rural markets where the brand was the strongest. To expand the market for Diet Mountain Dew, a campaign was created using the tagline "Do Diet Dew" and featured the "Dew Dudes"—four young slacker-type guys who live in a world in which only extreme stunts and Mountain Dew matter. Although originally developed for the diet product, the Dew Dudes helped solidify the association with action sports, as well as irreverence, and became the basis of the advertising for the entire Mountain Dew brand. The tagline evolved into "Do the Dew," which served as an umbrella theme for the Mountain Dew brand, and ads featuring the Dew Dudes became the basis of one of the best-known advertising campaigns of the past two decades.

Mountain Dew continued to build on its image as an irreverent brand that stands for individuality by continuing to embrace all things edgy, including extreme sports, videogaming, and other activities. In 2005 Mountain Dew began sponsoring the Dew Tour—a premier action sports tour that helps keep the brand connected to the action sports community. However, as the beverage market became more competitive, Mountain Dew looked for additional ways to connect with its loyal consumers, most of whom are males between the ages of 18 and 39 and are very active online.

In 2007 the Mountain Dew brand team gave its highly loyal consumer base a way to become more involved with the brand through an initiative called DEWmocracy. The goal of this program was to open up the product development process and have the brand's passionate fans create and choose a new Mountain Dew flavor. More than 1 million people participated in a series of interactive games on the Democracy.com website to develop every aspect of three alternatives for the new line extension, including color, flavor, graphics, and name. The three consumer-generated flavors were made available in stores across the country for a limited time, and approximately 500,000 votes were cast. The winner was Mountain Dew Voltage, a citrus flavor charged with raspberry and ginseng that was launched in January 2009 and became the first Mountain Dew made by fans for fans.

With one user-created beverage successfully launched, the Mountain Dew brand team launched a second DEWmocracy initiative that took the "crowd-sourcing" model several steps further and gave passionate fans even more control by taking advantage of the growing power of social media. DEWmocracy 2 kicked off in 2009 with a tiered grassroots campaign that included a mobile tour that created 222,712 sampling experiences and a contest that rewarded 50 Dew fanatics with home-tasting kits of seven potential flavors. Recipients of the kits were selected from fans who submitted video clips of up to 12 seconds explaining why they deserved a kit. The home tasters were given video cameras and encouraged to upload videos about their tasting experiences to Facebook and YouTube. Three finalist flavors emerged from the grassroots voting and feedback from brand fanatics.

Once the flavors were selected, DEW Labs, a brand community composed of the Mountain Dew brand's 4,000 most passionate fans, was created. Each member received samples of the three final flavors, chose a favorite, and joined the corresponding "Flavor Nation," which was charged with developing names, package designs, and colors for each. Consumers were asked to participate in the development of the products as well. Colors were selected via a live UStream event on Facebook, where Mountain Dew had half a million fans at the time. Consumers cast more than 7,000 votes, and the brand team devised a clever visual way to demonstrate the vote count that fit well with the culture of the Mountain Dew brand's irreverent fans—the votes triggered paint balls in the voters' preferred color to be shot at volunteers during a live event. To name their beverage, Flavor Nation members submitted lists of suggestions, then chose their three favorites. Once PepsiCo's legal department had vetted the name, the final

names were chosen via a "Twitter race" where each name was assigned a Twitter account and the one that attracted the most followers won. The three winners were Mtn Dew Typhoon, Mtn Dew Distortion, and Mtn Dew White Out.

Mountain Dew also turned over the creative component to fans, as agencies and individuals were invited to submit 12-second videos via 12seconds.tv outlining their ideas for marketing the three new flavor options. More than 200 ads were submitted, and six finalists were selected by consumers who cast more than 15,000 votes. The finalists created short pitch videos for the Flavor Nations, and three were selected to work closely with the DEW brand team and the Flavor Nations to create television spots for each flavor. The spots began airing nationally in April 2010 and marked the first use of traditional media for the campaign in 10 months of activity. The final phase of DEWmocracy involved having the Flavor Nations fight for the allegiance of DEW fans when their products hit the store shelves and rallying consumers around the country to vote for their products. Each nation had its own Facebook page and Twitter account to get the word out during the eight-week period that the products were available at retail.

Voting ran until early June, and the flavor receiving the most votes was Mtn Dew White Out. The DEW online community was once again engaged to help develop the launch plan for the new brand, which debuted as a permanent member of the Mountain Dew family on Labor Day 2010. DEWmocracy prevailed and Mtn Dew White Out became the second flavor of Mountain Dew created entirely by DEW drinkers for DEW drinkers.

The success of these programs has led Mountain Dew to go international—well, at least to Canada, where the DEWmocracy campaign will be implemented again (though in a slightly different format). Canadian DEWmocracy hopes to take advantage of the already strong social engagement with the brand on Facebook and Twitter by giving Canadian Dew consumers their own line extension. Can they Dew do it again?

Sources: "Mountain Dew Canada—Dewmocracy Coming March 18," www.bevwire.com, March 11, 2013; Natalie Zmuda, "Why Mtn Dew Let Skater Dudes Take Control of Its Marketing," Advertising Age, February 22, 2010, http://adage.com/print?article_id=14220; Natalie Zmuda, "New Pepsi 'Dewmocracy' Push Threatens to Crowd Out Shops," Advertising Age, November 2, 2009, http://adage.com/print?article_id=140120; "Dewmocracy Campaign Overview," www.dewmocracymediahub.com.

As you can see from the lead-in to this chapter, social media offer marketers a whole new way to do business and communicate with their existing and potential customers. While the Internet itself required marketers to rethink their IMC programs, the advent of Web 2.0, which led to even more capabilities, has altered the environment forever for new and old brands and large and small companies.

This chapter will examine the role of the Internet. We will examine the growth of the Internet, how companies use the various platforms therein, and its role in an IMC program as well as some of the advantages and disadvantages associated with this medium. We will also discuss the various new media options that have resulted from the development of the Internet and their roles in an IMC program. The chapter will conclude with a discussion of the measurement of these media.

# THE GROWTH OF THE INTERNET

### Why the Rapid Adoption of the Internet?

The unprecedented growth of the Internet—the digital revolution—has led to changes in the marketing environment forcing marketers to rethink almost everything they do. As the World Wide Web evolves, so too do marketing communications programs. There are now close to 2 billion Internet users worldwide, and the growth since the year 2000 is staggering. A number of reasons can be cited as to why this growth has been so rapid. One is consumers' increased desire for information that they are now able to obtain easily. The speed and convenience of acquiring this information, as well as the ability to control what and how much is received, has had great appeal. The ability to conduct e-commerce through one's personal computer is also very attractive as it now seems there is almost nothing that one can't find or buy on the Web. It is as though the Internet has no bounds, as every day one can find something new there.

Like the consumers', marketers' adoption of this medium has also soared. The ability to target customers effectively through the Net is attractive to marketers. The increased attention for accountability on the part of businesses has led to a view of the Internet as a medium that would provide more direct feedback on the value of marketing expenditures, customer satisfaction, trends, and the competition. As was true of direct marketing, companies liked the fact that, unlike traditional media, it was often easier to account for the ROI of their expenditures. In fact, in its earliest stages, a number of marketing companies perceived the Internet as a direct-response medium. While a large component of the Web is still that of e-commerce, today's marketers now employ the medium for numerous other communications and marketing objectives (as we will discuss shortly).

Today's World Wide Web has evolved into a different medium than anyone could have expected 10 years ago. Unlike other media, which are essentially unidirectional and responsible for the content provided and products and services offered for sale, the Internet is interactive, allowing for a two-way flow. Consumers not only control when and which messages and content they are exposed to, but now provide their own content, offer their own goods and services for sale, and provide feedback on the same as provided by others. As you will see, marketers are involving consumers in a way never seen before, through a variety of platforms that never existed just a few decades ago.

**YTC 15-01**

**Growth of the Internet**

youtube.com/10ebelch

### Web Objectives

When major corporations first began to conduct business on the Internet, they put up websites primarily for information purposes and a one-way flow of information resulted. Companies like Kmart and Maytag had sites that were really not much more than online catalogs, while those of other companies were designed for information purposes only. The role of the website quickly changed, however, as sites are now designed to accomplish a number of objectives and have become much more creative, by promoting brand images, positioning, and offering promotions, product information, and products and services for sale, with many allowing interactivity. In addition, these sites allow for consumers' feedback and input that can be directly used by marketers to keep their customers engaged. This resulted in marketers utilizing the Internet in an entirely new way, moving beyond the purely informational role. As you will see, the objective of disseminating information and selling products remains, but additional communications and sales objectives are also being pursued.

Unlike other media discussed thus far in the text, the Internet is actually a hybrid of media. In part, it is a communications medium, allowing companies to create awareness, provide information, and influence attitudes, as well as pursue other communications objectives. Banner ads, display ads, and commercials—some of which may also appear on television—are commonly used for this purpose. For others, it is also a direct-response medium, allowing the user to both purchase and sell products through e-commerce, like Amazon and Craigslist. With the advent of social media, marketers have increasingly pursued a third objective of building brand image and developing a more direct and involved relationship with customers through engagement with the brand. Thus, we will discuss each of the objectives in this chapter. Let's first look at some of the communications objectives these companies want to achieve.

**Create Awareness** Advertising on the Web can be useful in creating awareness of an organization as well as its specific product and service offerings. For small companies with limited budgets, the Web offers the opportunity to create awareness well beyond what might be achieved through traditional media. For example, a start-up company like the one shown in Exhibit 15–1 can almost immediately gain worldwide exposure at a reasonable cost—something that was not possible before the Internet. While a valuable tool for creating awareness—particularly for smaller companies that may have limited advertising budgets—the Internet is not likely to be the most effective of the IMC elements for achieving this objective for larger companies. Mass-media advertising may be more useful for this purpose, given its larger reach and lower cost per exposure (as the TV people will be glad to remind you!). Studies have demonstrated the effectiveness of TV to drive visitors to websites. Nevertheless, even larger well-established companies have the creation of and increase in awareness as a primary objective.

**EXHIBIT 15–1**

Start-up company SweetBling.com has benefited from the use of the Internet

**Generate Interest** A visit to RedBull.com will quickly demonstrate how a site can be used to generate interest. The site provides news, live streams, videos, and more from the "World of Red Bull" (Exhibit 15–2). The objectives of this site and many others like it are simple: Create interest that will bring visitors back to learn more about the products—and, of course, to sell stuff.

**Disseminate Information** One of the primary objectives for using the Web is to provide in-depth information about a company's products and services. Having a website has become a necessity, as more and more buyers expect that a company will have a site providing them with detailed information about its offerings, warranties, store locations, and so on. Think about the last time you tried to find information on a company on the Internet and it didn't have a website. It is extremely rare for this to happen, and if it did, you would likely be hesitant to pursue a relationship with the company. In the government sector, contracts are often put out to bid on the Internet. Information regarding requirements, specifications, submission dates, and

**EXHIBIT 15–2**

Red Bull has used its website to create a powerful brand image

**EXHIBIT 15–3**

Nikawater.org creates a favorable brand image

so forth is disseminated more quickly, to more potential candidates, and at a much lower cost via the Net than it is through other media. Want information on filing federal income taxes? The first place you would look would likely be www.irs.gov. Websites serve as a means of communicating information about a company's products and services, philanthropic efforts, contact information, and the company itself.

**Create an Image** Many websites are designed to reflect the image a company wants to portray. For example, check out the site www.nikawater.org (Exhibit 15–3). The site is an excellent example of a website used for image building. Visitors get a good feeling about the water company's concern for humanity. Interestingly, one of the difficulties traditional marketers have experienced is that of creating a brand image on the Internet. While some of these companies have been successful, others have not fared as well and have come to realize that branding and image-creating strategies must be specifically adapted to this medium.

**Create a Strong Brand** The Internet—as part of an integrated marketing communications program—can be a useful tool for branding. While originally many companies had difficulty using the Internet to establish their brand, this is no longer the case. Red Bull has used its site (shown earlier) as an integral part of its IMC campaign focusing on the "Red Bull Gives You Wings" image, positioning itself as a brand dedicated to excitement and daring through its motorsports, biking, surfing, and snowboarding news and videos as well as music and events sponsorships. Red Bull is one of the many companies that have "figured it out" in regard to successful branding.

**Stimulate Trial** Many marketers have found the Internet to be an effective medium for stimulating trial of their products or services. Often websites offer electronic coupons in an attempt to stimulate trial of their products. Others offer samples, promotions, and sweepstakes designed to encourage trial. Music sites, like iTunes.com, allow for a "sampling" of songs before you purchase, while some business-to-business sites allow you to test their software online before purchasing.

**Create Buzz** One of the many advantages of the Web is the ability to create buzz. The viral nature of social networking and other sites makes them attractive to marketers intending to spread the word and use word of mouth. In a very successful effort to go viral, Dove recently created a video employing a sketch artist to draw women's self-perceptions and the way others saw them based on the descriptions they provided, without his ever seeing them. Titled "Dove Real Beauty Sketches," the amazing difference between these perceptions made the point that women often suffer self-esteem issues needlessly. At the time of this writing, the video had been viewed over 100 millon times worldwide.

**Gain Consideration** Many marketers believe that the Internet is an effective medium for achieving communications objectives such as consideration and/or evaluation. Blogs and discussion boards are considered particularly useful for providing information useful in evaluating products and brands. The use of "mommy bloggers" and teen "haulers" has become a powerful marketing strategy used by H&M, JCPenney, Dove, Ann Taylor, and Timex, among others.

## E-Commerce

The Internet also offers the opportunity to sell directly to customers in both the consumer market and the business-to-business market.

**EXHIBIT 15–4**

eBay is one of the most popular e-commerce sites

This direct selling of goods and services has been labeled **e-commerce**. Sales through e-commerce are expected to reach over $327 billion in the United States by 2016[1] (Exhibit 15–4). Many of the sites already mentioned in this chapter have a sales component—as either a primary or secondary goal.

Many companies maintain their existing "brick-and-mortar" stores while also selling through the Internet. Ann Taylor, Macy's, and Nordstrom are placing more emphasis on online sales; Samsung has added kiosks inside its stores where consumers can order online.

We discussed e-commerce and strategies employed in this area in Chapter 14. Let's have a look at how the Internet can be used as part of an IMC program.

# THE INTERNET AND INTEGRATED MARKETING COMMUNICATIONS

LO 15-2

Up to this point, we have mentioned the need for using the Internet as part of an IMC program and the objectives sought. In this section, we discuss how the Web can be used with other program elements.

Wikipedia, among other sources, makes a distinction between Web 1.0 and Web 2.0. Web 1.0 is generally referred to as the first decade or so of the World Wide Web, ending with the "bursting of the dot-com bubble."[2] For the most part, Web 1.0 consists mainly of static sites resulting in a one-way flow of communication. Web 2.0 has led to dramatic changes in the World Wide Web, primarily as a result of decentralization of communications and interactivity, with information provided by users as contributors of content such as user-generated ads content and so on (Figure 15–1). In this chapter we are not concerned with the technical changes that have taken place, but rather the resulting impact on marketing communications. Everything we have discussed to this point still constitutes the way marketers use the Web; however, Web 2.0 has added some key components that have had a drastic impact on how the Internet is used in an IMC program; so we will discuss them separately, starting with Web 1.0.

**EXHIBIT 15–5**

Banner ad formats

## Advertising on the Internet—Web 1.0

Like broadcast or print, the Internet is an advertising medium. Companies and organizations working to promote their products and services must consider this medium as they would television, magazines, outdoor, and so on. Advertising on the Internet employs a variety of forms, including banners, sponsorships, pop-ups and pop-unders, interstitials, paid searches, behavioral targeting, contextual ads, and rich media. Web 1.0 is the terminology used to refer to the early evolution of the World Wide Web in which users could view web pages and interface with them but could not contribute to the content of the web page.

**Banners** The most common form of advertising on the web is **banner ads**. There were over 5.3 trillion such ads served to U.S. users in 2012—1 trillion more than in 2009.[3] Banner ads may be used for creating awareness or recognition, entering viewers into contests and sweepstakes, or direct-marketing objectives. Banner ads may take on a variety of forms, as shown in Exhibit 15–5, as well as a number

FIGURE 15–1

Differences in the Way
Organizations Have
Interacted with Customers
on the Web

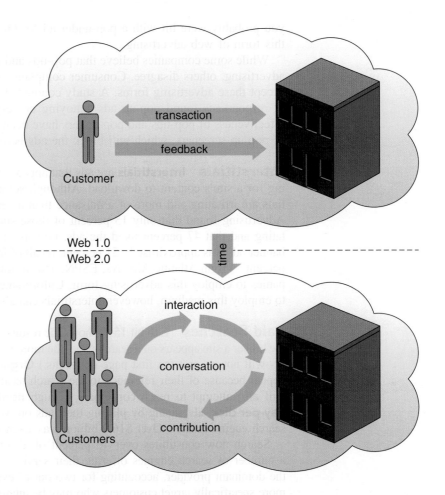

of names such as *leader boards, rectangles, side panels, skyscrapers,* or *verticals.* They can also be static, animated, or in flash. Initially banner ads constituted the vast majority of advertising on the Net, but studies indicating their questionable effectiveness have led some companies to reduce their usage. Reports on click-through rates vary, but most studies indicate a less than 1 percent response rate.[4] At the same time, a number of studies have shown that while viewers may not click through the banners, they can still be effective in driving consumers to search or visit the ad's website.[5,6] A study reported in the *Journal of Consumer Research* showed evidence that even with low click-through rates, banner ads may still create a favorable attitude toward the ads through repeated exposures.[7]

**Sponsorships**     Another common form of advertising is **sponsorships**. There are two types of sponsorships. *Regular sponsorships* occur when a company pays to sponsor a section of a site, for example, a *House Beautiful* magazine or *Cosmopolitan* magazine sponsorship on iVillage.com or a corporate sponsorship of a page on Forbes.com. A more involved agreement is the **content sponsorship**, in which the sponsor not only provides dollars in return for name association but also participates in providing the content itself. In some cases, the site is responsible for providing content and having it approved by the sponsor; in other instances, the sponsor may contribute all or part of the content.

**Pop-Ups/Pop-Unders**     When you access the Internet, you no doubt have seen a window or a creature of some sort appear on your screen in an attempt to get your attention. These advertisements are known as **pop-ups**, and they often appear when you access certain sites. Pop-ups are usually larger than banner ads but smaller than a full screen.

   **Pop-unders** are ads that appear underneath the web page and become visible only when the user leaves the site. For example, if you have ever visited a travel website, you probably were hit with a pop-under ad for Orbitz, one of the heaviest users of this form of web advertising.

While some companies believe that pop-ups and pop-unders are effective forms of advertising, others disagree. Consumer complaints have led some sites to no longer accept these advertising forms. A study conducted by TNS revealed that 93 percent of respondents found pop-up ads annoying or very annoying.[8] The frequency and effectiveness of pop-ups and pop-unders have been greatly reduced given the advent of pop-up screeners, which will block the ads before they appear on your screen.

**Interstitials**   **Interstitials** are ads that appear on your screen while you are waiting for a site's content to download. Although some advertisers believe that interstitials are irritating and more of a nuisance than a benefit, a study conducted by Grey Advertising found that only 15 percent of those surveyed felt that the ads were irritating and that 47 percent liked the ads. Perhaps more important, while ad recall of banner ads was approximately 51 percent, recall of interstitials was much higher, at 76 percent.[9] Virgin Atlantic Airways, ESPN, and Sprint are just a few of the many companies to employ this advertising form. Unfortunately for advertisers who may want to employ this medium, however, interstitials can also be blocked by pop-up blockers.

**Paid Searches**   Exhibit 15–6 shows the results of a **search** on Google. In general, the higher a site appears on a search page, the more visitors it will receive. (Often searchers will not go past the first page of results.) **Organic search results** are those that appear because of their relevance to the search terms, not advertisements. Advertisers will also attempt to reach consumers through **nonorganic** or **paid** search such as **pay-per-click** advertising by placing their ads on web pages that display results from search engine queries. Over $16.9 billion was spent on search advertising in 2012.[10]

Search now constitutes over 46 percent of all online spending.[11] While there are a number of search engines offering their services, Google (Exhibit 15–6) is by far the dominant provider, accounting for two out of every three searches. In an effort to more specifically target customers who may be interested in their offerings, advertisers employ **search engine optimization (SEO)**. SEO is the process of improving the volume of traffic driven to one's site by a search engine through unpaid (organic) results as opposed to paid inclusions. The belief is that the higher a site appears on the search results list, the more visitors it will receive. SEO considers how search engines work and edits its HTML and coding to increase its relevance to keywords and to remove barriers to the indexing activities of search engines.[12] SEO has now become an integral part of the Internet marketing strategy of companies and organizations of all sizes.

**EXHIBIT 15–6**

Results of a Google search for flowers

**Behavioral Targeting**   Another Internet advertising strategy that has seen rapid growth is **behavioral targeting**. Behavioral targeting is based on advertisers' targeting consumers by tracking their website surfing behaviors, such as which websites they have visited and/or searches they have made. By compiling clickstream data and Internet protocol (IP) information, segments of potential buyers can be identified and ads directed specifically to them. For example, by tracking an individual's visits to a number of automobile websites, an ad for cars or a dealership could be served to that individual in real time. As will be seen later in this chapter, behavioral targeting has been shown to be an effective, albeit controversial strategy.

Recently, advertisers have increased their use of **retargeting**. Once a user visits a website and leaves without purchasing the product, a specifically targeted ad will display on participating subsequent websites the user visits. For example, let's say you were shopping for a pair of shoes at Nordstrom online, but didn't purchase. The next time you visited a website such as Yahoo! or Microsoft, an ad for Nordstrom shoes would appear. Because advertisers find retargeting more successful than banner or display ads, their use is increasing. Zappos and Zipcar are just two frequent retargeters, and both foursquare and Facebook accept retargeted ads. Due to their rapid adoption, many advertisers are concerned that they may become as irritating as pop-up ads.

**Contextual Ads**   Advertisers who target their ads based on the content of the web page are using **contextual advertising**. Whereas behavioral advertising tracks surfing behaviors, contextual ad placements are determined by the content on the web page. For example, an advertiser may place an airline ad on a travel site, or a golf club ad on a golf site, or even in or near a story about golf on another site. As another example, Google's AdSense targets ads to match the content of a publisher's site. The ads come in a variety of formats including images and video ads and can be targeted to geographic or local markets.

Recently, some marketers and policymakers have become concerned due to the increased popularity of native advertising. As defined by *Wikipedia,* **native advertising** is "a web advertising in which the advertiser attempts to gain attention by providing valuable content in the context of the user's experience; it is similar in concept to an advertorial which is a paid placement attempting to look like an article. A native ad tends to be more obviously an ad than most advertorials while still providing interesting or useful information."[13]

The goal of native ads is to be less intrusive while catching the attention of the reader who is likely interested in the content matter he or she is reading. While these native ads have been shown to outperform the traditional banner ad, concern has been expressed over the fact that the ads sometimes appear as content, and not ads, leading the consumer to be misled.

**Rich Media**   The increased penetration of broadband into households has increased the attention given to streaming video. **Rich media**, as defined by *Wikipedia,* are "a broad range of interactive digital media that exhibit dynamic motion, taking advantage of enhanced sensory features such as video, audio and animation."[14] Others state that rich media include all content that is created in flash.[15] The successful adoption of music videos, sports clips, news, and more has led advertisers to create a variety of forms of streaming video advertising content.

Types of rich media include the following.

**Online Commercials**  The equivalent of traditional television commercials, **online commercials** are appearing more often on the Net. Some of these commercials appear before the content that the user is seeking. These ads, called **pre-rolls**, are becoming more commonly employed by online advertisers, with some requiring that you watch the ad prior to receiving the content. Some companies have created their own Web commercials to be shown only on the Internet, while others run the same spots they show on TV. A number of commercials were released online prior to their being shown on the 2013 Super Bowl—a break from tradition in which the TV commercials always appeared first. Another trend has been to have consumers develop their own commercials to be shown online or on TV—or both—to increase consumer engagement (remember the Mountain Dew example!). A number of companies have been successful in blending the two media, showing the commercial on TV and then directing interested viewers to the Web if they wish to see it again or to view longer versions. Online advertising spending continues to rise, and consumer acceptance of these ads is increasing.

**Video on Demand**  As described in Chapter 13, video clips of various entertainment activities (which include ads or are sponsored) are also available through the

Internet. College basketball games, FIFA World Cup highlights, and demonstrations on how to use the Apple iPhone are just a few of the many options available.

YTC 15–04

*Webisode Walking Dead*

youtube.com/10ebelch

**Webisodes** Short featured films created by the advertiser, such as those created by Jaquar and BMW, are examples of **webisodes**, in which companies create their own content to advertise their products. *The Walking Dead* and *The Office* are examples of ITV shows that now appear as webisodes. IKEA, Target, Sara Lee, and Honda are just a few of the companies that have employed webisodes, but the range of these efforts also includes small jewelers, baking companies, cereal producers, and others.

**Other Forms of Rich Media Advertising** Advertising interactive banner ads, expandable ads, and rich media ads placed in videogames, instant messaging, podcasts, and video ads within blogs are additional ways that rich media are currently employed.

# IMC Using Social and Other Media—Web. 2.0

LO 15-2

As noted earlier in the chapter, after the "dot-com bust" at the turn of the century, the World Wide Web underwent significant changes. These changes led to the adoption and the referral to the new Web as "Web 2.0." (Figure 15–2). As defined in *Wikipedia*:

> The term **Web 2.0** is commonly associated with Web applications that facilitate interactive information sharing, interoperability, user-centered design, and collaboration on the World Wide Web. A Web 2.0 site allows its users to interact with each other as contributors to the website's content, in contrast to websites where users are limited to the passive viewing of information that is provided to them.[16]

The birth of Web 2.0 has led to the development of many **new media**. As shown in Figure 15–3, these new media are designed for a number of purposes and contain a wide variety of materials for consumer use. While it is beyond the scope of this text to cover all of these new media, we will discuss many of them and their relevance to an IMC program. We will start our discussion with social networking sites, as the

**FIGURE 15–2**

Web 2.0 Is a Multifaceted Version of the Internet

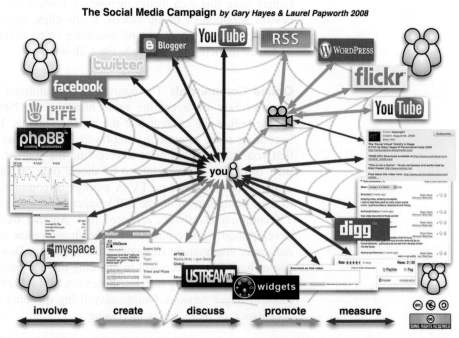

Source: Gary Hayes and Laurel Papworth, 2008.

| Types of New Media | Primary Purpose | Material | Examples |
|---|---|---|---|
| Forums and Chat Rooms | Discussion on topics, interest group sharing of information | Forum, Discussion boards | Hardwarezone.com Forums |
| E-Mail | Sending of electronic mail with file attachments | Web-based and non-web-based e-mail platforms | Hotmail Gmail Yahoo Mail |
| Social Networking Sites | Peer networking | Fan sites, alumni networks, personal news updates | Facebook Linkedin |
| Content Aggregators | Hosting of content for information and entertainment | Informative content, podcasts, videos, channels | YouTube Hulu |
| Virtual Reality | 3-D experience, alternate space | Simulated environments, experiences | Second Life |
| Online Gaming | Alternate fantasy, entertainment, gaming | MMORPG (massively multiplayer online role-playing games), multiplayer online games | World of Warcraft StarCraft II |
| Blogs | Opinions, information, viewpoints | Helpdesk, viewpoints, opinions | MrBrown.com Xiaxue.com |
| Portals | Aggregating news, communication tools | News studies, sponsored pages, ads | Asiaone.com Yahoo |
| Social News Sites | Peer-ranked news stories | News stories, popular blog content | Digg.com |

**FIGURE 15–3**

Types of New Media

YTC **15–05**

**Web 2.0 Social Media**

youtube.com/10ebelch

growth in this area has been literally astounding, and marketers have adopted these sites as an integral and critical part of their IMC programs.

**Social media** have been defined as "a group of Internet-based applications that build on the ideological and technological foundations of Web 2.0 and that allow the creation and exchange of user-generated content."[17] As can be seen in Figure 15–4 there are numerous ways for consumers to access these sites (desktops, laptops, tablets, smartphones, and connected devices), as well as a variety of reasons for using them, including sharing information, networking, and so forth. The most popular of these are **social networking sites**, which are platforms for networks or social relations among people who share interests, activities, backgrounds, or real-life connections. While there are hundreds of social networks in existence, a small number of these dominate in terms of membership. Prior to discussing each of these and how marketers have used them, let's first examine the characteristics of these platforms.

**Who Uses Social Media and Why** The use of social media is truly a worldwide phenomenon; there is a presence on every continent, and, interestingly while the "Big Four"—Facebook, Google+, YouTube, and Twitter—hold the largest market shares, over half of the top 15 sites are in China (where Facebook is not allowed).[18] China is the most socially engaged social media market, with over 84 percent of all Internet users using some form of social medium at least once a month.[19] As you will see when we discuss each of the Big Four (of the rest of the world) plus two (LinkedIn and Pinterest), the demographics of the users of these sites vary, as do the reasons for using them. Let's start off by examining why users of these sites do so, and who they are.

CHAPTER 15

**FIGURE 15–4**

Social Media Landscape

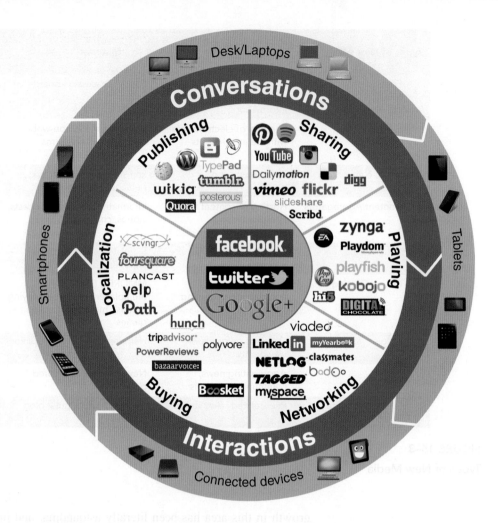

Although a number of motivations for using social media have been identified (sharing ideas, activities, and events with others; community involvement, etc.), marketers are most interested in why individuals use these platforms from a consumer behavior perspective. In a series of studies, Muntinga examined the motivations for using social media in a brand-related context.[20] (Consumers Online Brand-Related Activities—COBRAs). Specifically, the studies focused on why consumers (1) consume, (2) contribute to, and/or (3) create brand-related content. His results indicated that these COBRAs are driven by three primary motivations: (1) to gain information, (2) entertainment, and (3) remuneration. Gaining information included gathering prepurchase information, knowledge about brands, and new ideas. Entertainment involved enjoyment, relaxation, and passing time. Remuneration involved the potential to get something in return—for example, money, job-related benefits, or other rewards (social attraction, etc.). As will be seen throughout our further discussions, the ability for marketers to satisfy these motivations directly reflects their potential for success.

A Pew Research study recently showed that as many as 67 percent of all Internet users say that they use social networks, which places the number in the billions of users (Facebook alone has over 1 billion users).[21] While the networks are appealing to a range of demographics, they are particularly appealing to those between the ages of 18 and 29, and some are more appealing to women. As one might expect, the older age groups are less likely to engage in social media, particularly networks, though usage is on the increase in these segments as well.

Prior to examining these social media, let's examine how and why marketers use them in an IMC program. Again, the examples provided are but a sampling of the many ways marketers have used these media.

**How Marketers Use Social Media** In a recent study of 3,000 marketers conducted by Social Media Examiner, an amazing 97 percent of marketers say they now include social media in their marketing plans, with 86 percent stating that social media are important to their marketing success.[22] As can be seen in Figure 15–5, the primary reasons for using social media are to (1) drive traffic to one's site, (2) communicate with customers, and (3) gain brand exposure. The most important benefit these marketers believe they derive from the use of social media is increased exposure (89 percent). A close examination of Figure 15–5 indicates that marketers find different media more effective for achieving specific objectives. For example, Twitter is considered the best channel for direct communication with consumers, while LinkedIn may be better for connecting with specific groups (like professionals). At the same time, LinkedIn may be the least effective for driving traffic. Each site contributes in more than one way. Digital and Social Media Perspective 15–1 on page 512 shows how a few "older brands" have used social media.

Interestingly, although marketers strongly believe that social media are a necessary component in their marketing programs, they still feel uncertain as to how to use these media tactically and how to measure their effectiveness. Studies have shown that the ability to measure the effectiveness of these media is of major concern, and may hinder their increased adoption into marketing programs.[23]

Let's examine some of the more popular social media, and how marketers use them in their IMC programs. We start our discussion with the Big Four.

## The Big Four of Social Media

**Facebook** The largest of all social networks, Facebook has over 1 billion subscribers worldwide, covering six continents and 100 countries, 845 million of whom consider themselves active users. An estimated 67 percent of all Internet users state that they use Facebook across a range of demographics (Figure 15–6). While the site has been somewhat controversial over the years as a result of frequently changing its privacy agreements, and other privacy-related issues, businesses have found Facebook to be a valuable communications medium. In the study cited previously, 49 percent of those responding said that they considered Facebook to be the most important social platform for marketers. Facebook leads all other social media in display advertising revenues.

Just as individuals can exchange information by posting on a "wall," companies can as well by posting information about the company and/or its products, photos, promotions, events, news, and so on, Facebook also allows advertising that can be targeted to subsets of Facebook users based on demographic and geographic data and interests and activities. In addition, because Facebook knows what pages its members like and visit, what their interests are, and even who is in their social network, targeting can become even more precise—and, as you might expect, create even more privacy concerns. Facebook itself has evolved in an attempt to become an even more attractive medium for marketers by adding a number of new marketing tools, including sponsored stories, more targeted ads, and its Timeline format that asks for a member's complete lifetime history (and provides advertisers with even more data) as well as a number of metrics designed to attract advertisers.

In 2013 Facebook expanded the amount and type of data provided to marketers beyond that provided by users. The sites one visits outside of Facebook, loyalty program memberships, and even the types of products members buy in a brick-and-mortar store can now be obtained as a result of partnership agreements with other data providers including Acxiom, Datalogix, and Epsilon. As noted by Tim Peterson in *Adweek,* advertisers can now target "mortgage borrowing homemakers who own a minivan and buy baby food" or "dentists who live alone, own a BMW and buy big-and-tall clothes and diet foods."[24]

Facebook has become a "must have" medium for many marketers who have used the site in a variety of ways. Companies encourage Facebook members to "like" their brands and "share" information to gain exposure. Throughout this text we have shown numerous examples of how companies use this site. One such example is shown on Exhibit 15–7.

**FIGURE 15–5**

The Social Media Landscape

CMO.COM — Adobe

GOOD | OK | BAD

| | f (Facebook) | g+ (Google+) | (Twitter) | P (Pinterest) | in (LinkedIn) | YouTube |
|---|---|---|---|---|---|---|
| **CUSTOMER COMMUNICATION** | Facebook is an easy and efficient way to reach your entire demographic, but if you want to reach non-fans, you have to pay for sponsored posts. Facebook can be used to create and push content, or to help manage reputation. | Google+ still lacks the reach of Facebook and Twitter, but it does facilitate communication with customers—even if they are not in your circles. | Twitter is the best channel for direct communication with customers. Most under-24s prefer it as a forum for customer service. | Although businesses now have a presence on Pinterest, little opportunity exists for direct communication with costomers. | LinkedIn provides the opportunity to connect with customers through groups with specific interests connected to your brand. | Video enables customer involvement in the most unique way possible. Customers can be entertained, informed, and engaged—all at the same time. They also can respond directly through comments. |
| **BRAND EXPOSURE** | Facebook is one of the easiest, quickest, and most cost-effective ways to gain brand exposure. | Because you can reach people who are outside your circles, Google+ offers excellent brand exposure. Google+ accounts also appear in branded search reasults, which adds credibility and increased exposure. | Twitter is an easy and cost-effective way to gain exposure for your brand. | Visual content is viewed 70% more than written content. This makes Pinterest a powerful tool for brand exposure. What's more, about 25% of users have purchased a product/service they discovered on Pinterest. | LinkedIn provides impressive exposure to the business world, allowing you to promote personal and business brands to professional contacts and communities. | YouTube is a community. As such, it allows sharing, channel creation, and advertising, which is becoming more accepted by users—provided the video is worth watching. |
| **TRAFFIC TO YOUR SITE** | It's as simple as this: Fan page + 1 like = 20 new site visitors. | Google+ provides more worthwhile traffic. Users tend to stay on the sites whose links they follow. | Twitter has an unmatched ability to drive traffic directly to a site. | Pinned images contain links back to a site, which is why Pinterest tends to be one of the top three traffic referral sites. | LinkedIn is not a huge referral source for sites yet, but numbers are climbing. Connections and search engines can generate traffic. | YouTube can drive traffic to a site through links in a video and ads before a video begins. Popular channels and videos are highly effective in driving traffic. |
| **SEO** | Although social sharing might hold more weight in the future, right now only shared links from fan pages matter, not personal links. | The Google +1 button allows users to search both public and privately shared information. This has a knock-on effect for SEO and search engine ranking. | Google gives authority ranks for Twitter profiles, so link juice is limited. | Pinterest does not pass much link juice, and pinning does not allow follow links. | LinkedIn doesn't have a huge effect on individual content yet, but its profiles remain some of the easiest and most frequently SEO-ranked social profiles on the Web. | Active YouTube channels bump up SEO rankings. Integrating keywords, site maps, titles, and robot text files help judge relevance. |

## FIGURE 15–6

Percentage of Internet Users Who Use Facebook

| | | Use Facebook |
|---|---|---|
| **All Internet Users** (*n* = 860) | | **67%** |
| a | **Men** (*n* = 418) | **62** |
| b | **Women** (*n* = 442) | **72**[a] |
| **Age** | | |
| a | **18–29** (*n* = 164) | **86**[bcd] |
| b | **30–49** (*n* = 254) | **73**[cd] |
| c | **50–64** (*n* = 231) | **57**[d] |
| d | **65+** (*n* = 183) | **35** |
| **Education Attainment** | | |
| a | **Less than high school/high school grad** (*n* = 261) | **60** |
| b | **Some college** (*n* = 250) | **73**[a] |
| c | **College+** (*n* = 345) | **68** |
| **Household Income** | | |
| a | **Less than $30,000/yr** (*n* = 223) | **68** |
| b | **$30,000–$49,999** (*n* = 152) | **62** |
| c | **$50,000–$74,999** (*n* = 127) | **69** |
| d | **$75,000+** (*n* = 248) | **73** |
| **Urbanity** | | |
| a | **Urban** (*n* = 261) | **72** |
| b | **Suburban** (*n* = 442) | **65** |
| c | **Rural** (*n* = 157) | **63** |

Source: Pew Research Center's Internet & America Life Project Omnibus Survey, December 13–16, 2012. N-860 Internet users. Interviews ere conducted on landline and cell phones. The margin of error is +/− 2.9 percentage points for results based on internet users.

**Twitter** Twitter is an online social network microblogging network that enables users to send and receive text-based messages (tweets) up to 140 characters in length. Twitter has over 500 million registered users, but only 140 million who are active users (the others apparently just observe), adding 300,000 more users per day in 2012.[25] Like Facebook, Twitter has international appeal, with the largest base in the United States and Great Britain. Over half of all companies that use social media in their marketing plans use Twitter, given the finding that 50 percent of all users follow brands on Twitter and are likely to both buy and recommend brands they follow to others.[26]

Like Facebook, many marketers have found Twitter a useful tool for communicating with their customers and potential customers and, as noted in the CMO report shown earlier (Figure 15–5), may be the very best for establishing connections with customers. For example, a number of brands including AT&T, Capital One, Dove Men's Care, Nike, and Buick purchased promoted tweets in real time during the NCAA "March Madness" college basketball tourney. AT&T sent out

## EXHIBIT 15–7

An example of advertisements on Facebook

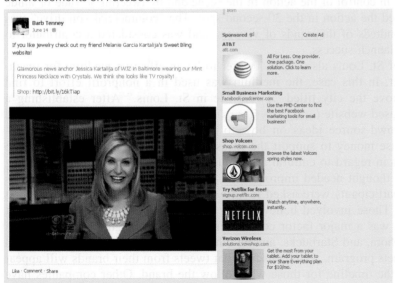

# Digital and Social Media Perspective 15–1 > > >

## "Old" Brands Use New Media to Reach Their Markets

There are a number of well known brands out there, but not many that have been around as long as these "old-timers." You no doubt have heard of them but may not have realized just how long they have been successfully marketed. Heinz (1869), Pillsbury (1869), Ivory Soap (1879), and Coca-Cola (1886)—the youngster—have been consumer favorites for well over a century because they are good products. They have also been around because they are successful marketers.

Throughout this text—as well as other marketing texts you have read—these brands have been cited as examples of how to do it. High product quality, solid public relations programs, and powerful advertising have all contributed to their success. But perhaps more than anything else, each of these brands has shown an ability to adapt to market changes that have taken place for almost 150 years. As consumers' media habits have changed, these companies have kept pace—and they continue to do so today. Consider these examples of adapting to the new digital and social world:

*Heinz* Even though Heinz Ketchup is already in 97 percent of U.S. households and holds 59 percent of the overall market, the Pittsburgh-based company is not resting on its laurels. While Heinz has made some slight product changes over the years, it continues to rely on the original product flavor as its standard. At the same time, Heinz has recognized that as the market changes it must change as well. So, when the company took the giant step (for Heinz) of introducing a new flavor—Heinz Ketchup Blended with Balsamic Vinegar—it did so very cautiously. Rather than a major announcement through advertising, the new product was introduced through the brand's Facebook page, allowing the loyal Heinz followers (over 825,000) to purchase it a month before it hit the grocery store shelves. Heinz hopes that the new "limited edition" tomato ketchup will generate buzz while rewarding loyalists at the same time.

*Pillsbury* The Pillsbury Doughboy has gone mobile. The long-standing favorite brand of moms is reaching out to younger moms with a TV spot linked to a mobile recipe center through the Shazam app. The television commercials will prompt viewers to use the app to get recipes for Pillsbury Crescents—a longtime American table staple—then save the recipes on their phones for later use (like when shopping!). The program is targeted to "Millennial Moms" who are tech savvy and almost always have their phones with them, hopefully while seeing the commercials on TV. The program is also promoted on Facebook. Pillsbury is just one of the General Mills brands using digital and social media, as the cake mix brand Betty Crocker has made good use of Twitter and Facebook as well.

*Coke* After an extensive round of research with teen panels, Coke thinks it has figured out what kids courtside photos through Twitter, encouraging fans to be engaged in the games while connecting with other viewers.

When Mercedes-Benz introduced its new A-Class automobile, a commercial was run on the popular TV show *X Factor* integrating the cast into a chase scene. Viewers were in control of the action in the scene and by tweeting #evade or #hide they determined the action in the 30-second spot. The "commercial you drive" was viewed by hundreds of thousands of viewers, and was considered a contributor to the product's launch success.

The City of St. Louis also found Twitter to be an effective medium for reaching its market. In this case, the medium was used in a nonprofit effort to find ways to improve the city titled "Tweet Me in St. Louis." After establishing a community-based website (www.rallystl.org), the organization used Facebook and Twitter to crowd-source ideas on how to improve the city as well as crowd-funding to raise money to support the ideas generated. The public was asked to tweet in ideas in regard to cultural arts, education, housing, or virtually anything else that they thought needed improvement. After the period for submitting ideas was closed, participants were asked to vote on the best ones—again by tweeting in their vote. Those involved believed that the simplicity of the ability to tweet in a response was a major factor contributing to the campaign's success. Virgin America, Sephora, and Starbucks, among others, have all used Twitter's enhanced promoted tweets program, which ensures that tweets from their brands will appear at the top of the timeline for those who follow the brand. Other companies have want from brands—fun, "snackable" digital experiences that center on mobile consumption. Coke unveiled "The AHHH Effect" initiative designed to reach the segment through a digital content only campaign that includes dozens of digital games and marketing content. The launch featured 17 digital experiences including games targeted to users on smartphones and tablets as well as desktops. Also included is a 15-second video and Twitter offerings. Future plans include the use of Facebook and Twitter to encourage the teens to create their own content for the brand, and to submit them for consideration. The 25 winners will be included in the "AHHH Effect" lineup. The content will be reviewed twice a week, as Coke knows it is hard to keep the attention of the younger generation.

*Ivory Soap* One of the eldest of the older brands, Ivory conducted a nationwide study of 1,000 moms to garner insights into what their lives are like. The research led to the creating of a new online community titled "The Soap Dish," located on Ivory's Facebook page. As part of the brand's makeover, which included a new package design and advertising campaign, Ivory is partnering with Emmy Award–winning actor and mom Melissa McCarthy on the branded community designed to appeal to younger moms. The Soap Dish is "a light-hearted social community that offers women an outlet to share in the everyday humor and honesty of their lives in an unapologetic manner," according to Procter & Gamble's press release.

If you think about it for a moment, these brands have been promoting their products for over a hundred years and

have managed to keep them successful by remaining current. Now they are adapting once again. Little doubt they will be successful!

Sources: Christopher Heine, "Coke Runs First All-Digital Effort, Focusing on Teens and Mobile," www.adweek.com, April 23, 2013; Kate Kaye, "Pillsbury Rolls Out Interactive Tools and Treats," www.clickz.com, December 5, 2011; Sheila Shayon, "Ivory Dishes on Facebook with Melissa McCarthy," www.brandchannel.com, December 13, 2011; Barry Silverstein, "Heinz Gets Sophisticated, and Social," www.brandchannel.com, October 26, 2011.

found that Twitter can be used to respond to customer complaints and/or inquiries, retweeting important information and monitoring the market to watch for opportunities or threats.

**EXHIBIT 15–8**

Google+ offers a search function

**Google+** Launched in 2011 by Google, Google+ was developed to be a direct competitor to Facebook, and is now the second largest social network in the world outside China. With over 500 million subscribers, Google+ allows users to develop their own profile and control the way it will appear across the entire Google network. It also allows for the development of a community, and offers a "hangout" where up to 10 users can video chat simultaneously. Its mobile capability allows one to stay connected on a smartphone while on the go and offers a search function (Exhibit 15–8). *Glamour Magazine* used Google+ to launch a monthlong series of custom Google+ Hangouts, giving its advertisers unique access, and exposure, to the title's more than 1.5 million Google+ followers. Knowing that advertisers are constantly seeing content, the publication invited select print digital advertisers to receive a custom Google+ Hangout that the magazine would produce on their behalf. The content ranged from beauty

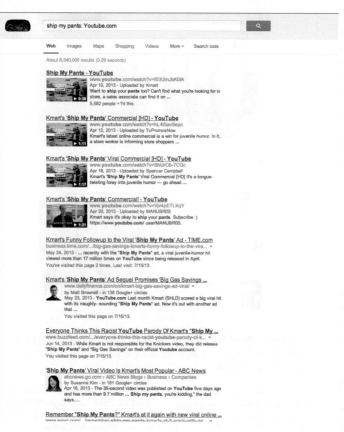

search bar shows "ship my pants: Youtube.com"

**EXHIBIT 15–9**

YouTube has become attractive to advertisers

**EXHIBIT 15–10**

Kmart's "Ship my Pants" commercial went viral

how-tos and shopping inspiration to live music and insider tips and was also posted on *Glamour*'s YouTube channel. Readers could also log on and participate using the hashtag #GLAMOURHangouts, while others allowed readers to watch and comment via Google+.

National Public Radio (NPR) also used Google+ Hangouts to promote its "Morning Edition Virtual Hangout," and a breast cancer organization established a hangout with doctors to inform people with the disease of options, advice, and so on. Others have found Google+ effective for reaching specific market segments like veterans or those in need of dental care. While Google+ has not reached the advertising revenue that Facebook has, the medium appears to have great potential as it offers many tools to advertisers that Facebook does not.

**YouTube** Another powerful social medium, YouTube is a content aggregator, hosting content for information and entertainment. Users can upload and share their own videos, as well as those placed by others (including companies). The growth of YouTube has been, and continues to be, phenomenal; there are now 6 billion hours of video being sent to more than 1 billion unique users per month around the world. In the United States, YouTube now reaches a larger audience of adults 18 to 34 than any single television network. Projections are that by 2018 YouTube could become as large as CBS or Viacom.[27]

What makes YouTube so effective for marketers is the ability to use the site as an advertising medium or as a search platform (Exhibit 15–9). Marketers can post videos of their products or brands that can be informational (how to build an IKEA bookcase) or entertaining (as noted, companies posted TV commercials on the YouTube site prior to showing them on the Super Bowl). Many companies have now established their own YouTube channel, which allows them to have a specifically branded URL and fully customized content. Volkswagen, Ford, and Quiksilver are just a few companies that have successfully employed this medium for entertainment purposes, while Home Depot, like IKEA, is just one of many that have used it for instruction and demonstration.

The potential for exposure on YouTube is one of the major attractions for marketers large and small. For example, the *Gangnam Style* video became the first YouTube video to reach a billion views and by 2013, the music video had been viewed over 1.59 billion times. At the same time, a small brand, Orabrush, that had no sales online or offline was able to successfully pull its product into large retail stores like Walmart as a result of its successful YouTube video. In less than two years the Orabush channel garnered over 38 million views, and consumers' demands for the tongue cleaner led to retail distribution. A Kmart ad titled "Ship My Pants" went viral on YouTube and was watched by almost 13 million viewers online—not to mention the additional word of mouth—in less than a week, providing the retailer with a great deal of well-needed buzz (Exhibit 15–10).

# Ethical Perspective 15–1 > > >

## Sometimes Going Viral Is Not a Good Thing

There is an old expression that "all publicity is good publicity, even if it is negative," a position that we do not particularly agree with. Just ask the myriad of products and brands that are no longer on the market due to negative publicity they have received and the following word of mouth that ensued.

The online version of getting free publicity and word-of-mouth communications is attempting to go viral. Success stories involving going viral like the *Gangnam Style* or *Ship My Pants* videos are the dream of many marketers, gaining exposure to the brand among millions of potential customers with a minimal investment. But sometimes the dream can become a nightmare if you are not careful.

Take Mountain Dew, for example. The highly successful user of social media has always had a strong following in the South and Midwest (as shown in the lead-in to this chapter) but has not done as well with the urban and Latino drinkers. No one would accuse Mountain Dew of being "Urban Cool." In an attempt to change this image, PepsiCo hired hip-hop singer Lil Wayne and street skateboarder Paul Rodriguez—favorites of the young and urban-hip crowd. The idea was to engage the fans of the two, and (hopefully) get them to try and switch to Mountain Dew. The new "This Is How We Dew" campaign targeted to teens and those in their 20s involved a TV campaign featuring Lil Wayne rapping over clips of concert footage and skateboarders. Additional promotions and a social media presence were also included.

But then something went wrong. Lil Wayne spouted some controversial lyrics in a remix of the rapper Future's "Karate Chop" song in which he made a reference to Emmett Till, the black teenage victim in a 1955 beating and murder that took place after he allegedly whistled at a white girl in Mississippi. The insensitive remarks went viral on social media sites—and not in a positive way. Till's parents were upset, and Mountain Dew almost immediately terminated its relationship with Lil Wayne. Even though Wayne apologized, as did PepsiCo, the damage to the image of both PepsiCo and Mountain Dew will be felt for some time.

Not long after, Mountain Dew did it again. This time it involved a video created by the hip-hop producer and rap artist Tyler, the Creator in which a battered white food server on crutches is asked to attempt to identify her assailant from a lineup of African American men and a goat.

During the attempt, the goat continuously talks to her with threatening remarks while a police officer drinking a Mountain Dew looks on. No sooner did the commercial go online than it went viral—again in a very nonfavorable way. Some critics referred to the commercial as "arguably the most racist commercial in history." The commercial was immediately pulled. Again Mountain Dew apologized.

But Mountain Dew is not alone. Ford, General Motors, Hyundai, and Reebok have also recently apologized to consumers for ads that have hinged on subjects like rape, race, and suicide—all attempting to go viral. Two creative directors at JWT India lost their jobs after creating commercials for the Ford Figo hatchback that showed women bound and gagged in the hatchback's trunk while celebrities Paris Hilton and Silvio Berlusconi sat behind the wheel. Though Ford never knew about or approved the ads, when they hit the Internet and went viral Ford apologized. Reebok dropped rapper Rick Ross after the brand came under fire for lyrics he used in the Rocko song "U.O.E.N.O" that referred to drugging a woman and then having sex with her without her knowledge. Hyundai UK pulled an ad depicting suicide, and GM pulled one referring to Chinese people in a derogatory manner.

Longtime advertising critic Bob Garfield believes that the situation is aggravated by the millennial "no holds barred" culture where "a sense of permissiveness exists." Nancy Hill, president and CEO of the American Association of Advertising Agencies, says "the race to retweet and to click 'thumbs up'" overwhelms the impulse to "take a step back and make sure the ad is crafted exactly the way you want it to be received." They, among many others, agree with Tor Myhren, chief creative officer at Grey, New York, who feels "it's the pressure to create 'viral' advertising, the urge to get more views online, that leads people to push the envelope."

Like publicity, all viral is not necessarily good viral.

Sources: Stuart Elliott and Tanzina Vega, "Trying to Be Hip and Edgy, Ads Become Offensive," www.nytimes.com, May 10, 2013; Joyce Chen, "Lil Wayne Dropped from Mountain Dew Endorsement Deal, Emmett Till's Family Reacts," www.usmagazine.com, May 5, 2013; Andrew Kirell, "Watch the Mountain Dew Ad Pulled after Critics Called It 'Arguably the Most Racist Commercial in History,'" www.mediaite.com, May 1, 2013; Andrew Kirell, "Mountain Dew Wants Some Street Cred," *Bloomberg Businessweek*, May 6, 2012, p. 24.

At the same time, marketers' obsession with "going viral" has led to major problems as well. The misfortunes of the brands discussed in Ethical Perspective 15–1 demonstrate what can happen when going viral becomes such an important goal that marketers lose site of other factors.

**Additional Social Media**   While the Big Four are the most commonly used social media, there are others that are important to marketers as well:

**Instagram** Instagram is an online photo-sharing and social networking site that allows users to post and edit pictures and share them on a variety of social

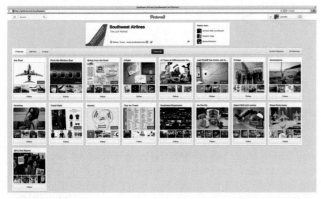

**EXHIBIT 15–11**
A number of companies have found Pinterest to be useful in their IMC programs

networks, such as Facebook or Twitter. The site is used more often by women, and has most appeal to 18-to-29 age group. Marketers have found Instagram useful for a variety of communications activities. For example, companies have posted news about events, new product introductions, and other company- or brand-related activities to increase exposure. Others have initiated very successful contests in which they engage consumers by having them post pictures related to their brands. In their #SonyLove contest, Sony asked people to first follow the company on Instagram and then post pictures of anything that represented "love" to them. One entry was chosen every day to win a $50 Sony Store gift card or other Sony merchandise based on their entry. Virgin America frequently surprises flyers with a gift and posts them in a picture on Instagram, or encourages its followers to do the same. Given the ability to post pictures to garner engagement, the variety of uses of this site for marketers seem almost endless.

**Pinterest** According to *Wikipedia,* Pinterest is a pinboard-style photo-sharing website that allows users to create and manage theme-based image collections such as events, interests, and hobbies. Users can browse other pinboards for images, "re-pin" images to their own pinboards, or "like" photos. Like Instagram, Pinterest is most attractive to females, as approximately 79 pecent of their users are women. As with Instagram, Sony has found this site to be quite useful in its marketing efforts as have numerous others such as Whole Foods, Southwest Airlines, and GE (Exhibit 15-11). Nordstrom has used Pinterest to post pictures of new product offerings, to make its blog more appealing, and to sponsor a bridal contest in which brides-to-be could win prizes including cash, a bridal consultant, and a hotel stay at a J.W. Marriott Resort. Many other marketers targeting women have found Pinterest to be an effective medium.

**LinkedIn** Another social networking site but with a different audience, LinkedIn now has over 200 million business professionals as members. While the site is primarily used by professionals to network, businesses have used banner ads on the site in an attempt to reach this professional audience to promote their products and services. LinkedIn offers marketers the opportunity to connect to customers with specific interests that may be related to their brand.

**Other Social Sites** As noted earlier, there are many, many more social media sites that are useful to marketers in their IMC programs. These sites have been used by marketers for marketing research, public relations, promotions, and a variety of other strategies.

YTC **15–06**
**Jim Henson Podcast**
youtube.com/10ebelch

**Podcasting**    **Podcasting** is a medium that uses the Internet to distribute audio or video files for downloading into iPods, iPads, and other portable devices. As the market for tablets and iPads grows, the attractiveness of this medium does as well. Radio stations, including Clear Channel Communications and National Public Radio, and television programs, such as *60 Minutes,* now podcast entire programs or video clips. As noted by Paul Verna, author of the report *Podcasting: Into the Mainstream,* this shift has resulted in the evolution of podcasting from a long tail medium to a Web 2.0 extension of popular, traditional media.[28] Traditional advertisers are adopting the medium, while others find it useful as well (Exhibit 15–12). For example, Durex, a condom manufacturer, has purchased product placements in podcasts—in part to reach young listeners with risque marketing messages while skirting FCC decency rules.

**EXHIBIT 15–12**
Podcasts have become popular with a number of advertisers

**EXHIBIT 15–13**
Yelp! guides potencional consumers uising augmented reality

**RSS**    **Really Simple Syndication (RSS)** is a specification that uses XML to organize and format web-based content in a standard way. Content owners create an RSS feed, which usually consists of titles and brief descriptions of about 10 articles elsewhere on the site. The difference between Web content and an RSS feed is that the latter can send out notifications whenever new material is available. Because the alerts can be customized to the viewers' preferences, advertisers have found it useful for disseminating information to those who may be most interested. For example, the *Washington Post* allows for advertising in its RSS feeds, and companies like American Express, Continental Airlines, and Verizon have all run ads through RSS feeds.

**Blogs**    A **blog** (or weblog) is a Web-based publication consisting primarily of periodic articles, normally presented in reverse chronological order. As noted, blogs may reflect the writings of an individual, a community, a political organization, or a corporation, and they offer advertisers a new way to reach their target audiences. For example, there are blogs about beer, current events, sports, raising children, and so on. In 2013 there were an estimated 93 million active blogs on the Internet. (This information came from a blog!)[29] Tumblr, the worldwide blog, hosts over 100 million blogs with over 44 billion posts.[30] Some marketers are excited about the potential of blogs to reach large or targeted audiences at a small cost. As a result, these marketers attempt to keep the bloggers happy by feeding them exclusives, releasing product news to them before it hits the mainstream, and so on. Others are a bit more skeptical, noting that there are a number of problems with the use of blogs, including the potential for deception and limited reach. Whether bloggers are full time professionals or just hobbyists, many of them write about brands they love or hate (or love to hate!), and their influence on consumers is on the increase, as they often use the information they obtain from blogs in their purchase decisions.

**Other 2.0 Media Forms**    There are numerous other 2.0 media forms also available to marketers including the use of virtual and augmented reality and QR codes.

**Augmented Reality**    While it may seem like something out of the future, **augmented reality** is very much here. The virtual reality world Second Life has not lived up to expectations, but there are now thousands of augmented reality apps that are currently being used by marketers and consumers alike, and the future promises much more. For example, Wikitude World Browser is widely regarded as one of the best of all augmented reality browsers. As one travels around any area, Wikitude will provide just about any geographically relevant information needed, including *Wikipedia* articles for landmarks, ATM locations, YouTube videos, tweets, foursquare locations, and so on. Yelp Monocle (Exhibit 15–13) uses cellphone GPS and compass data to display star rating and review count for

YTC **15-07**

**Second Life**

youtube.com/10ebelch

nearby businesses on top of the camera view in real time. Other AR apps can help one find subways, metros, and transit stops, calculate distances between locations, as well as provide many more forms of helpful information content. As noted in Chapter 14, companies are now incorporating augmented reality into their catalogs, brochures, and so on.

**QR Codes** While **QR codes** may not have reached the potential expected, many marketers have used them effectively. A large percentage of print ads now carry the bar codes, but consumers have not used them as frequently as expected. An example of a successful application of this technology was a joint effort between Disney and Cargill (Honeysuckle White and Shady Brook Farms meats) which used mobile bar codes to entice consumers to buy through a "Wreck-It Ralph" Blu-ray combo pack promotion. Cargill placed QR bar codes on 7 million packages of turkey products that, when scanned, took consumers to a website where they could get a $5 mail-in rebate over their mobile device. The very popular app Shazam is another good example of the use of a form of QR code, in which radio listeners can immediately identify a song, artist, and album title through their cell phones. Just as it seems that QR codes may be beginning to grow in popularity, they are being threatened by a new technology, near field communication (NFC). NFC enables marketers to deliver content through an embedded chip that allows wireless communications just by touching the material or being in close proximity to the NFC tag. Essentially, the NFC tag performs the same function as a QR code but with much less effort required on the part of the consumer.

## Sales Promotion on the Internet

Companies have found the Internet to be a very effective medium for disseminating sales promotions. Numerous companies tie in sales promotions to their websites and/or through other forms of digital and social media. According to a study by NCH Marketing Services, online coupons are now the second most highly redeemed form of coupon—behind only the instant on-package format, and much higher than traditional forms of couponing.[31] Ghiradelli engages in the use of sales promotions with its website as do many others (Exhibit 15–14). Numerous companies now print online coupons. Other examples include the use of trivia games, contests, sweepstakes, instant win promotions, and so on.

## Personal Selling on the Internet

The Internet has been both a benefit and a detriment to many of those involved in personal selling—particularly those in the business-to-business market. For some, the Internet has been a threat that might take away job opportunities. Companies have found that they can remain effective, or even increase effectiveness, by building a strong online presence. The high-cost and poor-reach disadvantages of personal selling are allowing these companies to reduce new hires and even cut back on their existing sales forces.

On the positive side, websites have been used quite effectively to enhance and support the selling effort. As noted earlier, digital and social media have become a primary source of information for millions of customers in the consumer and business-to-business markets. Visitors to websites can gain volumes of information about a company's products and services. In return, the visitors become a valuable resource for leads that both

**EXHIBIT 15–14**

Sales promotions are common on websites

internal and external salespersons can follow up, and they become part of a prospect database. Not only can potential customers learn about the company's offerings, but the selling organization can serve and qualify prospects more cost-effectively.

The Web can also be used to stimulate trial. For many companies, personal salespersons can reach only a fraction of the potential customer base. Through trial demonstrations or samples offered online, customers can determine if the offering satisfies their needs and, if so, request a personal sales call. In such cases both parties benefit from time and cost savings.

Companies have used the Internet to improve their one-on-one relationships with customers. By providing more information in a more timely and efficient manner, a company enables customers to learn more about what it has to offer. This increases the opportunity for cross-selling and customer retention. Twitter has become a powerful tool for consumers to voice their opinions of companies or complaints, while also allowing the involved company to respond quickly.

In a well-designed IMC program, the Internet and personal selling are designed to be complementary tools, working together to increase sales. It appears that more and more companies are coming to this realization.

## Public Relations on the Internet

The Internet is a useful medium for conducting public relations activities. Many sites devote a portion of their content to public relations activities, including the provision of information about the company, its philanthropic activities, annual reports, and more.

Companies, nonprofit organizations, and political parties have become quite adept at using the Internet for public relations purposes. An excellent example of the use of public relations on the Internet is provided by Chrysler (Exhibit 15–15). The site provides up-to-date news stories and other forms of content, photo images, and cross-references to other sites or media as well as press kits and a calendar of upcoming events. It also provides information about Chrysler automobiles and the corporation itself and allows for customer feedback and registration for updates. In addition, Daimler-Chrysler's homepage contains many of the articles written about the corporation, including awards won and philanthropic efforts achieved such as its concern for the environment and support for numerous causes.

Other examples of the effective use of public relations activities on the Internet are also available, as you will see in the chapter on public relations. The Web is a useful medium for conducting public relations activities, and its use for this function is on the increase.

At the same time, many philanthropic and nonprofit organizations have found the Internet to be a useful way to generate funds. As noted earlier, charitable organizations have also formed sites to handle public relations activities, provide information regarding the causes the charity supports, collect contributions, and so on. In an example of integrating the Internet with public relations and television, companies have found the Internet to be extremely useful for providing information in times of a crisis and for gathering feedback about their products and services and about themselves (particularly through blogs and RSS feeds).

**EXHIBIT 15–15**

Chrysler uses its website for public relations purposes

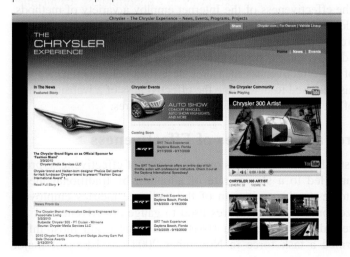

## Direct Marketing on the Internet

Our discussion of direct marketing and the Internet approached the topic from two perspectives: the use of direct-marketing tools for communications objectives and e-commerce (as discussed in Chapter 14). As we stated previously, many direct-marketing tools like direct mail, infomercials, and the like have been adapted to the Internet. At the same time, e-commerce—selling directly to the consumer via the Internet—has become an industry all its own.

# MOBILE

As dramatic an impact that the Internet had on companies' IMC programs, it almost pales in comparison to the changes brought about by **mobile**. Spawned by the rapid adoption of smartphones and tablets, mobile is now receiving strong attention from marketers, and ad revenues continue to climb, primarily through applications (apps). A study reported in *eMarketer* reported that by 2013 smartphone penetration in the United States would be over 50 percent. Projections are that in the 18-to-44 age bracket nearly 90 percent will own a smartphone by 2016.[32] As adoption of these phones increases, content consumption will grow right along with it, and so too will advertising spending to reach these users. (An interesting fact: In 2011 there were 3.2 billion toothbrushes sold annually around the world. There were 4.2 million global mobile users in the same year!)[33] Right along with the growth in adoption of smartphones is the adoption of tablets. By 2013 tablets were already generating a higher volume of website traffic than smartphones.[34] Numerous studies have shown that tablets have led to increases in search behavior and online purchasing and have dramatically changed the way we view television. While one might think tablets may be responsible for decreasing TV watching, this is not the case; more than half of those tablet owners surveyed indicated it had no impact, while many respondents under the age of 50 said it actually *increased* their TV viewing.[35] The amount of TV watching may not be changing much, but the way that it is being watched has. Younger consumers are much more likely to report that they watch TV with their tablet with them, posting, e-mailing, and texting friends as well as seeking information about program content and commercials while viewing.

Consumers also report that they use their mobile devices for in-store price comparisons (38 percent), browsing products (38 percent), and reading online product reviews (32 percent) as well as for making a product purchase (41 percent).[36] As discussed earlier, as the number of apps continues to increase, the uses for these apps in a marketing context is promising indeed. One can see why marketers see mobile as a golden opportunity!

# INTERNET METRICS

Companies measuring the effectiveness of the Internet employ a variety of methods, most of which can be done electronically. As you will see, a number of companies provide Internet measures as part of a package; that is, they provide audience measurement information (demographics, psychographics, etc.) as "up-front" information, as well as some of the effectiveness measures described below. First, we will discuss some of the measures used to determine the effectiveness of a website. Then, we will discuss some of the companies providing these measures.

## Audience Measures and Measures of Effectiveness

When the Internet industry first developed its own measures of effectiveness, problems with these measures led to a slower rate of adoption by traditional media buyers. In an attempt to respond to criticism of the audience metrics employed, as well as to standardize some of the measures used to gauge effectiveness of the Internet, the Interactive Advertising Bureau (IAB)—the largest and most influential trade group—formed a task force in November 2004 consisting of major

| Clicks |
| Post-click conversions |
| Cost per conversion |
| Unique visitors |
| Average frequency |
| Frequency to conversion ratios |
| Advertising exposure time |
| Ad interaction rate |
| View-through rate |
| Visits |
| Webpage eye tracking |
| Offline sales lift |
| Cross-media models |

**FIGURE 15–7**

Example Internet
Metrics

Source: IAB.net.

global corporations involved in advertising and research. The task force was created to examine and create standardized measures to measure advertising impact that could be used to assess the impact of ads and to eliminate confusion. The three key points of the new recommendations are detailed in a 20-page report available from IAB.net. Industry experts believe that the adoption of these guidelines, along with objective auditing, would make the Internet a more attractive medium for many of those who advertise in traditional media. The guidelines have the support of major online publishers, as well as the nearly 40 major proprietary online ad-server technologies and major associations worldwide.[37]

**Internet-Specific Measures** One of the perceived advantages of the Internet is a company's ability to measure commercial effectiveness, due in part to its ability to measure activity in real time. Figure 15–7 shows some of the measures that are currently used by companies. These measures include audience measures specific to the Internet and interactive industry. (For a detailed explanation of each of these terms, visit www.IAB.net.)

**Traditional Measures** In addition to the Internet-specific measures, companies employ a number of traditional marketing and communications measures. Some of these include the following.

- *Recall and retention.* A number of companies use traditional measures of recall and retention to test their Internet ads. These same measures have been used to pretest online commercials as well.
- *Surveys.* Survey research, conducted both online and through traditional methods, is employed to determine everything from site usage to attitudes toward a site.
- *Sales.* For the e-commerce marketers, a prime indicator of effectiveness is the volume of sales generated. Adding information regarding demographics, user behaviors, and so on, can increase the effectiveness of this measure.
- *Tracking.* Some companies now offer more traditional tracking measures such as brand awareness, ad recall, message association, and purchase intent.
- *ROI.* A study conducted by comScore, MySpace, and dunnhumby measured the ROI of online sales generated by a $1 million campaign on MySpace.[38]

The aforementioned measures reveal that the Internet has its own set of criteria for measuring effectiveness and is also borrowing from traditional measures; for example, brand recall has become a major area of focus. The American Association of Advertising Agencies and the Association of National Advertisers use a system called Advertising Digital Identification (Ad-Id). Ad-Id assigns advertising across all media a specific media code to facilitate cross-media buys. In 2008 Ad-Id became the official media coding standard.[39] The goal of the coalition is to develop cross-media standards employing impression comparisons that include the Internet. Many of the companies that provide research information in traditional media (Nielsen, Ipsos-ASI) are now extending their reach into the Internet world. Others (Insights.com, Forrester) have developed measures specifically for online users. Two of the commonly used Internet advertising effectiveness measurement companies used are comScore and Media Metrix. These companies offer a combination of effectiveness measures for marketers to use. Academics are also beginning to publish articles related to measuring effectiveness on the Internet. Studies on consumers' attitudes toward a site, response variations in e-mail surveys, and similarities between brick-and-mortar retailing and e-commerce are just a few of the many articles being published in academic journals to advance the measurement of Internet use.

In addition to the metrics provided here, there are numerous methods that have been suggested for measuring the effectiveness of social media. Note that the metrics

CHAPTER 15

shown in Figure 15–8 are not a complete list of effectiveness measures used, but they do provide an illustration of just some of the ways that marketers attempt to determine if they are accomplishing their goals when employing these media. Also keep in mind that many marketers are not enthralled with these measures, which has led to their reluctance to invest more monies in these new media, or to attempt to employ effectiveness measures at all.

Unfortunately, not all of the methods used to measure Internet activity and effectiveness are accurate. We discuss some of these problems next.

| SOCIAL MEDIA APPLICATION | BRAND AWARENESS | BRAND ENGAGEMENT | WORD OF MOUTH |
|---|---|---|---|
| Blogs | • number of unique visits<br>• number of return visits<br>• number of times bookmarked<br>• search ranking | • number of members<br>• number of RSS feed subscribers<br>• number of comments<br>• amount of user-generated content<br>• average length of time on site<br>• number of responses to polls, contests, surveys | • number of references to blog in other media (online/offline)<br>• number of reblogs<br>• number of times badge displayed on other sites<br>• number of "likes" |
| Microblogging (e.g., Twitter) | • number of tweets about the brand<br>• valence of tweets +/–<br>• number of followers | • v number of followers<br>• number of @replies | • number of retweets |
| Cocreation (e.g., NIKEID) | • number of visits | • number of creation attempts | • number of references to project in other media (online/offline) |
| Social bookmarking (e.g., StumbleUpon) | • number of tags | • number of followers | • number of additional taggers |
| Forums and Discussion Boards (e.g., Google Groups) | • number of page views<br>• number of visits<br>• valence of posted content +/– | • number of relevant topics/threads<br>• number of individual replies<br>• number of sign-ups | • incoming links<br>• citations in other sites<br>• tagging in social bookmarking<br>• offline references to the forum or its members<br>• in private communities: number of pieces of content (photos, discussions, videos); chatter pointing to the community outside of its gates<br>• number of "likes" |
| Product Reviews (e.g., Amazon) | • number of reviews posted<br>• valence of reviews<br>• number and valence of other users' responses to reviews (+/–)<br>• number of wish list adds<br>• number of times product included in users' lists (i.e., Listmanial on Amazon.com) | • length of reviews<br>• relevance of reviews<br>• valence of other users' ratings of reviews (i.e., how many found particular review helpful)<br>• number of wish list adds<br>• overall number of reviewer rating scores entered<br>• average reviewer rating score | • number of reviews posted<br>• valence of reviews<br>• number and valence of other users' responses to reviews (+/–)<br>• number of references to reviews in other sites<br>• number of visits to review site page<br>• number of times product included in users' lists (i.e., Listmanial on Amazon.com) |
| Social Networks (e.g., Bebo, Facebook, LinkedIn) | • number of members/fans<br>• number of installs of applications<br>• number of impressions<br>• number of bookmarks<br>• number of reviews/ratings and valence +/– | • number of comments<br>• number of active users<br>• number of "likes" on friends' feeds<br>• number of user-generated items (photos, threads, replies)<br>• usage metrics of applications/widgets<br>• impressions-to-interactions ratio<br>• rate of activity (how often members personalize profiles, bios, links, etc.) | • frequency of appearances in timeline of friends<br>• number of posts on wall<br>• number of reposts/shares<br>• number of responses to friend referral invites |
| Video and Photosharing (e.g., Flickr, YouTube) | • number of views of video/photo<br>• valence of video/photo ratings +/– | • number of replies<br>• number of page views<br>• number of comments<br>• number of subscribers | • number of embeddings<br>• number of incoming links<br>• number of references in mock-ups or derived work<br>• number of times republished in other social media and offline<br>• number of "likes" |

FIGURE 15–8

Relevant Metrics for Social Media Applications Organized by Key Social Media Objectives.

Source: MIT *Sloan Management Review* Fall 2010.

# ADVANTAGES AND DISADVANTAGES OF THE INTERNET, DIGITAL AND SOCIAL MEDIA

A number of advantages of the Internet can be cited:

1. *Target marketing.* A major advantage of the Internet, digital and social media is the ability to target very specific groups of individuals with a minimum of waste coverage. For those in the business-to-business market, the Internet resembles a combination trade magazine and trade show, as only those most interested in the products and/or services a site has to offer will visit the site (others have little or no reason to do so). In the consumer market, through personalization retargeting and other targeting techniques, sites are becoming more tailored to meet one's needs and wants.

2. *Message tailoring.* As a result of precise targeting, messages can be designed to appeal to the specific needs and wants of the target audience, much of which comes from behavior tracking. The interactive capabilities of social media make it possible to carry on one-to-one marketing with increased success in both the business and the consumer markets.

3. *Interactive capabilities.* Because these media are interactive, they provide strong potential for increasing customer involvement, engagement, and satisfaction and almost immediate feedback for buyers and sellers.

4. *Information access.* Perhaps the greatest advantage of the Internet is its availability as an information source. Internet users can find a plethora of information about almost any topic of their choosing merely by conducting a search. Once they have visited a particular site, users can garner a wealth of information regarding product specifications, costs, purchase information, and so on. Links will direct them to even more information if it is desired. Google and YouTube also offer a search function.

5. *Sales potential.* The sales numbers generated by Amazon and eBay alone (not to mention many, many more) demonstrate the incredible sales numbers being generated in both the business-to-business and the consumer segments. Forecasts are for continued growth in the future. In addition, the number of persons who shop online and then purchase offline has continued to increase.

6. *Creativity.* Creatively designed sites can enhance a company's image, lead to repeat visits, and positively position the company or organization in the consumer's mind. Visit some of the sites mentioned earlier to see what we mean. Consumer-generated social media leads to even more creativity.

7. *Exposure.* For many smaller companies, with limited budgets, the World Wide Web enables them to gain exposure to potential customers that heretofore would have been impossible (recall the example of the tongue cleaner). For a fraction of the investment that would be required using traditional media, companies can gain national and even international exposure in a timely manner.

8. *Speed.* For those requesting information on a company, its products, and/or its service offerings, the Internet is the quickest means of acquiring and providing this information. Well-designed sites keep this information current, and search allows for additional sources.

9. *Complement to IMC.* The Internet digital and social media complement and are complemented by other IMC media. As such, they serve as vital links in the integrative process. Marketers understand that these media support and are supported by traditional media.

While it is a potentially effective medium, the Internet also has its disadvantages, including the following:

1. *Measurement problems.* One of the greatest disadvantages of the Internet and new media is the lack of reliability of the research numbers generated. A quick review of forecasts, and other statistics offered by research providers will demonstrate a great deal of variance—leading to a serious lack of validity and

reliability. One company mentioned earlier, eMarketer, has attempted to reconcile such differences and explain the reasoning for the discrepancies (differences in methodologies employed), but the problem still exists. The actions taken by the IAB to standardize metrics will help in reducing some of this problem. But due to difficulties involved in both measuring and forecasting in this medium, it remains necessary to proceed with caution when using these numbers. In a study of 410 marketing executives published by McKinsey, the primary reason cited for not investing online was the lack of sufficient metrics.[40,41,42] As noted earlier, more recent studies indicate that this concern still exists.

2. *Clutter.* As the number of ads proliferates, the likelihood of one's ad being noticed drops accordingly. The result is that some ads may not get noticed, and some consumers may become irritated by the clutter. Studies show that banner ads have lost effectiveness for this very reason, while others show consistently declining click-through rates.

3. *Potential for deception.* The Center for Media Education has referred to the Web as "a web of deceit" in regard to advertisers' attempts to target children with subtle advertising messages. The center, among others, has asked the government to regulate the Internet. In addition, data collection without consumers' knowledge and permission, hacking, and credit card theft are among the problems confronting Internet users. Bloggers who endorse brands without revealing that they are being compensated to do so and native ads can also be misleading.

4. *Privacy.* One of the many issues of concern for Internet users is that of privacy. Perhaps of most concern is the collection of personal data which are subsequently provided to marketers, sometimes without the users' knowledge. While many younger users seem to be less worried, actions taken by websites like Facebook, among others, have led to user boycotts as well as calls for more regulation. The IAB has issued a policy on privacy to which it asks companies to adhere (see www.iab.net).

5. *Irritation.* Numerous studies have reported on the irritating aspects of some web tactics. These studies have shown consumers' discontent with clutter, e-mail spam, and pop-ups and pop-unders. There is also a growing sense of irritation with retargeting ads and pre-rolls. These irritating aspects can deter visitors from coming to and or returning to the sites, or result in negative attributes toward the advertiser.

Overall, the Internet offers marketers some very definite advantages over traditional media. At the same time, disadvantages and limitations render this medium as less than a one-stop solution. However, as part of an IMC program, the Internet is a very valuable tool.

## Summary

This chapter introduced you to the Internet and a variety of digital and social new media. It explained some of the objectives for these media and how they can be used in an IMC program.

The discussion of the Internet focused on understanding the growth of the Internet, the objectives sought when using the Internet, and Internet communications strategies. In addition, we discussed the role of the Internet in an IMC program, explaining how all the IMC program elements can be used with the Internet.

The chapter discussed a number of new online tools including paid search, behavioral targeting, contextual ads, rich media, and a number of Web 2.0 platforms including social media, social networks, user-generated content, blogs, RSS, and podcasting. We noted advantages of the Internet—including targeting markets, using interactive capabilities, and building relationships. In addition, we reviewed disadvantages—including high costs, unreliable measurements and statistics, and relatively low reach (compared to that of traditional media).

The Internet has been the most rapidly adopted medium of our time (until mobile). The growth of mobile, due to the adoption of smartphones and portable devices, and millions of applications has led to very rapid growth in advertising expenditures in this area. It holds great potential for both business-to-business and consumer marketers. However, contrary to popular belief, the Internet is not a stand-alone medium. Its role in an integrated marketing communications program strengthens the overall program as well as the effectiveness of the Internet itself.

## Discussion Questions

1.   Many marketers and policymakers believe the Internet and social media may constitute a "web of deceit." Explain what they mean by this comment. Provide examples as to why they have this feeling. (LO4)

2.   The drive to go viral has resulted in some major marketing mistakes. Explain why marketers are seemingly obsessed with going viral. Then explain some of the consequences that might occur should these efforts fail. (LO5)

3.   The new media discussed in this chapter offer some distinct advantages over traditional media, but also have some disadvantages. Discuss some of the advantages and disadvantages of traditional and new media. (LO4)

4.   Discuss the role of social media in an IMC program. What can these media best contribute in regard to helping marketers achieve communications objectives? (LO2)

5.   Policymakers are concerned that some bloggers may not be disclosing the fact that they are being compensated for product or brand endorsements. Explain why they may be concerned about this and why it may lead to negative impacts on the consumer. (LO5)

6.   The growth of Facebook has had a major impact on the way advertisers attempt to reach their customers. Discuss how Facebook has changed the media environment, citing examples. (LO2)

7.   Discuss why mobile has become an attractive medium for advertisers. Provide examples of how companies have used mobile. (LO2)

8.   There are indications that the popularity of blogs may have already reached the maturity stage. Take a position as to whether this is true or not, providing examples to support your opinion. (LO1)

9.   A trend among advertisers is to make more use of consumer-generated commercials to be placed on YouTube and similar sites. Discuss some of the advantages and disadvantages of employing this strategy. (LO4)

10.   Some marketers have argued that the strength of the Internet in an IMC program is at the midstage of the consumer funnel (knowledge consideration, etc.). Discuss whether you agree or disagree with this position, and support your position with examples. (LO1)

## LEARNING OBJECTIVES

(LO1) To understand the role of sales promotion in a company's integrated marketing communications program and to examine why it is increasingly important.

(LO2) To examine the various objectives of sales promotion programs.

(LO3) To examine the types of consumer- and trade-oriented sales promotion tools and the factors to consider in using them.

(LO4) To understand how sales promotion is coordinated with advertising.

(LO5) To consider potential problems and abuse by companies in their use of sales promotion.

# 16 Sales Promotion

## TAO TI SALES PROMOTION

Telford International Company Limited (Telford) is wholly owned and operated by the Fong family with 46 years of proven track record in services and strategic international and regional partnerships in the beverages, spirits, wine, and beer industries in Hong Kong. Telford also acquired sole distributorship of Tao Ti Green Tea from Taiwan in 1996; Honey Green Tea was the first Tao Ti product to be launched. From time to time, Telford introduces new products for Tao Ti. For instance, a new series of juice drinks named the "Orchard" or "Pak Gor Yuen" under the Tao Ti brand name was launched in 2002. In 2006, Telford also launched the Tao Ti Supreme Series. Telford insists all drinks in the six-product series of Tao Ti contain no added preservatives or artificial coloring.

Telford frequently undertakes sales promotion campaigns when launching new products. To be successful, both Telford and PHD Worldwide (Hong Kong)—the media and communications agency that handles Telford and Tao Ti accounts—think sales promotion activities should be compatible with the product's image and match the target customers' preferences and behaviors. The target customers of the Tao Ti Pak Gor Yuen juice product line are youngsters, in particular high school students who spend more time online—especially on social networking sites—than read traditional print media such as magazines or newspapers. For this reason, Tao Ti makes use of Facebook, YouTube, Mobile Ad, and WeChat to promote sales.

When the Tao Ti Pak Gor Yuen Watermelon Juice drink was launched in May 2013, various types of promotional tools were used on social networking sites (especially Facebook and YouTube) to increase sales volume. The sales promotional tools included:

(1) lucky draws which offered participants the chance to win two return tickets to Pattaya (in Thailand), a camera, 10 sets of "Beats Mixr" headphones, and bottles of watermelon juice or watermelon-shaped ukuleles;

(2) on-pack gifts of cutely designed miniature watermelons and watermelon coin bags;

(3) special offers of half-priced movie tickets; and

(4) a WeChat online campaign where 100 lucky customers had the chance to win a watermelon-shaped USB (4GB) pendrive by adding the TaoTiHKWeChat ID.

All the premium items were compatible with the product's image and appropriate for the target market. In fact, so sought after were the gifts that, for instance, all the USB pendrives were given away within two days of the sales promotion campaign because of their distinctive watermelon design and practical value.

The sales promotion campaign was very successful with sales doubling and it stimulated high public awareness of the new product within a very short period of time. According to the senior management of Telford, the success of the campaign was the result of a well-designed integrated marketing plan. On top of consumer-oriented and trade-related sales promotions, both above-the-line advertisements (5-second and 15-second TV advertisements and outdoor advertisements on Cross Harbour Tunnel billboards and bus shelter panels) and below-the-line chain-store point-of-sale displays (e.g., posters, cooler cards, shelf talkers, and stackings) were also used. The campaign also rode on social media channels which are very popular among the target customers. In addition, the company invited model and actress Dada Chan to endorse the watermelon juice. She is popular with young people and activities endorsed by her are bound to be commented on the Hong Kong Golden Forum (a leading discussion forum in Hong Kong) and various social media sites. The fact that the Facebook ad featuring Dada Chan running and drinking watermelon juice at a beach recorded over 600,000 views, 2,500 likes, 200 comments, and 100 shares is evident of her youth appeal.

In order to maintain the green and all natural image of Tao Ti, there are no preservatives in any of its drinks; only malic acid is added to enable the watermelon juice to be stored for a longer time. Unfortunately, there have been different views regarding the watermelon juice drink. Some people said the juice did not taste like watermelon. Telford is committed to making the necessary changes to the taste to suit customers' preferences. This example best illustrates that a well-designed marketing plan should go with a suitable product which customers prefer.

Movie coupon redemption programs are also frequently used by Telford when launching new products because many of its customers enjoy watching movies. For instance, free tickets to the movie *Blind Detective* were offered in conjunction with the launch of the Tao Ti Supreme series. Similarly, free movie passes for *Golden Chicken 3* and *Tales from the Dark* were offered during the launch of Balancy Herbal Cool. The coupon redemption program promoting the Pak Gor Yuen product line with an offer of tickets to the gala premiere of the movie *Nodame Cantabile* was most remarkable. The number of people taking up the free ticket offer rose 10 times compared with other movie coupon redemption programs. Its success can be traced to the fact that the two main characters of the movie, Hiroshi Tamaki and Juri Ueno, were invited to attend the gala premiere. It made the movie tickets more attractive. This example illustrates that integrating a sales promotion with event marketing can achieve better results.

Telford also undertakes other well-planned sales promotion activities to reinforce the brand image of Tao Ti. Green Tea is one of the core products under the brand. "Green Holiday" has been an annual sales promotion program since 1999; a lucky draw is organized as part of the promotion program and it is well-received by Tao Ti consumers and fans. The objective of "Green Holiday" is to promote a relaxed or leisurely lifestyle by allowing winners to visit some "green" and natural places so as to reinforce the brand's philosophy of "green living" and "natural taste."

A special edition of Honey Green Tea with a Green Holiday label is designed every year. During the sales promotion period, all a customer has to do is to purchase Tao Ti drinks and send back four bottle labels (the Green Holiday special label must be included) with personal information to enter the lucky draw and join the green holiday tours.

Tour destinations included Wolong Giant Panda Reserve in 1999, the rainforests of Taman Negara in Malaysia in 2003, Jigokudani Snow Monkeys Park in Japan in 2010, Phillip Island Nature Park in Australia in 2011, and Kyushu Natural Zoological Park in Japan in 2013. Around 5,000 to 8,000 people join the green holiday tour program every year. So far, more than 100 winners of the lucky draws have enjoyed these tours. Winners are more than happy to post the tour photos and videos and share their travel experiences with friends on various social media sites. This has helped Telford to gain publicity for its business.

To sum up, this Tao Ti case best illustrates that integrated marketing communication (IMC) activities such as sales promotion, event marketing, and advertising can assist a company to encourage existing customers to try its new products, attract new customers, boost sales volume, and reinforce brand image.

Sources: Tao Ti Facebook fan page, https://www.facebook.com/taotifans; Tao Ti website, http://www.tao-ti.com; "Tao Ti Pak Gor Yuen Watermelon Juice Ad ft. Dada Chan", YouTube videos, http://www.youtube.com/watch?v=mAGBE8p6xlo, http://www.youtube.com/watch?v=njuJBZwD8JA.

As discussed in the opening vignette, sales promotion is an effective way to move the products of companies off store shelves and into the hands of consumers. The integration of well-planned sales promotion activities with other IMC tools can assist companies to encourage existing customers to try their new products, attract new converts, increase sales volume, and strengthen brand image. They are using a variety of sales promotion methods targeted at both consumers and the wholesalers and retailers that distribute their products to stimulate demand. Most companies' IMC programs include consumer and trade promotions that are coordinated with their advertising, direct marketing, publicity/publications, and online/web-related marketing as well as their personal-selling efforts.

This chapter focuses on the role of sales promotion in a firm's IMC program. We examine how marketers use both consumer- and trade-oriented promotions to influence the purchase behavior of consumers as well as wholesalers and retailers. We explore the objectives of sales promotion programs and the various types of sales promotion tools that can be used at both the consumer and trade level. We also consider how sales promotion can be integrated with other elements of the promotional mix and look at problems that can arise when marketers become overly dependent on consumer and trade promotions, especially the latter.

# THE SCOPE AND ROLE OF SALES PROMOTION

**Sales promotion** has been defined as "a direct inducement that offers an extra value or incentive for the product to the sales force, distributors, or the ultimate consumer with the primary objective of creating an immediate sale."[1] Keep in mind several important aspects of sales promotion as you read this chapter.

First, sales promotion involves some type of inducement that provides an *extra incentive* to buy. This incentive is usually the key element in a promotional program; it may be a coupon or price reduction, the opportunity to enter a contest or sweepstakes, a money-back refund or rebate, or an extra amount of a product. The incentive may also be a free sample of the product, given in hopes of generating a future purchase or a premium such as the Mini Minion characters toy used by General Mills for Lucky Charms cereal (Exhibit 16–1). The Minion premium offer was part of promotional tie-in to the movie *Despicable Me 2* that included packaging themed to the movie, eight collectable Minion premiums, and product integrations.[2] Most sales promotion offers attempt to add some value to the product or service. While advertising appeals to the mind and emotions to give the consumer a reason to buy, sales promotion appeals more to the pocketbook and provides an incentive for purchasing a brand.

Sales promotion can also provide an inducement to marketing intermediaries such as wholesalers and retailers. A trade allowance or discount gives retailers a financial incentive to stock and promote a manufacturer's products. A trade contest directed toward wholesalers or retail personnel gives them extra incentive to perform certain tasks or meet sales goals.

A second point is that sales promotion is essentially an *acceleration tool,* designed to speed up the selling process and maximize sales volume.[3] By providing an extra incentive, sales promotion techniques can motivate consumers to purchase a larger quantity of a brand or shorten the purchase cycle of the trade or consumers by encouraging them to take more immediate action.

**EXHIBIT 16–1**

A premium offer is used to provide extra incentive to purchase Lucky Charms

Companies also use limited-time offers such as price-off deals to retailers or a coupon with an expiration date to accelerate the purchase process.[4] Sales promotion attempts to maximize sales volume by motivating customers who have not responded to advertising. The ideal sales promotion program generates sales that would not be achieved by other means. However, as we will see later, many sales promotion offers end up being used by current users of a brand rather than attracting new users.

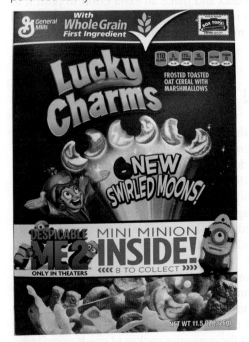

A final point regarding sales promotion activities is that they can be *targeted to different parties* in the marketing channel. As shown in Figure 16–1, sales promotion can be broken into two major categories: consumer-oriented and trade-oriented promotions. Activities involved in **consumer-oriented sales promotion** include sampling, couponing, premiums, contests and sweepstakes, refunds and rebates, bonus packs, price-offs, frequency programs, and event marketing. These promotions are directed at consumers, the end purchasers of goods and services, and are designed to induce them to purchase the marketer's brand.

As discussed in Chapter 2, consumer-oriented promotions are part of a promotional pull strategy; they work along with advertising to encourage consumers to purchase a particular brand and thus create demand for it. Consumer promotions are also used by retailers to encourage consumers to shop in their particular stores. Many grocery stores use their own coupons or sponsor contests and other promotions to increase store patronage.

**Trade-oriented sales promotion** includes dealer contests and incentives, trade allowances, point-of-purchase displays, sales training

**FIGURE 16–1**

Types of Sales Promotion
Activities

| Sales Promotion | |
|---|---|
| **Consumer-Oriented Promotions** | **Trade-Oriented Promotions** |
| Samples | Contests and dealer incentives |
| Coupons | Trade allowances |
| Premiums | Point-of-purchase displays |
| Contests/sweepstakes | Training programs |
| Refunds/rebates | Trade shows |
| Bonus packs | Cooperative advertising |
| Price-offs | |
| Loyalty programs | |
| Event marketing | |

programs, trade shows, cooperative advertising, and other programs designed to motivate distributors and retailers to carry a product and make an extra effort to push it to their customers. Many marketing programs include both trade- and consumer-oriented promotions, since motivating both groups maximizes the effectiveness of the promotional program.

# THE GROWTH OF SALES PROMOTION

While sales promotion has been part of the marketing process for a long time, its role and importance in a company's integrated marketing communications program have increased dramatically over the past decade. Consumer sales promotion–related spending increased from $56 billion in 1991 to more then $300 billion in 2013.[5] Marketers also spend an estimated $150 billion each year on promotions targeted at retailers and wholesalers. Consumer packaged goods (CPG) firms continue to be the core users of sales promotion programs and tools. However, sales promotion activity is also increasing in other categories, including health care, consumer electronics fast-food, retailing, and service industries.

Estimates are that marketers spend between 60 and 75 percent of their promotional budgets on sales promotion, with the remainder being allocated to media advertising.[6] Allocation of marketing budgets among consumer promotions, trade promotions, and media advertising varies by industry and company. For example, trade promotion accounts for nearly 50 percent of the budget for consumer packaged goods companies,

**EXHIBIT 16–2**
Advertisements often use promotions such as sweepstakes to draw attention

**EXHIBIT 16–3**
Aspen Marketing Services touts its IMC capabilities

with 27 percent going to consumer promotion and 24 percent to media advertising.[7] Moreover, a significant amount of the monies that marketers allocate to media advertising is spent on ads that deliver promotional messages regarding contests, games, sweepstakes, and rebate offers.[8] Surveys have shown that marketers devote about 17 percent of their ad budgets to promotional messages.[9] Promotional messages are also used to help attract attention to image-building ads. For example, the ad shown in Exhibit 16–2 shows how Channellock uses a sweepstakes promotion to help draw attention to an ad promoting the quality of its tools.

## Reasons for the Increase in Sales Promotion

The increases in the percentage of the IMC budget allocated to sales promotion over the years concerned many marketers who still viewed media advertising as the primary tool for brand building and saw sales promotion programs as little more than gimmicks that contributed little to brand equity. However, most have recognized that consumers may love their brands but often want an extra incentive to buy them. Marketers also know they must partner effectively with trade accounts, and this often means providing them with an additional incentive to stock and promote their brands and participate in various promotional programs.

A major reason for the increase in spending on sales promotion is that the promotion industry has matured over the past several decades. Increased sophistication and a more strategic role and focus have elevated the discipline and its role in the IMC program of many companies. In the past, sales promotion specialists would be brought in after key strategic branding decisions were made. Promotional agencies were viewed primarily as tacticians whose role was to develop a promotional program such as a contest or sweepstakes or a coupon or sampling program that could create a short-term increase in sales. However, many companies are now making promotional specialists part of their strategic brand-building team, a move that puts sales promotion on par with media advertising. Many promotional agencies have expanded their capabilities and expertise and now offer clients a variety of integrated marketing services that extend beyond just sales promotion. For example, Exhibit 16–3 shows how Aspen Marketing Services, one of the largest providers of integrated marketing and promotional services, promotes its capabilities, which include a variety of IMC tools.

There are also a number of other factors that have led to the increase in the importance of sales promotion and the shift in marketing dollars from media advertising to consumer and trade promotions. Among them are the growing power of retailers, declining brand loyalty, increased promotional sensitivity, brand proliferation, fragmentation of the consumer market, the short-term focus of many marketers, increased accountability, competition, clutter, and the growth of digital and social media.

**The Growing Power of Retailers** One reason for the increase in sales promotion is the power shift in the marketplace from manufacturers to retailers. For many years, manufacturers of national brands had the power and influence; retailers were just passive distributors of their products. Consumer-product manufacturers created consumer demand for their brands by using heavy advertising and some consumer-oriented promotions, such as samples, coupons, and premiums, and exerted pressure on retailers to carry the products. Retailers did very little research and sales analysis; they relied on manufacturers for information regarding the sales performance of individual brands.

In recent years, however, several developments have helped transfer power from the manufacturers to the retailers. With the advent of optical checkout scanners and sophisticated in-store computer systems, retailers gained access to data concerning how quickly products turn over, which sales promotions are working, and which products make money.[10] Retailers use this information to analyze sales of manufacturers' products and then demand discounts and other promotional support from manufacturers of lagging brands. Companies that fail to comply with retailers' demands for more trade support often have their shelf space reduced or even have their product dropped.

Another factor that has increased the power of retailers is the consolidation of the grocery store industry, which has resulted in larger chains with greater buying power and clout. These large chains have become accustomed to trade promotions and can pressure manufacturers to provide deals, discounts, and allowances. Consolidation has also given large retailers more money for advancing already strong private label initiatives, and sales promotion is the next step in the marketing evolution of private label brands. Private label brands in various packaged-good categories such as foods, drugs, and health and beauty care products are giving national brands more competition for retail shelf space and increasing their own marketing, including the use of traditional sales promotion tools. Private label food and beverage products now account for nearly 18 percent of sales in these categories and reached nearly $100 billion in 2012.[11] Well-marketed private label products are forcing national brand leaders, as well as second-tier brands, to develop more innovative promotional programs and to be more price-competitive.[12]

YTC 16–01

Walmart

youtube.com/10ebelch

One of the most significant developments among retailers is the tremendous growth of Walmart, which has become the largest company in the world as well as the most powerful retailer[13] (Exhibit 16–4). Walmart operates nearly 10,700 stores in 27 countries, including more than 4,200 in the United States, and had sales of $466 billion in fiscal 2013. It controls 20 percent of dry grocery, 29 percent of nonfood grocery, 30 percent of health and beauty aids, and 45 percent of general merchandise sales in the United States. Walmart accounts for a large share of the business done by every major U.S. consumer-products company and can use its power to influence the way marketers use sales promotions. Like many large retailers, Walmart often asks for account-specific promotions that are designed for and offered only through its stores. The company has been known to mandate that marketers forgo promotional offers and use the monies to reduce prices.[14]

**EXHIBIT 16–4**

Walmart is the world's largest and most powerful retailer

**Declining Brand Loyalty** Another major reason for the increase in sales promotion is that consumers have become less brand loyal and are purchasing more on the basis of price, value, and convenience. Some consumers are always willing to buy their preferred brand at full price without any type of promotional offer. However, many consumers are loyal coupon users and/or are conditioned to look for deals when they shop. They may switch back and forth among a set of brands they view as essentially equal. These brands are all perceived as being satisfactory and interchangeable, and consumers purchase whatever brand is on a special sale or for which they have a coupon.

**Increased Promotional Sensitivity** Marketers are making greater use of sales promotion in their marketing programs because consumers respond favorably to the incentives it provides. A major research project completed by Promotion Decisions, Inc. tracked the purchase behavior of over 33,000 consumers and their response to both consumer and trade promotions. The results showed that 42 percent of the total unit volume of the 12 packaged-good products analyzed was purchased with some type of incentive while 58 percent was purchased at full price. Coupons were particularly popular among consumers, as 24 percent of the sales volume involved the use of a coupon.[15]

Many marketers, as well as retailers, often condition consumers to wait for discounts through sales, special offers, and coupons, which make it very difficult to sell their merchandise at full price. Surveys have shown that consumers are 50 percent more price-sensitive than they were 25 years ago and for good reason.[16] Marketers issue more than 300 billion coupons each year, or nearly 1,000 per person. They also use rebates, buy-one-get-one-free offers, special sales events, price-off deals, and other discounts to attract price-sensitive consumers. Consumers are not naive; they know that manufacturers or retailers will offer some type of promotion that encourages them to wait for the next deal rather than purchasing a product at full price.

An obvious reason for consumers' increased sensitivity to sales promotion offers is that they save money. Another reason is that many purchase decisions are made at the point of purchase by consumers who are increasingly time-sensitive and facing too many choices. Some studies have found that up to 70 percent of purchase decisions are made in the store, where people are very likely to respond to promotional deals.[17] Buying a brand that is on special or being displayed can simplify the decision-making process and solve the problem of overchoice. Professor Leigh McAlister has described this process:

> As consumers go down the supermarket aisle they spend 3 to 10 seconds in each product category. They often don't know the regular price of the chosen product. However, they do have a sense of whether or not that product is on promotion. As they go down the aisle, they are trying to pensively fill their baskets with good products without tiresome calculations. They see a "good deal" and it goes in the cart.[18]

**Brand Proliferation** A major aspect of many firms' marketing strategies over the past decade has been the development of new products. The market has become saturated with new brands, most of which lack any significant advantages. According to the Global New Products Database, which monitors product innovation and retail success in consumer packaged goods markets worldwide, over 20,000 new products are added every month from 49 countries.[19] However, research shows that about 75 percent of consumer packaged goods and retail products fail in their first year—in large part because of ingrained consumer shopping habits.[20] Thus, companies increasingly depend on sales promotion to encourage consumers to try these brands. In Chapter 4, we saw how sales promotion techniques can be used as part of the shaping process to lead the consumer from initial trial to repeat purchase at full price. Marketers are relying more on samples, coupons, rebates, premiums, and other innovative promotional tools to achieve trial usage of their new brands and encourage repeat purchase (Exhibit 16–5).

**EXHIBIT 16–5**
Sales promotion tools such as coupons are often used to encourage trial of a new brand

Promotions are also important in getting retailers to allocate some of their precious shelf space to new brands. The competition for shelf space for new products in stores is enormous. Supermarkets carry an average of 30,000 products (compared with 13,067 in 1982). Retailers favor new brands with strong sales promotion support that will bring in more customers and boost their sales and profits. Many retailers require special discounts or allowances from manufacturers just to handle a new product. These slotting fees or allowances, which are discussed later in the chapter, can make it expensive for a manufacturer to introduce a new product.

**Fragmentation of the Consumer Market**  As the consumer market becomes more fragmented and traditional mass-media–based advertising less effective, marketers are turning to more segmented, highly targeted approaches. Many companies are tailoring their promotional efforts to specific regional markets. Sales promotion tools have become one of the primary vehicles for doing this, through programs tied into local flavor, themes, or events. For example, fast-food restaurants and take-out pizza chains such as Domino's spend a high percentage of their marketing budget on local tie-ins and promotions designed to build traffic and generate sales from their trade areas.

Marketers are also shifting more of their promotional efforts to direct and digital marketing, which often includes some form of sales promotion incentive. Many marketers use information they get from premium offers, trackable coupons, rebates, and sweepstakes to build databases for future direct-marketing efforts. As marketers continue to shift from media advertising to direct marketing, promotional offers will probably be used even more to help build databases. The technology is already in place to enable marketers to communicate individually with target consumers and transform mass promotional tools into ways of doing one-to-one marketing.

**Short-Term Focus**  Many businesspeople believe the increase in sales promotion is motivated by marketing plans and reward systems geared to short-term performance and the immediate generation of sales volume as discussed in the opening vignette to the chapter. Some think the packaged-goods brand management system has contributed to marketers' increased dependence on sales promotion. Brand managers use sales promotions routinely, not only to introduce new products or defend against the competition but also to meet quarterly or yearly sales and market share goals. The sales force, too, may have short-term quotas or goals to meet and may also receive requests from retailers and wholesalers for promotions. Thus, reps may pressure marketing or brand managers to use promotions to help them move the products into the retailers' stores.

Many managers view consumer and trade promotions as the most dependable way to generate short-term sales, particularly when they are price-related. The reliance on sales promotion is particularly high in mature and slow-growth markets, where it is difficult to stimulate consumer demand through advertising. This has led to concern that managers have become too dependent on the quick sales fix that can result from a promotion and that the brand franchise may be eroded by too many deals.

Professors Leonard Lodish and Carl Mela have conducted research that suggests many companies are too focused on short-term results because the profusion of scanner data allows brand and marketing managers, as well as retailers, to see how sales often spike in response to promotional discounts.[21] They note that managers became enamored with these short-term increases in sales, which resulted in the allocation of the majority of their marketing budgets to consumer and trade promotions. Another problem they note is that many brand managers stay in their positions for a short time period, which motivates them to focus on the use of promotional tactics that can have more of an immediate impact. They often view investing in advertising or product development as benefiting the performance of subsequent managers rather than their own. When asked about why they take a short-term perspective, marketing and brand managers point out that they are judged on quarterly sales because investors focus on these numbers, and the link between promotion and sales is obvious.

**Increased Accountability**  In addition to pressuring their marketing or brand managers and sales force to produce short-term results, many companies are demanding to know what they are getting for their promotional expenditures. Results from sales promotion programs are generally easier to measure than those from advertising. Many companies are demanding measurable, accountable ways to relate promotional expenditures to sales and profitability. For example, some companies use computerized sales information from checkout scanners in determining compensation for marketing personnel. Part of the pay managers receive depends on the sales a promotion generates relative to its costs.

Managers who are being held accountable to produce results often use price discounts or coupons, since they produce a quick and easily measured jump in sales. It takes longer for an ad campaign to show some impact, and the effects are more difficult to measure. Marketers are also feeling pressure from the trade as powerful retailers demand sales performance from their brands. Real-time data available from computerized checkout scanners make it possible for retailers to monitor promotions and track the results they generate on a daily basis.

**Competition**   Another factor that led to the increase in sales promotion is manufacturers' reliance on trade and consumer promotions to gain or maintain competitive advantage. The markets for many products are mature and stagnant, and it is increasingly difficult to boost sales through advertising. Exciting, breakthrough creative ideas are difficult to come by, and consumers' attention to mass-media advertising continues to decline. Rather than allocating large amounts of money to run dull ads, many marketers have turned to sales promotion.

Many companies are tailoring their trade promotions to key retail accounts and developing strategic alliances with retailers that include both trade and consumer promotional programs. A major development in recent years is **account-specific marketing** (also referred to as *comarketing*), whereby a manufacturer collaborates with an individual retailer to create a customized promotion that accomplishes mutual objectives. For example, Exhibit 16–6 shows an account-specific promotion the WD-40 Company ran in conjunction with the O'Reilly Auto Parts retail chain. The promotion included limited-edition, custom cans made to commemorate the 60th anniversary of WD-40's multiuse product, which has been made in the United States since 1953. The special cans were created as a salute to those who subscribe to the tradition of hard work and getting the job done.[22]

Estimates are that marketers will soon be spending more than half of their promotion budgets on account-specific marketing. A number of companies are developing promotional programs for major retail accounts such as supermarket chains, mass merchandisers, and convenience stores.

Retailers may use a promotional deal with one company as leverage to seek an equal or better deal with its competitors. Consumer and trade promotions are easily matched by competitors, and many marketers find themselves in a promotional trap where they must continue using promotions or be at a competitive disadvantage. (We discuss this problem in more detail later in the chapter.)

**EXHIBIT 16–6**
WD-40 developed an account-specific promotion for O'Reilly Auto Parts

**Clutter**   A promotional offer in an ad can break through the clutter that is prevalent in most media today. A premium offer may help attract consumers' attention to an ad, as will a contest or sweepstakes. Some studies have shown that readership scores are higher for print ads with coupons than for ads without them.[23] Promotional messages are prevalent in both magazine and newspaper ads. Sweepstakes, games, and contests are often advertised in magazine ads, while coupons and sales offers are common in newspaper advertising. As discussed below, promotional offers have also become commonplace in various forms of online advertising including social media and mobile marketing as a way of attracting the attention of consumers or encouraging them to take action.

**The Growth of Digital Marketing**   Another factor that has contributed to the increased use of sales promotion is the digital marketing revolution. Many marketers now use the various forms of online marketing to implement sales promotion programs as well as measure their effectiveness. Promotional offers such as coupons and discounts along with entry forms for contests and sweepstakes appear on their websites as well as their social media pages on Facebook, Twitter, and Tumblr. Sales promotion offers are also used by marketers as a way to encourage consumers to "like" their brands on Facebook or follow them on Twitter. Studies have shown that 40 percent of consumers say they "like" a company or brand on Facebook to receive discounts and promotions including free samples and coupons.[24] Research has also shown that nearly 90 percent of consumers say they follow brands on Twitter for the same reasons, as shown in Figure 16–2.

## Concerns about the Increased Role of Sales Promotion

Many factors have contributed to the increased use of sales promotion by consumer-product manufacturers. Marketing and advertising executives are concerned about how this shift in the allocation of the promotional budget affects brand equity. As noted in Chapter 2, *brand equity,* or consumer franchise, is an intangible asset of added value or goodwill that results from consumers' favorable image, impressions of differentiation, and/or strength of attachment to a brand. Some critics argue that sales promotion increases come at the expense of brand equity and every dollar that goes into promotion rather than advertising devalues the brand.[25] They say trade promotions in particular contribute to the destruction of brand franchises and equity as they encourage consumers to purchase primarily on the basis of price.

Marketers often struggle with the problem of determining the extent to which they should use promotions to help generate sales for their brands or drive traffic to their retail stores versus relying on advertising as a way to build their brand image and avoid discounting and price competition. Given a choice, many companies would prefer to minimize their reliance on promotions and discounts and compete on the basis of product quality and/or brand image. For example, a few years ago Macy's, which is one of the nation's premier retailers, embarked on a new strategy designed to wean consumers off the 15 to 20 percent coupons as well as the "one-day sales" which it had become very reliant on to drive store traffic. The new strategy also called for more advertising to let consumers know about Macy's makeover and build a strong brand image for the chain. A highly regarded and seasoned new chief marketing officer with extensive brand-building experience was hired to lead the new initiative to turn Macy's into a destination retailer.[26]

**FIGURE 16–2**

Reasons to Follow a Brand on Twitter

Macy's implemented its new strategy, but soon found that it was backfiring as consumers across the country turned their back on Macy's and sales dropped for four consecutive months. While some customers cited the merchandising changes as the reason they were no longer shopping at Macy's, it became clear to the company that its strategy of abruptly curtailing discounts and coupons was the primary factor. Macy's had to backtrack on its plan and revert to the previous strategy, which relied heavily on various forms of discounts as well as one-day and other types of short-term sales (Exhibit 16–7).

Proponents of advertising argue that marketers must maintain strong franchises if they want to differentiate their brands and charge a premium price for them. They say advertising is still the most effective way to build the long-term franchise of a brand: It informs consumers of a brand's features and benefits, creates an image, and helps build and maintain brand loyalty. However, many marketers are not investing in their brands as they take monies away from media advertising to fund short-term promotions. Professors Lodish and Mela suggest that managers need to develop and arm themselves with long-term measures of brand performance and use them to make smarter marketing decisions that will not undermine brand equity.[27] However, the temptation to look for the quick fix and sales spike from a promotion will always be there. And it is likely that many marketers will continue to yield to the temptation rather than try to sell their brands at full price, particularly when competitors are using promotional tactics to attract their customers.

Marketing experts generally agree that advertising plays an important role in building and maintaining a brand's image and position, which are core components of its equity. Many are concerned that if the trend toward spending more on sales promotion at the expense of media advertising continues, brands may lose the equity that advertising helped create and be forced to compete primarily on the basis of price. Many of these concerns are justified, but not all sales promotion activities detract from the value of a brand. It is important to distinguish between consumer franchise-building and nonfranchise-building promotions.

## Consumer Franchise-Building versus Nonfranchise-Building Promotions

Sales promotion activities that communicate distinctive brand attributes and contribute to the development and reinforcement of brand identity are **consumer franchise-building (CFB) promotions**.[28] Consumer sales promotion efforts cannot make consumers loyal to a brand that is of little value or does not provide them with a specific benefit. But they can make consumers aware of a brand and, by communicating its specific features and benefits, contribute to the development of a favorable brand image. Consumer franchise-building promotions are designed to build long-term brand preference and help the company achieve the ultimate goal of full-price purchases that do not depend on a promotional offer.

For years, franchise or image building was viewed as the exclusive realm of advertising, and sales promotion was used only to generate short-term sales increases. But now marketers are recognizing the image-building potential of sales promotion and paying attention to its CFB value. Surveys have found that nearly 90 percent of senior marketing executives believe consumer promotions can help build brand equity while nearly 60 percent think trade promotions can contribute.[29] Marketers recognize that the value of sales promotion extends well beyond quick-fix tactics

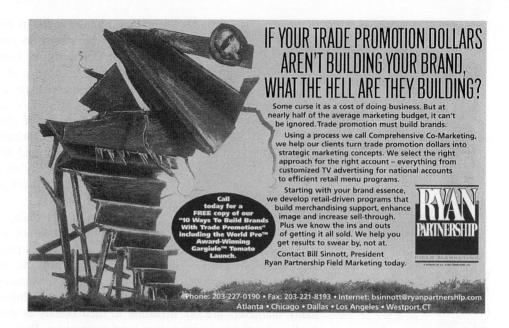

such as price-off deals. Most sales promotion agencies recognize the importance of developing consumer and trade promotions that can help build brand equity. For example, Exhibit 16–8 shows a classic ad for Ryan Partnership that stresses how the agency develops trade promotions that help build brand equity.

Companies can use sales promotion techniques in a number of ways to contribute to franchise building. Rather than using a one-time offer, many companies are developing frequency programs that encourage repeat purchases and long-term patronage. Many credit cards have loyalty programs where consumers earn bonus points every time they use their card to charge a purchase. These points can then be redeemed for various items. Most airlines and many hotel chains offer frequent-flyer or guest programs to encourage repeat patronage. Many retail stores have also begun using frequency programs to build loyalty and encourage repeat purchases.

**Nonfranchise-building (non-FB) promotions** are designed to accelerate the purchase decision process and generate an immediate increase in sales. These activities do not communicate information about a brand's unique features or the benefits of using it, so they do not contribute to the building of brand identity and image. Price-off deals, bonus packs, and rebates or refunds are examples of non-FB sales promotion techniques. Trade promotions receive the most criticism for being nonfranchise building—for good reason. First, many of the promotional discounts and allowances given to the trade are never passed on to consumers. Most trade promotions that are forwarded through the channels reach consumers in the form of lower prices or special deals and lead them to buy on the basis of price rather than brand equity.

Many specialists in the promotional area stress the need for marketers to use sales promotion tools to build a franchise and create long-term continuity in their promotional programs. Whereas non-FB promotions merely borrow customers from other brands, well-planned CFB activities can convert consumers to loyal customers. Short-term non-FB promotions have their place in a firm's promotional mix, particularly when competitive developments call for them. But their limitations must be recognized when a long-term marketing strategy for a brand is developed.

# CONSUMER-ORIENTED SALES PROMOTION

Marketers have been using various types of sales promotion for more than a hundred years and have found a variety of ways to give consumers an extra incentive to purchase their products and services. In this section, we examine the various sales promotion tools and techniques marketers can use to influence consumers. We study the consumer-oriented promotions shown in Figure 16–1 and discuss their advantages and limitations. First, we consider some objectives marketers have for sales promotion programs targeted to the consumer market.

## Objectives of Consumer-Oriented Sales Promotion

As the use of sales promotion techniques continues to increase, companies must consider what they hope to accomplish through their consumer promotions and how they interact with other promotional activities such as advertising, direct marketing, and personal selling. Not all sales promotion activities are designed to achieve the same objectives. As with any promotional-mix element, marketers must plan consumer promotions by conducting a situation analysis and determining sales promotion's specific role in the integrated marketing communications program. They must decide what the promotion is designed to accomplish and to whom it should be targeted. Setting clearly defined objectives and measurable goals for their sales promotion programs forces managers to think beyond the short-term sales fix (although this can be one goal).

While the basic goal of most consumer-oriented sales promotion programs is to induce purchase of a brand, the marketer may have a number of different objectives for both new and established brands—for example, obtaining trial and repurchase, increasing consumption of an established brand, defending current customers, targeting a specific market segment, or enhancing advertising and marketing efforts.

**Obtaining Trial and Repurchase**  One of the most important uses of sales promotion techniques is to encourage consumers to try a new product or service. While thousands of new products are introduced to the market every year, as many as 90 percent of them fail within the first year. Many of these failures are due to the fact that the new product or brand lacks the promotional support needed either to encourage initial trial by enough consumers or to induce enough of those trying the brand to repurchase it. Many new brands are merely new versions of an existing product without unique benefits, so advertising alone cannot induce trial. Sales promotion tools have become an important part of new brand introduction strategies; the level of initial trial can be increased through techniques such as sampling, couponing, and refund offers. The success of a new brand depends not only on getting initial trial but also on inducing a reasonable percentage of people who try the brand to repurchase it and establish ongoing purchase patterns. Promotional incentives such as coupons or refund offers are often included with a sample to encourage repeat purchase after trial. For example, Exhibit 16–9 shows an account-specific promotion Gillette used for its Fusion ProGlide razor. Razors were mailed to members of the Rite Aid drug chain wellness+ rewards program to encourage trial, while a $5 off coupon for cartridges was included to encourage consumers to continue to use the product.

**Increasing Consumption of an Established Brand**  Many marketing managers are responsible for established brands competing in mature markets, against established competitors, where consumer purchase patterns are often well set. Awareness of an established brand is generally high as a result of cumulative advertising effects, and many consumers have probably tried the brand. These factors can create a challenging situation for the brand manager. Sales promotion can generate some new interest in an established brand to help increase sales or defend market share against competitors.

**EXHIBIT 16–9**
Gillette used a product sample and coupon to promote trial and continued product use

**EXHIBIT 16–10**
Arm & Hammer used this FSI to promote a specific use for the product

Marketers attempt to increase sales for an established brand in several ways, and sales promotion can play an important role in each. One way to increase product consumption is by identifying new uses for the brand. Sales promotion tools like recipe books or calendars that show various ways of using the product often can accomplish this. One of the best examples of a brand that has found new uses is Arm & Hammer baking soda. Exhibit 16–10 shows a clever freestanding insert (FSI) that promotes the brand's fridge-freezer pack, which absorbs more odors in refrigerators and freezers.

Another strategy for increasing sales of an established brand is to use promotions that attract nonusers of the product category or users of a competing brand. Attracting nonusers of the product category can be very difficult, as consumers may not see a need for the product. Sales promotions can appeal to nonusers by providing them with an extra incentive to try the product, but a more common strategy for increasing sales of an established brand is to attract consumers who use a competing brand. This can be done by giving them an incentive to switch, such as a coupon, premium offer, bonus pack, or price deal. Marketers can also get users of a competitor to try their brand through sampling or other types of promotional programs. For example, MillerCoors used a Taste Challenge promotion to help regain market share for Miller Lite against Bud Light and other brands of light beer.[30] A key component of this integrated campaign was an interactive, on-premise promotion in bars, restaurants, and nightclubs where consumers were given the opportunity to compare the taste of Miller Lite against Bud Light (Exhibit 16–11).

**EXHIBIT 16–11**
Miller Lite's Taste Challenge was a very successful promotion for attracting users of competing brands

**Defending Current Customers**   With more new brands entering the market every day and competitors attempting to take away their customers through aggressive advertising and sales promotion efforts, many companies are turning to sales promotion programs to hold present customers and defend their market share. A company can use sales promotion techniques in several ways to retain its current customer base. One way is to load them with the product, taking them out of the market for a certain time. Special price promotions, coupons, or bonus packs can encourage consumers to stock up on the brand. This not only keeps them using the company's brand but also reduces the likelihood they will switch brands in response to a competitor's promotion.

**Targeting a Specific Market Segment**   Most companies focus their marketing efforts on specific market segments and are always looking for ways to reach their target audiences. Many marketers are finding that sales promotion tools such as contests and sweepstakes, events, coupons, and samplings are very effective ways to reach specific geographic, demographic, psychographic, and ethnic markets. Sales promotion programs can also be targeted to specific user-status groups such as nonusers or light versus heavy users. For example, MASS Hispanic, the promotional agency for Kimberly Clark's Kleenex brand of facial tissues, created an award-winning promotion whose objective was to increase the relevance of the brand and build a better connection with the Hispanic market. Another important goal of the promotion was to leverage the importance of package aesthetics to Hispanics, who are much more likely to purchase on the basis of package color and design than the general population.

The agency created a promotion called "Con Kleenex Expresa tu Hispanidad" (Express Your Hispanic Pride with Kleenex) where Hispanic consumers were invited to express their traditions and cultural pride through an art contest (Exhibit 16–12). The contest called on aspiring amateur Hispanic artists and consumers around the

**EXHIBIT 16–12**
Kimberly Clark used a contest targeted to Hispanic consumers to increase their involvement and connection to Kleenex

country to submit an original design expressing their Latino pride for the opportunity to win $5,000 plus the privilege of having the artwork appear on a boutique-size Kleenex tissue carton during Hispanic Heritage month. The back end of the promotion included a chance for consumers to participate in selecting a "People's Choice" winner and to purchase special cartons of Kleenex that were displayed in retail stores during Hispanic Heritage month. Over 30,000 consumers voted online to pick the best design and 18 of Kimberly Clark's key retail accounts provided special retail displays of the winning cartons, which led to a 476 percent increase in Kleenex sales in the stores during the promotional period.[31]

Promotion programs also can be developed to coincide with peak sales periods for certain products and services. For example, candy companies such as Mars and Hershey often develop sales promotions that are run right before Halloween while clothing and school supply companies targeting children and teens run promotions in late summer, when most of the back-to-school shopping occurs.

**Enhancing Integrated Marketing Communications and Building Brand Equity** A final objective for consumer-oriented promotions is to enhance or support the integrated marketing communications effort for a brand or company. While building and/or maintaining brand equity was traditionally viewed as something that was done through media advertising, it has also become an important goal for marketers as they develop their sales promotion programs. Companies are asking their advertising and promotion agencies to think strategically and develop promotional programs that can do more than simply generate short-term sales. They want promotions that require consumers to become more involved with their brands and offer a way of presenting the brand essence in an engaging way. Many marketers are recognizing that a well-designed and executed promotion can be a very effective way to engage consumers and to differentiate their brands. Sales promotion techniques such as contests or sweepstakes and premium offers are often used to draw attention to an advertising campaign, to increase involvement with the message and product or service, and to help build relationships with consumers. IMC Perspective 16–1 discusses a sweepstakes that McDonald's in Hong Kong uses to promote its set meals. The sweepstakes is a contest modeled after the famous Monopoly board game. It offers various types of prizes and the largest prize in 2013 was HK$1 million spending credits. Designed for maximum fun and excitement, reflecting the nature of the traditional Monopoly board game, the sweepstakes promotion plays an important role in the brand-building efforts of McDonald's.

# CONSUMER-ORIENTED SALES PROMOTION TECHNIQUES

## Sampling

Marketers use a variety of consumer-oriented sales promotion tools to accomplish the objectives just discussed. We will discuss how these various sales promotion tools are used and factors marketers must consider in using them, beginning with sampling.

**Sampling** involves a variety of procedures whereby consumers are given some quantity of a product for no charge to induce trial. Sampling is generally considered the most effective way to generate trial, although it is also the most expensive. As a sales promotion technique, sampling is often used to introduce a new product or brand to the market. However, sampling is used for established products as well.

# IMC Perspective 16–1 > > >

## McDonald's Monopoly Game in Hong Kong

McDonald's frequently undertakes sales promotion campaigns. For example, there are usually coupons and discounts for selected items on its menu. This fast-food giant is no stranger to innovative marketing tactics too. In Hong Kong and Macau, for example, one sales promotion activity has proven to be so successful that it has become a recurring feature since 2010.

In November 2010, McDonald's in Hong Kong and Macau launched a lucky draw based on the popular board game, Monopoly. The game has been localized with the properties named after well-known places in Hong Kong to enable Hong Kong consumers to identify with it. The game is simple: a customer gets two pairs of game pieces on purchasing a large Extra Value meal, while a regular Extra Value meal gets only one pair. In each pair, two sticky tickets are gifted. A ticket shows one property in Hong Kong.

Some of the prizes of the Monopoly game included the following:

1. *An instant prize.* A ticket may offer an instant prize. In 2010, the biggest prize offered was the Monopoly City Board Game, while the 2012 version included HK1,000 jewelry coupons.

Some companies do not use sampling for established products, reasoning that samples may not induce satisfied users of a competing brand to switch and may just go to the firm's current customers, who would buy the product anyway. This may not be true when significant changes (new and improved) are made in a brand.

Manufacturers of packaged-goods products such as food, health care items, cosmetics, and toiletries are heavy users of sampling since their products meet the three criteria for an effective sampling program:

1. The products are of relatively low unit value, so samples do not cost too much.
2. The products are divisible, which means they can be broken into small sample sizes that are adequate for demonstrating the brand's features and benefits to the user.
3. The purchase cycle is relatively short, so the consumer will consider an immediate purchase or will not forget about the brand before the next purchase occasion.

**Benefits and Limitations of Sampling**   Samples are an excellent way to induce trial as they provide consumers with a risk-free way to try new products. A major study conducted by the Promotion Marketing Association found that the vast majority of consumers receiving a sample either use it right away or save it to use sometime later.[32] Sampling generates much higher trial rates than advertising or other sales promotion techniques.

Getting people to try a product leads to a second benefit of sampling: Consumers experience the brand directly, gaining a greater appreciation for its benefits. This can be particularly important when a product's features and benefits are difficult to describe through advertising. Many foods, beverages, and cosmetics have subtle features that are most appreciated when experienced directly. Thus, marketers in these

**2.** *A collect-to-win prize.* If a consumer gets a full set of properties in the same color, he or she wins a prize.

**3.** *A lucky draw prize.* In the 2012 installment, the ticket with "Chance" can be used for weekly lucky draws through online or telephone registration, and hence a chance to win a fabulous prize.

The first game ran from December 2, 2010 to January 12, 2011. The top prize was HK$350,000 spending credits. Various types of advertisements were used to promote the Monopoly sweepstakes. These included the typical TV ads, print ads, and Internet ads. One of the most creative ad involved wrapping the floor of the MTR Central Station into a Monopoly board (MTR or mass transit railway is the underground train system in Hong Kong, and Central is one of the most crowded stations).

During a six-week campaign in 2010, McDonald's generated incremental sales of 7.1 percent and increased the number of consumers by 3.9 percent. There were over 550,000 visits to the campaign site, which was equivalent to 12.7 percent of Hong Kong's population. Consumers created their own online platforms where they exchanged information and discussed the game. Excitement on social media was high. On Facebook, over 9,500 fans were recruited in six weeks, with over 1.5 million views posted.

Due to favorable consumer reactions to the Monopoly sweepstakes, it has become a recurring event in Hong Kong. The latest Monopoly game ran from November 28 to December 31, 2013. Its coverage was similar to the previous installments. One minor revision was the introduction of the WeChat or Hotline daily draw. (WeChat is a smart phone application which allows users to send text messages, photos, videos, and audio clips to others.) The first prize was also increased to HK$1 million spending credits.

Sources: "McDonald's Adverts and Commercials Archive: McDonald's Monopoly," *Advertolog*, http://www.advertolog.com/mcdonalds/promo/mcdonalds-monopoly-15837705/; "Birth of 'McDonald's Monopoly 2011' Finale Drew Ultimate Winner," *Brand Daily*, http://www.brandqna.com.hk/bnitem.php?n=4f1eefb81e7c6; "McDonald's Monopoly Comes to Hong Kong," *Etchy*, http://www.alivenotdead.com/etchy/McDonalds-Monopoly-comes-to-Hong-Kong-profile-1125374.html; McDonald's Monopoly 2013, http://timable.com/zh-hk/event/209563.

**EXHIBIT 16–13**
Jack in the Box's "Free Fryday" promotion was an effective way to encourage consumers to try its new French fries

industries often use samples as a way to introduce consumers to their new products. For example, Jack in the Box, one of the major fast-food restaurant chains in the Western region of the United States, used a "Free Fryday" promotion to give consumers the opportunity to sample its new French fries (Exhibit 16–13). Nearly 70 percent of the respondents in the PMA survey indicated they have purchased a product they did not normally use after trying a free sample. The study also found that samples are even more likely to lead to purchase when they are accompanied by a coupon.

While samples are an effective way to induce trial, the brand must have some unique or superior benefits for a sampling program to be worthwhile. Otherwise, the sampled consumers revert back to other brands and do not become repeat purchasers. The costs of a sampling program can be recovered only if it gets a number of consumers to become regular users of the brand at full retail price.

Another possible limitation to sampling is that the benefits of some products are difficult to gauge immediately, and the learning period required to appreciate the brand may require supplying the consumer with larger amounts of the brand than are affordable. An example would be an expensive skin cream that is promoted as preventing or reducing wrinkles but has to be used for an extended period before any effects are seen.

**Sampling Methods**   One basic decision the sales promotion or brand manager must make is how the sample will be distributed. The sampling method chosen is important not only in terms of costs but also because it influences the type of consumer who receives the sample. The best sampling method gets the product to the best prospects for trial and subsequent repurchase. Some basic distribution methods include door-to-door, direct-mail, in-store, and on-package approaches.

**EXHIBIT 16–14**
Armor All uses on-package samples for related products

*Door-to-door sampling,* in which the product is delivered directly to the prospect's residence, is used when it is important to control where the sample is delivered. This distribution method is very expensive because of labor costs, but it can be cost-effective if the marketer has information that helps define the target market and/or if the prospects are located in a well-defined geographic area. For many years newspapers have been used to achieve mass distribution of samples since more than two-thirds of households receive a daily and/or Sunday paper. Many newspapers have distributed samples through poly bags, with a promotional message printed on them along with the sample. However, less than half of U.S. households now subscribe to a print newspaper, which reduces their value as a sampling method for marketers who want mass distribution of their samples.

*Sampling through the mail* is common for small, lightweight, nonperishable products. A major advantage of this method is that the marketer has control over where and when the product will be distributed and can target the sample to specific market areas. Many marketers are using information from geodemographic target marketing programs such as Nielsen's Prizm to better target their sample mailings. The main drawbacks to mail sampling are postal restrictions and increasing postal rates.

*In-store sampling* is increasingly popular, especially for food products. The marketer hires temporary demonstrators who set up a table or booth, prepare small samples of the product, and pass them out to shoppers. The in-store sampling approach can be very effective for food products, since consumers get to taste the item and the demonstrator can give them more information about the product while it is being sampled. Demonstrators may also give consumers a cents-off coupon for the sampled item to encourage immediate trial purchase. While this sampling method can be very effective, it can also be expensive and requires a great deal of planning, as well as the cooperation of retailers.

*On-package sampling,* where a sample of a product is attached to another item, is another common sampling method (see Exhibit 16–14). This procedure can be very cost-effective, particularly for multiproduct firms that attach a sample of a new product to an existing brand's package. A drawback is that since the sample is distributed only to consumers who purchase the item to which it is attached, the sample will not reach nonusers of the carrier brand. Marketers can expand this sampling method by attaching the sample to multiple carrier brands and including samples with products not made by their company.

*Event sampling* has become one of the fastest-growing and most popular ways of distributing samples. Many marketers are using sampling programs that are part of integrated marketing programs that feature events, media tie-ins, and other activities that provide consumers with a total sense of a brand rather than just a few tastes of a food or beverage or a trial size of a packaged-goods product. Event sampling can take place in stores as well as at a variety of other venues such as concerts, sporting events, and other places.

**Other Methods of Sampling** The four sampling methods just discussed are the most common, but several other methods are also used. Marketers may insert packets in magazines or newspapers (particularly Sunday supplements). Some tobacco and cereal companies send samples to consumers who call toll-free numbers to request them or mail in sample request forms. As discussed in Chapter 14, these sampling methods are becoming popular because they can help marketers build a database for direct marketing.

Many companies also use specialized sample distribution service companies. These firms help the company identify consumers who are nonusers of a product or users of a competing brand and develop appropriate procedures for distributing a sample to them. Many college students receive sample packs at the beginning of the semester that contain trial sizes of such products as mouthwash, toothpaste, headache remedies, and deodorant.

The Internet is yet another way companies are making it possible for consumers to sample their products, and it is adding a whole new level of targeting to the mix by giving consumers the opportunity to choose the samples they want. Several

**EXHIBIT 16–15**
Consumers can request samples from websites such as StartSampling.com

companies offer websites where consumers can register to receive free samples for products that interest them, including StartSampling and MyTownOffers. Exhibit 16–15 shows the homepage from the website of StartSampling.com promoting the samples and offers it makes available to consumers. The service asks consumers qualifying questions on product usage that can be used by marketers to target their samples and other promotional offers more effectively.

Marketers are also starting to use various forms of social media as a way to distribute samples. For example, Splenda used Facebook to distribute samples of a pocket-size spray form of its sweetener. The company used engagement ads to direct consumers to the Splenda Mist page, where they could sign up for a "first look" at the new product and provide the company with information about themselves. Splenda also used its Facebook page to solicit valuable feedback from consumers who received the samples.[33]

## Couponing

The oldest, most widely used, and most effective sales promotion tool is the cents-off coupon. Coupons have been around since 1895, when the C. W. Post Co. started using the penny-off coupon to sell its new Grape-Nuts cereal. In recent years, coupons have become increasingly popular with consumers, which may explain their explosive growth among manufacturers and retailers that use them as sales promotion incentives. Coupons are the most popular sales promotion technique as they are used by nearly all the packaged-goods firms.

Coupon distribution and use in the United States increased significantly during the recent recession as the number of coupons distributed reached a record 332 billion in 2010, with 3.3 billion being redeemed. As the economy recovered, the number of coupons distributed declined to 305 billion in 2012 with 2.9 billion being redeemed. According to NCH Marketing Services, a company that tracks coupon distribution and redemption patterns, over 90 percent of consumers in the United States use coupons and 13 percent say they always use them when they shop. The average face value of the 2.9 billion coupons distributed in 2012 was $1.27.[34]

Adding additional fuel to the coupon explosion of the past several decades has been the vast number of coupons distributed through retailers that are not even included in these figures. In some markets, a number of grocery stores make manufacturers' coupons even more attractive to consumers by doubling the face value.

**Advantages and Limitations of Coupons** Coupons have a number of advantages that make them popular sales promotion tools for both new and established products. First, coupons make it possible to offer a price reduction only to those consumers who are price-sensitive. Such consumers generally purchase *because* of coupons, while those who are not as concerned about price buy the brand at full value. Coupons also make it possible to reduce the retail price of a product without relying on retailers for cooperation, which can often be a problem. Coupons are generally regarded as second only to sampling as a promotional technique for generating trial. Since a coupon lowers the price of a product, it reduces the consumer's perceived risk associated with trial of a new brand. Coupons can encourage repurchase after initial trial. Many new products include a cents-off coupon inside the package to encourage repeat purchase.

Coupons can also be useful promotional devices for established products. They can encourage nonusers to try a brand, encourage repeat purchase among current users, and get users to try a new, improved version of a brand. Coupons may also help coax users of a product to trade up to more expensive brands. The product category where coupons are used most is disposable diapers, followed by cereal, detergent, and deodorant. Some of the product categories where coupons are used the least are carbonated beverages, candy, and gum.

But there are a number of problems with coupons. First, it can be difficult to estimate how many consumers will use a coupon and when. Response to a coupon is rarely immediate; it typically takes anywhere from two to six months to redeem one. A study of coupon redemption patterns by Inman and McAlister found that many coupons are redeemed just before the expiration date rather than in the period following the initial coupon drop.[35] Many marketers are attempting to expedite redemption by shortening the time period before expiration. The average length of time from issue date to expiration date for coupons in 2012 was 2.1 months for consumer packaged goods. However, coupons remain less effective than sampling for inducing initial product trial in a short period.

A problem associated with using coupons to attract new users to an established brand is that it is difficult to prevent the coupons from being used by consumers who already use the brand. Rather than attracting new users, coupons can end up reducing the company's profit margins among consumers who would probably purchase the product anyway. However, they can help retain users.

Other problems with coupons include low redemption rates and high costs. Couponing program expenses include the face value of the coupon redeemed plus costs for production, distribution, and handling of the coupons. Figure 16–3 shows the calculations used to determine the costs of a couponing program using an FSI (freestanding insert) in the Sunday newspaper and a coupon with a face value of $1.00. As can be seen from these figures, the cost of a couponing program can be very high. Marketers should track coupon costs very carefully to ensure their use is economically feasible.

Another problem with coupon promotions is misredemption, or the cashing of a coupon without purchase of the brand. Coupon misredemption or fraud occurs in a number of ways, including:

- Redemption of coupons by consumers for a product or size not specified on the coupon.
- Redemption of coupons by salesclerks in exchange for cash.
- Gathering and redemption of coupons by store managers or owners without the accompanying sale of the product.

**FIGURE 16–3**

Calculating Couponing Costs

| COST PER COUPON REDEEMED: AN ILLUSTRATION | |
|---|---|
| 1. Distribution cost<br>55,000,000 circulation × $6.25/M | $343,750 |
| 2. Redemptions at 1.5% | 825,000 |
| 3. Redemption cost<br>825,000 redemptions × $1.00 face value | $825,000 |
| 4. Retailer handling cost and processor fees<br>825,000 redemptions × $0.10 | $82,500 |
| 5. Creative costs | $1,500 |
| 6. Total program cost<br>Items 1 + 3 + 4 + 5 | $1,252,750 |
| Cost per coupon redeemed<br>Cost divided by redemption | $1.52 |
| 7. Actual product sold on redemption<br>(misredemption estimated at 20%)<br>825,000 × 80% | 660,000 |
| 8. Cost per product moved<br>Program cost divided by amount of product sold | $1.90 |

- Gathering or printing of coupons by criminals who sell them to unethical merchants, who, in turn, redeem them.
- Web-source coupon fraud, whereby phony coupons are produced and distributed online.

Coupon fraud and misredemption cost manufacturers an estimated $500 million a year in the United States alone. However, with the surge in Internet-related coupon fraud in recent years, this number is considered low. In 2007 the largest coupon clearinghouse in the United States was indicted for an alleged nine-year $250 million fraud against package-goods marketers. Consumers have also taken advantage of flaws in bar codes to fraudulently use coupons. However, a new bar coding system is being developed by the industry that will be harder to exploit and will simplify the use of coupons.[36]

Many manufacturers hold firm in their policy to not pay retailers for questionable amounts or suspicious types of coupon submissions. However, some companies are less aggressive, and this affects their profit margins. Marketers must allow a certain percentage for misredemption when estimating the costs of a couponing program. Ways to identify and control coupon misredemption, such as improved coding, are being developed, but it still remains a problem. Many retailers are tightening their policies regarding Internet coupons. For example, Walmart will not accept Internet coupons unless they have a valid expiration date, remit address, and bar code.

**Coupon Distribution**   Coupons can be disseminated to consumers by a number of means, including freestanding inserts in Sunday newspapers, direct mail, newspapers (either in individual ads or as a group of coupons in a cooperative format), magazines, and packages. Distribution through newspaper **freestanding inserts (FSIs)** is by far the most popular method for delivering coupons to consumers, accounting for 90 percent of all coupons distributed. An FSI is a four-color multipage printed advertising booklet that contains consumer packaged goods coupon offers delivered with newspapers (usually in Sunday editions). FSIs can also be delivered in direct-mail packages along with local retailer ads or can be cooperative booklets such as *RedPlum* or *SmartSource* as well as solo books done by companies. For example, Procter & Gamble uses its own *P&G brandSAVER* FSI booklet each month in newspapers throughout the country (Exhibit 16–16).

There are a number of reasons why FSIs are the most popular way of delivering coupons, including their high-quality four-color graphics, competitive distribution costs, national same-day circulation, market selectivity, and the fact that they can be competition-free due to category exclusivity (by the FSI company). Prices for a full-page FSI are currently about $6 to $7 per thousand, which makes FSI promotions very efficient and affordable. Because of their consumer popularity and predictable distribution, coupons distributed in FSIs are also a strong selling point with the retail trade.

The increased distribution of coupons through FSIs has, however, led to a clutter problem. Consumers are being bombarded with too many coupons, and although each FSI publisher offers product exclusivity in its insert, this advantage may be negated when there are three inserts in a Sunday paper. Redemption rates of FSI coupons have declined from 4 percent to only 1 percent and even lower for some products (Figure 16–4). These problems are leading many marketers to look at ways of delivering coupons that will result in less clutter and higher redemption rates, such as direct mail.

*Direct mail* accounts for about 2 percent of all coupons distributed. Most are sent by local retailers or through co-op mailings where a packet of coupons for many different products is sent to a household. These couponing programs include Metro-mail's Red Letter Day, Advo System's Super Coups, and Cox Target Media's Valpak. Cox Target Media redesigned the familiar Valpak blue

**EXHIBIT 16–16**
Procter & Gamble distributes its own FSI booklet

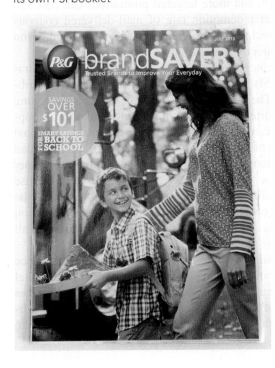

**FIGURE 16–4**

Coupon Average
Redemption Rates by
Media Type

| Media | Food Products | Nonfood Products |
|---|---|---|
| FSI | 1.0% | 0.6% |
| Magazine | 1.0 | 0.8 |
| Direct mail | 6.6 | 1.9 |
| Regular in-pack | 3.3 | 3.7 |
| Regular on-pack | 4.2 | 7.6 |
| Instant on-pack | 20.0 | 27.0 |
| Instant on-pack cross-ruff | 8.3 | 8.0 |
| Handout electronically dispensed | 8.8 | 7.0 |
| On-shelf distributed | 11.8 | 8.8 |
| All other handouts in store | 3.5 | 2.5 |
| All other handouts away from store | 5.3 | 2.0 |
| Internet home-printed | 16.8 | 10.0 |

Source: NCH Marketing Services, *Coupon Facts Report*, 2013.

envelope that delivers billions of coupons each year and uses advertising to improve the image of the direct-mail piece and increase consumers' use of the coupons distributed inside.

Direct-mail couponing has several advantages. First, the mailing can be sent to a broad audience or targeted to specific geographic or demographic markets such as teenagers, senior citizens, Hispanics, and other market segments. Firms that mail their own coupons can be quite selective about recipients. Another advantage of direct-mail couponing is a redemption rate that is higher than that for FSIs. Direct-mail couponing can also be combined with a sample, which makes it a very effective way to gain the attention of consumers.

The major disadvantage of direct-mail coupon delivery is the expense relative to other distribution methods. The cost per thousand for distributing coupons through co-op mailings ranges from $10 to $15, and more targeted promotions can cost $20 to $25 or even more. Also, the higher redemption rate of mail-delivered coupons may result from the fact that many recipients are already users of the brand who take advantage of the coupons sent directly to them.

The use of *newspapers* and *magazines* as couponing vehicles has declined dramatically since the introduction of FSIs as only 1 percent of coupons are distributed via newspapers and magazines. The advantages of newspapers as a couponing vehicle include market selectivity, shorter lead times with timing to the day, cooperative advertising opportunities that can lead to cost efficiencies, and promotional tie-ins with retailers. Other advantages of newspaper-delivered coupons are the broad exposure and consumer receptivity. Many consumers actively search the newspaper for coupons, especially on Sundays or "food day" (when grocery stores advertise their specials). This enhances the likelihood of the consumer at least noticing the coupon. Problems with newspapers as couponing vehicles include higher distribution costs, poor reproduction quality, clutter, and declining readership of newspapers; all contribute to low redemption rates.

The use of magazines as a couponing vehicle has also declined steadily since the introduction of FSIs. Magazines now account for around 1 percent of the total number of coupons distributed each year. Distribution of coupons through magazines can take advantage of the selectivity of the publication to reach specific target audiences, along with enhanced production capabilities and extended copy life in the

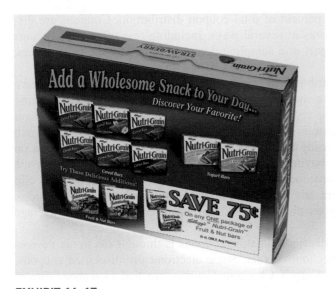

**EXHIBIT 16–17**

Kellogg Company uses an on-package coupon to encourage repurchase

home. However, the cost of distributing coupons through magazines is very high and redemption rates are low (just under 1 percent).

Placing coupons either *inside* or on the *outside* of the *package* is a distribution method that accounts for just over 1 percent of the coupons distributed. The in/on-package coupon has virtually no distribution costs and a much higher redemption rate than other couponing methods, averaging from 4 to 20 percent. An in/on-pack coupon that is redeemable for the next purchase of the same brand is known as a **bounce-back coupon**. This type of coupon gives consumers an inducement to repurchase the brand.

Bounce-back coupons are often used with product samples to encourage the consumer to purchase the product after sampling. They may be included in or on the package during the early phases of a brand's life cycle to encourage repeat purchase, or they may be a defensive maneuver for a mature brand that is facing competitive pressure and wants to retain its current users. The main limitation of bounce-back coupons is that they go only to purchasers of the brand and thus do not attract nonusers. A bounce-back coupon placed on the package for Kellogg Company's Nutri-Grain bars is shown in Exhibit 16–17.

Another type of in/on-pack coupon is the **cross-ruff coupon**, which is redeemable on the purchase of a different product, usually one made by the same company but occasionally through a tie-in with another manufacturer. Cross-ruff coupons have a redemption rate of 8 percent and can be effective in encouraging consumers to try other products or brands. Companies with wide product lines, such as cereal manufacturers, often use these coupons.

Yet another type of package coupon is the **instant coupon**, which is attached to the outside of the package so the consumer can rip it off and redeem it immediately at the time of purchase. Instant coupons have the highest redemption levels of all types of coupons, averaging around 20 percent for food products and 27 percent for nonfood items. However, the redemption level is much lower for instant cross-ruff coupons, as it averages around 8 percent. Instant coupons give consumers an immediate point-of-purchase incentive, and can be selectively placed in terms of promotion timing and market region. Exhibit 16–18 shows an instant cross-ruff coupon used by the California Milk Advisory Board for Real California Cheese as part of a promotional tie-in with Tia Rosa Tortillas. These types of coupons are often used to promote the purchase of complementary products. Some companies prefer instant coupons to price-off deals because the latter require more cooperation from retailers and can be more expensive, since every package must be reduced in price.

Another distribution method that has experienced strong growth over the past 10 years or so is **in-store couponing**, which includes all co-op couponing programs distributed in a retail store environment. This medium

**EXHIBIT 16–18**

An instant cross-ruff coupon is used to promote the purchase of complementary products now accounts for around 4 percent of total coupon distribution. Coupons are distributed to consumers in stores in several ways, including tear-off pads, handouts in the store (sometimes as part of a sampling demonstration), on-shelf dispensers, and electronic dispensers.

Most of the coupons distributed in stores are through instant coupon machines. These coupon dispensers are mounted on the shelf in front of the product being promoted and have blinking red lights to draw consumers' attention to the savings opportunity. These in-store coupons have several advantages: They can reach consumers when they are ready to make a purchase, increase brand awareness on the shelf, generate impulse buying, and encourage product trial. They also provide category exclusivity. In-store couponing removes the need for consumers to clip coupons from FSIs or print ads and then remember to bring them to the store. Redemption rates for coupons distributed by the instant coupon machine average about 9 to 12 percent.

Another popular way to distribute in-store coupons is through electronic devices such as kiosks or at the checkout counter. Some electronically dispensed coupons, such as Catalina Marketing Corp.'s Checkout Coupon, are tied to scanner data at each grocery store checkout. When the specified product, such as a competitive brand, is purchased, the consumer receives a coupon at the checkout for the company's brand. Companies also use this system to link purchases of products that are related. For example, a consumer who purchases a caffeine-free cola might be issued a coupon for a decaffeinated coffee.

Major advantages of electronically dispensed checkout coupons are that they are cost-effective and can be targeted to specific categories of consumers, such as users of competitive or complementary products. Since 65 to 85 percent of a manufacturer's coupons are used by current customers, marketers want to target their coupons to users of competitive brands. Redemption rates for electronically dispensed coupons average around 7 to 9 percent.

**Couponing Trends**  Coupons continue to be the most effective sales promotion tool for influencing consumers' purchase decisions, as evidenced by the 3 billion that are redeemed each year by U.S. consumers. The popularity of coupons reflects the fact that they are a way for the average household to save a considerable amount of money each year. Coupon use has remained high even after the recent recession; nearly 80 percent of consumers use coupons on a regular basis and some use them very heavily. In fact, the term *extreme couponing* has been coined to describe the activity of combining shopping skills with coupon use in an effort to save as much money as possible while shopping. The TLC network aired a popular reality show for several years titled *Extreme Couponing,* which focused on shoppers who save large amounts of money by using coupons (Exhibit 16–19).

**EXHIBIT 16–19**
*Extreme Couponing* is a popular reality TV show

The increased use of coupons also reflects the fact that more coupons are being distributed by marketers who are using them as a way to compete against lower-priced competitors as well as private label store brands.[37] While consumers are using more coupons, there are still a number of problems marketers are faced with in using them. The average U.S. household is still barraged with nearly 3,000 coupons per year and consumers redeem less than 2 percent of the hundreds of billions of coupons distributed.

Concerns over the cost and effectiveness of coupons have led some marketers to cut back on their use and/or change the way they use them. For example, marketers have reduced the duration period, with expiration dates of three months or less becoming more common. Marketers are also moving to greater use of multiple-item purchase requirements for coupons, particularly for grocery products where nearly 40 percent of the coupons use this tactic. The percentage of multiple purchase requirement coupons for health and beauty products has been declining and is now around 8 percent.[38] Critics argue that coupons cost too much to print, distribute, and process and that they do not benefit enough consumers. Former Procter & Gamble CEO Durk Jager echoed the sentiment of many consumer-product companies when he said, "Who can argue for a practice that fails 98 percent of the time?"[39]

Despite the growing sentiment among major marketers that coupons are inefficient and costly, very few companies, including Procter & Gamble, are likely to abandon them entirely. Although most coupons never get used, consumers use some of them and have come to expect them. With so many consumers eager for coupons, marketers will continue to accommodate them. However, companies as well as the coupon industry are looking for ways to improve on their use. For example, General Mills, Kellogg Company, and Post Cereals replaced brand-specific coupons with universal coupons good for any of their cereal brands. To make its couponing spending more efficient, Post began using universal coupons worth $1.50 off two boxes (matching the average cereal-coupon discount of 75 cents) and cut coupon distribution in half.

Some marketers and retailers are looking to the Internet as a medium for distributing coupons. Several companies now offer online couponing services. Catalina Marketing started Valupage.com as a way for marketers to reach consumers at home with promotions traditionally offered in-store, including coupons. Consumers can log on to the website, type in their zip code, and choose from a list of participating grocery stores in their area and download manufacturer- and retailer-sponsored coupons. A number of retailers, particularly supermarkets, are also using the Internet to distribute coupons to encourage consumers to shop at their stores. Cox Target Media also offers consumers the opportunity to access coupons online, through Valpak.com. The website makes the same coupons and offers available to consumers that come in the Valpak direct-mail envelope.

Another way to distribute coupons that is growing rapidly is through mobile marketing whereby coupons are sent directly to mobile phones. A number of marketers are working with Cellfire, a company that distributes coupons to mobile devices of consumers who sign up for its service.[40] Cellfire also has been partnering with a number of major grocery stores to offer mobile grocery coupons (Exhibit 16–20). Marketers are also using various social media channels, such as Facebook and Twitter, to deliver coupons. For example, Burger King ran a "Whopper Sacrifice" promotion on Facebook in which consumers were given a coupon for a free whopper in exchange for deleting 10 friends. Facebook eventually shut down the promotion, noting that it was a violation of the site's privacy policy, but not before nearly 24,000 coupons were awarded and 240,000 people were "unfriended."[41] Digital and Social Media Perspective 16–1 discusses daily deals a new form of couponing that has become popular by utilizing the growing popularity of social media and the power of group purchasing.

**EXHIBIT 16–20**
Cellfire distributes coupons to mobile phones

## Premiums

Premiums are a sales promotion device used by many marketers. A **premium** is an offer of an item of merchandise or service either free or at a low price that is an extra incentive for purchasers. Many marketers are eliminating toys and gimmicks in favor of value-added premiums that reflect the quality of the product and are consistent with its image and positioning in the market. Marketers spend over $4 billion a year on value-added premium incentives targeted at the consumer market. The two basic types of offers are the free premium and the self-liquidating premium.

Marketers have been bombarding consumers with coupons and other types of promotional discounts and offers for decades, with the vast majority of the more than 300 billion coupons being distributed through traditional methods such as FSIs in Sunday newspapers and direct-mail packets sent directly to consumers' homes. Marketers know that most of these coupons and promotional offers end up in the recycling bin of the more digitally oriented millennials who spend more time online, particularly on social media sites, than they do reading newspapers or sorting through direct-mail pieces. Thus, in recent years a number of companies have emerged that make coupons available to consumers online as well as through other methods, such as sending them directly to mobile devices.

While these online and mobile couponing methods provide marketers with a good way to reach tech-savvy consumers, a new form of couponing or discounting through online deals has become very popular over the past several years that capitalizes on the growing popularity of social media, as well as the power of group purchasing. The best known company competing in this new promotional space is Groupon, which was founded 2008 in Chicago and is rapidly expanding throughout the world. As of 2013 the company had 41 million active customers, more than 10,000 employees in 48 countries, and 500,000 merchants as partners. Groupon's original foundation was the daily deal whereby it offered discounted deals for various products and services on its website, Groupon.com, that had to be purchased that day to take advantage of the discount. The offer would remain available only if a certain number of people agreed to purchase it. However, Groupon no longer

uses a tipping point model and the deals it offers are now on from the start. Consumers can join the site for free and, once registered, receive e-mail notifications of discounted deals being offered in their market area each day.

The basis of Groupon's business model is that it uses collective buying power to offer deep discounts and provides a win-win for businesses as well as consumers. Consumers save money by shopping en masse and can learn about new businesses in their local markets, whereas businesses are exposed to a larger audience and gain new customers by offering discounts to people who might otherwise not purchase from them. Under the arrangement, Groupon makes money by having businesses that participate in the program pay them a percentage of their coupon sales, which can range from 30 to 50 percent. Consumers often spread the word about the Groupon deals among their friends and associates, with various forms of social media such as Facebook and Twitter often being the best way to do so.

The long-term viability of the daily deal market has been questioned by many analysts who argue that it is becoming saturated with competitors as many local companies such as newspapers have begun offering deals as well. There has already been a shakeout in the industry, with nearly a third of all daily deal sites shut down or sold; they have found the cost of acquiring customers as well as merchants to be too high. Critics have argued that merchants might tire of offering the deals since the percentage they have to pay companies like Groupon wipes out their profit margins. However, Groupon notes that its customers actually spend more money when using one of their deals than regular customers would, because they spend above and beyond the

**Free Premiums**   Free premiums are usually small gifts or merchandise included in the product package or sent to consumers who mail in a request along with a proof of purchase. In/on-package free premiums include toys, balls, trading cards, or other items included in cereal packages, as well as samples of one product included with another. Surveys have shown that in/on-package premiums are consumers' favorite type of promotion.[42]

Package-carried premiums have high impulse value and can provide an extra incentive to buy the product. However, several problems are associated with their use. First, there is the cost factor, which results from the premium itself as well as from extra packaging that may be needed. Finding desirable premiums at reasonable costs can be difficult, particularly for adult markets, and using a poor premium may do more harm than good.

Another problem with these premiums is possible restrictions from regulatory agencies such as the Federal Trade Commission and the Food and Drug Administration or from industry codes regarding the type of premium used. The National Association of Broadcasters has strict guidelines regarding the advertising of premium offers to children. There is concern that premium offers will entice children to request a

ANATOMY OF A GROUPON DEAL

**1** Deals sourced from high-quality merchants willing to provide discounts (e.g., $20 for $40 in value at local retailer)

**2** Groupon offers sent to subscribers via email or browsed by consumers on the website or mobile app
- 2300+ individual types of goods and services
- Running nearly 40,000 active deals in North America

Featured Merchants
Over 500,000 merchant partners

Consumers
41.7 million active customers (3/31)

**5** Groupon pays merchants
- **North America:** Groupon typically pays merchants and suppliers in installments within 60 days. Merchants with an ongoing deal in the Deal Bank typically receive payments on an ongoing basis throughout the term of the offering.
- **International:** Groupon typically pays merchants when the customer redeems the Groupon. Goods suppliers are typically paid within 60 days.

**4** Redeem goods or services from merchants

**3** Customers able to buy deals by location and keyword on the website and mobile app
- Local Deals
- Goods
- Live
- Getaways

cost of the deal. The marginal revenue is called "overspend" and is measured and aggregated into deal impact reports that are provided to merchants. The company also measures the number of merchants that choose to run additional deals with the company and claims the number is over 50 percent. Groupon has been successful in moving beyond its original business model of daily deals and become a marketplace for online deals used by many merchants on a continuous basis.

As part of its evolving strategy, Groupon has been moving from a demand-fulfillment model, such as where it helps fill empty seats in a restaurant on a slow night, to a demand-generation model, whereby customers will check its site or app for relevant deals. This means a shift from "pushing" deals to consumers through e-mails to "pulling" them to its website, Facebook page, or mobile app, where they can make then make a purchase. Groupon also plans to utilize more mobile marketing since more than 40 percent of its transactions now take place over smartphones and other mobile devices. More than 40 million people worldwide have downloaded the Groupon Mobile app,

which makes it possible for the company to use location-based marketing whereby deals are sent to consumers based on their proximity to a specific merchant such as a restaurant or retail store. The company also now offers a number of merchant services such as restaurant point-of-sales and mobile payment offerings.

Another opportunity for Groupon, as well as its competitors, is attracting more business from national brands rather than relying so much on local merchants. Groupon has done several deals with major companies such as Starbucks, Target, Fandanago, and American Apparel, while LivingSocial has partnered with major brands such as Whole Foods and McDonald's. Both companies have worked with major magazine and newspaper publishers such as *Elle, Marie Claire, Esquire, The New York Times,* and *The Wall Street Journal* to sell subscriptions via online deals. Groupon has become a marketplace for online deals and now offers discounts to consumers for direct product sales, travel, sporting events, and concerts. Its portfolio of businesses now includes Groupon Getaways, Groupon Goods, and a loyalty program called Groupon Rewards.

Groupon and other deal service sites recognize that it is important to provide consumers with good offers and make sure they understand the terms and conditions of the deals as well. Groupon's website offers a comment section for each deal, and consumers do not hesitate to note which offers they like and dislike. Business owners are also recognizing that they have to offer consumers attractive deals and be capable of handling a potential surge in business if the offer strikes a responsive chord with consumers. However, for most companies this is a problem they are more than happy to find ways to handle.

Sources: Elizabeth Spier, "Deal With It," *Fast Company*, May 2013, pp. 92–97, 119–121; "Deal-a-Day Market," *Adage Insights Trend Report*, October 1, 2012, pp.12–14; Shira Ovide and John Letzing, "Groupon Hits Growth Wall," *The Wall Street Journal*, September 14, 2012, pp. B1,2; Kunur Patel, "Groupon Takes Coupons into the Social-Media Age," *Advertising Age*, December 21, 2009, http://adage.com/print?article_id=141172.

**YTC 16–02**

**Groupon**
youtube.com/10ebelch

brand to get the promoted item and then never consume the product. The networks' policy on children's advertising is that a premium offer cannot exceed 15 seconds of a 30-second spot, and the emphasis must be on the product, not the premium.

Since most free mail-in premium offers require the consumer to send in more than one proof of purchase, they encourage repeat purchase and reward brand loyalty. But a major drawback of mail-in premiums is that they do not offer immediate reinforcement or reward to the purchaser, so they may not provide enough incentive to purchase the brand. Few consumers take advantage of mail-in premium offers; the average redemption rate is only 2 to 4 percent.[43]

Free premiums have become very popular in the restaurant industry, particularly among fast-food chains such as McDonald's and Burger King, which use premium offers in their kids' meals to attract children. McDonald's has become the world's largest toymaker on a unit basis, commissioning about 750 million toys per year for its Happy Meals (Exhibit 16–21). Many of the premium offers used by the fast-food giants have cross-promotional tie-ins with popular movies and can be very effective at generating incremental sales. McDonald's negotiates movie tie-in deals with a number of studios, including DreamWorks Animation SKG and Pixar Animation

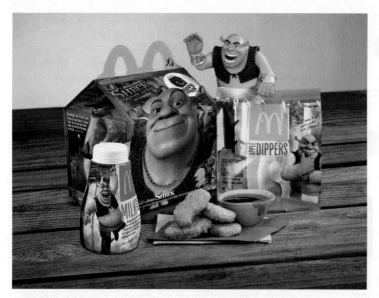

Studios, as well as Disney. McDonald's uses movie tie-ins as the basis for many of its Happy Meal promotions.

One of the fastest-growing types of incentive offers being used by marketers is airline miles, which have literally become a promotional currency. U.S. airlines make more than an estimated $2 billion each year selling miles to other marketers. Consumers are now choosing credit-card services, phone services, hotels, and many other products and services on the basis of mileage premiums for major frequent-flyer programs such as American Airlines's AAdvantage program or United Airlines's Mileage Plus program. Exhibit 16–22 shows how American Airlines promotes the value of AAdvantage miles as a promotional incentive that companies can offer to help attract and retain customers.

**EXHIBIT 16–21**
McDonald's Happy Meals use toys to help attract children

**Self-Liquidating Premiums** **Self-liquidating premiums** require the consumer to pay some or all of the cost of the premium plus handling and mailing costs. The marketer usually purchases items used as self-liquidating premiums in large quantities and offers them to consumers at lower-than-retail prices. The goal is not to make a profit on the premium item but rather just to cover costs and offer a value to the consumer.

In addition to cost savings, self-liquidating premiums offer several advantages to marketers. Offering values to consumers through the premium products can create interest in the brand and goodwill that enhances the brand's image. These premiums can also encourage trade support and gain in-store displays for the brand and the premium offer. Self-liquidating premiums are often tied directly to the advertising campaign, so they extend the advertising message and contribute to consumer franchise building for a brand. For example, Philip Morris offers Western wear, outdoor items, and other types of Marlboro gear through its Marlboro Country catalog, which reinforces the cigarette brand's positioning theme.

Self-liquidating premium offers have the same basic limitation as mail-in premiums: a very low redemption rate. Fewer than 10 percent of U.S. households have ever sent for a premium, and fewer than 1 percent of self-liquidating offers are actually redeemed.[44] Low redemption rates can leave the marketer with a large supply of items with a logo or some other brand identification that makes them hard to dispose of. Thus, it is important to test consumers' reaction to a premium incentive and determine whether they perceive the offer as a value. Another option is to use premiums with no brand identification, but that detracts from their consumer franchise-building value.

**EXHIBIT 16–22**
American Airlines promotes the value of AAdvantage miles as a purchase incentive

## Contests and Sweepstakes

Contests and sweepstakes are an increasingly popular consumer-oriented promotion. Marketers spent over $2 billion on these promotions in 2012. These promotions seem to have an appeal and glamour that such tools as cents-off coupons lack. Contests and sweepstakes are exciting because, as one expert has noted, many consumers have a "pot of gold at the end of the rainbow mentality" and think they can win the big prizes being offered.[45] The lure of sweepstakes and promotions has also been influenced by the "instant-millionaire syndrome" that has derived from huge cash prizes given by many state lotteries in recent years. Marketers are attracted to contests and sweepstakes as a way of generating attention and interest among a large number of consumers.

There are differences between contests and sweepstakes. A **contest** is a promotion where consumers compete for prizes or money on the basis of skills or ability. The company determines winners by judging the entries or ascertaining which entry comes closest to some predetermined criterion (e.g., picking the winning teams and total number of points in the Super Bowl or NCAA basketball tournament). Contests usually provide a purchase incentive by requiring a proof of purchase to enter or an entry form that is available from a dealer or advertisement. Some contests require consumers to read an ad or package or visit a store display to gather information needed to enter. Marketers must be careful not to make their contests too difficult to enter, as doing so might discourage participation among key prospects in the target audience.

A **sweepstakes** is a promotion where winners are determined purely by chance; it cannot require a proof of purchase as a condition for entry. Entrants need only submit their names for the prize drawing. While there is often an official entry form, handwritten entries must also be permitted. One form of sweepstakes is a **game**, which also has a chance element or odds of winning. Scratch-off cards with instant winners are a popular promotional tool. Some games occur over a longer period and require more involvement by consumers. Promotions where consumers must collect game pieces are popular among retailers and fast-food chains as a way to build store traffic and repeat purchases.

Because they are easier to enter, sweepstakes attract more entries than contests. They are also easier and less expensive to administer, since every entry does not have to be checked or judged. Choosing the winning entry in a sweepstakes requires only the random selection of a winner from the pool of entries or generation of a number to match those held by sweepstakes entrants. Experts note that the costs of mounting a sweepstakes are also very predictable. Companies can buy insurance to indemnify them and protect against the expense of awarding a big prize. In general, sweepstakes present marketers with a fixed cost, which is a major advantage when budgeting for a promotion.

Contests and sweepstakes can involve consumers with a brand by making the promotion product relevant or by connecting the prizes to the lifestyle, needs, or interests of the target audience. For example, Levi Strauss & Co. ran an innovative contest called the "Care to Air Challenge" which sought the world's most innovative, covetable, and sustainable air-drying solution for clothing (Exhibit 16–23). The contest was designed to address an important environmental issue by informing consumers that nearly 60 percent of the climate impact of owning a pair of jeans over their life cycle comes from the energy-intensive methods used for drying them. The contest offered consumers the chance to win $10,000 in prize money by submitting a photo and description of how they use clothesline designs or other innovative air drying solutions that are better for the environment and help reduce the carbon footprint.

The nature of contests and sweepstakes, as well as the way they are deployed, is changing as many companies are delivering them online rather than through traditional entry forms that are submitted via the mail or dropped in an entry box. Marketers are using the Internet for their contests and sweepstakes because of its cost efficiency, immediate data collection capabilities, and ability to keep consumers engaged. Promotions are being designed to ensure an engaging consumer experience by making them more entertaining and interactive and also developing prizes that are not only larger but more customized and experiential-based.[46] A number of companies are also integrating user-generated content into

**EXHIBIT 16–23**
Levi's "Care to Air" Contest ties in well to the product and the interests of the target market

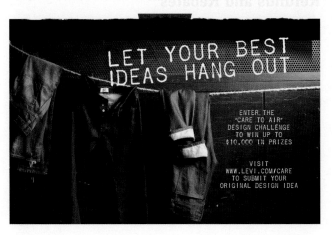

their contests, which are often promoted on their Facebook pages. Contests that rely on *crowd-sourcing* whereby consumers enter ideas and they are voted on by others are becoming increasingly popular. For example, Frito-Lay has run create-a-chip contests for Doritos as well as Lay's potato chips, while Samuel Adams has run contests asking consumers to create a crowd-sourced beer, and Arizona Beverages USA has prodded the public to create new iced tea flavors.[47]

### Problems with Contests and Sweepstakes

While the use of contests and sweepstakes continues to increase, there are some problems associated with these types of promotions. Many sweepstakes and/or contest promotions do little to contribute to consumer franchise building for a product or service and may even detract from it. The sweepstakes or contest often becomes the dominant focus rather than the brand, and little is accomplished other than giving away substantial amounts of money and/or prizes. Many promotional experts question the effectiveness of contests and sweepstakes. Some companies have cut back or even stopped using them because of concern over their effectiveness and fears that consumers might become dependent on them.

Another problem with contests and sweepstakes is the participation in them by hobbyists who submit entries but have no real interest in the product or service. Because most states make it illegal to require a purchase as a qualification for a sweepstakes entry, consumers can enter as many times as they wish. Entrants may enter a sweepstakes numerous times, depending on the nature of the prizes and the number of entries allowed. There are numerous websites on the Internet such as sweepsadvantage.com that inform consumers of all of the contests and sweepstakes being held, the entry dates, estimated probabilities of winning, how to enter, and solutions to any puzzles or other information that might be needed. The presence of the professional entrants not only defeats the purpose of the promotion but also may discourage entries from consumers who feel that their chances of winning are limited. Exhibit 16–24 shows a page from the website of the Contest.Bee, which provides consumers with information on contests and sweepstakes and how to enter them.

Numerous legal considerations affect the design and administration of contests and sweepstakes.[48] These promotions are regulated by several federal agencies, and each of the 50 states has its own rules. The regulation of contests and sweepstakes has helped clean up the abuses that plagued the industry for many years and has improved consumers' perceptions of these promotions. But companies must still be careful in designing a contest or sweepstakes and awarding prizes. Most firms use consultants that specialize in the design and administration of contests and sweepstakes to avoid any legal problems, but they may still run into problems with promotions, as discussed in IMC Perspective 16–2.

**EXHIBIT 16–24**
The Contest.Bee contains information on contests and sweepstakes

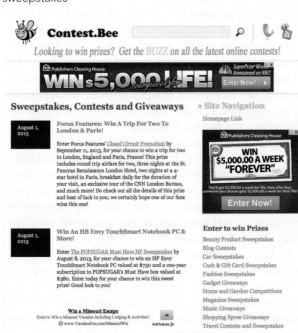

### Refunds and Rebates

**Refunds** (also known as *rebates*) are offers by the manufacturer to return a portion of the product purchase price, usually after the consumer supplies some proof of purchase. Consumers are generally very responsive to rebate offers, particularly as the size of the savings increases. Rebates are used by makers of all types of products, ranging from packaged goods to major appliances, cars, and computer software.

Packaged-goods marketers often use refund offers to induce trial of a new product or encourage users of another brand to switch. Consumers may perceive the savings offered through a cash refund as an immediate value that lowers the cost of the item, even though those savings are realized only if the consumer redeems the refund or rebate offer. Redemption rates for refund offers typically range from 1 to 3 percent for print and point-of-purchase offers and 5 percent for in/on-package offers.

Refund offers can also encourage repeat purchase. Many offers require consumers to send in multiple proofs of purchase. The size of the refund offer may even increase as the number of purchases gets larger. Some packaged-goods companies are switching away from cash refund offers to coupons or cash/coupon combinations. Using coupons in the refund offer enhances the likelihood of repeat purchase of the brand. For example, Exhibit 16–25 shows a coupon refund offer used by Pennzoil that can be redeemed on the next oil change.

**Evaluating Refunds and Rebates**   Rebates can help create new users and encourage brand switching or repeat purchase behavior, or they can be a way to offer a temporary price reduction. This offer can influence purchase even if the consumer fails to realize the savings, so the marketer can reduce price for much less than if it used a direct price-off deal.

Some problems are associated with refunds and rebates. Many consumers are not motivated by a refund offer because of the delay and the effort required to obtain the savings. They do not want to be bothered saving cash register receipts and proofs of purchase, filling out forms, and mailing in the offer.[49] A study of consumer perceptions found a negative relationship between the use of rebates and the perceived difficulties associated with the redemption process.[50] The study also found that consumers perceive manufacturers as offering rebates to sell products that are not faring well. Nonusers of rebates were particularly likely to perceive the redemption process as too complicated and to suspect manufacturers' motives. This implies that companies using rebates must simplify the redemption process and use other promotional elements such as advertising to retain consumer confidence in the brand.

When small refunds are being offered, marketers may find other promotional incentives such as coupons or bonus packs more effective. They must be careful not to overuse rebate offers and confuse consumers about the real price and value of a product or service. Also, consumers can become dependent on rebates and delay their purchases or purchase only brands for which a rebate is available. Many retailers have become disenchanted with rebates and the burden and expense of administering them.[51]

However, despite the complaints consumers and retailers may have about them, marketers are unlikely to eliminate the use of rebates as they are a very effective promotion tool. A well-promoted, high-value rebate can increase sales significantly, and eliminating them can have a negative impact on sales, particularly in product categories where consumers have come to expect them. Marketers also recognize that they can accomplish a perceived price reduction among consumers who plan to redeem the rebates but never do so and factor the redemption rates into their pricing structure.[52]

**EXHIBIT 16–25**
Pennzoil uses a refund offer that is tied to a future purchase

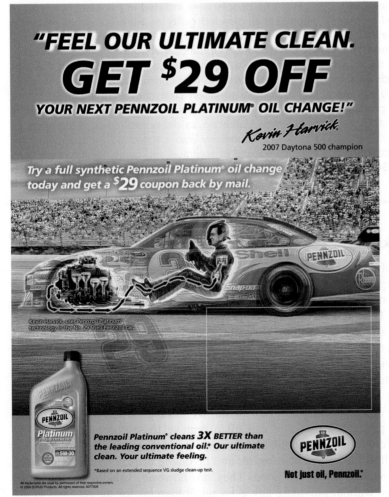

# Marketers and Consumers Learn the Perils of Promotions

Contests, sweepstakes, and premium offers are often used by marketers to give consumers an extra incentive to purchase their products. However, when these promotions don't go as planned, they can embarrass a company or even create legal problems. A number of high-profile companies known for their marketing excellence have experienced problems with promotions over the years. These botched promotions were embarrassing for the companies and resulted in the loss of goodwill as well as money.

Kraft was one of the first to learn how expensive it can be when a promotion goes awry. In 1989, a printing error resulted in the printing of too many winning game pieces for a match-and-win game promotion. Kraft canceled the promotion but still had to spend nearly $4 million to compensate the winners—versus the $36,000 budgeted for prizes. The snafu gave birth to the "Kraft clause," a disclaimer stating that a marketer reserves the right to cancel a promotion if there are problems and hold a random drawing if there are more winners than prizes.

A few years later, PepsiCo had a major problem when a bottle-cap promotion offering a grand prize of 1 million pesos (about $36,000) went wrong in the Philippines. Due to a computer glitch, the winning number appeared on more than 500,000 bottle caps, which would have made the company liable for more than $18 billion in prize money. When the error was discovered, Pepsi announced that there was a problem and quickly offered to pay $19 for each winning cap, which ended up costing the company nearly $10 million. The furor caused by the botched promotion prompted anti-Pepsi rallies, death threats against Pepsi executives, and attacks on Pepsi trucks and bottling plants.

Harrah's Entertainment, Inc. made a major couponing error that ended up costing the company nearly $6 million.

A mailing sent to its Total Rewards cardholders in its loyalty program included a coupon that members could redeem at Harrah's Joliet Casino near Chicago. Only a small number of the coupons were supposed to be worth $525 each; however, a printing error resulted in 11,000 coupons worth $525 being sent out. The coupons were barcoded, but most of the codes did not match the $525 printed on the coupon's face value and casino staff initially refused to honor the coupons when the bar codes did not match the face value. However, the Illinois gaming board ordered Harrah's to honor all of the coupons and most were eventually redeemed.

McDonald's also ran into a major problem when winning game pieces were embezzled from its popular Monopoly game promotion. McDonald's ran its first Monopoly game promotion in 1987 and began running it annually in 1991. However, in August 2001 the Federal Bureau of Investigation arrested eight people for embezzling winning game pieces from the Monopoly game as well as the company's "Who Wants to Be a Millionaire" sweepstakes in order to divert nearly $24 million worth of prizes to co-conspirators.

Fifty-one people were indicted in the case, nearly all of whom either pleaded guilty or were convicted following trial. Among those pleading guilty was the director of security for McDonald's promotional agency, Simon Marketing, who stole the winning tickets and conspired with the others to distribute them to a network of recruiters who solicited individuals to falsely claim they were legitimate game winners. Following the arrests McDonald's immediately fired Simon Marketing, as did several other of the agency's clients. The company also created an independent task force composed of antifraud and game security experts to review procedures for future promotions. McDonald's began

## Bonus Packs

**Bonus packs** offer the consumer an extra amount of a product at the regular price by providing larger containers or extra units (Exhibit 16–26). Bonus packs result in a lower cost per unit for the consumer and provide extra value as well as more product for the money. There are several advantages to bonus pack promotions. First, they give marketers a direct way to provide extra value without having to get involved with complicated coupons or refund offers. The additional value of a bonus pack is generally obvious to the consumer and can have a strong impact on the purchase decision at the time of purchase.

Bonus packs can also be an effective defensive maneuver against a competitor's promotion or introduction of a new brand. By loading current users with large amounts of its product, a marketer can often remove these consumers from the market and make them less susceptible to a competitor's promotional efforts. Bonus packs may result in larger purchase orders and favorable display space in the store if relationships with retailers are good. They do, however, usually require additional shelf space without providing any extra profit margins for the retailer, so the running the Monopoly promotion again in 2003, and it has again become very popular among consumers.

A recent example of a well-intended sales promotion tactic going awry involved an online coupon promotion that KFC was running in China in April 2010 in conjunction with Taobao.com, China's largest e-commerce site. KFC, which is China's largest fast-food chain with 2,000 outlets, planned to distribute coupons for three different menu items with each offering a 50 percent discount. The coupons could be downloaded on KFC's online store on Taobao.com at specific time periods. However, a problem arose when news of the discounts circulated around the Internet and the coupons were republished on other sites, where they were downloaded and redeemed at restaurants, far surpassing the volume anticipated by KFC. Store employees began refusing coupons, arguing that they were illegally produced from unauthorized sites, but the explanations varied from store to store, which added to the problem. Many consumers reacted, and some became violent, and police had to rush to some restaurants to restore order. KFC issued an apology for the problem, but the company's failure to honor the coupons damaged the brand's relationship with thousands of consumers, many of whom criticized KFC on blogs and social media sites in many cities around China.

Another area where marketers face potential problems is with contests that rely on user-generated content. Malibu Caribbean Rum ran a contest soliciting videos about its Malibu Banana Rum brand set to the tune of "Banana Boat Song," also known as "Day-O." It offered a prize of $25,000 or, if the winner preferred, a banana grove in a tropical location. Pernod Ricar, which owns the brand, stated it would consider the votes of YouTube users when it chose the winner. However, when the winner's name was posted and the finalists were not named publicly, some of the contest entrants complained on YouTube message boards that the contest had been rigged, a charge that the company vehemently denied. Frito-Lay also ran into a problem when one of the submissions in its popular "Crash the Super Bowl"

contests was a commercial showing a Catholic priest substituting Doritos for the Holy Eucharist during communion as a way of boosting church attendance. Frito-Lay had to pull the ad from the competition after receiving a number of complaints from Catholic groups and organizations.

Marketers are not the only ones who encounter problems with promotions as consumers who win contests and sweepstakes often learn that there may be unexpected tax consequences because the prizes are treated as income by the Internal Revenue Service.

A winner of a American Airlines "We know why you fly" contest faced major tax liability as the grand prize was 12 round-trip restricted coach tickets for two to anywhere in the world the airline flies. The contest's official rules explained that winners must pay federal and state income taxes, where applicable, on American's approximated retail value of the 24 tickets, which the airline valued at $2,200 per ticket or $52,800. The New York resident who won the contest was facing taxes on the tickets that could amount to nearly $19,000 and so declined the prize.

While marketers continue to use contests, sweepstakes, and games, they are taking precautions to safeguard them in an attempt to avoid the problems these companies encountered. Consumers who enter these promotions might also be well-advised to read the fine print to understand the tax liability associated with the prize and make sure they can really afford to win.

Sources: Normandy Madden, "KFC Gets Burned by Digital Coupon Promotion," *Advertising Age*, April 14, 2010, http://adage.com/print?article_id5143283; Kate McArthur, "McSwindle," *Advertising Age*, August 27, 2002, pp. 1, 22; Betsy Spethmann, "The Perils of Promotion," *Promo*, November 1996, pp. 22, 134; Melanie Trottman and Ron Lieber, "Contest Winner Declines 'Free' Airline Tickets," *The Wall Street Journal*, July 6, 2005; Betsy Spethmann, "Harrah's Coupon Error to Cost $2.8 Billion," promomagazine.com, November 23, 2005; "User-Generated Content: The Good, the Bad and the Ugly," *Yahoo! Advertising Solutions*, December 19, 2011, http://advertising.yahoo.com/blogs/advertising/user-generated-content-good-bad-ugly-193505793.html; Louise Story, "Outcome of Ad Contest Starts an Uproar on YouTube," *The New York Times*, June 27, 2007, www.nytimes.com/2007/06/27/technology/27malibu.ready.html.

marketer can encounter problems with bonus packs if trade relationships are not good. Another problem is that bonus packs may appeal primarily to current users who probably would have purchased the brand anyway or to promotion-sensitive consumers who may not become loyal to the brand.

## Price-Off Deals

Another consumer-oriented promotion technique is the direct **price-off deal**, which reduces the price of the brand. Price-off reductions are typically offered right on the package through specially marked price packs, as shown in Exhibit 16–27. Typically, price-offs range from 10 to 25 percent off the regular price, with the reduction coming out of the manufacturer's profit margin, not the retailer's. Keeping the retailer's margin during a price-off promotion maintains its support and cooperation.

Marketers use price-off promotions for several reasons. First, since price-offs are controlled by the manufacturer, it can make sure the promotional discount reaches the consumer rather than being kept by the trade. Like bonus packs, price-off deals usually present a readily apparent value to shoppers, especially when they

**EXHIBIT 16–26**

Bonus packs provide more value for consumers

have a reference price point for the brand and thus recognize the value of the discount.[53] So price-offs can be a strong influence at the point of purchase when price comparisons are being made. Price-off promotions can also encourage consumers to purchase larger quantities, preempting competitors' promotions and leading to greater trade support.

Price-off promotions may not be favorably received by retailers, since they can create pricing and inventory problems. Most retailers will not accept packages with a specific price shown, so the familiar $X$ amount off the regular price must be used. Also, like bonus packs, price-off deals appeal primarily to regular users instead of attracting nonusers. Finally, the Federal Trade Commission has regulations regarding the conditions that price-off labels must meet and the frequency and timing of their use.

## Loyalty Programs

One of the fastest-growing areas of sales promotion is the use of **loyalty programs** (also referred to as *continuity* or *frequency programs*). American Airlines was one of the first major companies to use loyalty programs when it introduced its AAdvantage frequent-flyer program in 1981. Since then frequency programs have become commonplace in a number of product and service categories, particularly travel and hospitality, as well as among retailers. Virtually every airline, car rental company, and hotel chain has some type of frequency program. American Airlines has more than 70 million members in its AAdvantage program, while Marriott International has enlisted more than 20 million business travelers into its Rewards program.

Many packaged-goods companies are also developing loyalty programs. Pillsbury, Nestlé, Kraft, and others have recently introduced continuity programs that offer consumers the opportunity to accumulate points for continuing to purchase their brands; the points can be redeemed for gifts and prizes. Loyalty programs have become particularly popular among grocery stores.[54] Nearly 7,000 supermarkets now have loyalty programs that offer members discounts, a chance to accumulate points that can be redeemed for rewards, newsletters, and other special services. Loyalty programs are also used by a variety of other retailers, including department stores, home centers, bookstores, and even local bagel shops. Many specialty retailers such as consumer electronics stores also have launched loyalty programs. For example, Best Buy launched its Rewards Zone program in 2003, and the program has grown to include more than 7 million members.

There are a number of reasons why loyalty programs have become so popular. Marketers view these programs as a way of encouraging consumers to use their products or services on a continual basis and as a way of developing strong customer loyalty. Many companies are also realizing the importance of customer retention and understand that the key to retaining and growing market share is building relationships with loyal customers.[55] Frequency programs also provide marketers with the opportunity to develop databases containing valuable information on their customers

**EXHIBIT 16–27**

Examples of price-off packages

that can be used to better understand their needs, interests, and characteristics as well as to identify and track a company's most valuable customers. These databases can also be used to target specific programs and offers to customers to increase the amount they purchase and/or to build stronger relationships with them. For example, the WD-40 Fan Club is a loyalty program for the brand which provides members with product information, usage tips, newsletters, downloads of games, and other benefits (Exhibit 16–28). The fan club has more than 100,000 members who educate each other about creative ways to use the solvent and serve as advocates for the brand.[56]

As frequency programs become more common, marketers will be challenged to find ways to use them as a means of differentiating their product, service, business, or retail store. The average American household belongs to 12 loyalty programs but is active in only 40 percent of them.[57] It has been argued that many

**EXHIBIT 16–28**

The WD-40 Fan Club is a popular customer loyalty program

of the loyalty programs developed by marketers are really short-term promotions that overreward regular users and do little to develop long-term loyalty.[58] A recent study by a loyalty marketing firm found that 66 percent of consumers say that discounts are the main reason they participate in loyalty programs. This study also found that many consumers drop out of loyalty programs because of the length of time it takes to accumulate reward points.[59] Marketers must find ways to make their loyalty programs more than just discount or frequent-buyer programs. This will require the careful management of databases to identify and track valuable customers and their purchase history and the strategic use of targeted loyalty promotions.

## Event Marketing

Another type of consumer-oriented promotion that has become very popular in recent years is the use of event marketing. It is important to make a distinction between *event marketing* and *event sponsorships,* as the two terms are often used interchangeably yet they refer to different activities. **Event marketing** is a type of promotion where a company or brand is linked to an event or where a themed activity is developed for the purpose of creating experiences for consumers and promoting a product or service. Marketers often do event marketing by associating their product with some popular activity such as a sporting event, concert, fair, or festival. However, marketers also create their own events to use for promotional purposes. For example, PepsiCo has created an irreverent brand image for its popular Mountain Dew brand by associating it with action sports. Extreme sports are about a nonconforming lifestyle from clothes to music, and young people respond to brands that make an authentic connection and become part of the action sports community. In 2005, the brand raised its involvement with action sports to a new level when it became a founding partner of the Dew Tour, a five-event series that features competition in skateboarding, BMX, and freestyle motocross and has expanded into winter sports as well with the Winter Dew Tour (Exhibit 16–29). From an event marketing perspective, an important part of the Dew Tour is the promotional opportunities associated with the various events. At each Dew Tour stop the company's event agency sets up the "Mountain Dew Green Label Experience" which is built around the action sports lifestyle and features custom art, interactive displays, athlete autograph sessions, lounges where fans can hang out and interact with their favorite extreme sport athletes, and the product sampling kitchen where they can try various Mountain Dew flavors, as well as other products.

An **event sponsorship** is an integrated marketing communications activity where a company develops actual sponsorship relations with a particular event and provides financial support in return for the right to display a brand name, logo, or advertising message and be identified as a supporter of the event. Event marketing often takes place as part of a company's sponsorship of activities such as concerts, the arts, social causes, and sporting events. Decisions and objectives for event sponsorships are often part of an organization's public relations activities and are discussed in the next chapter.

Event marketing has become a very popular part of the integrated marketing communications programs of many companies as they view them as excellent promotional opportunities and a way to associate their brands with certain lifestyles, interests, and activities. Events can be an effective

**EXHIBIT 16–29**

The Dew Tour provides Mountain Dew with event marketing opportunities way to connect with consumers in an environment where they are comfortable with receiving a promotional message. Moreover, consumers often expect companies to be part of events and welcome their participation as they make the events more entertaining, interesting, and exciting. Marketers can use events to distribute samples as well as information about their products and services or to actually let consumers experience their brands.

## Summary of Consumer-Oriented Promotions and Marketer Objectives

The discussion of the various sales promotion techniques shows that marketers use these tools to accomplish a variety of objectives. As noted at the beginning of the chapter, sales promotion techniques provide consumers with an *extra incentive* or *reward* for engaging in a certain form of behavior such as purchasing a brand. For some types of sales promotion tools the incentive the consumer receives is immediate, while for others the reward is delayed and is not realized immediately. Marketers often evaluate sales promotion tools in terms of their ability to accomplish specific objectives and consider whether the impact of the promotion will be immediate or delayed. Figure 16–5 outlines which sales promotion tools can be used to accomplish various objectives of marketers and identifies whether the extra incentive or reward is immediate or delayed.[60]

It should be noted that in Figure 16–5 some of the sales promotion techniques are listed more than once because they can be used to accomplish more than one objective. For example, loyalty programs can be used to retain customers by providing both immediate and delayed rewards. Shoppers who belong to loyalty programs sponsored by supermarkets and receive discounts every time they make a purchase are receiving immediate rewards that are designed to retain them as customers. Some loyalty promotions such as frequency programs used by airlines, car rental companies, and hotels offer delayed rewards by requiring that users accumulate points to reach a certain level or status before the points can be redeemed. Loyalty programs can also be used by marketers to help build brand equity. For example, when an airline or car rental company sends its frequent users upgrade certificates, the practice helps build relationships with these customers and thus contributes to brand equity.

| Consumer Reward Incentive | Marketing Objective | | |
| --- | --- | --- | --- |
| | Induce trial | Customer retention/loading | Support IMC program/ build brand equity |
| Immediate | • Sampling<br>• Instant coupons<br>• In-store coupons<br>• In-store rebates | • Price-off deals<br>• Bonus packs<br>• In- and on-package free premiums<br>• Loyalty programs | • Events<br>• In- and on-package free premiums |
| Delayed | • Media- and mail-delivered coupons<br>• Mail-in refunds and rebates<br>• Free mail-in premiums<br>• Scanner- and Internet-delivered coupons | • In- and on-package coupons<br>• Mail-in refunds and rebates<br>• Loyalty programs | • Self-liquidating premiums<br>• Free mail-in premiums<br>• Contests and sweepstakes<br>• Loyalty programs |

**FIGURE 16–5**

Consumer-Oriented Sales Promotion Tools for Various Marketing Objectives

While marketers use consumer-oriented sales promotions to provide current and/or potential customers with an extra incentive, they also use these promotions as part of their marketing program to leverage trade support. Retailers are more likely to stock a brand, purchase extra quantities, or provide additional support such as end-aisle displays when they know a manufacturer is running a promotion during a designated period. The development of promotional programs targeted toward the trade is a very important part of the marketing process and is discussed in the next section.

# TRADE-ORIENTED SALES PROMOTION

## Objectives of Trade-Oriented Sales Promotion

Like consumer-oriented promotions, sales promotion programs targeted to the trade should be based on well-defined objectives and measurable goals and a consideration of what the marketer wants to accomplish. Typical objectives for promotions targeted to marketing intermediaries such as wholesalers and retailers include obtaining distribution and support for new products, maintaining support for established brands, encouraging retailers to display established brands, and building retail inventories.

**Obtain Distribution for New Products** Trade promotions are often used to encourage retailers to give shelf space to new products. Manufacturers recognize that only a limited amount of shelf space is available in supermarkets, drugstores, and other major retail outlets. Thus, they provide retailers with financial incentives to stock and promote new products. While trade discounts or other special price deals are used to encourage retailers and wholesalers to stock a new brand, marketers may use other types of promotions to get them to push the brand. Merchandising allowances can get retailers to display a new product in high-traffic areas of stores, while incentive programs or contests can encourage wholesale or retail store personnel to push a new brand.

**Maintain Trade Support for Established Brands** Trade promotions are often designed to maintain distribution and trade support for established brands. Brands that are in the mature phase of their product life cycle are vulnerable to losing wholesale and/or retail distribution, particularly if they are not differentiated or face competition from new products. Trade deals induce wholesalers and retailers to continue to carry weaker products because the discounts increase their profit margins. Brands with a smaller market share often rely heavily on trade promotions, since they lack the funds required to differentiate themselves from competitors through media advertising.

Even if a brand has a strong market position, trade promotions may be used as part of an overall marketing strategy. For example, Heinz has relied heavily on trade promotions to hold its market share position for many of its brands. Many consumer packaged goods companies count on trade promotions to maintain retail distribution and support.

**Encourage Retailers to Display Established Brands** Another objective of trade-oriented promotions is to encourage retailers to display and promote an established brand. Marketers recognize that many purchase decisions are made in the store, and promotional displays are an excellent way of generating sales. An important goal is to obtain retail store displays of a product away from its regular shelf location. A typical supermarket has approximately 50 display areas at the ends of aisles, near checkout counters, and elsewhere. Marketers want to have their products displayed in these areas to increase the probability shoppers will come into contact with them. Even a single display can increase a brand's sales significantly during a promotion.

## Program Calendar FY13

**EXHIBIT 16–30**

WD-40's program calendar shows the retailers the marketing support planned for its products

Manufacturers often use multifaceted promotional programs to encourage retailers to promote their products at the retail level. For example, Exhibit 16–30 shows a program calendar the WD-40 Company provides to retailers showing the various marketing support programs the company planned to use during fiscal year 2013 for its new lawn and landscape lubricant products. The program included a variety of IMC tools including targeted advertising on television and in magazines; online videos, and e-newsletters; social media banners and blogs; trade publication and blogger outreach; and various types of consumer and trade promotions.

**Build Retail Inventories** Manufacturers often use trade promotions to build the inventory levels of retailers or other channel members. There are several reasons manufacturers want to load retailers with their products. First, wholesalers and retailers are more likely to push a product when they have high inventory levels rather than storing it in their warehouses or back rooms. Building channel members' inventories also ensures they will not run out of stock and thus miss sales opportunities.

Some manufacturers of seasonal products offer large promotional discounts so that retailers will stock up on their products before the peak selling season begins. This enables the manufacturer to smooth out seasonal fluctuations in its production schedule and passes on some of the inventory carrying costs to retailers or wholesalers. When retailers stock up on a product before the peak selling season, they often run special promotions and offer discounts to consumers to reduce excess inventories.

## Types of Trade-Oriented Promotions

Manufacturers use a variety of trade promotion tools as inducements for wholesalers and retailers. Next we examine some of the most often used types of trade promotions and some factors marketers must consider in using them. These promotions include contests and incentives, trade allowances, displays and point-of-purchase materials, sales training programs, trade shows, and co-op advertising.

**Contests and Incentives** Manufacturers may develop contests or special incentive programs to stimulate greater selling effort and support from reseller management or sales personnel. Contests or incentive programs can be directed toward managers who work for a wholesaler or distributor as well as toward store or department managers at the retail level. Manufacturers often sponsor contests for resellers and use prizes such as trips or valuable merchandise as rewards for meeting sales quotas or other goals.

Contests or special incentives are often targeted at the sales personnel of the wholesalers, distributors/dealers, or retailers. These salespeople are an important link in the distribution chain because they are likely to be very familiar with the market, more frequently in touch with the customer (whether it be another reseller or the ultimate consumer), and more numerous than the manufacturer's own sales organization. Manufacturers often devise incentives or contests for these sales personnel. These programs may involve cash payments made directly to the retailer's or wholesaler's sales staff to encourage them to promote and sell a manufacturer's product. These payments are known as **push money (pm)** or *spiffs*. For example, an appliance manufacturer may pay a $25 spiff to retail sales personnel for selling a certain model or size. In sales contests, salespeople can win trips or valuable merchandise for meeting certain goals established by the manufacturer. As shown in Figure 16–6, these incentives may be tied to product sales, new account placements, or merchandising efforts.

FIGURE 16–6

Three Forms of Promotion Targeted to Reseller Salespeople

- Product or Program Sales

  Awards are tied to the selling of a product, for example:

  Selling a specified number of cases

  Selling a specified number of units

  Selling a specified number of promotional programs

- New Account Placements

  Awards are tied to:

  The number of new accounts opened

  The number of new accounts ordering a minimum number of cases or units

  Promotional programs placed in new accounts

- Merchandising Efforts

  Awards are tied to:

  Establishing promotional programs (such as theme programs)

  Placing display racks, counter displays, and the like

While contests and incentive programs can generate reseller support, they can also be a source of conflict between retail sales personnel and management. Some retailers want to maintain control over the selling activities of their sales staffs. They don't want their salespeople devoting an undue amount of effort to trying to win a contest or receive incentives offered by the manufacturer. Nor do they want their people becoming too aggressive in pushing products that serve their own interests instead of the product or model that is best for the customer.

Many retailers refuse to let their employees participate in manufacturer-sponsored contests or to accept incentive payments. Retailers that do allow them often have strict guidelines and require management approval of the program.

**Trade Allowances** Probably the most common trade promotion is some form of **trade allowance**, a discount or deal offered to retailers or wholesalers to encourage them to stock, promote, or display the manufacturer's products. Types of allowances offered to retailers include buying allowances, promotional or display allowances, and slotting allowances.

**Buying Allowances** A buying allowance is a deal or discount offered to resellers in the form of a price reduction on merchandise ordered during a fixed period. These discounts are often in the form of an **off-invoice allowance**, which means a certain per-case amount or percentage is deducted from the invoice. A buying allowance can also take the form of *free goods;* the reseller gets extra cases with the purchase of specific amounts (for example, 1 free case with every 10 cases purchased).

Buying allowances are used for several reasons. They are easy to implement and are well accepted, and sometimes expected, by the trade. They are also an effective way to encourage resellers to buy the manufacturer's product, since they will want to take advantage of the discounts being offered during the allowance period. Manufacturers offer trade discounts expecting wholesalers and retailers to pass the price reduction through to consumers, resulting in greater sales. However, as discussed shortly, this is often not the case.

**Promotional Allowances** Manufacturers often give retailers allowances or discounts for performing certain promotional or merchandising activities in support of their brands. These merchandising allowances can be given for providing special displays away from the product's regular shelf position, running in-store promotional programs, or including the product in an ad. The manufacturer generally has

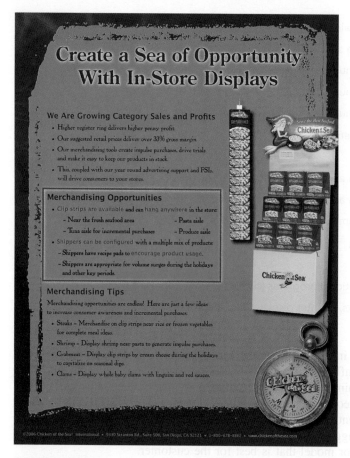

**EXHIBIT 16–31**

Chicken of the Sea encourages retailers to use in-store displays of its products

guidelines or a contract specifying the activity to be performed to qualify for the promotional allowance. The allowance is usually a fixed amount per case or a percentage deduction from the list price for merchandise ordered during the promotional period.

Exhibit 16–31 shows a trade promotional piece used by Chicken of the Sea International to inform retailers of the merchandising opportunities available for its products and to encourage them to use in-store displays. An important goal of the company's trade marketing efforts is to get retailers to set up more displays of its products in various areas of their stores where related products are sold.

**Slotting Allowances** In recent years, retailers have been demanding a special allowance for agreeing to handle a new product. **Slotting allowances**, also called *stocking allowances, introductory allowances,* or *street money,* are fees retailers charge for providing a slot or position to accommodate the new product. Retailers justify these fees by pointing out the costs associated with taking on so many new products each year, such as redesigning store shelves, entering the product into their computers, finding warehouse space, and briefing store employees on the new product.[61] They also note they are assuming some risk, since so many new product introductions fail.

Slotting fees can range from a few hundred dollars per store to $50,000 or more for an entire retail chain. Manufacturers that want to get their products on the shelves nationally can face several million dollars in slotting fees. Many marketers believe slotting allowances are a form of blackmail or bribery and say some 70 percent of these fees go directly to retailers' bottom lines.

Retailers can continue charging slotting fees because of their power and the limited availability of shelf space in supermarkets relative to the large numbers of products introduced each year. Some retailers have even been demanding **failure fees** if a new product does not hit a minimum sales level within a certain time. The fee is charged to cover the costs associated with stocking, maintaining inventories, and then pulling the product.[62] Large manufacturers with popular brands are less likely to pay slotting fees than smaller companies that lack leverage in negotiating with retailers.

In 1999, the Senate Committee on Small Business began taking action against the practice of using slotting fees in the grocery, drugstore, and computer software industries because of the fees' negative impact on small business.[63] The committee recommended that the Federal Trade Commission and Small Business Administration take steps to limit the use of slotting fees because they are anticompetitive. A study by Paul Bloom, Gregory Gundlach, and Joseph Cannon examined the views of manufacturers, wholesalers, and grocery retailers regarding the use of slotting fees. Their findings suggest that slotting fees shift the risk of new product introductions from retailers to manufacturers and help apportion the supply and demand of new products. They also found that slotting fees lead to higher retail prices, are applied in a discriminatory fashion, and place small marketers at a disadvantage.[64]

**Displays and Point-of-Purchase Materials** The next time you are in a store, take a moment to examine the various promotional materials used to display and sell products. Point-of-purchase (POP) displays are an important promotional tool because they can help a manufacturer obtain more effective in-store merchandising of products. Companies in the United States spend more than $19 billion a year on POP materials, including end-of-aisle displays, banners, posters, shelf cards, motion pieces, and stand-up racks, among others. Point-of-purchase displays are very important to marketers since many consumers make their purchase decisions in the store. In fact, some studies estimate that nearly two-thirds of a consumer's buying decisions are made in a retail store. Thus, it is very important for marketers to get the attention of consumers, as well as to communicate a sales or promotional message, through POP displays.

A measurement study from Point-of-Purchase Advertising International (an industry trade association) and the Advertising Research Foundation estimates that the cost-per-thousand-impressions figure for POPs is $6 to $8 for supermarket displays.[65] The CPM figure is based on findings that a grocery store display makes an average of 2,300 to 8,000 impressions per week, depending on store size and volume. Although this study has shown that POP displays are very effective at reaching consumers, difficulties in getting retail stores to comply with requests for displays often make it difficult for marketers to use them.[66] Moreover, many retailers are decreasing the amount of signage and displays they will accept as well as the messages they can communicate. Also, as account-specific promotions become more popular, some retailers are requiring customized POP materials. For example, 7-Eleven has taken over the responsibility for the production of all POP materials from vendors—who must still pay for them. The goal is to give 7-Eleven complete control over its in-store environment.

Despite these challenges, marketers recognize that point-of-purchase displays are an important part of their promotional programs. Many continue to develop innovative methods to display their products efficiently, make them stand out in the retail environment, and communicate a sales message to consumers. It should be noted that the importance of creative POP displays is not limited to grocery or convenience stores. Point-of-purchase displays are also important to companies that distribute their products through other types of retail outlets, such as home improvement, consumer electronic, and specialty retail stores. For example, Exhibit 16–32 shows an award-winning POP display created by E-B Display Co. to promote the SeaKlear family of pool and spa treatments. The display holds 16 different pool and spa products, and the unique octagonal shape allows for a 3608 shoppable display in a relatively small footprint. The display also has large graphic areas to educate consumers regarding specific uses and applications and help them make their purchase decisions.

Many manufacturers help retailers use shelf space more efficiently through **planograms**, which are configurations of products that occupy a shelf section in a store. Some manufacturers are developing computer-based programs that allow retailers to input information from their scanner data and determine the best shelf layouts by experimenting with product movement, space utilization, profit yields, and other factors.[67]

**Sales Training Programs**  Another form of manufacturer-sponsored promotional assistance is sales training programs for reseller personnel. Many products sold at the retail level require knowledgeable salespeople who can provide consumers with information about the features, benefits, and advantages of various brands and models. Cosmetics, appliances, computers, consumer electronics, and sporting equipment are examples of products for which consumers often rely on well-informed retail sales personnel for assistance.

Manufacturers provide sales training assistance to retail salespeople in a number of ways. They may conduct classes or training sessions that retail personnel can attend to increase their knowledge of a product or a product line. These training sessions present information and ideas on how to sell the manufacturer's product and may also include motivational components. Sales training classes for retail personnel are often sponsored by companies selling high-ticket items or complex products such as smartphones, cars, or ski equipment.

**EXHIBIT 16–32**
This award-winning point-of-purchase display plays an important role in the merchandising of SeaKlear pool and spa products

Another way manufacturers provide sales training assistance to retail employees is through their own sales force. Sales reps educate retail personnel about their product line and provide selling tips and other relevant information. The reps can provide ongoing sales training as they come into contact with retail sales staff members on a regular basis and can update them on changes in the product line, market developments, competitive information, and the like.

Manufacturers also give resellers detailed sales manuals, product brochures, reference manuals, and other material. Many companies provide DVDs or digital files for retail sales personnel that include product information, product-use demonstrations, and ideas on how to sell their product. These selling aids can often be used to provide information to customers as well.

**Trade Shows** Another important promotional activity targeted to resellers is the **trade show**, a forum where manufacturers can display their products to current as well as prospective buyers. According to the Center for Exhibition Industry Research, more than 100 million people attend the nearly 15,000 trade shows each year in the United States and Canada, and the number of exhibiting companies exceeds 1.3 million. In many industries, trade shows are a major opportunity to display one's product lines and interact with customers. They are often attended by important management personnel from large retail chains as well as by distributors and other reseller representatives.

A number of promotional functions can be performed at trade shows, including demonstrating products, identifying new prospects, gathering customer and competitive information, and even writing orders for a product. Trade shows are particularly valuable for introducing new products, because resellers are often looking for new merchandise to stock. Shows can also be a source of valuable leads to follow up on through sales calls or direct marketing. The social aspect of trade shows is also important. Many companies use them to entertain key customers and to develop and maintain relationships with the trade. An academic study demonstrated that trade shows generate product awareness and interest and can have a measurable economic return.[68] An example of a very high-profile trade show is the International Consumer Electronics Show (CES)® that is held in Las Vegas each January. The show is owned and produced by the Consumer Electronics Association (CEA)® and is often used as a platform for the announcement and release of new products such as computers, smartphones, HDTVs, and various other types of consumer electronic items. CES also receives extensive coverage from the media, which makes it a valuable promotional opportunity for markets launching new products. Exhibit 16–33 shows a picture from a recent CES.

**Cooperative Advertising** The final form of trade-oriented promotion we examine is **cooperative advertising**, where the cost of advertising is shared by more than one party. There are three types of cooperative advertising. Although the first two are not trade-oriented promotion, we should recognize their objectives and purpose. **Horizontal cooperative advertising** is advertising sponsored in common by a group of retailers or other organizations providing products or services to the market. For example, automobile dealers who are located near one another in an auto park or along the

**EXHIBIT 16–33**
The International CES is a very popular industry trade show

**EXHIBIT 16–34**
Qualcomm uses ingredient-sponsored advertising for its Snapdragon processor

YTC **16–03**

**Ingredient-Sponsored Advertising**
youtube.com/10ebelch

**EXHIBIT 16–35**
This Bridgestone Golf ad is an example of vertical cooperative advertising

same street often allocate some of their ad budgets to a cooperative advertising fund. Ads are run promoting the location of the dealerships and encouraging car buyers to take advantage of their close proximity when shopping for a new automobile.

**Ingredient-sponsored cooperative advertising** is supported by raw materials manufacturers; its objective is to help establish end products that include the company's materials and/or ingredients. Companies that often use this type of advertising include DuPont, which promotes the use of its materials such as Teflon and Kevlar; 3M, which promotes Thinsulate; and NutraSweet, whose artificial sweetener is an ingredient in many food products and beverages.

Perhaps the best-known, and most successful, example of this type of cooperative advertising is the "Intel Inside" program, sponsored by Intel Corporation, which the company has been using since 1991.[69] Under this program, computer manufacturers get back 5 percent of what they pay Intel for microprocessors in return for showing the "Intel Inside" logo in their advertising as well as on their PCs. The monies received from Intel must be applied to ads paid for jointly by the PC maker and Intel. Nearly 90 percent of the PC print ads run in the United States carry the "Intel Inside" logo, and the program has helped Intel grow its share of the microprocessor market from 56 percent in 1990 to nearly 80 percent. It is estimated that Intel spends several hundred million dollars each year on its cooperative advertising program. Intel recently made a significant change in the co-op program as companies that participate are now required to spend a minimum of 35 percent of the money that Intel provides on online marketing. The company made the mandated change in the media mix because its research shows that the major influences on consumers' purchasing decisions for personal computers come from some form of online media.[70]

Another technology company that uses ingredient-sponsored advertising is Qualcomm, which has been running a brand-building campaign for its Snapdragon processor that powers many smartphones and other mobile devices. The company runs ads in the United States and several other countries to promote the features and benefits of the Snapdragon processor and how it contributes to the performance of mobile devices. Exhibit 16–34 shows an ad for the Snapdragon processor.

The most common form of cooperative advertising is the trade-oriented form, **vertical cooperative advertising**, in which a manufacturer pays for a portion of the advertising a retailer runs to promote the manufacturer's product and its availability in the retailer's place of business. Manufacturers generally share the cost of advertising run by the retailer on a percentage basis (usually 50–50) up to a certain limit.

The amount of cooperative advertising the manufacturer pays for is usually based on a percentage of dollar purchases. If a retailer purchases $100,000 of product from a manufacturer, it may receive 3 percent, or $3,000, in cooperative advertising money. Large retail chains often combine their co-op budgets across all of their stores, which gives them a larger sum to work with and more media options.

Cooperative advertising can take several forms. Retailers may advertise a manufacturer's product in, say, a newspaper ad featuring a number of different products, and the individual manufacturers reimburse the retailer for their portion of the ad. Or the ad may be prepared by the manufacturer and placed in the local media by the retailer. Exhibit 16–35 shows a cooperative ad format for Bridgestone Golf that retailers in various market areas can use by simply inserting their store name and location.

Once a cooperative ad is run, the retailer requests reimbursement from the manufacturer for its percentage of the media costs. Manufacturers usually have specific requirements the ad must meet to qualify for co-op reimbursement, such as size, use of trademarks, content, and format. Verification that the ad was run is also required, in the form of a tearsheet (print) or an affidavit from the radio or TV station (broadcast) and an invoice.

As with other types of trade promotions, manufacturers have been increasing their cooperative advertising expenditures in recent years. Some companies have been moving money out of national advertising into cooperative advertising because they believe they can have greater impact with ad campaigns in local markets. There is also a trend toward more cooperative advertising programs initiated by retailers, which approach manufacturers with catalogs, promotional events they are planning, or advertising programs they have developed in conjunction with local media and ask them to pay a percentage of the cost. Manufacturers often go along with these requests, particularly when the retailer is large and powerful.[71]

# COORDINATING SALES PROMOTION WITH ADVERTISING AND OTHER IMC TOOLS

Those involved in the promotional process must recognize that sales promotion techniques usually work best in conjunction with advertising and other integrated marketing tools and that the effectiveness of an IMC campaign can be enhanced by consumer-oriented sales promotion efforts. Rather than separate activities competing for a firm's promotional budget, advertising and sales promotion should be viewed as complementary tools. When properly planned and executed to work together, advertising and sales promotion can have a *synergistic effect* much greater than that of either promotional mix element alone.

Proper coordination of sales promotion with other IMC tools is essential for the firm to take advantage of the opportunities offered by each and get the most out of its promotional budget. Successful integration of advertising and sales promotion requires decisions concerning not only the allocation of the budget to each area but also the coordination of the ad and sales promotion themes, proper media support for, and timing of, the various promotional activities, and the target audience reached.

## Budget Allocation

While many companies are spending more money on sales promotion than on media advertising, it is difficult to say just what percentage of a firm's overall promotional budget should be allocated to advertising versus consumer- and trade-oriented promotions. This allocation depends on a number of factors, including the specific promotional objectives of the campaign, the market and competitive situation, and the brand's stage in its life cycle.

Consider, for example, how allocation of the promotional budget may vary according to a brand's stage in the product life cycle. In the introductory stage, a large amount of the budget may be allocated to sales promotion techniques such as sampling and couponing to induce trial. In the growth stage, however, promotional dollars may be used primarily for advertising to stress brand differences and keep the brand name in consumers' minds.

When a brand moves to the maturity stage, advertising is primarily a reminder to keep consumers aware of the brand. Consumer-oriented sales promotions such as coupons, price-offs, premiums, and bonus packs may be needed periodically to maintain consumer loyalty, attract new users, and protect against competition. Trade-oriented promotions are needed to maintain shelf space and accommodate retailers' demands for better margins as well as them to promote the brand. A study on the synergistic effects of advertising and promotion examined a brand in the mature phase of its life cycle and found that 80 percent of its sales at this stage were due to sales promotions. When a brand enters the decline stage of the product life cycle, most of the promotional support will probably be removed and expenditures on sales promotion are unlikely.

## Coordination of Ad and Promotion Themes

To integrate the advertising and sales promotion programs successfully, the theme of consumer promotions should be tied in with the positioning platform for the company and/or their brand wherever possible. Sales promotion tools should attempt to communicate a brand's unique attributes or benefits and to reinforce the sales message or advertising campaign theme. In this way, the sales promotion effort contributes to the consumer franchise-building effort for the brand.

At the same time, media advertising and other IMC tools should be used to draw attention to a sales promotion program such as a contest, sweepstakes, or event or to a special promotion offer such as a price reduction or rebate program. An excellent example of this is the award-winning "Win 500 Flights" sweepstakes that was developed by MasterCard and its promotional agency, Armstrong Partnership. The sweepstakes was developed under the umbrella of MasterCard's "Priceless" campaign theme and thus was designed to deliver on the brand promise that MasterCard understands what matters most to consumers—in this case traveling for any reason at all. The primary objective of the integrated marketing campaign was to drive MasterCard use during the key summer travel season. Consumers using their MasterCard from July 1 to August 31 were automatically entered in the sweepstakes for a chance to win 500 airline tickets to anywhere that could be shared with family and friends. Media advertising including television, print, out-of-home, and online banner ads were used to promote the sweepstakes, along with an extensive public relations campaign. Exhibit 16–36 shows one of the print ads used to promote the "Win 500 Flights" sweepstakes.

**EXHIBIT 16–36**

MasterCard used media advertising to promote the "Win 500 Flights" sweepstakes

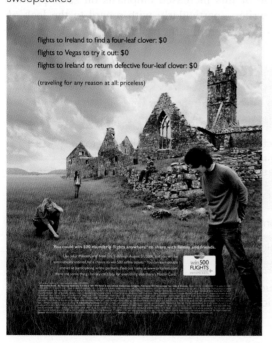

flights to Ireland to find a four-leaf clover: $0

flights to Vegas to try it out: $0

flights to Ireland to return defective four-leaf clover: $0

(traveling for any reason at all: priceless)

You could win 500 roundtrip flights anywhere™ to share with family and friends.

## Media Support and Timing

Media support for a sales promotion program is critical and should be coordinated with the media program for the ad campaign. Media advertising is often needed to deliver such sales promotion materials as coupons, sweepstakes, contest entry forms, premium offers, and even samples. It is also needed to inform consumers of a promotional offer as well as to create awareness, interest, and favorable attitudes toward the brand.

By using advertising in conjunction with a sales promotion program, marketers can make consumers aware of the brand and its benefits and increase their responsiveness to the promotion. Consumers are more likely to redeem a coupon or respond to a price-off deal for a brand they are familiar with than one they know nothing about. Moreover, product trial created through sales promotion techniques such as sampling or high-value couponing is more likely to result in long-term use of the brand when accompanied by advertising.[72]

Using a promotion without prior or concurrent advertising can limit its effectiveness and risk damaging the brand's image. If consumers perceive the brand as being promotion dependent or

**EXHIBIT 16–37**

Unilever coordinates the advertising and sales promotion for the Dove Men + Care line

of lesser quality, they are not likely to develop favorable attitudes and long-term loyalty. Conversely, the effectiveness of an ad can be enhanced by a coupon, a premium offer, or an opportunity to enter a sweepstakes or contest.

An example of the effective coordination of advertising and sales promotion is the introductory campaign Unilever developed for its Dove Men+Care line. Unilever sent samples of the body and face wash product to more than half the households in the United States along with high-value coupons and also used trade promotions targeted to retailers as part of its introductory marketing blitz. The sales promotion efforts were accompanied by heavy advertising in print and on television, including a commercial in the Super Bowl and a follow-up spot featuring New Orleans Saints quarterback Drew Brees, who won the game's MVP award, using the new product while showering.[73] The launch campaign included the use of additional IMC tools, including public relations, mobile marketing, and digital and social media. Unilever continues to coordinate advertising and sales promotion for the Dove Men + Care line with ads such as the one shown in Exhibit 16–37.

To coordinate their advertising and sales promotion programs more effectively, many companies are getting their sales promotion agencies more involved in the advertising and promotional planning process. Rather than hiring agencies to develop individual, nonfranchise-building types of promotions with short-term goals and tactics, many firms are having their sales promotion and advertising agencies work together to develop integrated promotional strategies and programs. Figure 16–7 shows how the role of promotional agencies is changing.

# SALES PROMOTION ABUSE

LO 16-5

The increasing use of sales promotion in marketing programs is more than a passing fad. It is a fundamental change in strategic decisions about how companies market their products and services. The value of this increased emphasis on sales promotion has been questioned by several writers, particularly with regard to the lack of adequate planning and management of sales promotion programs.[74]

| Traditional | New and Improved |
| --- | --- |
| 1. Primarily used to develop short-term tactics or concepts. | 1. Used to develop long- and short-term promotional strategies as well as tactics. |
| 2. Hired/compensated on a project-by-project basis. | 2. Contracted on annual retainer, following formal agency reviews. |
| 3. Many promotion agencies used a mix—each one hired for best task and/or specialty. | 3. One or two exclusive promotion agencies for each division or brand group. |
| 4. One or two contact people from agency. | 4. Full team or core group on the account. |
| 5. Promotion agency never equal to ad agency—doesn't work up front in annual planning process. | 5. Promotion agency works on equal basis with ad agency—sits at planning table up front. |
| 6. Not directly accountable for results. | 6. Very much accountable—goes through a rigorous evaluation process. |

**FIGURE 16–7**

The Shifting Role of the Promotion Agency

Are marketers becoming too dependent on this element of the marketing program? As was discussed earlier, consumer and trade promotions can be a very effective tool for generating short-term increases in sales, and many brand managers would rather use a promotion to produce immediate sales than invest in advertising and build the brand's image over an extended time. As the director of sales promotion services at one large ad agency noted: "There's a great temptation for quick sales fixes through promotions. It's a lot easier to offer the consumer an immediate price savings than to differentiate your product from a competitor's."[75]

Overuse of sales promotion can be detrimental to a brand in several ways. A brand that is constantly promoted may lose perceived value. Consumers often end up purchasing a brand because it is on sale, they get a premium, or they have a coupon, rather than basing their decision on a favorable attitude they have developed. When the extra promotional incentive is not available, they switch to another brand. A study by Priya Raghubir and Kim Corfman examined whether price promotions affect pretrial evaluations of a brand.[76] They found that offering a price promotion is more likely to lower a brand's evaluation when the brand has not been promoted previously compared to when it has been frequently promoted; that price promotions are used as a source of information about a brand to a greater extent when the evaluator is not an expert but does have some product or industry knowledge; and that promotions are more likely to result in negative evaluations when they are uncommon in the industry. The findings from this study suggest that marketers must be careful in the use of price promotions as they may inhibit trial of a brand in certain situations.

Alan Sawyer and Peter Dickson have used the concept of *attribution theory* to examine how sales promotion may affect consumer attitude formation.[77] According to this theory, people acquire attitudes by observing their own behavior and considering why they acted in a certain manner. Consumers who consistently purchase a brand because of a coupon or price-off deal may attribute their behavior to the external promotional incentive rather than to a favorable attitude toward the brand. By contrast, when no external incentive is available, consumers are more likely to attribute their purchase behavior to favorable underlying feelings about the brand.

Another potential problem with consumer-oriented promotions is that a **sales promotion trap** or spiral can result when several competitors use promotions extensively.[78] Often a firm begins using sales promotions to differentiate its product or service from the competition. If the promotion is successful and leads to a differential advantage (or even appears to do so), competitors may quickly copy it. When all the competitors are using sales promotions, this not only lowers profit margins for each firm but also makes it difficult for any one firm to hop off the promotional bandwagon.[79] This dilemma is shown in Figure 16–8.

A number of industries have fallen into this promotional trap. In the cosmetics industry, gift-with-purchase and purchase-with-purchase promotional offers were developed as a tactic for getting buyers to sample new products. But they have become a common, and costly, way of doing business.[80] In many areas of the country, supermarkets have gotten into the trap of doubling coupons, which cuts into their already small profit margins.

| All Other Firms | Our Firm | |
|---|---|---|
| | Cut back promotions | Maintain promotions |
| Cut back promotions | Higher profits for all | Market share goes to our firm |
| Maintain promotions | Market share goes to all other firms | Market share stays constant; profits stay low |

**FIGURE 16–8**

The Sales Promotion Trap

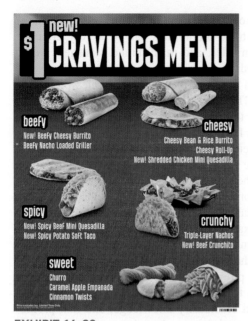

**EXHIBIT 16–38**

Taco Bell promotes its value menu

Fast-food chains have also fallen into the trap with promotions featuring popular menu items for 99 cents or one dollar. Fast-food companies such as McDonald's use their dollar menus to offer options to budget-conscious consumers and provide them with consistent everyday values. McDonald's has been ahead of many of its competitors in terms of promoting its value menu and has had popular items such as its double cheeseburger on the menu since its introduction in 2003. However, competitors such as Burger King and Wendy's have recently put popular items on their value meal menus in an effort to keep pace with the industry leader.[81] In 2013 Taco Bell introduced a "Cravings" value menu (Exhibit 16-38).

Marketers must consider both the short-term impact of a promotion and its long-term effect on the brand. The ease with which competitors can develop a retaliatory promotion and the likelihood of their doing so should also be considered. Marketers must be careful not to damage the brand franchise with sales promotions or to get the firm involved in a promotional war that erodes the brand's profit margins and threatens its long-term existence. Marketers are often tempted to resort to sales promotions to deal with declining sales and other problems when they should examine such other aspects of the marketing program as channel relations, price, packaging, product quality, or advertising.

After reading this chapter you can see that there are a number of factors that marketers must consider in developing and implementing effective sales promotion programs as they involve much more than just offering consumers an extra economic incentive to purchase a product. Priya Raghubir, Jeffrey Inman, and Hans Grande suggest that there are three aspects to consumer promotions, including economic, informative, and affective effects.[82] They note that in addition to economic effects, marketers must consider the information and signals a promotional offer conveys to the consumer as well as the affective influences. These include the consumer feelings and emotions aroused by exposure to a promotion or associated with purchasing the brand or company that is offering a deal. By considering all of these effects, managers can design and communicate consumer promotions more efficiently as well as more effectively.

## Summary

For many years, advertising was the major promotional-mix element for most consumer-product companies. Over the past two decades, however, marketers have been allocating more of their promotional dollars to sales promotion. There has been a steady increase in the use of sales promotion techniques to influence consumers' purchase behavior. The growing power of retailers, erosion of brand loyalty, increase in consumers' sensitivity to promotions, increase in new product introductions, fragmentation of the consumer market, short-term focus of marketing and brand managers, and increase in advertising clutter are some of the reasons for this increase.

Sales promotions can be characterized as either franchise building or nonfranchise building. The former contribute to the long-term development and reinforcement of brand identity and image; the latter are designed to accelerate the purchase process and generate immediate increases in sales.

Sales promotion techniques can be classified as either trade- or consumer-oriented. A number of consumer-oriented sales promotion techniques were examined in this chapter, including sampling, couponing, premiums, contests and sweepstakes, rebates and refunds, bonus packs, price-off deals, loyalty programs, and event marketing. The characteristics of these promotional tools were examined, along with their advantages and limitations. Various trade-oriented promotions were also examined, including trade contests and incentives, trade allowances, displays and point-of-purchase materials, sales training programs, trade shows, and cooperative advertising.

Advertising and sales promotion should be viewed not as separate activities but rather as complementary tools. When planned and executed properly, advertising and sales promotion can produce a synergistic effect that is greater than the response generated from either promotional-mix element alone. To accomplish this, marketers must coordinate budgets, advertising and promotional themes, media scheduling and timing, and target audiences.

Sales promotion abuse can result when marketers become too dependent on the use of sales promotion techniques and sacrifice long-term brand position and image for short-term sales increases. Many industries experience sales promotion traps when a number of competitors use promotions extensively and it becomes difficult for any single firm to cut back on promotion without risking a loss in sales. Overuse of sales promotion tools can lower profit margins and threaten the image and even the viability of a brand.

## Key Terms

## Discussion Questions

**1.** The chapter opener discusses the wide use of sales promotion tools by Telford International Company Limited (Telford) to promote new products. Do you expect customers to react negatively if Telford stops using sales promotion for its products? Suggest two more sales promotion activities that can be undertaken by Telford. Do you think the sales promotion campaign for the Tao Ti Pak Gor Yuen drinks should continue to use social media channels to reach the target market? (LO1)

**2.** Discuss the difference between consumer-oriented promotions and trade-oriented promotions and the role each plays in a marketer's IMC program. What are the various objectives for each category of sales promotion? (LO1,2,3)

**3.** What are some of the reasons marketing and brand managers are allocating more of their promotional budget to sales promotion rather than media advertising? Do you agree with critics who argue that the increased use of sales promotion is undermining brand equity for many once-powerful brands? (LO1)

**4.** Discuss how the Internet and the growing popularity of social media sites such as Facebook and Twitter are impacting marketers' use of sales promotion. (LO1,2)

**5.** What is the difference between a consumer franchise-building promotion and a nonfranchise-building promotion? Find an example of a promotion being used by a company that contributes to the equity of the brand and explain how it does so. (LO2)

**6.** IMC Perspective 16–1 discusses the Monopoly game contest McDonald's has adopted to promote its set meals in Hong Kong. Evaluate the effectiveness of this game as a consumer franchise-building promotion for McDonald's. (LO2)

**7.** Evaluate the effectiveness of coupons as a sales promotion tool. How would you respond to critics who argue that they are inefficient since less than 2 percent of coupons are redeemed? (LO3)

**8.** Discuss the type of company that would be likely to offer discounts to consumers using Groupon.com. What are the pros and cons of a company using this type of promotional offer? (LO3)

**9.** Discuss what marketers can do to avoid some of the promotional problems discussed in IMC Perspective 16–2. Do you think the problems that KFC experienced with its coupon promotion in China could have been avoided? (LO3)

**10.** A recent report by a rebate fulfillment service showed that the average redemption rate for a $50 rebate on a product that costs $200 is only 35 percent. Why do you think redemption rates for rebates are so low? How might these low redemption rates affect a marketer's decision regarding the use of rebates as a promotional tool? (LO3)

**11.** Discuss the various type of trade promotions used by marketers giving attention to the objectives as well as the pros and cons of each. (LO3)

**12.** What is meant by a sales promotion trap or spiral? Evaluate the promotional war that has developed in the fast-food industry as the various competitors promote their 99 cents or dollar menus. What are the options for companies in deciding whether to participate in the promotional war? (LO5)

## LEARNING OBJECTIVES

**LO1** To recognize the roles of public relations, publicity, and corporate advertising in the promotional mix.

**LO2** To know the difference between public relations and publicity and demonstrate the advantages and disadvantages of each.

**LO3** To understand the reasons for corporate advertising and its advantages and disadvantages.

**LO4** To know the methods for measuring the effects of public relations, publicity, and corporate advertising.

**LO5** To understand the different forms of corporate advertising.

# 17 Public Relations, Publicity, and Corporate Advertising

## HOI TIN TONG *GUILINGGAO* (OR TURTLE JELLY) SCANDALS

*Guilinggao* is a traditional Chinese health food. Commonly thought to be beneficial for skin health—particularly after repeated consumption—and muscle growth, its other supposed benefits include the ability to relieve itching, reduce acne, and improve blood circulation and kidney function. The common belief that it benefits the skin has made *guilinggao* a popular food among young women in Hong Kong.

Hoi Tin Tong, one of the chain stores selling *guilinggao*, has been successful in promoting it through heavy advertising and other sales promotion activities. It has also been successful at attracting customers through its online promotions. For example, in 2010, over 7,000 vouchers were sold through Groupon and sales increased to over 24,000 in two years.

Unfortunately, a series of adverse events hit Hoi Tin Tong in September 2013. A TV report aired in Huizhou, Guangdong (a province just north of Hong Kong), on September 11, 2013 showed an online video clip claiming that Hoi Tin Tong's *guilinggao* produced in Guangdong contained mold, and that the original pottery cups which held the jellies had been replaced by cheaper plastic cups for transport. The video had been viewed more than 10,000 times online before the TV report was aired.

In the video, workers in its outlets were shown cleaning mold off the *guilinggao* in pottery cups by washing them with tap water, and then boiling them for 30 minutes to kill the fungus. They were also shown using their bare hands to handle the *guilinggao* by moving the jellies from plastic to pottery cups. It has been claimed that *guilinggao* stored in pottery cups will stay fresher for a longer period of time and tastes better. A plastic cup of *guilinggao* was sold for HK$35 in Hong Kong (or RMB20 in Guangdong) while a pottery cup of *guilinggao* was sold for HK$50 (or RMB35 in Guangdong).

In the TV report, Choi Kwok Leung, who claimed to be a former senior staff of Hoi Tin Tong, admitted that he had posted the video online. He alleged that he disagreed with the production method of Hoi Tin Tong and had decided to expose it.

Hoi Tin Tong responded by holding two press conferences—one in Guangdong and the other in Hong Kong—on September 12, 2013. At the Hong Kong press conference, its founder, Ng Yiu Ming, denied any mold was found in its *guilinggao*. He also denied Hoi Tin Tong had used plastic cups. He called the video a fraud, as the steel tabletop featured in it was not found in any of Hoi Tin Tong outlets. He added that whenever the staff discover mold-contaminated jellies, the products would be discarded. He claimed that Hoi Tin Tong had been maligned, and that the company had lodged a report with the police over the matter.

Choi then confronted him with a white plastic cup and questioned if it belonged to Hoi Tin Tong, which Ng denied. It was only after Choi had shown journalists the minutes of a Hoi Ting Tong meeting—which disclosed more hygiene issues in the company's operations—that Ng finally admitted the white plastic cup did indeed belong to his company. However, he insisted that plastic cups were only used to carry out tests on the products. When told that some of Hoi Tin Tong's senior staff had admitted that the *guilinggao* for sale was transferred from plastic to pottery cups by workers using their bare hands, Ng replied that only a small portion of the product was involved.

At around the same time, another piece of bad news hit Hoi Tin Tong. A researcher from City University of Hong Kong had carried out a product test on the *guilinggao* produced by four companies, including Hoi Tin Tong, in August 2013. The researcher discovered that one Hoi Tin Tong sample did not contain turtle shell, a critical ingredient in *guilinggao*, while another two samples contained slight traces of it. In contrast, samples from the other three companies contained acceptable amounts of turtle shell.

Once again, Ng called a press conference to affirm that Hoi Tin Tong's products were indeed made from fresh turtle shell, and that was the reason why the test did not find any trace of it. His claim was dismissed by the researcher. Choi also insisted that Hoi Tin Tong did not use turtle shells because the company had failed to obtain approval to manufacture its health products in Huizhou. Due to stringent regulations, its plant in Huizhou did not dare use turtle shells to make its *guilinggao*. Later, the media reported that Hoi Tin Tong's operations in its Huizhou's plant were suspended in May 2013. After the scandals broke, many locals urged Hoi Tin Tong to make them a refund on their prepurchased *guilinggao* coupons.

Shortly after, the tide turned for Hoi Tin Tong. The Centre for Food Safety of Hong Kong took jelly samples from Hoi Tin Tong's outlets for testing. On September 17, 2013 Health Secretary Ko Wing Man announced that the Centre for Food Safety did not find any mold in the samples. Some Legislative Councillors in Hong Kong also supported Hoi Tin Tong (but their support might not have meant much as they had received contributions from Ng in their election campaigns). In October 2013, Hoi Tin Tong hired a biotechnology company to conduct tests to disprove claims that its *guilinggao* did not contain any turtle shell. The tests proved conclusive and the results were supported by customs officials who found it was present in the company's products.

In late December 2013 and early January 2014, Hoi Tin Tong embarked on a series of promotional campaigns to improve the company's image. A TV ad was launched showing Ng in conversation with a famous Hong Kong actor, Lo Hoi Pang, and reiterating that Hoi Tin Tong was "framed" in the September 2013 scandal. On January 10, 2014, Hoi Tin Tong launched a huge sales promotion when it gave away 100,000 cups of *guilinggao* and long queues were seen outside all its outlets. But *alas*, the event soon turned into a disaster when some recipients pointed out that the free gifts were produced in September 2013. It also did not help matters when footage of Lo using foul language in the TV ad was uploaded onto YouTube. Over 600,000 views and comments were posted online, mostly negative.

To complicate matters, Hoi Tin Tong *guilinggao* was shown to have replaced a critical ingredient, *tufuling* (土茯苓), with *xianfuling* (鲜茯苓). (The traditional meanings of the first two words of *guilinggao* are *turtle* and *tufuling*.) Some practitioners of Chinese medicine do not consider the latter to be as effective as the former, while others believe that it may even harm the health of consumers. Moreover, *xianfuling* is cheaper than *tufuling*. While Hoi Tin Tong did not call a press conference this time, Ng did release a brief statement in print ads apologizing to the locals with the words, "Sorry, I have not been clear in my words." In the eyes and expert opinion of several commentators and marketing practitioners, Hoi Tin Tong's crisis management was extremely poor and merited much more than just a terse statement of apology.

Sources: "Moldy *Guilinggao* Served to Guests after Washing and Re-steaming," *Apple Daily*, September 12, 2013; "Hoi Tin Tong Claims It Was Framed After Being Accused of Selling Moldy Paste," *Ming Pao*, September 12, 2013; "First, Moldy Jelly. Now It's Turtle Jelly—Minus the Turtle," *South China Morning Post*, September 13, 2013; "Power of Turtle Jelly Lies in Its Recipe: Hoi Tin Tong Founder," *South China Morning Post*, September 18, 2013; "Former Senior Official Confirms Hoi Tin Tong Sold Moldy *Guilinggao*," YouTube (2013), http://www.youtube.com/watch?v=LhDqc3RFPxA; "Hoi Tin Tong—Connecting with the Young," Groupon (2013), http://works.groupon.hk/en/case-studies/success-story2/; "Change in Hoi Tin Tong's Guilinggao Recipe Backfires," Apple Daily, January 10, 2014; "Hoi Tin Tong's Strike Back Backfires," Sky Post, January 27, 2014; "Hoi Tin Tong TV Ad," YouTube (2014), http://www.youtube.com/watch?v=2LL5u32VnhQ; "Foul Language in Hoi Tin Tong Ad," YouTube (2014), http://www.youtube.com/watch?v=uOTWy3CNvNA; "Guilinggao," Wikipedia (2014), http://en.wikipedia.org/wiki/Guilinggao.

LO 17-1

The opening vignette discusses the power of negative publicity. Negative publicity had an adverse effect on Hoi Tin Tong's sales and financial performance and it also hurts its image. A company must be careful in handling negative publicity. The misuse of positive publicity can also hurt a brand and/or a company. As you will see in this chapter, publicity is often out of the control of the marketer, but increasingly the management of publicity is being adopted as a marketing strategy. While attempts to generate positive publicity are nothing new, as these efforts increase, they signify changes in the public relations functions of companies and organizations. Although the importance and role of public relations in the IMC program may be argued, one thing is clear: The role of public relations in the communications program has changed. Like every other aspect of IMC, the public relations function has been changed by the Internet and other new media. Simply put, news travels faster and wider now for most companies and organizations. The role of public relations and the importance of managing publicity has taken an increased importance.

Publicity, public relations, and corporate advertising all have promotional program elements that may be of great benefit to marketers. They are integral parts of the overall promotional effort that must be managed and coordinated with the other elements of the promotional mix. However, these three tools do not always have the specific objectives of product and service promotion, nor do they always involve the same methods you have become accustomed to as you have read this text. Typically, these activities are designed more to change attitudes toward an organization or issue than to promote specific products or affect behaviors directly (though you will see that this role is changing in some organizations). This chapter explores the roles of public relations, publicity, and corporate advertising the advantages and disadvantages of each; and the process by which they are employed.

# PUBLIC RELATIONS

What is public relations? How does it differ from other elements of marketing discussed thus far? Perhaps a good starting point is to define what the term *public relations* has traditionally meant and then to introduce its new role.

## The Traditional Definition of PR

A variety of books define **public relations (PR)**, but perhaps the most comprehensive definition is that offered by the *Public Relations News* (the weekly newsletter of the industry):

> The management function which evaluates public attitudes, identifies the policies and procedures of an organization with the public interest, and executes a program of action (and communication) to earn public understanding and acceptance.[1]

Public relations is indeed a management function. The term *management* should be used in its broadest sense; it is not limited to business management but extends to other types of organizations, including nonprofit institutions.

In this definition, public relations requires a series of stages, including:

1. The determination and evaluation of public attitudes.
2. The identification of policies and procedures of an organization with a public interest.
3. The development and execution of a communications program designed to bring about public understanding and acceptance.

This process does not occur all at once. An effective public relations program continues over months or even years.

Finally, this definition reveals that public relations involves much more than activities designed to sell a product or service. The PR program may involve some of the promotional program elements previously discussed but use them in a different way. For example, companies may send press releases to announce new products or changes in the organization, companies may organize special events to create goodwill in the community, and companies may use advertising to state the firm's position on a controversial issue.

## The New Role of PR

An increasing number of marketing-oriented companies have established new responsibilities for public relations. In this new role PR takes on a much broader (and more marketing-oriented) perspective, designed to promote the organization as well as its products and/or services.

The way that companies and organizations use public relations might best be viewed as a continuum. On one end of the continuum is the use of PR from a traditional perspective. In this perspective, public relations is viewed as a nonmarketing function whose primary responsibility is to maintain mutually beneficial relationships between the organization and its publics. In this case, customers or potential customers are only part of numerous publics—employees, investors, neighbors, special-interest groups, and so on. Marketing and public relations are separate departments; if external agencies are used, they are separate agencies. At the other end of the continuum, public relations is considered primarily a marketing communications function. All noncustomer relationships are perceived as necessary only in a marketing context.[2] In these organizations, public relations reports to marketing. At the same time, for many companies the PR function is moving more and more toward a new role, which is much closer to a marketing function than a traditional one.

In the new role of public relations, managers envision both strong marketing and strong PR departments. Rather than each department operating independently, the two work closely together, blending their talents to provide the best overall image of the firm and its product or service offerings. As noted by Jonah Bloom, there has always been a cultural gulf separating the two departments, but today's information age demands the two camps work together. Bloom comments, "You'll struggle to peddle your eco-friendly detergent if your company is being slammed for pouring chemicals into a river."[3] In a poll conducted among members of the Public Relations Society of America (PRSA) and subscribers to *PR News,* 76 percent of respondents stated that they regularly work with the marketing department; 78 percent thought that the marketing department had a positive perception of the PR department, and an equal number indicated the same perception about marketing. While the degree of coordination differed by activity, the study clearly reflects coordination and cooperation.[4]

Writing in *Advertising Age,* William N. Curry notes that organizations must use caution in establishing this relationship because PR and marketing are not the same thing, and when one department becomes dominant, the balance required to operate at maximum efficiency is lost.[5] He says losing sight of the objectives and functions of public relations in an attempt to achieve marketing goals may be detrimental in the long run. Others take an even stronger view that if public relations and marketing distinctions continue to blur, the independence of the PR function will be lost, and it will become much less effective.[6] In fact, as noted by Cutlip and Center, marketing and public relations are complementary functions, "with each making unique but complementary contributions to building and maintaining the many relationships essential for organizational survival and growth. To ignore one is to risk failure in the other."[7] This position is consistent with our perception that public relations is an important part of the IMC process, contributing in its own way but also in a way consistent with marketing goals.

## Integrating PR into the Promotional Mix

Given the broader responsibilities of public relations, the issue is how to integrate it into the promotional mix. Companies have a number of ways in which they organize the marketing and public relations functions. Others may outsource the public relations to outside agencies. In this text we regard public relations as an IMC program element. This means that its broad role must include traditional responsibilities, as well as new ones.

Whether public relations takes on a traditional role or a more marketing-oriented one, PR activities are still tied to specific communications objectives. Assessing public attitudes and creating a favorable corporate image are no less important than promoting products or services directly.

## Marketing Public Relations Functions

Thomas L. Harris has referred to public relations activities designed to support marketing objectives as **marketing public relations (MPR)** functions.[8] Marketing objectives that may be aided by public relations activities include raising awareness, informing and educating, gaining understanding, building trust, giving consumers a reason to buy, and motivating consumer acceptance. MPR adds value to the integrated marketing program in a number of ways:

- *Building marketplace excitement before media advertising breaks.* The announcement of a new product, for example, is an opportunity for the marketer to obtain publicity and to dramatize the product, thereby increasing the effectiveness of ads. When Apple introduces any new product from the iPod to the iPad, a great deal of anticipation is created through public relations prior to the availability of the product. The result is that Apple receives a great deal of press coverage and word of mouth. It seems that upon release of any Apple product, consumers wait in lines—sometime for hours—to be the first to own the next innovation.
- *Improving ROI.* By reducing overall marketing costs, while at the same time delivering meaningful marketing outcomes, MPR helps improve ROI.
- *Creating advertising news where there is no product news.* Ads themselves can be the focus of publicity. There seems to be as much hype about the ads on the Super Bowl as there is for the game itself. TV commercials frequently find their ways to social sites on the Internet, where they are viewed time and time again and forwarded to others. (Remember the Kmart commercials in Chapter 15?)
- *Introducing a product with little or no advertising.* This strategy has been implemented successfully by a number of companies, including Hewlett-Packard, Segway, Ty, Crayola, and, of course, Apple. Among others, Gillette uses PR as the lead medium in every new product launch.
- *Providing a value-added customer service.* Butterball established a hotline where people can call in to receive personal advice on how to prepare their turkeys. The company handled 25,000 calls during the first holiday season. Many companies provide such services on their Internet sites. Chicken of the Sea provides recipes to visitors to its site (which, of course, suggest using Chicken of the Sea tuna).
- *Building brand-to-customer bonds.* The Pillsbury Bake-Off has led to strong brand loyalty among Pillsbury customers, who compete by submitting baked goods. The contest has taken place annually since 1949, and the winner now receives a $1 million prize! The winning recipes are posted on the Pillsbury website. Competitor Betty Crocker has used branded video to reach its MPR objectives and also has a helpful website (Exhibit 17–1).
- *Influencing the influentials.* That is, providing information to opinion leaders.
- *Defending products at risk and giving consumers a reason to buy.* By taking constructive actions to defend or promote a company's products, PR can actually give consumers a reason to buy the products. Energizer's national education campaign that urged consumers to change the batteries in their fire alarms when they reset their clocks in the fall resulted in a strong corporate citizen image and increased sales of batteries. Cessna's campaign to convince executives that there are legitimate reasons to buy corporate jets (Exhibit 17–2) is an excellent example of defending a product at risk. Figure 17–1 shows a few more examples.

As shown in Figure 17–2, Harris notes that there are a number of advantages of using MPRs.

One of the major threats of using an MPR structure, as expressed by Harris, is that public relations functions may become subservient to marketing efforts—a concern expressed by many opponents of MPR. However, if employed properly and used in conjunction with other traditional public relations practices as well as IMC elements, MPR can continue to be used effectively. Weiner also notes that the key to the successful use of MPRs is integration with IMC, though such a task may prove to be difficult to accomplish.

**EXHIBIT 17–1**
Betty Crocker's website is designed to create goodwill

CHAPTER 17

During the auto industry sales slump in 2009, top executives of Detroit's Big Three car companies went to the nation's capital to ask for a bailout. When the execs traveled on a $50 million private plane rather than drive, the lawmakers and press bashed them for it. Unfortunately, the backlash had a profound negative effect on jet manufacturers, as numerous orders were canceled or deferred. Production was cut by as much as 56 percent, and as much as one-third of the industry's workers were laid off. One company, Cessna, decided to fight back and give corporate America a reason to buy.

In a hard-hitting print campaign starting in *The Wall Street Journal* called "Rise," Cessna challenged business leaders to not be timid, and recognize private planes are not about ego, but about having the right tools to be productive. Cessna said it was time for the other side of the story to be told. In addition to *The Wall Street Journal*, the ads were run in national business newspapers and magazines as well as aviation trade journals, together with an extensive PR campaign. Four years later Cessna was still receiving requests for reprints of the ads, and sales were on the increase.

*Betty Crocker*

Faced with the objective of getting more cake bakers to visit its website, Betty Crocker worked with digital video agency Touchstorm to create a series of informational videos targeted to mothers who bake their children's birthday cakes. Analyzing search terms, the two determined that when mothers want information or help in baking cakes, they don't search on brand names, but rather on specific solution terms like "birthday cake." Given this information, a series of high-quality HD videos approximately five minutes in length were created and posted on the Betty Crocker website. To convey the idea that the videos were instructional and not promotional, there was little reference to the Betty Crocker brand. The videos were very engaging, with an average of 75 percent of the content being watched. To date, the videos have driven over 70 million visitors to the website and, more important, are building brand loyalty due to their instructional nature.

*Chrysler*

Chrysler's "Halftime in America" two-minute commercial shown on the Super Bowl raised both controversy and success for the American automaker. The emotional ad, featuring actor Clint Eastwood, had almost nothing to do with selling cars, but rather called for Americans to come together, putting aside politics and act as one for the betterment of the nation. Almost immediately, the ad became talk-show fodder with Republican commentator Karl Rove accusing Chrysler and Eastwood of supporting President Obama's reelection campaign (even though Eastwood is a Republican!). Chrysler's chief marketing officer denied any such intent, saying he was surprised at the controversy and claiming there was "zero political message" intent. Regardless, the single showing on TV led to more than 5 million views on YouTube, a 27 percent rise in consumers searching for information about Chrysler online while maintaining a 23 percent increase over the next few days. As noted by advertising professor John Durham at the University of San Francisco, "Chrysler and its dealers have to be in heaven right now."

**FIGURE 17–1**

Companies Use MPRs

**FIGURE 17–2**

Advantages and Disadvantages of MPRs

> **YTC** 17–01
>
> **Halftime in America**
> youtube.com/10ebelch

| Advantages |
| --- |
| ■ It is a cost-effective way to reach the market. |
| ■ It is a highly targeted way to conduct public relations. |
| ■ It benefits from the endorsement of independent and objective third parties who have no association with the product. |
| ■ It achieves credibility. |
| ■ It supports advertising programs by making messages more credible. |
| ■ It breaks through the clutter. |
| ■ It circumvents consumer resistance to sales efforts. |
| ■ There can be improved media involvement among consumers. |
| ■ It can create influence among opinion leaders and trendsetters. |
| ■ It can improve ROI. |

| Disadvantages |
| --- |
| ■ There is a lack of control over the media. |
| ■ It is difficult to tie in slogans and other advertising devices. |
| ■ Media time and space are not guaranteed. |
| ■ There are no standard effectiveness measures. |

Sources: Thomas L. Harris, "Marketing PR—The Second Century," *Reputation Management*, www.prcentral.com, January/February 1999, pp. 1–6.

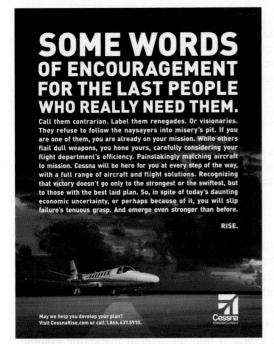

**EXHIBIT 17–2**

Cessna attempts to aid a product at risk

**EXHIBIT 17–3**

Netflix gained favor with an e-mail and personal letter explaining its actions to customers

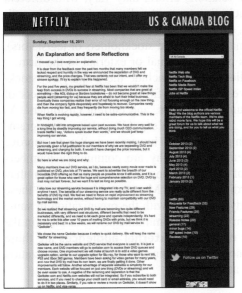

# THE PROCESS OF PUBLIC RELATIONS

The actual process of conducting public relations and integrating it into the promotional mix involves a series of both traditional and marketing-oriented tasks.

## Determining and Evaluating Public Attitudes

You have learned that public relations is concerned with people's attitudes toward the firm or specific issues beyond those directed at a product or service. The first question you may ask is why. Why is the firm so concerned with the public's attitudes?

One reason is that these attitudes may affect sales of the firm's products. A number of companies have experienced sales declines as a result of consumer boycotts. BP, Nestlé, Nokia, and Walmart are just a few companies that have had to respond to organized pressures. Likewise, the media must be concerned with the attitudes of the public. When *Fox News,* which is owned by News Corp, announced that it would air an interview with O. J. Simpson during sweeps titled "O. J. Simpson: If I Did It, Here's How It Happened" (in regard to accusations that he murdered his wife), a number of Fox affiliates immediately announced they would not carry the program, and media salespersons refused to sell advertising time. In addition, thousands of irate TV watchers e-mailed and phoned local Fox affiliates, as well as News Corp, causing them to pull the program in spite of an estimated loss of $10 million in revenue.[9]

On the other hand, companies can gain favorable impressions and positive attitudes from consumers by doing the right thing. Exhibit 17–3 shows a message sent by Netflix.com as an explanation for changing its product offerings and prices. The apology was used as an example of great customer service by bloggers and created positive attitudes for Netflix.

Second, no one wants to be perceived as a bad citizen. Corporations exist in communities, and their employees generally both work and live there. Negative attitudes carry over to employee morale and may result in a less-than-optimal working environment internally and in the community.

Due to their concerns about public perceptions, many privately held corporations, publicly held companies, utilities, and media survey public attitudes. The reasons for conducting this research are many, but include the following:

1. *It provides input into the planning process.* Once the firm has determined public attitudes, they become the starting point in the development of programs designed to maintain favorable positions or change unfavorable ones.
2. *It serves as an early warning system.* Once a problem exists, it may require substantial time and money to correct. By conducting research, the firm may be able to identify potential problems and handle them effectively before they become serious issues.
3. *It secures support internally.* If research shows a problem or potential problem exists, it will be much easier for the public relations arm to gain the support it needs to address this problem.
4. *It increases the effectiveness of the communication.* The better it understands a problem, the better the firm can design communications to deal with it.

## Establishing a PR Plan

For some companies, their PR programs involve little more than press releases, press kits for trade shows, and new product announcements.

CHAPTER 17

**FIGURE 17–3**

Ten Questions for
Evaluating Public
Relations Plans

1. Does the plan reflect a thorough understanding of the company's business situation?
2. Has the PR program made good use of research and background sources?
3. Does the plan include full analysis of recent editorial coverage?
4. Do the PR people fully understand the product's strengths and weaknesses?
5. Does the PR program describe several cogent, relevant conclusions from the research?
6. Are the program objectives specific and measurable?
7. Does the program clearly describe what the PR activity will be and how it will benefit the company?
8. Does the program describe how its results will be measured?
9. Do the research, objectives, activities, and evaluations tie together?
10. Has the PR department communicated with marketing throughout the development of the program?

Further, these tools are often not designed into a formal public relations effort but rather are used only as needed. In other words, no structured program for conducting PR is evident. As we noted earlier, the public relations process is an ongoing one, requiring formalized policies and procedures for dealing with problems and opportunities. Just as you would not develop an advertising and/or a promotions program without a plan, you should not institute public relations efforts haphazardly. Moreover, the PR plan needs to be integrated into the overall marketing communications program. Figure 17–3 provides some questions marketers should ask to determine whether their PR plan is workable.

Cutlip and Center suggest a four-step process for developing a public relations plan: (1) define public relations problems, (2) plan and program, (3) take action and communicate, and (4) evaluate the program.[10] The questions in Figure 17–3 and the four-step planning process tie in with the promotional planning process stressed throughout this text.

**EXHIBIT 17–4**

An example of a
newsletter used for
internal communication
by the College of Business
Administration at San Diego
State University

## Developing and Executing the PR Program

Because of the broad role that public relations may be asked to play, the PR program may need to extend beyond promotion. A broader definition of the target market, additional communications objectives, and different messages and delivery systems may be employed. Let us examine this process.

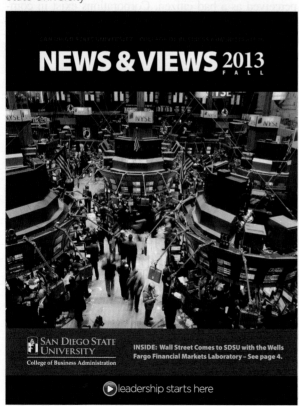

**Determining Relevant Target Audiences**   The targets of public relations efforts may vary, with different objectives for each. Some may be directly involved in selling the product; others may affect the firm in a different way (e.g., they may be aimed at stockholders or legislators). These audiences may be internal or external to the firm.

**Internal audiences** may include the employees, stockholders, and investors of the firm as well as members of the local community, suppliers, and current customers. As noted in Figure 17–1, Cessna's public relations programs were designed, in part, to reach buyers as well as to improve morale among employees. Why are community members and customers of the firm considered internal rather than external? According to John Marston, it's because these groups are already connected with the organization in some way, and the firm normally communicates with them in the ordinary routine of work.[11] **External audiences** are those people who are not closely connected with the organization (e.g., the public at large).

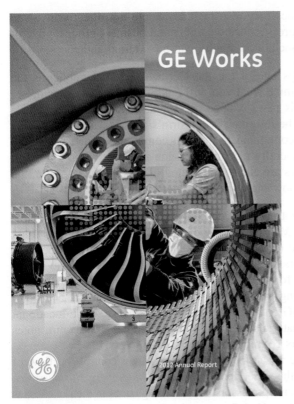

GE Works

2012 Annual Report

**EXHIBIT 17–5**

Annual reports serve a variety of purposes

**EXHIBIT 17–6**

Citgo demonstrates concern for the community

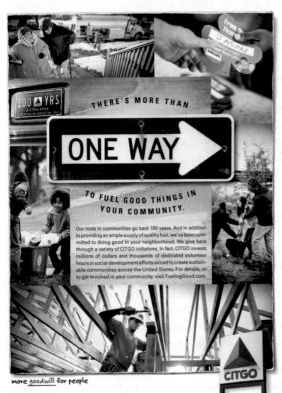

THERE'S MORE THAN

ONE WAY ➡

TO FUEL GOOD THINGS IN YOUR COMMUNITY.

Our roots in communities go back 100 years. And in addition to providing an ample supply of quality fuel, we've been committed to doing good in your neighborhood. We give back through a variety of CITGO initiatives. In fact, CITGO invests millions of dollars and thousands of dedicated volunteer hours in social development efforts aimed to create sustainable communities across the United States. For details, or to get involved in your community, visit FuelingGood.com.

*more goodwill for people*

CITGO

It may be necessary to communicate with these groups on an ongoing basis for a variety of reasons, ranging from ensuring goodwill to introducing new policies, procedures, or even products. A few examples may help.

**Employees of the Firm** Maintaining morale and showcasing the results of employees' efforts are often prime objectives of the public relations program. Organizational newsletters, notices on bulletin boards, awards ceremonies and events, direct mail, and annual reports are some of the methods used to communicate with these groups. Exhibit 17–4 shows one such internal communication used by the College of Business Administration at San Diego State University.

Personal methods of communicating may be as formal as an established grievance committee or as informal as an office Christmas party. Other social events, such as corporate bowling teams or picnics, are also used to create goodwill.

**Stockholders and Investors** You may think an annual report like the one in Exhibit 17–5 provides stockholders and investors only with financial information regarding the firm. While this is one purpose, annual reports are also a communications channel for informing this audience about why the firm is or is not doing well, outlining future plans, and providing other information that goes beyond numbers.

It has become very common for companies to use annual reports for public relations purposes—to generate additional investments, to bring more of their stocks "back home" (i.e., become more locally controlled and managed), and to produce funding to solve specific problems, as well as to promote goodwill.

**Community Members** People who live and work in the community where a firm is located or doing business are often the target of public relations efforts. Such efforts may involve ads informing the community of activities that the organization is engaged in, for example, reducing air pollution, cleaning up water supplies, or preserving wetlands. (The community can be defined very broadly.) As you can see in Exhibit 17–6, a number of oil companies are involved in this form of public relations by demonstrating to people that the organization is a good citizen with their welfare in mind.

**Suppliers and Customers** An organization wishes to maintain *goodwill* with its suppliers as well as its consuming public. If consumers think a company is not socially conscious, they may take their loyalties elsewhere. Suppliers may be inclined to do the same.

Sometimes sponsoring a public relations effort results in direct evidence of success. Certainly Betty Crocker achieved its goal of getting consumers to the website and getting engaged with the brand. Indirect indications of the success of PR efforts may include more customer loyalty, less antagonism, or greater cooperation between the firm and its suppliers or consumers.

Public relations efforts are often targeted to more than one group and are a direct result of concerns initiated in the marketplace. As noted earlier, along with potential consumers, trade association members, human resource directors, buyers, and suppliers often constitute the target audience for PR efforts.

Relevant audiences may also include people not directly involved with the firm. The press, educators, civic and business groups, governments, and the financial community can be external audiences.

**The Media** Perhaps one of the most critical external publics is the media, which determine what you will read in your newspapers or see on TV and how this news will be presented. Because of the media's power, they should be informed of the firm's actions. Companies issue press releases and communicate through conferences, interviews, and special events. The media are generally receptive to such information as long as it is handled professionally; reporters are always interested in good stories. In turn, the media are also concerned about how the community perceives them.

**Educators** A number of organizations provide educators with information regarding their activities. The Direct Marketing Association (DMA), the Promotional Products Association International (PPAI), and the Outdoor Advertising Association of America (OAAA), among others, keep educators informed in an attempt to generate goodwill as well as exposure for their causes. These groups and major corporations provide information regarding innovations, state-of-the-art research, and other items of interest. Marketing EDGE (formerly The Direct Marketing Educational Foundation (DMEF)) provides materials including case examples and lecture notes specifically designed for educators (Exhibit 17–7).

Educators are a target audience because, like the media, they control the flow of information to certain parties—in this case, people like you. *Bloomberg Businessweek* and *Fortune* magazines attempt to have professors use their magazines in their classes, as does *The Wall Street Journal, The New York Times,* and *Advertising Age,* among others. In addition to selling more magazines, such usage also lends credibility to the medium.

**Civic and Business Organizations** The local Jaycees, Kiwanis, and other nonprofit civic organizations also serve as gatekeepers of information. Companies' financial contributions to these groups, speeches at organization functions, and sponsorships are all designed to create goodwill. Corporate executives' service on the boards of nonprofit organizations also generates positive public relations.

**Governments** Public relations often attempts to influence government bodies directly at both local and national levels. Successful lobbying may mean immediate success for a product, while regulations detrimental to the firm may cost it millions. Imagine for a moment what FDA approval of a product can mean for sales, or what could happen to the beer and wine industries if TV advertising were banned. The pharmaceutical industry lobbied hard for permission to advertise prescription drugs directly to the consumer. Within the first five years of approval, an estimated 65 million consumers approached their doctors to inquire about the drugs as a result.[12] In turn, environmentalists, trade unions, and other groups with specific agendas will attempt to influence government legislation in their behalf.

**Financial Groups** In addition to current shareholders, potential shareholders and investors may be relevant target markets for PR efforts. Financial advisors, lending institutions, and others must be kept abreast of new developments as well as of financial information, since they offer the potential for new sources of funding. Press releases and corporate reports play an important role in providing information to these publics.

## Implementing the PR Program
Once the research has been conducted and the target audiences identified, the public relations program must be developed and delivered to the receivers. A number of PR tools are available for this purpose, including press releases, press conferences, exclusives, interviews, and community involvement.

**The Press Release** One of the most important publics is the press. To be used by the press, information must be factual, true, and of interest to the medium as well as to its audience. The source of the **press release** can do certain things to improve

News Release                                          April 22, 2013
                                                          No 35/13

*Tennis idol to become brand ambassador of the Stuttgart sports car manufacturer*

**Maria Sharapova to represent Porsche**

**Stuttgart**. Tennis megastar Maria Sharapova has taken on a new role: effective immediately, the 26-year-old world class player will be representing the sports car manufacturer, Porsche AG, as brand ambassador. The cooperation is initially signed for three years and involves a global communications campaign. The athlete is already very familiar with the vehicles from Zuffenhausen: as last year's winner of the Porsche Tennis Grand Prix in Stuttgart, Sharapova not only took home prize money, but also a white 911 Carrera S Cabriolet.

Born in Russia and living in the United States, Sharapova has achieved victories at all four Grand Slam tournaments in women's tennis and she was ranked number 1 for a total of 21 weeks.

"Maria Sharapova is an exceptional athlete. She combines top performance in her sports with elegance and power. These are precisely the qualities that are embroiled in our sports cars", as Matthias Mueller, CEO of Porsche AG, explained in today's introduction of the partnership. According to Mueller it was not easy to find the right person to be Porsche's ambassador. "Maria Sharapova is the perfect choice. Her profile and charisma are an ideal fit for Porsche. She is also highly respected around the world and enjoys an outstanding reputation."

| Porsche Cars North America, Inc. | 1 of 3 | Public Relations Department |
| 980 Hammond Drive, Suite 1000 | | Product Communications |
| Atlanta, GA 30328 USA | | Nick Twork |
| | | Phone +1.678.323.6975 |
| | | nick.twork@porsche.us |

**EXHIBIT 17–8**

Porsche press release

**EXHIBIT 17–9**

Lacrosse star Paul Rabil's foundation, gives back to the community

the likelihood that the "news" will be disseminated, such as ensuring that it reaches the right target audience, making it interesting, and making it easy to pass along (Exhibit 17–8).

The information in a press release won't be used unless it is of interest to the users of the medium it is sent to. For example, financial institutions may issue press releases to business trade media and to the editor of the business section of a general-interest newspaper. Organizations like the PRNewswire and PRLog.org provide services to help disseminate information.

**Press Conferences** We are all familiar with **press conferences** held by political figures. Although used less often by organizations and corporations, this form of delivery can be very effective. The topic must be of major interest to a specific group before it is likely to gain coverage. Usually major accomplishments (such as the awarding of the next Super Bowl or Olympics location), major breakthroughs (such as medical cures), emergencies, or catastrophes warrant a national press conference. On a local level, community events, local developments, and the like, may receive coverage. Companies often call press conferences when they have significant news to announce, such as the introduction of a new product or advertising campaign. Sports teams use this tool to attract fan attention and interest when a new star is signed.

**Exclusives** Although most public relations efforts seek a variety of channels for distribution, an alternative strategy is to offer one particular medium exclusive rights to the story if that medium reaches a substantial number of people in the target audience. Offering an **exclusive** may enhance the likelihood of acceptance. As you watch television over the next few weeks, watch for the various networks' and local stations' exclusives. Notice how the media actually use these exclusives to promote themselves.

**Interviews** When you watch TV or read magazines, pay close attention to the personal interviews. Usually someone will raise specific questions, and a spokesperson provided by the firm will answer them. Depending on how significant the issue is, sometimes even top management will get involved. When consumers protested Chick-fil-A's support of antigay Christian organizations, the president, Dan Cahy, stood by his decision in an interview with *The Baptist Press* newspaper.

**Community Involvement** Many companies and individuals enhance their public image through involvement in the local community. This involvement may take many forms, including membership in local organizations like the Kiwanis or Jaycees and contributions to or participation in community events (Exhibit 17–9).

**EXHIBIT 17–10**
Wawanesa Insurance promotes its J.D. Power Award

**The Internet** As discussed in Chapter 15, the Internet has become a means by which companies and organizations can disseminate public relations information. Just as in the print media, companies have used the Web to establish media relations and government, investor, and community relationships; to deal with crises; and even to conduct cause marketing. Companies have used their websites to address issues, as well as to provide information about products and services, archive press releases, link to other articles and sites, and provide lists of activities and events.

**Social Networks and Blogs** More and more companies and organizations are making use of social networks, blogs, and other Web 2.0 media (discussed in Chapter 15) for public relations purposes. It is now expected that companies will post information on their websites providing announcements and updates on product releases, recalls, or other issues. In addition, many of these companies are using 2.0 media to disseminate this information as well. NIVEA made valuable use of blogs, Facebook, Twitter, and other social media when some media accused it of running a racist ad. The company employed these media to apologize for the ad and to let consumers know it did not mean to offend anyone.[13]

An offensive rape scene ad to be run by Belvedere Vodka was pulled in just over one hour after consumer outrage over the ad went viral.[14] At the same time, these new media have required that the public relations functions for their organizations be constantly updated. Within hours after the release of the iPhone 4, information was circulating in regard to technical issues that led to dropped calls. The blogosphere was alive with information, requests, and proposals for solutions and even accusations that Apple knew about the problem before the phone's release.[15] In another instance, a mother reported a problem with Capri Sun to the manufacturer, Kraft Foods. When she did not receive a response after 10 days, she posted an account of her story on Kraft's Facebook page. In the seven hours it took Kraft to respond (an eternity in social media time!) Kraft was overwhelmed with negative comments, rumors, and even conspiracy theories about the cause of the problem, as well as Kraft's lack of response. The problem was subsequently addressed, but the public relations problem is reflective of how quickly these issues can occur in today's viral world.[16]

## Advantages and Disadvantages of PR

Like the other program elements, public relations has both advantages and disadvantages. Advantages include the following:

1. *Credibility*. Because public relations communications are not perceived in the same light as advertising—that is, the public does not realize the organization either directly or indirectly paid for them—they tend to have more credibility. The fact that the media are not being compensated for providing the information may lead receivers to consider the news more truthful and credible. For example, an article in newspapers or magazines discussing the virtues of aspirin may be perceived as much more credible than an ad for a particular brand of aspirin.

   Automotive awards presented in magazines such as *Motor Trend* have long been known to carry clout with potential car buyers. The influential J.D. Power awards are now offered for a variety of reasons (quality, customer satisfaction, service, etc.) in a variety of industries (automobile, financial services, airports, etc.). It has become a common practice for car companies and others to promote their achievements (Exhibit 17–10).

**EXHIBIT 17–11**

General Mills capitalizes on positive publicity

News about a product may in itself serve as the subject of an ad. Exhibit 17–11 demonstrates how General Mills used favorable publicity from a variety of sources to promote the importance of whole grain in a healthy diet and promote the use of whole grain in its cereals. Note that every cereal box prominently displays the whole-gain ingredients.

2. *Cost.* In both absolute and relative terms, the cost of public relations is very low, especially when the possible effects are considered. While a firm can employ public relations agencies and spend millions of dollars on PR, for smaller companies this form of communication may be the most affordable alternative available. As noted, many services exist to distribute this information at little or no cost. Many public relations programs require little more than the time and expenses associated with putting the program together and getting it distributed, yet they still accomplish their objectives.

3. *Avoidance of clutter.* Because they are typically perceived as news items, public relations messages are not subject to the clutter of ads. A story regarding a new product introduction or breakthrough is treated as a news item and is likely to receive attention.

4. *Lead generation.* Information about technological innovations, medical breakthroughs, and the like, results almost immediately in a multitude of inquiries. These inquiries may give the firm some quality sales leads.

5. *Ability to reach specific groups.* Because some products appeal to only small market segments, it is not feasible to engage in advertising and/or promotions to reach them. If the firm does not have the financial capabilities to engage in promotional expenditures, the best way to communicate to these groups is through public relations. Social networks and blogs have become extremely valuable in this regard.

6. *Image building.* Effective public relations helps develop a positive image for the organization. A strong image is insurance against later misfortunes. The strength of the Toyota brand name made it possible for Toyota to get through a series of crises involving mechanical problems.

Perhaps the major disadvantage of public relations is the potential for not completing the communications process. While public relations messages can break through the clutter of commercials, the receiver may not make the connection to the source. Many firms' PR efforts are never associated with their sponsors in the public mind.

Public relations may also misfire through mismanagement and a lack of coordination with the marketing department. When marketing and PR departments operate independently, there is a danger of inconsistent communications, redundancies in efforts, and so on.

The key to effective public relations is to establish a good program, worthy of public interest, and to manage it properly. To determine if this program is working, the firm must measure the effectiveness of the PR effort.

LO 17-4

## Measuring the Effectiveness of PR

As with the other promotional program elements, it is important to evaluate the effectiveness of the public relations efforts. In addition to determining the contribution of

**FIGURE 17–4**

Criteria for Measuring the
Effectiveness of PR

A system for measuring the effectiveness of the public relations program has been developed by Lotus HAL. The criteria used in the evaluation process follow:

- Total number of impressions over time
- Total number of impressions on the target audience
- Total number of impressions on specific target audiences
- Percentage of positive articles over time
- Percentage of negative articles over time
- Ratio of positive to negative articles
- Percentage of positive/negative articles by subject
- Percentage of positive/negative articles by publication or reporter
- Percentage of positive/negative articles by target audience

this program element to attaining communications objectives, the evaluation offers other advantages:

1. It tells management what has been achieved through public relations activities.
2. It provides management with a way to measure public relations achievements quantitatively.
3. It gives management a way to judge the quality of public relations achievements and activities.

As outlined in Figure 17–4 a number of criteria may be used to measure the effects of PR programs. Walter Lindenmann recommends that in measuring the effectiveness of a public relations campaign, one should consider whether the target audience (1) *received* the messages, (2) paid *attention* to them, (3) *understood* the messages, and (4) *retained* the messages in any shape or form.[17] Figure 17–5 shows the results of a study conducted in an attempt to determine how public relations professionals currently go about this process. (Note that the study was conducted in the EU, but as the authors indicate, the results may be generalized to the United States, the UK, and other developed countries because a similar usage pattern exists.)[18] Take a minute or two to examine the results of this study in respect to the criteria suggested by Lindenmann.

Mark Weiner, in discussing measures of effectiveness of MPRs, also suggests using the following methods:[19]

- *Media content analysis.* Systematically and objectively identifying the characteristics of messages that appear in the media, analyzing the content to determine trends and perceptions relevant to the product or brand.
- *Survey research.* Quantitatively assessing consumers' attitudes toward the product or brand.
- *Marketing-mix modeling.* Drawing data from multiple sources and integrating them to provide insight into the process.

In summary, the role of public relations in the promotional mix is changing. As PR has become more marketing oriented, the criteria by which the programs are evaluated have also changed. At the same time, nonmarketing activities will continue to be part of the public relations department and part of the basis for evaluation.

# PUBLICITY

**Publicity** refers to the generation of news about a person, product, or service that appears in broadcast or print media. To many marketers, publicity and public relations are synonymous. In fact, publicity is really a subset of the public relations effort.

But there are several major differences. First, publicity is typically a *short-term* strategy, while public relations is a concerted program extending over a period of time. Second, public relations is designed to provide positive information about

**FIGURE 17–5**  PR Measurement and Evaluation Tools: Frequency of Use and Perceived Effectiveness.

| PR measurement and evaluation tools | How often your organization has used the evaluation technique* | How effective in evaluating the impact of a PR programme is |
|---|---|---|
| Correlation between PR-related changes in coverages and changes in sales and market share | | |
| Regression-based "Marketing Mix Models" | | |
| Impact of PR programme on brand image among stakeholders | 57% | 96% |
| Impact of PR programme on corporate reputation among stakeholders | 54 | 98 |
| Media content analysis-related measures such as share of discussion/voice, key message penetration, tonality, etc. | 63 | 89 |
| Impressions/"Opportunity to see" | | |
| Penetration of key messages in target media | 70 | 91 |
| Clip reports/press cuttings books | 89 | 65 |
| Tracking the effectiveness of internal communications initiatives | 63 | 87 |
| Tracking the effectiveness of PR initiatives conducted via the Internet | | |
| Increasing target awareness of key messages or other key issues | 61 | 91 |
| Word of mouth/buzz creation | | |
| Improving volume of coverages versus competitors | | |
| Advertising value equivalencies (AVEs) | | |
| Reach/penetration of PR-generated coverage within target media | | |
| Correlation between PR-related boosts in coverage and positive changes in target behavior (e.g., website visitation, information requests, product inquiries, purchases) | | |
| Pre- and post-surveys as a way to measure the impact of events or changes in media coverage | 50 | 93 |
| Focus groups | | |
| Costs per thousand impressions generated by PR programme | | |
| "Gut feel" | | |

*Percentages reported only for variables where significant differences exist.

Source: Baskin et al., *Public Relations Review*, no. 36, 2010.

the firm and is usually controlled by the firm or its agent. Publicity, on the other hand, is not always positive and is not always under the control of, or paid for by, the organization. Both positive and negative publicity often originates from sources other than the firm.

In most organizations, publicity is controlled and disseminated by the public relations department. In this section, we discuss the role publicity plays in the promotional program and some of the ways marketers use and react to these communications.

## The Power of Publicity

LO 17-2

One of the factors that most set off publicity from the other program elements is the sheer power this form of communication can generate. Unfortunately for marketers, this power is not always realized in the way they would like it to be. Publicity can make or break a product or even a company. At one point, BP's stock dropped to less than one-half of what it was prior to the Gulf spill.

Why is publicity so much more powerful than advertising or sales promotion—or even other forms of public relations? First, publicity is highly credible. Unlike advertising and sales promotions, publicity is not usually seen as being sponsored by the company (in negative instances, it never is). So consumers perceive this information as more objective and place more confidence in it. In fact, media often take great measures to ensure their objectivity and promote the fact that they are not influenced by advertisers or other outside sources.

Publicity information may be perceived as endorsed by the medium in which it appears. For example, publicity regarding a breakthrough in the durability of golf balls will go far to promote them if it is reported by *Golf* magazine. *Car & Driver*'s award for car of the year reflects the magazine's perception of the quality of the auto selected.

Still another reason for publicity's power is its news value and the frequency of exposure it generates. When the publicity is positive, companies stand to benefit. When it is not, companies may suffer negative consequences such as lost sales, impacts on image, and even litigation, as shown in the opening vignette of this chapter.

The bottom line is that publicity is news, and people like to pass on information that has news value. Publicity thus results in a significant amount of free, credible, word-of-mouth information regarding the firm and its products.

**EXHIBIT 17–12**

Tree Top responds to the threat of negative publicity

## The Control and Dissemination of Publicity

In some of the examples cited previously, the control of publicity was not in the hands of the company. In some instances it is the firm's own blunder that allows information to leak out. Companies such as Toyota and BP could do nothing to stop the media from releasing negative information about them. When publicity becomes news, it is reported by the media, sometimes despite efforts by the firm. In these instances, the organization needs to react to the potential threat created by the news. Unfortunately, simply ignoring the problem will not make it go away.

A good example of one company's efforts to respond to adverse publicity is shown in Exhibit 17–12. Tree Top's problems began when all the major news media reported that the chemical Alar, used by some growers to regulate the growth of apples, might cause cancer in children. Despite published statements by reliable scientific and medical authorities (including the surgeon general) that Alar does not cause cancer, a few special-interest groups were able to generate an extraordinary amount of adverse publicity, causing concern among consumers and purchasing agents. A few school districts took apples off their menus, and even applesauce and juice were implicated.

**EXHIBIT 17–13**
Budweiser effectively responds to negative publicity.

YTC **17–02**
**Walmart News Release**
youtube.com/10ebelch

Tree Top ran the ad shown in Exhibit 17–12 to state its position and alleviate consumers' fears. It also sent a direct mailing to nutritionists and day care operators. The campaign was successful in assuring consumers of the product's safety and rebuilding their confidence.

Another example of effectively countering negative publicity is reflected in Budweiser's response to a class action lawsuit and negative publicity claiming that the brewer was watering down its beer, thereby reducing the alcoholic content and cheating consumers out of millions of dollars. Bud's response advertisement was particularly effective because it not only refuted the claim without giving it credence but at the same time turned the tables by indicating that not only does Bud maintain the brand's integrity, it also demonstrates the fact that they support causes by donating over 71 million cans of drinking water to those in need as shown in Exhibit 17–13.

Publicity can also work for marketers. Kids' toys frequently achieve significant sales due to high levels of positive publicity and word-of-mouth advertising. Sales of Cabernet Sauvignon increased an average of 45 percent in the month after a CBS *60 Minutes* report indicating that daily moderate consumption of red wine can reduce the risk of heart disease, and green tea sales skyrocketed when the word spread that consumption of the product was effective in preventing cancer. Products that contain antioxidents are now very popular due to their health benefits. There are many more examples of the positive impact publicity can have.

Marketers like to have as much control as possible over the time and place where information is released. One way to do this is with the **video news release (VNR)**, a publicity piece produced by publicists so that stations can air it as a news story. The videos almost never mention that they are produced by the subject organization, and most news stations don't mention it either. Many government agencies have used VNRs, as have the American Dental Association, GM, Motorola, and Nokia, among others. The use of VNRs without disclosing the source has led some consumer advocates to protest such actions. The Consumer Product Safety Commission has published guidelines for the appropriate use of VNRs at www. cpsp.gov.

In their efforts to manage publicity and public relations, marketers are continuously learning more about these activities. Courses are offered, websites are devoted to the topic, and books are written on how to manage publicity. These books cover how to make a presentation, whom to contact, how to issue a press release, and what to know about each medium addressed, including TV, radio, newspapers, magazines, the Internet, and direct-response advertising. They discuss such alternative media as news conferences, seminars, events, and personal letters, as well as insights on how to deal with government and other legislative bodies. Because this information is too extensive to include as a single chapter in this text, we suggest you peruse one of the many books available on this subject for additional insights.

## Advantages and Disadvantages of Publicity

Publicity offers the advantages of credibility, news value, significant word-of-mouth communications, and a perception of being endorsed by the media. Beyond the potential impact of negative publicity, other major problems arise from the use of publicity: lack of control, timing, and accuracy.

**Lack of Control**  In the viral world today, there is little control of what information is conveyed. Social networks, blogs, and so on, have expanded the number of recipients of messages, while at the same time opening up the information stream to sources that are not confined by standards that may be imposed on traditional media.

The result is that once public, the company or organization has lost control over the information. This can often become a costly experience. IMC Perspective 17–1 on page 598 demonstrates the power and speed of social media in spreading negative publicity with regard to Dolce & Gabbana in Hong Kong.

**Timing**  Timing of the publicity is not always completely under the control of the marketer. Unless the press thinks the information has very high news value, the timing of the press release is entirely up to the media—if it gets released at all. Thus, the information may be released earlier than desired or too late to make an impact.

**Accuracy**  There are numerous ways to generate publicity. Quite often these means are not in the company's control. Unfortunately, the information sometimes gets lost in translation; that is, it is not always reported the way the provider wishes it to be. As a result, inaccurate information, omissions, or other errors may result. Sometimes when you see a publicity piece that was written from a press release, you wonder if the two are even about the same topic.

### Measuring the Effectiveness of Publicity

The methods for measuring the effects of publicity are essentially the same as those discussed earlier under the broader topic of public relations. A well-respected model for measuring the effects of publicity has been developed by Ketchum Public Relations. Using Walter Lindenmann's criteria, the Ketchum Effectiveness Yardstick was perceived as the standard in the industry for decades and was used by numerous companies. While the Ketchum website makes no mention of the Yardstick communications program, the agency continues to provide effectiveness measures to its clients.

# CORPORATE ADVERTISING

LO 17-3

One of the more controversial forms of advertising is **corporate advertising**. Actually an extension of the public relations function, corporate advertising does not promote any one specific product or service. Rather, it is designed to promote the firm overall, by enhancing its image, assuming a position on a social issue or cause, or seeking direct involvement in something. Why is corporate advertising controversial? A number of reasons are offered:

1. *Consumers are not interested in this form of advertising.* Studies have shown that many consumers are not interested in corporate ads. At least part of this may be because consumers do not understand the reasons behind such ads. Of course, much of this confusion results from ads that are not very good from a communications standpoint.
2. *It's a costly form of self-indulgence.* Firms have been accused of engaging in corporate image advertising only to satisfy the egos of top management. This argument stems from the fact that corporate ads are not easy to write. The message to be communicated is not as precise and specific as one designed to position a product, so the top managersn often dictate the content of the ad, and the copy reflects their ideas and images of the corporation.
3. *The firm must be in trouble.* Some critics believe the only time firms engage in corporate advertising is when they are in trouble—either in a financial sense or in the public eye—and are advertising to attempt to remedy the problem. There are a number of forms of corporate advertising, each with its own objectives. These critics argue that these objectives have become important only because the firm has not been managed properly.
4. *Corporate advertising is a waste of money.* Given that the ads do not directly appeal to anyone, are not understood, and do not promote anything specific,

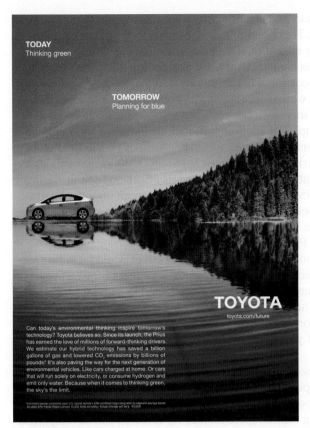

TODAY
Thinking green

TOMORROW
Planning for blue

TOYOTA
toyota.com/future

Can today's environmental thinking inspire tomorrow's technology? Toyota believes so. Since its launch, the Prius has earned the love of millions of forward-thinking drivers. We estimate our hybrid technology has saved a billion gallons of gas and lowered $CO_2$ emissions by billions of pounds.* It's also paving the way for the next generation of environmental vehicles. Like cars charged at home. Or cars that will run solely on electricity, or consume hydrogen and emit only water. Because when it comes to thinking green, the sky's the limit.

*Estimated savings compares each U.S. hybrid vehicle's EPA combined mpg rating with its segment average based on latest EPA Trends Report (driven 15,000 miles annually). Actual mileage will vary. ©2008

**EXHIBIT 17–14**

Toyota uses corporate image advertising for positioning

critics say the monies could be better spent in other areas. Again, much of this argument has its foundation in the fact that corporate image ads are often intangible. They typically do not ask directly for a purchase; they do not ask for investors. Rather, they present a position or try to create an image. Because they are not specific, many critics believe their purpose is lost on the audience and these ads are not a wise investment of the firm's resources.

Despite these criticisms and others, corporate advertising still enjoys wide usage. A variety of business-to-business and consumer-product companies continue to run corporate image ads, and numerous others have also increased expenditures in this area.

Since the term *corporate advertising* tends to be used as a catchall for any type of advertising run for the direct benefit of the corporation rather than its products or services, much advertising falls into this category. For purposes of this text (and to attempt to bring some perspective to the term), we use it to describe any type of advertising designed to promote the organization itself rather than its products or services.

## Objectives of Corporate Advertising

Corporate advertising may be designed with two goals in mind: (1) creating a positive image for the firm and (2) communicating the organization's views on social, business, and environmental issues. More specific applications include:

- Boosting employee morale and smoothing labor relations.
- Helping newly deregulated industries ease consumer uncertainty and answer investor questions.
- Helping diversified companies establish an identity for the parent firm rather than relying solely on brand names.[20]

As these objectives indicate, corporate advertising is targeted at both internal and external audiences and involves the promotion of the organization as well as its ideas.

## Types of Corporate Advertising

Marketers seek attainment of corporate advertising's objectives by implementing image, advocacy, or cause-related advertising. Each form is designed to achieve specific goals.

**Image Advertising**   One form of corporate advertising is devoted to promoting the organization's overall image. **Image advertising** may accomplish a number of objectives, including creating goodwill both internally and externally, creating a position for the company, and generating resources, both human and financial. A number of methods are used:

1. *General image or positioning ads.* As shown in Exhibit 17–14, ads are often designed to create an image of the firm in mind. The exhibit shows how Toyota is attempting to create an image of itself as an innovator and leader in caring for the environment. The ad is designed to demonstrate Toyota's concern for conservation today and preservation for the future.
2. *Sponsorships.* Firms often run corporate image advertising on TV programs or specials. For example, on the National Geographic Channel, a number of companies including Nikon, American Airlines, and others provide

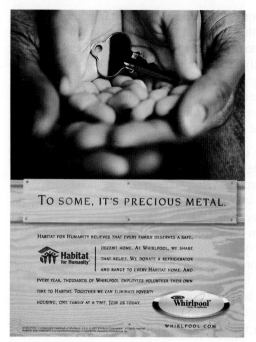

**EXHIBIT 17–15**

Whirlpool supports the fight to eliminate poverty housing

YTC 17–03

**The Girl Effect—Nike**

youtube.com/10ebelch

**FIGURE 17–6**

U.S. Olympic Sponsors and Partners

| |
|---|
| P&G |
| Coca-Cola |
| DOW |
| ATOS |
| McDonald's |
| Samsung |
| Visa |
| GE |
| Panasonic |
| Omega |

sponsorships to associate themselves with the quality programming shown. These and others also sponsor programs on public TV and other educational programs designed to promote the corporation as a good citizen. By associating itself with high-quality or educational programming, companies like Siemens and Starbucks as well as local sponsors hope for a carryover effect that benefits their own images.

Other examples of sponsorships include those run by American Express (Members Project), American Airlines (UNICEF), and Nike (The Girl Effect). Exhibit 17–15 shows Whirlpool's sponsorship of the Habitat for Humanity and its efforts to fight to eliminate poverty housing. Visa considers sponsorships an important part of its integrated marketing communications. It has sponsored the Olympics, the U.S. decathlon team, FIFA, NFL, NHL, The Toronto International Film Festival, and others. The sponsorships are designed to fulfill specific business objectives while providing support for the recipients. Figure 17–6 shows a few of the companies that decided an Olympic sponsorship would be good for them.

3. *Recruiting.* The associated ad presented in Exhibit 17–16 is a good example of corporate image advertising designed to attract new employees. If you want to talk about being a truck driver, respond to this ad.

4. *Generating financial support.* Some corporate advertising is designed to generate investments in the corporation. By creating a more favorable image, the firm makes itself attractive to potential stock purchasers and investors. More investments mean more working capital, more monies for research and development, and so on. In this instance, corporate image advertising is almost attempting to make a sale; the product is the firm.

While there is no concrete evidence that corporate image advertising leads directly to increased investment, many managers believe there is, and that there is a correlation between the price of stock and the amount of corporate advertising done. Firms that spend more on corporate advertising also tend to have higher-priced stocks (though a direct relationship is very difficult to substantiate).

This thing called *image* is not unidimensional. Many factors affect it. Figure 17–7 shows the results of three different rankings from three different sources. Note that none of the corporations appear on all three lists, which shows that companies can be respected and attain a strong corporate reputation in a number of ways. The most admired firms did not gain their positions merely by publicity and word of mouth (nor, we guess, did the least admired).

A positive corporate image cannot be created just from a few advertisements. Quality of products and services, innovation, sound financial practices, good corporate citizenship, and wise marketing are just a few of the factors that contribute to overall image. In addition, the type of product marketed and emotional appeal also contribute. The surveys cited above demonstrate that profits and stock performances have little to do with reputation and that once a reputation is acquired, it has lasting power. IMC Perspective 17–2 on page 602 discusses how Standard Chartered Bank in Hong Kong has successfully achieved recognition through its annual Standard Chartered Hong Kong Marathon.

**Event Sponsorships** As we noted in the last section, corporate sponsorships of charities and causes have become a popular form of public relations. While some companies sponsor specific events or causes with primarily traditional public relations objectives in mind, a separate and more marketing-oriented use of sponsorships is also on the increase. Such **event sponsorships** take on a variety of forms, as shown in Figure 17–8. Anything from apparel and equipment (Under Armour's sponsors men's and womens' teams in a variety of sports) to concerts, stadiums, and

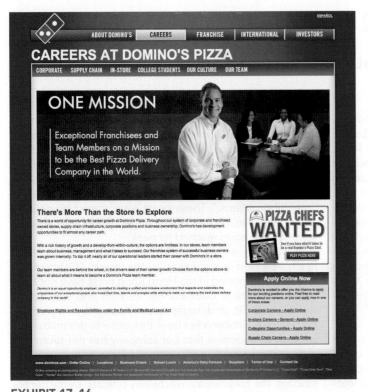

**EXHIBIT 17–16**

Corporate image advertising designed to attract employees

college football bowl games are now commonly used for corporate sponsorship. Like any other relationship, however, risks must be assumed by both sides in such agreements. For example, many companies that have had their names placed on stadiums—TWA Dome (St. Louis), PSINet (Baltimore), Fruit of the Loom (Miami)—have gone bankrupt, while others have had their images tarnished—Enron (Enron Field), MCI (MCI Center)—which is not good for the cities. A risk taken by a company in naming a stadium is the cost of hundreds of millions of dollars, which can cause stockholders and consumers concern over the value of such an investment. At the same time, naming a stadium can lead to increased name exposure—particularly for those companies that don't have strong brand recognition. For example, MetLife insurance, whose name is on the New York Jets and New York Giants stadium, believes it has been a very good investment, based on increased exposure alone. In addition, research has shown that 990 percent of fans can recall the name of the sponsors of their stadiums, and 35 percent say it causes them to have a more favorable impression of the brand.[21]

After seven straight years of growth, sponsorship spending decreased in 2009, due primarily to the state of the economy. Forecasts for 2013 show increases and expect renewed growth in all areas. Companies are expected to spend more than $533 billion on event sponsorships worldwide in 2013, with sports receiving the majority of event sponsorship monies.[22]

For example, the NASCAR Sprint Cup Series remains an attractive event to numerous companies, despite the increasing costs of sponsorship (Exhibit 17–17). Many companies are attracted to event sponsorships because effective IMC programs can be built around them, and promotional tie-ins can be made to local, regional, national, and even international markets. Companies are finding event sponsorships an excellent platform from which to build equity and gain affinity with target audiences as well as a good public relations tool. For example, Hertz Rental Cars recently signed a three-year deal with Penske Racing and expects it to be extended. Hertz CEO Mark Frissora considers it one of the best ways to spend his advertising dollars given the ability to reach his specific target market, as well as the number of impressions received for the investment. He also notes that 20 percent of NASCAR's fan base rented cars in 2012, and he wants them to think of Hertz when they do.[23]

**FIGURE 17–7**

Corporate Reputations

| World's Most Admired | Best Corporate Citizens | Global Rep Trak |
|---|---|---|
| 1. Apple | AT&T | BMW |
| 2. Google | Mattel, Inc. | Disney |
| 3. Amazon.com | Bristol-Myers Squibb | Rolex |
| 4. Coca-Cola | Eaton | Google |
| 5. Starbucks | Intel | Mercedes-Benz |

Sources: "World's Most Admired Companies 2013—Fortune," www.money.cnn.com; "CR's 100 Best Corporate Citizens 2013," www.cr.magazine.com; "Global Rep Trak 100," www.globalreptrak.com.

# IMC Perspective 17–1 > > >

## Dolce & Gabbana Faced the Wrath of the Hong Kong Public

In late December 2011, security guards hired by the Dolce & Gabbana (D&G) flagship store in Harbour City on Canton Road in Tsim Sha Tsui, Hong Kong prevented the locals from taking photographs outside the store. The incident was deemed offensive as the photo ban was restricted to locals, but not visitors from Mainland China.

This incident was reported in *Apple Daily* on January 5 and 6, 2012, and angry netizens took to posting their comments on D&G's fan page on Facebook. However, D&G deleted some of the comments. This incensed the public further and triggered off a strong backlash. Hundreds of negative comments were posted on D&G's New Year's greetings status update. An anti-D&G page was created by netizens on Facebook and over 20,000 "likes" were recorded within a week.

A "10,000 People Photograph D&G Event" was then organized to take place on January 8, 2012. The event was widely publicized via the anti-D&G Facebook page. On that day, a few thousand protesters gathered outside D&G's flagship store and took photographs. They also demanded that D&G issues a formal apology to the

Hong Kong public. This event was widely reported in the international media including *Forbes, News Week Japan, The Wall Street Journal, Repubblica,* and *The Telegraph.*

The situation worsened after a staff member at the D&G flagship store posted some controversial comments on her own Facebook page, by accusing protesters of having "mental problems." These posts were shared by netizens and reported in the media. The anger of the general public against D&G soon reached its peak.

It was only on the night of January 8, 2012 that D&G finally released a statement to the press: "Controversial statements reported in the Hong Kong press have not been made by Dolce & Gabbana nor its staff, and we strongly reject any racist or derogatory comments. It is regrettable that Dolce & Gabbana has been brought into this matter, but we wish to underline that our company has not taken part in any action aimed at offending the Hong Kong public."

This was the first response from D&G since the photo ban incident. The press release was heavily criticized by the general public who insisted that it was the worst they had ever seen. They were also angry with D&G for shifting the blame over the

FIGURE 17–8  North America (millions) Annual Sponsorship Spending in 1996–2013

| | 1996 | 1997 | 1998 | 1999 | 2002 | 2004 | 2008 | 2010 | 2013 |
|---|---|---|---|---|---|---|---|---|---|
| Sports | $3,540 | $3,840 | $4,556 | $5,100 | $6,430 | $7,690 | $11,600 | $11,600 | 13,790 |
| Entertainment tours/ attractions | 566 | 650 | 680 | 756 | 865 | 1,060 | 1,610 | 1,740 | 2,030 |
| Festivals, fairs, events | 512 | 558 | 612 | 685 | 834 | 792 | 754 | 781 | 849 |
| Causes | 485 | 535 | 544 | 630 | 828 | 991 | 1,500 | 1,610 | 1,780 |
| Arts | 323 | 354 | 408 | 460 | 610 | 612 | 832 | 841 | 920 |
| Total | $5,426 | $5,937 | $6,800 | $7,631 | $9,567 | $11,140 | $16,296 | $16,752 | 19,940 |

Sources: Adapted from *Cause Marketing Forum*, 2010; IEG, LLC, 2013.

**Advocacy Advertising**  A third major form of corporate advertising addresses social, business, or environmental issues. Such **advocacy advertising** is concerned with propagating ideas and elucidating controversial social issues of public importance in a manner that supports the interests of the sponsor.

While still portraying an image for the company or organization, advocacy advertising does so indirectly, by adopting a position on a particular issue rather than promoting the organization itself. An example of advocacy advertising sponsored by the American Heart Association and the American Stroke Association and advocating support for President Obama's health care program is shown in Exhibit 17–18. Advocacy advertising has increased in use over the past few years and has also met with increased criticism. An advertising campaign sponsored by the Santa Fe Natural Tobacco company was designed to create a more positive image of tobacco. The two-page ad began with a statement, "There are some things in our past you should incident to the media, and its unwillingness to apologize. On January 15, 2012, a week after the first protest, a few dozen people protested at the store and snapped photos.

At around 3.00 A.M. on January 18, 2012 D&G finally issued an official apology to the Hong Kong public. It went thus: "We understand that the events which unfolded in front of Dolce & Gabbana Boutique on Canton Road have offended the citizens of Hong Kong, and for this we are truly sorry and we apologise. The Dolce & Gabbana policy is to welcome the Hong Kong people and that of the whole world respecting the rights of each individual and of the local laws. Dolce & Gabbana wishes everyone a happy and prosperous year of the Dragon."

The corporate image of D&G was seriously affected following its poor handling of the crisis. It had responded too slowly, was not willing to apologize, had failed to investigate the claims at the early stage of the crisis, or to take cognizance of netizens' comments on Facebook. These factors ignited the public's anger and stoked strong reactions. Moreover, D&G was perceived to have pushed the blame for the incident onto the media, and for not enforcing a stricter code of conduct on its employees.

Another fault line in D&G's crisis management was its inadequacy in the use of social media to manage the incident. It seemed to have ignored the potential of social media to amplify events, to increase the likelihood of a crisis developing rapidly, and to disseminate information quickly to a wide audience. Throughout the incident, D&G had issued only two short, unsigned written statements to the press. No answers were provided to the questions raised, and no effort was made to initiate a dialog with the public. D&G should have monitored all its communication in real time. It also needed a spokesperson to communicate with the public after the incident and to offer an immediate response. Finally, when handling the crisis it ought to have paired its traditional public relations practices with the latest digital and social communication tools for a more effective response and management plan.

Sources: "Irate Locals Demand Apology from Dolce & Gabbana," *Apple Daily*, January 9, 2012, http://hk.apple.nextmedia.com/news/art/20120109/15964959; "What Luxury Brands Should Learn from Dolce & Gabbana's Hong Kong PR Disaster," *Jing Daily*, January 9, 2012, http://www.jingdaily.com/what-luxury-brands-should-learn-from-dolce-gabbanas-hong-kong-pr-disaster/13543; "Dolce & Gabbana Photo Ban Protest," the *Know Your Meme*, http://knowyourmeme.com/memes/events/dolce-gabbana-photo-ban-protest; Phila Siu and Diana Lee, "Get the Picture?," *The Standard*, January 9, 2012, http://www.thestandard.com.hk/news_detail.asp?pp_cat=30&art_id=118644&sid=35006726&con_type=3.

**EXHIBIT 17–17**
Hertz believes a NASCAR sponsorship is a good investment

know about," and continues on side two with statements that include the fact that the company has been supporting American farmers since the early 1990s, their tobacco is 100 percent additive-free, and it is all grown in the United States. The image of the tobacco industry in the United States has been a negative one for decades despite many attempts to change it. Santa Fe seems to be trying again.

Advocacy ads may be sponsored by a firm or by a trade association and are designed to tell readers how the firm operates or explain management's position on a

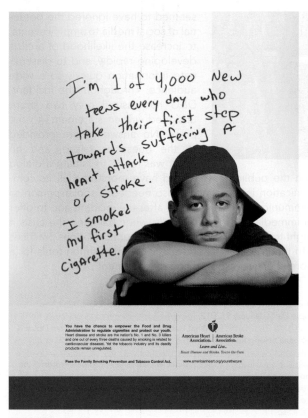

**EXHIBIT 17–18**

An example of an advocacy ad

particular issue. Sometimes the advertising is a response to negative publicity or to the firm's inability to place an important message through its regular public relations channels. At other times, the firm just wants to get certain ideas accepted or to have society understand its concerns.

Another form of advocacy advertising, **issue ads** are increasingly appearing in the media. While considered a form of advocacy advertising, issue ads may have no affiliation with a corporate or trade sponsor but may be sponsored by an organization to bring attention to what they consider to be an important issue. For example, after failed negotiations between the Humane Society of the United States and grocery store chain Trader Joe's, the animal welfare organization placed an issue ad (Exhibit 17–19). The response from Trader Joe's customers was enormous. And the company publicly announced that it would convert all of its brand eggs to cage free within three months. In 2007, the U.S. Supreme Court ruled that corporate and union sponsorships of issue ads (previously banned) must be permitted to run. Many believed this decision would lead to a significant increase in issue advertising.[24]

Advocacy advertising has been criticized by a number of sources. But as you can see in Exhibit 17–20, this form of communication has been around for a long time. AT&T engaged in issues-oriented advertising way back in 1908 and has continued to employ this form of communication into the 21st century. Critics contend that companies with large advertising budgets purchase too much ad space and time and that advocacy ads may be misleading, but the checks and balances of regular product advertising also operate in this area.

For example, a television commercial shown during the 2010 Super Bowl spawned a heated debate (not to mention lots of publicity). The commercial, sponsored by the conservative evangelical organization Focus on Family, included Heisman Trophy winner Tim Tebow and his mother and supported an antiabortion position. The ad was considered inappropriate by many in the media and the public, while others saw nothing controversial about it. In hindsight, it appears that the action off the field (that is, in the Super Bowl advertising community) was much greater than that generated by the ad itself.[25]

**Cause-Related Advertising** An increasingly popular method of image building is **cause-related marketing**, in which companies link with charities or nonprofit organizations as contributing sponsors. The company benefits from favorable publicity, while the charity receives much-needed funds. Proponents of cause marketing say that association with a cause may differentiate one brand or store from another, increase consumer acceptance of price increases, generate favorable publicity, and even win over skeptical officials who may have an impact on the company.[26] Indeed, a study by the Integer Group showed that association with a cause will impact consumers' purchase decisions—making them more likely to buy from the sponsor. Yoplait was the number 1 brand cited as being purchased as a result of its affiliation with causes.[27] Cause-marketing relationships can take a variety of forms. Making outright donations to a nonprofit cause, having companies volunteer for the cause, donating materials or supplies, running public service announcements, or even providing event refreshments are some of the ways companies get involved. Exhibit 17–21 shows an event titled "High Heels for Hope." The proceeds from this event went directly to the House of Ruth in Baltimore,

**EXHIBIT 17–19**

Issue ads are on the increase

**EXHIBIT 17–20**
AT&T has used advocacy ads for years

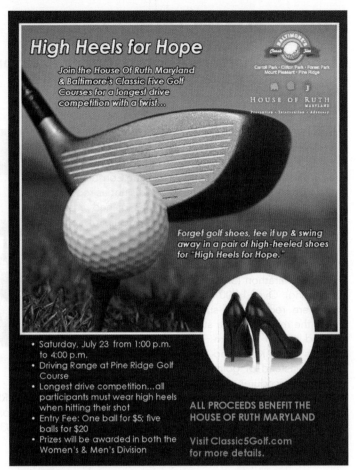

**EXHIBIT 17–21**
This ad was part of a campaign designed to stop domestic violence

Maryland—a cause supporting women and youth who have suffered from domestic violence. The campaign was targeted to those attempting to overcome the impact of domestic violence.

At the same time, not all cause marketing is a guarantee of success. Cause marketing requires more than just associating with a social issue, and it takes time and effort. Companies have gotten into trouble by misleading consumers about their relationships, and others have wasted money by supporting a cause that offered little synergism. One survey showed that more than 300 companies associated themselves with breast cancer concerns, but most became lost in sponsorship clutter. Another has shown that consumers are becoming more skeptical and are demanding more accountability from companies' cause-marketing efforts.[27] Others have simply picked the wrong cause—finding that their customers and potential customers either have little interest in or don't support the cause. In some cases, cause marketing is considered nothing more than shock advertising. Finally, the results of cause-marketing efforts can sometimes be hard to quantify.

## Advantages and Disadvantages of Corporate Advertising

A number of reasons for the increased popularity of corporate advertising become evident when you examine the advantages of this form of communication:

1. *It is an excellent vehicle for positioning the firm.* Firms, like products, need to establish an image or position in the marketplace. Corporate image ads are one way to accomplish this objective. A well-positioned product is much more likely

YTC 17–04

J and J "For All You Love"
youtube.com/10ebelch

# IMC Perspective 17–2 > > >

## Standard Chartered Hong Kong Marathon—From a Sporting Event to a Community Event

Standard Chartered Bank is one of three banks authorized by the Hong Kong Monetary Authority to issue currency notes in Hong Kong. Compared with the other two note-issuing banks, the Hongkong and Shanghai Banking Corporation and Bank of China, Standard Chartered Bank is not as reputable. However, Standard Chartered Bank has gained a strong reputation in at least one aspect: sponsorship of sporting events.

In 1997, the year when Hong Kong was returned to China, Standard Chartered Bank organized the Hong Kong-Shenzhen marathon (Shenzhen is a Chinese city bordering Hong Kong). Over 1,000 runners participated in the event. They were required to submit their passports the night before the marathon at a stadium in Hong Kong, and they received a chip in return. When they passed the border between Hong Kong and Shenzhen, they simply dropped the chip instead of going through the usual immigration clearance procedures.

Since that inaugural race, the marathon has been held in February every year. The participation rate has increased steadily over the years, even during the difficult years of 2003

(SARS epidemic) and 2009 (the financial tsunami). The number of participants rose from 13,574 in 2002 to over 18,386 in 2003, and from 42,577 in 2008 to 51,272 in 2009. Due to the

to achieve success than is one with a vague or no image. The same holds true of the firm. Stop and think for a moment about the image that comes to mind when you hear the name Apple, Johnson & Johnson, or Procter & Gamble.

Now what comes to mind when you hear Unisys, USX, or Navistar? How many consumer brands can you name that fall under ConAgra's corporate umbrella? (Hunts, Chef Boyardee, Pam, Slim-Jims, and many others.) While we are not saying these latter companies are not successful—because they certainly are—we are suggesting their corporate identities (or positions) are not as well entrenched as the identities of those first cited. Companies with strong positive corporate images have an advantage over competitors that may be enhanced when they promote the company overall.

2. *It takes advantage of the benefits derived from public relations.* As the PR efforts of firms have increased, the attention paid to these events by the media has lessened (not because they are of any less value, but because there are more events to cover). The net result is that when a company engages in a public relations effort, there is no guarantee it will receive press coverage and publicity. Corporate image advertising gets the message out, and though consumers may not perceive it as positively as information from an objective source, the fact remains that it can communicate what has been done.

3. *It reaches a select target market.* Corporate image advertising should not be targeted to the general public. It is often targeted to investors and managers of other firms rather than to the general public. It doesn't matter if the general public does not appreciate this form of communication, as long as the target market does (remember the Hertz–Penske relationship?). In this respect, this form of advertising may be accomplishing its objectives.

huge turnout at every race, there is now a cap on the number of participants. In 2014, that number was 73,000.

The race attracts not only the locals, but runners from all over the world. In 2012, it was recognized by the International Association of Athletics Federation (IAAF) as a Bronze Label event. In 2013, it was upgraded to Silver Label Road Race status by the IAAF.

Many organizations, companies, and universities have formed teams to join the marathon. Many famous movie stars and other celebrities in Hong Kong have also jumped on the bandwagon. The Standard Chartered marathon has been transformed from being a sporting event into a carnival. Many runners take photos at the marathon to show their participation. This reflects the fact that the runners are proud of having run the marathon. The number of races in the event has increased from only a marathon and a half marathon in 1997 to include 10-kilometer races and 3-kilometer or 10-kilometer wheelchair races in recent years. As the number of participants is huge, there are numerous categories within each type of race. Furthermore, many prizes are offered such as Leaders Cup, Disciplined Forces Cups, and District Council Cup Results which pique interest in the various events.

The race has been a very successful public relations exercise for Standard Chartered Bank. For example, a 2008 survey had found public awareness of the bank's sponsorship was 90 percent while awareness about the marathon was 98 percent, and 90 percent of respondents agreed that the marathon demonstrated Standard Chartered Bank's support for community events.

Currently, Standard Chartered Bank also sponsors marathons in other cities around the world: Bangkok, Dubai, Jersey (the largest of the British-owned Channel Islands), Kuala Lumpur, Mumbai (India), Nairobi (Kenya), Singapore, and Taipei.

Sources: Hong Kong Standard Chartered Marathon website, http://www .hkmarathon.com; Internationalist Awards for Innovation in Media 2008, "Gold Winner: Standard Chartered Bank, 'Are You Ready?'—Marathon Campaign," http://www.internationalist-awards.com/inter-media-2008/ Standard.html; "Standard Chartered Marathon," Wikipedia (2014), http:// zh.wikipedia.org/wiki/%E6%B8%A3%E6%89%93%E9%A6%AC%E6%8B% 89%E6%9D%BE.

Some of the disadvantages of corporate advertising were alluded to earlier in the chapter. To these criticisms, we can add the following:

1. *Questionable effectiveness.* There is no strong evidence to support the belief that corporate advertising works. Many doubt the data cited earlier that demonstrated a correlation between stock prices and corporate image advertising as some studies show little support for this effect.
2. *Constitutionality and/or ethics.* Some critics contend that since larger firms have more money, they can control public opinion unfairly. This point was resolved in the courts in favor of the advertisers. Nevertheless, many consumers still see such advertising as unfair given the great disparities that sometimes exist in financial resources available to some but not others, and immediately take a negative view of the sponsor.

A number of valid points have been offered for and against corporate advertising. Two things are certain: (1) No one knows who is right, and (2) the use of this communications form continues to increase.

## Measuring the Effectiveness of Corporate Advertising

As you can tell from our discussion of the controversy surrounding corporate advertising, there needs to be methods for evaluating whether or not such advertising is effective:

■ *Attitude surveys.* One way to determine the effectiveness of corporate advertising is to conduct attitude surveys to gain insights into both the public's and investors' reactions to ads. A study conducted by Janas Sinclair and Tracy Irani on advocacy advertising in the biotechnology industry employed a survey research methodology to demonstrate that public accountability was a good predictor of corporate trustworthiness, and this and the attitude toward the advertiser would predict consumers' attitude toward the ad, biotechnology, and purchase intentions.[28] The Phase II study conducted by market research firm Yankelovich, Skelly & White is one of the best-known applications of this measurement method.[29] The firm measured recall and attitude toward corporate advertisers and found that corporate advertising is more efficient in building recall for a company name than is product advertising alone. Frequent corporate advertisers rated better on virtually all attitude measures than those with low corporate ad budgets.

- *Studies relating corporate advertising and stock prices.* A number of studies have examined the effect of various elements of corporate advertising (position in the magazine, source effects, etc.) on stock prices. These studies have yielded conflicting conclusions, indicating that while the model for such measures seems logical, methodological problems may account for at least some of the discrepancies.

- *Focus group research.* Focus groups have been used to find out what investors want to see in ads and how they react after the ads are developed. As with product-oriented advertising, this method has limitations, although it does allow for some effective measurements.

While the effectiveness of corporate advertising has been measured by some of the methods used to measure product-specific advertising, reported research in this area has not kept pace with that of the consumer market. The most commonly offered reason for this lack of effort is that corporate ads are often the responsibility of those in the highest management positions in the firm, and these parties do not wish to be held accountable. It is interesting that those who should be most concerned with accountability are the most likely to shun this responsibility!

## Summary

This chapter examined the role of the promotional elements of public relations, publicity, and corporate advertising. We noted that these areas are all significant to the marketing and communications effort and are usually considered differently from the other promotional elements. The reasons for this special treatment stem from the facts that (1) they are typically not designed to promote a specific product or service, and (2) in many instances it is harder for the consumer to make the connection between the communication and its intent.

Public relations was shown to be useful in its traditional responsibilities as well as in a more marketing-oriented role. In many firms, PR is a separate department operating independently of marketing; in others, it is considered a support system. Many large firms have an external public relations agency, just as they have an outside ad agency.

In the case of publicity, another factor enters the equation: lack of control over the communication the public will receive. In public relations and corporate advertising, the organization remains the source and retains much more control. Publicity often takes more of a reactive than a proactive approach, yet it may be more instrumental (or detrimental) to the success of a product or organization than all other forms of promotion combined.

While not all publicity can be managed, the marketer must nevertheless recognize its potential impact. Press releases and the management of information are just two of the factors under the company's control. Proper reaction and a strategy to deal with uncontrollable events are also responsibilities.

Corporate advertising was described as controversial, largely because the source of the message is top management, so the rules for other advertising and promoting forms are often not applied. This element of communication definitely has its place in the promotional mix. But to be effective, it must be used with each of the other elements, with specific communications objectives in mind.

Finally, we noted that measures of evaluation and control are required for each of these program elements, just as they are for all others in the promotional mix. We presented some methods for taking such measurements and some evidence showing why it is important to use them. As long as the elements of public relations, publicity, and corporate advertising are considered integral components of the overall communications strategy, they must respect the same rules as the other promotional-mix elements to ensure success.

## Key Terms

public relations (PR) p. 579
marketing public relations
    (MPR) p. 580
internal audiences p. 584
external audiences p. 584
press release p. 586

press conference p. 587
exclusive p. 587
publicity p. 590
video news release (VNR) p. 593
corporate advertising p. 594
image advertising p. 595

event sponsorship p. 596
advocacy advertising p. 598
issue ads p. 600
cause-related marketing p. 600

## Discussion Questions

1.  As described in the chapter lead-in, Hoi Tin Tong suffered as a result of the negative publicity it received for its main product, *guilinggao*. Discuss what Hoi Tin Tong had done right and wrong to ward off the negative impact of bad press. (LO2)

2.  Research studies have indicated that cause marketing can actually lead to an increased intention to purchase a brand. Explain why this is the case and provide examples that you feel may pertain. (LO5)

3.  Putting one's name on a stadium can be an expensive proposition, and the prices continue to increase. Discuss whether this would be a good investment for a company, and why or why not. Give examples of companies for which this might be a good investment. (LO3)

4.  The chapter discusses cause marketing, advocacy advertising, and issue ads. Explain the differences between these forms of communication and give examples of each. (LO5)

5.  Social media have had a profound impact on the power of publicity. Explain what this means and whether you believe it to be true or not. Provide examples to support your position. (LO2)

6.  Describe the conflict between traditional PR agencies and those that see PR as more of a marketing function. Cite reasons why each of these groups holds the position it does. Who is right? (LO1)

7.  Some marketers consider corporate advertising a waste of time and money. What are some of the reasons they feel this way? Take a position pro or con corporate advertising and defend it. (LO3)

8.  Explain how social networks can both help and hurt companies in regard to publicity. (LO1)

9.  Discuss some of the advantages and disadvantages of public relations. Now do the same for MPRs. (LO3)

10.  Why do companies get involved in event sponsorships? Is this an effective strategy? Give examples of event sponsorships that were successful and some that were not. (LO5)

For PepsiCo's Frito-Lay division, Neuro-Focus tested women's responses to Baked Lays. The research helped shape an ad campaign and new single-serve packaging.

To analyze the tech giant's global image, NeuroFocus tapped Chinese and American brains.

NeuroFocus measured viewers' responses to pilots and new shows; of course its corporate parent, Nielsen, measures how many people are watching.

Which olive-oil label appealed most to consumers? NeuroFocus tested several options to find one that set brains afire.

Advertisers want the best on-air display they can get; NeuroFocus helped the cable net make its sponsor splashes more noteworthy.

NeuroFocus helped its PayPal division find a more refined corporate identity than "safe, simple, wow!"

## LEARNING OBJECTIVES

**LO1** To understand reasons for measuring promotional program effectiveness.

**LO2** To know the various measures used in assessing promotional program effectiveness.

**LO3** To understand the requirements of proper effectiveness research.

**LO4** To evaluate alternative methods for measuring promotional program effectiveness.

# 18 Measuring the Effectiveness of the Promotional Program

## ARE MARKETERS MAKING DECISIONS IN THE DARK?

For years it has been a struggle for managers to get an idea of how well their advertising programs were working. To make matters worse, when they have taken efforts to determine the effectiveness of their programs, they often got pushback from their ad agencies, which argued (and still do!) that it is difficult to measure how ads are contributing to the overall marketing program, and that measuring could actually lead to *lower* effectiveness by stifling creativity. But then, shareholders and others arguing for some of the monies being spent on advertising began to have an impact and marketers started to pay more attention to metrics that might provide them with data to make better management decisions. With the advent of new media, it seems that marketers are (or at least some feel that they are) regressing to a time long ago, as it is so difficult to measure the contribution that these new media are making to the overall marketing program.

What makes this issue even more important is a recent study conducted by Marketing Budgets Report, in which 54 percent of the companies responding indicated that they expect to increase marketing spending this year in both online and off-line channels—but at a rate of almost 4 to 1 in online. At the same time only about half of these companies say they feel they have a good understanding of marketing effectiveness in either channel. Agencies are even more skeptical, with 36 percent indicating that their clients' understanding of the effects is either "poor" or "very poor." Both of these numbers show a decrease from the last study.

What makes these numbers even more interesting is that marketers and the consumers they are trying to reach also don't agree on what works. In a survey conducted by Adobe, marketers indicated that they believed online ads were more effective than TV ads. But 67 percent of consumers claimed that TV ads worked better. And while marketers continue to shift advertising dollars to digital, consumers say they like seeing ads in print magazines (45 percent), and on TV (23 percent) more than on their favorite websites (11 percent), in social media (3 percent), or in digital magazines (2 percent). While both groups felt that the ads created by professionals are more effective than those created by consumers, marketers were more likely to take this position. Paid search ads—highly touted by marketers—were considered less effective by consumers, who believe that outdoor works much better than the marketers do.

As we said at the beginning, the lack of agreement on the effectiveness of advertising—whether online or off-line—is nothing new. While traditional advertisers have debated the issue for decades, those involved with online ads have been discussing the problem as well. A study conducted in 2009 showed that the inability to understand how advertising works was considered the major impediment to integrating digital into the IMC program. Although most marketers feel that this situation has improved, few believe that they have a good grasp of how effective ads are or how well they contribute to an integrated program.

So what's the answer? As you will see in this chapter, marketers are trying a variety of methods to try to find out. Many of these measures are new, some have been around for a while, and some are a combination of old and new. New techniques like eye tracking and neuroscience applications are being used alongside traditional recall and attitude measurement techniques. More and more retailers are using attribution modeling to attempt to determine how various media touch points are performing, and there has been an increase in measuring the effectiveness of emotional versus cognitive ads, the impact of creativity, storytelling versus hard sell, and so on.

While the marketers have disagreed on both the value of measuring effectiveness and how to measure for a long time, few these days argue for the need to determine the former. Now if we can just figure out how to do it!

Sources: Laurie Sullivan, "Marketing Budgets Rise, Determining Multi-Channel ROI, Metrics Remains a Challenge," www.mediapost.com, February 5, 2013; Laurie Sullivan, "Retailers Use Attribution Modeling to Measure the Touchpoints Driving Sales," www.emarketer.com, May 28, 2013; Laurie Sullivan, "Consumers, Marketers Disagree on Effective Ads," www.emarketer.com, November 13, 2012; Karlene Lukovitz, "Survey: Metrics Biggest Integration Obstacle," www.mediapostnews.com, April 23, 2009.

As noted throughout this text, the increased emphasis on accountability is forcing many companies to evaluate, or reevaluate, their IMC plans. Both clients and agencies are continually striving to determine whether their communications are working and how well they are working relative to other options. As can be seen in the lead-in to this chapter, researchers are not confident in the metrics they are currently using and are searching for new methods designed to assist in this endeavor. Companies and organizations continue to work together in an attempt to provide answers to these questions and to develop new ways to measure communications effectiveness.

Measuring the effectiveness of the promotional program is a critical element in the promotional planning process. Research allows the marketing manager to evaluate the performance of specific program elements and provides input into the next period's situation analysis. It is a necessary ingredient to a continuing planning process, yet it is often not carried out.

In this chapter, we discuss some reasons firms should measure the effectiveness of their IMC programs, as well as why many decide not to. We also examine how, when, and where such measurements can be conducted. Most of our attention is devoted to measuring the effects of advertising because much more time and effort have been expended developing evaluation measures in advertising than in the other promotional areas. We will, however, discuss measurement in other areas of the IMC program as well. You'll recall that we addressed the methods used to evaluate many of the other promotional elements in previous chapters.

It is important to understand that in this chapter we are concerned with research that is conducted in an evaluative role—that is, to measure the effectiveness of advertising and promotion and/or to assess various strategies before implementing them. This is not to be confused with research discussed earlier in the text to help develop the promotional program, although the two can (and should) be used together, as you will see. While evaluative research may occur at various times throughout the promotional process (including the development stage), it is conducted specifically to assess the effects of various strategies. We begin our discussion with the reasons effectiveness should be measured as well as some of the reasons firms do not do so.

# ARGUMENTS FOR AND AGAINST MEASURING EFFECTIVENESS

Almost any time one engages in a project or activity, whether for work or for fun, some measure of performance occurs. In sports you may compare your golf score against par or your time on a ski course to other skiers' performance. In business, employees are generally given objectives to accomplish, and their job evaluations are based on their ability to achieve these objectives. Advertising and promotion should not be an exception. It is important to determine how well the communications program is working and to measure this performance against some standards.

## Reasons to Measure Effectiveness

Assessing the effectiveness of ads both before they are implemented and after the final versions have been completed and fielded offers a number of advantages:

1.  *Avoiding costly mistakes.* The top three advertisers in the United States spent over $6 billion in advertising and promotion in 2012. The top 10 spent a total of over $15.3 billion.[1] This is a lot of money to be throwing around without some understanding of how well it is being spent. If the program is not achieving its objectives, the marketing manager needs to know so he or she can stop spending (wasting) money on it.

    Just as important as the out-of-pocket costs is the opportunity loss due to poor communications. If the advertising and promotions program is not accomplishing its objectives, not only is the money spent lost but so too is the potential gain that could result from an effective program. Thus, measuring the effects of advertising does not just save money. It also helps the firm maximize its investment.

2.  *Evaluating alternative strategies.* Typically a firm has a number of strategies under consideration. For example, there may be some question as to the degree to which each medium should be used or whether one message is more effective than another. Or the decision may be between two promotional program elements. A key issue for the manager is to be able to determine how effective each one was. Numerous companies have also reallocated monies to nontraditional media. A number of studies have revealed that advertisers said they planned to spend more monies in digital and social media in the coming years.[2,3] The question is, should research be spent on traditional, on social, digital, or advertising or other media and/or in what combination? Research may be designed to help the manager determine which strategy is most likely to be effective.

3.  *Increasing the efficiency of advertising in general.* You may have heard the expression "can't see the forest for the trees." Sometimes advertisers get so close to the project they lose sight of what they are seeking, and because they know what they are trying to say, they expect their audience will also understand. They may use technical jargon that not everyone is familiar with. Or the creative department may get too creative or too sophisticated and lose the meaning that needs to be communicated. How many times have you seen an ad and asked yourself what it was trying to say, or how often have you seen an ad that you really like, but you can't remember the brand name? Conducting research helps companies develop more efficient and effective communications. An increasing number of clients are demanding accountability for their promotional programs and putting more pressure on the agencies to produce. As IMC Perspective 18–1, discussing the Ogilvy Award winners, demonstrates, effective research can be used for both of these purposes.

4.  *Determining if objectives are achieved.* In a well-designed IMC plan, specific communication objectives are established. If objectives are attained, new ones need to be established in the next planning period. An assessment of how program elements led to the attainment of the goals should take place, and/or reasons for less-than-desired achievements must be determined. Research should address whether the strategy delivers the stated objectives and how appropriate the measures used to make this assessment are.

## Reasons Not to Measure Effectiveness

While it seems obvious that it makes sense to measure effectiveness, the fact remains that in too many instances this is not done. Whereas advertisers know that it is important to measure effectiveness, with as many as 90 percent considering it a priority, many do not do so, or if they do, they are not confident of the results. On the positive side, 54 percent of these managers say they plan to increase their expenditures in this area.[4]

# IMC Perspective 18–1 > > >

## The 2013 Ogilvy Award Winners

GLAD® is a registered trademark of the Glad Products Company and is used with permission. © 2013 The Glad Products Company. Reprinted with permission.

One of the most prestigious awards an advertising agency and its client can receive is an Ogilvy Award. The award is named for longtime advertising executive David Ogilvy, who was always a strong advocate of the use of research in advertising. Sponsored by the Advertising Research Foundation, the awards are given for excellence in advertising research and/or the creative use of research in the advertising development process.

Following are a few of the 2013 winners:

**Grand Ogilvy Award Winner:** "P&G London 2012 Olympic Games "Thank You Mom" Procter & Gamble

The campaign was designed as a way to unite P&G and its brands through a global Olympic sponsorship. The campaign was designed to provide a heartwarming umbrella that would connect the individual P&G brands and the Olympics movement together in the minds of consumers through a highly emotional insight to life that linked P&G and Olympic values. The "Thank You Mom" campaign was created to speak to moms and anyone with a mom by honoring the role mothers play in helping their kids reach their full potential and showing how moms have the hardest job in the world—but also the best job. The "Thank You Mom" ads illustrated the role and viewpoint of moms in a way that moved billions of people all over the world. The campaign did this in context of the Olympic games and other media and included 32 brands in over 50 countries.

Just some of the results of the campaign indicated that (1) consumers' perceptions of P&G went from cold and distant to "deeply human and personal"; (2) the ads were perceived as the strongest Olympic-sponsored ads ever; (3) P&G gained equity in every market measured; and (4) the campaign won Cannes and Emmy Awards. Some managers at P&G believe it will forever change the way that P&G advertises.

**Research Achievement Award:** "Slim Jim Center for Spice Loss" (ConAgra)

Long a favorite of teenage males, purchases of Slim Jims dropped off significantly once teens turned 18. The goal of the campaign was to extend the favorable brand image and consumption of teens throughout their next life stage of 18 to 29, while increasing the consumption

---

YTC 18-01

P&G "Thank You Mom"

youtube.com/10ebelch

Companies give a number of reasons for not measuring the effectiveness of advertising and promotions strategies:

1. *Cost.* Perhaps the most commonly cited reason for not testing (particularly among smaller firms) is the expense. In one of the surveys cited, it was noted that while some companies spend as much as 25 percent of their revenue on marketing and advertising, 70 percent of them spend less than 2 percent on measuring effectiveness.[5] Good research can be expensive in terms of both time and money. Many managers decide that time is critical and they must implement the program while the opportunity is available. Many believe the monies spent on research could be better spent on improved production of the ad, additional media buys, and the like.

   While the first argument may have some merit, the second does not. Imagine what would happen if a poor campaign were developed or the incentive program did not motivate the target audience. Not only would you be spending money without the desired effects, but the effort could do more harm than good. Spending more money to buy media does not remedy a poor message or substitute for an improper promotional mix. For example, one of the nation's leading brewers watched its test-market sales for a new brand of beer fall short of expectations. The problem, it thought, was an insufficient media buy. The solution, it decided, was to buy all the TV time available that matched its target among teens at the same time. The new tongue-in-cheek campaign, "Man Medicine," introduced the world to the Slim Jim Center for Spice Loss, a medical-type organization whose trained professionals treated males suffering from the negative effects of unmanly behavior. Essentially, the campaign can best be described through a medical solution lens: Disorder = Male Spice Loss. Cause = The newfound pressures of adult responsibility. Symptoms = Plummeting gaming and diminished zombie survival skills. Cure = Slim Jim products. Depending on the symptoms, patients were prescribed a number of Slim Jim products to restore manliness. It was an idea designed to both attract an older audience and still deliver the irreverent humor that teenage guys expect from Slim Jim. Ads were placed on TV, digital online video, Xbox, and social media.

The success of the campaign was measured by increased relevance, purchase intent, and consumption in both targeted segments. Most importantly, Slim Jim was able to show these increases with no additional media spending.

A third award winner included Glad:

**Research Innovation:** "Stronger Stand Against Waste" (Glad)

Most of the time (one would guess!) consumers aren't sitting around thinking about trash bags. At the same time, Glad found out through research that consumers do think about what goes into a bag and its impact on the environment. This insight led the way for Glad's "Stronger Stand Against Waste" campaign. The campaign showcased Glad's new stronger bag, made with less plastic, by visually bringing to life the collective magnitude of impact that just one person with the help of just one bag can make on the environment.

After significantly improving the trash bags themselves by reducing the amount of plastic used in manufacturing, and making them stronger, Glad went a step further with the goal of targeting mothers in their 30s who manage the household, care for the family, and value brands and products that help them in these endeavors. Because many of these women were already Glad buyers, the brand had to move carefully so as not to threaten their existing relationships. To do this, Glad and its advertising and research agencies developed the campaign "Small Changes That Can Make a Big Difference." To convey the idea that the Glad bags were now stronger while made with less plastic, television commercials showed that the plastic saved could cover all of Manhattan or Mt. Rainier or fill 200 garbage trucks. A "waste-less" website was developed, as was an app to provide insights on recycling and composting. PR initiatives and a "One Bag" initiative encouraging consumers to use one less bag at a college football game were also included in the IMC program.

Research indicated that the campaign exceeded virtually every objective. Advertising efficiency (defined by showing that consumers would be willing to pay more for sustainable products in a down economy, and become even more engaged in environmental issues) was increased by 540 percent, whereas the amount of waste reduction was increased by 121 percent. Unique visitors to Glad.com increased by 616 percent, with repeat visits increasing by 575 percent. Glad's research included focus groups and neuroresearch and other methodologies to guide the company in its endeavor, and it attributes much of its success to this research.

Source: "2013 Ogilvy Awards," www.thearf.org, 2013.

audience. After two months sales had not improved, and the product was abandoned in the test market. Analysis showed the problem was not in the media but rather in the message, which communicated no reason to buy. Research would have identified the problem, and millions of dollars and a brand might have been saved. The moral: Spending research monies to gain increased exposure to the wrong message is not a sound management decision.

2. *Research problems.* A second reason cited for not measuring effectiveness is that it is difficult to isolate the effects of promotional elements. Each variable in the marketing mix affects the success of a product or service. Because it is often difficult to measure the contribution of each marketing element directly, some managers become frustrated and decide not to test at all. They say, "If I can't determine the specific effects, why spend the money?" Only 50 percent of companies surveyed feel they have a good understanding of the ROI they get from advertising (online or off-line). This number was down from a survey taken just a year before.[6]

This argument also suffers from weak logic. While we agree that it is not always possible to determine the dollar amount of sales contributed by promotions, research can provide useful results and, as shown throughout this text, most have metrics to evaluate their performance. As demonstrated by the Ogilvy Award–winning strategies discussed in IMC Perspective 18–1,

FIGURE 18–1

Metrics Used by
CMOs Worldwide to
Measure the Value of
Social Media Marketing
Activities, 2010 and 2011
(% of respondents)

| % of respondents | | |
| --- | --- | --- |
| | **2010** | **2011** |
| Site traffic | 68.0% | 68.0% |
| Conversion | 32.6 | 65.7 |
| Number of fans/members | 59.4 | 62.9 |
| Number of positive customer mentions | 52.6 | 62.9 |
| Number of contributors | 42.9 | 50.3 |
| Revenues | 29.1 | 49.7 |
| Number of page views | 50.9 | 43.4 |
| Number of posts | 40.0 | 42.3 |
| Number of mentions | 41.1 | 41.1 |
| Average order value | 22.3 | 23.4 |
| Reduced returns | 12.0 | 16.0 |
| Increased channel sales | 4.0 | 14.9 |
| Reduced call volume | 11.4 | 11.4 |
| Other | 2.9 | 6.9 |
| Do not track metrics | 18.3 | 6.9 |

Note: n =175.
Source: Bazaarvoice and The CMO Club 'CMOs on Social Marketing
Plans for 2011.' provided to eMarketer; eMarketer calculations
January 27,2011.

communications effectiveness can be measured and may carry over to sales or other behaviors, such as engagement.

3. *Disagreement on what to test.* The objectives sought in the promotional program may differ by industry, by stage of the product life cycle, or even for different people within the firm. There are numerous ways to measure these and not always a consensus as to what measure should be used. The sales manager may want to see the impact of promotions on sales, top management may wish to know the impact on corporate image, and those involved in the creative process may wish to assess recall and/or recognition of the ad. Lack of agreement on what to test often results in no testing. A study conducted by the AAAA and ANA revealed that many marketers were dissatisfied with their efforts to integrate traditional and digital media, and there is a need to develop appropriate metrics for doing so. At the same time there is much disagreement as to what to measure. As shown in Figure 18–1 a variety of metrics are used in measuring the effectiveness of social media alone, and these measures continue to change.

Again, there is little rationale for this position. With the proper design, many or even all of the above might be measured. Since every promotional element is designed to accomplish specific objectives while contributing to the overall program, research can be used to measure its effectiveness in doing so.

4. *The objections of creative.* It has been argued by many (and denied by others) that the creative department does not want its work to be tested and many agencies are reluctant to submit their work for testing. This is sometimes true. Ad agencies' creative departments argue that tests are not true measures of the creativity and effectiveness of ads; applying measures stifles their creativity; and the more creative the ad, the more likely it is to be successful. They want permission to be creative without the limiting guidelines marketing may impose. The Chiat/Day ad shown in Exhibit 18–1 reflects how many people in the advertising business feel about this subject.

**To advertisers interested in 'day after recall', we submit a case history:**

*'My friends... each of you is a single cell in the great body of the State. And today, that great body has purged itself of parasites.*

*We have triumphed over the unprincipled dissemination of facts. The thugs and wreckers have been cast out. And the poisonous weeds of disinformation have*

*been consigned to the dustbin of history... Let each and every cell rejoice! For today we celebrate the first glorious anniversary of the Information Purification Directives.*

*We have created, for the first time in all history, a garden of pure ideology where each worker may bloom secure from the pests of contradictory and confusing truths.*

*Our Unification of Thought is more powerful a weapon than any fleet or army on earth. We are one people. We are one will.*

*One resolve. One cause. Our enemies shall talk themselves to death. And we will bury them with their own confusion.*

*We shall prevail!*

*Title and Voice Over: On January 24, Apple Computer will introduce Macintosh.*

*And you'll see why 1984 won't be like '1984.'*

On January 22, 1984, one commercial for Apple Computer ran on network television.

With all due respect to Burke, we didn't bother to test it.

Unlike a lot of advertising agencies, we prefer a different form of measurement:

When the product mentioned in the commercial, Apple's new Macintosh,' was unveiled on January 24, over 200,000 people lined up to see it in person.

Within 6 hours, they bought $3,500,000 worth of Macintosh computers. And left cash deposits for $1,000,000 more.

ABC, CBS, NBC and CNN featured the commercial in network news segments.

Dan Rather covered it at night. Bryant Gumbel covered it at dawn.

The BBC ran it in England.

Associated Press put it on the wire.

27 TV stations in major U.S. markets

ran it on local news programs.

Steven Spielberg called.

As did *The New York Times, The Wall Street Journal, The Washington Post,* the *Philadelphia Inquirer, USA Today,* the *Boston Globe,* the *Los Angeles Times,* the *San Francisco Chronicle* and, of course, the *San Jose Mercury News.*

Not to mention *Time, Newsweek, Fortune, Forbes, Business Week* and, of course, *Advertising Age.*

Apple is now producing one Macintosh every 27 seconds. And selling one every 20 seconds.

Not bad for one 60-second spot on the Super Bowl.

**Chiat/Day**

Los Angeles, San Francisco, New York

**EXHIBIT 18–1**

Chiat/Day expresses its opinion of recall tests

At the same time, the marketing manager is ultimately responsible for the success of the product or brand. Given the substantial sums being allocated to advertising and promotion, it is the manager's right, and responsibility, to know how well a specific program—or a specific ad—will perform in the market. Interestingly, in a study examining the 200 most awarded commercials over a two-year span, it was shown that 86 percent were deemed effective in achieving their goals, versus only 33 percent for other ads—proving that creative ads are effective.[7]

5. *Time.* A final reason given for not testing is a lack of time. Managers believe they already have too much to do and just can't get around to testing, and they don't want to wait to get the message out because they might miss the window of opportunity.

Planning might be the solution to the first problem. Although many managers are overworked and time poor, research is just too important to skip.

The second argument can also be overcome with proper planning. While timeliness is critical, getting the wrong message out is of little or no value and may even be harmful. There will be occasions where market opportunities require choosing between testing and immediate implementation. But even then some testing may help avoid mistakes or improve effectiveness.

# CONDUCTING RESEARCH TO MEASURE ADVERTISING EFFECTIVENESS

## What to Test

We now examine how to measure the effects of communications. This section considers what elements to evaluate, as well as where and how such evaluations should occur.

In Chapter 5, we discussed the components of the communications model (source, message, media, receiver) and the importance of each in the promotional program. Marketers need to determine how each is affecting the communication process. Other decisions made in the promotional planning process must also be evaluated.

**Source Factors** An important question is whether the spokesperson being used is effective and how the target market will respond to him or her. Or a product spokesperson may be an excellent source initially but, owing to a variety of reasons, may lose impact over time. As shown in Chapter 17, negative publicity can easily change the value of a source. The fact that so many of the companies using Lance Armstrong as a spokesperson terminated their contracts with him was based on the expectation that the target audiences would no longer have positive perceptions of him. The list of celebrities who have fallen out of favor is a long one.

**Message Variables** Both the message and the means by which it is communicated are bases for evaluation. For example, in the beer example discussed

LO 18-2

earlier, the message never provided a reason for consumers to try the new product. In other instances, the message may not be strong enough to pull readers into the ad by attracting their attention or clear enough to help them evaluate the product. Sometimes the message is memorable but doesn't achieve the other goals set by management. For example, one study examined what effect sexually themed print ads would have on viewers. Among the numerous results was that men favor sex appeals more than women do and that recall of the brands was lower for sexual ads than for nonsexual ones. Whereas men responded that sexual ads have "high stopping power" for them, their lower brand recall seems to indicate that they are paying more attention to other aspects of the ad than the marketers would prefer.[8] A number of companies are now attempting to determine the specific reactions that viewers have to product and brand messages, including excitement, engagement stress, and anxiety responses.[9]

**Media Strategies**   Research may be designed in an attempt to determine which media class (for example, broadcast versus print), subclass (newspapers versus magazines), or specific vehicles (which newspapers or magazines) generate the most effective results. Likewise, how does one digital medium compare relative to others, or to traditional media? Perhaps most importantly, how does each medium contribute to the achievement of overall IMC objectives?

An important factor is the **vehicle option source effect**, "the differential impact that the advertising exposure will have on the same audience member if the exposure occurs in one media option rather than another." People perceive ads differently depending on their context.[10]

Another factor to consider in media decisions involves scheduling. The evaluation of flighting versus pulsing or continuous schedules is important, particularly given the increasing costs of media time. As discussed in Chapter 10, there is evidence to support the fact that continuity may lead to a more effective media schedule than does flighting. Likewise, there may be opportunities associated with increasing advertising weights in periods of downward sales cycles or recessions. The manager experimenting with these alternative schedules and/or budget outlays should attempt to measure their differential impact.

As more and more companies and organizations move toward an integrated media mix, it becomes increasingly important to attempt to determine the individual contributions of various media as well as their synergistic effect. As you will see later in this chapter, progress is being made in this regard, but making such a determination is not a simple task.

**Budgeting Decisions**   A number of studies have examined the effects of budget size on advertising effectiveness and the effects of various ad expenditures on sales. Many companies have also attempted to determine whether increasing their ad budget directly increases sales. This relationship is often hard to determine, perhaps because using sales as an indicator of effectiveness ignores the impact of other marketing-mix elements. More definitive conclusions may be possible if other dependent variables, such as the communications objectives stated earlier, are used.

## When to Test

Virtually all test measures can be classified according to when they are conducted. **Pretests** are measures taken before the campaign is implemented; **posttests** occur after the ad or commercial has been in the field. A variety of pretests and posttests are available to the marketer, each with its own methodology designed to measure some aspect of the advertising program. Figure 18–2 classifies these testing methods.

**FIGURE 18–2**

Classification of Testing Methods

| PRETESTS | | |
|---|---|---|
| *Laboratory Methods* | | |
| Consumer juries | Theater tests | Readability tests |
| Portfolio tests | Rough tests | Comprehension and reaction tests |
| Physiological measures | Concept tests | |
| *Field Methods* | | |
| Dummy advertising vehicles | On-air tests | |
| POSTTESTS | | |
| *Field Methods* | | |
| Recall tests | Single-source systems | Recognition tests |
| Association measures | Inquiry tests | Tracking studies |

**Pretesting**   Pretests may occur at a number of points, from as early on as idea generation to rough execution to testing the final version before implementing it. More than one type of pretest may be used. For example, concept testing (which is discussed later in this chapter) may take place at the earliest development of the ad or commercial, when little more than an idea, basic concept, or positioning statement is under consideration. In other instances, layouts of the ad campaign that include headlines, some body copy, and rough illustrations are used. For TV commercials, storyboards and animatics may be tested. In these tests specific shortcomings may be identified, and changes made to enhance certain executional elements. As noted by Cramphorn, the best reason to pretest is to identify winners, to enhance good ads, and to eliminate bad ones. He notes that it is important to know the probable effect the ad will have before committing to its use.[11]

The methodologies employed to conduct pretests vary. In focus groups, participants freely discuss the meanings they get from the ads, consider the relative advantages of alternatives, and even suggest improvements or additional themes. In addition to or instead of the focus groups, consumers are asked to evaluate the ad on a series of rating scales. (Different agencies use different measures.) In-home interviews, mall intercept, Internet surveys, or laboratory methods may be used to gather the data.

The advantage of pretesting at this stage is that feedback is relatively inexpensive. Any problems with the concept or the way it is to be delivered are identified before large amounts of money are spent in development. Sometimes more than one version of the ad is evaluated to determine which is most likely to be effective.

Due to the fact that it costs so much less to find out that an ad may not work prior to making it public, rather than after doing so, it certainly makes sense to pretest.

The disadvantage is that mock-ups, storyboards, or animatics may not communicate nearly as effectively as the final product. The mood-enhancing and/or emotional aspects of the message are very difficult to communicate in this format. Another disadvantage is time delays. Many marketers believe being first in the market offers them a distinct advantage over competitors, so they forgo research to save time and ensure this position—even though this may be a risky strategy.

**Posttesting**   Posttesting is also common among both advertisers and ad agencies (with the exception of testing commercials for wearout). Posttesting is designed to (1) determine if the campaign is accomplishing the objectives sought and (2) serve as input into the next period's situation analysis.

## Where to Test

In addition to when to test, decisions must be made as to *where*. These tests may take place in either laboratory or field settings.

**Laboratory**   In **laboratory tests**, people are brought to a particular location where they are shown ads and/or commercials. The testers either ask questions about them or measure participants' responses by other methods—for example, pupil dilation, eye tracking, or galvanic skin response.

The major advantage of the lab setting is the *control* it affords the researcher. Changes in copy, illustrations, formats, colors, and the like can be manipulated inexpensively, and the differential impact of each assessed. This makes it much easier for the researcher to isolate the contribution of each factor.

The major disadvantage is the lack of *realism*. Perhaps the greatest effect of this lack of realism is a **testing bias**. When people are brought into a lab (even if it has been designed to look like a living room), they may scrutinize the ads much more closely than they would at home. A second problem with this lack of realism is that it cannot duplicate the natural viewing situation, complete with the distractions or comforts of home. Looking at ads in a lab setting may not be the same as viewing at home on the couch, with the spouse, kids, dog, cat, and parakeet chirping in the background. (A bit later you will see that some testing techniques have made progress in correcting this deficiency. No, they did not bring in the dogs and the parakeets.) Overall, however, the control offered by this method probably outweighs the disadvantages, which accounts for the frequent use of lab methods.

**Field Tests**   **Field tests** are tests of the ad or commercial under natural viewing situations, complete with the realism of noise, distractions, and the comforts of home. Field tests take into account the effects of repetition, program content, and even the presence of competitive messages.

The major disadvantage of field tests is the lack of control. It may be impossible to isolate causes of viewers' evaluations. If atypical events occur during the test, they may bias the results. Competitors may attempt to sabotage the research. And field tests usually take more time and money to conduct, so the results are not available to be acted on quickly. Thus, realism is gained at the expense of other important factors. It is up to the researcher to determine which trade-offs to make.

## How to Test

Our discussion of what should be tested, when, and where was general and designed to establish a basic understanding of the overall process as well as some key terms. In this section, we discuss more specifically some of the methods commonly used at each stage. First, however, it is important to establish some criteria by which to judge ads and commercials.

Conducting evaluative research is not easy. Twenty-one of the largest U.S. ad agencies have endorsed a set of principles aimed at "improving the research used in preparing and testing ads, providing a better creative product for clients, and controlling the cost of TV commercials."[12] This set of nine principles, called **Positioning Advertising Copy Testing (PACT)**, defines *copy testing* as research "that is undertaken when a decision is to be made about whether advertising should run in the marketplace. Whether this stage utilizes a single test or a combination of tests, its purpose is to aid in the judgment of specific advertising executions."[13] The nine principles of good copy testing are shown in Figure 18–3.

As you can see, advertisers and their clients are concerned about developing *appropriate* testing methods. Adherence to these principles may not make for perfect testing, but it goes a long way toward improving the state of the art and alleviates at least one of the testing problems cited earlier.

**FIGURE 18–3**

Positioning Advertising
Copy Testing (PACT)

1. Provide measurements that are relevant to the objectives of the advertising.
2. Require agreement about how the results will be used in advance of each specific test.
3. Provide multiple measurements (because single measurements are not adequate to assess ad performance).
4. Be based on a model of human response to communications—the reception of a stimulus, the comprehension of the stimulus, and the response to the stimulus.
5. Allow for consideration of whether the advertising stimulus should be exposed more than once.
6. Require that the more finished a piece of copy is, the more soundly it can be evaluated and require, as a minimum, that alternative executions be tested in the same degree of finish.
7. Provide controls to avoid the biasing effects of the exposure context.
8. Take into account basic considerations of sample definition.
9. Demonstrate reliability and validity.

# THE TESTING PROCESS

Testing may occur at various points throughout the development of an ad or a campaign: (1) concept generation research; (2) rough, prefinished art, copy, and/or commercial testing; (3) finished art or commercial pretesting; and (4) market testing of ads or commercials (posttesting).

## Concept Generation and Testing

Figure 18–4 describes the process involved in advertising **concept testing**, which is conducted very early in the campaign development process in order to explore the targeted consumer's response to a potential ad or campaign or have the consumer evaluate advertising alternatives. Positioning statements, copy, headlines, and/or illustrations may all be under scrutiny. The material to be evaluated may be just a headline or a rough sketch of the ad. The colors used, typeface, package designs, and even point-of-purchase materials may be evaluated.

One of the more commonly used methods for concept testing is focus groups, which usually consist of 8 to 10 people in the target market for the product. Companies have tested everything from product concepts to advertising concepts using focus groups. For most companies, the focus group is the first step in the research process. The number of focus groups used varies depending on group consensus, strength of response, and/or the degree to which participants like or dislike the concepts. Some

**FIGURE 18–4**

Concept Testing

| *Objective:* |
| --- |
| Explores consumers' responses to various ad concepts as expressed in words, pictures, or symbols. |
| *Method:* |
| Alternative concepts are exposed to consumers who match the characteristics of the target audience. Reactions and evaluations of each are sought through a variety of methods, including focus groups, direct questioning, and survey completion. Sample sizes vary depending on the number of concepts to be presented and the consensus of responses. |
| *Output:* |
| Qualitative and/or quantitative data evaluating and comparing alternative concepts. |

FIGURE 18–5

Weaknesses Associated
with Focus Group Research

- The results are not quantifiable.
- Sample sizes are too small to generalize to larger populations.
- Group influences may bias participants' responses.
- One or two members of the group may steer the conversation or dominate the discussion.
- Consumers become instant "experts."
- Members may not represent the target market. (Are focus group participants a certain type of person?)
- Results may be taken to be more representative and/or definitive than they really are.

companies use 50 or more groups to develop a campaign, although fewer than 10 are usually needed to test a concept sufficiently.

While focus groups continue to be a favorite of marketers, they are often overused. The methodology is attractive in that results are easily obtained, directly observable, and immediate. A variety of issues can be examined, and consumers are free to go into depth in areas they consider important. Also, focus groups don't require quantitative analysis. Unfortunately, many managers are uncertain about research methods that require statistics; and focus groups, being qualitative in nature, don't demand much skill in interpretation. Weaknesses with focus groups are shown in Figure 18–5. Clearly, there are appropriate and inappropriate circumstances for employing this methodology.

Another way to gather consumers' opinions of concepts is mall intercepts, where consumers in shopping malls are approached and asked to evaluate rough ads and/or copy. Rather than participating in a group discussion, individuals assess the ads via questionnaires, rating scales, and/or rankings. New technologies allow for concept testing over the Internet, where advertisers can show concepts simultaneously to consumers throughout the United States, garnering feedback and analyzing the results almost instantaneously. In addition, online focus groups are being used more often to do concept testing (Exhibit 18–2). Internet methods are becoming increasingly popular given the cost savings and time efficiencies associated with these research methods, and some research firms now offer hybrid studies that involve a combination of online and traditional measures.

## Rough Art, Copy, and Commercial Testing

Because of the high cost associated with the production of an ad or commercial (many network commercials cost hundreds of thousands of dollars to produce), advertisers are increasingly spending more monies testing a rendering of the final ad at early stages. Slides of the artwork posted on a screen or animatic and photomatic roughs may be used to test at this stage. (See Figure 18–6 for an explanation of terminology.) Because such tests can be conducted inexpensively, research at this stage is becoming ever more popular.

EXHIBIT 18–2

Online focus groups are used
for concept testing

Virtual Focus Facility: Observer View

But cost is only one factor. The test is of little value if it does not provide relevant, accurate information. Rough tests must indicate how the finished commercial would perform. Studies have demonstrated that these testing methods are reliable and the results typically correlate well with the finished ad.

Most of the tests conducted at the rough stage involve lab settings, although some on-air field tests are also available. Popular tests include comprehension and reaction tests and consumer juries. Again, the Internet allows field settings to be employed at this stage.

A *rough* commercial is an unfinished execution that may fall into three broad categories:

| Animatic Rough | Photomatic Rough | Live-Action Rough |
|---|---|---|
| Succession of drawings/cartoons | Succession of photographs | Live motion |
| Rendered artwork | Real people/scenery | Stand-in/nonunion talent |
| Still frames | Still frames | Nonunion crew |
| Simulated movement: | Simulated movements: | Limited props/minimal opticals |
|    Panning/zooming of frame/rapid sequence |    Panning/zooming of frame/rapid sequence | Location settings |

| A Finished Commercial Uses: |
|---|
| Live motion/animation |
| Highly paid union talent |
| Full union crew |
| Exotic props/studio sets/special effects |

**FIGURE 18–6**

Rough Testing Terminology

1. *Comprehension and reaction tests.* One key concern for the advertiser is whether the ad or commercial conveys the meaning intended. The second concern is the reaction the ad generates. Obviously, the advertiser does not want an ad that evokes a negative reaction or offends someone. **Comprehension and reaction tests** are designed to assess these responses (which makes you wonder why some ads are ever brought to the marketplace).

   Tests of comprehension and reaction employ no one standard procedure. Personal interviews, group interviews, and focus groups have all been used for this purpose, and sample sizes vary according to the needs of the client; they typically range from 50 to 200 respondents.

2. *Consumer juries.* This method uses consumers representative of the target market to evaluate the probable success of an ad. **Consumer juries** may be asked to rate a selection of layouts or copy versions presented in pasteups on separate sheets. The objectives sought and methods employed in consumer juries are shown in Figure 18–7.

**FIGURE 18–7**

Consumer Juries

| Objective: |
|---|
| Potential viewers (consumers) are asked to evaluate ads and give their reactions to and evaluation of them. When two or more ads are tested, viewers are usually asked to rate or rank order the ads according to their preferences. |

| Method: |
|---|
| Respondents are asked to view ads and rate them according to either (1) the order of merit method or (2) the paired comparison method. In the former, the respondent is asked to view the ads and then rank them from one to *n* according to their perceived merit. In the latter, ads are compared only two at a time. Each ad is compared to every other ad in the group, and the winner is listed. The best ad is that which wins the most times. Consumer juries typically employ 50 to 100 participants. |

| Output: |
|---|
| An overall reaction to each ad under construction as well as a rank ordering of the ads based on the viewers' perceptions. |

While the jury method offers the advantages of control and cost effectiveness, serious flaws in the methodology limit its usefulness:

- *The consumer may become a self-appointed expert.* One of the benefits sought from the jury method is the objectivity and involvement in the product or service that the targeted consumer can bring to the evaluation process. Sometimes, however, knowing they are being asked to critique ads, participants try to become more *expert* in their evaluations, paying more attention and being more critical than usual. The result may be a less than objective evaluation or an evaluation on elements other than those intended.
- *The number of ads that can be evaluated is limited.* Whether *order of merit* or *paired comparison* methods are used, the ranking procedure becomes tedious as the number of alternatives increases. Consider the ranking of 10 ads. While the top two and the bottom two may very well reveal differences, those ranked in the middle may not yield much useful information.

  In the paired comparison method, the number of evaluations required is calculated by the formula

  $$\frac{n(n-1)}{2}$$

  If six alternatives are considered, 15 evaluations must be made. As the number of ads increases, the task becomes even more unmanageable.
- *A halo effect is possible.* Sometimes participants rate an ad good on all characteristics because they like a few and overlook specific weaknesses. This tendency, called the **halo effect**, distorts the ratings and defeats the ability to control for specific components. (Of course, the reverse may also occur—rating an ad bad overall due to only a few bad attributes.)
- *Preferences for specific types of advertising may overshadow objectivity.* Ads that involve emotions or pictures may receive higher ratings or rankings than those employing copy, facts, and/or rational criteria. Even though the latter are often more effective in the marketplace, they may be judged less favorably by jurists who prefer emotional appeals.

Some of the problems noted here can be remedied by the use of ratings scales instead of rankings. But ratings are not always valid either. Thus, while consumer juries have been used for years, questions of bias have led researchers to doubt their validity. As a result, a variety of other methods (discussed later in this chapter) are more commonly employed.

## Pretesting of Finished Ads

Pretesting finished ads is one of the more commonly employed studies among marketing researchers and their agencies. At this stage, a finished advertisement or commercial is used; since it has not been presented to the market, changes can still be made.

Many researchers believe testing the ad in final form provides better information. Several test procedures are available for print and broadcast ads, including both laboratory and field methodologies.

Print methods include portfolio tests, analyses of readability, and dummy advertising vehicles. Broadcast tests include theater tests and on-air tests. Both print and broadcast may use physiological measures.

### Pretesting Finished Print Messages
A number of methods for pretesting finished print ads are available. One is *Gallup & Robinson's Impact System,* described in Figure 18–8. The most common of these methods are portfolio tests, readability tests, and dummy advertising vehicles.

**Portfolio Tests Portfolio tests** are a laboratory methodology designed to expose a group of respondents to a portfolio consisting of both control and test ads.

**FIGURE 18–8**

Gallup & Robinson's Impact
System

*Objective:*

Understanding the performance of individual advertising executions or testing finished products. Evaluation of print advertising in magazines or newspapers. Can also be used to pretest rough advertising executions or posttesting finished products.

*Method:*

Interviewers contact potential respondents door to door or by telephone and screen for qualification.

*Output:*

Scores include recall, idea communication, persuasion, brand rating, and ad liking. Diagnostics in regard to ad reactions and brand attributes are also reported.

Respondents are then asked what information they recall from the ads. The assumption is that the ads that yield the *highest recall* are the most effective.

While portfolio tests offer the opportunity to compare alternative ads directly, a number of weaknesses limit their applicability:

1. Factors other than advertising creativity and/or presentation may affect recall. Interest in the product or product category, the fact that respondents know they are participating in a test, or interviewer instructions (among others) may account for more differences than the ad itself.
2. Recall may not be the best test. Some researchers argue that for certain types of products (those of low involvement) ability to recognize the ad when shown may be a better measure than recall.

One way to determine the validity of the portfolio method is to correlate its results with readership scores once the ad is placed in the field. Whether such validity tests are being conducted or not is not readily known, although the portfolio method remains popular in the industry.

**Readability Tests** The communications efficiency of the copy in a print ad can be tested without reader interviews. This test uses the **Flesch formula**, named after its developer, Rudolph Flesch, to assess readability of the copy by determining the average number of syllables per 100 words. Human interest appeal of the material, length of sentences, and familiarity with certain words are also considered and correlated with the educational background of target audiences. Test results are compared to previously established norms for various target audiences. The test suggests that copy is best comprehended when sentences are short, words are concrete and familiar, and personal references are drawn.

The Flesch Kincaid Reading Ease Score method eliminates many of the interviewee biases associated with other tests and avoids gross errors in understanding. The norms offer an attractive standard for comparison. Other readibility measures also exist, including the SMOG Readibility Formula and the Fry Graph Readibility Formula.

Disadvantages are also inherent, however. The copy may become too mechanical, and direct input from the receiver is not available. Without this input, contributing elements like creativity cannot be addressed. To be effective, this test should be used only in conjunction with other pretesting methods.

**New Print Pretesting Measures** In an effort to improve upon the traditional print pretest measures, a number of companies have introduced new methodologies or improved upon existing methods. Many of these involve hybrid measures that either measure effectiveness in different ways, or in different channels. For example, Ipsos ASI Next*Connect has introduced an online copy testing tool (Figure 18–9) that can test ads on digital or traditional media. Consumers are recruited to complete an online

**FIGURE 18–9**

Ipsos-ASI's Next* Connect

| *Objective:* |
|---|
| To assist advertisers in copy testing of print advertisements to determine the print ad's individual executions or multiple campaign elements across any platform impact on the brand |
| *Method:* |
| Consumers are recruited to complete an online survey where they are exposed to a variety of messages and results are compared against those from a control group not exposed to any ads. |
| *Output:* |
| Standard scores, related recall, persuasion, and specific diagnostics. |

survey where they are exposed to a variety of ad messages. The results are compared against a control group that was not exposed to the advertising. The methodology allows for testing ads in finished or rough formats, for individual executions or multiple campaign elements, and determine ads' impact in traditional and new media.

The PreTesting Groups' People Reader methodology measures the time a respondent spends with a print ad or on the iPad by providing consumers with two mocked-up magazines, telling them that the publisher is interested in their opinions of the magazines. The magazines contain a number of ads targeted toward the interests of the consumers. Unknown to the consumers, as they go through the magazines, hidden cameras record where their eyes go on the page, how long they stay on the page reading the ad, and the stopping power of the ad. The studies can be conducted in person or online and can measure recall, main idea communication, and more.

Millward Brown offers its own trademarked methodology as well, called Link. According to the company, Link uses a comprehensive set of diagnostic questions to evoke viewer reactions to the ads. Nonverbal measures including eye tracking can also be used to determine consumers' enjoyment, comprehension, involvement, and other reactions to the ads. The three key metrics provided include awareness, persuasion, and short-term sales likelihood.

While other methods and measures are available, the most popular form of pretesting of print ads now involves a series of measures. The tests can typically be used for rough and/or finished ads and are most commonly conducted in a lab or online.

**Pretesting Finished Broadcast Ads** A variety of methods for pretesting broadcast ads are available. The tests can typically be used for rough and/or finished ads and are most commonly conducted in a lab or online: As noted, most of the companies that offer pretesting of print ads have expanded their services to include TV and other platforms. For example, MSW•ARS Research provides offerings that allow the advertiser to evaluate the impact of advertising messages and campaigns composed of any combination of touch points, including broadcast (television and radio), outdoor, and digital. The company provides research solutions in brand strategy, all stages of creative development from concept to fully finished ads, campaign evaluation across all channels, advertising and brand equity tracking, and additional consulting services.

**Theater Tests** In the past, one of the most popular laboratory methods for pretesting finished commercials was **theater testing**. In theater tests participants are invited to view pilots of proposed TV programs. In some instances, the show is actually being tested, but more commonly a standard program is used so audience responses can be compared with normative responses established by previous viewers. Sample sizes range from 250 to 600 participants, with 300 being most typical.

The methods of theater testing operations vary, though all measure brand preference changes. For example, many of the services now use programs with the

**FIGURE 18–10**

GfK AD*VANTAGE/ACT
Methodology

AD*VANTAGE/ACT surveys are based on tests carried out in a studio. The number of respondents is typically about *n* = 125, normally composed of category users defined by the client. Each participant is shown a TV program, with commercial breaks that include the test commercial, and then asked questions about the program (Exhibit 18–3). The closed- and open-ended questions are recorded via a touch-screen system. Key measures include (1) visibility (Will the commercial be remembered?); (2) branding (Will the brand be remembered?); (3) communications (What visuals and messages will be remembered?); (4) brand enhancement (Does the ad promote a positive feeling toward the brand?); and (5) persuasion (Will the commercial inspire nonusers to try the product, and will it enhance brand loyalty among existing customers?). The diagnostics include measures of viewers' awareness, comprehension, uniqueness, and involvement of the commercial. The AD*VANTAGE/ACT methodology also allows for scene-by-scene analysis, and can be used to test all traditional forms of advertising as well as digital.

commercials embedded for viewing in one's home or office rather than in a theater. Others establish viewing rooms in malls and/or hotel conference rooms. Some do not take all the measures listed here; others ask the consumers to turn dials or push buttons on a keypad to provide the continual responses. An example of one methodology is shown in Figure 18–10 (you may remember GfK from Chapter 10).

Those opposed to theater tests cite a number of disadvantages. First, they say the environment is too artificial. The recruiting and lab testing conditions are likely to lead to testing effects, and consumers are exposed to commercials they might not even notice in a more natural environment. Second, the contrived measure of brand preference change seems too phony to believe. Critics contend that participants will see through it and make changes just because they think they are supposed to. Finally, the group effect of having others present and overtly exhibiting their reactions may influence viewers who did not have any reactions themselves.

**EXHIBIT 18–3**

AD*VANTAGE/ACT scores care place in a studio

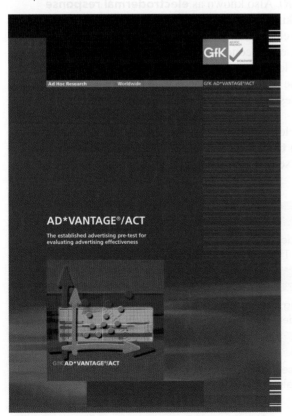

Proponents argue that theater tests offer distinct advantages. In addition to control, the established norms (averages of commercials' performances) indicate how one's commercial will fare against others in the same product class that were already tested. Further, advocates say the brand preference measure is supported by actual sales results.

Despite the limitations of theater testing, most major consumer-product companies have used it to evaluate their commercials. This method may have shortcomings, but it allows them to identify strong or weak commercials and to compare them to other ads.

**On-Air Tests** Some of the firms conducting theater tests also insert the commercials into actual TV programs in certain test markets. Typically, the commercials are in finished form, although the testing of ads earlier in the developmental process is becoming more common. This is referred to as an **on-air test** and often includes single-source ad research (discussed later in this chapter). Information Resources, Ipsos-ASI, MSW•ARS, and Nielsen are well-known providers of on-air tests.

On-air testing techniques offer all the advantages of field methodologies, as well as all the disadvantages. The most commonly employed metric used in an on-air test is **recall**, that is, the number of persons able to recall the ad and/or its message. In an examination of real-world advertising tests reported in the *Journal of Advertising Research*, Hu et al.

conclude that recall and persuasion pretests, while often employed, do not fare well in respect to reliability and/or validity.[14] Nevertheless, most of the testing services have offered evidence of both validity and reliability for on-air pretesting of commercials. Both Ipsos-ASI and MSW•ARS claim their pretest and posttest results yield the same recall scores 9 out of 10 times—a strong indication of reliability and a good predictor of the effect the ad is likely to have when shown to the population as a whole.

In summary, on-air pretesting of finished or rough commercials offers some distinct advantages over lab methods and some indications of the ad's likely success. Whether the measures used are as strong an indication as the providers say remains in question.

**Physiological Measures** A less common method of pretesting finished commercials involves a laboratory setting in which physiological responses are measured. These measures indicate the receiver's *involuntary* response to the ad, theoretically eliminating biases associated with the voluntary measures reviewed to this point. (Involuntary responses are those over which the individual has no control, such as heartbeat and reflexes.) Physiological measures used to test both print and broadcast ads include pupil dilation, galvanic skin response, eye tracking, and brain waves:

1. *Pupil dilation.* Research in **pupillometrics** is designed to measure dilation and constriction of the pupils of the eyes in response to stimuli. Dilation is associated with action; constriction involves the body's conservation of energy.

   Advertisers have used pupillometrics to evaluate product and package design as well as to test ads. Pupil dilation suggests a stronger interest in (or preference for) an ad or implies arousal or attention-getting capabilities. Other attempts to determine the affective (liking or disliking) responses created by ads have met with less success.

   Because of high costs and some methodological problems, the use of pupillometrics has waned over the past decade. But it can be useful in evaluating certain aspects of advertising.

2. *Galvanic skin response (GSR).* Also known as **electrodermal response (EDR)**, GSR measures the skin's resistance or conductance to a small amount of current passed between two electrodes. Response to a stimulus activates sweat glands, which in turn increases the conductance of the electrical current. Thus, GSR/EDR activity might reflect a reaction to advertising. While there is evidence that GSR/EDR may be useful to determine the effectiveness of ads, difficulties associated with this testing method have resulted in its infrequent use at this time.

3. *Eye tracking.* As seen in the lead-in to this chapter, a methodology that is more commonly employed is **eye tracking** (Figure 18–11), in which viewers are asked to view an ad while a sensor aims a beam of infrared light at the eye.

**FIGURE 18–11**

Eye Movement Research

| *Objective:* |
| --- |
| Track viewers' eye movements to determine what viewers read or view in print ads and where their attention is focused in TV commercials, websites, or billboards. |
| *Method:* |
| Fiber optics, digital data processing, and advanced electronics are used to follow eye movements of viewers and/or readers as they process an ad. |
| *Output:* |
| Relationship among what readers see, recall, and comprehend. Scan movement paths on print ads, billboards, commercials, print materials, and websites. (Can also be used to evaluate package designs.) |

**EXHIBIT 18-4**

Eye tracking is becoming more commonly used

The beam follows the movement of the eye and shows the exact spot on which the viewer is focusing (Exhibit 18-4). The continuous reading of responses demonstrates which elements of the ad are attracting attention, how long the viewer is focusing on them, and the sequence in which they are being viewed.

Eye tracking can identify strengths and weaknesses in an ad. For example, attractive models or background action may distract the viewer's attention away from the brand or product being advertised. The advertiser can remedy this distraction before fielding the ad. In other instances, colors or illustrations may attract attention and create viewer interest in the ad.

Eye tracking has increasingly been used to measure the effectiveness of websites and online ads and, as noted earlier, e-mails. Using eye tracking to examine how consumers view homepages, Steve Outing and Laura Roel were able to determine that (1) eyes first fixate on the upper left of the screen, (2) dominant headlines draw attention first, and (3) larger type promotes scanning, while small type encourages reading. The study drew other conclusions as well—too many to mention here.[15] Digital and Social Media Perspective 18-1 details some other applications of eye tracking.

4. *Brain waves.* **Electroencephalographic (EEG) measures** can be taken from the skull to determine electrical frequencies in the brain. These electrical impulses are used in two areas of research, alpha waves and hemispheric lateralization:

- **Alpha activity** refers to the degree of brain activation. People are in an alpha state when they are inactive, resting, or sleeping. The theory is that a person in an alpha state is less likely to be processing information (recall correlates negatively with alpha levels) and that attention and processing require moving from this state. By measuring a subject's alpha level while viewing a commercial, researchers can assess the degree to which attention and processing are likely to occur.

- **Hemispheric lateralization** distinguishes between alpha activity in the left and right sides of the brain. It has been hypothesized that the right side of the brain processes visual stimuli and the left processes verbal stimuli. The right hemisphere is thought to respond more to emotional stimuli, while the left responds to logic. The right determines recognition, while the left is responsible for recall. If these hypotheses are correct, advertisers could design ads to increase learning and memory by creating stimuli to appeal to each hemisphere. However, some researchers believe the brain does not function laterally and an ad cannot be designed to appeal to one side or the other.

- Using technologies originally designed for the medical field such as positron emission tomography (PET), functional magnetic resonance imaging (fMRI), and electroencephalography (EEG), neuroscientists have teamed up with marketers to examine physiological reactions to ads and brands through brain scan imaging. By monitoring the brain activity directly, scientists are learning how consumers make up their minds by measuring chemical activity and/or changes in the magnetic fields of the brain as well as how they react to commercials.

While EEG research has engaged the attention of academic researchers for some time, recently the technology has gained in attractiveness to practioners as well.

An increased emphasis on accountability and the pressure to determine an ad's effectiveness, along with the explosion of new media and changes and improvements to existing media, are just some of the reasons why marketers continue to seek new ways to examine how their messages are performing. As a result, new research methodologies are being developed, and existing technologies are being adapted to assist in making this determination. (Recall our earlier discussion of neurosciences.) Some of these are proving to be quite successful.

For example, there is a new methodology called "mouse hovering" in which a heat-mapping technology collects data as to where users have "moused" over an ad and for how long. The start-up company claims that the data will help advertisers better understand which parts of the ad users engage with and how intensely. Given that click-throughs are more important to direct marketers than those attempting to use the Internet for branding purposes, Moat—the developer of the technology—believes that its method of determining effectiveness is of more value than counting clicks. A competitor of Moat, RealVu, addresses this same problem from a different perspective, focusing on display advertising on the Internet. Rather than using heat-mapping technology, RealVu measures the seconds a user is actually exposed to an ad. While both companies agree that click-throughs are not effective measures of Internet advertising, they don't necessarily agree what is the best measure.

A methodology that seems to be gaining more and more acceptance in marketing circles has actually been around for quite some time. The usefulness of eye tracking technology for measuring advertising effectiveness is not news for marketers. Back in the late 1970s and early 1980s, advertising researchers were employing this technology to determine where viewers were focusing when they looked at ads and/or TV commercials. One story is that one of the original Tab diet soft-drink commercials was changed when viewers focused on the female swimsuit model instead of the product. The commercial was supposedly changed to have her hold the can in front of her body to attract attention. For whatever reason, while proven to be useful, eye tracking never went away, but no one seemed to pay much attention it. Now all of that is changing.

One company heavily involved with using eye tracking to determine advertising effectiveness is Tobii. An international company with offices located in the United States, Norway, Germany, Japan, and China, Tobii was founded as a result of a research project at the Royal Institute of Technology in Stockholm, Sweden, and employs eye tracking for a variety of nonmarketing purposes, as well as for measuring ad effectiveness. The company offers its research services for studying online marketing, including determining the effectiveness of banner ads, e-mail campaigns, newsletters, and in-game advertising. More traditional testing includes copy testing print ads in the creative stage; assessing the impact of out-of-home-ads in bars, airports, grocery stores, and so on; determining the effectiveness of product placements and TV commercials; and even testing promotional products.

The increased emphasis on accountability and desire to determine an ad's effectiveness, along with the explosion of new media and changes to existing media platforms, are just some of the reasons marketers have found a number of new applications for eye tracking. In addition to the effectiveness measures offered by Tobii and others, companies have used this methodology for:

- *Retail (interior displays/window design):* Eye tracking studies enabling interior designers to choose color, lighting, architecture, and so on, so as to subtly influence the customer's mood. This includes the use of eye catchers to attract passers-by and arouse their curiosity.
- *Package design:* Optimizing the look and feel of the packaging as well as the attention-getting capabilities.
- *Advertisements:* Allowing the advertiser to determine what customers see and to determine the effectiveness of copy and visuals.

In addition to those examples cited earlier in the chapter and throughout this text, companies like the $4.2 billion Nielsen Company—the world's largest audience measurement company—have invested in neuroscience measurement as *Fortune* 500 companies increasingly seek these services. Neuroscience measures have been used to determine viewers' responses to Super Bowl commercials, differences in responses to drinking Coke and Pepsi, political ads, and movie trailers to name just a few of the many applications.

## Market Testing of Ads

The fact that the ad and/or campaign has been implemented does not mean there is no longer a need for testing. The pretests were conducted on smaller samples and

- *Online marketing:* From Web design to viewers' attention to display ads, marketers are finding eye tracking a valuable tool to enhance effectiveness.

Researchers use eye movements to tell specifically where viewers are looking, to see if they are reading or scanning, and what catches their first view. They can also tell how much time the viewers spend looking at a specific stimulus and the order in which they view others (if they do!). For example:

- An eye tracking study conducted by Oneupweb asked participants to navigate Facebook, Twitter, and YouTube as they normally would. The study revealed that 65 percent of them engaged with a sponsor within 10 seconds of beginning their search, when asked to search for Pepsi on both Facebook and YouTube (Twitter was not included as it has no search tool). On Facebook, the results showed that their first attention was paid to the sponsored ads, and others were barely, if at all, viewed, while on YouTube, the top six organic results and the first sponsored ad got all the attention. The conclusion? Sponsored ads work better than expected.

- In another Internet study, Jakob Nielsen and Kara Pernice, authors of the book *Eyetracking Web Usability*, tracked how people navigate websites when looking for information. Searches included how to deal with heartburn, shopping for baby presents, and picking cell phone features, among others. Their results indicate that to be effective, an ad should be simple, with those that had only text or text and a separate image being most effective, while those that imposed text on top of images or included animation fared the worse. While the study showed that people saw 36 percent of the ads on the pages they visited, the time spent viewing them was only one-third of a second. One of the most surprising results was the fact that text-only ads scored best. When asked for an explanation, the authors hypothesized that unlike television which is a passive medium, the Web is all about taking action, searching, clicking, and so forth. On the Web, it is the value of content that makes it attractive.

- In a scarier application, a Canadian company now offers an eye tracking device that can determine when someone looks at a billboard, where the person looks, and for how long, without one even knowing it—up to 33 feet. It then provides Google-like metrics that greatly improve on existing methods of data collection.

- In Germany, a pre- and posttest research study was designed to measure participants' perceptions and recall of ads through a virtual reality situation in which one drives a van down the street with advertisements on both sides. The eye tracking and survey results are then combined to determine viewers' unaided/aided recall, recognition and design aspects of the ads. And yes, they can do it at different speeds!

Part of the reason why eye tracking measures have not hit the mainstream is the high cost and obtrusiveness of the measurement equipment (usually the participants have to wear headgear, whether in a lab setting or in the field—for example, walking through a department store or supermarket looking weird). There was also the question about whether the fact that the participants knew they were in a study influenced their behaviors. However, P&G, working with an external eye tracking firm, believes that eye tracking has saved the company substantial amounts of money by allowing P&G to cancel website display ads that are not being seen. The information is gathered from a panel of 14 million consumers using webcams to track their eye movements while on a site, and is then fed back to P&G's creative department indicating what works best.

Maybe eye tracking is here to stay!

Sources: Christopher Heine, "P&G Slashes Wasteful Display Ad Budgets Using Eye Tracking," www.adweek.com, May 30, 2013; "Advertising Research and Eye Tracking," www.tobii.com, June 10, 2013; Barbara Kiviat, "Why We Look at Some Web Ads and Not Others," www.time.com, November 8, 2009; Nathania Johnson, "Eye Tracking Study Shows Sponsored Ads Attract Social Media Searchers," July 19, 2009, blog.searchenginewatch.com; Dan Skeen, "Eye-Tracking Device Lets Billboards Know When You Look at Them," www.wired.com, June 12, 2007; G. Theuner, K. Pischke, and T. Bley, "Analysis of Advertising Effectiveness with Eye Tracking," *Proceedings of Measuring Behavior 2008*, Maastricht, The Netherlands, August 26–29, 2008, pp. 229–230.

YTC **18–02**

**Tobii Eye Tracking**

youtube.com/10ebelch

may in some instances have questionable merit, so the marketer must find out how the ad is doing in the field. In this section, we discuss methods for posttesting an ad. Some of the tests are similar to the pretests discussed in the previous section and are provided by the same companies.

**Posttests of Print Ads**   A variety of print posttests are available, including inquiry tests, recognition tests, and recall tests.

**Inquiry Tests**   Used in both consumer and business-to-business market testing, **inquiry tests** are designed to measure advertising effectiveness on the basis of inquiries generated from ads appearing in various print media, often referred to as "bingo cards" such as the one shown in Exhibit 18–5. While still used, the response

EXHIBIT 18–5

Reader response cards are popular in business-to-business markets

**TARGET** MARKETING  Receive the information you need to market smarter instantly!
Go to: **www.targetonline.com** and click on free information.

**Or...** Fill out this card and either FAX your request today: 215-238-5388 or mail.

**Free Subscription**

Do you wish to receive (continue to receive) a FREE subscription to TARGET MARKETING? ☐ YES ☐ NO

Signature_____ Date_____
Name (please print) _____ Title _____
Company Name _____
Address _____
City/State/Zip _____
Telephone_____ FAX _____
Email Address: _____

1. **TYPE OF BUSINESS AT THIS LOCATION: (Check One)**
   04 ☐ Catalogers, Mail Order Companies
   05 ☐ Retailers, Wholesaler/Distributor
   06 ☐ On-line Merchant
   03 ☐ Financial Services: Banks, Insurance, Credit Cards, Investment
   21 ☐ Fund Raisers: Non-Profit Groups, Charities
   33 ☐ High Technology: Internet Services, Computers, Software, Telecommunications, Office Equipment
   12 ☐ Manufacturers, Package Goods and Other Business-to-Business Marketers
   31 ☐ Non Financial Services Marketers: Associations, Clubs, Educational, Government Agencies, Health Care, Membership Organizations, Personnel Services, Real Estate, Utilities, Communications, Tourism and Travel
   13 ☐ Publishers: Magazines, Books, Newsletters, Newspapers, Book & Record Clubs On-line publications
   01 ☐ Advertising/DM Agencies, Freelance Creative and Consultants
   09 ☐ Mailing List Professionals: Brokers, Compilers, Owners
   20 ☐ Other: (Please Specify) _____

2. **JOB FUNCTION: (Check One)**
   10 ☐ Corporate and General Management (Excluding Sales, Marketing and Advertising Management)
   02 ☐ Marketing, List and Sales Management
   01 ☐ Advertising Promotion and Public Relations Management
   08 ☐ Operational, Technical and Telemarketing Management
   06 ☐ Circulation Management
   11 ☐ Other: (Please Specify) _____

3. **MY FIRM'S MARKETING ACTIVITY: (Check All That Apply)**
   1 ☐ Catalog           5 ☐ Consumer
   2 ☐ Direct Mail        6 ☐ Business-to-Business
   09 ☐ Internet          7 ☐ International
   3 ☐ Telemarketing      8 ☐ None of the Above
   10 ☐ Alternate Media

4. **IN THE PERFORMANCE OF YOUR JOB, CHECK THE ONE THAT BEST DESCRIBES YOUR PURCHASING AUTHORITY: (Check One)**
   1 ☐ Authorize/Approve Purchase
   2 ☐ Recommend/ Specify Purchase
   3 ☐ No Purchasing Authority

**Free Information**

Circle the free info number for the products and services that interest you

| | | | | | | | | | | | |
|---|---|---|---|---|---|---|---|---|---|---|---|
|001|002|003|004|005|006|007|008|009|010|011|012|
|013|014|015|016|017|018|019|020|021|022|023|024|
|025|026|027|028|029|030|031|032|033|034|035|036|
|037|038|039|040|041|042|043|044|045|046|047|048|
|049|050|051|052|053|054|055|056|057|058|059|060|
|061|062|063|064|065|066|067|068|069|070|071|072|
|073|074|075|076|077|078|079|080|081|082|083|084|
|085|086|087|088|089|090|091|092|093|094|095|096|
|097|098|099|100|101|102|103|104|105|106|107|108|
|109|110|111|112|113|114|115|116|117|118|119|120|
|121|122|123|124|125|126|127|128|129|130|131|132|
|133|134|135|136|137|138|139|140|141|142|143|144|
|145|146|147|148|149|150|151|152|153|154|155|156|
|157|158|159|160|161|162|163|164|165|166|167|168|
|169|170|171|172|173|174|175|176|177|178|179|180|

**For Information on Product/Service Categories**

To request information on any of the following areas of interest, check the appropriate free information number:

| | |
|---|---|
|501 ☐ Agencies/Consultants/Creative Services|530 ☐ Internet Services|
|502 ☐ Alternate Media/Delivery|513 ☐ Lettershop Services|
|503 ☐ Broadcast Media/Services|514 ☐ Lists-Business-to-Business|
|504 ☐ Call Center Equipment|515 ☐ Lists-Consumer|
|505 ☐ Credit/Collection Services|528 ☐ Lists-E-mail|
|506 ☐ Database Management Systems/Services/Software|516 ☐ Lists-International|
| |517 ☐ List Services|
|507 ☐ Delivery Services|518 ☐ Mailing Equipment/Services|
|529 ☐ E-mail Marketing|520 ☐ Paper|
|508 ☐ Envelopes/Order Forms/Labels|521 ☐ Premiums/Promotional Products|
|509 ☐ Fulfillment Services/Operations|522 ☐ Prepress Equipment/Services|
|510 ☐ Int'l Call Centers|523 ☐ Printers|
|511 ☐ Int'l Delivery Services|527 ☐ Printing Systems/Equipment|
|512 ☐ Int'l DM Agencies|524 ☐ Telemarketing Services|
|525 ☐ International DM Services| |

RS0110

card is employed less often today as viewers can seek information merely by searching on the URL provided in the ad. The inquiry may take the form of the number of coupons returned, phone calls generated, or direct inquiries through reader cards. If you called in a response to an ad in a local medium recently, perhaps you were asked how you found out about the company or product or where you saw the ad. This is a very simple measure of the ad's or medium's effectiveness.

More complex methods of measuring effectiveness through inquiries may involve (1) running the ad in successive issues of the same medium, (2) running **split-run tests**, in which variations of the ad appear in different copies of the same newspaper or magazine, and/or (3) running the same ad in different media. Each of these methods yields information on different aspects of the strategy. The first measures the *cumulative* effects of the campaign; the second examines specific elements of the ad or variations on it. The final method measures the effectiveness of the medium rather than the ad itself.

While inquiry tests may yield useful information, weaknesses in this methodology limit its effectiveness. For example, inquiries may not be a true measure of the attention-getting or information-providing aspects of the ad. The reader may be attracted to an ad, read it, and even store the information but not be motivated to inquire at that particular time. Time constraints, lack of a need for the product or service at the time the ad is run, and other factors may limit the number of inquiries. But receiving a small number of inquiries doesn't mean the ad was not effective; attention, attitude change, awareness, and recall of copy points may all have been achieved. At the other extreme, a person with a particular need for the product may respond to any ad for it, regardless of specific qualities of the ad.

Major advantages of inquiry tests are that they are inexpensive to implement and they provide some feedback with respect to the general effectiveness of the ad or medium used. But they are usually not very effective for comparing different versions or specific creative aspects of an ad.

FIGURE 18–12

The *GfK Starch Ad Readership Report*

**Objective:**

Determining recognition of print ads and providing insight into the involvement readers have with specific ads.

**Method:**

Personal interviewers screen readers for qualifications and determine exposure and readership to specific issues of newspapers, consumer magazines, and business and professional publications. Samples include a minimum of 200 males and females, as well as specific audiences where required. Participants are asked to go through the magazines, looking at the ads, and provide specific responses.

**Output:**

*Starch Ad Readership Reports* generate three recognition scores:

- Noting score—the percentage of readers who remember seeing the ad.
- Brand-associated score—the percentage of readers who recall seeing or reading any part of the ad identifying the product or brand.
- Read-most score—the percentage of readers who report reading at least half of the copy portion of the ad. Ad norms provide a benchmark to provide a comparison to other ads in the issue.

These conventional scores have now been supplemented by additional measures, including brand disposition, purchase behavior or intention, actions taken, and publication and advertising engagement.

**Recognition Tests** Perhaps the most common posttest of print ads is the **recognition method**, most closely associated with GfK-Starch. The *Starch Ad Readership Report*, which has existed for over 85 years, lets the advertiser assess the impact of an ad in a single issue of a magazine, over time, and/or across different magazines. Starch measures hundreds of thousands of print ads representing more than 180 consumer magazines per year and provides a number of measures of an ad's effectiveness. In addition to the traditional *Starch Ad Readership Report,* Starch now offers syndicated and private studies, pretesting, out-of-home studies and more. The measures used in the Starch test methodology are shown in Figure 18–12. An example of a Starch scored ad is shown in Exhibit 18–6.

Starch claims that (1) the pulling power of various aspects of the ad can be assessed through the control offered, (2) the effectiveness of competitors' ads can be compared through the norms provided, (3) alternative ad executions can be tested, and (4) readership scores are a useful indication of consumers' *involvement* in the ad or campaign. (The theory is that a reader must read and become involved in the ad before the ad can communicate. To the degree that this readership can be shown, it is a direct indication of effectiveness.)

Of these claims, perhaps the most valid is the ability to judge specific aspects of the ad. Some researchers have criticized other aspects of the Starch recognition method (as well as other recognition measures) on the basis of problems of false claiming, interviewer sensitivities, and unreliable scores:

1. *False claiming.* Research shows that in recognition tests, respondents may claim to have seen an ad when they did not. False claims may be a result of having seen similar ads elsewhere, expecting that such an ad would appear in the medium, or wanting to please the questioner. Interest in the product category also increases reporting of ad readership. Whether this

**EXHIBIT 18–6**

An ad scoring very high on the Starch rating scale.

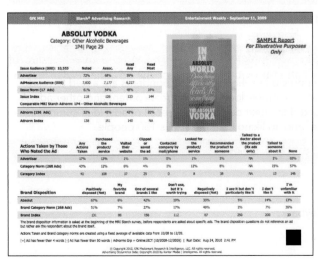

false claiming is deliberate or not, it leads to an overreporting of effectiveness. On the flip side, factors such as interview fatigue may lead to an underreporting bias—that is, respondents not reporting an ad they did see.

2. *Interviewer sensitivities.* Any time research involves interviewers, there is a potential for bias. Respondents may want to impress the interviewer or fear looking unknowledgeable if they continually claim not to recognize an ad. There may also be variances associated with interviewer instructions, recordings, and so on, regardless of the amount of training and sophistication involved.

3. *Reliability of recognition scores.* Starch admits that the reliability and validity of its readership scores increase with the number of insertions tested, which essentially means that to test just one ad on a single exposure may not produce valid or reliable results.

In sum, despite critics, the Starch readership studies continue to dominate the posttesting of print ads. The value provided by norms and the fact that multiple exposures can improve reliability and validity may underlie the decisions to employ this methodology. In addition, the long-standing reliability and trustworthiness of the organization definitely comes into play.

**Recall Tests** There are several tests to measure recall of print ads. Perhaps the best known of these are the Ipsos-ASI Next*Correct test and the Gallup & Robinson Magazine Impact Research Service (MIRS) described in Figure 18–13. (A number of other companies, including Millward Brown and Decision Analyst, offer similar services.) These **recall tests** are similar to those discussed in the section on pretesting broadcast ads in that they attempt to measure recall of specific ads.

In addition to having the same interviewer problems as recognition tests, recall tests have other disadvantages. The reader's degree of involvement with the product and/or the distinctiveness of the appeals and visuals may lead to higher-than-accurate recall scores, although in general the method may lead to lower levels of recall than actually exist (an error the advertiser would be happy with). Critics contend the test is not strong enough to reflect recall accurately, so many ads may score as less effective than they really are, and advertisers may abandon or modify them needlessly.

On the plus side, it is thought that recall tests can assess the ad's impact on memory. Proponents of recall tests say the major concern is not the results themselves but how they are interpreted. Previous studies have shown that the correlation between ad recall and recognition is very high in both newspapers and magazines.

**FIGURE 18–13**

Gallup & Robinson Magazine Impact Research Service (MIRS)

| *Objective:* |
|---|
| Tracking recall of advertising (and client's ads) appearing in magazines to assess performance and effectiveness. |
| *Method:* |
| Test magazines are placed in participants' homes and respondents are asked to read the magazine that day. Test ads are embedded with editorial content and other ads. A telephone interview is conducted the next day to assess recall of ads, idea communication, persuasion, brand rating, and ad liking. Sample size is 150 people. |
| *Output:* |
| Measures provided:<br>■ Norms.<br>■ Vertatin respondent playback.<br>■ Performance summary.<br>■ Diagnostics. |

**Posttests of Broadcast Commercials**  A variety of methods exist for posttesting broadcast commercials. The most common provide a combination of day-after recall tests, persuasion measures, and diagnostics. Test marketing and tracking studies, including single-source methods, are also employed.

**Day-After Recall Tests**  The most popular method of posttesting employed in the broadcasting industry for decades was the *Burke Day-After Recall test.* While a number of companies offered day-after recall methodologies, the "Burke test" for all intents and purposes became the generic name attached to these tests. While popular, day-after recall tests also had problems, including limited samples, high costs, and security issues (ads shown in test markets could be seen by competitors). Because of their common usage, numerous studies have been conducted to determine the efficacy of DAR tests. While these studies have been conducted quite some time ago, the conclusions seem to be relevant today and merit consideration here. In addition, the following disadvantages with recall tests were also suggested:

1. DAR tests may favor unemotional appeals because respondents are asked to verbalize the message. Thinking messages may be easier to recall than emotional communications, so recall scores for emotional ads may be lower.[16] A number of other studies have also indicated that emotional ads may be processed differently from thinking ones; some ad agencies, for example, Leo Burnett and BBDO Worldwide among others, have gone so far as to develop their own methods of determining emotional response to ads.[17]
2. Program content may influence recall. The programs in which the ad appears may lead to different recall scores for the same brand. The net result is a potential inaccuracy in the recall score and in the norms used to establish comparisons.
3. A prerecruited sample may pay increased attention to the program and the ads contained therein because the respondents know they will be tested the next day. This effect would lead to a higher level of recall than really exists.
4. In addition, studies have shown that recall is a measure that the ad has been received, but not necessarily accepted, and not predictive of sales.[18,19]

The major advantage of day-after recall tests is that they are field tests. The natural setting is supposed to provide a more realistic response profile. These tests are also popular because they provide norms that give advertisers a standard for comparing how well their ads are performing. In addition to recall, a number of different measures of the commercial's effectiveness are now offered, including persuasive measures and diagnostics. (The Burke test itself no longer exists under that name.)

**Persuasive Measures**  As noted earlier in our discussion of pretesting broadcast commercials a number of research firms now offer measures of a commercial's persuasive effectiveness day. Some of the services offer additional persuasion measures, including purchase, intent, and frequency-of-purchase criteria.

**Diagnostics**  In addition to measuring recall and persuasion, copy testing firms also provide diagnostic measures. These measures are designed to garner viewers' evaluations of the ads, as well as how clearly the creative idea is understood and how well the proposition is communicated. Rational and emotional reactions to the ads are also examined. A number of companies offer diagnostic measures, including Gallup & Robinson and Millward Brown, among many others.

**Comprehensive Measures**  While each of the measures just described provides specific input into the effectiveness of a commercial, many advertisers are interested in more than just one specific input. Thus, some companies provide comprehensive approaches in which each of the three measures just described can be obtained through one testing program. Figure 18–14 describes one such comprehensive program, Ipsos-ASI's Next*TV test (Exhibit 18–7).

**FIGURE 18–14**

Ipsos-ASI's Next*TV

| Objectives: |
|---|
| To assist advertisers in testing of their commercials through multiple measures to determine (1) the potential of the commercial for impacting sales, (2) how the ad contributes to brand equity, (3) how well it is in line with existing advertising strategies and objectives, and (4) how to optimize effectiveness. |

| Method: |
|---|
| Consumers are recruited to evaluate a TV program, with ads embedded into the program as they would be on local prime-time television. Consumers view the commercial on a video-based system that self-erases in their homes to simulate actual field conditions. (The option to use local cable television programs with commercial inserts is also provided.) |

| Output: |
|---|
| Related recall (day-after recall) scores; multiple persuasion scores, including brand preference shifts, purchase intent and frequency, in-market sales effectiveness, copy effect, comprehensive diagnostics to determine what viewers take away from the ad and how creative elements contribute to or distract from advertising effectiveness, and comparison to norms. |

**Test Marketing** Many companies conduct tests designed to measure their advertising effects in specific test markets before releasing them nationally. The markets chosen are representative of the target market. For example, a company may test its ads in Portland, Oregon; San Antonio, Texas; or Buffalo, New York, if the demographic and socioeconomic profiles of these cities match the product's market. A variety of factors may be tested, including reactions to the ads (for example, alternative copy points), the effects of various budget sizes, or special offers. The ads run in finished form in the media where they might normally appear, and effectiveness is measured after the ads run.

The advantage of test marketing of ads is realism. Regular viewing environments are used and the testing effects are minimized. A high degree of control can be attained if the test is designed successfully. For example, an extensive test market study was designed and conducted by Seagram and Time, Inc., over a period of three years to measure the effects of advertising frequency on consumers' buying habits.

**EXHIBIT 18–7**

Ipsos-ASI offers a comprehensive testing measure

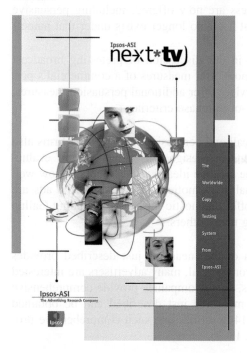

This study demonstrated just how much could be learned from research conducted in a field setting but with some experimental controls. It also showed that proper research can provide strong insights into the impact of ad campaigns. (Many advertising researchers consider this study one of the most conclusive ever conducted in the attempt to demonstrate the effects of advertising on sales.)

The Seagram study also reveals some of the disadvantages associated with test market measures, not the least of which are cost and time. Few firms have the luxury to spend three years and hundreds of thousands of dollars on such a test. In addition, there is always the fear that competitors may discover and intervene in the research process.

A number of companies, including Procter & Gamble and Toyota, have test-marketed interactive commercials. Reckitt—the world's largest manufacturer of household cleaning products—and Whirlpool have joined efforts to test *i*TV ads. Customers were offered three different enticements to interact with the campaign: (1) register to win a Whirlpool dishwasher, (2) register for free samples of Finish Dishwater Freshener, or (3) order money-off coupons for Finish Dishwater Tablets. After eight months of testing, Reckitt reported that the target goal of 35,000 responses was exceeded.[20] Sears and Ford have both tested the impact of ads placed on Gemstar—*TV Guide*'s interactive program guide—while Chrysler has experimented with online gaming to generate leads and stimulate buzz.[21]

Test marketing can provide substantial insight into the effectiveness of advertising if care is taken to minimize the negative aspects of such tests.

**Single-Source Tracking Studies** Since the 1980s the focus of many research efforts has been on single-source tracking methods. **Single-source tracking methods** track the behaviors of consumers from the television set to the supermarket checkout counter. Participants in a designated area who have cable TV and agree to participate in the studies use optical scanning equipment that identifies their household and gives the research company their demographics. The households are split into matched groups; one group receives an ad while the other does not, or alternate ads are sent to each. Their purchases are recorded from the bar codes of the products bought. Commercial exposures are then correlated with purchase behaviors.

Earlier we mentioned the use of single-source ad research in pretesting commercials. The single-source method can also be used effectively to posttest ads, allowing for a variety of dependent measures and tracking the effects of increased ad budgets and different versions of ad copy—and even ad effects on sales.

A 10-year study conducted by Information Resources' BehaviorScan service demonstrated long-term effects of advertising on sales. The study examined copy, media schedules, ad budgets, and the impact of trade promotions on sales in 10 markets throughout the United States and concluded that advertising can produce sales growth as long as two years after a campaign ends.[22] (The study also concluded that results of copy recall and persuasion tests were unlikely to predict sales reliably.) A number of single-source methods have been used, among them BehaviorScan (Information Resources) and The Nielsen Company's ScanTrack.

Many advertisers believe these single-source measures will change the way research is conducted due to the advantages of control and the ability to measure directly the ads' effects on sales. A number of major corporations and ad agencies are now employing this method, including companies and their agencies in the automotive, entertainment, financial services, packaged goods, and pharmaceutical industries among others.

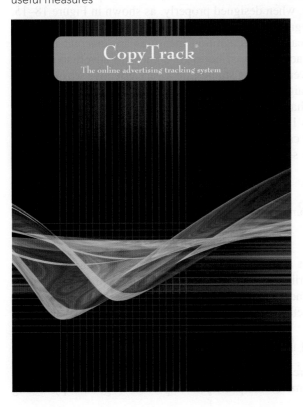

While single-source testing is a valuable tool, it still has some problems. One researcher says, "Scanner data focus on short-term sales effects, and as a result capture only 10 to 30 percent of what advertising does."[23] Others complain that the data are too complicated to deal with, as an overabundance of information is available. Still another disadvantage is the high cost of collecting single-source data. While the complexity of single-source data resulted in a slow adoption rate, this method of tracking advertising effectiveness became widely adopted in the 1990s by the research companies mentioned earlier (Gallup & Robinson, Millward Brown, and Ipsos ASI).

**Tracking Print/Broadcast Ads** One of the more useful and adaptable forms of posttesting involves tracking the effects of the ad campaign by taking measurements at regular intervals. **Tracking studies** have been used to measure the effects of advertising on awareness, recall, interest, and attitudes toward the ad and/or brand as well as purchase intentions. (Ad tracking may be applied to both print and broadcast ads but is much more common with the latter.) Personal interviews, phone surveys, mall intercepts, and even mail surveys have been used. Sample sizes typically range from 250 to 500 cases per period (usually quarterly or semiannually). Tracking studies yield perhaps the most valuable information available to the marketing manager for assessing current programs and planning for the future. (See Exhibit 18–8.)

**FIGURE 18–15**

Factors That Make or Break
Tracking Studies

1. Properly defined objectives
2. Alignment with sales objectives
3. Properly designed measures (e.g., adequate sample size, maximum control over interviewing process, adequate time between tracking periods)
4. Consistency through replication of the sampling plan
5. Random samples
6. Continuous interviewing (that is, not seasonal)
7. Evaluate measures related to behavior (attitudes meet this criterion; recall of ads does not)
8. Critical evaluative questions asked early to eliminate bias
9. Measurement of competitors' performance
10. Skepticism about questions that ask where the advertising was seen or heard (TV always wins)
11. Building of news value into the study
12. "Moving averages" used to spot long-term trends and avoid seasonality
13. Data reported in terms of relationships rather than as isolated facts
14. Integration of key marketplace events with tracking results (e.g., advertising expenditures of self and competitors, promotional activities associated with price changes in ad campaigns, introductions of new brands, government announcements, changes in economic conditions)

The major advantage of tracking studies is that they can be tailored to each specific campaign and/or situation. A standard set of questions can track effects of the campaign over time or through the consumer purchase funnel. In a study by the research organization Yankelovich and the Television Bureau of Advertising (TVB), it was shown that the effectiveness of advertising depends on the product category and where the consumer is in the purchase funnel. The advertising medium impact varied as the consumer moved through the stages.[24] The effects of various media can also be determined, although with much less effectiveness. Tracking studies have also been used to measure the differential impact of different budget sizes, the effects of flighting, brand or corporate image, and recall of specific copy points. As you will see later in the chapter, however, it is often difficult to quantify some of the measures suggested. Finally, when designed properly, as shown in Figure 18–15, tracking studies offer a high degree of reliability and validity.

Some of the problems of recall and recognition measures are inherent in tracking studies, since many other factors may affect both brand and advertising recall. Despite these limitations, however, tracking studies are a very effective way to assess the effects of advertising campaigns.

In summary, you can see that each of the testing methods considered in this chapter has its strengths and its limitations. You may wonder: Can we actually test advertising effectiveness? What can be done to ensure a valid, reliable test? The next section of this chapter suggests some answers.

# ESTABLISHING A PROGRAM FOR MEASURING ADVERTISING EFFECTS

There is no surefire way to test advertising effectiveness. However, in response to pressures to determine the contribution of ads to the overall marketing effort, steps are being taken to improve this measurement task. Let's begin by reviewing the major problems with some existing methods and then examine possible improvements.

## Problems with Current Research Methods

When current testing methods are compared to the criteria established by PACT (see Figure 18–3), it is clear that some of the principles important to good copy testing can be accomplished readily, whereas others require substantially more effort. For example, principle 6 (providing equivalent test ads) should require a minimum of effort. The researcher can easily control the state of completion of the test communications. Also fairly easy are principles 1 and 2 (providing measurements relative to the objectives sought and determining *a priori* how the results will be used).

We have seen throughout this text that each promotional medium, the message, and the budget all consider the marketing and communications objectives sought. The integrated marketing communications planning model establishes the roles of these elements. So by the time one gets to the measurement phase, the criteria by which these programs will be evaluated should simply fall into place.

Slightly more difficult are principles 3, 5, and 8, although again these factors are largely in the control of the researcher. Principle 3 (providing multiple measurements) may require little more than budgeting to make sure more than one test is conducted. At the most, it may require considering two similar measures to ensure reliability. Likewise, principle 5 (exposing the test ad more than once) can be accomplished with a proper research design. Finally, principle 8 (sample definition) requires little more than sound research methodology; any test should use the target audience to assess an ad's effectiveness. You would not use a sample of nondrinkers to evaluate new liquor commercials.

The most difficult factors to control—and the principles that may best differentiate between good and bad testing procedures—are PACT requirements 4, 7, and 9. Fortunately, however, addressing each of these contributes to the attainment of the others.

The best starting point is principle 4, which states the research should be guided by a model of human response to communications that encompasses reception, comprehension, and behavioral response. It is the best starting point, in our opinion, because it is the principle least addressed by practicing researchers. If you recall, Chapter 5 proposed a number of models that could fulfill this principle's requirements. Yet even though these models have existed for quite some time, few if any common research methods attempt to integrate them into their methodologies. Most current methods do little more than provide recall scores, despite the fact many researchers have shown that recall is a poor measure of effectiveness. Models that do claim to measure such factors as attitude change or brand preference change are often fraught with problems that severely limit their reliability. An effective measure must include some relationship to the communications process.

It might seem at first glance that principle 7 (providing a nonbiasing exposure) would be easy to accomplish. But lab measures, while offering control, are artificial and vulnerable to testing effects. And field measures, while more realistic, often lose control. The Seagram and Time study may have the best of both worlds, but it is too large a task for most firms to undertake. Some of the improvements associated with the single-source systems help solve this problem. In addition, properly designed ad tracking studies provide truer measures of the impact of the communication. As technology develops and more attention is paid to this principle, we expect to see improvements in methodologies soon.

Last but not least is principle 9, the concern for reliability and validity. Most of the measures discussed are lacking in at least one of these criteria, yet these are two of the most critical distinctions between good and bad research. If a study is properly designed, and by that we mean it addresses principles 1 through 8, it should be both reliable and valid.

## Essentials of Effective Testing

Simply put, good tests of advertising effectiveness must address the nine principles established by PACT. One of the easiest ways to accomplish this is by following the decision sequence model in formulating promotional plans.

- *Establish communications objectives.* We have stated that except for a few instances (most specifically direct-response advertising), it is nearly impossible to show the direct impact of advertising on sales. So the marketing objectives established for the promotional program are not usually good measures of communication effectiveness. For example, it is very difficult (or too expensive) to demonstrate the effect of an ad on brand share or on sales. On the other hand, attainment of communications objectives can be measured and leads to the accomplishment of marketing objectives.

- *Use a consumer response model.* Early in this text we reviewed the hierarchy of effects models and cognitive response models, which provide an understanding of the effects of communications and lend themselves to achieving communications goals. Many companies including Honda, General Motors, Sprint, and others use hierarchy models to establish objectives and assess effectiveness.

- *Use both pretests and posttests.* From a cost standpoint—both actual cost outlays and opportunity costs—pretesting makes sense. It may mean the difference between success or failure of the campaign or the product. But it should work in conjunction with posttests, which avoid the limitations of pretests, use much larger samples, and take place in more natural settings. Posttesting may be required to determine the true effectiveness of the ad or campaign.

- *Use multiple measures.* Many attempts to measure the effectiveness of advertising focus on one major dependent variable—perhaps sales, recall, or recognition. As noted earlier in this chapter, advertising may have a variety of effects on the consumer, some of which can be measured through traditional methods and others that require updated thinking (recall the discussion on physiological responses). For a true assessment of advertising effectiveness, a number of measures may be required. The Ogilvy Award winners mentioned earlier all employed multiple measures to track the effects on communications objectives.

- *Understand and implement proper research.* It is critical to understand research methodology. What constitutes a good design? Is it valid and reliable? Does it measure what we need it to? There is no shortcut to this criterion, and there is no way to avoid it if you truly want to measure the effects of advertising.

A major study sponsored by the Advertising Research Foundation (ARF), involving interviews with 12,000 to 15,000 people, addressed some of these issues.[25] While we do not have the space to analyze this study here, note that the research was designed to evaluate measures of copy tests, compare copy testing procedures, and examine some of the PACT principles. Information on this study has been published in a number of academic and trade journals and by ARF.

# MEASURING THE EFFECTIVENESS OF OTHER PROGRAM ELEMENTS

Throughout this text, we have discussed how and when promotional program elements should be used, the advantages and disadvantages of each, and so on. In many chapters we have discussed measures of effectiveness used to evaluate these programs. In the final section of this chapter, we add a few measures that were not discussed earlier.

## Measuring the Effectiveness of Sales Promotions

Sales promotions are not limited to retailers and resellers of products. Sports marketers have found them a very effective way to attract crowds and have been able to measure their relative effectiveness by the number of fans attending games. Major League Baseball teams have seen their attendance increase for those games in which promotions are offered.

A number of organizations measure sales promotions. One firm, MarketSource, provides marketers with a basis for measuring the effectiveness of their sampling

**FIGURE 18-16**

Measuring the Effects of FSIs

A study by Promotion Decisions Inc. examined the actual purchase data of users and nonusers of 27 coupon promotions in its National Shopper Lab (75,000 households) over a period of 18 months. The findings:

- FSI coupons generated significant trial by new and lapsed users of a product (53%).
- Repeat purchase rates were 11.8% higher among coupon redeemers than nonredeemers.
- 64.2% of repeat volume among coupon redeemers was without a coupon.
- There was no significant difference in share of volume between buyers who used coupons and those who did not.
- Coupons returned between 71% and 79% of their cost within 12 weeks.
- Full-page ads provided higher redemption rates, incremental volume, redemption by new users, and a higher number of repeat buyers than half-page ads.
- Consumers who used coupons were brand loyal.

programs. While too involved to discuss in detail here, the program calculates a breakeven rate by dividing the sampling investment by the profit for the user. If the conversions exceed the breakeven rate, the sampling program is successful.[26] Promotion Decisions Inc. examines the impact of freestanding inserts (FSIs) (Figure 18–16).

Other measures of sales promotions are also available. Schnucks (St. Louis), Smitty's Super Valu (Phoenix), and Vons (Los Angeles) have all used pretests with effects measured through scanner data. Others have employed this methodology to examine brand and store switching, alternative promotions, price discounts, and merchandising techniques.[27] Other advertisers use awareness tracking studies and count the number of inquiries, coupon redemptions, and sweepstakes entries. They also track sales during promotional and nonpromotional periods while holding other factors constant. The Nielsen Company's ScanTrack methodology helps marketers answer the questions regarding how many promotions to do and how this promotion compares to competitors', and what overall sales lift is associated with individual promotions using scanner data.

One recent technological development designed to track the effectiveness of sales promotions at the point of sale is offered by Shopper Trak. Shopper Trak places sensors in the store that track whether a person is coming or going, calculate the shopper's height (to differentiate between adults and children), and gauge traffic patterns. The system helps retailers evaluate the effectiveness of promotions or displays located throughout the store.[28]

## Measuring the Effectiveness of Nontraditional Media

In Chapter 13, we noted that one of the disadvantages of employing nontraditional media is that it is usually difficult to measure the effectiveness of the programs. But some progress has been made, as shown in these examples:

- *The effects of shopping cart signage.* Earlier we discussed sales increases that occurred when shopping cart signage was used. We have also noted throughout this chapter that while increasing sales is a critical goal, many other factors may contribute to or detract from this measure. (It should be noted that these results are provided by the companies that sell these promotional media.) At least one study has examined the effectiveness of shopping cart signage on data besides sales.[29] This study used personal interviews in grocery stores to measure awareness of, attention to, and influence of this medium. Interestingly, it suggests shopping carts are much less effective than the sign companies claim.
- *The effectiveness of ski resort–based media.* In Chapter 13, we discussed advertising on ski chair lifts and other areas to attempt to reach selective demographic groups. Now the Traffic Audit Bureau (TAB) is tracking the effectiveness of this form of advertising to give advertisers more reliable criteria on which to

base purchase decisions. The TAB data verify ad placements, while the media vendors have employed Experian Simmons Market Research and Nielsen Media Research to collect ad impressions and advertising recall information.[30] These measures are combined with sales tracking data to evaluate the medium's effectiveness.

- *The effects of in-store radio and television.* Interactive Market Systems (IMS) introduced software that enables clients to measure the effectiveness of in-store radio. The company planned to introduce similar software designed to measure in-store television advertising effectiveness.[31]

- *The effectiveness of other media.* A number of companies provide effectiveness measures to determine the impact of package designs, POP displays, trade show exhibits, and the like. Nielsen Entertainment and Massivemedia now offer a service to measure videogame advertising effectiveness.[32] While it is not possible to list them all here, suffice it to say that if one wants to measure the impact of various IMC elements, the resources are available.

## Measuring the Effectiveness of Sponsorships

In earlier chapters we discussed the growth in sponsorships and the reasons why organizations have increased their investments in this area. Along with the increased expenditures have come a number of methods for measuring the impact of sponsorships. Essentially, measures of sponsorship effectiveness can be categorized as exposure-based methods or tracking measures:[33]

- *Exposure methods.* Exposure methods can be classified as those that monitor the quantity and nature of the media coverage obtained for the sponsored event and those that estimate direct and indirect audiences. While commonly employed by corporations, scholars have heavily criticized these measures. For example, Michel Pham argues that media coverage is not the objective of sponsorships and should not be considered as a measure of effectiveness. He argues that the measures provide no indication of perceptions, attitude change, or behavioral change and should therefore not be considered as measures of effectiveness.[34]

- *Tracking measures.* These measures are designed to evaluate the awareness, familiarity, and preferences engendered by sponsorship based on surveys. A number of empirical studies have measured recall of sponsors' ads, awareness of and attitudes toward the sponsors and their products, and image effect, including brand and corporate images.

A number of companies now measure the effectiveness of sports and other sponsorships. For example, companies assign a value referred to as media equivalency and assign a monetary value to the amount of exposure the sponsor receives during the event. They review broadcasts and add up the number of seconds a sponsor's product name or logo can be seen clearly (for example, on signs or shirts). A total of 30 seconds is considered the equivalent of a 30-second commercial. (Such measures are of questionable validity.)

As with all other IMC touch points, marketers would like to measure the ROI of event sponsorships. But—like these other means of communication—this is usually not possible, so the focus will be on other more communication-oriented objectives. Figure 18–17 shows a Sponsorship Performance Matrix used by effectiveness measurement company SponsorMap. The vertical axis of this matrix measures the passion the target audience feels toward the sponsoring organization. The more emotionally attached to the property (sporting team, event, etc.), the higher the Passion Index. The horizontal axis measures sponsor appreciation—the Gratitude Index. According to SponsorMap, companies can achieve more appreciation by being more active, thus creating more goodwill. As can be seen in Figure 18–17, the sponsor would want to be in the upper right-hand corner to achieve maximum effectiveness.

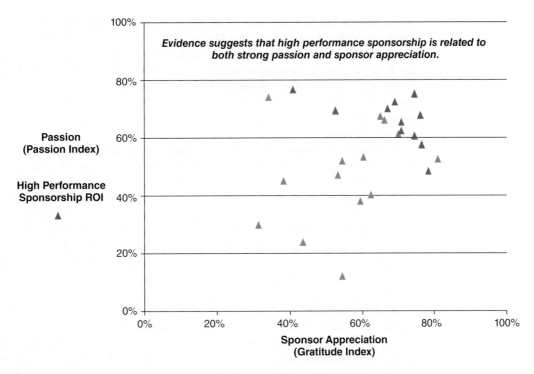

100%

*Evidence suggests that high performance sponsorship is related to both strong passion and sponsor appreciation.*

80%

Passion
(Passion Index)

60%

High Performance
Sponsorship ROI

▲

40%

20%

0%

0%    20%    40%    60%    80%    100%

Sponsor Appreciation
(Gratitude Index)

**FIGURE 18–17**

Sponsorship Performance
Matrix

Performance Research measures impact on brand awareness and image shifts. Tracking the number of website visits and buzz generated are also criteria that have been used.

While each of these measures has its advantages and disadvantages most do not go far enough. As noted by John Nardone and Ed See, most marketers limit their sponsorship evaluations to brand awareness and impressions. The key question that needs to be asked, they say, is "how do you do sponsorships that build brand equity and maintain financial responsibility?"[35] We suggest using several in assessing the impact of sponsorships. In addition to those mentioned here, the eight-step process suggested in Figure 18–18 could be used to guide these evaluations.

## Measuring the Effectiveness of Other IMC Program Elements

Many of the organizations mentioned in this chapter offer research services to measure the effectiveness of specific promotional program elements. As we noted at the outset of this chapter, the increased use of integrated marketing communications

**FIGURE 18–18**

Eight Steps to Measuring
Event Sponsorship

1. Narrowly define objectives with specifics.
2. Establish solid strategies against which programming will be benchmarked and measure your programming and effectiveness against the benchmark.
3. Set measurable and realistic goals; make sure everything you do supports them.
4. Enhance, rather than just change, other marketing variables.
5. Don't pull Marketing Plan 101 off the shelf. Programming should be crafted to reflect the particulars of your company's constituencies and target audiences.
6. Define the scope of your involvement. Will it involve multiple areas within the company? Who internally and externally constitutes the team?
7. Think "long term." It takes time to build brand equity. Also, think of leveraging your sponsorship through programming for as long as possible, before and after the event.
8. Build evaluation and a related budget into your overall sponsoring program. Include items such as pre- and postevent attitude surveys, media analyses, and sales results.

programs has led to more interest in determining the synergistic effects of all program elements. A review of the Ogilvy Award winners from 1993 to date demonstrates the increased integration of additional media (as opposed to specifically the best advertising campaign) and the value of measuring their contribution to the program's success. Also departing from the specific focus on advertising are the awards given by the London-based *Institute of Practitioners,* which has opened the competition to nontraditional media as well as public relations, sales promotions, and other entries.[36]

As noted throughout the chapter, a number of studies have been implemented to determine the combined effects of two or more media as well as their synergistic impact. The number of studies being designed to specifically measure synergistic effects continues to increase—most of which demonstrate a higher effectiveness when multiple media are employed. For example, after receiving negative publicity from a number of sources, Walmart increased its public relations activities and its advertising designed to enhance its corporate image. In less than a year, Walmart was able to show significant improvement in its image, which the company directly attributes to the combined use of the two program elements.[37]

Other companies are applying traditional advertising effectiveness measures offered by companies such as Millward Brown and Nielsen Media Research to their online advertising to assess their overall communications effects.[38] One very effective approach to measuring the impact of the IMC program is that provided by the marketing communications research company Integration. Based on the belief that integrated marketing communications improve both the efficiency and the effectiveness of a campaign. Integration contends that most traditional measurement techniques focus only on the former of these (see Figure 18–19). Noting the increased demand for marketing managers to prioritize the media vehicles used to promote their brands, Integration developed Market ContactAudit to measure both the efficiency and the effectiveness of media used to establish contacts with consumers. By measuring consumers' understanding, evaluation, and perceptions of the contacts and their association with the brand, the Market ContactAudit allows marketers to assess the overall effectiveness as well as the relative contribution of individual IMC elements.[39]

All the advertising effectiveness measures discussed here have their inherent strengths and weaknesses. They offer the advertiser some information that may be useful in evaluating the effectiveness of promotional efforts. While not all promotional efforts can be evaluated effectively, progress is being made.

**FIGURE 18–19**

Measuring Effectiveness, Not Only Efficiency

The most important issue for IMC planning is identifying the most appropriate contact mix, that is, which contacts to prioritize.

| Questions: Are we. . . | |
| --- | --- |
| Being effective: | 1. Doing the right things? |
| Being efficient: | 2. Doing things right? |
| **Current techniques measure only efficiency** | |
| Reach, frequency, GRPs (media surveys) | |
| Weight of market activity (stochastic) | |
| **MCA by integration measures effectiveness and efficiency** | |
| Influence of contacts | |
| Consumer brand experience | |

## Summary

This chapter introduced you to issues involved in measuring the effects of advertising and promotions. These issues include reasons for testing, reasons companies do not test, and the review and evaluation of various research methodologies. We arrived at a number of conclusions: (1) Advertising research to measure effectiveness is important to the promotional program, (2) not enough companies test their ads, and (3) problems exist with current research methodologies. In addition, we reviewed the criteria for sound research and suggested some ways to accomplish effective studies.

All marketing managers want to know how well their promotional programs are working. This information is critical to planning for the next period, since program adjustments and/or maintenance are based on evaluation of current strategies. Problems often result when the measures taken to determine such effects are inaccurate or improperly used.

This chapter demonstrated that testing must meet a number of criteria (defined by PACT) to be successful. These evaluations should occur both before and after the campaigns are implemented.

A variety of research methods were discussed, many provided by syndicated research firms such as Ipsos-ASI, MSW•ARS, Millward Brown, and the Nielsen Co. All of these companies have expanded their service offerings to assist in the evaluation of online and other advertising platforms. Many companies have developed their own testing systems. There has been an increase in testing through the Internet.

Single-source research data were discussed. These single-source systems offer strong potential for improving the effectiveness of ad measures in the future, since commercial exposures and reactions may be correlated to actual purchase behaviors.

It is important to recognize that different measures of effectiveness may lead to different results. Depending on the criteria used, one measure may show that an ad or promotion is effective while another states that it is not. This is why clearly defined objectives and the use of multiple measures are critical to determining the true effects of an IMC program.

## Key Terms

vehicle option source effect p. 614
pretests p. 614
posttests p. 614
laboratory tests p. 616
testing bias p. 616
field tests p. 616
Positioning Advertising Copy Testing (PACT) p. 616
concept testing p. 617
comprehension and reaction tests p. 619

consumer juries p. 619
halo effect p. 620
portfolio tests p. 620
Flesch formula p. 621
theater testing p. 622
on-air test p. 623
recall p. 623
pupillometrics p. 624
electrodermal response (EDR) p. 624
eye tracking p. 624

electroencephalographic (EEG) measures p. 625
alpha activity p. 625
hemispheric lateralization p. 625
inquiry tests p. 627
split-run tests p. 628
recognition method p. 629
recall tests p. 630
single-source tracking methods p. 633
tracking studies p. 633

## Discussion Questions

1. Most managers believe that they should be measuring the effectiveness of their advertising programs. However, studies have shown that they usually do not do so. Cite some of the reasons why managers should measure effectiveness and why they do not. (LO1)

2. Marketers have turned to physiological measures in an attempt to determine the effectiveness of their advertising. Discuss some of the methods now being used and the advantages and disadvantages of each. (LO3)

3. How have marketers employed the methodology of eye tracking? Give examples of companies that have employed this methodology. When does eye tracking seem to be most useful? (LO3)

4. Describe the *Starch Ad Readership Report* and the measures provided therein. Discuss how Starch has had to adapt this report due to changing market conditions, and the new metrics now provided. (LO2)

5. Explain why different metrics may be more useful to marketers in determining the effectiveness of their advertising at different times. Give examples of which metrics

may be useful as consumers go through the purchase decision process. (LO4).

6. Explain why it is so difficult to measure the effectiveness of an IMC program that uses multiple program elements. (LO3)

7. Discuss the various types of pretests that advertisers employ. Why do marketers pretest ads? What are some reasons why marketers may not pretest? (LO2)

8. What are some of the problems with existing effectiveness measures? Discuss the essentials of effective testing methods. (LO3)

9. The Ogilvy Awards are given to companies and their agencies that have successfully employed research to develop and measure the effectiveness of their campaigns. Google the Ogilvy Awards, pick any of the award winners, and discuss why that program was successful. (LO1)

10. Cite examples where advertisers may be able to develop successful ads without the benefit of pretesting. Why would an advertiser decide to make the decision not to pretest? (LO2)

## LEARNING OBJECTIVES

**LO1** To examine the importance of international marketing and the role of international advertising and promotion.

**LO2** To review the various factors in the international environment and how they influence advertising and promotion decisions.

**LO3** To consider the pros and cons of global versus localized marketing and advertising.

**LO4** To examine the various decision areas of international advertising.

**LO5** To understand the role of other promotional-mix elements in the international integrated marketing communications program.

# 19 International Advertising and Promotion

## EXPECT AMAZING FROM THE 2022 FIFA WORLD CUP QATAR™

The Fédération Internationale de Football Association (FIFA) World Cup™ is the largest single-event sporting competition in the world. The tournament, which is held once every four years, is FIFA's flagship event, involving the national soccer (or football, as it is referred to in most countries) teams from 32 qualifying nations. The FIFA World Cup™ is also the world's most widely viewed sporting event. Nearly 3 billion people worldwide tune in to the monthlong tournament on television, and over 3 million spectators usually attend the 64 matches played.

One of the goals of FIFA in awarding hosting rights is to promote the game of football around the globe, as well as in the host nation and region. The 2010 FIFA World Cup™ was played in South Africa, while the 2014 tournament will be hosted by Brazil, followed by Russia in 2018. And in 2022, the small country of Qatar will become the first Middle Eastern and Arab nation to host the prestigious event.

Qatar is the smallest nation, both by population and by area, ever to have been awarded the right to host the FIFA World Cup™; the country is approximately the size of the state of Connecticut and has a population of 2 million. Qatar recognized that its size could be perceived as a shortcoming in competing against Australia, Japan, South Korea and the United States, the four other nations that bid for the right to host the 2022 FIFA World Cup™. Rather than shying away from the issue, Qatar decided to turn its size into a positive by positioning itself as an environmentally and socially friendly host nation for the FIFA World Cup™. As an example, the bid detailed how all of the stadiums, as well as nearly 90,000 hotel rooms and other amenities, would be within a 60-kilometer (37.3 miles) radius and easily accessible by public transportation from Doha, Qatar's capital. It also noted how the new, state-of the-art stadiums would rely on solar power as part of a commitment to host the first ever carbon neutral FIFA World Cup™, and use innovative cooling systems to provide maximum comfort for players and fans. The bid also outlined how most of the stadiums would be constructed using modular components, so that they could be disassembled after the tournament and donated to developing countries, contributing to the tournament's legacy and leaving Qatar with stadiums suitable for its size.

Qatar's effort to win the right to host the 2022 FIFA World Cup™ entailed hard work and innovation, as well as an integrated marketing campaign designed to deliver the message of how this small country planned to transform various perceived challenges into unique assets. The process began with a positioning platform, developed in conjunction with the Y&R Dubai advertising agency, built around the tagline "Expect Amazing." The tagline was designed to communicate its intentions and dare people to believe in Qatar and its bid to host the FIFA World Cup™. The "Expect Amazing" campaign was officially launched in December 2009, one year before FIFA would make its decision to award hosting rights, with a TV commercial called "Puzzles." The goal of the spot was to gain global support for the bid by showcasing Qatar as a beautiful and vibrant country that welcomed people of all nations and was capable of hosting the World Cup. In addition, Qatar launched its official bid website in late 2009. The website included a blog that allowed football fans to learn what was happening behind the scenes and kept them informed of the latest news so they would feel like partners in the bidding process. Social media, including Facebook, Twitter, and a YouTube channel, was also used to engage fans and supporters and provide another digital platform for what became known as the Qatar 2022 marketing effort.

The next phase of the campaign included a social responsibility initiative called "Generation Amazing." Football tournaments were held for underprivileged children from various countries in the Middle East and Asia, including Nepal, Pakistan, Lebanon, Syria, and Qatar. A select group of participants, chosen based on their football and leadership skills, were taken to South Africa to attend the 2010 FIFA World Cup™. A documentary was created by London film production company New Moon to capture the experiences of the children and posted on the Qatar 2022 Bid's YouTube channel to help generate publicity for the cause. Leading up to the 2010 FIFA World Cup™, another video, called "Stadiums," was created and posted on YouTube, showcasing several of the stadiums that had been designed to host the football matches. That video received more than 2 million views on the Qatar 2022 Bid's YouTube channel and helped generate buzz across various other social media channels. Throughout the campaign, Qatar repeatedly grabbed the spotlight by introducing various legendary soccer players as ambassadors for its bid. It did so to great effect in September 2010, just two months before FIFA was to make its decision, when it announced that Zinedine Zidane, a French soccer superstar of Algerian origin who played for the French national team as well as top European Premier League teams such as Real Madrid and Juventus, had joined as an ambassador. The announcement and accompanying TV ad gained huge interest for Qatar's bid. The finale of the marketing campaign occurred in November 2010, just a few weeks before the FIFA decision, when Qatar hosted a friendly soccer match between Brazil and Argentina, two of the world's top teams, showcasing the country and its ability to host the type of big international soccer matches for which the FIFA World Cup™ is rightfully known.

While Qatar utilized an excellent integrated marketing program to draw attention to its desire to host the FIFA World Cup™, there were a number of other key strategic components to its bid. Qatar repeatedly emphasized the diversity of its population and the country's geographic location as a crossroads between the East and West. To demonstrate its diversity, Qatar's final presentation to the FIFA Executive Committee, the organization's voting body, was delivered in three different languages: French, Spanish, and English, punctuated by three videos produced by New York–based creative agency Radical Media that drove home the bid's message that the Executive Committee had the chance to make history by bringing the FIFA World Cup™ to the Middle East for the first time. The last speaker at the final bid presentation was Her Highness Sheikha Moza, the wife of the country's then-emir, who challenged the Executive Committee, asking them, "When do you think is the right time for the World Cup to come to the Middle East?" She also noted the significant impact that Qatar's hosting of the FIFA World Cup™ would have on the Middle East region and the world as a whole.

On December 2, 2010, FIFA's president pulled Qatar's name from an envelope, awarding hosting rights for the 2022 FIFA World Cup™ to Qatar, a small Middle Eastern nation that had defied the odds. Following the decision, the Qatar 2022 Supreme Committee (Q22) was created by Qatar's government to deliver the infrastructure required for this high-profile sporting event, while also achieving the social, economic, and environmental goals laid out during the bid. Qatar views hosting the FIFA World Cup™ as a catalyst for driving growth and economic development and an opportunity to leave a lasting legacy for Qatar, the Middle East, and beyond. The country's hosting plans are closely aligned to the Qatar National Vision 2030, which has the goal of transforming Qatar into an advanced country by 2030, capable of sustaining its development and providing a high standard of living for all of its people for generations to come. Q22 also recognizes that major sporting events such as the FIFA World Cup™ provide a unique opportunity to increase focus, awareness, and unity within society, and is actively promoting increased participation in sports, especially for women, and healthy lifestyles.

Over the next eight years, Q22 must develop and implement an effective integrated marketing communications program that addresses the delivery of infrastructure, including the progress being made and the opportunities being created for firms in Qatar and around the world. The committee is also focused on raising awareness, addressing concerns, and building positive perceptions of Qatar as a culturally rich, dynamic, stable, and vibrant nation in the Gulf region. During the bidding process Qatar told the world to "Expect Amazing." Now it is time for the country to "Deliver Amazing" as it strives to host a successful FIFA World Cup™ in 2022.

Sources: Vivienne Walt, "Qatar Takes Over The World," *Fortune*, September 2, 2013, pp. 90–95; *Qatar 2022 Strategic Plan*, Qatar 2022 Supreme Committee; *Building Towards 2022*, Qatar 2022 Supreme Committee; Tarek Nasr, "Qatar 2022 World Cup Bid—A Marketing Case Study, http://blog.enterplanet360.com/2010/12/qatar-2022-world-cup-bid-a-marketing-case-study/, December 7, 2010.

---

YTC 19–01

Qatar 2022

youtube.com/10ebelch

The primary focus of this book so far has been on integrated marketing communications programs for products and services sold in the U.S. market. Many American companies have traditionally devoted most of their marketing efforts to the domestic market, since they often lack the resources, skills, or incentives to go abroad. This is changing rapidly, however, as U.S. corporations recognize the opportunities that foreign markets offer for new sources of sales and profits as well as the need to market their products internationally. Many companies are striving to develop global brands that can be advertised and promoted the world over.

In this chapter, we look at international advertising and promotion and the various issues marketers must consider in communicating with consumers around the globe. We examine the environment of international marketing and how companies often must adapt their promotional programs to conditions in each country. We review the debate over whether a company should use a global marketing and advertising approach or tailor it specifically for various countries.

We also examine how firms organize for international advertising, select agencies, and consider various decision areas such as creative strategy and media selection. While the focus of this chapter is on international advertising, we also consider other promotional-mix elements in international marketing, including sales promotion, publicity/public relations, and digital and social media. Let's begin by discussing some of the reasons international marketing has become so important to companies.

# THE IMPORTANCE OF INTERNATIONAL MARKETS

LO 19-1

One of the major developments in the business world over the past two decades has been the globalization of markets. The emergence of a largely borderless world has created a new reality for all types of companies. Today, world trade is driven by global competition among global companies for global consumers.[1] With the development of faster communication, transportation, and financial transactions, time and distance are no longer barriers to global marketing. Products and services developed in one country quickly make their way to other countries, where they are finding enthusiastic acceptance. Consumers around the world wear Nike shoes and Calvin Klein jeans, eat at McDonald's, shave with Gillette razors, use Dell computers, listen to music on Apple iPods, drink Coca-Cola and Pepsi Cola soft drinks and Starbucks coffee, talk on cellular phones made by Nokia, Samsung, and Apple, and drive cars made by global automakers such as Ford, Honda, Toyota, and Volkswagen.[2]

Companies are focusing on international markets for a number of reasons. Many companies in the United States and Western Europe recognize that their domestic markets offer them limited opportunities for expansion because of slow population growth, saturated markets, intense competition, and/or an unfavorable marketing environment. For example, soft-drink consumption in the United States has been declining over the past decade as consumers turn to healthier beverages such as juices, teas, and fortified waters. The industry has also been under pressure from public health groups and regulatory agencies in both the United States and the European Union because of concerns over the consumption of sugared soft drinks and childhood obesity.[3] Thus companies like PepsiCo and Coca-Cola are looking to international markets in Asia, Africa, and Latin America for growth opportunities.[4]

Many companies must focus on foreign markets to survive. Most European nations are relatively small in size and without foreign markets would not have the economies of scale to compete against larger U.S. and Japanese companies. For example, Swiss-based Nestlé and Netherlands-based Unilever are two of the world's largest consumer-product companies because they have learned how to market their brands to consumers in countries around the world. Three of the world's major marketers of cellular telephones are from small countries. Nokia is based in Finland, and Samsung and LG are based in Korea. Australia's tourist industry is a major part of its economy and relies heavily on visitors from other countries. Tourism Australia, the federal government agency responsible for the country's international and domestic tourism marketing, recently launched a $250 million global campaign called "There's Nothing Like Australia," which is designed to attract visitors by showcasing the diversity of places to visit and experiences available across the country. The campaign was built with the involvement of the Australian people by having them share their favorite place in the world. The

YTC 19-02
Tourism Australia
youtube.com/10ebelch

CHAPTER 19

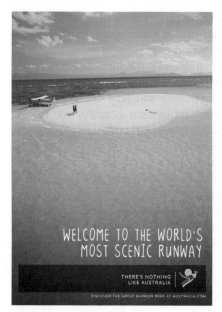

**EXHIBIT 19–1**

Tourism Australia promotes the country as a travel destination with the "There's Nothing Like Australia" campaign

**EXHIBIT 19–2**

The WD-40 Co. gets much of its sales growth from foreign markets such as Latin America

fully integrated campaign uses digital, print, broadcast, and outdoor media as well as direct marketing and point-of-sale ads in travel agencies. During the first phase of the campaign, Australians were invited to share their personal stories of where they live and holiday in Australia as a way to promote the country as a travel destination. Australians uploaded nearly 30,000 stories and images to the website developed for the campaign (www.nothinglikeaustralia.com). For the second phase of the campaign Tourism Australia used the entries to create an interactive digital map of the country that included all of the places and experiences Australians think are special about their country. The various entries were also used to create a series of print ads used in the campaign, such as the one shown in Exhibit 19–1. In 2012 the agency developed the next generation of the campaign with a 90-second signature commercial featuring scenes from 20 different destinations in the country, such as the Great Barrier Reef, Kangaroo Island, Sydney, and Melbourne. The commercial is featured on the Tourism Australia website as well as on various social media sites such as YouTube and popular digital platforms in China, which is Australia's fastest-growing and highest-value tourist market.[5]

Companies are also pursuing international markets because of the opportunities they offer for growth and profits. The dramatic economic, social, and political changes around the world in recent years have opened markets in Eastern Europe and China. China's joining of the World Trade Organization in 2001 has provided foreign competitors with access to 1.3 billion potential Chinese consumers, and Western marketers are eager to sell them a variety of products and services.[6] The growing markets of the Far East, Latin America, Africa, and other parts of the world present tremendous opportunities to marketers of consumer products and services as well as business-to-business marketers.

Many companies in the United States, as well as in other countries, are also pursuing international markets out of economic necessity as they recognize that globalization is revolutionizing the world far more radically and rapidly than industrial development and technological changes of previous eras. In his influential book *The World Is Flat: A Brief History of the Twenty-First Century,* Thomas L. Friedman discusses how the economic flattening of the earth is being stimulated by technology that is breaking down barriers that historically inhibited and restricted international trade. He notes that companies in the United States can prosper only if they are able to compete in the global marketplace that encompasses the 95 percent of the world's population that lives beyond our borders.[7]

Most major multinational companies have made the world their market and generate much of their sales and profits from abroad. Gillette sells more than 800 products in over 200 countries while Colgate-Palmolive generates almost 80 percent of its over $17 billion in sales from outside North America and Procter & Gamble gets 60 percent of its revenue outside the United States. Starbucks sells lattes around the world as its name and image connect with consumers in Europe and Asia as well as North America. The company has coffee shops in more than 60 countries and operates nearly 6,000 international outlets from Beijing to Sydney to London. Starbucks' projected growth plan includes establishing 20,000 stores worldwide, with at least 5,000 locations outside the United States. China is expected to become its second largest market as the company plans to have 1,500 stores in the country by 2015. Starbucks has also recently entered India through a joint venture with Tata Global beverages to capitalize on the rising coffee consumption in the world's second largest country.[8]

International markets are important to small and midsize companies as well as the large multinational corporations. Many of these firms can compete more effectively in foreign markets, where they may face less competition or appeal to specific market segments or where products have not yet reached the maturity stage of their life cycle. For example, the WD-40 Co. has saturated the U.S. market with its lubricant product and now gets much of its sales growth from markets in Europe, Asia, Latin America, China, and Australia (Exhibit 19–2).

Another reason it is increasingly important for U.S. companies to adopt an international marketing orientation is that imports are taking a larger and larger share of the domestic market for many products. The United States has been running a continuing **balance-of-trade deficit**; the monetary value of our imports exceeds that of our exports. American companies are realizing that we are shifting from being an isolated, self-sufficient, national economy to being part of an interdependent *global economy*. This means U.S. corporations must defend against foreign inroads into the domestic market as well as learn how to market their products and services to other countries.

While many U.S. companies are becoming more aggressive in their pursuit of international markets, they face stiff competition from large multinational corporations from other countries. Some of the world's most formidable marketers are European companies such as Unilever, Nestlé, Siemens, Philips, and Renault, as well as the various Japanese car and electronic manufacturers and packaged-goods companies such as Suntory, Shiseido, and Kao.

# THE ROLE OF INTERNATIONAL ADVERTISING AND PROMOTION

Advertising and promotion are important parts of the marketing program of firms competing in the global marketplace. An estimated $198 billion was spent on advertising in the United States in 2013, with much of this money being spent by multinational companies headquartered outside this country. Advertising expenditures outside the United States have increased by nearly 60 percent since 1990, reaching an estimated $365 billion in 2013, as global marketers based in the United States, as well as European and Asian countries, increase their worldwide advertising. Figure 19–1 shows the top 10 companies in terms of worldwide advertising spending.

In addition, estimates are that another $500 billion is spent on sales promotion efforts targeted at consumers, retailers, and wholesalers around the world. The United States is still the world's major advertising market, accounting for over one-third of the estimated $563 billion in worldwide ad expenditures. Nearly 90 percent of the money spent on advertising products and services around the world is concentrated in the United States and Canada along with the industrialized countries of Western Europe and the Pacific Rim, including Japan, South Korea, and Australia. However,

**FIGURE 19–1**

Top 10 Companies by Worldwide Advertising Spending

| Rank | Advertiser | Headquarters | MEASURED MEDIA SPENDING (MILLIONS US DOLLARS) | | |
|------|-----------|--------------|-----------|-----------------|----------------|
| | | | Worldwide | Outside the U.S. | U.S. Spending |
| 1 | Procter & Gamble Co. | Cincinnati, Ohio | $11,247 | $8,113 | $3,134 |
| 2 | Unilever | Rotterdam/London | 7,358 | 6,754 | 604 |
| 3 | L'Oreal | Clichy, France | 5,553 | 4,173 | 1,380 |
| 4 | General Motors | Detroit, Michigan | 3,334 | 1,560 | 1,774 |
| 5 | Nestlé | Vevey, Switzerland | 2,977 | 1,975 | 882 |
| 6 | Coca-Cola Co. | Atlanta, Georgia | 2,906 | 2,516 | 390 |
| 7 | Toyota Motor Corp. | Toyota City, Japan | 2,828 | 1,740 | 1,088 |
| 8 | Volkswagen | Wolfsburg, Germany | 2,823 | 2,312 | 511 |
| 9 | McDonald's Corp. | Oak Brook, Illinois | 2,647 | 1,684 | 963 |
| 10 | Reckitt Benckiser | Slough, Berkshire U.K. | 2,616 | 2,182 | 434 |

Source: "Global Marketers 2012," *Advertising Age*, December 10, 2012, pp. 17–18.

advertising spending is increasing rapidly of in markets outside North America, Europe, and Japan such as India, China and Brazil.[9]

More and more companies recognize that an effective promotional program is important for companies competing in foreign markets. As one international marketing scholar notes:

> Promotion is the most visible as well as the most culture bound of the firm's marketing functions. Marketing includes the whole collection of activities the firm performs in relating to its market, but in other functions the firm relates to the market in a quieter, more passive way. With the promotional function, however, the firm is standing up and speaking out, wanting to be seen and heard.[10]

Many companies have run into difficulties developing and implementing advertising and promotion programs for international markets. Companies that promote their products or services abroad face an unfamiliar marketing environment and customers with different sets of values, customs, consumption patterns, and habits, as well as differing purchase motives and abilities. Languages vary from country to country and even within a country, such as India or Switzerland. Media options are quite limited in many countries, owing to lack of availability or limited effectiveness. These factors demand different creative and media strategies as well as changes in other elements of the advertising and promotional program for foreign markets.

# THE INTERNATIONAL ENVIRONMENT

Just as with domestic marketing, companies engaging in international marketing must carefully analyze the major environmental factors of each market in which they compete, including economic, demographic, cultural, and political/legal variables. Figure 19–2 shows some of the factors marketers must consider in each category

**FIGURE 19–2**

Forces in the International Marketing Environment

when analyzing the environment of each country or market. These factors are important in evaluating the potential of each country as well as designing and implementing a marketing and promotional program.

## The Economic Environment

A country's economic conditions indicate its present and future potential for consuming, since products and services can be sold only to countries where there is enough income to buy them. This is generally not a problem in developed countries such as the United States, Canada, Japan, and most of Western Europe, where consumers generally have higher incomes and standards of living. Thus, they can and want to purchase a variety of products and services. Developed countries have the **economic infrastructure** in terms of the communications, transportation, financial, and distribution networks needed to conduct business in these markets effectively. By contrast, many developing countries lack purchasing power and have limited communications networks available to firms that want to promote their products or services to these markets.

For most companies, industrialized nations represent the greatest marketing and advertising opportunities. But most of these countries have stable population bases, and their markets for many products and services are already saturated. Many marketers are turning their attention to parts of the world whose economies and consumer markets are growing. Markets in Asia, as well as in Europe and South America, were stagnant for a number of years, which led to reductions in advertising spending in most countries. However, these markets are experiencing strong economic growth, which is resulting in greater consumer spending as well as increases in advertising. Over the past several years, advertising spending in the BRIC nations, which include Brazil, Russia, India, and China, has grown four times faster than the world average and is expected to reach nearly $70 billion by 2013. Brazil is experiencing stable, solid economic growth after a period of high inflation and economic volatility as is Russia. Much of Brazil's growth is coming from an emerging lower middle class that now represents nearly half of the company's population. Marketers of products such as consumer electronics, mobile phones, and automobiles are targeting this emerging middle class as their disposable income rises in the growing Brazilian economy.[11]

China and India in particular are two countries that are transforming the global economy. The two countries together account for a third of the world's population, and they both have had economic growth rates ranging from 6 to 10 percent over the past several years, which is much greater than other countries in the world. Each country has the fundamentals to sustain the high growth rates, including young populations, high savings, and a growing number of consumers who have the ability to purchase, as well as the need for, many products.[12]

Marketers of products such as mobile phones, TVs, personal computers, cars, as well as luxury items such as jewelry and designer clothing are focusing more attention on consumers in India and China.[13] The growing middle class in these countries is also creating growth opportunities for marketers of consumer packaged-goods products, who are focusing a great deal of attention and spending more on advertising to reach these consumers. For example, China has become Nike's second largest market, and the company is spending large amounts of money there on media advertising, promotions, events, and sponsorship of sports teams and athletes such as track star and Olympic gold medalist Liu Xiang (Exhibit 19–3). China has become the third largest advertising market in the world, trailing only the United States and Japan.

Many multinational companies are also turning their attention to third-world countries where consumer markets are slowly emerging. Package-goods

**EXHIBIT 19–3**

Nike uses track star Liu Xiang as an endorser in China

CHAPTER 19

# Global Perspective 19–1 > > >

## Marketing to Consumers at the Bottom of the Pyramid

Most multinational companies generate the majority of their sales and profits by selling products and services to consumers and businesses in highly developed countries. When they do venture into developing nations such as China, India, Indonesia, or Vietnam, they have traditionally focused on urban areas where incomes are higher and communication, transportation, and distribution systems are available to implement their marketing programs. The holy grail for companies in developing markets has always been the emerging middle class to whom companies want to deliver "mass prestige" by delivering high-quality brands. However, many multinational marketers have begun turning their attention to the 4 billion consumers who live in the remote, rural communities of developing countries. These people are yearning for a better way of life and are eager to become consumers for a variety of products.

Marketers also recognize the opportunity this market presents, as over the next 20 years the number of upper-middle to upper-income consumers will decline slightly while the developing world will acquire another 2 billion people. Thus, companies that want to achieve their growth objectives must be able to compete at the lower end of the economic spectrum just as aggressively as they do at the higher end. For example, McDonald's has set a goal of acquiring 800 million new customers by 2015 and is shifting its emphasis from Western countries to markets in Asia and Africa. A number of other companies are also targeting the emerging consumer markets in Africa, which is one of the fastest-growing economic regions in the world. Nokia and Coca-Cola have distribution networks in nearly every African country, while Unilever has a presence in 20 African nations. Africa's population is young, growing, and migrating to metropolitan centers.

The emerging practice of targeting billions of poor consumers in developing countries has been given various labels such as business-to-4-billion, selling to the "bottom of the pyramid," or selling to premarkets; a number of companies are recognizing that they can turn a profit while having a positive effect on people not normally considered potential consumers. However, they also realize that it is a tremendous challenge to market to these consumers. Many of the world's poor live in severe poverty, subsisting on less than $2,000 a year, and are illiterate or nearly so. They often live in tiny villages in remote areas that are completely beyond the reach of mass media and common distribution channels. Their access to and ability to use products is determined by the available infrastructure—water, roads, electricity—or lack thereof. Clearly marketers have to package, price, and distribute their products differently as well as find innovative ways to communicate with these consumers. For example, Coca-Cola has created a network of microdistribution centers to reach informal distribution channels, such as vendors and family-run businesses to reach retailers in both rural and urban areas in many parts of Africa. More than 2,800 small businesses use bicycles and manual pushcarts to deliver products over unpaved roads to rural villages.

So how do global marketers like Procter & Gamble, Unilever, Wrigley, Samsung, Nokia, Coca-Cola, and many others market products such as toothpaste, shampoo, soft drinks, and gum—as well as cell phones and TVs—to consumers in these developing countries? They often start by examining the daily lives of these consumers including their needs, aspirations, and habits to better understand what they may want as consumers. For example, P&G is one of the multinational companies targeting what the company calls the "$2 a day" consumer based on his or her average income. As part of its $2-a-day initiative, P&G has launched

companies such as Procter & Gamble and Unilever sell products such as soap, toothpaste, shampoo, and laundry detergents to consumers in remote villages. Often they adapt their products for these markets by making them available in single-use sachets that cost the equivalent of pennies rather than dollars and can be easily distributed and sold through the small kiosks found in rural villages. Global Perspective 19–1 discusses the opportunities these markets present as well as the challenges of marketing to them.

## The Demographic Environment

Major demographic differences exist among countries as well as within them. Marketers must consider income levels and distribution, age and occupation distributions of the population, household size, education, and employment rates. In some countries, literacy rates are also a factor; people who cannot read will not respond well to print ads. Demographic data can provide insight into the living standards and lifestyles in a particular country to help companies plan ad campaigns.

Demographic information can reveal the market potential of various foreign markets. India's population was nearly 1.3 billion in 2013, half of whom are under the a loosely structured project team to approach this low-end consumer from a new perspective. Rather than trying to develop products first or rely on market research alone, the team spends days or weeks in the field trekking through the jungles of Brazil, the slums of India, and the farming villages in rural China. The group has found that women living in remote villages of China on 900 renminbi a year (about $135) still care about beauty and their appearance and are willing to pay for products like Rejoice shampoo rather than washing their hair with laundry soap flakes.

In many cases, advertising agencies are following or often leading their clients into these rural areas. For example, Lowe & Partners office in India, Lowe Lintas, formed Linterland Rural Initiatives, an integrated marketing division designed to provide specialized marketing and communication services to rural India. Linterland works with companies and helps them understand how specialized forms of marketing communications, such as events, road shows, and sampling, are needed to reach the 700 million people who are spread out in nearly a million villages across India that are virtually untouched by mass media. Linterland uses its network of more than 8,500 individual field workers to coordinate and help deliver marketing messages on behalf of a number of consumer-product companies.

While packaged-goods retailers have been selling products such as shampoo, soap, and toothpaste to rural villagers

for years, many companies are now trying to sell them products such as cell phones, TVs, computers, and even cars. Companies such as Nokia, Lenovo, and Samsung are generating strong sales in emerging markets such as China and India as well as Africa with low-cost models aimed at first-time mobile phone users. Nokia focuses on phone models priced from $20 to $50 and adjusts profit targets to reflect the lower prices. Word of mouth is still the supreme marketing tool for reaching consumers in these rural markets, followed by education and product demonstrations. However, advertising along with traditional promotional tactics such as price cuts and discounts are also still important. Integrated marketing agencies such as Linterland and Ogilvy Outreach work with schoolteachers, village heads, and local health workers to get them to relay their clients' marketing messages. For example, in Kaler, a small town of 300 families in India's northeastern Punjab region, Hyundai was able to reach the marketer's dream—the village headman, an opinion leader whose advice is sought on marriages, on crops, and increasingly, on which TV set or car to buy.

Many developing countries are becoming more stable and open to trade and direct foreign investment, while education levels are also improving. Although investment in these markets still requires a long-term perspective, many companies are recognizing that the billions of people in the third world are eager to become consumers and represent a major growth opportunity. However, the real opportunity for marketers is not in just changing the package sizes and price points of the products they sell in the West. It is in understanding consumers in these developing markets, innovating to meet their needs, and selling them quality products at prices they can afford.

Sources: Musta Chironga, Acha Leke, Susan Lund, and Arend van Wamelen, "Cracking the Next Growth Market: Africa," *Harvard Business Review*, May 2011, pp. 117–122; Jennifer Reingold, "Can P&G Make Money in Places Where People Earn $2 a Day?," *Fortune*, January 17, 2011, pp. 86–91; Antonio Regalado, "McCann Offers Peek at Lives of Latin America's Poor," *The Wall Street Journal*, December 8, 2008, p. B6; Michelle Kristula-Green, "How to Market to Asia's Masses," *Advertising Age*, August 6, 2007, pp. 14–15.

YTC **19-03**

**Bottom of the Pyramid**

youtube.com/10ebelch

age of 25. Only China has a larger population. Latin America remains one of the world's largest potential markets, although the meager income of most consumers in the region is still a problem. Brazil, the largest consumer market in South America, now has a population of 200 million and is a growing market for many products and services.[14] More than 50 percent of the Latin American market is younger than age 26, and 30 percent is under 15. Moreover, children are the fastest-growing segment of that market. These numbers have caught the attention of international advertisers such as Mattel, PepsiCo, Coca-Cola, Burger King, and others. Indonesia also has a very young population, with more people under the age of 16 than the United States, and they are very receptive to Western ways and products.

## The Cultural Environment

Another important aspect of the international marketing environment is the culture of each country. Cultural variables marketers must consider include language, customs, tastes, attitudes, lifestyles, values, and ethical/moral standards. Nearly every country exhibits cultural traits that influence not just the needs and wants of consumers but how they go about satisfying them.

**EXHIBIT 19–4**

The tagline used in this TaylorMade ad had to be changed for Asian countries because of translation problems

Marketers must be sensitive not only in determining what products and services they can sell foreign cultures but also in communicating with them. Advertising is often the most effective way to communicate with potential buyers and create markets in other countries. But it can also be one of the most difficult aspects of the international marketing program because of problems in developing messages that will be understood in various countries.

International advertisers often have problems with language. The advertiser must know not only the native tongue of the country but also its nuances, idioms, and subtleties. International marketers must be aware of the connotations of words and symbols used in their messages and understand how advertising copy and slogans are translated. Marketers often encounter problems in translating their advertising messages and brand names into various languages. The ad for TaylorMade Burner Irons golf clubs shown in Exhibit 19–4 is one example. In the United States and other English speaking countries, the tagline the advertising used is "The Set Is Dead." However, in Asian countries such as Japan and Korea, the word *dead* in the tagline did not translate well so it was changed to "The Set Is History," which made the meaning of phrase easier to understand.

When the Colgate-Palmolive Co. launched its Colgate Max Fresh toothpaste brand in China, the company found that the brand name did not translate well, which led to it being changed to Icy Fresh. Colgate also had to change the description of the dissolvable mini breath strips that were part of the formulation of the product to cooling crystals since the concept of breath strips had no relevance to Chinese consumers.

Advertisers can encounter problems with the connotative meaning of signs and symbols used in their messages. For example, the thumbs-up sign, which signifies affirmation to most Americans, has offensive meaning in some countries such as Russia and Poland if the palm of the hand is visible but is acceptable if the back of the hand is shown. There can also be problems associated with the symbolic meanings of colors. In Japan, as in many Asian countries, white is a color for mourning rather than black, and purple is associated with death in many Latin American countries. An American ad campaign using various shades of green was a disaster in Malaysia, where the color symbolizes death and disease.

Problems arising from language diversity and differences in signs and symbols can usually be best solved with the help of local expertise. Marketers should consult local employees or use an ad agency knowledgeable in the local language that can help verify that the advertiser is saying what it wants to say. Many companies turn to agencies that specialize in translating advertising slogans and copy into foreign languages.[15]

Tastes, traditions, and customs are also an important part of cultural considerations. The customs of a society affect what products and services it will buy and how they must be marketed. In France, cosmetics are used heavily by men as well as women, and advertising to the male market is common. There are also cultural differences in the grooming and hygiene habits of consumers in various countries. For example, though many U.S. consumers use products like deodorant and shampoo daily, consumers in many other Western countries are not as fanatical about personal hygiene, so consumption of products such as deodorants and mouthwash is much lower than in the United States.

Another aspect of culture that is very important for international marketers to understand is values. **Cultural values** are beliefs and goals shared by members of a society regarding ideal end states of life and modes of conduct. Society shapes consumers' basic values, which affect their behavior and determine how they respond to various situations. For example, cultural values in the United States place a major emphasis on individual activity and initiative, while many Asian societies stress cooperation

**EXHIBIT 19–5**

New Balance shoes have become very popular in France

**EXHIBIT 19–6**

New Balance created a new version of the 576 shoe dedicated to France

and conformity to the group. Values and beliefs of a society can also affect its members' attitudes and receptivity toward foreign products and services.[16] Values such as *ethnocentrism,* which refers to the tendency for individuals to view their own group or society as the center of the universe, or nationalism often affect the way consumers in various countries respond to foreign brands or even advertising messages.[17] For many years, consumers in many European countries were reluctant to buy American brands and there was even a backlash against American imagery. In fact, many U.S. companies doing business in Europe were careful not to flaunt their American roots.

One European country, in particular, where American-made products were not well received for many years is France. The French have always been very protective of their culture; for example, they have quotas for French-language shows on TV and music on the radio. As historian Richard Pells notes: "France, like the U.S., has traditionally seen itself as a country with a mission and a country whose culture and civilization is worthy of being exported around the world."[18] However, in recent years many American brands have become popular in France, particularly among younger consumers. For example, the French subsidiary of New Balance, the Boston-based athletic shoe and apparel company, experienced strong growth in France when its 576 model became *de rigueur* among the fashion elite in the late 1990s (Exhibit 19–5). As sales took off, New Balance kept the nubuck shoes coming in a variety of solid colors and also kept the prices high and distribution limited to perpetuate the luxury goods image of the 576.[19] The shoe has remained popular over the past decade, and in 2010 New Balance released a new version of the popular shoe called the 576 "France" which comes in the country's national colors and even has the French flag in the form of embroidery on the heel (Exhibit 19–6). This new 576 marked the first time New Balance had dedicated a shoe to a country.[20]

In recent years, U.S. brands have become popular in many other European countries as well as in Asia. Marketers attribute the rising popularity of many U.S.-made products to the worldwide distribution of American music, films, and TV shows; the growth of the Internet; and the increase in travel to the United States. These factors have made consumers in foreign countries more familiar with American culture, values, and lifestyle.[21]

Japan is one of the more difficult markets for many American advertisers to understand because of its unique values and customs.[22] For example, the Japanese have a very strong commitment to the group; social interdependence and collectivism are as important to them as individualism is to most Americans. Ads stressing individuality and nonconformity have traditionally not done well in Japan, but westernized values have become more prevalent in Japanese advertising in recent years.[23]

However, the Japanese dislike ads that confront or disparage the competition and tend to prefer soft rather than hard sells.[24] A study found that Japanese and American magazine ads tend to portray teenage girls in different ways and that the differences correspond to each country's central concepts of self and society. In many American ads teens are associated with images of independence, rebelliousness, determination, and even defiance that are consistent with the American value of individuality. In contrast, Japanese ads tend to portray a happy, playful, childlike, girlish image that is consistent with the Japanese culture's sense of self, which is more dependent on others.[25] Another study examined gender-role portrayals in Japanese magazine advertising and found that some of the previously used hard-line stereotyping of both men and women has softened considerably since the 1980s. Men are not associated as much with stereotypical male traits, while women are shown in more positive ways. The researchers suggest that this may reflect the westernization of the depictions of men and women in Japan.[26]

As advertisers turn their attention to China, more consideration is also being given to understanding the cultural system and values of the world's most populous country. Chinese values are centered on Confucianism, which stresses loyalty and interpersonal relationships. Chinese culture also emphasizes passive acceptance of fate by seeking harmony with nature; inner experiences of meaning and feeling; stability and harmony; close family ties; and tradition.[27] A study of advertising appeals used in China found that advertising reflects these traditional Chinese cultural values. Chinese advertisers tend to base their advertising strategies on creating liking for a product through image and emotional appeals rather than information-laden ads. However, the study also found subtle changes in appeals to cultural values used by advertisers, particularly for ads targeting younger consumers. Youth and modernity appeals were found to be prevalent, reflecting the westernization, as well as the modernization, trend in China.[28] Marketing is just beginning to emerge in China, and advertising is a relatively new social phenomenon, so it will be important for marketers to develop a better understanding of Chinese cultural values and their implication for communications strategy.[29]

Nike recently ran into a problem over a commercial that aired in China showing NBA basketball star LeBron James winning a battle with a Chinese dragon and a kung fu master. The commercial was banned by government regulators who stated that it created indignant feelings among Chinese television viewers because it showed an American sports icon defeating the dragon, a symbol of Chinese culture, and the martial arts master, a symbol of national pride. A statement posted on the website of China's State Administration for Radio, Film, and Television stated that the ad violated the regulation that "all advertisements must uphold national dignity and interest, and respect the motherland's culture." Nike's China marketing director said that it was not the company's intention to show disrespect to the Chinese culture, explaining that the ad was meant to inspire youth to overcome internal fear and obstacles in order to improve themselves. Toyota Motor Co. of Japan also had to retract and issue an apology for an ad that ran in magazines and newspapers in China depicting stone lions, a traditional sign of Chinese power, saluting and bowing to a Prado Land Cruiser sport utility vehicle.[30] A recent study examined perceptions of offensive advertising among Chinese consumers living in Hong Kong and Shanghai. The study found that the central issue related to whether an ad was perceived as offensive by the type of execution and creative tactics used or by the offensiveness of the product or service being advertised. The researchers noted that despite the sophistication and modernization of these two major cities, consumers there remain conservative and, to some extent collectivist, as susceptibility to interpersonal influence affects this evaluation of offensive advertising. They recommended that marketers remain cautious when developing advertising for China and should not take too many risks with offensive advertising.[31] Global Perspective 19–2 discusses the challenges and opportunities marketers face in China.

Religion is another aspect of culture that affects norms, values, and behaviors. For example, in many Arab countries, advertisers must be aware of various taboos resulting from conservative applications of the Islamic religion. Alcohol and pork cannot be advertised. Human nudity is forbidden, as are pictures of anything sacred, such as images of a cross or photographs of Mecca. The faces of women may not be shown in photos, so cosmetics use drawings of women's faces in ads. In conservative Islamic countries, many religious authorities are opposed to advertising on the grounds that it promotes Western icons and culture and the associated non-Islamic consumerism. Restrictions on advertising still exist in some countries such as Iran, which has particularly averse feelings toward Western-style advertising. However, Western-style ads have become more prevalent in many Middle Eastern countries such as Egypt and Lebanon.

Both Coca-Cola and PepsiCo have taken their cola wars to the Middle East and have been engaged in a battle to win the soft drink allegiance of Arabs, especially

YTC 19–04
**Nike China**
youtube.com/10ebelch

**EXHIBIT 19–7**

Pepsi targets young consumers in the Middle East with its "Yalla Now" campaign

the youth, in countries such as Lebanon, Saudi Arabia, Egypt, and Qatar. To reach the youth market, the two companies have used a variety of integrated marketing tools including media advertising, sponsorship of sports teams as well as sporting and musical events, and talent shows as well as branded entertainment. In 2013 Pepsi developed a regional adaptation of its global "Live Now" campaign for the Middle East and North Africa. The integrated campaign is called "Yalla Now" and targets a new progressive generation of Arabs by aligning the Pepsi brand with music and living for the moment. The campaign is designed to engage young consumers through social media including Facebook and Twitter as well as branded entertainment such as sponsorship of the *X Factor Arabia* television show (Exhibit 19–7).[32]

## The Political/Legal Environment

The political and legal environment in a country is one of the most important factors influencing the advertising and promotional programs of international marketers. Regulations differ owing to economic and national sovereignty considerations, nationalistic and cultural factors, and the goal of protecting consumers not only from false or misleading advertising but, in some cases, from advertising in general. It is difficult to generalize about advertising regulation at the international level, since some countries are increasing government control of advertising while others are decreasing it. Government regulations and restrictions can affect various aspects of a company's advertising program, including:

- The types of products that may be advertised.
- The content or creative approach that may be used.
- The media that all advertisers (or different classes of advertisers) are permitted to employ.
- The amount of advertising a single advertiser may use in total or in a specific medium.
- The use of foreign languages in ads.
- The use of advertising material prepared outside the country.
- The use of local versus international advertising agencies.
- The specific taxes that may be levied against advertising.

A number of countries ban or restrict the advertising of various products. Cigarette advertising is banned in some or all media in numerous countries besides the United States including, Argentina, Canada, France, Italy, Norway, Sweden, and Switzerland. The Australian government limits tobacco advertising to point of purchase. The ban also excludes tobacco companies from sponsoring sporting events.

In 2012 Australia's high court upheld the country's Plain Packaging Act making it the first country to ban brand logos on all tobacco packages. The new law

**EXHIBIT 19–8**

Australia bans brand logos on tobacco packages and requires graphic images of negative health effects

requires tobacco and cigarettes to be sold in plain green packages that feature graphic pictures of the negative health effects of smoking such as blindness; mouth, throat, and lung cancer; and the dangers of second-hand smoke (Exhibit 19–8). The new law is being challenged by tobacco companies through the World Trade Organization; they have concerns that it could set a marketing precedent that is adopted by other countries.[33] In Malaysia, a government ban on cigarette-related advertising and sponsorship was initiated

# Global Perspective 19–2 > > >

## The Marketing Challenges and Opportunities of China

For many years marketers could only dream of selling their products to China's 1.3 billion consumers. However, with the end of the Cultural Revolution in 1979 and its massive modernization drive over the past three decades, China has become one of the fastest-growing consumer markets in the world. Advertising, once banned as a capitalist scourge, is now encouraged by the Chinese government, which views it as a catalyst that can accelerate China's economic development. Underlying the growth of advertising in China is the tremendous economic growth of the country, particularly in the urban areas that are home to more than a third of the country's population. There is also a new spirit of consumption, as reform in China has brought about dramatic increases in the purchasing power and size of the middle class. The average disposable income of Chinese consumers continues to rise and demand is increasing for many other products, including personal computers, mobile phones, automobiles, clothing, and fast food.

As China continues to develop, companies from the United States as well as other countries have been working to penetrate the Chinese market and for good reason. China's gross domestic product (GDP) in 2012 was $8.3 trillion, making it the world's second largest economy after the United States. Some studies suggest that China's economy is larger, and its consumer purchasing power greater, than the U.S. economy after accounting for cost-of-living differences and currency values. China has become the world's largest automotive market with 19.3 million vehicles being sold in the country in 2012 versus 14 million in the United States and 12 million in the European Union. The newly emerging middle class in China is very brand conscious and demand for popular Western products from the United States and Europe, as well as goods from Japan and Korea, is increasing. For example, Chinese consumers prefer foreign brands associated with technological innovation, status, and fashion while local brands prevail for more functional commoditized purchases such as washing machines, air conditioners, and refrigerators. China has become the largest market in the world for luxury brands; sales of opulent goods from companies such as Louis Vuitton, Prada, Rolex, and others rose by 19 percent in 2012 and have tripled over the past five years.

While imported products are extremely popular among consumers, Chinese companies are fighting back by developing strong brands in many product categories. Traditionally, Chinese companies competed on price, but many are trying to move away from the low end of the market by developing higher-end products with more brand equity. A number of Chinese companies are striving to improve their brand images including the Haier Group, which is the leading home appliance brand in the world and has forged a marketing partnership with the National Basketball Association; TCL, which makes TVs and mobile phones; and Tsingtao, China's leading brand of beer. Li-Ning (named after its founder, a former Chinese Olympic athlete) is a fast-growing maker of athletic shoes and apparel, which is sponsoring up-and-coming young Chinese athletes to grow its brand recognition. The company is also trying to penetrate the U.S. market by signing Miami Heat star guard Dwyane Wade as an endorser to join its other NBA endorser, Evan Turner of the Philadelphia 76ers.

The pent-up demand of China's 1.3 billion emerging consumers makes entering the market a no-brainer for most multinational companies. However, the realities of entering the market are much more difficult as China's diverse customer base encompasses a broad range of economic disparity and cultural complexity. China lacks the marketing infrastructure that companies take for granted in the West. The country lacks quality consumer research data as well as distribution systems and it has very fragmented state-owned media. It is generally accepted that there are four socioeconomic consumer tiers in China, although some marketers and their ad agencies now

---

in 2003 in an effort to curb the rising number of smokers in the country.[34] In China, tobacco and liquor advertising are banned except in hotels for foreigners. In Europe there has been a long-standing ban on advertising for prescription-drug products, which is designed to keep government-subsidized health care costs under control. The European Union (EU) has argued that advertising increases the marketing budgets of drug companies and results in higher prices. The ban prevents prescription-drug companies from mentioning their products even on their websites or in brochures, although some relaxation of these restrictions is being considered by the European Commission for drugs used to treat AIDS, diabetes, and respiratory ailments.[35]

The advertising of tobacco and liquor is banned in India, although many companies have tried to get around the ban by using what are known as "surrogate advertisements." Instead of promoting tobacco and liquor products, these TV commercials and print ads market unrelated products that the company also happens to manufacture—such as CDs, playing cards, and bottled water—that carry the same brand name and allow them to build brand awareness. The Indian government has been clamping down on surrogate TV ads in response to complaints by health activists, which is leading marketers to look to other ways to promote their brands such divide the country into eight tiers. The tiers are based on size, sophistication, purchasing habits, attitudes, and disposable income of the population. Tier 1 is the most affluent and includes the major cities of Beijing, Shanghai, Guangzhou, and Shenzen. Tier 2 has about 30 cities, mostly provincial capitals with more than 5 million people. Increased urban development, China's high-speed rail system, and a growing middle class are making second-tier cities rife with opportunities.

Multinational companies are recognizing that they must move beyond the prosperous tier 1 cities and coastal regions if they are to have a future in China. Thus, companies are moving into the middle and lower tiers that include thousands of towns as well as China's smallest villages where 70 percent of the overall market resides. Procter & Gamble now sells brands such as Crest and Tide in 2,000 cities and 11,000 towns and villages. P&G has become the country's largest consumer-products company and now sells more tubes of toothpaste in China than it does in the United States. Distribution systems are a critical success factor for packaged-goods companies; the CEO of Coca-Cola has noted that the company needs 11 million points of distribution to reach its goal of being "with an arm's reach" of every Chinese consumer.

Advertisers are finding that television is the most effective way to reach China's masses—over 95 percent of Chinese consumers have a TV and they are more influenced by commercials than consumers in the West. However, China has only one national network, state-owned CCTV, which airs 16 channels 24 hours a day, seven days a week. Since there is only one national network, advertisers have little leverage when purchasing television time. They also find that it can be very challenging to develop TV ads that can communicate effectively

with such a broad and diverse target audience that ranges from sophisticated urban dwellers to rural farmers. The Internet and social media have also become important IMC tools in China as they are used by consumers to learn about brands. Social media are used extensively by consumers to share information about brands, and some experts suggest they have become substitutes for government enforcement of quality control.

Advertising agencies are also finding that doing business in China can be very challenging. Local clients are demanding and agency relationships last less than three years on average. Many multinational marketers are also breaking with global agency alignments in China and are working with local agencies as they expand deeper into the country. Nearly 75 percent of China's ad billings are in the hands of local agencies, which are becoming stronger and expanding their capabilities. One industry consultant noted that being a top executive for a multinational agency network in China is the toughest job in advertising as it is a market in transition with little or no account loyalty.

Multinational companies recognize that the enormous size of the Chinese market, along with its strong economic development and growth, make it imperative for them to be there. However, they also know that there are many challenges and obstacles to overcome if they are going to be successful in the world's largest consumer market.

Sources: Manuela Mesco, "Unfashionably Late to China," *The Wall Street Journal*, March 26, 2013, http://search.proquest.com/docview/1319502349?accountid=13758; Hilary Masell Oswald, "A New Vantage Point," *Marketing News*, April 2013, pp. 38–42; Joan Voight, "The Great Brand of China," *Adweek*, October 29, 2012, p. 22; Christine Birkner, "Eastern Influence," *Marketing News*, September 15, 2012, pp. 10–15.

**YTC 19–05**

**Marketing in China**

youtube.com/10ebelch

as the branding of sports teams, concerts, and other entertainment events. They are also lobbying the Indian government for more flexibility in enforcing the crackdown such as allowing liquor ads on late-night television programs.[36]

Many countries restrict the media that advertisers can use as well as the extent to which ads can appear in the media. In the EU, legislation limits the commercial time to 12 minutes per hour and some countries require less frequent but longer advertising breaks that can be as long as 6 minutes. In 1999, the European Commission threw out an appeal against Greece's national ban on toy advertising on daytime television. Thus, advertisers can advertise toys on TV only during the evening hours.[37] Some of the most stringent advertising regulations in the world are found in Scandinavian countries. Commercial TV advertising did not begin in Sweden until 1992, and both Sweden and Denmark limit the amount of time available for commercials. Both Sweden and Norway prohibit domestic advertising that targets children as their governments believe that young people are not able to differentiate between advertising and programming and are not capable of understanding the selling intent of commercials.[38] Saudi Arabia opened its national TV system to commercial advertising in 1986, but advertising is not permitted on the state-run radio system. Advertising in magazines and newspapers in the country is subject to government and religious restrictions.[39]

**EXHIBIT 19–9**
Diet Coke must use a different name in some countries

Many governments have rules and regulations that affect the advertising message. For example, comparative advertising is legal and widely used in the United States and Canada but is illegal in some countries, such as Korea and Belgium. In Europe, the European Commission has developed a directive to standardize the basic form and content of comparative advertising and develop a uniform policy. In 2012 the EU updated its Directive on Misleading and Comparative Advertising that specifies the conditions under which comparative advertising is permitted and requires marketers to make sure their advertisements are not misleading: compare "like with like"—goods and services meeting the same needs or intended for the same purpose; objectively compare important features of the products or services concerned; do not discredit other companies' trademarks; and do not create confusion among traders.[40] Comparative advertising is used on a limited basis in many EU countries, such as the United Kingdom.

Many Asian and South American countries have also begun to accept comparative ads. However, Brazil's self-regulatory advertising codes are so strict that few advertisers have been able to create a comparative message that has been approved.[41] Many countries restrict the types of claims advertisers can make, the words they can use, and the way products can be represented in ads. In Greece, specific claims for a product, such as "20 percent fewer calories," are not permitted in an advertising message.[42]

Copyright and other legal restrictions make it difficult to maintain the same name from market to market. For example, Diet Coke is known as Coca-Cola Light in Germany, France, and many other countries because of legal restrictions prohibiting the word *diet* (Exhibit 19–9).

China has also begun cracking down on advertising claims as consumer groups slowly become a more powerful force in the country. For years, government regulation of advertising was less stringent than in developed markets and many companies were very aggressive with their advertising claims. However, government officials have begun enforcing a 1995 law that stipulates that statistical claims and quotations "should be true and accurate with sources clearly indicated." In 2005, the Chinese government launched a crackdown on false and illegal ads with a focus on cosmetic, beauty, health, and pharmaceutical products.[43]

An area that is receiving a great deal of attention in Europe, as well as in the United States, is the marketing and advertising of food products that are considered to contribute to childhood obesity. The European Health Commission has called on advertisers of a variety of food products to set their own regulations to curb the advertising of so-called junk food to the 450 million consumers in the European Union. The commission has also recommended that these companies do not advertise directly to children and has even threatened to ban advertising icons such as Ronald McDonald and Tony the Tiger.[44]

# GLOBAL VERSUS LOCALIZED ADVERTISING

The discussion of differences in the marketing environments of various countries suggests that each market is different and requires a distinct marketing and advertising program. However, in recent years a great deal of attention has focused on the concept of **global marketing**, where a company uses a common marketing plan for all countries in which it operates, thus selling the product in essentially the same way everywhere in the world. **Global advertising** falls under the umbrella of global marketing as a way to implement this strategy by using the same basic advertising approach in all markets.

The debate over standardization versus localization of marketing and advertising programs began years ago.[45] But the idea of global marketing was popularized by Professor Theodore Levitt, who says the worldwide marketplace has become homogenized and consumers' basic needs, wants, and expectations transcend geographic, national, and cultural boundaries.[46] One writer described Levitt's position on global marketing as follows:

> Levitt's vision of total worldwide standardization is global marketing at the extreme. He argues that, thanks to cheap air travel and new telecommunications technology, consumers the world over are thinking—and shopping—increasingly alike. According to Levitt, the New Republic of Technology homogenizes world tastes, wants, and possibilities into global marketing proportions, which allows for world standardized products.[47]

Not everyone agrees with Levitt's global marketing theory, particularly with respect to advertising. Many argue that products and advertising messages must be designed or at least adapted to meet the differing needs of consumers in different countries.[48] We will consider the arguments for and against global marketing and advertising, as well as situations where it is most appropriate.

## Advantages of Global Marketing and Advertising

**YTC 19–06**
**Global Marketing**
youtube.com/10ebelch

A global marketing strategy and advertising program offers certain advantages to a company, including the following:

- Economies of scale in production and distribution.
- Lower marketing and advertising costs as a result of reductions in planning and control.
- Lower advertising production costs.
- Abilities to exploit good ideas on a worldwide basis and introduce products quickly into various world markets.
- A consistent international brand and/or company image.
- Simplification of coordination and control of marketing and promotional programs.

Advocates of global marketing and advertising contend that standardized products are possible in all countries if marketers emphasize quality, reliability, and low prices. They say people everywhere want to buy the same products and live the same way. Product standardization results in lower design and production costs as well as greater marketing efficiency, which translates into lower prices for consumers. Product standardization and global marketing also enable companies to roll out products faster into world markets, which is becoming increasingly important as product life cycles become shorter and competition increases.

A number of companies, including IBM, DeBeers, Merrill Lynch, British Airways, and American Express, have successfully used the global advertising approach. Gillette has used the "Best a Man Can Get" as its global advertising theme for over a decade and has launched a number of new razor products including the Sensor, Mach3, and Fusion using a global approach.[49] Gillette uses the same advertising theme in each country and maintains websites with similar content and layout, with only language differences.

Frito-Lay launched its first global campaign in 2013 for Doritos, which is the world's largest tortilla/corn-chip brand. Doritos had a different look and feel across the 37 countries where the brand is sold as 25 packaging variations existed and different advertising approaches were used in various markets. Packaging for Doritos was standardized across all markets and the global campaign themed "For the Bold" was developed that included digital and television advertising, promotions on Facebook and Twitter, and sponsorship of concerts. The creative approach used in the campaign included humorous TV and print executions focusing on bold choices made to enjoy Doritos such as the ad shown in Exhibit 19–10. Frito-Lay's vice president of marketing explained the move to a global campaign: "With the rise of social media and technology, our world is smaller and more connected than ever before. We have found that our consumers across the world share very similar passions and interests,

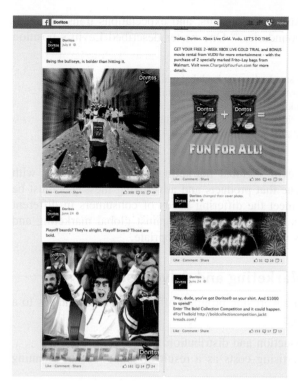

**EXHIBIT 19–10**

Doritos uses global advertising to create a consistent image for the brand in various countries

**EXHIBIT 19–11**

Domino's Pizza used its humorous Moon Branch Project promotion in Japan

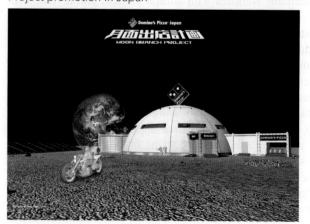

but until now may not have had a consistent way of speaking about the Doritos brand. The campaign is our way of connecting these fans worldwide, as we now provide a consistent storyline, and look and feel from the Doritos brand."[50]

## Problems with Global Advertising

Opponents of the standardized global approach argue that very few products lend themselves to global advertising.[51] Differences in culture, market, and economic development; consumer needs and usage patterns; media availabilities; and legal restrictions make it extremely difficult to develop an effective universal approach to marketing and advertising. Advertising may be particularly difficult to standardize because of cultural differences in circumstances, language, traditions, values, beliefs, lifestyle, music, and so on. Moreover, some experts argue that cultures around the world are becoming more diverse, not less so. Thus, advertising's job of informing and persuading consumers and moving them toward using a particular brand can be done only within a given culture.

Consumer usage patterns and perceptions of a product may vary from one country to another, so advertisers must adjust their marketing and advertising approaches to different problems they may face in different markets. For example, while eating pizza is viewed as a casual affair in the United States and many other countries, in Japan it is perceived as an upscale meal that is consumed more on special occasions. Domino's Pizza entered the Japanese market in 1985 and has been focusing on creating more usage occasions such as Valentine's Day and Mother's Day by delivering its pizza in heart-shaped, pink boxes. The company has also used clever promotions such as one where the chain offered 2.5 million yen (about $30,000) for one hour's work at a Domino's store. For another popular offbeat promotion Domino's announced that it was working with space agency JAXA (the Japanese equivalent of NASA), Honda, and other high-profile companies to build the first-ever pizza store on the moon.[52] The CEO of Domino's Japan participated in the promotion by appearing in a full spacesuit, customized with a Domino's patch, and displaying a big picture of the Moon Branch Project (Exhibit 19–11).

Laundry detergent is another example of a product category where there are differences across various markets that make the use of a global campaign difficult.[53] For example, the U.S. market is well behind Western Europe's with regard to washing machine technology and the degree of involvement in washing clothes. In countries such as Germany top-of-the line front loading machines are the norm, and clothes are washed in water at very high temperatures, which requires highly specialized laundry detergents. Europe accounts for 45 percent of the world's $41 billion in annual spending on laundry products despite having only 11 percent of the population.[54] In other parts of the world such as China and Brazil, the shift to washing machines is a function of economic development and many consumers still cling to traditional laundry habits. Companies that compete in the laundry detergent market such as Unilever, Henkel, and Procter & Gamble have to adapt their products, as well as their integrated marketing programs, to account for differences in technology, water usage, and cultural preferences in various markets (Exhibit 19–12).

Many experts believe that marketing a standardized product the same way all over the world can turn off consumers,

**EXHIBIT 19–12**

Marketers of laundry products must adapt their products and IMC programs to account for differences in various countries

**EXHIBIT 19–13**

Advertising for Colgate toothpaste uses a consistent visual image, but the copy may vary for different markets

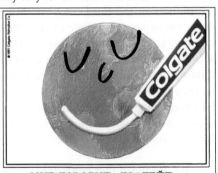

МИР ГОВОРИТ «КОЛГЕЙТ»–
ПОДРАЗУМЕВАЕТ ЗУБНАЯ ПАСТА.
МИР ГОВОРИТ ЗУБНАЯ ПАСТА–
ПОДРАЗУМЕВАЕТ «КОЛГЕЙТ».

Для людей в более чем 160 странах      защищают их от кариеса.
мира зубная паста «Колгейт» вот           С помощью пасты «Колгейт» вы и
уже 100 лет является синонимом       ваша семья смогут сохранить зубы
высочайшего качества. Люди боль-     здоровыми. Вашей семье также по-
ше доверяют пасте «Колгейт», чем     нравится освежающий вкус ментола.
другим пастам, потому что она со-          Чистите зубы пастой «Колгейт»
держит кальций и фтор, которые      и вы убедитесь сами, что «Колгейт»
способствуют укреплению зубов и      означает качество.

ЗУБНАЯ ПАСТА НОМЕР ОДИН В МИРЕ.

*Translation:*

COLGATE. WHAT THE WORLD CALLS TOOTHPASTE.

THE WORLD SAYS COLGATE, THE WORLD MEANS TOOTHPASTE.
THE WORLD SAYS TOOTHPASTE, THE WORLD MEANS COLGATE.

In the 100 years since it was first introduced, Colgate toothpaste has come to mean superior quality to people in over 160 countries. In fact, more families trust Colgate than any other toothpaste in the world because it contains calcium and fluoride for stronger teeth and unsurpassed cavity protection. Colgate will also help keep your family's teeth healthy. And it has a fresh, minty taste they'll love. Brush with Colgate. And see for yourself that, when the world says "Colgate," they mean quality.

THE NUMBER ONE TOOTHPASTE IN THE WORLD.

alienate employees, and blind a company to diversities in customer needs. Multinational companies can also encounter problems when they use global advertising as local managers in countries or regions often resent the home office standardizing the advertising function and mandating the type of advertising to be used in their markets. Sir Martin Sorrell, chair of the United Kingdom–based WPP Group, argues that there are limits to global advertising and that the one-size-fits-all pendulum has gone too far. He urges his executives to focus on consumer needs in the countries they serve and advocates the use of country managers to build contacts and adapt campaigns to local markets.[55]

Some major companies are moving away from a completely standardized approach. For example, the Colgate-Palmolive Co. has used global advertising for many of its brands, including the Colgate, Palmolive, and Ajax product lines, and continues to endorse the use of global appeals. Under its current marketing strategy, however, advertising is often modified for a specific country or region, particularly where local creativity can improve the advertising over the global standard. An example of this approach is the advertising used for Colgate toothpaste in Russia (see Exhibit 19–13). The globe/smile image is used as the visual in nearly every country where Colgate is marketed, but the copy varies.

Some marketing experts claim much of the attention to the advantages of global advertising stems from large ad agencies trying to increase business by encouraging clients to use one agency to handle their marketing communications worldwide.[56] Many large multinational companies are indeed consolidating their business with one or a few agencies that have offices around the world and offer international advertising capabilities. However, the consolidations are often driven by the client's increasing emphasis on global markets.[57]

## When Is Globalization Appropriate?

While globalization of advertising is viewed by many in the advertising industry as a difficult task, some progress has been made in learning what products and services are best suited to worldwide appeals:[58]

1. Brands or messages that can be adapted for a visual appeal, avoiding the problems of trying to translate words into dozens of languages.
2. Brands that are promoted with image campaigns that play to universal needs, values, and emotions.
3. High-tech products and new products coming to the world for the first time, not steeped in the cultural heritage of a country.
4. Products with nationalistic flavor if the country has a reputation in the field.
5. Products that appeal to a market segment with universally similar tastes, interests, needs, and values.

Many companies and brands rely on visual appeals that are easily adapted for use in global advertising campaigns. These companies are often marketing products in the secondary category, such as jewelry, cosmetics, liquor, and cigarettes, that appeal to universal needs, values, and emotions and lend themselves to global campaigns. Marketers recognize that emotions such as joy, sentiment, excitement, and pleasure are

**EXHIBIT 19–14**
Campari uses global advertising to position the brand as the sophisticated choice of upscale consumers

**EXHIBIT 19–15**
High-tech products such as the HTC One smartphone often use global advertising campaigns

universal as are needs/values such as self-esteem, status, and achievement. Thus, it is common for global advertising campaigns to use emotional and image appeals. As one advertising executive notes:

> What it all boils down to is that we are all human. We share the gift of emotional response. We feel things. And we feel them in remarkably similar ways. We speak different languages, we observe different customs, but we are wired to each other and to an ultimate power source that transcends us in a way that makes us subject to a common emotional spectrum.[59]

A number of companies whose products appeal to universal needs, values, and emotions use global advertising. For example, the Lambesis agency created a global advertising campaign for the Italian liqueur brand Campari that celebrated its status as the sophisticated choice of upscale drinkers. The campaign celebrates Campari's passionate brand history with iconic high-fashion images used in posterlike print ads and fine art calendars as well as TV commercials featuring actress Jessica Alba. The "Club Campari" global campaign runs in over 30 countries in print, television, and outdoor media as well as online. However, in developing this campaign the agency had to account for differences in the way the brand is viewed in different countries, such as Germany where it is enjoyed while watching sunsets; Brazil where it is often consumed poolside and has a very upbeat image; and Italy where Campari has more of a progressive and cinematic image. The TV commercial developed by Lambesis, which is shown in Exhibit 19–14, effectively combines these various perceptions and images of the brand.

High-tech products such as mobile phones, personal computers, plasma and LCD televisions, videogames, and MP3 players are products in the third category. Many of the marketers of high-tech products use global campaigns to promote their brands. For example, Taiwan-based HTC recently developed a global campaign for its HTC One smartphone that focused on testimonials from real people rather than actors.[60] One of the spots featured a photographer using an HTC One phone to shoot a fashion model as they're both falling at 126 miles an hour in the Arizona desert. Pictures taken on the phone were run in print ads in U.S. publications such as *Wired, Sports Illustrated, People,* and *Us Weekly* as well as publications in other countries (Exhibit 19–15).

Products in the fourth category are those that come from countries with national reputations for quality and/or a distinctive image that can be used as the basis for global advertising. These products capitalize on the **country-of-origin effect,** which refers to consumers' general perceptions of quality for products made in a given country.[61] Examples include Swiss watches, French wine, and German beer or automobiles. Many U.S. companies are taking advantage of the cachet American products have acquired among consumers in Europe and other international markets. For example, Jeep promotes itself as "the American legend" in Europe and Japan. Brown-Forman has been using an American theme for its Jack Daniel's and Southern Comfort liquor brands since it began selling them in foreign markets more than two decades ago. A number of studies have shown a pronounced effect of country of origin on the quality perceptions of products, with the reputation of specific countries impacting consumers' evaluative judgments of brands.[62] Thus, companies and brands that originate in countries associated with quality may want to take advantage of this in their advertising. However, some marketing experts argue that in today's world of globalization, consumers are only vaguely aware of the country of origin for many of the brands they buy.[63] Thus, marketers need to understand whether product origin is relevant to the consumers in their target market. A study conducted among a representative sample of 1,000 college students from over 375 universities across the United States found that the vast majority of them were unaware of the country of origin of most brands. However, while the students were not aware of where the brands came from, they did have definite opinions about which countries produce the best products. When students were asked whether they believe a country makes quality products, Japan was rated the highest at 82 percent, followed by the United States at 78 percent, Germany at 77 percent, and Italy at 74 percent. Countries rated the lowest for product quality were Russia, Mexico, and Vietnam.[64]

In the final category for which globalization is appropriate are products and services that can be sold to common market segments around the world, such as those identified by Salah Hassan and Lea Katsansis.[65] One such segment is the world's elite—people who, by reason of their economically privileged position, can pursue a lifestyle that includes fine jewelry, expensive clothing, quality automobiles, and the like. Marketers of high-quality products such as Bally leather goods, Cartier jewelry, Godiva chocolates, and Louis Vuitton luggage can use global advertising to appeal to the elite market segment around the world. Well-known international brands competing in the luxury goods marketplace often present a singular image of prestige and style to the entire world.

An example of a marketer of luxury products that uses global advertising is Swiss watchmaker TAG Heuer, which targets upscale consumers, many of whom are world travelers. Thus, the company feels that it is important to have a consistent advertising message and image in each country. Creative elements of TAG Heuer ads such as the layout, logo, pictures of the product, slogan, and tagline remain clear, consistent, and visually recognizable at first glance all over the world. The only element of the ad that changes from country to country is the celebrity ambassador who appears in the ad. For example, TAG Heuer's new campaign uses Formula 1 champions Sergio Perez and Jenson Button in Europe. In India, the ambassadors include racing champion Karun Chandhok and Bollywood actor Shah Rukh Khan while in the United States the ambassadors include Cameron Diaz, Maria Sharapova, and Leonardo DiCaprio (Exhibit 19–16).

**EXHIBIT 19–16**
TAG Heuer uses a global campaign featuring different celebrity ambassadors for various countries

Another segment of global consumers who have similar needs and interests and seek similar features and benefits from products and services is teenagers. There are more than 200 million teens in Europe, Latin America, and the Pacific Rim countries of Asia whose lifestyles are converging with those of the 40 million teens in the United States and Canada to create a vast, free-spending global market.[66] Teens now have intense exposure to television, magazines movie, music, travel, and global advertising from companies such as Levi Strauss, Benetton, Nike, Coca-Cola, Pepsi, and many others.

## Global Products, Local Messages

While the pros and cons of global marketing and advertising continue to be debated, many companies are taking an in-between approach by standardizing their products and basic marketing strategy but localizing their advertising messages. This approach recognizes similar desires, goals, needs, and uses for products and services but tailors advertising to the local cultures and conditions in each market. Some agencies call this approach "think globally, act locally" while others describe it as "global vision with a local touch."

Although some marketers use global ads with little or no modification, most companies adapt their messages to respond to differences in language, market conditions, and other factors. Many global marketers use a strategy called **pattern advertising**: their ads follow a basic approach, but themes, copy, and sometimes even visual elements are adapted to differences in local markets. For example, Unilever's Dove soap uses the same basic advertising and positioning theme globally, but models from Australia, France, Germany, and Italy are used to appeal to women in those countries. The TAG Heuer ads shown in Exhibit 19–16 are an example of pattern advertising. The basic creative approach is the same, although minor changes are sometimes made for a country such as the choice of brand ambassadors.

Another way global marketers adapt their campaigns to local markets is by producing a variety of ads with a similar theme and format and allowing managers in various countries or regions to select those messages they believe will work best in their markets. Some companies are also giving local managers more autonomy in adapting global campaign themes to local markets. For example, Coca-Cola developed a new model for its global advertising and brand communication model: Rather than authorizing the heads of individual markets to run their own advertising, various regions of the world are consolidated into a series of hubs or clusters. Although the company provides local marketing support for each cluster, a global team oversees creative work that can be used in various markets, thus allowing for fewer creative executions. Coca-Cola's chief creative officer notes that the new structure "allows us to feel more like global brands with local relevance."[67]

Although many marketers are striving to develop global brands, research suggests most are doing so by using a localized approach. A study of international advertising strategies of successful U.S. multinational corporations found that only 9 percent used totally standardized global advertising for all foreign markets, while 37 percent used all localized advertising. The remaining 54 percent used a combination strategy, standardizing portions of their advertising but adapting it for local markets.[68] Marketers said a major risk of the global approach was a lack of communication owing to cultural differences. Another study found that most U.S. consumer durable goods manufacturers used a localized advertising approach—but most used some standardized messages.[69]

A more recent study of international advertising decision makers found that "think globally, act locally" still appears to be the dominant strategy of international advertisers, but with a slight revision: "think globally, act regionally."[70] Most of the respondents in this survey said their companies' worldwide headquarters play a dominant role in determining their international advertising messages so they are consistent worldwide. However, there is a trend toward giving regional offices the autonomy to adapt the global theme for their local markets.

Most managers believe it is important to adapt components of their advertising messages—such as the language, models, scenic backgrounds, message content, and symbols—to reflect the culture and frame of reference of consumers in various countries. For example, global branding expert Nigel Hollis notes that research conducted by Millward Brown found that, all things being equal, brands that are identified with local culture will perform better than others.[71] He notes several reasons why it is important for brands to have a strong degree of identity to local culture and advises that the key to global brand success is to connect with consumers at the local level while capitalizing on the advantages offered by operating on a global scale.[72] Many companies are making these tactical adjustments to their advertising messages while still pursuing global strategies that will help them project a consistent global image and turn their products and services into global brands. Global Perspective 19–3 discusses how global marketers are facing more competition from local companies.

# DECISION AREAS IN INTERNATIONAL ADVERTISING

Companies developing advertising and promotional programs for international markets must make certain organizational and functional decisions similar to those for domestic markets. These decisions include organization style, agency selection, creative strategy and execution, and media strategy and selection.

## Organizing for International Advertising

One of the first decisions a company must make when it decides to market its products to other countries is how to organize the international advertising and promotion function. This decision is likely to depend on how the company is organized overall for international marketing and business. Three basic options are centralization at the home office or headquarters, decentralization of decision making to local foreign markets, or a combination of the two.

**Centralization**   Many companies prefer to *centralize* the international advertising and promotion function so that all decisions about agency selection, creative strategy and campaign development, media strategy, and budgeting are made at the firm's home office.

Complete centralization is likely when market and media conditions are similar from one country to another, when the company has only one or a few international agencies handling all of its advertising, when the company can use standardized advertising, or when it desires a consistent image worldwide. Centralization may also be best when a company's international business is small and it operates through foreign distributors or licensees who do not become involved in the marketing and promotional process.

Many companies prefer the centralized organizational structure to protect their foreign investments and keep control of the marketing effort and corporate and/or brand image. Centralization can save money, since it reduces the need for staff and administration at the local subsidiary level. As the trend toward globalized marketing and advertising strategies continues, more companies are likely to move more toward centralization of the advertising function to maintain a unified world brand image rather than presenting a different image in each market. Some foreign managers may actually prefer centralized decision making, as it removes them from the burden of advertising and promotional decisions and saves them from defending local decisions to the home office. However, many marketing and advertising managers in foreign markets oppose centralized control. They say the structure is too rigid and makes it difficult to adapt the advertising and promotional program to local needs and market conditions.

# Global Perspective 19–3 > > >

## Global Brands Turn Their Attention to Local Competitors

It has been more than 30 years since former Harvard marketing professor Theodore Levitt popularized the idea of globalization in his classic article titled "The Globalization of Markets" which appeared in the *Harvard Business Review* in 1983. Levitt argued that the world was becoming a global marketplace where people have the same basic needs, wants, desires, and tastes no matter where they live, and called on companies to develop global marketing strategies and true global brands that could be sold under one name around the world. Many multinational companies heeded the call for globalization, and their advertising agencies were given the charge of helping them turn their products into global brands that could be promoted with the same basic advertising theme and approach worldwide.

A number of U.S.-based companies such as Procter & Gamble, Coca-Cola, IBM, Microsoft, PepsiCo, Dell, Nike, and Disney have been successful in turning many of their products and services into global brands. Companies based outside the United States such as Nestlé, Unilever, Nokia, Toyota, Samsung, IKEA, and Nintendo have done so as well; the small size of their domestic markets has necessitated that they be adroit at marketing their brands abroad. However, while many companies refer to themselves and/or their various products and services as "global brands," the number that is truly global in scope is actually quite small. Experts note that a true global brand is one that does more than use the same basic product, name, packaging, and advertising around the world. In his book *The Global Brand*, Nigel Hollis, executive vice president and chief global

analyst for the Millward Brown Group, defines a global brand as one that has transcended its cultural origins to develop strong relationships with consumers across different countries and cultures. Hollis also notes that the number of truly global brands is quite small, with only around 5 percent of the world's brands marketed in more than six countries.

Most of the world's global brands have taken a long time to establish themselves across multiple countries and cultures and to develop strong connections with consumers in various regions. Hollis notes that for most of the leading global brands, there is a strong relationship between the length of time in a market with how well accepted the brand is there. The longer the brand has been around and the more people have grown up with it, the more localized the brand is in terms of how it competes in the market and how it is perceived by consumers. A number of global marketers of packaged goods such as Procter & Gamble, Unilver, and Colgate-Palmolive have been gaining market share in markets such as Latin America, China, and India. However, all of the BRIC countries (Brazil, Russia, India, and China) have feisty and savvy local companies that are proving to be formidable competitors. These local competitors often understand the consumers in their markets better as well as the local distribution systems. Moreover, some of these companies have their own international ambitions and want to expand beyond their home countries. For example, Hypermarcas in Brazil and India's Dabur have plans to expand beyond their local markets. Competition from local companies in the BRIC countries is not limited to packaged-goods products. Tata

**Decentralization** Under a *decentralized* organizational structure, marketing and advertising managers in each market have the authority to make their own advertising and promotional decisions. Local managers can select ad agencies, develop budgets, conduct research, approve creative themes and executions, and select advertising media. Companies using a decentralized approach put a great deal of faith in the judgment and decision-making ability of personnel in local markets. This approach is often used when companies believe local managers know the marketing situation in their countries the best. They may also be more effective and motivated when given responsibility for the advertising and promotional program in their markets. Decentralization also works well in small or unique markets where headquarters' involvement is not worthwhile or advertising must be tailored to the local market.

International fragrance marketer Chanel, Inc. uses a decentralized strategy. Chanel found that many of its fragrance concepts do not work well globally and decided to localize advertising. For example, the U.S. office has the option of using ads created by the House of Chanel in Paris or developing its own campaigns for the U.S. market. Chanel executives in the United States think that the French concept of prestige is not the same as Americans' and the artsy ads created in France do not work well in this country.[73]

**Combination** While there is an increasing trend toward centralizing the international advertising function, many companies combine the two approaches. The home office, or headquarters, has the most control over advertising policy, guidelines, and operations in all markets. The international advertising manager works closely with

Nano is being marketed as India's "first car for everyone" and has a price that is appropriate for the developing automobile market in India of just $2,000. "The People's Car" is ultrasmall as well; it is only 10 feet long from bumper to bumper and is very fuel efficient.

Nike and adidas face strong competition from Li-Ning in China, which has 8,000 stores across the country, as well as Anta, which is another strong Chinese athletic shoe and apparel brand. Li-Ning adopted many of its competitors' tactics by becoming the official partner of the National Basketball Association in China and by signing sponsorship deals with the national basketball teams of Spain and Argentina and deals with several tennis pros and track athletes. A very strong international company based in China is Lenovo, which purchased IBM's personal computer division in 2005 and by 2013 was battling with HP to become the world's leading PC company. Lenovo's primary strength is in its home market as well as in emerging markets such as India. Over the past several years Lenovo focused heavily on its domestic market, particularly China's rural areas and third-, fourth-, and fifth-tier cities, which represent a potential market of nearly 700 million first-time computer buyers. Lenovo developed an innovative integrated marketing program called "PCs for Rural China" that reaches consumers in these areas by presenting free feature films in more than 3,000 villages and small towns. However, Lenovo has taken its "For Those Who Do" umbrella theme globally and is targeting young consumers around the world. For example, in Mexico and Latin

America Lenovo has held a competition called "Los Doers," and in India and Russia the company has created a "Do Network" that engages young doers with projects such as the YouTube Space Lab partnership where high school students compete to have their experiments conducted aboard the International Space Stations.

Multinational companies will continue their efforts to turn many of their products and services into global brands. However, they are learning that they must now compete against regional and local brands that are improving their product and service quality and have stronger emotional connections to consumers. This means marketers must develop advertising and IMC programs that travel well and transcend markets or adapt them to make them more in tune with local consumers and cultures. While the world seems to be getting smaller every day, cultural perceptions of brands and marketing still vary from country to country and can often be worlds apart.

Sources: Beth Snyder Bulik, "What Do You Do When Your Business Outpaces Your Brand? Lenovo May Soon Have the Answer," *Advertising Age*, January 9, 2012, p. 12; Jack Neff, "Emerging-Market Growth War Pits Global Brand Giants against Scrappy Local Rivals," *Advertising Age*, June 13, 2011, p. 4; Ann Marie Kerwin, "A World of Inspirational Problem-Solving, Savvy Brands and Smart Marketing," *Advertising Age*, June 1, 2010, pp. 4–5; Normandy Madden, "Lenovo Sets Its Sights Back to Local," *Advertising Age*, June 22, 2009, http://adage.com/print?article_id=137481; Normandy Madden, "Two Chinese Brands Break onto World Scene," *Advertising Age*, June 15, 2009, p. 17; Nigel Hollis, *The Global Brand* (New York: Palgrave Macmillan, 2008).

YTC 19-07
Lenovo
youtube.com/10ebelch

local or regional marketing managers and personnel from the international agency (or agencies) and sets advertising and promotional objectives, has budgetary authority, approves all creative themes and executions, and approves media selection decisions, especially when they are made on a regional basis or overlap with other markets.

Advertising managers in regional or local offices submit advertising plans and budgets for their markets, which are reviewed by the international advertising manager. Local managers play a major role in working with the agency to adapt appeals to their particular markets and select media.

The combination approach allows for consistency in a company's international advertising yet permits local input and adaptation of the promotion program. Most consumer-product companies find that local adaptation of advertising is necessary for foreign markets or regions, but they want to maintain control of the overall worldwide image they project. For example, Levi Strauss in 2010 hired its first global chief marketing officer to oversee the company's marketing operations in over 60 countries and try to make the Levi's brand more competitive against premium denim lines such as True Religion, Seven For All Mankind, and Joe's Jeans.[74] However, the company still provides a great deal of autonomy to regional marketing directors.

## Agency Selection

One of the most important decisions for a firm engaged in international marketing is the choice of an advertising agency. The company has three basic alternatives in

CHAPTER 19

selecting an agency to handle its international advertising. First, it can choose a major agency with both domestic and overseas offices. Many large agencies have offices all over the world and have become truly international operations. Some Western agencies have opened offices in Eastern Europe and Russia to create ads for the multinational companies participating in the free-market economies that are developing in these countries. Many agencies are moving their offices from Hong Kong to Shanghai to be closer to the world's largest consumer market on the mainland of China.[75]

Many American companies prefer to use a U.S.-based agency with foreign offices; this gives them greater control and convenience and also facilitates coordination of overseas advertising. Companies often use the same agency to handle international and domestic advertising. As discussed in Chapter 3, the flurry of mergers and acquisitions in the ad agency business in recent years, both in the United States and in other countries, has created large global agencies that can meet the international needs of global marketers. A number of multinational companies have consolidated their advertising with one large agency. The consolidation trend began in 1994 when IBM dismissed 40 agencies around the world and awarded its entire account to Ogilvy & Mather Worldwide.[76] A year later, Colgate-Palmolive consolidated all of its global advertising with New York–based Young & Rubicam. The move, which followed the worldwide restructuring of Colgate's manufacturing and distribution system, marked the first time a large multibrand advertiser put all of its billings with one agency.[77]

There are a number of reasons why global marketers consolidate their advertising with one agency. Many companies recognize they must develop a consistent global image for the company and/or its brands and speak with one coordinated marketing voice around the world. For example, IBM officials felt the company had been projecting too many images when its advertising was divided among so many agencies. The consolidation enabled IBM to present a single brand identity throughout the world while taking advantage of one of the world's best-known brand names (Exhibit 19–17).

Companies are also consolidating their global advertising in an effort to increase cost efficiencies and gain greater leverage over their agencies. When a major client puts all of its advertising with one agency, that company often becomes the agency's most important account. And, as one IBM executive notes, "You become a magnet for talent and attention."[78] Consolidation can also lead to cost-efficiencies. For example, Levi Strauss has consolidated most of its advertising for various regions with the Wieden + Kennedy agency, which has offices around the world, while the WPP Group's Wunderman was chosen as the company's first global digital agency to give the company greater global reach and more operational efficiency in the digital arena.[79]

Advertising executives also noted that a major reason for all of the account consolidation is that agencies now have the ability to communicate and manage globally. The Internet, e-mail, and airline connections make it much easier to manage accounts around the globe. Of course, placing an entire global advertising account with one agency can be risky. If the agency fails to deliver an effective campaign, the client has no backup agency to make a fast rebound and the search for a new agency can be very time-consuming. Clients who consolidate also face the problem of selling the idea to regional offices, which often previously enjoyed their own local agency relationships. However, it appears that more and more companies are willing to take these risks and rely on one agency to handle their advertising around the world.

A second alternative for the international marketer is to choose an agency that rather than having its own foreign offices or branches is affiliated with agencies in other countries or belongs to a network of foreign agencies.

**EXHIBIT 19–17**
IBM uses the Ogilvy & Mather agency to handle all of its global advertising

# HOW TO COMPETE IN THE ERA OF "SMART".

For five years, IBMers have been working with companies, cities and communities to build a Smarter Planet. We've seen enormous advances, as leaders have begun using the vast supply of Big Data to transform their enterprises and institutions through mobile technology, social business and the cloud.

Big Data has changed how these leaders work, how they make decisions and how they serve their customers. And the ability to harness Big Data is giving their enterprises a new competitive edge in today's era of "smart".

but as individuals. And that's changing how companies serve customers. Call centers, once evaluated by how quickly they got callers off the phone, are training employees to engage more with customers by starting conversations and serving individuals.

*Social networks shift value in the workplace from knowledge that people possess to knowledge that they can communicate.*

*Police in Memphis used Big Data and analytics to verify patterns of criminal activity, which helped them change their strategy.*

**DECISIONS BASED ON ANALYTICS, NOT ON INSTINCT.** Decision makers once viewed their intuition and experience as the keys to formulating strategy and assessing risk. But analytics increasingly helps them discern real patterns and anticipate events.

A decade ago, the Memphis Police Department developed an analytics platform that created multilayer maps to identify patterns of criminal

activity. The department then changed its patrolling strategy, reducing crime by 24 percent.

**THE SOCIAL NETWORK IS THE NEW PRODUCTION LINE.** In this knowledge economy, the exchange of ideas has become the new means of production. The advent of social and mobile technology is shifting the competitive edge from having workers who amass knowledge to having workers who impart it.

Cemex, a $15 billion cement maker, wanted to create its first global brand of concrete, which required a coordination of stakeholders from each country. Cemex didn't build

a new lab. It built a social business network. Employees in 50 countries formed one global active community whose collaboration helped launch its first global brand in a third of the anticipated time.

FROM YOU AS A SEGMENT TO YOU AS YOU.
The age of Big Data and analytics is revealing customers not as demographic "segments"

*Effective marketing no longer aims publicity at broad demographic groups—it opens conversations with individuals.*

**FINDING SUCCESS ON A SMARTER PLANET.** An organisation that adopts these principles is a Smarter Enterprise. But using emerging technology is only part of the story. The real challenge now is to use these new insights to change entrenched work practices. To learn more about the new principles of the Smarter Enterprise, visit us at ibm.com/smarterplanet/in

LET'S BUILD A SMARTER PLANET.

 IBM.

IBM, the IBM logo, ibm.com, Smarter Planet and the planet icon are trademarks of International Business Machines Corp, registered in many jurisdictions worldwide. A current list of IBM trademarks is available on the Web at www.ibm.com/legal/copytrade.shtml. © International Business Machines Corporation 2013.

A domestic agency may acquire an interest in several foreign agencies or become part of an organization of international agencies. The agency can then sell itself as an international agency offering multinational coverage and contacts. Many of the large agency holding companies such as the WPP Group, Publicis Groupe, Omincom, and the Interpublic Group own agencies throughout the world that can handle their clients' advertising in various countries.

The advantage of this arrangement is that the client can use a domestic-based agency yet still have access to foreign agencies with detailed knowledge of market conditions, media, and so on in each local market. There may be problems with this approach, however. The local agency may have trouble coordinating and controlling independent agencies, and the quality of work may vary among network members. Companies considering this option must ask the local agency about its ability to control the activities of its affiliates and the quality of their work in specific areas such as creative and media.

The third alternative for the international marketer is to select a local agency for each national market in which it sells its products or services. Since local agencies often have the best understanding of the marketing and advertising environment in their country or region, they may be able to develop the most effective advertising.

Some companies like local agencies because they may provide the best talent in each market. In many countries, smaller agencies may, because of their independence, be more willing to take risks and develop the most effective, creative ads. Choosing local agencies also increases the involvement and morale of foreign subsidiary managers by giving them responsibility for managing the promotion function in their markets. Some companies have the subsidiary choose a local agency, since it is often in the best position to evaluate the agency and will work closely with it.

**Criteria for Agency Selection**  The selection of an agency to handle a company's international advertising depends on how the firm is organized for international marketing and the type of assistance it needs to meet its goals and objectives in foreign markets. Figure 19–3 lists some criteria a company might use in selecting an agency. In a study conducted among marketing directors of European companies, creative capability was ranked the most important factor in selecting an advertising agency network, followed by understanding the market, understanding marketing goals, and ability to produce integrated communications. Size of the agency and agency reputation were cited as important criteria by less than 2 percent of the respondents.[80] Another recent study found that most clients choose an agency based on its creative reputation and the creative presentation it had made. However, a large number of clients felt their agencies lacked international expertise and account coordination ability.[81]

Some companies choose a combination of the three alternatives just discussed because their involvement in each market differs, as do the advertising environment and situation in each country. Several experts in international marketing and advertising advocate the use of international agencies by international companies, particularly those firms moving toward global marketing and striving for a consistent

FIGURE 19–3

Criteria for Selecting an Agency to Handle International Advertising

- Ability of agency to cover relevant markets
- Quality of agency work
- Market research, public relations, and other services offered by agency
- Relative roles of company advertising department and agency
- Level of communication and control desired by company
- Ability of agency to coordinate international campaign
- Size of company's international business
- Company's desire for local versus international image
- Company organizational structure for international business and marketing (centralized versus decentralized)
- Company's level of involvement with international operations

*anima sana in corpore sano*

**ASICS**
*sound mind, sound body*

**EXHIBIT 19–18**
ASICS used a global campaign that relied heavily on visual imagery and was easily translated into different languages

**YTC 19–08**
**Creative**
youtube.com/10ebelch

**EXHIBIT 19–19**
Television ads for Las Vegas were adapted for the Mexican market

corporate or brand image around the world. The trend toward mergers and acquisitions and the formation of mega-agencies with global marketing and advertising capabilities suggests the international agency approach will become the preferred arrangement among large companies.

## Creative Decisions

Another decision facing the international advertiser is determining the appropriate advertising messages for each market. Creative strategy development for international advertising is basically similar in process and procedure to that for domestic advertising. Advertising and communications objectives should be based on the marketing strategy and market conditions in foreign markets. Major selling ideas must be developed and specific appeals and execution styles chosen.

An important factor in the development of creative strategy is the issue of global versus localized advertising. If the standardized approach is taken, the creative team must develop advertising that will transcend cultural differences and communicate effectively in every country. For example, Asics used a global advertising campaign for several years called "The Cleansing Power of Sport" which used exercise, and more specifically running, as a cleansing metaphor. As shown in Exhibit 19–18, the campaign's pervading theme was executed by showing a runner sprinting through walls of water as words such as *fear, stress, insecurity,* and *doubt,* rendered in various languages, fall away from his body. For the campaign to work globally, the message had to be visually iconic and easily translatable. Adapting the image-based print ads for different countries and languages was not very difficult or expensive, and the final campaign was translated into more than a dozen languages.[82]

When companies follow a **localized advertising strategy,** the creative team must determine what type of selling idea, ad appeal, and execution style will work in each market. A product may have to be positioned differently in each market depending on consumers' usage patterns and habits. For example, the Las Vegas Convention and Visitors Authority took its popular "What Happens Here, Stays Here" campaign to several foreign markets, including the United Kingdom and Mexico. Research conducted by the ad agency found that the creative ads were not provocative enough for the United Kingdom, needed to be toned down for Mexico, and could be left alone for western Canada.[83] However, French Canadians in the eastern part of the country are more European-like in their sensibilities and the agency plans to develop alternative taglines and stories for a French-language campaign there. Mexicans were more comfortable with story lines that fit with family customers and were not sexually provocative. For example, one spot featured a young man meeting a group of friends in a Mexican bar and trying to tell them about his first trip to Las Vegas but being too excited to find the right words (Exhibit 19–19).

Marketers must also figure out what type of advertising appeal or execution style will be most effective in each market. Emotional appeals such as humor may work well in one country but not in another because of differences in cultural backgrounds and consumer perceptions of what is or is not funny. While humorous appeals are popular in the United States and Britain, they are not used often in Germany, where consumers do not respond favorably to them. German advertising typically uses rational appeals that are text-heavy and contain arguments for a product's superiority.[84] France, Italy, and Brazil are more receptive to sexual appeals and nudity in advertising than are most other societies. The French government recently stepped up its efforts to convince advertisers and their ad agencies to tone down the use of sexual imagery and violence in their advertising.[85] France's Truth in Advertising Commission, which is the main self-regulatory body, has issued new standards regarding the presentation of human beings in advertising.

Countries such as Japan, Brazil, and Thailand appreciate creativity: Humorous and irreverent ads are often needed to catch the attention of consumers. In Thailand, which has become the creative nerve center of Asian advertising, the unusual blend of culture, religion, politics, and language influences the advertising. Thailand's *sabi-sabai* ("take it easy") attitude is partly a product of the country's Buddhist religion, which teaches disciples to forgive and look on the sunny side of life, as well as the country's heritage as a peaceful kingdom. Thailand has a very high literacy rate but few people read as a leisure activity, which results in most ads being visual in nature rather than based upon language.[86] Many marketers have found that ads that are more humorous, irreverent, or adventurous break through the clutter and attract the attention of Thai consumers.

Another country where there is a major emphasis on creativity is India where consumers are not as cynical toward advertising as they are in many other countries, such as the United States.[87] Multinational marketers are recognizing that they must create ads specifically for the Indian market rather than trying to adapt campaigns being used globally or in their domestic markets.

In China, marketers must deal with a very decentralized market with distinct differences in culture, language, food preferences, and lifestyles among the various regions and 2,000 cities. In general, the Chinese place a high emphasis on group and family values. Advertisers must be careful when using humor and sexual appeal, particularly for national campaigns, as language and values vary greatly from province to province. Human interest stories are used as the basis for ads in southern China but less so in cities such as Beijing and Shanghai where residents prefer more information-based ads.[88]

## Media Selection

One of the most challenging areas for international marketers is media strategy and selection. Companies generally find major differences in the media available outside their home markets, and media conditions may vary considerably from one country to another. In less developed countries such as Vietnam, Kenya, and Egypt, most consumers do not have contact with a marketer's advertising and promotion efforts until they enter a store. Packaging and other point-of-purchase elements, rather than media advertising, will have the greatest impact on purchase decisions. On the other hand, advertising bombards consumers in the more affluent countries of Europe, the Pacific Rim, and North America through a variety of print and broadcast as well as interactive media. Media planners face a number of problems in attempting to communicate advertising and promotional messages to consumers in various countries. First, the types of media available are different in different countries. Many homes in developing countries do not have TV sets. For example, in many South and Central African nations (such as Uganda, Tanzania, Kenya, and Zimbabwe), radio is the dominant medium and access to TV sets is very limited. For many years, access to television was limited in countries such as Vietnam, and outdoor advertising was the best way to reach consumers along with point-of-purchase material. However, the number of households with televisions is growing rapidly in less developed countries such as India and Vietnam, as are other media such as the Internet.

The amount of time people spend watching television also varies from one country to the next. In the United States, the average person spends nearly 4.5 hours a day watching television. However, in Europe average daily viewing averages 3.5 hours and ranges from a low of 2.4 hours in Switzerland to a high of 3.9 hours in Greece. Many European countries have hundreds of channels available to cable households or homes with satellite connections.

In some countries, TV advertising is not accepted or the amount of commercial time is severely limited. For example, in Germany advertising is not permitted after 8 P.M. on government-owned channels and is prohibited on Sundays and holidays.

However, the restrictions do not apply to Germany's privately owned television stations, which can devote up to 20 percent of their airtime to commercials. In the Netherlands, TV spots are limited to 5 percent of airtime and must be booked up to a year in advance. Programs also do not have fixed time slots for ads, making it impossible to plan commercial buys around desired programs. In some countries, the limited number of channels and demand for commercial time result in extremely high levels of advertising clutter.

The number of TV sets is increasing tremendously in India, but there is still controversy over TV advertising. Commercials are restricted to only 10 percent of programming time and must appear at the beginning or end of a program. Australia lifted a ban on cable TV advertising in 1997. However, some cable channels won't accept any advertising, and Australian consumers will not tolerate as much advertising on cable channels as on free TV networks.[89]

The characteristics of media differ from country to country in terms of coverage, cost, quality of reproduction, restrictions, and the like. In some countries, media rates are negotiable or may fluctuate owing to unstable currencies, economic conditions, or government regulations. For example, in China TV stations charge a local rate for Chinese advertisers, a foreign rate, and a joint venture rate. Although its 1.19 billion TV viewers make China the world's largest television market, the medium is strictly controlled by the Communist Party. State-owned China Central Television (CCTV) controls the national networks. Politics frequently intrude into program selection and scheduling: A show might be delayed for several months to coincide with a key political event, or programs from foreign countries may be pulled off the air.[90] CCTV has developed its own version of an up-front market, as an auction is held each November to sell advertising time on prime-time programming for the coming year. The annual auction is generally considered a barometer for China's media market as local and regional channels will often hold off setting their advertising rates to see the level of demand for advertising time. While CCTV is China's only national broadcaster, it accounts for just 12 percent of the total television advertising revenue in China, with the remainder going to local TV channels, provincial satellite channels, and provincial TV stations.[91]

Another problem international advertisers face is obtaining reliable media information such as circulation figures, audience profiles, and costs. Many countries that had only state-owned TV channels are now experiencing a rapid growth in commercial channels, which is providing more market segmentation opportunities. However, reliable audience measurement data are not available, and media buyers often rely on their instincts when purchasing TV time. A number of research companies are developing audience measurement systems for countries in Eastern Europe, Russia, and China. In China, AGB Nielsen Media Research monitors TV-viewing audiences in 11 of China's biggest cities including Beijing, Shanghai, and Guangzhou as well as in the rural parts of several provinces, using nearly 10,000 households with people meters.[92] Audience measurement information is also available from CSM Media Research, a company that is a joint venture between CTR Market Research (the leading market research company in China) and TNS Group, a global market information company based in London.

The goal of international advertisers is to select media vehicles that reach their target audience most effectively and efficiently. Media selection is often localized even for a centrally planned, globalized campaign. Local agencies or media buyers generally have more knowledge of local media and better opportunities to negotiate rates, and subsidiary operations can maintain control and adapt to media conditions and options in their market. Media planners have two options: using national or local media or using international media.

**Local Media**   Many advertisers choose the local media of a country to reach its consumers. Print is the most used medium worldwide, since TV commercial time and the number of homes with TV sets are limited in many countries. Many

**EXHIBIT 19–20**

*Jelly* is a popular fashion magazine in Japan

**EXHIBIT 19–21**

International editions of *Cosmopolitan* magazine are distributed in more than 100 countries in 35 languages

countries have magazines that are circulated nationwide as well as national or regional newspapers that carry advertising directed to a national audience. Most countries also have magazines that appeal to special interests or activities, allowing for targeting in media selection. For example, Japan has numerous fashion magazines such as *Jelly,* which focuses on runway fashions, as well as street fashion and culture (Exhibit 19–20).

Although restrictions and regulations have limited the development of TV as a dominant advertising medium in many countries, it is a primary medium for obtaining nationwide coverage in most developed countries and offers tremendous creative opportunities. Restrictions on television may be lessening in some countries, and time availability may increase. For example, the number of TV stations and television advertising in Italy have exploded in the past decade since government restrictions against private broadcasting were lifted. Advertising groups are using economic, legal, and political pressure to get more television commercial time from reluctant European governments. The increase in TV channels through direct broadcasting by satellite to many European households (discussed later in this section) is hastening this process.

In addition to print and television, local media available to advertisers include radio, direct mail, billboards, cinema, and transit advertising. These media give international advertisers great flexibility and the opportunity to reach specific market segments and local markets within a country. Most international advertisers rely heavily on national and local media in their media plans for foreign markets.

**International Media** The other way for the international advertiser to reach audiences in various countries is through international media that have multimarket coverage. The primary focus of international media has traditionally been magazines and newspapers. A number of U.S.-based consumer-oriented publications have international editions, including *Time, Reader's Digest,* and *National Geographic* as well as the newspaper *USA Today.* Hearst Magazines International oversees the publication of Hearst's leading consumer magazines around the world. Hearst publishes nearly 300 international editions for distribution in more than 80 countries including *Esquire, Good Housekeeping, Seventeen,* and *Elle.* Hearst also publishes *Cosmopolitan,* which with 64 international editions is the largest selling young women's magazine and has more editions than any other magazine in the world (Exhibit 19–21).[93] Other U.S.-based publications with foreign editions include *Bloomberg Businessweek, Fortune,* and *The Wall Street Journal.*

A number of U.S.-based publishers are looking for growth by taking their brands to other countries where the number of magazines is still growing and the Internet has less of an impact on advertising revenue. The CEO of Hearst Magazines International has noted that the BRIC countries—Brazil, Russia, India, and China—offer good growth opportunities based on the level of competition, as well as growth in GDP and advertising spending.[94] Over the past several years Hearst has started new editions of magazines such as *Cosmopolitan, Harper's Bazaar,* and *Esquire* in India, Vietnam, Spain, and Australia. Another major publisher, Time Inc., has launched new editions of *Sports Illustrated* and *InStyle* in China; *People* and *Sports Illustrated* in India; *Fortune* in Korea; and *InStyle* in Thailand. However, publishing companies must still overcome a number of challenges in foreign countries such as underdeveloped distribution systems, cultural differences, and low cover prices and advertising rates that make it difficult to generate enough revenue to make the magazines profitable.[95]

International publications offer advertisers a way to reach large audiences on a regional or worldwide basis. Readers of these publications are usually upscale, high-income individuals who are desirable target markets for many products and services. There are, however, several problems with these international media that can limit their attractiveness to many advertisers. Their reach in any one foreign country may be low, particularly for specific segments of a market. Also, while they deliver desirable audiences to companies selling business or upscale consumer products and services, they do not cover the mass consumer markets or specialized market segments very well. Other U.S.-based publications in foreign markets do offer advertisers ways to reach specific market segments.

While print remains the dominant medium for international advertising, many companies are turning their attention to international commercial TV. Package-goods companies in particular view TV advertising as the best way to reach mass markets and effectively communicate their advertising messages. Satellite technology has helped spread the growth of TV in other countries and made global television networks a reality. For example, MTV Networks International has a variety of brands that span the globe and are seen in over 500 million households in 160 countries, including its flagship MTV network as well as VH1 and Nickelodeon. MTV is still the premier media platform for marketers trying to reach young consumers in countries throughout the world, including Europe, Asia, and Latin America.

A major development affecting broadcasting in Europe, Asia, and Latin America is **direct broadcast by satellite (DBS)** to homes and communities equipped with small, low-cost receiving dishes. A number of satellite networks operate in these regions and beam entertainment programming across several countries. The satellite network market is dominated by the global media conglomerate News Corporation, which was founded by Rupert Murdoch and owns a number of media properties in the United States, including the Fox Broadcasting Company. News Corp has a controlling interest in British Sky Broadcasting (BSkyB), which beams more than 300 channels to 10 million subscribers in Britain, and also owns STAR, which is the world's largest satellite network, stretching from the Middle East to India and South Korea and reaching more than 300 million viewers in 53 countries. In 2009 News Corp restructured its Asian broadcast businesses into three units—STAR India, STAR Greater China, and Fox International Channels (FIC). The changes are designed to support continued growth of each unit by deploying resources into local markets. For example, Exhibit 19–22 shows an ad for STAR India, which has become the leading television company in India with 60 channels

**EXHIBIT 19–22**
STAR India reaches more than 400 million people every week

India and UK's No. 1 South Asian channel*

Diya Aur Baati Hum

Mon - Fri **9**pm

India StarPlus

www.startv.com/usa

*TAM and BARB

in 10 languages that reach more than 400 million people every week across India and 65 other countries around the world.[96] News Corp also owns part of Phoenix Satellite Television, which reaches several provinces in China and has greater reach than any other foreign channel, particularly among upscale educated viewers in urban areas such as Houg Koug, Beijing, Shanghai, and Guangzhou.[97]

Advances in satellite and communications technology, the expansion of multinational companies with global marketing perspectives, and the development of global ad agencies mean advertisers' use of television as a global medium is likely to increase.

# THE ROLES OF OTHER PROMOTIONAL-MIX ELEMENTS IN INTERNATIONAL MARKETING

This chapter has focused on advertising, since it is usually the primary element in the promotional mix of the international marketer. However, as in domestic marketing, promotional programs for foreign markets generally include such other elements as sales promotion, public relations, and digital and social media. The roles of these other promotional-mix elements vary depending on the firm's marketing and promotional strategy in foreign markets.

Sales promotion and public relations can support and enhance advertising efforts; the latter may also be used to create or maintain favorable images for companies in foreign markets. For some firms, personal selling may be the most important promotional element and advertising may play a support role. This final section considers the roles of some of these other promotional-mix elements in the international marketing program.

## Sales Promotion

Sales promotion activity in international markets is growing due in part to the transfer of promotion concepts and techniques from country to country and in part to the proliferation of media. The growth also stems from the liberalization of trade, the rise of global brands, the spread of cable and satellite TV, and the deregulation and/or privatization of media. Sales promotion and direct-response agencies have been becoming more common, particularly in Europe and more recently in South American, Asian, and Middle Eastern countries. In many less developed countries, spending on sales promotion often exceeds media spending on TV, radio, and print ads.

As we saw in Chapter 16, sales promotion is one of the fastest-growing areas of marketing in the United States. Companies increasingly rely on consumer- and trade-oriented sales promotion to help sell their products in foreign markets as well. Many of the promotional tools that are effective in the United States, such as free samples, premiums, event sponsorships, contests, coupons, and trade promotions, are also used in foreign markets. For example, Häagen-Dazs estimates it gave out more than 5 million free tastings of its ice cream as part of its successful strategy for entering the European market. Since taste is the major benefit of this premium product, sampling was an appropriate sales promotion tool for entering foreign markets. The WD-40 Company uses samples in the United States as well as foreign markets to educate consumers about the versatility of the product and encourage trial. The sample shown in Exhibit 19–23, which uses the front headline "One Can. One Thousand

Uses," was translated into 20 different languages. This makes it possible for the distributors in different countries to use a sampling tool in their local languages. Nestlé introduced its Nescafe brand to China by conducting the world's largest coffee-sampling program. Nescafe samples were passed out across 150 cities in China using 18 teams throughout the country. The sampling program helped increase sales by over 150 percent in the predominantly tea-drinking country.[98]

Unlike advertising, which can be done on a global basis, sales promotions must be adapted to local markets. Kamran Kashani and John Quelch noted several important differences among countries that marketers must consider in developing a sales promotion program.[99] They include the stage of economic development, market maturity, consumer perceptions of promotional tools, trade structure, and legal restrictions and regulations:

- *Economic development.* In highly developed countries such as the United States, Canada, Japan, and Western European nations, marketers can choose from a wide range of promotional tools. But in developing countries they must be careful not to use promotional tools such as in- or on-package premiums that would increase the price of the product beyond the reach of most consumers. Free samples and demonstrations are widely used as effective promotional tools in developing countries. But coupons, which are so popular with consumers in the United States, are rarely used because of problems with distribution and resistance from retailers. In the United States and Britain, most coupons are distributed through newspapers (including FSIs) or magazines. Low literacy rates in some countries make print media an ineffective coupon distribution method, so coupons are delivered door to door, handed out in stores, or placed in or on packages. The use of coupons by both marketers as well as consumers is much greater in the United States than other countries as more than 300 billion coupons were distributed and nearly 3 billion redeemed in 2012. Coupon distribution and redemption in other countries drops dramatically from the levels seen in the United States, as the United Kingdom is the second largest user of coupons with just over 6 billion distributed and less than 100 million redeemed.

- *Market maturity.* Marketers must also consider the stage of market development for their product or service in various countries when they design sales promotions. To introduce a product to a country, consumer-oriented promotional tools such as sampling, high-value coupons, and cross-promotions with established products and brands are often effective. The competitive dynamics of a foreign market are also often a function of its stage of development. More competition is likely in well-developed mature markets, which will influence the types of sales promotion tools used. For example, there may be competitive pressure to use trade allowances to maintain distribution or consumer promotions that will maintain customer loyalty, such as bonus packs, price-off deals, or coupons.

- *Consumer perceptions.* An important consideration in the design of sales promotion programs is how they are perceived by consumers as well as the trade. Consumer perceptions of various sales promotion tools vary from market to market. For example, Japanese women are less likely to take advantage of contests, coupons, or other promotions than are women in the United States. Premium offers in particular must be adapted to the tastes of consumers in various markets. A study by Huff and Alden examined consumers' opinions toward the use of coupons and sweepstakes in three Asian countries: Taiwan, Malaysia, and Thailand. The study found differences among the three countries, with consumers in Taiwan having more negative attitudes and lower levels of use of both sweepstakes and coupons than consumers in Malaysia and Thailand.[100]

- *Trade structure.* In areas with highly concentrated retailing systems, such as northern Europe, the trade situation is becoming much like the United States and Canada as pressure grows for more price-oriented trade and in-store promotions. In southern Europe, the retail industry is highly fragmented and there is less trade pressure for promotions. The willingness and ability of channel members to accommodate sales promotion programs must also be considered. Retailers in many countries do not want to take time to process coupons, post promotional displays, or deal with premiums or packaging that require special handling or storage. In countries like Japan or India, where retailing structures are highly fragmented, stores are too small for point-of-purchase displays or in-store sampling. In most Asian countries simple price-cut promotions that are supported by direct-mail leaflets and newspaper advertising are the primary promotional vehicles.[101]

■ *Regulations.* An important factor affecting the use of sales promotions in foreign countries is the presence of legal restrictions and regulations. Laws affecting sales promotions are generally more restrictive in other countries than in the United States. Some countries ban contests, games, or lotteries, while others restrict the size or amount of a sample, premium, or prize. For example, fair-trade regulations in Japan limit the maximum value of premiums to 10 percent of the retail price; in France the limit is 5 percent. Canada prohibits games of pure chance unless a skill element is used to determine the winner. In Japan the amount of a prize offer is limited to a certain percentage of the product tied to the promotion.[102] In some countries, a free premium must be related to the nature of the product purchased. Many countries have strict rules when it comes to premium offers for children, and some ban them altogether.

Variations in rules and regulations mean marketers must often develop separate consumer sales promotion programs for each country. Many companies have found it difficult to do any promotions throughout Europe because sales promotion rules differ so much from one country to another. While the treaty on European Union may result in a more standardized legal environment in Europe, laws regarding sales promotion are still likely to vary. This is why many companies use local agencies or international sales promotion companies to develop sales promotion programs for foreign markets.

## Public Relations

Many companies involved in international marketing are recognizing the importance of using public relations to support and enhance their marketing and advertising efforts.[103] Public relations activities are needed to deal with local governments, media, trade associations, and the general public, any of which may feel threatened by the presence of a foreign multinational. The job of PR agencies in foreign markets is not only to help the company sell its products or services but also to present the firm as a good corporate citizen concerned about the future of the country.

Companies generally need a favorable image to be successful in foreign markets. Those perceived negatively may face pressure from the media, local governments, or other relevant publics or even boycotts by consumers. Often, public relations is needed to deal with specific problems a company faces in international markets. For example, NutraSweet had problems getting its low-calorie sweetener into some markets because of strong sugar lobbies in Australia, Canada, and Europe. These lobbies encouraged the foreign press to pick up some unfavorable news about the product from the U.S. media. The company retained Burson-Marsteller, the second largest PR company in the world, to help design factual ads about the product and to conduct other PR activities to counter the problems and get the facts out about NutraSweet.

Häagen-Dazs encountered a public relations problem in India, which resulted from miscommunications in posters used to promote the company's first retail outlet in Delhi. The messages on the posters read: "Exclusive Preview for International Travelers. Access restricted only to holders of international passports," and were intended to create a cosmopolitan image and to suggest that you can experience international places such as the French Riviera by enjoying Häagen-Dazs. The controversy arose when the web editor of the *Times of India* posted a blog criticizing the company after a friend was refused entry to the new store and e-mailed him a photo of the ad which the editor posted. The post generated more than 1,000 comments from Indians who were offended by the ad. Häagen-Dazs executives indicated that the people were barred from entering the store only because it was too crowded and apologized for the wording of the ad. The company also terminated its relationship with the advertising agency that created the teaser message. This public relations problem encountered by Häagen-Dazs serves as a reminder to companies doing business in India that the level of national pride is very high in the country and that it has a number of social activists and nongovernment organizations (NGOs) that can utilize social media to quickly create public relations problems for companies.[104]

McDonald's and a number of other companies have had to deal with public relations problems arising from concerns over the nutritional value of their food. The latest controversy erupted in response to a report showing child obesity in France had doubled to 16 percent in 10 years. Concerns over the problem of childhood obesity have spread to other European countries and other food companies such as Kraft and Kellogg are also being criticized. As noted earlier, the European Union called on the food industry to regulate so-called junk-food advertising aimed at consumers across the continent.[105]

Yum! Brand's KFC division ran into a public relations problem in late 2012 in China, which is the restaurant chain's largest market, when Chinese media reported that several KFC suppliers used hormones and antibiotics to shorten the maturation cycle of chickens. The Chinese state television network (CCTV) ran an investigative piece on large-scale chicken farmers in the country, highlighting concerns over their practices; the food scare resulted in a 6 percent decline in sales for several months in KFC restaurants. In response to the PR crisis, KFC eliminated more than 1,000 farms from its supplier networks to ensure food safety and also pledged to step up self-inspections as well as enhance communication with the government and public.[106] As part of its response KFC used its various social media sites in the country such as Sina Weibo and Renren to respond to detail steps the company was taking to ensure the safety of its chicken, engage key media opinion leaders, and restore consumer confidence.[107]

## Digital and Social Media

### Worldwide Growth of the Internet
The Internet is coming of age as a global marketing medium and is becoming an important IMC tool for companies around the world, both large and small. Marketers are using the Internet to promote their companies, build their brands, and engage in e-commerce transactions in their own countries as well as across borders. As more homes and offices become connected to the Internet, its importance as an integrated marketing communications tool and way of transacting business will increase tremendously for companies selling consumer products and services as well as business-to-business marketers.

During its formative years the Internet was largely a North American phenomenon. By the end of the 90s, nearly 54 percent of all online users were in North America and English was the language used on three-fourths of all websites and nearly all e-commerce sites, even though it is the primary language of only 8 percent of the world's population. However, this is changing rapidly. As of 2013, there were more than 2.4 billion Internet users around the world, with the largest number of users residing in Asia, followed by Europe and North America. China is now the country with the largest number of people online, with an estimated 538 million users, followed by the United States with 220 million, and Japan with 96 million.[108] While the United States has the second highest number of users, its ranks 27th in terms of Internet penetration as a percentage of the population at 78 percent. The country that ranks the highest in Internet users is Iceland (98 percent), followed by Norway (97 percent) and Sweden (93 percent). Other countries ranking higher than the United States include Netherlands, Australia, United Kingdom, Germany, and Canada.

As noted, China now has the world's largest Internet population. There are key differences in the demographic and usage behavior of China's "digital elite" as they are younger, better educated, and more likely to be employed full-time versus Internet users in other countries. They also spend more time online and are more involved with Web 2.0 activities such as participating in blogs and chats, posting product ratings and reviews, and using social media. They are also more likely to access the Internet from mobile devices. The look, feel, and features of many Chinese websites are similar to those in the United States and Europe, and China has search (Baidu)

**EXHIBIT 19–24**

TaylorMade Golf develops a website specifically for specific countries

**EXHIBIT 19–25**

Mixi was the leading social networking site in Japan

and e-commerce (Taobao) sites that function like Google and eBay.[109] Baidu dominates online search in China today as Google closed its China site in March 2010 because of censorship by the Chinese government and intrusion from hackers. Google's retreat from China is only partial as it has retained many of its operations there and continues to offer online mapping and music services. Though Google removed its servers from China, users on the mainland have been able to conduct searches through its Hong Kong website. It is expected that Google will work to resolve its disagreements with the Chinese government as the company will not want to turn its back on what has become the world's largest Internet and continues to grow.[110]

Internet usage is also very high in other Asian countries such as Taiwan and South Korea. While English is the dominant language of the Internet, most multinational companies are developing websites in a variety of languages as Internet penetration increases and more consumers around the world go online for information and entertainment.

## Use of Digital and Social Media in International Marketing

Digital media are becoming an integral part of the IMC program of marketers at a global, regional, and local level as Internet penetration increases in countries around the world and marketers become more adept using social media, mobile marketing, and other forms of digital communication. Most multinational marketers now have websites for specific countries and/or regions which allow them to tailor the information they provide to the needs, interests, lifestyles, and subtleties of consumers in these markets. For example, Exhibit 19–24 shows a page from the website used by the TaylorMade Golf Company in Japan. Markets are also using mass media advertising to drive consumers to their websites, where they provide them with detailed information about their products and services, encourage them to participate in online promotions, or allow them to make purchases. Business-to-business marketers are also using their websites as well as social media to provide customers with information and conduct business with them.

The use of social media is also becoming prevalent in countries around the world, and marketers are making social networking sites an integral part of their IMC programs. Facebook has become the first truly global social networking brand and now has more than 1 billion users around the world. As discussed in Digital and Social Media Perspective 19–1, Facebook has become the leading social networking site in the United States as well as most other countries. Over the past few years it has become very popular in Brazil and replaced Orkut, which is owned by Google, as the most popular social media site in the country. However, Facebook has very little presence in China, where it is banned by the Chinese government along with several other social media sites, including Twitter. Its penetration is also very low in other countries such as Korea and Russia, as local social networking sites are thriving in these countries. One country where Facebook has overtaken a popular local social networking site is Japan; in 2012 it reached 15 million active users in the country, surpassing Japanese social network Mixi (Exhibit 19–25). It is reported that several factors helped Facebook become very

# Digital and Social Media Perspective 19–1 > > >

## Facebook Goes Global—Almost

In October 2012, Facebook reached a milestone when the popular social media site reached the 1 billion user mark. Not just 1 billion profiles—which could include repeats, fake users, or bots—but 1 billion *active* users who log on to their accounts at least once per month. The milestone means one in seven people on planet Earth have a Facebook account, and the number keeps growing daily. While Facebook began in the United States and has grown rapidly here, its growth rate of 161 percent from 2009 to 2012 in this country was among the lowest rates of any country with more than 5 million users during that same period. As of 2013, over 85 percent of Facebook's worldwide users are from countries other than the United States. And, in much the same way that culture and traditions in everyday life vary from country to country, Facebook usage differs around the world as well.

One particular market where Facebook, and overall social media usage, has exploded is Brazil, which is currently second behind the United States in number of Facebook users and among the top five most active countries on Twitter. While the average time spent on Facebook dropped 2 percent globally in 2012 to 361 average minutes per month, Brazilians increased their Facebook usage by 208 percent to 535 minutes per month. Average time spent per month on YouTube also increased in Brazil by 5 percent during the same period, making it one of the video-sharing site's top five markets by revenue. One explanation as to why social media usage in Brazil is increasing so rapidly is culture. Brazilians are known for their gregarious behavior in public spaces such as elevators and restaurants, their openness, and their passion for sharing information and pictures with friends and family.

Brazilians, like an increasing number of mobile social media users in the United States, also show a propensity for being glued to social media platforms during sporting events and TV shows, as they are able to converse and share feelings in real time while watching.

Another reason for significant social media growth in Brazil is the very nature of its emerging economy, particularly the middle class's increasing access to the Internet at home and on mobile devices, and the expanding credit market among middle-class consumers. Brazilian consumers have shown an unusually strong willingness to make purchases online using credit cards, leading to increases in online advertising spending, which is expected to more than double in the next five years. These developments are being watched very closely by Facebook and Twitter, both of whom have launched in-country operations in Brazil and plan to capitalize on online and mobile advertising opportunities on their respective platforms.

Another market of great interest to Facebook is India, where the number of users has growth from 8 million in 2010 to 65 million users by the end of 2012. While countries like Brazil represent significant opportunities for Facebook, India is the mother lode given its population of over 1 billion people. Currently about 100 million people have Internet access in India and most go online via desktops and wired connections. In the coming years, however, Web access will become increasingly available to 900 million-plus mobile phone users. However, only about 10 percent urban Indians have smartphones and ownership of the devices is miniscule in rural areas. Facebook is working hard to develop mobile platforms for lower-end phones that

popular in Japan, including the popularity of the movie *The Social Network* and the huge number of social media interactions that occurred following the Tōhoku earthquake and the Fukushima nuclear disaster.[111]

Twitter has also become a global brand and is experiencing rapid growth around the world. As of 2013 the microblogging site had nearly 300 million active users, which represents a growth rate of over 700 percent since 2009. An estimated 36 percent of the global Internet population has a Twitter account and 21 percent use Twitter actively on a monthly basis.[112] The way people around the world are using Twitter is also changing. Research shows that usage is becoming much more commercial, with consumers posting comments about brands, using branded apps, and asking friends about products. It is likely that global marketers will continue to find sell for under $50. The company has also added support for Hindi and seven other Indian languages over the past year and is working with software developers to get them to come up with more India-specific content that has high viral potential. One important aspect of this mobile marketing development in the country is coming up with new ways to allow advertisers to reach mobile users on low-tech phones. For example, some marketers in India have found that voice ads reach users better on low-end mobile devices.

Facebook is staying somewhat quiet about its India strategy, probably because it wants the freedom to experiment and make mistakes. The company hopes that lessons it learns in India will carry over to other emerging markets such as Indonesia, parts of Africa, and the aforementioned Brazil, where it already has a strong presence. And then there's China, which remains completely untapped by Facebook due to government censorship. Like India, China represents another tremendous growth opportunity based on its population of 1.3 billion people and the fact that the Chinese are avid users of social media. However, more than 2,600 Internet sites are banned in China, including certain Google products, YouTube, Twitter, and WordPress. Even if China were to welcome Mark Zuckerberg and his social platform with open arms, there's no guarantee that Facebook wouldn't suffer the same fate as other Western Internet giants such as Google, eBay, and Twitter, all of whom have had lackluster experiences in the world's largest Internet market. Chinese culture; the size, scope, and pace of China's Internet market; government protection and influence; and late entrance to a market already full of social media copycats are just a few of the challenges Facebook faces in China.

One of the most popular social media sites in China is a micro-blog called Sina Weibo that was launched by Chinese portal giant Sina.com in 2009. Sina Weibo, which is closer to Twitter than Facebook in terms of the user experience, has more than 300 million users. Another popular social media network is Renren, which has 154 million users. While Facebook has been able to find its way into nearly every country in the world, penetrating the "great firewall of China" is likely to remain a challenge. Facebook founder Mark Zuckerberg has said that the company will use a strategy of surround and conquer, so to speak, noting that the company will focus on other places in the world where it can connect people more easily without having to deal with the difficult issues it would face in China, such as government restrictions and censorship. However, Facebook as well as other social media sites like Twitter may be encouraged by the fact that there are already over 63 million Facebook users in China while Twitter has 35 million users, even though both are officially banned there. Chinese users of the platforms are using virtual private networks, (VPNs), virtual cloud networks (VCNs), or connections that are routed internationally to access the sites. Of course this still leaves well over a billion people to go in the world's largest country.

Sources: Loretta Chao, "Brazil: The Social Media Capital of the Universe," *The Wall Street Journal*, February 5, 2013, pp. B1,B5; Amol Sharma, "India, a New Facebook Testing Ground," *The Wall Street Journal*, October 20, 2012, pp. B1,B5; Bruce Einhorn, "China Great Firewall Can't Stop Facebook," *San Francisco Chronicle*, September 30, 2012, www.sfgate.com/technology/article/China-Great-Firewall-can-t-stop-Facebook-3907518.php; Normandy Madden, "What Will Facebook Find If It Ventures into China?," *Advertising Age*, June 13, 2011, pp. 12, 14.

ways to leverage Twitter as an IMC tool through the use of Promoted Tweets as well as hashtag campaigns

As the digital revolution continues, marketers will be making greater use of digital and social media in their global as well as regional and local IMC programs. The use of social networking sites will become more prevalent, and marketers are also expected to increase their use of mobile marketing techniques as more consumers are now using their mobile devices to access and surf the Internet. Spending on mobile advertising is increasing in the United States, as well as in many other countries where mobile devices are popular, including many Asian countries. As consumers become more reliant on the Internet and various forms of digital media for information, entertainment, and socializing, marketers must develop ways to reach them through these contact points.

## Summary

Many U.S. companies are recognizing not only the opportunities but also the necessity of marketing their products and services internationally because of saturated markets and intense competition from both domestic and foreign competitors. Advertising and promotion are important parts of the international marketing program of a multinational corporation. Advertising is generally the most cost-effective way to communicate with buyers and create a market in other countries.

International marketers must carefully analyze the major environmental forces in each market where they compete, including economic, demographic, cultural, and political/legal factors. These factors are important not only in assessing the potential of each country as a market but also in designing and implementing advertising and promotional programs.

In recent years, much attention has focused on global marketing, where a standard marketing program is used in all markets. Part of global marketing is global advertising, where the same basic advertising approach is used in all markets. Opponents of the global (standardized) approach argue that differences in culture, market and economic conditions, and consumer needs and wants make a universal approach to marketing and advertising impractical. Many companies use an in-between approach,

standardizing their basic marketing strategy but localizing advertising messages to fit each market.

There are a number of important decision areas in the development of advertising and promotional programs for international markets. These include organization, agency selection, creative strategy and execution, and media strategy and selection.

Sales promotion, personal selling, public relations, and the Internet are also part of the promotional mix of international marketers. Sales promotion programs usually must be adapted to local markets. Factors to consider include stage of market development, market maturity, consumer perceptions of promotional tools, trade structure, and legal restrictions and regulations. PR programs are also important to help international marketers develop and maintain favorable relationships with governments, media, and consumers in foreign countries. The use of digital and social media such as the Internet, social networking sites, and mobile marketing is becoming an important part of international marketers' IMC programs. Internet penetration is increasing rapidly in most countries, and as more consumers go online, marketers are developing websites for various countries and also using other forms of digital and social media to reach them.

## Key Terms

balance-of-trade deficit p. 647
economic infrastructure p. 649
cultural values p. 652
global marketing p. 658

global advertising p. 658
country-of-origin effect p. 662
pattern advertising p. 664
localized advertising strategy p. 670

direct broadcast by satellite (DBS)
p. 674

## Discussion Questions

1. Discuss how global marketers might use the 2022 FIFA World Cup soccer tournament that will be held in Qatar as an integrated marketing communications opportunity. What types of companies are best suited to use the World Cup as an IMC opportunity? (LO1, 2)

2. What are some of the challenges the Q2022 Supreme Committee will face in promoting the World Cup in Qatar? Discuss the various IMC tools that can be used to promote the World Cup in countries around the world. (LO1, 2)

3. Why are international markets so important to companies located in the United States as well as other nations? Discuss the various factors that companies must consider in developing IMC programs for various countries. (LO1)

4. Global Perspective 19–1 discusses how many multinational companies are focusing more attention on the 4 billion consumers who live in the remote, rural communities of developing countries. Discuss the challenges companies face in marketing their products to the world's

poorest consumers. How do they have to adapt their IMC programs for these countries? (LO2)

5. Why are so many multinational companies expanding into China? What challenges do marketers and their advertising agencies face in developing IMC programs for the Chinese market? (LO2)

6. What are some of the cultural variables that marketers must consider in developing advertising and promotional programs in a foreign market? Choose one of these cultural variables and discuss how it has created a problem or challenge for a company in developing an advertising and promotional program in a specific country. (LO2)

7. What is meant by a country-of-origin effect? Discuss the implications of the survey conducted among college students in the United States which found that they have limited knowledge of the country-of-origin of most brands. Does this mean country-of-origin is not important to students? (LO3)

8. What is meant by a global market segment? Provide an example of a company that has identified a global market segment and advertises its product or service the same way around the world to this market. (LO3)

9. Discuss the evolving role of the Internet and other digital and social media in the IMC program of international marketers. How can marketers make effective use of digital and social media in marketing their products and services in various countries? (LO5)

10. Why do you think social media sites such as Facebook and Twitter are becoming so popular in countries around the world? Discuss the importance of social media sites in the IMC programs of international marketers. (LO5)

## LEARNING OBJECTIVES

**LO1** To examine how advertising is regulated, including the role and function of various regulatory agencies.

**LO2** To examine self-regulation of advertising and evaluate its effectiveness.

**LO3** To consider how advertising is regulated by federal and state government agencies, including the Federal Trade Commission.

**LO4** To examine rules and regulations that affect sales promotion, direct marketing, and marketing on the Internet.

# 20 Regulation of Advertising and Promotion

## MARKETERS OF TONING SHOES ACCUSED OF DECEPTIVE ADVERTISING

For years Nike dominated the $1.7 billion women's athletic footwear market; by 2009 its market share in the category reached 37 percent. However, within a year Nike's share dropped to just under 30 percent as its sales declined by 7 percent even though the women's athletic-shoe market was experiencing double-digit sales growth. It was no mystery where all of the women abandoning Nike were going to purchase their athletic shoes—most were switching to Skechers and Reebok. Skechers tripled its market share during the same period, from 5.5 to 16.5 percent, and Reebok nearly did the same, jumping from 3.3 to 8 percent.

The reason women were moving to Skechers and Reebok was because both companies were investing heavily in product development and advertising for a new type of athletic footwear called toning shoes that promised women they could get in shape and firm up their leg muscles and butts simply by walking in them. However, Nike refused to enter the toning-shoe market as it was skeptical about the claims being made for the products and said the shoes did not fit with the company's performance-focused brand image. And as it turns out, Nike made a wise decision; the Federal Trade Commission charged both Skechers and Reebok with deceptive advertising based on the claims they were making for their shoes.

The toning-shoe market was in its infancy in 2009; there were a few brands that had achieved a cultlike following such as MBT, Ryn, and FitFlop before Reebok and Skechers entered the market. The idea behind the oddly shaped shoes was that they could simulate walking on a soft surface, causing the wearer to use muscles not normally used when walking on hard surfaces. They created instability, which would force the wearer to engage certain muscles to maintain balance. The benefits resulting from the shoes were purported to include weight loss, greater muscle tone, reduced cellulite, and firmer butts. Skechers put a spotlight on the

toning-shoe category by running an ad on the 2010 Super Bowl that featured testimonials by NFL Hall of Fame quarterback Joe Montana as well as consumers. The company ran another Super Bowl spot in 2011 featuring celebrity Kim Kardashian and was also running ads with Brooke Burke, who was endorsing its Shape Up shoes. Skechers's ads included claims such as "Shape up while you walk" and "Get in shape without setting foot in a gym." The ads also told women that wearing the shoes would help tone their butt, leg, and abdominal muscles, burn calories, fight cellulite, improve posture and circulation, and reduce joint stress. By early 2011 the toning-shoe category reached $1.1 billion in sales with Skechers controlling nearly 60 percent of the market.

Reebok also invested heavily in what became known as the "derriere-enhancing" shoes as the sales for the category skyrocketed. Reebok was a leading brand in the women's athletic-shoe category during the 1980s, when it dominated the aerobics-shoe market. Reebok saw the toning-shoe category as a way to once again focus on the female market and reconnect with women who still had favorable feelings about the company. The company put its energy behind its EasyTone line that was marketed with claims such as "Get a better butt" and "EasyTone shoes help tone your butt and legs with every step." Reebok's ads and website claimed that its shoes generated more muscle activity in the gluteus maximus as well as users' hamstrings and calves. Reebok spent over $30 million in advertising for EasyTone in the United States alone in 2010 and also launched a global campaign that included the introduction of the EasyTone apparel line. By the end of 2010 Reebok had a 33 percent share of the toning-shoe market and claimed to have sold 5 million pairs of the shoes in the United States and double that globally. The CEO of Reebok's parent company adidas said: "The explosion of growth in this space in such a short period of time eclipses nearly everything I have witnessed in the industry over the last 25 years."

Skechers and Reebok continued to invest heavily in advertising while other athletic-shoe companies such as Avia and New Balance also introduced their brands of toning shoes. However, although the market continued to grow, many in the medical profession were skeptical about the efficacy claims being made for toning shoes, arguing that they were "far-fetched" and "utter nonsense" and could not be supported. Some doctors also expressed concern that the shoes could be dangerous and lead to injuries resulting from their instability. Based on these concerns, the Federal Trade Commission (FTC), along with attorneys general from nearly all 50 states, launched an investigation of the toning-shoe category and the advertising claims being made by Reebok and Skechers.

Following an investigation, the FTC alleged that the testing conducted by Reebok did not substantiate certain claims used in the advertising of its EasyTone line of toning shoes. In the fall of 2011 the FTC announced that Reebok had agreed to a $25 million settlement to resolve charges that it deceptively advertised its toning shoe and apparel. Reebok issued a statement saying that it was standing behind its shoes and agreed to the settlement only to avoid a protracted legal battle. As part of the settlement, Reebok is barred from making claims that toning shoes or apparel strengthens muscles or that using the products will result in a specific percentage or amount of muscle toning or strengthening, unless the claims can be supported by scientific evidence.

A few months later, in May 2012, the FTC announced that Skechers had agreed to pay $40 million to settle charges that it deceived consumers with weight-loss and toning claims related to its Shape Up shoes and other toning products. The FTC charged that specific muscle activation results related to the use of the shoes that were used as the basis of advertising claims made by Skechers were "cherry-picked" from a study and the company failed to substantiate its advertising claims. The FTC also noted that Skechers's ads included an endorsement from a chiropractor who was married

to a marketing executive in the company and that the independent clinical study conducted by the chiropractor did not produce the results claimed. The $40 million settlement was one of the largest ever agreed to with the FTC and barred Skechers from making any claims about strengthening, weight loss, or any other health or fitness-related benefits from its toning shoes, unless they are true and backed by scientific evidence.

Both Reebok and Skechers were required to put most of the $65 million into a fund intended to return money to consumers who bought their toning products. The funds are to be made available to consumers either directly from the FTC or through a court-approved class-action lawsuit. In May 2013 a federal judge approved a $40 million class-action settlement between Skechers and consumers who bought the company's toning shoes whereby approved claims would result in repayment of up to $84 a pair, depending on the price of the shoes.

Sales of toning shoes in the U.S. market have declined by 50 percent following the negative publicity resulting from the deceptive advertising claims and settlements. However, Reebok has not given up on the toning-shoe category; the company claims there is still a market for the shoes and announced that it was enhancing its testing protocol and tweaking its advertising claims. While the company rolled out a new campaign in Europe and Asia in 2012 using the tagline "A beautiful way to reduce body fat," it has not run the ads in the United States. Yet.

Sources: Natalie Zmuda, "Reebok Bounces Back in Toning Category after FTC Settlement," *Advertising Age*, April 22, 2012, http://adage.com/article/news/reebok-toning-body-fat-reduction-claim/234272/; Natalie Zmuda, "Skechers Pays $40 Million to Settle Toning Claims FTC: Settlement May Be Largest Payout Ever to Consumers," *Advertising Age*, May 16, 2012, http://adage.com/article/news/skechers-pays-40-million-settle-toning-claims/234799/; Natalie Zmuda, "Reebok Agrees to $25M Settlement over Butt-Shaping Shoes," *Advertising Age*, September 28, 2011, http://adage.com/article/news/ftc-calls-butt-shaping-shoes-bogus-reebok-stands-claims/230082/; Michael McCarthy, "A Revolutionary Sneaker, or Overhyped Gimmick?" *USA Today*, June 30, 2010, pp. A1,A2; Jeremy Mullman, "Nike Women's Biz Gets Pounded as Toning Footwear Kicks Butt," *Advertising Age*, June 2, 2010, p. 3.

LO 20-1   Suppose you are the advertising manager for a consumer-products company and have just reviewed a new commercial your agency created. You are very excited about the ad. It presents new claims about your brand's superiority that should help differentiate it from the competition. However, before you approve the commercial you need answers. Are the claims verifiable? Did researchers use proper procedures to collect and analyze the data and present the findings? Do research results support the claims? Were the right people used in the study? Could any conditions have biased the results?

YTC **20–01**

**Toning Shoes**

youtube.com/10ebelch

Before approving the commercial, you have it reviewed by your company's legal department and by your agency's attorneys. If both reviews are acceptable, you send the ad to the major networks, which have their censors examine it. They may ask for more information or send the ad back for modification. (No commercial can run without approval from a network's Standards and Practices Department.)

Even after approval and airing, your commercial is still subject to scrutiny from such state and federal regulatory agencies as the state attorney general's office and the Federal Trade Commission. Individual consumers or competitors who find the ad misleading or have other concerns may file a complaint with the National Advertising Division of the Council of Better Business Bureaus. Finally, disparaged competitors may sue if they believe your ad distorts the facts and misleads consumers. If you lose the litigation, your company may have to retract the claims and pay the competitor damages, sometimes running into millions of dollars.

After considering all these regulatory issues, you must ask yourself if the new ad can meet all these challenges and is worth the risk. Maybe you ought to continue with the old approach that made no specific claims and simply said your brand was great.

Regulatory concerns can play a major role in the advertising decision-making process. Advertisers operate in a complex environment of local, state, and federal rules and regulations. Additionally, a number of advertising and business-sponsored associations, consumer groups and organizations, and the media attempt to promote honest, truthful, and tasteful advertising through their own self-regulatory programs and guidelines. The legal and regulatory aspects of advertising are very complex. Many parties are concerned about the nature and content of advertising and its potential to offend, exploit, mislead, and/or deceive consumers.

Advertising has also become increasingly important in product liability litigation involving products that are associated with consumer injuries. In many of these cases the courts have been willing to consider the impact of advertising on behavior of consumers that leads to injury-causing situations. Thus advertisers must avoid certain practices and proactively engage in others to ensure that their ads are comprehended correctly and do not misrepresent their products or services.[1] As discussed in the chapter opener, the consequences can be quite severe when companies become involved in legal proceedings regarding their advertising claims.

Numerous guidelines, rules, regulations, and laws constrain and restrict advertising. These regulations primarily influence individual advertisers, but they can also affect advertising for an entire industry. For example, cigarette advertising was banned from the broadcast media in 1970, and many groups are pushing for a total ban on the advertising of tobacco products.[2] Legislation now being considered would further restrict the advertising of alcoholic beverages, including beer and wine.[3] Advertising is controlled by internal self-regulation and by external state and federal regulatory agencies such as the Federal Trade Commission (FTC), the Federal Communications Commission (FCC), the Food and Drug Administration (FDA), and the U.S. Postal Service. And state attorneys general have become more active in advertising regulation. While only government agencies (federal, state, and local) have the force of law, most advertisers also abide by the guidelines and decisions of internal regulatory bodies. In fact, internal regulation from such groups as the media and the National Advertising Review Board probably has more influence on advertisers' day-to-day operations and decision making than government rules and regulations.

Decision makers on both the client and agency side must be knowledgeable about these regulatory groups, including the intent of their efforts, how they operate, and how they influence and affect advertising and other promotional-mix elements. In this chapter, we examine the major sources of advertising regulation, including efforts by the industry at voluntary self-regulation and external regulation by government agencies. We also examine regulations involving sales promotion, direct marketing, and marketing on the Internet.

# SELF-REGULATION

For many years, the advertising industry has practiced and promoted voluntary **self-regulation**. Most advertisers, their agencies, and the media recognize the importance of maintaining consumer trust and confidence. Advertisers also see self-regulation as a way to limit government interference, which, they believe, results in more stringent and troublesome regulations. Self-regulation and control of advertising emanate from all segments of the advertising industry, including individual advertisers and their agencies, business and advertising associations, and the media.

## Self-Regulation by Advertisers and Agencies

Self-regulation begins with the interaction of client and agency when creative ideas are generated and submitted for consideration. Most companies have specific guidelines, standards, and policies to which their ads must adhere. Recognizing that their ads reflect on the company, advertisers carefully scrutinize all messages to ensure they are consistent with the image the firm wishes to project. Companies also review their ads to be sure any claims made are reasonable and verifiable and do not mislead or deceive consumers. Ads are usually examined by corporate attorneys to avoid potential legal problems and their accompanying time, expense, negative publicity, and embarrassment.

Internal control and regulation also come from advertising agencies. Most have standards regarding the type of advertising they either want or are willing to produce, and they try to avoid ads that might be offensive or misleading. Most agencies will ask their clients to provide verification or support for claims the clients might want to make in their advertising and will make sure that adequate documentation or substantiation is available. However, agencies will also take formal steps to protect themselves from legal and ethical perils through agency–client contracts. For example, many liability issues are handled in these contracts. Agencies generally use information provided by clients for advertising claims, and in standard contracts the agency is protected from suits involving the accuracy of those claims. Contracts will also absolve the agency of responsibility if something goes wrong with the advertised product and consumers suffer damages or injury or other product liability claims arise.[4] However, agencies have been held legally responsible for fraudulent or deceptive claims and in some cases have been fined when their clients were found guilty of engaging in deceptive advertising.[5] Many agencies have a creative review board or panel composed of experienced personnel who examine ads for content and execution as well as for their potential to be perceived as offensive, misleading, and/or deceptive. Most agencies also employ or retain lawyers who review the ads for potential legal problems. Exhibit 20–1 shows the homepage for the Olshan law firm in New York City, which specializes in advertising and integrated marketing communications law.

**EXHIBIT 20–1**

The Olshan firm specializes in advertising and integrated marketing communications law

## Self-Regulation by Trade Associations

Like advertisers and their agencies, many industries have also developed self-regulatory programs. This is particularly true in industries whose advertising is prone to controversy, such as liquor and alcoholic beverages, drugs, and various products marketed to children. Many trade and industry associations develop their own advertising guidelines or codes that member companies are expected to abide by.

The Wine Institute, the U.S. Brewers Association, and the Distilled Spirits Council of the United States all have guidelines that member companies are supposed to follow in advertising alcoholic beverages.[6] No specific law prohibits the advertising of hard liquor on radio or television. However, such advertising was effectively banned for over five decades as a result of a code provision by the National Association of Broadcasters and by agreement of liquor manufacturers and their self-governing body, the Distilled Spirits Council of the United States (DISCUS). However, in November 1996, DISCUS amended its code of good practice and overturned its self-imposed ban on broadcast advertising.[7] IMC Perspective 20–1 discusses the reasons why the council decided to overturn the ban, as well as the increase in TV advertising for distilled spirits that has resulted from its decision. Other industry trade associations with advertising codes and guidelines include the Toy Industry Association, the Motion Picture Association of America, and the Pharmaceutical Research and Manufacturers of America.

Many professions also maintain advertising guidelines through local, state, and national organizations. For years professional associations like the American Medical Association (AMA) and the American Bar Association (ABA) restricted advertising by their members on the basis that such promotional activities lowered members' professional status and led to unethical and fraudulent claims. However, such restrictive codes have been attacked by both government regulatory agencies and consumer groups. They argue that the public has a right to be informed about a professional's services, qualifications, and background and that advertising will improve professional services as consumers become better informed and are better able to shop around.[8]

In 1977, the Supreme Court held that state bar associations' restrictions on advertising are unconstitutional and that attorneys have First Amendment freedom of speech rights to advertise.[9] Many professional associations subsequently removed their restrictions, and advertising by lawyers and other professionals is now common (Exhibit 20–2).[10] In 1982, the Supreme Court upheld an FTC order permitting advertising by dentists and physicians.[11]

Research shows that consumers generally favor increased use of professional advertising. However, professionals continue to have reservations. They worry that advertising has a negative impact on their image, credibility, and dignity and see benefits to consumers as unlikely.[12] Still, advertising by professionals is increasing, particularly among newcomers to medicine, dentistry, and law. Associations such as the AMA and the ABA developed guidelines for members' advertising to help maintain standards and guard against misleading, deceptive, or offensive ads.

**EXHIBIT 20–2**

Advertising is often used by attorneys to promote their services

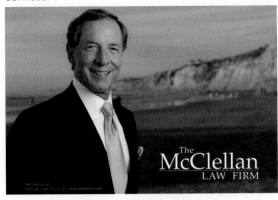

The McClellan Law Firm handles the most complex cases in the most creative way

Catastrophic Personal Injury | Products Liability | Business Litigation | Intellectual Property

By limiting the number of cases and taking a team-based approach,
The McClellan Law Firm devotes all of our time, energy and resources to your case.
• Over 95 verdicts and settlements in excess of $1million—more than any other San Diego Lawyer
• Only San Diego lawyer inducted into the Inner Circle of Advocates
• 2012 San Diego Product Liability Litigation Lawyer of the Year by Best Lawyers
• 2012 Daniel T. Broderick III Award winner
• Fellow, American College of Trial Lawyers
• Top 50 San Diego Super Lawyers list 2007-2013
• Designated Tier 1 Personal Injury law firm by U.S. News & World Report

(619) 231-0505
www.mcclellanlaw.com

1144 State Street | San Diego CA 92101 | Tel: 619.231.0505 | Fax: 619.544.0540
Highest referral fees paid in accordance with Rules of Professional Conduct

The issue of professional advertising, particularly by attorneys, is still debated. Some traditional law firms resist using advertising, particularly on TV, due to concern that it might hurt the profession's image. Many in the legal profession worry that ads soliciting personal injury victims only worsen the public's perception of attorneys. A sizable faction within the American Bar Association (ABA) blames the legal profession's image problem on sleazy ads. The ABA's Commission on Advertising held a series of public hearings on what, if any, restrictive measures to recommend to state ethics panels. Some states restrict the content of attorney ads and the way they can be delivered and require a disclaimer urging consumers not to base their attorney selection on an advertisement. Many attorneys are incensed over efforts to restrict their rights to promote themselves because they use advertising to help build their practices. Several cases are currently being litigated, but ultimately the Supreme Court may have to decide just how far states can go in curtailing advertising.

Although industry associations are concerned with the impact and consequences of members' advertising, they have no legal way to enforce their guidelines. They can only rely on peer pressure from members or other nonbinding sanctions to get advertisers to comply.

# IMC Perspective 20–1 > > >

## Liquor Advertising Makes It to Network Television

If you are watching a late-night television show on one of the four major networks, like *Saturday Night Live* on NBC, *Late Night with Jimmy Fallon* on ABC, or the *Late Show with David Letterman* on CBS, it is very likely you will see a commercial for a hard liquor brand such as Jägermeister, Grey Goose, or Wild Turkey. The airing of a commercial for a hard liquor brand may not seem like a very big deal to you; it may be seen as just other commercial trying to sell you something. However, the airing of hard liquor ads on a network TV show represents a major victory for the distilled spirits industry, which has argued there should be a level playing field for alcohol advertising and that liquor should be viewed the same way as beer and wine. It is also a very big deal to many public health groups that argue that liquor is more dangerous than beer or wine because of its higher alcohol content. They were successful in keeping advertising for spirits off the major networks until recently.

For more than five decades, distilled spirits were not advertised on television or radio because of a self-imposed ban by members of the Distilled Spirits Council of the United States (DISCUS). Council members agreed in 1936 to avoid radio advertising and extended the ban to TV in 1948. But Seagram, the second largest distiller in the world at the time, ended the U.S. spirits industry's long-standing ban on broadcast advertising in June 1996 by airing commercials for its Crown Royal Canadian Whiskey brand on an affiliate in Corpus Christi, Texas.

Seagram issued a statement that it was ending the liquor industry's decades-old practice of not advertising on TV because DISCUS's voluntary code of good practice placed spirits at a competitive disadvantage to beer and wine, which did not have any such restrictions. Seagram also argued that the ban had become outdated because radio and TV have become more targeted and that it could pinpoint its advertising message to people of legal drinking age. A number of distillers, eager to turn around the long, slow decline in hard liquor sales, watched Seagram test the water with its TV ads before rolling out their own commercials. Some held discussions with TV stations but waited for a formal amendment to the DISCUS code of good practice before proceeding. The

amendment came in November 1996, when DISCUS members voted unanimously to overturn the self-imposed ban on broadcast ads. The DISCUS president noted that spirits makers wanted to break down the public perception that spirits are stronger or more dangerous than beer and wine and thus deserving of harsher social and political treatment.

After the DISCUS ban was lifted, the four major broadcast TV networks as well as major cable networks such as ESPN and MTV continued to refuse liquor ads, prompting consumer and public interest groups to applaud their actions. In fact, it has been argued that it was really the refusal by TV stations and networks to accept liquor advertising that had kept them off the air rather than the DISCUS code. However, the major networks cannot control the practices of affiliate stations they do not own and many of them began accepting liquor ads, as did local cable channels and independent broadcast stations. By the fall of 2001, DISCUS estimated that about 400 local stations and cable channels were permitting or considering spirit ads, although most had restrictions that the ads had to air after 9 P.M.

In December 2001 NBC, which was owned by the General Electric Co. at the time, announced it would become the first broadcast network to accept hard liquor advertising. NBC planned to limit the liquor ads to programs where at least 85 percent of viewers are 21 or older, such as during late-night time slots. However, NBC was not joined by the three other major broadcast networks—ABC, CBS, and Fox—in its decision to accept liquor commercials. NBC's decision engendered a considerable amount of controversy and criticism from members of Congress, federal regulators, the American Medical Association, and many public advocacy groups. Critics expressed concern that airing liquor ads on TV would glamorize drinking and encourage children and teenagers to drink. Facing a widening backlash over its decision, in March 2002 NBC announced that it was dropping its plans to accept liquor advertising.

While the national broadcast networks continued their self-imposed ban for the remainder of the decade, the amount of liquor advertising on television continued to increase as more cable and local broadcast stations began accepting

## Self-Regulation by Businesses

LO 20-2

A number of self-regulatory mechanisms have been established by the business community in an effort to control advertising practices.[13] The largest and best known is the **Better Business Bureau (BBB)**, which promotes fair advertising and selling practices across all industries. The BBB was established in 1916 to handle consumer complaints about local business practices and particularly advertising. Local BBBs are located in most large cities throughout the United States and supported entirely by dues of the more than 100,000 member firms.

Local BBBs receive and investigate complaints from consumers and other companies regarding the advertising and selling tactics of businesses in their area. Each the commercials. By 2010 television grabbed $142 million in advertising from liquor brands, which was about 34 percent of all media advertising for the category. And in 2009 Absolut, the Swedish vodka that used aggressive advertising and marketing over the past three decades to become one of the world's leading spirit brands, took the bold step of breaking the voluntary ban of spirits advertising on network television by airing a prime-time commercial during the third hour of the Grammy Awards. The commercial ran on CBS-owned-and-operated stations in 15 of the top markets reaching 31 percent of U.S. TV households and marked the first time a commercial for a distilled spirits product aired on any CBS-owned station. According to a CBS representative, local station managers are responsible for determining the suitability of the commercials they air and determined that the soft-sell Absolut spot was tasteful and appropriate for their late-evening audiences.

Following the initial network airing on the Grammy's, Absolut ran the ad on network TV in a number of local markets and it was not long before the other networks began airing liquor ads on their late-night shows. In November 2011 CBS began airing ads for Bacardi Ltd.'s Grey Goose vodka nationally on *Late Night with David Letterman,* and in 2012 Brown-Forman began airing ads for Southern Comfort whiskey on all of the network late-night talk shows as well as *Saturday Night Live.* Industry consultant Arthur Shapiro noted, "The world has changed since 2001. People are more accepting of spirits advertising. The industry draws the distinction between network, cable or spot. The consumer doesn't care." The decision by the networks to run liquor ads was also not surprising; the recession took its toll on advertising spending and local advertising has been particularly hard hit, making it difficult to turn away a new source of advertising revenue. The major networks also have to compete against cable networks and have been shifting their ad budgets to the Internet as well as online video options such as YouTube.

The broadcast networks are not opening their doors all the way to advertising for hard liquor as most of the ads

do not air before 11 P.M., unlike on cable, where many networks allow them anytime. However, as might be expected, public advocacy groups remain opposed to the network's softening of its stance, arguing that youth exposure to liquor ads on TV has already increased 30-fold since 2001, driven by the ads appearing on cable. George Hacker, the director of the alcohol policies project at the Center for Science in the Public Interest (CSPI), predicted that brands that advertise on network TV would certainly be held up to scorn and noted that the group was less than delighted by the expansion of spirits advertising into network television. The former executive director of the Center on Alcohol Marketing and Youth at Georgetown University called the move a step backward and refuted the argument that it is acceptable to run the ads on late-night programs, noting that many young people have TVs in their rooms and this is a heavy viewing time for the groups most at risk.

David Jernigan, the director of Johns Hopkins University's Center on Alcohol Marketing and Youth, is also critical of the network's changes in policy, stating, "It's basically death by a thousand cuts in terms of voluntary bans." However, the acceptance of ads from the networks is a victory for the distilled spirits industry, which has sought parity with beer and wine since it lifted its ban. The senior vice president of DISCUS stated, "Just as the federal government doesn't distinguish between beer and wine and spirits, most of these broadcasters are recognizing that alcohol is alcohol." The FTC also has said there is no basis for treating liquor ads differently than advertising for other types of alcohol. Thus, it appears that TV advertising for distilled spirits is here to stay and it's likely that you will see a lot more liquor ads on network TV shows as well as on cable.

Sources: E. J. Schultz, "Hard Time: Liquor Advertising Pours into TV," *Advertising Age,* May 14, 2012, pp. 1, 41; Mike Esterl, "Liquor Ads Win Airtime," *The Wall Street Journal,* August 2, 2012, p. B6; Stuart Elliott, "Facing Outcry, NBC Ends Plan to Run Liquor Ads," *The New York Times,* March 21, 2002, p. C1.

YTC 20-02
**Liquor Advertising**
youtube.com/10ebelch

local office has its own operating procedures for handling complaints; generally, the office contacts the violator and, if the complaint proves true, requests that the practice be stopped or changed. If the violator does not respond, negative publicity may be used against the firm or the case may be referred to appropriate government agencies for further action.

While BBBs provide effective control over advertising practices at the local level, the parent organization, the **Council of Better Business Bureaus**, plays a major role at the national level, as the third-party administrator of the advertising industry self-regulatory system. Policies and procedures for industry self-regulation are established by the Advertising Self-Regulatory Council (ASRC). The system includes three investigative units—the National Advertising Division of the Council

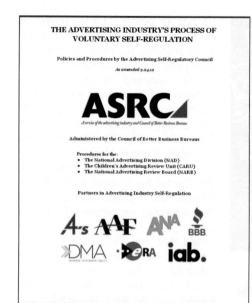

**EXHIBIT 20–3**

The ASRC partners with various advertising and marketing organizations to create an effective self-regulatory system

of Better Business Bureaus (NAD), the Children's Advertising Review Unit (CARU), and the Electronic Retailing Self-Regulation Program (ERSP)—and an appellate unit, the **National Advertising Review Board (NARB)**. Staffed primarily by attorneys, NAD, CARU, and ERSP review advertising claims that are national in scope. CARU reviews advertising directed to children under the age of 12, and ERSP examines advertising claims in direct-response advertising, including infomercials and home shopping channels.

## The Advertising Self-Regulatory Council and the NAD/NARB

In 1971 four associations—the American Advertising Federation (AAF), the American Association of Advertising Agencies (AAAA), the Association of National Advertisers (ANA), and the Council of Better Business Bureaus—joined forces to establish the National Advertising Review Council (NARC). In 2009, the CEOs of three other major marketing organizations—the Direct Marketing Association (DMA), Electronic Retailing Association (ERA), and the Interactive Advertising Bureau—joined the NARC Board of Directors and in 2012 the organization changed its name to the **Advertising Self-Regulatory Council (ASRC)**.

The ASRC's mission is to sustain high standards of truth and accuracy in national advertising. NAD has examined advertising for truth and accuracy since 1971 and has published more than 5,000 decisions, focusing on areas that include product performance claims, superiority claims against competitive products, and all kinds of scientific and technical claims. The ASRC has a process that it follows for self-regulation and follows a specific set of policies and procedures that can be found on its website (Exhibit 20–3).

Federal law requires that advertisers possess substantiation for their advertising claims before the claims are published. After initiating or receiving a complaint, NAD requests the advertiser's substantiation, reviews the information, and reaches a determination. In cases where the substantiating evidence does not support the claim, NAD recommends that the advertiser modify or discontinue the claim. When an advertiser or a challenger disagrees with the NAD's findings, NAD's decision can be appealed to the NARB for additional review.

The NAD's advertising monitoring program is the source of many of the cases it reviews (Figure 20–1). It also reviews complaints from consumers and consumer groups, trade associations, local BBBs, and competitors. For example, the NAD received a complaint from the Center for Science in the Public Interest, a consumer advocacy group, over an ad run by Campbell Soup for the company's V8 vegetable juice that suggested a link between the tomato-based product and a reduced risk of cancer. Though

**FIGURE 20–1**

Sources of NAD Cases and Decisions, 2012

| Sources | Number | Percentage | Decisions | Number | Percentage |
|---|---|---|---|---|---|
| Competitor challenges | 79 | 71% | Modified/discontinued | 41 | 37% |
| NAD monitoring | 20 | 18 | Substantiated/modified/discontinued | 35 | 31 |
| Local BBB challenges | 11 | 10 | Administratively closed | 10 | 9 |
| Consumer challenges | 1 | 1 | Compliance | 14 | 13 |
| Total | 111 | 100% | Substantiated | 7 | 6 |
| | | | Referred to government | 4 | 4 |
| | | | Total (28 cases pending) | 111 | 100% |

the NAD decided that Campbell provided competent and reliable evidence to support certain claims, it recommended that the company modify language stating "for prostate cancer, a lower risk is apparent when five or more servings (of tomato products) are consumed per week." Campbell agreed to change the wording of the ad.[14]

Lawyers at the NAD routinely scour magazines, newspapers, radio, television, and social media to find misleading advertisements. The NAD staff recently challenged an ad for CoverGirl mascara featuring singer Taylor Swift, arguing that it was misleading because her eyelashes had been enhanced after the fact to look fuller. The fine print under the photo of Swift read that her lashes had been "enhanced in post-production." However, the NAD considered the express claims made in the ad which indicated that the mascara would give eyelashes "2x more volume" and that the product was "20 percent lighter" than the most expensive mascara. The NAD attorneys argued that the photograph stood as a product demonstration and at issue was what one's lashes would look like when using the product. Procter & Gamble, the parent company of the CoverGirl brand, fully cooperated with the NAD and voluntarily discontinued making the challenged claims as well as the photograph.[15]

During the 1970s and 80s, many of the complaints to the NAD came from consumers. However, with the increased use of comparative advertising, the majority of the complaints are now coming from marketers that are challenging competitors' comparisons with their brands.[16] For example, the online dating service eHarmony filed a complaint with the NAD over advertising used by competitor Chemistry.com, which claimed that it could use "the latest science of attraction to predict which single men and women one will have a relationship and dating chemistry."[17] Chemistry.com's matchmaking system was developed by an anthropologist who studies mate selection and uses responses to an extensive survey to determine people who might be attracted to one another.

In the Chemistry.com case, the NAD concluded that the dating service could not substantiate many of the advertising claims and ruled that the company should discontinue them. Chemistry's parent company, Match.com, issued a statement saying that it disagreed with some of the NAD's findings but would discontinue the claims at issue.[18]

Advertisers that disagree with NAD's findings have an automatic right to appeal NAD's decision to the National Advertising Review Board. The NARB is made up of 70 professionals from three different categories: National Advertisers (40 members), Advertising Agencies (20 members), and Public members (10), which includes academics and former members of the public sector.

In 2003, for example, Millennium Import Company, importers of Belvedere and Chopin vodka, filed a complaint with the NAD over advertising used by Sidney Frank Importing for its popular Grey Goose vodka brand that claimed it is the world's best-tasting vodka. Millennium argued that the claims were based on the results of a 1998 taste test and communicated a false message to consumers that Grey Goose currently ranked substantially higher than Belvedere in taste testing. After reviewing the case, the NAD ruled in favor of Millennium and Sidney Frank appealed the decision to the NARB, which concurred with the NAD's decision and found the advertising claim for Grey Goose inaccurate and misleading for consumers. Sidney Frank refused to comply with the NAD's and NARB's directive to discontinue or modify their ads, and the self-regulatory agency referred the matter to the Federal Trade Commission. Millennium also filed a lawsuit against Sidney Frank in 2004 accusing the company of false advertising and was successful in gaining an injunction preventing Grey Goose from using the claim.[19]

Although the self-regulatory system has no power to order an advertiser to modify or stop running an ad and no sanctions it can impose, advertisers who participate in NAD/CARU/ERSP or NARB proceedings generally comply. When companies refuse to participate in a self-regulatory proceeding or do not comply with the terms of a decision, their disputed advertising may be referred to the most appropriate federal agency for further review. For example, the NAD criticized Reebok in early 2011 for exaggerating the health and performance benefits of its EasyTone shoe line and warned the company to discontinue the claims. However, Reebok contended that its EasyTone shoes are the only fitness shoes with a built-in balance bar design on the soles to create instability, so that users' muscles would have to work harder and continued to run ads for the product.[20] As discussed in the chapter opener, the FTC became involved in the case, which resulted in Reebok paying a $25 million settlement to resolve the charges.

In 2012, of the 111 cases handled by the NAD, 41 were modified or discontinued; 35 were substantiated, modified, or discontinued; 14 complied with the NAD; 10 were administratively closed; 7 were substantiated and 4 were referred to the government (Figure 20–1).[21]

CARU's activities include the review and evaluation of child-directed advertising in all media, as well as online privacy issues that affect children. The CARU also provides a general advisory service for advertisers and agencies and has developed self-regulatory guidelines for children's advertising. CARU recognizes that the special nature and needs of a youthful audience require particular care and diligence on the part of advertisers. As such, CARU's Self-Regulatory Guidelines for Children's Advertising go beyond truthfulness and accuracy to address children's developing cognitive abilities.

In 2004, the NARC became involved in the self-regulation of electronic retailing when it initiated the Electronic Retailing Self-Regulation Program (ERSP). The program is sponsored by the Electronic Retailing Association (ERA), although it works independently of the ERA to create an unbiased self-regulatory system. The mission of the ERSP is to enhance consumer confidence in electronic retailing, to discourage advertising and marketing in the electronic retailing industry that contains unsubstantiated claims, and to demonstrate a commitment to meaningful and effective self-regulation. The majority of claims reviewed under the ERSP program are for direct-response TV ads, including long- and short-form infomercials. Reviews apply to all aspects of a marketing campaign, including radio and Internet marketing. Spam e-mails along with Internet pop-up ads that lead to further e-commerce are in the ERSP's purview as well as advertising on TV shopping channels.[22]

In 2012 the ASRC implemented a new self-regulatory program, the Internet-Based Advertising Accountability Program, which regulates online behavioral advertising (OBA) across the Internet.[23] OBA uses information collected across multiple unaffiliated websites to predict a user's preferences and display ads most likely to interest consumers. The new program was developed at the urging of leading industry associations and is based on the seven Self-Regulatory Principles for Online Behavioral Advertising. The principles correspond with tenets proposed by the Federal Trade Commission in 2009, and also address public education and industry accountability issues raised by the FTC. The principles, which are shown in Figure 20–2, are designed to address consumer concerns about the use of personal information for interest-based advertising and focus on transparency and consumer-control issues. The NAD monitors companies engaged in OBA while the Accountability Program is charged with providing objective, independent, and vigorous oversight and enforcement of the principles.

The NAD also works with various industries to help them develop more effective self-regulatory programs. For example, the National Advertising Review Council and the Council for Responsible Nutrition (CRN), a trade association representing dietary supplement manufacturers and ingredient suppliers, developed a dietary supplement advertising review program. The goal of the program was to increase consumer confidence in the truth and accuracy of advertising claims for dietary supplement products and to encourage fair competition within the industry. The year before the monitoring initiative began, the NAD opened less than 10 cases involving dietary supplement advertising. However, during the first three years of the program the NAD opened more than 75 cases, with almost all resulting in voluntary compliance. In 2009 the NAD received a $959,000 grant from the CRN Foundation to extend the program Self-Regulatory through 2014.[24]

**FIGURE 20–2**

Self-Regulatory Principles for Online Behavioral Advertising

**The Education Principle** calls for organizations to participate in efforts to educate individuals and businesses about online behavioral advertising and the Principles.

**The Transparency Principle** calls for clearer and easily accessible disclosures to consumers about data collection and use practices associated with online behavioral advertising. It will result in new, enhanced notice on the page where data is collected through links embedded in or around advertisements, or on the Web page itself.

**The Consumer Control Principle** provides consumers with an expanded ability to choose whether data is collected and used for online behavioral advertising purposes. This choice will be available through a link from the notice provided on the Web page where data is collected.

**The Consumer Control Principle** requires "service providers", a term that includes Internet access service providers and providers of desktop applications software such as Web browser "tool bars" to obtain the consent of users before engaging in online behavioral advertising, and take steps to de-identify the data used for such purposes.

**The Data Security Principle** calls for organizations to provide appropriate security for, and limited retention of data, collected and used for online behavioral advertising purposes.

**The Material Changes Principle** calls for obtaining consumer consent before a Material Change is made to an entity's Online Behavioral Advertising data collection and use policies unless that change will result in less collection or use of data.

**The Sensitive Data Principle** recognizes that data collected from children and used for online behavioral advertising merits heightened protection, and requires parental consent for behavioral advertising to consumers known to be under 13 on child-directed Web sites. This Principle also provides heightened protections to certain health and financial data when attributable to a specific individual.

**The Accountability Principle** calls for development of programs to further advance these Principles, including programs to monitor and report instances of uncorrected non-compliance with these Principles to appropriate government agencies. The CBBB and DMA have been asked and agreed to work cooperatively to establish accountability mechanisms under the Principles.

Source: Advertising Self-Regulatory Council, Accountability Program, www.asrcreviews.org/2011/12/about-the-accountability-program/.

The Advertising Council, working through the NAD/CARU/ERSP and NARB, is a valuable and effective self-regulatory body. Cases brought to it are handled at a fraction of the cost (and with much less publicity) than those brought to court and are expedited more quickly than those reviewed by a government agency such as the FTC. The system also works because judgments are made by the advertiser's peers, and most companies feel compelled to comply. Firms may prefer self-regulation rather than government intervention in part because they can challenge competitors' unsubstantiated claims and win a more rapid resolution.[25]

**Advertising Associations**   Various groups in the advertising industry also favor self-regulation. The two major national organizations, the American Association of Advertising Agencies and the American Advertising Federation, actively monitor and police industrywide advertising practices. The AAAA, which is the major trade association of the ad agency business in the United States, has established standards of practice and its own creative code. It also issues guidelines for specific types of advertising such as comparative messages (Figure 20–3). The AAF consists of advertisers, agencies, media, and numerous advertising clubs. The association has standards for truthful and responsible advertising, is involved in advertising legislation, and actively influences agencies to abide by its code and principles.

CHAPTER 20

The Board of Directors of the American Association of Advertising Agencies recognizes that when used truthfully and fairly, comparative advertising provides the consumer with needed and useful information.

However, extreme caution should be exercised. The use of comparative advertising, by its very nature, can distort facts and, by implication, convey to the consumer information that misrepresents the truth.

Therefore, the Board believes that comparative advertising should follow certain guidelines:

1. The intent and connotation of the ad should be to inform and never to discredit or unfairly attack competitors, competing products, or services.
2. When a competitive product is named, it should be one that exists in the marketplace as significant competition.
3. The competition should be fairly and properly identified but never in a manner or tone of voice that degrades the competitive product or service.
4. The advertising should compare related or similar properties or ingredients of the product, dimension to dimension, feature to feature.
5. The identification should be for honest comparison purposes and not simply to upgrade by association.
6. If a competitive test is conducted, it should be done by an objective testing source, preferably an independent one, so that there will be no doubt as to the veracity of the test.
7. In all cases the test should be supportive of all claims made in the advertising that are based on the test.
8. The advertising should never use partial results or stress insignificant differences to cause the consumer to draw an improper conclusion.
9. The property being compared should be significant in terms of value or usefulness of the product to the consumer.
10. Comparatives delivered through the use of testimonials should not imply that the testimonial is more than one individual's thought unless that individual represents a sample of the majority viewpoint.

Source: Reprinted with permission.

## Self-Regulation by Media

The media are another important self-regulatory mechanism in the advertising industry. Most media maintain some form of advertising review process and, except for political ads, may reject any they regard as objectionable. Some media exclude advertising for an entire product class; others ban individual ads they think offensive or objectionable. For example, *Reader's Digest* does not accept advertising for tobacco or liquor products. A number of magazines in the United States and other countries refused to run some of Benetton's shock ads on the grounds that their readers would find them offensive or disturbing (Exhibit 20–4).[26]

Newspapers and magazines have their own advertising requirements and restrictions, which often vary depending on the size and nature of the publication. Large, established publications, such as major newspapers or magazines, often have strict standards regarding the type of advertising they accept. Some magazines, such as *Parents* and *Good Housekeeping*,

**EXHIBIT 20–4**

A number of magazines refused to run this Benetton ad

regularly test the products they advertise and offer a "seal of approval" and refunds if the products are later found to be defective. Such policies are designed to enhance the credibility of the publication and increase the reader's confidence in the products it advertises.

Advertising on television and radio has been regulated for years through codes developed by the industry trade association, the National Association of Broadcasters (NAB). Both the radio code (established in 1937) and the television code (1952) provided standards for broadcast advertising for many years. Both codes prohibited the advertising of certain products, such as hard liquor. They also affected the manner in which products could be advertised. However, in 1982, the NAB suspended all of its code provisions after the courts found that portions (dealing with time standards and required length of commercials in the TV code) were in restraint of trade. While the NAB codes are no longer in force, many individual broadcasters, such as the major TV networks, have incorporated major portions of the code provisions into their own standards.[27]

The four major television networks have the most stringent review process of any media. All four networks maintain standards and practices divisions, which carefully review all commercials submitted to the network or individual affiliate stations. Advertisers must submit for review all commercials intended for airing on the network or an affiliate.

A commercial may be submitted for review in the form of a script, storyboard, animatic, or finished commercial (when the advertiser believes there is little chance of objection). A very frustrating, and often expensive, scenario for both an agency and its client occurs when a commercial is approved at the storyboard stage but then is rejected after it is produced. Commercials are rejected for a variety of reasons, including violence, morbid humor, sex, politics, and religion. Network reviewers also consider whether the proposed commercial meets acceptable standards and is appropriate for certain audiences. For example, different standards are used for ads designated for prime-time versus late-night spots or for children's versus adults' programs (see Figure 20–4). Although most of these guidelines for children's advertising remain in effect, several networks have loosened their rules on celebrity endorsements.[28]

**FIGURE 20–4**

A Sampling of the TV Networks' Guidelines for Children's Advertising

Each of the major TV networks has its own set of guidelines for children's advertising, although the basics are very similar. A few rules, such as the requirement of a static "island" shot at the end, are written in stone; others, however, can sometimes be negotiated. Many of the rules below apply specifically to toys. The networks also have special guidelines for kids' food commercials and for kids' commercials that offer premiums.

Must not overglamorize product

No exhortative language, such as "Ask Mom to buy . . ."

No realistic war settings

Generally no celebrity endorsements

Can't use "only" or "just" in regard to price

Show only two toys per child or maximum of six per commercial

Five-second "island" showing product against plain background at end of spot

Animation restricted to one-third of a commercial

Generally no comparative or superiority claims

No costumes or props not available with the toy

No child or toy can appear in animated segments

Three-second establishing shot of toy in relation to child

No shots under one second in length

Must show distance a toy can travel before stopping on its own

**EXHIBIT 20–5**

This humorous "Got milk?" commercial had to be modified slightly to satisfy network censors

The four major networks receive nearly 50,000 commercials a year for review; nearly two-thirds are accepted, and only 3 percent are rejected. Most problems with the remaining 30 percent are resolved through negotiation, and the ads are revised and resubmitted.[29] Most commercials run after changes are made. For example, censors initially rejected a humorous "Got milk?" spot that showed children watching an elderly neighbor push a wheelbarrow. Suddenly, the man's arms rip off, presumably because he doesn't drink milk. The spot was eventually approved after it was modified so that the man appears unhurt after losing his limbs and there was no expression of pain (Exhibit 20–5).[30]

Network standards regarding acceptable advertising change constantly. The networks first allowed lingerie advertisers to use live models rather than mannequins in 1987. Advertising for contraceptives is now appearing on some stations. The networks also loosened long-standing restrictions on endorsements and competitive advertising claims.[31] Network standards will continue to change as society's values and attitudes toward certain issues and products change. Also, many advertising people believe these changes are a response to competition from independent and cable stations, which tend to be much less stringent in their standards and practices. However, since television is probably the most carefully scrutinized and frequently criticized of all forms of advertising, the networks must be careful not to offend their viewers and detract from advertising's credibility.

For example, a number of advertisers such as Go Daddy have had ads created for the Super Bowl rejected because the big game has a very large audience that ranges from children to older adults and the networks ruled that the sexually suggestive ads were inappropriate for the tenor of the event.[32] CBS rejected a commercial that ManCrunch, a gay dating website, wanted to air on the Super Bowl showing two young men watching a football game and rooting for their teams and then becoming passionate when their hands meet inside a bowl of chips (Exhibit 20–6). In its rejection letter CBS stated that the ad was not within the network's broadcast standards for Super Bowl Sunday and that it had difficulty verifying ManCrunch's credit status. While CBS indicated that it was open to working with the company on alternative submissions, some gay rights groups complained that the network was discriminating against the company as well as gays by not accepting the ad.[33]

**EXHIBIT 20–6**

CBS rejected a commercial that ManCrunch wanted to run on the Super Bowl

## Appraising Self-Regulation

The three major participants in the advertising process—advertisers, agencies, and the media—work individually and collectively to encourage truthful, ethical, and responsible advertising. The advertising industry views self-regulation as an effective mechanism for controlling advertising abuses and avoiding the use of offensive, misleading, or deceptive practices, and it prefers this form of regulation to government intervention. Self-regulation of advertising has been effective and in many instances probably led to the development of more stringent standards and practices than those imposed by or beyond the scope of legislation. Moreover, over 90 percent of advertisers comply with NAD decisions since failure to do so can result in government action, which can be very expensive to companies and result in more punitive measures.[34]

A senior vice president and general counsel at Kraft Foods, while praising the NAD, summarized the feelings of many advertisers toward self-regulation. In his testimonial he stated: "NAD is superior to its competition, which is regulation by the government or regulation by the courts. Accurate, prompt, and inexpensive decisions year in and year out have earned NAD its well-deserved credibility with the industry and with regulators." Former Federal Trade Commission chair Timothy Murris has described the NAD as a "model of self-regulation." Deborah Platt Majoras, who was the FTC chair from 2004 until 2008, also praised the National Advertising Review Council for running a model program covering national advertising as well as a number of other areas.

C. Lee Peeler, president-CEO of the Advertising Self-Regulatory Council, recently wrote: "With more than four decades of experience, the self-regulatory system built by the advertising industry and administered by the Council of Better Business Bureaus is the gold standard against which other self-regulation is judged."[35] He notes that the self-regulatory system protects consumers from misleading advertising by acting quickly and decisively against misleading advertising claims; it points the way on new media issues, providing advertisers with guidance that helps avoid missteps; it provides a fast, efficient, and expert forum that levels the playing field for all advertisers by holding them to high standards of truthfulness and requiring claim substantiation; and it provides the intellectual capital for the development of strong, new self-regulation programs. Exhibit 20–7 shows a page from the ASRC website summarizing the value of the NAD.

There are, however, limitations to self-regulation, and the process has been criticized in a number of areas. For example, the NAD may take six months to a year to resolve a complaint, during which time a company often stops using the commercial anyway. Budgeting and staffing constraints may limit the number of cases the NAD/NARB system investigates and the speed with which it resolves them. Financial support remains an important challenge for the ASCR as its programs are supported by less than 140 national corporations through partnership with the Council of Better Business Bureaus. Support for self-regulatory programs is much smaller in the United States than many other countries despite the fact that the advertising market in the United States is much larger.[36] And some critics believe that self-regulation is self-serving to the advertisers and advertising industry and lacks the power or authority to be a viable alternative to federal or state regulation. However, while the FTC does not always pursue the cases referred by the NAD, the threat of referral serves as an important deterrent.[37]

Many do not believe advertising can or should be controlled solely by self-regulation. They argue that regulation by government agencies is necessary to ensure that consumers get accurate information and are not misled or deceived. Moreover, since advertisers do not have to comply with the decisions and recommendations of self-regulatory groups, it is sometimes necessary to turn to the federal and/or state government.

**EXHIBIT 20–7**
The NAD is an effective alternative to government intervention and/or litigation.

CHAPTER 20

# FEDERAL REGULATION OF ADVERTISING

LO 20-3

Advertising is controlled and regulated through federal, state, and local laws and regulations enforced by various government agencies. The federal government is the most important source of external regulation since many advertising practices come under the jurisdiction of the **Federal Trade Commission (FTC)**. In addition, depending on the advertiser's industry and product or service, other federal agencies such as the Federal Communications Commission, the Food and Drug Administration, the U.S. Postal Service, and the Bureau of Alcohol, Tobacco, Firearms and Explosives may have regulations that affect advertising. We will begin our discussion of federal regulation of advertising by considering the basic rights of marketers to advertise their products and services under the First Amendment.

## Advertising and the First Amendment

Freedom of speech or expression, as defined by the First Amendment to the U.S. Constitution, is the most basic federal law governing advertising in the United States. For many years, freedom of speech protection did not include advertising and other forms of speech that promote a commercial transaction. However, the courts have extended First Amendment protection to **commercial speech**, which is speech that promotes a commercial transaction. There have been a number of landmark cases over the past three decades where the federal courts have issued rulings supporting the coverage of commercial speech by the First Amendment.

In a 1976 case, *Virginia State Board of Pharmacy v. Virginia Citizens Consumer Council,* the U.S. Supreme Court ruled that states cannot prohibit pharmacists from advertising the prices of prescription drugs, because such advertising contains information that helps the consumer choose between products and because the free flow of information is indispensable.[38] As noted earlier, in 1977 the Supreme Court ruled that state bar associations' restrictions on advertising are unconstitutional and attorneys have a First Amendment right to advertise their services and prices.[39] In another landmark case in 1980, *Central Hudson Gas & Electric Corp. v. New York Public Service Commission,* the Supreme Court ruled that commercial speech was entitled to First Amendment protection in some cases. However, the Court ruled that the U.S. Constitution affords less protection to commercial speech than to other constitutionally guaranteed forms of expression. In this case the Court established a four-part test, known as the **Central Hudson Test**, for determining restrictions on commercial speech.[40] In a more recent case, the Supreme Court's 1996 decision in *44 Liquormart, Inc. v. Rhode Island* struck down two state statutes designed to support the state's interest in temperance. The first prohibited the advertising of alcoholic beverage prices in Rhode Island except on signs within a store, while the second prohibited the publication or broadcast of alcohol price ads. The Court ruled that the Rhode Island statutes were unlawful because they restricted the constitutional guarantee of freedom of speech, and the decision signaled strong protection for advertisers under the First Amendment.[41]

In the cases regarding advertising, the U.S. Supreme Court has ruled that freedom of expression must be balanced against competing interests. For example, the courts have upheld bans on the advertising of products that are considered harmful, such as tobacco. The Court has also ruled that only truthful commercial speech is protected, not advertising or other forms of promotion that are false, misleading, or deceptive.

In an important case involving Nike, the California Supreme Court issued a ruling that is likely to impact the way companies engage in public debate regarding issues that affect them. Nike was sued for false advertising under California consumer protection laws for allegedly making misleading statements regarding labor practices and working conditions in its foreign factories. Nike argued that statements the company made to defend itself against the charges should be considered political speech, which is protected by the First Amendment, rather than commercial speech, which is subject to advertising regulations. However, the California high court ruled that statements made by the company to defend itself against the allegations were commercial in nature and thus subject to the state's consumer protection regulations. Nike appealed the case to the U.S. Supreme Court, which sent it back to California for trial to determine if the company's statements were deceptive and misleading. However, Nike settled the case rather than risking a long and costly court battle. While the ruling in this case only applies to California, it is important as the courts ruled that speech in the form of press releases or public statements by company representatives can be considered commercial and subject to consumer protection laws.[42]

The job of regulating advertising at the federal level and determining whether advertising is truthful or deceptive is a major focus of the Federal Trade Commission. We now turn our attention to federal regulation of advertising and the FTC.

## Background on Federal Regulation of Advertising

Federal regulation of advertising originated in 1914 with the passage of the **Federal Trade Commission Act** (FTC Act), which created the FTC, the agency that is today the most active in, and has primary responsibility for, controlling and regulating advertising. The FTC Act was originally intended to help enforce antitrust laws, such as the Sherman and Clayton Acts, by helping restrain unfair methods of competition. The main focus of the first five-member commission was to protect competitors from one another; the issue of false or misleading advertising was not even mentioned. In 1922, the Supreme Court upheld an FTC interpretation that false advertising was an unfair method of competition, but in the 1931 case *FTC v. Raladam Co.,* the Court ruled the commission could not prohibit false advertising unless there was evidence of injury to a competitor.[43] This ruling limited the power of the FTC to protect consumers from false or deceptive advertising and led to a consumer movement that resulted in an important amendment to the FTC Act.

In 1938, Congress passed the **Wheeler-Lea Amendment**. It amended section 5 of the FTC Act to read: "Unfair methods of competition in commerce and unfair or deceptive acts or practices in commerce are hereby declared to be unlawful." The amendment empowered the FTC to act if there was evidence of injury to the public; proof of injury to a competitor was not necessary. The Wheeler-Lea Amendment also gave the FTC the power to issue cease-and-desist orders and levy fines on violators. It extended the FTC's jurisdiction over false advertising of foods, drugs, cosmetics, and therapeutic devices. And it gave the FTC access to the injunctive power of the federal courts, initially only for food and drug products but expanded in 1972 to include all products in the event of a threat to the public's health and safety.

In addition to the FTC, numerous other federal agencies are responsible for, or involved in, advertising regulation. The authority of these agencies is limited, however, to a particular product area or service, and they often rely on the FTC to assist in handling false or deceptive advertising cases.

## The Federal Trade Commission

The FTC is responsible for protecting both consumers and businesses from anti-competitive behavior and unfair and deceptive practices. The major divisions of the FTC include the bureaus of competition, economics, and consumer protection. The Bureau of Competition seeks to prevent business practices that restrain competition and is responsible for enforcing antitrust laws. The Bureau of Economics helps the FTC evaluate the impact of its actions and provides economic analysis and support to antitrust and consumer protection investigations and rule makings. It also analyzes the impact of government regulation on competition and consumers. The Bureau of Consumer Protection's mandate is to protect consumers against unfair, deceptive, or fraudulent practices. This bureau also investigates and litigates cases involving acts or practices alleged to be deceptive or unfair to consumers. The Division of Advertising Practices protects consumers from deceptive and unsubstantiated

**EXHIBIT 20–8**

The Division of Advertising Practices protects consumers from deceptive and unsubstantiated advertising claims

advertising and enforces the provisions of the FTC Act that forbid misrepresentation, unfairness, and deception in general advertising at the national and regional level (Exhibit 20–8). The Division of Marketing Practices engages in activities that are related to various marketing and warranty practices such as fraudulent telemarketing schemes, 900-number programs, and disclosures relating to franchise and business opportunities.

The FTC has had the power to regulate advertising since passage of the Wheeler-Lea Amendment. However, not until the early 1970s—following criticism of the commission in a book by "Nader's Raiders" and a special report by the American Bar Association citing its lack of action against deceptive promotional practices— did the FTC become active in regulating advertising.[44] The authority of the FTC was increased considerably throughout the 1970s. The Magnuson-Moss Act of 1975, an important piece of legislation, dramatically broadened the FTC's powers and substantially increased its budget. The first section of the act dealt with consumers' rights regarding product warranties; it allowed the commission to require restitution for deceptively written warranties where the consumer lost more than $5. The second section, the FTC Improvements Act, empowered the FTC to establish **trade regulation rules (TRRs)**, industrywide rules that define unfair practices before they occur.

During the 1970s, the FTC made enforcement of laws regarding false and misleading advertising a top priority. Several new programs were instituted, budgets were increased, and the commission became a very powerful regulatory agency. However, many of these programs, as well as the expanded powers of the FTC to develop regulations on the basis of "unfairness," became controversial. At the root of this controversy is the fundamental issue of what constitutes unfair advertising.

## The Concept of Unfairness

Under section 5 of the FTC Act, the Federal Trade Commission has a mandate to act against unfair or deceptive advertising practices. However, this statute does not define the terms *unfair* and *deceptive,* and the FTC has been criticized for not doing so itself. While the FTC has taken steps to clarify the meaning of *deception,* people have been concerned for years about the vagueness of the term *unfair.*

Controversy over the FTC's authority to regulate unfair advertising practices began in 1978, when the agency relied on this mandate to formulate its controversial "kid vid" rule restricting advertising to children.[45] This interpretation caused widespread concern in the business community that the term *unfair* could be used to encompass anything FTC commissioners might find objectionable. For example, in a 1980 policy statement the FTC noted that "the precise concept of consumer unfairness is one whose precise meaning is not immediately obvious." Consequently, in 1980 Congress responded by suspending the children's advertising rule and banning the FTC from using unfairness as a legal basis for advertising rulemaking.

The FTC responded to these criticisms in December 1980 by sending Congress a statement containing an interpretation of unfairness. According to FTC policy, the basis for determining **unfairness** is that a trade practice (1) causes substantial physical or economic injury to consumers, (2) could not reasonably be avoided by consumers, and (3) must not be outweighed by countervailing benefits to consumers or competition. The agency also stated that a violation of public policy (such as other government statutes) could, by itself, constitute an unfair practice or could be used to prove substantial consumer injury. Practices considered unfair are claims made without prior substantiation, claims that might exploit such vulnerable groups as children and older adults, and instances where consumers cannot make a valid choice because the advertiser omits important information about the product or competing products mentioned in the ad.[46]

The FTC's statement was intended to clarify its interpretation of unfairness and reduce ambiguity over what might constitute unfair practices. However, efforts by the FTC to develop industrywide trade regulation rules that would define unfair practices and have the force and effect of law were limited by Congress in 1980 with the passage of the FTC Improvements Act. Amidst calls to end the stalemate over the FTC's regulation of unfair advertising by having the agency work with Congress to define its advertising authority, in 1994 Congress and the advertising industry agreed on a definition of unfair advertising that is very similar to the FTC's 1980 policy statement discussed earlier. However, the new agreement requires that before the FTC can initiate any industrywide rule, it has to have reason to believe that the unfair or deceptive acts or practices are prevalent.[47]

The FTC does have specific regulatory authority in cases involving deceptive, misleading, or untruthful advertising. The vast majority of advertising cases that the FTC handles concern deception and advertising fraud, which usually involve knowledge of a false claim.

## Deceptive Advertising

In most economies, advertising provides consumers with information they can use to make consumption decisions. However, if this information is untrue or misleads the consumer, advertising is not fulfilling its basic function. Moreover, a study by Peter Drake and Robin Ritchie found that deceptive advertising engenders mistrust, which negatively affects consumers' responses to subsequent advertising from the same source as well as second-party sources. They note that deceptive advertising can seriously undermine the effectiveness and credibility of advertising and marketing in general by making consumers defensive toward future advertising and should be of concern to all marketers.[48] But what constitutes an untruthful or deceptive ad? Deceptive advertising can take a number of forms, ranging from intentionally false or misleading claims to ads that, although true, leave some consumers with a false or misleading impression.

The issue of deception, including its definition and measurement, receives considerable attention from the FTC and other regulatory agencies. One of the problems regulatory agencies deal with in determining deception is distinguishing between false or misleading messages and those that, rather than relying on verifiable or substantiated objective information about a product, make subjective claims or statements, a practice known as puffery. **Puffery** has been legally defined as "advertising or other sales presentations which praise the item to be sold with subjective opinions, superlatives, or exaggerations, vaguely and generally, stating no specific facts."[49] The use of puffery in advertising is common. For example, Bayer aspirin calls itself the "wonder drug that works wonders," Nestlé claims "Nestlé makes the very best chocolate," Snapple advertises that its beverages are "made from the best stuff on Earth," and BMW uses the tagline "The Ultimate Driving Machine." Superlatives such as *greatest, best,* and *finest* are puffs that are often used.

Puffery has generally been viewed as a form of poetic license or allowable exaggeration. The FTC takes the position that because consumers expect exaggeration or inflated claims in advertising, they recognize puffery and don't believe it. But some studies show that consumers may believe puffery and perceive such claims as true.[50] One study found that consumers could not distinguish between a verifiable fact-based claim and puffery and were just as likely to believe both types of claims.[51] Ivan Preston argues that puffery has a detrimental effect on consumers' purchase decisions by burdening them with untrue beliefs and refers to it as "soft-core deception" that should be illegal.[52]

Advertisers' battle to retain the right to use puffery was supported in the latest revision of the Uniform Commercial Code in 1996. The revision switches the burden of proof to consumers from advertisers in cases pertaining to whether certain claims were meant to be taken as promises. The revision states that the buyer must prove that an affirmation of fact (as opposed to puffery) was made, that the buyer was aware of the advertisement, and that the affirmation of fact became part of the agreement with the seller.[53]

One of the most intense battles regarding the use of puffery was fought by Papa John's and Pizza Hut and went all the way to the United States Supreme Court.[54] The central issue in the case was Papa John's use of the tagline "Better Ingredients. Better Pizza." Pizza Hut filed a lawsuit against Papa John's claiming that the latter's ads were false and misleading because it had failed to prove its sauce and dough were superior. Following a long-drawn-out legal battle that lasted nearly five years and cost the two companies millions of dollars, the U.S. Supreme Court issued a decision in support of the use of puffery as the basis for a comparative advertising claim. The advertising industry was relieved that the Supreme Court ruled in favor of Papa John's because a ruling against the puffery defense could have opened the door for other challenges and a redrawing of the blurry line between so-called puffery and outright false advertising.[55]

As an interesting by-product of the case, Domino's Pizza decided to take advantage of the appellate court ruling that Papa John's slogan was considered puffery and ran TV commercials showing the company's head chef, Brian Solano, standing outside a federal court of appeals building in New Orleans talking about Papa John's and its slogan. In the spot Solano says: "For years Papa John's has been telling us they have better ingredients and better pizza. But when challenged in this court, they stated their slogan is puffery." He then turns to a lawyer standing next to him and asks him: "What's puffery?" Reading from a law book, the lawyer says: "Puffery. An exaggerated statement based on opinion. Not fact" (Exhibit 20–9). Solano then says, "Here's what's not puffery" and goes on to explain how Domino's beat Papa John's in a national taste test. The spot ends with Solano stating, "Our pizza tastes better and that's not puffery, that's proven.[56]

Since unfair and deceptive acts or practices have never been precisely defined, the FTC is continually developing and refining a working definition in its attempts to regulate advertising. The traditional standard used to determine deception was whether a claim had the "tendency or capacity to deceive." However, this standard was criticized for being vague and all-encompassing.

In 1983, the FTC, under Chair James Miller III, put forth a new working definition of **deception**: "The commission will find deception if there is a misrepresentation, omission, or practice that is likely to mislead the consumer acting reasonably in the circumstances to the consumer's detriment."[57] There are three essential elements to this definition of deception.[58] The first element is that the representation, omission, or practice must be *likely to mislead* the consumer. The FTC defines *misrepresentation* as an express or implied statement contrary to fact, whereas a *misleading omission* occurs when qualifying information necessary to prevent a practice, claim, representation, or reasonable belief from being misleading is not disclosed.

The second element is that the act or practice must be considered from the perspective of *the reasonable consumer.* In determining reasonableness, the FTC considers the group to which the advertising is targeted and whether their interpretation of or reaction to the message is reasonable in light of the circumstances. The standard is flexible and allows the FTC to consider factors such as the age, education level, intellectual capacity, and frame of mind of the particular group to which the message or practice is targeted. For example, advertisements

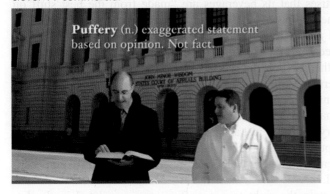

YTC 20–03

**Domino's Puffery**

youtube.com/10ebelch

**EXHIBIT 20–9**

Domino's poked fun at Papa John's puffery defense in a clever TV commercial

Puffery (n.) exaggerated statement based on opinion. Not fact.

targeted to a particular group, such as children or older adults, are evaluated with respect to their effect on a reasonable member of that group.

The third key element to the FTC's definition of deception is *materiality*. According to the FTC a "material" misrepresentation or practice is one that is likely to affect a consumer's choice or conduct with regard to a product or service. What this means is that the information, claim, or practice in question is important to consumers and, if acted upon, would be likely to influence their purchase decisions. In some cases the information or claims made in an ad may be false or misleading but would not be regarded as material since reasonable consumers would not make a purchase decision on the basis of this information.

Miller's goal was to help the commission determine which cases were worth pursuing and which were trivial. Miller argued that for an ad to be considered worthy of FTC challenge, it should be seen by a substantial number of consumers, it should lead to significant injury, and the problem should be one that market forces are not likely to remedy. However, the revised definition may put a greater burden on the FTC to prove that deception occurred and that the deception influenced the consumers' decision-making process in a detrimental way.

Determining what constitutes deception is still a gray area. Two of the factors the FTC considers in evaluating an ad for deception are (1) whether there are significant omissions of important information and (2) whether advertisers can substantiate the claims made for the product or service. The FTC has developed several programs to address these issues.

**Affirmative Disclosure**   An ad can be literally true yet leave the consumer with a false or misleading impression if the claim is true only under certain conditions or circumstances or if there are limitations to what the product can or cannot do. Thus, under its **affirmative disclosure** requirement, the FTC may require advertisers to include certain types of information in their ads so that consumers will be aware of all the consequences, conditions, and limitations associated with the use of a product or service. The goal of affirmative disclosure is to give consumers sufficient information to make an informed decision. An ad may be required to define the testing situation, conditions, or criteria used in making a claim. For example, fuel mileage claims in car ads are based on Environmental Protection Agency (EPA) ratings since they offer a uniform standard for making comparisons. Cigarette ads must contain a warning about the health risks associated with smoking.

An example of an affirmative disclosure ruling is the FTC's case against Campbell Soup for making deceptive and unsubstantiated claims. Campbell's ads, run as part of its "Soup is good food" campaign, linked the low-fat and low-cholesterol content of its soup with a reduced risk of heart disease. However, the advertising failed to disclose that the soups are high in sodium, which may increase the risk of heart disease. In a consent agreement, Campbell agreed that, for any soup containing more than 500 milligrams of sodium in an 8-ounce serving, it will disclose the sodium content in any advertising that directly or by implication mentions heart disease in connection with the soup. Campbell also agreed it would not imply a connection between soup and a reduction in heart disease in future advertising.[59]

Another area where the Federal Trade Commission is seeking more specificity from advertisers is in regard to country-of-origin claims. The FTC has been working with marketers and trade associations to develop a better definition of what the "Made in the USA" label means. The 50-year-old definition used until 1998 required full manufacturing in the United States, using U.S. labor and parts, with only raw materials from overseas.[60] Many companies argue that in an increasingly global economy, it is becoming very difficult to have 100 percent U.S. content and remain price-competitive. However, the FTC argues that advertising or labeling a product

**EXHIBIT 20–10**

New Balance promotes its commitment to U.S. manufacturing

**EXHIBIT 20–11**

The U.S. Champagne Bureau is running ads calling for clarification of the region of origin on wine labels

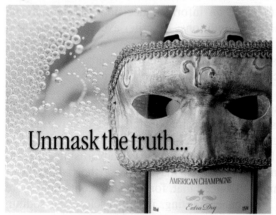

Unmask the truth...

AMERICAN CHAMPAGNE
★
Extra Dry

**No more cover-ups.**

It's not just subprime mortgages and derivative insurance that bury honesty in legal mumbo jumbo. A legal loophole allows some U.S. wines to masquerade as something they're not.

There are many fine sparkling wines, but only those from **Champagne** can use that region's name. Names of American wine regions like Napa Valley and Willamette are also misused.

Consumer groups agree: deceptive wine labeling must stop. Tell Congress to protect consumers. Sign the petition at www.champagne.us.

Champagne *only* comes
from Champagne, France.

as "Made in the USA" can provide a company with a competitive advantage. For many products some consumers do respond to the claim, as they trust the quality of domestic-made products and/or feel patriotic when they buy American. For example, athletic-shoe-maker New Balance is a company that promotes its commitment to domestic manufacturing and the fact that 25 percent of its products are made in the United States (Exhibit 20–10).

In December 1998, the FTC issued new guidelines for American-made products. The guidelines spell out what it means by "all or virtually all" in mandating how much U.S. content a product must have to wear a "Made in USA" label or be advertised as such. According to the new FTC guidelines, all significant parts and processing that go into the product must be of U.S. origin and the product should have no or very little foreign content. Companies do not have to receive the approval of the FTC before making a "Made in USA" claim. However, the commission does have the authority to take action against false and unsubstantiated "Made in USA" claims just as it does with other advertising claims.[61]

Another interesting example of a case involving product origin claims is in the wine industry. The U.S. Champagne Bureau launched its "Unmask the Truth" ad campaign which has the goals of rallying consumers and demanding lawmakers protect place-of-origin names on wine sold in the United States. The ad, which is shown in Exhibit 20–11, features a mask over a sparkling wine bottle mislabeled "American Champagne" and asks consumers to voice their support for truthful labeling regarding where wine comes from. The campaign is designed to address a loophole in federal law that allows some U.S. sparkling wine producers to mislead consumers by labeling their products "Champagne" even though they do not come from the Champagne region of France. The trade association argues that names of American wine regions such as Napa Valley and Williamette also risk being misused.[62]

**Advertising Substantiation**   A major area of concern to regulatory agencies is whether advertisers can support or substantiate their claims. For many years, there were no formal requirements concerning substantiation of advertising claims. Many companies made claims without any documentation or support such as laboratory tests or clinical studies. In 1971, the FTC's **advertising substantiation** program required advertisers to have supporting documentation for their claims and to prove the claims are truthful.[63] Broadened in 1972, this program now requires advertisers to substantiate their claims before an ad appears. Substantiation is required for all express or implied claims involving safety, performance, efficacy, quality, or comparative price.

The FTC's substantiation program has had a major effect on the advertising industry, because it shifted the burden of proof from the commission to the advertiser. Before the substantiation program, the FTC had to prove that an advertiser's claims were unfair or deceptive.

Ad substantiation seeks to provide a basis for believing advertising claims so consumers can make rational and informed decisions and companies are deterred from making claims they cannot adequately support. The FTC takes the perspective that it is illegal and unfair to consumers for a firm to make a claim for a product without having a "reasonable basis" for the claim.

In their decision to require advertising substantiation, the commissioners made the following statement:

> Given the imbalance of knowledge and resources between a business enterprise and each of its customers, economically it is more rational and imposes far less cost on society, to require a manufacturer to confirm his affirmative product claims rather than impose a burden on each individual consumer to test, investigate, or experiment for himself. The manufacturer has the ability, the know-how, the equipment, the time and resources to undertake such information, by testing or otherwise, . . . the consumer usually does not.[64]

Many advertisers respond negatively to the FTC's advertising substantiation program. They argue it is too expensive to document all their claims and most consumers either won't understand or aren't interested in the technical data. Some advertisers threaten to avoid the substantiation issue by using puffery claims, which do not require substantiation.

Generally, advertisers making claims covered by the substantiation program must have available prior substantiation of all claims. However, in 1984, the FTC issued a new policy statement that suggested after-the-fact substantiation might be acceptable in some cases and it would solicit documentation of claims only from advertisers that are under investigation for deceptive practices.

In a number of cases, the FTC has ordered advertisers to cease making inadequately substantiated claims. In 1993, the FTC took on the weight-loss industry when it filed a complaint charging that none of five large, well-known diet program marketers had sufficient evidence to back up claims that their customers achieved their weight-loss goals or maintained the loss. Three of the companies agreed to publicize the fact that most weight loss is temporary and to disclose how long their customers kept off the weight they lost. The agreement required the companies to substantiate their weight-loss claims with scientific data and to document claims that their customers keep off the weight by monitoring a group of them for two years[65] (Exhibit 20–12).

Recently the FTC has stepped up its action against false and unsubstantiated claims in ads and infomercials. A few years ago, the commission fined the Home Shopping Network $1.1 million for making unsubstantiated advertising claims for two weight-loss products, an acne treatment, and a dietary supplement for menopause and premenstrual syndrome. Under the settlement Home Shopping is enjoined from making product claims about curing and treating diseases without "reliable scientific evidence."

In early 2013 the FTC issued a very important ruling against POM Wonderful LLC—the maker of juices, teas, and fruit—upholding an initial finding by an administrative law judge that the company had made a number of unsubstantiated claims for its pomegranate juice. One of the ads run by the company showed a bottle with a noose around its neck and the headline "Cheat Death" while the ad copy claimed that the juice "can help prevent premature aging, heart disease stroke, Alzheimer's, even cancer. Eight ounces a day is all you need." The ruling by FTC commissioners stated that POM's claims must be backed by two randomized, controlled clinical trials, which is the same type of evidence the FDA requires when approving new drugs.[66] POM indicated it would appeal the ruling, arguing that the FTC was taking an unprecedented step in holding food companies to the same standard as pharmaceuticals. However, the FTC countered that its standards for food health claims are not nearly as stringent as those of the FDA for drugs. The FTC ruling in the case suggests that the commission plans to take a more aggressive approach toward health claims made by food companies and marketers of natural products and may require more substantiation to support any health-related claims they make.[67]

**EXHIBIT 20–12**

Weight-loss program marketers are now required to substantiate their claims as a result of an FTC ruling

# The FTC's Handling of Deceptive Advertising Cases

**Consent and Cease-and-Desist Orders**   Allegations of unfair or deceptive advertising come to the FTC's attention from a variety of sources, including competitors, consumers, other government agencies, or the commission's own monitoring and investigations. Once the FTC decides a complaint is justified and warrants further action, it notifies the offender, who then has 30 days to respond. The advertiser can agree to negotiate a settlement with the FTC by signing a **consent order**, which is an agreement to stop the practice or advertising in question. This agreement is for settlement purposes only and does not constitute an admission of guilt by the advertiser. Most FTC inquiries are settled by consent orders because they save the advertiser the cost and possible adverse publicity that might result if the case went further.

If the advertiser chooses not to sign the consent decree and contests the complaint, a hearing can be requested before an administrative law judge employed by the FTC but not under its influence. The judge's decision may be appealed to the full five-member commission by either side. The commission either affirms or modifies the order or dismisses the case. If the complaint has been upheld by the administrative law judge and the commission, the advertiser can appeal the case to the federal courts.

The appeal process may take some time, during which the FTC may want to stop the advertiser from engaging in the deceptive practice. The Wheeler-Lea Amendment empowers the FTC to issue a **cease-and-desist order**, which requires that the advertiser stop the specified advertising claim within 30 days and prohibits the advertiser from engaging in the objectionable practice until after the hearing is held. Violation of a cease-and-desist order is punishable by a fine of up to $10,000 a day. Figure 20–5 summarizes the FTC complaint procedure.

**Corrective Advertising**   By using consent and cease-and-desist orders, the FTC can usually stop a particular advertising practice it believes is unfair or deceptive. However, even if an advertiser ceases using a deceptive ad, consumers may still remember some or all of the claim. To address the problem of residual effects, in the 1970s, the FTC developed a program known as **corrective advertising**. An advertiser found guilty of deceptive advertising can be required to run additional advertising designed to remedy the deception or misinformation contained in previous ads.

The impetus for corrective advertising was another case involving Campbell Soup, which when making a photo for an ad placed marbles in the bottom of a bowl of vegetable soup to force the solid ingredients to the surface, creating a false impression that the soup contained more vegetables than it really did. (Campbell Soup argued that if the marbles were not used, all the ingredients would settle to the bottom, leaving an impression of fewer ingredients than actually existed!) While Campbell Soup agreed to stop the practice, a group of law students calling themselves SOUP (Students Opposed to Unfair Practices) argued to the FTC that this would not remedy false impressions created by prior advertising and contended Campbell Soup should be required to run advertising to rectify the problem.[68]

Although the FTC did not order corrective advertising in the Campbell case, it has done so in many cases since then. Profile Bread ran an ad stating each slice contained fewer calories than other brands, but the ad did not mention that slices of Profile bread were thinner than those of other brands. Ocean Spray cranberry juice was found guilty of deceptive advertising because it claimed to have more "food energy" than orange or tomato juice but failed to note it was referring to the technical definition of food energy, which is calories. In each case, the advertisers were ordered to spend 25 percent of their annual media budgets to run corrective ads. The STP Corporation was required to run corrective advertising for claims regarding the ability of its oil additive to reduce oil consumption. Many of the

**FIGURE 20–5**

FTC Complaint Procedure

corrective ads run in the STP case appeared in business publications to serve notice to other advertisers that the FTC was enforcing the corrective advertising program. The texts of the corrective messages required in each of these cases are shown in Figure 20–6.

Corrective advertising is probably the most controversial of all the FTC programs.[69] Advertisers argue that corrective advertising infringes on First Amendment

| Profile Bread | Ocean Spray | STP |
|---|---|---|
| "Hi, [celebrity's name] for Profile Bread. Like all mothers, I'm concerned about nutrition and balanced meals. So, I'd like to clear up any misunderstanding you may have about Profile Bread from its advertising or even its name.<br><br>"Does Profile have fewer calories than any other breads? No. Profile has about the same per ounce as other breads. To be exact, Profile has seven fewer calories per slice. That's because Profile is sliced thinner. But eating Profile will not cause you to lose weight. A reduction of seven calories is insignificant. It's total calories and balanced nutrition that count. And Profile can help you achieve a balanced meal because it provides protein and B vitamins as well as other nutrients.<br><br>"How does my family feel about Profile? Well, my husband likes Profile toast, the children love Profile sandwiches, and I prefer Profile to any other bread. So you see, at our house, delicious taste makes Profile a family affair."<br><br>(To be run in 25 percent of brand's advertising, for one year.) | "If you've wondered what some of our earlier advertising meant when we said Ocean Spray Cranberry Juice Cocktail has more food energy than orange juice or tomato juice, let us make it clear: we didn't mean vitamins and minerals. Food energy means calories. Nothing more.<br><br>"Food energy is important at breakfast since many of us may not get enough calories, or food energy, to get off to a good start. Ocean Spray Cranberry Juice Cocktail helps because it contains more food energy than most other breakfast drinks.<br><br>"And Ocean Spray Cranberry Juice Cocktail gives you and your family Vitamin C plus a great wake-up taste. It's . . . the other breakfast drink."<br><br>(To be run in one of every four ads for one year.) | As a result of an investigation by the Federal Trade Commission into certain allegedly inaccurate past advertisements for STP's oil additive, STP Corporation has agreed to a $700,000 settlement. With regard to that settlement, STP is making the following statement:<br><br>"It is the policy of STP to support its advertising with objective information and test data. In 1974 and 1975 an independent laboratory ran tests of the company's oil additive which led to claims of reduced oil consumption. However, these tests cannot be relied on to support the oil consumption reduction claim made by STP.<br><br>"The FTC has taken the position that, in making the claim, the company violated the terms of a consent order. When STP learned that the test did not support the claim, it stopped advertising containing that claim. New tests have been undertaken to determine the extent to which the oil additive affects oil consumption. Agreement to this settlement does not constitute an admission by STP that the law has been violated. Rather, STP has agreed to resolve the dispute with the FTC to avoid protracted and prohibitively expensive litigation." |

**FIGURE 20–6**

Examples of Corrective Advertising Messages

rights of freedom of speech. In one of the most publicized corrective advertising cases ever, involving Listerine mouthwash, Warner-Lambert tested the FTC's legal power to order corrective messages.[70] For more than 50 years Warner-Lambert had advertised that gargling with Listerine helped prevent colds and sore throats or lessened their severity because it killed the germs that caused these illnesses. In 1975, the FTC ruled these claims could not be substantiated and ordered Warner-Lambert to stop making them. In addition, the FTC argued that corrective advertising was needed to rectify the erroneous beliefs that had been created by Warner-Lambert as a result of the large amount of advertising it had run for Listerine over the prior 50 years.

Warner-Lambert argued that the advertising was not misleading and, further, that the FTC did not have the power to order corrective advertising. Warner-Lambert appealed the FTC decision all the way to the Supreme Court, which rejected the argument that corrective advertising violates advertisers' First Amendment rights. The powers of the FTC in the areas of both claim substantiation and corrective advertising were upheld. Warner-Lambert was required to run $10 million worth of corrective ads over a 16-month period stating, "Listerine does not help prevent colds or sore throats or lessen their severity."

Since the Supreme Court ruling in the Listerine case, there have been several other situations where the FTC has ordered corrective advertising on the basis of the "Warner-Lambert test," which considers whether consumers are left with a latent impression that would continue to affect buying decisions and whether corrective ads are needed to remedy the situation.

In a more recent case involving Novartis Consumer Health Corp.'s Doan's Pills, the FTC sent a strong message to advertisers and agencies that it will require marketers to run corrective ads to remedy any misleading impressions that were created through unsubstantiated advertising claims.[71] In this case, Novartis was ordered to spend $8 million, or the equivalent of the average annual ad budget for Doan's Pills over an eight-year period, on corrective ads to remedy any impressions that might exist from previous advertising that the brand is more effective than other analgesics for relieving back pain. Novartis was ordered to include the statement "Although Doan's is an effective pain reliever, there is no evidence that Doan's is more effective than other pain relievers for back pain" on packaging and in ads until $8 million was spent on the campaign. Novartis appealed the FTC decision ordering corrective advertising. However, the U.S. Court of Appeals unanimously upheld the FTC's right to demand corrective advertising in this case. Also at issue in the appeal was the FTC's standard for determining whether a lingering false impression exists from deceptive advertising and whether the commission has to prove that the years of advertising created the false impression or could assume that years of advertising would have done so. The courts described the evidence of lingering effect the FTC had amassed as "thin and somewhat fragmentary," but upheld the commission's decision based on the record as a whole.[72]

The appeals court decision in this case has very important implications for the FTC as well as for advertisers. The ruling reaffirmed the commission's authority to order corrective advertising and gave it greater freedom to use the remedy, whereas a loss could have limited its authority to do so. The ruling also has repercussions for advertisers who expressed concern over the FTC's contention that "corrective advertising is not a drastic remedy" but is an appropriate method for restoring the status quo. Advertisers fear that this is a sign the FTC will be more willing to apply the remedy in future cases. However, FTC officials indicated that the ruling would not substantially change its request for corrective ads. This appears to be the case thus far.

However, in 2009 another federal agency, the FDA, ordered Bayer to run a six-month, $20 million corrective advertising campaign for Yaz, the company's birth-control product. The FDA ruled that Bayer's marketing and advertising for Yaz, which is the leading nongeneric in the birth-control market, was deceptive and made false claims regarding its efficacy for acne and premenstrual syndrome. Bayer was ordered to spend nearly a third of the $66.7 million it spent in measured media the prior year on corrective ads and was also required to submit all of its advertising for Yaz to the FDA for approval for the next six years.[73]

## Developments in Federal Regulation by the FTC

YTC 20-04
Yaz Corrective ad
youtube.com/10ebelch

Over the past decade the FTC has focused its attention on the enforcement of existing regulations, particularly in areas such as telemarketing and Internet privacy.[74] The FTC also has focused on eliminating false e-mail advertising and has stepped up its enforcement against senders of deceptive or misleading claims via e-mail. The commission also scrutinized the use of testimonial ads more carefully, particularly with respect to the use of a "results not typical" disclosure in situations where the outcomes are more likely to vary substantially than be typical for most consumers.[75] The FTC has been active in bringing enforcement action against deceptive health claims and companies and principals in the mortgage lending industry for deceptive and unfair practices in servicing mortgage loans. The FTC has also become more involved in the area of environmental marketing

CHAPTER 20

and the use of "green" claims for carbon offset, landfill reduction, and sustainable packaging.[76]

Under the Obama administration, the FTC has become very active in the regulation of advertising as well as of other marketing practices. The administration, has asked Congress to grant the agency increased powers to protect consumers from deceptive practices by unscrupulous providers of financial services and products. The FTC has noted that it intends to step up its efforts to stop fraud that targets financially distressed consumers. It has joined forces with a number of states and other federal agencies to take action against mortgage modification and foreclosure rescue scams; phony debt reduction and credit repair operations; and payday lenders, get-rich-quick schemes, and bogus government grants. To better protect consumers, the FTC is also seeking to streamline the its rulemaking procedures, asking for power to bring charges directly against aiders and abettors of financial fraud and expanding the commission's remedial powers.

The FTC is focusing attention on protecting consumers' online privacy and the collection of sensitive information, particularly for those using social media such as Facebook and Twitter. In 2009 it passed a new set of guidelines for online endorsements that requires bloggers to disclose any "material connection" to an advertiser.[77] The FTC also released its Self-Regulatory Principles for Online Behavioral Advertising in 2009 which were discussed earlier in the chapter and shown in Figure 20–2. In its 2013 Annual Highlights, the commission outlined its major initiatives and achievements, which included protecting consumer privacy, both online and off, as well as challenging deceptive advertising and marketing practices such as health claims made by food marketers (Exhibit 20–13). Over the next several years the FTC is expected to increase its efforts to enforce federal privacy laws, particularly in the expanding world of smartphones and mobile apps.[78] The commission will continue to be the primary regulator of advertising and marketing practices in the United States, although the direction of the FTC is likely to be influenced by the political party of the presidential administration.

While the FTC is the major regulator of advertising for products sold in interstate commerce, several other federal agencies and departments also regulate advertising and promotion.

## Additional Federal Regulatory Agencies

**The Federal Communications Commission** The FCC, founded in 1934 to regulate broadcast communication, has jurisdiction over the radio, television, telephone, and telegraph industries. The FCC has the authority to license broadcast stations as well as to remove a license or deny renewal to stations not operating in the public's interest. The FCC's authority over the airways gives it the power to control advertising content and to restrict what products and services can be advertised on radio and TV. The FCC can eliminate obscene and profane programs and/or messages and those it finds in poor taste. While the FCC can purge ads that are deceptive or misleading, it generally works closely with the FTC in the regulation of advertising.

Many of the FCC's rules and regulations for TV and radio stations have been eliminated or modified. The FCC no longer limits the amount of television time that can be devoted to commercials. (But in 1991, the Children's Television Act went into effect. The act limits advertising during children's programming to 10.5 minutes an hour on weekends and 12 minutes an hour on weekdays.)

Under the Reagan administration, the controversial Fairness Doctrine, which required broadcasters to provide time for opposing

**LO 20-3**

**EXHIBIT 20–13**
The FTC issues an annual highlights report on its activities and initiatives

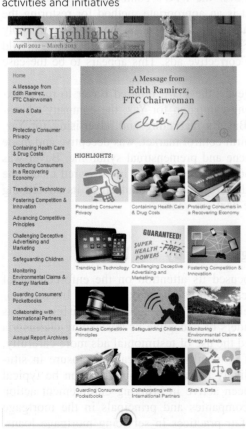

viewpoints on important issues, was repealed on the grounds that it was counterproductive. It was argued that the Fairness Doctrine actually reduced discussion of important issues because a broadcaster might be afraid to take on a paid controversial message in case it might be required to provide equal free exposure for opposing viewpoints. It was under this doctrine that the FCC required stations to run commercials about the harmful effects of smoking before passage of the Public Health Cigarette Smoking Act of 1970, which banned broadcast advertising of cigarettes. Many stations still provide time for opposing viewpoints on controversial issues as part of their public service requirement, not necessarily directly related to fairness.

The FCC has become very active in enforcing laws governing the airing of obscene, indecent, and profane material. For example, in 2004, the commission fined "shock jock" Howard Stern $495,000 for broadcasting indecent content and also levied fines against Clear Channel Communications, the nation's largest owner of radio stations, which carried his syndicated show. Concern over Stern's constant battling with the FCC led to a decision by Clear Channel to drop his daily radio show.[79] Stern subsequently signed a contract with Sirius Satellite radio, the subscription-based radio service, where his show is not subject to FCC regulations. The FCC also stepped up its enforcement of obscenity in the wake of the controversy following the baring of Janet Jackson's breast during the halftime show of the 2004 Super Bowl (Exhibit 20–14).[80] These incidents resulted in federal legislation dramatically increasing the amount both radio and television networks and stations can be fined for broadcast obscenity violations.

**EXHIBIT 20–14**
Janet Jackson's "wardrobe malfunction" during the 2004 Super Bowl halftime show led to greater enforcement of obscenity laws by the FCC

The FCC has also recently become involved in issues affecting the area of publicity and public relations. In 2005, the commission issued a missive insisting that broadcasters screen video news releases to ensure that they clearly disclose "the nature, source and sponsorship" of the material. The crackdown is designed to address a marketing practice whereby prepackaged promotional videos sent to TV stations by companies, organizations, and government agencies are represented as news stories.[81] And, as discussed in IMC Perspective 20–2, the FCC is also currently considering the regulation of the use of product placements in television shows.

**The Food and Drug Administration**   Now under the jurisdiction of the Department of Health and Human Services, the FDA has authority over the labeling, packaging, branding, ingredient listing, and advertising of packaged foods and drug products, as well as cosmetics. The FDA is authorized to require caution and warning labels on potentially hazardous products and also has limited authority over nutritional claims made in food advertising. This agency has the authority to set rules for promoting these products and the power to seize food and drugs on charges of false and misleading advertising.

Like the FTC, the Food and Drug Administration has become a very aggressive regulatory agency in recent years. The FDA has cracked down on a number of commonly used descriptive terms it believes are often abused in the labeling and advertising of food products—for example, *natural, light, no cholesterol, fat free,* and *organic.* The FDA has also become tougher on nutritional claims implied by brand names that might send a misleading message to consumers. For example, Great Foods of America was not permitted to continue using the HeartBeat trademark under which it sold most of its foods. The FDA argued the trademark went too far in implying the foods have special advantages for the heart and overall health.

Many changes in food labeling are a result of the Nutritional Labeling and Education Act, which Congress passed in 1990. Under this law the FDA established legal definitions for a wide range of terms (such as *low fat, light,* and *reduced calories*) and required straightforward labels for all foods beginning in early 1994

CHAPTER 20

# IMC Perspective 20–2 > > >

## Product Placements May Face Regulation

Product placements are nearly as old as television itself; they date back to the early days of TV when the hosts of popular shows such as *Milton Berle's Texaco Star Theater* and *Mutual of Omaha's Wild Kingdom* promoted the sponsor's products. During his tenure as host of *General Electric Theater* from 1954 to 1962, future U.S. president Ronald Reagan commonly plugged the show's sponsor in introductions, segues, and closing comments by delivering a friendly message about the company that usually ended with the tagline "Progress is our most important product." The mentioning of these companies was never considered a problem as they sponsored the production of the program and they were very aboveboard in promoting themselves. However, the number of product placements has increased dramatically over the years and the way brands are integrated into TV shows has also changed, which has led to concern over the practice by various consumer advocacy groups.

Unlike some countries, the United States does not prohibit product placements in the broadcast or motion picture industries. However, the use of undisclosed commercial messages in broadcasting has been regulated for more than 75 years as section 317 of the Communications Act of 1934, which requires broadcasters to disclose "any money, service or valuable consideration" that is paid to, or promised to, or charged by the broadcaster in exchange for product placements. However, broadcasters do not have to disclose product placements when they are offered without charge or for a nominal fee. The Federal Communications Commission (FCC) is the governmental agency that has the responsibility to prescribe the appropriate rules and regulations needed to carry out the sponsorship identification requirements. The FCC has basically interpreted the purpose of section 317 to be that the viewers in the TV audience must be clearly informed that what they are viewing has been paid for and that the entity paying for the broadcast must be clearly identifiable.

While there are a number of requirements and conditions associated with section 317, broadcasters usually have been considered in compliance with the regulation by placing an announcement in the credits at the beginning or end of the program stating that "promotional consideration paid for by (name of sponsor)" which remains on the screen long enough to be read or heard by the average viewer. This single disclosure has been the common practice in the industry, but a number of consumer groups have argued that more stringent regulation is needed. They argue that product placements have become more prevalent and also steal their in nature as marketers work with producers of TV shows to integrate their brands into their programs. Product placements have definitely become more ubiquitous according to numbers from Nielsen IAG, which tracks the number of show segments in which a brand placement appears. The television programs with the most product placements include *American Idol*, *The Biggest Loser*, *Celebrity Apprentice*, *Dancing with the Stars*, and *X Factor* while the top brands with TV product placements are AT&T, Coca-Cola, Apple, and Ford. Many of these programs have between 10 to 15 product placements per show.

Although the FCC has enforcement authority against certain forms of product placement, some consumer advocacy groups have argued that more regulation of the practice is needed. Those expressing concern over product placements range from consumer advocacy groups to pediatricians who seek to protect children from the promotion of sugary cereals. One of the leading critics of product placement is Commercial Alert, a nonprofit organization co-founded by consumer activist Ralph Nader, which argues that product placements are inherently deceptive because so many viewers do not realize they are, in fact, advertisements. Another activist group that opposes the product placements is Free Press. Corie Wright, an attorney and policy advisor for the group, argues that the practice is deceptive, stating that "product placements don't allow us to have the usual veil of skepticism we have when we watch a standard commercial."

Critics are concerned not just by the prevalence of products appearing in shows but also by the various forms of integration whereby brands are actually written into plotlines such as a *30 Rock* episode where Alec Baldwin sang the praises of Cisco teleconferencing equipment. In 2012 the show's producers and the NBC ad-sales staff reached out to Kraft regarding a live episode celebrating the history of live TV that was in the offing and their desire to use a sponsor in a sketch that was around in the medium's early days. A product

(Exhibit 20–15). In its current form the act applies only to food labels, but it may soon affect food advertising as well. The FTC would be asked to ensure that food ads comply with the new FDA standards.

The FDA has also become increasing active in policing health-related claims for food products. General Mills received a warning letter from the FDA for violations stemming from claims the company has been making that eating Cheerios cereal can reduce cholesterol by 4 to 6 percent in six weeks. The FDA charged that the claims placement deal was signed whereby Kraft cheese "singles" got a mention in a fictional *Kraft Product Placement Comedy Hour* during which the brand was touted as "the cheese that won World War II." The first ad in the next commercial break was for, no surprise, Kraft Singles.

Critics argue that the promotion of brands is no longer confined to the commercial breaks and that commercials and content are becoming one and the same and difficult to distinguish from one another. Some are calling on the FCC to require the TV networks to disclose product placements by using some form of onscreen notification system. Proposals range from requiring programs to run text along the bottom of the screen when a product appears in a scene, to using a flashing red light to alert viewers that a marketer is promoting a product. Some point to a system that is being used in the United Kingdom, which began allowing product placements for the first time in 2011 after the European Union approved their use in 2009 but left it up to the individual countries to make their own decisions. Regulators in the UK require the use of an onscreen symbol, the form of a large *P* at the beginning and end of programs to alert audiences to the paid product placements that are embedded in the shows. The logo must appear for a minimum of three seconds at the start and end of a program so that viewers know that the show contains product placement. It must also appear after commercial breaks before the return to the program.

In 2008 the FCC published a Notice of Inquiry and a Notice of Proposed Rulemaking to seek public comment on the call for more stringent regulations. The FCC is proposing more frequent and more obvious disclosures during programming with product placement, extension of product integration regulations to cable television, and additional restrictions for children's programming. While little has been done thus far, the television industry is already up in arms as are the marketers who use product placements. Subway's chief marketing officer opposes disclosures except at the end of a program arguing that "we'd rather seem like a natural part of the show rather than punch the viewer in the nose with a message like, 'Hey, this is paid for.'" Producers

of television programs as well as the major broadcast and cable networks are also concerned because paid product placements are an important source of revenue that help underwrite the costs of TV shows. Marketers also view product placements as a way to deliver branding messages to consumers who are becoming more difficult to reach during commercial breaks, particularly when they can record a show on a DVR and fast-forward through the commercials when watching it.

Proponents of product placements also point to the fact that the FTC, which has broad jurisdiction over advertising practices, has declined to regulate their use. The FTC position has been that it has no basis for doing so since product placements rarely make objective, material claims about a product when used within a show. The FTC has also stated that it would be difficult to develop a "one-size-fits-all" rule or guide that could effectively regulate product placements. Proponents note that the FTC's position supports their argument that further restrictions on product placement are unnecessary since they are not causing any injury to consumers.

Ultimately, it may be consumers who decide the fate of product placements. The time may come when we yearn for a return to the traditional model of television whereby ads appear during commercial breaks rather than having brands appearing in shows or being integrated into the plotlines. However, until then, it is likely that marketers will continue to look for clever ways to integrate their brands into the TV shows and leave it up to the consumers to figure out why they are there.

Sources: Brian Steinberg, "How '30 Rock' Pitched Kraft on Product Placement in Rare Outreach," *Advertising Age*, http://adage.com/article/tuning-in/30-rock-pitched-kraft-product-placement/234486/; Torin Douglas, "Product Placement Ban on British TV Lifted," *BBC News*, February 28, 2011, www.bbc.co.uk/news/uk-12593061; Brian Steinberg, "Don't Like Product Placement? Here's Why It's Your Fault," *Advertising Age*, February 11, 2010, http://adage.com/print?article_id=142069; Daniel Hertzberg, "Blasting Away at Product Placement," *Bloomberg Businessweek*, October 26, 2010, p. 60; Richard J. Wegener, *Product Placement & Government Regulation: FCC vs. FTC*, paper presented at Promotional Marketing Association's 30th Annual Promotion Marketing Conference, November 20, 2008.

made for the product based on clinical studies would make it a drug, not a food, because it is intended for use in the prevention, mitigation, and treatment of disease. General Mills has been working with the FDA to resolve the issue as the cholesterol-reduction claims are an important part of the brand's positioning and used as the basis for much of its advertising.[82] However, the company did remove the specific cholesterol reduction claim and replaced it with a more general statement that the toasted oats "can help reduce cholesterol" and "along with a diet low in saturated

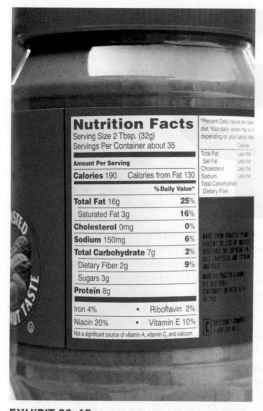

**EXHIBIT 20–15**

The Nutritional Labeling and Education Act requires that labels be easy for consumers to understand

fat and cholesterol may reduce the risk of heart disease."[83] In recent years the FDA has issued complaints against a number of food companies for violation of the federal Food, Drug, and Cosmetic Act. The violations include unauthorized health or nutrient-content claims, and unauthorized use of words such as *healthy,* which have strict, regulated definitions. In a letter issued to food companies the FDA commissioner noted, "Today, consumers' ready access to reliable information about the calorie and nutrient content of food is even more important, given the prevalence of obesity and diet-related diseases in the United States."[84]

Another regulatory area where the FDA has been heavily involved is the advertising and promotion of tobacco products. In 1996, President Bill Clinton signed an executive order declaring that nicotine is an addictive drug and giving the FDA broad jurisdiction to regulate cigarettes and smokeless tobacco. Many of the regulations resulting from this order were designed to keep teenagers from smoking.[85] However, the tobacco industry immediately appealed the order. While continuing to fight its legal battle with the federal government over the FDA regulations, the tobacco makers did agree to settle lawsuits brought by 46 states against the industry in late 1998 by signing the Master Settlement Agreement. This settlement was considered a better deal for the tobacco industry, as many of the onerous cigarette marketing restrictions contained in the original FDA proposal settlement were missing. The agreement allows large outdoor signs at retailers, whereas the original proposal banned all outdoor ads. The original deal banned all use of humans and cartoons in ads, while the current settlement bans only cartoons and even permits their use on cigarette packs. And while the original proposal eliminated sports sponsorships, the current agreement allows each company to continue one national sponsorship.[86]

An important provision of the Master Settlement Agreement was that the tobacco companies agreed not to target youth (those under the age of 18) in the advertising, promotion, and marketing of tobacco products either directly or indirectly. However, over the past several years there has been considerable debate over whether tobacco companies are complying with the agreement. Much of this debate centers on what is called the 15 percent rule, under which the tobacco companies voluntarily pledged not to advertise in magazines that have more than 15 percent of their readers under the age of 18. Some major tobacco companies such as Philip Morris have stopped advertising in magazines that have a substantial number of youth readers, such as *People, Sports Illustrated, Spin,* and *Rolling Stone.* However, other tobacco companies still advertise in these publications, and it appears that there remains a number of battles to fight in the war over the marketing and advertising of cigarettes.[87]

In 2000, the United States Supreme Court ruled that the Food and Drug Administration did not have the authority to regulate tobacco as a drug and that Congress would have to specifically enact legislation to allow the FDA to regulate tobacco. As a result, all FDA tobacco regulations were dropped. However, in June 2009 Congress passed a tobacco-control bill giving the FDA sweeping new powers over the packaging, manufacturing, and marketing of tobacco products, and it was signed into law by President Obama shortly thereafter. The Family Smoking Prevention and Tobacco Control Act calls for restrictions on marketing and sales to youths, including a ban on all outdoor tobacco advertising within 1,000 feet of schools and playgrounds; a ban on all remaining tobacco-brand sponsorships of sports and entertainment events; a ban on free giveaways of nontobacco products with the purchase of a tobacco product; a limit on advertising in publications with significant teen readership as well as limiting outdoor and point-of-sale advertising, except in adult-only facilities, to black-and-white ads only; and a restriction on ads on vending machines and self-service displays to adult-only facilities.[88]

Immediately following the passage of the landmark legislation, six tobacco companies along with several other entities, including the Association of National Advertisers and the American Civil Liberties Union, filed a lawsuit in federal court challenging the constitutionality of the new law. The suit argues that the marketing and advertising restrictions laid out in the bill fail to comply with free-speech protections provided by the First Amendment.[89] In January 2010, the federal court ruled that the ban on the use of colors and illustrations does indeed violate the First Amendment, but upheld the remaining parts of the new law. While additional appeals by the tobacco companies are expected, the new law will have a significant impact on the marketing and advertising of tobacco products.

A number of consumer advocacy groups as well as health departments in many states run ads warning consumers against the dangers of smoking and tobacco-related diseases. For example, the American Legacy Foundation, which was established as part of the 1998 tobacco settlement and is dedicated to reducing tobacco use, has run a number of hard-hitting ads warning consumers of the risk of smoking. One of the most successful programs developed by the ALF has been truth®, which was launched in 2000 and is the largest national youth smoking prevention campaign. Truth® exposes the tactics of the tobacco industry, the truth about addiction, the health effects and consequences of smoking, and is designed to allow teens to make informed choices about tobacco use by giving them the facts about the industry and its products. Truth® is a fully integrated campaign which includes advertising in media that are popular with youth, a summer travel tour that allows teens to engage firsthand with the campaign, and a website (www.thetruth.com) that contains a number of distinctive interactive elements (Exhibit 20–16). IMC Perspective 20–3 discusses how funding for the American Legacy Foundation has been reduced significantly in recent years as a result of a provision in the Master Settlement Agreement regarding the collective market share of the four major tobacco companies. It also discusses how some countries are now requiring graphic images on cigarette packs as a way to deter smoking and the possibility of this practice spreading to other markets.

Another area where the Food and Drug Administration has become more involved is the advertising of prescription drugs. Tremendous growth in direct-to-consumer (DTC) drug advertising has occurred since the FDA issued new guidelines making it easier for pharmaceutical companies to advertise prescription drugs to consumers. In 2007, Congress passed legislation giving the FDA more power to regulate DTC drug advertising. The bill gives the FDA the power to require drug companies to submit TV ads for review before they run, but it can only recommend changes, not require them. The bill also granted the FDA the power to impose fines on a drug company if its ads are found to be false and misleading. The fines can amount to $250,000 a day for the first violation in any three-year period and up to $5,000 for any subsequent violation.[90] In 2009, Pfizer agreed to pay $2.3 billion to settle the largest fraudulent health care marketing case in history. The government accused Pfizer of making false and misleading claims of safety and efficacy to promote Bextra for unapproved uses and for dosages above the approved level from 2002 through April 2005. Pfizer also was forced to stopping running TV commercials for its blockbuster drug Lipitor after the government and other critics charged that the ad misrepresented the credentials of Dr. Robert Jarvik, who endorsed

**EXHIBIT 20–16**
truth® has been a very effective youth smoking prevention campaign

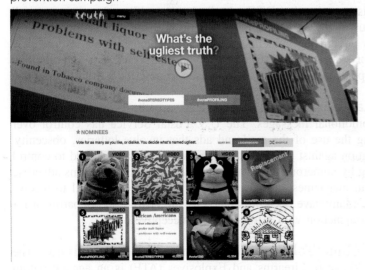

# IMC Perspective 20-3 > > >

## The Never-Ending Battle against Smoking Gets Graphic

Federal government agencies, such as the Centers for Disease Control and Prevention and the Food and Drug Administration, as well as public health agencies in nearly every state have been working to deter people from smoking for decades. In addition to the efforts of federal and state agencies, a myriad of public health groups have been attacking smokers from every angle, including levying heavy taxes on cigarettes; using graphic ads to depict the risks and consequences of smoking; showing how nonsmokers are impacted by secondhand smoke; banning smoking in public places; and attaching a social stigma to those who continue to smoke in hopes of getting them to quit. The efforts of all these initiatives to deter smokers are summarized quite well by *Advertising Age* journalist Matthew Creamer, who writes: "To be a smoker in 2012 is not only to ignore the biological reality that the habit will knock years off your life but also shrug off the cultural stigmas—the dwindling number of smoke-friendly public places, the dirty looks—and the fact that heavily-taxed smokes are priced at a point only a one-percenter could easily afford."

While most nonsmokers might wonder why anyone would ever take up the habit, the reality is that smoking is an addictive behavior and is still a major public health problem in most countries; it costs billions of dollars to treat diseases that result from prolonged tobacco use. Smoking began to decline steadily in the United States following the initial warnings by the Surgeon General in 1964 and the requirement to put warning labels on cigarette packages in 1969. The percentage of adults who smoke declined to around 20 percent over the next 40 years, but since 2005 the changes have been minimal. The all-important youth smoking rates have also declined; a Monitoring the Future Survey released in December 2012 showed that among 12th graders, the smoking rate has declined from a peak of 36.5 percent in 1997 to 17.1 percent in 2012.

Many experts attribute the decline in smoking to the barrage of antismoking ads that consumers have been exposed to over the years; there have been a number of studies showing that these ads are effective. A study published in the *American Journal of Preventive Medicine* did a cost-effectiveness study of the critically acclaimed truth® campaign, which focuses on deterring smoking among youth, and found that $324 million spent on the campaign averted about $1.9 billion in medical costs. The truth® campaign, along with many other antismoking advertising efforts, was sponsored by the American Legacy Foundation, which was created in 1998 as part of the Master Settlement Agreement with the four major tobacco companies and given the charge to reduce tobacco use. However, the foundation's funding is just a fraction of what it was 10 years ago because the agreement required the big four tobacco companies that signed it to fund Legacy through 2003 only if their collective market share fell below 99.05 percent, which it did in 2001. Under the settlement, payments to states continue but only about 2 percent of the $25 billion goes to fight tobacco use as many budget-strapped states have cut back their antitobacco advertising programs.

Many public health experts are concerned that reductions in antismoking advertising efforts will make it difficult to continue to reduce tobacco use and the costs that come with it. Some experts argue that the FDA needs to do more to deter smoking and suggests that the agency look

---

the drug. The ad represented Jarvik as a medical expert, when most of his career was spent on the invention of the artificial heart.[91]

The FDA can also require that DTC ads disclose specific safety risks as well as clear, conspicuous, and neutral statements about any side effects. In 2009, the FDA published new advertising guidelines that caution companies not to downplay a drug's risks and/or side effects by using tactics to distract viewers such as loud music or using a typeface smaller than the one used to describe a drug's benefits.

**The U.S. Postal Service** Many marketers use the U.S. mail to deliver advertising and promotional messages. The U.S. Postal Service has control over advertising involving the use of the mail and ads that involve lotteries, obscenity, or fraud. The regulation against fraudulent use of the mail has been used to control deceptive advertising by numerous direct-response advertisers. These firms advertise on TV or radio or in magazines and newspapers and use the U.S. mail to receive orders and payment. Many have been prosecuted by the Post Office Department for use of the mail in conjunction with a fraudulent or deceptive offer.

**Bureau of Alcohol, Tobacco, Firearms and Explosives** The Bureau of Alcohol, Tobacco, Firearms and Explosives (ATF) is an agency within the Treasury Department that enforces laws, develops regulations, and is responsible to what is being done in other countries to deal with the problem. For example, in late 2012 Australia's high court upheld the Plain Packaging Act, making it the first country to ban brand logos on all tobacco packages. The ruling requires tobacco and cigarettes to be sold in plain green packages that show large, nauseatingly graphic images such as diseased lungs, gangrenous limbs, and rotting teeth. Brand names must be printed in a uniform font on a background legally mandated as "drab dark brown." The goal of the new law is to show that the health consequences of smoking are horrific and to dissuade consumers, particularly young ones, from making a cigarette purchase. The legislation is also designed to take away the brand identity and image of cigarette brands such as Marlboro which have been built through years of advertising and other forms of marketing.

Australia is not the only country that has turned to cigarette packages as a way to deter smoking, although its law is the first barring almost all branding. Mandatory picture warnings were first introduced in Canada in 2001 and are now used in 47 countries, including the United Kingdom, Brazil, and Turkey. Legislation requiring the use of graphic images on cigarette packages was supposed to go into effect in the United States in October 2012 but was challenged by the tobacco companies on First

Amendment grounds and is unlikely to be resolved until decided on by the U.S. Supreme Court.

Australia's new law is being closely watched by tobacco companies as well as antismoking advocates in countries around the world who are hoping for a domino effect whereby it spreads to other countries if it proves to be effective in deterring smoking. However, tobacco companies are not the only ones watching what happens down under; there is concern that it could set a precedent that might eventually spread to other industries where there are public health concerns such as alcohol or food and beverages that are high in sugar. Marketers who have invested billions of dollars to build their brands over the years are not likely to sit back and watch this equity be taken away from them. It will be very interesting to see what the future holds with regard to restriction on the marketing of tobacco as well as many other products in the United States as well as other countries.

Sources: David Fickling, "The Marlboro Man's Grisly Replacement," *Bloomberg Businessweek*, October 12, 2012, pp. 25–26; Rich Thomaselli, "Will Australia's Cigarette Branding Ban Spread beyond Borders, Tobacco?" *Advertising Age*, August 19, 2012, http://adage.com/article/news/australia-s-cigarette-brand-ban-prompt-domino-effect/236761/; Matthew Creamer, "Anti-Smoking Campaigns Work, So Don't Quit Now," *Advertising Age*, January 16, 2012, pp. 1, 18–19.

for tax collection for the liquor industry. ATF regulates and controls the advertising of alcoholic beverages. The agency determines what information can be provided in ads as well as what constitutes false and misleading advertising. It is also responsible for including warning labels on alcohol advertising and banning the use of active athletes in beer commercials. ATF can impose strong sanctions for violators. The advertising of alcoholic beverages has become a very controversial issue, with many consumer and public interest groups calling for a total ban on the advertising of beer, wine, and liquor.

## The Lanham Act

While most advertisers rely on self-regulatory mechanisms and the FTC to deal with deceptive or misleading advertising by their competitors, many companies are filing lawsuits against competitors they believe are making false claims. One piece of federal legislation that has become increasingly important in this regard is the Lanham Act. This act was originally written in 1947 as the Lanham Trade-Mark Act to protect words, names, symbols, or other devices adopted to identify and distinguish a manufacturer's products. The **Lanham Act** was amended to encompass false advertising by prohibiting "any false description or representation including words or other symbols tending falsely to describe or represent the same." While the FTC Act did not give individual advertisers the opportunity to sue a competitor for deceptive advertising, civil suits are permitted under the Lanham Act.

More and more companies are using the Lanham Act to sue competitors for their advertising claims, particularly since comparative advertising has become so common. Wilkinson Sword and its advertising agency were found guilty of false advertising and ordered to pay $953,000 in damages to the Gillette Co. Wilkinson had run TV and print ads claiming its Ultra Glide razor and blades produced shaves "six times smoother" than Gillette's Atra Plus blades. This case marked the first time an agency was held liable for damages in connection with false claims made in a client's advertising.[92] Although the agency was later found not liable, the case served as a sobering reminder to agencies that they can be drawn into litigation over advertising they create for their clients. To deal with this problem, many agencies insist on indemnification clauses in contracts with their clients.

Suing competitors for false claims was made even easier with passage of the TradeMark Law Revision Act of 1988. According to this law, anyone is vulnerable to civil action who "misrepresents the nature, characteristics, qualities, or geographical origin of his or her or another person's goods, services, or commercial activities." This wording closed a loophole in the Lanham Act, which prohibited only false claims about one's own goods or services. While many disputes over comparative claims are never contested or are resolved through the NAD, more companies are turning to lawsuits for several reasons: the broad information discovery powers available under federal civil procedure rules, the speed with which a competitor can stop the offending ad through a preliminary injunction, and the possibility of collecting damages.[93] However, companies do not always win their lawsuits. Under the Lanham Act you are required to prove five elements to win a false advertising lawsuit containing a comparative claim.[94] You must prove that:

- False statements have been made about the advertiser's product or your product.
- The ads actually deceived or had the tendency to deceive a substantial segment of the audience.
- The deception was "material" or meaningful and is likely to influence purchasing decisions.
- The falsely advertised products or services are sold in interstate commerce.
- You have been or likely will be injured as a result of the false statements, by either loss of sales or loss of goodwill.

Over the years there has been a significant increase in the use of comparative advertising, and it has resulted in more and more companies' suing one another under the Lanham Act. The Campbell Soup Co. advertised that its Prego brand of spaghetti sauce was thicker than Van Den Bergh Food's Ragu brand. Van Den Bergh sued to have Campbell's comparative ads for Prego halted but lost the case in district court as well as in appeals court. Campbell capitalized on its victory by creating an ad based on it. The ad tweaked Ragu by showing snippets of the comparison ads and then a shot of Prego with a breadstick standing up in the sauce (Exhibit 20–17). The tagline was, "Ragu took us to court. We made our case stand. Just like our breadstick." The two companies finally declared a truce in the spaghetti sauce wars in late 1999.[95]

In another suit brought under the Lanham Act, PepsiCo sued rival Coca-Cola over the advertising for a new version of the latter's Powerade brand sports drink. The issue in the case was an ad campaign promoting Powerade Ion4 as the "complete sports drink" and better than PepsiCo's Gatorade because it contains four electrolytes while Gatorade contains only two. PepsiCo argued that the Powerade superiority claims were false as there was no evidence that the rival brand was better than Gatorade, and that Powerade had the

**EXHIBIT 20–17**
Comparative claims involving the Prego and Ragu brands of spaghetti sauce resulted in a lawsuit

extra electrolytes in only trace amounts anyway. The case ended up in court, where a federal judge denied PepsiCo's request that Coca-Cola stop running the comparative ads (because it had already done so). The judge also ruled that the company had not presented sufficient evidence that brand equity or sales of Gatorade had suffered or that Powerade's campaign had caused irreparable injury to PepsiCo. However, the judge did find evidence of possible misconduct by Coca-Cola for referring to Gatorade as incomplete despite concerns from one of its research scientists about the claim. Coca-Cola dropped the comparative claims for Powerade and both sides claimed victory in the case.[96]

**EXHIBIT 20–18**

TaylorMade ran this ad to challenge rival Callaway's claim of having the number one driver on the PGA Tour

Marketers using comparative ads have to carefully consider whether their messages have the potential to mislead consumers or may overstate their brand's performance relative to that of competitors. In some cases, a competitor may run an ad challenging a rival's claim if they feel that it misleading or is not based on accurate information. For example, Exhibit 20–18 shows an ad run recently by the TaylorMade Golf Company challenging rival Callaway's claim of its driver being the number one driver used on the Professional Golf Association tour. The ad provides information to substantiate TaylorMade's claim that it is the number one driver on tour. A study by Michael J. Barone and his colleagues provides a framework for developing measures to assess the misleading effects that may arise from various types of comparative advertising.[97]

# STATE REGULATION

In addition to the various federal rules and regulations, advertisers must also concern themselves with numerous state and local controls. An important early development in state regulation of advertising was the adoption in 44 states of the *Printers Ink* model statutes as a basis for advertising regulation. These statutes were drawn up in 1911 by *Printers Ink,* for many years the major trade publication of the advertising industry. Many states have since modified the original statutes and adopted laws similar to those of the Federal Trade Commission Act for dealing with false and misleading advertising. For example, in California, the Business and Professional Code prohibits "unlawful, unfair, or fraudulent" business practices and "unfair, deceptive, untrue, or misleading advertising."

In addition to recognizing decisions by the federal courts regarding false or deceptive practices, many states have special controls and regulations governing the advertising of specific industries or practices. As the federal government became less involved in the regulation of national advertising during the 1980s, many state attorneys general (AGs) began to enforce state laws regarding false or deceptive advertising. For example, the attorneys general in New York and Texas initiated investigations of Kraft ads claiming the pasteurized cheese used in Cheez Whiz was real cheese.[98] The well-publicized "monster truck" deceptive advertising case involving Volvo and its advertising agency that occurred in the early 90s was initiated by the attorney general's office in the state of Texas.[99]

LO 20-3

The **National Association of Attorneys General (NAAG)** moved against a number of national advertisers as a result of inactivity by the FTC during the Reagan administration. In 1987, the NAAG developed enforcement guidelines on airfare advertising that were adopted by more than 40 states. The NAAG has also been involved in other regulatory areas, including car-rental price advertising as well as advertising dealing with nutrition and health claims in food ads. The NAAG's foray into regulating national advertising raises the issue of whether the states working together can create and implement uniform national advertising standards that will, in effect, supersede federal authority. An American Bar Association panel concluded that the Federal Trade Commission is the proper regulator of national advertising and recommended the state AGs focus on practices that harm consumers within a single state.[100] This report also called for cooperation between the FTC and the state attorneys general. In recent years state attorneys general have been working with the FTC and other federal government agencies on false advertising cases. For example, 27 state attorneys general worked with the FDA in the deceptive advertising case for Bayer's Yaz birth control pill that resulted in corrective advertising. A group of state attorneys general also worked with the FTC in a recent case against the makers of Airborne, a multivitamin and herbal supplement whose labels and ads falsely claimed that the product cures and prevents colds. Airborne had been making the false claims since 1999 and agreed to refund the money to consumers who had bought the product, as part of a $23.3 million class action settlement.[101]

Advertisers are concerned about the trend toward increased regulation of advertising at the state and local levels because it could mean that national advertising campaigns would have to be modified for every state or municipality. Yet the FTC takes the position that businesses that advertise and sell nationwide need a national advertising policy. While the FTC recognizes the need for greater cooperation with the states, the agency believes regulation of national advertising should be its responsibility.[102] Just in case, the advertising industry is still keeping a watchful eye on changes in advertising rules, regulations, and policies at the state and local levels.

# REGULATION OF OTHER PROMOTIONAL AREAS

So far we've focused on the regulation of advertising. However, other elements of the promotional mix also come under the surveillance of federal, state, and local laws and various self-regulatory bodies. This section examines some of the rules, regulations, and guidelines that affect sales promotion, direct marketing, and marketing on the Internet.

## Sales Promotion

Both consumer- and trade-oriented promotions are subject to various regulations. The Federal Trade Commission regulates many areas of sales promotion through the Marketing Practices Division of the Bureau of Consumer Protection. Many promotional practices are also policed by state attorneys general and local regulatory agencies. Various aspects of trade promotion, such as allowances, are regulated by the Robinson-Patman Act, which gives the FTC broad powers to control discriminatory pricing practices.

**Contests and Sweepstakes**  As noted in Chapter 16, numerous legal considerations affect the design and administration of contests and sweepstakes, and these promotions are regulated by a number of federal and state agencies. There are two important considerations in developing contests (including games) and sweepstakes. First, marketers must be careful to ensure their contest or sweepstakes is not classified as a *lottery,* which is considered a form of gambling and violates the Federal Trade Commission Act and many state and local laws. A promotion is considered a lottery if a prize is offered, if winning a prize depends on chance and not skill, and if the participant is required to give up something of value in order to participate. The latter requirement is referred to as *consideration* and is the basis on which most contests, games, and sweepstakes avoid being considered lotteries.

**EXHIBIT 20–19**

Marketers are required to provide consumers with full details of a contest or sweepstakes

Generally, as long as consumers are not required to make a purchase to enter a contest or sweepstakes, consideration is not considered to be present and the promotion is not considered a lottery.

The second important requirement in the use of contests and sweepstakes is that the marketer provide full disclosure of the promotion. Regulations of the FTC, as well as many state and local governments, require marketers using contests, games, and sweepstakes to make certain all of the details are given clearly and to follow prescribed rules to ensure the fairness of the game.[103] Disclosure requirements include the exact number of prizes to be awarded and the odds of winning, the duration and termination dates of the promotion, and the availability of lists of winners of various prizes (Exhibit 20–19). The FTC also has specific rules governing the way games and contests are conducted, such as requirements that game pieces be randomly distributed, that a game not be terminated before the distribution of all game pieces, and that additional pieces not be added during the course of a game.

A number of states have responded to concerns over fraud on the part of some contest and sweepstakes operators and have either passed or tightened prize notification laws, requiring fuller disclosure of rules, odds, and the retail value of prizes. And many of the states are following through with tougher enforcement of these laws. For example, New York passed a law requiring that the odds of winning a sweepstakes "must be conspicuously disclosed in the same type face, size and boldness and adjacent to the most prominent listing of the prizes on the front of the first page of the offer." The state law also prohibits statements that someone is a "winner" or that his or her name "has been selected" when no prize has been won. The law carries a fine of $1,000 per incident, which could be $1,000 per letter received by New York residents. Some of the most ambitious legal actions are taking place in individual states, where prosecutors are taking sweepstakes and contest companies to court for misleading and deceptive practices.[104]

Many marketers are now using the Internet and social media sites such as Facebook, YouTube, and Twitter to run their contests and sweepstakes. This is creating additional issues that marketers must consider such as whether automated or repetitive electronic submissions will be accepted, how the contest website will detect violations, and restrictions on length, size, or format of content submitted. If the contest or sweepstakes is being marketed using e-mail, marketers must comply with online-data-privacy laws as well as the Can Spam Act, which is discussed later in the chapter. If the online entry form collects personal information from persons under the age of 13 (including e-mail addresses), marketers must comply with the Children's Online Privacy Protection Act.[105]

Marketers that post audiovisual entries on YouTube or feature a contest on Facebook or Twitter must comply with each site's guidelines for on-site promotions. For contests that involve user-generated content, such as photos, videos, or short stories, the rules must contain specific language granting the company the necessary rights and licenses to use the content. Marketers that want to use the content for marketing purposes should obtain a liability and publicity release from every individual who appears in the photos or videos that are displayed on their website.[106] The Internet and social media provide marketers with a greater opportunity to promote their contests and sweepstakes to specific target audiences and make the administration of these promotions more efficient and cost-effective. However, they also bring a host of additional legal factors that must be considered by companies.

**Chapter 20** REGULATION OF ADVERTISING AND PROMOTION    723

**Premiums**   Another sales promotion area subject to various regulations is the use of premiums. A common problem associated with premiums is misrepresentation of their value. Marketers that make a premium offer should list its value as the price at which the merchandise is usually sold on its own. Marketers must also be careful in making premium offers to special audiences such as children. While premium offers for children are legal, their use is controversial; many critics argue that they encourage children to request a product for the premium rather than for its value. The Children's Advertising Review Unit has voluntary guidelines concerning the use of premium offers. These guidelines note that children have difficulty distinguishing a product from a premium. If product advertising contains a premium message, care should be taken that the child's attention is focused primarily on the product. The premium message should be clearly secondary. Conditions of a premium offer should be stated simply and clearly. "Mandatory" statements and disclosures should be stated in terms that can be understood by the child audience.[107] However, a recent study of children's advertising commissioned by CARU found the single most prevalent violation involved devoting virtually an entire commercial message to information about a premium. CARU guidelines state that advertising targeted to children must emphasize the product rather than the premium offer.[108]

**Trade Allowances**   Marketers using various types of trade allowances must be careful not to violate any stipulations of the Robinson-Patman Act, which prohibits price discrimination. Certain sections of the Robinson-Patman Act prohibit a manufacturer from granting wholesalers and retailers various types of promotional allowances and/or payments unless they are made available to all customers on proportionally equal terms.[109] Another form of trade promotion regulated by the Robinson-Patman Act is vertical cooperative advertising. The FTC monitors cooperative advertising programs to ensure that co-op funds are made available to retailers on a proportionally equal basis and that the payments are not used as a disguised form of price discrimination.

As noted in Chapter 16, another trade promotion area where the FTC is becoming involved is the use of slotting fees or allowances paid to retailers for agreeing to handle a new product. In 1999, the Senate Committee on Small Business charged retailers in the grocery, drugstore, and computer software industries with illegally using slotting fees to lock out competitors and prevent consumers from having their choice of the best products. Packaged-goods marketers and retailers have argued that examining slotting fees alone is unfair since they are just part of a wide variety of inducements marketers use to secure the best shelf space. The FTC is investigating the use of slotting fees as anticompetitive weapons that make it difficult for small-size companies to secure retail shelf space.[110] In 2000, the FTC launched its first direct attack on slotting fees when it accused McCormick & Co., the leading spice maker, of offering discriminatory discounts on its products to several grocery chains. McCormick agreed to settle a complaint that the discounts were a way of paying some retailers disproportionately more in slotting fees than others. The FTC charged that the slotting fees were a way for McCormick to gain more shelf space at the expense of smaller rivals. The practice that was deemed illegal by the FTC is a standard way of doing business in the grocery trade as well as other industries, and some legal experts have argued that this case could impact the use of slotting fees in the future.[111]

**Direct Marketing**   As we saw in Chapter 14, direct marketing is growing rapidly. Many consumers now purchase products directly from companies in response to TV and print advertising or direct selling. The Federal Trade Commission enforces laws related to direct marketing, including mail-order offers, the use of 900 telephone numbers, and direct-response TV advertising. The U.S. Postal Service enforces laws dealing with the use of the mail to deliver advertising and promotional messages or receive payments and orders for items advertised in print or broadcast media.

A number of laws govern the use of mail-order selling. The FTC and the Postal Service police direct-response advertising closely to ensure the ads are not deceptive or misleading and do not misrepresent the product or service being offered. Laws also forbid mailing unordered merchandise to consumers, and rules govern the use of "negative option" plans whereby a company proposes to send merchandise to consumers and expects payment unless the consumer sends a notice of rejection or cancellation.[112] FTC rules also encourage direct marketers to ship ordered merchandise promptly. Companies that cannot ship merchandise within the time period stated in the solicitation (or 30 days if no time is stated) must give buyers the option to cancel the order and receive a full refund.[113]

Another area of direct marketing facing increased regulation is telemarketing. With the passage of the Telephone Consumer Protection Act of 1991, marketers who use telephones to contact consumers must follow a complex set of rules developed by the Federal Communications Commission. These rules require telemarketers to maintain an in-house list of residential telephone subscribers who do not want to be called. Consumers who continue to receive unwanted calls can take the telemarketer to state court for damages of up to $500. The rules also ban telemarketing calls to homes before 8:00 A.M. and after 9:00 P.M., automatic dialer calls, and recorded messages to emergency phones, health care facilities, and numbers for which the call recipient may be charged. They also ban unsolicited junk fax ads and require that fax transmissions clearly indicate the sender's name and fax number.[114]

The Federal Trade Commission has also been actively involved with the regulation of advertising that encourages consumers to call telephone numbers with a 900 prefix, whereupon they are automatically billed for the call. While there are many legitimate uses for 900-number technology, it has also been heavily used for sleazy sex operations, contest scams, and other unscrupulous activities.[115] One area of particular concern to the FTC has been ads targeting children and encouraging them to call 900 numbers. In 1993, the FTC issued its 900-Number Rule for advertising directed at children. The rule restricts advertisers from targeting children under the age of 12 with ads containing 900 numbers unless they provide a bona fide educational service. The rule also requires that 900-number ads directed at those under the age of 18 must contain a "clear and conspicuous" disclosure statement that requires the caller to have parental/guardian permission to complete the call. The rule also obligates advertisers to disclose the cost of the call and give the caller the opportunity to hang up without incurring any costs.[116]

The FTC enacted the 900-Number Rule under the provision that it would be reviewed within four years to consider its costs and benefits.[117] This review was undertaken and the rule was retained and revised, although under a new name. The name was changed to the Pay-Per-Call Rule, and in 1998 the rule was revised to give the FTC the authority to broaden its scope and add new provisions. Among other things, the new provisions combat telephone bill cramming, which is the placing of unauthorized charges on consumers' phone bills.[118]

In 2003, Congress approved a Federal Trade Commission proposal for the formation of a National Do Not Call Registry allowing consumers to opt out of most commercial telemarketing.[119] Consumers can place their home phone numbers, as well as personal cell phone numbers, on the National Do Not Call Registry (Exhibit 20–20). Commercial telemarketers must pay a fee to access the registry and generally are prohibited from calling the listed numbers. Telemarketers have three months to comply once a number goes on the list, and a consumer's registration lasts

**EXHIBIT 20–20**

The National Do Not Call Registry protects consumers from calls by telemarketers five years. Political and charitable solicitation calls are not affected by the regulation, and telemarketers can call consumers with whom they have an established relationship. Marketers face penalties of $11,000 per incident for calling someone on the list. The Federal Trade Commission, the Federal Communications Commission, and individual states are enforcing the National Do Not Call Registry, which contained move than 217 million phone numbers as of the end of 2012.[120]

The National Do Not Call Registry affects the direct-marketing industry as it greatly reduces the number of households that telemarketers can call. As might be expected, the direct-marketing industry is strongly opposed to the registry, arguing that it violates their First Amendment rights and, further, that such a program is not needed. The Direct Marketing Association (DMA), which is the primary trade group for the direct-marketing industry, has argued that consumers already have a number of do-not-call options. They can ask to be excluded from an individual company's telemarketing list at the same time they can sign up with state lists or pay $5 to sign up on the voluntary national list maintained by the Direct Marketing Association. The DMA argues that the national registry imposes more bureaucracy on the direct-marketing industry and that the same goal can be achieved by the industry itself with better education and enforcement.

The Direct Marketers Association and the American Teleservices Association, which represent callers, challenged the legality of the registry on the grounds that it took away their rights to First Amendment–protected speech and that it was excessive and poorly drafted, with competitive marketers forced to abide by different rules. However, in February 2004, the U.S. Court of Appeals upheld the registry's validity, ruling that it is a valid commercial speech regulation. The appellate court said that because the registry doesn't affect political or charitable calls and because there is a danger of abusive telemarketing and invasion of consumer privacy from telemarketers, the government has a right to regulate its use.[121]

Direct marketers have been adjusting their telemarketing strategies to deal with the restrictions imposed by the Do Not Call Registry. They are focusing more attention on generating leads through promotional efforts such as sweepstakes and direct-mail programs, prompting consumers to opt in and agree to receive calls from direct marketers.[122] Some industry experts as well as academics argue that the Do Not Call Registry may actually improve telemarketing practice and the general efficiency of the business because direct marketers must focus more attention on consumers who are receptive to receiving their telemarketing calls.[123] However, there is also concern that some companies are finding loopholes in the rules governing the Do Not Call Registry. For example, one technique that has emerged is the use of a marketing tool called a "lead card," which invites a recipient to mail a reply card for free information. However, the cards often fail to warn consumers that by sending a reply, they are giving up their right to avoid telephone solicitations from the sender—even if their phone numbers are listed on the Do Not Call list.[124]

Another tactic being used by some companies to avoid the Do Not Call Registry is to use sweepstakes entry forms as a way to harvest consumers' telephone numbers for telemarketing purposes. When done correctly, this may be a legitimate direct-marketing tool; however the FTC has cracked down on some companies that have violated Do Not Call regulations by calling phone numbers obtained via sweepstakes entry forms. Companies that want to collect telemarketing leads through a sweepstakes entry form must clearly and conspicuously disclose that their entry-form information will be used for telemarketing purposes and include a statement to be signed by consumers expressing agreement under the Do Not Call provision.[125]

The direct-marketing industry is also scrutinized by various self-regulatory groups, such as the Direct Marketing Association and the Direct Selling Association, that have specific guidelines and standards member firms are expected to adhere to and abide by. However, some critics argue that these self-regulatory groups are not doing

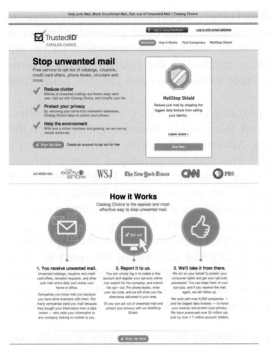

**EXHIBIT 20–21**

Catalog Choice offers consumers a way to opt out of receiving unwanted direct mail

**YTC 20–05**

**Catalog Choice**

youtube.com/10ebelch

enough to keep consumers from receiving unwanted marketing messages, such as calls from telemarketers and direct-mail offers and solicitations. Thus, it is likely that they will continue to call for more government intervention and regulations.

Direct mail is an area that has been under attack as many consumers are tired of seeing their mailboxes bulging with catalogs as well other forms of direct mail and want to take action. Some states have considered legislation that would create state-run do-not-mail registries that would allow consumers to keep unsolicited direct mail out of their mailboxes. However, none of the proposed do-not-mail bills have made it beyond the hearing stage and it may take years before any type of legislation is enacted. A number of advocacy groups are not waiting for the government to address the problem, though, and are taking steps to help consumers reduce the amount of unwanted direct mail they are receiving. Several of these initiatives have been started by groups that are interested in reducing the environmental impact created by the direct-mail industry.

One initiative having a significant impact in terms of reducing the amount of direct mail is Catalog Choice, which was launched in October 2007 with the mission of reducing the number of repeat and unsolicited catalog mailings, and promoting the adoption of sustainable industry best practices (Exhibit 20–21).[126] The company offers an online service that allows people to compile a list of catalogs, coupons, credit-card offers, and other types of direct mail they do not want to receive. The company then contacts the retailers with a request to take the person's name off their mailing list or makes a downloadable file available that merchants can then feed into their direct-mail database. Several hundred merchants and marketers have agreed to abide by the site's opt-out requests, including major companies such as Lands' End, Office Depot, and REI. In 2012 Catalog Choice was acquired by TrustedID, a company that delivers privacy, security, and reputation management services to proactively help protect against credit and identity theft—safeguarding individuals, families, and businesses.

## Marketing on the Internet

The rapid growth of the Internet as a marketing tool has created a new area of concern for regulators. The same consumer protection laws that apply to commercial activities in other media apply to online as well. The Federal Trade Commission Act, which prohibits "unfair or deceptive acts or practices," encompasses Internet advertising, marketing, and sales. Claims made in Internet ads or on websites must be substantiated, especially when they concern health, safety, or performance, and disclosures are required to prevent ads from being misleading and to ensure that consumers receive material information about the terms of a transaction. There are several areas of particular concern with regard to marketing on the Internet. These include privacy issues, online marketing to children, and the use of spam or unsolicited e-mails for commercial purposes.

The major privacy issue regarding the Internet that has emerged involves undisclosed profiling whereby Web marketers can profile a user on the basis of name, address, demographics, and online/offline purchasing data. Marketers have suggested that profiling offers them an opportunity to target specific niches and reach consumers with custom-tailored messages. However, the FTC has stated that Internet sites that claim they don't collect information but permit advertisers to surreptitiously profile viewer sites are violating consumer protection laws and are open to a charge of deception.[127] In 1999, DoubleClick, the company that is the leader in selling and managing online advertising as well as tracking Web

CHAPTER 20

**EXHIBIT 20-22**

The Network Advertising Initiative website provides consumers with information about online advertising practices

**YTC 20-06**

**COPPA**

youtube.com/10ebelch

users and now owned by Google, set off a controversy by connecting consumers' names, addresses, and other personal information with information it collects about where consumers go on the Internet. The controversy resulted in the company being investigated by the Federal Trade Commission and lawsuits being filed in some states.[128]

In response to the profiling controversy, companies that collect Internet usage data and information joined together under the banner of the Network Advertising Initiative (NAI) to develop a self-regulatory code.[129] The NAI has developed a set of privacy principles in conjunction with the Federal Trade Commission that provides consumers with explanations of Internet advertising practices and how the practices affect both consumers and the Internet itself. The NAI has also launched a website (www.networkadvertising.org) that provides consumers with information about online advertising practices and gives them the choice to opt out of targeted advertising delivered by NAI member companies (Exhibit 20–22). The privacy debate is likely to escalate, and it is expected that legislation will be introduced to force companies to seek consumers' approval before sharing personal information captured from their websites.

While various proposals are aimed at protecting the privacy rights of adults, one of the biggest concerns is over restricting marketers whose activities or websites are targeted at children. These concerns over online marketing to children led to the passage of the **Children's Online Privacy Protection Act (COPPA) of 1998**, which the FTC began enforcing in April 2000.[130] This act places tight restrictions on collecting information from children via the Internet and requires that websites directed at children and young teens have a privacy policy posted on their home page and areas of the site where information is collected. The law also requires websites aimed at children under age 13 to obtain parental permission to collect most types of personal information and to monitor chat rooms and bulletin boards to make sure children do not disclose personal information there. When the law was enacted in 2000, it was left to the FTC to determine how to obtain the required permission, and the FTC temporarily allowed websites to let parents simply return an e-mail to approve certain information. Since then no other solution to the permission issue has surfaced, and the FTC has made the solution permanent.[131] However, the issue continues to be an area of concern as many marketers close their websites to children under the age of 13, but children under this age will often lie about their ages to gain access to the sites. The prevalence of social media is adding to the problem as many young people want access to fan clubs, blogs, and other websites that allow online interaction.[132]

On July 1, 2013, the FTC began enforcing updates to the COPPA that are designed to bring the law in line with changes that have occurred in the market, including the explosive growth of mobile device usage among kids and the data collection that goes along with it. The changes include the categorization of geolocation information, photos, and videos as personal information, requiring parental consent before such data are collected on children under age 13. The changes also extended the COPPA to cover persistent device identifiers such as IP addresses and mobile device IDs that allow companies to track a user across various personal devices but do not cover mobile app stores.[133]

Concerns over consumer privacy have become a major issue among the government and various regulatory agencies such as the FTC.[134] The federal government is currently considering a number of privacy-related laws, many of which would have an impact on marketing and advertising over the Internet. The FTC has requested that marketers voluntarily step up the disclosures they make about data they collect and seek permission from consumers before tracking their Internet surfing behavior.[135] Many marketers adhere to the Digital Alliance Ad Choices program, which is a self-regulatory initiative that was implemented by the Advertising Self-Regulatory Council as part of its Internet Advertising Accountability Program discussed earlier in the chapter. However, critics have argued that the program only blocks behavioral ad targeting rather than actually stopping behavioral data collection. There continue to be calls for the FTC to oversee the development of a Do-Not-Track program that would prohibit websites or mobile app operators from compiling or disclosing personal data to third parties for targeted marketing purposes.[136]

Concerns over privacy have increased with the explosion in the popularity of social media sites such as Facebook, Twitter, and others. In June 2010 the FTC settled a complaint against Twitter charging it deceived consumers and put their privacy at risk by failing to safeguard their personal information, marking the agency's first such case against a social networking service. The FTC ordered Twitter to establish a security program subject to government monitoring for the next 10 years. Twitter agreed to the terms in exchange for the FTC not pursuing a civil lawsuit against the company.[137] Facebook has also announced significant changes to its privacy policies giving users more control over their content, reducing the amount of their information that is available to others, and also making it easier to control whether applications and websites can access their information.[138]

The FTC has also taken action to address the issue of endorsements made through social media sites and blogs and ensure that the same rules apply in this context as they do in traditional advertising and infomercials. In 2009 the agency passed a new set of guidelines for online endorsements that require online endorsers and bloggers to disclose any "material connection" to an advertiser. Under the new guidelines, paid endorsers who post on social media sites such as Facebook or post product reviews on marketer sites such as Amazon can be held liable if they do not identify themselves as such.[139]

Another Internet-related area receiving regulatory attention is **spamming**, which is the sending of unsolicited multiple commercial electronic messages. Spamming has become a major problem; studies show that the typical Internet user spends the equivalent of 10 working days a year dealing with incoming spam.[140] Spam also costs businesses billions of dollars every year in terms of lost worker productivity and network maintenance. Moreover, most of these messages are fraudulent or deceptive in one or more respects.

A number of states have enacted antispamming legislation, and a comprehensive federal antispam bill, the Controlling the Assault of Non-Solicited Pornography and Marketing Act of 2003 (CAN-SPAM Act), went into effect on January 1, 2004. The act's general requirements for commercial e-mails include the following requirements:

- A prohibition against false or misleading transmission information.
- Conspicuous notice of the right to opt out and a functioning Internet-based mechanism that a recipient may use to request to not receive future commercial e-mail messages from the sender.
- Clear and conspicuous identification that the message is an advertisement.
- A valid physical postal address for the sender.

Violations of the CAN-SPAM law include both civil and criminal penalties, including a fine of $250 (calculated on a per e-mail basis) up to a maximum of $2 million. While the CAN-SPAM Act carries severe penalties for violators, thus far it has done little to stop unsolicited e-mail messages. Spammers have been able to stay one step ahead of law enforcement officials by operating offshore and by constantly moving the Internet hosting source.[141]

YTC 20-07
Online Advertising Regulation
youtube.com/10ebelch

# Summary

Regulation and control of advertising stem from internal regulation or self-regulation as well as from external control by federal, state, and local regulatory agencies. For many years the advertising industry has promoted the use of voluntary self-regulation to regulate advertising and limit government interference with and control over advertising. Self-regulation of advertising emanates from all segments of the advertising industry, including advertisers and their agencies, business and advertising associations, and the media.

The Advertising Self Regulatory Council, the primary self-regulatory mechanism for national advertising, has been very effective in achieving its goal of voluntary regulation of advertising and other forms of marketing communication. Various media also have their own advertising guidelines. The major television networks maintain the most stringent review process and restrictions.

Traditionally, the federal government has been the most important source of external regulation, with the Federal Trade Commission serving as the major watchdog of advertising in the United States. The FTC protects both consumers and businesses from unfair and deceptive practices and anticompetitive behavior. The FTC became very active in the regulation of advertising during the 1970s when it began several new programs and policies, including affirmative disclosure, advertising substantiation, and corrective advertising. Since 1980 the FTC has not been allowed to implement industrywide rules that would define unfair advertising practices. However, the advertising industry and Congress are nearing agreement on a definition of unfairness, and this power may be restored to the FTC.

In 1983, the FTC developed a new working definition of deceptive advertising. Recently the FTC has become more active in policing false and deceptive advertising. Under the Lanham Act, many companies are taking the initiative by suing competitors that make false claims. Many states, as well as the National Association of Attorneys General, are also active in exercising their jurisdiction over false and misleading advertising.

A number of laws also govern the use of other promotional-mix elements, such as sales promotion and direct marketing. The Federal Trade Commission regulates many areas of sales promotion as well as direct marketing. Various consumer-oriented sales promotion tools such as contests, games, sweepstakes, and premiums are subject to regulation. Recently many states have become very active in the regulation of contests and sweepstakes. Trade promotion practices, such as the use of promotional allowances and vertical cooperative advertising, are regulated by the Federal Trade Commission under the Robinson-Patman Act. The FTC also enforces laws in a variety of areas that relate to direct marketing and mail-order selling as well as the Internet, while the FCC has rules governing telemarketing companies.

The rapid growth of the Internet as a marketing tool has created a new area of concern for regulators. The same consumer protection laws that apply to commercial activities in other media apply online as well. Major areas of concern with regard to advertising and marketing on the Internet are privacy, online marketing to children, and spamming or the sending of unsolicited commercial e-mail messages. Concerns over online marketing to children have led to the passage of the Children's Online Privacy Protection Act, which the FTC began enforcing in early 2000. The federal government passed the CAN-SPAM Act, which went into effect on January 1, 2004, and was updated in 2013. This legislation sets stringent requirements for commercial e-mail messages. The Federal Trade Commission has become increasingly concerned over privacy issues related to the increasing popularity of social media and is requiring various sites to protect the privacy of users. The FTC also has issued new guidelines covering online endorsements that require endorsers and bloggers to disclose any material connection to an advertiser.

# Key Terms

self-regulation p. 688
Better Business Bureau (BBB) p. 690
Council of Better Business
 Bureaus p. 691
National Advertising Review Board
 (NARB) p. 692
Advertising Self-Regulatory Council
 (ASRC) p. 692
Federal Trade Commission
 (FTC) p. 700

commercial speech p. 700
Central Hudson Test p. 700
Federal Trade Commission Act p. 701
Wheeler-Lea Amendment p. 701
trade regulation rules (TRRs) p. 702
unfairness p. 702
puffery p. 703
deception p. 704
affirmative disclosure p. 705
advertising substantiation p. 706

consent order p. 708
cease-and-desist order p. 708
corrective advertising p. 708
Lanham Act p. 719
National Association of Attorneys
 General (NAAG) p. 721
Children's Online Privacy Protection
 Act (COPPA) of 1998 p. 728
spamming p. 729

## Discussion Questions

1. The chapter opener discusses how Skechers and Reebok were fined for making advertising claims for their toning shoes that the Federal Trade Commission argues were false and misleading and unsubstantiated. Evaluate the claims made by these companies in their toning-shoe ads from a deceptive advertising perspective. Why do you think they agreed to pay money to settle their cases rather than appeal them? (LO1, 2)

2. Discuss the need for regulation of advertising and other IMC tools. Do you advocate more or less regulation of advertising and other forms of promotion by governmental agencies such as the Federal Trade Commission and the Food and Drug Administration? (LO1, 3)

3. Discuss the role the Advertising Self-Regulatory Council plays in the self-regulation of advertising. Discuss the arguments for and against self-regulation as an effective way of protecting consumers from misleading or deceptive advertising as well as companies competing against one another. (LO2)

4. IMC Perspective 20–1 discusses the battle that marketers of hard liquor have waged to advertise on television and the broadcast networks in particular. Do you agree with the DISCUS argument that advertising for hard liquor should be treated the same as advertising for beer and wine? Should advertising for spirits be confined to late-night programs on the networks or should the ads be permitted to run earlier in the evening as well? (LO2)

5. What are the three essential elements required to prove deception under the definition used by the Federal Trade Commission? (LO3)

6. Find several examples of advertising claims or slogans that are based on puffery rather than substantiated claims. Discuss whether you feel these advertising claims can be defended on the basis of puffery. (LO3)

7. IMC Perspective 20–2 discusses how the Federal Communications Commission is considering more stringent regulation of product placements in television shows. Evaluate the arguments for and against more stringent regulation of product placements by the FCC. (LO3)

8. Discuss the Lanham Act and how it affects advertising. What elements are necessary to win a false or deceptive advertising claim under the Lanham Act? (LO3)

9. Do you think the U.S. Drug Administration should consider adopting the type of cigarette packaging being used in Australia that requires graphic images and removes all branding elements? How effective do you think this type of packaging would be in reducing cigarette smoking? (LO3)

10. Discuss how the Do Not Call Registry developed by the Federal Trade Commission is impacting the direct-marketing industry. What arguments might direct marketers make in their efforts to have this program rescinded? (LO4)

11. Do you agree with the new guidelines from the Federal Trade Commission requiring bloggers and endorsers to disclose any material connection to an advertiser? How might this impact companies that use social media in their IMC programs? (LO4)

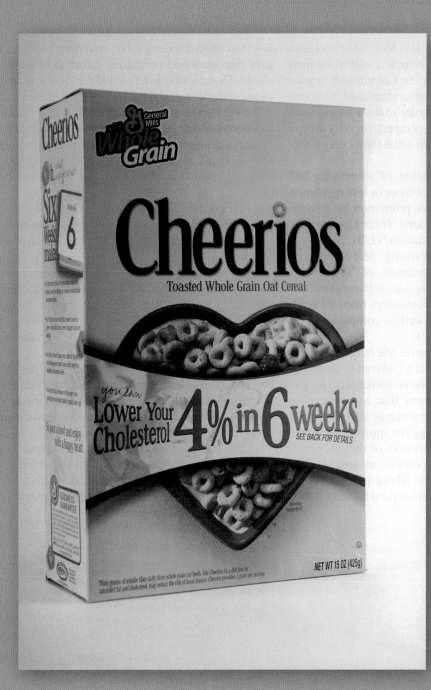

## LEARNING OBJECTIVES

**LO1** To consider various perspectives concerning the ethical aspects of advertising and promotion.

**LO2** To consider various perspectives concerning the social aspects of advertising and promotion.

**LO3** To evaluate the social criticisms of advertising.

**LO4** To examine the economic role of advertising and its effects on consumer choice, competition, and product costs and prices.

# 21 Evaluating the Social, Ethical, and Economic Aspects of Advertising and Promotion

## SOMETIMES DOING THE RIGHT THING PAYS OFF

"The times, they are a changing." These famous song lyrics were written by singer Bob Dylan over 40 years ago to reflect that events were taking place in America that would change the future of the country. At the time, Dylan probably hoped—but never realized—that these words would become prophetic. Well, for many of us, but not all.

A relatively unassuming commercial called "Just Checking" featuring an interracial family with a little girl expressing concern for her father's health was aired in 2013—almost exactly 40 years to the day of Dylan's song release—by Cheerios. Yes, Cheerios, the cereal, not some edgy brand trying to get attention. (The iconic Cheerios brand has been around since 1945!) And, even though the United States has had a black president for two terms, there are still many out there who apparently haven't gotten Dylan's message. The response to the commercial, which was viewed over 2 million times on YouTube, received such racist and vitriolic feedback that General Mills had to disable the comments section of the posting. As noted by media and pop culture columnist Barbara Lippert, "A progressive-looking commercial collides with the ugliness of the Internet." At the same time, it should be reported that while comments referring to Nazis, "troglodytes," and even "racial genocide" were way too frequent, there were also many positive reactions to the commercial commending the brand for being progressive, timely, and considerate. Within a few days, Cheerio's Facebook page was flooded with positive comments praising the ad, with more than a million "likes," and YouTube ratings reflected over 21,000 "thumbs up" compared to less than 1,500 "thumbs down."

So what do you do if you are General Mills? Well—according to most marketing experts—the right thing. Other than disabling the comments section on the YouTube video, Cheerios stood by the spot, keeping it on the air, as well as on YouTube. As noted by Camille Gibson, vice president of marketing for Cheerios, in an e-mail comment, "There are many kinds of families, and Cheerios celebrates them all." Gibson explained that the comments section on the YouTube video was disabled because Cheerios is a family brand and not all of the comments were family-friendly.

Praise from the marketing community was overwhelmingly positive. (While some skeptics wondered if "Just Checking" was an attempt to get attention, they were few and far between.) Allen Adamson, managing director of Landor Associates, told *CBS News* that he applauded General Mills for standing by the ad, noting that "the traditional approach depicting the old 'Leave It to Beaver family, while offending no one, is not very realistic." Meagan Hatcher-Mays, a celebrity fashion columnist, in a post on Jezebel commented, "this commercial is a huge step for interracial families like mine who want to be seen in public together and maybe eat some heart-healthy snacks." Numerous others took the same position, commending and cheering on Cheerios marketers for their actions.

But in marketing, we also have to look at the bottom line. How did the commercial impact the cereal? Besides the millions of exposures the brand received on the YouTube video, the publicity surrounding the ad and the brand was enormous. In addition to the positive articles generated in the business media such as *Adweek* and Brandchannel.com, Gibson appeared on *The Today Show* and was interviewed by *USA Today*. CBS network and numerous other local stations covered the controversy. Cross-web exposure increased by 77 percent in the week following the story's breaking, and the ad tested the highest of six new Cheerios ads, garnering attention and likability scores of 9 and 11 percent, respectively, which put it above the 90-day norm for cereals.

So while all of the negativity generated by the commercial actually resulted in many good things for both society and Cheerios, the fact remains that all is not well that ends well. As noted by Charles Malik Whitfield, the father in the ad, "Let's not pretend racism doesn't exist. Let's not pretend that we've come so far." We wonder what Bob Dylan would think.

Sources: Christopher Heine, "Cheerios' Interracial Ad Spiked Its Online Branding by 77%," www.adweek.com, June 7, 2013; Bruce Horovitz, "Hate Talk Won't Derail Mixed-Race Cheerios Ad," www.USAtoday.com, June 3, 2013; Morgan Whitaker, "Interracial Family in Cheerios Ad Sparks Online Backlash," www.morganwinn.com, June 3, 2013; Sheila Shayon, "General Mills Cheered for Defying Racial Backlash over Cheerios Ad," www.brandchannel.com, June 6, 2013; Stacy Lambe, "An Internet High-Five to Cheerios for Showcasing Diverse Families," www.qeerty.com, June 2, 2013.

> **YTC 21–01**
>
> **Cheerios "Just Checking"**
>
> youtube.com/10ebelch

*If I were to name the deadliest subversive force within capitalism, the single greatest source of its waning morality—I would without hesitation name advertising. How else should one identify a force that debases language, drains thought, and undoes dignity?*[1]

Based on the negative reaction to the Cheerios commercial discussed in the lead-in to this chapter, it would seem that there may be many others who question the morality of advertising. Their opposition to interracial portrayals would seem to indicate that they, too, think that advertising is not necessarily in the best interests of society.

The primary focus of this text has been on the role of advertising and promotion as marketing activities used to convey information to, and influence the behavior of, consumers. We have been concerned with examining the advertising and promotion function in the context of a business and marketing environment and from a perspective that assumes these activities are appropriate. However, as you can see in this quote from economist Robert Heilbroner, not everyone shares this viewpoint. Advertising and promotion are the most visible of all business activities and are prone to scrutiny by those who are concerned about the methods marketers use to sell their products and services.

Proponents of advertising argue that it is the lifeblood of business—it provides consumers with information about products and services and encourages them to improve their standard of living. They say advertising produces jobs and helps new firms enter the marketplace. Companies employ people who make the products and provide the services that advertising sells. Free-market economic systems are based on competition, which revolves around information, and nothing delivers information better and at less cost than advertising.

Not everyone, however, is sold on the value of advertising. Critics argue that most advertising is more propaganda than information; it creates needs and faults consumers never knew they had. Ads suggest that children need cell phones, that our bodies should be leaner, our faces younger, and our houses cleaner. They point to the sultry, scantily clad bodies used in ads to sell everything from perfume to beer to power tools and argue that advertising promotes materialism, insecurity, and greed.

One of the reasons advertising and other forms of integrated marketing communications are becoming increasingly criticized is because they are so prevalent. Not only are there more ads than ever, but there are more places where these ads appear. Advertising professor David Helm notes: "Between the stickered bananas and the ads over the urinals and the ones on the floor of the supermarkets, we're exposed to 3,000 commercial messages a day. That's one every 15 seconds, assuming we sleep for 8 hours, and I'd guess right now there's someone figuring out how to get us while our eyes are closed."[2]

As marketers intensify their efforts to get the attention of consumers, resentment against their integrated marketing communications efforts is likely to increase. Concern is growing that there may be a consumer backlash as integrated marketing efforts move to new heights and marketers become increasingly aggressive. The growing practice of placing ads and logos everywhere seems a desperate last attempt to make branding work according to the old rules. As telemarketing, advertising in

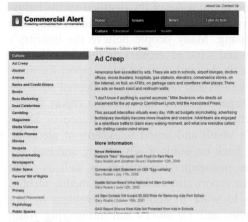

**EXHIBIT 21-1**

Commercial Alert, a project
of Public Citizen, is concerned
with the excessive amount
of marketing messages
consumers receive

the digital and social media, in movie theaters, in classrooms, and seemingly everywhere else continues at a frenzied pace, the value of the messages decreases. The system seems headed for a large implosion. Groups such as Commercial Alert are concerned about intrusion of advertising and other types of marketing messages into all aspects of consumers' lives. In addition to their concerns about the pervasiveness of commercially related messages, the organization is also concerned with other ad-related issues, as can be seen in Exhibit 21–1. Consumer advocacy groups also argue that many companies are obliterating the line between marketing communications and entertainment by creating and delivering ads and other messages that appear to be part of popular culture but have a persuasive intent.[3] (You may recall our earlier discussion on native ads.)

Advertising is a very powerful force, and this text would not be complete without a look at the criticisms regarding its social and economic effects as well as some defenses against these charges. We consider the various criticisms of advertising and promotion from an ethical and social perspective and then appraise the economic effects of advertising.

# ADVERTISING AND PROMOTION ETHICS

LO 21-1

In the previous chapter, we examined the regulatory environment in which advertising and promotion operate. While many laws and regulations determine what advertisers can and cannot do, not every issue is covered by a rule. Marketers must often make decisions regarding appropriate and responsible actions on the basis of ethical considerations rather than on what is legal or within industry guidelines. **Ethics** are moral principles and values that govern the actions and decisions of an individual or group.[4]

A particular action may be within the law and still not be ethical. A good example of this involves target marketing. No laws restrict tobacco companies from targeting advertising and promotion for new brands to African Americans. However, given the high levels of lung cancer and smoking-related illnesses among the black population, many people would consider this an unethical business practice. The same holds true for ads targeting children.

Throughout this text we have presented a number of ethical perspectives to show how various aspects of advertising and promotion often involve ethical considerations. Ethical issues must be considered in integrated marketing communications decisions. And advertising and promotion are areas where a lapse in ethical standards or judgment can result in actions that are highly visible and often very damaging to a company.

The role of advertising in society is controversial and has sometimes resulted in attempts to restrict or ban advertising and other forms of promotion to certain groups or for certain products. College students are one such group. The level of alcohol consumption and binge drinking by college students has become a serious problem. Alcohol-related problems have proliferated on college campuses in recent years and have resulted in many negative consequences, including death.[5] Several studies have shown that there has been a significant increase in binge drinking among college students and have advocated a ban on alcohol-related advertising and promotion to this segment.[6] Many colleges and universities have imposed restrictions on the marketing of alcoholic beverages to their students. These restrictions include banning sponsorships or support of athletic, musical, cultural, or social events by alcoholic-beverage companies and limiting college newspaper advertising to price and product information ads.

A great deal of attention is being focused on the issue of whether alcoholic-beverage companies target not only college students but underage drinkers as well. As noted in Chapter 20, the actions of beer, wine, and liquor marketers are being

**EXHIBIT 21–2**

This ad is part of a campaign to drink responsibly by the Alberta Gaming and Liquor Commission

**YTC 21-02**

**Alberta Drink Responsibly**

youtube.com/10ebelch

**EXHIBIT 21–3**

Belvedere Issued an Apology for its Ad that some considered offensive to women.

closely scrutinized in the wake of the distilled-spirits industry's decisions to reverse its long-standing ban on television and radio advertising. Many people believe the industry's push to join beer and wine advertisers on television is testing the public's attitudes and may lead to support for more government restrictions and regulations on alcohol advertising.[7] The U.S. surgeon general has issued a report stating that alcohol is the most widely used substance of abuse among America's youth and urged marketers of alcoholic beverages to cut back on outdoor advertising and end any remaining college newspaper advertising as well as event sponsorships.[8] The report also called on the media, alcohol marketers, and colleges and universities to work to address the problem by not glamorizing underage alcohol use in movies and TV shows and minimizing youth exposure to alcohol advertising through the media as well as on the Internet.

Companies marketing alcoholic beverages such as beer and liquor recognize the need to reduce alcohol abuse and drunken driving, particularly among young people, as do government agencies. Many of these companies have developed programs and ads designed to address this problem. The same is true in Canada, where The Alberta Gaming and Liquor Commission (Alberta, Canada) has been running an advertising campaign that uses ads such as the one shown in Exhibit 21–2 to encourage drinkers to consume responsibly. The campaign also includes an age-verification splash page, a Facebook page, and images on Pinterest, Instagram, and Twitter. The Beer Institute and Distilled Spirits Council of the U.S. marketing codes also ban college newspaper ads, prohibit rite-of-passage ad appeals, and limit some outdoor ads. Both groups also require that ads be placed in media where 70 percent of the audience is 21 or older.

Criticism often focuses on the actions of specific advertisers. Groups like the National Organization for Women and Women Against Pornography have been critical of advertisers for promoting sexual permissiveness and objectifying women in their ads. These groups have now been joined by the general public. For example, the makers of Belvedere brand vodka recently came under criticism for an ad that many considered offensive to women. The ad depicted a woman looking horrified while a man grabs her from behind. The text read, "Unlike some people, Belvedere always goes down smoothly." Almost immediately after the ad was posted on the company's Facebook page Belvedere felt the backlash, as social media sites lit up with negative comments about the advertisement's trivialization of rape. Bloggers and those in traditional media followed, calling the ad disgusting, "one of the worst pieces of promotional material ever published," and more. Shortly afterward, the female actor in the ad sued Belvedere, alleging emotional distress and unlawful use of her image (the image was taken from an online video company site that had no knowledge of its being used).[9] While Belvedere removed the post and issued numerous apologies, the backlash continued for some time (Exhibit 21–3). NOW protests ads such as this on the Love Your Body: Offensive Ads section of its website.

Another company that has received a great deal of criticism for its advertising over the years is Benetton. For nearly two decades the Italian-based clothing company ran numerous "shock" ads containing controversial images such as a black woman nursing a white baby, an AIDS patient and his family moments before his death, and a priest kissing a nun. Oliviero Toscani, Benetton's former creative director who developed most of these ads, noted that the controversial images were designed to raise public awareness of social issues and position the company as a cutting-edge, socially conscious marketer.[10] The company's most controversial ads, at least in the United States, were those used in its "Death Row" campaign that ran in 2000. The campaign, aimed at drawing attention to the use of capital punishment in the United States, featured ads showing piercing portraits of death-row inmates (Exhibit 21–4).

The campaign created a storm of controversy; the state of Missouri sued Toscani and Benetton for misrepresenting themselves while interviewing four

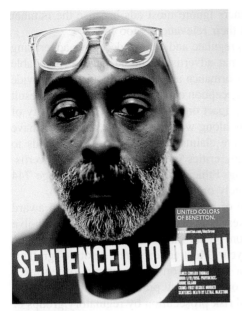

**EXHIBIT 21–4**
Benetton's "Death Row" ads created a major controversy

death-row inmates featured in the campaign. Protests from the families of the inmates' victims and threatened boycotts from enraged consumers resulted in Sears dropping the Benetton line. A year later the lawsuit was settled when Benetton agreed to write letters of apology to the four Missouri families whose relatives were murdered by the inmates featured in the ads and to make a donation to the Missouri Crime Victims Compensation Fund.[11] Since 2000, Benetton had toned down its advertising, alternating between conventional product campaigns and ads focusing on socially relevant issues such as volunteerism and famine. After a bit of a lull, the international clothing retailer ran an ad depicting Pope Benedict XVI kissing a Muslim imam as part of its "UNHATE" campaign (Exhibit 21–5). In addition to this ad, digitally altered images of President Obama kissing President Hugo Chavez of Venezuela and Israeli Prime Minister Benjamin Netanyahu with Palestinian Authority President Mahmoud Abbas were also part of the campaign. While a spokesperson for the Benetton Group said, "We reiterate that the meaning of this campaign is exclusively to combat the culture of hatred in all its forms," the ads were pulled after the Vatican threatened legal action to protect the pope's image.[12]

As you read this chapter, remember that the various perspectives presented reflect judgments of people with different backgrounds, values, and interests. You may see nothing wrong with the ads for cigarettes or beer or sexually suggestive ads. Others, however, may oppose these actions on moral and ethical grounds. While we attempt to present the arguments on both sides of these controversial issues, you will have to draw your own conclusions as to who is right or wrong.

# SOCIAL AND ETHICAL CRITICISMS OF ADVERTISING

Much of the controversy over advertising stems from the ways many companies use it as a selling tool and from its impact on society's tastes, values, and lifestyles. Specific techniques used by advertisers are criticized as deceptive or untruthful, offensive or in bad taste, and exploitative of certain groups, such as children. We discuss each of these criticisms, along with advertisers' responses. We then turn our attention to criticisms concerning the influence of advertising on values and lifestyles, as well as charges that it perpetuates stereotyping and that advertisers exert control over the media.

**EXHIBIT 21–5**
Benetton's "UNHATE" campaign has initiated a new controversy

## Advertising as Untruthful or Deceptive

One of the major complaints against advertising is that many ads are misleading or untruthful and deceive consumers. A number of studies have shown a general mistrust of advertising among consumers.[13] These studies have shown that consumers don't find most commercials to be honest and do not trust them. In a recent *Adweek Media/Harris* Poll, 65 percent of those surveyed said they trust advertising only sometimes, 18 percent most of the time, and 13 percent never.[14]

A study conducted by Forrester Research found that consumers mistrust ads for most types of products and rely on word of mouth from friends and family as the most trusted source of information. Brand websites were rated the second most trusted source of information with 8 percent of consumers reporting that they completely trust brand websites versus only 1 to 2 percent for most other media. The study found that consumers ignore most ads because the number and intrusiveness of them is too high and their relevance is too low.[15]

Attempts by industry and government to regulate and control deceptive advertising were discussed in Chapter 20. We noted that advertisers should have a reasonable basis for making a claim about product performance and may be required to provide evidence to support their claims. However, deception can occur more subtly as a result of how consumers perceive the ad and its impact on their beliefs.[16] The difficulty of determining just what constitutes deception, along with the fact that advertisers have the right to use puffery and make subjective claims about their products, tends to complicate the issue. But a concern of many critics is the extent to which advertisers are *deliberately* untruthful or misleading. Ethical Perspective 21–1 on page 744 discusses a TV advertisement that deliberately omitted important information.

Sometimes advertisers have made false or misleading claims or failed to award prizes promoted in a contest or sweepstakes. However, these cases usually involve smaller companies and only a tiny portion of the hundreds of billions of dollars spent on advertising and promotion each year. Most advertisers do not design their messages with the intention to mislead or deceive consumers or run sweepstakes with no intention of awarding prizes. Not only are such practices unethical, but the culprits would damage their reputation and risk prosecution by regulatory groups or government agencies. National advertisers invest large sums of money to develop loyalty to, and enhance the image of, their brands. These companies are not likely to risk hard-won consumer trust and confidence by intentionally deceiving consumers.

The problem of untruthful or fraudulent advertising and promotion exists more at the local level and in specific areas such as mail order, telemarketing, and other forms of direct marketing. Yet there have been many cases where large companies were accused of misleading consumers with their ads or promotions. For example, automobile companies Kia and Hyundai were the targets of class-action suits in 2013 when the Environmental Protection Agency found both manufacturers guilty of posting inflated fuel economy estimates on their vehicles since 2010.[17] Some companies test the limits of industry and government rules and regulations to make claims in an attempt to give their brands an advantage in highly competitive markets.

While many critics of advertising would probably agree that most advertisers are not out to deceive consumers deliberately, they are still concerned that consumers may not be receiving enough information to make an informed choice. They say advertisers usually present only information that is favorable to their position and do not always tell consumers the whole truth about a product or service.

Many believe advertising should be primarily informative in nature and should not be permitted to use puffery or embellished messages. Others argue that advertisers have the right to present the most favorable case for their products and services and should not be restricted to just objective, verifiable information.[18] They note that consumers can protect themselves from being persuaded against their will and that the various industry and government regulations suffice to keep advertisers from misleading consumers. Figure 21–1 shows the advertising ethics and principles of the American Advertising Federation, which many advertisers use as a guideline in preparing and evaluating their ads.

## Advertising as Offensive or in Bad Taste

Another common criticism of advertising is that ads are offensive, tasteless, irritating, boring, obnoxious, and so on. A number of studies have found that consumers feel most advertising insults their intelligence and that many ads are in poor taste.[19]

**Sources of Distaste**   Consumers can be offended or irritated by advertising in a number of ways. Some object when certain products or services such as contraceptives or personal hygiene products are advertised at all. Most media did not accept ads for condoms until the AIDS crisis forced them to reconsider their restrictions. The major TV networks gave their affiliates permission to accept condom advertising in 1987, but the first condom ad did not appear on network TV until 1991.

| Principle 1 | Advertising, public relations, marketing communications, news, and editorial all share a common objective of truth and high ethical standards in serving the public. |
| --- | --- |
| Principle 2 | Advertising, public relations, and all marketing communications professionals have an obligation to exercise the highest personal ethics in the creation and dissemination of commercial information to consumers. |
| Principle 3 | Advertisers should clearly distinguish advertising, public relations and corporate communications from news and editorial content and entertainment, both online and offline. |
| Principle 4 | Advertisers should clearly disclose all material conditions, such as payment or receipt of a free product, affecting endorsements in social and traditional channels, as well as the identity of endorsers, all in the interest of full disclosure and transparency. |
| Principle 5 | Advertisers should treat consumers fairly based on the nature of the audience to whom the ads are directed and the nature of the product or service advertised. |
| Principle 6 | Advertisers should never compromise consumers' personal privacy in marketing communications, and their choices as to whether to participate in providing their information should be transparent and easily made. |
| Principle 7 | Advertisers should follow federal, state and local advertising laws, and cooperate with industry self-regulatory programs for the resolution of advertising practices. |
| Principle 8 | Advertisers and their agencies, and online and offline media, should discuss privately potential ethical concerns, and members of the team creating ads should be given permission to express internally their ethical concerns. |

EXHIBIT 21–6

Many of the broadcast
networks now accept ads for
condoms during prime time
that promote health-related
uses

In 1994, the U.S. Department of Health's Centers for Disease Control and Prevention (CDC) began a new HIV prevention campaign that included radio and TV commercials urging sexually active people to use latex condoms. The commercials prompted strong protests from conservative and religious groups, which argued that the government should stress abstinence in preventing the spread of AIDS among young people. NBC and ABC agreed to broadcast all the commercials, while CBS said it would air certain spots.[20]

Advertising for condoms has now been appearing on TV for almost 20 years, but only in late-night time slots or on cable networks. However, in 2005, the broadcast networks agreed to accept commercials for condoms during prime time by agreeing to run heath-oriented ads for the Trojan brand.[21] The tone of the Trojan advertising was informational and provided facts and figures designed to raise viewers' consciousness and awareness about the potential consequences of unprotected sex among those who are sexually active (Exhibit 21–6). In 2007 both CBS and Fox rejected a commercial for Trojan condoms because of concerns about the creative content of the ad. Fox

CHAPTER 21

**EXHIBIT 21–7**
American Apparel was branded as "sexist" over their ads

YTC **21–03**
SKYY "Passion for Perfection"
youtube.com/10ebelch

**EXHIBIT 21–8**
SKYY Vodka ads have been criticized by conservative groups

indicated that it rejected the ad because contraceptive advertising must stress health-related uses rather than the prevention of pregnancy.[22]

There has been found to be a strong product class effect with respect to the types of ads consumers perceived as distasteful or irritating. The most irritating commercials tend to be for feminine hygiene products; ads for women's undergarments and hemorrhoid products were close behind. Another study found that consumers are more likely to dislike ads for products they do not use and for brands they would not buy.[23] Ads for personal products have become more common on television and in print, and the public is more accepting of them. However, advertisers must still be careful of how these products are presented and the language and terminology used. There are still many rules, regulations, and taboos advertisers must deal with to have their TV commercials approved by the networks.[24]

Another way advertising can offend consumers is by the type of appeal or the manner of presentation. For example, many people object to appeals that exploit consumer anxieties. Fear appeal ads, especially for products such as deodorants, mouthwash, and dandruff shampoos, are often criticized for attempting to create anxiety and using a fear of social rejection to sell these products. Some ads for home computers were also criticized for attempting to make parents think that if their young children couldn't use a computer, they would fail in school.

**Sexual Appeals** The advertising appeals that have received the most criticism for being in poor taste are those using sexual appeals such as suggestiveness and/or nudity. In a longitudinal study of TV viewers in Australia, Michael Ewing found that the issue resulting in the most complaints to the country's advertising Standards Bureau involved sex, sexuality, and/or nudity—almost three times more than any other issue.[25] Similar attitudes have been demonstrated in other countries as well. These techniques are often used to gain consumers' attention and may not even be appropriate to the product being advertised. Even if the sexual appeal relates to the product, people may be offended by it.

A common criticism of sexual appeals is that they can demean women (or men) by depicting them as sex objects (such as the Belvedere ad discussed earlier). Ads for cosmetics and lingerie are among the most criticized for their portrayal of women as sex objects and for being implicitly suggestive. For example, American Apparel has been branded "sexist" over ads depicting men in full attire but women half naked except for their unisex shirts (Exhibit 21–7).[26]

Critics have been particularly concerned about the use of sexual appeals in the advertising of products such as cigarettes, liquor, and beer. Sexual appeals and risqué images have long been used in advertising for alcoholic beverages. SKYY Spirits has used provocative, sexually oriented ads to promote its popular namesake vodka brand. Some of its ads, which use stylized images placing the brand's distinctive blue bottle in suggestive situations, have been criticized by conservative groups (Exhibit 21–8). However, a company spokesperson has responded to the criticisms by noting, "Style is a maker of interpretation and like with all art we appreciate all points of view."[27]

Attitudes toward the use of sex in advertising is a polarizing issue as opinions regarding its use vary depending upon the individual's values and religious orientation, as well as by

## FIGURE 21–2

Attitudes toward Sex in Advertising: Men versus Women

Source: From Media Analyzer.

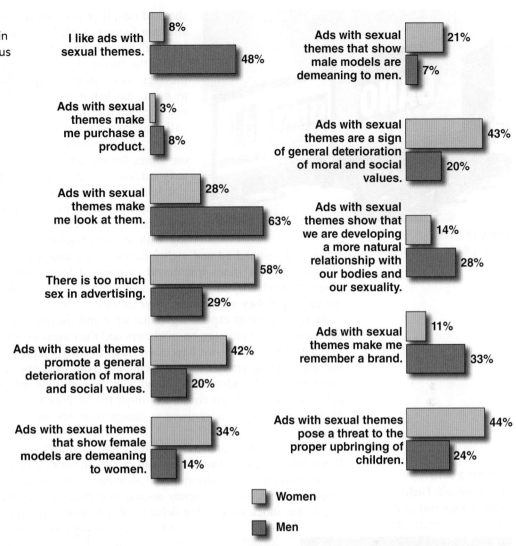

**I like ads with sexual themes.**
Women: 8%
Men: 48%

**Ads with sexual themes that show male models are demeaning to men.**
Women: 21%
Men: 7%

**Ads with sexual themes make me purchase a product.**
Women: 3%
Men: 8%

**Ads with sexual themes are a sign of general deterioration of moral and social values.**
Women: 43%
Men: 20%

**Ads with sexual themes make me look at them.**
Women: 28%
Men: 63%

**Ads with sexual themes show that we are developing a more natural relationship with our bodies and our sexuality.**
Women: 14%
Men: 28%

**There is too much sex in advertising.**
Women: 58%
Men: 29%

**Ads with sexual themes make me remember a brand.**
Women: 11%
Men: 33%

**Ads with sexual themes promote a general deterioration of moral and social values.**
Women: 42%
Men: 20%

**Ads with sexual themes that show female models are demeaning to women.**
Women: 34%
Men: 14%

**Ads with sexual themes pose a threat to the proper upbringing of children.**
Women: 44%
Men: 24%

Women
Men

age, education, and gender. One study found major differences between men and women in their attitudes toward sex in advertising.[28] As you can see in Figure 21–2, while almost half of men said they liked sexual ads, only 8 percent of women felt the same way. Most men (63 percent) indicated that sexual ads have high stopping power and get their attention, but fewer women thought the same (28 percent). Also, most women (58 percent) said there is too much sex in advertising versus only 29 percent of the men. Women were also much more likely than men to say that sexual ads promote a deterioration of moral and social values and that they are demeaning of the models used in them.

**Shock Advertising** With the increasing clutter in the advertising environment, advertisers continue to use sexual appeals and other techniques that offend some people but catch the attention of consumers and may even generate publicity for their companies. In recent years, there has been an increase in what is often referred to as **shock advertising**, in which marketers use nudity, sexual suggestiveness, or other startling images to get consumers' attention. As discussed earlier in the chapter, shock advertising is nothing new; companies such as Benetton and Calvin Klein have been using this tactic in their ads since the 1980s. However, a number of other marketers have been criticized for using shock techniques in their ads as well as in other promotional materials. Mexican beer brand Tecate recently

**EXHIBIT 21–9**
Tecate's Billboard gained
attention and criticism

shocked people passing by its billboard in Los Angeles and San Francisco when the advertisement displayed a tree with the word *baño* (Spanish for "bathroom") overlaying the image (Exhibit 21–9). The tongue-in-cheek message was meant to imply that it is easier for guys to go to the bathroom. While Tecate said the ad was not intended for the U.S. market, and took it down, one still wonders what it was meant to accomplish. Clothing retailer Abercrombie & Fitch has been criticized numerous times for the content and images used in its quarterly catalogs, which have included sex tips from porn star Jenna Jameson, a spoof interview with a shopping mall Santa portrayed as a pedophile, and nude photos. A few years ago the retailer promoted its Christmas catalog with an advertisement across the plastic covering stating, "Two-hundred and eighty pages of sex and Xmas fun" (Exhibit 21–10).[29] Officials in four states threatened or pursued legal action against the company, which responded by implementing a policy of carding would-be buyers of the catalog to ensure they are at least 18 years old.

Many advertising experts argue that what underlies the increase in the use of shock advertising is the pressure on marketers and their agencies to do whatever it takes to get their ads noticed—we have seen this in earlier chapters. However, critics argue that the more advertisers use the tactic, the more shocking the ads have to be to get attention. How far advertisers can go with these appeals will probably depend on the public's reaction. When consumers think the advertisers have gone too far, they are likely to pressure the advertisers to change their ads and the media to stop accepting them.

While marketers and ad agencies often acknowledge that their ads push the limits with regard to taste, they also complain about a double standard that exists for advertising versus editorial television program content. The creative director for Abercrombie & Fitch's agency argued that there is a double standard and hypocrisy in the shock advertising debate: "When advertising uses sex, everybody complains—when editorial does it, nobody cares."[30] Advertisers and agency creative directors argue that even the most suggestive commercials are bland compared with the content of many television programs.

**EXHIBIT 21–10**
Abercrombie & Fitch's
catalogs were criticized over
the use of sex and nudity

## Advertising and Children

Another controversial topic advertisers must deal with is the issue of advertising to children. TV and the Internet are two vehicles through which advertisers can reach children easily. Estimates are that children between the ages of 6 and 12 in the United States spend slightly over 7.4 hours a week online. At least four other countries children spend even more time there[31] (Figure 21–3) of TV a week. A study conducted by the Kaiser Family Foundation found that children ages 2 to 7 are exposed to an average of 13,904 TV ads a year for all products, while the comparable numbers are 30,155 ads for 8- to 12-year-olds and 28,655 for teens between the ages of 13 and 17.[32] Approximately 80 percent of all advertising targeted to children falls within four product categories: toys, cereals, candy, and fast-food restaurants.[33] Advertisers spend billions of dollars a year to reach children because TV is an important source of information for them and influences their direct purchases as well as their influence over other family

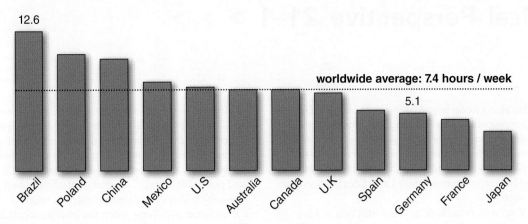

worldwide average: 7.4 hours / week

12.6

5.1

Brazil Poland China Mexico U.S Australia Canada U.K Spain Germany France Japan

**FIGURE 21–3**

Children's Time Spent on the Internet

Source: The Marketing Store, "The New Definition of Childhood."

members. In addition, if the child continues to use the product into adulthood, his or her lifetime value as a customer increases significantly. Perhaps this is why Camel cigarettes—once again—has come under fire for marketing to youth. Interestingly, but not surprisingly, the most popular brand of cigarettes among teens just happens to be Camel.[34] Concern has also been expressed about marketers' use of other promotional vehicles and techniques such as radio ads, point-of-purchase displays, premiums in packages, and the use of commercial characters as the basis for TV shows.

Critics argue that children, particularly young ones, are especially vulnerable to advertising because they lack the experience and knowledge to understand and critically evaluate the purpose of persuasive advertising appeals. Research has shown that preschool children cannot differentiate between commercials and programs, do not perceive the selling intent of commercials, and cannot distinguish between reality and fantasy.[35] The study also concluded that children must understand how advertising works in order to use their cognitive defenses against it effectively. Because of children's limited ability to interpret the selling intent of a message or identify a commercial, critics charge that advertising to them is inherently unfair and deceptive and should be banned or severely restricted.

At the other extreme are those who argue that advertising is a part of life and children must learn to deal with it in the **consumer socialization process** of acquiring the skills needed to function in the marketplace. They say existing restrictions are adequate for controlling children's advertising and that marketplace knowledge plays an important role in adolescents' skepticism toward advertising. They contend that greater knowledge of the marketplace appears to give teens a basis by which to evaluate ads and enables them to recognize the persuasion techniques used by advertisers.[36]

Children are also protected from the potential influences of commercials by network censors and industry self-regulatory groups such as the Council of Better Business Bureaus' Children's Advertising Review Unit (CARU). CARU has strict self-regulatory guidelines regarding the type of appeals, product presentation and claims, disclosures and disclaimers, the use of premiums, safety, and techniques such as special effects and animation. The CARU guidelines for advertising addressed to children under 12 are presented in Figure 21–4, and Commercial Alert's Parents' Bill of Rights is shown Figure 21–5.

As we saw in Chapter 20, the major networks also have strict guidelines for ads targeted to children. For example, in network TV ads, only 10 seconds can be devoted to animation and special effects; the final 5 seconds are reserved for displaying all the toys shown in the ad and disclosing whether they are sold separately and whether accessories such as batteries are included.[37]

Concerns over advertising and other forms of promotion directed at children diminished somewhat during the late 90s and the early part of the new decade. However, the issue has once again begun receiving a considerable amount of

In 2009, the Hong Kong Broadcasting Authority (HKBA)—an organization responsible for licensing and regulating the broadcasting industry in Hong Kong—received complaints that a television advertisement of Lake Silver was misleading. Lake Silver is a property development project in Hong Kong of MTR Corporation and Sino Land Cooperation and Development.

The TV ad was broadcast on four stations in May 2009: Home Channel of Asia Television Limited (ATV); Jade and Pearl Channels of Television Broadcasts Limited (TVB); Cable News Channel of Hong Kong Cable Television Limited (HKCTV); and Now Business News Channel of PCCW Media Limited (Now TV). The duration of the Lake Silver advertisement was about one minute. The advertisement showed forests, lakes, and other natural scenery in a hyper-real way. There were shots of a beautiful girl on a yacht in the middle of a sea and a collection of palaces. The end shot of this TV ad showed seven properties arranged in an L-shaped configuration and located in a bay surrounded by trees. A voiceover narrated: "Palace by the sea, Lake Silver." An Italian song performed by Andrea Bocelli, *Con Te Partiro*, was used as a jingle for this TV ad.

After taking into consideration all the relevant information, HKBA concluded that property landscape was an important determinant of the value and popularity of a property. Though advertising can be expressed in imaginative ways, the information conveyed must be accurate and not misleading. The end shot of the Lake Silver TV ad—which showed seven properties located in the bay surrounded by trees—gave the impression that Lake Silver was surrounded by green trees only, and that there was no other building nearby. However, according to the sales brochure of Lake Silver, there were other development projects around it. The contention of the complaints was that audiences would be misled into thinking that this end shot was a true description of the property. Therefore, the TV ad was considered to have intentionally omitted important information and conveyed a false impression.

The four TV stations were advised by HKBA to observe closely the relevant provisions in the Generic Code of Practice on Television Advertising Standards. In particular, the following paragraphs in Chapter 3 of the Generic Code of Practice were considered relevant to the case:

attention as various groups are calling for restrictions on advertising targeted to children. The American Psychological Association (APA), the nation's largest organization of psychologists, issued a report criticizing the increasing commercialization of childhood and calling for new curbs on marketing aimed at children.[38] The APA report faulted marketers for taking advantage of an ever-fragmenting media landscape of cable channels and the Internet to target children. The report noted that marketing activities focused on America's youth have reached unprecedented levels and called for restrictions on advertising in TV programming that appeals primarily to children under the age of eight and a total ban on advertising in programs aimed at very young children in this group. The report also found that the Internet is a particularly effective, and thus potentially harmful, means of sending advertising messages to children as websites often blur or even ignore the boundaries between commercial and noncommercial content. Marketing and advertising trade groups have been critical of the report and continue to defend their right to advertise on the basis that parents of younger children, rather than the children themselves, make purchase decisions.[39]

In addition to concerns over the increasing amount of advertising targeted to children, there are a number of other issues that consumer groups and regulatory agencies have raised with respect to young people. These include an increase in the

(1) Paragraph 1: "television advertising should be legal, clean, honest and truthful"; and

(2) Paragraph 9: "no advertisements may contain any descriptions, claims or illustrations which expressly or by implication depart from truth or mislead about the product or service advertised or about its suitability for the purpose recommended."

Sources: "Lake Silver TV Ad," YouTube video, http://www.youtube.com/watch?v=NYbE3oOqMAc; "TV Ad of Lake Silver is Misleading," *Hong Kong Economic Journal*, November 2009, http://forum.hkej.com/node/40116; "Misleading Property TV Ad Censured," *Oriental Daily News*, November 3, 2009, http://orientaldaily.on.cc/cnt/news/20091103/00176_023.html; "Lake Silver TV Ad is Misleading," *property.mpfinance.com*, November 2, 2009, http://property.mpfinance.com/cfm/pa3.cfm?File=20091102/pab01/p11757.txt.

number of ads encouraging children to call 900 numbers, the increase in the number of toy-based programs on TV, and general concerns over the content of children's programming, particularly with regard to violence. The marketing of violent entertainment to minors and the advertising practices and rating systems of the film, music, and electronic game industries are also being monitored very carefully. The issue of what young consumers are watching, listening to, and playing and how much violence that entertainment contains became an area of great concern following a flurry of shootings at schools.

As discussed in the previous chapter, there is also growing concern over how marketers are using the Internet to communicate with and sell to children. Studies have claimed that advertisers avoid many of the regulations designed to protect children by advertising on the Internet instead of traditional media. Noting that the Internet is less regulated, one study claims that advertising regulators are failing to protect children who are the targets of aggressive marketing through ads as well as in Internet games.[40] Another study demonstrated that children and youth can be reached through games, ads, brand pages, and social networking sites, and as a result, marketers have increased their efforts to reach these groups.[41] The study argues that these efforts may be even more fruitful than TV given the stronger attraction to online activities. A study by Group M revealed that advertising expenditures

YTC 21–04
CARU
youtube.com/10ebelch

CHAPTER 21

**FIGURE 21–4**

Children's Advertising
Review Unit Principles

Six basic principles underlie these guidelines for advertising directed to children:

1. Advertisers should always take into account the level of knowledge, sophistication, and maturity of the audience to which their message is primarily directed. Younger children have a limited capability for evaluating the credibility of information they receive. They also may lack the ability to understand the nature of the personal information they disclose on the Internet. Advertisers, therefore, have a special responsibility to protect children from their own susceptibilities.
2. Realizing that children are imaginative and that make-believe play constitutes an important part of the growing-up process, advertisers should exercise care not to exploit unfairly the imaginative quality of children. Unreasonable expectations of product quality or performance should not be stimulated either directly or indirectly by advertising.
3. Products and content inappropriate for children should not be advertised or promoted directly to children.
4. Recognizing that advertising may play an important part in educating the child, advertisers should communicate information in a truthful and accurate manner and in language understandable to young children with full recognition that the child may learn practices from advertising which can affect his or her health and well-being.
5. Advertisers are urged to capitalize on the potential of advertising to influence behavior by developing advertising that, wherever possible, addresses itself to positive and beneficial social behavior, such as friendship, kindness, honesty, justice, generosity, and respect for others.
6. Care should be taken to incorporate minority and other groups in advertisements in order to present positive and pro-social roles and role models wherever possible. Social stereotyping and appeals to prejudice should be avoided.

These Principles embody the philosophy upon which CARU's mandate is based. The Principles, and not the Guidelines themselves, determine the scope of our review. The Guidelines effectively anticipate and address many of the areas requiring scrutiny in child-directed advertising, but they are illustrative rather than limiting. Where no specific Guideline addresses the issues of concern to CARU, it is these broader Principles that CARU applies in evaluating advertising directed to the uniquely impressionable and vulnerable child audience.

Source: From Children's Advertising Review Unit.

targeted to children online doubled between the years 2006 and 2011, and were expected to increase again in 2012, with the fastest growth being on mobile ads.[42]

Advertising to children will remain a controversial topic. Some groups feel that the government is responsible for protecting children from the potentially harmful effects of advertising and other forms of promotion, while others argue that parents are ultimately responsible for doing so. A survey of 12,500 young people up to 18 years of age conducted for *Advertising Age* regarding their attitudes toward advertising and various media found that two-thirds of those surveyed believed the main goal of advertising is to make them buy things, while only 11 percent felt that its objective is to provide information.[43]

It is important to many companies to communicate directly with children. However, only by being sensitive to the naiveté of children as consumers will they be able to do so freely and avoid potential conflict with those who believe children should be protected from advertising and other forms of promotion.

## Social and Cultural Consequences

Concern is often expressed over the impact of advertising on society, particularly on values and lifestyles. While a number of factors influence the cultural values, lifestyles, and behavior of a society, the overwhelming amount of advertising and

# Commercial Alert's
# PARENTS' BILL OF RIGHTS

*We the Parents*

WHEREAS, the nurturing of character and strong values in children is one of the most important functions of any society;

WHEREAS, the primary responsibility for the upbringing of children resides in their parents;

WHEREAS, an aggressive commercial culture has invaded the relationship between parents and children, and has impeded the ability of parents to guide the upbringing of their own children;

WHEREAS, corporate marketers have sought increasingly to bypass parents, and speak directly to children in order to tempt them with the most sophisticated tools that advertising executives, market researchers and psychologists can devise;

WHEREAS, these marketers tend to glorify materialism, addiction, hedonism, violence and anti-social behavior, all of which are abhorrent to most parents;

WHEREAS, parents find themselves locked in constant battle with this pervasive influence, and are hard pressed to keep the commercial culture and its degraded values out of their children's lives;

WHEREAS, the aim of this corporate marketing is to turn children into agents of corporations in the home, so that they will nag their parents for the things they see advertised, thus sowing strife, stress and misery in the family;

WHEREAS, the products advertised generally are ones parents themselves would not choose for their children: violent and sexually suggestive entertainment, video games, alcohol, tobacco, gambling and junk food;

WHEREAS, this aggressive commercial influence has contributed to an epidemic of marketing-related diseases in children, such as obesity, type 2 diabetes, alcoholism, anorexia and bulimia, while millions will eventually die from the marketing of tobacco;

WHEREAS, corporations have latched onto the schools and compulsory school laws as a way to bypass parents and market their products and values to a captive audience of impressionable and trusting children;

WHEREAS, these corporations ultimately are creatures of state law, and it is intolerable that they should use the rights and powers so granted for the purpose of undermining the authority of parents in these ways;

-------------------------------------------------------------------------------------

THEREFORE, BE IT RESOLVED, that the U.S. Congress and the fifty state legislatures should right the balance between parents and corporations and restore to parents some measure of control over the commercial influences on their children, by enacting this Parents' Bill of Rights, including,

-------------------------------------------------------------------------------------

Leave Children Alone Act. This act bans television advertising aimed at children under 12 years of age. (federal)

Child Privacy Act. This act restores to parents the ability to safeguard the privacy of their own children. It gives parents the right to control any commercial use of personal information concerning their children, and the right to know precisely how such information is used. (federal, state)

Advertising to Children Accountability Act. This act helps parents affix individual responsibility for attempts to subject their children to commercial influence. It requires corporations to disclose who created each of their advertisements, and who did the market research for each ad directed at children under 12 years of age. (federal)

Commercial-Free Schools Act. Corporations have turned the public schools into advertising free-fire zones. This act prohibits corporations from using the schools and compulsory school laws to bypass parents and pitch their products to impressionable schoolchildren. (federal, state)

Fairness Doctrine for Parents. This act provides parents with the opportunity to talk back to the media and the advertisers. It makes the Fairness Doctrine apply to all advertising to children under 12 years of age, providing parents and community with response time on broadcast TV and radio for advertising to children. (federal)

Product Placement Disclosure Act. This law gives parents more information with which to monitor the influences that prey upon their children through the media. Specifically, it requires corporations to disclose, on packaging and at the outset, any and all product placements on television and videos, and in movies, video games and books. This prevents advertisers from sneaking ads into media that parents assume to be ad-free. (federal)

Child Harm Disclosure Act. Parents have a right to know of any significant health effects of products they might purchase for their children. This act creates a legal duty for corporations to publicly disclose all information suggesting that their product(s) could substantially harm the health of children. (federal)

Children's Food Labeling Act. Parents have a right to information about the food that corporations push upon their children. This act requires fast food restaurant chains to label contents of food, and provide basic nutritional information about it. (federal, state)

Children's Advertising Subsidy Revocation Act. It is intolerable that the federal government actually rewards corporations with a big tax write-off for the money they spend on psychologists, market researchers, ad agencies, media and the like in their campaigns to instill their values in our children. This act eliminates all federal subsidies, deductions and preferences for advertising aimed at children under 12 years of age. (federal)

-------------------------------------------------------------------------------------

Please make copies of the Parents' Bill of Rights, and give or mail them to your members of Congress, state legislators and candidates. Ask them to turn the provisions into law. Distribute this at day care centers, schools, churches, synagogues, coffee shops, grocery stores and other places where parents gather. Call 503.235.8012 to volunteer or to find out how you can help enact the Parents' Bill of Rights into law.

Commercial Alert • www.commercialalert.org • 4110 SE Hawthorne Blvd. #123, Portland, OR 97214-5246 • 503.235.8012

**FIGURE 21–5**

Commercial Alert's Parents' Bill of RightsCommercial Alert, www.commercialalert.org.

CHAPTER 21

# Ethical Perspective 21–2 > > >

## Baby Milk Powder Advertisements in Hong Kong Guilty of Exaggerated Claims

In Hong Kong, many baby milk powder brands emphasize the benefits of drinking powdered milk through advertising. In April 2011, the Society of Hospital Pharmacists of Hong Kong (SHPHK) announced that some advertisements of baby milk powder brands were found to have greatly exaggerated the benefits of their products, after testing the nutritional elements of seven brands.

For example, Frisco had claimed that babies experienced easier bowel movements after drinking its milk powder which contained probiotics, prebiotics, and water-soluble dietary fiber. SHPHK stoutly refuted its claim, citing a lack of evidence that showed bowel movements of babies were actually improved by these ingredients in Frisco's product.

Many brands also resorted to the use of seemingly academic terms to emphasize the benefits of drinking their milk powder products. For example, some brands had claimed that their milk powder products contain docosahexaenoic acid (DHA) and phosphatidylcholine (PhD), which will boost intelligence and creativity. In its response, SHPHK clarified that DHA might only have

---

its prevalence in the mass media lead many critics to argue that advertising plays a major role in influencing and transmitting social values. In his book *Advertising and Social Change,* Ronald Berman says:

> The institutions of family, religion, and education have grown noticeably weaker over each of the past three generations. The world itself seems to have grown more complex. In the absence of traditional authority, advertising has become a kind of social guide. It depicts us in all the myriad situations possible to a life of free choice. It provides ideas about style, morality, behavior.[44]

Mike Hughes, president and creative director of the Martin Agency, notes that advertising has a major impact on society: "Ads help establish what is cool in society; their messages contribute to the public dialogue. Gap ads show white, black and Hispanic kids dancing together. Hilfiger ads showed it's cool for people to get along. IKEA showed a gay couple." He argues that advertising agencies have a social and ethical responsibility to consider the impact of the advertising messages they create for their clients.[45] Gap, JCPenney, McDonald's, Levis, and Amazon Kindle have all produced ads that are lesbian, gay, bisexual, and transgender friendly.[46]

While there is general agreement that advertising is an important social influence agent, opinions as to the value of its contribution are often negative. Advertising is criticized for encouraging materialism, manipulating consumers to buy things they do not really need, perpetuating stereotypes, and controlling the media.

the body. Thus, its efficacy in boosting the immune system of babies is doubtful.

Concerned over what it perceived to be exaggerated claims made by various baby milk powder brands, SHPHK has suggested to the Hong Kong government the setting up of a regulatory body to review milk powder advertisements prior to publication. In response, the milk powder manufacturers banded together to form the Hong Kong Infant and Young Child Nutrition Association (HKIYCNA). In 2011, it drafted the HKIYCNA Code of Practice for the Marketing of Infant Formula.

In October 2012, the Hong Kong authorities drafted the Hong Kong Code of Marketing and Quality of Formula Milk and Related Products, and Food Products for Infants and Young Children (in short, "the HK Code"). The public consultation period lapsed at the end of February 2013. As of early 2014, the HK Code has yet to be adopted even though the consultation period ended over a year ago.

short-term effects while its long-term effects are not significant. PhD was a term created by milk powder manufacturers, and more research is needed before its claim of beneficial effects can be corroborated.

Furthermore, it was claimed that the ingredient beta-glucan in milk powder can enhance a baby's immunity. However, only beta-glucan injections have been proven to prolong the lives of cancer patients. There is no evidence that beta-glucan, when taken orally, can be absorbed into

Sources: Department of Health, the Government of the Hong Kong Special Administrative Region, "The Hong Kong Code," http://www.fhs.gov.hk/english/news/hkcode/hkcode.html; Hong Kong Infant and Young Child Nutrition Association website, http://hkiycna.hk/en/code_of_practice.php; "The Pharmacists Society Revealed that Baby Milk Powder Ads Have Five Untrue Claims," *MingPao*, April 11, 2011; "Baby Milk Powder Suppliers Regulate Themselves by Determining Code of Practice," *MingPao*, October 19, 2011; "Regulating Baby Milk Powder Ads: Only Hearsay?," *MingPao*, February 3, 2014, http://happypama.mingpao.com/cfm/parenting3.cfm?File=20140203/newa/gha2.txt.

**Advertising Encourages Materialism**   Many critics claim advertising has an adverse effect on consumer values by encouraging **materialism**, a preoccupation with material things rather than intellectual or spiritual concerns. They argue that a major contributor to materialism is advertising that

- Seeks to create needs rather than merely showing how a product or service fulfills them.
- Surrounds consumers with images of the good life and suggests the acquisition of material possessions leads to contentment and happiness and adds to the joy of living.
- Suggests material possessions are symbols of status, success, and accomplishment and/or will lead to greater social acceptance, popularity, sex appeal, and so on.

Advertising for products such as expensive automobiles and luxury goods like clothing, jewelry, and alcoholic beverages is often criticized for promoting materialistic values (Exhibit 21–11).

This criticism of advertising assumes that materialism is undesirable and is sought at the expense of other goals. But many believe materialism is an acceptable part of the **Protestant ethic**, which stresses hard work and individual effort and initiative and views the accumulation of material possessions as evidence of success. Others

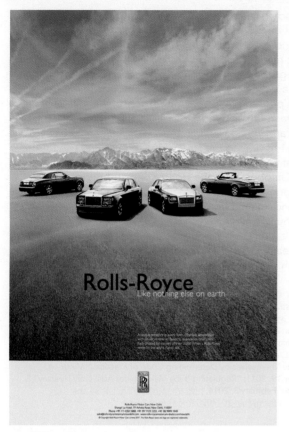

Rolls-Royce
Like nothing else on earth

**EXHIBIT 21–11**
Critics argue that advertising contributes to materialistic values

**EXHIBIT 21–12**
The advertising industry argues that advertising reflects society

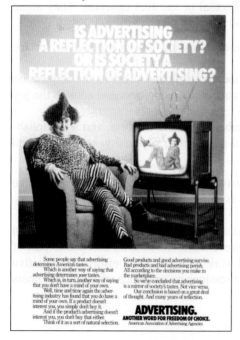

argue that the acquisition of material possessions has positive economic impact by encouraging consumers to keep consuming after their basic needs are met. Many Americans believe economic growth is essential and materialism is both a necessity and an inevitable part of this progress.

It has also been argued that an emphasis on material possessions does not rule out interest in intellectual, spiritual, or cultural values. Defenders of advertising say consumers can be more interested in higher-order goals when basic needs have been met and point out that consumers may purchase material things in the pursuit of nonmaterial goals. For example, a person may buy an expensive stereo system to enjoy music rather than simply to impress someone or acquire a material possession.

Even if we assume materialism is undesirable, there is still the question of whether advertising is responsible for creating and encouraging it. While many critics argue that advertising is a major contributing force to materialistic values, others say advertising merely reflects the values of society rather than shaping them.[47] They argue that consumers' values are defined by the society in which they live and are the results of extensive, long-term socialization or acculturation.

The argument that advertising is responsible for creating a materialistic and hedonistic society is addressed by Stephen Fox in his book *The Mirror Makers: A History of American Advertising and Its Creators.* Fox concludes advertising has become a prime scapegoat for our times and merely reflects society. Regarding the effect of advertising on cultural values, he says:

To blame advertising now for those most basic tendencies in American history is to miss the point. It is too obvious, too easy, a matter of killing the messenger instead of dealing with the bad news. The people who have created modern advertising are not hidden persuaders pushing our buttons in the service of some malevolent purpose. They are just producing an especially visible manifestation, good and bad, of the American way of life.[48]

The ad shown in Exhibit 21–12 was developed by the American Association of Advertising Agencies and suggests that advertising is a reflection of society's tastes and values, not vice versa. The ad was part of a campaign that addressed criticisms of advertising.

Individuals from a variety of backgrounds are concerned over the values they see driving our society. They believe that materialism, greed, and selfishness increasingly dominate American life and that advertising is a major reason for these undesirable values. The extent to which advertising is responsible for materialism and the desirability of such values are deep philosophical issues that will continue to be part of the debate over the societal value and consequences of advertising.

**Advertising Makes People Buy Things They Don't Need** A common criticism of advertising is that it manipulates consumers into buying things they do not need. Many critics say advertising should just provide information useful in making purchase decisions and should not attempt to persuade. They view information advertising (which reports price, performance, and other objective criteria) as desirable but persuasive advertising (which plays on consumers' emotions, anxieties, and psychological needs and desires such as status, self-esteem, and attractiveness) as unacceptable. Persuasive advertising is criticized for fostering discontent among consumers and encouraging them to purchase products and services to solve deeper problems.

Defenders of advertising offer a number of rebuttals to these criticisms. First, they point out that a substantial amount of advertising is essentially informational in nature. Also, it is difficult to separate desirable informational advertising from undesirable persuasive advertising. Shelby Hunt, in examining the *information-persuasion dichotomy,* points out that even advertising that most observers would categorize as very informative is often very persuasive. He says, "If advertising critics really believe that persuasive advertising should not be permitted, they are actually proposing that no advertising be allowed, since the purpose of all advertising is to persuade."[49]

Defenders of advertising also take issue with the argument that it should be limited to dealing with basic functional needs. In our society, most lower-level needs recognized in Maslow's hierarchy, such as the need for food, clothing, and shelter, are satisfied for most people. It is natural to move from basic needs to higher-order ones such as self-esteem and status or self-actualization. Consumers are free to choose the degree to which they attempt to satisfy their desires, and wise advertisers associate their products and services with the satisfaction of higher-order needs.

Proponents of advertising offer two other defenses against the charge that advertising makes people buy things they do not really need. First, this criticism attributes too much power to advertising and assumes consumers have no ability to defend themselves against it. Second, it ignores the fact that consumers have the freedom to make their own choices when confronted with persuasive advertising. While they readily admit the persuasive intent of their business, advertisers are quick to note it is extremely difficult to make consumers purchase a product they do not want or for which they do not see a personal benefit. If advertising were as powerful as the critics claim, we would not see products with multimillion-dollar advertising budgets failing in the marketplace. The reality is that consumers do have a choice and they are not being forced to buy. Consumers ignore ads for products and services they do not really need or that fail to interest them (see Exhibit 21–13).

**EXHIBIT 21–13**

The AAAA responds to the claim that advertising makes consumers buy things they do not need

**DESPITE WHAT SOME PEOPLE THINK, ADVERTISING CAN'T MAKE YOU BUY SOMETHING YOU DON'T NEED.**

Some people would have you believe that you are putty in the hands of every advertiser in the country.

They think that when advertising is put under your nose, your mind turns to oatmeal.

It's mass hypnosis. Subliminal seduction. Brain washing. Mind control. It's advertising.

And you are a pushover for it.

It explains why your kitchen cupboard is full of food you never eat. Why your garage is full of cars you never drive.

Why your house is full of books you don't read, TV's you don't watch, beds you don't use, and clothes you don't wear.

You don't have a choice. You are forced to buy.

That's why this message is a cleverly disguised advertisement to get you to buy land in the tropics.

Got you again, didn't we? Send in your money.

**ADVERTISING**
ANOTHER WORD FOR FREEDOM OF CHOICE.
American Association of Advertising Agencies

## Advertising and Stereotyping

Advertising is often accused of creating and perpetuating stereotypes through its portrayal of women, ethnic minorities, and other groups.

**Women** The portrayal of women in advertising is an issue that has received a great deal of attention through the years. Advertising has received much criticism for stereotyping women and failing to recognize the changing role of women in our society. Critics have argued that advertising often depicts women as preoccupied with beauty, household duties, and motherhood or shows them as decorative objects or sexually provocative figures. The various research studies conducted through the years show a consistent picture of gender stereotyping that has varied little over time. Portrayals of adult women in American television and print advertising have emphasized passivity, deference, lack of intelligence and credibility, and punishment for high levels of effort. In contrast, men have been portrayed as constructive, powerful, autonomous, and achieving.[50]

Research on gender stereotyping in advertising targeted to children has found a pattern of results similar to that reported for adults. A study found sex-role stereotyping in television advertising targeted at children in the United States as well as in Australia.[51] Boys are generally shown as being more knowledgeable, active, aggressive, and instrumental than girls. Nonverbal behaviors involving dominance and control are associated more with boys than girls. Advertising directed toward children has also been shown to feature more boys than girls, to position boys in more dominant, active roles, and to use male voiceovers more frequently than female ones.[52] A study examining race and gender stereotyping of children's advertising on the Turner Cartoon Network found that the primary target for most of the commercials was active, white boys. Girls were portrayed in traditional roles and shown performing limited passive, indoor activities, while boys were shown in the outdoor world engaging in more exciting and active things.[53]

Feminist groups such as the National Organization for Women (NOW) and the Sexual Assault Prevention and Awareness Center argue that advertising that portrays women as sex objects contributes to violence against women. These groups often protest to advertisers and their agencies about ads they find insulting to women and have even called for boycotts against offending advertisers. NOW has also been critical of advertisers for the way they portray women in advertising for clothing, cosmetics, and other products. The organization feels that many of these ads contribute to the epidemic of eating disorders and smoking among women and girls who hope such means will help them control their weight.[54]

While sexism and stereotyping still exist, advertising's portrayal of women is improving in many areas. Many advertisers have begun to recognize the importance of portraying women realistically. The increase in the number of working women has resulted not only in women having more influence in family decision making but also in more single-female households, which means more independent purchasers.

Researchers Steven Kates and Glenda Shaw-Garlock argue that the transformed social positioning of women in North American society is perhaps the most important social development of this century.[55] They note that as women have crossed the boundary from the domestic sphere to the professional arena, expectations and representations of women have changed as well. For example, a number of magazines, such as *Ms.* and *Working Mother,* now incorporate and appeal to the sociocultural shifts in women's lives. Many advertisers are now depicting women in a diversity of roles that reflect their changing place in society. In many ads, the stereotypic character traits attributed to women have shifted from weak and dependent to strong and autonomous. The ad for NetworkSolutions shown in Exhibit 21–14 is an example of how advertisers are changing the way they portray women in their ads. One reason for the changes in the way women are portrayed in advertising is the emergence of females in key agency roles. Women advertising executives are likely to be more sensitive to the portrayal of their own gender and to strengthen the role of women beyond stereotypical housewives or a position of subservience to men.[56]

**EXHIBIT 21–14**

Many advertisers now portray women in powerful roles

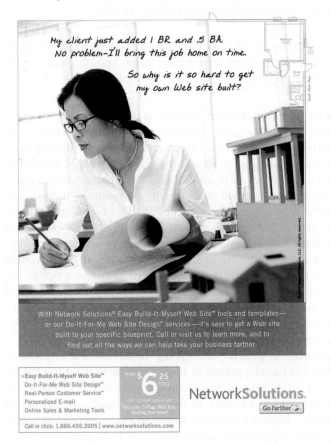

**African Americans and Hispanics** African Americans and Hispanics have also been the target of stereotyping in advertising. For many years, advertisers virtually ignored all nonwhite ethnic groups as identifiable subcultures and viable markets. Ads were rarely targeted to these ethnic groups, and the use of blacks and Hispanics as spokespeople, communicators, models, or actors in ads was very limited.

One study of minorities in magazine print ads showed that 83.8 percent of all models used were Caucasian, 9.5 percent African American, and 6.6 percent Asian American. While this study concluded

**EXHIBIT 21–15**

Banana Republic broke ground with this ad showing an interracial couple

that Asian Americans were overrepresented relative to the percentage of this ethnicity in the United States, it also showed that the variety of roles in which they were depicted and the variety of magazines were restricted. Asians were more likely to appear in science, business, and technology media and typically in nonworking decorative roles.[57] The study was consistent with a previous study conducted by Taylor et al. five years earlier.[58] A study conducted in the UK indicated that black, Asian, or other ethnic minority groups appeared in only 5 percent of 35,000 commercials aired, even though these groups constituted 13 percent of the UK population.[59]

Ads are increasingly likely to be racially integrated. As seen in the lead-in to this chapter, advertisers have begun breaking the taboo against suggesting interracial attraction. For example, Banana Republic, and many other retailers, commonly run interracial ads (Exhibit 21–15). Advertisers are also finding that advertising developed specifically for the African American market, such as the Levi's ad shown in Exhibit 21–16, is an effective way of reaching this ethnic market. A study by Corliss L. Green found that ads targeting African Americans through racially targeted media, especially with race-based products, benefit from featuring African American models with a dominant presence in the ad.

There is little question that advertising has been guilty of stereotyping women and ethnic groups in the past and, in some cases, still does so. But as the role of women changes, advertisers are changing their portrayals to remain accurate and appeal to their target audience. Advertisers are also trying to increase the incidence of minority groups in ads while avoiding stereotypes and negative role portrayals. They are being careful to avoid ethnic stereotyping and striving to develop advertising that has specific appeals to various ethnic groups. Increases in the size and purchasing power of ethnic minorities are leading companies to give more attention to multicultural marketing.

**EXHIBIT 21–16**

Many marketers are creating ads specifically for the African American market

**Other Groups** While the focus here has been on women and ethnic minorities, some other groups feel they are victims of stereotyping by advertisers. Many groups in our society are battling against stereotyping and discrimination, and companies must consider whether their ads might offend them. Creative personnel in agencies sometimes feel restricted as their ideas are squelched out of concern that they might offend someone or be misinterpreted. However, advertisers must be sensitive to the portrayal of specific types of people in their ads, for both ethical and commercial reasons. For example, both Volkswagen and General Motors received protests from mental health groups over commercials considered insensitive to the problem of suicide. The Volkswagen spot showed a young man about to commit suicide by jumping off a roof after he is seen expressing his unhappiness with the state of the world, but ultimately opts not to do so after he learns that there are three VW models available for under $17,000. Volkswagen ended up pulling the spot after receiving protests from a number of suicide prevention groups.[60] The General Motors ad, which premiered on the Super Bowl, created a controversy by showing

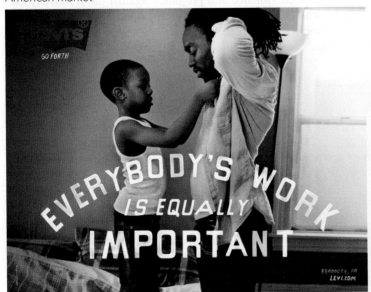

a robot that gets fired for dropping a bolt on the assembly line, takes a succession of lesser jobs, and eventually jumps off a bridge in despair. GM agreed to change the ad, which was designed to show the company's obsession with product quality, after discussing concerns about it with the American Foundation for Suicide Prevention.[61]

One area where significant changes have taken place recently is in advertising targeted to gay consumers. In 1995 IKEA broke new ground with a TV commercial featuring a gay couple shopping for furniture. For years beer companies targeted this market by placing ads in local gay media to support or sponsor AIDS awareness, Gay Pride festivals, and the Gay Games. A number of beer companies, including Anheuser-Busch and Miller Coors, now run gay-specific, brand-specific ads in national gay publications.

More advertisers are turning to gay themes in their mainstream commercials, though often subtly. (Interestingly, sometimes ads are perceived as targeting gays when that was not the intention, resulting in very positive feedback from this segment nevertheless.) However, few run these ads on network television; they limit them to spot TV and local stations in more gay-friendly cities such as New York, Los Angeles, and San Francisco. The Miller Brewing Co. took a bold step by airing one of the first gay-themed commercials on network television. One ad was for Miller Lite beer and showed a gay couple holding hands in a straight bar to the dismay of two women who are interested in them. Levi Strauss recently created a spot with alternative endings, one of which was designed to appeal to the gay market. The spot featured a young, attractive male in his second-floor apartment slipping on his Levi's. The motion of yanking up his jeans inexplicably causes the street below his apartment to get pulled up as well, crashing through his floor and bringing with it an attractive female in a telephone booth who he walks away with. In a version of the ad that aired on Logo, MTV's gay cable network seen in more than 27 million homes, an attractive man is in the phone booth and the two men run off together in the same manner as their heterosexual counterparts.[62]

A commercial that was not well received by the gay community was a spot for Snickers candy bars that also aired during the 2007 Super Bowl. The "mechanics" spot depicted two auto mechanics who end up sharing a Snickers bar and an inadvertent kiss and then ripping out chest hair to do something "manly" (Exhibit 21–17). Snickers also created a microwebsite featuring alternative endings to the commercial, such as the mechanics beating each other with wrenches as well as other players from the Super Bowl teams reactions to them. Gay-rights groups complained to the parent company of Snickers, Masterfoods USA—a subsidiary of Mars—that the spots were homophobic and encouraged violence and prejudice against gays. Masterfoods noted that the commercial was only trying to be humorous and attract the attention of the core Snickers consumer. However, the company agreed to stop running the ad and removed the website.[63]

**Advertising and the Media** The fact that advertising plays such an important role in financing the media has led to concern that advertisers may influence or even control the media. It is well documented that *economic censorship* occurs, whereby the media avoid certain topics or even present biased news coverage, in acquiescence to advertiser demands.[64] In fact, Professors Lawrence Soley and Robert Craig say, "The assertion that advertisers attempt to influence what the public sees, hears, and reads in the mass media is perhaps the most damning of all criticisms of advertising, but this criticism isn't acknowledged in most advertising textbooks."[65] We will address this important issue in this book by considering arguments on both sides.

YTC **21–05**

**Snickers Super Bowl Ad**

youtube.com/10ebelch

**EXHIBIT 21–17**

Snickers offended the gay community with its Super Bowl commercial

**Arguments Supporting Advertiser Control** Advertising is the primary source of revenue for nearly all the news and entertainment media in the United States. Some critics charge that the media's dependence on advertisers' support makes them susceptible to various forms of influence, including exerting control over the editorial content of magazines and newspapers; biasing editorial opinions to favor the position of an advertiser; limiting coverage of a controversial story that might reflect negatively on a company; and influencing the news and program content of television.

Newspapers and magazines receive nearly 70 percent of their revenue from advertising; commercial TV and radio derive virtually all their income from advertisers. Small, financially insecure newspapers, magazines, or broadcast stations are the most susceptible to pressure from advertisers, particularly companies that account for a large amount of the media outlet's advertising revenue. In some local markets, automobile and furniture advertisers may constitute as much as 80 percent of the TV stations' ad revenues. As you might imagine, the stations may tread lightly when reporting news that does not portray these industries positively. A local newspaper may be reluctant to print an unfavorable story about a car dealer or supermarket chain on whose advertising it depends. For example, a few years ago more than 40 car dealers canceled their ads in the *San Jose Mercury News* when the paper printed an article titled "A Car Buyer's Guide to Sanity." The dealers objected to the tone of the article, which they felt implied consumers should consider car dealers unethical adversaries in the negotiation process.[66] A recent study by Soontae An and Lori Bergen surveyed advertising directors at 219 daily newspapers in the United States and found frequent conflicts between the business side and editorial side of the newspaper operations. Advertising directors at small newspapers or chain-owned newspapers were more likely to endorse scenarios where editorial integrity was compromised to please, or refrain from offending, their advertisers.[67]

While larger, more financially stable media should be less susceptible to an advertiser's influence, they may still be reluctant to carry stories detrimental to companies that purchase large amounts of advertising time or space. For example, since cigarette commercials were taken off radio and TV in 1970, tobacco companies have allocated most of their budgets to the print media. The tobacco industry outspends all other national advertisers in newspapers, and cigarettes constitute the second-largest category of magazine advertising (behind transportation). This has led to charges that magazines and newspapers avoid articles on the hazards of smoking to protect this important source of ad revenue.[68]

Individual TV stations and even the major networks also can be influenced by advertisers. Programming decisions are made largely on the basis of what shows will attract the most viewers and thus be most desirable to advertisers. Critics say this often results in lower-quality television as educational, cultural, and informative programming is usually sacrificed for shows that get high ratings and appeal to the mass markets. It is well recognized that advertisers often avoid TV shows that deal with controversial issues. Most advertisers also have contract stipulations allowing them to cancel a media buy if, after prescreening a show, they are uncomfortable with its content or feel sponsorship of it may reflect poorly on their company.

Advertisers have also been accused of pressuring the networks to change their programming. Many advertisers have withdrawn commercials from programs that contain too much sex or violence, often in response to threatened boycotts of their products by consumers if they advertise on these shows. For example, groups such as the American Family Association have been fighting sex and violence in TV programs by calling for boycotts. A number of companies, including Procter & Gamble, Mars Inc., and Kraft Foods, pulled their advertising from certain shows while others have not responded to their actions.

**Arguments against Advertiser Control** The commercial media's dependence on advertising means advertisers can exert influence on their character, content, and coverage of certain issues. However, media executives offer several reasons why advertisers do not exert undue influence over the media.

First, they point out it is in the best interest of the media not to be influenced too much by advertisers. To retain public confidence, they must report the news fairly and accurately without showing bias or attempting to avoid controversial issues. Media executives point to the vast array of topics they cover and the investigative reporting they often do as evidence of their objectivity. They want to build a large audience for their publications or stations so that they can charge more for advertising space and time.

Media executives also note that an advertiser needs the media more than they need any individual advertiser, particularly when the medium has a large audience or does a good job of reaching a specific market segment. Many publications and stations have a broad base of advertising support and can afford to lose an advertiser that attempts to exert too much influence. This is particularly true for the larger, more established, financially secure media. For example, a consumer-product company would find it difficult to reach its target audience without network TV and could not afford to boycott a network if it disagreed with a station's editorial policy or program content. Even the local advertiser in a small community may be dependent on the local newspaper, since it may be the most cost-effective media option available.

Most magazine and newspaper publishers insist they do not allow advertiser pressure to influence their editorial content. They argue that they have long regarded the formal separation of their news and business departments as essential to their independence and credibility. This separation is often referred to as "The Wall" and is often spoken of with a mixture of reverence and trepidation.[69] Many magazines and newspapers have traditionally discouraged employees on the publishing side—including advertising, circulation, and other business departments—from interacting with those on the editorial side, who write and edit the articles. This is done by separating editorial and advertising offices, barring the sales force from reading articles before they are printed, and prohibiting editorial employees from participating in advertising sales calls.

Most print media are very concerned over maintaining the concept of The Wall and ensuring that decisions on the writing, editing, and publishing of stories are made on journalistic merit rather than on whether they will attract or repel advertisers. However, the new economics of the publishing industry is making it difficult to maintain the separation: Competition from TV, direct media, and the Internet is increasing, and newspaper and magazine readership and revenues continue to decline. There have been several well-publicized situations in recent years where major magazines and newspapers were found to have given favorable editorial consideration to an advertiser.[70] However, the media usually hold their ground when challenged by companies that threaten to pull their advertising, or even do so, when they find editorial coverage objectionable. For example, in April 2005 General Motors canceled all of its advertising in the *Los Angeles Times* after a series of articles in the newspaper were unflattering to the automaker. GM, which was spending an estimated $21 million in the *Times* each year, claimed that "factual errors and misrepresentations" in various articles led it to withdraw its advertising in the paper. The paper had run several articles that were critical of certain GM vehicles, and also suggested that some senior GM executives should be dismissed because of the company's sales and profit woes. GM's advertising boycott of the *Los Angeles Times* lasted four months and was finally ended after executives from the two sides met to resolve their differences.[71] At the same time, more recent negative reports regarding the false mileage claims of Kia and Hyundai resulted in no backlash against the media.

The media in the United States are basically supported by advertising; this means we can enjoy them for free or for a fraction of what they would cost without advertising. The alternative to an advertiser-supported media system is support by users through higher subscription costs for print media and increased rates for cable and satellite TV access. Note that the decrease in newspaper subscriptions has led some

## WITHOUT ADVERTISING, YOUR NEWSPAPER WOULD COST YOU A BUNDLE.

Did you know that every ad in your newspaper helps pay for the rest of the essential pages? The fact is, your paper would cost you about $5.00 a day without advertisements. A price that would make news indeed.

Advertising. That's the way it works.

INTERNATIONAL ADVERTISING ASSOCIATION

The global partnership of advertisers, agencies and media.

**EXHIBIT 21–18**
This ad points out how advertising lowers the cost of newspapers for consumers

YTC 21–06
**Drugfree.org**
youtube.com/10ebelch

**EXHIBIT 21–19**
The Partnership at Drugfree .org helps families address teen drug abuse

papers to reduce their publication schedules and begin charging or increasing rates for online subscriptions. The ad in Exhibit 21–18, part of a campaign by the International Advertising Association, explains how advertising lowers the cost of print media for consumers. Another alternative is government-supported media like those in many other countries, but this runs counter to most people's desire for freedom of the press. Although not perfect, our system of advertising-supported media provides the best option for receiving information and entertainment.

## Summarizing Social Effects

We have examined a number of issues and have attempted to analyze the arguments for and against them. Many people have reservations about the impact of advertising and promotion on society. The numerous rules, regulations, policies, and guidelines marketers comply with do not cover every advertising and promotional situation. Moreover, what one individual views as distasteful or unethical may be acceptable to another.

Negative opinions regarding advertising and other forms of promotion have been around almost as long as the field itself, and it is unlikely they will ever disappear. However, the industry must address the various concerns about the effects of advertising and other forms of promotion on society. Advertising is a very powerful institution, but it will remain so only as long as consumers have faith in the ads they see and hear every day. Many of the problems discussed here can be avoided if individual decision makers make ethics an important element of the IMC planning process.

The primary focus of this discussion of social effects has been on the way advertising is used (or abused) in the marketing of products and services. It is important to note that advertising and other IMC tools are also used to promote worthy causes and to deal with problems facing society (drunk driving, drug abuse, and the obesity crisis, among others). For example, the Partnership at Drugfree.org (formerly the Partnership for a Drug Free America) has created a website and uses social media, as well as print and TV ads to drive awareness and action around teen substance abuse (Exhibit 21–19).

The Partnership is funded primarily by donations from individuals, corporations, foundations, and the public sector. The organization has also partnered with the U.S. Office of National Drug Control Policy (ONDCP), and their joint campaign, "Above the influence.com." Above the Influence (ATI) won an Effie Award given for sustainability for its long-term effectiveness. Youth who are aware of ATI advertising are consistently more likely to have stronger anti-drug beliefs compared to those unaware of campaign advertising. However, concern with the misuse and abuse of prescription drugs is increasing and The Partnership created The Medicine Abuse Project, using ads to address this problem. As an example, when the organizations discovered that Urban Outfitters, the national retail store popular with teens, was selling products made to look like prescription pill bottles that made light of prescription drug misuse and abuse, they launched an advocacy effort and petition to ask the company to remove these products from their stores and website. The successful effort led Urban Outfitters to halt sales of the products. Campaigns for nonprofit organizations and worthy causes are often developed pro bono by advertising agencies, and free advertising time and space are donated by the media. Exhibit 21–20 shows an ad from a very successful public service campaign for the Boys & Girls Clubs of America featuring San Francisco 49ERS football star Patrick Willis. The campaign is designed to establish an image to

**EXHIBIT 21-20**
This ad campaign for the Boys & Girls Club is an example of the pro bono work often done by advertising agencies for nonprofit organizations

**HOW TO BE A POWER HITTER IN ANY ECONOMY.**

Advertising is a powerful business tool in any economic environment. Consider this: In lean times, competition increases, and it's the companies who continue to advertise that increase the demand for their products. These are the survivors, the leaders, the all-stars of branding.

**ADWEEK**
www.adweek.com

**EXHIBIT 21-21**
This ad promotes the economic value of advertising

distinguish the Boys & Girls Clubs from other public service groups and to encourage adults to organize clubs, and is sponsored by numerous companies, organizations, and media.

# ECONOMIC EFFECTS OF ADVERTISING

LO 21-4

Advertising plays an important role in a free-market system like ours by making consumers aware of products and services and providing them with information for decision making. Advertising's economic role goes beyond this basic function, however. It is a powerful force that can affect the functioning of our entire economic system (Exhibit 21-21).

Advertising can encourage consumption and foster economic growth. It not only informs customers of available goods and services but also facilitates entry into markets for a firm or a new product or brand; leads to economies of scale in production, marketing, and distribution, which in turn lead to lower prices; and hastens the acceptance of new products and the rejection of inferior products.

Critics of advertising view it as a detrimental force that not only fails to perform its basic function of information provision adequately but also adds to the cost of products and services and discourages competition and market entry, leading to industrial concentration and higher prices for consumers. In Hong Kong, milk powder manufacturers aim to inform consumers about the ingredients in their products and the health benefits. However, it is clear from their advertisements that once in a while they are not averse to exaggerating the nutritional claims (see Ethical Perspective 21-2 on page 748).

"We spent over 40 million dollars to kill a rubber chicken."

Richard Branson, Chairman, Virgin Atlantic Airways.

AAAA
American Association of Advertising Agencies

**EXHIBIT 21–22**

Virgin Atlantic Airways chair Richard Branson acknowledges the importance of advertising

In their analysis of advertising, economists generally take a macroeconomic perspective: They consider the economic impact of advertising on an entire industry or on the economy as a whole rather than its effect on an individual company or brand. Our examination of the economic impact of advertising focuses on these broader macro-level issues. We consider its effects on consumer choice, competition, and product costs and prices.

## Effects on Consumer Choice

Some critics say advertising hampers consumer choice, as large advertisers use their power to limit our options to a few well-advertised brands. Economists argue that advertising is used to achieve (1) **differentiation**, whereby the products or services of large advertisers are perceived as unique or better than competitors', and (2) brand loyalty, which enables large national advertisers to gain control of the market, usually at the expense of smaller brands.

Larger companies often end up charging higher prices and achieve a more dominant position in the market than smaller firms that cannot compete against them and their large advertising budgets. When this occurs, advertising not only restricts the choice alternatives to a few well-known, heavily advertised brands but also becomes a substitute for competition based on price or product improvements.

Heavily advertised brands dominate the market in certain product categories, such as soft drinks, beer, and cereals. But advertising generally does not create brand monopolies and reduce the opportunities for new products to be introduced to consumers. In most product categories, a number of different brands are on the store shelves and thousands of new products are introduced every year. In 2013, there were over 110 brands of bottled water on the market. The opportunity to advertise gives companies the incentive to develop new brands and improve their existing ones. When a successful new product such as a smartphone or tablet is introduced, competitors quickly follow and use advertising to inform consumers about their brand and attempt to convince them it is superior to the original. Companies like Virgin Atlantic Airways recognize that advertising has been an important part of their success (Exhibit 21–22).

## Effects on Competition

One of the most common criticisms economists have about advertising concerns its effects on competition. They argue that power in the hands of large firms with huge advertising budgets creates a **barrier to entry**, which makes it difficult for other firms to enter the market. This results in less competition and higher prices. Economists note that smaller firms already in the market find it difficult to compete against the large advertising budgets of the industry leaders and are often driven out of business. Take the U.S. wireless market as an example. While there are a number of wireless providers, the market is dominated by seven major providers. Verizon and AT&T hold the major share of the market, with an estimated 222 million subscribers between them. These companies are also two of the largest advertisers, spending approximately $2.3 and $2.4 billion a year, respectively. As you might imagine, to try to break into this market would be extremely difficult if not impossible.

Large advertisers clearly enjoy certain competitive advantages. First, there are **economies of scale** in advertising, particularly with respect to factors such as media costs. Firms such as Procter & Gamble and PepsiCo, which spend several billion dollars a year on advertising and promotion, are able to make large media buys at a reduced rate and allocate them to their various products.

Large advertisers usually sell more of a product or service, which means they may have lower production costs and can allocate more monies to advertising, so they can afford the costly but more efficient media like network television. Their large

CHAPTER 21

**EXHIBIT 21–23**

SPANX has been successful even with no advertising

YTC 21-07

**SPANX Founder Sara Blakely**

youtube.com/10ebelch

advertising outlays also give them more opportunity to differentiate their products and develop brand loyalty. To the extent that these factors occur, smaller competitors are at a disadvantage and new competitors are deterred from entering the market.

While advertising may have an anticompetitive effect on a market, there is no clear evidence that advertising alone reduces competition, creates barriers to entry, and thus increases market concentration. High levels of advertising are not always found in industries where firms have a large market share. These findings run contrary to many economists' belief that industries controlled by a few firms have high advertising expenditures, resulting in stable brand shares for market leaders.

Defenders of advertising say it is unrealistic to attribute a firm's market dominance and barriers to entry solely to advertising. There are a number of other factors, such as price, product quality, distribution effectiveness, production efficiencies, competitive strategies and even government legislation. For many years, products such as Coors beer and Hershey chocolate bars were dominant brands even though these companies spent little on advertising. Hershey did not advertise at all until 1970. For 66 years, the company relied on the quality of its products, its favorable reputation and image among consumers, and its extensive channels of distribution to market its brands. Industry leaders often tend to dominate markets because they have superior product quality and the best management and competitive strategies, not simply the biggest advertising budgets.[72] SPANX is another good example. The billion-dollar company was started without a single cent being spent on advertising—primarily because founder Sara Blakely didn't have any money to buy it. Starting the company with only $5,000, Blakely relied on word of mouth and endorsements from celebrities like Oprah, Brooke Shields, Julia Roberts and Gwyneth Paltrow, and other marketing factors like packaging and product benefits. Even today, SPANX does not advertise[73] (Exhibit 21–23).

While market entry against large, established competitors is difficult, companies with a quality product at a reasonable price often find a way to break in. Moreover, they usually find that advertising actually facilitates their market entry by making it possible to communicate the benefits and features of their new product or brand to consumers.

## Effects on Product Costs and Prices

A major area of debate among economists, advertisers, consumer advocates, and policymakers concerns the effects of advertising on product costs and prices. Critics argue that advertising increases the prices consumers pay for products and services. First, they say the large sums of money spent on advertising a brand constitute an expense that must be covered and the consumer ends up paying for it through higher prices. As discussed in the previous chapter, concern has been expressed that the tremendous increase in direct-to-consumer drug advertising by pharmaceutical companies is driving up the cost of prescription drugs. Critics argue that the millions of dollars spent on advertising and other forms of promotion are an expense that must be covered by charging higher prices.[74]

A second way advertising can result in higher prices is by increasing product differentiation and adding to the perceived value of the product in consumers' minds. The fundamental premise is that advertising increases the perceived differences between physically homogeneous products and enables advertised brands to command a premium price without an increase in quality.

Critics of advertising generally point to the differences in prices between national brands and private-label brands that are physically similar, such as aspirin or tea bags, as evidence of the added value created by advertising. They see consumers'

## ADVERTISING MAKES THINGS COST MORE, RIGHT?

We admit it. Advertising has a tremendous impact on prices. But you may be surprised by what *kind* of impact.

In addition to being informative, educational and sometimes entertaining, advertising can actually lower prices.

It works like this: Advertising spurs competition which holds down prices. And since advertising also creates a mass market for products, it can bring down the cost of producing each product, a savings that can be passed on to consumers.

Moreover, competition created by advertising provides an incentive for manufacturers to produce new and better products.

Which means advertising can not only reduce prices, but it can also help you avoid lemons.

**ADVERTISING**
ANOTHER WORD FOR FREEDOM OF CHOICE.
American Association of Advertising Agencies

**EXHIBIT 21–24**
This ad refutes the argument that reducing advertising expenditures will lead to lower prices

willingness to pay more for heavily advertised national brands rather than purchasing the lower-priced, nonadvertised brand as wasteful and irrational. The prescription drug industry is again a very good example of this, as critics argue that the increase in advertising is encouraging consumers to request brand-name drugs and steering them away from lower-priced generics.[75] However, consumers do not always buy for rational, functional reasons. The emotional, psychological, and social benefits derived from purchasing a national brand are important to many people. Moreover, say researchers Albion and Farris,

Unfortunately there seems to be no single way to measure product differentiation, let alone determine how much is excessive or attributable to the effects of advertising . . . Both price insensitivity and brand loyalty could be created by a number of factors such as higher product quality, better packaging, favorable use experience and market position. They are probably related to each other but need not be the result of advertising.[76]

Proponents of advertising offer several other counterarguments to the claim that advertising increases prices. They acknowledge that advertising costs are at least partly paid for by consumers. But advertising may help lower the overall cost of a product more than enough to offset them. For example, advertising may help firms achieve economies of scale in production and distribution by providing information to and stimulating demand among mass markets. These economies of scale help cut the cost of producing and marketing the product, which can lead to lower prices—if the advertiser chooses to pass the cost savings on to the consumer. The ad in Exhibit 21–24, from a campaign sponsored by the American Association of Advertising Agencies, emphasizes this point.

Advertising can also lower prices by making a market more competitive, which usually leads to greater price competition. It has been shown that for some products, advertising has helped to keep the costs down. Finally, advertising is a means to market entry rather than a deterrent and helps stimulate product innovation, which makes markets more competitive and helps keep prices down.

Overall, it is difficult to reach any firm conclusions regarding the relationship between advertising and prices. After an extensive review of this area, Farris and Albion concluded, "The evidence connecting manufacturer advertising to prices is neither complete nor definitive . . . consequently, we cannot say whether advertising is a tool of market efficiency or market power without further research."[77]

### Summarizing Economic Effects

Economists' perspectives can be divided into two principal schools of thought that make different assumptions regarding the influence of advertising on the economy.[78] Figure 21–6 summarizes the main points of the "advertising equals market power" and "advertising equals information" perspectives.

**Advertising Equals Market Power**    The belief that advertising equals market power reflects traditional economic thinking and views advertising as a way to change consumers' tastes, lower their sensitivity to price, and build brand loyalty among buyers of advertised brands. This results in higher profits and market power for large advertisers, reduces competition in the market, and leads to higher prices and fewer choices for consumers. Proponents of this viewpoint generally have negative attitudes regarding the economic impact of advertising.

**Advertising Equals Information**    The belief that advertising equals information takes a more positive view of advertising's economic effects. This model sees advertising as providing consumers with useful information, increasing their

| Advertising = Market Power | Advertising | Advertising = Information |
| --- | --- | --- |
| Advertising affects consumer preferences and tastes, changes product attributes, and differentiates the product from competitive offerings. | Advertising | Advertising informs consumers about product attributes but does not change the way they value those attributes. |
| Consumers become brand loyal and less price sensitive and perceive fewer substitutes for advertised brands. | Consumer buying behavior | Consumers become more price sensitive and buy best "value." Only the relationship between price and quality affects elasticity for a given product. |
| Potential entrants must overcome established brand loyalty and spend relatively more on advertising. | Barriers to entry | Advertising makes entry possible for new brands because it can communicate product attributes to consumers. |
| Firms are insulated from market competition and potential rivals; concentration increases, leaving firms with more discretionary power. | Industry structure and market power | Consumers can compare competitive offerings easily and competitive rivalry increases. Efficient firms remain, and as the inefficient leave, new entrants appear; the effect on concentration is ambiguous. |
| Firms can change higher prices and are not as likely to compare on quality or price dimensions. Innovation may be reduced. | Market conduct | More informed consumers pressure firms to lower prices and improve quality; new entrants facilitate innovation. |
| High prices and excessive profits accrue to advertisers and give them even more incentive to advertise their products. Output is restricted compared with conditions of perfect competition. | Market performance | Industry prices decrease. The effect on profits due to increased competition and increased efficiency is ambiguous. |

**FIGURE 21–6**

Two Schools of Thought on Advertising's Role in the Economy

price sensitivity (which moves them toward lower-priced products), and increasing competition in the market. Advertising is viewed as a way to communicate with consumers and tell them about a product and its major features and attributes. More informed and knowledgeable consumers pressure companies to provide high-quality products at lower prices. Efficient firms remain in the market, whereas inefficient firms leave as new entrants appear. Proponents of this model believe the economic effects of advertising are favorable and think it contributes to more efficient and competitive markets.

There is considerable evidence that advertising does provide the information consumers need to make purchase decisions. Avery Abernethy and George Franke performed a meta-analysis of studies examining the information content of advertising and found that more than 84 percent of 91,000 ads analyzed in these studies contain at least one information cue. The most commonly provided types of information included performance, availability, components, price, and quality, all of which are important to consumers in making an informed choice.[79]

It is unlikely the debate over the economic effects and value of advertising will be resolved soon. Many economists will continue to take a negative view of advertising and its effects on the functioning of the economy, while advertisers will continue to view it as an efficient way for companies to communicate with their customers and an essential component of our economic system. The International Advertising Association has been running a campaign for several years to convince consumers around the world of the economic value of advertising. Ads like the one shown in Exhibit 21–25 are used in countries where consumers may be less familiar with the concept of advertising. The goal of the campaign is to get consumers in these countries to recognize the role advertising plays in contributing to their economic well-being.

# WHEN ADVERTISING DOES ITS JOB, MILLIONS OF PEOPLE KEEP THEIRS.

Good advertising doesn't just inform. It sells. It helps move product and keep businesses in business. Every time an ad arouses a consumer's interest enough to result in a purchase, it keeps a company going strong. And it helps secure the jobs of the people who work there.

## Advertising. That's the way it works.

INTERNATIONAL
ADVERTISING
ASSOCIATION

The global partnership of advertisers, agencies and media

**EXHIBIT 21–25**
This ad is part of a global campaign by the International Advertising Association to educate consumers about the economic value of advertising

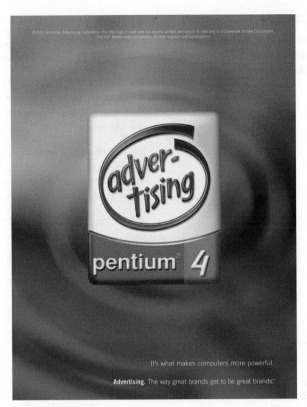

**EXHIBIT 21–26**
The AAF promotes the value of advertising in building strong brands

The advertising industry in the United States continually promotes the value of advertising. Major advertising associations, such as the American Association of Advertising Agencies (AAAA), the American Advertising Federation (AAF), along with trade associations for various media, often run campaigns reminding the general public of advertising's contributions to the economy as well as to consumers' social well-being. However, sometimes the industry must also remind advertisers themselves of the value of advertising. Recently the American Advertising Federation, which is the advertising industry's primary trade organization, decided to take action to change the way advertising is viewed by companies. The AAF decided that the best way to get marketers to recognize the value of advertising was to practice what it preaches, and thus an integrated marketing communications campaign was developed to redefine advertising in the eyes of corporate executives.

The campaign was targeted at corporate executives who were responsible for establishing and maintaining budget levels for advertising. The theme of the campaign, "Advertising. The way great brands get to be great brands," cautions corporate executives not to neglect their brand development. The Great Brands campaign promoted the economic power of advertising by featuring companies synonymous with quality advertising and for whom advertising has played a critical role in building brand equity. Exhibit 21–26 shows one of the ads from the campaign featuring Intel, the market leader for computer chips and microprocessors.

Figure 21–7, excerpts from a speech given by famous ad executive Leo Burnett, summarizes the perspective of most advertising people on the economic effects of advertising. Advertising and marketing experts agree that advertising and promotion play an important role in helping to expand consumer demand for new products and services and in helping marketers differentiate their existing brands.

To me it means that if we believe to any degree whatsoever in the economic system under which we live, in a high standard of living and in high employment, advertising is the most efficient known way of moving goods in practically every product class.

My proof is that millions of businessmen have chosen advertising over and over again in the operations of their business. Some of their decisions may have been wrong, but they must have thought they were right or they wouldn't go back to be stung twice by the same kind of bee.

It's a pretty safe bet that in the next 10 years many Americans will be using products and devices that no one in this room has even heard of. Judging purely by past performance, American advertising can be relied on to make them known and accepted overnight at the lowest possible prices.

Advertising, of course, makes possible our unparalleled variety of magazines, newspapers, business publications, and radio and television stations.

It must be said that without advertising we would have a far different nation, and one that would be much the poorer—not merely in material commodities, but in the life of the spirit.

Leo Burnett

Source: Excerpts from a speech given by Leo Burnett on the American Association of Advertising Agencies' 50th anniversary, April 20, 1967.

## Summary

Advertising is a powerful institution and has been the target of considerable criticism regarding its social and economic impact. The criticism of advertising concerns the specific techniques and methods used as well as its effect on societal values, tastes, lifestyles, and behavior. Critics argue that advertising is deceptive and untruthful; that it can be offensive, irritating, or in poor taste; and that it exploits certain groups, such as children. Many people believe advertising should be informative only and advertisers should not use subjective claims, puffery, embellishment, or persuasive techniques.

Advertising often offends consumers by the type of appeal or manner of presentation used; sexually suggestive ads and nudity receive the most criticism. Advertisers say their ads are consistent with contemporary values and lifestyles and are appropriate for the target audiences they are attempting to reach. Advertising to children is an area of particular concern, since critics argue that children lack the experience, knowledge, and ability to process and evaluate persuasive advertising messages

rationally. Although an FTC proposal to severely restrict advertising to children was defeated, it remains an issue.

The pervasiveness of advertising and its prevalence in virtually all media have led critics to argue that it plays a major role in influencing and transmitting social values. Advertising has been charged with encouraging materialism; manipulating consumers to buy things they do not really want or need; perpetuating stereotypes through its portrayal of certain groups such as women, minorities, and older adults; and controlling the media.

Advertising has also been scrutinized with regard to its economic effects. The basic economic role of advertising is to give consumers information that helps them make consumption decisions. Some people view advertising as a detrimental force that has a negative effect on competition, product costs, and consumer prices. Economists' perspectives regarding the effects of advertising follow two basic schools of thought: the advertising equals market power model and the advertising equals information model. Arguments consistent with each perspective were considered in analyzing the economic effects of advertising.

## Key Terms

ethics p. 735
shock advertising p. 741
consumer socialization process p. 743

materialism p. 749
Protestant ethic p. 750
differentiation p. 759

barrier to entry p. 759
economies of scale p. 759

## Discussion Questions

1. The chapter presents both sides of the argument as to whether the government should get involved in the battle of obesity by passing regulations, restrictions, and/or taxes. Present both sides of the argument and take a position, providing support for your opinion. (LO3)

2. There seems to be a relaxed atmosphere regarding the use of ethnic groups, interracial couples, and gay and lesbian themes in advertising. Explain the benefits and pitfalls inherent in this strategy. (LO2)

3. Camel cigarettes continues to go in the face of government regulations in its efforts to market cigarettes to children. Give some of the reasons why you think Camel continues to do so. What could be done to put an end to these practices? (LO4)

4. Do you consider the TV ad of Lake Silver (see Ethical Perspective 21–1) to be deceptive? (LO1)

5. Economists argue that advertising can be a barrier to entry for many companies that simply cannot come up with the money required to initiate an effective advertising campaign. At the same time, SPANX has succeeded without spending any money at all to promote the product. Explain how a company like SPANX can be successful with little or no advertising. (LO4)

6. What are shock ads? Do you think they are designed to create sales, or to bring attention to specific issues? Do they work? (LO2)

7. Over the years, and again very recently, there have been calls to eliminate or severely restrict advertising to children. Discuss the social and ethical issues as to whether advertising to children should be permitted. Support your position. (LO1)

8. Groups such as Commercial Alert are concerned about the intrusion of advertising and other types of marketing messages into all aspects of consumers' lives. Discuss some of the reasons consumer watchdog groups are critical of advertising and other types of marketing practices. (LO2)

9. Discuss how attitudes toward the use of sex in advertising differ between men and women. Discuss the implications of these attitudinal differences for marketers who are developing ads for each sex. (LO1)

10. The chapter discusses how many marketers are struggling with their multicultural marketing efforts and suggests that one reason may be the lack of diversity in advertising agencies. What are some of the reasons for the low number of minorities, such as African Americans, working in advertising? How can the industry address this problem? (LO2)

# 22 Personal Selling

## LEARNING OBJECTIVES

**LO1** To understand the role of personal selling in the integrated marketing communications program.

**LO2** To know the advantages and disadvantages of personal selling as a promotional program element.

**LO3** To understand how personal selling is combined with other elements in an IMC program.

**LO4** To know methods used to determine the effectiveness of the personal selling effort.

GO TO WWW.MHEDUCATION.ASIA/OLC/BELCH TO ACCESS CHAPTER 22.

# GLOSSARY OF ADVERTISING AND PROMOTION TERMS

*Note: Numbers in parentheses after term indicate chapter(s) where term is discussed.*

**absolute cost (10)**   The actual total cost of placing an ad in a particular media vehicle.

**account executive (3)**   The individual who serves as the liaison between the advertising agency and the client. The account executive is responsible for managing all of the services the agency provides to the client and representing the agency's point of view to the client.

**account planner (3)**   Advertising agency personnel who gather information that is relevant to a client's product or service and can be used in the development of the creative strategy as well as other aspects of an IMC campaign.

**account planning (8)**   The process of conducting research and gathering all relevant information about a client's product, service, brand, and consumers in the target audience for use in the development of creative strategy as well as other aspects of an IMC campaign.

**account-specific marketing (16)**   Development of customized promotional programs for individual retail accounts by marketers.

**ad execution–related thoughts (5)**   A type of thought or cognitive response a message recipient has concerning factors related to the execution of the ad, such as creativity, visual effects, color, and style.

**adjacencies (11)**   Commercial spots purchased from local television stations that generally appear during the time periods adjacent to network programs.

**advergames (13)**   Online games designed to promote a product and/or brand.

**advertainment (13)**   Media combining the use of advertising and entertainment (for example, in-game advertising, advergaming).

**advertising (1)**   Any paid form of nonpersonal communication about an organization, product, service, or idea by an identified sponsor.

**advertising agency (3)**   A firm that specializes in the creation, production, and placement of advertising messages and may provide other services that facilitate the marketing communications process.

**advertising appeal (9)**   The basis or approach used in an advertising message to attract the attention or interest of consumers and/or influence their feelings toward the product, service, or cause.

**advertising campaign (8)**   A comprehensive advertising plan that consists of a series of messages in a variety of media that center on a single theme or idea.

**advertising creativity (8)**   The ability to generate fresh, unique, and appropriate ideas that can be used as solutions to communication problems.

**advertising manager (3)**   The individual in an organization who is responsible for the planning, coordinating, budgeting, and implementing of the advertising program.

**Advertising Self-Regulatory Council (ASRC) (20)**   An organization founded by the Council of Better Business Bureaus and various advertising industry groups to promote high standards of truth, accuracy, morality, and social responsibility in national advertising.

**advertising substantiation (20)**   A Federal Trade Commission regulatory program that requires advertisers to have documentation to support the claims made in their advertisements.

**advocacy advertising (17)**   Advertising that is concerned with the propagation of ideas and elucidation of social issues of public importance in a manner that supports the position and interest of the sponsor.

**aerial advertising (13)**   A form of outdoor advertising where messages appear in the sky in the form of banners pulled by airplanes, skywriting, and on blimps.

**affect referral decision rule (4)**   A type of decision rule where selections are made on the basis of an overall impression or affective summary evaluation of the various alternatives under consideration.

**affiliates (11)**   Local television stations that are associated with a major network. Affiliates agree to preempt time during specified hours for programming provided by the network and carry the advertising contained in the program.

**affirmative disclosure (20)**   A Federal Trade Commission program whereby advertisers may be required to include certain types of information in their advertisements so consumers will be aware of all the consequences, conditions, and limitations associated with the use of the product or service.

**affordable method (7)**   A method of determining the budget for advertising and promotion where all other budget areas are covered and remaining monies are available for allocation.

**AIDA model (5)**   A model that depicts the successive stages a buyer passes through in the personal-selling process, including attention, interest, desire, and action.

**alpha activity (18)**   A measure of the degree of brain activity that can be used to assess an individual's reactions to an advertisement.

**alternative media (13)**   A term commonly used in advertising to describe support media.

**animatic (8, 18)**   A preliminary version of a commercial whereby video of the frames of a storyboard is produced along with an audio soundtrack.

**arbitrary allocation (7)**   A method for determining the budget for advertising and promotion based on arbitrary decisions of executives.

**attitude toward the ad (5)**   A message recipient's affective feelings of favorability or unfavorability toward an advertisement.

**attractiveness (6)**   A source characteristic that makes him or her appealing to a message recipient. Source attractiveness can be based on similarity, familiarity, or likability.

**augmented reality (15)**   A view of the real-world environment supplemented by computer-generated sensory input.

**average frequency (10)**   The number of times the average household reached by a media schedule is exposed to a media vehicle over a specified period.

**average quarter-hour (AQH) figure (11)**   The average number of persons listening to a particular station for at least 5 minutes during a 15-minute period. Used by Arbitron in measuring the size of radio audiences.

**average quarter-hour rating (AQH RTG) (11)**   The average quarter-hour figure estimate expressed as a percentage of the population being measured. Used by Arbitron in measuring the size of radio audiences.

**balance-of-trade deficit (19)** A situation where the monetary value of a country's imports exceeds its exports.

**banner ad (15)** An ad on a webpage that may be "hot-linked" to the advertiser's site.

**barrier to entry (21)** Conditions that make it difficult for a firm to enter the market in a particular industry, such as high advertising budgets.

**behavioral targeting (15)** A basis for target marketing based on consumers' website surfing behaviors.

**behavioristic segmentation (2)** A method of segmenting a market by dividing customers into groups based on their usage, loyalties, or buying responses to a product or service.

**below-the-line media (13)** A term used to refer to support media whose costs are not assigned directly to advertising and/or promotional budgets.

**benchmark measures (7)** Measures of a target audience's status concerning response hierarchy variables such as awareness, knowledge, image, attitudes, preferences, intentions, or behavior. These measures are taken at the beginning of an advertising or promotional campaign to determine the degree to which a target audience must be changed or moved by a promotional campaign.

**benefit segmentation (2)** A method of segmenting markets on the basis of the major benefits consumers seek in a product or service.

**Better Business Bureau (BBB) (20)** An organization established and funded by businesses that operate primarily at the local level to monitor activities of companies and promote fair advertising and selling practices.

**billings (3)** The amount of client money agencies spend on media purchases and other equivalent activities. Billings are often used as a way of measuring the size of advertising agencies.

**bleed pages (12)** Magazine advertisements where the printed area extends to the edge of the page, eliminating any white margin or border around the ad.

**blog (15)** Also known as a weblog, a blog is a web-based publication consisting primarily of periodic articles written and provided in reverse chronological order. Blogs may reflect the writings of an individual, community political organization, or corporation.

**body copy (9)** The main text portion of a print ad. Also often referred to as copy.

**bonus packs (16)** Special packaging that provides consumers with extra quantity of merchandise at no extra charge over the regular price.

**bounce-back coupon (16)** A coupon offer made to consumers as an inducement to repurchase the brand.

**brand development index (BDI) (10)** An index that is calculated by taking the percentage of a brand's total sales that occur in a given market as compared to the percentage of the total population in the market.

**brand equity (2)** The intangible asset of added value or goodwill that results from the favorable image, impressions of differentiation, and/or the strength of consumer attachment of a company name, brand name, or trademark.

**brand identity (2)** the combination of the name, logo, symbols, design, packaging, image and associations held by consumers toward a brand.

**brand loyalty (4)** Preference by a consumer for a particular brand that results in continual purchase of it.

**brand manager (3)** The person responsible for the planning, implementation, and control of the marketing program for an individual brand.

**branded entertainment (13)** The combined use of an audiovisual program (such as TV, radio, podcast, or videocast) and a brand to market a product or service. The purpose of a branded entertainment program is to entertain, while at the same time provide the opportunity for brands or products to be promoted.

**buildup approach (7)** A method of determining the budget for advertising and promotion by determining the specific tasks that have to be performed and estimating the costs of performing them. See objective and task method.

**buzz marketing (5)** the use of various activities that generate conversations and word-of-mouth communication about a particular topic such as a company, brand or marketing activity

**cable television (11)** A form of television where signals are carried to households by wire rather than through the airways.

**campaign theme (8)** The central message or idea that is communicated in all advertising and other promotional activities.

**carryover effect (7)** A delayed or lagged effect whereby the impact of advertising on sales can occur during a subsequent time period.

**category development index (CDI) (10)** An index that is calculated by taking the percentage of a product category's total sales that occur in a given market area as compared to the percentage of the total population in the market.

**category management system (3)** An organizational system whereby managers have responsibility for the marketing programs for a particular category or line of products.

**cause-related marketing (17)** Image-related advertising in which companies link with charities or nonprofit organizations as contributing sponsors.

**cease-and-desist order (20)** An action by the Federal Trade Commission that orders a company to stop engaging in a practice that is considered deceptive or misleading until a hearing is held.

**Central Hudson Test (20)** A four-part test used by the courts for determining restrictions on commercial speech.

**central route to persuasion (5)** One of two routes to persuasion recognized by the elaboration likelihood model. The central route to persuasion views a message recipient as very active and involved in the communications process and as having the ability and motivation to attend to and process a message.

**centralized system (3)** An organizational system whereby advertising along with other marketing activities such as sales, marketing research, and planning are divided along functional lines and are run from one central marketing department.

**channel (5)** The method or medium by which communication travels from a source or sender to a receiver.

**Children's Online Privacy Protection Act (COPPA) of 1998 (20)** Federal legislation which places restrictions on information collected from children via the Internet and requires that websites directed at children have a privacy policy posted on their home page and areas of the site where information is collected.

**city zone (12)** A category used for newspaper circulation figures that refers to a market area composed of the city where the paper is published and contiguous areas similar in character to the city.

**classical conditioning (4)** A learning process whereby a conditioned stimulus that elicits a response is paired with a neutral stimulus that does not elicit any particular response. Through repeated exposure, the neutral stimulus comes to elicit the same response as the conditioned stimulus.

**classified advertising (12)** Advertising that runs in newspapers and magazines that generally contains text only and is arranged under subheadings according to the product, service, or offering. Employment, real estate, and automotive ads are the major forms of classified advertising.

**clients (3)** The organizations with the products, services, or causes to be marketed and for which advertising agencies and other marketing promotional firms provide services.

**clipping service (7)** A service that clips competitors' advertising from local print media, allowing the company to monitor the types of advertising that are running or to estimate their advertising expenditures.

**clutter (6, 11)** The nonprogram material that appears in a broadcast environment, including commercials, promotional messages for shows, public service announcements, and the like.

**COBRAS (15)** Consumers' Online Brand-Related Activities–studies examining the motivations of consumers for using social media in a brand-related context. Specifically the studies focus on why consumers consume, contribute to, and create brand-related content.

**cognitive dissonance (4)** A state of psychological tension or postpurchase doubt that a consumer may experience after making a purchase decision. This tension often leads the consumer to try to reduce it by seeking supportive information.

**cognitive responses (5)** Thoughts that occur to a message recipient while reading, viewing, and/or hearing a communication.

**collateral services (3)** Companies that provide companies with specialized services such as package design, advertising production, and marketing research.

**combination rate (12)** A special space rate or discount offered for advertising in two or more periodicals. Combination rates are often offered by publishers who own both morning and evening editions of a newspaper in the same market.

**commercial ratings (11)** Measures of the average viewership of a television commercial both live and up to three days after the ads are played back on a digital video recorder (DVR).

**commercial speech (20)** Speech that promotes a commercial transaction.

**commission system (3)** A method of compensating advertising agencies whereby the agency receives a specified commission (traditionally 15 percent) from the media on any advertising time or space it purchases.

**communication (5)** The passing of information, exchange of ideas, or process of establishing shared meaning between a sender and a receiver.

**communication objectives (1, 7)** Goals that an organization seeks to achieve through its promotional program in terms of communication effects such as creating awareness, knowledge, image, attitudes, preferences, or purchase intentions.

**communications task (7)** Under the DAGMAR approach to setting advertising goals and objectives, something that can be performed by and attributed to advertising such as awareness, comprehension, conviction, and action.

**comparative advertising (6, 9)** The practice of either directly or indirectly naming one or more competitors in an advertising message and usually making a comparison on one or more specific attributes or characteristics.

**competitive advantage (2)** Something unique or special that a firm does or possesses that provides an advantage over its competitors.

**competitive parity method (7)** A method of setting the advertising and promotion budget based on matching the absolute level of percentage of sales expenditures of the competition.

**compliance (6)** A type of influence process where a receiver accepts the position advocated by a source to obtain favorable outcomes or to avoid punishment.

**comprehension and reaction tests (18)** Advertising testing to ensure receivers comprehend the message and to gauge their reaction to the same.

**computer simulation models (7)** Quantitative-based models that are used to determine the relative contribution of advertising expenditures on sales response.

**concave-downward function model (7)** An advertising/sales response function that views the incremental effects of advertising on sales as decreasing.

**concentrated marketing (2)** A type of marketing strategy whereby a firm chooses to focus its marketing efforts on one particular market segment.

**concept testing (18)** A method of pretesting alternative ideas for an advertisement or campaign by having consumers provide their responses and/or reactions to the creative concept.

**conditioned response (4)** In classical conditioning, a response that occurs as a result of exposure to a conditioned stimulus.

**conditioned stimulus (4)** In classical conditioning, a stimulus that becomes associated with an unconditioned stimulus and capable of evoking the same response or reaction as the unconditioned stimulus.

**consent order (20)** A settlement between a company and the Federal Trade Commission whereby an advertiser agrees to stop the advertising or practice in question. A consent order is for settlement purposes only and does not constitute an admission of guilt.

**consumer behavior (4)** The process and activities that people engage in when searching for, selecting, purchasing, using, evaluating, and disposing of products and services so as to satisfy their needs and desires.

**consumer franchise-building (CFB) promotions (16)** Sales promotion activities that communicate distinctive brand attributes and contribute to the development and reinforcement of brand identity.

**consumer juries (18)** A method of pretesting advertisements by using a panel of consumers who are representative of the target audience and provide ratings, rankings, and/or evaluations of advertisements.

**consumer-oriented sales promotion (16)** Sales promotion techniques that are targeted to the ultimate consumer such as coupons, samples, contests, rebates, sweepstakes, and premium offers.

**consumer socialization process (21)** The process by which an individual acquires the skills needed to function in the marketplace as a consumer.

**contact (or touch) point (1)** Each and every opportunity a consumer has to see or hear about a company and/or its brands or have an encounter or experience with it.

**content sponsorship (15)** The sponsor not only provides dollars in return for name association on the Internet but also participates in the provision of content itself.

**contest (16)** A promotion whereby consumers compete for prizes or money on the basis of skills or ability, and winners are determined by judging the entries or ascertaining which entry comes closest to some predetermined criteria.

**contextual advertising (15)** Internet advertising placed on the basis of the content of the webpage.

**continuity (10)** A media scheduling strategy where a continuous pattern of advertising is used over the time span of the advertising campaign.

**contribution margin (7)** The difference between the total revenue generated by a product or brand and its total variable costs.

**controlled-circulation basis (12)** Distribution of a publication free to individuals a publisher believes are of importance and responsible for making purchase decisions or are prescreened for qualification on some other basis.

**cooperative advertising (16)** Advertising program in which a manufacturer pays a certain percentage of the expenses a retailer or distributor incurs for advertising the manufacturer's product in a local market area.

**copywriter (3, 8)** Individual who helps conceive the ideas for ads and commercials and writes the words or copy for them.

**corporate advertising (17)** Advertising designed to promote overall awareness of a company or enhance its image among a target audience.

**corrective advertising (20)** An action by the Federal Trade Commission whereby an advertiser can be required to run advertising messages designed to remedy the deception or misleading impression created by its previous advertising.

**cost per order (CPO) (14)** A measure used in direct marketing to determine the number of orders generated relative to the cost of running the advertisement.

**cost per ratings point (CPRP) (10)** A computation used by media buyers to compare the cost-efficiency of broadcast programs that divides the cost of commercial time on a program by the audience rating.

**cost per thousand (CPM) (10)** A computation used in evaluating the relative cost of various media vehicles that represents the cost of exposing 1,000 members of a target audience to an advertising message.

**cost-plus system (3)** A method of compensating advertising agencies whereby the agency receives a fee based on the cost of the work it performs plus an agreed-on amount for profit.

**Council of Better Business Bureaus (20)** The parent office of local offices of the Better Business Bureau. The council assists in the development of codes and standards for ethical and responsible business and advertising practices.

**counterargument (5)** A type of thought or cognitive response a receiver has that is counter or opposed to the position advocated in a message.

**country-of-origin effect (19)** The impact on consumers' perceptions of products and/or brands that results from where the products are manufactured.

**coverage (10)** A measure of the potential audience that might receive an advertising message through a media vehicle.

**creative boutique (3)** An advertising agency that specializes in and provides only services related to the creative aspects of advertising.

**creative brief (8)** A document that specifies the basic elements of the creative strategy such as the basic problem or issue the advertising must address, the advertising and communications objectives, target audience, major selling idea or key benefits to communicate, campaign theme or appeal, and supportive information or requirements.

**creative execution style (9)** The manner or way in which a particular advertising appeal is transformed into a message.

**creative strategy (8)** A determination of what an advertising message will say or communicate to a target audience.

**creative tactics (8)** A determination of how an advertising message will be implemented so as to execute the creative strategy.

**credibility (6)** The extent to which a source is perceived as having knowledge, skill, or experience relevant to a communication topic and can be trusted to give an unbiased opinion or present objective information on the issue.

**Cross-Platform Campaign Ratings (11)** An audience measurement from the Nielsen Co. that measures the number of people who watch an ad only on television, the number who view it online, and the overlap between the two.

**cross-ruff coupon (16)** A coupon offer delivered on one product that is redeemable for the purchase of another product. The other

product is usually one made by the same company but may involve a tie-in with another manufacturer.

**cultural values (19)** Refers to beliefs and goals shared by members of a society regarding ideal end-states of life and modes of conduct.

**culture (4)** The complexity of learned meanings, values, norms, and customs shared by members of a society.

**cume (11)** A term used for cumulative audience, which is the estimated total number of different people who listened to a radio station for a minimum of five minutes during a particular daypart.

**customer lifetime value (CLV) (14)** an estimate of the total lifetime profit that can be generated from a specific customer.

**DAGMAR (7)** An acronym that stands for defining advertising goals for measured advertising results. An approach to setting advertising goals and objectives developed by Russell Colley.

**daily inch rate (10)** A cost figure used in periodicals based on an advertisement placed one inch deep and one column wide (whatever the column inch).

**dayparts (11)** The time segments into which a day is divided by radio and television networks and stations for selling advertising time.

**decentralized system (3)** An organizational system whereby planning and decision-making responsibility for marketing, advertising, and promotion lies with a product/brand manager or management team rather than a centralized department.

**deception (20)** According to the Federal Trade Commission, a misrepresentation, omission, or practice that is likely to mislead the consumer acting reasonably in the circumstances to the consumer's detriment.

**decoding (5)** The process by which a message recipient transforms and interprets a message.

**demographic segmentation (2)** A method of segmenting a market based on the demographic characteristics of consumers.

**departmental system (3)** The organization of an advertising agency into departments based on functions such as account services, creative, media, marketing services, and administration.

**designated market areas (DMAs) (11)** The geographic areas used by the Nielsen Station Index in measuring audience size. DMAs are nonoverlapping areas consisting of groups of counties from which stations attract their viewers.

**differentiated marketing (2)** A type of marketing strategy whereby a firm offers products or services to a number of market segments and develops separate marketing strategies for each.

**differentiation (21)** A situation where a particular company or brand is perceived as unique or better than its competitors.

**digital billboards (13)** Billboards using digital imagery that changes every 6 to 8 seconds.

**digital-interactive agency (3)** Agencies that specialize in the development and strategic use of various digital and interactive marketing tools such as websites for the Internet,, banner ads, search engine optimization, mobile marketing, and social media campaigns.

**digital out-of-home media (13)** Traditional out-of-home media (billboards, transit ads, etc.), now presented in a digital format.

**direct broadcast by satellite (DBS) (19)** A television signal delivery system whereby programming is beamed from satellites to special receiving dishes mounted in the home or yard.

**direct channel (2)** A marketing channel where a producer and ultimate consumer interact directly with one another.

**direct headline (9)** A headline that is very straightforward and informative in terms of the message it is presenting and the target audience it is directed toward. Direct headlines often include a specific benefit, promise, or reason for a consumer to be interested in a product or service.

**direct marketing (1, 14)** A system of marketing by which an organization communicates directly with customers to generate a response and/or transaction.

**direct-marketing agency (3)** A company that provides a variety of direct-marketing services to their clients, including database management, direct mail, research, media service, creative, and production.

**direct-response advertising (1, 14)** A form of advertising for a product or service that elicits a sales response directly from the advertiser.

**direct-response media (14)** Media used to seek a direct response from the consumer, including direct mail, television, print, digital, and other media.

**direct selling (14)** The direct personal presentation, demonstration, and sale of products and services to consumers usually in their homes or at their jobs.

**directional medium (13)** Advertising media that are not used to create awareness or demand for products or services but rather to inform customers as to where purchases can be made once they have decided to buy. The Yellow Pages are an example of a directional medium.

**display advertising (12)** Advertising in newspapers and magazines that uses illustrations, photos, headlines, and other visual elements in addition to copy text.

**dissonance/attribution model (5)** A type of response hierarchy where consumers first behave, then develop attitudes or feelings as a result of that behavior, and then learn or process information that supports the attitude and behavior.

**divergence (8)** the extent to which an advertisement contains certain creative elements that are novel, different or unusual

**duplicated reach (10)** Individuals exposed to the same commercial on two or more media vehicles.

**e-commerce (15)** Direct selling of goods and services through the Internet.

**e-mail (14)** Messages sent electronically over the Internet.

**economic infrastructure (19)** A country's communications, transportation, financial, and distribution networks.

**economies of scale (7, 21)** A decline in costs with accumulated sales or production. In advertising, economies of scale often occur in media purchases as the relative costs of advertising time and/or space may decline as the size of the media budget increases.

**effective reach (10)** A measure of the percentage of a media vehicle's audience reached at each effective frequency increment.

**80–20 rule (2)** The principle that 80 percent of sales volume for a product or service is generated by 20 percent of the customers.

**elaboration likelihood model (ELM) (5)** A model that identifies two processes by which communications can lead to persuasion—central and peripheral routes.

**electrodermal response (EDR) (18)** A measure of the resistance the skin offers to a small amount of current passed between two electrodes. Used as a measure of consumers' reaction level to an advertisement.

**electroencephalographic (EEG) measures (18)** Measures of the electrical impulses in the brain that are sometimes used as a measure of reactions to advertising.

**emotional appeals (9)** Advertising messages that appeal to consumers' feelings and emotions.

**encoding (5)** The process of putting thoughts, ideas, or information into a symbolic form.

**ethics (21)** Moral principles and values that govern the actions and decisions of an individual or group.

**ethnographic research (8)** A research technique that involves observing or studying consumers in their natural environment.

**evaluative criteria (4)** The dimensions or attributes of a product or service that are used to compare different alternatives.

**event marketing (16)** A type of promotion where a company or brand is linked to an event, or where a themed activity is developed for the purpose of creating experiences for consumers and promoting a product or service.

**event sponsorship (16, 17)** A type of promotion whereby a company develops sponsorship relations with a particular event such as a concert, sporting event, or other activity.

**exchange (1)** Trade of something of value between two parties such as a product or service for money. The core phenomenon or domain for study in marketing.

**exclusive (17)** A public relations tactic whereby one particular medium is offered exclusive rights to a story.

**external analysis (1)** The phase of the promotional planning process that focuses on factors such as the characteristics of an organization's customers, market segments, positioning strategies, competitors, and marketing environment.

**external audiences (17)** In public relations, a term used in reference to individuals who are outside of or not closely connected to the organization such as the general public.

**external search (4)** The search process whereby consumers seek and acquire information from external sources such as advertising, other people, or public sources.

**eye tracking (18)** A method for following the movement of a person's eyes as he or she views an ad or commercial. Eye tracking is used for determining which portions or sections of an ad attract a viewer's attention and/or interest.

**failure fee (16)** A trade promotion arrangement whereby a marketer agrees to pay a penalty fee if a product stocked by a retailer does not meet agreed-upon sales levels.

**fear appeals (6)** An advertising message that creates anxiety in a receiver by showing negative consequences that can result from engaging in (or not engaging in) a particular behavior.

**Federal Trade Commission (FTC) (20)** The federal agency that has the primary responsibility for protecting consumers and businesses from anticompetitive behavior and unfair and deceptive practices. The FTC regulates advertising and promotion at the federal level.

**Federal Trade Commission Act (20)** Federal legislation passed in 1914 that created the Federal Trade Commission and gave it the responsibility to monitor deceptive or misleading advertising and unfair business practices.

**fee–commission combination (3)** A type of compensation system whereby an advertising agency establishes a fixed monthly fee for its services to a client and media commissions received by the agency are credited against the fee.

**feedback (5)** Part of the message recipient's response that is communicated back to the sender. Feedback can take a variety of forms and provides a sender with a way of monitoring how an intended message is decoded and received.

**field of experience (5)** The experiences, perceptions, attitudes, and values that senders and receivers of a message bring to a communication situation.

**field tests (18)** Tests of consumer reactions to an advertisement that are taken under natural viewing situations rather than in a laboratory.

**financial audit (3)**   An aspect of the advertising agency evaluation process that focuses on how the agency conducts financial affairs related to serving a client.

**first cover (12)**   The outside front cover of a magazine

**fixed-fee method (3)**   A method of agency compensation whereby the agency and client agree on the work to be done and the amount of money the agency will be paid for its services.

**flat rate (12)**   A standard newspaper advertising rate where no discounts are offered for large-quantity or repeated space buys.

**Flesch formula (18)**   A test used to assess the difficulty level of writing based on the number of syllables and sentences per 100 words.

**flighting (10)**   A media scheduling pattern in which periods of advertising are alternated with periods of no advertising.

**focus groups (8)**   A qualitative marketing research method whereby a group of 10 to 12 consumers from the target market is led through a discussion regarding a particular topic such as a product, service, or advertising campaign.

**fourth cover (12)**   The outside back cover position of a magazine where an ad can be placed

**frequency (10)**   The number of times a target audience is exposed to a media vehicle(s) in a specified period.

**frequency programs (16)**   A type of promotional program that rewards customers for continuing to purchase the same brand of a product or service over time (also referred to as continuity or loyalty programs).

**freestanding insert (FSI) (16)**   A four-color multipage printed advertising booklet that contains consumer-packaged-goods coupon offers delivered with newspapers (usually in Sunday editions). FSIs can also be delivered in direct-mail packages along with local retailer ads or can be cooperative booklets such as *RedPlum* or *SmartSource* as well as solo books done by companies.

**full-service agency (3)**   An advertising agency that offers clients a full range of marketing and communications services, including the planning, creating, producing, and placing of advertising messages and other forms of promotion.

**functional consequences (4)**   Outcomes of product or service usage that are tangible and can be directly experienced by a consumer.

**game (16)**   A promotion that is a form of sweepstakes because it has a chance element or odds of winning associated with it. Games usually involve game card devices that can be rubbed or opened to unveil a winning number or prize description.

**gatefolds (12)**   An oversize magazine page or cover that is extended and folded over to fit into the publication. Gatefolds are used to extend the size of a magazine advertisement and are always sold at a premium.

**general advertising rates (12)**   Rates charged by newspapers to display advertisers outside the paper's designated market areas and to any classification deemed by the publisher to be general in nature.

**general preplanning input (8)**   Information gathering and/or market research studies on trends, developments, and happenings in the marketplace that can be used to assist in the initial stages of the creative process of advertising.

**geographic segmentation (2)**   A method of segmenting a market on the basis of different geographic units or areas.

**global advertising (19)**   The use of the same basic advertising message in all international markets.

**global marketing (19)**   A strategy of using a common marketing plan and program for all countries in which a company operates, thus selling the product or services the same way everywhere in the world.

**gross ratings points (GRPs) (10)**   A measure that represents the total delivery or weight of a media schedule during a specified time period. GRPs are calculated by multiplying the reach of the media schedule by the average frequency.

**group system (3)**   The organization of an advertising agency by dividing it into groups consisting of specialists from various departments such as creative, media, marketing services, and other areas. These groups work together to service particular accounts.

**halo effect (18)**   The tendency for evaluations of one attribute or aspect of a stimulus to distort reactions to its other attributes or properties.

**headline (9)**   Words in the leading position of the advertisement; the words that will be read first or are positioned to draw the most attention.

**hemispheric lateralization (18)**   The notion that the human brain has two relatively distinct halves or hemispheres with each being responsible for a specific type of function. The right side is responsible for visual processing while the left side conducts verbal processing.

**heuristics (4)**   Simplified or basic decision rules that can be used by a consumer to make a purchase choice, such as buy the cheapest brand.

**hierarchy of effects model (5)**   A model of the process by which advertising works that assumes a consumer must pass through a sequence of steps from initial awareness to eventual action. The stages include awareness, interest, evaluation, trial, and adoption.

**hierarchy of needs (4)**   Abraham Maslow's theory that human needs are arranged in an order or hierarchy based on their importance. The need hierarchy includes physiological, safety, social/love and belonging, esteem, and self-actualization needs.

**hit (15)**   The number of times that a specific component of a website is accessed.

**horizontal cooperative advertising (16)**   A cooperative advertising arrangement where advertising is sponsored in common by a group of retailers or other organizations providing products or services to a market.

**households using television (HUT) (11)**   The percentage of homes in a given area that are watching television during a specific time period.

**identification (6)**   The process by which an attractive source influences a message recipient. Identification occurs when the receiver is motivated to seek some type of relationship with the source and adopt a similar position in terms of beliefs, attitudes, preferences, or behavior.

**image advertising (8, 17)**   Advertising that creates an identity for a product or service by emphasizing psychological meaning or symbolic association with certain values, lifestyles, and the like.

**image transfer (11)**   A radio advertising technique whereby the images of a television commercial are implanted into a radio spot.

**incentive-based system (3)**   A form of compensation whereby an advertising agency's compensation level depends on how well it meets predetermined performance goals such as sales or market share.

**index number (10)**   A ratio used to describe the potential of a market. The index number is derived by dividing the percentage of users in a market segment by the percentage of population in the same segment and multiplying by 100.

**indirect channel (2)**   A marketing channel where intermediaries such as wholesalers and retailers are utilized to make a product available to the customer.

**indirect headlines (9)** Headlines that are not straightforward with respect to identifying a product or service or providing information regarding the point of an advertising message.

**infomercials (14)** Television commercials that are very long, ranging from several minutes to an hour. Infomercials are designed to provide consumers with detailed information about a product or service.

**information processing model (5)** A model of advertising effects developed by William McGuire that views the receiver of a message as an information processor and problem solver. The model views the receiver as passing through a response hierarchy that includes a series of stages including message presentation, attention, comprehension, acceptance or yielding, retention, and behavior.

**informational/rational appeals (9)** Advertising appeals that focus on the practical, functional, or utilitarian need for a product or service and emphasize features, benefits, or reasons for owning or using the brand.

**ingredient-sponsored cooperative advertising (16)** Advertising supported by raw material manufacturers with the objective being to help establish end products that include materials and/or ingredients supplied by the company.

**inherent drama (8)** An approach to advertising that focuses on the benefits or characteristics that lead a consumer to purchase a product or service and uses dramatic elements to emphasize them.

**in-house agency (3)** An advertising agency set up, owned, and operated by an advertiser that is responsible for planning and executing the company's advertising program.

**ink-jet imaging (12)** A printing process where a message is reproduced by projecting ink onto paper rather than mechanical plates. Ink-jet imaging is being offered by many magazines to allow advertisers to personalize their messages.

**innovation adoption model (5)** A model that represents the stages a consumer passes through in the adoption process for an innovation such as a new product. The series of steps includes awareness, interest, evaluation, trial, and adoption.

**inquiry tests (18)** Tests designed to measure advertising effectiveness on the basis of inquiries or responses generated from the ad such as requests for information, number of phone calls, or number of coupons redeemed.

**inside cards (13)** A form of transit advertising where messages appear on cards or boards inside of vehicles such as buses, subways, or trolleys.

**instant coupons (16)** Coupons attached to a package that can be removed and redeemed at the time of purchase.

**in-store couponing (16)** The distribution of coupons in retail stores through various methods such as tear-off pads, handouts, and on-shelf or electronic dispensers.

**in-store media (13)** Advertising and promotional media that are used inside of a retail store such as point-of-purchase displays, ads on shopping carts, coupon dispensers, and display boards.

**integrated marketing communications (IMC) (1)** A strategic business process used to develop, execute, and evaluate coordinated, measurable, persuasive brand communications programs over time with consumers, customers, prospects, employees, associates, and other targeted relevant external and internal audiences. The goal is to both generate short-term financial returns and build long-term brand and shareholder value.

**integrated marketing communications management (1)** The process of planning, executing, evaluating, and controlling the use of various promotional-mix elements to effectively communicate with a target audience.

**integrated marketing communications objectives (7)** Statements of what various aspects of the integrated marketing communications program will accomplish with respect to factors such as communication tasks, sales, market share, and the like.

**integrated marketing communications plan (1)** A document that provides the framework for developing, implementing, and controlling an organization's integrated marketing communications program.

**integration processes (4)** The way information such as product knowledge, meanings, and beliefs is combined to evaluate two or more alternatives.

**interactive media (1, 10)** A variety of media that allows the consumer to interact with the source of the message, actively receiving information and altering images, responding to questions, and so on.

**interconnects (11)** Groups of cable systems joined together for advertising purposes.

**internal analysis (1)** The phase of the promotional planning process that focuses on the product/service offering and the firm itself, including the capabilities of the firm and its ability to develop and implement a successful integrated marketing communications program.

**internal audiences (17)** In public relations, a term used to refer to individuals or groups inside of the organization or with a close connection to it.

**internal search (4)** The process by which a consumer acquires information by accessing past experiences or knowledge stored in memory.

**internalization (6)** The process by which a credible source influences a message recipient. Internalization occurs when the receiver is motivated to have an objectively correct position on an issue and the receiver will adopt the opinion or attitude of the credible communicator if he or she believes the information from this source represents an accurate position on the issue.

**interstitial (15)** An advertisement that appears in a window on your computer screen while you are waiting for a webpage to load.

**issue advertising (issue ads) (17)** A form of advocacy advertising in which the advertiser wishes to bring attention to what they consider to be an important issue.

**jingles (9)** Songs about a brand or company that usually carry the advertising theme and a simple message.

**laboratory tests (18)** Tests of consumer reactions to advertising under controlled conditions.

**Lanham Act (20)** A federal law that permits a company to register a trademark for its exclusive use. The Lanham Act was amended to encompass false advertising and prohibits any false description or representation including words or other symbols tending falsely to describe or represent the same.

**layout (9)** The physical arrangement of the various parts of an advertisement including the headline, subheads, illustrations, body copy, and any identifying marks.

**local advertising (11)** Advertising done by companies within the limited geographic area where they do business.

**localized advertising strategy (19)** Developing an advertising campaign specifically for a particular country or market rather than using a global approach.

**low-involvement hierarchy (5)** A response hierarchy whereby a message recipient is viewed as passing from cognition to behavior to attitude change.

**loyalty programs (16)** Programs designed to encourage repeat purchase or patronage of a specific brand of a product or service.

**magazine networks (12)** A group of magazines owned by one publisher or assembled by an independent network that offers advertisers the opportunity to buy space in a variety of publications through a package deal.

**mailing list (14)** The database from which names are generated, and the ability to segment markets and, of course the offer.

**major selling idea (8)** The basis for the central theme or message idea in an advertising campaign.

**marginal analysis (7)** A principle of resource allocation that balances incremental revenues against incremental costs.

**market opportunities (2)** Areas where a company believes there are favorable demand trends, needs, and/or wants that are not being satisfied, and where it can compete effectively.

**market segmentation (2)** The process of dividing a market into distinct groups that have common needs and will respond similarly to a marketing action.

**market segments (2)** Identifiable groups of customers sharing similar needs, wants, or other characteristics that make them likely to respond in a similar fashion to a marketing program.

**marketing (1)** The activity, set of institutions, and processes for creating, communicating, delivering, and exchanging offerings that have value for customers, clients, partners, and society at large.

**marketing channels (2)** The set of interdependent organizations involved in the process of making a product or service available to customers.

**marketing mix (1)** The controllable elements of a marketing program including product, price, promotion, and place.

**marketing objectives (1, 7)** Goals to be accomplished by an organization's overall marketing program such as sales, market share, or profitability.

**marketing plan (1)** A written document that describes the overall marketing strategy and programs developed for an organization, a particular product line, or a brand.

**marketing public relations (MPR) (17)** Public relations activities designed to support marketing objectives and programs.

**mass media (5)** Nonpersonal channels of communication that allow a message to be sent to many individuals at one time.

**materialism (21)** A preoccupation with material things rather than intellectual or spiritual concerns.

**media buying services (3)** Independent companies that specialize in the buying of media, particularly radio and television time.

**media objectives (10)** The specific goals an advertiser has for the media portion of the advertising program.

**media organizations (3)** One of the four major participants in the integrated marketing communications process whose function is to provide information or entertainment to subscribers, viewers, or readers while offering marketers an environment for reaching audiences with print and broadcast messages.

**media planning (10)** The series of decisions involved in the delivery of an advertising message to prospective purchasers and/or users of a product or service.

**media specialist companies (3)** Companies that specialize in the buying of advertising media time and space, particularly for radio and television.

**media strategies (10)** Plans of action for achieving stated media objectives such as which media will be used for reaching a target audience, how the media budget will be allocated, and how advertisements will be scheduled.

**media vehicle (10)** The specific program, publication, or promotional piece used to carry an advertising message.

**medium (10)** The general category of communication vehicles that are available for communicating with a target audience such as broadcast, print, direct mail, and outdoor.

**message (5)** A communication containing information or meaning that a source wants to convey to a receiver.

**mnemonics (4)** Basic cues such as symbols, rhymes, and associations that facilitate the learning and memory process.

**mobile (15)** Type of services accessed through a portable communications device.

**mobile billboards (13)** An out-of-home medium in which advertisements are able to be transported to different locations (signs painted on automobiles, trailers pulling billboards, and the like).

**motivation research (4)** Qualitative research designed to probe the consumer's subconscious and discover deeply rooted motives for purchasing a product.

**motive (4)** Something that compels or drives a consumer to take a particular action.

**multiattribute attitude model (4)** A model of attitudes that views an individual's evaluation of an object as being a function of the beliefs that he or she has toward the object on various attributes and the importance of these attributes.

**multiplexing (11)** An arrangement where multiple channels are transmitted by one cable network.

**narrowcasting (11)** The reaching of a very specialized market through programming aimed at particular target audiences. Cable television networks offer excellent opportunities for narrowcasting.

**National Advertising Review Board (NARB) (20)** A part of the National Advertising Division of the Council of Better Business Bureaus. The NARB is the advertising industry's primary self-regulatory body.

**National Association of Attorneys General (NAAG) (20)** An organization consisting of state attorneys general that is involved in the regulation of advertising and other business practices.

**national spot advertising (11)** All nonnetwork advertising done by a national advertiser in local markets.

**native advertising (12, 15)** Web advertising in which the advertiser attempts to gain attention by providing content in the context of the user's experience.

**needledrop (9)** A term used in the advertising industry to refer to music that is prefabricated, multipurpose, and conventional and can be used in a commercial when a particular normative effect is desired.

**negotiated commission (3)** A method of compensating advertising agencies whereby the client and agency negotiate the commission structure rather than relying on the traditional 15 percent media commission.

**new media (15)** A term used to describe the proliferation of media resulting from the advent of Web 2.0.

**Nielsen Television Index (11)** A service that provides daily and weekly estimates of the size and composition of national television viewing audiences for the network shows.

**noise (5)** Extraneous factors that create unplanned distortion or interference in the communications process.

**nonfranchise-building (non-FB) promotions (16)** Sales promotion activities that are designed to accelerate the purchase decision process and generate an immediate increase in sales but do little or nothing to communicate information about a brand and contribute to its identity and image.

**nonmeasured media (13)** A term commonly used in the advertising industry to describe support media.

**nonorganic (paid) search results (15)** Internet search results that are impacted by advertisements paid for by marketers.

**nontraditional media (13)** Newer media, including various forms of support media such as entertainment marketing, guerrilla marketing, product placements, and the like, as well as Internet and interactive media, such as blogs, podcasts, and more.

**objective and task method (7)** A build-up approach to budget setting involving a three-step process: (1) determining objectives, (2) determining the strategies and tasks required to attain these objectives, and (3) estimating the costs associated with these strategies and tasks.

**off-invoice allowance (16)** A promotional discount offered to retailers or wholesalers whereby a certain per-case amount or percentage is deducted from the invoice.

**on-air tests (18)** Testing the effectiveness of television commercials by inserting test ads into actual TV programs in certain test markets.

**one-sided message (6)** Communications in which only positive attributes or benefits of a product or service are presented.

**one-step approach (14)** A direct-marketing strategy in which the medium is used directly to obtain an order (for example, television direct-response ads).

**online commercials (15)** The equivalent of traditional television commercials that appear on the net.

**open-rate structure (12)** A rate charged by newspapers in which discounts are available based on frequency or bulk purchases of space.

**operant conditioning (instrumental conditioning) (4)** A learning theory that views the probability of a behavior as being dependent on the outcomes or consequences associated with it.

**organic search results (15)** Search results that appear due to the relevance of the search terms, not advertisements.

**out-of-home advertising (13)** The variety of advertising forms including outdoor, transit, skywriting, and other media viewed outside the home.

**outside posters (13)** Outdoor transit posters appearing on buses, taxis, trains, subways, and trolley cars.

**participations (11)** The situation where several advertisers buy commercial time or spots on network television.

**pass-along rate (10)** An estimate of the number of readers of a magazine in addition to the original subscriber or purchaser.

**pass-along readership (12)** The audience that results when the primary subscriber or purchaser of a magazine gives the publication to another person to read, or when the magazine is read in places such as waiting rooms in doctors' offices.

**pattern advertising (19)** Advertisements that follow a basic global approach although themes, copy, and sometimes even visual elements may be adjusted.

**payout plan (7)** A budgeting plan that determines the investment value of the advertising and promotion appropriation.

**pay-per-click (15)** Advertisement payment method in which advertisers' costs are based on the number of times the ad is clicked on during a search.

**people meter (11)** An electronic device that automatically records a household's television viewing, including channels watched, number of minutes of viewing, and members of the household who are watching.

**percentage charges (3)** The markups charged by advertising agencies for services provided to clients.

**percentage-of-sales method (7)** A budget method in which the advertising and/or promotions budget is set based on a percentage of sales of the product.

**perception (4)** The process by which an individual receives, selects, organizes, and interprets information to create a meaningful picture of the world.

**peripheral route to persuasion (5)** In the elaboration likelihood model, one of two routes to persuasion in which the receiver is viewed as lacking the ability or motivation to process information and is not likely to be engaging in detailed cognitive processing.

**personal selling (1, 10)** Person-to-person communication in which the seller attempts to assist and/or persuade prospective buyers to purchase the company's product or service or to act on an idea.

**persuasion matrix (6)** A communications planning model in which the stages of the response process (dependent variables) and the communications components (independent variables) are combined to demonstrate the likely effect that the independent variables will have on the dependent variables.

**planogram (16)** A planning configuration of products that occupy a shelf section in a store that is used to provide more efficient shelf space utilization.

**podcasting (15)** A medium using the Internet to distribute files for downloading into iPods and other MP3 players.

**pop-under (15)** Ads that pop up as the user is leaving the website.

**pop-ups (15)** Advertisement windows on the Internet usually larger than a banner ad and smaller than a full screen.

**Portable People Meter (PPM) (11)** A wearable pager-sized device that electronically traces what consumers listen to on the radio by detecting inaudible identification codes that are embedded in the programming.

**portfolio tests (18)** A laboratory methodology designed to expose a group of respondents to a portfolio consisting of both control and test print ads.

**positioning (2)** The art and science of fitting the product or service to one or more segments of the market in such a way as to set it meaningfully apart from competition.

**Positioning Advertising Copy Testing (PACT) (18)** A set of principles endorsed by 21 of the largest U.S. ad agencies aimed at improving the research used in preparing and testing ads, providing a better creative product for clients, and controlling the cost of TV commercials.

**posttests (18)** Ad effectiveness measures that are taken after the ad has appeared in the marketplace.

**preferred position rate (12)** A rate charged by newspapers that ensures the advertiser the ad will appear in the position required and/or in a specific section of the newspaper.

**premium (16)** An offer of an item of merchandise or service either free or at a low price that is used as an extra incentive for purchasers.

**preprinted inserts (12)** Advertising distributed through newspapers that is not part of the newspaper itself, but is printed by the advertiser and then taken to the newspaper to be inserted.

**pre-roll ad (15)** Video display advertisements that play on an Internet site before the video requested appears.

**press conference (17)** The calling together of the press to announce significant news and/or events.

**press release (17)** Factual and interesting information released to the press.

**pretests (18)** Advertising effectiveness measures that are taken before the implementation of the advertising campaign.

**price-off deal (16)** A promotional strategy in which the consumer receives a reduction in the regular price of the brand.

**primacy effect (6)** A theory that the first information presented in the message will be the most likely to be remembered.

**primary circulation (12)** The number of copies of a magazine distributed to original subscribers.

**problem detection (8)** A creative research approach in which consumers familiar with a product (or service) are asked to generate an exhaustive list of problems encountered in its use.

**problem recognition (4)** The first stage in the consumer's decision-making process in which the consumer perceives a need and becomes motivated to satisfy it.

**product integrations (13)** The act of integrating the product into television program content.

**product placement (13)** A form of advertising and promotion in which products are placed in television shows and/or movies to gain exposure.

**product- or service-specific preplanning input (8)** Specific studies provided to the creative department on the product or service, the target audience, or a combination of the two.

**product symbolism (2)** The meaning that a product or brand has to consumers.

**program rating (10, 11)** The percentage of TV households in an area that are tuned to a program during a specific time period.

**promotion (1)** The coordination of all seller-initiated efforts to set up channels of information and persuasion to sell goods and services or to promote an idea.

**promotional mix (1)** The tools used to accomplish an organization's communications objective. The promotional mix includes advertising, direct marketing, sales promotion, publicity/public relations, and personal selling.

**promotional products marketing (13)** The advertising or promotional medium or method that uses promotional products such as ad specialties, premiums, business gifts, awards, prizes, or commemoratives.

**promotional pull strategy (2)** A strategy in which advertising and promotion efforts are targeted at the ultimate consumers to encourage them to purchase the manufacturer's brand.

**promotional push strategy (2)** A strategy in which advertising and promotional efforts are targeted to the trade to attempt to get them to promote and sell the product to the ultimate consumer.

**Protestant ethic (21)** A perspective of life that stresses hard work and individual effort and initiative and views the accumulation of material possessions as evidence of success.

**psychoanalytic theory (4)** An approach to the study of human motivations and behaviors pioneered by Sigmund Freud.

**psychographic segmentation (2)** Dividing the product on the basis of personality and/or lifestyles.

**psychosocial consequences (4)** Purchase decision consequences that are intangible, subjective, and personal.

**public relations (PR) (1, 17)** The management function that evaluates public attitudes, identifies the policies and procedures of an individual or organization with the public interest, and executes a program to earn public understanding and acceptance.

**public relations firm (3)** An organization that develops and implements programs to manage a company's publicity, image, and affairs with consumers and other relevant publics.

**publicity (1, 17)** Communications regarding an organization, product, service, or idea that are not directly paid for or run under identified sponsorship.

**puffery (20)** Advertising or other sales presentations that praise the item to be sold using subjective opinions, superlatives, or exaggerations, vaguely and generally, stating no specific facts.

**pulsing (10)** A media scheduling method that combines flighting and continuous scheduling.

**pupillometrics (18)** An advertising effectiveness methodology designed to measure dilation and constriction of the pupils of the eye in response to stimuli.

**purchase intention (4)** The predisposition to buy a certain brand or product.

**push money (PM) (16)** Cash payments made directly to the retailers' or wholesalers' sales force to encourage them to promote and sell a manufacturer's product.

**QR codes (15)** Short for *quick response code*; an optically machine-readable label attached to an item or advertisement that records information, which can be revealed to the viewer through an imaging device, which translates the code into content.

**qualitative audit (3)** An audit of the advertising agency's efforts in planning, developing, and implementing the client's communications programs.

**qualitative media effect (6)** The positive or negative influence the medium may contribute to the message.

**ratings point (11)** A measurement used to determine television viewing audiences in which one ratings point is the equivalent of 1 percent of all of the television households in a particular area tuned to a specific program.

**reach (10)** The number of different audience members exposed at least once to a media vehicle (or vehicles) in a given period.

**readers per copy (10)** A cost comparison figure used for magazines that estimates audience size based on pass-along readership.

**Really Simple Syndication (RSS) (15)** (*see* RSS)

**recall (18)** An advertising effectiveness score indicating the number of persons who remember an ad.

**recall tests (18)** Advertising effectiveness tests designed to measure advertising recall.

**receiver (5)** The person or persons with whom the sender of a message shares thoughts or information.

**recency (10)** The idea that advertising will have the most effect on someone who is in the market for the product and that planners should attempt to reach that consumer as close as possible to their purchase decision.

**recency effect (6)** The theory that arguments presented at the end of the message are considered to be stronger and therefore are more likely to be remembered.

**recency planning (10)** Media planning that attempts to reach the consumer in the period of time just before their purchase decision.

**recognition method (18)** An advertising effectiveness measure of print ads that allows the advertiser to assess the impact of an ad in a single issue of a magazine over time and/or across alternative magazines.

**reference group (4)** A group whose perspectives, values, or behavior is used by an individual as the basis for his or her judgments, opinions, and actions.

**refund (16)** An offer by a manufacturer to return a portion of a product's purchase price, usually after the consumer supplies a proof of purchase.

**refutational appeal (6)** A type of message in which both sides of the issue are presented in the communication, with arguments offered to refute the opposing viewpoint.

**reinforcement (4)** The rewards or favorable consequences associated with a particular response.

**relative cost (10)** The relationship between the price paid for advertising time or space and the size of the audience delivered; it is used to compare the prices of various media vehicles.

**relevance (8)** The degree to which the various elements of an advertisement are meaningful, useful, or valuable to the consumer.

**reminder advertising (9)** Advertising designed to keep the name of the product or brand in the mind of the receiver.

**repositioning (2)** The changing of a product or brand's positioning.

**resellers (2)** Intermediaries in the marketing channel such as wholesalers, distributors, and retailers.

**response (5)** The set of reactions the receiver has after seeing, hearing, or reading a message.

**retail or local advertising rates (12)** Rates newspapers charge to advertisers that conduct business or sell goods and services within the paper's designated market area.

**retail trading zone (12)** The market outside the city zone whose residents regularly trade with merchants within the city zone.

**retargeting (15)** Resending an ad to a website visitor who previously visited the site seeking information but did not purchase, in an attempt to make a sale.

**rich media (15)** A term for advanced technology used in Internet ads, such as a streaming video, which allows interaction and special effects.

**ROI (7)** Return on investment is a measure used to determine the returns received on advertising and other IMC element investments.

**ROI budgeting method (return on investment) (7)** A budgeting method in which advertising and promotions are considered investments, and thus measurements are made in an attempt to determine the returns achieved by these investments.

**RSS (15)** Really Simple Syndication is a specification that uses XML to organize and format web-based content in a standard way to provide RSS feeds, which consist of titles and brief descriptions of other online articles.

**run of paper (ROP) (12)** A rate quoted by newspapers that allows the ad to appear on any page or in any position desired by the medium.

**S-shaped response curve (7)** A sales response model that attempts to show sales responses to various levels of advertising and promotional expenditures.

**sales promotion (1, 16)** Marketing activities that provide extra value or incentives to the sales force, distributors, or the ultimate consumer and can stimulate immediate sales.

**sales promotion agency (3)** An organization that specializes in the planning and implementation of promotional programs such as contests, sweepstakes, sampling, premiums, and incentive offers for its clients.

**sales promotion trap (16)** A spiral that results when a number of competitors extensively use promotions. One firm uses sales promotions to differentiate its product or service and other competitors copy the strategy, resulting in no differential advantage and a loss of profit margins to all.

**salient attributes (2)** Attributes considered important to consumers in the purchase decision process.

**salient beliefs (4)** Beliefs concerning specific attributes or consequences that are activated and form the basis of an attitude.

**sampling (16)** A variety of procedures whereby consumers are given some quantity of a product for no charge to induce trial.

**scatter market (11)** A period for purchasing television advertising time that runs throughout the TV season.

**schedules of reinforcement (4)** The schedule by which a behavioral response is rewarded.

**script (9)** A written version of the commercial that provides a detailed description of its video and audio content.

**search (15)** Looking for a term, company, and so forth on the Internet.

**search engine optimization (SEO) (15)** The process of improving ranking in search engine results.

**second cover (12)** The inside front cover position of a magazine where a print ad can be placed

**seeding (5)** The process of identifying and choosing the initial group of consumers who will be used to start the diffusion or spreading of a message.

**selective attention (4)** A perceptual process in which consumers choose to attend to some stimuli and not others.

**selective binding (12)** A computerized production process that allows the creation of hundreds of copies of a magazine in one continuous sequence.

**selective comprehension (4)** The perceptual process whereby consumers interpret information based on their own attitudes, beliefs, motives, and experiences.

**selective exposure (4)** A process whereby consumers choose whether or not to make themselves available to media and message information.

**selective learning (5)** The process whereby consumers seek information that supports the choice made and avoid information that fails to bolster the wisdom of a purchase decision.

**selective perception (4)** The perceptual process involving the filtering or screening of exposure, attention, comprehension, and retention.

**selective retention (4)** The perceptual process whereby consumers remember some information but not all.

**selectivity (12)** The ability of a medium to reach a specific target audience.

**self-liquidating premiums (16)** Premiums that require the consumer to pay some or all of the cost of the premium plus handling and mailing costs.

**self-regulation (20)** The practice by the advertising industry of regulating and controlling advertising to avoid interference by outside agencies such as the government.

**sensation (4)** The immediate and direct response of the senses (taste, smell, sight, touch, and hearing) to a stimulus such as an advertisement, package, brand name, or point-of-purchase display.

**shaping (4)** The reinforcement of successive acts that lead to a desired behavior pattern or response.

**share of audience (11)** The percentage of households watching television in a special time period that are tuned to a specific program.

**shock advertising (21)** Advertising in which marketers use nudity, sexual suggestiveness, or other startling images to get consumers' attention.

**single-source tracking method (18)** A research method designed to track the behaviors of consumers from the television set to the supermarket checkout counter.

**situational determinants (4)** Influences originating from the specific situation in which consumers are to use the product or brand.

**sleeper effect (6)** A phenomenon in which the persuasiveness of a message increases over time.

**slogan (or tagline) (8)** A statement or phrase consisting of a few words that succinctly expresses the company image, identity, and/or positioning a company or brand wants to communicate.

**slotting allowance (16)** Fees that must be paid to retailers to provide a "slot" or position to accommodate a new product on the store shelves.

**social class (4)** Relatively homogeneous divisions of society into which people are grouped based on similar lifestyles, values, norms, interests, and behaviors.

**social media (1, 15)** Online means of communication and interactions among people that are used to create, share, and exchange content such as information, insights, experiences, perspectives, and even media themselves.

**social network (15)** A network of business or social contacts.

**social networking sites (15)** Online platforms for networks or social relations among people who share interests, activities, backgrounds, or real-life connections.

**source (5, 6)** The sender—person, group, or organization—of the message.

**source bolsters (5)** Favorable cognitive thoughts generated toward the source of a message.

**source derogations (5)** Negative thoughts generated about the source of a communication.

**source power (6)** The power of a source as a result of his or her ability to administer rewards and/or punishments to the receiver.

**spam (14)** Unsolicited commercial e-mail.

**spamming (20)** The sending of unsolicited multiple commercial electronic messages.

**specialized marketing communication services (3)** Organizations that provide marketing communication services in their areas of expertise including direct marketing, public relations, and sales promotion firms.

**specialty advertising (13)** An advertising, sales promotion, and motivational communications medium that employs useful articles of merchandise imprinted with an advertiser's name, message, or logo.

**split-run test (18)** An advertising effectiveness measure in which different versions of an ad are run in alternate copies of the same newspaper and/or magazine.

**split runs (12)** Two or more versions of a print ad are printed in alternative copies of a particular issue of a magazine.

**sponsorship (11)** When the advertiser assumes responsibility for the production and usually the content of a television program as well as the advertising that appears within it.

**sponsorships (15)** When advertisers sponsor content on a website, it is considered a sponsorship.

**spot advertising (11)** Commercials shown on local television stations, with the negotiation and purchase of time being made directly from the individual stations.

**standard advertising unit (SAU) (12)** A standard developed in the newspaper industry to make newspaper purchasing rates more comparable to other media that sell space and time in standard units.

**standard learning model (5)** Progression by the consumers through a learn-feel-do hierarchical response.

**station reps (11)** Individuals who act as sales representatives for a number of local stations and represent them in dealings with national advertisers.

**storyboard (8)** A series of drawings used to present the visual plan or layout of a proposed commercial.

**strategic marketing plan (2)** The planning framework for specific marketing activities.

**subcultures (4)** Smaller groups within a culture that possess similar beliefs, values, norms, and patterns of behavior that differentiate them from the larger cultural mainstream.

**subheads (9)** Secondary headlines in a print ad.

**subliminal perception (4)** The ability of an individual to perceive a stimulus below the level of conscious awareness.

**superagencies (3)** Large external agencies that offer integrated marketing communications on a worldwide basis.

**superstations (11)** Independent local stations that send their signals via satellite to cable operators that, in turn, make them available to subscribers (WWOR, WPIX, WGN, WSBK, WTBS).

**support advertising (14)** A form of direct marketing in which the ad is designed to support other forms of advertising appearing in other media.

**support argument (5)** Consumers' thoughts that support or affirm the claims being made by a message.

**support media (13)** Those media used to support or reinforce messages sent to target markets through other more "dominant" and/or more traditional media.

**survey of buying power index (10)** An index that provides information regarding population, effective buying income, and total retail sales in an area.

**sweeps (10, 11)** The times of year in which television audience measures are taken (February, May, July, and November).

**sweepstakes (16)** A promotion whereby consumers submit their names for consideration in the drawing or selection of prizes and winners are determined purely by chance. Sweepstakes cannot require a proof of purchase as a condition for entry.

**syndicated programs (11)** Shows sold or distributed to local stations.

**target CPM (TCPM) (10)** A relative cost comparison that calculates CPMs based on the target audience as opposed to the overall audience.

**target marketing (2)** The process of identifying the specific needs of segments, selecting one or more of these segments as a target, and developing marketing programs directed to each.

**target ratings points (TRPs) (10)** The number of persons in the primary target audience that the media buy will reach—and the number of times.

**teaser advertising (9)** An ad designed to create curiosity and build excitement and interest in a product or brand without showing it.

**telemarketing (14)** Selling products and services by using the telephone to contact prospective customers.

**television household (11)** Defined by Nielsen as a home with at least one operable TV/monitor with the ability to deliver video via traditional means of antennae, cable set-top-box or satellite receiver and/or with a broadband connection.

**television network (11)** The provider of news and programming to a series of affiliated local television stations.

**terminal posters (13)** Floor displays, island showcases, electronic signs, and other forms of advertisements that appear in train or subway stations, airline terminals, and the like.

**testing bias (18)** A bias that occurs in advertising effectiveness measures because respondents know they are being tested and thus alter their responses.

**theater testing (18)** An advertising effectiveness pretest in which consumers view ads in a theater setting and evaluate these ads on a variety of dimensions.

**third cover (12)** the inside back cover position of a magazine where a print ad can be placed

**top-down approaches (7)** Budgeting approaches in which the budgetary amount is established at the executive level and monies are passed down to the various departments.

**total audience (television) (11)** The total number of homes viewing any five-minute part of a television program.

**total audience/readership (12)** A combination of the total number of primary and pass-along readers multiplied by the circulation of an average issue of a magazine.

**tracking studies (18)** Advertising effectiveness measures designed to assess the effects of advertising on awareness, recall, interest, and attitudes toward the ad as well as purchase intentions.

**trade advertising (2)** Advertising targeted to wholesalers and retailers.

**trade allowance (16)** A discount or deal offered to retailers or wholesalers to encourage them to stock, promote, or display a manufacturer's product.

**trade-oriented sales promotion (16)** A sales promotion designed to motivate distributors and retailers to carry a product and make an extra effort to promote or "push" it to their customers.

**trade regulation rules (TRRs) (20)** Industrywide rules that define unfair practices before they occur. Used by the Federal Trade Commission to regulate advertising and promotion.

**trade show (16)** A type of exhibition or forum where manufacturers can display their products to current as well as prospective buyers.

**transformational ad (9)** An ad that associates the experience of using the advertised brand with a unique set of psychological characteristics that would not typically be associated with the brand experience to the same degree without exposure to the advertisement.

**transit advertising (13)** Advertising targeted to target audiences exposed to commercial transportation facilities, including buses, taxis, trains, elevators, trolleys, airplanes, and subways.

**two-sided message (6)** A message in which both good and bad points about a product or claim are presented.

**two-step approach (14)** A direct-marketing strategy in which the first effort is designed to screen or qualify potential buyers, while the second effort has the responsibility of generating the response.

**undifferentiated marketing (2)** A strategy in which market segment differences are ignored and one product or service is offered to the entire market.

**unduplicated reach (10)** The number of persons reached once with a media exposure.

**unfairness (20)** A concept used by the Federal Trade Commission to determine unfair or deceptive advertising practices. Unfairness occurs when a trade practice causes substantial physical or economic injury to consumers, could not be avoided by consumers, and must not be outweighed by countervailing benefits to consumers or competition.

**unique selling proposition (USP) (8)** An advertising strategy that focuses on a product or service attribute that is distinctive to a particular brand and offers an important benefit to the customer.

**up-front market (11)** A buying period that takes place prior to the upcoming television season when the networks sell a large part of their commercial time.

**user-generated content (9)** Advertising and/or other forms of content provided by consumers or other nonprofessional sources.

**value (1)** The customer's perception of all of the benefits of a product or service weighed against the costs of acquiring and consuming it.

**vehicle option source effect (18)** The differential impact the advertising exposure will have on the same audience member if the exposure occurs in one media option rather than another.

**vertical cooperative advertising (16)** A cooperative arrangement under which a manufacturer pays for a portion of the advertising a retailer runs to promote the manufacturer's product and its availability in the retailer's place of business.

**video news release (VNR) (17)** News stories produced by publicists so that television stations may air them as news.

**video on demand (15)** Video clips of various entertainment activities, which include ads or are sponsored, are also available through the Internet.

**viral marketing (5)** The act of propagating marketing-relevant messages through the help and cooperation of individual consumers.

**voiceover (9)** A message or action on the screen in a commercial that is narrated or described by a narrator who is not visible.

**want (4)** A felt need shaped by a person's knowledge, culture, and personality.

**waste coverage (10)** A situation where the coverage of the media exceeds the target audience.

**wearout (6)** The tendency for a television or radio commercial to lose its effectiveness when it is seen and/or heard repeatedly.

**Web 1.0 (15)** A term used to describe the original version of the Internet, which consisted of primarily a one-way flow of communication.

**Web 2.0 (15)** Web applications that facilitate interactive information sharing, interoperability, user-centered design, and interactivity.

**webisodes (15)** Short featured films created by the advertiser.

**Wheeler-Lea Amendment (20)** An act of Congress passed in 1938 that amended section 5 of the FTC Act to read that unfair methods of competition in commerce and unfair or deceptive acts or practices in commerce are declared unlawful.

**word-of-mouth (WOM) communications (5)** Social channels of communication such as friends, neighbors, associates, co-workers, or family members.

**Yellow Pages (13)** A telephone directory providing names of companies that provide specific products and/or services.

**zapping (11)** The use of a remote control device to change channels and switch away from commercials.

**zero-based communications planning (7)** An approach to planning the integrated marketing communications program that involves determining what tasks need to be done and what marketing communication functions should be used to accomplish them and to what extent.

**zipping (11)** Fast-forwarding through commercials during the playback of a program previously recorded on DVR.

# ENDNOTES

## Chapter One

1. Bob Garfield, *The Chaos Scenario* (Nashville, TN: Stielstra Publishing, 2009).
2. "2013 Ad Spending Forecast +.7% as Digital Growth More Than Offsets Legacy Declines," *Jack Myers Media Business Report* (Rhinebeck, NY: M.E.D.I.Advisory Group LLC, January 4, 2013).
3. Ibid.
4. Jonathan Barnard, "ZenithOptimedia Releases September 2012 Advertising Expenditure Forecasts," October 1, 2012, www.zenithoptimedia.com/zenithoptimedia-releases-september-2012-advertising-expenditure-forecasts/.
5. Suzanne Vranica, "Global Ad-Spending Outlook Dims," *The Wall Street Journal*, December 4, 2012, p. B4.
6. "AMA Approves New Marketing-Definition," *Marketing News*, March 1, 1985, p. 1.
7. Richard P. Bagozzi, "Marketing as Exchange," *Journal of Marketing* 39 (October 1975), pp. 32–39.
8. Lisa M. Keefe, "Marketing Defined," *Marketing News*, January 15, 2008, pp. 28–29.
9. Frederick E. Webster Jr., "Defining the New Marketing Concept," *Marketing Management* 3, no. 4 (1993), pp. 22–31.
10. Adrienne Ward Fawcett, "Integrated Marketing—marketers Convinced: Its Time Has Arrived," *Advertising Age*, November 6, 1993, pp. S1–S2.
11. "Do Your Ads Need a SuperAgency?" *Fortune*, April 27, 1991, pp. 81–85; Faye Rice, "A Cure for What Ails Advertising?" *Fortune*, December 16, 1991, pp. 119–22.
12. Scott Hume, "Campus Adopts 'New' Advertising," *Advertising Age*, September 23, 1991, p. 17.
13. Don E. Schultz, "Integrated Marketing Communications: Maybe Definition Is in the Point of View," *Marketing News*, January 18, 1993, p. 17.
14. Ibid.
15. Joep P. Cornelissen and Andrew R. Lock, "Theoretical Concept or Management Fashion? Examining the Significance of IMC," *Journal of Advertising Research*, September/October 2000, pp. 7–15.
16. Philip J. Kitchen, Joanne Brignell, Tao Li, and Graham Spickett Jones, "The Emergence of IMC: A Theoretical Perspective," *Journal of Advertising Research*, March 2004, pp. 19–30.
17. Don E. Schultz, "IMC Receives More Appropriate Definition," *Marketing News*, September 15, 2004, pp. 8–9.
18. Cornelissen and Lock, "Theoretical Concept or Management Fashion?"
19. Harlan E. Spotts, David R. Lambert, and Mary L. Joyce, "Marketing Déjà Vu: The Discovery of Integrated Marketing Communications," *Journal of Marketing Education* 20, no. 3 (December 1998), pp. 210–18.
20. Tom Duncan and Sandra E. Moriarty, "A Communication-Based Model for Managing Relationships," *Journal of Marketing* 62, no. 2 (April 1998), pp. 1–13.
21. Anthony J. Tortorici, "Maximizing Marketing Communications through Horizontal and Vertical Orchestration," *Public Relations Quarterly* 36, no. 1 (1991), pp. 20–22.
22. Emily Steel, "Advertising's Brave New World: Different Lineup of Players Emerges with Online's Rise," *The Wall Street Journal*, May 25, 2007, p. B1.
23. W. Glynn Mangold and David J. Faulds, "Social Media: The New Hybrid Element of the Promotion Mix," *Business Horizons* 52, no. 4 (July/August 2009), pp. 52, 357–65.
24. Matthew Creamer, "Marketing's Five-Year Plan," *Advertising Age*, October 8, 2012, pp. 20–22.
25. Nat Ives, "Consumers Bugged by Many Ads," *Advertising Age*, December 1, 2008, http://adage.com/article/media/consumers-bugged-ads/132867/.
26. Natalie Zmuda, "Inside Gatorade's Social Media 'Mission Control,'" *Advertising Age*, September 28, 2010, http://adage.com/article/news/video-inside-gatorade-s-social-media-mission-control/146149/.
27. Bob Garfield, "The Chaos Scenario 2.0: The Post Advertising Age," *Advertising Age* March 26, 2007, pp. 1, 12–14; Sergio Zyman, *The End of Marketing as We Know It* (New York: HarperBusiness, 1999); Joe Cappo, "Agencies: Change or Die," *Advertising Age*, December 7, 1992, p. 26.
28. Kevin Lane Keller, "The Brand Report Card," *Harvard Business Review* 78, no. 1 (January/February 2000), pp. 3–10.
29. Kevin Lane Keller, "Conceptualizing, Measuring, and Managing Customer-Based Brand Equity," *Journal of Marketing* 57 (January 1993), pp. 1–22.
30. Michael L. Ray, *Advertising and Communication Management* (Englewood Cliffs, NJ: Prentice Hall, 1982).
31. Ralph S. Alexander, ed., *Marketing Definitions* (Chicago: American Marketing Association, 1965), p. 9.
32. "TV Costs & CPM Trends," Television Bureau of Advertising, 2013, www.tvb.org/trends/4718/4709.
33. Jessica E. Vascellaro and Sam Schechner, "TV Lures Ads as Audiences Scatter," *The Wall Street Journal*, September 21, 2011, pp. B1, B2; Kenneth Hein, "Study: TV Ads More Effective Than Ever," *Adweek*, February 25, 2009, www.adweek.com/news/television/study-tv-ads-more-effective-ever-98506.
34. Rance Crain, "Why Business-to-Business Advertising Is Increasingly Also Aimed at Consumers," *Advertising Age*, June 17, 2012, http://adage.com/article/rance-crain/b-b-advertising-increasingly-aimed-consumers/235413/.
35. Barbara Conners, "Use CRM Data to Build Relevance—and Avoid Message Overload," *Advertising Age*, August 13, 2013, http://adage.com/article/datadriven-marketing/making-crm-data-work-avoiding-offer-overload/243441/.
36. *Internet World Stats: Usage and Population Statistics—2012,* n.d., www.internetworldstats.com/stats.htm.
37. Todd Powers, Dorothy Advincula, Manila S. Austin, Stacy Graiko, and Jasper Snyder, "Digital and Social Media in the Purchase Decision Process: A Special Report from the Advertising Research Foundation," *Journal of Advertising Research* 52, no. 4 (December 2012), pp. 479–89.
38. Rita Chang, "Marketers Say Hello to Long-Awaited Mobile Technology," *Advertising Age*, March 16, 2009, http://adage.com/article/digital/long-awaited-mobile-technology-2-d-barcodes/135248/; Alice Z. Cuneo, "Mobile Marketing Based on Place Is Finally Making Strides," *Advertising Age*,

March 31, 2008, p. 24; Alice Z. Cuneo, "Wireless Giants Leap into Third-Screen Marketing," September 11, 2006, http://adage.com/article/digital/wireless-giants-leap-screen-marketing/111748/.

39. Jason Del Rey, "Will Mobile's Massive Growth Ever Equal Real Revenue?," *Advertising Age*, October 1, 2012, http://adage.com/article/digital/mobile-s-massive-growth-equal-real-revenue/237511/.

40. Jennifer Valentino-Devries and Jeremy Singer-Vine, "They Know What You're Shopping For," *The Wall Street Journal*, December 7, 2012, pp. C1, C2.

41. Jennifer Valentino-Devries, Jeremy Singer-Vine, and Ashkan Soltani, "Websites Vary Prices, Deals Based on Users' Information," *The Wall Street Journal*, December 24, 2012, pp. A1, A10.

42. "2009 Promo Industry Trends Report," *Promo*, http://promomagazine.com/09-industry-trends-report/.

43. Natalie Zmuda, "Coca-Cola Addresses Obesity Head On in New Ads," *Advertising Age*, January 14, 2013, http://adage.com/article/news/coca-cola-addresses-obesity-ads/239163/.

44. Kate Linebaugh and Norihiko Shirouzu, "Toyota Halts Sales over Safety Issue," *The Wall Street Journal*, January 26, 2010, p. B2.

45. Hans Greimel and Mark Rechtin, "Toyota Adopts 'Devil's Advocate' in Quest to Restore Quality, Confidence," *Advertising Age*, January 21, 2011, http://adage.com/article/news/toyota-s-devil-s-advocate-policy-restore-quality/148415/; Kathy Jackson, "Toyota Sales Strategy Threatens Pricing Power," *Advertising Age*, March 22, 2010, http://adage.com/print?article_id=142997.

46. H. Frazier Moore and Bertrand R. Canfield, *Public Relations: Principles, Cases, and Problems*, 7th ed. (Burr Ridge, IL: Irwin, 1977), p. 5.

47. Jooyoung Kim, Hye Jin Yoon, and Sun Young Lee, "Integrating Advertising and Publicity, *Journal of Advertising* 39, no. 1 (Spring 2010), pp. 97–114; Paul Holmes, "Marketers See a Greater Role for Public Relations in the Marketing Mix," *Advertising Age*, January 24, 2005, C4–C10; Jack Neff, "Ries' Thesis: Ads Don't Build Brands, PR Does," *Advertising Age*, July 15, 2002, pp. 14–15.

48. Tom Duncan, *Principles of Advertising & IMC*, 2nd ed. (New York: McGraw-Hill/Irwin, 2005).

49. Ibid.

50. Geoffrey A. Fowler, "Facebook: One Billion and Counting," *The Wall Street Journal*, October 4, 2012, http://online.wsj.com/news/articles/SB10000872396390443635404578036164027386112.

51. Karlene Lukovitz, "Naked Juice Launches Viral Eco Campaign," *MediaPost News: Marketing Daily*, September 14, 2009, http://mediapost.com/publications/?fa=articles=113460.

## Chapter Two

1. Stuart Elliott, "It's a Fine Broth of a Campaign," November 2, 2009, www.nytimes.com/2009/11/02/business/media/02adnewsletter1.html?_r=0.

2. Cheryl Krauss, "Luxury Goods Market Predicted to Grow Six to Seven Percent in 2012, Defying Global Turmoil and Spreading to New Markets, according to Spring Update of Bain & Company's Luxury Goods Worldwide Market Study," May 15, 2012, www.bain.com.

3. Ben Bouckley, "Beverages Show More 'Brand Momentum' Than Soup for Campbell's," May 22, 2012, www.beveragedaily.com.

4. Ted Goldammer, *The Beer Brewer's Handbook,* 2nd ed. (Apex, 2012).

5. Meghan Casserly, "Dells Revamped 'Della' Site for Women," *Forbes,* May 22, 2009, www.forbes.com.

6. Linda Lowen, "Beating the Odds—Verizon Grants Help Domestic Violence Survivors Gain Independence," March 1, 2012, www.about.com.

7. Thomas A. Hargett, "Former Wachovia Reps Preyed on Elderly, SEC Says," December 20, 2010, www.istockanalyst.com.

8. "AARP's Audience," www.advertise.AARP.org.

9. The 2012 Statistical Abstract, U.S. Census Bureau, 2012.

10. Jamie Beckland, "The End of Demographics: How Marketers Are Going Deeper with Personal Data," June 30, 2011, www.mashable.com.

11. Edward M. Tauber, "Research on Food Consumption Values Finds Four Market Segments: Good Taste Still Tops," *Marketing News,* May 15, 1981, p. 17; Rebecca C. Quarles, "Shopping Centers Use Fashion Lifestyle Research to Make Marketing Decisions," *Marketing News,* January 22, 1982, p. 18; "Our Auto, Ourselves," *Consumer Reports,* June 1985, p. 375.

12. Judith Graham, "New VALS2 Takes Psychological Route," *Advertising Age,* February 13, 1989, p. 24.

13. Beckland, "The End of Demographics."

14. *Ayer's Dictionary of Advertising Terms* (Philadelphia: Ayer Press, 1976).

15. Andrew M. Carlo, "The Comfort Zone," *Home Channel News,* May 24, 2004, pp. 3, 29; Davis A. Aaker and John G. Myers, *Advertising Management,* 3rd ed. (Englewood Cliffs, NJ: Prentice Hall, 1987), p. 125.

16. Jack Trout and Al Ries, "Positioning Cuts through Chaos in the Marketplace," *Advertising Age,* May 1, 1972, pp. 51–53.

17. Jack Trout, "Branding Can't Exist without Positioning," *Advertising Age,* March 14, 2005, p. 28.

18. David A. Aaker and J. Gary Shansby, "Positioning Your Product," *Business Horizons,* May/June 1982, pp. 56–62.

19. Aaker and Myers, *Advertising Management.*

20. Natalie Zmuda, "Gatorade Not Just for Elite Athletes Anymore," *Advertising Age,* January 30, 2009, http://adage.com/article/news/gatorade-repositions-starting-super-bowl-ads/134226/.

21. Jonathan Hall, "Sports Drink Sales Get into Shape," July 12, 2011, www.bevindustry.com.

22. J. Paul Peter and Jerry C. Olson, *Consumer Behavior* (Burr Ridge, IL: Irwin, 1987), p. 505.

23. Michael R. Solomon, "The Role of Products as Social Stimuli: A Symbolic Interactionism Perspective," *Journal of Consumer Research,* December 10, 1983, pp. 319–29.

24. Don. E. Schultz, Stanley I. Tannenbaum, and Robert F. Lauterborn, *Integrated Marketing Communications* (Lincolnwood, IL: NTC Publishing Group, 1993), p. 72.

25. Peter and Olson, *Consumer Behavior,* p. 571.

26. Jack Neff, "Study: TV Spots Reduce Consumers' Sensitivity to Price Change," *Advertising Age,* October 10, 2007.

27. Roger A. Kerin, Steven W. Hartley, Eric N. Berkowitz, and William Rudelius, *Marketing,* 8th ed. (Burr Ridge, IL: Irwin/McGraw-Hill, 2006).

28. David W. Stewart, Gary L. Frazier, and Ingrid Martin, "Integrated Channel Management: Merging the Communication and Distribution Functions of the Firm," in *Integrated Communication: Synergy of Persuasive Voices,* Esther Thorson and Jeri Moore, eds. (Mahwah, NJ: Erlbaum, 1996), pp. 185–215.

# Chapter Three

1. Jack Neff, "P&G Redefines the Brand Manager," *Advertising Age*, October 13, 1997, pp. 1, 18, 20.
2. Thomas J. Cosse and John E. Swan, "Strategic Marketing Planning by Product Managers—room for Improvement?," *Journal of Marketing* 47 (Summer 1983), pp. 92–102.
3. "Behind the Tumult at P&G," *Fortune*, March 7, 1994, pp. 74–82; "Category Management: New Tools Changing Life for Manufacturers, Retailers," *Marketing News*, September 25, 1989, pp. 2, 19.
4. Timothy Dewhirst and Brad Davis, "Brand Strategy and Integrated Marketing Communications," *Journal of Advertising* 34, no. 4 (Winter 2005), pp. 81–92.
5. Cosse and Swan, "Strategic Marketing Planning by Product Managers."
6. Victor P. Buell, *Organizing for Marketing/Advertising Success* (New York: Association of National Advertisers, 1982).
7. Jean Halliday, "GM Puts Final Nail in Coffin of Brand-Management Effort," *Advertising Age*, April 5, 2004, p. 8.
8. Jack Neff, "Why It's Time to Do Away with the Brand Manager," *Advertising Age*, October 12, 2009, http://adage.com/print?article_id=139593; Tom Hinkes, "Our Biggest Brands Can No Longer Be Managed by Nerds," *Advertising Age*, March 17, 2010, http://adage.com/article/cmo-strategy/biggest-brands-longer-managed-nerds/142841/.
9. Jenna Schnuer, "How to Manage Your Brand's Social Life," *Advertising Age*, April 23, 2012, http://adage.com/article/digital/manage-brand-s-social-life/234309/.
10. Rupal Parekh, "Thinking of Pulling a CareerBuilder? Pros and Cons of Bringing an Account In-House," *Advertising Age*, May 18, 2009, http://adage.com/article/agency-news/pros-cons-house-careerbuilder/136701/.
11. Ibid.
12. Bruce Horovitz, "Some Companies Say the Best Ad Agency Is No Ad Agency at All," *Los Angeles Times,* July 19, 1989, sec. IV, p. 5.
13. Suzanne Vranica, "Google, Expanding Its Reach, Taps into Madison Avenue," *The Wall Street Journal*, September 19, 2007, p. B3.
14. Shareen Pathak, "72andSunny Picks Up Google Chrome Assignment: A Look Back at the Brand's Recent Messaging Via BBH," *Advertising Age*, February 22, 2013, http://adage.com/article/agency-news/72andsunny-picks-google-chrome-assignment/239983/.
15. Joan Voight, "The Outsiders," *Adweek*, October 4, 2004, pp. 32–35.
16. "Best Buy Awards Accounts to BBDO and Crispin Porter," *The New York Times*, June 18, 2007, p. C6.
17. "Prominent In-House Agencies: Content Factory, Yellow Tag Productions, Fidelity Communications & Advertising," *Advertising Age*, April 25, 2011, p. 9.
18. Aaron Baar and Noreen O'Leary, "Second City, Second Thoughts," *Adweek*, May 14, 2007, pp. 8–9.
19. Alice Z. Cuneo, "Not So Golden Anymore," *Advertising Age*, January 24, 2005, pp. 1, 53; Kate MacArthur, "Chicago Blues," *Advertising Age*, September 10, 2001, pp. 1, 12; Anthony Vagnoni, "Gotham Regains Some Lost Luster as Center of U.S. Agency Creativity," *Advertising Age*, April 12, 1999, pp. 1, 10.
20. Sally Goll Beatty, "Global Needs Challenge Midsize Agencies," *The Wall Street Journal*, December 14, 1995, p. B9.
21. Bradley Johnson, "Agency Report 2013," *Advertising Age*, April 29, 2013, pp. 32–33.
22. Ibid.
23. Bob Lammons, "A Good Account Exec Makes a Big Difference," *Marketing News*, June 3, 1996, p. 12.
24. Matthew Creamer, "The Demise of the Suit," *Advertising Age*, March 13, 2006, pp. 1, 41.
25. Phil Johnson, "A Vision for the Future of Account Management," *Advertising Age*, March 24, 2010, http://adage.com/article/small-agency-diary/account-management-entrepreneurs-suits/142947.
26. Jon Steel, *Truth, Lies & Advertising: The Art of Account Planning* (New York: Wiley, 1998).
27. Quote in Alice Z. Cuneo, "Account Planners at a Crossroads," *Advertising Age*, July 30, 2007, http://adage.com/article/news/account-planners-a-crossroads/119558/.
28. "Ad Age Picks the Agencies to Watch in 2013," *Advertising Age*, January 28, 2013, http://adage.com/article/special-report-agency-alist-2013/ad-age-picks-agencies-watch-2013/239400/.
29. Anthony Vagnoni, "Small Fries," *Advertising Age*, March 2, 2002, pp. 20–22.
30. E.J. Schultz, "Heineken Selects Starcom MediaVest for Global Media," *Advertising Age*, May 2, 2012, http://adage.com/article/agency-news/heineken-selects-starcom-mediavest-global-media/234499/.
31. David Beals, *Trends in Agency Compensation,* 14th ed. (New York: Association of National Advertisers, 2007).
32. David Beals, *Global Agency Compensation: Key Findings Report* (New York: Association of National Advertisers, 2012).
33. Kate Maddox, "Fee-Based Model Dominant in Global Agency Compensation," *BtoB Magazine*, September 17, 2012, www.btobonline.com/article/20120917/AGENCIES/309179973/fee-based-model-dominant-in-global-agency-compensation.
34. Chris Kuenne, "Why Ad Agencies Need to Embrace Value-Based Compensation," *Advertising Age*, March 22, 2010, http://adage.com/article/agency-news/ad-agencies-embrace-based-compensation/142915/.
35. Beals, *Global Agency Compensation.*
36. Jack Neff and Bradley Johnson, "P&G Pushes More Performance Pay," *Advertising Age*, May 10, 2004, pp. 1, 2; Kathryn Kranhold, "P&G Expands Its Program to Tie Agency Pay to Brand Performance," *The Wall Street Journal*, September 16, 1999, p. B12.
37. Jeremy Mullman and Natalie Zmuda, "Coke Pushes Pay-for-Performance Model," *Advertising Age*, April 27, 2009, http://adage.com/print?article_id=136266.
38. Rupal Parekh, "Jockey Tells ANA Its 'Accountable Comp' Agency Model Works," *Advertising Age*, May 9, 2012, http://adage.com/article/agency-news/jockey-tells-ana-accountable-comp-agency-model-works/234655/.
39. Rupal Parekh, "ANA Survey: 52% of Marketers Will Ask Agencies to Lower Internal Costs," *Advertising Age*, April 2, 2012, http://adage.com/article/cmo-strategy/survey-majority-marketers-shops-lower-costs/233880/.
40. Ibid.
41. Jack Neff, "ANA Survey: Agency-Performance Reviews Are Now Business as Usual, *Advertising Age*, September 14, 2009, http://adage.com/article/agency-news/ana-survey-agency-performance-reviews-business-usual/138983/.

42. *Report on the Agency-Advertiser Value Survey*, American Association of Advertising Agencies and Assocation of National Advertisers, August 2007.

43. Tim Williams and Ronald Baker, "New Value-Based Comp Model Needed," *Advertising Age,* June 11, 2007, http://adage.com/article/cmo-strategy/based-comp-model-needed/117143/.

44. Teressa Iezzi, "What's to Become of Long-Term Marketer, Agency Relationships?," *Advertising Age*, March 26, 2007, p. 17; Joanne Lipman, "Study Shows Clients Jump Ship Quickly," *The Wall Street Journal*, May 21, 1992, p. B6.

45. Alexandra Bruell and Maureen Morrison, "Exxon Consolidates Global Ad Duties with Omnicom and Interpublic," *Advertising Age*, November 3, 2011, http://*adage*.com/article/agency-news/exxon-consolidates-global-duties-omnicom-interpublic/230804/.

46. Rupal Parekh, "Why Carmichael Lynch Resigned Harley after 31 Years," *Advertising Age*, August 30, 2010, http://adage.com/article/agency-news/advertising-carmichael-lynch-resigned-harley-davidson/145638/.

47. Rupal Parekh, "Why the Client–Agency Bond Just Isn't What It Used to Be," *Advertising Age*, February 14, 2011, http://adage.com/article/agency-news/long-term-ad-agency-client-bonds-a-rarity/148787/.

48. David Kiley, "Innocean Strives to Be Known as More Than Hyundai Agency," *Advertising Age,* April 25, 2011, pp. 8, 9.

49. Maureen Morrison, "Marketing Executives Reveal What They Want from Strong Client–Agency Relationship," *Advertising Age*, July 18, 2012, http://adage.com/article/cmo-strategy/marketers-ad-agency-relationships/236100/; "How to Be a Better Agency Client," *Advertising Age*, January 9, 2012, pp. 8, 9; Kathleen Sampley, "Love's Labors Lost: Behind the Breakups," *Adweek*, August 1, 2005, p. 8; Fred Beard, "Marketing Client Role Ambiguity as a Source of Dissatisfaction in Client–Ad Agency Relationships," *Journal of Advertising Research*, September/October 1996, pp. 9–20; Paul Michell, Harold Cataquet, and Stephen Hague, "Establishing the Causes of Disaffection in Agency–Client Relations," *Journal of Advertising Research* 32, no. 2 (1992), pp. 41–48; Peter Doyle, Marcel Corstiens, and Paul Michell, "Signals of Vulnerability in Agency–Client Relations," *Journal of Marketing* 44 (Fall 1980), pp. 18–23; Daniel B. Wackman, Charles Salmon, and Caryn C. Salmon, "Developing an Advertising Agency–Client Relationship," *Journal of Advertising Research* 26, no. 6 (December 1986–January 1987), pp. 21–29.

50. Joan Voight and Wendy Melillo, "Study: Clients Want Multiple Partners," *Adweek*, May 14, 2007, pp. 20–21.

51. Alvin J. Silk, "Conflict Policy and Advertising Agency–Client Relations: The Problem of Competing Clients Sharing a Common Agency," *Working Knowledge, Harvard Business School Working Paper Number 12-104*, May 31, 2012, http://hbswk.hbs.edu/item/7021.html.

52. Suzanne Vranica, "Pinched Firms Woo Rivals' Happy Clients," *The Wall Street Journal*, March 4, 2002, p. B8.

53. Jack Neff, "Why Spec Creative Should Go Away but Won't," *Advertising Age*, January 9, 2012, pp. 10, 11.

54. Jennifer Comiteau, "What Agencies Think of Search Consultants," *Adweek*, August 4, 2003, pp. 14–16.

55. Fred K. Beard, "Exploring the Use of Advertising Agency Review Consultants," *Journal of Advertising Research* 42, no. 1 (January/February) 2002, pp. 39–50.

56. "Ad Age Picks the Agencies to Watch in 2013," *Advertising Age*, January 28, 2013, http://adage.com/article/special-report-agency-alist-2013/ad-age-picks-agencies-watch-2013/239400/.

57. Jack Neff, "Ries' Thesis: Ads Don't Build Brands, PR Does," *Advertising Age*, July 15, 2002, pp. 14–15; Prema Nakra, "The Changing Role of Public Relations in Marketing Communications," *Public Relations Quarterly* 1 (1991), pp. 42–45.

58. Betsy Spathmann, "Sudden Impact," *Promo*, April 1999, pp. 42–48.

59. Quoted in Laura Q. Hughes and Kate MacArthur, "Soft Boiled," *Advertising Age*, May 28, 2001, pp. 3, 54.

60. Study cited in Michael Bush, "Memo to Marketers: It's Your Fault If Your Shops Flounder," *Advertising Age*, March 29, 2010, http://adage.com/article/cmo-strategy/marketers-fault-ad-agencies-flounder/143010/ .

61. Kunur Patel, "Adland's Identity Crisis Leaves Clients' Heads Spinning," *Advertising Age*, April 25, 2011, p. 4.

62. William N. Swain, "Perceptions of IMC after a Decade of Development: Who's at the Wheel and How Can We Meaasure Success?," *Journal of Advertising Research*, March 2004, pp. 46–67; Philip J. Kitchen and Don E. Schultz, "A Multi-Country Comparison of the Drive for IMC," *Journal of Advertising Research* 39, no. 1 (January 1999), pp. 21–38.

63. David N. McArthur and Tom Griffin, "A Marketing Management View of Integrated Marketing Communications," *Journal of Advertising Research* 37, no. 5 (September/October) 1997, pp. 19–26; Adrienne Ward Fawcett, "Integrated Marketing—marketers Convinced: Its Time Has Arrived," *Advertising Age*, November 6, 1993, pp. S1–S2.

64. Claire Atkinson, "Tracking the Challenges of Integrated Marketing," *Television Weekly*, March 17, 2003, p. 11.

65. Voight and Melillo, "Study: Clients Want Multiple Partners."

66. Quoted in Michael Bush, "Memo to Marketers: It's Your Fault If Your Shops Flounder."

## Chapter Four

1. Dirk Zeims, "The Morphological Approach for Unconscious Consumer Motivation Research," *Journal of Advertising Research* 44, no. 2 (June 2004), pp. 210–15.

2. Jeffrey Ball, "But How Does It Make You Feel?," *The Wall Street Journal*, May 3, 1999, p. B1.

3. Jagdish N. Sheth, "The Role of Motivation Research in Consumer Psychology" (Faculty Working Paper, University of Illinois, Champaign, 1974); Bill Abrams, "Charles of the Ritz Discovers What Women Want," *The Wall Street Journal*, August 20, 1981, p. 29; Ernest Dichter, *Getting Motivated* (New York: Pergamon Press, 1979).

4. Ball, "But How Does It Make You Feel?"

5. Gary Strauss, "TV Sex: Uncut, Unavoidable," *USA Today*, January 20, 2010, p. 1.

6. Joanne Lipman, "Leaders Turning Up Their Noses at 'Scent Strips' Ads in Magazines," *The Wall Street Journal*, December 6, 1989, p. 1.

7. Gord Hotchkiss, "4,000 Ads a Day, and Counting," November 14, 2007, www.mediapost.com/publications/article/68986/.

8. Gordon W. Allport, "Attitudes," in *Handbook of Social Psychology*, C.M. Murchison, ed. (Winchester, MA: Clark University Press, 1935), p. 810.

9. Robert B. Zajonc and Hazel Markus, "Affective and Cognitive Factors in Preferences," *Journal of Consumer Research* 9, no. 2 (June 1982), pp. 123–31.

10. Joel B. Cohen, Paul W. Minniard, and Peter R. Dickson, "Information Integration: An Information Processing Perspective," in *Advances in Consumer Research* (vol. 7), Jerry C. Olson, ed. (Ann Arbor, MI: Association for Consumer Research, 1980), pp. 161–70.

11. James F. Engel, "The Psychological Consequences of a Major Purchase Decision," in *Marketing in Transition*, William S. Decker, ed. (Chicago: American Marketing Association, 1963), pp. 462–75.

12. Leon G. Schiffman and Leslie Lazar Kannuk, *Consumer Behavior*, 4th ed. (Englewood Cliffs, NJ: Prentice Hall, 1991), p. 192.

13. Gerald J. Gorn, "The Effects of Music in Advertising on Choice: A Classical Conditioning Approach," *Journal of Marketing* 46 (Winter 1982), pp. 94–101.

14. James J. Kellaris, Anthony D. Cox, and Dena Cox, "The Effect of Background Music on Ad Processing: A Contingency Explanation," *Journal of Marketing* 57, no. 4 (Fall 1993), p. 114.

15. Brian C. Deslauries and Peter B. Everett, "The Effects of Intermittent and Continuous Token Reinforcement on Bus Ridership," *Journal of Applied Psychology* 62 (August 1977), pp. 369–75.

16. Lyman E. Ostlund, "Role Theory and Group Dynamics," in *Consumer Behavior: Theoretical Sources*, Scott Ward and Thomas S. Robertson, eds. (Englewood Cliffs, NJ: Prentice Hall, 1973), pp. 230–75.

## Chapter Five

1. Wilbur Schram, *The Process and Effects of Mass Communications* (Urbana: University of Illinois Press, 1955).

2. Ibid.

3. Maureen Morrison, "Starbucks' New Logo Signals Intent to 'Think Beyond Coffee,'" *Advertising Age*, January 5, 2011, http://adage.com/article/news/starbucks-logo-signals-intent-coffee/148020/.

4. Andrew Hampp and Rupal Parekh, "Gap to Scrap New Logo, Return to Old Design Plans to Announce Change of Company Facebook Page," *Advertising Age*, October 11, 2010, http://adage.com/article/news/gap-scrap-logo-return-design/146417/.

5. Joseph T. Plummer, "Word-of-Mouth—a New Advertising Discipline?," *Journal of Advertising Research* 47, no. 4 (December 2007), pp. 385–86; Dee T. Allsop, Bryce R. Bassett, and James A. Hoskins, "Word-of-Mouth Research; Principles and Applications," *Journal of Advertising Research* 47, no. 4 (December 2007), pp. 398–411; Robert E. Smith and Christine A. Vogt, "The Effects of Integrating Advertising and Negative Word-of-Mouth Communications on Message Processing and Response," *Journal of Consumer Psychology* 4, no. 2 (1995), pp. 133–51; Barry L. Bayus, "Word of Mouth: The Indirect Effect of Marketing Efforts," *Journal of Advertising Research* 25, no. 3 (June/July 1985), pp. 31–39.

6. Kate Niederhoffer, Rob Mooth, David Wiesenfeld, and Jonathon Gordon, "The Origin and Impact of CPG New-Product Buzz: Emerging Trends and Implications," *Journal of Advertising Research*, December 2007, pp. 420–26; Catharine P. Taylor, "Pssst! How Do You Measure Buzz?," *Adweek*, October 24, 2005, pp. 26–28; Robert Brenner, "I Sold It through the Grapevine," *BusinessWeek*, May 26, 2006, pp. 32–34; Garry Khermouch and Jeff Green, "Buzz Marketing," *BusinessWeek*, July 30, 2001, pp. 50–56.

7. E.J. Schultz, "Why 'Crash the Super Bowl' Hasn't Burned Out for Doritos," *Advertising Age*, January 24, 2013, http://adage.com/article/special-report-super-bowl/crash-super-bowl-burned-doritos/239373/; Michael Learmoth, "Doritos, Google, Super Bowl Ads Storm Chart," *Advertising Age*, February 18, 2010, http://adage.com/article/the-viral-video-chart/doritos-google-super-bowl-ads-storm-viral-video-chart/142151/ .

8. Christopher Heine, "Frito-Lay Likes the Data from Doritos' 'Crash the Super Bowl,'" *Adweek*, February 7, 2013, www.adweek.com/news/technology/frito-lay-likes-data-doritos-crash-super-bowl-147127.

9. Yuping Liu-Thompkins, "Seeding Viral Content," *Journal of Advertising Research* 52, no. 4 (December 2012), pp. 465–78.

10. Ibid.

11. H.C. Chiu, Y.C. Hsieh, Y.H. Kao, and M. Lee, "The Determinants of Email Receivers' Disseminating Behaviors on the Internet," *Journal of Advertising Research* 47, no. 4 (December 2007), pp. 524–34; T. Sun, S.Y.G. Wu, and M. Kuntaraporn, "Online Word-of-Mouth (or Mouse): An Exploration of Its Antecedents and Consequences," *Journal of Computer-Mediated Communication* 11, no. 4 (2006).

12. J.Y.C. Ho and M. Dempsey, "Viral Marketing Motivations to Forward Online Content," *Journal of Business Research* 63, no. 9/10 (2010), pp. 1000–06; Z. Katona, P. Zubcsek, and M. Sarvary, "Network Effect and Personal Influences: Diffusion of an Online Social Network," *Journal of Marketing Research* 48, no. 3 (2011), pp. 425–43; M. Trusov, A.V. Bodpati, and R.E. Bucklin, "Determining Influential Users in Internet Social Networks," *Journal of Marketing Research* 47, no. 4 (2010), pp. 643–58.

13. Liu-Thompkins, "Seeding Viral Content."

14. Natalie Zmuda, "Vitaminwater Look to Boost Trial, Awareness with Olympics Campaign," *Advertising Age*, July 25, 2012, http://adage.com/article/news/vitaminwater-boost-awareness-olympics-campaign/236311/.

15. Ed Keller and Brad Fay, "The Role of Advertising in Word of Mouth," *Journal of Advertising Research* 49, no. 2 (June 2009), pp. 154–58; Ed Keller and Jon Berry, "Word-of-Mouth: The Real Action Is Offline," *Advertising Age*, December 4, 2006, p. 20.

16. Ed Keller and Brad Fay, "Word-of-Mouth Advocacy," *Journal of Advertising Research*, December 2012, pp. 459–64.

17. Ibid.

18. Ed Keller and Brad Fay, *The Face-to-Face Book: Why Real Relationships Rule in a Digital Marketplace* (New York: Free Press, 2012), pp. 103–06.

19. Larry Yu, "How Companies Turn Buzz into Sales," *MIT Sloan Management Review*," Winter 2005, pp. 5–6.

20. Suzanne Vranica, "Getting Buzz Marketers to Fess Up," *The Wall Street Journal*, February 9, 2005, p. B9.

21. Ibid.

22. Keller and Fay, "Word-of-Mouth Advocacy."

23. Quote by Gordon S. Bower in *Fortune*, October 14, 1985, p. 11.

24. Meg James, "Over 50 and out of Favor," *The Los Angeles Times*, May 10, 2005, pp. A1, A10.

25. Thomas V. Bonoma and Leonard C. Felder, "Nonverbal Communication in Marketing: Toward Communicational Analysis," *Journal of Marketing Research*, May 1977, pp. 169–80.

26. Jacob Jacoby and Wayne D. Hoyer, "Viewer Miscomprehension of Televised Communication: Selected Findings," *Journal of Marketing* 46, no. 4 (Fall 1982), pp. 12–26; Jacob Jacoby and Wayne D. Hoyer, "The Comprehension and Miscomprehension of Print Communications: An Investigation of Mass Media Magazines," *Advertising Education Foundation Study*, New York, 1987.

27. E.K. Strong, *The Psychology of Selling* (New York: McGraw-Hill, 1925), p. 9.

28. Brent Adamason, Matthew Dixon, and Nicholas Toman, "The End of Solution Sales," *Harvard Business Review* 90, no. 7/8 (July/August 2012), pp. 60–68.

29. Robert J. Lavidge and Gary A. Steiner, "A Model for Predictive Measurements of Advertising Effectiveness," *Journal of Marketing* 24 (October 1961), pp. 59–62.

30. Thomas Barry, "The Development of the Hierarchy of Effects: An Historical Perspective," *Current Issues & Research in Advertising* 10, no. 2 (1987), pp. 251–95.

31. Everett M. Rogers, *Diffusion of Innovations* (New York: Free Press, 1962), pp. 79–86.

32. "Shiny New Things: What Digital Adopters Want, How to Reach Them, and Why Every Marketer Should Pay Attention," *Advertising Age Insights White Paper*, March 15, 2010.

33. Ibid.

34. William J. McGuire, "An Information Processing Model of Advertising Effectiveness," in *Behavioral and Management Science in Marketing*, Harry J. Davis and Alvin J. Silk, eds. (New York: Ronald Press, 1978), pp. 156–80.

35. Michael L. Ray, "Communication and the Hierarchy of Effects," in *New Models for Mass Communication Research*, P. Clarke, ed. (Beverly Hills, CA: Sage, 1973), pp. 147–75.

36. Herbert E. Krugman, "The Impact of Television Advertising: Learning without Involvement," *Public Opinion Quarterly* 29 (Fall 1965), pp. 349–56.

37. Scott A. Hawkins and Stephen J. Hoch, "Low-Involvement Learning: Memory without Evaluation," *Journal of Consumer Research* 19, no. 2 (September 1992), pp. 212–25.

38. Harry W. McMahan, "Do Your Ads Have VIP?" *Advertising Age*, July 14, 1980, pp. 50–51.

39. Robert E. Smith, "Integrating Information from Advertising and Trial: Processes and Effects on Consumer Response to Product Information," *Journal of Marketing Research* 30 (May 1993), pp. 204–19.

40. DeAnna S. Kempf and Russell N. Laczniak, "Advertising's Influence on Subsequent Product Trial Processing," *Journal of Advertising* 30, no. 3 (Fall 2001), pp. 27–38.

41. Judith L. Zaichkowsky, "Conceptualizing Involvement," *Journal of Advertising* 15, no. 2 (1986), pp. 4–14; Anthony G. Greenwald and Clark Leavitt, "Audience Involvement in Advertising: Four Levels," *Journal of Consumer Research* 11, no. 1 (June 1984), pp. 581–92; Richard Vaughn, "How Advertising Works: A Planning Model," *Journal of Advertising Research* 20, no. 5 (October 1980), pp. 27–33; Richard Vaughn, "How Advertising Works: A Planning Model Revisited," *Journal of Advertising Research* 26, no. 1 (February/March 1986), pp. 57–66.

42. Todd Powers, Dorothy Advincula, Manila S. Austin, Stacy Graiko, and Jasper Snyder, "Digital and Social Media in the Purchase Decision Process," *Journal of Advertising Research*, December 2012, pp. 479–89.

43. Roxane Divol, David Edelman, and Hugo Sarrazin, "Demystifying Social Media," *McKinsey Quarterly*, April 2012, www.mckinsey.com/insights/marketing_sales/demystifying_social_media.

44. Ibid.

45. David Court, Dave Elzinga, Susan Mulder, and Ole Jorgen Vetvik, "The Consumer Decision Journey," *McKinsey Quarterly*, June 2009, www.mckinsey.com/insights/marketing_sales/the_consumer_decision_journey.

46. Ibid.

47. Jerry C. Olson, Daniel R. Toy, and Phillip A. Dover, "Mediating Effects of Cognitive Responses to Advertising on Cognitive Structure," in *Advances in Consumer Research* (vol. 5), H. Keith Hunt, ed. (Ann Arbor, MI: Association for Consumer Research, 1978), pp. 72–78.

48. Anthony A. Greenwald, "Cognitive Learning, Cognitive Response to Persuasion and Attitude Change," in *Psychological Foundations of Attitudes*, A.G. Greenwald, T.C. Brock, and T.W. Ostrom, eds. (New York: Academic Press, 1968); Peter L. Wright, "The Cognitive Processes Mediating Acceptance of Advertising," *Journal of Marketing Research* 10 (February 1973), pp. 53–62; Brian Wansink, Michael L. Ray, and Rajeev Batra, "Increasing Cognitive Response Sensitivity," *Journal of Advertising* 23, no. 2 (June 1994), pp. 65–76.

49. Peter Wright, "Message Evoked Thoughts, Persuasion Research Using Thought Verbalizations," *Journal of Consumer Research* 7, no. 2 (September 1980), pp. 151–75.

50. Scott B. Mackenzie, Richard J. Lutz, and George E. Belch, "The Role of Attitude toward the Ad as a Mediator of Advertising Effectiveness: A Test of Competing Explanations," *Journal of Marketing Research* 23 (May 1986), pp. 130–43; Rajeev Batra and Michael L. Ray, "Affective Responses Mediating Acceptance of Advertising," *Journal of Consumer Research* 13 (September 1986), pp. 234–49; Tim Ambler and Tom Burne, "The Impact of Affect on Memory of Advertising," *Journal of Advertising Research* 29, no. 3 (March/April 1999), pp. 25–34.

51. Ronald Alsop, "TV Ads That Are Likeable Get Plus Rating for Persuasiveness," *The Wall Street Journal*, February 20, 1986, p. 23.

52. David J. Moore and William D. Harris, "Affect Intensity and the Consumer's Attitude toward High Impact Emotional Advertising Appeals," *Journal of Advertising* 25, no. 2 (Summer 1996), pp. 37–50; Andrew A. Mitchell and Jerry C. Olson, "Are Product Attribute Beliefs the Only Mediator of Advertising Effects on Brand Attitude?," *Journal of Marketing Research* 18 (August 1981), pp. 318–32.

53. David J. Moore, William D. Harris, and Hong C. Chen, "Affect Intensity: An Individual Difference Response to Advertising Appeals," *Journal of Consumer Research* 22 (September 1995), pp. 154–64; Julie Edell and Marian C. Burke, "The Power of Feelings in Understanding Advertising Effects," *Journal of Consumer Research* 14 (December 1987), pp. 421–33.

54. Richard E. Petty and John T. Cacioppo, "Central and Peripheral Routes to Persuasion: Application to Advertising," in *Advertising and Consumer Psychology*,

Larry Percy and Arch Woodside, eds. (Lexington, MA: Lexington Books, 1983), pp. 3–23.

**55.** Ibid.

**56.** Richard E. Petty, John T. Cacioppo, and David Schumann, "Central and Peripheral Routes to Advertising Effectiveness: The Moderating Role of Involvement," *Journal of Consumer Research* 10 (September 1983), pp. 135–46.

**57.** Demetrios Vakratsas and Tim Ambler, "How Advertising Works: What Do We Really Know?" *Journal of Marketing* 63 (January 1999), pp. 26–43.

**58.** Bruce F. Hall, "A New Model for Measuring Advertising Effects," *Journal of Advertising Research* 42, no. 2 (March/April 2002), pp. 23–31.

**59.** Thomas E. Barry, "In Defense of the Hierarchy of Effects: A Rejoinder to Weilbacher," *Journal of Advertising Research*, May/June 2002, pp. 44–47.

**60.** William M. Weilbacher, "Point of View: Does Advertising Cause a 'Hierarchy of Effects'?," *Journal of Advertising Research* 41, no. 6 (November/December 2001), pp. 19–26.

## Chapter Six

**1.** William J. McGuire, "An Information Processing Model of Advertising Effectiveness," in *Behavioral and Management Science in Marketing,* Harry J. Davis and Alvin J. Silk, eds. (New York: Ronald Press, 1978), pp. 156–80.

**2.** Dennis Thompsett, "Kardashians Know How to Attract Their Target Audience," *Owen Sound Sun Times,* May 2, 2012, www.owensoundsuntimes.com/2012/05/02/kardashians-know-how-to-attract-their-target-audience.

**3.** Kate Niedeerhoffer, Rob Mooth, David Wiesenfeld, and Jonathon Gordon, "The Origin and Impact of CPG New-Product Buzz: Emerging Trends and Implications," *Journal of Advertising Research* 47, no. 4 (December 2007), pp. 420–26.

**4.** Herbert C. Kelman, "Processes of Opinion Change," *Public Opinion Quarterly* 25 (Spring 1961), pp. 57–78.

**5.** William J. McGuire, "The Nature of Attitudes and Attitude Change," in *Handbook of Social Psychology* (2nd ed.), G. Lindzey and E. Aronson, eds. (Cambridge, MA: Addison-Wesley, 1969), pp. 135–214; Daniel J. O'Keefe, "The Persuasive Effects of Delaying Identification of High- and Low-Credibility Communicators: A Meta-Analytic Review," *Central States Speech Journal* 38 (1987), pp. 63–72.

**6.** Rebecca Ohanian, "The Impact of Celebrity Spokespersons' Image on Consumers' Intention to Purchase," *Journal of Advertising Research* 21 (February/March 1991), pp. 46–54.

**7.** Clinton Amos, Gary Holmes, and David Strutton, "Exploring the Relationship between Celebrity Endorser Effects and Advertising Effectiveness," *International Journal of Advertising* 27, no. 2 (2008), pp. 209–34.

**8.** "E-Score Celebrity Special Report–Year End 2012," E-Poll Market Research, www.epollresearch.com/marketing/E-score%20Celebrity%20YE%202012%202013-03-19-01-sl.pdf

**9.** David P. Hamilton, "Celebrities Help 'Educate' Public on New Drugs," *The Wall Street Journal*, April 22, 2002, p. B1.

**10.** James Bandler, "How Companies Pay TV Experts for On-Air Product Mentions," *The Wall Street Journal*, April 19, 2005, pp. A1, A12.

**11.** Michael Learmonth, "FTC Cracks Down on Blogger Payola, Celebrity Tweets," *Advertising Age*, October 5, 2009, http://adage.com/article/digital/ftc-regulates-social-media-endorsements-blogger-payola/139457/.

**12.** Karen Benezra and Jennifer Gilbert, "The CEO as Brand," *Chief Executive* 174 (January 2002), www.chiefexecutive.net.

**13.** "Business Celebrities," *Business-Week*, June 23, 1986, pp. 100–07.

**14.** Bruce Horovitz and Theresa Howard, "Wendy's Loses Its Legend," *USA Today*, January 9, 2002, pp. 1B, 2B.

**15.** Karlene Lukovitz, "Ads Starring CEOs: What Makes Winners, Losers?," *Marketing Daily*, March 13, 2012, www.mediapost.com/publications/article/170057/?print#axzz2i1DzzuMl.

**16.** Frank Green, "Masters of the Pitch," *San Diego Union-Tribune*, January 30, 2000, pp. 1, 6.

**17.** Barbara Lippert, "A Winner out of the Gates," *Adweek*, September 22, 2008, p. 28.

**18.** Emily Bryson York and Brooke Capps, "Dave Disciples Flip Wigs over Trendy Wendy," *Advertising Age*, September 3, 2007, pp. 1, 22; Kate MacArthur, "Wendy's Unveils New Brand Spokesperson," *Advertising Age,* February 18, 2004, http://adage.com/article/news/wendy-s-unveils-brand-spokesman/39467/.

**19.** Rupal Parekh and Kunur Patel, "Ten Things to Think Hard about before Featuring the Chairman in Advertising," *Advertising Age*, September 14, 2009, htpp://adage.com/print?article_id=138984.

**20.** Erick Reidenback and Robert Pitts, "Not All CEOs Are Created Equal as Advertising Spokespersons: Evaluating the Effective CEO Spokesperson," *Journal of Advertising* 20, no. 3 (1986), pp. 35–50; Roger Kerin and Thomas E. Barry, "The CEO Spokesperson in Consumer Advertising: An Experimental Investigation," in *Current Issues in Research in Advertising*, J.H. Leigh and C.R. Martin, eds. (Ann Arbor: University of Michigan, 1981), pp. 135–48; J. Poindexter, "Voices of Authority," *Psychology Today*, August 1983.

**21.** Green, "Masters of the Pitch."

**22.** A. Eagly and S. Chaiken, "An Attribution Analysis of the Effect of Communicator Characteristics on Opinion Change," *Journal of Personality and Social Psychology* 32 (1975), pp. 136–44.

**23.** For a review of these studies, see Brian Sternthal, Lynn Philips, and Ruby Dholakia, "The Persuasive Effect of Source Credibility: A Situational Analysis," *Public Opinion Quarterly* 42 (Fall 1978) pp. 285–314.

**24.** Brian Sternthal, Ruby Dholakia, and Clark Leavitt, "The Persuasive Effects of Source Credibility: Tests of Cognitive Response," *Journal of Consumer Research* 4, no. 4 (March 1978), pp. 252–60; Robert R. Harmon and Kenneth A. Coney, "The Persuasive Effects of Source Credibility in Buy and Lease Situations," *Journal of Marketing Research* 19 (May 1982), pp. 255–60.

**25.** For a review, see Noel Capon and James Hulbert, "The Sleeper Effect: An Awakening," *Public Opinion Quarterly* 37 (1973), pp. 333–58.

**26.** Darlene B. Hannah and Brian Sternthal, "Detecting and Explaining the Sleeper Effect," *Journal of Consumer Research* 11, no. 2 (September 1984), pp. 632–42.

**27.** H.C. Triandis, *Attitudes and Attitude Change* (New York: Wiley, 1971).

**28.** J. Mills and J. Jellison, "Effect on Opinion Change Similarity between the Communicator and the Audience He Addresses," *Journal of Personality and Social Psychology* 9, no. 2 (1969), pp. 153–56.

**29.** Arch G. Woodside and J. William Davenport Jr., "The Effect of Salesman Similarity and Expertise on Consumer Purchasing Behavior," *Journal of*

*Marketing Research* 11 (May 1974), pp. 198–202; Paul Busch and David T. Wilson, "An Experimental Analysis of a Salesman's Expert and Referent Bases of Social Power in the Buyer–Seller Dyad," *Journal of Marketing Research* 13 (February 1976), pp. 3–11.

30. Jeff Graham, "Whassup with All Those Award Wins?," *Advertising Age*, August 21, 2000, http://adage.com/article/cracks-in-the-foundation/defense-whassup/56775/.

31. Louise Story, "Seeing Stars," *The New York Times*, October 12, 2006, p. C1; Rich Thomaselli, "Searching for Michael Jordan," *Advertising Age*, September 5, 2005, p. 12.

32. George E. Belch and Michael A. Belch, "A Content Analysis Study of the Use of Celebrities in Magazine Advertising," *International Journal of Advertising* 32, no. 3 (2013), pp. 369–89.

33. Sejung Marina Choi, Wei-Na Lee, and Hee-Jung Kim, "Lessons from the Rich and Famous: A Cross-Cultural Comparison of Celebrity Endorsement in Advertising," *Journal of Advertising* 34, no. 2 (Summer 2005), pp. 85–99.

34. Kurt Badenhausen, "The World's Highest-Paid Athletes," *Forbes*, June 18, 2012, www.forbes.com/sites/kurtbadenhausen/2012/06/18/mayweather-tops-list-of-the-worlds-100-highest-paid-athletes/.

35. Elena Gorgan, "Angelina Jolie Dumped by St. John for Overshadowing the Brand," *Softpedia*, January 9, 2010, http://news.softpedia.com/news/Angelina-Jolie-Dumped-by-St-John-for-Overshadowing-the-Brand-131636.shtml.

36. Jason Stein, "Inside Chrysler's Celine Dion Advertising Disaster," *Advertising Age,* November 24, 2003, http://adage.com/article/news/inside-chrysler-s-celine-dion-advertising-disaster/38897/.

37. Valerie Folkes, "Recent Attribution Research in Consumer Behavior: A Review and New Directions," *Journal of Consumer Research* 14 (March 1988), pp. 548–65; John C. Mowen and Stephen W. Brown, "On Explaining and Predicting the Effectiveness of Celebrity Endorsers," in *Advances in Consumer Research* (vol. 8), K.B. Monroe, ed. (Ann Arbor, MI: Association for Consumer Research, 1981), pp. 437–41.

38. Bruce Horovitz, "Armstrong Rolls to Market Gold," *USA Today*, May 4, 2000, pp. 1, 2B.

39. Stephen Rae, "How Celebrities Make Killings on Commercials," *Cosmopolitan*, January 1997, pp. 164–67.

40. Lee Hawkins and Suzanne Vranica, "McDonald's Bets LeBron James Won't Be a Tiger," *The Wall Street Journal,* February 1, 2010, http://online.wsj.com/news/articles/SB10001424052748704343104575033378169040057.

41. Charles Atkin and M. Block, "Effectiveness of Celebrity Endorsers," *Journal of Advertising Research* 23, no. 1 (February/March 1983), pp. 57–61.

42. Brian D. Till and Terence A. Shimp, "Endorsers in Advertising: The Case of Negative Celebrity Information," *Journal of Advertising* 27, no. 1 (Spring 1998), pp. 67–82.

43. Mallory Russell, "Kobe Bryant and Lionel Messi Go Head-to-Head for Turkish Airlines," *Advertising Age*, December 11, 2012, http://adage.com/article/the-viral-video-chart/kobe-bryant-lionel-messi-head-head-turkish-airlines/238716/; "Vitamin Water Planning Full Marketing Campaign around Kobe Bryant," *Sports Business Daily*, May 13, 2008, www.sportsbusinessdaily.com/article/120800; Rich Thomaselli, "Kobe Kept on the Marketing Bench," *Advertising Age*, September 13, 2004, p. 16.

44. Stephanie Thompson, "Heroin Chic OK, Cocaine Use Not," *Advertising Age*, September 26, 2005, pp. 3, 80.

45. Cathy Yingling, "Beware the Lure of Celebrity Endorsers," *Advertising Age*, September 24, 2007, http://adage.com/article/cmo-strategy/beware-lure-celebrity-endorsers/120560/; James Tenser, "Endorser Qualities Count More Than Ever," *Advertising Age*, November 8, 2004, pp. S2, S4.

46. Rich Thomaselli, "GM Ending Tiger Woods Endorsement Deal," *Advertising Age*, November 24, 2008, http://adage.com/article/news/gm-ending-tiger-woods-endorsement-deal/132810/.

47. Rich Thomaselli, "Tiger Woods' Agent: No More Car Sponsors for Tiger," *Advertising Age*, December 1, 2008, http://adage.com/article/agency-news/woods-agent-car-sponsors-tiger/132877/.

48. Anita Elberse and Jeroen Verleun, "The Economic Value of Celebrity Endorsements," *Journal of Advertising Research* 52, no. 2 (June 2012), pp. 149–65.

49. E.J. Schultz and Rupal Parekh, "Justin Timberlake Is the New Face of Bud Light Platinum," *Advertising Age*, February 7, 2013, http://adage.com/article/news/justin-timberlake-face-bud-light-platinum/239672/.

50. Shareen Pathak, "Beyonce Just Latest to Become Brand Ambassador, but Do These Deals Actually Work?" *Advertising Age*, December 17, 2012, http://adage.com/article/news/beyonce-latest-brand-ambassador-deals-work/238795/.

51. Natalie Zmuda, "Beverage Brand Swaps Equity for Met's Endorsements," *Advertising Age*, April 20, 2009, http://adage.com/article/news/beverage-brand-sonu-swaps-equity-mets-endorsements/136085/.

52. Dean Crutchfield, "Celebrity Endorsements Still Push Product," *Advertising Age*, September 22, 2010, http://adage.com/article/cmo-strategy/marketing-celebrity-endorsements-push-product/146023/.

53. Kevin Plank, "Under Armour's Founder on Learning to Leverage Celebrity Endorsements," *Harvard Busienss Review*, May 2012, pp. 45–48.

54. Dave McCaughan, "The Fine Art of Matching a Celebrity with a Brand," *Advertising Age*, April 16, 2007, p. 34; Betsy Cummings, "Star Power," *Sales and Marketing Management*, April 2001, pp. 52–59; Michael A. Kamins, "An Investigation into the 'Match-Up' Hypothesis in Celebrity Advertising," *Journal of Advertising* 19, no. 1 (1990), pp. 4–13.

55. Grant McCracken, "Who Is the Celebrity Endorser? Cultural Foundations of the Endorsement Process," *Journal of Consumer Research* 16, no. 3 (December 1989), pp. 310–21.

56. Ibid., p. 315.

57. Stephen Williams, "Fiat Enlists Ultimate Bad Boy for Its Ads: Charlie Sheen, *Advertising Age,* March 1, 2012, http://adage.com/article/adages/fiat-enlists-ultimate-bad-boy-ads-charlie-sheen/233045/.

58. "Electrolux Taps Kelly Ripa to Launch New Premium Kitchen Appliance Line in North America," *PR Newswire*, April 14, 2008.

59. B. Zafer Erdogan, Michael J. Baker, and Stephen Tagg, "Selecting Celebrity Endorsers: The Practitioner's Perspective," *Journal of Advertising Research* 41, no. 43 (May/June 2001), pp. 39–48.

60. For an excellent review of these studies, see Marilyn Y. Jones, Andrea J.S. Stanaland, and Betsy D. Gelb, "Beefcake and Cheesecake: Insights for Advertisers," *Journal of Advertising* 27, no. 2 (Summer 1998), pp. 32–51; W.B. Joseph, "The Credibility of Physically Attractive Communicators," *Journal of Advertising* 11, no. 3 (1982), pp. 13–23.

61. Michael Solomon, Richard Ashmore, and Laura Longo, "The Beauty Match-Up Hypothesis: Congruence between Types of Beauty and Product Images in Advertising," *Journal of Advertising* 21, no. 4, pp. 23–34; M.J. Baker and Gilbert A. Churchill Jr., "The Impact of Physically Attractive Models on Advertising Evaluations," *Journal of Marketing Research* 14 (November 1977), pp. 538–55.

62. Robert W. Chestnut, C.C. La Chance, and A. Lubitz, "The Decorative Female Model: Sexual Stimuli and the Recognition of the Advertisements," *Journal of Advertising* 6 (Fall 1977), pp. 11–14; Leonard N. Reid and Lawrence C. Soley, "Decorative Models and Readership of Magazine Ads," *Journal of Advertising Research* 23, no. 2 (April/May 1983), pp. 27–32.

63. Amanda B. Bower, "Highly Attractive Models in Advertising and the Women Who Loathe Them: The Implications of Negative Affect for Spokesperson Effectiveness," *Journal of Advertising* 30, no. 3 (Fall 2001), pp. 51–63; Amanda B. Bower and Stacy Landreth, "Is Beauty Best? Highly versus Normally Attractive Models in Advertising," *Journal of Advertising* 30, no. 1 (2001), pp. 1–12.

64. Jack Neff, "In Dove Ads, Normal Is the New Beautiful," *Advertising Age*, September 27, 2004, pp. 1, 80.

65. Michelle Jeffers, "Behind Dove's 'Real Beauty,'" *Adweek*, September 12, 2005, pp. 34–35.

66. Herbert E. Krugman, "On Application of Learning Theory to TV Copy Testing," *Public Opinion Quarterly* 26 (1962), pp. 626–39.

67. C.I. Hovland and W. Mandell, "An Experimental Comparison of Conclusion Drawing by the Communicator and by the Audience," *Journal of Abnormal and Social Psychology* 47 (July 1952), pp. 581–88.

68. Alan G. Sawyer and Daniel J. Howard, "Effect of Omitting Conclusions in Advertisements to Involved and Uninvolved Audiences," *Journal of Marketing Research* 28 (November 1991), pp. 467–74.

69. Paul Chance, "Ads without Answers Make Brain Itch," *Psychology Today* 9 (1975), p. 78.

70. Connie Pechmann, "Predicting When Two-Sided Ads Will Be More Effective Than One-Sided Ads," *Journal of Marketing Research* 24 (November 1992), pp. 441–53; George E. Belch, "The Effects of Message Modality on One- and Two-Sided Advertising Messages," in *Advances in Consumer Research* (vol. 10), Richard P. Bagozzi and Alice M. Tybout, eds. (Ann Arbor, MI: Association for Consumer Research, 1983), pp. 21–26.

71. Robert E. Settle and Linda L. Golden, "Attribution Theory and Advertiser Credibility," *Journal of Marketing Research* 11 (May 1974), pp. 181–85; Edmund J. Faison, "Effectiveness of One-Sided and Two-Sided Mass Communications in Advertising," *Public Opinion Quarterly* 25 (Fall 1961), pp. 468–69.

72. Martin Eisend, "Two-Sided Advertising: A Meta-Analysis," *International Journal of Research in Marketing* 23 (June 2006), pp. 187–98.

73. Paul Farhi, "Behind Domino's Mea Culpa Ad Campaign," *The Washington Post*, January 12, 2010, p. C7.

74. Alan G. Sawyer, "The Effects of Repetition of Refutational and Supportive Advertising Appeals," *Journal of Marketing Research* 10 (February 1973), pp. 23–37; George J. Szybillo and Richard Heslin, "Resistance to Persuasion: Inoculation Theory in a Marketing Context," *Journal of Marketing Research* 10 (November 1973), pp. 396–403.

75. Andrew A. Mitchell, "The Effect of Verbal and Visual Components of Advertisements on Brand Attitudes and Attitude toward the Advertisement," *Journal of Consumer Research* 13 (June 1986), pp. 12–24; Julie A. Edell and Richard Staelin, "The Information Processing of Pictures in Advertisements," *Journal of Consumer Research* 10, no. 1 (June 1983), pp. 45–60; Elizabeth C. Hirschmann, "The Effects of Verbal and Pictorial Advertising Stimuli on Aesthetic, Utilitarian and Familiarity Perceptions," *Journal of Advertising* 15, no. 2 (1986), pp. 27–34.

76. Jolita Kisielius and Brian Sternthal, "Detecting and Explaining Vividness Effects in Attitudinal Judgments," *Journal of Marketing Research* 21, no. 1 (1984), pp. 54–64.

77. H. Rao Unnava and Robert E. Burnkrant, "An Imagery-Processing View of the Role of Pictures in Print Advertisements," *Journal of Marketing Research* 28 (May 1991), pp. 226–31.

78. Susan E. Heckler and Terry L. Childers, "The Role of Expectancy and Relevancy in Memory for Verbal and Visual Information: What Is Incongruency?" *Journal of Consumer Research* 18, no. 4 (March 1992), pp. 475–92.

79. Michael J. Houston, Terry L. Childers, and Susan E. Heckler, "Picture-Word Consistency and the Elaborative Processing of Advertisements," *Journal of Marketing Research* 24 (November 1987), pp. 359–69.

80. William L. Wilkie and Paul W. Farris, "Comparative Advertising: Problems and Potential," *Journal of Marketing* 39 (1975), pp. 7–15.

81. For a review of comparative advertising studies, see Fred K. Beard, "Practitioner View of Comparative Advertising," *Journal of Advertising Research* 53, no. 3 (September 2013), pp. 313–23; Cornelia Pechmann and David W. Stewart, "The Psychology of Comparative Advertising," in *Attention, Attitude and Affect in Response to Advertising*, E.M. Clark, T.C. Brock, and D.W. Stewart, eds. (Hillsdale, NJ: Erlbaum, 1994), pp. 79–96; Thomas S. Barry, "Comparative Advertising: What Have We Learned in Two Decades?" *Journal of Advertising Research* 33, no. 2 (1993), pp. 19–29.

82. Emily Bryson York, "Brand vs. Brand: Attack Ads on the Rise," *Advertising Age*, October 27, 2008, http://adage.com/article/news/brand-brand-attack-ads-rise/132028/.

83. Beth Snyder Bulik, "Marketer of the Decade: Apple," *Advertising Age*, October 18, 2010, http://adage.com/article/special-report-marketer-of-the-year-2010/marketer-decade-apple/146492/.

84. Michael Learmonth, "Samsung Tops Red Bull, Google, Apple and Nike as Viral Brand of 2012," *Advertising Age*, December 20, 2012, http://adage.com/article/the-viral-video-chart/samsung-tops-red-bull-google-apple-nike-viral-brand-2012/238847/.

85. Rupal Parekh, "Microsoft Changes 'Laptop Hunters' Ad after Apple Complains," *Advertising Age*, July 23, 2009, http://adagecom/print?article_id=138117.

86. Patrick Meirick, "Cognitive Responses to Negative and Comparative Political Advertising," *Journal of Advertising* 31, no. 1 (Spring 2002), pp. 49–59.

87. Bruce E. Pinkleton, Nam-Hyun Um, and Erica Weintraub Austin, "An Exploration of the Effects of Negative Political Advertising on Political Decision Making," *Journal of Advertising* 31, no. 1 (Spring 2002), pp. 13–25.

88. Bruce E. Pinkleton, "The Effects of Negative Comparative Political Advertising on Candidate Evaluations and Advertising Evaluations: An

Exploration," *Journal of Advertising* 26, no. 1 (1997), pp. 19–29.

89. Michael L. Ray and William L. Wilkie, "Fear: The Potential of an Appeal Neglected by Marketing," *Journal of Marketing* 34 (January 1970), pp. 54–62.

90. Brian Sternthal and C. Samuel Craig, "Fear Appeals Revisited and Revised," *Journal of Consumer Research* 1 (December 1974), pp. 22–34.

91. Punam Anand Keller and Lauren Goldberg Block, "Increasing the Persuasiveness of Fear Appeals: The Effect of Arousal and Elaboration," *Journal of Consumer Research* 22, no. 4 (March 1996), pp. 448–60.

92. John F. Tanner Jr., James B. Hunt, and David R. Eppright, "The Protection Motivation Model: A Normative Mode of Fear Appeals," *Journal of Marketing* 55 (July 1991), pp. 36–45.

93. Ibid.

94. Sternthal and Craig, "Fear Appeals Revisited and Revised."

95. Herbert Jack Rotfeld, "The Textbook Effect: Conventional Wisdom, Myth and Error in Marketing," *Journal of Marketing* 64 (April 2000), pp. 122–27.

96. The Meth Project, http://foundation. methproject.org/About-Us/index.php.

97. Andrea C. Morales, Eugenia C. Wu, and Gavan J. Fitzsimons, "How Disgust Enhances the Effectiveness of Fear Appeals," *Journal of Marketing Research*, June 2012, pp. 383–93.

98. For a discussion of the use of humor in advertising, see C. Samuel Craig and Brian Sternthal, "Humor in Advertising," *Journal of Marketing* 37 (October 1973), pp. 12–18.

99. Bobby J. Calder and Brian Sternthal, "A Television Commercial Wearout: An Information Processing View," *Journal of Marketing Research* 17 (May 1980), pp.173–87.

100. Dottie Enroco, "Humorous Touch Resonates with Consumers," *USA Today*, May 13, 1996, p. 3B.

101. Yong Zhang, "Response to Humorous Advertising: The Moderating Effect of Need for Cognition," *Journal of Advertising* 25, no. 1 (Spring 1996), pp. 15–32; Marc G. Weinberger and Charles S. Gulas, "The Impact of Humor in Advertising: A Review," *Journal of Advertising* 21 (December 1992), pp. 35–59.

102. Marc G. Weinberger and Leland Campbell, "The Use of Humor in Radio Advertising," *Journal of Advertising Research* 31 (December/January 1990–91), pp. 44–52.

103. Yong Zhang and George M. Zinkhan, "Responses to Humorous Ads," *Journal of Advertising*, Winter 2006, pp. 113–27.

104. Thomas J. Madden and Marc G. Weinberger, "Humor in Advertising: A Practitioner View," *Journal of Advertising Research* 24, no. 4 (August/September 1984), pp. 23–26.

105. Harold C. Cash and W.J.E. Crissy, "Comparison of Advertising and Selling: The Salesman's Role in Marketing," *Psychology of Selling* 12 (1965), pp. 56–75.

106. Marshall McLuhan, *Understanding Media: The Extensions of Man* (New York: McGraw-Hill, 1966).

107. Marvin E. Goldberg and Gerald J. Gorn, "Happy and Sad TV Programs: How They Affect Reactions to Commercials," *Journal of Consumer Research* 14, no. 3 (December 1987), pp. 387–403.

108. Andrew B. Aylesworth and Scott B. MacKenzie, "Context Is Key: The Effect of Program-Induced Mood on Thoughts about the Ad," *Journal of Advertising* 27, no. 2 (Summer 1998), pp. 17–32.

109. Michael T. Elliott and Paul Surgi Speck, "Consumer Perceptions of Advertising Clutter and Its Impact across Various Media," *Journal of Advertising Research* 38, no. 1 (January/February 1998), pp. 29–41; Peter H. Webb, "Consumer Initial Processing in a Difficult Media Environment," *Journal of Consumer Research* 6, no. 3 (December 1979), pp. 225–36.

110. Sam Thielman, "You Endure More Commercials When Watching Cable Networks," *Adweek*, June 23, 2013, www.adweek.com/news/television/you-endure-more-commercials-when-watching-cable-networks-150575.

111. Katy Bachman, "Clutter Makes TV Ads Less Effective," *Adweek*, February 9, 2010, www.adweek.com/aw/content_display/news/media/e3i4f-e3d67e44c8b3ad4c3fcbfe797fc862.

112. Steve McClellan, "Buyers, Now Try to Skirt Clutter with Sponsor Deals," *Adweek*, October 31, 2005, p. 9.

## Chapter Seven

1. Mya Frazier, "GEICO's Big Spending Pays Off, Study Says," *Advertising Age,* June 26, 2007, http://adage.com/article/news/geico-s-big-spending-pays-study/118844/.

2. Nina M. Lentini, "Heinz Credits Marketing Strategy for 19% Profit Hike," November 30, 2007, www.mediapost publications.com.

3. Donald S. Tull, "The Carry-Over Effect of Advertising," Journal of Marketing, April 1965, pp. 46–53.

4. Darral G. Clarke, "Econometric Measurement of the Duration of Advertising Effect on Sales," Journal of Marketing Research 23 (November 1976), pp. 345–57.

5. Philip Kotler, Marketing Decision Making: A Model Building Approach (New York: Holt, Rinehart & Winston, 1971), Ch. 5.

6. Becky Ebenkamp, "You Can Teach an Old Hot Dog Brand Some New Design Tricks," Brandweek, September 28, 2009.

7. Stephanie Thompson, "Kellogg's Roars Back with Out of Box Ads," Advertising Age, May 3, 2004, pp. 4–5.

8. Noreen O'Leary, "Why the New Caribou Coffee Logo Features Less Caribou," Brandweek, March 1, 2010, p. 7.

9. Russell H. Colley, *Defining Advertising Goals for Measured Advertising Results* (New York: Association of National Advertisers, 1961).

10. Don E. Schultz, Dennis Martin, and William Brown, *Strategic Advertising Campaigns*, 2nd ed. (Lincolnwood, IL: Crain Books, 1984).

11. Michael L. Ray, "Consumer Initial Processing: Definitions, Issues, Applications," in *Buyer/Consumer Information Processing*, G. David Hughes, ed. (Chapel Hill: University of North Carolina Press, 1974); David A. Aaker and John G. Myers, *Advertising Management*, 2nd ed. (Englewood Cliffs, NJ: Prentice Hall, 1982), pp. 122–23.

12. Aaker and Myers, *Advertising Management.*

13. Steven W. Hartley and Charles H. Patti, "Evaluating Business-to-Business Advertising: A Comparison of Objectives and Results," *Journal of Advertising Research* 28 (April/May 1988), pp. 21–27.

14. Study cited in Robert F. Lauterborn, "How to Know If Your Advertising Is Working," *Journal of Advertising Research* 25 (February/March 1985), pp. RC9–RC11.

15. Don E. Schultz, "Integration Helps You Plan Communications from Outside-In," *Marketing News*, March 15, 1993, p. 12.

16. Thomas R. Duncan, "To Fathom Integrated Marketing, Dive!," *Advertising Age*, October 11, 1993, p. 18.

17. G. Tellis and K Tellis, "Research on Advertising in a Recession," *Journal of*

*Advertising Research* 49, no. 3 (2009), 304–27. Retrieved from Communication & Mass Media Complete database.

18. Robert L. Steiner, "The Paradox of Increasing Returns to Advertising," *Journal of Advertising Research*, February/March 1987, pp. 45–53.

19. David A. Aaker and James M. Carman, "Are You Overadvertising?" *Journal of Advertising Research* 22, no. 4 (August/September 1982), pp. 57–70.

20. Julian A. Simon and Johan Arndt, "The Shape of the Advertising Response Function," *Journal of Advertising Research* 20, no. 4 (1980), pp. 11–28.

21. Melvin E. Salveson, "Management's Criteria for Advertising Effectiveness," in *Proceedings to the 5th Annual Conference, Advertising Research Foundation* New York, 1959, p. 25.

22. Boonghee Yoo and Rujirutana Mandhachitara, "Estimating Advertising Effects on Sales in a Competitive Setting," *Journal of Advertising Research* 43, no. 3 (2003), pp. 310–20.

23. Dan Lippe, "Media Scorecard: How ROI Adds Up," *Advertising Age*, June 20, 2005, pp. S-6, S-42.

24. Mike Beirne and Kenneth Hein, "Marketers' Mantra: It's ROI, or I'm Fired!," *Brandweek*, October 18, 2004, pp. 14–15.

25. Joe Mandese, "Half of Media Buys Driven by ROI, TV, Online Dominate," April 20, 2005, www.mediapost.com/publications/article/29392/half-of-media-buys-driven-by-roi-tv-online-domin.html.

26. Wayne Friedman, "ROI Measurement Still Falls Short," *TelevisionWeek*, January 31, 2005, p. 19.

27. Hillary Chura, "Advertising ROI Still Elusive Metric," *Advertising Age*, July 26, 2004, p. 8.

28. James O. Peckham, "Can We Relate Advertising Dollars to Market Share Objectives?," in *How Much to Spend for Advertising*, M.A. McNiven, ed. (New York: Association of National Advertisers, 1969), p. 30.

29. George S. Low and Jakki Mohr, "Setting Advertising and Promotion Budgets in Multi-Brand Companies," *Journal of Advertising Research* 39, no. 1 (January/February 1999), pp. 667–78.

30. John P. Jones, "Ad Spending: Maintaining Market Share," *Harvard Business Review* 68, no. 1 (January/February 1990), pp. 38–42; James C. Schroer, "Ad Spending: Growing Market Share," *Harvard Business Review* 68, no. 1 (January/February 1990), pp. 44–48.

31. Randall S. Brown, "Estimating Advantages to Large-Scale Advertising," *Review of Economics and Statistics* 60 (August 1978), pp. 428–37.

32. Kent M. Lancaster, "Are There Scale Economies in Advertising?" *Journal of Business* 59, no. 3 (1986), pp. 509–26.

33. Johan Arndt and Julian Simon, "Advertising and Economics of Scale: Critical Comments on the Evidence," *Journal of Industrial Economics* 32, no. 2 (December 1983), pp. 229–41; Aaker and Carman, "Are You Overadvertising?"

34. George S. Low and Jakki J. Mohr, "The Budget Allocation between Advertising and Sales Promotion: Understanding the Decision Process," *AMA Educators' Proceedings, Summer 1991* (Chicago: American Marketing Association 1991), pp. 448–57.

## Chapter Eight

1. Jeremy Mullman and Stephanie Thompson, "Burnett's Stumble Continues as Altoids Slips Away," *Advertising Age*, January 5, 2007, http://adage.com/article/agency-news/burnett-s-stumble-continues-altoids-slips/114094/.

2. "DDB Cut from Bud Light Review, Move Ends 30-Year Relationship with Brand in U.S.," *Advertising Age*, October 11, 2011.

3. Douglas West, Albert Caruana, and Kannika Leelapanyalert, "What Makes Win, Place, or Show: Judging Creativity in Advertising at Award Shows," *Journal of Advertising Research* 53, no. 3 (2013), pp. 324–38; Bob Garfield, "Award Winners' Edge: That's Entertainment," *Advertising Age*, August 3, 2004, pp. 16–17; Brent Bouchez, "Trophies Are Meaningless," *Advertising Age*, July 30, 2001, p. 16; Vanessa O'Connell, "Ad Slump Deflates Awards Show," *The Wall Street Journal*, May 21, 2002, p. B2; Jennifer Pendleton, "Awards-Creatives Defend Pursuit of Prizes," *Advertising Age*, April 25, 1988, pp. 1, 7.

4. Elizabeth C. Hirschman, "Role-Based Models of Advertising Creation and Production," *Journal of Advertising* 18, no. (1989), pp. 42–53.

5. Ibid., p. 51.

6. Cyndee Miller, "Study Says 'Likability' Surfaces as Measure of TV Ad Success," *Marketing News*, January 7, 1991, pp. 6, 14; Ronald Alsop, "TV Ads That Are Likeable Get Plus Rating for Persuasiveness," *The Wall Street Journal*, February 20, 1986, p. 23.

7. Brian D. Till and Daniel W. Baack, "Recall and Persuasion: Does Creativity Matter?," *Journal of Advertising* 34, no. 3 (2005), pp. 47–57.

8. Robert E. Smith, Scott B. MacKenzie, Xiaojing Yang, Laura Buchholz, William K. Darley, and Xiaojing Yang, "Modeling the Determinants and Effects of Creativity in Advertising," *Marketing Science* 26, no. 6 (2007), pp. 819–33; Robert E. Smith and Xiaojing Yang, "Toward a General Theory of Creativity in Advertising: Examining the Role of Divergence," *Marketing Theory* 4, no. 1/2 (2004), pp. 29–55.

9. Deborah J. MacInnis and Bernard J. Jaworski, "Information Processing from Advertisement: Toward an Integrative Framework," *Journal of Marketing* 53, no. 4 (October 1989), pp. 1–23.

10. Personal correspondence with Douglas Van Praet.

11. Robert E. Smith, Jiemiao Chen, and Xiaojing Yang, "The Impact of Advertising Creativity on the Hierarchy of Effects," *Journal of Advertising* 37, no. 4 (Winter 2008), pp. 47–61.

12. Smith et al., "Modeling the Determinants and Effects of Creativity in Advertising."

13. Swee Hoon Ang, Yih Hwai Lee, and Siew Meng Leong, "The Ad Creativity Cube: Conceptualization and Initial Validation," *Journal of the Academy of Marketing Science* 35, no. 23 (2007), pp. 220–32; Arthur J. Kover, Stephen M. Goldenberg, and William L. James, "Creativity vs. Effectiveness? An Integrative Classification for Advertising," *Journal of Advertising Research* 35 (November/December 1995), pp. 29–38.

14. Smith et al., "Modeling the Determinants and Effects of Creativity in Advertising."

15. For an interesting discussion on the embellishment of advertising messages, see William M. Weilbacher, *Advertising*, 2nd ed. (New York: Macmillan, 1984), pp. 180–82.

16. David Ogilvy, *Confessions of an Advertising Man* (New York: Atheneum, 1963); Hanley Norins, *The Compleat Copywriter* (New York: McGraw-Hill, 1966).

17. Hank Sneiden, *Advertising Pure and Simple* (New York: ANACOM, 1977).

18. Quoted in Valerie H. Free, "Absolut Original," *Marketing Insights*, Summer 1991, p. 65.

19. Jeff Jensen, "Marketer of the Year," *Advertising Age*, December 16, 1996, pp. 1, 16.

20. Ann Christine Diaz, "Creativity's Agency of the Year," *Advertising Age*, January 28, 2013, p. 24; Cathy Taylor, "Risk Takers: Wieden & Kennedy," *Adweek's Marketing Week*, March 23, 1992, pp. 26, 27.

21. "Residence Inn by Marriott Unleashes New Campaign, Spotlights Room to Work, Play and Chill," March 8, 2012, http://news.marriott.com/2012/03/residence-inn-by-marriott-the-hotel-brand-that-originated-the-extended-stay-category-in-1975-today-premiered-a-wild-new-adv.html.

22. Anthony Vagnoni, "Creative Differences," *Advertising Age*, November 17, 1997, pp. 1, 28, 30.

23. Jonathon Cranin, "Has Advertising Gone the Way of the Costra Nostra?," *Advertising Age*, June 6, 2005.

24. Vagnoni, "Creative Differences."

25. Cranin, "Has Advertising Gone the Way of the Costra Nostra?"

26. Arthur J. Kover, "Copywriters' Implicit Theories of Communication: An Exploration," *Journal of Consumer Research* 21, no. 4 (March 1995), pp. 596–611.

27. Sheila L. Sasser and Scott Koslow, "Desparately Seeking Advertising Creativity," *Journal of Advertising* 37, no. 4 (Winter 2008), pp. 5–19.

28. James Webb Young, *A Technique for Producing Ideas*, 3rd ed. (Chicago: Crain Books, 1975), p. 42.

29. Graham Wallas, *The Art of Thought* (New York: Harcourt Brace, 1926).

30. Debra Goldman, "Origin of the Species: Has the Planner Finally Evolved into the Agency's Most Potent Creature?" *Adweek*, April 10, 1995, pp. 28–38.

31. Jon Steel, *Truth, Lies & Advertising: The Art of Account Planning* (New York: Wiley, 1998).

32. Sandra E. Moriarty, *Creative Advertising: Theory and Practice* (Englewood Cliffs, NJ: Prentice Hall, 1986).

33. E.E. Norris, "Seek Out the Consumer's Problem," *Advertising Age*, March 17, 1975, pp. 43–44.

34. Thomas L. Greenbaum, "Focus Groups Can Play a Part in Evaluating Ad Copy," *Marketing News*, September 13, 1993, pp. 24–25.

35. Emily Steel, "The New Focus Groups: Online Networks, Proprietary Panels Help Consumer Companies Shape Product Ads," *The Wall Street Journal*, January 14, 2008, p. B6.

36. Jennifer Comiteau, "Why the Traditional Focus Group Is Dying," *Adweek*, October 31, 2005, pp. 24–25, 32; Stephanie Thompson, "'Tipping Point' Guru Takes on Focus Groups," *Advertising Age*, January 24, 2005, pp. 4, 54; Malcolm Gladwell, *Blink: The Power of Thinking without Thinking* (New York: Little, Brown, 2004).

37. David Kiley, "Shoot the Focus Group," *BusinessWeek*, November 14, 2005, pp. 120–21.

38. Thompson, "'Tipping Point' Guru Takes on Focus Groups."

39. Eric J. Arnould and Melanie Wallendorf, "Market-Oriented Ethnography: Interpretation Building and Marketing Strategy Formulation," *Journal of Marketing Research* 31 (November 1994), pp. 388–96.

40. "There's Life to Be Done—the Chevrolet Silverado Turnaround," *2012 David Ogilvy Awards*, Advertising Research Foundation, http://thearf.org/ogilvy-12.php.

41. "White Gold," 2009 Bronze Effie Winner, Effie Awards, www.effie.org/winners/showcase/2009/3686.

42. "In the NFL There Are No Sick Days," Vick's DayQuil and Vicks NyQuil," *2012 David Ogilvy Awards*, Advertising Research Foundation, http://thearf.org/ogilvy-12.php.

43. Stephen Winzenburg, "Your Advertising Slogans Are Crummy. Can't You Do Better?," *Advertising Age*, January 14, 2008, p. 15; John Mathes, "Taglines That Stick; Here's How to Create an Effective Brand Summation Line. How Long Should It Be? Is It the Same as Your Brand Positioning? How Often Do You Need to Refresh It?," *ABA Bank Marketing*, December 1, 2008, pp. 22–25.

44. Chiranjeev Kohli, Lance Leuthesser, and Rajneesh Suri, "Got Slogan? Guidelines for Creating Effective Slogans," *Business Horizons* 50 (2007), pp. 415–22.

45. Ibid.

46. John Sutherland, Lisa Duke, and Avery Abernethy, "A Model of Marketing Information Flow," *Journal of Advertising* 22, no. 4 (Winter 2004), pp. 39–52.

47. A. Jerome Jeweler, *Creative Strategy in Advertising* (Belmont, CA: Wadsworth, 1981).

48. John O'Toole, *The Trouble with Advertising*, 2nd ed. (New York: Random House, 1985), p. 131.

49. David Ogilvy, *Ogilvy on Advertising* (New York: Crown, 1983), p. 16.

50. Julie Halpert "Chrysler Group Is Ad Age's Marketer of the Year," *Advertising Age*, November 25, 2012, http://adage.com/article/special-report-marketer-alist-2012/chrysler-group-ad-age-s-marketer-year/238443/.

51. Christine Birkner, "Success by Association," *Marketing News*, April 30, 2012, pp. 14–18.

52. Arthur J. Kover, "Copywriters' Implicit Theories of Communication: An Exploration," *Journal of Consumer Research* 21 (4), (March 1995), pp. 596–611.

53. John R. Rossiter, "Defining the Necessary Components of Creative, Effective Ads," *Journal of Advertising Research* 37, no. 4 (Winter 2008), pp. 139–44.

54. Rosser Reeves, *Reality in Advertising* (New York: Knopf, 1961), pp. 47, 48.

55. Shelly Branch and Frances A. McMorris, "Irate Firms Take Comparisons to Court," *The Wall Street Journal*, December 22, 1999, p. B8.

56. Jeremy Mullman, "Hey, Those A-B Brands Look Like Miller Beers," *Advertising Age*, June 11, 2009, http://adage.com/article/news/beer-marketing-a-b-brands-miller-beers/137260/; Jeremy Mullman, "Miller Lightens Its Load: Will Go National with MGD 64 by Fall," *Advertising Age*, http://adage.com/article/news/miller-lightens-load-national-mgd-64-fall/127945/.

57. Ogilvy, *Confessions*.

58. Martin Mayer, *Madison Avenue, U.S.A.* (New York: Pocket Books, 1958).

59. Jeremy Mullman, "Hallmark Reminds Consumers That Little Things Mean a Lot," *Advertising Age*, http://adagecom/print?article_id=135625.

60. Al Ries and Jack Trout, *Positioning: The Battle for Your Mind* (New York: McGraw-Hill, 1985); Jack Trout and Al Ries, "The Positioning Era Cometh," *Advertising Age*, April 24, 1972, pp. 35–38; May 1, 1972, pp. 51–54; May 8, 1972, pp. 114–16.

61. Jack Trout, "Brands Can't Exist without Positioning," *Advertising Age*, March 14, 2005, p. 28.

62. Jean Halliday, "Sometimes Oil and Oil Don't Mix," *Advertising Age*, March 4, 2002, pp. 4, 62.

63. Rajeev Batra, John G. Myers, and David A. Aaker, *Advertising Management*, 5th ed. (Upper Saddle River, NJ: Prentice Hall, 1996).

64. Anthony Vagnoni, "They Might Be Giants," *Advertising Age*, April 27, 1998, pp. 1, 20, 24.

65. Anthony Vagnoni, "Goodby, Silverstein Do 'Intelligent Work' with a Sales Pitch," *Advertising Age*, April 27, 1998, pp. 20, 24.

66. Anthony Vagnoni, "Having Ad Bosses Focus on the Work Key to Cult of Clow," *Advertising Age*, April 27, 1998, pp. 22, 24.

67. Ira Teinowitz, "Agencies Using Creativity to Save Themselves," *Advertising Age*, April 9, 2008, http://adage.com/article/news/agencies-creativity-save/126275/.

68. Eleftheria Parpis, "U.S. Agency of the Year—2007: Goodby Silverstein," *Adweek*, January 7, 2008, p. 20.

69. Rupal Parkeh," Lee Clow on Advertising, Then and Now," *Advertising Age*, June 11, 2013, http://adage.com/article/agency-news/lee-clow-advertising/241987/.

## Chapter Nine

1. Sandra E. Moriarty, *Creative Advertising: Theory and Practice*, 2nd ed. (Englewood Cliffs, NJ: Prentice Hall, 1991), p. 76.

2. William M. Weilbacher, *Advertising*, 2nd ed. (New York: Macmillan, 1984), p. 197.

3. William Wells, John Burnett, and Sandra Moriarty, *Advertising* (Englewood Cliffs, NJ: Prentice Hall, 1989), p. 330.

4. Hamish Pringle and Peter Field, "Why Emotional Messages Beat Rational Ones," *Advertising Age*, March 2, 2009, http://adage.com/article/cmo-strategy/emotional-messages-beat-rational/134920/; Stuart J. Agres, "Emotion in Advertising: An Agency Point of View," in *Emotion in Advertising*: *Theoretical and Practical Explanations*, Stuart J. Agres, Julie A. Edell, and Tony M. Dubitsky, eds. (Westport, CT: Quorom Books, 1991).

5. Edward Kamp and Deborah J. Macinnis, "Characteristics of Portrayed Emotions in Commercials: When Does What Is Shown in Ads Affect Viewers?" *Journal of Advertising Research* 22, no. 4 (November/December 1995), pp. 19–28.

6. For a review of research on the effect of mood states on consumer behavior, see Meryl Paula Gardner, "Mood States and Consumer Behavior: A Critical Review," *Journal of Consumer Research* 12, no. 3 (December 1985), pp. 281–300.

7. Cathy Madison, "Researchers Work Advertising into an Emotional State," *Adweek*, November 5, 1990, p. 30.

8. Hamish Pringle and Peter Field, *Brand Immortality: How Brands Can Live Long and Prosper* (London: Kogan Page Limited, 2009).

9. Pringle and Field, "Why Emotional Messages Beat Rational Ones."

10. Natalie Zmuda, "'Dear Dreamers': JC Penney Uses Oscars to Launch Emotional Ad Campaign," *Advertising Age*, February 24, 2013, http://adage.com/article/news/dear-dreamers-jc-penney-s-oscar-ads-aim-emotion/239998/.

11. Christopher P. Puto and William D. Wells, "Informational and Transformational Advertising: The Different Effects of Time," in *Advances in Consumer Research* (vol. 11), Thomas C. Kinnear, ed. (Ann Arbor, MI: Association for Consumer Research, 1984), p. 638.

12. Ibid.

13. E.J. Schultz, "Corona Light Ditches the Beach in New Spot," *Advertising Age*, April 11, 2011, http://adage.com/article/news/corona-light-ditches-beach-commercial/226928/.

14. David Ogilvy and Joel Raphaelson, "Research on Advertising Techniques That Work and Don't Work," *Harvard Business Review*, July/August 1982, p. 18.

15. "New American Airlines TV Commercials Created by TIM Advertising Capture 'Smart Travelers' Perspective," *PR Newswire*, March 22, 2010.

16. *Topline*, no. 4 (September 1989), McCann-Erickson, New York.

17. Natalie Zmuda, "Mastercard's Priceless Evolution: How the Brand Put a New Twist on Its 15-Year-Old Campaign," *Advertising Age*, October 11, 2012, http://adage.com/article/special-report-ana-annual-meeting-2012/mastercard-s-priceless-evolution/237706/.

18. Xiang Fang, Surendra Singh, and Rohini Ahluwalia, "An Examination of Different Explanations for the Mere Exposure Effect," *Journal of Consumer Research* 34 (June 2007), pp. 97–103.

19. Robert Zajonc, "Attitudinal Effects of Mere Exposure," *Journal of Personality and Social Psychology Monographs*, no. 2 (Pt. 2), pp. 1–27.

20. John Young, "Making Online Ad Suck Less in 8 Easy Steps," *Advertising Age*, April 10, 2010, http://adage.com/article/digitalnext/making-online-ads-suck-8-easy-steps/143368/.

21. Quote by Irwin Warren, cited in Enrico, "Teaser Ads Grab Spotlight," *USA Today*, July 6, 1995, pp. 1B, 2B.

22. Colin Campbell, Leyland F. Pitt, Michael Parent, and Pierre R. Berthhon, "Understanding Consumer Conversations around Ads in a Web2.0 World," *Journal of Advertising* 40, no. 1 (Spring 2011), pp. 87–102; E.J. Schultz, "Why 'Crash the Super Bowl' Hasn't Burned Out for Doritos," *Advertising Age*, January 24, 2013, http://adage.com/article/special-report-super-bowl/crash-super-bowl-burned-doritos/239373/.

23. Christopher Heine, "New Ford Fiesta Campaign Will Be Entirely User-Generated," *Adweek*, February 19, 2013, www.adweek.com/news/advertising-branding/ford-campaign-will-be-all-user-generated-147384.

24. Ginny Marvin, "User-Generated Video Ad Units Come to Facebook Newsfeeds through New Partnership," *Marketing Land*, May 16, 2013, http://marketingland.com/user-generated-video-ad-units-coming-to-facebook-newsfeeds-through-new-partnership-44078.

25. Martin Mayer, *Madison Avenue, U.S.A.* (New York: Pocket Books, 1958), p. 64.

26. Chris Reidy, "Gillette Rolls Out Shaving Products Designed for Men with Sensitive Skin," *Boston Globe*, February 14, 2013, www.boston.com/businessupdates/2013/02/14/gillette-rolls-out-shaving-products-designed-for-men-with-sensitive-skin/va3MCX5AoS9ueUx9NvqinO/story.html.

27. Sally Beatty, "P&G to Ad Agencies: Please Rewrite Our Old Formulas," *The Wall Street Journal*, November 5, 1998, pp. B1, B10; Alecia Swasy, "P&G Tries Bolder Ads—with Caution," *The Wall Street Journal*, May 7, 1990, pp. B1, B7.

28. Lynn Coleman, "Advertisers Put Fear into the Hearts of Their Prospects," *Marketing News*, August 15, 1988, p. 1.

29. Ibid.

30. Ann Christine Diaz, "Chipotle and CAA Add a Film Grand Prix to Collection of Top Honors," *Advertising Age*, June 23, 2012, http://adage.com/article/special-report-cannes-2012/chipotle-caa-add-a-film-grand-prix-collection-top-honors/235603/.

31. Theresa Howard, "Aflac Duck Gives Wings to Insurer's Name Recognition," *USA Today*, May 17, 2001, p. B9.

32. Piet Lievy, "Keeping It Interesting," *Marketing News*, October 20, 2009.

33. Barbara B. Stern, "Classical and Vignette Television Advertising: Structural Models, Formal Analysis, and Consumer Effects," *Journal of Consumer Research* 20, no. 4 (March 1994), pp. 601–15; John Deighton, Daniel Romer, and Josh McQueen, "Using Drama to Persuade," *Journal of Consumer Research* 15, no. 3 (December 1989), pp. 335–43.

34. Moriarty, *Creative Advertising*, p. 77.

35. Mario Pricken, *Creative Advertising* (New York: Thames & Hudson, 2009).

36. W. Keith Hafer and Gordon E. White, *Advertising Writing*, 3rd ed. (St. Paul, MN: West Publishing, 1989), p. 98.

37. Carol Marie Cooper, "Who Says Talk Is Cheap?," *The New York Times*, October 22, 1998, pp. C1, C5; Wendy Brandes, "Star Power Leaves Some Voice-Over Artists Speechless," *The Wall Street Journal*, June 2, 1995, p. B6.

38. David Allan, "A Content Analysis of Music Placement in Prime-Time Advertising," *Journal of Advertising Research*, September 2008, pp. 404–14.

39. Linda M. Scott, "Understanding Jingles and Needledrop: A Rhetorical Approach to Music in Advertising," *Journal of Consumer Research* 17, no. 2 (September 1990), pp. 223–36.

40. Kineta Hung, "Framing Meaning Perceptions with Music: The Case of Teaser Ads," *Journal of Advertising* 30, no. 3 (Fall 2001), pp. 39–49; Russell I. Haley, Jack Richardson, and Beth Baldwin, "The Effects of Nonverbal Communications in Television Advertising," *Journal of Advertising Research* 24, no. 4 (July/August 1984), pp. 11–18.

41. Maureen Morrison, "Kia to Bring Back Hamsters for New Campaign," *Advertising Age*, July 26, 2012, http://adage.com/article/special-report-small-agency-awards-2012/kia-bring-back-hamsters-campaign/236351/.

42. Steve Oakes, "Evaluating Empirical Research into Music in Advertising: A Congruity Perspective," *Journal of Advertising Research*, March 2007, pp. 38–50.

43. Gerald J. Gorn, "The Effects of Music in Advertising on Choice Behavior: A Classical Conditioning Approach," *Journal of Marketing* 46 (Winter 1982), pp. 94–100.

44. Donna DeMarco, "TV Ads Go Pop: Advertisers Marry Modern Music with Their Products," *The Washington Times*, May 12, 2002, p. A1.

45. Matthew Boyle, "The Accidental Hero," *BusinessWeek*, November 5, 2009, www.businessweekcom/print/magazine/content/09_46/b4155058815908.htm.

46. Stephanie Thompson, "Promotions: Nostalgia Bolognese," *Brandweek*, April 14, 1997.

47. Quote from Suzanne Vranica, "P&G Dusts Off a Familiar Tune," *The Wall Street Journal*, March 3, 2005, p. B2.

48. Andrew Hampp, "A Reprise for Jingles on Madison Avenue, Brands, Agencies Rediscovering Power of Original Tunes in Ad Campaigns," *Advertising Age*, September 6, 2010, http://adage.com/article/madisonvine-news/a-reprise-jingles-madison-avenue/145744/.

49. Ken Wheaton, "Stop the Presses: Cee Lo Green, Purrfect Remix Meow Mix Jinge," *Advertising Age*, May 4, 2012, http://adage.com/article/adages/cee-lo-green-remix-a-song-a-rented-cat/234574/.

50. Vranica, "P&G Dusts Off a Familiar Tune."

51. "Results of 4A's 2011 Television Production Costs Survey," American Association of Advertising Agencies, Bulletin #7480, January 22, 2013.

52. Jack Neff, "Industry Explores New Compensation Model for Talent," *Advertising Age*, May 3, 2010, http://adage.com/article/news/industry-explores-compensation-model-talent-fees/143638/.

53. Jack Neff, "Why P&G Won't Win Many Cannes Lions," *Advertising Age*, June 13, 2005, pp. 3, 45; Beatty, "P&G to Ad Agencies."

54. Meg James, "Over 50 and out of Flavor," *Los Angeles Times*, May 10, 2005, pp. A1, A10.

55. Rupel Parekh, "Brand Awareness Was Only Half the Battle for Aflac," *Advertising Age*, June 22, 2009, http://adage.com/article/cmo-strategy/aflac-s-jeff-charney-insurance-brand-awareness/137392/; Suzanne Vranica, "Aflac Partly Muzzles Iconic Duck," *The Wall Street Journal*, December 2, 2004, p. B8.

56. Jack Neff, "Method Pulls 'Shiny Suds' Ad after Sexism Complaints," *Advertising Age*, December 2, 2009, http://adage.com/article/news/method-pulls-shiny-suds-ad-sexism-complaints/140830; Bob Garfield, "Why Method Did Right in Pulling the Plug on 'Shiny Suds,'" *Advertising Age*, December 7, 2009, http://adage.com/article/ad-review/method-pulling-plug-shiny-suds/140894/.

## Chapter Ten

1. Jamie Turner, "Top 52 Social Media Platforms Every Marketer Should Know," April 9, 2010, www.60secondmarketer.com.

2. Ronald D. Geskey, *Media Planning & Buying in the 21st Century*, 2nd ed. (2020 Marketing Communications, LLC, 2013), Rochester, MI.

3. Matthew Creamer, "Ad Groups Back Switch from 'Frequency' to 'Engagement,'" *Advertising Age*, July 21, 2005, http://adage.com/article/news/ad-groups-back-switch-frequency-engagement/46348/.

4. Jeff Cusack, "Chuck Shows the Value of Audience Engagement," May 1, 2009, www.filmindustry.suite101.com.

5. Beth Snyder Bullik, "How Personality Can Predict Media Usage," *Advertising Age*, May 4, 2009, http://adage.com/article/news/personality-predict-media-usage/136408/.

6. Chuck Ross, "Study Finds for Continuity vs. Flights," *Advertising Age*, April 19, 1999, p. 2.

7. Joseph W. Ostrow, "Setting Frequency Levels: An Art or a Science?" *Journal of Advertising Research* 24 (August/September 1984), pp. 9–11.

8. David Crane, "Arnold vs Calbuzz, eMeg's Ad Buy; Memo to Media," March 10, 2010, www.calbuzz.com.

9. Scott Walker, "Ratings and TV Advertising Sales," April 2, 2008, www.tvadvertising.suite101.com.

10. David Berger, "How Much to Spend," *Foote, Cone & Belding Internal Report*, in *Advertising*, Michael L. Rothschild (Lexington, MA: Heath, 1987), p. 468.

11. David W. Olson, "Real World Measures of Advertising Effectiveness for New Products," *Speech to the 26th Annual Conference of the Advertising Research Foundation*, New York, March 18, 1980.

12. Joseph W. Ostrow, "What Level Frequency?" *Advertising Age*, November 1981, pp. 13–18.

13. Jack Myers, "More Is Indeed Better," *MediaWeek*, September 6, 1993, pp. 14–18.

14. Jim Surmanek, "One-Hit or Miss: Is a Frequency of One Frequently Wrong?" *Advertising Age*, November 27, 1995, p. 46.

15. Erwin Ephron, "Back to the Future," April 14, 2010, www.ephrononmedia.com.

16. Ostrow, "What Level Frequency?"

17. Erwin Ephron, "Recency Planning," March 18, 1998, www.ephrononmedia.com.

18. Erwin Ephron, "Sitting on the Shelf," October 1, 2009, www.ephrononmedia.com.

## Chapter Eleven

1. Radio Advertising Bureau, "Why Radio," 2013, www.rab.com/whyradio/.

2. Tim Nudd, "How Subaru Fell in Love and Never Looked Back," *Adweek*, April 13, 2013, www.adweek.com/news/advertising-branding/how-subaru-fell-love-and-never-looked-back-148475.

3. "Network Television Cost and CPM Trends," *Trends in Media,* Television Bureau of Advertising, www.tvb.org/rcentral.

4. Rebecca Dana and Stephane King, "Answer to Vexing Question: Who's Not Watching Ads," *The Wall Street Journal*, October 17, 2009, p. B2; Lex van Meurs, "Zapp! A Study on Switching Behavior during Commercial Breaks," *Journal of Advertising Research*, January/February 1998, pp. 43–53; John J. Cronin, "In-Home Observations of Commercial Zapping Behavior," *Journal of Current Issues and Research in Advertising* 17, no. 2 (Fall 1995), pp. 69–75.

5. "Results of 4A's 2011 Television Production Costs Survey," American Association of Advertising Agencies, Bulletin #7480, January 22, 2013.

6. Laurel Wentz, "Behind the Five Most Creative U.S. Hispanic Ideas," *Advertising Age*, May 1, 2013, http://adage.com/article/hispanic-marketing/creative-u-s-hispanic-ideas/241197/; Brian Grow, "Hispanic Nation," *BusinessWeek*, March 15, 2004, pp. 58–70.

7. "Network Television Commercial Activity by Length of Commercial."

8. Emily Fredrix, "TV Ads Shrink to Match Attention Spans," *Toronto Star*, October 28, 2010, p. C1; Steve McClellan, "Buyers, Nets Try to Skirt Clutter with Sponsor Deals," *Adweek*, October 31, 2005, p. 9.

9. John J. Cronin and Nancy Menelly, "Discrimination vs. Avoidance: 'Zipping' of Television Commercials," *Journal of Advertising* 21, no. 2 (June 1992), pp. 1–7.

10. Suzanne Vranica, "TiVo Serves Up Portrait of the Ad-Zappers," *The Wall Street Journal*, November 8, 2007, p. B5.

11. Cronin, "In-Home Observations of Commercial Zapping Behavior."

12. Carrie Heeter and Bradley S. Greenberg, "Profiling the Zappers," *Journal of Advertising Research* 25, no. 2 (April/May 1985), pp. 9–12; Fred S. Zufryden, James H. Pedrick, and Avu Sandaralingham, "Zapping and Its Impact on Brand Purchase Behavior," *Journal of Advertising Research* 33, no. 1 (January/February 1993), pp. 58–66; Patricia Orsini, "Zapping: A Man's World," Spring Television Report, *Adweek's Marketing Week*, April 8, 1991, p. 3.

13. van Meurs, "Zapp! A Study on Switching Behavior during Commercial Breaks."

14. Alan Ching Biu Tse and Rub P. W. Lee, "Zapping Behavior during Commercial Breaks," *Journal of Advertising Research* 41, no. 3 (May/June 2001), pp. 25–29.

15. Danny King, "Nielsen Report: Many DVR Viewers Play the Commercials," *Daily Finance*, December 21, 2010, www.dailyfinance.com/2010/12/21/nielsen-report-many-dvr-viewers-play-the-commercials/.

16. Keach Hagey, "CBS Quashes Award for DVR," *The Wall Street Journal*, January 15, 2013, p. B3.

17. Brian Steinberg, "ABC Tests Ad Packages Including 'On-Demand' Viewers," *Advertising Age*, March 22, 2012, http://adage.com/article/media/abc-tests-ad-packages-including-demand-viewers/233462/; Brooks Barnes, "ABC, Cox Bar Ad Skipping in Video on Demand," *The Wall Street Journal*, May 8, 2007, p. B8.

18. Linda F. Alwitt and Paul R. Prabhaker, "Identifying Who Dislikes Television Advertising: Not by Demographics Alone," *Journal of Advertising Research* 34, no. 6 (November/December 1994), pp. 30–42.

19. Banwari Mittal, "Public Assessment of TV Advertising: Faint Praise and Harsh Criticism," *Journal of Advertising Research* 34, no. 1 (1994), pp. 35–53.

20. Lucy L. Henke, "Young Children's Perceptions of Cigarette Brand Advertising Symbols: Awareness, Affect, and Target Market Identification," *Journal of Advertising* 24, no. 4 (Winter 1995), pp. 13–28.

21. "Nielsen: Global Consumers' Trust in 'Earned' Advertising Grows in Importance," *Nielsen Newswire*, April 10, 2012, www.nielsen.com/us/en/press-room/2012/nielsen-global-consumers-trust-in-earned-advertising-grows.html.

22. Brian Steinberg, "How Fox Went from Small Outcast to Broadcast Powerhouse," *Advertising Age*, April 18, 2011, pp. 2–3.

23. Bill Mann, "What's with CW? Result of Merger between WB and UPN Targets 18-and-Ups," *The Press Democrat*, December 16, 2007, p. D8.

24. Brooks Barnes and Miram Jordan, "Big Four TV Networks Get a Wake-Up Call—in Spanish," *The Wall Street Journal*, May 2, 2005, pp. B1, B6.

25. Fernando Rodriguez, "Six Things Advertisers Need to Know about the Growing Hispanic Market," *Advertising Age*, July 26, 2012, http://adage.com/article/the-big-tent/advertisers-reach-growing-u-s-hispanic-market/236336/.

26. Brian Steinberg, "TV Ad Prices: 'Idol' No Match for Football," *Advertising Age*, October 21, 2012, http://adage.com/article/media/tv-ad-prices-idol-match-football/237874/.

27. Brian Steinberg, "TV Nets Notice Uptick in 'Just in Time' Ad Buying," *Advertising Age*, September 7, 2009, http://adage.com/article/media/tv-networks-notice-uptick-scatter-advertising-buying/138856/.

28. Jeanine Poggi, "Why Cable Has Become More Like Broadcast TV," *Advertising Age*, May 14, 2012, p. 16; Brian Steinberg, "Broadcast TV or Cable, It's All the Same to Consumers," *Advertising Age,* March 23, 2009, http://adage.com/print?article_id=135246.

29. Gary Levin, "Arbitron Exits from Ratings Race," *Advertising Age*, October 25, 1993, p. 4.

30. A.J. Frutkin, "Do Sweeps Still Matter?," Mediaweek.com, April 30, 2007.

31. "Measuring TV Audience," *Broadcast Engineering*, October 1, 2007, p. 26.

32. Brian Steinberg and Andrew Hampp, "Commecial Ratings? Nets Talk TiVo Instead," *Advertising Age*, June 4, 2007, pp. 1, 60.

33. Steve McClellan, "Taking the 'Break' out of Commercial Pods," *Adweek*, March 16, 2007, p. 9.

34. Brian Steinberg, "Marketers Demanding Ratings for Each TV Ad," *Advertising Age*, February 23, 2009, http://adage.com/article/media/c3-marketers-demanding-ratings-tv-ad/134785/.

35. Wayne Friedman, "Given Ratings, C7 May Usurp C3 Model," MediaDailyNews, November 13, 2012, www.mediapost.com/publications/article/187200/given-ratings-c7-may-usurp-c3-model.html?print#axzz2imBtBmUn.

36. Brian Steinberg, "CBS Chief Acknowledges C7 Rating May Not Come until 2014, *Advertising Age*, March 5, 2013, http://adage.com/article/media/cbs-chief-acknowledges-c7-ratings-2014/240159/.

37. Steinberg, "Marketers Demanding Ratings for Each TV Ad."

38. "Nielsen Appoints Client Advisory Committees for Its Anytime Anywhere Media Measurement (A2/M2) Initiative," *PR Newswire*, October 16, 2006.

39. Kate Fitzgerald, "Campus Viewing Stirs a Romp," *Advertising Age*, April 9, 2007, http://adage.com/article/special-report-upfront07/campus-viewing-stirs-a-rumpus/115950/.

40. "Does College Play a Role in Media Consumption?," *Nielsen Newswire*, January 10, 2013, www.nielsen.com/us/en/newswire/2013/does-college-play-a-role-in-media-consumption.html.

41. Andrew Hampp, "Nielsen Adds Ratings for Away-From-Home TV Networks," *Advertising Age*, April 14, 2010, http://adage.com/article/media/nielsen-adds-ratings-home-tv-networks/143308/.

42. Richard Lawler, "Nielsen Ratings Expand Definition of TV Households to Include Internet-Only Viewers," *Engadget*, February 21, 2013, www.engadget.com/about/.

43. Brian Steinberg, "Nielsen Plans to Expand Ratings from TV to Broadband Views," *Advertising Age*, February 21, 2013, http://adage.com/article/media/nielsen-plans-expand-ratings-tv-broadband-views/239961/; Jeanine Poggi, "Nielsen Marries TV, Online Ratings," *Advertising Age,* October 1, 2012, p. 8.

44. Radio Advertising Bureau, "Why Radio."

45. Ibid.

46. *Radio Marketing Guide* (New York: Radio Advertising Bureau, 2010), www.rab.com.

47. Verne Gay, "Image Transfer: Radio Ads Make Aural History," *Advertising Age*, January 24, 1985, p. 1.

48. *The Benefits of Synergy: Moving Money into Radio* (New York: Radio Ad Effectiveness Lab, Inc., December 2004), www.radioadlal.com.

49. Avery Abernethy, "Differences between Advertising and Program Exposure for Car Radio Listening," *Journal of Advertising Research* 31, no. 2 (April/May 1991), pp. 33–42.

50. *Radio Marketing Guide.*

51. Martin Peers, "Radio Produces Both Gains and Skeptics," *The Wall Street Journal*, January 1, 1999, p. B6.

52. Andrew Hampp, "Liberty Media Rides in to Rescue Sirius XM," *Advertising Age*, February 17, 2009, http://adage.com/article/media/liberty-media-rides-rescue-sirius-xm/134661/.

53. Ben Sisario, "With iTunes Radio, Apple Takes Aim at Pandora," *The New York Times*, September 10, 2013, www.nytimes.com/2013/09/11/business/media/with-itunes-radio-apple-takes-aim-at-pandora.html?_r=0.

54. Heather Green, Tom Lowry, Catherine Young, and David Kiley, "The New Radio Revolution," *BusinessWeek*, March 14, 2005, pp. 32–35.

55. Ibid.

56. Andrew Hampp, "Contextual Radio Ads: Clear Channel's New Pitch to National Marketers," *Advertising Age*, January 15, 2010, http://adage.com/article/media/radio-clear-channel-rolls-contextual-radio-advertising/141533/.

57. Jon Fine, "A Better Measure of Old Media," *BusinessWeek,* July 9, 2007, p. 20.

58. "Media Rating Council Grants Accreditation to Four Additional Arbitron Portable People Meter Markets," *PR Newswire*, February 5, 2013, www.prnewswire.com/news-releases/media-rating-council-grants-accreditation-to-four-additional-arbitron-portable-people-meter-markets-189901731.html; Steve Carney, "Don't Touch That Radio Dial—Arbitron Is Listening," *Los Angeles Times*, August 24, 2011, http://articles.latimes.com/2011/aug/24/entertainment/la-et-radio-ratings-20110824.

59. David McLaughlin, "Nielsen's $1.26 Billion Arbitron Purchase Cleared by U.S.," *Bloomberg Businessweek*, September 20, 2013, www.bloomberg.com/news/2013-09-20/nielsens-1-26-billion-arbitron-purchase-cleared-by-u-s-.html.

# Chapter Twelve

1. An excellent resource on the role of magazines as advertising media vehicles is the Association of Magazine Media website at www.magazine.org/ and the Newspaper Association of America at www.naa.org/.

2. Herbert E. Krugman, "The Measurement of Advertising Involvement," *Public Opinion Quarterly* 30 (Winter 1966–67), pp. 583–96.

3. *Magazine Media: MPA Factbook 2013/2014* (New York: Association of Magazine Media), www.magazine.org/insights-resources/research-publications.

4. Ibid.

5. *Mr. Magazine: Launch Monitor*, www.mrmagazine.com/.

6. Tim Nudd, "Lexus Print Ad Roars to Life, with a Little Help from an iPad," *Adweek*, October 10, 2012, www.adweek.com/adfreak/lexus-print-ad-roars-life-little-help-ipad-144349.

7. Tim Nudd, "VW's Green Print Ad Includes Pre-Paid Mailing Label to Recycle Magazine," *Adweek*, September 4, 2012, www.adweek.com/adfreak/vws-green-print-ad-includes-pre-paid-mailing-label-recycle-magazine-143320.

8. David Gianatasio, "The CW Embeds a Live Twitter Feed Inside Its 'EW' Print Ad," *Adweek*, September 28, 2012, www.adweek.com/adfreak/cw-embeds-live-twitter-feed-inside-its-ew-print-ad-144048.

9. Brian Steinberg, "Gimmicky Magazine Inserts Aim to Grab Page Flippers," *The Wall Street Journal*, August 8, 2005, pp. B1, B2.

10. Scott Donaton and Pat Sloan, "Ad 'Printaculars' under Scrutiny," *Advertising Age*, February 12, 1990, p. 3.

11. *Magazine Media: MPA Factbook 2013/2014*.

12. Ibid.

13. Sarah Ellison, "Good Housekeeping Touts Its Test Lab to Seek New Readers' Seal of Approval," *The Wall Street Journal*, October 11, 2006, pp. B1, B4.

14. Sara Rosengren and Micael Dahlén, "Judging a Magazine by Its Advertising," *Journal of Advertising Research* 53, no. 1 (March 2013), pp. 61–70.

15. Steve Fajen, "Numbers Aren't Everything," *Media Decisions* 10 (June 1975), pp. 65–69.

16. *Magazines: The Medium of Action: A Comprehensive Guide and Handbook 2009/2010* (New York: Magazine Publishers of America), www.magazine.org/handbook.

17. *Magazine Media: MPA Factbook 2013/2014*.

18. Sally Goll Beatty, "Philip Morris Starts Lifestyle Magazine," *The Wall Street Journal*, September 16, 1996, pp. B1, B8.

19. Jack Neff, "P&G Extends Online Custom Publishing," *Advertising Age*, March 22, 2004, pp. 24–25.

20. Jon Fine, "Audit Bureau to Change How It Counts Circulation," *Advertising Age*, July 17, 2001, http://adage.com/article/news/audit-bureau-change-counts-circulation/30030/.

21. "ASME Guidelines for Editors and Publishers Updated September 2013," *American Society of Magazine Editors*,

www.magazine.org/asme/editorial-guidelines.

22. Study cited in Jim Surmanek, *Media Planning: A Practical Guide* (Lincolnwood, IL: Crain Books, 1985).

23. "How Advertising Readership Is Influenced by Ad Size," Report no. 110.1, *Cahners Advertising Research*, Newton, MA; "Larger Advertisements Get Higher Readership," *LAP Report no. 3102*, McGraw-Hill Research, New York; "Effect of Size, Color and Position on Number of Responses to Recruitment Advertising," *LAP Report no. 3116*, McGraw-Hill Research, New York.

24. "Almost Everything You Want to Know about Positioning in Magazines," study by Roper Starch Worldwide, Inc. 1999.

25. "Readership by Advertising Unit Type," *Magazine Dimensions,* 2001, Media Dynamics, Inc., www.magazine.org/resources/fact_sheets/adv.

26. Nat Ives, "Why Ad Pages Won't Ever Fully Return to Mags," *Advertising Age*, July 27, 2009, http://adage.com/article/media/magazines-ad-pages-fully-return/138131/.

27. Nat Ives, "Sporting News Ends Print Edition after 126 Years," *Advertising Age*, December 11, 2012, http://adage.com/article/media/sporting-news-ends-print-edition-126-years/238719/; Michael Learmonth, "Newsweek to End Print Edition in Quest to Cut Losses," *Advertising Age*, October 18, 2012, http://adage.com/article/media/newsweek-end-print-edition/237833/.

28. Katy Bachman, "Magazines, Newspaper Brace for Exigent Postal Rate Hike," *Adweek*, August 29, 2013, www.adweek.com/news/press/magazines-newspapers-brace-exigent-postal-rate-hike-152010.

29. "Ad Age's Magazine A-List: Marie Claire Is Magazine of the Year," *Advertising Age*, October 14, 2012, http://adage.com/article/media/ad-ages-magazine-a-list-marie-claire-magazine-year/237716/; Emma Bazilian, "Advertisers Keep It Real with Marie Claire Pub," *Adweek,* April 2, 2012, p. 14.

30. Nat Ives, "Mags March Calmly into Face of Chaos," *Advertising Age*, April 23, 2007, http://adage.com/article/media/mags-march-calmly-face-chaos/116231/.

31. Nat Ives, "Magazines to Sell Subscriptions within Facebook's News Feed," *Advertising Age,* May 12, 2010, http://adage.com/article/media/magazines-sell-subscriptions-facebook-news-feed/143813/.

32. Rupal Parekh, "Daily-Deal Sites Offer Dose of Growth for Magazine Circulation," *Advertising Age*, February 27, 2012, p. 17; Nat Ives, "Many Magazines That Cut Subscription Prices Lose Subscribers Anyway," *Advertising Age*, February 5, 2010, http://adage.com/article/media/magazines-cheaper-subscriptions-win-subscribers/141945/.

33. *Magazine Media: MPA Factbook 2013/2014.*

34. "Newspaper Readership and Audience by Age and Gender," *Newspaper Assocation of America*, March 2013, www.naa.org/en/Trends-and-Numbers/Readership.aspx/.

35. Ann Marie Kerwin, "After a Long Lobbying Effort, 'New York Times' Wins New Ad Status," *Advertising Age*, February 22, 1999, p. 24.

36. Ann Marie Kerwin, "Big-City Dailies Eye National Stage," *Advertising Age*, February 22, 1999, p. 24.

37. Hanna Liebman, "NAA Network Ready to Roll," *MediaWeek*, December 13, 1993, p. 18.

38. "The American Newspaper Media Industry Revenue Profile 2012," *Newspaper Association of America*, April 8, 2013, www.naa.org/Trends-and-numbers/newspaper-Revenue/newspaper-media-Industry-Revenue-Profile-2012.aspx.

39. Nat Ives, "Newspaper Subscribers Stick around Longer, Pay More," *Advertising Age*, September 30, 2009, http://adage.com/article/media/media-news-newspaper-subscribers-cancel-pay/139346/.

40. "Newspaper Readership and Audience by Age and Gender."

41. Rick Edmonds, Emily Guski, Tom Rosentiel, and Amy Mitchell, "Newspaper: By the Numbers," *The State of the News Media 2012*, The Pew Research Center's Project for Excellence in Journalism, March 18, 2013, http://stateofthemedia.org/.

42. Ibid.

43. "Smart Is the New Sexy," Newspaper Association of America, www.naa.org/smart-is-the-new-sexy-ads.aspx.

44. Jane Sasseen, Katerina-Eva Matsa, and Amy Mitchell, "News Magazines: Embracing Their Digital Future," *The State of the News Media 2013,* The Pew Research Center's Project for Excellence in Journalism, http://stateofthemedia.org/2013/news-magazines-embracing-their-digital-future/.

45. Julia Angwin, "Newspapers Set to Jointly Sell Ads on Web Sites," *The Wall Street Journal*, January 10, 2007, pp. A1, A8.

46. Rebecca McPheters, "Magazines and Newspapers Need to Build Better Apps," *Advertising Age*, January 13, 2012, http://adage.com/article/media/viewpoint-magazines-newspapers-build-apps/232085/.

## Chapter Thirteen

1. Outdoor Advertising Association of America, 2013.

2. Product Acceptance & Research, 2007.

3. David Kaplan, "Agency Offers In-Store Insight: End-Aisles, Print Surpass TV," June 23, 2005, www.mediapost.com.

4. Point of Purchase Advertising Institute, 2010.

5. Outdoor Advertising Association of America, 2013.

6. Ibid.

7. Mukesh Bhargava and Naveen Donthu, "Sales Response to Outdoor Advertising," *Journal of Advertising Research* 39, no. 3 (July/August 1999).

8. American Public Transportation Association, 2010.

9. Andrew Hampp, "Outdoor Ad Industry Finally Gets Its Improved Metrics," *Advertising Age*, March 30, 2010, http://adage.com/article/media/outdoor-ad-industry-finally-improved-metrics/143049/.

10. Promotional Products Association International, 2013.

11. Ibid.

12. Ibid.

13. Ibid.

14. Ibid.

15. Yellow Pages Association, 2013.

16. Ibid.

17. Ibid.

18. Ibid.

19. "Catch a Commercial at the Movies," October 29, 2007. www.mediapost.com.

20. Sarah McBride, "In Theaters: Commercials Aplenty," *The Wall Street Journal*, February 8, 2007.

21. Erik Sass, "Movie Metrics: Cinema Ads Click with Viewers," April 13, 2010, www.mediapost.com.

22. Cliff Marks, "American Moviegoers— those Wonderful People out There in the Dark," March 13, 2013, www.printthis.clickability.com.

23. Hank Kim, "Regal Pre-Movie Package Boosts Recall," *Advertising Age*, June 7, 2004, p. 21.

24. Joe Mandese, "And the Winner Is . . . Cinema Ads: Brain Research Shows They're More Emotionally Engaging Than TV Spots," February 27, 2012, www.mediapost.com.

25. Sarah McBride, "Cinema Surpassed DVD Sales in 2009," January 4, 2010, http://online.wsj.com/news/articles/SB10001424052748704789404574636531903626624.

26. Katy Bachman, "Taco Bell Goes Cinematic with Ad Campaign," June 28, 2009, www.mediaweek.com.

27. "Online Viewers Are More Likely Than the Typical Adult to Go to the Movies," *Adweek,* February 20, 2012, p. 17.

28. "PQ Media Global Product Placement Spending Forecast 2012–2016," March 26, 2013, www.pqmedia.com.

29. Shahnaz Mahmud, "Branded Content, Mobile to Grow," *Adweek*, August 8, 2007.

30. Michael Belch and Cristel A. Russell, "A Managerial Investigation into the Product Placement Industry," *Journal of Advertising Research*, March 2005, pp. 73–92.

31. Emma Hall, "UK Gives Product Placement Go-Ahead for February—with Conditions," *Advertising Age*, December 21, 2010, http://adage.com/article/global-news/product-placement-uk-start-date-official-rules/147786/.

32. David G. Kennedy, "Coming of Age in Consumerdom," *American Demographics,* April 2004, p. 14

33. Marc Graser, "Movie Placement Creates Demand for Nonexistent Shoe," *Advertising Age*, January 31, 2005, http://adage.com/article/news/movie-placement-creates-demand-nonexistent-shoe/42006/.

34. Jim Edwards, "Will Product Placement Get Its Own Dot-Comeuppance?," *Brandweek*, July 25, 2005, p. 13.

35. Brian Steinberg, "'Modern Family' Featured an Ipad, but ABC Didn't Collect," *Advertising Age*, April 1, 2010, http://adage.com/article/media/modern-family-ipad-abc-collect/143105/.

36. Kennedy, "Coming of Age in Consumerdom."

37. Kaplan, "Product Placement: Well-Placed among Consumers," March 25, 2005, www.mediapost.com/publications/article/28530/.

38. Abe Sauer, "Marlboro Washes Up in Jersey Shore: Best Anti-Smoking Ad Ever?" July 19, 2011, www.brandchannel.com.

39. Gail Schiller, "Tie-ins Often Sobering for Liquor Firms," *Hollywood Reporter,* August 1, 2005, pp. 1–3; MarinInstitute.org, 2006.

40. Katy Bachman, "Study: Industry's Found Sneaky Way to Keep Advertising Junk Food to Kids," August 2, 2011, www.adweek.com.

41. John Consoli, "80% TV Viewers Approve Product Placement," March 28, 2005, www.inside brandedentertainment.com.

42. Kennedy, "Coming of Age in Consumerdom."

43. Harris Interactive, "Attitudes of US Children and Teens toward Advertising Tactics, by Age, May 2006," *eMarketer*, 2006.

44. Steve McClellan, "Branded Entertainment Finding Its Place(ment)," March 28, 2005, www.insidebrandedentertainment.com.

45. Belch and Russell, "A Managerial Investigation into the Product Placement Industry."

46. Lorin Cipolla, "Guerilla Marketing Goes Mainstream," February 17, 2004, www.promomagazine.com.

47. Betsy Spethmann, Patrica Odell, Tim Parry, and Amy Johannes, "Guerilla Marketing Grows Up," January 12, 2005, www.PROMOXtra.com.

48. David Gianatasio, "Prankvertising: Are Outrageous Marketing Stunts Worth the Risks?" April 1, 2013, www.adweek.com.

49. "ESA Facts," May 22, 2010, www.theesa.com.

50. "Outcast Sees High Recall for At-the-Pump Network: Nielsen," May 6, 2009, www.mediabuyerplanner.com.

51. PRN.com.

## Chapter Fourteen

1. Direct Marketing Association, 2013.

2. *Direct Marketing Association Statistical Fact Book* (New York: Direct Marketing Association, 2013).

3. Ibid.

4. Ibid.

5. Bureau of Labor Statistics, 2010.

6. Erik Sass, "Survey Results Make a Case for Direct Mail," *MediaPost,* June 12, 2007.

7. *Direct Marketing Association Statistical Fact Book.*

8. Ibid.

9. Ibid.

10. Juliette Kopecky, "An Investigation into the ROI of Direct Mail versus E-mail Marketing," January 10, 2013, www.hubspot.com.

11. Elaine Underwood, "Is There a Future for the TV Mall?," *Brandweek*, March 25, 1996, pp. 24–26.

12. www.responsemagazine.com, April 2013.

13. *Direct Marketing Association Statistical Fact Book.*

14. Marianna Morello, "Print Media + DRTV = Retail Success," *Response*, September 2002, p. 6.

15. David Kaplan, "OnStar Positions New TV Ad Format: The 'Documercial,'" April 14, 2005, www.mediapost.com/publications/article/29204/?print.

16. expoTV.com, 2010.

17. Jessica Dickler, "Home Shopping Networks Go High-End," July 19, 2011, www. Money.cnn.com.

18. *Direct Marketing Association Statistical Fact Book.*

19. Direct Selling Association, 2013.

20. *Direct Marketing Association Statistical Fact Book.*

## Chapter Fifteen

1. "E-retail Spending to Increase 62% by 2016," February 27, 2012, www.verticalwebmedia.com.

2. Wikipedia.org.

3. Brian Morrissey, "15 Alarming Stats about Banner Ads," March 21, 2013, www.digiday.com.

4. Ibid.

5. Anita Davis, "Banner Ads Drive Search Behavior: Study," May 13, 2009, www.brandrepublic.asia.

6. Tessa Wegert, "Banner Ads: Beyond the Click," May 18, 2009, www.emarketer.com.

7. Xiang Fang, Surendra Singh, and Rohini Ahluwalia, "An Examination of Different Explanations for the Mere Exposure Effect," *Journal of Consumer Research*, June 2007.

8. "Consumers Unhappy with Web Site Simply Go Away," August 23, 2005, www.mediapost.com/publications/article/33195/.

9. Cong Li and Robert Meeds, "Different Forced-Exposure Levels of Internet Advertising: An Experimental Study of Pop-Up Ads and Interstitials," *American Academy of Advertising Conference Proceedings,* 2005, pp. 200–08.

10. "US Digital Ad Spending to Top $37 billion in 2012 as Market Consolidates," September 20, 2012, www.emarketer.com.

11. Ibid.

12. Wikipedia.org, 2013.

13. Ibid.

14. Ian Schafer, "What Is Rich Media, Really?," September 23, 2005, www.clickz.com/clickz/column/1692953/what-is-rich-media-really.

15. Wikipedia.org, 2013

16. Ibid.

17. Ibid.

18. "Top 15 Most Popular Social Networking Sites/October 2013," October 2013, www.ebizmba.com.

19. "China Internet Watch," May 16, 2013, www.chinainternetwatch.com.

20. Daniel Muntinga, "Catching COBRAS," The Foundation for Scientific Research on Commercial Communication, Amsterdam, The Netherlands, 2013.

21. Joanna Brenner, "Pew Internet: Social Networking," February 14, 2013, www.pewinternet.org.

22. Michael Steizner, "2013 Social Media Marketing Industry Report," May 2, 2013, www.socialmediaexaminer.com.

23. Karlene Lukovitz, "Survey: Metrics Biggest Integration Obstacle," April 24, 2009, www.mediapost.com/publications/article/104704/?print.

24. Tim Peterson, "Facebook Opens up Ad Targeting to Minivan-Driving, Baby Food–Buying Homemakers," April 10, 2013, www.adweek.com.

25. "Twitter Statistics," May 7, 2013, www.statisticbrain.com.

26. Ibid.

27. "Could YouTube Become as Big as CBS or Viacom?" May 3, 2013, www.variety.com.

28. "Podcasting Goes Mainstream," March 4, 2009, www.emarketer.com.

29. "Internet 2012 in Numbers," January 16, 2013, www.royalpingdom.com.

30. Ibid.

31. NCH Marketing Resource Center, 2011, www.nchmarketing.com.

32. "Smartphone Population Gains Users, Young and Old," April 25, 2012, www.emarketer.com.

33. Jamie Turner, "Mobile Phones vs. Toothbrushes," October 18, 2011, www.60secondmarketer.com.

34. "Tablet Traffic Overtakes Smartphones," Marach 2013, www.warc.com.

35. "Together, TV and Tablets Drive Brand Searches," December 6, 2012, www.emarketer.com.

36. "The Effect of Mobile on the Path to Purchase," February, 29, 2012, www.emarketer.com.

37. "Measurement Guidelines and Measurement Certification," 2006, www.iab.net.

38. Jack Neff, "Study: ROI May Be Measurable in Facebook, MySpace After All," *Advertising Age*, April 13, 2009, http://adage.com/article/digital/study-cpg-roi-measurable-facebook-myspace/135940/.

39. 39. "Measurement Guidelines and Measurement Certification."

40. Steve Latham, "Why Marketers Are Not Investing Online," *MediaPost*, February 13, 2008.

41. "Brands Failing to Measure Social Results," August 12, 2012, www.warc.com. Gavin O'Malley, "Excessive Online Ads Curbed by Metric Standard," August 16, 2012, www.mediapost.com.

## Chapter Sixteen

1. Louis J. Haugh, "Defining and Redefining," *Advertising Age*, February 14, 1983, p. M44.

2. Wendy Goldman Getzier, "McDonald's, General Mills among Despicable Me 2 Marketing Minions," *kidscreen*, May 21, 2013, http://kidscreen.com/2013/05/21/mcdonalds-general-mills-among-despicable-me-2-marketing-minions/.

3. Scott A. Nielsen, John Quelch, and Caroline Henderson, "Consumer Promotions and the Acceleration of Product Purchases," in *Research on Sales Promotion: Collected Papers*, Katherine E. Jocz, ed. (Cambridge, MA: Marketing Science Institute, 1984).

4. J. Jeffrey Inman and Leigh McAlister, "Do Coupon Expiration Dates Affect Consumer Behavior?" *Journal of Marketing Research* 31 (August 1994), pp. 423–28.

5. "2013 Ad Spending Forecast +.7% as Digital Growth More Than Offsets Legacy Declines," *Jack Myers Media Business Report* (Rhinebeck, NY: M.E.D.I.Advisory Group LLC, January 4, 2013).

6. "2009 Promo Industry Trends Report," *Promo*, December 1, 2009, http://promomagazine.com/09-industry-trends-report/index.html.

7. Betsy Spethman, "Is Promotion a Dirty Word?," *Promo,* March 2001, pp. 64–72.

8. "Clutter: Extras, Extras!," August 1, 2001, www.promomagazine.com.

9. Ibid.

10. Ellen Byron and Suzanne Vranica, "Scanners Check Out Who's Browsing," *The Wall Street Journal*, September 27, 2006, p. B2.

11. Matthew Boyle, "Brand Killers," *Fortune*, August 11, 2003, pp. 89–100.

12. Hank Schultz, "Private Label Sales Hit $98 Billion on 6% Growth, Report Says," October 30, 2012, FoodNavigator–USA, www.foodnavigator-usa.com/Markets/Private-label-sales-hit-98-billion-on-6-growth-report-says.

13. "Fortune 500," http://money.cnn.com/magazines/fortune/fortune500/2013/full_list/.

14. Andy Serwer, "Bruised in Bentonville," *Fortune*, April 18, 2005, pp. 84–89.

15. *The Effects of Promotion Stimuli on Consumer Purchase Behavior* (Glenview, IL: FSI Council, 1999).

16. *Coupon Trends–2012 Year-End Report* (Winston-Salem, NC: 2013).

17. Betsy Spethman, "Tuning in at the Shelf," *Promo 13th Annual Source Book*, 2006, pp. 22, 24.

18. Leigh McAlister, "A Model of Consumer Behavior," *Marketing Communications*, April 1987.

19. *Mintel's Global New Products Database*, www.gnpd.com/sinatra/gnpd/frontpage/.

20. Joan Schneider and Julie Hall, "Why Most Product Launches Fail," *Harvard Business Review*, April 2011, http://hbr.org/2011/04/why-most-product-launches-fail/.

21. Leonard M. Lodish and Carl F. Mela, "If Brands Are Built over Years, Why Are They Managed over Quarters?" *Harvard Business Review* 85, no. 7/8 (July/August 2007), pp. 104–12.

22. "Special 'Made in the U.S.A.' WD-40 Smart Straw Cans Celebrate Hard Work, Heritage," *WD-40 Product News and Information*, http://wd40.com/news/in-the-news/JUN0313/.

23. Nielsen Clearing House, *NCH Reporter,* no. 1 (1983).

24. Amy Porterfield, "Study Reveals Why Consumers Fan Facebook Pages," *Social Media Examiner*, October 29, 2010, www.socialmediaexaminer.com/study-reveals-why-consumers-fan-facebook-pages/.

25. Lodish and Mela, "If Brands Are Built over Years, Why Are They Managed over Quarters?"

26. Michael Barbaro, Karen Ann Cullotta, and Christopher Maag, "Given Fewer Coupons to Clip, Bargain Hunters Snub Macy's," *The New York Times*, September 29, 2007, www.nytimes.com/2007/09/29/business/29coupons.html?_r=0p.

27. Lodish and Mela, "If Brands Are Built over Years, Why Are They Managed over Quarters?"

28. R.M. Prentice, "How to Split Your Marketing Funds between Advertising

and Promotion Dollars," *Advertising Age*, January 10, 1977, pp. 41–42, 44.

29. Betsy Spethman, "Money and Power," *Brandweek*, March 15, 1993, p. 21.

30. "Miller Taste Challenge," 2005 Reggie Awards, Promotion Marketing Association, www.baalink.org/.

31. "Con Kleenex Expresa Tu Hispanidad Art Contest," 2010 Reggie Awards Multi-Cultural/Ethnic, www.baalink. org/?reggieawards.

32. "Trial and Conversion VI: Consumers' Reactions to Samples and Demonstrations," Promotional Marketing Association, Inc., 2002.

33. Natalie Zmuda, "Facebook Turns Focus Group with Splenda Product-Sampling App," *Advertising Age*, July 13, 2009, http://adage.com/article?article_id=137851.

34. *2013 NCH Coupon Facts Report* (Deerfield, IL: NCH Marketing Services).

35. Inman and McAlister, "Do Coupon Expiration Dates Affect Consumer Behavior?"

36. Emily Fredrix, "Big Firms Sue Coupon Clearinghouse," *The Washington Post*, October 6, 2007, www.washingtonpost.com/wpdyn/content/article/2007/10/05/AR2007100502304.html; Karen Holt, "Coupon Crimes," *Promo*, April 2004, pp. 23–26, 70.

37. *2013 NCH Coupon Facts Report.*

38. Ibid.

39. Jack Neff, "Coupons Get Clipped," *Advertising Age*, November 1, 2001, pp. 1, 47.

40. "Kroger Expands Mobile Grocery Coupon Program," *Adweek*, January 28, 2009, www.adweek.com/news/advertising-branding/kroger-expands-mobile-grocery-coupon-program-105158; Stehpanie Kang, "Coupons Gain New Market on Cellphones," *The Wall Street Journal*, September 11, 2007, p. B8.

41. Emily Bryson York, "BK 'Sacrifices' Whopper Facebook Application," *Advertising Age*, January 15, 2009, http://adage.com/article/news/bk-sacrifices-whopper-facebook-application/133800/.

42. Survey by Oxtoby-Smith, Inc., cited in "Many Consumers View Rebates as a Bother," *The Wall Street Journal*, April 13, 1989, p. B1.

43. William R. Dean, "Irresistible but Not Free of Problems," *Advertising Age*, October 6, 1980, pp. S1–S12.

44. William A. Robinson, "What Are Promos' Weak and Strong Points?" *Advertising Age*, April 7, 1980, p. 54.

45. Richard Sale, "Serving Up Sweeps," *Promo*, August 1999, pp. 70–78; "Sweepstakes Fever," *Forbes*, October 3, 1988, pp. 164–66.

46. "Next-Tech," *Promo*, July 2005, pp. 24–27.

47. David Kiefaber, "Lay's Crowdsourced Potato-Chip Finalists: Cheesy Garlic Bread, Chicken & Waffles, Sriracha," *Adweek*, February 11, 2013, www.adweek.com/adfreak/lays-crowdsourced-potato-chip-finalists-cheesy-garlic-bread-chicken-waffles-sriracha-147197; David Kiefaber, "Sam Adams Crowdsourcing Its Next Beer," *Adweek*, January 20, 2012, www.adweek.com/adfreak/sam-adams-crowdsourcing-its-next-beer-137619.

48. Bob Woods, "Picking a Winner," *Promo*, August 1998, pp. 57–62; Richard Sale, "Sweeping the Courts," *Promo*, May 1998, pp. 148–52, 422–45; Maxine S. Lans, "Legal Hurdles Big Part of Promotions Game," *Marketing News*, October 24, 1994, pp. 15–16.

49. Kimberly Palmer, "Why Shoppers Love to Hate Rebates," January 18, 2008, www.usnews.com.

50. Peter Tat, William A. Cunningham III, and Emin Babakus, "Consumer Perceptions of Rebates," *Journal of Advertising Research* 28, no. 4 (August/September 1988), pp. 45–50.

51. "Rebates: Get What You Deserve," *Consumer Reports*, September 2009, p. 7; Brian Grow, "The Great Rebate Runaround," *BusinessWeek*, December 5, 2005, pp. 34–37.

52. Grow, "The Great Rebate Runaround."

53. Edward A. Blair and E. Lair Landon, "The Effects of Reference Prices in Retail Advertisements," *Journal of Marketing* 45, no. 2 (Spring 1981), pp. 61–69.

54. Betsy Spethman, "Switching Loyalty," *Promo*, July 2002, pp. 40–45.

55. "Retailers Should Overhaul Loyalty Programs: Survey," promomagazine.com, August 22, 2007.

56. "WD-40 Fan Club Celebrates 10th Anniversary," *WD-40 Product News and Information*, March 8, 2011, http://wd40.com/news/in-the-news/wd-40-fan-club-celebrates-10th-anniversary/.

57. "Top of Wallett," promomagazine.com, July 1, 2007.

58. Spethman, "Switching Loyalty."

59. Kathleen M. Joyce, "Keeping the Faith," *Promo's 12th Annual Source Book 2005*, p. 24.

60. Adapted from Terrence A. Shimp, *Advertising, Promotion, and Supplemental Aspects of Integrated Marketing Communication*, 6th ed. (Mason, OH: South-Western, 2003), p. 524.

61. William L. Wilkie, Debra M. Desrochers, and Gregory T. Gundlach, "Marketing Research and Public Policy: The Case of Slotting Fees," *Journal of Marketing & Public Policy* 21, no. 2 (Fall 2002), pp. 275–88; Frank Green, "Battling for Shelf Control," *San Diego Union-Tribune*, November 19, 1996, pp. C1, C6, C7.

62. "Want Shelf Space at the Supermarket? Ante Up," *BusinessWeek*, August 7, 1989, pp. 60–61.

63. Ira Teinowitz, "Senators Berate Industry Abuse of Slotting Fees," *Advertising Age*, September 20, 1999, pp. 3, 66.

64. Paul N. Bloom, Gregory T. Gundlach, and Joseph P. Cannon, "Slotting Allowances and Fees: Schools of Thought and Views of Practicing Managers," *Journal of Marketing* 64, April 2000, pp. 92–108.

65. "Crunching the Numbers," *Promo*, May 1, 2001, pp. 49–50.

66. Matthew Kinsman, "No Pain, No Gain," *Promo*, January 2002, pp. 26–28.

67. Tom Steinhagen, "Space Management Shapes Up with Planograms," *Marketing News*, November 12, 1990, p. 7.

68. Srinath Gopalakrishna, Gary L. Lilien, Jerome D. Williams, and Ian K. Sequeria, "Do Trade Shows Pay Off?" *Journal of Marketing* 59 (July 1995), pp. 75–83.

69. Beth Snyder Bulik, "Inside the 'Intel Inside' Campaign," *Advertising Age*, September 21, 2009, http://adage.com/article/news/advertising-inside-inside-intel-campaign/139128/.

70. Stuart Elliott, "'Intel Inside' Ad Campaign Shifts Focus to the Web," *International Herald Tribune*, October 11, 2007, www.iht.com.

71. Cynthia Rigg, "Hard Times Means Growth for Co-op Ads," *Advertising Age*, November 12, 1990, p. 24.

72. Edwin L. Artzt, "The Lifeblood of Brands," *Advertising Age*, November 4, 1991, p. 32.

73. Jack Neff and Rupal Parekh, "Dove Takes Its New Men's Line to the Super Bowl," *Advertising Age*, January 5, 2010, http://adage.com/print?article_id=141312.

74. Lodish and Mela, "If Brands Are Built over Years, Why Are They Managed over Quarters?"; Jack Neff, "The New Brand Management," *Advertising Age*, November 8, 1999, pp. S2, S18; Benson P. Shapiro, "Improved Distribution

with Your Promotional Mix," *Harvard Business Review*, March/April 1977, p.116; Roger A. Strang, "Sales Promotion—Fast Growth, Faulty Management," *Harvard Business Review*, July/August 1976, p. 119.

75. Quote by Thomas E. Hamilton, director of sales promotion service, William Esty Advertising, cited in Felix Kessler, "The Costly Couponing Craze," *Fortune*, June 9, 1986, p. 84.

76. Priya Raghubir and Kim Corfman, "When Do Price Promotions Affect Pretrial Brand Evaluations?" *Journal of Marketing Research* 36 (May 1999), pp. 211–22.

77. Alan G. Sawyer and Peter H. Dickson, "Psychological Perspectives on Consumer Response to Sales Promotion," in *Research on Sales Promotion: Collected Papers*, Katherine E. Jocz, ed. (Cambridge, MA: Marketing Science Institute, 1984).

78. William E. Myers, "Trying to Get Out of the Discounting Box," *Adweek*, November 11, 1985, p. 2.

79. Leigh McAlister, "Managing the Dynamics of Promotional Change," in *Looking at the Retail Kaleidoscope, Forum IX* (Stamford, CT: Donnelley Marketing, April 1988).

80. "Promotions Blemish Cosmetic Industry," *Advertising Age*, May 10, 1984, pp. 22–23, 26; Cliff Edwards, "Everyone Loves a Freebie—except Dell's Rivals," *BusinessWeek*, July 22, 2002, p. 41.

81. "Taco Bell '$1 Cravings' Value Menu to Likely Go National," *The Huffington Post*, May 2, 2013, www.huffington-post.com/2013/05/02/taco-bell-1-cravings_n_3203491.html; Lauren Shepherd, "Customers Getting More Burger for the Buck," *San Diego Union-Tribune*, February 13, 2008, pp. C1, C3.

82. Priya Raghubir, J. Jeffrey Inman, and Hqans Gande, "The Three Faces of Consumer Promotions," *California Management Review*, Summer 2004, pp. 23–42.

## Chapter Seventeen

1. www.publicrelationsnewspr.com.

2. Scott M. Cutlip, Allen H. Center, and Glen M. Broom, *Effective Public Relations,* 11th ed. (Upper Saddle River, NJ: Prentice Hall, 2012).

3. Jonah Bloom, "The Cultural Gulf That Separates Marketing and PR," *Advertising Age*, March 11, 2007.

4. "PR News/PRSA Survey," *PR News,* May 25, 2005, p. 1.

5. N. Curry, "PR Isn't Marketing," *Advertising Age*, December 18, 1991, p. 18.

6. Martha M. Lauzen, "Imperialism and Encroachment in Public Relations," *Public Relations Review* 17, no. 3 (Fall 1991), pp. 245–55.

7. Cutlip, Center, and Broom, *Effective Public Relations.*

8. Thomas L. Harris, "How MPR Adds Value to Integrated Marketing Communications," *Public Relations Quarterly*, Summer 1993, pp. 13–18.

9. Wayne Friedman, "Fox's O.J Dilemma: An $8M Question," *MediaPost*, November 20, 2006.

10. Cutlip, Center, and Broom, *Effective Public Relations.*

11. John E. Marston, *Modern Public Relations* (New York: McGraw-Hill, 1979).

12. "Pfizer Announces Improvements to Consumer Advertising for Prescription Medicines," *Pfizer News Release,* 2005, www.pfizer.com.

13. Ken Wheaton, "Nivea Pulls Ad, Apologizes after Racism Accusations," *Advertising Age*, August 18, 2011, http://adage.com/article/the-big-tent/nivea-pulls-ad-apologizes-racism-accusations/229368/.

14. Alana Horowitz, "Belvedere Vodka Ad under Fire for Rape Implications," March 25, 2012, www.huffingtonpost.com/2012/03/25/belvedere-vodka-rape-ad_n_1377975.html.

15. L. Chang, "Did Apple Fail to Detect iPhone 4g Antenna Problem Beforehand?" June 26, 2010, www.lanewsmonitor.com.

16. Laura Crovo, "The Art of Kraft-ing a Social Media Response," June, 24, 2010, www.mghus.com.

17. Walter K. Lindenmann, "Public Relations Research for Planning and Evaluation," 2006, www.instituteforpr.org.

18. Otis Baskin, Joe Hahn, Samuel Seaman, and Dan Reines, "Perceived Effectiveness and Implementation of Public Relations Measurement and Evaluation Tools among European Providers and Consumers of PR Services," *Public Relations Review* 36 (2010), pp. 105–11.

19. Mark Weiner, "Marketing PR Revolution," *Communication World,* January/February 2005, pp. 1–5.

20. Jaye S. Niefeld, "Corporate Advertising," *Industrial Marketing*, July 1980, pp. 64–74.

21. "Naming Rights, Naming Wrongs," October 2013, www.performanceresearch.com.

22. "2013 Sponsorship Outlook: Spending Increase Is Double-edged Sword," January 7, 2013, www.sponsorship.com.

23. Mark J. Miller, "NACAR Sponsors: Hertz Backs Penske as Teams Look to Get Back on Track," January 24, 2013, www.brandchannel.com.

24. Wayne Friedman, "Supreme Court OKs Corporate-Sponsored Issue Ads," *MediaPost*, June 27, 2007.

25. Stuart Elliott, "An Advocacy Ad Stirs a National Debate," February 1, 2010, www.nytimes.com.

26. Harvey Meyer, "When the Cause Is Just," *Journal of Business Strategy*, November/December 1999, pp. 27–31.

27. Jackie Jones, "Consumers Expect More Accountability in Cause Marketing," September 27, 2011, www.responsemagazine.com.

28. Janas Sinclair and Tracy Irani, "Advocacy Advertising for Biotechnology," *Journal of Advertising*, Fall 2005, pp. 59–74.

29. Bob Donath, "Corporate Communications," *Industrial Marketing*, July 1980, pp. 53–57.

## Chapter Eighteen

1. "100 Leading National Advertisers Index," *Advertising Age,* June 24, 2013, http://adage.com/article/datacenter-advertising-spending/100-leading-national-advertisers-index/106348/.

2. "US Total Media Ad Spend Inches Up, Pushed by Digital," August 22, 2013, www.emarketer.com.

3. "In 2013, Mobile, Social Lead Shift from Traditional Media to Digital," February 19, 2013, www.emarketer.com.

4. Laurie Sullivan, "Marketing Budgets Rise, Determining Multichannel ROI, Metrics Remains a Challenge," February 5, 2013, www.mediapost.com.

5. Ibid.

6. Ibid.

7. Noreen O'Leary, "Does Creativity Count?" *Adweek*, December 11, 2000, pp. 30–34.

8. Tim Nudd, "Does Sex Really Sell?," *Adweek*, October 17, 2005, pp. 14–17.

9. Stephen McClellan, "WPP Invests in Affectiva, Mining Emotional Metrics," July 20, 2011, www.mediapost.com.

10. David A. Aaker and John G. Myers, *Advertising Management*, 3rd ed.

(Englewood Cliffs, NJ: Prentice Hall, 1987), p. 474.

11. Spike Cramphorn, "What Advertising Testing Might Have Been, If We Had Only Known," *Journal of Advertising Research* 44, no. 2 (June 2004), pp. 170–80.

12. "21 Ad Agencies Endorse Copy-Testing Principles," *Marketing News* 15 (February 19, 1982), p. 1.

13. Ibid.

14. Ye Hu, Leonard Lodish, Abba Krieger, and Babak Hayati, "An Update of Real-World TV Advertising Tests," *Journal of Advertising Research*, June 2009, pp. 201–06.

15. Steve Outing and Laura Ruel, "The Best of Eyetrack III: What We Saw When When We Looked through Their Eyes," 2004, www.poynterextra.org.

16. Hubert A. Zielske, "Does Day-After Recall Penalize 'Feeling Ads'?," *Journal of Advertising Research* 22, no. 1 (1982), pp. 19–22.

17. Arthur J. Kover, "Why Copywriters Don't Like Advertising Research—and What Kind of Research Might They Accept," *Journal of Advertising Research* 36 (March/April 1996), pp. RC8–RC10; Gary Levin, "Emotion Guides BBDO's Ad Tests," *Advertising Age*, January 29, 1990, p. 12.

18. Terry Haller, "Day-After Recall to Persist Despite JWT Study; Other Criteria Looming," *Marketing News*, May 18, 1979, p. 4.

19. Joel Dubow, "Recall Revisited: Recall Redux," *Journal of Advertising Research* 34, no. 3 (May/June 1994), p. 92.

20. Ravi Chandiramani, "Reckitt Launches Debut iTV Campaign for Finish," *Marketing*, January 10, 2002, p. 9.

21. Kipp Cheng, "IPG Platform Gains Major Advertisers," *Adweek*, July 23, 2001, p. 5.

22. Gary Levin, "Tracing Ads' Impact," *Advertising Age*, November 12, 1990, p. 49.

23. Jeffrey L. Seglin, "The New Era of Ad Measurement," *Adweek's Marketing Week*, January 23, 1988, p. 24.

24. "Yankelovich Study Shows Advertising's Effects Vary, Depending on Category and Purchase Funnel Stage," April 16, 2009, www.tvb.org.

25. Russell I. Haley and Allan L. Baldinger, "The ARF Copy Research Validity Project," *Journal of Advertising Research*, April/May 1991, pp. 11–32.

26. Glenn Heitsmith, "Something for Nothing," *Promo*, September 1993, pp. 30, 31, 93.

27. Ibid.

28. "Journeying Deeper into the Minds of Shoppers," *BusinessWeek*, February 4, 1991, p. 85.

29. David W. Schumann, Jennifer Grayson, Johanna Ault, Kerri Hargrove, Lois Hollingsworth, Russell Ruelle, and Sharon Seguin, "The Effectiveness of Shopping Cart Signage: Perceptual Measures Tell a Different Story," *Journal of Advertising Research* 31 (February/ March 1991), pp. 17–22.

30. June Bryan Kim, "Research Makes Ski Run Easier," *Advertising Age*, August 18, 1991, p. 30.

31. Steve McClellan, "New Software to Track In-Store Radio," *Adweek*, October 10, 2005, p. 10.

32. Bettina Cornwell and Isabelle Maignan, "An International Review of Sponsorship Research," *Journal of Advertising* 38, no. 1 (March 1998), pp. 1–23.

33. Michel Tuan Pham, "The Evaluation of Sponsorship Effectiveness: A Model and Some Methodological Considerations," Gestion 2000, pp. 47–65.

34. Ibid.

35. John Nardone and Ed See, "Measure Sponsorship to Drive Sales-Shift Gears: Move Beyond Perceiving Them as Mere Brand Builders and Instead Assess ROI," *Advertising Age*, March 5, 2007.

36. "2008 David Ogilvy Awards Finalists," *The ARF*, 2008.

37. Teresa F. Lindeman, "Good Wal-Mart, Bad Wal-Mart; Retail Giant Hopes to Combat Negative Publicity," *Knight Ridder Tribune Business News*, April 10, 2005, pp.1–6.

38. "Advertisers Demand More Accountability for Digital Media," *Center for Media Research*, February 22, 2007, pp. 1–2.

39. Marek Winearz, "The Market Contact Audit," 2010, www.integration-imc.com.

# Chapter Nineteen

1. Richard S. Post and Penelope N. Post, *Global Brand Integrity Management* (New York: McGraw-Hill, 2008); David A. Aaker and Erich Joachimsthaler, "The Lure of Global Branding," *Harvard Business Review*, November/ December 1999, pp. 137–44.

2. David Kiley and Burt Helm, "The Great Trust Offensive," *BusinessWeek*, September 28, 2009, pp. 38–42.

3. Emma Hall, "As Regulation Increases, WFA Must Decide What's Worth Protecting," *Advertising Age*, March 12, 2013, http://adage.com/article/ cmo-interviews/pernod-ricard-cmo-riley-leads-wfa-amid-regulation-concerns/240222/.

4. Geoff Colvin, "Indra Nooyi's Challenge," *Fortune*, June 11, 2012, pp. 149–56; Mutsa Chironga, Acha Leke, Susan Lund, and Arend van Wamelen, "Cracking the Next Growth Market: Africa," *Harvard Business Review*, May 2011, pp. 117–22.

5. "There's Nothing Like Australia," *Tourism Australia*, June 17, 2012, www.tourism.australia.com/events/News-events-7309.aspx.

6. Joan Voight, "The Great Brand of China," *Adweek*, October 29, 2012, p. 22; Christine Birkner, "Eastern Influence," *Marketing News*, September 15, 2012, pp. 10–15; Normandy Madden, "China Ad Opportunities to Grow with WTO Deal," *Advertising Age International*, January 2000, p. 6.

7. Thomas H. Friedman, *The World Is Flat* (New York: Farrar, Straus and Giroux, 2005).

8. Anita Chang Beattie, "Can Starbucks Make China Love Joe?" *Advertising Age*, November 4, 2012, http://adage.com/china/article/china-news/can-starbucks-make-china-love-coffee/238101/.

9. "Global Marketers 2012," *Advertising Age*, December 10, 2012, pp. 17–18.

10. Vern Terpstra, *International Marketing*, 4th ed. (New York: Holt, Rinehart & Winston/Dryden Press, 1987), p. 427.

11. Claudia Penteado, "Emerging Lower Middle Class Fires Up Marketers in Brazil," *Advertising Age*, June 14, 2010, p. 12.

12. Bradley Johnson, "Where's the Growth in Marketing? Follow the BRIC Road," *Advertising Age*, December 4, 2011, http://adage.com/article/global-news/growth-marketing-follow-bric-road/231359/.

13. Manuela Mesco, "Unfashionably Late to China," *The Wall Street Journal*, March 26, 2013, http://search.proquest.com/docview/1319502349?accoun tid=13758.

14. Noreen O'Leary, "The Rise of BRIC," *Adweek*, February 4–11, 2008, pp. 32–37, 65; Noreen O'Leary, "Bright Lights, Big Challenges," *Adweek*, January 15, 2007, 22–33.

15. Mark Lasswell, "Lost in Translation," *Business 2.0*, Auguest 2004, pp. 68–70.

16. George E. Belch and Michael A. Belch, "Toward Development of a Model

and Scale for Assessing Consumer Receptivity to Foreign Products and Global Advertising," in *European Advances in Consumer Research* (vol. 1), Gary J. Bamossy and W. Fred van Raaij, eds. (Provo, UT: Association for Consumer Research, 1993), pp. 52–57.

17. Subhash Sharma, Terrence Shimp, and Jeongshin Shin, "Consumer Ethnocentrism: A Test of Antecedents and Moderators," *Journal of the Academy of Marketing Science,* Winter 1995, pp. 26–37.

18. Shelly Pannill, "The Road to Richesse," *Sales & Marketing Management,* November 1999, pp. 89–96.

19. Ibid.

20. L. Ruano, "New Balance 576 'France' Release Recap," May 9, 2010, http://hypebeast.com/2010/05/balance-576-france-release-recap.

21. Steve Hamm, "Borders Are So 20th Century," *BusinessWeek,* September 22, 2003, pp. 68–73.

22. For an excellent discussion of various elements of Japanese culture such as language and its implications for promotion, see John F. Sherry Jr. and Eduardo G. Camargo, "May Your Life Be Marvelous: English Language Labelling and the Semiotics of Japanese Promotion," *Journal of Consumer Research* 14, no. 2 (September 1987), pp. 174–88.

23. Barbara Mueller, "Reflections on Culture: An Analysis of Japanese and American Advertising Appeals," *Journal of Advertising Research,* June/July 1987, pp. 51–59.

24. Barbara Mueller, "Standardization vs. Specialization: An Examination of Westernization in Japanese Advertising," *Journal of Advertising Research* 31, no. 1 (January/February 1992), pp. 15–24; Johny K. Johansson, "The Sense of Nonsense: Japanese TV Advertising," *Journal of Advertising* 23, no. 1 (March 1994), pp. 17–26.

25. Michael L. Maynard and Charles R. Taylor, "Girlish Images across Cultures: Analyzing Japanese versus U.S. Seventeen Magazine Ads," *Journal of Advertising* 28, no. 1 (Spring 1999), pp. 39–49.

26. John B. Ford, Patricia Kramer Voli, Earl D. Honeycutt Jr., and Susan L. Casey, "Gender Role Portrayals in Japanese Advertising: A Magazine Content Analysis," *Journal of Advertising* 27, no. 1 (Spring 1998).

27. Francis Hsu, *Americans and Chinese: Passage to Differences* (Honolulu: University Press of Hawaii, 1981).

28. Carolyn A. Lin, "Cultural Values Reflected in Chinese and American Television Advertising," *Journal of Advertising* 30, no. 4 (2001), pp. 83–94.

29. Don E. Schultz, "New Systems Make China Next Hot Spot," *Marketing News,* January 7, 2002, p. 5.

30. Geoffrey A. Fowler, "China Bans Nike's LeBron Ad as Offensive to Nation's Dignity," *The Wall Street Journal,* December 7, 2004, p. B4.

31. Gerard Prendergast, Wah-Leung Cheung, and Douglas West, "How Far Is Too Far? The Antecedents of Offensive Advertising in Modern China," *Journal of Advertising Research* 48, no. 4 (December 2008), pp. 484–95.

32. Iain Akerman, "Pepsi Launches Major Ad Campaign with 'Yalla Now,'" *Campaign Middle East,* March 11, 2013, http://campaignme.com/2013/03/11/14427/pepsi-launches-major-ad-campaign-with-yalla-now/.

33. Rich Thomaselli, "Will Australia's Cigarette Branding Ban Spread beyond Borders, Tobacco?" *Advertising Age,* August 19, 2012, http://adage.com/article/news/australia-s-cigarette-brand-ban-prompt-domino-effect/236761/.

34. "Malaysia Bans 'Sly' Tobacco Ads," *Marketing News,* September 1, 2002, p. 7.

35. Vanessa Fuhrmans, "In Europe, Prescription-Drug Ads Are Banned—and Health Costs Lower," *The Wall Street Journal,* March 15, 2002, pp. B1, B4.

36. Niraj Sheth, "India Liquor, Tobacco Firms Shift Tack," *The Wall Street Journal,* May 6, 2008, p. B8.

37. Jeremy Slate, "EC Lets Stand Toy Ad Ban," *Advertising Age International,* August 1999, pp. 1, 11.

38. Sam Loewenberg, "Effort in EU to Ban TV Ads Aimed at Kids Gains Steam," *Los Angeles Times,* July 9, 2001, p. C3.

39. Safran S. Al-Makaty, G. Norman van Tubergen, S. Scott Whitlow, and Douglas S. Boyd, "Attitudes toward Advertising in Islam," *Journal of Advertising Research* 36, no. 3 (May/June 1996), pp. 16–26; Marian Katz, "No Women, No Alcohol: Learn Saudi Taboos before Placing Ads," *International Advertiser,* February 1986, pp. 11–12.

40. "Misleading Advertising," *European Commission,* http://ec.europa.eu/justice/consumer-marketing/unfair-trade/false-advertising/; Naveen Donthu, "A Cross-Country Investigation of Recall of and Attitude

toward Comparative Advertising," *Journal of Advertising* 27, no. 2 (Summer 1998), pp. 111–22.

41. Derek Turner, "Coke Pops Brazilian Comparative Ad," *Advertising Age,* September 9, 1991, p. 24.

42. J. Craig Andrews, Steven Lysonski, and Srinivas Durvasula, "Understanding Cross-Cultural Student Perceptions of Advertising in General: Implications for Advertising Educators and Practitioners," *Journal of Advertising* 20, no. 2 (June 1991), pp. 15–28.

43. Jonathan Cheng, "China Demands Concrete Proof of Ad Claims," *The Wall Street Journal,* July 8, 2005, pp. B1, B4.

44. Stephanie Thompson, "Europe Slams Icons as Food Fights Back," *Advertising Age,* January 31, 2005, pp. 1, 38.

45. Robert D. Buzzell, "Can You Standardize Multinational Marketing?" *Harvard Business Review,* November/December 1968, pp. 102–13; Ralph Z. Sorenson and Ulrich E. Wiechmann, "How Multinationals View Marketing," *Harvard Business Review,* May/June 1975, p. 38.

46. Theodore Levitt, "The Globalization of Markets," *Harvard Business Review,* May/June 1983, pp. 92–102; Theodore Levitt, *The Marketing Imagination* (New York: Free Press, 1986).

47. Anne B. Fisher, "The Ad Biz Gloms onto Global," *Fortune,* November 12, 1984, p. 78.

48. Maduh Agrawal, "Review of a 40-Year Debate in International Advertising," *International Marketing Review* 12, no. 1 (1995), pp. 26–48; William L. James and John S. Hill, "International Advertising Messages, to Adapt or Not to Adapt (That Is the Question)," *Journal of Advertising Research* 31 (June/July 1991), pp. 65–71; Keith Reinhard and W.E. Phillips, "Global Marketing: Experts Look at Both Sides," *Advertising Age,* April 15, 1988, p. 47; Anthony Rutigliano, "The Debate Goes On: Global vs. Local Advertising," *Management Review,* June 1986, pp. 27–31.

49. Jack Neff, "Gillette Signs Three Sports Giants for Global Effort," *Advertising Age,* February 5, 2007, http://adage.com/article/news/gillette-signs-sports-giants-global-effort/114822/; Bernhard Warner, "IQ News: Gillette's Mach 3 Media Hits Web: Eureopean Site Next?," *AdweekOnline,* August 24, 1998.

50. E.J. Schultz, "Doritos Launches First Global Campaign," *Advertising Age,*

March 6, 2013, http://adage.com/article/news/doritos-launches-global-campaign/240173/.

51. Kevin Goldman, "Professor Who Started Debate on Global Ads Still Backs Theory," *The Wall Street Journal*, October 13, 1992, p. B8.

52. Anita Chang Beattie, "In Japan, Pizza Is Recast as a Meal for Special Occasions," *Advertising Age*, April 2, 2012, p. 16.

53. Jack Neff, "The Dirt on Laundry Trends around the World," *Advertising Age*, June 14, 2010, p. 8.

54. Ibid.

55. Eric White and Jeffrey A. Trachtenberg, "One Size Doesn't Fit All," *The Wall Street Journal*, October 1, 2003, pp. B1, B2.

56. Joanne Lipman, "Marketers Turn Sour on Global Sales Pitch," *The Wall Street Journal*, May 12, 1988, p. 1.

57. Sally Goll Beatty, "Global Needs Challenge Midsize Agencies," *The Wall Street Journal*, December 14, 1995, p. B9.

58. Criteria cited by Edward Meyer, CEO, Grey Advertising, in Rebecca Fannin, "What Agencies Really Think of Global Theory," *Marketing & Media Decisions*, December 1984, p. 74.

59. Quote cited in Reinhard and Phillips, "Global Marketing," p. 47.

60. Kunur Patel, "HTC Goes All-In on 'One' Phone in Battle with Apple, Samsung," *Advertising Age*, March 30, 2012, http://adage.com/article/digital/htc-phone-battle-apple-samsung/233843/.

61. Durairaj Maheswaran, "Country of Origin as a Stereotype: Effects on Product Evaluations," *Journal of Consumer Research*, September 1994, pp. 354–65.

62. Paul Chao, "The Moderating Effects of Country of Assembly, Country of Parts, and Country of Design on Hybrid Product Evaluations," *Journal of Advertising* 20, no. 4 (Winter 2001), pp. 67–82.

63. Beth Snyder Bulik, "Ditch the Flags, Kids Don't Care Where You Come From," *Advertising Age*, June 4, 2007, pp. 1, 59.

64. Ibid.

65. Salah S. Hassan and Lea P. Katsanis, "Identification of Global Consumer Segments: A Behavioral Framework," *Journal of International Consumer Marketing* 3, no. 2 (1991), pp. 11–28.

66. Arundhati Parmar, "Global Youth United," *Marketing News*, October 28, 2002, pp. 1, 49; "Ready to Shop until They Drop," *BusinessWeek*, June 22, 1998, pp. 104–10; "Teens Seen as the First Truly Global Consumers," *Marketing News*, March 27, 1995, p. 9; Shawn Tully, "Teens: The Most Global Market of All," *Fortune*, May 16, 1994, pp. 90–97.

67. Teressa Iezzi, "Emotional Juice," *Creativity*, March 2004, pp. 10, 30–32.

68. Robert E. Hite and Cynthia L. Fraser, "International Advertising Strategies of Multinational Corporations," *Journal of Advertising Research* 28, no. 4 (August/September 1988), pp. 9–17.

69. Ali Kanso, "International Advertising Strategies: Global Commitment to Local Vision," *Journal of Advertising Research*, January/February 1992, pp. 10–14.

70. Jan Jaben, "Ad Decision-Makers Favor Regional Angle," *Advertising Age International*, May 1995, pp. i3,16.

71. Nigel Hollis, *The Global Brand* (New York: Palgrave Macmillan, 2008).

72. Nigel Hollis, "Global Brands, Local Cultures," *Research World*, July/August 2009, pp. 20–24; Piet Levy, "10 Minutes with Nigel Hollis," *Marketing News*, August 30, 2009, pp. 18–19.

73. Penelope Rowlands, "Global Approach Doesn't Always Make Scents," *Advertising Age International*, January 17, 1994, pp. i1, 38.

74. Natalie Zmuda, "Levi's Names Jaime Szulc Its First Global CMO," *Advertising Age*, August 26, 2009, http://adage.com/article/cmo-strategy/levi-s-names-jaime-szulc-global-cmo/138659/.

75. Normandy Madden, "Shanghai Rises as Asia's Newest Marketing Capital," *Advertising Age*, October 14, 2002, pp. 1, 13.

76. Kevin Goldman, "Global Companies Hone Agency Rosters," *The Wall Street Journal*, July 25, 1995, p. B8.

77. Sally Goll Beatty, "Young & Rubicam Is Only One for Colgate," *The Wall Street Journal*, December 1, 1995, p. B6.

78. Goldman, "Global Companies Hone Agency Rosters."

79. Natalie Zmuda and Alexandra Bruell, "Levi's Taps Wunderman as First Global Digital Shop," *Advertising Age*, January 4, 2012, http://adage.com/article/agency-news/levi-s-taps-wunderman-global-digital-shop/231887/.

80. "Advertising Is Indeed Going Global," *Market Europe*, October 1997, pp. 8–10.

81. Anne-Marie Crawford, "Clients and Agencies Split over Ad Superstars," *Ad Age Global* 1, no. 9 (May 2001), p. 16.

82. Eleftheria Parpis, "Asics: Sound Mind, Sound Body," *Adweek*, February 22, 2010, www.adweek.com/news/advertising-branding/asics-sound-mind-sound-body-107080.

83. Joan Voight, "Exporting Las Vegas," *Adweek*, September 3, 2007, pp. 14–15.

84. Erin White, "German Ads Get More Daring, but Some Firms Aren't Pleased," *The Wall Street Journal*, November 22, 2002, p. B6.

85. Larry Speer, "French Government Attacks 'Sexist' Ads," *Ad Age Global*, May 2001, p. 7.

86. Normandy Madden," Looking for the Next Brazil? Try Thailand," *Advertising Age,* April 11, 2005, p. 22.

87. Stephanie King, "Indian Ads Come into Their Own," *The Wall Street Journal*, December 12, 2007, p. B4.

88. Normandy Madden, "Two Chinas," *Advertising Age*, August 16, 2004, pp. 1, 22.

89. Rochell Burbury, "Australia Ends Ban on Cable TV Spots," *Advertising Age International*, March 1997, p. i22.

90. Leslie Chang, "Cracking China's Huge TV Market," *The Wall Street Journal*, August 1, 2000, pp. B1, B4.

91. "To Cope with New Rules, China TV Station Holds Ad Auction Do-Over," *Advertising Age*, December 9, 2011, http://adage.com/article/global-news/china-tv-station-holds-ad-auction-cope-rules/231492/.

92. Jane Lanhee Lee, "TV Marketers Aim to Reap Rural China's Fertile Land," *The Wall Street Journal*, July 30, 2007, p. B2.

93. Hearst International Magazines, www.hearst.com/magazines/hearst-magazines-international.php.

94. Nat Ives, "For Pubs, Going Global Comes with Challenges," *Advertising Age*, June 14, 2010, p. 17.

95. Ibid.

96. Normandy Madden, "Murdoch Restructures Star TV," *Advertising Age*, August 26, 2009, http://adage.com/china/article/china-news/news-corp-restructures-broadcast-businesses-in-asia/138656/.

97. Ronal Grover and Tom Lowry, "Rupert's World," *BusinessWeek*, January 19, 2004, pp. 51–60.

98. Noreen O'Leary, "The Lay of the Land," *Adweek*, February 5, 2007, pp. 14–21.

99. Kamran Kashani and John A. Quelch, "Can Sales Promotion Go Global?" *Business Horizons*, May/June 1990, pp. 37–43.

100. Lenard C. Huff and Dana L. Alden, "An Investigation of Consumer Response

to Sales Promotion in Developing Markets: A Three Country Analysis," *Journal of Advertising Research* 26, no. 1 (May/June 1998), pp. 47–56.

101. "Global Consumers Go Sale Searching and Coupon Clipping," *Nielsen*, October 12, 2011, www.nielsen.com/us/en/newswire/2011/global-consumers-go-sale-searching-and-coupon-clipping.html.

102. Douglas J. Wood and Linda A. Goldstein, "A Lawyer's Guide to Going Global," *Promo Magazine*, Special Report, August 1998, p. S11.

103. "Foreign Ads Go Further with PR," *International Advertiser*, December 1986, p. 30.

104. Laurel Wentz, "Haagen-Dazs Teaser Ad Offends Indians," *Advertising Age*, December 29, 2009, http://adage.com/article/global-news/marketing-haagen-dazs-teaser-ad-offends-indians/141246/.

105. Loewenberg, "Effort in EU to Ban TV Ads Aimed at Kids Gains Steam."

106. Laurie Burkitt, "KFC Apologizes amid Probe," *The Wall Street Journal*, January 11, 2013, p. B7.

107. Laurie Burkitt and Julie Jargon, "China Woes Put Dent in Yum Brand," *The Wall Street Journal*, January 9, 2013, p. B3.

108. *Internet World Stats: Usage and Population Statistics: 2013*, www.internetworldstats.com/stats.htm.

109. Cate Riegner, "Wired China: The Power of the World's Largest Internet Population," *Journal of Advertising Research* 48, no. 4 (December 2008), pp. 496–505.

110. V. V. V., "Mr Kim, Tear Down That Wall; Mr Xi, Carry On," *The Economist*, January 11, 2013, www.economist.com/blogs/analects/2013/01/google-china; David Wolf, "With Google out, Will Baidu Reign in China?" *Advertising Age*, March 16, 2010, http://adage.com/article/global-news/google-baidu-reign-china/142825/.

111. Jonathan Espinosa, "Facebook Overtakes Japanese Social Network Mixi in Japan," *Inside Facebook*, September 13, 2012, www.insidefacebook.com/2012/09/13/facebook-overtakes-japanese-social-network-mixi-in-japan/.

112. Tom, "Twitter Now the Fastest Growing Social Platform in the World," *Global Web Index*, January 28, 2013, https://www.globalwebindex.net/twitter-now-the-fastest-growing-social-platform-in-the-world/.

## Chapter Twenty

1. Fred W. Morgan and Jeffrey J. Stoltman, "Advertising and Product Liability Litigation," *Journal of Advertising* 26, no. 2 (Summer 1997), pp. 63–75.

2. Ira Teinowitz, "Curb Proposal Raises Tobacco Marketers' Ire," *Advertising Age*, March 18, 2002, p. 70; Myron Levin, "U.S. to Pursue Lawsuit to Curb Cigarette Marketing," *Los Angeles Times*, March 12, 2002, pp. C1, C15.

3. Christopher Lawton, "Beer Industry Tests FTC's Patience," *The Wall Street Journal*, February 2, 2005, p. B2.

4. Alice Z. Cuneo, "Of Contracts and Claims; Agencies Face Liability Issues," *Advertising Age*, January 31, 2000, p. 25.

5. Steven W. Colford and Raymond Serafin, "Scali Pays for Volvo Ad: FTC," *Advertising Age*, August 26, 1991, p. 4; Alice Z. Cuneo, "Can an Agency Be Guilty of Malpractice?" *Advertising Age*, January 31, 2000, pp. 24–25.

6. Priscilla A. LaBarbera, "Analyzing and Advancing the State of the Art of Advertising Self-Regulation," *Journal of Advertising* 9, no. 4 (1980), pp. 27–38.

7. Ian P. Murphy, "Competitive Spirits: Liquor Industry Turns to TV Ads," *Marketing News*, December 2, 1996, pp. 1, 17.

8. John F. Archer, "Advertising of Professional Fees: Does the Consumer Have a Right to Know?" *South Dakota Law Review* 21 (Spring 1976), p. 330.

9. Bates v. State of Arizona, 97 S. Ct. 2691. 45, *U.S. Law Week* 4895 (1977).

10. Charles Laughlin, "Ads on Trial," *Link*, May 1994, pp. 18–22; "Lawyers Learn the Hard Sell—and Companies Shudder," *BusinessWeek*, June 10, 1985, p. 70.

11. Bruce H. Allen, Richard A. Wright, and Louis E. Raho, "Physicians and Advertising," *Journal of Health Care Marketing* 5 (Fall 1985), pp. 39–49.

12. Robert E. Hite and Cynthia Fraser, "Meta-Analyses of Attitudes toward Advertising by Professionals," *Journal of Marketing* 52, no. 3 (July 1988), pp. 95–105.

13. LaBarbera, "Analyzing and Advancing the State of the Art of Advertising Self-Regulation."

14. Shelly Branch, "Campbell Is in the Soup on V8 Ad," *The Wall Street Journal*, April 26, 2002, p. B4.

15. Tanzina Vega, "CoverGirl Withdraws 'Enhanced' Taylor Swift Ad," *The New York Times*, December 21, 2011, http://mediadecoder.blogs.nytimes.com/2011/12/21/covergirl-withdraws-enhanced-taylor-swift-ad/?_r=0.

16. Jack Neff, "Household Brands Counterpunch," *Advertising Age*, November 1, 1999, p. 26.

17. Jessica E. Vascellaro, "Regulators Say Love Ain't 'Chemistry' After All," *The Wall Street Journal*, September 17, 2007, p. B5.

18. Ibid.

19. "Millennium Import Company, Importers of Belvedere and Chopin Vodkas, File Motion for Preliminary and Permanent Injunction Against Grey Goose," *Business Wire*, January 26, 2004, p. 1.

20. "NAD Weighs in on Toning Shoes, FTC Announces $25 Million Settlement," *Better Business Bureau: Consumer News and Opinion*, September 29, 2011, www.bbb.org/blog/2011/09/nad-weighs-in-on-toning-shoes-ftc-announces-25-million-settlement-2/.

21. *NAD/CARU Case Reports, Summary of NAD/CARU/NARB/ERSP Case Work* (National Advertising Division, Council of Better Business Bureaus) 35, no. 1 (January 2013), p. 2.

22. "The Electronic Retailing Self-Regulation Program: Policy and Procedures," National Advertising Review Council, www.narcpartners.org/ersp.

23. Advertising Self-Regulatory Council, Accountability Program, www.asrcreviews.org/category/ap/about-the-accountability-program/.

24. Linda Bean, "CRN Foundation Announces Five-Year Grant to NAD," November 9, 2009, www.bbb.org/us/post/crn-foundation-announces-five-year-grant-to-nad-859.

25. Dorothy Cohen, "The FTC's Advertising Substantiation Program," *Journal of Marketing* 44, no. 1 (Winter 1980), pp. 26–35.

26. Rupal Parekh, "Netanyahu, Abbas Smooch in Benetton Ad," *Advertising Age*, November 16, 2011, http://adage.com/article/agency-news/netanyahu-abbas-smooch-latest-benetton-ad-campaign/231037/; Eric J. Lyman, "The True Colors of Toscani," adageglobal.com, August 2001, www.ericjlyman.com/adageglobal.html.

27. Lynda M. Maddox and Eric J. Zanot, "The Suspension of the National Association of Broadcasters' Code and Its Effects on the Regulation of

Advertising," *Journalism Quarterly* 61 (Summer 1984), pp. 125–30, 156.

28. Joe Mandese, "ABC Loosens Rules," *Advertising Age*, September 9, 1991, pp. 2, 8.

29. Avery M. Abernethy and Jan LeBlanc Wicks, "Self-Regulation and Television Advertising: A Replication and Extension," *Journal of Advertising Research* 41, no. 3 (May/June 2001), pp. 31–37; Eric Zanot, "Unseen but Effective Advertising Regulation: The Clearance Process," *Journal of Advertising* 14, no. 4 (1985), p. 48.

30. Joanne Voight and Wendy Melillo, "To See or Not to See?" *Adweek*, March 11, 2002, p. 30.

31. Mandese, "ABC Loosens Rules."

32. Hoag Levins, "Fox Killed Second Airing of Super Bowl Godaddy Ad," *Advertising Age*, February 8, 2005, http://adage.com/article/news/fox-killed-airing-super-bowl-godaddy-ad/45076/.

33. Jermey Mullman and Ken Wheaton, "Mancrunch Swears This Isn't a Super Bowl Stunt (Updated)," *Advertising Age*, January 20, 2010, http://adage.com/article/adages/mancrunch-super-bowl-a-natural-place-advertise/141816/.

34. Irina Slutsky, "Nine Things You Can't Do in Advertising If You Want to Stay on Right Side of the Law," *Advertising Age*, March 6, 2011, http://adage.com/article/news/advertising-regulation-nad-case-rulings-remember/149226/.

35. C. Lee Peeler, "Four Decades Later, Ad Industry's Self-Regulation Remains the Gold Standard," *Advertising Age*, March 13, 2013, http://adage.com/article/guest-columnists/40-years-adland-s-regulation-remains-gold-standard/240245/.

36. Steven W. Colford, "Speed Up the NAD, Industry Unit Told," *Advertising Age*, May 1, 1989, p. 3.

37. Linda Goldstein, "The NAD Sets Precedent for Others in Media, Marketing," *Advertising Age*, March 6, 2011, http://adage.com/article/guest-columnists/nad-sets-precedent-media-marketing/149217/.

38. Virginia State Board of Pharmacy v. Virginia Citizens Consumer Council, 425 U.S. 748, 96 S. Ct. 1817, 48 L. Ed. 2d 346 (1976).

39. Bates v. State of Arizona.

40. Central Hudson Gas & Electric v. Public Service Commission, 447 U.S. 557, 100 S. Ct. 2343, 65 L. Ed. 2d 341 (1980).

41. Liquormart, Inc. v. Rhode Island, 517 U.S. 484 (1996).

42. Erik L. Collins, Lynn Zoch, and Christopher S. McDonald, "When Professional Worlds Collide: Implications of Kasky v. Nike for Corporate Reputation Management," *Public Relations Review* 30, no. 4 (November 2004), pp. 411–18; Anne Gearan, "High Court Passes Up Decision on Nike Case," *San Diego Union-Tribune,* June 27, 2003, p. C1.

43. FTC v. Raladam Co., 258 U.S. 643 (1931).

44. Edward Cox, R. Fellmeth, and J. Schultz, "The Consumer and the Federal Trade Commission" (Washington, DC: American Bar Association, 1969); American Bar Association, *Report of the American Bar Association to Study the Federal Trade Commission* (Washington, DC: The Association, 1969).

45. *FTC Staff Report on Advertising to Children* (Washington, DC: Government Printing Office, 1978).

46. Federal Trade Commission Improvement Act of 1980, Pub. L. No. 96-252.

47. Bruce Silverglade, "Does FTC Have an 'Unfair' Future?" *Advertising Age*, March 26, 1994, p. 20.

48. Peter R. Darke and Robin J. Ritchie, "The Defensive Consumer: Advertising Deception, Defensive Processing, and Distrust," *Journal of Marketing Research* 44 (February 2007), 114–27.

49. Ivan L. Preston, *The Great American Blow-Up: Puffery in Advertising and Selling* (Madison: University of Wisconsin Press, 1975), p. 3.

50. Isabella C.M. Cunningham and William H. Cunningham, "Standards for Advertising Regulation," *Journal of Marketing* 41 (October 1977), pp. 91–97; Herbert J. Rotfeld and Kim B. Rotzell, "Is Advertising Puffery Believed*?*" *Journal of Advertising* 9, no. 3 (1980), pp. 16–20.

51. Herbert J. Rotfeld and Kim B. Rotzell, "Puffery vs. Fact Claims—really Different?," in *Current Issues and Research in Advertising,* James H. Leigh and Claude R. Martin Jr., eds. (Ann Arbor: University of Michigan, 1981), pp. 85–104.

52. Preston, *The Great American Blow-Up.*

53. Chuck Ross, "Marketers Fend Off Shift in Rules for Ad Puffery," *Advertising Age,* February 19, 1996, p. 41.

54. Louise Kramer, "Jury Finds Papa John's Ads Misled," *Advertising Age,* November 22, 1999, http://adage.com/article/news/jury-finds-papa-john-s-ads-misled/60251/.

55. Apryl Duncan, "Better Pizza? Bigger Lawsuit," *About Advertising,* http://advertising.about.com/od/foodrelatedadnews/a/papajohns.htm.

56. Emily Bryson York, "Domino's Claims Victory with Pizza Makeover Strategy," *Advertising Age*, May 20, 2010, http://advertising.about.com/od/foodrelatedadnews/a/papajohns.htm.

57. Federal Trade Commission, "Policy Statement on Deception," 45 ATRR 689 (October 27, 1983), at p. 690.

58. For an excellent discussion and analysis of these three elements of deception, see Gary T. Ford and John E. Calfee, "Recent Developments in FTC Policy on Deception," *Journal of Marketing* 50, no. 3 (July 1986), pp. 86–87.

59. Ray O. Werner, ed., "Legal Developments in Marketing," *Journal of Marketing* 56 (January 1992), p. 102.

60. Ira Teinowitz, "FTC Strives to Clarify 'Made in USA' Rules," *Advertising Age*, April 29, 1996, p. 12.

61. Kalpana Srinivasan, "FTC Spells Out Tough Standards for 'Made in USA,'" *Marketing News*, January 18, 1999, p. 18.

62. "Champagne Bureau; Ad Campaign Urges Consumers to 'Unmask the Truth' about Champagne & Wine Place Names," *Marketing Weekly News*, December 26, 2009, p. 41.

63. Cohen, "The FTC's Advertising Substantiation Program."

64. *Trade Regulation Reporter,* Par. 20,056 at 22,033, 1970–1973 Transfer Binder, Federal Trade Commission, July 1972.

65. John E. Califee, "FTC's Hidden Weight-Loss Ad Agenda," *Advertising Age*, October 25, 1993, p. 29; Chester S. Galloway, Herbert Jack Rotfeld, and Jeff I. Richards, "Holding Media Responsible for Deceptive Weight-Loss Advertising," *West Virginia Law Review* 107, no. 2 (Winter 2005), pp. 353–84; Herbert Jack Rotfeld, "Desires versus the Reality of Self-Regulation," *The Journal of Consumer Affairs* 27, no. 2 (Winter 2003), pp. 424–27.

66. Alicia Mundy, "FTC Bars Pom Juice's Health Claims," *The Wall Street Journal*, January 16, 2013, http://online.wsj.com/article/SB10001424127887323468604578245740405648024.html.

67. Ibid.

68. For an excellent description of the Campbell Soup corrective advertising

case, see Dick Mercer, "Tempest in a Soup Can," *Advertising Age*, October 17, 1994, pp. 25, 28–29.

69. William L. Wilkie, Dennis L. McNeill, and Michael B. Mazis, "Marketing's 'Scarlet Letter': The Theory and Practice of Corrective Advertising," *Journal of Marketing* 48 (Spring 1984), pp. 11–31.

70. Warner-Lambert Co. v. Federal Trade Commission, CCH P61, 563A-D.C., August 1977 and CCH P61, 646 CA-D.C., September 1977.

71. Bruce Ingersoll, "FTC Orders Novartis to Correct Claims," *The Wall Street Journal*, May 28, 1999, p. B2; Ira Teinowitz, "Doan's Decision Worries Marketers," *Advertising Age*, May 31, 1999, p. 74.

72. Ira Teinowitz, "Doan's Decision Sets Precedent for Corrective Ads," September 4, 2000, http://adage.com/article/news/doan-s-decision-sets-precedent-corrective-ads/31813/.

73. Rich Thomaselli, "What Bayer Campaign Means for Pharma Ads," *Advertising Age*, February 16, 2009, http://adage.com/article/news/bayer-campaign-means-pharma-ads/134624/.

74. "Brill Tells DMA That FTC Is 'Ramping Up Enforcement,'" *Advertising Age*, March 13, 2013, http://adage.com/article/digital/brill-tells-dma-ftc-ramping-enforcement/240330/.

75. Ira Teinowitz, "Beales Makes Regulation Academic as FTC Director," *Advertising Age*, December 10, 2001, p. 66.

76. Laurie Sullivan, "FTC Pushes up Hearings on Environmental Marketing Guides," November 29, 2007, www.mediapost.com/publications/article/71725/?print.

77. Michael Bush, "Blogger Be Warned: FTC May Monitor What You Say," *Advertising Age*, April 13, 2009, http://adage.com/article/news/bloggers-warned-ftc-monitor/135938/.

78. Ira Teinowitz, "FTC to Marketers: Self-Regulate Behavioral Targeting," *Advertising Age*, February 12, 2009, http://adage.com/article/digital/ftc-marketers-regulate-targeting-online-ads/134587/.

79. Ira Teinowitz, "Howard Stern to Abandon FM Radio," *Advertising Age*, October 6, 2004, http://adage.com/article/media/howard-stern-abandon-fm-radio-move-sirius/41266/; Ira Teinowitz, "Clear Channel Drops Howard Stern," *Advertising Age*, February 26, 2004, http://adage.com/article/media/clear-channel-drops-howard-stern-fcc-indecency-fine/39530/.

80. Ira Teinowitz, "FCC to Probe Super Bowl Halftime Breast Incident," *Advertising Age*, February 2, 2004, http://adage.com/article/media/fcc-probe-super-bowl-halftime-show-wardrobe-malfunction/39341/.

81. Ira Teinowitz and Matthew Creamer, "Fake News Videos Unmasked in FCC Crackdown," *Advertising Age*, April 18, 2005, http://adage.com/article/news/fake-news-videos-unmasked-fcc-crackdown/102925/.

82. Rich Thomaselli, "Cheerios First in FDA Firing Line. Who's Next?," *Advertising Age*, May 18, 2009, http://adage.com/print?article_id=136704.

83. E.J. Schultz, "Did FDA Cross the Line in Its 2009 Cheerios-Case Finding?" *Advertising Age*, March 6, 2011, http://adage.com/article/news/fda-cross-line-2009-cheerios-case-finding/149236/.

84. Emily Bryson York, "FDA Demands Changes to Food and Beverage Product Labels," *Advertising Age*, March 3, 2010, http://adage.com/article/news/fda-demands-food-beverage-product-labels/142460/.

85. Sheryl Stolberg, "Clinton Imposes Wide Crackdown on Tobacco Firms," *Los Angeles Times*, August 24, 1996, pp. A1, A10.

86. Joy Johnson Wilson, Summary of the Attorneys General Master Tobacco Settlement Agreement, National Conference of State Legislators, www.academic.udayton.edu/health/syllabi/tobacco/summary.

87. Charles King III and Michael Siegel, "The Master Settlement Agreement with the Tobacco Industry and Cigarette Advertising in Magazines," *The New England Journal of Medicine* 345 (August 16, 2001), pp. 504–11.

88. Rich Thomaselli, "FDA Set to Take Control of Tobacco Regulation," *Advertising Age*, June 11, 2009, http://adage.com/article/news/marketing-curbs-expected-fda-controls-tobacco/137253/.

89. Rich Thomaselli, "ANA Mounts Suit to Block Tobacco Legislation," *Advertising Age*, June 16, 2009, http://adage.com/article/news/advertising-ana-aims-block-tobacco-legislation/137355/.

90. Jisu Huh and Rita Langteau, "Presumed Influence of Direct-to-Consumer (DTC) Prescription Drug Advertising on Patients: The Physician's Perspective," *Journal of Advertising* 36, no. 3 (Fall 2007), pp. 151–72; Sejung Marina Choi and Wei-Na Lee, "Understanding the Impact of Direct-to-Consumer (DTC) Pharmaceutical Advertising on Patient–Physician Interaction," *Journal of Advertising* 36, no. 3 (Fall 2007), pp. 137–49.

91. Rich Thomaselli, "Pfizer to Pay $2.3 Billion in Fraudulent-Marketing Suit," *Advertising Age*, September 2, 2009, http://adage.com/article/news/pfizer-pay-2-3-billion-fraudulent-marketing-suit/138763/.

92. Jan Joben, "A Setback for Competitive Ads?" *Business Marketing*, October 1992, p. 34.

93. Bruce Buchanan and Doron Goldman, "Us vs. Them: The Minefield of Comparative Ads," *Harvard Business Review*, May/June 1989, pp. 38–50.

94. Maxine Lans Retsky, "Lanham Have It: Law and Comparative Ads," *Marketing News*, November 8, 1999, p. 16.

95. Judann Pollack, "Prego Prevails in Battle over Comparative Ad," *Advertising Age*, September 1, 1996, p. 12; Michael Fumento, "Free-a-the-Papa!" *Forbes*, February 21, 2000, p. 53.

96. Natali Zmuda and Rupal Parekh, "Judge Rules in Powerade–Gatorade Court Battle, but Dispute Lives On," *Advertising Age*, August 6, 2009, http://adage.com/article/news/sports-drinks-powerade-gatorade-dispute-lives/138327/.

97. Michael J. Barone, Randall L. Rose, Paul W. Minniard, and Kenneth C. Manning, "Enhancing the Detection of Misleading Comparative Advertising," *Journal of Advertising Research* 39, no. 5 (September/October 1999), pp. 43–50.

98. "Deceptive Ads: The FTC's Laissez-Faire Approach Is Backfiring," *BusinessWeek*, December 2, 1985, p. 136.

99. Jennifer Lawrence, "State Ad Rules Face Showdown," *Advertising Age*, November 28, 1988, p. 4.

100. Steven Colford, "ABA Panel Backs FTC over States," *Advertising Age*, April 10, 1994, p. 1.

101. "Airborne to Pay $23.3 Million for False Advertising," *Natural Standard Blog*, March 21, 2008, http://blog.naturalstandard.com/natural-standard-blog/2008/03/airborne.

102. S.J. Diamond, "New Director Putting Vigor Back into FTC," *Los Angeles Times*, March 29, 1991, pp. D1, D4.

103. Federal Trade Commission, "Trade Regulation Rule: Games of Chance

in the Food Retailing and Gasoline Industries," 16 CFR, Part 419 (1982).

104. Richard Sale, "Sweeping the Courts," *Promo*, May 1998, pp. 42–45, 148–152. Ira Teinowitz and Carol Krol, "Multiple States Scrutinize Sweepstakes Mailings," *Advertising Age*, February 9, 1998, p. 41; Mark Pawlosky, "States Rein in Sweepstakes, Game Operators," *The Wall Street Journal*, July 3, 1995, pp. B1, B3.

105. Steven Winters and Joann Kohl, "Keep Your Online Sweepstakes and Contests on the Right Side of the Law," *Advertising Age*, March 6, 2011, http:// adage.com/article/guest-columnists/ online-sweepstakes-legal/149206/.

106. Ibid.

107. *Children Advertising Review Unit Self Regulatory Guidelines for Children's Advertising*, Council of Better Business Bureaus, 2003, www.caru. org/guidelines/index.

108. Steven W. Colford, "Top Kid TV Offender: Premiums," *Advertising Age*, April 29, 1991, p. 52.

109. Federal Trade Commission, "Guides for Advertising Allowances and Other Merchandising Payments and Services," 16 CFR, Part 240 (1983).

110. William L. Wilkie, Debra M. Desrochers, and Gregory T. Gundlach, "Marketing Research and Public Policy: The Case of Slotting Fees," *Journal of Marketing & Public Policy* 21, no. 2 (Fall 2002), pp. 275–88.

111. Ira Teinowitz, "FTC, McCormick Reach Accord on Slotting Fees," *Advertising Age*, March 13, 2000, p. 75.

112. Federal Trade Commission, "Trade Regulation Rule: Use of Negative Option Plans by Sellers in Commerce," 16 CFR, Part 42 (1982).

113. For a more thorough discussion of legal aspects of sales promotion and mail-order practices, see Dean K. Fueroghne, *Law & Advertising* (Chicago: Copy Workshop, 1995).

114. Mary Lu Carnevale, "FTC Adopts Rules to Curb Telemarketing," *The Wall Street Journal*, September 18, 1992, pp. B1, B10.

115. Scott Hume, "900 Numbers: The Struggle for Respect," *Advertising Age*, February 18, 1991, p. S1.

116. *Federal Register*, "Rules and Regulations," August 9, 1993, 42364–42406.

117. "Commission to Seek Public Comment on 900-Number Rule Revisions," *Federal Trade Commission Press Release*, October 23, 1998; Russell

N. Laczniak, Les Carlson, and Ann Walsh, "Antecedents of Mothers' Attitudes toward the FTC's Rule for 900-Number Advertising Directed at Children," *Journal of Current Issues and Research in Advertising* 21, no. 2 (Fall 1999), pp. 49–58.

118. "US FTC: FTC Workshop to Address Proposed Changes to Its Pay-per-Call-Rule," *M2 Presswire*, May 20, 1999.

119. Ira Teinowitz, "Congress Approves National 'Do Not Call,'" *Advertising Age*, February 13, 2003, http://adage. com/article/news/congress-approves-national-call/36837/.

120. Maggie Shader, "National Do-Not-Call List Hits 217 Million Phone Numbers, FTC Wants to Stop Illegal Robocalls," *Consumer Reports*, October 18, 2012, www.consumerreports.org/cro/ news/2012/10/national-do-not-call-list-hits-217-million-phone-numbers-ftc-wants-to-stop-illegal-robocalls/ index.htm.

121. Ira Teinowitz, "'Do Not Call' Law Upheld as Constitutional," *Advertising Age*, February 17, 2004, http://adage.com/article/news/ call-law-upheld-constitutional/39453/.

122. Ira Teinowitz, "'Do Not Call' Does Not Hurt Direct Marketers," *Advertising Age*, April 11, 2005, pp. 3, 95.

123. Herbert Jack Rotfeld, "Do-Not-Call as the US Government's Improvement to Telemarketing Efficiency," *Journal of Consumer Marketing* 21, no. 4 (2004), pp. 242–44.

124. Jennifer Levitz and Kelly Greene, "Marketers Use Trickery to Evade No-Call Lists," *The Wall Street Journal*, October 26, 2007, p. A1, A8.

125. Natasha Shabani, "Are You Using Sweepstakes to Skirt the Do-Not-Call List?," *Advertising Age*, April 12, 2010, http://adage. com/article/guest-columnists/ sweepstakes-skirt-call-list/143190/.

126. Jenny Rough, "Saving Trees and Your Sanity by Managing Junk Mail," *The Examiner*, February 14, 2010, p. 31; Steven Swanson, "Up to Here in Catalogs?," There Is a Solution Online," *Tribune Business News*, November 4, 2007.

127. Ira Teinowitz and Jennifer Gilbert, "FTC Chairman: Stop Undisclosed Profiling on Net," *Advertising Age*, November 8, 1999, p. 2.

128. Andrea Petersen, "DoubleClick Reverses Course after Privacy Outcry," *The Wall Street Journal*, March 3,

2000, pp. B1, B6; Jennifer Gilbert and Ira Teinowitz, "Privacy Debate Continues to Rage," *Advertising Age*, February 7, 2000, pp. 44, 46.

129. "NAI Launches Privacy-Awareness Web Site," *Advertising Age*, May 28, 2001, http://adage.com/article/news/nai-launches-privacy-awareness-web-site/11226/; "Online Advertisers Launch Two Consumer Privacy Tools," *Network Advertising Initiative*, May 23, 2001, www.networkadvertising.org/ aboutnai.

130. James Heckman, "COPPA to Bring No Surprises, Hefty Violation Fines in April," *Marketing News*, January 31, 2000, p. 6.

131. Ira Teinowitz, "FTC Proposal on Kids' Privacy Raises Ire of Watchdog Groups," *Advertising Age*, March 14, 2005, http://adage.com/article/digital/ ftc-proposal-kids-privacy-raises-ire-watchdog-groups/102494/.

132. Kate Kaye, "In Wake of Privacy Laws, Kids' Site See Ad Revenue Plummet," *Advertising Age*, August 23, 2013, http://adage.com/article/privacy-and-regulation/kids-sites-freaking-privacy-laws/243795/.

133. Kate Kaye, "FTC Aims to Bring Child Privacy Law into 21st Century," *Advertising Age*, December 19, 2012, http://adage.com/article/digital/ftc-aims-bring-child-privacy-law-21st-century/238842/.

134. Cotton Delo, "FTC Privacy Report Urges Congress to Pass Data-Security Legislation," *Advertising Age*, March 26, 2012, http://adage.com/article/ digital/ftc-urges-congress-pass-data-security-legislation/233719/; Larry Dobrow, "Privacy Issues Loom for Marketers," *Advertising Age*, March 13, 2006, http://adage.com/ article/100-leading-media-companies/ privacy-issues-loom-companies-mar-keting-kids-online/107066/.

135. Ira Teinowitz, "Why Ignoring New Voluntary FTC Privacy Guidelines Could Be Perilous," *Advertising Age*, December 28, 2007, http://adage.com/ article/digital/ignoring-voluntary-ftc-privacy-guidelines-perilous/122814/; Betsy Spethmann, "Private Eyes," *Promo*, January 2002, pp. 37–43; "Protecting Consumers' Privacy: 2002 and Beyond," Remarks of FTC chairm Timothy J. Muris at the Privacy 2001 Conference, Cleveland, Ohio, October 4, 2001, www.ftc.gov/ speeches/muris/privisp1002.

136. Kate Kaye, "Do-Not-Track Show Will Go on at W3C—for Now Group Names Two New Co-Chairs," *Advertising Age*, September 20, 2013, http://adage.com/article/privacy-and-regulation/track-show-w3c/244285/; Ira Teinowitz, "Consumer Groups Push Obama for 'Do Not Track' List," *Advertising Age*, December 16, 2008, http://adage.com/article/news/consumer-groups-push-obama-track-list/133329/.

137. Bryon Acohido, "FTC Tells Twitter to Protect the Private Data of Its Users," *USA Today*, June 25, 2010, p. 3B.

138. Vindu Goel, "Facebook to Update Privacy Policy, but Adjusting Settings Is No Easier," *The New York Times: Bits*, August 29, 2013, http://bits.blogs.nytimes.com/2013/08/29/facebook-to-update-privacy-policy-but-adjusting-settings-is-no-easier/; Bryon Acohido, "FTC Tells Twitter to Protect the Private Data of Its Users," *USA Today*, June 25, 2010, p. 3B; Mark Zuckerberg, "Making Control Simple," *The Facebook Blog*, May 26, 2010, http://blog.facebook.com/blog.php?post=391922327130.

139. Abbey Klaassen and Michael Learmonth, "What You Need to Know about the New FTC Endorsement Rules—and Why," *Advertising Age*, October 12, 2009, http://adage.com/article/digital/ftc-endorsement-rules/139595/.

140. Ira Teinowitz, "U.S. House Passes Anti-Spam Measure in Dawn Session," *Advertising Age*, November 23, 2003, http://adage.com/article/digital/u-s-house-passes-anti-spam-measure-dawn-session/38896/; Lisa Takeuchi Cullen, "Some More Spam, Please," *Time*, November 11, 2002, pp. 58–62.

141. Tom Zeller Jr., "Federal Law Hasn't Curbed Junk E-mail," *San Diego Union-Tribune*, February, 1, 2005, pp. C1, C5.

# Chapter Twenty-One

1. Robert L. Heilbroner, "Demand for the Supply Side," *New York Review of Books* 38 (June 11, 1981), p. 40.

2. David Helm, "Advertising's Overdue Revolution," speech given to the Adweek Creative Conference, October 1, 1999.

3. Claire Atkinson, "FTC and FCC Nearing Product-Placement Decisions," *Advertising Age*, October 29, 2004, http://adage.com/article/news/ftc-fcc-nearing-product-placement-decisions/41433/; Daniel Eisenberg, "Its an Ad, Ad, Ad World," *Time*, September 2, 2002, pp. 38–41.

4. Eric N. Berkowitz, Roger A. Kerin, Steven W. Hartley, and William Rudelius, *Marketing,* 7th ed. (Burr Ridge, IL: Irwin/McGraw-Hill, 2003), p. 21.

5. Je Eun Lee, Meichum Kuo, and Hang Lee, "College Binge Drinking in the 1990's: A Continuing Problem. Results of the Harvard School of Public Health 1999 College Alcohol Study," *Journal of American Collegiate Health* 48, no. 5 (2000), pp. 199–210; Jim O'Hara, "New Study Shows Underage Youth a Target of Alcohol Marketing: Youth Are More Likely to See Alcohol Advertising Than Adults," *U.S. Newswire*, September 24, 2002.

6. Jennifer Christie, Dan Fisher, John C. Kozup, Scott Smith, Scott Burton, and Elizabeth H. Creyer, "The Effects of Bar-Sponsored Beverage Promotions across Binge and Nonbinge Drinkers," *Journal of Public Policy & Marketing* 20, no. 2 (Fall 2001), pp. 240–53.

7. Mike Beirne, "In the Name of Responsibility," *Brandweek*, May 12, 2003, pp. 32–36; Ira Teinowitz, "BoozeHounded," *Advertising Age*, March 25, 2002, pp. 1, 27.

8. Ira Teinowitz, "Underage-Drinking Report Calls for Voluntary Alcohol Cutbacks," *Advertising Age,* March 6, 2007, http://adage.com/article/news/underage-drinking-report-calls-voluntary-alcohol-ad-cutbacks/115414/.

9. Ron Dicker, "Belvedere Lawsuit: Alicyn Packard, Actress in Controversial Belvedere Ad, Sues Company," April 2, 2012, www.huffingtonpost.com.

10. Stephanie Bentley, "Benetton Risks Fresh Outrage," *Marketing Week*, September 13, 1996, p. 9; Gary Levin, "Benetton Ad Lays Bare the Bloody Toll of War," *Advertising Age*, February 21, 1994, p. 38.

11. Jerry Della Famina, "Benetton Ad Models Are Dressed to Kill Sales," *The Wall Street Journal*, March 20, 2000, p. A34.

12. Francis X Rocca, "Clothing Retailer Benetton Pulls Pope-Kissing Ad," *USA Today,* November 17, 2011, http://usatoday30.usatoday.com/news/religion/story/2011-11-16/pope-kiss-benetton/51245428/1.

13. Stephanie O'Donohoe, "Attitudes to Advertising: A Review of British and American Research," *International Journal of Advertising* 14 (1995), pp. 245–61.

14. Samantha Braverman, "Young Adults More Trusting of Advertising," November 5, 2010, www.harrisinteractive.com.

15. Patricia Odell, "Consumer Feel Assaulted by Ads: Forrester," *Promo Xtra,* September 21, 2004, www.promo-maazine.com/news.

16. Gita Venkataramini Johar, "Consumer Involvement and Deception from Implied Advertising Claims," *Journal of Marketing Research* 32 (August 1995), pp. 267–79; J. Edward Russo, Barbara L. Metcalf, and Debra Stephens, "Identifying Misleading Advertising," *Journal of Consumer Research* 8 (September 1981), pp. 119–31.

17. Zach Bowman, "Hyundai, Kia Admit Exaggeratged Mileage Claims, Will Compensate Owners," November 2, 2012, www.autoblog.com.

18. Shelby D. Hunt, "Informational vs. Persuasive Advertising: An Appraisal," *Journal of Advertising*, Summer 1976, pp. 5–8.

19. "The Take on You," *Adweek*, September 24, 2007, pp. 14–15; Banwari Mittal, "Public Assessment of TV Advertising: Faint Praise and Harsh Criticism," *Journal of Advertising Research* 34, no. 1 (January/February 1994), pp. 35–53; J.C. Andrews, "The Dimensionality of Beliefs toward Advertising in General," *Journal of Advertising* 18, no. 1 (1989), pp. 26–35.

20. Helen Cooper, "CDC Advocates Use of Condoms in Blunt AIDS-Prevention Spots," *The Wall Street Journal,* January 5, 1994, p. B1.

21. Jack Neff, "Trojan Ads Ready for Prime Time: NBC," *Advertising Age*, May 16, 2005, p. 3.

22. Claude Brodesser-Akner, "Sex on TV Is OK as Long as It's Not Safe," *Advertising Age,* September 17, 2007, http://adage.com/article/news/sex-tv-long-safe/120489/.

23. Stephen A. Greyser, "Irritation in Advertising," *Journal of Advertising Research* 13 (February 1973), pp. 3–10.

24. Joan Voight and Wendy Melillo, "Rough Cut," *Adweek*, March 11, 2002, pp. 27–29; Joanne Lipman, "Censored Scenes: Why You Rarely See Some Things in Television Ads," *The Wall Street Journal*, August 17, 1987, p. 17.

25. Michael T. Ewing, "The Good News about Television: Attitudes Aren't

Getting Worse," *Journal of Advertising Research*, March 2013, p. 89.

26. Martha De Lacey, "American Apparel Branded 'Sexist' over 'Sleazy' Ads for Unisex Shirt with Half-Naked Women in G-Strings . . . but Fully Clothed Men," May 16, 2013, www.dailymail.com.

27. James B. Arndorfer, "Skyy Hit the Limit with Racy Ad: Critics," *Advertising Age*, February 7, 2005, p. 6.

28. Tim Nudd, "Does Sex Really Sell?," *Adweek*, October 17, 2005, pp. 14–17.

29. Leanne Potts, "Retailers, Ads Bare Flesh for Bottom Line," *Albuquerque Journal*, December 20, 2002, p. D1.

30. Rebecca Quick, "Is Ever-So-Hip Abercrombie & Fitch Losing Its Edge with Teens?" *The Wall Street Journal*, February 22, 2000, pp. B1, B4.

31. The Marketing Store, "The New Definition of Childhood," March 2012, www.themarketingstore.com.

32. "Food for Thought: Television Food Advertising to Children in the United States," Kaiser Family Foundation Report, March 2007, www.kff.org.

33. Dale Kunkel, "Children and Television Advertising," in *The Handbook of Children and Media*, D.G. Singer and J.L. Singer, eds. (Thousand Oaks, CA: Sage, 2001), pp. 375–94.

34. Mark J. Miller, "Camel Cigarettes under Fire for Targeting Kids—again," May 31, 2013, www.brandchannel.com.

35. Merrie Brucks, Gary M. Armstrong, and Marvin E. Goldberg, "Children's Use of Cognitive Defenses against Television Advertising: A Cognitive Response Approach," *Journal of Consumer Research* 14, no. 4 (March 1988), pp. 471–82.

36. Tamara F. Mangleburg and Terry Bristol, "Socialization and Adolescents' Skepticism toward Advertising," *Journal of Advertising* 27, no. 3 (Fall 1998), pp. 11–21.

37. Ronald Alsop, "Watchdogs Zealously Censor Advertising Targeted to Kids," *The Wall Street Journal*, September 5, 1985, p. 35.

38. *Report of the APA Task Force on Advertising and Children*, February 20, 2004, www.apa.org.

39. Tiffany Meyers, "Marketing to Kids Comes under Fresh Attack," *Advertising Age*, February 21, 2005, pp. S2, S8.

40. Robert Booth, "Junk Foods Avoid Ad Ban by Targeting Children Online," April 28, 2013, www.guardian.co.uk.

41. Betsy McKay, "Soda Marketers Will Cut Back Sales to Schools," *The Wall Street Journal*, August 17, 2005, pp. B1, B3.

42. Betsy McKay, "Are Your Children Ready for the Internet's Advertising Onslaught," April 2012, www.webroot.com.

43. Dan Lippe, "What Children Say about Media and Advertising," *Advertising Age*, February 4, 2002, http://adage.com/article/news/children-media-advertising/33709/.

44. Ronald Berman, *Advertising and Social Change* (Beverly Hills, CA: Sage, 1981), p. 13.

45. Quoted in Voight, "The Consumer Rebellion."

46. Glennisha Morgan, "Amazon Kindle Backs Gay Marriage with New Commercial," February 21, 2013, www.huffingtonpost.com.

47. Morris B. Holbrook, "Mirror Mirror on the Wall, What's Unfair in the Reflections on Advertising," *Journal of Marketing* 5 (July 1987), pp. 95–103; Theodore Levitt, "The Morality of Advertising," *Harvard Business Review*, July/August 1970, pp. 84–92.

48. Stephen Fox, *The Mirror Makers: A History of American Advertising and Its Creators* (New York: Morrow, 1984), p. 330.

49. Hunt, "Informational vs. Persuasive Advertising."

50. Daniel J. Brett and Joanne Cantor, "The Portrayal of Men and Women in U.S. Television Commercials: A Recent Content Analysis and Trends of 15 Years," *Sex Roles* 18, no. 9/10 (1998), pp. 595–608; John B. Ford and Michael La Tour, "Contemporary Perspectives of Female Role Portrayals in Advertising," *Journal of Current Issues and Research in Advertising* 28, no. 1 (1996), pp. 81–93.

51. Beverly A. Browne, "Gender Stereotypes in Advertising on Children's Television in the 1990s: A Cross-National Analysis," *Journal of Advertising* 27 no. 1 (Spring 1998), pp. 83–96.

52. Richard H. Kolbe, "Gender Roles in Children's Advertising: A Longitudinal Content Analysis," in *Current Issues and Research in Advertising*, James H. Leigh and Claude R. Martin Jr., eds. (Ann Arbor: University of Michigan, 1990), pp. 197–206.

53. Debra Merskin, "Boys Will Be Boys: A Content Analysis of Gender and Race in Children's Advertisements on the Turner Cartoon Network," *Journal of Current Issues and Research in Advertising* 24, no. 1 (Spring 2002), pp. 51–60.

54. Cate Terwilliger, "'Love Your Body Day' Auraria Event Takes Aim at 'Offensive' Images, Ads," *Denver Post*, September 23, 1999, p. E3.

55. Steven M. Kates and Glenda Shaw-Garlock, "The Ever Entangling Web: A Study of Ideologies and Discourses in Advertising to Women," *Journal of Advertising* 28, no. 2 (Summer 1999), pp. 33–49.

56. Suzanne Vranica, "Stereotypes of Women Persitst in Ads," *The Wall Street Journal*, October 17, 2003, p. B4.

57. Thomas H. Stevenson, "How Are Blacks Portrayed in Business Ads?" Industrial Marketing Management 20 (1991), pp. 193–99; Helen Czepic and J. Steven Kelly, "Analyzing Hispanic Roles in Advertising," in *Current Issues and Research in Advertising,* James H. Leigh and Claude R. Martin Jr., eds. (Ann Arbor: University of Michigan, 1983), pp. 219–40; R.F. Busch, Allan S. Resnik, and Bruce L. Stern, "A Content Analysis of the Portrayal of Black Models in Magazine Advertising," in *American Marketing Association Proceedings: Marketing in the 1980s,* Richard P. Bagozzi, ed. (Chicago: American Marketing Association, 1980); R.F. Busch, Allan S. Resnik, and Bruce L. Stern, "There Are More Blacks in TV Commercials," *Journal of Advertising Research* 17 (1977), pp. 21–25.

58. Malgorzata Kolling (Skorek), "Portrayal of Asian Americans in U.S. Magazines," in *One World Periphery Reads the Other: Knowing the "Oriental" in the Americas and the Iberian Peninsula,* I. Lopez-Calvo, ed. (Newcastle, England: Cambridge Scholars Publishing, 2010), pp. 330–45.

59. Charles R. Taylor, Stacy Landreth, and Hae-Kyong Bang, "Asian Americans in Magazine Advertising: Portrayals of the 'Model Minority,'" *Journal of Macromarketing*, October 2005, pp. 163–73.

60. Bruce Horovitz, "Mental Health Groups Slam Volkswagen Ad," *USA Today*, February 15, 2007, p. B1.

61. Brooke Capps, "Suicide Prevention Group Tells GM to Yank Robot Spot," *Advertising Age*, February 7, 2007, http://adage.com/article/news/suicide-prevention-group-tells-gm-yank-robot-spot/114866/.

62. Andrew Hampp, "An Ad in Which Boy Gets Girl . . . or Boy," *Advertising Age*, August 6, 2007, http://adage.com/article/news/ad-boy-girl-boy/119705/.

63. Stephanie Thompson, "Mars Pulls Snickers Super Bowl Spot," *Advertising Age*, February 6, 2007, http://adage.com/article/special-report-super-bowl07/mars-pulls-snickers-super-bowl-spot/114843/.

64. Jef I. Richards and John H. Murphy, II, "Economic Censorship and Free Speech: The Circle of Communication between Advertisers, Media and Consumers," *Journal of Current Issues and Research in Advertising* 18, no. 1 (Spring 1996), pp. 21–33.

65. Lawrence C. Soley and Robert L. Craig, "Advertising Pressure on Newspapers: A Survey," *Journal of Advertising*, December 1992, pp. 1–10.

66. Mark Simon, "Mercury News Ad Dispute Cooling Off: Advertisers Return While Reporters Stew," *San Francisco Business Chronicle*, July 15, 1994, p. B1.

67. Soontae An and Lori Bergen, "Advertiser Pressure on Daily Newspapers," *Journal of Advertising* 36, no. 2 (Summer 2007), pp 111–21.

68. Janet Guyon, "Do Publications Avoid Anti-Cigarette Stories to Protect Ad Dollars?" *The Wall Street Journal*, November 22, 1982, pp. 1, 20; Elizabeth M. Whelan, "When Newsweek and Time Filtered Cigarette Copy," *The Wall Street Journal*, November 1, 1984, p. 3; "RJR Swears Off Saatchi and Nabisco Is in a Sweat," *BusinessWeek*, April 18, 1988, p. 36.

69. David Shaw, "An Uneasy Alliance of News and Ads," *Los Angeles Times*, March 29, 1998, pp. A1, A28.

70. Steven T. Goldberg, "Do the Ads Tempt the Editors?" *Kiplingers Personal Finance*, May 1996, pp. 45–49.

71. Nat Ives, "GM Ends 'L.A.Times' Boycott, Resumes Advertising," *Advertising Age*, August 2, 2005, http://adage.com/article/media/gm-ends-l-a-times-boycott-resumes-advertising/46441/.

72. Robert D. Buzzell, Bradley T. Gale, and Ralph G. M. Sultan, "Market Share—a Key to Profitability," *Harvard Business Review*, January/February 1975, pp. 97–106.

73. Clare O'Connor, "How Spanx Became a Billion-Dollar Business without Advertising," *Forbes,* March 12, 2012, www.forbes.com.

74. Paul W. Farris and Mark S. Albion, "The Impact of Advertising on the Price of Consumer Products," *Journal of Marketing* 44, no. 3 (Summer 1980), pp. 17–35.

75. Buron, "Reining in Drug Advertising."

76. Farris and Albion, "The Impact of Advertising on the Price of Consumer Products,"

77. Ibid., p. 30.

78. Ibid.

79. Avery M. Abernethy and George R. Franke, "The Information Content of Advertising: A Meta-Analysis," *Journal of Advertising* 25, no. 2 (Summer 1996), pp. 1–17.

# PHOTO CREDITS

## Chapter 1

Opener: Courtesy of Gatorade, Inc.; p. 5: Courtesy of Gatorade, Inc.; p. 7: Courtesy of The American Red Cross; p. 9: Courtesy of Montblanc Inc.; p. 11: Google and the Google logo are registered trademarks of Google Inc., used with permission; p. 12: Courtesy of Gatorade, Inc.; p. 15: © Oleksiy Maksymenko/age fotostock; p. 17: © Crain Communications Inc., Courtesy of Ad Age; p. 19(top): Advertisement courtesy of American Advertising Federation; p. 19(bottom): Courtesy of GE; p. 21: Courtesy of Under Armour, Inc.; p. 23: Courtesy of Red Laser/eBay Inc.; p. 25: © Neilson Barnard/Getty Images; p. 26(top): Courtesy of Chicken of The Sea International; p. 26(bottom): American Honda Motor Company; p. 29: Image via Yelp.com; p. 31: © Starbucks; p. 35: Naked Juice Company.

## Chapter 2

Opener: Car2go N.A., LLC; p. 44: Courtesy of Manischewitz; p. 45(top): © PRNewsFoto/Mercedes-Benz USA/AP Images; p. 45(bottom): © 2013 SoBe ®; p. 46(top): Courtesy of Campbell Soup Company; p. 46(bottom): Copywriter and CEO: David Adamson; Art Director: Serena Halsey; Creative Director: Alexander Van Walsum; Agency: Juggernaut Advertising; p. 48: Used with permission from MillerCoors LLC; p. 50(top): Cheerwine is a registered trademark of the Carolina Beverage Corporation; p. 50(bottom): Courtesy of iVillage; p. 51: © The McGraw-Hill Companies, Inc./Mark Dierker, photographer; p. 52: Courtesy of Telemundo Media and Gap, Inc.; p. 53: Courtesy of AT&T Intellectual Property. Used with permission; p. 55(top): Hilton Worldwide, Inc.; p. 55(bottom): © PRNewFoto/Burt's Bees/AP Images; p. 56(top): Published with permission; 5-hour ENERGY ® is a registered trademark of International IP Holdings, LLC (www.5hourenergy.com); p. 56(bottom): © PRNewsFoto/Iconix Brand Group, Inc./AP Images; p. 57(top): Reprinted with permission. © Intuit, Inc. All Rights Reserved; p. 57(bottom): © Church & Dwight Co., Inc. Use of image is with the express written permission of Church & Dwight Co., Inc. Princeton, New Jersey; p. 58(top left): Courtesy of Campbell Soup Company; p. 58(top right): Courtesy of DC Shoes, Inc.; p. 58(bottom left): © PRNewsFoto/United Through Reading/AP Images; p. 58(bottom right): © PRNewsFoto/Gatorade/AP Images; p. 59: © Jason LaVeris/Getty Images; p. 61(top): Courtesy of Rolex Watch U.S.A., Inc.; p. 61(bottom): Courtesy of the WD-40 Company; p. 62: Image courtesy of "Christian Dior Parfums".

## Chapter 3

Opener: "The Force" commercial is used with permission of Volkswagen Group of America, Inc.; p. 70: © National Geographic Images; p. 73: Courtesy of The Procter & Gamble Company; p. 75: Courtesy of The Procter & Gamble Company; p. 76: © Crain Communications Inc., Courtesy of Ad Age; p. 80: © TongRo/ImageStock/Alamy RF; p. 81(top): © Crain Communications Inc., Courtesy of Ad Age; p. 81(bottom): Courtesy of Mentus; p. 83: © John Kuczala/Stone/Getty Images; p. 87: Courtesy of Droga5, LLC; p. 88: Courtesy of Initiative; p. 96: Hyundai Motor America; p. 99(top): Courtesy of Volkswagen® Group of America, Inc.; p. 99(bottom): Courtesy of Anderson Direct Marketing; p. 100: Courtesy of Don Jagoda Associates, Inc.; p. 101: Courtesy of Volkswagen® Group of America, Inc.; p. 102: © Wildfire Interactive, Inc.

## Chapter 4

Opener: Illustration of brain, © Bryan Christie Design, Courtesy of AdWeek; p. 111: Courtesy of Tommy Bahama; p. 112(top): Image reproduced courtesy of GlaxoSmith Kline; p. 112(bottom): Courtesy of Developlus, Inc.; p. 113: © NetPhotos/Alamy; p. 114(left): © Volvo Cars of North America, LLC; p. 114(right): Copyright © 2012. Jaguar Land Rover North America, LLC. All Rights Reserved; p. 116: Photographer: John Higginson, Associate Creative Director: Fabio Simoes Pinto\Molly Grubbs, Art Producer: Lisa Matthews. Agency: Team One Advertising; p. 117(top): Courtesy of Angie's List Inc.; p. 117(bottom): Courtesy of PepsiCo; p. 118: Courtesy of The American Association of Advertising Agencies; p. 119: Courtesy of Alberto-Culver Company; p. 120: © Walter Daran/Time Life Pictures/Getty Images; p. 121: Courtesy of www.TexasWideOpenForBusiness.com; p. 123: Courtesy of Michelin North America, Inc.; p. 124: ©PRNewsFoto/Levi Strauss & Co./AP Images; p. 126: Used with permission from Ally Bank; p. 127: TD Ameritrade, Inc. and McGraw-Hill Higher Education are separate unaffiliated companies and are not responsible for each other's services or policies. © 2012 TD Ameritrade IP Company, Inc. Used with permission. For illustrative purposes only; p. 129: © PRNewsFoto/Elizabeth Arden, Inc./AP Images; p. 130: Courtesy of Kyocera Corporation; p. 132(bottom left): Liya Kebede @ Viva Paris for L'Oreal Paris; p. 132(bottom right): Markwins Beauty Products 2008, National Ad Campaign for Tropez Cosmetics, Designed by Jane Hjellum; p. 134(top): American Eurocopter Corp.; p. 134(bottom left): Courtesy of The United States Army; p. 134(bottom right): Quality Social.

## Chapter 5

Opener: Ford Motor Company/Team Detroit, Inc.; p. 144: The California Milk Processor Board; p. 146: © PRNewsFoto/Citizen Watch Company/AP Images; p. 147: Courtesy of Coach, Inc.; p. 149: Courtesy of Frito-Lay North America, Inc.; p. 150: Courtesy of Seeding, a division of Pomegranate, Inc.; p. 151: Courtesy of Procter & Gamble; p. 153: © Ken Stinnett Photography; p. 155: © 2011 Scott Adams. Used By permission of UNIVERSAL UCLICK. All rights reserved; p. 159: VISTAKON®, Division of Johnson & Johnson Vision Care, Inc.; p. 160: Courtesy of Advertising Age; p. 161: Microsoft's Surface tablet is an innovative new product. Photo by Alex Strohl; p. 163(top): American Honda Motor Company; p. 163(bottom): Discover; p. 164: © H.J. Heinz Company, used with permission; p. 165: © Eveready Battery Company, Inc. Printed with permission; p. 169: © The Procter & Gamble Company. Used by permission; p. 170: Courtesy of Petco Animal Supplies, Inc.; p. 173: Courtesy of AdWeek; p. 175: Courtesy of Old World Industries.

## Chapter 6

Opener: © Spencer Platt/Getty Images; p. 184: © PRNewsFoto/MilkPEP/AP Images; p. 185: Courtesy of Unilever Home and Personal Care-USA; p. 186: © NC1 WENN Photos/Newscom; p. 188: Papa John's International; p. 191: © PRNewsFoto/Cole Haan/AP Images; p. 192: Image courtesy of Breitling. © Anthony Mandler; p. 193: Courtesy of Saatchi & Saatchi LA and Toyota Motor Sales U.S.A, Inc.; p. 194: © PRNewsFoto/YES! Golf/AP Images; p. 195: © The McGraw-Hill Companies/Mark Dierker, photographer; p. 197: Courtesy of Electrolux; p. 200: Courtesy of Unilever Home and Personal Care-USA; p. 201: Courtesy of Take Pride in America; p. 202: Courtesy of the Meth Project, The Partnership at Drugfree.org; p. 203: Domino's Pizza LLC; p. 204: Avocados From Mexico; p. 205(top): Nestle Waters North America; p. 205(bottom): © 2013 Procter & Gamble, Inc.; p. 206(top): © A.Miller/WENN Photos/Newscom; p. 206(bottom): © Richard B. Levine/Newscom; p. 207: Courtesy of Seagate Technology LLC; p. 209(top): ©Obama for America/AP Images; p. 209(bottom): Courtesy of the Meth Project, The Partnership at Drugfree.org; p. 210: Courtesy of Australasian New Car Assessment Program (ANCAP); p. 212: Courtesy of Facebook; p. 214: Image courtesy of Travel + Leisure; Photo by Simon Watson.

## Chapter 7

Opener: "Display By The Numbers," Bizo Inc.; p. 222(left): Standard Bank Group; p. 222(right): All Rights Reserved and owned by Qatar Foundation; p. 226(top): Courtesy of Kayem Foods Inc.; p. 226(bottom): © 2010 Mercury Insurance Group. All rights reserved.; p. 227(top): Courtesy of J.C. Penney Company, Inc.; p. 227(bottom): Consolidated Edison Co. of New York, Inc.; p. 228: © 2010 Caribou Coffee Company, Inc.; p. 231: Hyundai Motor America; p. 232: Courtesy of Performics, www.performics.com; p. 236: © San Diego Zoo Global; p. 238: Courtesy of The American Association of Advertising Agencies; p. 240: © Apic/Hulton Archive/Getty Images.

## Chapter 8

Opener: © 2013 Tacori; p. 265: Courtesy of BMW of North America, LLC; p. 267: Courtesy Cannes Lions International Advertising Festival.

Cannes Lions 2010 Grand Prix Winner; p. 268: Altoids and all affiliated designs owned by and used courtesy of the Wm. Wrigley Jr. Company; p. 269: © PRNewsFoto/Kellogg Company/AP Images; p.270: Courtesy of Volkswagen® Group of America, Inc.; p. 273(top): © PRNewsFoto/ Nike, Inc./AP Images; p. 273(bottom): Reprinted with permission of Marriott International, Inc.; p.275: Courtesy of Safeway Inc.; p. 278(top): © The McGraw-Hill Companies/Mark Dierker, photographer; p. 278(bottom): BrandAsset Valuator is used by BAV Consulting to manage brands; p. 280: Courtesy of AFLAC Incorporated; p. 281(top): © California Fluid Milk Processor Board; p. 281(bottom): Photo © Andy Lyons/Getty Images; Ad Courtesy of Procter & Gamble, Inc.; p. 282: Courtesy of Skyy Spirits, LLC; p. 285: Courtesy of Kumail Hemani; p. 286: © 2009 Tacori; p. 288: Chrysler and Imported From Detroit are registered trademarks of Chrysler Group LLC; p. 289: Courtesy Colgate-Palmolive Company; p. 291: Siemens AG 2013. All Rights Reserved; p. 292(top): Bebe Stores, Inc. All Rights Reserved; p. 292(bottom): Courtesy Hallmark; p. 293(top): Courtesy of GE; p. 293 (bottom all): Courtesy of Shell Oil Products, US; p. 295: Courtesy of Under Armour, Inc.

## Chapter 9

Opener: DORITOS and DORITOS Logo are trademarks owned by Frito-Lay North America, Inc. ©2014 Taco Bell and Live Más are trademarks owned by Taco Bell Corporation, Inc.; p. 302(left): Courtesy of Bridgestone Americas, Inc.; p. 302(right): The RED BULL marks are registered trademarks of Red Bull GmbH. © Red Bull GmbH, all rights reserved; p. 303(top): Courtesy of HP; p. 303(bottom): Courtesy of TaylorMade Golf Company; p. 304: PRNewsFoto/National Milk Mustache "got milk?" Campaign/AP Images; p. 305: Courtesy of J.C. Penney Corporation, Inc.; p. 306(top): Crown Imports, LLC; p. 306(bottom): Courtesy of McCann Worldgroup; p. 308(top): Courtesy of MasterCard Worldwide, created by McCann Erickson Worldwide; p. 308(bottom): Courtesy of General Mills and Paul Nelson; p. 309(top): Courtesy of Under Armour, Inc.; p.309(bottom): Ford Motor Company/Team Detroit, Inc.; p. 312(top): Courtesy of Procter & Gamble; p. 312(bottom): Courtesy of Kinerase. Kinerase is a registered trademark of Valeant Pharmaceuticals International; p. 313(top): Photo and Ad by Arnell; p. 313(bottom): Courtesy of Jenny Craig; p. 314: Makers of Listerine; p. 315: "Back to the Start" Cannes Lions Film Grand Prix Winner 2012; p. 316: © Ethan Miller/WireImage/Getty Images; p. 317(left): Courtesy of Singapore Airlines; p. 317(right): Bebe Stores, Inc. All Rights reserved; p. 318: © NetPhotos/Alamy; p. 320: Courtesy of General Motors and Leo Burnett Detroit; p. 321: © American Express; p. 322(left): Courtesy of American Indian College Fund; p. 322(right): Courtesy of GEICO; p. 323(top): © PRNewsFoto/ Minnesota Partnership for Action Against Tobacco (MPAAT)/AP Images; p. 323(bottom): © The Coca-Cola Company; p. 324: Kia Motors America; p. 331: © The Advertising Archives; p. 332: Courtesy of Skyy Spirits, LLC; p.333: Courtesy of TaylorMade Golf Company.

## Chapter 10

Opener: Courtesy of Samsung Global; p. 339: © American Broadcasting Companies, Inc.; p. 350: MindSet Media LLC.

## Chapter 11

Opener: © Cal Sport Media/AP Images; p. 376: Courtesy of Subaru of America, Inc.; p. 378: Courtesy of AdWeek and Google; p. 380: Courtesy of Oxygen Media LLC; p. 381: © TiVo, TiVo's Trademark and copyrighted material are used by McGraw-Hill Higher Education under license; p. 382: Courtesy of GSN; p. 385: © PRNewsFoto/ M-Go/AP Images; p. 386(top): Courtesy of The CW Television Network; p. 386(bottom): Courtesy of Univision Communications Inc.; p.388: Courtesy of Syndicated Network Television Association; p. 393: The Time Warner Cable Media webpage and all Time Warner Cable indicia reproduced thereon are © and ™ of Time Warner Cable and/or Time Warner Inc., used with permission; p. 394: Courtesy of The Travel Channel, www.travelchannel.com; p. 395: © ABC/Photofest; p. 396: Courtesy ESPN; p. 399(top): Copyrighted information of The Nielsen Company, licensed for use herein; p. 399(bottom): Courtesy of WJZ-TV; p.401: © Comedy Central/ PhotoFest; p. 402: Courtesy of Radio Advertising Bureau; p. 404: Courtesy of Radio Advertising Bureau; p. 406: Courtesy of Radio Advertising Bureau; p.407(top): Courtesy of Arbitron; p. 407: © The McGraw-Hill Companies/Mark Dierker, photographer; p.409: Courtesy of The Dan Patrick Show; p. 411: Courtesy of Arbitron.

## Chapter 12

Opener: © The Oklahoma Publishing Co., p. 419: Courtesy of Magazines Publishers Association; p. 420: Courtesy of Virgo Publishing, LLC; p.421(top): Courtesy of TransWorld Snowboarding; p. 421(bottom): Photo courtesy of BEEF Magazine; p. 422: Courtesy of Samir Husni, Ph.D. – Mr. Magazine™; p. 423: Courtesy of City and Regional Magazine Association; p. 424: Photographer: John Higginson, Associate Creative Director: Fabio Simoes Pinto\Molly Grubbs, Art Producer: Lisa Matthews. Agency: Team One Advertising; p. 425(top): Courtesy of The CW Television Network; p. 425(bottom): Courtesy of WD-40 Company; p. 426: Reproduction of the Good Housekeeping Seal for this textbook use only is granted by permission of Good Housekeeping magazine. Published by Hearst Communications, Inc.; p. 427: Courtesy of MPA-The Association of Magazine Media; p. 430: The Procter & Gamble Company; p. 432: Reprinted with permission of Alliance for Audited Media; p. 433: Courtesy of Rolling Stone Magazine, © Wenner Media; p. 434: Courtesy of Ivy League Magazine Network; p. 435: © The McGraw-Hill Companies/Mark Dierker, photographer; p. 437: Courtesy of the Wall Street Journal; p. 440(top): © Parade Publications Inc.; p. 440(bottom): Courtesy of the San Diego Union Tribune; p. 441: Courtesy of Callaway Golf Company; p. 442(top): Chicago Tribune Media Group; p.442(bottom): Courtesy of the San Diego Union Tribune; p. 444: Courtesy of the Los Angeles Times; p. 446: Newspaper National Network LP; p. 449: Newspaper Association of America.

## Chapter 13

Opener: © Eric McCandless/ABC via Getty Images; p. 457(top left): Courtesy of Outdoor Advertising Association of America; p. 457 (top right): Used with permission of PR Newswire; Reuters Sign provided through a partnership with Times Square2; p. 457(bottom): © David R. Frazier/Photolibrary, Inc. RF; p. 458(top): Courtesy of Outdoor Advertising Association of America; p. 458 (bottom left): Courtesy of Mickey Belch; p. 458(bottom right): Courtesy of Outdoor Advertising Association of America; p.461(all): Courtesy of Outdoor Advertising Association of America; p. 467: © David J. Green/Alamy; p. 469: © The Jersey Journal/Landov Images; p. 475(top): KFC Corporation; p. 475(bottom): © AP Images; p. 476: © Charlie Neuman/Zuma Press.

## Chapter 14

Opener: Courtesy of The Phoenix Coyotes; p. 483: Advertisement used with permission of Bose® Corporation; p. 484: Photo image provided by Costco Wholesale; p. 485: Courtesy of Pinehurst and Acura; p. 486(top): Maserati North America, Inc.; p. 486(bottom): © Jude Buffum; p. 487: Used with permission of Inter IKEA Systems B.V.; p. 488(top): Copyrighted information of The Nielsen Company, licensed for use herein; p. 488(bottom): Courtesy of Road Runner Sports-World's Largest Running Store; p. 489: © Executive Visions Inc./PRNewFoto/ AP Images; p.490: PedEgg by Telebrands; p. 491: Image courtesy of CUTCO Cutlery Corp.

## Chapter 15

Opener: © 2009 PepsiCo, Inc. Used with permission; p. 500: Courtesy: SweetBling.com; p. 501(top): The RED BULL marks are registered trademarks of Red Bull GmbH. © Red Bull GmbH, all rights reserved; p. 501(bottom): Courtesy of Nika Water; p. 502(top): These materials have been reproduced with the permission of eBay Inc. © 2013 EBAY INC. All Rights Reserved; p. 502(bottom): Courtesy of Darrell Coomes, HeyBannerBanner. com; p. 504: Google and the Google logo are registered trademarks of Google Inc., used with permission; p. 511: Courtesy of Jessica Kartalija; p. 513(top): Courtesy of The Procter & Gamble Company; p. 513(bottom): Google and the Google logo are registered trademarks of Google Inc., used with permission; p. 514(top): Google and the Google logo are registered trademarks of Google Inc., used with permission; p. 514(bottom): Kmart 2013; p. 516: Southwest Airlines; p. 517(top): © Rob Kim/Landov Images; p. 517(bottom): Image via Yelp.com; p. 518: © PRNewsFoto/Ghirardelli Chocolate Company/AP Images; p. 519: Chrysler is a registered trademark of Chrysler Group LLC.

## Chapter 16

Opener: Courtesy of Telford International Co., Ltd.; p. 529: © The McGraw-Hill Companies/Mark

Dierker, photographer; p. 531(top): Channellock, Inc. Meadville, PA USA; p. 531(bottom): Courtesy of Aspen Marketing Services; p. 532: © The McGraw-Hill Companies, Inc./John Flournoy, photographer; p. 533: BumbleBee Foods LLC; p. 535: Courtesy of WD-40 Company; p. 537: © The McGraw-Hill Companies/Jill Braaten, photographer; p. 538: Courtesy of Ryan Partnership; p. 539: © The McGraw-Hill Companies, Inc./Mark Dierker, photographer; p. 540(top): © Church & Dwight Co., Inc. Use of image is with the express written permission of Church & Dwight Co., Inc. Princeton, New Jersey; p. 540(bottom): Courtesy Miller Brewing Company; p. 541: Kimberly-Clark Corp.; p. 542: © Machiavel/Dreamstime; p. 543(top): © Steven Cukrov/Dreamstime; p. 543 (bottom): Courtesy of © Jack In The Box Inc. 2010; p. 544: ArmorAll Products Corporation; p. 545: Image supplied by StartSampling, Inc. For further information about the company and its services, please see www.startsampling.com; p. 547: © The McGraw-Hill Companies, Inc./Mark Dierker, photographer; p. 549(top): © The McGraw-Hill Companies/Jill Braaten, photographer; p. 549(bottom): California Milk Advisory Board; p. 550: © The McGraw-Hill Companies/Mark Dierker, photographer; p. 551: Image provided by Cellfire, Inc.; p. 553: Groupon, Inc.; p. 554(top): PRNewsFoto/ DreamWorks Animation SKG, Inc./AP Images; p. 554(bottom): © The McGraw-Hill Companies/ Mark Dierker, photographer; p. 555: Courtesy of Levi's; p. 556: Courtesy of ContestBee, www. contestbee.com; p. 557: Used with permission from Penzoil/Quaker State Company; p. 560(top): ArmorAll Products Corporation; p. 560(bottom): KAO Brands Company; p. 561(top): Courtesy of the WD-40 Company; p. 561(bottom): Courtesy of Mountain Dew, © 2009 PepsiCo, Inc. Used with permission.; p. 564: Courtesy of the WD-40 Company; p. 566: Courtesy of Chicken of The Sea International; p. 567: Courtesy of SeaKlear; p. 568: © Consumer Electronics Association; p. 569(top): © 2013 QUALCOMM Incorporated; p. 569(bottom): Courtesy of Bridgestone Golf Inc.; p. 571: Courtesy of MasterCard; p. 572: Courtesy of Unilever; p. 574: Courtesy of Taco Bell Corporation, Inc.

## Chapter 17

Opener: Oliver Strewe/Lonely Planet Images/ Getty; p. 581: Used with permission of General Mills Marketing Inc. (GMMI); p. 583(top): Cessna Aircraft Company, A Textron Inc. Company; p. 584: Courtesy of San Diego State University College of Business Administration; p. 585(top): Courtesy of GE; p. 585(bottom): Ad courtesy of CITGO Petroleum Corporation; p. 586: Courtesy of Marketing EDGE; p. 587(top): Porsche; p. 587(bottom): Courtesy of Paul Rabil Foundation; p. 588: Courtesy of Wawanesa Insurance; p. 589: Used with permission of General Mills Marketing Inc. (GMMI); p. 592: Tree Top Inc.; p. 593: © PRNewsFoto/Anheuser-Busch/AP Images; p. 595: © The Advertising Archives; p. 596: WHIRLPOOL is a registered trademark of Whirlpool, U.S.A. © 2005 Whirlpool Corporation. All rights reserved. HABITAT FOR HUMANITY is a registered trademark of Habitat for Humanity International, Inc.; p. 597: Domino's Pizza LLC; p. 598: Jason Lawler/ Flickr Vision/Getty; p. 599(top): Jason Lawler/

Flickr Vision/Getty; p. 599(bottom): © Tom Pennington/Getty Images; p.600 (top): © 2013 American Heart Association, Inc.; p. 600(bottom): Courtesy of Trader Joe's; p. 601(left): Courtesy of AT&T Archives and History Center; p. 601(right): House Of Ruth Maryland; p. 602: © Mike Kwok/ Dreamstime; p. 603: © Koh Sze Kiat/Dreamstime.

## Chapter 18

Opener: Illustration by Superexpresso; p. 610: GLAD® is a registered trademark of the Glad Products Company and is used with permission. © 2013 The Glad Products Company. Reprinted with permission; p. 613: Courtesy of Chiat/Day/ Mogo Inc. Advertising; p. 618: Image provided by InsideHeads.com, conducting online focus groups since 1998; p. 623: Courtesy of GfK; p. 625: Courtesy of SensoMotoric Instruments (SMI); p. 628: With permission from Target Marketing/ NAPCO; p. 629: Courtesy of GfK MRI Starch Advertising Research; p. 632: Courtesy of Ipsos-ASI, Inc.; p. 633: Decision Analyst.

## Chapter 19

Opener: Courtesy of Supreme Committee for Qatar 2022; p. 646(top): Courtesy Australian Tourist Commission ™ © The Brand Australia Trademark is the subject of copyright and is a trademark of the Australia Tourist Commission, 2013; p. 646(bottom): Used by permission of WD-40 Company; p. 649: © Newscom Images; p. 651: © Linterland 2006; p. 652: © 2010 Taylor Made Golf Company, Inc. All rights reserved. TaylorMade is a part of the Adidas Group; p. 653(all): Courtesy of New Balance Athletic Shoe, Inc.; p. 655(top): © The McGraw-Hill Companies, Inc./Mark Dierker, photographer; p. 655(bottom): © Reuters/Australian Government/Landov; p. 657: © Imaginechina/ Corbis; p. 658: © Francis Dean/Dean Pictures/ Newscom; p. 660(top): Courtesy of Frito-Lay North America, Inc.; p. 660(bottom): Domino's Pizza LLC; p. 661 (top): Courtesy of Advertising Age; p. 661(bottom): Courtesy The Colgate-Palmolive Company; p. 662(top): © Davide Campari-Milano S.P.A. All rights Reserved; p. 662(bottom): Made by Mother, www.motherlon-don.com; p. 663: Tag Heuer; p. 667: Courtesy of Lenovo; p. 668: Courtesy of International Business Machines Corp.; p. 670(top): © Asics Corporation; p. 670(bottom): Courtesy of Las Vegas Convention and Visitors Authority; p. 673(top): © McGraw-Hill Companies/Mark Dierker, photographer; p. 673(bottom): Hearst Magazines International; p. 674: Star TV, USA (image - Diya Aur Baati Hum); p. 675: Courtesy WD-40 Company; p. 679(top): Courtesy of TaylorMade Golf Company; p. 679(bottom): Courtesy of mixi, Inc.; p. 681: © NetPhotos/Alamy.

## Chapter 20

Opener: © Kevan Brooks/AdMedia/Newscom; p. 688: Courtesy of Olshan Frome Wolosky LLP; p. 689: The McClellan Law Firm (Photo by J.Kat Photo, Inc./www.jkatphoto.com; p. 691: © The Center on Alcohol Marketing and Youth; p. 692: Courtesy of Advertising Self-Regulatory Council;

p. 696: © Fotogramma/Ropi/ ZUMAPRESS. com/Newscom; p. 698(top): Courtesy California Milk Advisory Board; p. 698(bottom): www.man-crunch.com; p. 699: Courtesy of Advertising Self-Regulatory Council; p. 702: Courtesy of Federal Trade Commission; p. 704: Domino's Pizza LLC; p. 706(top): © flicker/inspectedbyNo27; p. 706(bottom): Courtesy of The Champagne Bureau; p. 707: © PRNewsFoto/Atkins Nutritionals Inc./AP Images; p. 712: Courtesy of Federal Trade Commission; p. 713(top): © Frank Micelotta/Getty Images; p. 715: © Ofcom; p. 716: © Dennis MacDonald/ Alamy RF; p. 717: Courtesy of Legacy ®; p. 719: © Commonwealth of Australia; p. 720: Courtesy Campbell Soup Company; p. 721: Courtesy of the TaylorMade Golf Company, Inc.; p. 723: Used with permission from Penzoil/Quaker State Company; p. 725: Courtesy of Federal Trade Commission; p. 727: Courtesy of TrustedID; p. 728: © 2012 Network Advertising Initiative.

## Chapter 21

Opener: © The McGraw-Hill Companies/Jill Braaten, photographer; p. 735: Public Citizen; p. 736(top): Alberta Gaming And Liquor Commission; p. 736(bottom): Courtesy of RAINN, www.rainn. org; p. 737(top): Courtesy Cannes Lions International Advertising Festival; p. 737(bottom): © ROPI/ ZUMAPRESS/Newscom; p. 739: © Church & Dwight; p. 740(top): © Jonathan Nackstrand/AFP/ Getty Images; p. 740(bottom): Courtesy of Skyy Vodka and Lambesis; p. 742(top): Jose Ybarra; p. 742(bottom): © Splash News/Newscom; p. 745: © Arseniy Rogov/Dreamstime; p. 748: Bloomberg via Getty Images; p. 749: Mike Clarke/AFP/Getty Images; p. 750: © Rolls Royce Motor Cars New Delhi; p. 750(bottom): © American Association of Advertising Agencies; p. 751: © American Association of Advertising Agencies; p. 752: Courtesy of Network Solutions. © Copyright 2005 Network Solutions. All rights reserved; p. 753(top): © Igor Studenkov/Flickr; p. 753(bottom): © PRNewsFoto/The Levi's brand/ AP Images; p. 754: © PRNewsFoto/Masterfoods USA/AP Images; p. 757(top): Courtesy International Advertising Association; p. 757(bottom): © The Partnership at Drugfree.org; p. 758(left): Courtesy of Boys & Girls Clubs of America; p. 758(right): Courtesy of ADWEEK; p. 759: © American Association of Advertising Agencies; p. 760: Spanx, Inc.; p. 761: © American Association of Advertising Agencies; p. 763(left): © American Association of Advertising Agencies; p. 763(right): Courtesy of the American Advertising Federation.

## Chapter 22

Opener: © Vicente Barceló Varona/Alamy RF; p. 5: Courtesy of ©DePuy Synthes Companies; p. 8: Copyright © 2007 SAS Institute Inc. All Rights Reserved. Reproduced with permission of SAS Institute Inc., Cary, NC. USA; p. 10: Courtesy of CDW; p. 11: Salesgenie.com, a division of infoUSA Marketing, Inc.; p. 16: © 2013 Dell Inc. All Rights Reserved; p. 17: Courtesy of U-Haul and American Red Cross; p. 18: Reality Works Group, www.realityworksgroup.com; p. 19(top): © Justin Sullivan/Getty Images; p. 19(bottom): Courtesy of GoToMeeting®; p. 20: Webmarketing 123, Inc.

# NAME AND COMPANY INDEX

Kohl's, 340
Kohl's Department Stores, 56, 284
Koslow, Scott, 275
Kotex, 193
Kover, Arthur, 275, 289
*Kraft Food & Family,* 430
Kraft Foods, 26, 69, 87, 118, 170, 240, 389, 430, 459, 558, 560, 588, 678, 699, 714–715, 721, 755
Kristula-Green, Michelle, 651
Krugman, Dean, 15, 362
Krugman, Herbert, 164
Kudrow, Lisa, 324
Kyocera, 129, 130

# L

La Comunidad, 87
Labrecque, Jeff, 187
*Ladies' Home Journal,* 422, 429
Lady Gaga, 326, 469–470
Lafayette, Jon, 220
Lahr, John, 172
Lambe, Stacy, 734
Lambert, Miranda, 184
Lambesis, 263–264, 286, 323, 662
Lancaster, Kent, 259
Land Rover, 441
Landor Associates, 145, 733
Lands' End, 21, 727
LaNeve, Mark, 319
Las Vegas Convention and Visitors Authority (LVCVA), 670
Laswell, Mark, 145
Lavidge, Robert, 158, 230
La-Z-Boy, 59
Learmouth, Michael, 25, 142, 331
Led Zeppelin, 326
Lee, Ang, 85
Lee, Spike, 85
Leke, Acha, 651
Lenovo Group, 651, 667
Leo Burnett Co., 80, 94, 266, 278, 292, 295, 318, 325, 631
Leo Burnett Worldwide, 80
Leo Burnett/Worldwide Arc, 101
Lepore, Nanette, 59
Letzing, John, 553
Leuthesser, Lance, 283
Levi Strauss & Co., 124, 274, 305, 474, 555, 664, 667, 668, 748, 753, 754
Levitt, Theodore, 658–659, 666
Levy, Doug, 16, 17
Levy, Piet, 291
Lexus, 51, 116, 337, 423–424
LG Electronics, 459, 645
Li, Shan, 459
Liberty Media, 397
Lieber, Ron, 559
LIEFA, 470

Lifetime Television, 395
Lil Wayne, 326, 327, 515
Lincoln, Abraham, 208
Lindenmann, Walter, 590, 594
Lindstrom, Martin, 109, 120
Li-Ning, 656, 667
LinkedIn, 11, 14, 22, 136, 154, 155, 507, 509, 510, 516, 522
Linterland Rural Initiatives, 651
Liodice, Bob, 95
Lippert, Barbara, 267, 733
Liquidation Channel, 489–490
Listerine, 314, 710
Living Social, 435, 553
L.L. Bean, 21
LMFAO, 324
Lodish, Leonard, 534, 537
Loechner, Dack, 257
Logo, 754
Lohan, Lindsey, 490
Lollipop Bling, 128, 129, 362
Long, Justin, 205
Lopez, Hernan, 311
Lopez, Jennifer, 191
L'Oréal, 18, 55, 109, 132, 340, 418, 647
*Los Angeles Magazine,* 422
*Los Angeles Times,* 439, 444, 756
Lou, Linda, 476
Louis Vuitton, 453, 656, 663
Low, George, 254, 259
Lowe & Partners, 651
Lowe Lintas, 651
Lowe's Home Improvement Warehouse, 241
Lucci, Susan, 490
Lukovitz, Karlene, 52, 608
lululemon, 16, 24, 294
Lund, Susan, 651
Lux, 186

# M

Macinnis, Deborah J., 304
MacKenzie, Scott, 214
Macy's, 18, 283, 340, 502, 527, 536–537
Madden, Normandy, 559, 667, 681
Maddox, Kate, 257
Madell, Dawn Sutter, 327
Madonna, 59, 187, 326
Magazine Impact Research Service (MIRS), 630
Mail Pouch Tobacco, 456
Major League Baseball (MLB), 3, 5, 307, 378, 384, 397, 636
Major League Soccer (MLS), 3
Majoras, Deborah Platt, 699
Maker's Mark, 577
Malibu Caribbean Rum, 559
Mallon, Ken, 311
Maltby, Emily, 145

ManCrunch, 698
Mandhachitara, Rujirutana, 248
Mangano, Terry, 52
Manischewitz Co., 44
Manning, Eli, 3
Manning, Peyton, 3
Marcarelli, Paul, 193
Marcus Thomas, LLC, 116
*Marie Claire,* 435, 553
Marin Institute, 472
Marketing Budgets Report, 607
Marketing EDGE, 586
Marketing Evaluations, Inc., 198, 199
*Marketing News,* 278, 437
The Marketing Store, 743
MarketSource, 636–637
Marlboro, 94, 283, 292, 295, 471, 554, 719
Marley, Bob, 325
Marriott International, 54, 273, 291, 560. *see also* J.W. Marriott Resort
Mars, Inc., 284, 379, 541, 754, 755
Martin, Andrew, 42
Martin, Nancee, 155
Martin Agency, 748
Martson, John, 584
Mary Kay Cosmetics, 62, 491
Maserati, 485, 486
Maslow, Abraham, 113–114
MASS Hispanic, 540–541
Massivemedia, 638
Masta, Katerina-Eva, 419
MasterCard, 173, 307–308, 483, 571
Masterfoods USA, 754
Masters of Snowboarding, 470
Match.com, 693
Mathes, John, 284, 285
Matt & Kim, 327
Mattel, 87, 597, 651
*Maxim,* 366, 422, 429
Mayer, John, 292
Mayer, Martin, 310
Maytag, 292, 315, 499
Mayzlin, Diane, 152
MBT, 685
McAlister, Leigh, 533, 546
McArthur, Kate, 559
McCann Erickson Worldwide, 80, 84, 94, 116, 306–308, 327
McCarthy, Melissa, 513
McCarthy, Michael, 374, 686
McCaughan, Dave, 187
McClellan, Steve, 351
McCormick & Co., 724
McCracken, Grant, 196, 197
McDonald's, 13, 18, 45, 57, 62, 94, 109, 146, 192, 193, 194, 265, 283, 284, 288, 289, 292, 304, 340, 377, 456, 460, 474, 541, 553–554, 558–559, 574, 596, 645, 647, 650, 678, 748
McFarland, John, 42
McGreevy, Patrick, 476

McGuire, William, 160
MCI, 597
McKinsey & Co., 167, 524
*McKinsey Quarterly,* 219
McLaren Automotive, 486
McLuhan, Marshall, 214
McMahan, Harry, 164
McNiven, Michael D., 15
MEC Sensor, 459
Media Analysis Plus, 359
Media Metrix, 521
MediaAnalyzer Software & Research, 172–173, 741
MediaCom, 219
Mediamark Research, 353. *see also* GfK MRI
Mela, Carl, 534, 537
*Men's Health,* 435
*Men's Journal,* 419, 435
Mentus, 81
Meow Mix, 326
Mercedes-Benz, 51, 55, 67, 438, 441, 512, 597
Mercury Insurance Group, 226
Meredith National Media, 419
Merrill Lynch, 659
Mesco, Manuela, 657
Messi, Lionel, 191, 194
Method, 333–334
MetLife, 193, 597
Metromail Corp., 547
*Metropolitan,* 434
Michelin, 60, 123
Mickelson, Phil, 191, 441
Microsoft, 13, 14, 15, 22, 95, 161, 188, 205, 206, 273, 326, 331, 340, 377, 475, 489, 505, 666
Microsoft Network (MSN), 14
Middleton, Kate, 308
Millennium Import Co., 693
Miller, James, III, 704, 705
Miller, Mac, 327
Miller, Mark J., 59
Miller Brewing Co., 96, 205, 206, 754. *see also* MillerCoors
MillerCoors, 48, 87, 274, 280, 290, 378, 540, 754
Millward Brown, 310, 379, 622, 630, 631, 633, 640, 665, 666
Mindset Media, 351
Mindshare, 25
Mindshare Worldwide, 84
Miscavige, David, 439
Mitchell, Amy, 416, 419
Mitsubishi Motors, 327
Mixi, 679
Mlodinow, Leonard, 120
Moat, 626
*Modern Maturity,* 422
Moeller, Jon, 240
Mohan, Geoffrey, 351

Mohr, Jakki, 254, 259
Mondelez International, 87
*Money,* 418
Monster.com, 415, 448
Montag, Heidi, 59
Montana, Joe, 685
*Montana Farmer Stockman,* 420
Montana Meth Project (MMP), 202, 208–210
Montblanc, 9
Monty, Scott, 142
Moore, Demi, 324
Moore, Timothy, 120
Morales, Andrea, 210
Morgan, Tracy, 68
Moriarty, Sandra, 277, 317
Morrison, Jim, 326
Morrison, Maureen, 68, 300
Moss, Kate, 194
*Motor Trend,* 117, 337, 588
Motorola, 493, 593
Mountain Dew, 497–498, 505, 515, 561
The Movie Channel, 391, 471
Moxie, 50
Moza, Sheikah, 644
MPA, 42
*Ms.,* 422, 752
MSN, 14
MSW•ARS Research, 622, 623, 624
MTV, 11, 19, 59, 87, 294, 295, 325, 354, 385, 393, 394, 395, 401, 470, 690, 754
MTV2, 381
MTV Networks International, 674
Mukherjee, Anindita, 17
Mulder, Susan, 220
Mullman, Jeremy, 182, 686
Muntinga, D. G., 508
Murdoch, Rupert, 674
Murray, Michael, 330
Murris, Timothy, 699
Mustafa, Isaiah, 266, 267
Mutual of Omaha, 714
Muzak, 474
Myers, Jack, 359
Myers, John G., 55, 56, 57
Myers Reports, 359
Myhren, Tor, 515
MySpace, 14, 281, 521

## N

Nader, Ralph, 714
Nakashima, Ryan, 385
Naked Juice, 34–35
Nardone, John, 639
NASCAR, 5, 351, 407, 597
Nasr, Tarek, 644
National Basketball Association (NBA), 3, 5, 194, 397, 470, 656, 667
National Collegiate Athletic Association. *see* NCAA

*National Enquirer,* 362
National Football League (NFL), 3, 5, 281, 374, 378, 384, 396, 397, 596
*National Geographic,* 70, 420, 429, 673
National Geographic Channel, 395, 595
National Hockey League (NHL), 3, 5, 307, 596
*National Hog Farmer,* 420
*National Law Review,* 421
National Newspaper Network, 446, 449
National Public Radio (NPR), 514, 516
National Shopper Lab, 637
Nationwide Insurance, 124, 318, 324
Nature Valley, 308
Navistar, 602
NBA. *see* National Basketball Association (NBA)
NBC, 11, 299, 337, 343, 374, 384, 385, 386, 391, 397, 453, 473, 690, 714, 739
NBC Universal, 385
NCAA, 337, 373, 374, 511, 555
NCH Marketing Services, 518, 545, 548
*Nebraska Farmer,* 420
NEC, 459
Neff, Jack, 77, 95, 171, 182, 241, 267, 667
Neiman Marcus, 55, 62, 339, 486
Nelson, Erin Mulligan, 42
Nelson, Willie, 315
Nespresso, 187
Ness, Leona, 470
Nestlé, 52, 73, 560, 583, 645, 647, 666, 676, 703
Netanyahu, Benjamin, 737
Netflix, 14, 382, 385, 583
Network Solutions, 752
NetZero, 14
NeuroFocus, 109
New Balance, 193–194, 653, 686, 706
New Castle Brown Ale, 87
New York Giants, 479, 597
New York Interconnect, 393
New York Jets, 479–480, 597
New York Life, 125
*The New York Times,* 109, 187, 205, 362, 416, 437, 553, 586
*The New York Times Sunday Magazine,* 438–439
New York Titans, 479
News Channel 1, 476
News Corp., 340, 583, 674, 675
*Newspaper Advertising Source,* 444, 445
*Newsweek,* 331, 418, 434
NextMedium, 473
Nexus, 78
NFL. *see* National Football League (NFL)
NHL. *see* National Hockey League (NHL)
Nicholls, Charles, 487
Nickelodeon, 674
Nicks, Stevie, 59
Nicoderm, 112, 325
Nielsen, Jakob, 627

TCL, 656
TD Ameritrade, 127, 353
Team Detroit, 141
Team One, 337, 423–424
Tebow, Tim, 600
Tecate, 741–742
Ted Bates Agency, 289, 295
*Teen People,* 434
Tegler, Eric, 142
Telecommunications Research and Action
        Center, 489
Telemundo, 52, 385
Television Bureau of Advertising, 634
Telford International Company Limited
        (Telford), 527
Tellis, G., 238
Tellis, K., 238
Terrell, Tammi, 325
Texaco, 389, 714
*Texas Monthly,* 422
Thaler, Linda, 187
theLadders, 415
Theron, Charlize, 186
Theuner, G., 627
Theus, Kathryn, 120
Thomas, Dave, 188, 189
Thomaselli, Rich, 719
Thompson, Robert, 474
Thorpe, John, 84
3M, 569
Thurner, Rob, 311
Tia Rosa Tortillas, 549
Tiffany & Co., 191, 263
Till, Emmett, 515
Timberlake, Justin, 195
Time Inc., 418, 419, 632, 635, 674
*Time Magazine,* 19, 183, 331, 339,
        363–364, 365, 366, 417, 418, 419,
        422, 428, 429, 431, 434, 673
Time Warner, Inc., 18, 340, 384, 395, 397,
        418, 470
*Times of India,* 677
Timex, 501
Tinkham, Spencer F., 15
TiVo Inc., 381, 470
T.J. Maxx, 527
TLC (The Learning Channel), 550
T-Mobile, 22, 474
TNS Group, 504, 672
TNT, 337, 393, 397, 470
Tobii, 626
Tommy Bahama, 111
Tommy Hilfiger, 748
Tom's Shoes, 123
Toronto International Film
        Festival, 596
Toscani, Oliviero, 736
Toshiba, 87
Totes Isotoner, 195
Touchstorm, 582
Tourism Australia, 645–646
Townshend, Pete, 59

Toyota Motor Co., 13, 18, 26, 67, 70, 142,
        193, 213, 340, 343, 377, 453, 476,
        589, 592, 632, 645, 647, 654, 666
Toys R Us, 325
Trader Joe's, 600
Traffic Audit Bureau (TAB), 463,
        637–638
Tragos, Bill, 271
*Transworld Snowboarding,* 420, 421
*Travel & Leisure,* 214, 362
Travel Channel, 394, 470
Travelocity, 104
Tree Top, 592–593
Trek, 182
Trident, 87
TripAdvisor, 28
Trojan, 739
Tropez, 132
Tropicana Products Inc., 117, 119
Trottman, Melanie, 559
Trout, Jack, 55, 292–293
Trudeau, Kevin, 489
Trump, Donald, 385
TrustedID, 727
Truth in Advertising Commission,
        670–671
Tsingtao, 656
Tumblr, 77, 295, 517, 536
Tupperware, 21, 62, 491
Turkish Airlines, 194
Turner, Evan, 656
Turner Broadcasting, 374, 401, 470
Turner Cartoon Network, 752
*TV Guide,* 331, 632
TWA, 597
24 Hour Fitness, 182
Twitter, 5, 11, 14, 16, 17, 22, 25, 68, 77,
        102, 136, 141–142, 149, 150, 151,
        154, 155, 167, 171, 182, 188, 203,
        267, 295, 300, 384–385, 406, 424,
        459, 498, 507, 509, 510, 511–513,
        516, 519, 522, 536, 551, 552, 588,
        627, 643, 655, 679, 680–681, 712,
        723, 729, 736
Ty, 581
Tyler, The Creator, 515
Tyme ATMs, 474

## U

U2, 326
UM (Universal McCann), 84
Under Armour, 16, 21, 24, 75, 195, 283,
        293, 294–295, 309, 596
Unerman, Sue, 219, 220
UNICEF, 596
Unilever, 18, 73, 87, 102, 155, 170,
        198–199, 265, 266, 275, 340, 572,
        645, 647, 649, 650, 660, 664, 666
Unisys, 602
United Airlines, 554
U.S. Champagne Bureau, 706

U.S. Soccer Foundation, 52
United Way, 460
Universal McCann (UM), 84, 337
University of Florida, 3
Univision, 385, 386
UPN (United Paramount Network), 384
Upper Deck, 194
UPS, 182, 288
Urban Outfitters, 757
US Airways, 125
*Us Weekly,* 419, 435, 662
USA Network, 393
*USA Today,* 379, 437, 453, 673, 733
*USA Weekend,* 438
USAA Insurance, 17, 319
USX, 602

## V

Vagnoni, Anthony, 294
Vakratsas, Demetrios, 175–176
Van Cleef & Arpels, 486
Van Den Bergh Foods, 720
Van Praet, Douglas, 109, 110, 270
Van Wamelen, Arend, 651
*Vanity Fair,* 339, 366, 470
Vega, Tanzina, 515
Venetian Resort, 459
Venice, Deborah L., 145
Verizon, 18, 22, 50, 193, 236, 249, 265, 324,
        339, 340, 376, 377, 456, 459, 517, 759
Verleun, Jeroen, 195
Verna, Paul, 516
Vernor's, 50
Versace, 60
Vert, Inc., 461
Vertis, 484
Vetvik, Ole Jorgen, 220
VH1, 11, 59, 337, 393, 395, 674
Viacom, 109, 340, 384, 408, 514
*Vibe,* 434
Vicary, James, 109, 114, 120
Vick, Michael, 181
Vicks, 281
Victoria's Secret, 482, 483, 487
Virgin, 188
Virgin America, 291, 512, 516
Virgin Atlantic Airways, 504, 759
Visa, 110, 181, 307, 321, 324, 483, 596
Vitaminwater. *see* Glacéau Vitaminwater
Vizio, 374, 385
VML, 5
VO5, 119
Vocalpoint, 151
*Vogue,* 435
Voight, Joan, 657
Volkswagen, 54, 67–68, 99, 101, 270, 327,
        424, 514, 596, 645, 647, 753–754
Volvo, 87, 114, 721
Vonn, Lindsey, 181
Vons, 637
Vranica, Suzanne, 241, 374, 385

# SUBJECT INDEX

## A

Ability, 173
Absolute cost, 363
Account executives, 83
Account planners, 84
Account planning, 84, 276–277
Account-specific marketing, 535
Actual state, 111
Ad agency review consultants, 98
Ad execution-related thoughts, 171
Adaptive brand marketing, 76–77
Adjacencies, 390
Ad-to-consumer relevance, 269–270
Advergames, 470
Advertainment, 470
Advertiser-supported syndication, 388
Advertising, 17–20
  advocacy, 598–600
  business-to-business. *see* Business-to-
    business advertising
  classifications of, 20
  classified, 415, 440, 447–448
  corporate. *see* Corporate advertising
  creativity. *see* Advertising creativity;
    Creative strategy
  criticisms of, 734–735, 737–758
    deception/untruthfulness, 737–738
    economic censorship, 754–757
    manipulation, 750
    materialism, 749–750
    offensiveness/bad taste, 738–742
    stereotyping, 751–754
  deceptive. *see* Deceptive advertising
  direct marketing combined with, 483
  direct-response, 21, 250
  economic effects of, 758–764
  economies of scale in, 258–259
  expenditures on, 6, 12
  global. *see* Global advertising
  growth of, 6–7
  image. *see* Image advertising
  international. *see* International
    advertising/promotion
  leading advertisers, U.S., 18
  local, 20
  national, 20
  native, 436, 438–439, 505
  organizing for. *see* Organization for
    advertising/promotion
  political, 206, 208–209
  primary-demand, 20
  product pricing and, 62
  professional, 20
  reminder, 308–309
  retail, 20

role of, 63–64
sales promotion combined with, 571
selective-demand, 20
social/cultural impact. *see* Social/
  Cultural impact of advertising
subliminal, 119, 120
teaser, 309
trade, 20, 63
value of, 18–19, 761–764
Advertising agencies, 69–70, 79–99
  account planning, 84, 276–277
  account services, 83
  art department, 85
  billings, 79
  budget allocation and, 255–257
  client-agency communication, 286–287
  compensation, 88–92
    commission system, 88–89
    cost-plus system, 90
    fixed-fee method, 89–90
    future of, 91–92
    incentive-based, 90–91
    percentage charges, 91
  creative boutiques, 86–87
  creative services, 85
  departmental system, 86
  evaluating, 92–99
  financial audits of, 92
  full-service, 82
  gaining/losing clients, 94–99
  group system, 86
  IMC services, 102–104
  in-house, 75–79
  international, 667–670
  management/finance, 85–86
  marketing services, 83–85
  media department, 84–85
  media rebates, 94–95
  media specialist companies, 87–88
  organization/structure of, 86
  procurement department, 94–95
  production department, 85
  qualitative audits of, 92
  reasons for using, 81–82
  research department, 83–84
  role of, 81–82
  superagencies, 80–81
  top ten, U.S., 80
  traffic department, 85
  types of, 82–88
  value added by, 92–93
  youth bias in, 153–155
Advertising appeals, 204–211, 301–309.
  *see also* Creative execution styles
  attack ads, 206, 208–209
  comparative. *see* Comparative
    advertising

competitive advantage, 302
emotional, 303–308
favorable price, 302
fear, 206–210
feature, 301–302
humor, 210–211
informational/rational, 301–303,
  306–308
news, 303
offensive/distasteful, 713, 738–742, 754
product/service popularity, 303
refutation, 203–204
reminder advertising, 308–309
sexual, 172–173, 740–741
shock ads, 736–737, 741–742
teaser advertising, 309
transformational ads, 305–306
user-generated content, 148–149, 309,
  555–556, 559
Advertising campaigns, 282–284
Advertising creativity, 268–271. *see also*
  Creative strategy
  DAGMAR and, 232
  defined, 269
  determinants of, 269–271
  in digital/social media, 310–311
  divergence, 269–271
  effectiveness measurement and, 612–613
  hard-sell advertising vs., 274
  importance of, 265–268
  perspectives on, 268–269
  relevance, 269–271
  standards for, 271, 272
Advertising managers, 71–72
Advertising Research Foundation (ARF),
  98, 109, 166, 167–168, 220, 280, 341
Advertising Self-Regulatory Council
  (ASRC), 691–695, 699, 729
Advertising substantiation, 706–707
Advertorials, 438
Advocacy advertising, 598–600
Aerial advertising, 457
Affect, response process, 176
Affect referral decision rule, 124
Affective stage, 161
Affiliates, 383, 385–386
Affirmative disclosure, 705–706
Affordable method, 243–244
African-Americans, stereotyping of,
  752–753
AIDA model, 158, 159
Alberta Liquor and Gaming
  Commission, 736
Alcoholic beverage advertising
  college students/underage drinkers,
    735–736
  international restrictions, 656–657

# C

Cable television, 391–395
California Supreme Court, 700–701
Campaign theme, 283
Cannes Lions Awards, 98–99
CAN-SPAM Act, 723, 729
Carryover effect, 225
Catalogs, 486–487
Category development index (CDI), 349–350
Category management system, 73–75
Cause-related marketing, 600–601
Cease-and-desist orders, 708
Celebrity endorsement, 175, 190–200
  audience receptivity, 192–194
  foreign ads, 186–187
  infomercials, 490
  likability, 190–191
  meaning transfer model, 196–197
  overexposure, 192
  product overshadowing, 191
  return on investment, 194–195
  risk in using, 181–182, 194
  selection of endorser, 197–200
  typecasting of actors, 192–193
Celebrity voiceovers, 324
Cell phones. *see* Mobile marketing; Smartphones
Centers for Disease Control and Prevention (CDC), 718, 739
*Central Hudson Gas & Electric Corp. v. New York Public Service Commission,* 700
Central Hudson Test, 700
Central route to persuasion, 173–174
Centralized system, 71–73, 79, 665
Channels
  communication. *see* Communication channels
  marketing, 62–63
Chat rooms, 507
Children
  advertising self-regulation, 694, 697
  CARU advertising principles, 746
  ethical issues, 742–746
  food marketing, 658
  Internet marketing, 728, 744–746
  network guidelines, 697
  900-Number Rule, 725
  online privacy, 723, 728
  Parents' Bill of Rights, 747
  premium guidelines, 552–553, 724
  teenagers, 655, 664, 735–736
Children's Advertising Review Unit (CARU), 692, 694, 724, 743, 746
Children's Online Privacy Protection Act (COPPA) of 1998, 723, 728
Children's Television Act, 712
Cinema advertising, 251, 467–468
City and Regional Magazine Association, 422, 423

City zone, 444
Classical conditioning, 128–129
Classified advertising, 415, 440, 447–448
Clients, 69
  client-agency communication, 286–287
  creative output evaluation/approval by, 329–334
  gaining and losing, 94–99
  organizing for advertising/promotion, 70–79, 104
CLIO Awards, 99
Clipping service, 248
Clutter, 215
  magazines, 429–430
  newspapers, 444
  radio, 408
  sales promotion, 535
  television, 215, 380–381
COBRAs (Consumers Online Brand-Related Activities), 508
Cognition, response process, 176
Cognitive dissonance, 126
Cognitive learning theory, 131
Cognitive orientation, 127
Cognitive responses, 169–172
Cognitive stage, 161
Collateral services, 70, 102
Comarketing, 535
Combination rates, 447
Commercial ratings, 400
Commercial speech, 700–701
Commission system, 88–89
Common ground, 153
Communication, 140–178
  analysis of, 35
  basic model of, 145–156
  channels of. *see* Communication channels
  cognitive processing of, 168–175
  decoding, 153–155
  encoding, 146–147
  feedback, 156, 160–161
  message. *see* Message
  nature of, 143–144
  noise, 155–156
  problems in foreign markets, 144–145, 652
  receiver, 153–158
  response, 156. *see also* Response process
  source. *see* Source
Communication channels, 147–153, 211–215
  clutter, 215
  context/environment effects, 214
  mass media. *see* Mass media
  nonpersonal, 147–148, 211–213
  personal, 148–149, 211–213
Communication effects pyramid, 228
Communication objectives, 35, 221–222, 227–230

communications effects pyramid, 228
  effective testing and, 635–636
  IMC objectives, 223–224, 233–235
  marketing objectives vs., 223–224
  problems with, 229–230
  sales-oriented objectives vs., 224–230
Communications Act of 1934, 714
Communications situation, 135
Communications task, 230
Company-created touch points, 27
Comparative advertising, 205–206, 312–313
  AAAA guidelines, 696
  in foreign markets, 658
  lawsuits arising from, 720–721
Competitive advantage, 45, 290
Competitive advantage appeals, 302
Competitive analysis, 34, 44–46
Competitive parity method, 248–249
Compliance, 200
Comprehension and reaction tests, 619
Computer simulation models, 254
Conative stage, 161
Concave-downward function model, 240, 242
Concentrated marketing, 54–55
Concept testing, 617–618
Conditioned response, 128
Conditioned stimulus, 128
Condom advertising, 739–740
Consent orders, 708
Consequences, 121–122
Consider stage, 167
Consumer, family, 135
Consumer behavior, 108–138
  alternative approaches, 136–137
  attitudes, 122–123
  behavioral learning theory, 127–131
  cognitive learning theory, 131
  culture, 132
  decision-making. *see* Decision-making process
  defined, 110
  environmental influences, 131–135
  ethnographic research, 280
  generational differences, 133
  new methodologies/insights, 137
  overview, 110–111
  reference groups, 134–135
  research, 109–110
  response process. *see* Response process
  situational determinants, 135
  social class, 132–133
  subcultures, 132, 133
Consumer Electronics Association (CEA), 568
Consumer era, 16
Consumer franchise-building (CFB) promotions, 537–538, 575
Consumer juries, 619–620

Daily newspapers, 436, 443
Data mining, 136
Database, 21, 51
David Ogilvy Award. *see* Ogilvy Award
Day-after recall tests, 631
Dayparts, 390–391, 409
Decentralized system, 73–75, 79, 666
Deception, 704–705
Deceptive advertising, 685–686, 703–711, 737–738
  advertising substantiation, 706–707
  affirmative disclosure, 705–706
  cease-and-desist orders, 708
  consent orders, 708
  corrective advertising, 708–711
  country-of-origin claims, 705–706
  FTC remedies for, 708–711
  infomercial endorsements, 489
  puffery, 703–704
Decision maker(s), family, 135
Decision rules, 123–124
Decision-making process, 111–127
  alternative evaluation, 119–122
  attitudes, 122–123
  decision rules, 123–124
  evaluative criteria/consequences, 121–122
  evoked set, 119, 121
  in families, 134–135
  information search, 117
  integration processes, 123–124
  model of, 111
  motivation, 113–116, 173
  perception, 117–119
  postpurchase evaluation, 125–126
  problem recognition, 111–113
  purchase decision, 124–125
  purchase funnel, 159, 219, 229
  social media and, 166–168, 234–235
  variations in, 126–127
Decoding, 153–155
Decorative models, 198–199
Demographic segmentation, 49, 50–51
Demographic selectivity, 422–423
Demonstration advertising, 312
Departmental system, 86
Dependent variables, 183
Designated market areas (DMAs), 399
Differentiated marketing, 54
Differentiation, 759
Digital adopters, 160
Digital out-of-home media, 457, 458–459
Digital pay plans, 416
Digital video recorders (DVRs), 381–382, 400
Digital/Interactive agencies, 101–102
Digital/Interactive media, 22–23. *see also* Internet; Internet marketing; Social media
  adaptive brand marketing, 76–77

budget allocation for, 24–25, 256–257
catalog stores and, 487
characteristics of, 367
for consumer-packaged goods, 170–171
creativity needed for, 310–311
IMC and, 14–15, 154–155
international marketing, 678–681
older brands and, 512–513
out-of-home, 457, 458–459
print media disruption, 415–416, 418–419
purchase decisions and, 166–168, 219–220
television watching and, 384–385
Direct broadcast satellite (DBS) services, 674–675
Direct channels, 62–63
Direct headlines, 321
Direct mail, 485–486
  attacks against, 727
  characteristics of, 367
  coupon delivery by, 547–548
  regulation, 724–725
  sample delivery by, 544
Direct marketing, 21, 478–495
  advantages/disadvantages, 492–494
  advertising combined with, 483
  broadcast media and, 488
  catalogs, 486–487
  defined, 480–482
  direct e-mail, 488
  direct mail. *see* Direct mail
  direct selling, 484, 491, 501–502
  e-commerce, 501–502
  effectiveness measurement, 492
  growth of, 482–483
  home shopping, 489–490
  in IMC program, 483–484
  infomercials, 489, 490
  Internet and, 501–502, 519–520
  objectives, 484–485
  one-step approach, 485
  personal selling combined with, 484
  print media and, 490–491
  public relations combined with, 483–484
  regulation, 724–727
  sales promotion combined with, 484
  short-form programs (TV spots), 488–489
  sporting events and, 479–480
  support media combined with, 484
  telemarketing. *see* Telemarketing
  two-step approach, 485
  U.S. expenditures by medium/market, 481–482
Direct-marketing agencies, 99–100
Direct Marketing Association (DMA), 341, 480, 482, 487, 493, 586, 692, 726
Direct selling, 484, 491, 501–502
Direct Selling Association, 726

Direct source, 184
Directional medium, 467
Direct-response advertising, 21, 250, 488
Direct-response media, 482
Disassociative reference groups, 134
Display advertising, 439–440
Dissatisfaction, 112, 125
Dissonance/attribution model, 162–163
Distilled Spirits Council of the United States (DISCUS), 688–689, 690, 691, 736
Distribution channels, 62–63
Divergence, 269–271
Division of Advertising Practices, 701–702
Division of Marketing Practices, 702, 722
Door-to-door sampling, 544
Dramatization, 317–318
Duplicated reach, 357
DVRs, 381–382, 400

# E

Early adopters, 159–160
Earned media, 167
E-commerce, 501–502
Economic censorship, 754–757
Economic impact, of advertising, 758–764
  competition, 759–760
  consumer choice, 759
  information, 761–762
  market power, 761, 762
  product costs/prices, 760–761
Economic infrastructure, 649
Economies of scale, 258–259, 759–760
Effective reach, 359–361
Effectiveness measurement, 606–641
  arguments for/against, 608–613
  audience measurement. *see* Audience measurement
  branded entertainment, 473
  budgeting decisions, 614
  Burke Day-After Recall test, 631
  comprehension/reaction tests, 619
  comprehensive measures, 631–632
  concept testing, 617–618
  consumer juries, 619–620
  corporate advertising, 603–604
  cost of, 610–611
  creativity and, 612–613
  day-after recall tests, 631
  diagnostics, 631
  direct marketing, 492
  effective testing essentials, 635–636
  field tests, 615, 616
  Flesch formula, 621
  focus groups, 604, 618
  how to test, 616–617
  IMC impact, 639–640
  inquiry tests, 627–628
  Internet marketing, 520–522, 626–627

Integrated marketing communications (IMC)—*Cont.*
    importance of, 11–13
    management of, 30
    objectives, 223–224, 233–235
    participants, 69–70, 71
    planning process. *see* Planning process
    promotional mix. *see* Promotional mix
    pros and cons of, 103–104
    radio and, 404–406
    responsibility for, 104
    word-of-mouth marketing and, 151–153
Integrated marketing communications management, 30
Integrated marketing communications plan, 30. *see also* Planning process
Integration processes, 123–124
Interactive Advertising Bureau (IAB), 341, 692
Interactive agencies, 101–102
Interactive media. *see* Digital/Interactive media
Interconnects, 393
Intermittent reinforcement schedule, 130
Internal analysis, 31, 34
Internal audiences, 584–585
Internal Revenue Service (IRS), 559
Internal search, 117
Internalization, 185
International Advertising Association (IAA), 757, 762–763
International advertising/promotion, 642–683
    agency selection, 667–670
    alcoholic beverage advertising, 656–657
    celebrity endorsements, 186–187
    centralization of, 665
    in China, 649, 654, 656–657, 671, 672, 678–679, 681
    combined systems, 666–667
    communication problems, 144–145, 652
    creative decisions, 670–671
    cultural environment, 648, 651–655
    decentralization of, 666
    demographic environment, 648, 650–651
    in developing countries, 650–651
    digital/social media and, 678–681
    economic environment, 648–649, 676–677
    in France, 653
    global approach. *see* Global advertising
    global marketing, 658
    in India, 649, 656–657, 671, 672, 680–681
    international markets, importance of, 645–647
    in Japan, 653, 679–680
    local media, 672–673
    magazines, 673–674
    media selection, 671–675
    in the Middle East, 654–655

newspapers, 673–674
    organizing for, 665–667
    political/legal environment, 648, 655–658, 677
    public relations, 677–678
    religion and, 654
    role of, 647–648
    sales promotion, 675–677
    television, 671–675
    tobacco advertising, 655–657
    top ten companies, by spending, 647
Internet, 496–525. *see also* Internet marketing
    changes in, 14–15
    growth of, 499–502, 678–679
    IMC programs and, 502–522
    online radio, 402, 408, 411
    regulatory issues, 727–729
    Web 2.0. *see* Web 2.0
Internet marketing, 22–23. *see also* Internet
    advantages, 523
    augmented reality, 517–518
    banner ads, 308–309, 502–503
    behavioral targeting, 136, 504–505, 694, 695
    blogs, 507, 517, 522, 588, 729
    children and, 723, 728, 744–746
    Children's Online Privacy Protection Act (COPPA) of 1998, 723, 728
    classified/employment ads, 415, 448
    contests/sweepstakes, 555–556, 723
    contextual ads, 505
    couponing, 518, 547, 551, 552–553, 559
    direct marketing, 519–520
    disadvantages, 523–524
    e-commerce, 501–502
    effectiveness measurement, 250, 520–522, 626–627
    expenditures on, 6
    interstitials, 504
    native advertising, 436, 438–439, 505
    new media, 506–507
    objectives, 499–501
        awareness creation, 500
        brand strengthening, 501
        buzz creation, 501
        consideration, gaining, 501
        image creation, 501
        information dissemination, 500–501
        interest generation, 500
        product trial, 501
    online ads, 308–309
    online commercials/prerolls, 505
    online deals, 552–553
    online endorser guidelines, 188, 729
    paid search advertising, 11, 22, 504
    personal selling, 518–519
    podcasting, 516–517
    pop-ups/pop-unders, 503–504
    privacy issues, 712, 723, 727–729
    public relations, 519, 588
    QR codes, 116, 518

Really Simple Syndication (RSS), 517
    regulatory issues, 727–729
    rich media, 505–506
    sales promotion, 518, 536
    sampling, 544–545
    social media. *see* Social media
    spam, 488, 729
    sponsorships, 503
    video-on-demand (VOD), 505–506
    Web 1.0 advertising, 502–506
    Web 2.0 advertising, 506–518
    webisodes, 506
Internet reporter report, 346
Interstitials, 504
Interviews, 587
Intrinsic touch points, 28
Introductory allowances, 566
Involvement, 127
Issue ads, 600

## J

Jingles, 325–326
Joint Policy Committee on Broadcast Relations, 328
Junk mail. *see* Direct mail

## K

Key benefit claim, 289

## L

Laboratory tests, 615, 616
Lanham Act, 719–721
Layouts, 85, 323
Leader boards, 503
Likability, source, 189, 190–191, 198–199
LinkedIn, 510, 516. *see also* Name and Company Index
Local advertising, 20, 387
Local advertising rates, 445–446
Local people meters, 399
Localized advertising strategy, 670
Love and belonging needs, 114
Low-involvement hierarchy, 164–165
Loyalty programs, 560–561

## M

Made in the USA labeling, 705–706
Magazine advertising. *see also* Magazines; Print advertising
    decline in, 415
    effectiveness measurement, 620–622, 627–630
    native advertising, 436, 438–439
    purchasing space, 433–434
    rates for, 433–434
    relative cost of, 363–366, 428

Magazine networks, 434
Magazines, 417–436. *see also* Magazine
    advertising
    advantages, 421–427
    audience information, 432–433
    business publications, 421
    characteristics of, 367
    circulation, 430–431
    circulation management, 435
    classifications of, 418–421
    clutter, 429–430
    competition among, 429–430
    consumer, 419–420
    consumer receptivity/engagement,
        426–427
    as couponing vehicle, 548–549
    creative flexibility, 424–425
    digital app editions, 419, 431, 436
    digital disruption of, 418–419
    direct marketing and, 490–491
    disadvantages, 428–430
    editorial platform strength, 434–435
    farm publications, 420
    future for, 434–436
    international, 673–674
    lead time, 428
    online delivery, 435–436, 438–439
    permanence, 425
    prestige, 426
    reach/frequency limitations, 428
    readership, 431–432
    reproduction quality, 423–424
    role of, 417
    selectivity, 421–423
    services offered by, 427
    top, 420, 429
    total audience, 431–432
Magnuson-Moss Act, 702
Mailing lists, 486
Major selling idea, 288–296
Marginal analysis, 238–239
Market niches, 157
Market opportunities, 44
Market segmentation, 47–53
    baby boomers, 50–51, 133
    bases for, 48–53
    behavioristic, 51–53
    benefit segmentation, 53
    buying situations, 49
    coverage alternatives, 54–55
    defined, 48
    demographic, 49, 50–51
    80-20 rule, 53
    gay consumers, 754
    geographic, 48–50
    Hispanics, 52, 540–541
    market selection, 46, 53–55
    millennials (gen Y), 12, 41–42, 133,
        141–142
    personality, media usage and, 350–351
    PRIZM social groups, 54

    process of, 53
    psychographic, 49, 51
    segment potential, evaluating, 55
    socioeconomic, 49
    U.S. beer market, 47
Market segments, 44, 157
Marketer-induced problem recognition, 112
Marketing, 7–8, 40–65
    AMA definition, 7
    buzz, 148. *see also* Viral marketing
    cause-related, 600–601
    competitive analysis, 34, 44–46
    exchange concept and, 7
    global, 658
    interactive. *see* Digital/Interactive media
    Internet. *see* Internet marketing
    opportunity analysis, 44
    process model, 43
    program development/planning. *see*
        Marketing planning program
    strategy/analysis, 43–46
    target marketing. *see* Target marketing
        process
    value and, 7–8
Marketing channels, 62–63
Marketing mix, 8
Marketing objectives, 35, 223–224
Marketing plan, 30
Marketing planning program, 60–63
    distribution channel decisions, 62–63
    packaging, 61
    price decisions, 61–62
    product decisions, 60–61
    push vs. pull strategies, 63
Marketing public relations (MPR), 580–582
Marketing research, 102
    motivation, 114–116
    neuroscience, 109–110
    privacy issues, 136
    product/service-specific, 278–279
Marketing/promotions process model, 43
Mass markets, 157–158
Mass media, 147–148, 157–158
    broadcast media. *see* Broadcast media
    information processing and, 213–214
    print media. *see* Print media
Master recording, 325
Master Settlement Agreement,
    716–717, 719
Materialism, 749–750
Meaning transfer model, 196–197
Media
    advertiser control of, 754–757
    characteristics of, 366–367
    digital. *see* Digital/Interactive media
    mass. *see* Mass media
    relative costs of, 363–366
    self-regulation, 696–698
    social. *see* Social media
    support. *see* Support media
    usage of, personality and, 350–351
Media department, 84–85

Media objectives, 339, 351–352
Media organizations, 70
Media plan, 341
Media planning, 336–352
    activities, 342
    awards, 337–338
    defined, 339
    effectiveness measurement
        difficulties, 343
    evaluation/follow-up, 366
    geographic considerations, 347–351
    inconsistent terminologies, 341–343
    insufficient information, 341
    integration focus, 337–338
    internal/external factors, 347
    market analysis, 344–351
    media characteristics, 366–367
    national advertisers ranked by
        spending, 340
    objectives, 339, 351–352
    overview, 338–343
    personality and media usage, 350–351
    problems in, 341–343
    stages of, 344
    strategy development/implementation.
        *see* Media strategy
    target market identification, 344–347
    terminology, 339
    time pressures, 343
Media rebates, 94–95
Media specialist companies, 87–88
Media strategy, 36, 339, 352–366
    budget considerations, 363–366
    creative aspects, 362
    flexibility, 362–363
    geographic coverage, 354
    media mix, 352
    mood, 362
    reach vs. frequency, 355–362
    recency planning, 361–362
    scheduling methods, 354–355
    target market coverage, 352–354
Media vehicle, 339
Medium, 339
Mere exposure effect, 308
Message, 147, 200–211
    appeals. *see* Advertising appeals
    cognitive responses to, 169
    conclusion drawing, 202
    effectiveness measurement, 613–614
    order of presentation, 201
    refutation, 203–204
    sidedness of, 202–203
    structure, 200–204
    verbal vs. visual, 204
Mexican Hass Avocado Importers
    Association, 204
Micromarketing, 11
Millennials (gen Y), 12, 41–42, 133,
    141–142
Mnemonics, 119
Mobile billboards, 458–459

Promotion agencies, 572
Promotional allowances, 565–566
Promotional mix, 16–27
  advertising. *see* Advertising
  digital marketing. *see* Digital/Interactive
    media
  direct marketing. *see* Direct marketing
  Internet marketing. *see* Internet
    marketing
  personal selling. *see* Personal selling
  public relations. *see* Public relations
  publicity. *see* Publicity
  sales promotion. *see* Sales promotion
Promotional Products Association
    International (PPAI), 464, 466, 586
Promotional products marketing, 464–466
Promotional pull strategy, 63
Promotional push strategy, 63
Protestant ethic, 749
Psychoanalytic theory, 114, 115–116
Psychographic segmentation, 49, 51
Psychosocial consequences, 121
Public Health Cigarette Smoking Act, 713
Public relations, 26–27, 579–590. *see also*
    Corporate advertising; Publicity
  advantages/disadvantages, 588–589
  community involvement, 587
  direct marketing combined with,
    483–484
  effectiveness measurement, 250, 589–
    590, 591
  exclusives, 587
  in foreign markets, 677–678
  gaining clients by, 98
  Internet and, 519, 588
  interviews, 587
  marketing public relations (MPR),
    580–582
  new role of, 579–580
  press conferences, 587
  press releases, 586–587
  process of, 583–590
    development and execution, 584–588
    plan evaluation, 583–584
    program implementation, 586–588
    public attitude evaluation, 583
    target audience determination,
      584–586
  in promotional mix, 580
  ROI measurability, 250
  social media and, 588
  target audiences, 584–586
    civic/business organizations, 586
    community members, 585
    educators, 586
    employees, 585
    external, 584, 586
    financial groups, 586
    governments, 586
    internal, 584–585
    the media, 586

    stockholders/investors, 585
    suppliers/customers, 585
    traditional definition, 579
Public relations firms, 100–101
Public Relations Society of America
    (PRSA), 580
Public service announcements (PSAs), 17,
    215
Publicity, 25–26, 590–594
  accuracy, 594
  advantages/disadvantages, 593–594
  control/dissemination of, 592–593
  effectiveness measurement, 594
  lack of control of, 593–594
  negative, 515, 578
  power of, 592
  timing, 594
  video news release (VNR), 593
Puffery, 703–704
Pulsing, 354–355
Pupillometrics, 624
Purchase funnel, 159, 219, 229
Purchase intention, 124
Purchase situation, 135
Purchasing agent, family, 135
Push money (pm), 564

## Q

QR codes, 116, 518
Q-scores, 198, 199
Qualitative audits, 92
Qualitative media effect, 214
Qualitative research, 102, 137, 279–281
Quality, positioning by, 56
Quantitative research, 102

## R

Radio, 375, 402–411, 455
  advantages, 402–406
  Arbitron, 410–411
  audience information, 409–411
  buying procedures, 406, 408–409
  characteristics of, 367
  clutter, 408
  cost/efficiency of, 402–403
  creative limitations of, 406
  digital media competition, 407–408
  emotional attributes for, 403
  flexibility, 404
  format profiles by age group, 405
  fragmentation and, 406
  IMC opportunities, 404–406
  Internet, 402, 408, 411
  limitations, 406–408
  limited research data for, 406–407
  listener attention, limited, 407
  local, 409–410
  mental imagery, 404

  network, 408–409
  RADAR, 411
  receptivity, 403
  ROI measurability, 251
  satellite, 407–408
  selectivity, 404
  spot, 409
  time classifications, 409
Random information catching, 164
Ratings point, 398
Rational appeals, 301–303, 306–308
Reach, 339
  duplicated, 357
  effective, 359–361
  gross ratings points and, 357–359
  level needed, 355–356
  objectives, 357
  unduplicated, 357
Readability tests, 621
Readers per copy, 365–366
Readership, magazine, 431–432
Really Simple Syndication (RSS), 517
Rebates, 556–557
Recall, 623–624
Recall tests, 630, 631
Receiver, 153–158. *see also* Response
    process
Recency, 361–362
Recency effect, 201
Recency planning, 361–362
Recessions, advertising in, 236–238,
    240–241
Recognition method, 629–630
Rectangles, 503
Reference groups, 134–135
Referrals, gaining clients by, 97
Refunds, 556–557
Refutational appeal, 203–204
Regulation, 684–731
  alcoholic beverage advertising,
    471–472, 688–689, 690–691
  federal. *see* Federal regulation
  in foreign markets, 648, 655–658, 677
  self-regulation. *see* Self-regulation
  state and local, 721–722, 723
  tobacco advertising, 471–472, 655–657,
    716–717
Reinforcement, 129–130
Related products, problem recognition
    and, 112
Relationship era, 16–17
Relative cost, 363–366
Relevance, 269–271
Reminder advertising, 121, 308–309
Repetition, 128
Repetitive person-to-person selling, 491
Repositioning, 58–60
Reputation, gaining clients by, 98–99
Research department, 83–84
Residuals, 328
Response, 156

Social media—*Cont.*
  IMC and, 14–15, 154–155
  Instagram, 515–516. *see also* Name and
    Company Index
  international marketing, 678–681
  LinkedIn, 510, 516. *see also* Name and
    Company Index
  in marketing plans, 509
  negative publicity, 515, 578
  older brands and, 512–513
  Pinterest, 510, 516. *see also* Name and
    Company Index
  privacy issues, 136, 712, 729
  public relations and, 588
  purchase decision-making, 166–168,
    219–220, 234–235
  reasons for using, 507–508
  sample distribution by, 536, 545
  Super Bowl advertising, 148–149,
    378–379
  Twitter, 511–513. *see also* Name and
    Company Index
  user-generated content, 148–149, 309,
    555–556, 559
  users of, 507–508
  viral marketing. *see* Viral marketing
  YouTube, 510, 514–515. *see also* Name
    and Company Index
Social needs, 114
Social networking sites, 507. *see also*
  Social media
Socioeconomic segmentation, 49
Software applications. *see* Apps
Solicitations, gaining clients by, 97–98
Source, 145–147, 184–197
  attractiveness, 189–197
  celebrities. *see* Celebrity endorsement
  cognitive responses, 169–170
  corporate leaders, 188–189
  credibility, 185–189
  decorative models, 198–199
  direct, 184
  effectiveness measurement, 613
  encoding, 146–147
  expertise, 185
  familiarity, 189
  identification, 189–190
  indirect, 184
  likability, 189, 190–191, 198–199
  similarity, 189, 190
  trustworthiness, 186–188
Source bolsters, 170
Source derogations, 170
Source power, 199–200
Spam, 488, 729
Special-audience newspapers, 437–438
Specialized marketing communication services, 70, 99–102
Specialty advertising, 464
Spiffs, 564
Split runs, 427
Split-run tests, 628

Sponsorships, 389–390
  annual spending, North America, 598
  content, 470, 503
  corporate advertising, 595–596
  effectiveness measurement, 251, 638–639
  event, 561, 596–597
  Internet advertising, 503
  Olympics, 596, 610
Spot advertising, 387, 390, 393, 409
S-shaped response curve, 240–241, 242
Standard advertising units (SAUs), 446
Standard Chartered Hong Kong
  Marathon, 602
*Standard Directory of Advertising
  Agencies,* 79
Standard learning model, 162
Starch readership studies, 629–630
Station posters, 461–462
Station reps, 387
Stimulus-response orientation (S-R),
  127–128
Stocking allowances, 566
Stopping power, 191
Storyboards, 85, 282, 329
Straight sell execution style, 311–312
Strategic marketing plan, 43
Street furniture, 455, 460
Street money, 566
Students Opposed to Unfair Practices
  (SOUP), 708
Subcultures, 132, 133
Subheads, 321–322
Subliminal perception, 119, 120
Super Bowl ads, 376
  Apple's "1984" ad, 330–331
  "Crash the Super Bowl" contest,
    148–149, 309, 559
  "Halftime in America," 582
  "Live Más" campaign, 300
  offensive/distasteful, 713, 754
  "Punch Dub," 68
  using social media, 148–149, 378–379
Superagencies, 80–81
Superstations, 391
Support advertising, 488
Support arguments, 169
Support media, 452–477
  branded entertainment. *see* Branded
    entertainment
  miscellaneous alternative media,
    474–475
  nontraditional, 468–475
  out-of-home. *see* Out-of-home
    advertising
  product placements. *see* Product
    placements
  promotional products marketing,
    464–466
  scope of, 454
  traditional, 455–468
  video game ads, 250, 474
  Yellow Pages, 466–467

Survey of buying power index, 347, 348
Sustainable competitive advantage, 290
Sweeps periods, 341, 399–400
Sweepstakes, 554–556, 722–723
Syndicated Network Television
  Association (SNTA), 388
Syndicated programs, 387–389, 409

# T

Tablet computers, 15, 22, 520
Taglines, 283, 284–285
Target audiences
  identifying, 157–158
  public relations, 584–586
Target customers, 527
Target CPM (TCPM), 365
Target marketing, 46
Target marketing process, 46–55
  market identification, 46–47, 344–347
  market positioning. *see* Positioning
  market segmentation. *see* Market
    segmentation
  market selection, 46, 53–55
  target market coverage, 352–354
Target ratings points (TRPs), 358
Teaser advertising, 309
Technical evidence execution style, 312
Teenagers, 655, 664, 735–736
Telemarketing, 484, 491
  National Do Not Call Registry, 491,
    494, 725–726
  personal selling and, 484
  regulation, 725–726
Telephone Consumer Protection
  Act, 725
Television, 374–402. *see also* Television
  advertising
  advantages, 375–378
  advertiser influence, 754–757
  affiliates, 383, 385–386
  audience measurement, 396–402, 672
  A2/M2 initiative, 401
  Cross-Platform Campaign
    Ratings, 401
  designated market areas
    (DMAs), 399
  developments in, 400–402
  households using television (HUT),
    398
  local audience information, 399–400
  national audience information,
    398–399
  Nielsen Television Index, 398–399
  people meters, 398–399
  program rating, 397–398
  ratings point, 398
  share of audience, 398
  sweeps ratings, 399–400
  television households, 397
  total audience, 398

cable, 391–395
characteristics of, 367
digital media and, 14, 384–385, 520
in foreign markets, 671–675
genres, most engaging, 343
limitations, 378–383
satellite, 674–675
smart TVs, 385
Spanish-language networks, 385
zero-TV homes, 384, 401–402
Television advertising, 158, 375–391, 393.
    *see also* Television
    advantages, 375–378
    audio component, 324–327
    buying time, 383–402
        local advertising, 387
        network advertising, 383–387
        participations, 390
        sponsorship, 389–390
        spot advertising, 387, 390
        syndicated programs, 387–389
        time period/program selection,
            390–391
    on cable television, 393
    captivity/attention, 376–377, 381–383
    clutter, 215, 380–381
    college sports, 373–374
    cost of, 327–328, 379, 386
    coverage/cost effectiveness of, 376, 379
    creative tactics, 323–329
    creativity/impact, 375–376
    direct-response, 488
    distrust/negative evaluation, 383
    effectiveness measurement, 250,
        622–626, 631–634. *see also*
        Effectiveness measurement
    fleeting message, 380
    flexibility, 377–378
    infomercials, 489
    international restrictions, 671–672, 673
    jingles, 325–326
    limitations, 378–383
    music, 324–327
    needledrop, 324
    online commercials/prerolls, 505
    planning/production, 326–329
    posttests, 631–634
    pretests, 622–626
    ROI measurability, 250
    selectivity, 377–378, 379–380
    self-regulation, 697–698
    short-form programs, 488–489
    top national advertisers, 377
    tracking studies, 633–634
    video component, 324
    viewer attention, 376–377, 381–383
    voiceover, 324
    zipping/zapping of, 381–382
Television Bureau of Advertising, 219, 278
Television households, 397
Television networks, 383–387, 392
Terminal posters, 461–462

Test marketing, 632–633
Testimonials, 313
Testing bias, 616
Text messaging, 14–15
Text perspective/organization, 36–38
Theater testing, 622–623
Third cover, 433
Tobacco advertising, 655–657, 716–717
    Master Settlement Agreement,
        716–717, 719
    product placements, 471–472
Top-down approaches, 243–250
Top-of-mind awareness, 121
Total audience/readership, 398, 431–432
Touch points, 27–29, 219–220
Toy Industry Association, 689
Tracking studies, 633–634
Trade advertising, 20, 63
Trade allowances, 565–566, 724
Trade regulation rules (TRRs), 702
Trade shows, 568
Trademark Law Revision Act, 720
Trade-oriented sales promotion, 24,
        529–530, 563–570
    building retail inventories, 564
    buying allowances, 565
    contests, 564–565
    cooperative advertising, 568–570
    established brand support/display,
        563–564
    incentives, 564–565
    new products, 563
    objectives, 563–564
    planograms, 567
    point-of-purchase displays, 566–567
    promotional allowances, 565–566
    sales training programs, 567–568
    slotting allowances, 566, 724
    trade allowances, 565–566
    trade shows, 568
    types of, 564–570
Traffic department, 85
Transformational ads, 305–306
Transit advertising, 455, 460–463
Trustworthiness, 186–188
truth® antismoking campaign, 717, 719
Tweens, 133
Twitter, 510, 511–513. *see also* Name and
    Company Index
Two-sided message, 202–203
Two-step approach, 485

# U

Unconditioned response, 128
Unconditioned stimulus, 128
Undifferentiated marketing, 54
Unduplicated reach, 357
Unexpected touch points, 28
Unfairness, 702–703
Uniform Commercial Code, 703–704

Unique selling proposition (USP), 289–290
United Nations, 87
U.S. Air Force, 471
U.S. Army, 134, 288
U.S. Brewers Association, 688
U.S. Department of Health and Human
    Services, 713, 739
U.S. Department of Justice, 381
U.S. Postal Service, 482, 687, 700, 718,
    724–725
U.S. Supreme Court, 600
    cigarette packaging, 719
    commercial speech, 700–701
    corrective advertising, 710–711
    FDA tobacco regulation, 716
    professional advertising, 689
    puffery, 704
U.S. Surgeon General, 736
U.S. Treasury Department, 718
Universal Advertising Standards, 271, 272
Up-front market, 386–387
Usage imagery, 316
Usage situation, 135
User imagery, 316
User-generated content (UGC), 148–149,
    309, 555–556, 559

# V

VALS, 51, 53, 493
VALS 2, 51
Value, 7–8
Value-based compensation, 90
Vehicle option source effect, 614
Vertical cooperative advertising, 569–570
Verticals, 503
Video game ads, 250, 474
Video news release (VNR), 593
Video-on-demand (VOD), 382, 400,
    470–471, 505–506
Viral marketing, 149–153, 266–267, 501
    guerrilla tactics, 473–474
    negative publicity, 515
    seeding, 150–151
    word-of-mouth vs., 148–149
*Virginia State Board of Pharmacy v.
    Virginia Citizens Consumer Council,*
    700
Virtual reality, 507
Visual elements, 322–323
Visual image personality (VIP), 164–165
Voice-over, 324

# W

"The Wall," 756
Wants, 112
Waste coverage, 352–353, 462
Wearout, 210–211, 212–213, 462
Web 1.0, 502–506
Web 2.0, 14, 22, 502, 503, 506–518

Webisodes, 506
Weblogs. *see* Blogs
Weekly newspapers, 437
Wheeler-Lea Amendment, 701, 708
Wikitude World Browser, 517
Women, stereotyping of, 751–752
Women Against Pornography, 736
Word of Mouth Marketing Association
    (WOMMA), 152
Word-of-mouth (WOM), 148–153. *see*
    *also* Viral marketing

Work plan, 284
World Trade Organization, 646, 655
World Wide Web (WWW). *see* Internet;
    Web 1.0; Web 2.0

# Y

Yellow Pages, 447, 466–467
YouTube, 510, 514–515. *see also* Name
    and Company Index

# Z

Zapping, 381–382
Zero-based communications planning, 234
Zero-TV homes, 384, 401–402
Zipping, 381